The
Historical Atlas
of the
World at War

A CARTOGRAPHICA BOOK

This updated edition published in 2010 by
CHARTWELL BOOKS, INC.
A division of BOOK SALES, INC.
276 Fifth Avenue Suite 206
New York, New York 10001
USA

ISBN 13: 978-0-7858-2745-0
ISBN 10: 0-7858-2745-5

QUMHA16

This book is produced by
Cartographica Ltd
6 Blundell Street
London N7 9BH

Publisher: Sarah Bloxham
Project Editor: Samantha Warrington
Production Manager: Rohana Yusof
Design: Andrew Easton

Cartography:
Red Lion Mapping

Printed in Singapore by
Star Standard Industries Pte Ltd.

THE
HISTORICAL ATLAS
OF THE
WORLD AT WAR

B. LEWIS AND RUPERT MATTHEWS

CHARTWELL
BOOKS, INC.

Contents

MAP LIST

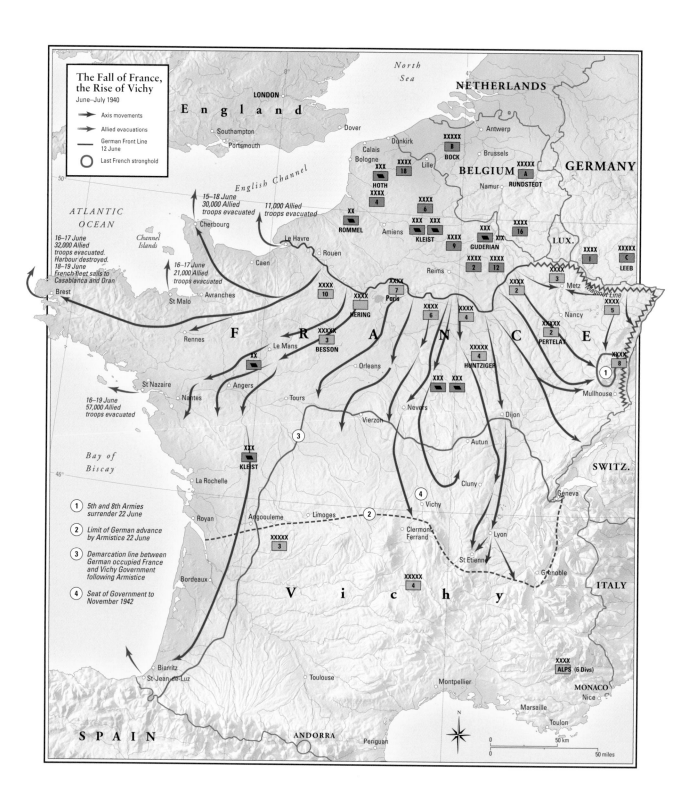

The Fall of France,
the Rise of Vichy
June–July 1940

→ Axis movements

→ Allied evacuations

— German Front Line
12 June

◯ Last French stronghold

England

LONDON

Southampton

Portsmouth

Dover

English Channel

North Sea

NETHERLANDS

Antwerp

Calais
Bologne

Dunkirk

Brussels

BELGIUM

GERMANY

Namur

XXXXX
B
BOCK

XXXXX
A
RUNDSTEDT

Lille

XXX
18
HOTH

XXXX
4

XX
ROMMEL

Amiens

XXXX
6

XXX XXX
KLEIST

XXXX
9

XXX
GUDERIAN

XIX

XXXX
2

XXXX
12

XXXX
16

LUX.

XXXX
1

XXXXX
C
LEEB

XXXX
3

Metz

Maginot Line

XXXX
2

Nancy

XXXX
5

*ATLANTIC
OCEAN*

50°

16–17 June
32,000 Allied
troops evacuated.
Harbour destroyed.
18–19 June
French fleet sails to
Casablanca and Oran

Brest

*Channel
Islands*

15–18 June
30,000 Allied
troops evacuated

11,000 Allied
troops evacuated

16–17 June
21,000 Allied
troops evacuated

Cherbourg

Le Havre

Rouen

Caen

St Malo

Avranches

XXXX
10

XXXX
NERING

XXXX
7
Paris

Reims

XXXX
6

XXXX
4

XXXXX
PERTELAT

F   R   A   N   C   E

Rennes

Le Mans

XXXXX
3
BESSON

XX

Angers

Orleans

XXXXX
4
HUNTZIGER

XXX XXX

XXXX
8

◯
1

Mullhouse

St Nazaire

16–19 June
57,000 Allied
troops evacuated

Nantes

Tours

Vierzon

Nevers

Dijon

Autun

SWITZ.

*Bay of
Biscay*

46°

XXX
KLEIST

◯
3

Cluny

◯
4
Vichy

Lyon

Geneva

La Rochelle

Royan

Angouleme

Limoges

◯
2

Clermont
Ferrand

St Etienne

Grenoble

ITALY

1 5th and 8th Armies
surrender 22 June

2 Limit of German advance
by Armistice 22 June

3 Demarcation line between
German occupied France
and Vichy Government
following Armistice

4 Seat of Government to
November 1942

Bordeaux

XXXXX
3

V   i   c   h   y

XXXXX
4

XXXX
ALPS (6 Divs)

Biarritz
St-Jean-de-Luz

Toulouse

Montpellier

Marsaille

MONACO
Nice

Toulon

S   P   A   I   N

ANDORRA

Periguan

N

0   50 km

0   50 miles

KEY TO MAPS

Military movements

→ attack

➤ retreat

✈ bombers

✳ explosion

✈ airfield

Military units/types

⊠ infantry

armoured

motorized infantry

⊠ airlanding and Luftwaffe field

airborne

artillery

Military units/size

XXXXX army group

XXXX army

XXX corps

XX division

X brigade

III regiment

II battalion

I company

General military symbols

— XXXXX — army group boundary

— XXXX — army boundary

— XXX — corps boundary

pocket or position

paratroop drop

sunken ship

mobile gun

anti-tank gun

light machine gun

heavy machine gun /other infantry weapon

gun emplacement

gun in casement

heavy AA gun

light AA gun

20mm anti-aircraft gun

German strongpoints

pillbox for guns

concrete shelter

shelter with cupola

sea mine

land mine

✕✕✕✕✕✕ barbed wire

major defensive line

entrenchment

radar station

church

Geographical symbols

buildings

urban area

road

railway

river

seasonal river

canal

border

bridge or pass

marsh/swamp

rocks and beach

woodland

INTRODUCTION: THE ROOTS OF WAR

EARTH HAS ALWAYS BEEN A CHALLENGING PLACE IN WHICH TO LIVE. SURVIVAL IN THIS DEMANDING ENVIRONMENT HAS REQUIRED GREAT EFFORTS TO CLAIM A SHARE OF EARTH'S RESOURCES, EFFORTS THAT HAVE BRED VIOLENT RIVALRIES WHICH, IN THEIR TURN, HAVE BRED WAR.

A Polynesian war club, formed from a single piece of wood. The handle is carved to provide a secure grip and ends in a boss to prevent the club slipping from the hand in the heat of battle. Clubs were among the first types of weapons.

The history of warfare and the history of humanity have run parallel to each other for thousands of years — and for a vital reason: for most of the time humans have lived on Earth, war has been virtually the only way to ensure the most important function known to Nature: survival and with that, adequate supplies of the means of survival, most importantly food and water. The weapons of war were always ready at hand, for they were little different from the weapons used for hunting. The spears, arrows, and other missiles that could kill animals for food could just as easily dispatch rivals challenging for that food. As far back as the Old Stone Age, which began around 2.5 million years ago, groups of men fought each other, using crude stone implements, large animal bones or lengths of wood, and did so not only for food or water, but also for women, the best hunting grounds, or the most congenial cave-homes.

From the start, weapons of war belonged to one of two types. The first was the "shock" weapon which in prehistoric times comprised the hand-held club — a large animal bone or length of wood — and was used in close quarter combat. The second, the more versatile of the two weapons, was the missile in the form of small, smooth rocks which hunters could hurl at their prey or at a human enemy. The effectiveness of a missile was greatly increased by the sling-shot, which was usually made of leather. The flinging action of the slingshot enabled a missile to be thrown at increased distances and with greater speed and accuracy. Both types of weapons gradually evolved over time, and the club was still being used in 18th and 19th-century America where the Indians deployed the tomahawk. Some clubs acquired sharpened edges and so became the precursors of the sword. Small stone missiles developed into the throwing stick, which in its turn evolved into sharp-ended darts, boomerangs, and javelins. Later still, the heavy pike or thrusting spear developed from the javelin. The arrow, a longer variant of the dart, gained greater force when combined with the bow, which made its appearance in the later years of the Stone Age. As weapons grew more deadly and damaging, warriors acquired defenses against them. In fact, the entire history of warfare illustrates a trade-off between defenses designed to counteract offensive weapons and offensive weapons designed to deal more effectively with the new defenses. The chief personal defense in primitive warfare was the shield which, before the Bronze Age and the advent of metal weapons, comprised a simple wooden framework covered in leather hide. Some of these early shields were made entirely of wood, although in Asia, wickerwork shields were common. Special protection for the head, torso, or legs were made of leather, wickerwork, wood, or padded, sometimes quilted, cloth.

The discovery of metals, which began with gold in around 6000BC, represented a quantum leap in warfare technology and had a similar effect on everyday life. Copper, discovered in around 4,200BC, replaced stone axe-heads. In around 1,750BC, when tin was mixed with copper to produce bronze, warfare acquired a much harder alloy that went on to make spears, arrows, daggers, swords, shields, helmets, and other body armor. Even more durable were weapons made of iron though these did not come into everyday use until after 1,200BC when iron deposits were discovered on Earth. Previously, the only source — and a very rare one — had been the iron provided by meteorites which occasionally landed from the Heavens, and through primitive religious belief acquired a magical, even mystical, reputation. At first, all metals were in short supply and were therefore used economically. Rather than use them for entire weapons, metals served to make sharp points and edges on existing weaponry. Metals were also the ideal means of smashing surfaces, breaking non-metallic weapons, or making short work of enemies with inadequate defenses. As time went on, it became possible to produce all-metal weapons. The first were daggers. Then came the sword. At the start, sword blades were long and thin. They remained so for as long as metallurgy was insufficiently developed to allow the working of hard, malleable metals, a technique that did not become available until around 2000BC in the Bronze Age. This time period also saw the rise of the intensely aggressive Assyrian Empire, the world's first military state, which is thought to have introduced the sword onto the battlefield. In addition, metals greatly improved the effectiveness of body armor and were used to reinforce and give a new flexibility to breastplates and helmets. Greaves, which protected the lower legs, were soon made entirely of metal, at first of bronze and iron.

One of the most significant uses of bronze was for the production of weaponry. This illustration shows an example of bronze weaponry found in Romania. It was a much more durable material than copper, allowing the production of much more deadly weapons.

CHAPTER 1 — WARFARE IN THE ANCIENT WORLD: Tribal War

TRIBAL CONFLICT WAS THE INITIAL FORM OF WARFARE AND IT AROSE AS SOON AS RIVAL GROUPS OF PEOPLE BEGAN CONTESTING THE SAME ADVANTAGES. LAND, FOOD, WATER, AND DOMINATION WERE AMONG THE MOTIVES AND WAR WAS THE WAY TO SECURE THEM.

All war has long been, and still is, tribal war. The term can describe virtually any form of hostility between small, local groups, rival countries, and even transcontinental alliances such as those that contested the two World Wars of the 20th century. Of course, these extensive conflicts required populations large enough to supply armies capable of sustaining prolonged hostilities. It has long been held, though also disputed, that widespread warfare was unlikely in prehistoric times when the world was so sparsely populated that a fighting group probably included no more than around 20 or 30 men. Even so, the effectiveness of small-group warfare was evidenced in the Armana "letters," tablets inscribed in Akkadian cuneiform, the writing of ancient Mesopotamia. The Armana "letters" are an archive of correspondence on clay tablets, mostly diplomatic, between the Egyptian administration and its representatives in Canaan and Amurru during the New Kingdom. In the 14th century BC, Armana was the capital of the Egyptian Pharoah Akhenaten and some of the "letters" record the devastation and terror caused by only 20 marauders in settlements of the ancient Middle East. Today, tribal societies that still live much as they did in paleolithic times provide more clues to what prehistoric existence was like. In the Amazonian jungle of South America, for example, or the more remote Pacific islands, there are isolated tribes that regularly raid neighboring settlements and steal land, women, slaves, and goods just as their forebears probably did thousands of years ago. Intense violence is frequently involved. Many a fearsome reputation can be built that way and it may be that in prehistoric times, such reputations served as a form of psychological defense against other tribes with similarly combative ideas.

Prehistoric warfare may have become ritualized, featuring set-piece actions designed to indicate essential qualities. Masculinity was doubtless one of them. After all, in ancient times, the survival of a tribe depended on the strength, courage, and enterprise of its males whose ability to hunt or fend off attack was essential to tribal survival. In some primitive tribes still extant today, ritual fighting remains an important ingredient of their culture. The Amazonian Yanomamo, for instance, perform duels in which aggression is indicated by chest-beating and side-slapping. They also fight with clubs and throw spears as preludes to all-out war.

Paleolithic cave paintings as found in southwest France, Spain, South Africa, Australia, and elsewhere do not specifically depict scenes of battle between humans: the "enemy" is represented by animals being hunted for food, even though the clubs and spears used as early as 35,000BC could serve equally well as the weapons of early warfare. Clubs and spears characterized close combat conflict rather than the wider-ranging hostilities that went to make and prolong all-out battles. Just as prehistoric Man discovered that distance made hunting animals safer and the surrounding of prey from a short way off more productive, so new weapons developed in around 12,000BC gave the same advantages to warfare. Bows and arrows, slings, and maces expanded the scope and power of warfare and allowed concerted attacks to be made in more security than had ever been possible with close quarter fighting. This was particularly true of bows and arrows which later became the "artillery" of medieval armies, allowing archers to fire at an enemy from out-of-range positions on the battlefield. It was at this juncture that prehistoric battle scenes began to appear on cave walls and ceilings, painted there for the same reason as the earlier hunting pictures: to ensure success and victory. The warfare depicted was clearly organized, illustrating warriors arrayed opposite each other in extended battle lines. Tactics such as flanking movements and one force moving in to envelop another also decorated prehistoric caves.

The move from cave-homes and temporary shelters to villages and small towns that occurred in the Neolithic, or New Stone, Age was prompted by the change from the peripatetic hunter-gatherer society to the more settled existence offered by farming. In the Middle East this occurred in around 9500BC and over time, spread westward. But permanent settlement presented its problems. The Neolithic world was no paradise of peace and plenty. Settlements required defenses and needed to be built in defensible locations. Unfortunately, this was precisely what did not occur, or at least occur frequently enough, and proof of internecine warfare and its attendant brutalities soon began to accrue. The first archaeological record of what may have been a prehistoric battle, dating from around 9000BC was discovered on the River Nile near the border between Egypt and the Sudan. Cemetery 117, as the place is known, contained a vast number of corpses which, from the mass of arrowheads embedded in them, must have died in an overwhelming onslaught of fire from Neolithic archers. Nearly half the bodies were female, suggesting a massacre of civilians. Another massacre, this time in Neolithic Europe, may have occurred even earlier, in around 9500BC at Talheim in southern Germany. The Talheim Death Pit, so-called, was discovered in 1983 and contained 34 people who had been tied up before being killed by a blow to the head. The thousands of fortifications constructed by the Maoris on the South Pacific Islands they inhabited in around 5500BC, some time before they colonized New Zealand, gave another indication that war had become endemic in prehistoric life. These defenses were intended to protect people and livestock from invaders, and were generally successful in doing so, even though they left the homes, fields, and crops beyond them open to attack and depredation. It was clear that as civilization developed, greater was the potential for war.

WARS OF SETTLEMENT AND CITIES

CIVILIZATION AND HISTORY ARE SAID TO HAVE BEGUN WITH SUMER, A COMPLEX OF SEVERAL MESOPOTAMIAN CITIES FIRST ESTABLISHED AFTER THE 5TH MILLENNIUM BC IN WHAT IS NOW SOUTHERN IRAQ. UNFORTUNATELY, THE SEPARATE CITY ARRANGEMENT INEVITABLY LED TO QUARRELS AND WAR.

The first inhabitants of Mesopotamia came from Asia Minor or the Caucasus Mountains of southern Russia in around 4000BC. Although two mighty rivers, the Tigris and Euphrates, flowed through Mesopotamia, the fertility of the region varied considerably. The north was hilly, with soil enriched by seasonal rains. There was plenty of timber available and metals and fine stone could be mined in the mountains. The south was less favored, featuring wide, barren marshes with few natural resources. This imbalance deprived Mesopotamia of the stability enjoyed by Ancient Egypt, where civilization developed at much the same time. While Egypt, which was universally blessed by the bounty of the River Nile, evolved into a unified kingdom, Mesopotamia split into 23 major and minor cities, all independent of each other and soon at loggerheads. There were the usual conflicts over the availability of land and water, but other motives also entered the argument. There were boundary disputes or attempts to monopolize the Tigris and Euphrates for the irrigation and transport facilities they offered. Rival cities quarreled over access to the timber or the metal and stone deposits of the north, while some, like Kish or Lagash, sought to dominate the entire region for their own benefit. The upshot was that the city-states of Sumer were almost continuously at war for some 2,000 years. In this context, military technology developed with such rapidity that the techniques of Sumerian warfare became the most sophisticated in the then-known world. The most important innovation introduced by the Sumerians

All the early civilizations were situated close to water — Egypt by the Nile, Mesopotamia by the Tigris and Euphrates, and elsewhere, the Chinese civilization by the Yangtse-Kiang, Mohenjo-daro by the Indus River. This map shows why: the rivers were oases of survival in the midst of deserts.

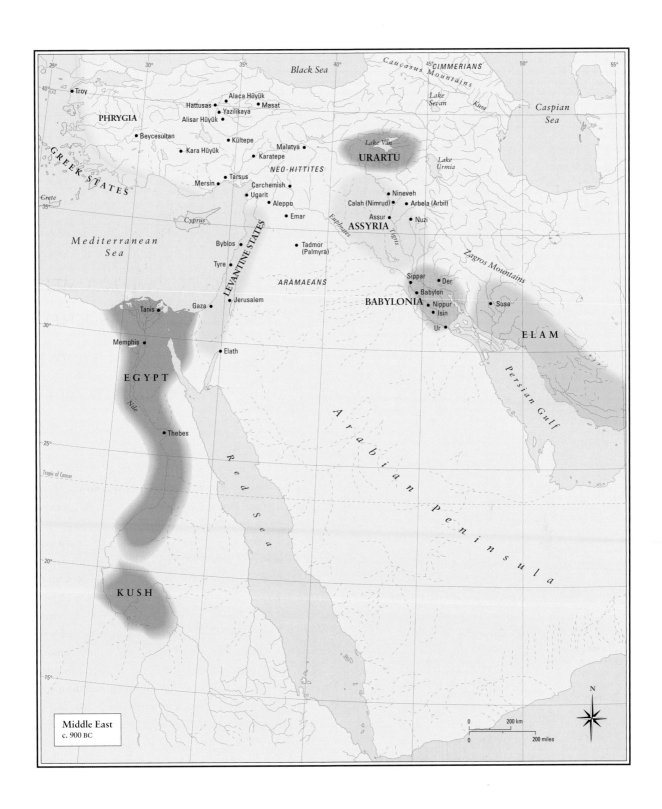

Middle East
c. 900 BC

was the chariot. This made its first appearance in around 3000BC as a somewhat cumbersome vehicle with four solid wooden wheels drawn by wild asses. It was more likely to be used for transportation than for attack purposes, but there was also a lighter, two-wheeled version, pulled by four asses, which sometimes carried a spearman together with a charioteer. The wheels were still made of solid wood and were covered in skins. Some 1,500 years on, in around 2500BC, the solid wheels were replaced by spoked wheels. Thanks to victorious Sumerian kings and generals who depicted their triumphs on intricately carved stelae (tall commemorative stones), it is possible many thousands of years later to see what a Sumerian army looked like going into battle and how its leader, in this case King Eannatum of Lagash, appeared riding in his chariot.

The war between the Sumerian cities of Lagash and Umma in 2525BC was the first to be recorded in detail. The stele erected by the victor, King Eannatum of Lagash, depicted features of his army, its equipment, and its weaponry. The Stele of the Vultures was so called because it showed these savage birds of prey, together with lions, tearing at the bodies of defeated Umman soldiers. King Eannatum was depicted in the thick of the fighting, leading his infantry who trampled on their fallen enemies as they advanced. On their heads, King Eannatum's spearmen wore copper helmets which were probably lined with leather or a cap. The war with Umma was not the first in which this protection was used, for in the so-called Death Pits of Ur, another Sumerian city, archeologists discovered evidence dating from around 2500BC: the bodies of soldiers with their helmets still on their heads. Next to the chariot, the helmet was a major innovation among the many introduced in Sumerian times. Helmets were vital, even this early on in the history of warfare, and one particularly terrible weapon made them so: the mace, which was probably the first unfailingly effective weapon of war ever introduced. The mace had a wooden handle with a heavy stone or metal ball attached to it by a chain, and could crack open an unprotected skull at a single stroke. In time, the helmet proved so effective that the mace lost much of its terror and was used less and less on ancient battlefields. Sumerian foot-soldiers were equipped with sickle-shaped swords with blades forged in a crescent shape. In the battle between Lagash and Umma, this sword was a comparatively recent development and as such, was particularly terrifying for soldiers facing it for the first time.

Hardly less formidable than the sword was the bronze socket-axe, a murderously damaging weapon with a narrow blade held inside a strong socket, which made it possible for any soldier wielding it to cut right through bronze plate armor. The axe was so fearsome and successful that it outlived the armies of Sumeria by many centuries and remained a major military weapon for the next 2,000 years. Ironically, it was the Sumerians themselves who introduced bronze plate armor and another form of body protection, the armored cloak. In the Stele of the Vultures, a fragmented limestone stele found in Ngirsu (modern Telloh), Iraq, King Eannatum of Lagas, was shown very well equipped for going to battle, with a socket-axe in his hand. In an illustration on another panel, he carried a sickle-bladed sword. The Stele of the Vultures was erected as a monument of the victory of Eannatum over Enakelle of Umma.

Another weapon which had its power increased by Sumerian ingenuity was the simple bow. Its replacement, the Sumerian composite bow, was possibly invented about 30 years before the start of the war between Lagash and Umma. It differed from the simple, all-wood bow in that it was made from different materials — wood, horn, sinew — that were laminated together under pressure. This

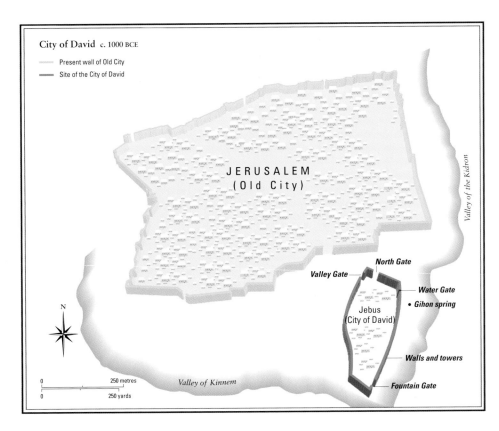

City of David c. 1000 BCE

····· Present wall of Old City
▬▬ Site of the City of David

JERUSALEM
(Old City)

Valley of the Kidron

North Gate

Valley Gate

Water Gate

• Gihon spring

Jebus
(City of David)

Walls and towers

Fountain Gate

N

0 — 250 metres
0 — 250 yards

Valley of Kinnem

Jebus was one of the names for the city later called Jerusalem. The name meant "fastness" or "waterless hill" and Jerusalem certainly acquired the reputation of being impregnable. It is mentioned many times in the Bible, and is identified with Jerusalem in the book of Judges (Chapter 19 Verse 10).

construction gave the composite bow much greater strength and enabled it to exert up to three times the "pull" of the simple bow that had been in use since prehistoric times. Its advantage was that it combined added firepower with smaller size and could therefore be used in restricted circumstances, on horseback, or from the wickerwork basket that lined the cart of a chariot. Arrows fired by the composite bow could pierce leather or bronze armor, though in this case from a distance, and like the socket axe, long outlived its beginnings: it was still being used on the battlefield 1,500 years later.

The Stele of the Vultures also revealed that Sumerian soldiers fought in phalanxes. These were six files deep, fronted by a row of eight men. This formation was still being employed centuries later in Ancient Greece and suggests that King Eannatum's army was a standing professional force. Fighting in phalanx formation required a great deal of discipline and much training so that strategy and tactics could be orchestrated as the needs of battle dictated. This made Eannatum's army radically different from earlier forces which comprised civilians turned soldier for the purpose of fighting a battle and afterwards returning to their normal work. Another indication was that the equipment of a professional army had to be standardized, which meant that the choice of weaponry was no longer left to individual combatants who had formerly provided their own. The professional army, by contrast, was equipped at the expense of the rulers whose battles they fought.

THE FIRST EMPIRES

IN THE THIRD AND FOURTH MILLENIA BC, MESOPOTAMIA WAS AN
ATTRACTIVE ENVIRONMENT FOR THE SETTING UP OF EMPIRES. ITS
ADVANCED TECHNOLOGY, SCIENCE, AND AGRICULTURE, LUCRATIVE
TRADE ROUTES, AND WELL-DEVELOPED CITIES OFFERED GREAT
PRESTIGE TO IMPERIAL-MINDED CONQUERORS.

The first Mesopotamian ruler with imperial ambitions was Lugalzaggisi of Umma who conquered several Sumerian cities — Kish, Lagash, Ur, Nippur, Larsa, and Uruk — before setting himself up as king in Uruk in 2296BC. Lugalzaggisi claimed that Enlil, the leading Mesopotamian god, had given him all the lands between the Mediterranean and the Persian Gulf. This was quite a claim, for in Lulalzaggisi's time, the Mediterranean represented the western edge of the world. Lugalzaggisi did not last long, around 25 years, before a conqueror far mightier than he arrived on the scene. In around 2271BC, Sargon of Akkad destroyed the walls of Uruk, seized Lugalzaggisi, put him in a neck-stock, and had him taken to Enlil's temple in Nippur.

Sargon was a man of humble origins. As an infant, he was purportedly found floating in a basket along the river Euphrates by a gardener who brought him up to follow the same line of work. But Sargon was never going to be a gardener. A man of extraordinary energy and ambition, he rose to become cupbearer to the King of the Sumerian city of Kish. Subsequently, he overthrew and replaced his royal benefactor before setting out on the conquest of an empire. Sargon's defeat of Lugalzaggisi gave him a readymade nucleus which he afterward expanded into the vast Akkadian Empire that stretched as far as the Mediterranean sea from Elam in the far west of present-day Iran and across Mesopotamia, Syria, Anatolia (Turkey), and the Arabian peninsula. This mammoth enterprise involved 34 wars and occupied much of Sargon's 56-year reign. The record in the Chronicle of the Early Kings, an ancient Babylonian text that described Sargon's exploits in glowing terms: "(He) had neither rival nor equal. His splendor over the lands, it diffused. He crossed the sea in the east....he conquered the western land to its farthest

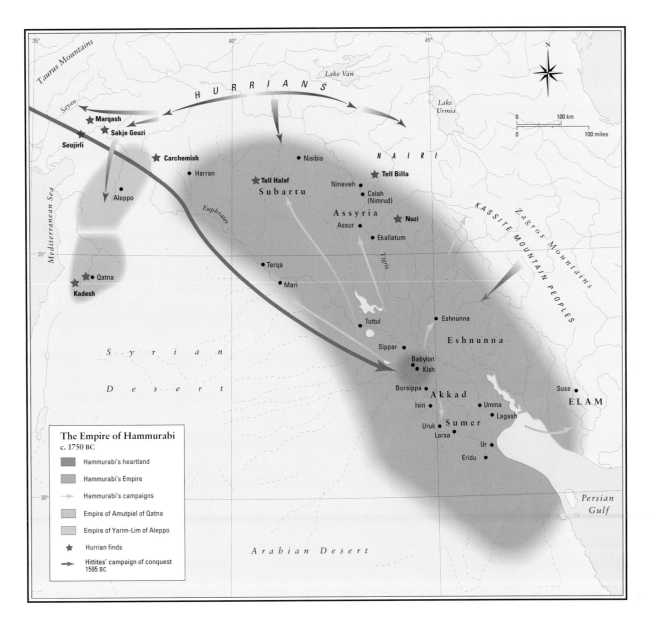

The Empire of Hammurabi
c. 1750 BC

- Hammurabi's heartland
- Hammurabi's Empire
- Hammurabi's campaigns
- Empire of Amutpiel of Qatna
- Empire of Yarim-Lim of Aleppo
- ★ Hurrian finds
- Hittites' campaign of conquest 1595 BC

point... he set up his statues there and ferried... booty across on barges... he marched to Kazallu and turned Kazallu into a ruin heap, so that there was not even a perch for a bird left."

After Sargon's death, aged 85, in 2215BC, his empire lasted for three centuries. Its successor, the First Babylonian Empire, which controlled the whole of Mesopotamia, was the work of another remarkable ruler, Hammurabi. Though known best for formulating the first written codes of law, Hammurabi was also a highly successful warrior whose armies overran all the major city-states in Mesopotamia except for Aleppo and Qanta in the west. After that, the whole of Mesopotamia was united under Hammurabi's rule.

Hammurabi was the first ruler of the Babylonian Empire. At the start of his reign in around 1792BC, Hammurabi's territory extended over a limited area around Bablyon itself. When he died in around 1750BC, a series of wars against neighboring states had given him hegemony over the whole of Mesopotamia.

But after his death in 1750BC, his successors proved unable to exercise similar power and Hammurabi's empire fell to Hittite raiders in around 1600BC.

The Hittites were the most renowned charioteers in the ancient world. Their chariots featured lighter, eight-spoked wheels and held three warriors instead of two. Hittite expertise earned them numerous victories, notably at the Battle of Kadesh in 1299BC in which 5,000 chariots participated. Kadesh, the largest conflict of its type ever fought, led to the Hittite conquest of Syria. The Hittites also made their mark on military history by introducing iron weapons — the hardest and strongest weapons yet — in the early 13th century BC. But though they conquered large areas in Asia Minor and Mesopotamia, the Hittites failed to hold them for long. Instead, they remained essentially raiders and marauders and consequently minor players in the great imperial game that was played out in Mesopotamia in ancient times. They were too preoccupied with internal squabbles and indeterminate struggles with the Egyptians or the Mitanni of northwest Mesopotamia to establish the firm, centralized rule that successful empire-building required. In about 2000BC, when the Hittites first made their presence felt in and around Mesopotamia, their eventual nemesis, Assyria, also rose to power. In time, the Assyrians conquered an empire extending from the Caspian Sea to the Black Sea, across Mesopotamia and northern Arabia into Upper Egypt. Assyria was the world's first military state, infinitely superior in organization, tactics, and siege-craft to any of its contemporaries. Much of this dominance rested on the Assyrian use of iron rather than bronze for weapons, armor, and chariots. Already, by 1000BC, two centuries after the Hittites introduced iron weapons, this new, much stronger metal enjoyed a monopoly of Assyrian army equipment.

Tiglath-Pileser III, King of Assyria from 745BC to 727BC, is considered to be one of the most successful military commanders in history, conquering most of the world known to the ancient Assyrians before his death. The empire grew significantly due to his miliatry reforms. He saw to it that Assyrian superiority was maintained by systematic improvements to weaponry. This, combined with stringent training in the use of weapons, ensured that his army, which could number 50,000 men at one time, kept well ahead of its rivals. Assyrian bowmen, firing iron-tipped arrows with deadly accuracy, routinely slaughtered their enemies and Assyrian expertise at the massed chariot charge enabled them to crash through the enemy infantry, leaving a host of corpses littering the battlefield. The chariots, the main striking force, were closely co-ordinated with archers, cavalry, and close-packed spearmen to provide the irresistible advance that was typical of the later stages of an Assyrian battle plan. By the time the situation reached that point, another Assyrian victory was assured.

Actual fighting, though, was not the whole story. The Assyrians were probably the first to use psychological warfare against their enemies, inducing in them a fear so extreme that they were physically and mentally unable to carry on fighting. When Assyrians captured a town or city, they usually smashed the place to ruins and killed entire populations or carried them off into slavery. By this means, the very name of Assyria became a byword for cruelty and ferocity. However, as history, particularly military history, has so often proved, the mightiest of powers eventually crumbles and by 612BC, after three centuries of supremacy, the Assyrians' turn came when their capital, Nineveh, was destroyed by the Babylonians and Medians. But their fearsome reputation lived on through the centuries. "The Assyrian came down like a wolf on the fold" wrote the 19th century English poet Lord Byron.

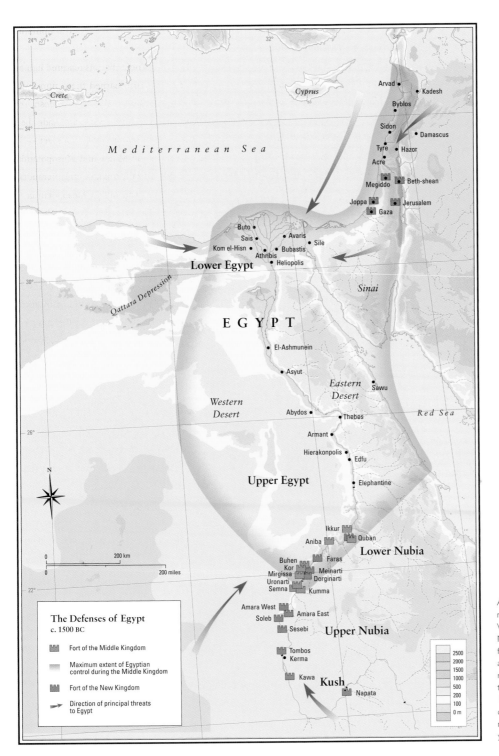

The Defenses of Egypt
c. 1500 BC

⌗ Fort of the Middle Kingdom

⬛ Maximum extent of Egyptian
control during the Middle Kingdom

⌗ Fort of the New Kingdom

→ Direction of principal threats
to Egypt

Ancient Egypt enjoyed strong natural defenses — the Western and Sinai desert, the Mediterranean coast, and the first cataract of the river Nile at Aswan. More defenses were required, though, and during the Middle Kingdom (c.2040-1782BC) numerous forts were constructed, each of them measuring around nearly 24,000 yards square.

OFFENSE, DEFENSE: SIEGE WARFARE IN ANCIENT TIMES

SIEGE WARFARE BECAME INEVITABLE ONCE TOWNSPEOPLE FELT THREATENED BY THEIR NEIGHBORS AND BUILT DEFENSIVE WALLS TO KEEP THEM OUT. THE NEXT STAGE, ALSO INEVITABLE, WAS THE DEVELOPMENT OF SPECIAL WEAPONS TO SCALE, BREACH, OR BREAK DOWN THE DEFENSIVE WALLS.

Towns and cities acquired walls for protection against attack as early as Neolithic times. The town of Jericho, first settled some 11,000 years ago, was once surrounded by a massive wall 10 ft (3m) thick and probably half a mile long. Archeologists excavating it more than half a century ago reckoned that it was surrounded by a moat 10 ft (3m) deep which included a circular tower 33 ft (10m) wide and 28 ft (8.5m) high — and all of it constructed with primitive flint tools. The size of the effort and the time involved must have been colossal, but it was also unavoidable after the introduction of projectile weapons like bows and arrows and slings. At this early stage, town walls were built of mud bricks, strengthened with stone, pieces of wood, or both. Jericho's wall was not the only huge structure of this kind. The walls of Uruk, for instance, were 6 miles (9.6km) long, and 40 ft (12m) high. But size was not only a practical deterrent to an attacking force. Uruk's mighty walls, rearing up into the sky above the Sumerian plain, stood as an indication of strength and power and the fighting qualities of its defenders.

The siege as strategy had already been used by the Sumerians when the Assyrians took it up and improved existing techniques. Accompanying the Assyrian armies were large siege trains containing specialized equipment. Among this equipment were materials designed for building movable wooden towers which, in action, were draped in wetted leather hides to protect them from flaming arrows fired by defenders. Soldiers sited at the tops of the towers unleashed a blizzard of arrows designed to keep defenders away from the walls and prevent them from dropping stones on their attackers. In the meantime, other archers, protected by a phalanx of shields held by spearmen, fired their own flaming arrows in a high trajectory over the walls to land apparently out of the sky in the streets and terrorize the town's inhabitants. The siege trains also carried the crude, but mighty, battering rams. Usually consisting of an entire tree trunk fitted at the front with a sharpened iron tip, they were used to pound their way through a town's gates or other entrances to allow the attacking force to storm in. A more insidious technique was mining, which involved digging into the masonry of a city wall until a cavity was created, then temporarily supporting the wall with wooden props. Before moving out, the miners set fire to the props which eventually crumbled, allowing the wall to collapse.

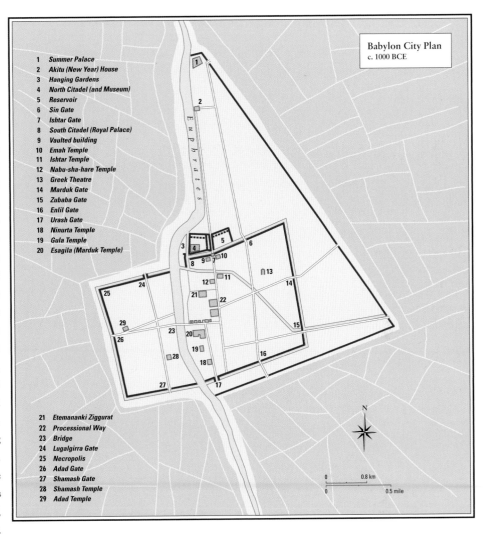

Babylon City Plan
c. 1000 BCE

1 Summer Palace
2 Akitu (New Year) House
3 Hanging Gardens
4 North Citadel (and Museum)
5 Reservoir
6 Sin Gate
7 Ishtar Gate
8 South Citadel (Royal Palace)
9 Vaulted building
10 Emah Temple
11 Ishtar Temple
12 Nabu-sha-hare Temple
13 Greek Theatre
14 Marduk Gate
15 Zubaba Gate
16 Enlil Gate
17 Urash Gate
18 Ninurta Temple
19 Gula Temple
20 Esagila (Marduk Temple)

21 Etemananki Ziggurat
22 Processional Way
23 Bridge
24 Lugalgirra Gate
25 Necropolis
26 Adad Gate
27 Shamash Gate
28 Shamash Temple
29 Adad Temple

0   0.8 km
0   0.5 mile

Defenders standing at the top of the wall fell down with it, as their foothold suddenly disappeared.

Most often though, results in siege warfare were not speedily obtained. The military history of Ancient Egypt records several unduly prolonged sieges. The Egyptians, like the Assyrians and other military leaders in ancient times, far preferred to face their foes on the battlefield and secure a decision in less time and at less cost. But however much they preferred to avoid the siege, this form of warfare also exhausted and demoralized the besieged. Food stocks ran low and could not easily be replenished. The only recourse then was to eat anything that could be chewed and swallowed, such as shoe-leather, or to kill and consume horses, domestic pets, or rats: people could also turn cannibal in situations like this. In addition, disease could run riot inside a surrounded town, where there was nowhere to run to obtain immunity. Eventually, the inhabitants might grow so weak and desperate that they surrendered, and so the city or town would be taken.

Babylon's days of glory commenced in around 1894BC, when its first ruling dynasty was founded. The city acquired 1,332 temples, splendid palaces, immensely strong defensive walls and towers, 24 streets built on a grid system, and the famous Processional Way that was lined with 120 lions in glazed brick.

The Glory of Persia

IN 728BC, THE PERSIAN EMPIRE WAS FOUNDED ON THE PERSIAN PLATEAU BY THE MEDES. FROM THEN ON, ITS RAPID GROWTH WAS MASTERMINDED BY TWO BRILLIANT KINGS OF THE ACHAEMENID DYNASTY. THE FIRST WAS CYRUS THE GREAT.

Cyrus the Great, who began the Persian Empire's rise as the richest, most militarily successful and most extensive in the ancient world, spent almost his entire reign conquering, and afterward, unifying other empires. According to the Greek historian Herodotus, Cyrus "brought into subjection every nation without exception" between his assumption of power in Persia in 559BC and his death in battle in Afghanistan 30 years later. The secret of Cyrus' success was what he himself termed "diversity in counsel, unity in command" whether that principle applied to his tolerant government, his concern for his subjects' welfare, or his style of military leadership. Cyrus' cousin, Darius I, who became ruler of Persia in 521BC, faced six major rebellions during his 35-year reign, yet still managed to "hold the empire together," to quote his own words. In actual fact, he did much more than this. It was Darius who extended the empire all the way east to the Indus Valley of northwest India, and west into Thrace and Macedon on the borders of Ancient Greece. With that, Persia took its place among the major powers of the ancient world.

Although Darius I made his own important contribution to the glory of Persia, what he did was mainly to perfect the military developments made before him by his cousin Cyrus. Cyrus' first task was to instill concepts of discipline and regular training into his troops. This way, he could bring under control the habit long ago adopted by the infantry to operate in a formless mass or make individual attacks whenever opportunity presented itself. Cyrus ordered stringent training and drilling procedures to eliminate these practices which thus far, had made it extremely difficult to organize maneuvers or get troops to act in unison. When properly trained, the infantry was able to outflank the enemy; something the mass assault, however impressive, had rarely been able to achieve. With their short spears, large bows, cane arrows, and daggers hanging from their belts, the new-style Persian infantry was more impressive, more soldierly, and less like a wild rabble. They also had a feeling of pride, fellowship, and common loyalty.

The enemies Cyrus faced often employed horses on the battlefield, which gave them the advantage of a quick escape when danger presented itself, and the ability to strike at foot-soldiers on the ground. The Persians were very adaptable and soon acquired the horsemanship that enabled them to field a phalanx of heavy cavalry ridden by archers who became the best in the ancient world. Under Cyrus II, Cyrus' son and successor Cambyses II who conquered Egypt in 525BC, and Darius I, the Persians had achieved much military glory in a series of successful campaigns that had brought them the largest empire the world had seen up to their time. But sadly, inevitably, the party came to an end after Xerxes I, Darius' son, attacked Greece in 484BC with a huge army backed up by a fleet provided by the Phoenicians of northern Canaan. The Greeks presented the Persians with a particularly tough and stubborn enemy, fanatically devoted to their city-state homelands and to the freedom their topography had enabled them to enjoy. It was no coincidence that democracy, in its early form, first arose among the individualistic Greeks. The Persians were already familiar with the exploits of the hoplites, the well-trained, highly disciplined Greek heavy infantry, since they had themselves employed them as foreign mercenaries in their own armies. Now, facing them in the service of Xerxes as enemies, the Persians were at the business end of

By 560BC, the Kingdom of Egypt had been established for over 2,500 years. The Kingdom of Lydia arose in the 12th century BC. The Median Empire, founded c.715BC, was ruled by the first Iranian dynasty and the New Babylonian Empire, founded c.612BC became the most powerful state in the ancient world.

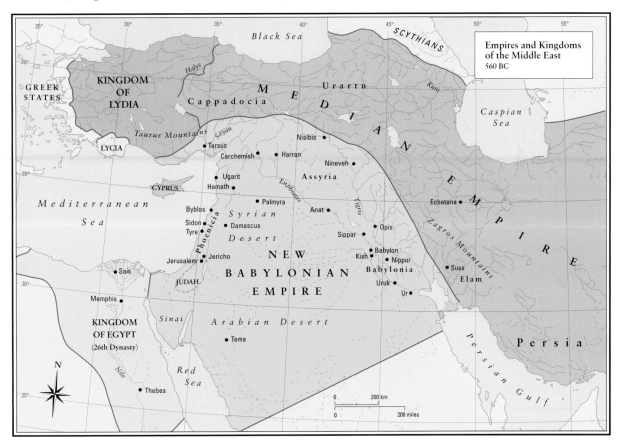

the hoplites' spears which measured up to 10 ft (3m) long, and were pointed directly at them in a long, bristling line. The hoplites were well protected by helmets, breastplates, greaves, and large round shields. They were also superbly fit, honed to peak condition by combat or competitive sports that developed their strength, endurance, and confidence. The hoplites' task, which they frequently accomplished, was to advance to the sound of war flutes, break through the enemy's battle line, and throw his troops into disarray. Once they reached this stage, the hoplites produced their 2ft (60cm) long double-edged swords and set about dispatching their opponents. This was the prospect that confronted Xerxes' army

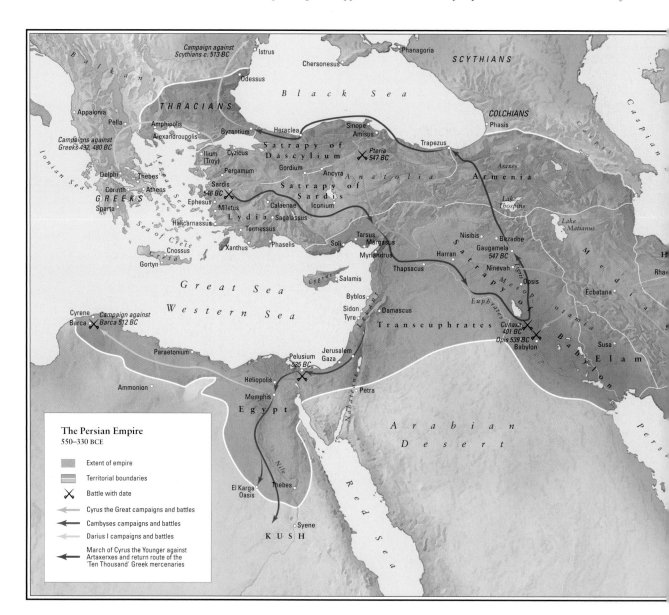

The Persian Empire
550–330 BCE

Extent of empire

Territorial boundaries

✕ Battle with date

◄— Cyrus the Great campaigns and battles

◄— Cambyses campaigns and battles

◄— Darius I campaigns and battles

◄— March of Cyrus the Younger against Artaxerxes and return route of the 'Ten Thousand' Greek mercenaries

in 480BC, when they were defeated by Leonidas, king of the city-state of Sparta, at the narrow mountain pass of Thermopylae. Leonidas, his 300 Spartan soldiers and 700 Thespians all died, but the Persians did not pass. Xerxes got his revenge at Athens, which he destroyed, but was again beaten in 480BC at Salamis, the first naval battle ever recorded. After this Xerxes withdrew to the Hellespont (Dardanelles) where in 479BC he received the dire news that his general Mardonius had been thrashed by the Greeks at the battle of Platea. At that, Xerxes retreated. The Persian Empire was perhaps the greatest in the ancient world.

The Achaemenid Persian Empire founded by Cyrus the Great was the most extensive empire in the ancient world, stretching from southeast Europe to the border of India in the east. It comprised several conquests: the Medean Empire together with the former territory of the Babylonians, Phoenicians, Lydians, and Assyrians.

SUN TZU: THE ART OF WAR

NO ONE KNOWS WHETHER SUN TZU WAS A TRUE HISTORICAL FIGURE OR NOT. WHAT IS CERTAIN IS THAT HIS MILITARY TREATISE, *THE ART OF WAR*, WAS AND REMAINS A HUGELY INFLUENTIAL WORK ON THE CONDUCT OF WAR, POLITICS, AND BUSINESS.

One tradition surrounding Sun Tzu — and there were many — describes him as an eminent general in the service of the King of Wu, who ruled in China between about 544BC and 496BC. Another places him a good deal later, for according to his biography written in the 2nd century BC, Sun was born in Qi, one of the seven nations that fought for control of China during the Warring States period of 476-221BC. *The Art of War* reflected Sun's experience of hostilities as a successful commander which he distilled into a philosophy of war with particular reference to winning battles and stage-managing conflicts. Sun's book still stands as a masterpiece on strategy and later became required reading for those applying for military appointments in the Chinese army. Over the centuries, *The Art of War* has proved an invaluable guide to generations of generals, including Napoleon Bonaparte in the 19th century and the Chinese Communist leader Mao Zedong in the mid-20th. More recently, Sun's precepts were still being used to plan campaigns in the first Gulf War.

Sun Tzu began *The Art of War* by setting out the five constant factors that were essential to the laying of initial plans. The first was the moral law, which inspired people to follow their leader "undismayed by any danger." The next was Heaven, which Sun interpreted as "night and day, cold and heat, times and seasons." The third constant was Earth, its distances, dangers, and security, open ground and narrow passes and the chances it offered for death or survival. After that came the commander of an army and the qualities that made him a good leader — wisdom, sincerity, benevolence, courage, and strictness. The fifth and last constant was method and discipline which included the ordering of an army into divisions, sub-divisions, the gradations of rank, and the practical considerations: the maintenance of roads in a condition suitable for supplying the army and a tight hold on the purse strings to better ensure control

The last chapter of *The Art of War*, written in the 6th century BC by the Chinese military strategist Sun Tzu, deals with the usefulness of spies in warfare. Sun Tzu outlines the tasks of different spies, all of whom can equip a commander with valuable foreknowledge of the enemy.

of military expenditure.

"All warfare," Sun continued "is based on deception. Hence, when able to attack, we must seem unable; when using our forces, we must seem inactive; when we are near, we must make the enemy believe we are far away; when far away, we must make him believe we are near." Exploiting an enemy's weaknesses could be turned into a positive asset, Sun believed. Therefore a pretence of weakness could encourage him to grow arrogant and so be rushed into making mistakes.

Further on in his book, Sun Tzu warned against the destruction of an enemy, his towns, his cities, his army. Far better, he advised, to break an enemy's resistance, ruin his plans, or prevent his forces from linking up. Above all, Sun counseled, avoid besieging walled cities, a wasteful, time-consuming procedure which was the worst strategy of all. Sun went on to explain the disadvantages of siege warfare — the lengthy preparations, the building of ramps against town walls, the wear and tear on a general's patience who, Sun wrote "unable to contain his irritation, will launch his men to the assault like swarming ants, with the result that one third of his men are slain, while the town still remains untaken."

Sun Tzu set out five essentials for victory: knowing when and when not to fight; knowing how to handle both superior and inferior forces; leading an army united in its fighting spirit; being prepared while waiting to take the enemy unprepared; and serving a sovereign who does not interfere with his army's military capacity. At the same time, though, Sun warned against complacency and regarding victory as easy to achieve. "You can be sure of succeeding in your attacks only if you attack places which are undefended," he wrote. "You can ensure the safety of your defense only if you hold positions that cannot be attacked."

"Military tactics," Sun Tzu concluded "are like unto water; for water in its natural course runs away from places and hastens downward. So, in war, the way is to avoid that which is strong and to strike at what is weak."

Sun Tzu is still read today.

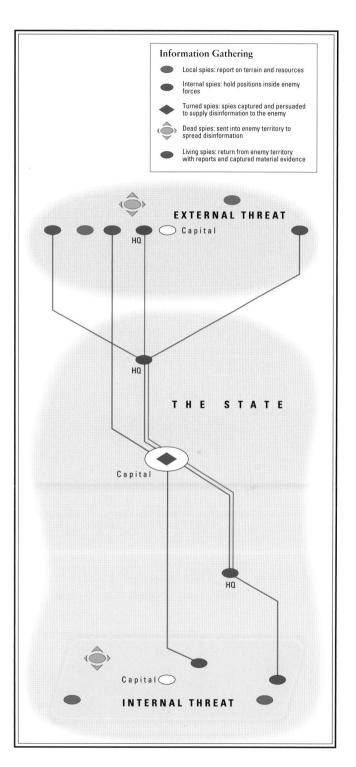

Information Gathering

Local spies: report on terrain and resources

Internal spies: hold positions inside enemy forces

Turned spies: spies captured and persuaded to supply disinformation to the enemy

Dead spies: sent into enemy territory to spread disinformation

Living spies: return from enemy territory with reports and captured material evidence

EXTERNAL THREAT

Capital

HQ

HQ

THE STATE

Capital

HQ

Capital

INTERNAL THREAT

Warfare in the Classical Age

THE RIVALRIES AMONG THE ANCIENT GREEKS OFTEN TOOK THEM TO THE BRINK OF WAR. QUARRELS AMONGST THEMSELVES WERE NOT NECESSARILY SERIOUS, BUT ONCE THEY WERE CONFRONTED WITH POWERFUL PERSIAN INVADERS, THE PICTURE WAS DRASTICALLY CHANGED.

The first Greco-Persian war of 492-490BC and the second, in 480-479BC (see page 25) gave the Greeks frightening examples of foreign invasion and the danger it posed to everything they held dear: their gods, their culture, their democracy, and above all, their independence. Instead, the Greeks found themselves in danger of becoming absorbed in the mighty, far-flung Persian empire whose western frontier, in Anatolia, was only a few miles away across the Aegean Sea. In response, the Greeks did what was least expected of such inveterate rivals: some city-states joined together, and presented a united front against the Persians whose king, Darius I, was resolved to conquer Greece. Darius gathered an immense force for a land-sea expedition which was also a punitive venture, a means of punishing the Greek city-states of Athens and Eritrea for supporting the Ionian revolt against Persian rule. This revolt, in central coastal Anatolia, took place between 499BC and 493BC, but collapsed after its prime mover, the city of Miletus, was besieged and sacked and its forces were thrashed at the battle of Lade Island in 494BC.

The triumphant Darius proved surprisingly conciliatory. He allowed the establishment of democratic rule in some Ionian cities. The Greek ethos predominated in Ionia, as the Persian aristocracy was encouraged to participate in Greek religious practices, intermarry with Greeks, and give their children Greek rather than Persian names. This was a giant propaganda exercise to win over the city-states of the Greek mainland and persuade their citizens that nothing really important was going to change if they transferred their allegiance to the Persian Empire. After allowing sufficient time for these temptations to sink in, Darius sent heralds to Greece to demand the submission of the city-states. Most of them readily gave in, but Athens, Darius' prime target, together with Sparta, the most militant of the city-states, were among the leading exceptions.

With that, Darius once again resorted to total war, only to find that luck and the gods were on the side of the Greeks. In 492BC, a campaign by Darius' general Mardonius met with disaster. His fleet was wrecked in a violent storm off the coast of Mount Athos in Macedonia. In a raid by

A sculpture from Ancient Persopolis. The mighty city of Persopolis was built by Darius I who lead several campaigns against the well-defended Ancient Greek city-states.

a Thracian tribe, the general was injured and was obliged to withdraw. Darius tried again in 491BC, this time gathering a massive force of close on 50,000 men for an amphibious landing near Marathon, some 20 miles (32km) northeast of Athens. When the Athenians learned of the impending invasion, they sent an urgent message to the Spartans, asking for help. The Spartans proved willing, but were delayed by a religious festival and arrived too late to take part in the ensuing battle of Marathon. Meanwhile, a small force from the city of Plataea joined the Athenians and together, they routed the Persians at Marathon with a double envelopment of their center: according to the Ancient Greek historian Herodotus, 6,400 Persians were killed while the survivors ran for their ships in a headlong effort to get away.

The infuriated Darius planned his revenge, but died, in 486BC, before he could achieve it. The task was taken up by his son and successor, King Xerxes I, in 480BC, (see page 25). However he too was forced to play "Goliath" to the Greek "David" as the Spartan heroics at Thermopolyae and the triumph of the Greek fleet at Salamis, both in 480BC, destroyed the Persians' war effort. Further clashes, notably the naval battles at Eurymedon in 466BC and at another Salamis, this time in Cyprus, in 450BC, obliged the Persians to make peace with the Greeks at Callias in 448BC. Their triumph in the Greco-Persian wars may have been unexpected, but it was, all the same, a close-run thing. This was a fact which the Greeks were wise enough to realize and it changed their attitude to war. First of all, it was clearly impossible for a single city-state to overcome the might of the Persian armies with their huge manpower and economic, strategic, and geographic strength. Success in such circumstances could be achieved only by alliances between the city-states and a pooling of resources. This would serve to increase available manpower and finances, permit warfare on a greater and more diversified scale, and enlarge the scope of strategy and tactics.

In theory, therefore, the armies of Ancient Greece could become a force to be reckoned with and a positive deterrent to future invaders. Unfortunately, this was not the first result to come out of the reorganizing of the Greek armed forces. Instead, the Greeks returned to their rivalries and jealousies as Athens and Sparta and their allies muscled up to each other in a long and horrifically destructive civil war between themselves.

THE ANCIENT GREEKS AT WAR

IN ANCIENT GREECE, THE CITY-STATES OF ATHENS AND SPARTA WERE OFTEN AT LOGGERHEADS, DUE MAINLY TO THE TOTAL DIFFERENCE IN THEIR ETHOS. THE ATHENIANS WERE ARTISTIC, AND MATERIALISTIC. THE SPARTANS WERE MILITARY MARTINETS. THE UPSHOT WAS RIVALRY AND WAR.

O nce the danger posed by the Persians was over, it took Athens and Sparta no more than a year to revert to their dislike and disapproval of each other. The city of Athens had been destroyed during the second Greco-Persian war, a disaster that secretly pleased the Spartans who abhorred the Athenians for their self-indulgent love of luxury, and money-making. The rebuilding of Athens after the war dismayed the Spartans, since it helped stimulate the city's commercial eminence and wealth. The Athenians hated Spartan asceticism and their ruthless, militaristic disposition. Each city had a specific grudge against the other — Athens over Sparta's cruel suppression of helots (serfs), Sparta over Athens' autocratic control over its allies in the Delian League and the creation of a virtual empire from the territory of League members.

Delian League states were spread around the Aegean coast of Greece and Anatolia. Sparta, too, had its allies, in the Peloponnesian League, a less extensive grouping which shared with Sparta the island of Lakonia in southeastern Greece. Members of this League included Corinth, whose economic rivalry with Athens sparked off the first of the Peloponnesian Wars in 460BC. Aegina, another state in the Peloponnesian League, joined in, but its ships were overwhelmed by the Athenian fleet in 458BC and the city was besieged and captured in the following year.

It was at this stage that Sparta stepped in, renounced the alliance with Athens that had made them allies in the Greco-Persian wars, and in 457BC, engaged the Athenians at the battle of Tanagra, near Thebes. According to the contemporary Greek historian Thucydides, the Athenians fielded "their whole army, supported by 1,000 troops from Argos and by contingents from their other allies, making up altogether a force of 14,000 men." Tanagra was nevertheless a disaster for the Athenians, who were

Although, as the map shows, Greece was full of extremely difficult, mountainous country, it was by no means impervious to invasion. Among the earliest invaders, the Dorian people have been blamed for the destruction of the Mycenean civilization in around 1100BC. Other invaders included the extensive armies of the Persians and the Romans.

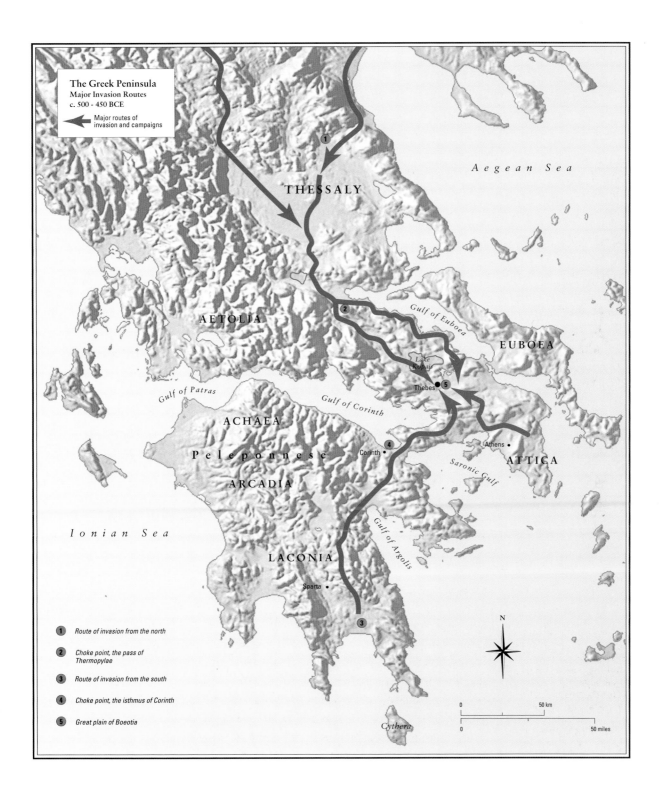

The Greek Peninsula
Major Invasion Routes
c. 500 - 450 BCE

Major routes of
invasion and campaigns

THESSALY

Aegean Sea

AETOLIA

Gulf of Euboea

EUBOEA

Lake
Kopais

Thebes

Gulf of Patras

Gulf of Corinth

ACHAEA

Peleponnese

Corinth

Athens

ARCADIA

Saronic Gulf

ATTICA

Ionian Sea

Gulf of Argolis

LACONIA

Sparta

N

Cythera

① Route of invasion from the north

② Choke point, the pass of
Thermopylae

③ Route of invasion from the south

④ Choke point, the isthmus of Corinth

⑤ Great plain of Boeotia

0   50 km

0   50 miles

smashed to defeat.

Despite some successes over the next ten years, the war severely weakened the Athenians. Athens was soon threatened by revolts inside the Delian League, lost its hold on its territories in mainland Greece, and had its once renowned Navy decimated to such an extent that it could barely retain its control of the seas. Pericles, renowned statesman and "first citizen" of Athens, realized that Athenian strength lay not in military adventures but in trade and the planting of colonies overseas. In 445 BC, he managed to mastermind a 30-year peace.

Peace lasted only a third of that time and by 432BC, Sparta and Athens were fighting the second Peloponnesian War. The Athenians won several victories, notably their destruction of cities along the Peloponnesian coast, but the Spartans had the last word: in 422BC, their general, Brasidas, mounted a surprise attack at Amphipolis and crushed the Athenian forces. Unfortunately, the terms of the Peace of Nicias that followed in 421BC proved so unacceptable that alliances which had held good for some 40 years fell apart. Both sides forged new links and Athens took the field again in 418BC backed by its new allies — Argos, Mantinea, and Elis. But the Spartans soon made mincemeat of that: their King, Agis, invaded Argos and Mantinea, and the allies were decisively beaten.

At this low point in the Athenians' fortunes, a new leader, Alcibiades, appeared on the scene: forget the Peloponnesian League, he told Athenians, a better, more lucrative target was Sicily, which many Greeks considered a land of opportunity. In 415BC, Alcibiades prepared an expedition against Syracuse, Sicily's richest city. Alcibiades' fleet included 136 triremes and 136 transports to carry some 5,000 hoplites and a force of light troops. But before he could reach Sicily, Alcibiades' political enemies trumped up charges of sacrilege against him, accusing him of mutilating statuettes of the Greek god Hermes. Alcibiades abandoned the expedition and fled to Sparta where he turned traitor and advised the Spartans to reinforce the defenses of Syracuse. The Spartans took his advice, and the upshot was that an Athenian army preparing to besiege Syracuse was thwarted in 414BC. Worse was to follow. The following year, forces from the Greek state of Corinth got together with Syracuse and annihilated the Athenian navy. Afterwards the remnants of the Athenian army were pursued and captured, their generals Nicias and Demosthenes were executed, and the survivors became slaves.

Three years later, the feckless Alcibiades switched allegiances once again. In 410BC, he was leading a restored and much strengthened Athenian Navy against the Peloponnesian fleet and scored an overwhelming victory at the battle of Cyzicus. Two years after that, Alcibiades led an Athenian force in the capture of Byzantium (now Istanbul in Turkey) on the shore of the Bosphorus. However, Alcibiades was soon running out of triumphs. In 406BC, he encountered Lysander, the Spartan commander who turned out to be his nemesis. Four times Lysander refused enticements to fight, waiting to wear down the Athenians' watchfulness. And the very moment they relaxed, Lysander struck, attacking 200 vessels of the Athenian fleet which were moored for the night at Aegospotami, near the Hellespont (Dardanelles). Destruction was total. The Spartans destroyed the Athenian fleet in its entirety and most of the crews were slaughtered. It was the end. Lysander's triumph at Aegospotami was the signal for a Spartan siege of Athens whose inhabitants were starved into submission within six months. Athens surrendered in the spring of 404BC and the Peloponnesian Wars were over. The same year, the faithless Alcibiades was assassinated.

In 490BC, Darius I of Persia (Darius the Great) landed his troops at a bay near Marathon, 20 miles (32km) northeast of Athens. The Athenians marched an army to the site and blocked both exits from the plain of Marathon, attacked the Persians and routed Darius' infantry.

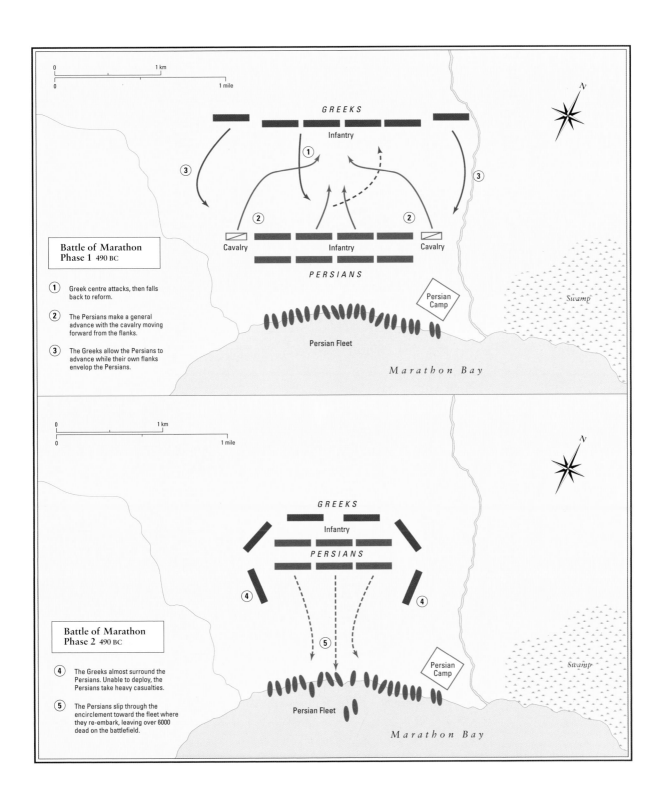

Battle of Marathon
Phase 1 490 BC

(1) Greek centre attacks, then falls back to reform.

(2) The Persians make a general advance with the cavalry moving forward from the flanks.

(3) The Greeks allow the Persians to advance while their own flanks envelop the Persians.

Battle of Marathon
Phase 2 490 BC

(4) The Greeks almost surround the Persians. Unable to deploy, the Persians take heavy casualties.

(5) The Persians slip through the encirclement toward the fleet where they re-embark, leaving over 6000 dead on the battlefield.

THE AGE OF ALEXANDER

ALEXANDER THE GREAT WAS A MILITARY GENIUS. DESPITE THE LAPSE OF 2,330 YEARS SINCE HIS PREMATURE DEATH AT AGE 32, HIS INSPIRED AND INNOVATIVE STRATEGIES AND TACTICS STAND AS EXAMPLES OF A STYLE OF WARFARE THAT IS STILL APPLICABLE TODAY.

Alexander, aged 20, became King of Macedon in 336BC after the assassination of his father, Philip. Philip had managed to bring most of the city-states of mainland Greece under Macedonian hegemony. Alexander also inherited his father's position as Captain-General. The Persians were threatening Greece at this time, and despite Alexander's youth, all the Greek city-states — apart from Sparta — elected him to lead their army as Captain-General of the Hellenes (Greeks). For Darius, King of Persia, the idea that the inexperienced Alexander could challenge the mighty Persian Empire was a joke. So much so that Alexander and his army had penetrated deep inside Persian territory before Darius woke up to the danger they represented. He acted too late. Alexander scored a stunning victory with a double strike at the battle of the Granicus River in 334BC. The Macedonian cavalry and light infantry assaulted the Persian line from the left while Alexander and his personal bodyguards charged through on horseback to smash the Persian center. The cavalry surged through the resultant gap to rout the Persian infantry and cavalry. This first demonstration of unorthodox warfare was repeated in several battles over the next four years. The pattern became so obvious that many Persian towns surrendered without a fight rather than risk the destruction, looting and death, or enslavement that was often the price of defeat in ancient times. Naturally, this option was not open to King Darius. Instead, he kept on trying to overcome Alexander. Once or twice, he came close, but never succeeded. For example, at the siege of Halicarnassus in 334BC, Alexander's forces were obliged to retreat when faced with bombardment from the defenders' catapults, but hit back by breaking through the city walls. After vanquishing the Persians again in two more sieges — at Tyre and Gaza — Alexander proceeded into Syria. He met Darius again at Gaugamela in 331BC,

At Gaugamela in AD 331, King Darius III of Persia expected to triumph over Alexander the Great by sheer weight of numbers. But Alexander ordered an attack on the Persian center, which weakened it, and his 1,000 Agrarians demolished Darius' chariots. Darius' battle line fell apart and he fled the battlefield.

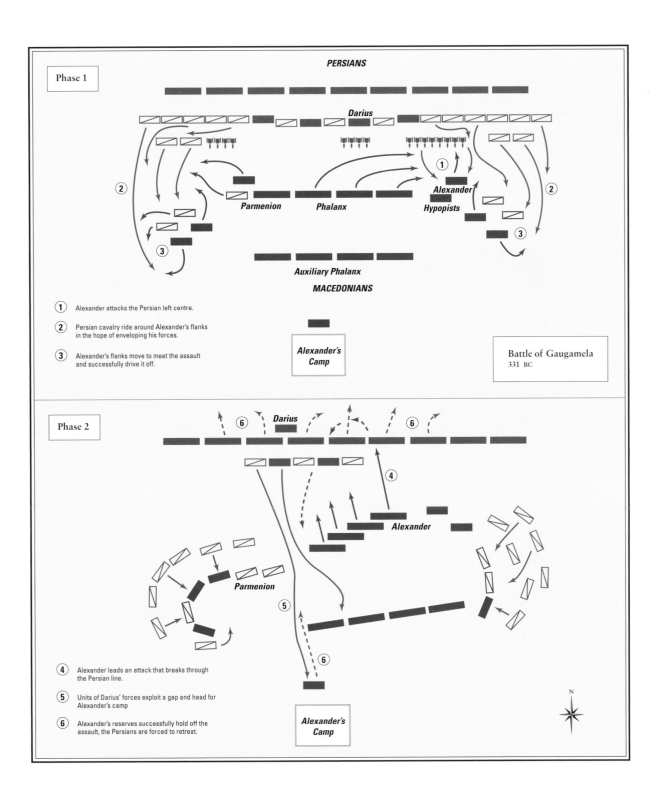

Phase 1

PERSIANS

Darius

Alexander

Parmenion   *Phalanx*

Hypopists

Auxiliary Phalanx

MACEDONIANS

① Alexander attacks the Persian left centre.

② Persian cavalry ride around Alexander's flanks in the hope of enveloping his forces.

③ Alexander's flanks move to meet the assault and successfully drive it off.

Alexander's Camp

Battle of Gaugamela
331 BC

Phase 2

Darius

Alexander

Parmenion

④ Alexander leads an attack that breaks through the Persian line.

⑤ Units of Darius' forces exploit a gap and head for Alexander's camp

⑥ Alexander's reserves successfully hold off the assault, the Persians are forced to retreat.

Alexander's Camp

N

where the Persian king massed a huge army, including a mighty force of chariots. But Alexander's Agrianarians, 1,000 ferocious mountain men, weakened the Persian center. Alexander then charged at the center and forced a way through. As he fled, Darius was intercepted and stabbed to death by Bassus, the satrap (provincial governor) of Bactria. Alexander was now effectively ruler of the Persian

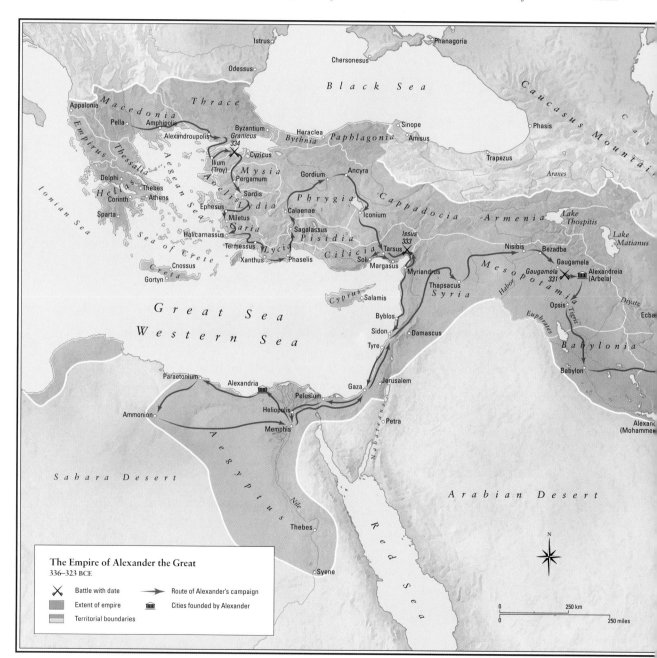

The Empire of Alexander the Great
336–323 BCE

✗ Battle with date

⬛ Extent of empire

⬛ Territorial boundaries

➔ Route of Alexander's campaign

🏛 Cities founded by Alexander

Empire, but he wanted much more than that. He longed to rule the whole world which, in his time, "ended" in eastern India, and managed to conquer much territory there. Eventually, Alexander's army had campaigned across 11,000 miles (18,000 km) in eight years. Weary and far from home, Alexander turned back for Greece, but never got there. He died in Babylon in 323BC, probably from malaria.

Alexander the Great was the supreme military prodigy of the ancient world. He led his army along a trail of conquest that earned him a far-flung empire.

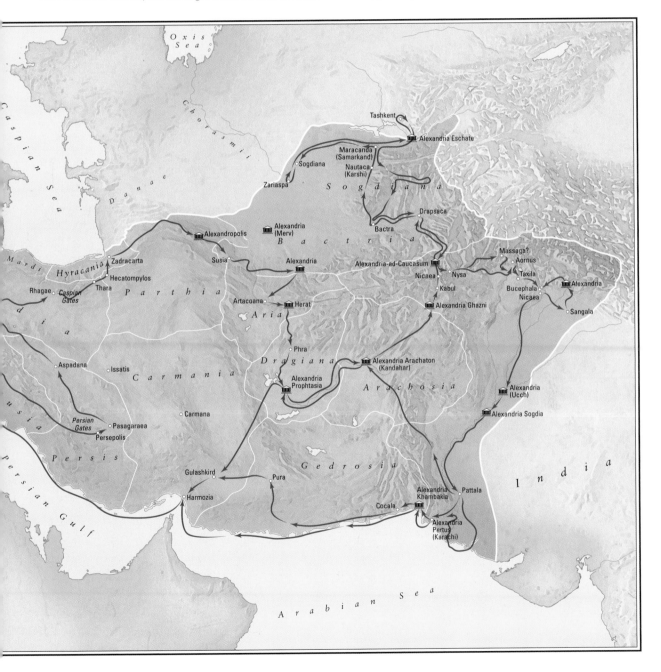

The Emergence of Rome

ROME WAS THE MIGHTIEST POWER IN THE ANCIENT WORLD, WITH THE MOST SUCCESSFUL ARMY, AND, EVENTUALLY, THE GREATEST LAND EMPIRE EVER KNOWN IN EUROPE. TRADITIONALLY, ROME WAS FOUNDED IN 753BC BUT ITS BEGINNINGS COULD NOT HAVE BEEN MORE HUMBLE.

The city began as two small villages high above the River Tiber on the Palatine Hill, one of the seven hills of Rome. Located along the Mediterranean sea, as early as the 10th century BC, this little township was to grow into one of the largest empires of the ancient world. The earliest Romans lived in simple huts made of wood and wickerwork plastered with clay and thatched with straw. On the rich pastureland surrounding their villages, the Romans planted their crops and tended their flocks. They were not just farmers, but soldier-farmers. Ancient Italy, like Ancient Greece, was a collection of settlements divided among at least eight assorted groups. Rome was one of the Latin states, and the smallest of them. In Greece, a similar diversity had led to constant rivalry and war. Italy had potential to be the same, but the Romans, a disciplined and practical people, saw to it that the peninsula took a different route. The Latin states had strong trade and cultural links within the Latin League, but this was not good enough for the ambitious, expansionist Romans. They aimed for mastery and in 341BC, a war broke out among the Latins. Within three years, the Romans emerged as victors, but victors of an unusual kind. Instead of oppressing their defeated enemies, they offered them Roman citizenship and the status of allies rather than subjects. A conquered enemy turned ally could be a positive advantage. They could colonize an ally's territory, so offering more living space than the Roman's own, increasingly crowded city could provide. In addition, defeated troops furnished more soldiers for the Roman Army rather than requiring the Romans to spend time, money, and blood to keep a vanquished foe in order.

By 250BC a professional standing army had evolved with the Roman legion at its core. In an effort to build on its already considerable might, the army's cavalry was expanded and the reliance on hand-to-hand combat reduced. The cavalry were eventually one-quarter of the typical Roman army.

The Ancient Romans soon learned that Italy was full of rivals. Their response was to make their army a crack fighting force. The new Roman Army overcame all its rivals until, by 270BC, Roman territory covered Italy from Rimini in the north to the Straits of Messina in the south.

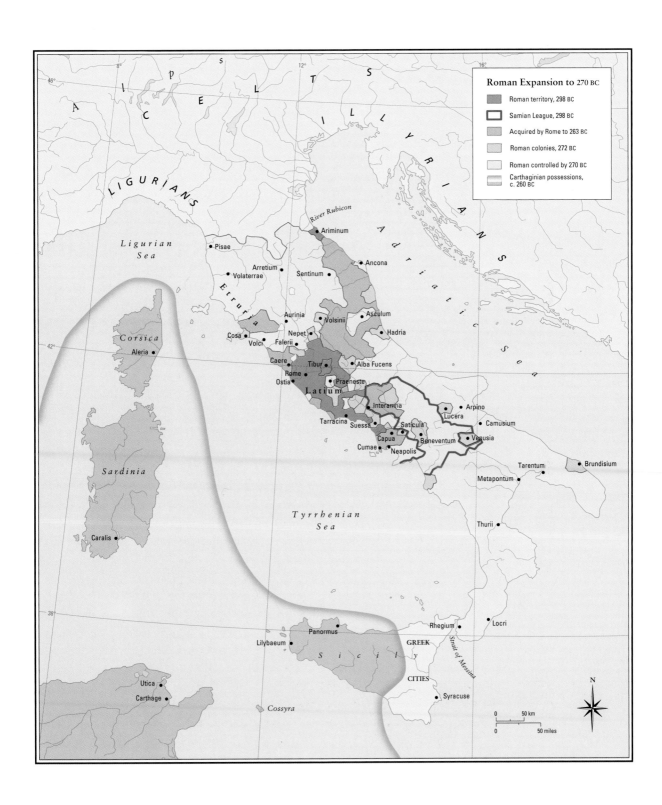

Roman Expansion to 270 BC

- Roman territory, 298 BC
- Samian League, 298 BC
- Acquired by Rome to 263 BC
- Roman colonies, 272 BC
- Roman controlled by 270 BC
- Carthaginian possessions, c. 260 BC

A L P S

C E L T S

I L L Y R I A N S

LIGURIANS

Ligurian Sea

River Rubicon

• Ariminum

• Pisae

Arretium •
Volaterrae •

Sentinum •

• Ancona

Etruria

Aurinia •

• Volsinii

• Asculum

Cosa •
Volci •

Nepet •

Falerii

• Hadria

Corsica

Aleria •

Caere •

Tibur •

• Alba Fucens

Rome •
Ostia •

Latium

Praeneste

Interamna •

• Arpino

• Lucera

Sardinia

Tarracina •

Suessa •

Saticula •

• Camusium

Benevbentum •

• Venusia

Capua •

Cumae •

Neapolis •

• Tarentum

• Metapontum

• Brundisium

Caralis •

Tyrrhenian Sea

Adriatic Sea

• Thurii

Utica •

Panormus •

Lilybaeum •

Sicily

Rhegium •

• Locri

GREEK

CITIES

Strait of Messina

Carthage •

Cossyra

• Syracuse

N

0   50 km

0   50 miles

The strong discipline of the early Roman Army accounted for most of their success. Many of their enemies tended to use the "mass rush" technique, each man hurtling toward his opponents brandishing his weapons and shouting terrifying war cries. This could be very frightening, but the Romans did not frighten easily. Their legions kept in close, strong phalanx formation and as the enemy came within fighting distance, the Romans lunged out at them and drove them back. Through these sophisticated fighting methods followed by magnanimity in victory, Rome's power gradually spread from the banks of the Tiber until, by around 275BC, it covered almost all of Italy, from Pisa and Rimini in the north to the Straits of Messina and Brindisi in the south. From there, Italy served as a springboard for Roman expansion overseas.

By temperament as well as training, the Romans were well suited to the task of building, preserving, and organizing an empire. They may not have been the most imaginative people and, in fact, borrowed their art, architecture, and even their gods from the more artistic and inspirational Greeks, but they majored in method, organization, and the other sturdy qualities that empire-building — and successful soldiering — required. Soldiers were the most admired and most honored of men and acquiring military glory was an important aim. Their role models were the legendary heroes of Rome who were either fearless warriors or men who were willing to sacrifice everything that was dear to them, even life itself, for the sake of Rome and its ideals.

Inevitably, the Roman army sometimes lost battles, but never a war, and fought to a pattern that brought them much of their success. Protected by elliptical or oblong shields made of wood, hemp, and leather, studded with a sharp central boss and rimmed with a strip of iron, the Romans advanced towards their opponents in strong formation, waiting for the moment to start hurling their iron-tipped javelins (*pilum*). These javelins were over 6ft (3m) long and each soldier carried two. When the javelins had duly confused and alarmed the enemy, the Romans charged at them with their short swords, or *gladius*. At times, the Romans found themselves in a tight spot and for that, they employed special battle tactics. One of them was the *testudo* (tortoise): the Romans made themselves into an armored column with overlapping shields that formed the "roof" and sides, and from beneath its safety stabbed out at their attackers. The testudo later developed another role, as protection for soldiers handling battering rams during sieges. The ram was slung from the beams of the "roof" and the whole thing was equipped with a wheeled platform. The Romans were also protected by their armor, wearing a metal breastplate made from overlapping strips of metal stretching from his neck to his waist. Their helmets covered the entire head, ending at the back in a flange, a flat rim that jutted outwards to protect the base of the skull.

The Romans made regular use of engines of war, which in time became a standard part of a legion's equipment. Each legion possessed up to ten catapults and, for hurling larger missiles into a besieged city, 60 ballistae. A really big ballista could throw a stone weighing 50lb (23kg) over a distance of 400 yd (366m). Missiles from these monster machines could easily kill anyone unlucky enough to be caught in their path and destroy or severely damage anything they struck. But the machines were difficult to move and would normally be used from one position during a siege or battle. More mobile was the smaller scorpion which required a small crew of only two soldiers. The scorpion was a very large bow whose wooden arms were drawn back by winches to fire a very large arrow.

"Legion" can describe the entire Roman army, or more specifically, the heavy infantry of the army at the time of the late Republic (before 27BC). The consular army was the force commanded by the consuls who were elected annually as heads of the Republican government of Rome and as magistrates.

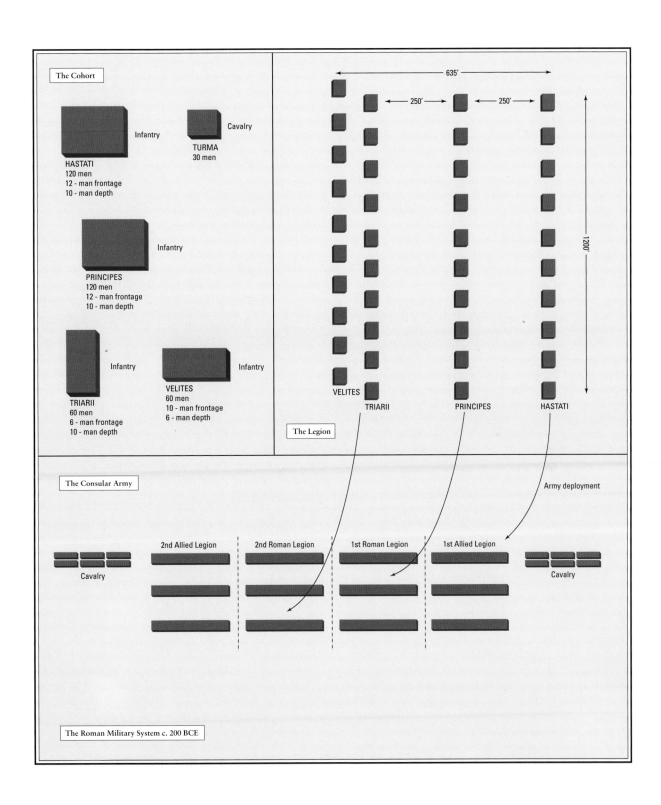

The Cohort

Infantry
HASTATI
120 men
12 - man frontage
10 - man depth

Cavalry
TURMA
30 men

Infantry
PRINCIPES
120 men
12 - man frontage
10 - man depth

Infantry
TRIARII
60 men
6 - man frontage
10 - man depth

Infantry
VELITES
60 men
10 - man frontage
6 - man depth

The Legion

635'
250'
250'
1200'

VELITES
TRIARII
PRINCIPES
HASTATI

The Consular Army

Army deployment

Cavalry
2nd Allied Legion
2nd Roman Legion
1st Roman Legion
1st Allied Legion
Cavalry

The Roman Military System c. 200 BCE

THE THREE PUNIC WARS

AFTER ROME WON THE PUNIC WARS AGAINST THE CARTHAGINIANS, THEY RECEIVED MORE THAN VICTORY: THEY ALSO INHERITED THE CARTHAGINIAN EMPIRE, BASED IN PRESENT DAY TUNISIA, ONE OF THE LONGEST-LASTING AND LARGEST IN THE ANCIENT MEDITERRANEAN.

The Romans came face to face with the Carthaginians in around 275BC, when their conquests in Italy reached the Straits of Messina in the southwest of the peninsula. There, only 10 miles (16km) of water separated them from Punic (Phoenician) settlers on the island of Sicily, who soon became their rivals. Carthage, meaning "new town," had been founded by the Phoenicians, by tradition in 814BC, which made it some 60 years older than Rome, and the two cities and their inhabitants were very much alike. The Carthaginians, too, went in for conquest and were fearless, adventurous, hardworking and warlike. Where the Romans were superior on land, the Carthaginians were their equals at sea.

In 508BC and 507BC, before they acquired their empire, which included Sardinia, Corsica, the Balearic Islands, parts of Spain, and most of Sicily, the Carthaginians had signed treaties with the Romans. But in 264BC, conflict arose between them at Messina in northeast Sicily, and what began as a trivial quarrel exploded into a full-scale war, the First Punic War, which lasted for 23 years. At the start, the Romans had nothing like the naval strength or skill of the Carthaginians. To remain in contention, they had to build their first fleet in 260BC. The Romans were virtual novices at naval warfare, so it came as a huge shock to the Carthaginians when this new fleet won its first battle. In 256BC, the Romans routed the entire Carthaginian fleet off Licata in southern Sicily and in 241BC, they rowed out in a violent storm to sink or capture most of the Carthaginian ships in a battle off western Sicily. This last triumph settled the First Punic War. The Carthaginians, who had lost Corsica to the Roman armies, and had their power greatly weakened in Sicily and Spain, sued for peace.

The peace terms forced the Carthaginians to hand over Sicily to the Romans, as well as the Lipari

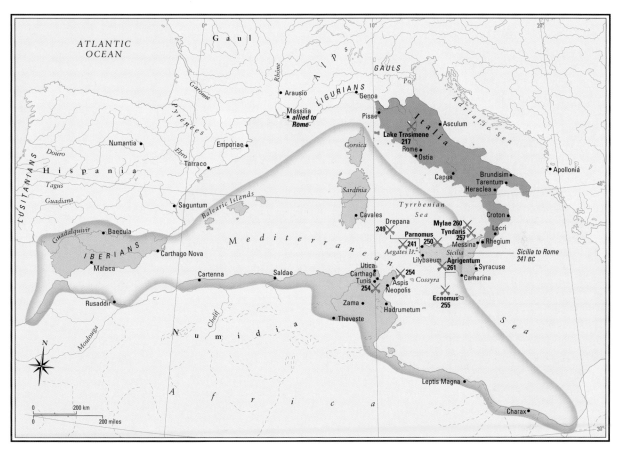

First Punic War
264–241 BC

◼ Controlled by Rome 264 BC

◼ Carthaginian Empire 264 BC

◻ Controlled by Carthage 241 BC

✕ Major battle

Islands and the sum of 3,200 talents. Suffering defeat and surrendering land and money was bad enough, but the greatest loss for the Carthaginians was loss of naval supremacy in the Mediterranean. The shame and fury this created fed a fierce desire for vengeance. Before long, the Carthaginians were building up a new base in Spain for a new attack on Rome. In Spain, they gradually regained the power they had lost, brought men and equipment over from Carthage, and penetrated inland toward Spain's rich gold and silver mines. This made the Romans very suspicious. So did the fact that this activity was being masterminded by a man of real ability, Hamilcar Barca. Hamilcar was determined to avenge the defeat of Carthage and made his son, Hannibal, swear a solemn oath of eternal enmity with Rome. In 221 BC, when Hannibal was 26 years old, he took over command in Spain and in him, the Romans faced a truly formidable foe. Hannibal was a military genius. He was also a hot-tempered young man who had seethed with anger in 238 BC when the Romans made Carthage give up Sardinia and pay another hefty fine of 1,200 talents. Hannibal's fury escalated even further when the Carthaginians were forced to limit their power in Spain to the region south of the River Ebro. Hannibal's resentment and Rome's suspicions led to war once more, in 218 BC, the year in which Hannibal overran the Greek colony of Saguntum (Murviedro) in Spain. Saguntum was a Roman ally, but when Roman ambassadors demanded

The Romans and Carthaginians, both warlike, adventurous, and expansionist, were natural rivals. However, the Romans were the more powerful of the two and in the first Punic War, they beat the Carthaginians at sea, where the Carthaginians had, till then, been supreme. The Romans also captured the Carthaginian island of Corsica.

In the Second Punic War, the Carthaginian leader Hannibal invaded Italy by crossing the Alps but was stopped by the Roman general Fabius Maximus, who adopted a guerrilla strategy.

Second Punic War
218–201 BC

Carthaginian Empire 218 BC

Roman Empire 218 BC

Scipio's campaign
218–210 BC

Roman campaign against
Macedonia 216–211 BC

Movements of Carthaginian
fleet 215–209 BC

Hannibal's campaign
216–203 BC

Hasdrubal's campaign
208–207 BC

Mago's campaign
205–203 BC

Major battle

that Hannibal hand over the town to them, he refused. The infuriated Romans declared war. Hannibal won several victories. The worst defeat for the Romans came at Cannae in 216BC. The Romans planned to win by driving straight through the center of Hannibal's army. He allowed them to do so, but while the Romans were pressing forward, packed closely together and blinded by hot clouds of dry dust, Hannibal's cavalry wheeled in from behind and closed them in a trap. Out of 60,000 Roman soldiers, only 10,000 managed to escape. The survivors suffered the appalling shame of bending down to pass under a yoke of spears.

When news of the disaster at Cannae reached Rome, a mood of despair permeated the city. But despair was short lived and was soon replaced by a typically Roman determination to resist Hannibal. In any case, the situation was not as bad as it appeared. Roman armies in Spain were preventing reinforcements from Carthage from reaching Hannibal and Rome's central Italian allies remained loyal. Without their help, Hannibal had no hope of capturing Rome. Soon, Hannibal and his forces became wanderers in Italy. On the way, they were constantly harassed by Roman guerilla forces. Under their patient general, Quintus Fabius Maximus, the Romans watched the Carthaginians from a distance, ready to pounce on any isolated detachment, slowly wearing their enemies down. Meanwhile,

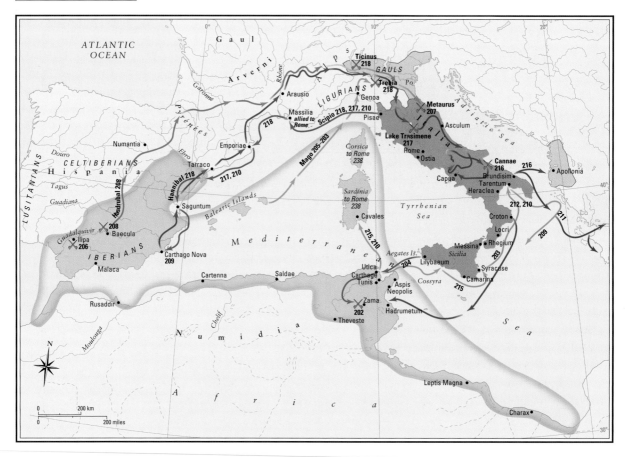

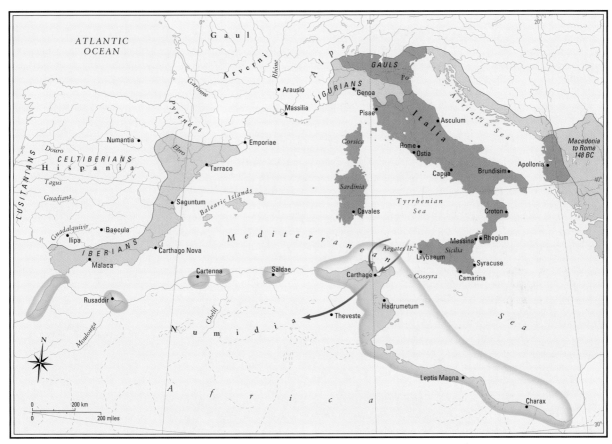

Third Punic War
149–146 BC

▮ Roman Empire c. 200 BC

▮ Roman expansion to 149 BC

▮ Carthaginian Empire
c. 149 BC

→ Carthaginian attacks on
Numidia 150 BC

➤ Roman attacks and siege
on Carthage 147–146 BC

in 204BC, other Roman forces landed on the North African coast to make a direct attack on the city of Carthage itself. Finally, the exhausted Hannibal sailed home in 203BC, to help defend his city. He failed. The Romans, led by Scipio Africanus, used Hannibal's own strategy at Cannae to defeat the Carthaginians. The terms of the treaty that ended the second Punic War in 201BC were extremely harsh. The Carthaginians were forced to give up all their colonies, their war elephants , and all but ten of their warships. The Romans took 100 hostages and exacted a fine of 200 silver talents a year for 50 years. The Carthaginians were not permitted to sign treaties and could not make alliances or fight wars unless the Romans gave permission.

Carthage was left in a state of total humiliation and pitiful weakness, but even so, the Romans remained suspicious, with Senator Cato declaring: "Delenda est Carthago (Carthage must be destroyed)." Ultimately, in the Third Punic War, the Romans destroyed Carthage so completely that nothing remained of it. They besieged the city in 149BC and after it fell three years later, burned it to a mass of ashes and rubble. Finally, they ploughed over the land where Carthage had once stood and sowed salt on the site, in this way casting a symbolic curse on it forever. Of the city's 250,000 inhabitants, only 50,000 survived the siege and they were sold into slavery.

Cato, a Roman senator, ended every speech he made with the words: "Carthago delenda est" — Carthage must be destroyed. Cato got his way with the Third Punic War of 149BC-146BC in which Carthage was totally destroyed. 200,000 of its inhabitants died, and the surviving 50,000 were sold into slavery.

Pax Romana

PAX ROMANA — THE ROMAN PEACE — WAS AN OASIS OF CIVILIZATION IN A BRUTAL WORLD. ON THE FACE OF IT, THE PEACE ALLOWED CITIZENS OF THE ROMAN EMPIRE TO ENJOY SECURITY, PROSPERITY, AND COMFORT. BUT THIS WAS NOT ALWAYS THE CASE.

P ax Romana could never have existed without the Roman Army. Danger was never far away and the legions' task was to police the frontiers of the Empire, fending off barbarians who constantly tried to break in. In reality, the Empire was an armed camp. However, the soldiers on guard duty had no chance of sharing the benefits they enabled other Romans to enjoy. Living conditions were simple and rough, with the men living in stone or wooden barracks, surrounded by strong stone walls and defensive ditches. Patrols guarded the camp and its four gates, ready at any moment to light the fire, which, by night, served as a warning of danger. By day, the signal was a column of smoke.

On the march, soldiers carried their weapons, food, and cooking utensils as well as saws and sickles. When legionaries camped for the night, they constructed an earth wall and dug a wide ditch for protection against attack. Danger could lurk on every riverbank, in every wood, around every hill, and in every valley. For at least one Roman commander, Quintilus Varus, this danger turned to total disaster. In 9AD, Varus was leading three legions — around 60,000 men — through densely wooded hill country between the rivers Rhine and Vistula when the Cherusci, a German tribe, attacked and killed them all. Except for Quintilus Varus who, rather than become a prisoner of barbarians, committed suicide in the Roman fashion, by falling on his sword.

Potentially, every Roman soldier faced this fate throughout the 20 years' service he gave to the Army. In exchange, he got his pay, his clothing, his weapons and after he retired — if he lived long enough, that is — a gratuity of 3,000 denarii (around US $888) and perhaps a plot of land to farm. Although a soldier's pay was hardly princely — only 300 denarii a year (US $22) — some soldiers still managed to put away savings in the banks run by their legions. A soldier's food was not particularly palatable. A legionary's diet consisted of vegetables and porridge, washed down with bitter-tasting wine. Meat was

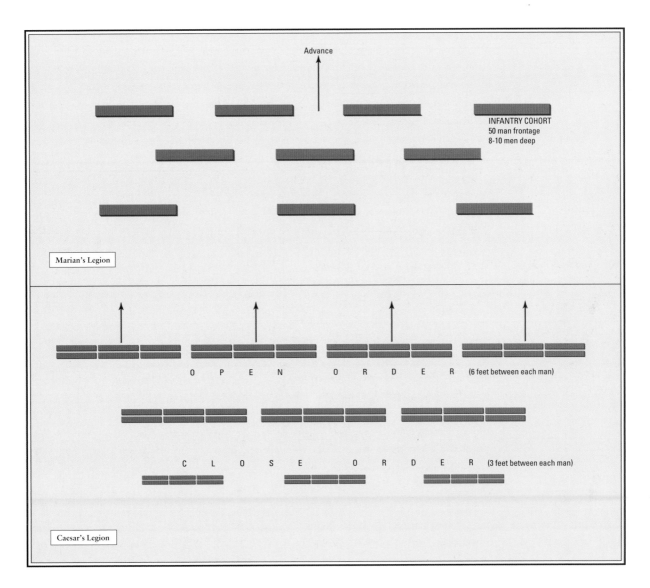

Advance

INFANTRY COHORT
50 man frontage
8-10 men deep

Marian's Legion

O P E N   O R D E R   (6 feet between each man)

C L O S E   O R D E R   (3 feet between each man)

Caesar's Legion

something they rarely ate, and even when they did, it was usually the tough meat of old animals. Local people often hid the younger, tastier animals when the Roman Army was anywhere near the vicinity.

Considering the thousands of miles of frontier territory it had to defend, the Roman Army was surprisingly small, only about 600,000 men. Their task was a lonely one, carried out far from Rome and, indeed, any other civilized place. Consequently, Roman soldiers had to be very self-sufficient. If weapons, shields, or anything else they used was damaged, they did the repairs themselves. Roman soldiers were also smiths, toolmakers, carpenters, stonemasons, and engineers. They built mile upon mile of roads, and hundreds of bridges and aqueducts. They constructed defensive barriers like Hadrian's Wall in northern Britain and the massive legionary fortresses in particularly troublesome places. These

Maintaining Pax Romana depended on the excellence of the Roman Army. Gaius Marius and Julius Caesar (whose legion formations are shown above) were instrumental in strengthening the Army. Marius standardized its training and made the army service a career. Caesar increased its efficiency and led it to many great victories.

strongholds were dauntingly impressive, sometimes covering as much as 50 acres of land. They might contain barracks housing a full legion, double-size granaries, an engineering workshop, and a hospital.

Despite its many drawbacks and the long years spent far from home, the military life had considerable appeal for many Romans. The ordinary soldier who did all the hard, back-breaking work may not have been quite so impressed by the glory of it all as were the generals, the officers, and the wealthy families who sent their sons into the Army. Nevertheless, the humble legionary often took pride in his work and in belonging to the finest, best equipped, most efficient, and most accomplished army in the world.

From time to time, their success was displayed in Rome, where even the thrills of chariot racing and gladiatorial combat could not rival the splendor of the military triumph. As a victorious general led his men through the streets, the buildings were decked with garlands and enthusiastic crowds would clap and cheer and yell: "*Io triumphe!*" (Hail conqueror!). Magistrates and senators headed the procession, with trumpeters behind them, followed by the booty and arms captured from the vanquished enemy. After them came sacrificial animals, usually white oxen with gilded horns, and then a batch of prisoners. Next came the "star" of the show, the Triumphator, riding in a four-horse chariot, clad in purple and gold robes, carrying in his right hand a laurel branch and in his left, an eagle-topped ivory scepter. Above his head, a slave held the golden crown of the god Jupiter and whispered in the Triumphator's ear: "Remember thou art mortal!" to remind him of his own impermanence.

A Triumph was one of the most magnificent spectacles to be seen in Ancient Rome. It was also a colorful reminder of how the mighty Roman armies were preserving Pax Romana and the civilized

standards of living their efforts made possible. This work was vital, for when the Empire in Europe came to an end after 476AD, one of the main reasons was that the Army was no longer strong enough to defend its frontiers and prevent it from being overrun by barbarians.

Roman emporers also isssued coins with Pax on the reverse, and patronized literature praising the benefits of Pax Romana. To preserve Pax Romana, they believed, was to keep the Empire safe.

Although Rome was an armed camp, with borders guarded by the Roman Army, life inside during Pax Romana was remarkably pleasant.

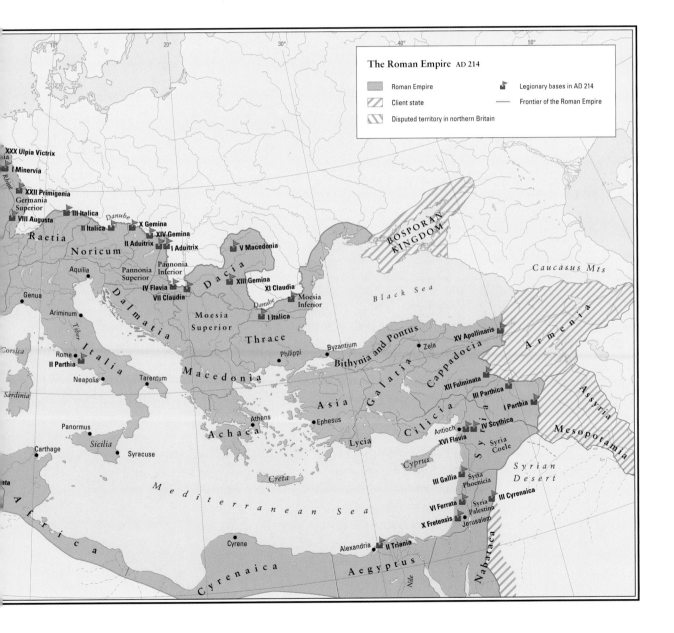

Barbarians in the Roman Army

TRADITIONALLY, SOLDIERS IN THE ROMAN ARMY HAD COME FROM THE RANKS OF ROMAN CITIZENS AND SUBJECTS FROM THE EMPIRE. BUT BY THE EARLY 3RD CENTURY AD, THIS POOL OF RECRUITS BEGAN TO DIMINISH, AND THE ARMY HAD TO LOOK ELSEWHERE.

The frequent foreign wars fought by their Army gave Romans the chance to experience what other forces could do on the battlefield. This, in turn, showed the Romans how to augment their own military expertise by recruiting rather than fighting them. This applied particularly to the barbarian tribes and the effectiveness of their cavalry. Nomads and raiders they might be, but tribes like the Huns or the Goths knew how to combine horsemanship with battle tactics in a way that made them superior to the Roman cavalry. Although overall, the Roman Army was a supreme fighting machine, their cavalry was a weak spot and in this respect, they had much to learn from their barbarian opponents. This, combined with reduced numbers of Roman recruits, led to what has been termed the "barbarization" of the Roman Army. Although this practice was more noticeable in the Army's later days, there was nothing novel about it. In the 1st century BC, the legendary Julius Caesar had gone out of his way to recruit German mercenaries for his war against Vercingetorix, the chieftain of the Arverni who led a revolt against Roman rule in Gaul (France). Augustus, the first Roman Emperor, filled the ranks of his imperial bodyguard with Germans. These choices were no coincidence. Julius Caesar and possibly Augustus, too, believed that civilization made men soft. It followed, then, that the best fighters were unspoiled by the civilized life.

For Caesar, Augustus, and his successors Tiberius and Caligula, hiring barbarians was something of a luxury, for in their time, at least 65 out of every 100 legionaries were recruited in Italy. It was only later, by the mid 2nd century AD that this percentage dwindled to a mere one in every 100. It was ironic, but this presented a great opportunity for Germans and other barbarians to acquire the benefits of civilization for themselves. The Roman way of life meant security and ease, rather than the hard struggle for existence as it was lived outside the frontiers of the Empire. So, the barbarians learned Latin, adopted Roman manners, ate Roman foods, aspired to be Roman citizens, enjoyed Roman comforts, like the public baths, and looked forward to retirement with a plot of land to call their own. Ironically, in time, they, too, would become "softened" by civilization and in their turn faced barbarians who had stayed at home and remained in their indigenous state.

Two centuries after the first Roman emperors, a succession of military crises intensified Rome's reliance on barbarian troops. Particularly important were the horse archers: they were needed to counteract the use of this type of unit by virtually all the opponents who were attacking the Empire's borders by the

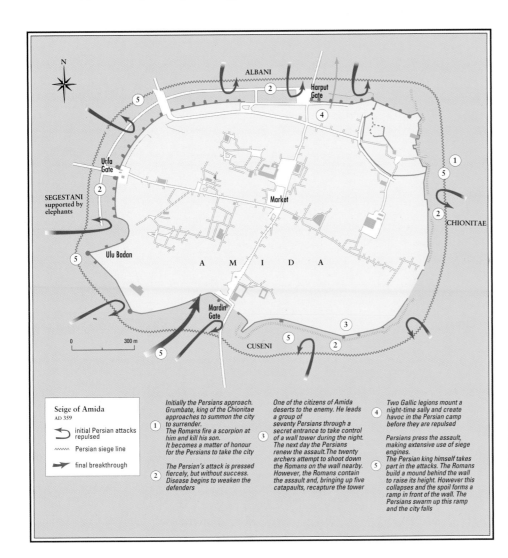

Seige of Amida
AD 359

↪ initial Persian attacks repulsed

〰 Persian siege line

➡ final breakthrough

1 Initially the Persians approach. Grumbate, king of the Chionitae approaches to summon the city to surrender. The Romans fire a scorpion at him and kill his son. It becomes a matter of honour for the Persians to take the city

2 The Persian's attack is pressed fiercely, but without success. Disease begins to weaken the defenders

3 One of the citizens of Amida deserts to the enemy. He leads a group of seventy Persians through a secret entrance to take control of a wall tower during the night. The next day the Persians renew the assault. The twenty archers attempt to shoot down the Romans on the wall nearby. However, the Romans contain the assault and, bringing up five catapaults, recapture the tower

4 Two Gallic legions mount a night-time sally and create havoc in the Persian camp before they are repulsed

5 Persians press the assault, making extensive use of siege engines. The Persian king himself takes part in the attacks. The Romans build a mound behind the wall to raise its height. However this collapses and the spoil forms a ramp in front of the wall. The Persians swarm up this ramp and the city falls

The 73-day siege of Amida took place in 358AD during a prolonged struggle between Persia and Rome. The siege, in which Amida was strongly defended by a Roman garrison obstructed the Persian invasion of Armenia and, though the Romans were forced to surrender, the Persians suffered very heavy losses.

late 3rd and early 4th centuries. Consequently, several horse-archer units were included in the radical facelift the Roman Army received under Diocletian and Constantine I, who ruled as emperors between 284AD and 337AD. Between them, they doubled the Army until its manpower reached 600,000. They divided their forces into *limitanei* (frontier troops) who were stationed along the imperial borders, and the *comitatenses* (mobile field forces) who were earmarked for frontal assaults against an enemy. In a typical battle plan, the task of the *limitanei* was to delay an enemy advance which allowed them to penetrate Roman lines until they became trapped and therefore ripe for destruction by the *comitatenses*. Before the reforms, barbarian troops were classed as auxiliary to the Roman Army. Now, though, they became *foederati*, or allies who fought for Rome in return for a pledge giving them the right to settle in Roman territory.

The *foederati* cavalry were light cavalry units led by Roman officers and were most frequently used for scouting out enemy positions, covering the movements of the main body of Roman soldiers, and pursuing the enemy once they had been put to flight. The archers recruited by the Romans were, effectively, the artillery of the ancient armies and were designed to shoot from a distance: their role was to support other troops in battle, but not to take part in close-quarter hand-to-hand fighting. These archers wore no armor, to make sure they could move fast across the battlefield. The Sarmatian auxilia from the west of Scythia in the steppes north of the Black Sea, did wear armor, made of bronze or iron metalplates sewn onto leather garments. They were universally known — and feared — as ferocious fighters. Originally nomadic pastoralists, their horse-riding skills were legendary and made them ideal for the shock-cavalry role the Romans assigned to them.

The Equitas Sagitarii (mounted horse archers) were the all-round fighters of the Romans, new-style cavalry. The one drawback in employing them was that they used composite bows. The simple bow was made from a single piece of wood and only had to be dried out after getting wet to become an effective weapon again. But getting wet could ruin a composite bow. The damp penetrated the glue that held its various layers together and once that had gone too far, the composite bow simply fell apart. Nevertheless, the Equites were a valuable adjunct to the Roman Army. They were trained to fight as medium cavalry, using swords in hand-to-hand combat. Another

non-Roman cavalry unit, the *alae* was deployed on the wings of the Army and served to prevent a determined enemy from outflanking the Romans' battle line.

The Roman requirement for increasing mobility to meet growing threats, especially in the east European steppe, involved a greater and greater deployment of cavalry. The Romans, copying their Persian opponents, covered the cavalryman and his steed with coats of chain mail, which gave a real degree of protection from lighter weapons. Despite the increasing role for the cavalry, the Roman army still maintained garrisons and mobile armies at various bases around their Empire. The typical legion now stood at 6,000 men composed of ten cohorts, two of which were 1,000 strong, the other eight 500 in strength. By the end of the 4th century, the army had around 300,000 men.

By the 4th century AD, the Roman Empire was in constant danger of attack from barbarian tribes — Germans, Visigoths, and Anglo-Saxons on the east coast of Britannia (Britain). All were attempting to invade Roman territory in order to share the benefits of Roman civilization that existed within its borders.

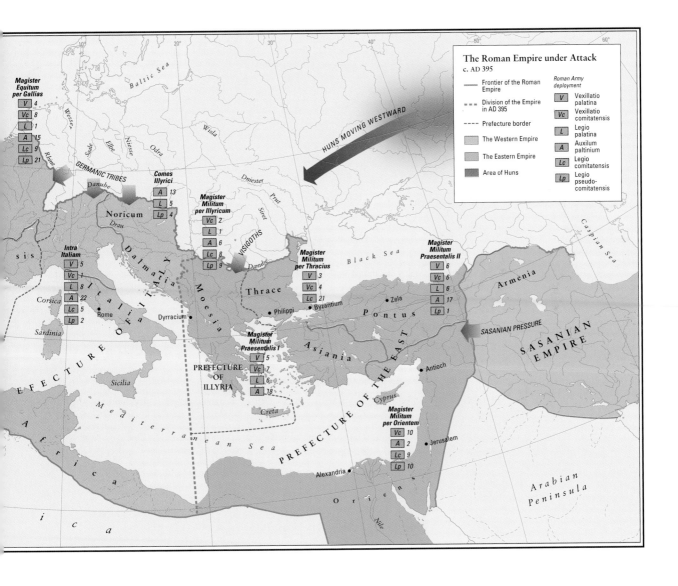

THE FALL OF THE WESTERN ROMAN EMPIRE

WHEN THE ROMAN EMPIRE IN THE WEST COLLAPSED AROUND AD476, ROME WAS VULNERABLE IN SEVERAL WAYS, APART FROM THE WEAKNESS OF THE ROMAN ARMY. THE GOVERNMENT WAS INEFFECTUAL. SOME EMPERORS WERE EXTRAVAGANT, OTHERS CORRUPT. TAXATION WAS PUNITIVE. DISCONTENT WAS WIDESPREAD.

Serious signs of decay appeared in Rome in AD410 when the Visigoths under Alaric attacked the city and ravaged it for three terrifying days. They robbed, they burned, they destroyed, they spread murder through the streets and left behind them smoking ruins and scores of dead. This was not the first time a disaster like this had overtaken Rome — the barbarian Gauls from France had done much the same in 390BC — but on that occasion, the Romans recovered, rebuilt their city, made its protective walls stronger than ever before, and reorganized their army into the most efficient fighting force the ancient world had yet known. By AD410 however, the pride, energy, and determination that had once made the Romans conquerors and overlords of a vast empire no longer seemed to exist. Too many Romans seemed to prefer the soft life of luxury and leisure. Too many of the Emperors were weak and corrupt and heavy taxation was required to keep the ever more costly state running.

By Alaric's time, attacks were not met with defiance, but with appeasement. Immediately before the Visigoth attack on Rome, for example, the Senate tried to buy them off with gold. But the Visigoths were after a great deal more than gold. Moreover, they were only one among many barbarian tribes who, for many years, had been demanding that the Romans let them settle inside the territory of the Empire. Others included the Huns, Vandals, Suebi, and Allemanni who inhabited the untamed, uncivilized regions beyond the rivers Rhine and Danube. Hoping to avoid a wholesale onslaught, the Romans eventually allowed the Visigoths into the Empire in AD376, but only on the condition that they came unarmed and

Pax Romana came to an end gradually during the 5th century AD as the Roman Army grew less and less able to hold the frontiers against incursions by barbarian tribes who wanted their share of Roman prosperity. Ironically, it was the barbarian invasions and the resulting chaos that destroyed that prosperity.

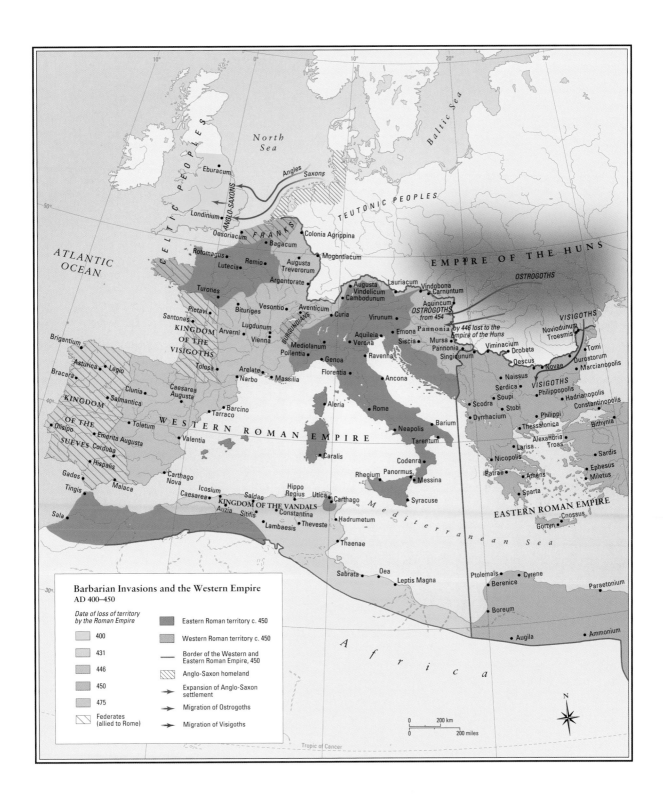

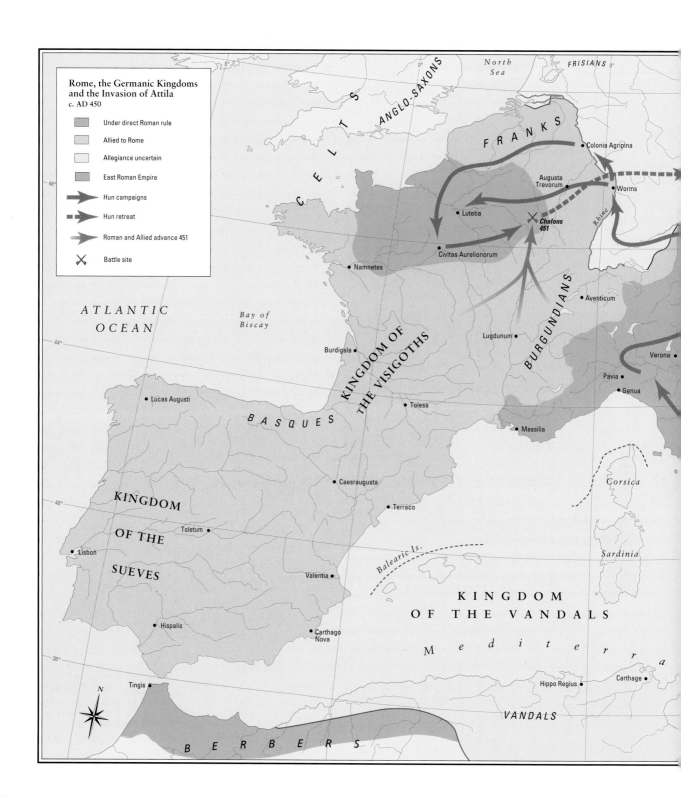

Rome, the Germanic Kingdoms
and the Invasion of Attila
c. AD 450

Under direct Roman rule

Allied to Rome

Allegiance uncertain

East Roman Empire

Hun campaigns

Hun retreat

Roman and Allied advance 451

Battle site

North Sea

FRISIANS

C E L T S

ANGLO-SAXONS

F R A N K S

Colonia Agripina

Augusta Trevorum

Worms

Rhine

Lutetia

Chalons 451

Civitas Aurelionorum

Namnetes

Aventicum

Lugdunum

B U R G U N D I A N S

Verona

Pavia

Genua

ATLANTIC OCEAN

Bay of Biscay

Burdigala

KINGDOM OF THE VISIGOTHS

B A S Q U E S

Tolesa

Massilia

Corsica

Lucas Augusti

KINGDOM

OF THE

SUEVES

Caesraugusta

Toletum

Terraco

Balearic Is.

Sardinia

Lisbon

Valentia

KINGDOM
OF THE VANDALS

Hispalis

Carthago Nova

M e d i t e r r a

n e a

Tingis

N

Hippo Regius

Carthage

V A N D A L S

B E R B E R S

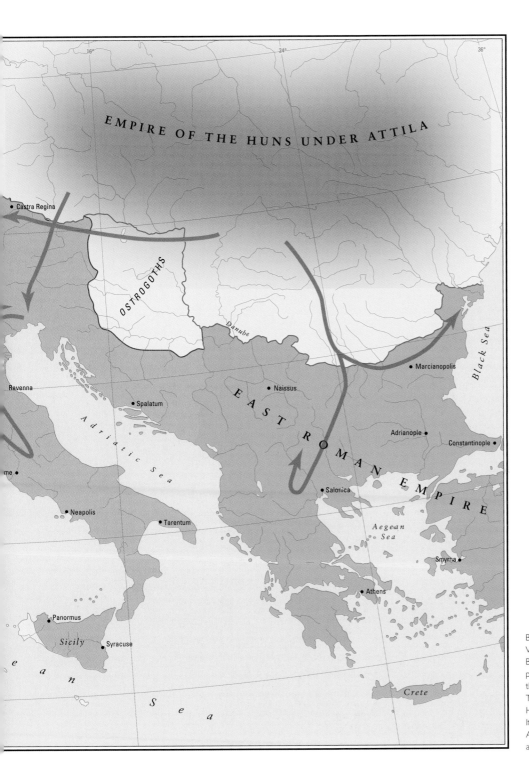

By AD450, the Ostrogoths, Visigoths, Vandals, Huns, and Burgundians had formed powerful kingdoms that seriously threatened the security of Rome. This was particularly true of the Huns who were about to invade Italy in AD452 when their leader, Attila, was miraculously dissuaded and turned back by Pope Leo I.

sent their children as hostages for their good behavior. But the Roman generals did not keep their part of the bargain. Enraged at this betrayal, the Visigoths swept across the Danube and plundered, burned, and slaughtered their way to Adrianople in Turkey. The Roman Army, once supreme and mighty, was unable to hold them back.

Some 45 years after Alaric, in AD455, the Vandals led by Gaiseric invaded Rome. Even before the Vandals got there, many Romans hastily evacuated the city. The Emperor Petronius Maximus was expected to organize resistance to the Vandals, or at least put up some sort of fight. But he, too, elected to abandon Rome, and urged the Senate to flee with him.

The people of Rome were infuriated by their emperor's craven cowardice. So were his personal bodyguard and most of his friends, all of whom deserted him. As he rode out of the city, Petronius was greeted with a shower of stones. One of them struck him on the head and killed him. A raging mob mutilated his body and then threw it into the River Tiber. Three days later, on June 2, AD455, Gaiseric and the Vandals reached Rome. Yet again the Romans experienced terror, rapine, rape, destruction, and wholesale killing as the Vandals ran wild through the streets. Two weeks later, they departed, leaving half the city destroyed and burning and littered with wreckage and dead bodies. The Vandals also took with them a vast amount of loot. The ten short-lived emperors who succeeded Petronius Maximus over the next 20 years did little to reverse the fortunes of Rome as, remorselessly, the city slid toward catastrophe. But without a strong, loyal army and senate behind them, their chances of success were, in any case, extremely small.

There was, then, very little to stop the Suebi, Allemmanni, and the Ostrogoths from the East who flooded across the Roman frontiers and overwhelmed the Roman Army in an unstoppable tide. By around AD476, the end was fast approaching. In that year, the emperor — the last in a long line — was a child, who by one of the great ironies of history bore the name of the first king and first emperor of Rome, Romulus Augustus. The young emperor was a puppet in the hands of his father, Orestes, who, on 31 October AD475, had driven out his predecessor, Basilicus, and replaced him with his young son. For the next few months, Orestes ruled Italy in the name of Romulus Augustus. Then, Orestes' soldiers mutinied against him and joined Odoacer, a German who later became the first non-Roman ruler of Italy. Odoacer executed Orestes on 28 August, AD476, but spared Romulus Augustus because of his extreme youth. Romulus was given a pension and was sent to live with his family in Campania, southern Italy. There were no more Emperors in Rome after Romulus Augustus. But a part of the empire still survived. In AD293, the Emperor Diocletian realized that the vast Roman territories were too extensive for one ruler to control. So, he divided them into the Western Empire, centered on Rome, and Eastern or Byzantine Empire based in Constantinople (now Istanbul). The separation proved fortuitous. For a while the Western Empire went down to disaster and ruin, the Byzantine continued, and flourished for almost 1,000 years. But the Empire in the West was gone. The splendid roads, aqueducts, and bridges built by the Roman army became neglected. The public baths, monuments, fora (the central meeting places in Roman towns and cities), the fountains, and beautifully laid-out houses fell into ruins. Above all, the Roman way of life disappeared as people reverted to the rougher, more primitive agricultural existence of the barbarian tribes. It would take centuries before some semblance of the highly civilized life enjoyed by the Romans would be possible again.

At the battle of Chalons in northeast France in AD451, Attila the Hun confronted the Romans, who counted the forces of the Visigothic King Theodoric I among their allies. Attila's diviners had foretold disaster for the Huns at Chalons and when the Visigoths attacked, he retreated to his camp.

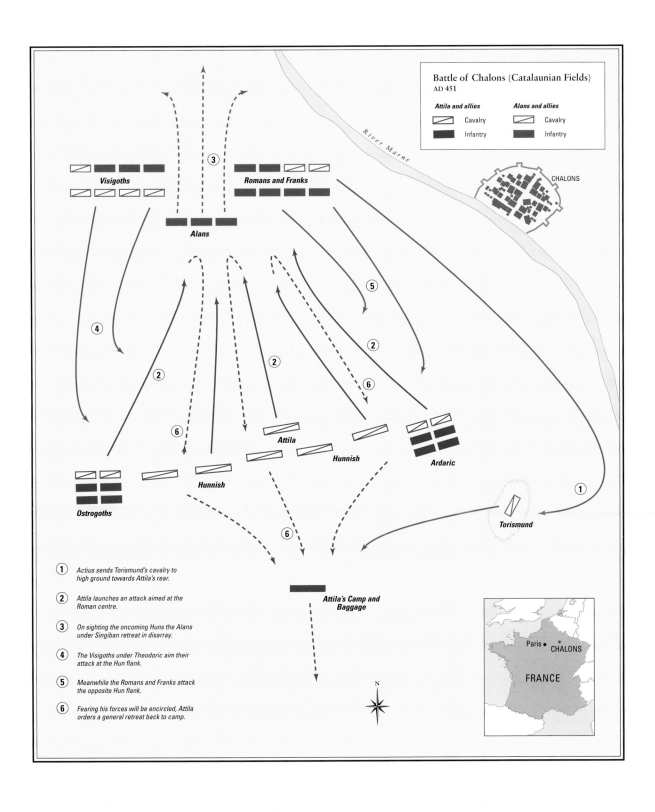

Battle of Chalons (Catalaunian Fields)
AD 451

Attila and allies

Cavalry

Infantry

Alans and allies

Cavalry

Infantry

River Marne

CHALONS

Visigoths

Romans and Franks

Alans

Torismund

Ostrogoths

Hunnish

Attila

Hunnish

Ardaric

Attila's Camp and Baggage

1. Actius sends Torismund's cavalry to high ground towards Attila's rear.

2. Attila launches an attack aimed at the Roman centre.

3. On sighting the oncoming Huns the Alans under Singiban retreat in disarray.

4. The Visigoths under Theodoric aim their attack at the Hun flank.

5. Meanwhile the Romans and Franks attack the opposite Hun flank.

6. Fearing his forces will be encircled, Attila orders a general retreat back to camp.

N

Paris • CHALONS

FRANCE

CHAPTER II — WARFARE IN THE DARK AGES: THE BYZANTINE EMPIRE

OVER 1,200 YEARS AFTER IT BEGAN AS TWO SMALL VILLAGES ABOVE THE RIVER TIBER, DISASTER HAD FINALLY OVERTAKEN ROME. YET PART OF ROME'S POWER PERSISTED IN THE EASTERN EMPIRE AND ITS MAGNIFICENT CAPITAL CITY.

C onstantinople, formerly Byzantium, took its name from Emperor Constantine I who built the city between AD324 and AD330. Byzantium offered an excellent deep-water harbor and its position, not far from the mouth of the Danube, made it an appropriate place to keep guard on the barbarians who infested that river. In addition, Byzantium stood at the meeting point where two important trade routes crossed — the land route from Europe to Asia and the sea route from the Aegean to the Black Sea. When its transformation was complete, the one-time small trading town had become a magnificent metropolis. It was full of superbly decorated palaces, splendid statues, great broad squares, and arrow-straight streets. There was a public stadium, the Hippodrome, a court of justice, and double walls with 192 watchtowers and ten gates. By AD330, it was a storehouse of fine arts, intricately carved marble, colorful mosaics, and gold finishes. Constantine, the first Christian emperor, had also provided the city with dozens of churches and monuments depicting Christ dressed in imperial purple, surrounded by his saints.

Overleaf: The Byzantine Empire, the Roman Empire in the East Territories that had been lost to the Byzantine Empire and were reclaimed during the reign of Emperor Justinian I. Among them was a large part of Italy which Justinian's general Belisarius retrieved from the barbarian Goths between AD535 and AD540 Belisarius held Rome for a whole year, despite massive Gothic attacks.

Adopting Christianity did not mean that the Byzantines repudiated wealth and the means of acquiring it. On the contrary, they became as rich and as fond of luxury as the Romans had once been. The eastern Roman Empire remained the greatest commercial power in the world for some 900 years but unfortunately, like the Romans, the Byzantines also took a similar road to disaster. After the 11th century, the strength of the Byzantine Army began to fade, and in the 13th century, a great deal of Byzantine trade was lost to new Italian trading cities like Venice and Genoa. The end came on May 29, 1453, the day the Ottoman Turkish Muslims captured Constantinople. The Turks scaled the city's great walls, and ran wild, destroying works of art, wrecking churches, and massacring the inhabitants. Byzantines were sold as slaves. Among the victims was the last Byzantine emperor, Constantine XI. The Turks mutilated his body so brutally that his subjects recognized it only by the imperial red shoes left on his feet.

In AD330 the first Christian Emperor of Rome, Constantine I, moved his capital from Rome to Constantinople (formerly Byzantium). It was a wise move, for in around AD476, when the "western" Empire centred around Rome fell, the "eastern" Byzantine Empire around Constantinople survived and continued for another thousand years.

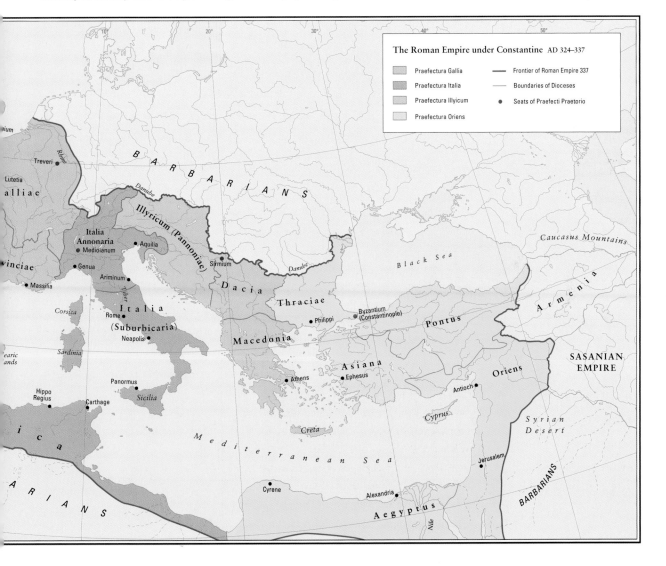

The Roman Empire under Constantine AD 324–337

- Praefectura Gallia
- Praefectura Italia
- Praefectura Illyicum
- Praefectura Oriens
- —— Frontier of Roman Empire 337
- —— Boundaries of Dioceses
- ● Seats of Praefecti Praetorio

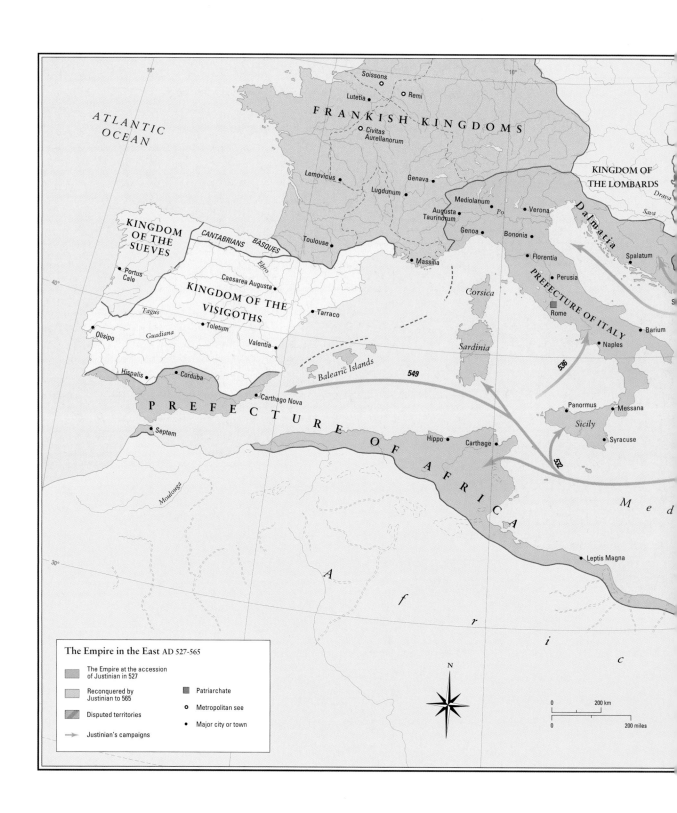

ATLANTIC
OCEAN

FRANKISH KINGDOMS

Soissons
Lutetia   Remi
Civitas
Aurellanorum

KINGDOM OF
THE LOMBARDS
Drava

Lemovicus   Genava

Lugdunum   Mediolanum   Po   Verona   Sava   Dalmatia
Augusta   Bononia
Taurinorum   Genoa   Spalatum
KINGDOM   CANTABRIANS   BASQUES   Florentia
OF THE   Toulouse   Perusia
SUEVES   Massilia   PREFECTURE OF ITALY
Portus   Caesarea Augusta   Corsica   Rome   Barium
Cale   KINGDOM OF THE   Naples
VISIGOTHS   Tarraco   536
Olisipo   Tagus   Guadiana   Toletum
Valentia   Sardinia
Hispalis   Corduba   Balearic Islands   549
Carthago Nova   Panormus   Messana
Septem   Sicily
P R E F E C T U R E   Syracuse
O F   A F R I C A
Hippo   Carthage   552
Moulouga   M e d

A

Leptis Magna
f

r

i

c

The Empire in the East AD 527-565

- The Empire at the accession of Justinian in 527
- Reconquered by Justinian to 565
- Disputed territories
- → Justinian's campaigns
- ■ Patriarchate
- ○ Metropolitan see
- • Major city or town

N

0   200 km
0   200 miles

Dnieper

Dniester

Bug

Prut

Siret

Kuma

Caspian Sea

30°

40°

50°

**GDOM OF
E GEPIDS**

Viminacium

Occupied by
epids 539–51

Ratiaria

Danube

Moesia

Marcianopolis

Cherson

Black Sea

Sebastopolis

LAZICA

IBERIA

Justina
Prima

Serdica

Philippopolis

Adrianopole

Sinope

Trebizond

Thracia

Scupi

Stobi

Thessalonica

Traianopolis

Constantinople

Chalcedon

Nicomedia

Cyzicus

Nicaea

Heraclea

Pontica

Sebastia

ARMENIA

Amida

PERSIAN

EMPIRE

Galatia

Cappadocia

Caesarea

Melitene

Edessa

Dura

Nisibis

F ILLYRICUM

Corinth

A s i a n a

Sardes

Hierapolis

Ephesus

Lapdicea

Aphrodisias

Perga

Tyana

Anazarbus

Tarsus

Hierapolis

Tigris

Seleucia

Antioch

Beroea

Circesium

Euphrates

Crete

Gortyn

Cyprus

Syria

Apamea

Emesa

LAKHMID
ARABS

erranean Sea

Damascus

Busra

PREFECTURE OF ORIENS

GHASSANID
ARABS

Jerusalem

Gaza

Alexandria

Heliopolis

Memphis

Aila

Arabian
Peninsula

EGYPT

Nile

Panopolis

Red Sea

Philae

THE BYZANTINE MILITARY SYSTEM

THE BYZANTINE EMPIRE EVOLVED FROM THE ROMAN EMPIRE IN THE SAME WAY THAT THE BYZANTINE ARMY GREW OUT OF THE LATER ROMAN ARMY. THE BYZANTINES, TOO, FACED BARBARIAN INVASIONS, BUT ALSO CONFRONTED A SINGLE FOE OF PHENOMENAL POWER AND WEALTH: ISLAM.

The Byzantine Empire was no stranger to war when its Islamic (Muslim) rival appeared on the scene in the mid-7th century AD. Having swept through Egypt, North Africa, Palestine, Syria-Mesopotamia, the Muslims left no doubt that they were an enemy like no other: inspired with a fiery fervor for their new faith, they resolved to conquer the Middle East and then spread their faith around the world. The Byzantines were now first in the front line and lost so much of their empire to the Muslims that their territory was halved and what was left was under severe threat. The Byzantines' traditional military strategy had been largely defensive and relied, like the Romans, on legions of infantry. In the new situation, there was more emphasis on the cavalry and, in a drastic reorganization, the army adopted the Thema system. Under this system, the Byzantine armies were concentrated in Asia Minor, where the former imperial provinces were rearranged into administrative divisions. Each division enjoyed a degree of autonomy in both military and civil matters and managed their affairs through their own local governments. At the start, there were five Themes, centered in Armenia, Anatolia, northwestern Asia Minor, Thrace, and Illyricum where the Army occupied the southern coast of Asia Minor and the Aegean Islands.

"Thematic," soldiers received grants of land to enable them to support their families and provide themselves with weapons. Members of the local community also had a duty to contribute to ensure that in the event of war the farmer-turned-warrior presented himself to his *Strategos* (overall commander)

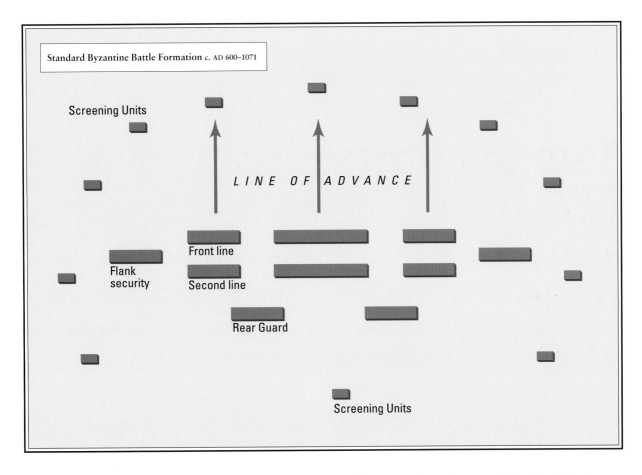

properly armed and equipped for training and combat. The "Thematic" soldier's area of operations was his own region where he would be motivated to defend his own town, farm, family, and community. Regional defense was not, on its own, the most suitable means of dealing with the Muslim armies, which rapidly overwhelmed their enemies, giving them little or no time to coordinate a defense. The central government also provided for a professional standing army known as the Tagmata. The Tagmata represented an élite of heavily armored shock-effect cavalry which, together with crack infantry regiments, combined to confront the Muslims with a force up to 20,000 strong. They spearheaded counter-offensive warfare against Muslim invaders who had already been exhausted by the persistent hit-and-run tactics employed by the "Thematic" soldiers.

Many historians regard the Battle of Yarmuk as being one of the most significant battles in history, because it marked the first great wave of Muslim conquest outside the Arabian Peninsula. The battle was fought between the Muslim Arabs and the Byzantine Roman Empire and took place northeast of the Sea of Galilee. It heralded the rapid advance of Islam into Christian Palestine, Syria, and Mesopotamia. At the end the Byzantine army were surrounded and unable to use their weapons. Most were killed or captured.

Using this standard battle formation, Byzantine armies were just as successful in war as their western Roman counterparts. Among many brilliant Byzantine generals, the most famous was Belisarius, who thrashed the Persians so thoroughly that they vowed never to wage a full-scale war against the Empire while Belisarius was alive.

The Sassanid Empire in Persia

THE SASSANIDS, WHO SEIZED POWER IN AD224 BELONGED TO THE LAST NATIVE DYNASTY IN PERSIA BEFORE CONQUEST BY THE MUSLIM ARABS SOME FOUR CENTURIES LATER. THE SASSANID ARMY WAS SO EFFECTIVE THAT THE ROMANS CONSIDERED THEM AS EQUALS.

The Sassanid Persian Empire was the last Iranian empire. It succumbed in AD651 to invasion by the Muslim Arab Caliphate after resisting for 14 years. By the time it fell, the Sassanid Empire had lasted for more than four centuries as one of the most powerful states in western Asia.

The Sassanid Empire covered an area of 1,351,358 sq miles (3, 500, 000 sq km), encompassing the territory of modern Iran and Iraq and extending as far as Pakistan in the east and the coast of Arabia in the south. The Sassanid capital, Ctesiphon, grew into a magnificent city, adorned by cultural wonders in art, architecture, textiles, and sculpture. There was a stable government, and an efficient tax system that enabled the king to afford decent pay for his soldiers and the best military equipment. The Sassanid rulers gave themselves the grandiose title of Shahanshah (King of Kings), and the Roman Emperors referred to them as "my brother." The Romans, of course, knew military brilliance when they saw it, and they had ongoing experience of Sassanid expertise to confirm it. The Sassanids first challenged the Romans on the field of battle in AD231 and they organized themselves for battle in much the same way. After the fall of the Western Roman Empire in around AD476, the Byzantines continued the rivalry with the Sassanids. In around AD570, the Byzantine emperor Maurice, himself no mean warrior, wrote of Sassanid military tactics in his manual of war, the Strategikon that they had "an orderly approach" to battle, attacking with "calmness and determination" rather than "in a disorderly fashion." The Romans never resolved their rivalry with the Sassanids but the Byzantines were more successful. Sassanid defeat at the hands of the Byzantine Emperor Heraclius in AD627 initiated a rapid decline, worsened by a weakening of central control over the Sassanid provinces. During those years, the Sassanid Empire was repeatedly assaulted by the army of Islam and finally succumbed after the Muslims captured Ctesiphon in AD638 and virtually destroyed the Sassanid Army three years later.

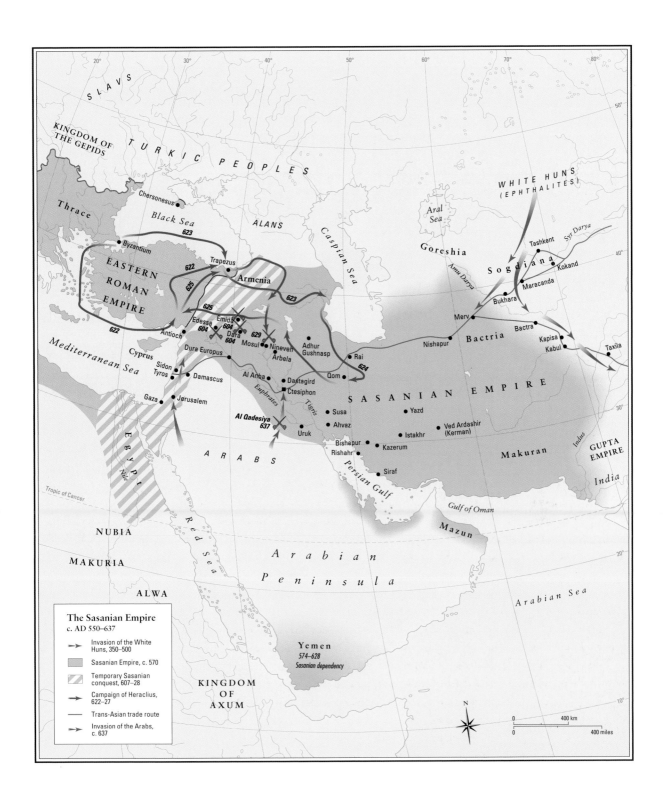

The Sasanian Empire
c. AD 550–637

→ Invasion of the White
  Huns, 350–500

▨ Sasanian Empire, c. 570

▨ Temporary Sasanian
  conquest, 607–28

→ Campaign of Heraclius,
  622–27

— Trans-Asian trade route

→ Invasion of the Arabs,
  c. 637

The Hindu Military System to AD600

HINDU WARFARE CHANGED LITTLE IN THE 12 CENTURIES UP TO AD600. IN PARTICULAR, BOWS AND ARROWS REMAINED THE PRINCIPAL WEAPON. WHILE CAVALRY WAS INTRODUCED IN RESPONSE TO PERSIAN INVASIONS, IT NEVER BECAME THE MIGHTY FORCE SEEN IN OTHER ANCIENT ARMIES.

The Gupta Empire in India was comparatively short-lived, it lasted from only AD320 to around AD550, when it was destroyed by the Huna or Indo-Hephthalites. While it lasted, though, the Gupta Empire covered a considerable part of northern and central India and was renowned for its science, mathematics, and astronomy.

Although, before 600BC, the Hindus employed some chariots, their armies consisted almost entirely of infantry using bows and arrows as their chief weapon. The classical literature of India, notably the *Rigveda* and the *Mahabharata* made little or no mention of cavalry, for in much of India, the climate was not suitable for breeding horses of suitable quality. A century or so later, the Hindus were obliged to introduce cavalry and the weapons they used most, the sword and the lance, following the damaging invasions of the Persian kings Cyrus I, in 537BC and Darius I between 517BC and 509BC. War elephants made their first appearance on Indian battlefields in the 6th century BC. They were still being used over the next 2,500 years, although the chariot faded out long before that. The demise of the chariot in Indian warfare seems to have started with Chandragupta Maurya, who, after 323BC, conquered almost all of India and created a permanent military which reportedly comprised 600,000 infantry, 30,000 cavalry, and 9,000 elephants. It was during Chandragupta's reign as first Maurya emperor that the Arthasastra (political manual) was written by his friend Kautilya. The manual's military coverage included the composition of armies, how various branches of the military should function, the duties of officers, the rules of field operations, siegecraft and fortifications but contained little or nothing about chariots. Another military classic, the Siva-Dhanur-veda, appeared some 800 years later, in the 6th century AD. This book served to show that very little had changed in Indian warfare since the days of Chandragupta.

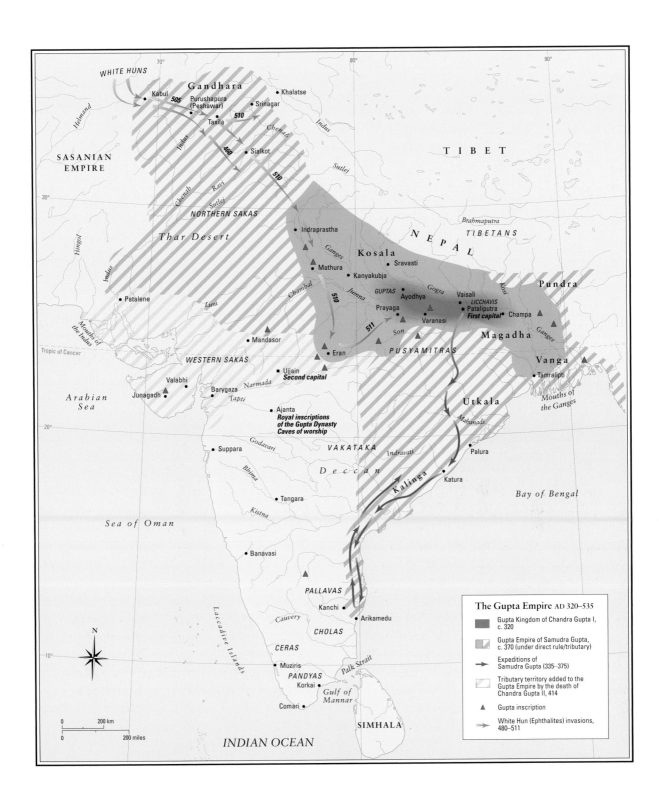

WHITE HUNS

Gandhara

SASANIAN
EMPIRE

• Kabul *505*
Purushapura
(Peshawar)
• Khalatse
• Taxila *510*
• Srinagar
460
• Sialkot
510

Helmand
Indus
Chenab

TIBET

Indus

Sutlej

Brahmaputra

NORTHERN SAKAS

Thar Desert

Chenab Ravi Sutlej

NEPAL

TIBETANS

• Indraprastha

Ganges

Kosala

• Mathura
• Sravasti
• Kanyakubja

GUPTAS
510
Ayodhya
Gogra
Vaisali

• Patalene

Hingol
Indus
Luni

Chambal

Jumna
Prayaga
• Varanasi

LICCHAVIS
Pataliputra
First capital •
Champa •

Son

511

• Mandasor

Pundra

Kosi

Ganges

Magadha

Vanga

Tropic of Cancer

WESTERN SAKAS

PUSYAMITRAS

• Eran

Mouths of
the Indus

• Ujjain
Second capital

Valabhi

Narmada

• Barygaza

• Tamralipti

Junagadh •

Tapti

*Royal inscriptions
of the Gupta Dynasty
Caves of worship*

• Ajanta

Utkala

Mahanadi

Mouths of
the Ganges

Arabian
Sea

Godavari

VAKATAKA

Indravati

• Palura

• Suppara

Bhima

Deccan

Kalinga

• Katura

• Tangara

Kistna

Bay of Bengal

Sea of Oman

• Banavasi

Laccadive Islands

Cauvery

PALLAVAS

Kanchi •
• Arikamedu

CHOLAS

CERAS

• Muziris

PANDYAS

Korkai •

Gulf of
Mannar

Palk Strait

Comari •

N

0   200 km
0   200 miles

SIMHALA

INDIAN OCEAN

The Gupta Empire AD 320–535

Gupta Kingdom of Chandra Gupta I,
c. 320

Gupta Empire of Samudra Gupta,
c. 370 (under direct rule/tributary)

Expeditions of
Samudra Gupta (335–375)

Tributary territory added to the
Gupta Empire by the death of
Chandra Gupta II, 414

▲ Gupta inscription

White Hun (Ephthalites) invasions,
480–511

CHAPTER III — MEDIEVAL WARFARE: THE RISE OF ISLAM

IN THE 7TH CENTURY AD, MUSLIM ARMIES CREATED ONE OF THE MOST RAPIDLY ACQUIRED EMPIRES IN ALL HISTORY. SWEEPING NORTH OUT OF ARABIA AFTER AD633, THEY CONQUERED PERSIA, SYRIA, EGYPT, AND LIBYA BY AD650. THIS, THOUGH, WAS ONLY JUST THE BEGINNING.

The Prophet Mohamed, founder of the Muslim religion, Islam, died in AD632, only a year before his followers began their surge across the Middle East. He is regarded by followers of Islam as a prophet and a messenger of God, the last and the greatest law-bearer. He was also regarded by Muslims as an agent of divine action. Born in AD570, Mohamed was destined to follow in the family footsteps and become a merchant. But around the age of 30, according to Muslim tradition, he began to receive revelations from the Angel Gabriel which disclosed to him the Word of Allah, the One and Only true God. The Word was that the idols who worshipped at the shrine in Mecca must be destroyed and replaced as a focus of faith by Allah. Furthermore, the rich should give to the poor, an idea that naturally alarmed the affluent. Mohamed made his first converts in Mecca but was forced to run for his life in AD622 through the mounting hostility of his enemies. Accompanied by a small band of followers, Mohamed fled to the town of Yathrib. This journey, known as the Hegira, marked the start of the Muslim era and led to Yathrib being renamed Medina, the "city of the Prophet." The Muslim concept of *jihad* (holy war) came into force at the same time, and from then on, Islam was set on a course of conquest and conversion.

Holy war began in December AD623 when the Muslims defeated a Meccan army. They continued in AD627 by breaking the Meccan siege of Medina. In AD629, Mohamed was in control of Mecca. Only a year later, he had spread his power over the whole of Arabia. Mohamed's death on June 8, AD632 was the signal to extend the holy war beyond the bounds of Arabia. The Muslims achieved their first victories over their nearest and weakest enemies. Years of near-continuous conflict had exhausted the Byzantine and Persian empires and in AD636, the Byzantines were unable to throw back the onslaught the Muslims launched against them at the Yarmuk River in Syria. The Muslims were inspired to victory at Yarmuk by their dynamic new faith, and the assurance, given by Mohamed that any man killed fighting the infidel (unbeliever) was assured of a place in Heaven. This meant that the Muslims had a total disregard for death. As a result, their victories were often won at a horrific cost in lives. Yarmuk was the precursor to a series of Muslim victories which in the west, extended their empire along the North African coast and its immediate hinterland all the way to Spain by the early 8th century BC, and in the east, reached the frontier of China some 50 years later. The Muslim armies suffered setbacks and usually came off second best when confronted by strongly led, well equipped, and disciplined forces. In 717—718AD, for instance, the Byzantines, by this time in greater strength and spirit than at Yarmuk, frustrated the Muslim siege of Constantinople. Another example was the victory of Charles Martel, commander of a Frankish army, when he repulsed the Muslims' attempt to invade France at the battle of Tours in AD732.

The Muslims' secret weapon was their morale and the strength they derived from their faith. During their early conquests, much of the terrain over which the Muslims fought their enemies was desert. Most Muslims were familiar with the landscape and were able to navigate the trackless sands more easily than the enemy. With their expert handling of camels they could achieve mobility in an environment that was disorientating to non-desert dwellers. These advantages bred in Muslims a superior resilience and an endurance that enabled them to survive in some of the harshest and most unforgiving conditions in the world. From there, it was a simple matter to convert the lessons of camel warfare to the use of cavalry. Due to their expert use of cavalry they were so successful, in fact, that by the 8th century AD, the armies of Islam had become the most accomplished in the Middle East, despite only simple weapons, such as bows and arrows, the short, curved scimitar sword, and the spear. This was because they knew how to use cavalry to hit their opponents at their weakest point and throw an enemy into disarray by pouring a blizzard of arrows into their ranks. Then, after a little over a century, the Muslims' run of triumphs came to an abrupt end, not on the battlefield but in the corridors of power. In AD750, the Umayyad ruling dynasty was overthrown by a new ruling house, the Abbasids. They took over the Caliphate, the civil and religious government of Islam, and set up a lavish court in Baghdad. The Umayyads still ruled from Cordoba in Spain but Islam was now deeply divided. With this, there was a loss of the unity that was so vital to success and with that, Muslim military expansion was over.

An Islamic banner captured at the Battle of Las Navas de Tolosa. The Arabic transcription translates as "I take refuge in God... In the name of God, the Merciful, the Compassionate, God bless him and give him peace."

The Islamic Conquest of Spain

THE SPEED OF CONQUEST WITH WHICH THE MUSLIMS CREATED THEIR EMPIRE REACHED HISPANIA (SPAIN) IN AD711. THE TIDE OF MILITARY SUCCESS SWEPT ON SO FAST THAT AFTER ONLY SEVEN YEARS MOST OF THE IBERIAN PENINSULA WAS UNDER MUSLIM RULE.

The ten or fifteen thousand invaders of the Christian Visigoth kingdom in Hispania (Spain) in AD711 were Berber Moors from northwest Africa, only recently converted to Islam. This did nothing to lessen their zeal after they landed, possibly at Gibraltar, under the command of Tariq ibn Ziyad. They arrived at a particularly propitious time: the Visigoth royal family, which had been in control of Hispania since the end of Roman rule in the 5th century AD was distracted by dynastic squabbles, and seeing the Berber vessels plying back and forth across the straits between southern Spain and the Moroccan coast, mistook them for the trading ships that regularly made the voyage. The Berber fleet was, in fact, transporting two armies totaling 19,000 men, together with their equipment, to a site close by the Salado River on the shore of a lagoon.

The Visigoth King Roderick realized his error when his army, reportedly 90,000 strong, confronted Tariq's forces at Guadalete on July 19, AD711. Despite their apparently vast superiority in numbers, Roderick's men were routed and the king himself fled the battlefield. He was drowned while attempting to escape across the nearby River Guadalquivir. In 1712, some 18,000 Berber Moors besieged the city of Merida, near Badajoz in western Spain, near what is now the Portuguese frontier. This time, though, the Visigoth army came out to challenge the invaders on the open plain around Merida. They put up a vigorous defense which cost them hundreds of casualties, but nevertheless succumbed to famine and were forced to surrender. This was virtually the end of effective Visigoth resistance and three years later, an event in Damascus, the capital of Syria, underlined how very thoroughly they had been thrashed by the Moorish invaders. In February AD715, Musa ibn Nusair, Governor of Ifriqiya (Africa) put on an impressive show when he paraded through the streets of the Syrian capital scores of Visigoth kings and princes, together with a mass of other royal personages and thousands of other captives. Furthermore, these captives were seen to offer homage to the commander of Damascus. By AD718, the Muslim invaders had overrun the greater part of Hispania which they renamed al-Andalus. The same year, the

The Muslim Moors from North Africa never succeeded in overrunning the whole of Spain, and it was from a narrow corridor of territory in the far north that the eventual Christian kingdoms were able to reconquer the peninsula.

first Emir of al-Andalus, Abd al-Aziz ibn Musa, was appointed and shortly afterward, he married Egilona Balthes, the widow of the vanquished King Roderick.

Greatly emboldened by their rapid success in al-Andalus, the Moors crossed the Pyrenees mountains and irrupted into southern France. Here, though, they encountered the Franks who proved far more energetic opponents than the Visigoths. The Moors were heavily defeated by the renowned Angevin warrior Charles Martel at the battle of Tours in AD732, and their attempt to conquer western Europe ended then and there.

However, there was glory enough for the Moors in al-Andalus where they established magnificent centers of learning and made significant advances in astronomy, architecture, medicine, science, geography, literature, music, and philosophy. In AD948, the geographer Ibn Hawkal enthused over the Moorish city of Cordoba, in terms of amazement: "The amount of coins in circulation!" he wrote. "The variety of crops grown! The people! The textiles! The gardens! The mosques!" There were 600 public baths in Cordoba, palaces that were the height of luxury, paved streets with lighting and a population numbering around 250,000. By the time Ibn Hawkal visited Cordoba, the city was the capital of one of the great Caliphates of Islam, the government based on the Muslim religion and the principle of the Ummah, the world-wide Islamic nation.

Yet behind all this achievement, al-Andalus faced a determined challenge from the Christian kingdoms that still existed in the north of Spain, in Galicia, Asturias, Cantabria, and the Basque country. Immediately after the Moorish conquest, Pelagius, a Visigoth noble, inaugurated the *Reconquista* (the Re-conquest) by raiding the city of Leon. This established a pattern for the Reconquista, which comprised pinprick raids, pillaging, and plundering. Around the turn of the 9th century, King Alfonso II of Asturias began using these tactics to discomfit the Moors and filch parts of the north from them while pushing the border of Asturias southward. Bases in Castile, Galicia, and Léon were fortified and the sparsely inhabited countryside was repopulated. The idea was to provide inhabitants to defend the retrieved territory should the Moors attempt to reclaim it. Such attempts were, however, crippled by civil wars among the Moors which resulted, by 1031, in the appearance of 34 small, quarrelsome, and therefore weak taifa kingdoms. Even the Cordoba Caliphate was de-stabilized, robbing the Moors of the chance to present a united front against the slow, but steady, advance of the Christian Reconquista.

This process became inexorable and from time to time flared into pitched battle. The most important of these battles took place on

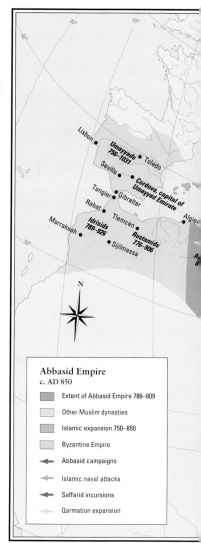

Abbasid Empire
c. AD 850

Extent of Abbasid Empire 786–809

Other Muslim dynasties

Islamic expansion 750–850

Byzantine Empire

Abbasid campaigns

Islamic naval attacks

Saffarid incursions

Qarmation expansion

July 16, 1212 at Las Navas de Tolosa, where a Christian coalition of Castile, Aragon, Portugal, and Navarre confronted the forces of the Almohads, a Berber dynasty which took over al-Andalus in 1170. At Las Navas, the leader of the coalition, King Alfonso VIII of Castile, led his army across the mountain range defending the Almohad camp, slipping through the Despeñaperros Pass in the Andalusian mountains. Taken completely by surprise, the Almohads were smashed, and the Christian forces killed so many of them that afterward, some 100,000 corpses littered the battlefield. In 1294, King Sancho IV of Castile and Léon captured Tarifa which commanded the Straits of Gibraltar, leaving Granada, Almeria, and Malaga as the only cities left to the Moors in Spain. The final showdown that ended Moorish rule in Spain followed two centuries later, in 1492 (see pages 142—143).

The Abbasid Empire, which lasted from AD750 to 1258, represented the third of the Islamic Caliphates and enjoyed a "golden age" of science, literature, philosophy, and technology. It eventually fell to Mongol conquerors who sacked the Empire's capital Baghdad in 1258. Even so, the religious authority of the Caliphate continued.

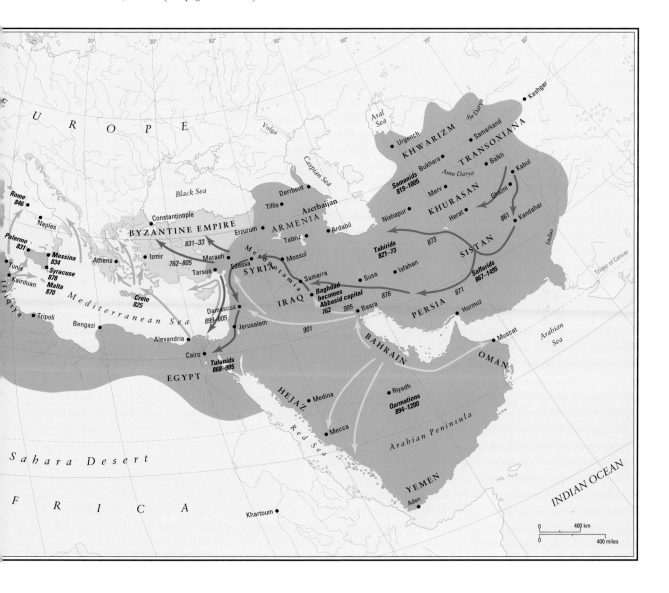

THE BYZANTINES AT WAR

THE BYZANTINE ARMY WAS A WORTHY SUCCESSOR TO THE ROMAN ARMY. BACKED BY THE MOST LUCRATIVE ECONOMIES IN THE ANCIENT WORLD, THE BYZANTINES WERE ABLE TO FIELD EXTREMELY POWERFUL, WELL ORGANIZED, AND EFFECTIVE FORCES.

Like Rome, the Byzantine Empire enjoyed a Pax Romana. The brilliant Byzantine success in trade and the arts could hardly have flourished for as long as it did without a long period of peace. And, as in Rome, the Byzantine peace was assured for many centuries in the same fashion, by a strong, well-led army, which fought numerous wars to keep the enemies of the Empire at bay. The basic strength of the Byzantine military lay in its heavy cavalry which was composed of *cataphractoi*, a name derived from the Ancient Greek word for "covered". Byzantine *cataphractoi* were horsemen covered in full metal scale armor, including a conical iron helmet. They rode horses similarly protected over the head, neck and chest. *Cataphractoi* carried a variety of weapons — bows and arrows, long lance, sword, and dagger sometimes with an axe attached to the saddle. Customary strategy for the heavy cavalry was a grimly effective maneuver — charging the enemy at high speed and crashing through the opposition.

Developing skill in archery was part of *cataphract* training, an essential of military proficiency strongly emphasized in the 6th century AD by Flavius Belisarius, one of the most famous and successful of all Byzantine generals. Belisarius defeated the Vandals of North Africa in AD533, and between AD535 and AD540, won back part of Italy from the Goths on behalf of his emperor, Justinian I. He also held Rome for a year despite massive assaults by the Goths. An important part of Belisarius' success derived from the training he gave his cavalry to shoot arrows accurately from the saddle while riding at high speed. Their technique was to draw their bowstrings along the forehead about opposite to the right ear and then let fly: this gave an arrow tremendous force in flight. Byzantine bowmen who made up most of the light infantry wore armored corselets and greaves up to the knee to safeguard their legs and carried small shields to protect their faces and necks.

In battle, the Byzantine bowmen could be formidable. In AD543, during the Byzantines' second war against them, the Sassanid Persians were so dismayed when Belisarius' archers routed 40,000 of their soldiers that they are said to have vowed never to wage another full-scale war against the Empire for as long as the renowned general lived. Belisarius died in AD565 at the great age, for his time, of 60 years. The Sassanids, it seems, kept their vow, for their next major war against the Byzantines did not begin until AD572.

The Byzantines were even more heavily armored than the Romans. Although chain mail was used, the Byzantines seem to have preferred lamellar armor, consisting of small strips of iron or toughened leather laced together to form a continuous flexible sheet. The Byzantine heavy cavalry, known as cataphracts, wore full body armor and gave protection to their horses with quilts made from lameller armor.

The Persians were by no means the only opponents who found the Byzantines disconcerting adversaries. Byzantine prowess was incomparable. Like their Roman predecessors, they were the best military force in their time, but it was not for nothing that the adjective "byzantine'" became, and remains, a dictionary definition for devious and underhand procedures. In order to win battles, the Byzantines made regular use of bribery and trickery and were experts at psychological warfare. Bogus propaganda was often used to maintain the morale of their own soldiers, and false rumors were spread among opponents by letters sent to enemy commanders persuading them that their own officers were conspiring against them. On the battlefield, a favorite Byzantine ploy was to pretend to retreat when, in reality, they were drawing their foes toward dangerous terrain — a ravine or a waterlogged marsh, for example — where they could be easily trapped and overcome.

This detail shows Justinian I, 483-565, who was Byzantine emperor from 527. He recovered North Africa from the Vandals, southeast Spain from the Visigoths and Italy from the Ostrogoths, largely owing to the skills of General Belisarius (c. 505-565), who led the imperial armies.

Nor did the Byzantines shrink from using a terror weapon, one which in its day produced the same dread as the nuclear weapons of modern times. The formula for the Byzantines' famous Greek Fire was a closely guarded secret. Invented in around AD672, Greek Fire was first used in battle in the following year, when the Byzantines destroyed a Muslim fleet attacking Constantinople. In 718AD, another Muslim fleet suffered the same fate when Greek Fire was poured down from the city's walls and totally consumed both ships and crews.

Even those who used Greek Fire knew no more than their own part in the process: they remained in the dark about its other workings so that none of them could betray the whole system to anyone else. Even today, no one knows the exact ingredients that went into making Greek Fire. Suggestions have included quicklime or calcium oxide which can use moisture to generate heat and makes whatever catches fire, including human bodies, burn fast. Another candidate has been napalm which in one of its many varieties, is a thick liquid that sticks to the skin and once stuck, keeps on burning intensively.

Other possibilities are naphtha, a flammable oil, sulfur, and niter, later used to manufacture gunpowder. Whatever the recipe, Greek Fire could not be extinguished once it was ablaze. Pouring water on the flames was useless, for far from putting it out, water actually encouraged Greek Fire to burn more fiercely. This, of course, gave the Byzantines an advantage when they used Greek Fire during naval battles where it was sprayed or poured on enemies from siphons, earthenware pots, or grenades.

Greek fire was still in use in 1103, when a sea battle took place between the Byzantines and a fleet from the Italian city of Pisa. The Byzantine historian Anna Komnene recorded what happened when the two sides met. A tube ending in the head of a lion or other beast wrought in brass or iron, had been fixed to the bows of each galley "so that the animals might seem to vomit flames..." The fleet came up with the Pisans between Rhodes and Patara... Count Eleeman... rammed the stern of a Pisan vessel so that the bows of his ship became stuck in its steering-oar tackle. Then, shooting forth The Fire, he set it ablaze, after which he pushed off and successfully discharged his tube into three other vessels, all of which were soon in flames. "The Pisans," Komnene concluded "fled in disorder, having had no previous knowledge of the device".

Although they were this ruthless in war, the Byzantine forces nevertheless observed a strict code of honor. Their commanders were forbidden to harm ambassadors or negotiators, break signed treaties, mistreat women, or attack enemy stretcher-bearers carrying the dead and wounded from the battlefield. A courageous foe, when captured, had to be treated generously and with respect. The toughness of the Byzantine military was buttressed by a chain of command first established in the reign of the Emperor Diocletian, the so-called "Augustus of the east", who reigned between AD286 and AD305. The *Magister Militum* (Chief of the Military) headed the Army and below him came the *Comes*, his Deputy and the *Dux* (Leader). After them, the chain of command continued with the *Praefectus Praetorio*, (Chief of Staff) *Vicarius* (Second in Command), and *Praeses* (Governor).

Guidance was provided in ten manuals which between them explored virtually every aspect of war. The best known was the *Strategikon* written in the 6th century AD and attributed to the Emperor Maurice whose reign, between AD582 and AD602, was almost entirely occupied with fighting on all the frontiers of his empire. In the 12 volumes of the *Strategikon*, Maurice outlined his preferred strategies — ambushes, ruses, night raids — and guidance on how to understand an enemy, by studying his fighting methods, customs and home ground. Three centuries later, another Byzantine emperor, Leo VI who reigned between AD895 and AD912, produced a new edition of the *Strategikon*, but with some important updates. Where Maurice pre-dated the marauding Muslims, Emperor Leo was closely involved with them. His additions reflected the strategies and tactics required to deal with them and also with another persistent foe, the Magyars of Hungary. Leo also provided new chapters on naval warfare. A later 10th century emperor, Nikephorus II Phokas, who reigned between AD963 and AD969 provided an extension of Leo's methods against the Muslims in *De Velittione Bellica*, a manual on guerrilla warfare which included an analysis of the skirmish, reconnaissance, the use of terrain at night, and how to prepare against enemy raids, large-scale invasions, and sieges.

In general, medieval battles tended to be brief and relatively unsophisticated, and that for much of this period the most elaborate tactics were those of the Byzantine armies. However, this did not protect them from setbacks and losses at the hands of their enemies.

Opposite page: The Byzantine Empire, like its western Roman counterpart, depended on its army for survival against its enemies. As the map shows, the danger came mainly from the east and the vast territory of the Abbasid Empire, the third of the Islamic caliphates dedicated to spread Muslim rule worldwide.

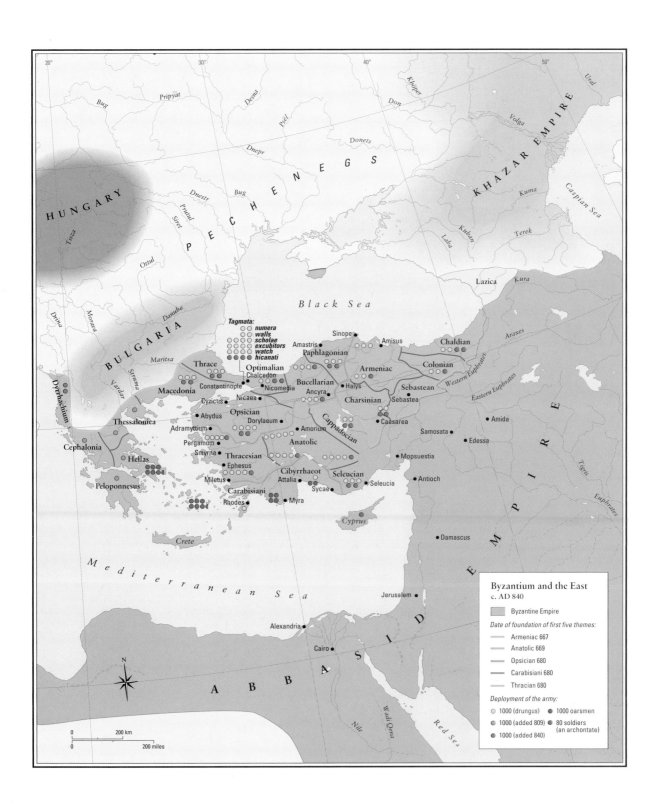

Byzantium and the East
c. AD 840

Byzantine Empire

Date of foundation of first five themes:

Armeniac 667

Anatolic 669

Opsician 680

Carabisiani 680

Thracian 680

Deployment of the army:

○ 1000 (drungus) ● 1000 oarsmen

● 1000 (added 809) ● 80 soldiers (an archontate)

● 1000 (added 840)

Tagmata:
○ numera
○ walls
○ scholae
○ excubitors
○ watch
● hicanati

FRONTIERS OF THE ISLAMIC EMPIRE

AFTER AD750, WHEN INTERNAL DISSENT AND DIVISION BROUGHT AN END TO THE LIGHTNING EXPANSION OF THE ISLAMIC EMPIRE, ITS TERRITORY COVERED A VAST AREA. IT STRETCHED NEARLY 3,900 MILES (6,300 KM) FROM SPAIN AND NORTH AFRICA IN THE WEST TO THE BORDERS OF CHINA IN THE EAST.

The vast swathe of conquest, achieved in only 117 years, brought the Muslims up against frontiers that had once been seen as virtually inviolate. This was particularly true of lands at the extremities of the Empire, in Spain and China, where the idea that the distant Arabians, primitively armed, could reach that far seemed quite impossible. Spain, which had been ruled by "barbarian" Visigoths since the fall of the western Roman Empire in around AD476, remained immune until after AD705, when the Muslim armies at last managed to push past the fierce resistance put up by the Berbers. However, the Berbers did prove susceptible to Islam and their conversion in large numbers eventually facilitated the Muslim drive through Algeria and Tunisia to Morocco on the Atlantic coast. The next step was the conquest of Spain, which was effected after AD711 by the Muslim Moors, many of whom were ironically, of Berber descent. Moorish Spain, known to its conquerors as al-Andalus, lasted, though not in its entirety, until 1492. By AD718, it reached as far north as the Pyrenees mountains, but no farther. The Moorish advance was halted at the Battle of Tours in AD732 by a Frankish army led by the formidable Christian warrior Charles Martel.

By that time, the Islamic armies had scored better success in central Asia, where in AD727, they embarked on a war with the Khazar kingdom north of Persia and pushed their conquests all the way to the Caucasus mountains. From there, the next destination was China. The Islamic armies defeated the Chinese at the Battle of Talas in Kirghiyztan in AD751: this victory terminated Chinese control west of the Pamir and Tien Shan mountains and extended the Islamic Empire eastward to the frontier of China.

Among the empires shown, the Angevin in western Europe was small but significant. The Angevin Empire comprised the inheritance of King Henry II and included the Duchy of Normandy and Kingdom of England (through his mother) the counties of Anjou, Touraine, and Maine (through his father), and Aquitaine (through his wife).

Eurasia c. 1200
- ■ Major city
- Angevin Empire and possessions
- ─ Holy Roman Empire
- Byzantine Empire
- Jin Empire
- Southern Song Empire
- Kingdom of Srivijaya
- Other states

The Muslims went no farther in China itself, but to the south, along the Islamic frontier with India, it was a different story. In AD712, the Ummayed General Muhamed bin Qasim brought Muslim rule to northwest India by conquering the provinces of Sindh and Multan in the southern Punjab. This set the stage for invasions from Central Asia which, between the 10th and 15th centuries AD, established new Muslim empires on the Indian sub-continent. Eventually, after 1526, these were absorbed into the Muslim Mughal Empire which dominated the whole of India by around 1700. Although, over time, the medieval Islamic Empire broke up into separate states, in a sense it has survived to this day: for with the exception of Christian Spain, all of them retained the faith of Islam.

CHARLEMAGNE

THE DARK AGES ARE OFTEN DEPICTED AS A TIME WHEN EUROPE WAS TRAPPED IN AN UNENDING CYCLE OF WAR AND DESTRUCTION. BUT THE PERIOD HAD ITS GLORIES, AND ONE OF THEM WAS THE REIGN OF THE HOLY ROMAN EMPEROR, CHARLEMAGNE.

The Dark Ages saw a ferociously fought struggle between the Christians of Europe and their Muslim and pagan enemies. This was reflected in contemporary histories, which depicted Christian warriors as the saviors of Europe. The most prominent of these saviors was Charlemagne — Charles the Great — whose achievements not only included a renaissance of learning, art, education, architecture and industry, but military exploits that gained him high status in the pantheon of Christian heroes.

As a military leader, Charlemagne forged an orderly army out of a swarm of men running or riding into battle, wielding swords and uttering blood-curdling war cries. This, Charlemagne realized, was not the way to achieve the victories or conquests he had in mind. To this end, he disciplined his infantry and cavalry so that they responded to orders issued by superior officers — something unknown in European warfare since the fall of the Ancient Roman Empire and its army.

Feeding and supplying his armies was another problem Charlemagne needed to solve. For the kind of warfare he had in mind, it was too haphazard for the Franks to plunder and forage at random. Instead, Charlemagne organized supply trains carrying enough food and equipment to keep his army operational for weeks. He also reintroduced the siege train, as once used by the Romans, and included archers to give his armies long-range capability. *Burgs*, or fortified posts, were built and liberally stocked with supplies. These innovations enabled Charlemagne's armies to campaign up to 1,000 miles (1,600 km) away from France, maintain long sieges, and operate throughout winter weather, another procedure unknown in western Europe since Roman times.

After Charlemagne became King of the Franks in AD768, he expanded his territory over most of central and Western Europe. On Christmas Day, AD800 he was crowned first Holy Roman Emperor by Pope Leo III. His most important function was as protector of the papacy and in this role, Charlemagne went to war with the Lombards of northern Italy, who were refusing to return papal cities to the jurisdiction of Rome. In AD773, Charlemagne took an army across the Alps into Italy and drove the Lombards back to Pavia, which he promptly besieged. The siege lasted until the Spring of AD774, when Charlemagne captured the Lombard king, Desiderius, appropriated Desiderius' kingdom, and added it to his own territories.

In AD777, Charlemagne tackled the Muslim Moors, who had invaded southern Spain 66 years before. They had now reached the far north of Spain, where they established the Caliphate of Cordoba. This was far too close for comfort to Frankish territory in southern France. Dealing with them appeared easy at first. Squabbles among the Moors had led the Muslim rulers of Zaragoza, Gerona, Barcelona, and Huesca to take the unusual step of offering homage to Charlemagne in return for military assistance. Seeing

An early wood-cut showing Charlegmane being crowned on Christmas Day, AD800. Charlegmane was the first Holy Roman Emperor, having earned the position through his military skill in conquering much of Europe.

an opportunity to add to his domains, and spread Christianity into pastures new, Charlemagne agreed. Homage was duly given, but on his way back to France, the rearguard and baggage train of Charlemagne's army was ambushed while crossing the Pass of Roncesvalles in the Pyrenees mountains. Trapped and helpless in a narrow defile by Muslim dissidents and Christian Basques, scores of Charlemagne's men were killed and the baggage train was destroyed. Some years later, in AD800, Charlemagne avenged the dead of Roncesvalles when he thrashed the Basques and drove the Moors south as far as the River Ebro, 100 miles from the Pyrenees. Charlemagne's wars against the Moors in Spain and the Mediterranean continued throughout his reign. His armies captured Gerona and gradually spread Frankish control along the coast of Catalonia until they captured Tarragona in AD809 and Tortosa in AD811. In AD812, the Emir al-Hakam I of Valencia, which the Franks were threatening, sought to mollify them by recognizing their conquests.

Charlemagne's fight against the Moors in Spain was paralleled by constant warfare against the pagan Saxons in Germany. The Saxon wars covered 30 years and 18 campaigns before Charlemagne, riding at the head of his elite Scara bodyguard, his famous sword *Joyeuse* (joyful) in his hand, finally overcame this stubborn enemy and, for good measure, converted them to Christianity. Pagan Vikings from Denmark, first attacked Charlemagne's domains across the River Elbe in AD809. They were repulsed after three years' hard campaigning and the Frankish fleet was put on guard along the coast of Charlemagne's empire to make them keep their distance. Charlemagne died in AD814 and sadly, his great Empire and its accomplishments did not survive him for long. According to Frankish laws of heredity, his hard-won territory was divided between his sons, all of whom lacked his authority and charisma. Although the title of Holy Roman Emperor continued among Charlemagne's descendants until AD962, when it passed to German kings, its days of glory were gone.

Warrior Societies: Vikings and Magyars

THE "DARK AGES" WAS A TERM COINED IN THE 1330S BY THE ITALIAN POET PETRARCH TO DESCRIBE THE EARLY MIDDLE AGES, WHEN THE LAW, ORDER, AND SECURITY ONCE PROVIDED BY THE ROMANS HAD GONE AND BARBARIAN RAIDERS RAMPAGED ACROSS EUROPE.

When the western Roman Empire ceased to exist in around AD476, Europeans lost all the reassurances to which they had for centuries become accustomed, and Dark Age Europe lay at the mercy of raiders like the Vikings of Scandinavia or the Magyars (Hungarians). The Christian church became a major victim of robbery, rapine, and slaughter. The Vikings reached Britain on 8 January AD793. The Vikings landed at Lindisfarne, a center of Christian worship in Northern England, and caused untold damage and destruction. Before leaving, the Vikings butchered or drowned most of the monks who had survived the initial assault and carried off the rest as slaves. News of the slaughter and devastation on Lindisfarne sent a shudder of horror across Christian Europe, where similar atrocities were soon occurring as bands of Vikings spread death and destruction along the coasts of France, Spain, and Italy and crossed the Mediterranean Sea to do the same in North Africa. A major part of the shock the Viking raids created came from their ability to navigate out of sight of land — which was thought to be impossible. Viking seafaring expertise was unmatched and their skill also allowed them to navigate along rivers. This was how they could sail their longships down the River Rhine and River Elbe to raid Germany. Other Vikings headed up the River Rhône or penetrated deep into northeastern France by way of the River Loire, heading for the fabulous booty to be found in the rich abbeys of the region.

To the east, Swedish Vikings also used rivers to reach destinations that lay far inland, conquering parts of Russia. From there, in AD941 they raided the Byzantine capital, Constantinople. Unfortunately for

The Vikings were the most feared raiders of the Dark Ages because of their superb seafaring skills, which enabled them to go anywhere they wanted. They could sail along rivers and out into the open ocean, cross the inimical North Sea out of sight of land and even circumnavigate the whole of Europe.

Viking Europe
c. 910

→ Viking invasions

them, the Byzantine fleet was waiting for them and used the dreaded Greek Fire to repulse the attack.

While Swedish Vikings were moving south to settle in what is now the Ukraine, seven "hordes" (tribes) of Magyars came into Russia from another direction, the east, to arrive by around AD830 in the Steppes of the Urals and the Caucasus. Magyar ferocity came to the attention of the Byzantines, who used them as mercenaries. Magyars were also enlisted by the German King Arnulf for his fight against the Slavs of Moravia, but eventually, they met their match in the Pechenegs who lived in the Ural mountains of Russia and were even more savage than the Magyars themselves.

The Pechenegs evicted the Magyars from their settlements and gave them such a thrashing that they were forced to migrate westward, seeking a new home. They found it in the Carpathian Mountains of central and eastern Europe, a territory later extended after 900AD when the Magyars acquired the former Roman province of Pannonia (modern Hungary). After that, no one was immune from Magyar marauding which reached as far as Denmark, Spain, and Portugal, and they became the terror of Europe.

The Magyars gained a bloodthirsty reputation as inveterate plunderers, rapists, and killers. So much so that when they decided to convert to Christianity, no established Church would admit them. Finally, after many attempts, the Eastern Orthodox Church proved braver than the rest and allowed them to join. On Christmas Day in the year AD1000, Stephen I (St. Stephen) was formally crowned by Pope Sylvester II as King of Hungary, and with that his realm became a Christian country.

The Magyars probably originated in the Ural Mountains of Russia and migrated into eastern Europe in the 5th century AD. After AD889 they moved into the River Danube basin and settled in Hungary. From there, the Magyars became the terror of Europe, staging raids all over the continent.

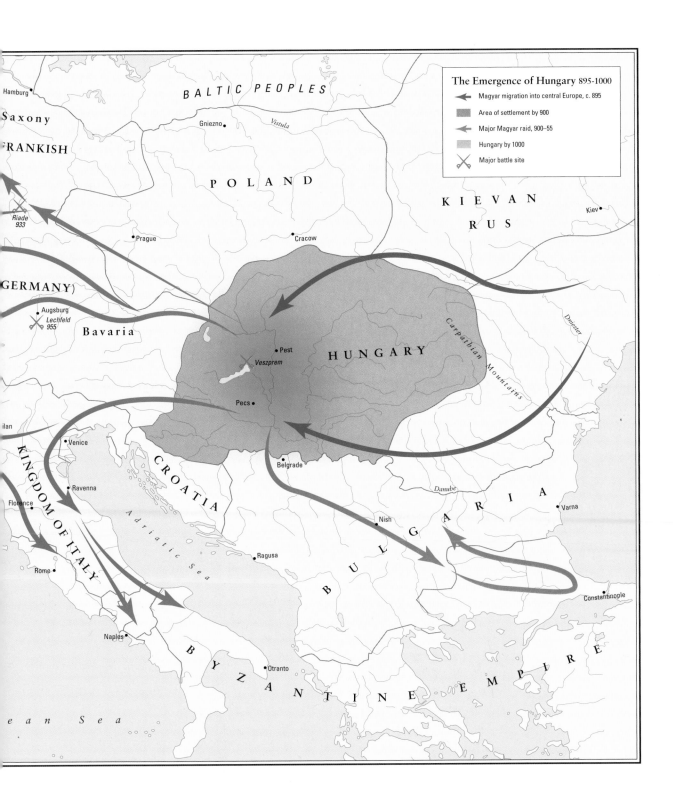

The Emergence of Hungary 895-1000

- Magyar migration into central Europe, c. 895
- Area of settlement by 900
- Major Magyar raid, 900–55
- Hungary by 1000
- Major battle site

VIKING WARFARE TO AD1000

THE VIKINGS WERE MORE THAN MERE RAIDERS; STRIKING THEIR TARGETS, SEIZING THEIR BOOTY, AND RETURNING FOR MORE IN THE NEXT RAIDING SEASON. THEY WERE ALSO ADVENTURERS AND WARRIORS INTENT ON CONQUERING AND SETTLING THE LANDS THEY RAIDED.

T he wide-ranging raids staged by the Vikings of Scandinavia after the late 8th century AD brought them not only great wealth, but gave them a tantalizing glimpse of the world beyond their own ice-bound, mist-wrapped shores. Tempting tales circulated in Europe about Britain's mineral wealth, the temperate British climate, its fertile soil, well-stocked fields, rich grazing land, and forests teeming with animal life. These conditions were in stark contrast to Scandinavia, a place where survival of the fittest was the basic law of life and nature and hard work was required to wrest a living from the unforgiving soil. Inevitably, these harsh conditions bred a race of fearless warriors and adventurers who were willing to use their superlative seamanship to venture far beyond their own shores and seize the better chances offered by lands farther south.

The urge to emigrate and settle down did not, of course, mean that the Vikings gave up raiding. All the more so because even the threat of a Viking raid brought them easy money as the terrified English gave them Danegeld to go away. The Viking forces were very successful in establishing communities in Europe, particularly in France, where they occupied the duchy that came to be known as Normandy, and in England, where assaults by the "great heathen army" of Vikings from Denmark gave them control of vast territory in the north and east by around AD871. The Viking takeover of land was as brutal as it was straightforward: drive away established settlers, seize their farms and fields, their homes, possessions and animals, and move in and exploit these new acquisitions for themselves.

The great military advantage that enabled the Vikings to make war and plant new settlements far from home lay in their superlative warships, which could be propelled at speed by 30 pairs of oars. In these sturdy, clinker-built longboats, with their double-thick coarse woolen sails mounted on tree-trunk

England and Danelaw
902–19

English Kingdoms or under English control c. 902

Extent of Danelaw c. 902

The Five Boroughs of Danelaw

Other major fortified towns

English fortified towns (*burh*) established by 916

Wessex border after the annexation of Mercia c. 919

Major Scandinavian movements

Major English movements

Major battle site

① 903: Danes attack English Mercia and Wessex

② 903: English reprisal attack defeated

③ 909: English army ravages Kingdom of York

④ 910: Danes launch reprisal raid, they are badly defeated at Tettenhall

⑤ 914: Viking raids launch from Brittany, defeated by English

⑥ 917: Danish King of East Anglia killed in battle of Tempsford after which Danish resistence crumbles. The English conquest of Danelaw completed under the leadership of Wessex

⑦ 918: Norse chieftain based in Dublin took control of the English-ruled Earldom of Northumbria and then seized control of the Kingdom of York

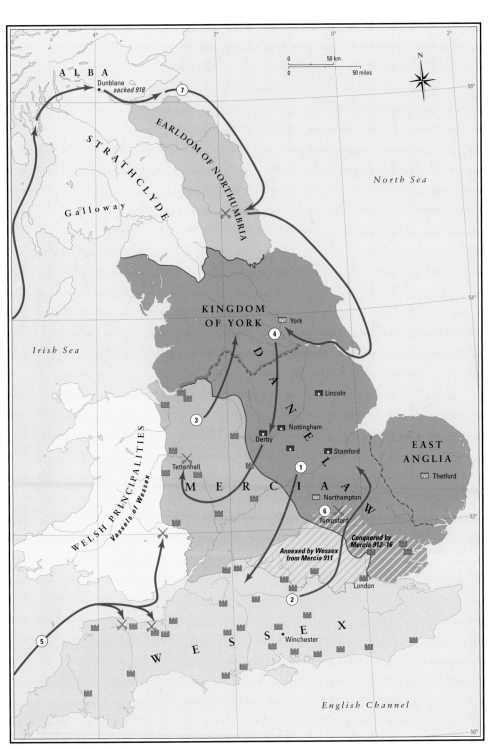

masts up to 41 ft (12.5m) high, the Vikings could travel anywhere they chose, reaching destinations far inland like the port of Dorstadt in Germany, 50 miles (80 km) from the sea, whose inhabitants thought themselves safe. Viking warships could be identified while they were still far offshore, from their slim lines and the rows of circular shields, some 3 ft (1m) across, which were carried along their sides. These weapons were the personal property of free Vikings, each of whom was expected to own their own spears, swords, battle-axes and bows and arrows. In this aggressive world, training in the use of weapons began at an early age, usually as soon as a young Viking grew strong enough to handle them with ease. Weapons were used not only in war, but also for hunting and sports.

Weapons were also regarded as a sign of wealth and status. The wooden Viking spears measured up to 9ft (3m) in length and were usually made of ash, with iron blades shaped like long spikes or broad leaves. The skilled spearman was a much admired warrior, capable, it was said, of throwing spears with both hands at once and even catching an incoming spear in mid-air and throwing it back. The Viking battleaxe, which was introduced in the late 10th century, was a particularly formidable weapon, but also an inconvenient one. Since it was double-handed, it was impossible for a warrior to hold a shield at the same time. Instead, his "shield" was a line of fellow warriors standing in front of him sheltering him until the moment was right for him to rush out, whirling his weapon above his head and setting about the enemy with terrifying ferocity. For protection, Viking warriors wore mail coats made of interlocking rings with thick padding underneath. Armor was probably confined in battle to leaders since it was very costly and time-consuming to make and the same also applied to the often elaborate Viking helmets: one Viking grave discovered at Gjermundbu in Norway featured a visor shaped like a pair of spectacles and a four-section dome with a spike at the crown. Horns — probably a Hollywood invention — were not in fact worn on Viking helmets. In battle, the Vikings would line up with overlapping shields forming a "wall". Another line

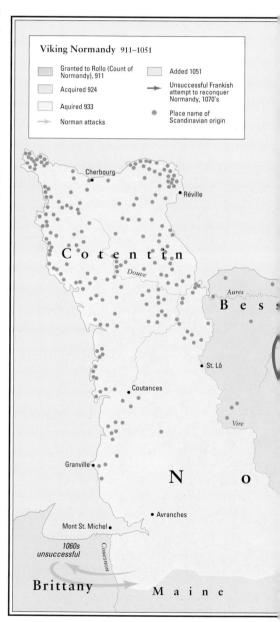

Viking Normandy 911–1051

Granted to Rollo (Count of Normandy), 911

Acquired 924

Aquired 933

Norman attacks

Added 1051

Unsuccessful Frankish attempt to reconquer Normandy, 1070's

Place name of Scandinavian origin

of warriors stood in support behind them. Vikings did not usually fight in tight formations, preferring instead the wild onrush, which often terrified opponents. However, one way to defeat enemies was the *svinlylking*: a wedge of up to 30 warriors that could charge and hopefully blast through the opposition by sheer weight of numbers. There were also some groups made up of Vikings who worked themselves up into a frenzy, known as *berserker*. They believed Odin, their war god, protected them and so they had no need to wear armor.

In AD911, the French king, Charles III, granted the Viking Rollo lands in the lower Seine area of northern France, and the Channel Islands. Rollo became Count of Rouen and swore feudal alliegance to the French king. His descendants called themselves Dukes of Normandy.

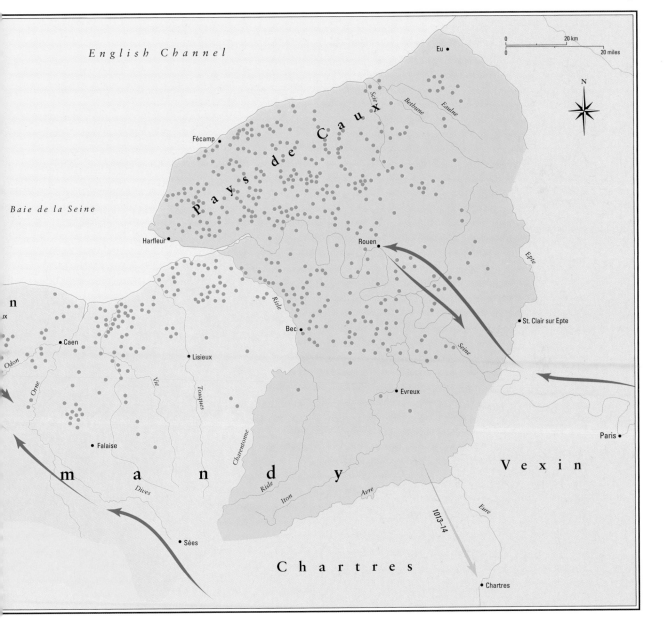

EUROPE: THE NORMANS

OVER 1,200 YEARS AFTER IT BEGAN AS TWO SMALL VILLAGES ON A HILL ABOVE THE RIVER TIBER, DISASTER HAD FINALLY OVERTAKEN ROME. YET PART OF ROME'S POWER PERSISTED IN THE EASTERN EMPIRE AND ITS MAGNIFICENT CAPITAL CITY, CONSTANTINOPLE.

Opposite: In the 11th century, Normandy was second only to France in the size of its territory. Henry II, king of England, later controlled not only Normandy, but Brittany, Anjou, Maine and Touraine, together with Poitou and Aquitaine.

Overleaf: England was by no means the Normans' only target for conquest. The urge for settling overseas that had characterised their Viking ancestors frequently asserted itself in the 11th century as Normans set out to conquer Sicily, invade the Papal States in Italy, and confront the Muslims long before the Crusades began.

Overleaf: The Battle of Hastings steered British history in a new direction. Before the battle on 14 October, 1066, England was being linked to Scandinavia, through persistent Viking raids and settlements. But the Normans, the victors at Hastings, altered this connection to give England a north–European future instead.

The Normans, or "Northmen," were originally Vikings who settled in the northern French territory later known as Normandy. Like their Scandinavian ancestors, they were ferocious warriors, but more interested in conquering and ruling than in raiding. There was an unusual sequel to the victory of King Charles III of France at the battle of Chartres where he vanquished a Viking invasion force in AD911. Instead of consolidating his triumph and driving the Vikings from his territory or paying them to leave, the King offered their leader, Rollo, a deal: he promised to give the Vikings lands in what later became the Duchy of Normandy in exchange for their feudal allegiance, their conversion to Christianity, and the task of fighting off other Vikings who attempted to attack the north of France. Although local imperatives were uppermost in the King's mind, his decision had far-reaching consequences for France and, in fact, for the whole of western Europe. What King Charles had done was to establish the Vikings as a permanent presence in continental Europe, legitimized by membership of the feudal system, and with their own territory which they soon proceeded to expand. Less than 150 years after Charles made his deal with the Normans — as Rollo's Vikings were soon known — they earmarked southern Italy as a useful hunting ground for new conquests. This brought the Norman knights into direct conflict with Pope Leo XI whose Papal States lay in central Italy to the north of lands the knights acquired in a series of military expeditions. The crunch came in 1053 at Civitella in southern Italy, where the Normans defeated the Pope's forces. The Normans assaulted the Pope's cavalry while other knights charged the papal infantry from the rear and the last two formations attacked at the front. This way, the Normans had the papal forces inescapably trapped. Subsequently, southern Italy became a base for the Normans to eject the Byzantines from Italy and cross the Straits of Messina to do the same

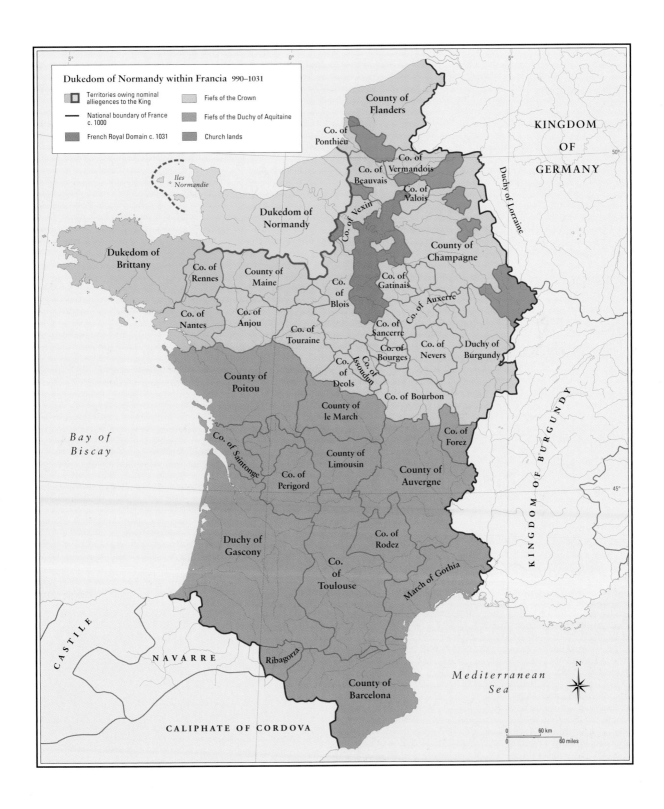

Dukedom of Normandy within Francia 990–1031

- Territories owing nominal alliegences to the King
- National boundary of France c. 1000
- French Royal Domain c. 1031
- Fiefs of the Crown
- Fiefs of the Duchy of Aquitaine
- Church lands

KINGDOM OF GERMANY

County of Flanders

Co. of Ponthieu

Co. of Vermandois

Co. of Beauvais

Co. of Valois

Co. of Vexin

Duchy of Lorraine

Iles Normandie

Dukedom of Normandy

County of Champagne

Dukedom of Brittany

Co. of Rennes

County of Maine

Co. of Blois

Co. of Gatinais

Co. of Auxerre

Co. of Nantes

Co. of Anjou

Co. of Touraine

Co. of Sancerre

Co. of Bourges

Co. of Nevers

Duchy of Burgundy

Co. of Issoudun

Co. of Deols

Co. of Bourbon

County of Poitou

County of le March

KINGDOM OF BURGUNDY

Bay of Biscay

Co. of Saintonge

County of Limousin

Co. of Forez

Co. of Perigord

County of Auvergne

County of Toulouse

Duchy of Gascony

Co. of Rodez

March of Gothia

CASTILE

NAVARRE

Ribagorza

Mediterranean Sea

County of Barcelona

CALIPHATE OF CORDOVA

N

0   60 km
0   60 miles

to the Muslim Arabs in Sicily. The task was extremely prolonged, but after more than 30 years, in 1093, the whole of southern Italy and Sicily were in Norman hands. Norman knights were probably the most formidable warriors in 11th-century Europe. The knights, who carried an 8ft (2.5m) long lance and a flat sword, rode heavy warhorses, and wore chain mail armor, helmets and long, weighty kite-shaped shields. During close combat, the knights stood up in their stirrups, giving them added power as they slashed opponents with their swords.

In 1066, Duke William of Normandy brought his army to England to claim the English throne, which he believed had been promised him by the Anglo-Saxon King Edward the Confessor. But after Edward died on January 5, 1066, he was succeeded by his brother-in-law Harold Godwinson. Nine months later, an infuriated William arrived at Hastings on the English south coast to unseat the usurper. The Normans and Anglo-Saxons met on October 14 at Hastings where Harold's 20,000 infantry confronted the invaders with their customary shield "wall." Harold's housecarls stood at the highest point along a ridge on Senlac Hill at the centre of his defensive line, with his infantry densely massed perhaps some 20 men deep

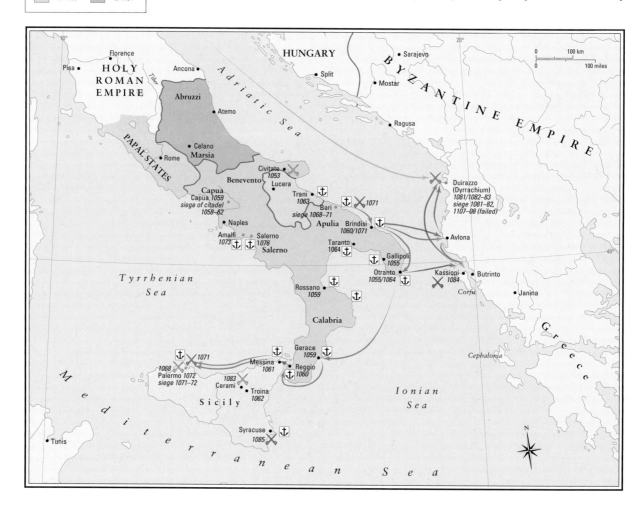

over a distance of some 1,200 ft (400 m) on either side. At first, the Norman archers, crossbowmen, pikemen and even their cavalry, made little impression on the English formations. Standing on Senlac Hill, the English had the advantage of greater height and showered the Normans below them with rocks and javelins. At this, the Norman infantry panicked and beat a hasty retreat. Suddenly, a rumor sprang up to say that Duke William had been killed and the rest of the Norman ranks, disheartened, began to fall apart. William, who was very much alive, made a dramatic gesture to refute the rumor. Removing his helmet, he rode along the infantry lines so that every man could see his face. When the Norman infantry had began to break apart, the English came down from Senlac Hill to pursue them. This was their great mistake. As the Normans rallied on realizing that Duke William was safe, the pursuers were overwhelmed. Duke William now resorted to an old Byzantine trick and ordered his cavalry to pretend to withdraw. The English were fooled into following, only to be slaughtered as the Normans turned on them. Meanwhile, the Norman archers rained arrows on the English ranks, using high-angle fire so that the missiles would fall out of the sky on the enemy massed below. For several hours, the English were attacked by the Norman archers who alternated their assaults with repeated cavalry charges. Harold Godwinson was killed by an arrow that reportedly struck him in the eye. With that, most of the English soldiers lost heart and began to melt away. The Battle of Hastings was over.

On Christmas Day, 1066, Duke William was crowned King William I at Westminster Abbey in London and England became another Norman possession.

(1) *The Norman army advanced soon after dawn with the front rank of archers opening with an ineffective fire on English ranks.*

(2) *Norman infantry advanced through the archers and attacked the English shield wall but were beaten off with heavy losses.*

(3) *The Norman cavalry then attacked but were again beaten back. The Norman left fell back in panic.*

(4) *Breaking ranks, the English right wing chased the retreating Norman cavalry. Duke William rallied his cavalry and attacked the dispersed English right wing.*

(5) *The English centre was again attacked by Norman cavalry and infantry and again drove them off. William feigned retreat, the English finally broke ranks to pursue. William counter-attacked killing many English. However, the line still stood. Eventually, after further attacks by all arms, the English gave ground. Harold was mortally wounded and lay dying while the English resistance gradually crumbled.*

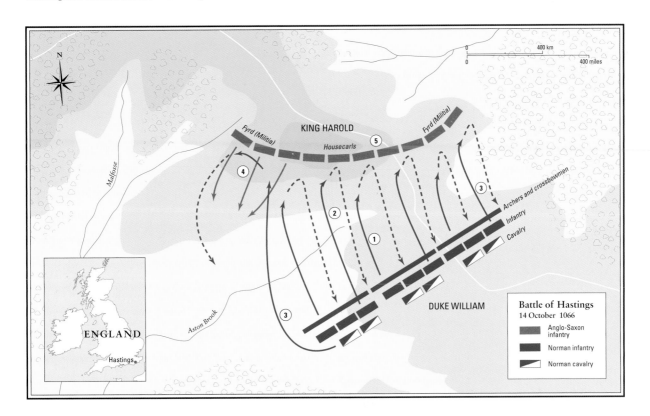

WESTERN EUROPE: THE EMERGENCE OF THE KNIGHT

IN MEDIEVAL EUROPE, THE ARMORED KNIGHT ON HORSEBACK WAS THE MOST ADMIRED OF WARRIORS, THE EPITOME OF MILITARY SKILL, CHIVALRY, COURTESY, PHYSICAL STRENGTH, AND AGILITY. HE WAS, AND STILL IS, THE MOST ROMANTICIZED FIGURE IN THE ENTIRE HISTORY OF WARFARE.

For a young man in medieval times, the route to knighthood was a long and arduous one. It began at the age of seven years, when a boy who came from a family with sufficient wealth to afford the expense involved in training, began his service as page to the squire of a knight. The squire was there to serve the knight and also undertake the prolonged period of training that would qualify him to be a knight in his turn. Despite his youth, a page had to become adept at some of a knight's skills, such as tilting a lance at a target while sitting astride a wooden horse. He also fought his fellow pages with a wooden, covered, or blunt-ended sword, while carrying a wooden shield for protection. In addition, pages practiced throwing the javelin, archery, and wrestling. Skilled horsemanship was, of course, essential, for no one unable to handle a horse in battle conditions could ever become a knight. One of the most important of these horsemanship skills was the ability to balance while engaged in mounted combat and for pages, the relevant practice was provided by fighting on piggyback.

After seven years, the page graduated to become a squire and in the next seven years learned how to perfect and augment the skills he had learned as a page. Sword-fighting practice continued, but other training became much more dangerous. This particularly applied to the use of a lance to practice with a quintain. A quintain was a dummy covered by a shield, sometimes with heavy sandbags attached, suspended from a swinging pole. The squire would gallop toward the quintain and hit the shield with his lance, making the whole contraption spin around at speed. He had to duck to avoid the rotating dummy or risk being knocked out of the saddle. To make this exercise more difficult, a test called "Running the Rings" was sometimes employed in which the quintain was replaced by a ring: the squire had to place the tip of his lance in the center of the ring, a technique that required great accuracy but could mean the difference between life and death on some future battlefield.

At age 21, the squire ceased to be an apprentice-knight, and became instead a knight-in-training, taking skills already learned to higher, more professional levels. At this point, the training also included feats of physical prowess that demanded great strength and agility. One was to leap into the saddle wearing full armor without touching the stirrups. Another required the knight to roll over on the ground and jump to his feet, again wearing full armor. These were not just athletic stunts: the ability to move fast and get out of the way of an opponent's weapon could mean surviving or being killed in battle. A frequent practice-ground for knights-in-training was the tournament, where they were able to hone their expertise with the two-handed sword, the battle-axe, the mace, dagger, and lance. Jousting at the tournament was basically a rehearsal for war, but it also served as the most thrilling sport of medieval times and drew crowds of excited spectators. They came to watch two fully-armored knights gallop toward each other on beautifully caparisoned horses, lances at the ready, to meet in a mighty clash of steel on steel. One or other of them, sometimes both, might be thrown out of the saddle and be sent crashing to the ground. Needless to say, tournaments were dangerous. Death at the tournament was not uncommon, which was why they met with great disapproval from the Church and were banned from time to time.

The Church had its own ethical interest in the training of knights, for in addition to physical and fighting attainments, knighthood stood for honor, chivalry, loyalty, fearlessness, and Christian devotion. The ceremony that finally qualified a young man to be a knight was imbued through and through with religious significance. It was preceded by a ten-hour vigil in chapel, during which the soon-to-be knight prayed before the altar where a sword and shield had been placed. He took a ritual bath to ensure that his body was properly cleansed. The public part of the ceremony that followed involved taking the Oath of Knighthood, which included vows never to have dealings with traitors and to hear Mass and make an offering in Church every day. The accolade of knighthood was conferred by the *colée*, a blow struck with the flat of the hand or the side of a sword that was supposed to be the last the new knight would have to suffer without responding. His sponsors girded on his sword and put on his spurs, and with that, the ceremony was complete.

Knights fighting during the Battle of Najera, 1367. Fought during a civil war in Castile, this minor battle gives an example of the type of armor used in the later 14th century.

THE CRUSADES

ON 27 NOVEMBER, 1095, AT CLERMONT, FRANCE, POPE URBAN II
ISSUED AN URGENT CALL TO ARMS. CHRISTIANS IN THE HOLY LAND
WERE BEING ATTACKED BY MUSLIMS. A CRUSADE WAS NEEDED TO
RESCUE THEM AND RETRIEVE THE HOLY LAND FOR CHRIST.

P ope Urban's call to crusade was the most significant event of its kind to occur in Christian
Europe during the Middle Ages. It generated enormous enthusiasm among the barons and
bishops who heard him speak at Clermont. A wave of emotion swept through the audience,
as several listeners leapt to their feet shouting "Dieu le veult! Dieu le veult! God wills it! God wills it!"
The enthusiasm spread throughout Europe as the message was publicized in cities, towns, and villages
and before long, great crusading armies were formed in southern Italy and France. Duke Robert of
Normandy, son of King William I of England, went as far as pawning his duchy for almost $40,000
in order to 'take the Cross' as going on crusade was termed. But the widespread fervor the crusade
provoked was not all that it seemed. Many knights were thrilled at the prospect of serving the cause of
Christ, but others were in it for military glory and adventure, and some for the chances the Holy Land
offered for personal gain.

During 1096 and the early months of 1097, great armed hosts rode and marched across Europe,
pennons flying, the fiery red cross of the crusader emblazoned on their surcoats. Local chiefs, pilgrims,
and priests joined in, so that the ranks of knightly crusaders swelled to greater and greater numbers.
They arrived in Constantinople in separate groups, but by May 1097, the last of them had reached the
capital of the Byzantine Empire. The emperor, Alexius I, furnished supplies, ships, and guides to take
the crusaders through the unknown territory that lay across the Bosphorus strait in Asia Minor. By
mid-summer 1097, they had arrived in Anatolia. Despite the exhausting heat, the flies, and the lack of
sufficient food and water, the crusaders scored speedy success. By June 1097, they had put an end to
the resistance of the Turkish Muslims in Asia Minor and afterward drove the Turks from the cities of
Edessa and Antioch, where they set up the first crusader states. Jerusalem on the other hand, which the

During and after the First
Crusade, four states were
created along the Mediterranean
coast of the Holy Land. Antioch,
founded in 1098, lasted until
1268. Edessa, also founded in
1098, lasted until 1144, Jerusalem
was founded in 1099 and lasted
until 1291, and Tripoli, founded in
1104, lasted until 1289.

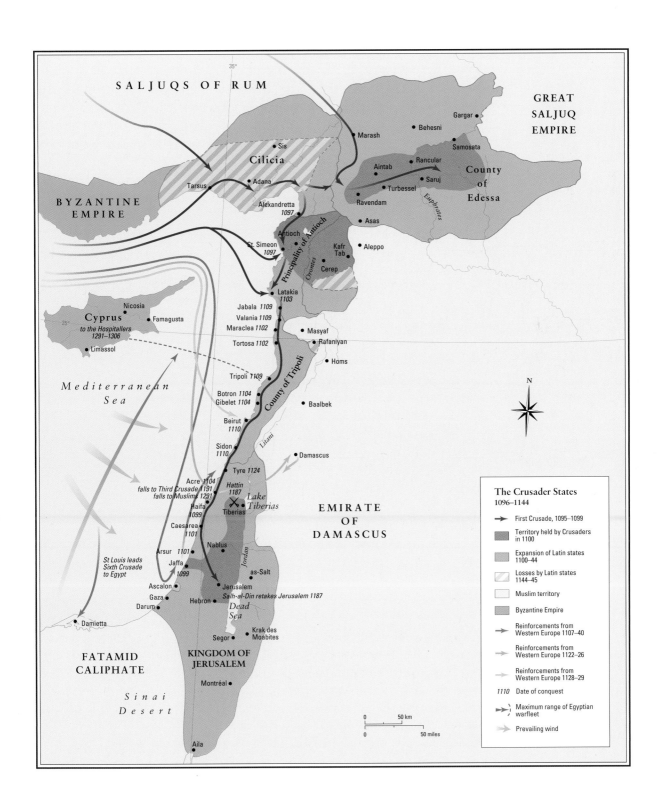

SALJUQS OF RUM

GREAT
SALJUQ
EMPIRE

Gargar

Behesni

Marash

Samosata

Sis

Cilicia

Aintab   Rancular

County
of
Edessa

Tarsus   Adana   Saruj

Turbessel

Alexandretta
1097   Ravendam

BYZANTINE
EMPIRE

Asas

Antioch

St. Simeon
1097   Kafr
Tab   Aleppo

Principality of Antioch

Cerep

Orontes

Latakia
1103

Jabala 1109

Valania 1109

Maraclea 1102   Masyaf

Tortosa 1102   Rafaniyan

Nicosia

Cyprus   Famagusta

Homs

to the Hospitallers
1291–1306

Limassol

Tripoli 1109

Mediterranean
Sea

Botron 1104
Gibelet 1104

County of Tripoli

Baalbek

Beirut
1110

Sidon
1110   Litani   Damascus

Tyre 1124

Acre 1104
falls to Third Crusade 1191   Hattin
falls to Muslims 1291   1187   Lake
Tiberias

EMIRATE
OF
DAMASCUS

Haifa
1099   Tiberias

Caesarea
1101

Arsur 1101   Nablus

Jaffa
1099   as-Salt

St Louis leads
Sixth Crusade
to Egypt

Ascalon   Jerusalem

Gaza   Hebron   Salh-al-Din retakes Jerusalem 1187

Darum   Dead
Sea

Damietta

FATAMID
CALIPHATE   KINGDOM OF
JERUSALEM

Segor   Krak des
Moabites

Sinai
Desert

Montréal

N

Aila

The Crusader States
1096–1144

➤ First Crusade, 1095–1099

▮ Territory held by Crusaders
in 1100

▮ Expansion of Latin states
1100–44

▨ Losses by Latin states
1144–45

☐ Muslim territory

▮ Byzantine Empire

➤ Reinforcements from
Western Europe 1107–40

➤ Reinforcements from
Western Europe 1122–26

➤ Reinforcements from
Western Europe 1128–29

1110 Date of conquest

➤ Maximum range of Egyptian
warfleet

➤ Prevailing wind

0   50 km

0   50 miles

crusaders reached on June 7, 1099, was a much more difficult proposition. Located high in the Judean mountains, Jerusalem remained inaccessible and for five weeks, its Muslim and Jewish defenders resisted the determined crusader siege. It was only when the crusaders decided to build huge siege machines resembling castle towers on wheels that the situation began to change.

On July 15, 1099, in the sizzling afternoon heat, a giant tower was wheeled toward the north wall of Jerusalem. Amid a shower of arrows and spears flung down by the defenders, the crusaders lowered a bridge from the top of the tower onto the battlements. They surged over the bridge and swarmed through Jerusalem's narrow streets, killing every Muslim and Jew they could find. The massacres went on for three whole days. By the time the crusaders gathered in the Church of the Resurrection to give thanks to God for their victory, Jerusalem was littered with bodies, stained with blood, and choked with the smoke of burning houses, mosques, and synagogues.

In the 12 years after the fall of Jerusalem, the crusaders captured the Mediterranean coastline of Syria, Lebanon, and Palestine and moved inland to overrun Judea, Samaria, Galilee and most of the land across the river Jordan. However, the Saracens never gave up attacking crusader territory at every possible opportunity and gradually, in time, crusader power weakened. In 1144, the Saracens captured the crusader state of Edessa, provoking a rescue mission. This was the Second Crusade which turned out to be an embarrassing failure. In 1148, the Crusade died after the Christian army ran short of water and had to give up. Worse was to come in 1187, after the Sultan of Egypt and Syria, Saladin, led 80,000 Saracens in rapid sweep through Palestine, conquering all the way until they captured Jerusalem.

The fall of Jerusalem was greeted in Europe as an appalling tragedy. The call to crusade went out once more and attracted three of the greatest monarchs in Europe: King Frederick I Barbarossa of Germany (who was drowned on his way to the Holy Land), King Philip II Augustus of France, and King Richard I Lionheart of England, a great hero whose life was dedicated to soldiering. Richard was

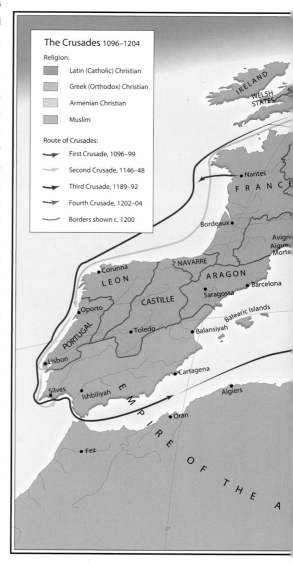

The Crusades 1096–1204

Religion:
- Latin (Catholic) Christian
- Greek (Orthodox) Christian
- Armenian Christian
- Muslim

Route of Crusades:
- First Crusade, 1096–99
- Second Crusade, 1146–48
- Third Crusade, 1189–92
- Fourth Crusade, 1202–04
- Borders shown c. 1200

so keen that he put his kingdom up for sale to raise the immense amount of money that crusading required. On June 8 1191, Richard reached the port of Acre, where a ten-month crusader siege had reached stalemate. To complicate matters, the besiegers were themselves besieged, by Saladin's army. Richard and Philip of France soon got to work with mangonels, battering rams, and other siege engines. Saladin tried several times to relieve the garrison inside Acre but failed and finally decided to negotiate a truce. Richard, Philip, and their elated crusaders took possession of the city on July 12, 1191. Soon afterward, though, Philip decided to return home to France, leaving Richard on his own to fulfill the next task: an attack on Jerusalem.

Richard and his army left Acre for Jerusalem at the end of August 1191, with Saladin and his

The first of the Crusades, which began in 1096, was undoubtedly the most successful, winning considerable territory from the Muslim Saracens and setting up several crusader states in the Holy Land. Later, the crusading ideal became debased and reached a nadir with the attack on Christian Byzantium in 1204, during the Fourth Crusade.

army shadowing them all the way. Saladin, who was familiar with local conditions, knew that Richard's forces would become sick, hungry, and exhausted in the tremendous heat long before he could reach Jerusalem. Saladin was right. Richard came close enough to Jerusalem to glimpse its towers and spires, but realized that his men were too weak to have a chance of capturing the city. The king reportedly wept and covered his eyes with his shield. "If my hand cannot take it," he said "my eyes shall not see it."

After King Richard left the Holy Land, crusading, once considered a noble, valiant undertaking, fell into disrepute. Five more crusades took place and all but the last were thoroughly ignominious. For example, in the Fourth Crusade of 1201-1204, the crusaders went nowhere near the Holy Land, but virtually turned pirate and attacked and sacked the Christian city of Zara. Next, they assaulted Constantinople, causing such intense outrage that all the participants were excommunicated by the pope.

As for the eighth and final crusade of 1270, it ended in fearful tragedy after the crusader leader, King Louis IX of France (St. Louis), planned to land in Tunisia, conquer Muslim-ruled Egypt, then march on to the Holy Land and retrieve Jerusalem. The crusaders never got there. After going ashore at Tunis, Louis fell ill with dysentery — some accounts suggest that he contracted bubonic plague — and died on 26 August, 1270. As he lay dying, it was said that he whispered in heartbroken tones: "Jerusalem! Jerusalem!".

By this time, crusading had become so thoroughly discredited that for many people, it was little more than a bad joke. Although candidates for crusading still existed, they were regarded, at best, as fools and at worst, greedy opportunists. Meanwhile in the Holy Land, the crusading ideal

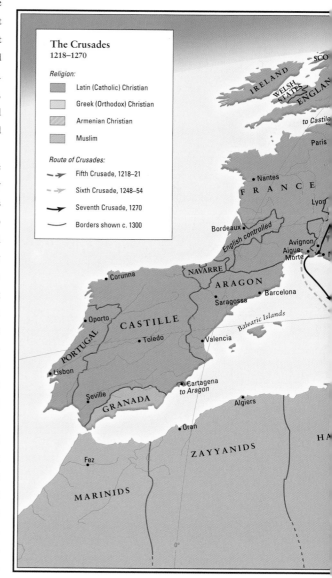

weakened so far that Sultan Baybars of Egypt was able to eject the crusaders from Caesarea, Haifa, Arsuf, Jaffa, Antioch, and the castles of Safed and Belfort. By 1271, Baybars' forces overwhelmed the last three inland crusader castles: Safita, Krak des Chevaliers, and Montfort. For a while, the crusaders managed to maintain a presence in the Holy Land, but only by resorting to the tiny island of Arwad, 2 miles (3.2 km) off the Mediterranean coast. They finally surrendered in 1303, so bringing two centuries of crusading adventure to an end.

The Crusades had a lasting effect on medieval Europe, not least in that much of the Islamic knowledge in areas such as science, medicine, and architecture was transferred to the Western world.

After the crusaders' initial success, the Muslim Saracens began to fight back. Their greatest triumph was the recapture of Jerusalem in 1187. Over the ensuing years, the Saracens pressured the crusader states until, by 1270, they had shrunk to mere enclaves along the Mediterranean coast of the Holy Land.

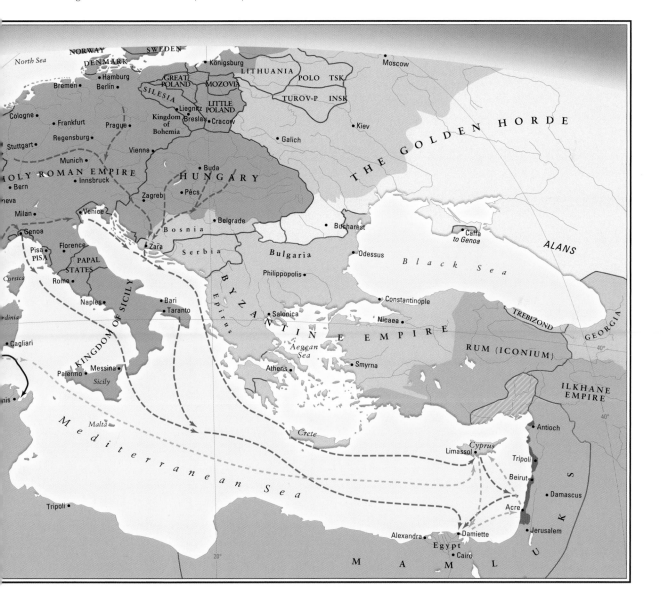

SAMURAI JAPAN

THE SAMURAI WARRIORS OF JAPAN ACHIEVED POWER IN 1192, WHEN
THEIR LEADER, MINAMOTO YORITOMO, BECAME THE FIRST SHOGUN,
A TITLE MEANING "BARBARIAN-SUBDUING GENERALISSIMO." SAMURAI
DOMINANCE LASTED FOR NEARLY 700 YEARS, BEFORE SUCCUMBING
TO THE LURE OF WESTERN-STYLE MODERNIZATION.

When the Shoguns assumed power in Japan, the country had long been in a constant state of internecine war, and would remain so for many centuries to come. A military-style feudal government, with the Shogun at its head, seemed the only answer to this situation and in time, samurai values came to permeate Japanese society. An extraordinary code of conduct, *Bushido* (the Way of the Warrior) developed among the samurai, imposing ultimate obedience, honor, duty and loyalty and a standard of self-sacrifice that required *seppuku*, or suicide, as the price for the slightest shortfall in the performance of duty. The samurai were hardly less rigorous with the obeisance they felt was their due. Anyone suspected of showing insufficient respect or not falling flat on their faces fast enough when a samurai passed by was likely to be executed on the spot.

Codes of conduct have not been unusual among the military, but none went as far as the strict requirements of *Bushido*. Westerners have found it difficult to understand the samurai willingness to kill themselves in the cause of duty. The Japanese, however, found it easier to accept because of their very different view of the value of life. They had a more fatalistic attitude, regarding their time on Earth as only a passing thing, impermanent and therefore not of enormous importance. One Japanese haiku, or "song-poem," put it this way:

The fleeting glory of the flowering trees testified that all that flourishes must decay.
The proud do not last forever, their life is like a summer night's dream.
Warriors, too, must fall in the end, for they are like a lamp at the mercy of the wind...

Ideally, the samurai wanted death to come to them in battle, for this was an honor that would enable them to reach the peace and security of *yomi-nokumi*, the Beyond. Failing to reach the Beyond was far more fearful for them than dying, for it meant being condemned to join other discontented spirits wandering the endless road called *muryogo-no-michi*.

The samurai equipped themselves for battle in suits of armor that covered every part of their bodies. Samurai armor was made of lacquered steel plates, with gauntlets covering their hands and greaves to protect their legs up to the knee. Their steel helmets had visors with wings on either side to proof them against sword thrusts to the head. The samurai carried two swords. One of them, called *daitoor katana* measured more than 2 ft (60cm) in length. The other, shorter, sword called *shoto* or *wkizashi*, was half that size. Further samurai weapons were bows and arrows and the *naginata*, a long pole with a curved blade at the end, resembling the European halberd. The earlier Samurai were expert at fighting both on horseback and on the ground, constantly practicing armed and unarmed combat. One martial combat involved *so-jutsu*, or spear fighting. The samurai also practiced *iai-jutsu*, the art of drawing a sword from its scabbard, *kyo-jutsu*, bow and arrow fighting or *kyuba no machi*, the art of using the bow on horseback. They used their swords for close quarter fighting and, when they got the chance, for beheading their enemies. At first, samurai swords were straight, similar in design to Korean and Chinese swords, but later they preferred the curve-bladed sword which was sharper and tougher. The sword-smith or *muramasa* forged weapons for the samurai through a long process that began with hammering an iron and carbon blade into shape on an anvil using fire and water. Once the blade was forged, it was tested on a corpse or the live body of a condemned criminal. The results of the test were often inscribed on a piece of metal called a *nakago* which joined the sword blade to the hilt. Samurai also applied cosmetics to their faces to make themselves look ferocious and frighten their enemies. This was a very old military practice, dating far back into ancient history, and was so out of tune with the modern world that cosmetics were among the first samurai equipment to be banned by imperial decree. This came about after 1853 when the United States demanded that Japan, which had isolated itself from the outside world for over two centuries, must shed its feudal practices and modernize. There were revolts and violent protests as the samurai fought fanatically for their ancient traditions and customs, but to no avail. The samurai and their way of life disappeared as the Japanese rushed to catch up with the 19th century and emerge into the 20th as a fully-fledged modern nation.

The Samurai warrior was a highly-trained, deadly-accurate mounted bowman. This Japanese knight was protected from retaliation by an elaborate suit of armor quite different in appearance and manufacture to his European counterpart.

THE RISE OF THE MONGOLS 1190-1206

THE MONGOLS WERE THE MOST SURPRISING IMPERIALISTS IN THE WORLD. THEY WERE PASTORAL NOMADS AND YET, UNDER THEIR LEADER GENGHIS KHAN, THEY CONQUERED AN EMPIRE SOME 4,500 MILES (7,250 KM) WIDE, FROM THE BLACK SEA TO THE YELLOW SEA.

Ghengis Khan, future founder of the Mongol Empire, began life in modest guise: he was born, in 1162, as Timujen, son of Yesukhai, chief of the Borjigin, one of the assorted Mongol tribes of Central Asia. The malevolent nature of Central Asian tribes was brought home to Timujen in 1171, when his father was murdered by Tatars, who had long been enemies of the Mongols. Eleven years later, raiders from the Bjartskular tribe, once allies of the Borjigin, captured and enslaved Timujen. He managed to escape and hid himself away in a narrow fissure by a river. Soon afterward, Timujen was joined by the Mongol warriors Jelme and Arslan and by his three brothers and half-brother. Timujen's escape from the Bjartskular gained him a certain fame which fed his reputation as a courageous leader and the man who could unite the Mongol nation. This appeared to be a total impossibility, for the Mongol world was a morass of internecine warfare, raiding, stealing, and murderous vendettas like the enmity that had brought about the death of Timujen's father. Alliances between Mongol tribes were traditionally cemented by inter-tribal marriages and in 1178, Timujen himself made a union to Borte of the Olkut-hun tribe. There was, though, another route to Mongol unity and Timujen took it when he offered to become an ally of Toghrul, the Khan of the Kerait tribe, who had been his father's *anda* (blood brother). Toghrul soon proved his usefulness when he provided 20,000 Kerait warriors to help Timujen retrieve his wife Borte, who was abducted by another rival tribe, the Merkits, soon after their marriage.

This rescue resulted in the total defeat of the Merkits, who were among the first of many conquered tribes in what Timujen intended should become a small, but significant, Mongol confederation.

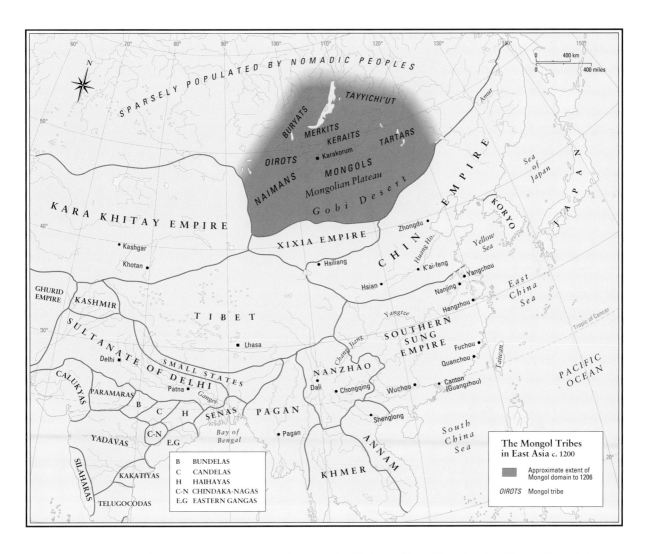

The Mongol Tribes in East Asia c. 1200

Approximate extent of Mongol domain to 1206

OIROTS Mongol tribe

B	BUNDELAS
C	CANDELAS
H	HAIHAYAS
C-N	CHINDAKA-NAGAS
E.G	EASTERN GANGAS

Timujen went on to bring the Naimans, Tanguts, Jin, and Tatars under his leadership and introduced several innovations until then unknown in Mongol society, and promised to make his followers rich through a share in the spoils of future wars, an incentive that helped to ensure obedience. With each victory, Timujen integrated conquered enemies into his own, Borjigin, tribe and even used his mother, Hoelun, as an adoption agency for orphans whose parents had been killed in the latest war. These magnanimous arrangements encouraged loyalty in conquered tribes and made it easier for them to accept Timujen's Yassa code of behavior. The code was designed to eliminate the brutal and divisive habits that had kept the Mongols at each other's throats for centuries. There was to be no stealing of livestock from other tribes, no abduction of women, or enslaving of other Mongols. Rules for the military were strict, as befitted a people who had long been prone to violence, vengeance, and vendetta. Every man, with rare exceptions, must join the army, weapons of war must be kept in good order; officers and

The Mongols comprised several, very quarrelsome tribes. The great dream of Timujen (Ghengis Khan) was to unite all the Mongols, whatever their differences because that way, he believed, they would gain strength and become conquerors. Considering the eventual size of the Mongol Empire, Timujen had good reason for his belief.

chieftains who failed in their duty would be executed and so would soldiers found looting an enemy's belongings without permission. Timujen was also determined to stamp out the local squabbles that had once disrupted the territories he conquered. Timujen finally succeeded in uniting the Mongols by 1206. His next ambition was the conquest of most of Central Asia. The first priority was to perfect the best-organized, best-trained, and best-disciplined army the world had ever seen. It was not, however, the huge "horde" or wild mob filling the landscape from horizon to horizon, as would be imagined by the Mongols' European opponents, but a much smaller, systematically structured force that was high on quality. Mongol armies consisted entirely of cavalry, about 40 percent of it heavy cavalry destined to provide shock action on the battlefield. These cavalrymen, whose chief weapon was the lance, wore complete armor, usually made of leather or mail, with a casque helmet. Heavy cavalry horses were also protected by leather armor. The light-cavalry units, comprising the other 60 percent of the Mongol army, wore no armor, apart from a helmet, and carried two quivers-full of arrows. Their chief weapons were the javelin, the lasso, and the reflex bow which was roughly the same length as the English longbow and equally devastating in action. The light cavalry was intended to provide the fighting force with reconnaissance, screening, supporting fire, and after the battle, mopping up operations and pursuit of a fleeing enemy. All Mongol cavalry, both heavy and light, carried the curve-bladed scimitar or a battleaxe. Born to the nomadic way of life, Mongol cavalrymen were entirely at home with life on horseback and had little care for luxury or creature comforts. They were, in addition, inured to hardship and extremes of weather and knew how to keep themselves fit, strong and mobile in the most demanding conditions.

Campaigns against an enemy usually began with the Mongol *toumans* (divisions of about 10,000 men) advancing on a broad front to seek out the enemy. When found, a small enemy force would be attacked straight away, but if it was too large, the main Mongol army would be called up to provide an active screen of cavalry. One Mongol ruse was to pretend to retreat, change onto the spare horses kept in reserve behind the main force, then return to the battle with new vigor. In battle, the Mongol cavalry squadrons were arranged in five single-rank lines. The first two lines were filled by the heavy cavalry, the next three by the light cavalry, with other light cavalry units reconnoitering and screening in front of them. Gaps were left in the lines of heavy cavalry to allow the light cavalry to move through to blast oncoming enemy forces with javelins and arrows. All this was designed to confuse, intimidate, and scatter the enemy and often succeeded in doing so. Once the enemy was softened up by these tactics, the heavy Mongol cavalry moved into action to complete their destruction. Timujen and his commanders gave as much attention to the "backroom" strategies of war as they did to battlefield tactics. The Mongols were not the first, but they were arguably the most clever exponents of the intelligence and spy network, and of sophisticated supply and messenger route systems or *yams*. Ruses, stratagems, and similar tricks had a long history in war well before the Mongols. They continued the tradition, though without the chivalry that would make European knights shrink from playing dirty tricks even on an enemy. One wintertime stratagem was to test the strength of the ice covering marshes or rivers by getting the local inhabitants to take their cattle onto the ice and see what happened. Another, less dangerous, deception was to start fires as a means of creating a smokescreen to deceive the enemy or conceal Mongol troop movements.

The Mongol conquests were terrifyingly rapid. Their strategy was first to stage raids that enabled them to observe the "target" and then move in with a full-scale invasion. By this means, it took them only 17 years to conquer a huge swathe of Russian territory.

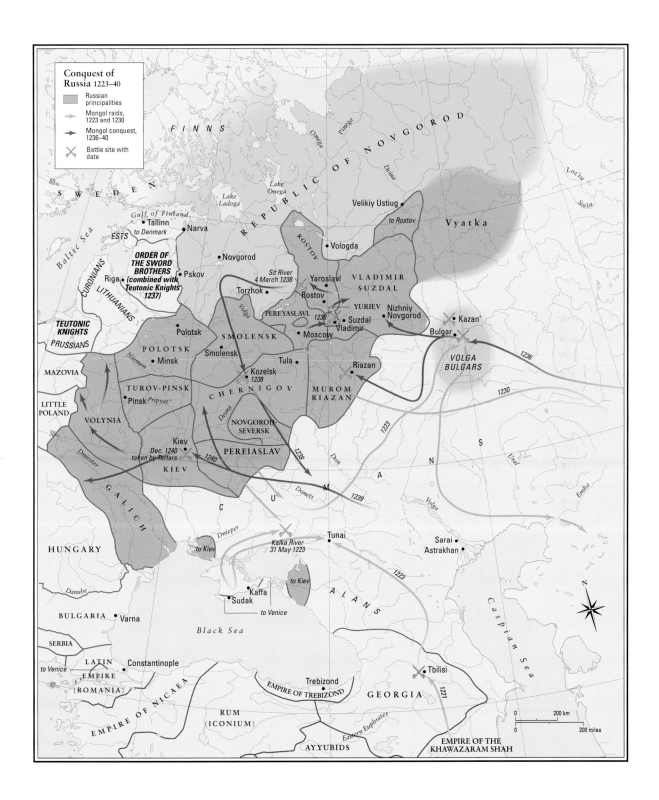

Conquest of Russia 1223–40

Russian principalities

Mongol raids, 1223 and 1230

Mongol conquest, 1236–40

Battle site with date

FINNS

REPUBLIC OF NOVGOROD

Vyatka

SWEDEN

Lake Onega

Lake Ladoga

Velikiy Ustiug

to Rostov

Gulf of Finland

Tallinn

to Denmark

Narva

ESTS

Baltic Sea

Riga

ORDER OF THE SWORD BROTHERS *(combined with Teutonic Knights 1237)*

CURONIANS

LITHUANIANS

TEUTONIC KNIGHTS

PRUSSIANS

MAZOVIA

LITTLE POLAND

Pskov

Novgorod

ROSTOV

Vologda

Sit River 4 March 1238

Yaroslavl

Torzhok

Rostov

VLADIMIR SUZDAL

YURIEV

Nizhniy Novgorod

PEREYASLAVL 1238 Suzdal

Vladimir

Kazan'

Bulgar

Polotsk

SMOLENSK

Moscow

POLOTSK

Smolensk

Tula

Riazan

VOLGA BULGARS

Minsk

Niemen

CHERNIGOV

MUROM RIAZAN

1236

TUROV-PINSK

Pinsk *Pripyat*

Kozelsk 1238

VOLYNIA

NOVGOROD-SEVERSK

1230

Kiev Dec. 1240 *taken by Tartars*

PEREIASLAV

1240

KIEV

1238

Don

Volga

Ural

GALICH

Dniester

Dnieper

1239

Donets

C U M A N S

Embla

HUNGARY

to Kiev

Kalka River 31 May 1223

Tunai

Sarai

Astrakhan

1223

Kaffa

Sudak

to Venice

to Kiev

A L A N S

Caspian Sea

BULGARIA

Varna

Black Sea

SERBIA

LATIN EMPIRE (ROMANIA)

to Venice

Constantinople

EMPIRE OF NICAEA

Trebizond

EMPIRE OF TREBIZOND

GEORGIA

Tbilisi

1221

RUM (ICONIUM)

Eastern Euphrates

AYYUBIDS

EMPIRE OF THE KHAWAZARAM SHAH

0   200 km

0   200 miles

THE MONGOL CAMPAIGNS OF 1207-1279

IN 1206, TEMUJIN WAS CROWNED IN THE KHURULTAI, THE MONGOL "PARLIAMENT," AS GENGHIS KHAN, THE ALL-ENCOMPASSING RULER, AND AT ONCE EMBARKED ON CREATING A MONGOL EMPIRE. HIS FIRST TARGET WAS THE CONQUEST OF TWO EMPIRES IN CHINA.

Ghengis Khan's concept of war was forthright and brutal. "Happiness," he said "lies in conquering one's enemies, in driving them in front of oneself, in taking their property, in savoring their despair." On this evidence, he must have been a happy man after smashing the power of the Western Hsia empire in China by 1209 and forcing its emperor to acknowledge his suzerainty. Genghis' next war, against the Chin Empire, took his three armies as far as the Great Wall in 1213. From there, the Mongols rampaged through northern China and then besieged, captured, and looted Beijing in 1215. The Chin emperor, too, was forced to bow to Mongol suzerainty. The Khwarezmian Empire, centered on Persia, became Genghis' next victim and in the battle of Jand in 1219, an army of 200,000 Khwarezmians was brought to a standstill by 30,000 Mongols. Afterward, the Mongol forces advanced so rapidly through his territory, spreading destruction and terror wherever they went, that in 1220, Alud-Din Mohammed, the Khwarezmian shah, fled south with his family and a small bodyguard. Mohammed died, reportedly broken-hearted, the following year.

The Mongols swept on, through present day Turkey, reaching the Caucasus in 1221 and invading Russia the following year. The "hordes" of Genghis Khan were now nearing the doorstep of Europe and when news spread across the continent that they had reached the Russian steppes, panic gripped towns and cities even as far away as London.

This time, however, the hysteria proved unjustified. Whatever the temptations of Europe, more urgent

Mongols Invasion of Europe 1240–43

← Main attack

← Flank attack

← Reconnaissance and minor raids

✕ Battle site

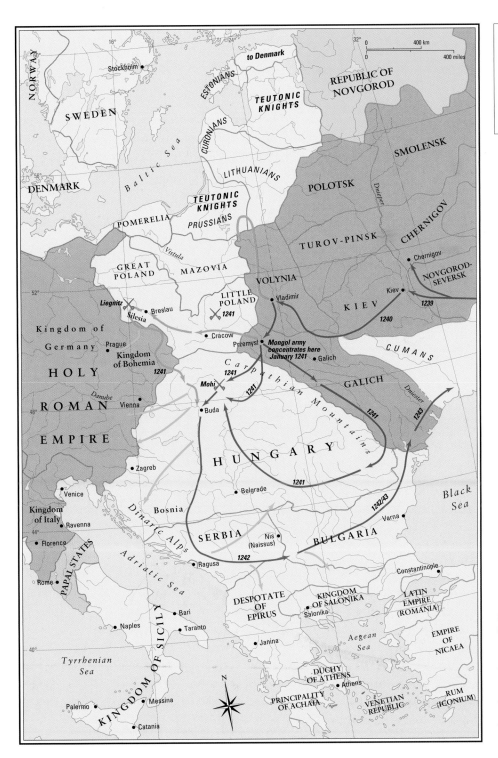

In the 12th century, the Mongols appeared to be unstoppable. Irrupting out of their native Mongolia, they had swept across Asia and the east and by the mid-13th century they invaded southeast Europe. Before they finally halted, the Mongols were marauding across Hungary and threatening the Holy Roman Empire.

distractions supervened. Mstislav, the Prince of Kiev, made a stand against the Mongols in 1223, only to see his army of 80,000 virtually annihilated. In 1225, the Hsia and Chin attempted a rebellion in China that took the Mongols two years to suppress. Soon after that was accomplished, in 1227, Genghis Khan died on his way home to Mongolia.

During 18 arduous years of campaigning and conquest that had brought triumph and territory to the Mongols, Ghengis' four sons — Jochi, Chagatei, Ogedai and Tolui — had all proved brilliant commanders of their father's armies. But, in Genghis' estimation only his third son, Ogedai, was also sufficiently charismatic and politically astute to carry on his work of empire-building. The *khurultai* agreed and soon after his father's death, Ogedai was declared Great Khan of the Mongol Empire.

The death of Ghengis Khan left areas of China still unconquered, but Ogedai did not immediately resume operations in eastern Asia. Instead, he concentrated on another piece of unfinished business: the invasion of eastern Europe. Ogedai took his time. He already had on hand a reconnaissance of Russia which he had carried out in 1223, and augmented that with further intelligence probes until he was ready to move. In December 1237, ten years after the death of Genghis Khan, Ogedai ordered the Mongol armies to cross the frozen River Volga. Now commanded by Subotei, Genghis Khan's and Ogedai's greatest general, the Mongols swept through Moscow and Kaluga, 100 miles (160 km) to the southwest. The destruction was locust-like: in the first few months of 1238, the northern principalities of Russia were obliterated. Eastern and southern Russia followed. In November 1240, once more exploiting frozen rivers and snowbound countryside to aid mobility, the Mongols irrupted into the Ukraine, destroyed Kiev, and overran all areas southeast of the Carpathian mountains and northwest of the Black Sea. Within a few months in early 1241, the Mongols completed the conquest of the Ukraine and all of Russia.

After leaving 30,000 men to control these conquests, Ogetai's grandsons Subotei and Kaidu led an army, 120,000 strong, into Poland and Hungary. Neither the Poles nor the Hungarians stood a chance. On April 9, 1241, Kaidu smashed the 40,000-strong force with which Prince Henry of Silesia attempted to stand in the Mongols' way at Liegnitz. The survivors fled from the battlefield, but the Mongols did not pursue them. They had no need, for the job was done. The whole of north-central Europe from Baltic Sea to the Carpathian mountains had been devastated, its defenders totally subdued and no longer any danger to the rapidly advancing Mongols. That done, Kaidu turned his attention to marching south to link up with the main body of the Mongol army in Hungary and for good measure, laying waste to Moravia on the way. Two days after Liegnitz, on April 11, Subotai disposed of a Hungarian force at the Sajo river, some 100 miles (160 km) northeast of Budapest. The Mongol onslaught was so terrifying that thousands of Hungarians panicked and fled, discarding their weapons and armor as they ran in order to get away as fast as they could. But the Mongols

Mongol Conquests
1206–59

OIROTS Original tribe

Homeland of the Mongol tribes

Mongol Empire, 1206

Mongol Empire, 1236

Mongol Empire, 1259

Area paying tribute or under loose Mongol control

→ Mongol campaign

✳ City sacked by Mongols

were waiting for them. Closing in from all sides, they butchered almost every fugitive, killing a total of up to 70,000 men. Subotei spent the ensuing summer perfecting plans to invade Italy, Austria, and Germany but his campaign was brought to a halt in late December 1241 when news arrived that Ogetai was dead. This meant the Mongol armies had to withdraw, for by Mongol custom the death of the khan required his family and his forces "wherever they might be" to return home to choose a new leader. Europe, it seems, was fortuitously saved, for the Mongols never returned. Instead, they turned their attention to completing Genghis Khan's initial ambition: the conquest of China.

Ultimately, the Mongols not only achieved their objective but their ruler, Kublai Khan, another of Ghengis' grandsons, established the Yuan dynasty of China in 1279 as well as adding Korea, Tibet, Arabia, and the Middle East to the largest land empire that has ever existed.

The Mongols conquered an empire that was several times larger than their own home territory. In the west, they reached as far as the Byzantine Empire and so terrified Europeans that Londoners panicked when they heard the Mongols had reached the steppes of Russia.

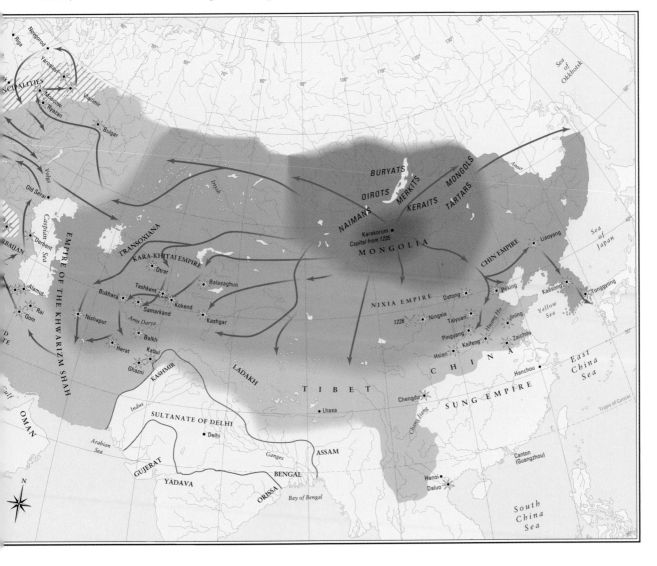

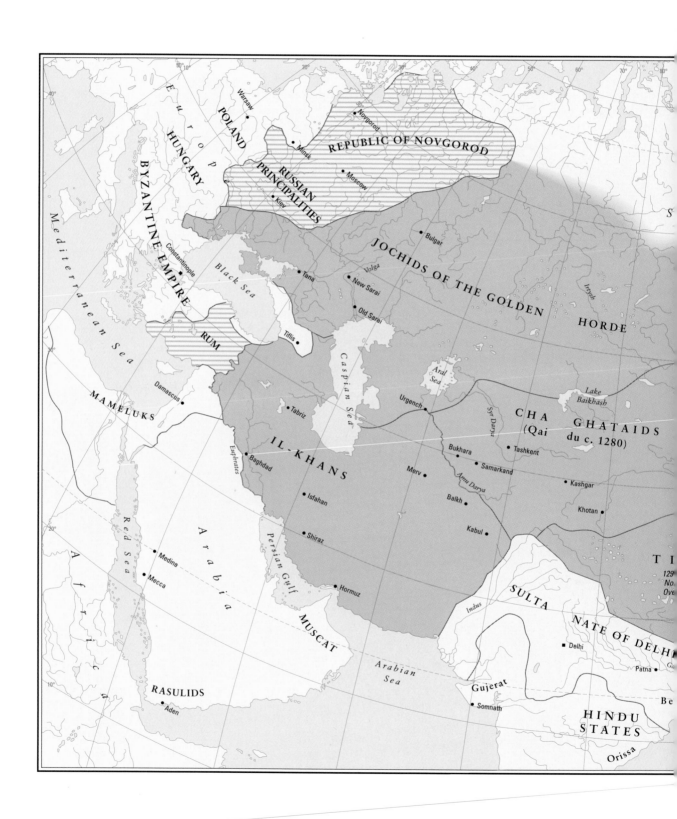

Warsaw

POLAND

HUNGARY

E u r o p e

Novgorod

REPUBLIC OF NOVGOROD

Minsk

RUSSIAN PRINCIPALITIES

Moscow

Kiev

BYZANTINE EMPIRE

Constantinople

Black Sea

Tana

Bulgar

Volga

New Sarai

JOCHIDS OF THE GOLDEN HORDE

Irtysh

S

Mediterranean Sea

RUM

Tiflis

Old Sarai

Caspian Sea

Aral Sea

Lake Baikhash

MAMELUKS

Damascus

Tabriz

Urgench

CHA GHATAIDS (Qai du c. 1280)

Euphrates

Baghdad

IL-KHANS

Merv

Bukhara

Samarkand

Tashkent

Syr Darya

Amu Darya

Kashgar

Isfahan

Balkh

Khotan

A r a b i a

Shiraz

Kabul

Red Sea

Persian Gulf

Hormuz

Medina

Mecca

A f r i c a

MUSCAT

Indus

SULTA

TI

129
No.
Ove

NATE OF DELHI

Delhi

Arabian Sea

Gujerat

Patna

Ga

Be

RASULIDS

Aden

Somnath

HINDU STATES

Orissa

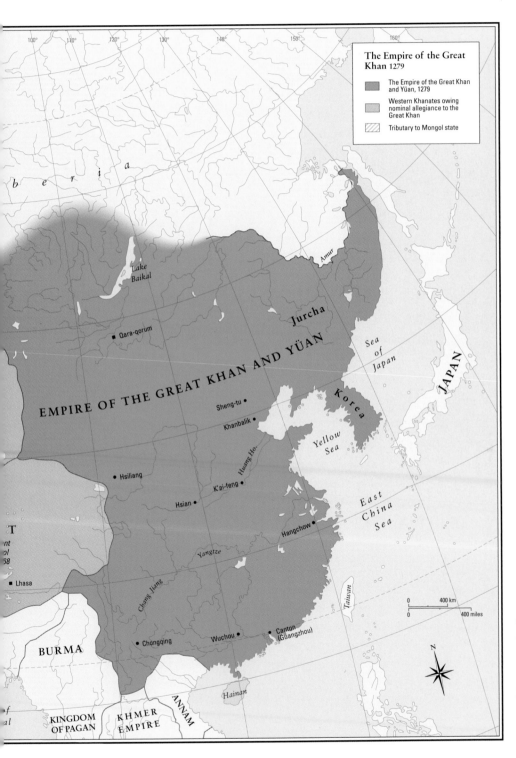

The Empire of the Great Khan 1279

The Empire of the Great Khan and Yüan, 1279

Western Khanates owing nominal allegiance to the Great Khan

Tributary to Mongol state

The conquest of China, completed by Ogedai, the second Great Khan after his father Genghis, covered half of the vast Mongol Empire. In 1271, Genghis' grandson, Kublai Khan, initiated the Yuan dynasty in China and it was at his court that Marco Polo saw the fabulous riches of "Cathay."

A War of Religion: The Cathars of France

WARS OF RELIGION WERE AMONG THE MOST VICIOUS FORMS OF CONFLICT, FUELED AS THEY WERE BY IGNORANCE, FEAR, AND SUPERSTITION. THE FATE OF THE CATHARS, A CHRISTIAN SECT LABELED AS HERETICS BY THE MEDIEVAL CHURCH, WAS A TYPICAL EXAMPLE OF THIS PREJUDICE.

The Cathars first appeared in the Languedoc region of modern southwest France in around 1143. With their belief that the world, created by Satan, was irredeemably evil, they were naturally regarded as subversive heretics. In 1204, Pope Innocent III began a campaign to persuade the Cathars to recant. He was wasting his time and soon resorted to the only alternative: a crusade. Termed the Albigensian Crusade after the town of Albi, a Cathar stronghold in Languedoc, it was prosecuted with maximum brutality. On 22 July, 1208, at Béziers on the River Orb in southwestern France, the Albigensians invaded churches and slaughtered their way through the entire congregations. Finally, they looted and pillaged Béziers and set it alight. Ten days later, the Albigensians attacked Carcassonne and butchered its defenders. In the next 20 years, these horrors were repeated over and over again until it was reckoned that almost one million Cathars had been killed. This, though, did not eliminate them and in many cases served only to strengthen their heretical beliefs. Inevitably, in 1231, the crusade to wipe them out entered a new and even more deadly phase as a new pope, Gregory IX, reinvented the Bishops' Inquisition, a method of dealing with heretics first introduced in 1184. Dominican priests were hired as inquisitors and quickly became notorious for their cruelty. Before long, the Inquisition became a byword for torture, terror, and unimaginable suffering. For example, in Toulouse, one elderly Cathar lady who was already dying was tricked into betraying herself. As her horrified relatives watched, knowing they would be the next victims of the Inquisition, she was tied to her bed, carried out into the street, and thrown onto a bonfire, bed and all, where she burned to ashes.

Ever since 1204, when it was specifically constructed for the purpose, Cathars had fled to the shelter of the fortress of Montségur to escape the persecutions. From its dizzying height of 3000ft. above the surrounding hills and valleys, Montségur served this purpose for nearly 40 years. It was so high up in the Pyrenees mountains that it was believed to be inaccessible but in 1244, a new Pope, Innocent IV, shattered that belief. There were some 500 refugees inside Montségur when papal crusaders scaled the precipitous Roc de la Tour and burst in on the defenders. The Cathar guards, unable to fight back swiftly enough, were killed in an instant or thrown over the cliff edge to their deaths. After that, the fortress quickly surrendered. Given a choice between recanting and death, most of the Cathars chose martyrdom. On 13 March, 1244, 21 men and women requested the consolamentum, the Cathar equivalent of the Last Rite given to Catholics, in which they were enjoined to lead chaste, ascetic lives. Those lives had only three more days to run.

In the meadows below Montségur, a patch of ground surrounded by a palisade was being prepared for a bonfire of burnings, using wood chopped down from the nearby forests. Rows of stakes were set in the ground, ropes to tie the Cathars were piled up, torches to light the fires were stacked and ladders were propped up against the palisades. Early on the morning of 16 March, a procession of 221 Cathars began to wind down the path that led from the summit of Montségur to the bottom of the slope. The leaders went barefoot, wearing nothing but their coarsely woven robes. When they reached the burning ground, they climbed the ladders and were bound together onto the stakes in pairs, back to back. The rest followed until row upon row of men and women filled the enclosure. When all was ready, Archbishop Amiel gave the signal for flaming brands to be thrown in among them. The soft murmur of prayers was audible, only to be drowned out by the sinister crackle of fire as it climbed up the stakes and set everyone and everything alight. As the blaze grew and the human forms at its centre disappeared, the crackle turned to a roar and smoke, thick, black and choking, began to fill the valleys, dirty the meadow grass that grew between them and finally curl up into the sky.

The medieval city of Carcassone, one of the great fortified trading centers of Languedoc. The Cathars were expelled from here in 1209.

THE HUNDRED YEARS' WAR

IN THE SO-CALLED HUNDRED YEARS' WAR, WHICH ACTUALLY TOOK PLACE BETWEEN 1337 AND 1453, THE THRONE OF FRANCE WAS CONTESTED BY TWO EUROPEAN DYNASTIES — THE FRENCH HOUSE OF VALOIS AND THE ENGLISH HOUSE OF PLANTAGENET.

T he Anglo-French quarrel began in 1328, when Philip VI of Valois was crowned King of France in preference to his niece, the posthumous daughter of Philip's cousin King Charles IV. Although the ancient Salic Law was cited, barring females or males descended from females from ascending the French throne, the real motive appears to have been to destroy the claims of King Edward III of England, whose mother Isabella was the sister of the dead king, Charles IV. Hostilities were initially provoked in 1337 when Philip declared forfeit the rich, wine-producing English fiefs (feudal estates) in Gascony. In response, Edward III sent raiding parties into north and southwestern French territory and in 1338, declared himself the rightful King of France. The only appreciable action before a truce was agreed was the naval battle of Sluys on 24 June, 1340 where an English fleet virtually annihilated Philip's ships with missiles from siege engines and archers firing clouds of arrows from the English decks. The archers' action was a foretaste of the much more hard-fought battles of the War. The first English success was the capture of Caen in Normandy, but for over six weeks, the French avoided battle until King Edward reached the River Somme. After Crécy, the English seized Calais, but the deadly plague pandemic, later known as the Black Death, intervened after 1347 to put an end to the fighting for the next eight years.

The Hundred Years' War resumed in 1355 with English raids across northern France led by King Edward's sons Edward, the Black Prince and John of Gaunt. Though immensely damaging, the raids were only a prelude to the second major land battle of the War which took place at Poitiers, 100 miles (160 km) from Nantes in western France on September 19, 1356. History repeated itself. Eventually, the French attack was repulsed, but with very heavy losses on both sides. The English followed their victory at Poitiers with desultory raids, until, in 1360, a Peace was signed in which the French recognized Calais

Among the English forces at the Battle of Crécy in 1346, an encounter early on in the Hundred Years' War, the longbowmen were the farthest away from their French and Genoese opponents. But their reach was so great that their clouds of deadly arrows were decisive in winning the battle.

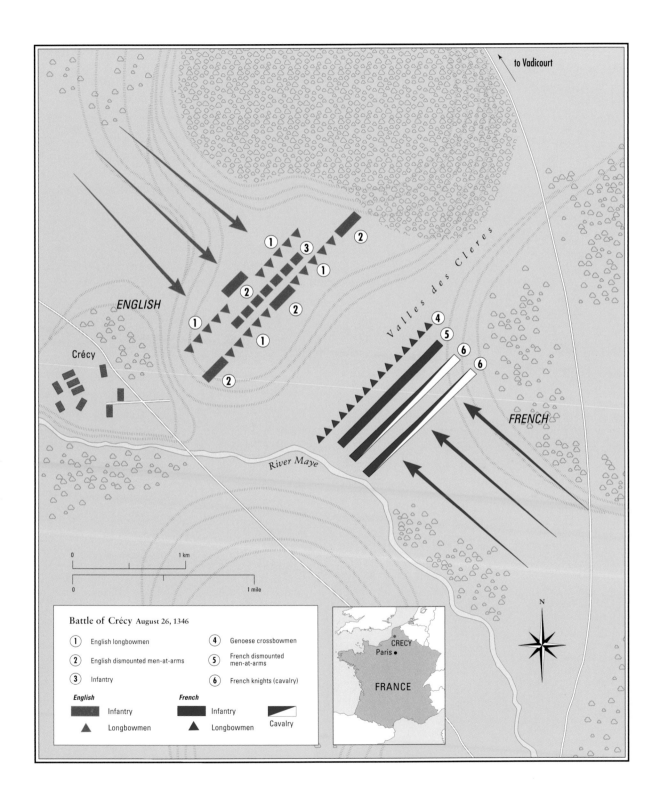

to Vadicourt

Valles des Cleres

ENGLISH

Crécy

FRENCH

River Maye

0   1 km

0   1 mile

N

Battle of Crécy August 26, 1346

① English longbowmen
② English dismounted men-at-arms
③ Infantry
④ Genoese crossbowmen
⑤ French dismounted men-at-arms
⑥ French knights (cavalry)

English
    Infantry
▲ Longbowmen

French
    Infantry
▲ Longbowmen
    Cavalry

CRÉCY
Paris ●

FRANCE

and Ponthieu as English possessions. Fighting nevertheless continued, interspersed with occasional truces, until the Peace of Paris in 1396, when the new kings of England and France, Richard II, grandson of Edward III and Charles VI, grandson of Jean II, agreed to a 30-year period of peace. But peace ran out far sooner, after another King of England, Edward III's great-grandson, Henry V, revived the old monarch's claim to the French throne. Henry V was one of England's most vigorous rulers and its greatest warrior-king. He was also young and eager for military glory. In 1415, six years after he acceded to the English throne, Henry set out across the Channel to claim his second crown. It was a cunningly timed move, for Charles VI, still King of France, but prone to bouts of madness, was susceptible to the threat which the young English monarch presented. In the spring of 1415, Henry formally declared war on the French King Charles VI. The following August 10, he sailed for France with an army of 12,000 men that included some 2,000 men-at-arms and 6,000 bowmen. Three days later, the English were in action at Harfleur in eastern Normandy, where they besieged the castle and its small garrison of 400 defenders. A significant feature of the siege, which ended with a French surrender on September 22, was the English use of a new form of warfare — guns and gunpowder — which wrought critical damage on Harfleur's walls.

Next, King Henry set out for Calais, some 140 miles (225 km) away along the northern coast of France, which he hoped to reach while managing to evade the French army. He failed. On October 24, Henry found that some 30,000 men commanded by the Constable of France, Charles d'Albret were waiting for the English near the castle of Agincourt, 30 miles (48 km) southeast of Boulogne. Henry was forced to fight in very unfavorable circumstances. His army was hungry, exhausted from a long march, and many of his men were still suffering from the "bloody flux" (dysentery) that had dogged them during the long and grueling siege of Harfleur. They were also outnumbered by more than three to one, with only 900 men-at-arms and 8,000 archers fit to do battle. The battlefield at Agincourt was cramped into a narrow defile only 1,000 yd (914 m) wide with thick woodland on both sides and the nearby plowed fields sodden with rain. The French knights were keen to fight the English so Henry decided to lure them in and ordered a cautious advance of about half a mile. The ruse worked. Unable to contain themselves, the French knights dismounted and headed for the English front line. However, they failed to take account of the weight of armor they were wearing, which left them barely mobile as they struggled in thick mud and within range of the English longbowmen. A massacre followed. Around 5,000 knights were killed and another 1,000 were taken prisoner. Reportedly, Henry's forces lost only 13 men-at-arms and about 1000 infantry, though it was likely that the toll was far greater than that. Henry's unexpected triumph at Agincourt brought him two significant prizes. In May 1420, he married Catherine, daughter of Charles VI of France, who was then persuaded — or frightened — into declaring the English king to be his heir, disinheriting Charles' son, the Dauphin Charles, whose supporters, including the famous Joan of Arc, were determined to see him claim his birthright. By then, Henry was well on the way to conquering the whole of northern France, but disaster intervened when he died of the "bloody flux" on 31 August, 1422, aged 35. Seven weeks later, Charles VI died, too, and Henry's nine-month old son, also Henry, became king of both England and France. Yet English power in France was on the wane. The Dauphin was crowned King Charles VII at Rheims cathedral in 1429, and after a long series of defeats at the hands of the French, English rule in France collapsed in 1453.

The victory won by King Henry V at Agincourt shocked his French opponents who had presumed that their mounted knights represented a far superior force. They had, of course, reckoned without the deadly power of the English longbowmen and their ability to cut down armored knights from a distance.

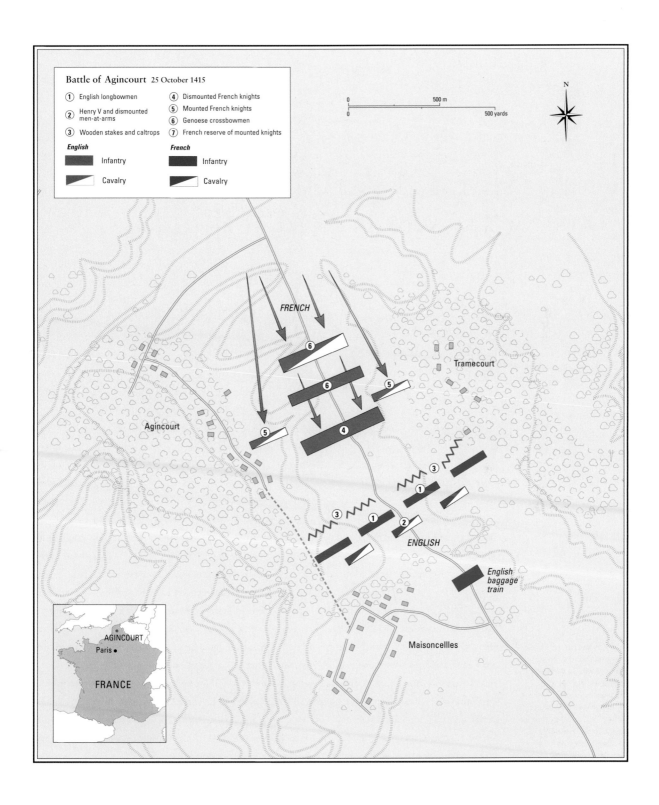

Battle of Agincourt 25 October 1415

① English longbowmen
② Henry V and dismounted men-at-arms
③ Wooden stakes and caltrops
④ Dismounted French knights
⑤ Mounted French knights
⑥ Genoese crossbowmen
⑦ French reserve of mounted knights

English
　Infantry
　Cavalry

French
　Infantry
　Cavalry

500 m
500 yards

N

FRENCH

Tramecourt

Agincourt

ENGLISH

English
baggage
train

AGINCOURT
Paris

FRANCE

Maisoncelles

THE RISE OF GUNPOWDER: CANNON AND ARQUEBUS

THE FIRST RECORD OF A GUN IN EUROPEAN WARFARE WAS AN ILLUSTRATION IN A MANUSCRIPT OF 1327 SHOWING A SMALL, POT-BELLIED CONTAINER CALLED "VASI." IT DID NOT LOOK MUCH, BUT "VASI" REVOLUTIONIZED WAR AS IT WAS FOUGHT IN EUROPE.

Gunpowder, or at least some kind of explosive, was reputedly used by the Chinese in around 1161 in fireworks. A century later, it appears that the news about explosives had reached Europe, for in around 1260, the English monk Roger Bacon recorded a recipe involving mixing together seven parts of saltpeter, five parts of charcoal, and five parts of sulfur. "With such a mixture," Bacon wrote, "you will produce a bright flash and a thundering noise, if you know the trick."

Within another 60 years or so, many people had come to "know the trick" and they did not use it for fireworks, either. The first recorded instance in Western Europe of the serious, that is military, use of fireworks was at the siege of Metz in 1324 during the feudal conflict called "The Four Lords War." In the manuscript written three years later, the vasi, or *pot de fer* (iron pot), was shown lying on its side with an arrow sticking out of its muzzle. At the other end stood a soldier with a red-hot rod poised over the firing hole. At this very early stage, gunpowder was used in battle as an alternative to mechanical methods of propulsion — torsion, tension, or counterweights for firing arrows and stones. These, of course, were the same missiles as those dispatched by catapults, mangonels, and other engines of war. It was probably a *pot de fer* that was used at the siege of Metz and the new weapon must have impressed the military of the time, for by the mid-14th century, it began to appear on European battlefields with some regularity. For example, in 1340, during the Hundred Years' War, the French employed arrow-firing "bombards," probably of the vasi-type, against an English army at the Battle of Quesnoi. The French, however, had been pre-empted the year before, by the English who had used a new weapon — the ribauldequin, a volley gun, which was fired in a similar manner to the modern machine gun or a battery of rockets.

When the early cannon got down to the business of firing shot instead of arrows, like the vasi, they were given the shape they have retained to the present day. The vital difference, though, was in the metals used: they had to become stronger as the power of the weapons increased.

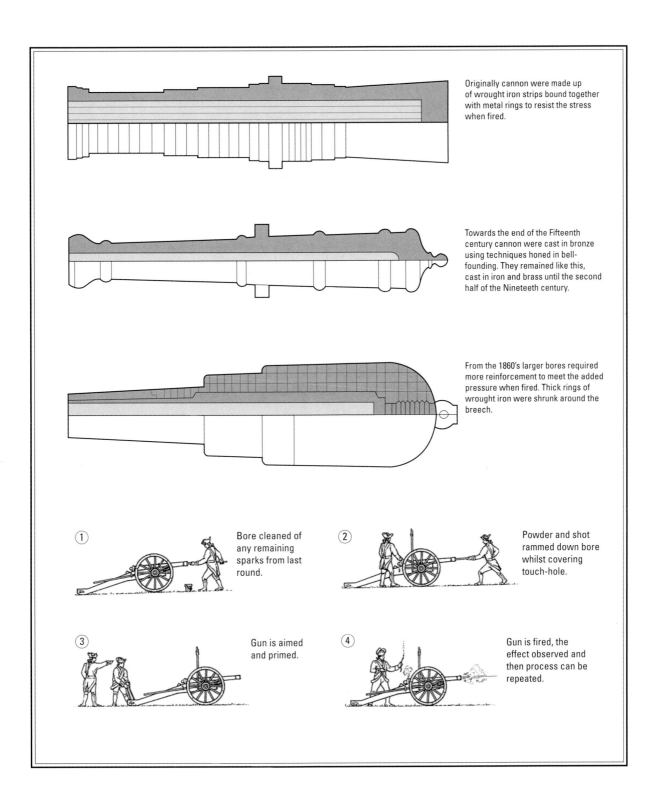

Originally cannon were made up of wrought iron strips bound together with metal rings to resist the stress when fired.

Towards the end of the Fifteenth century cannon were cast in bronze using techniques honed in bell-founding. They remained like this, cast in iron and brass until the second half of the Nineteeth century.

From the 1860's larger bores required more reinforcement to meet the added pressure when fired. Thick rings of wrought iron were shrunk around the breech.

① Bore cleaned of any remaining sparks from last round.

② Powder and shot rammed down bore whilst covering touch-hole.

③ Gun is aimed and primed.

④ Gun is fired, the effect observed and then process can be repeated.

The ribauldequin comprised a number of small-caliber iron barrels laid parallel to each other on a cart or a platform. When they were fired in unison, opponents were showered with iron shot. The English ribauldequin, as used during the Hundred Years' War by the army of King Edward III, had 12 barrels.

It was not long, though, before guns began to take on their more familiar appearance as long-barreled weapons, which they have retained to this day. Most early guns of this type were fairly small and were made of bronze, brass, or wrought iron. But they tended to be unreliable and in fact posed more danger to the soldiers using them than to their opponents. There were two main problems here. More than one gun, even when correctly fired, blew apart as the black powder exploded because it was not made strongly enough to contain the power generated by the detonation. More than one gunner managed to destroy himself, his equipment, his crew, and anyone else who happened to be nearby when he applied a naked light to the black explosive mixture. The most skilful and experienced gunner faced great hazards because he usually had to mix his gunpowder on the battlefield itself. When transported over long distances, the ingredients in ready-mixed powder tended to separate, with the heavy sulfur falling to the bottom and the lighter charcoal resting on the top. In this state, gunpowder was virtually useless. There was nothing else to do but to mix the powder in battle conditions, where a stray spark or a match lit nearby could ignite the highly inflammable materials a gunner was using.

Before the end of the 14th century, gun makers had discovered how to cast larger and stronger guns. By this time, the average bombard — as guns were now termed — measured some 20 ft (6 m) in length and could fire a cannon ball weighing up to 300 lbs. Artillery guns like these — and they were not even the largest ones — were powerful enough to batter down castles and reduce to ruins the walls of fortified towns. This is what happened at the French town of Harfleur in 1415, during the later stages of the Hundred Years' War when the army of the English king, Henry V, bombarded one of its walls with a battery of ten large guns. After four weeks, the town gate and its barbican, the double tower above it, was almost totally demolished. The English gunners finished the job by firing one last shell, an incendiary, to set the woodwork alight. Subsequently, Henry's army took Harfleur by storm. Some 40 years later, in 1453, the Ottoman Turks demolished the walls of Constantinople, capital of the Byzantine Empire, with 70 powerful cannon. One of them was a bronze gun nearly 27 ft (8 m) long, which fired a missile weighing 1,250 lb (567 kg).

Like the castle, the medieval knight was on the way out as an effective participant in war. The knight was being replaced by the soldier with the hand-held gun firing shot which, in time, was able to penetrate the knight's thick plate armor. Hand-held guns made the same primitive, not very efficient, debut in war as the artillery, and started on their way toward revolutionizing warfare at the same time. The first hand-held guns, which came into use soon after 1325, solved a problem posed by the cannon: they were too cumbersome and too heavy to be easily moved. This was why the hand-held versions were, in effect, miniature cannons attached to long sticks and were frequently called "hand bombards."

Firing the first hand bombards was every bit as dangerous as firing larger artillery guns. The barrel, which might be up to 12 in (30 cm) long, was filled three-fifths full with gunpowder. The gunpowder was then rammed down and a wooden wad and a small cannon ball inserted. The gunner ignited the charge, either by poking a red-hot wire through the touch-hole or by setting it alight with a hot coal held between tongs.

The Battle of Formigny, fought in 1450 in the last stages of the Hundred Years' War, showed that the French had learned from their defeats at Crécy (1346) and Agincourt (1415). They parked two long-barreled culverins out of longbow range and bombarded each flank of the English army.

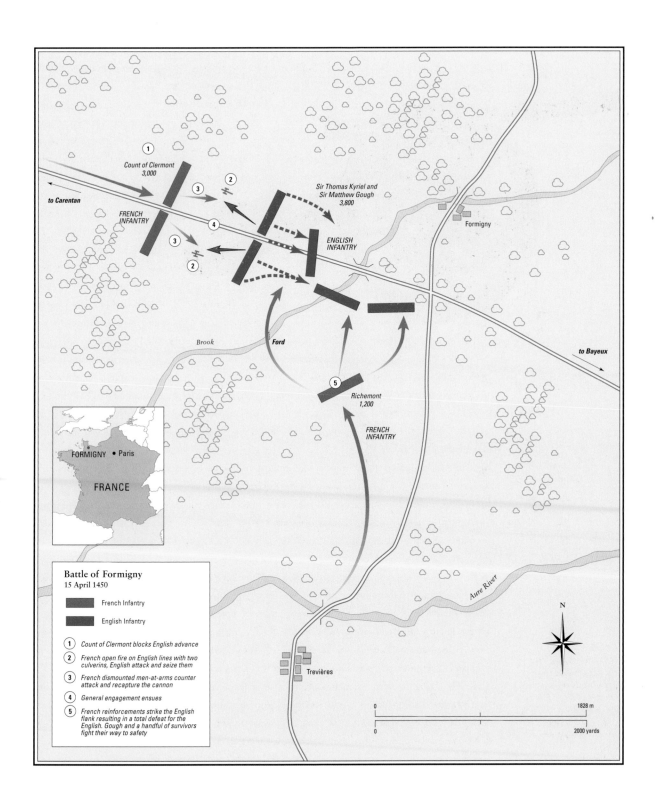

Count of Clermont
3,000

to Carentan

FRENCH
INFANTRY

Sir Thomas Kyriel and
Sir Matthew Gough
3,800

Formigny

ENGLISH
INFANTRY

Brook

Ford

to Bayeux

Richemont
1,200

FRENCH
INFANTRY

FORMIGNY ● Paris

FRANCE

Aure River

Trevières

N

Battle of Formigny
15 April 1450

French Infantry

English Infantry

1 Count of Clermont blocks English advance

2 French open fire on English lines with two
culverins, English attack and seize them

3 French dismounted men-at-arms counter
attack and recapture the cannon

4 General engagement ensues

5 French reinforcements strike the English
flank resulting in a total defeat for the
English. Gough and a handful of survivors
fight their way to safety

0   1828 m

0   2000 yards

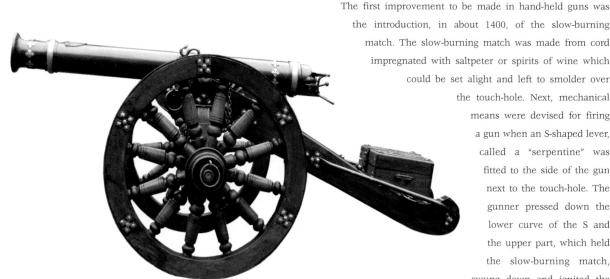

A medieval cannon weapon. Cannons revolutionized warfare in the middle ages, reducing the need for close combat between ranks of infantry.

The first improvement to be made in hand-held guns was the introduction, in about 1400, of the slow-burning match. The slow-burning match was made from cord impregnated with saltpeter or spirits of wine which could be set alight and left to smolder over the touch-hole. Next, mechanical means were devised for firing a gun when an S-shaped lever, called a "serpentine" was fitted to the side of the gun next to the touch-hole. The gunner pressed down the lower curve of the S and the upper part, which held the slow-burning match, swung down and ignited the gunpowder. The first gun equipped with the serpentine was a fairly light gun, the arquebus. Unfortunately, it had the disadvantage of being very slow. The arquebus took so long to load and prime that arquebusiers were able to fire, on average, no more than once about every 15 minutes. In the same time, a contemporary English longbowman could discharge more than 200 arrows. During the long intervals between firing, the arquebusiers had to be protected against enemy cavalry by soldiers armed with 18ft (6 m) pikes.

Nevertheless, despite its drawbacks, the arquebus could be effective if concentrated in sufficient numbers. This was triumphantly demonstrated by the Spaniards in 1503 during the Battle of Cerignola against the French in Italy. During the battle, the French cavalry charged the Spanish ranks three times. The first two onslaughts were quickly broken up by the Spaniards' heavy artillery fire. At the third attempt, the French headed for what looked like a modest line of arquebusiers protected, as usual, by pikemen. The French were in for a shock. The arquebusiers, who were equipped with the latest hand guns, waited until the French were within range and then opened fire, plastering the oncoming cavalry with shot. Dozens of Frenchmen were mown down and the French army was forced to withdraw. Cerignola afterward went down as the first battle in history won by hand-held guns alone.

The Battle of Fornovo, fought on July 6, 1495, was the first big battle of the Italian Wars. King Charles VIII of France claimed the Kingdom of Naples and conquered it by February 1495, but the League of Venice (Venice, Milan, and Mantua) defeated him at Fornovo and expelled him from Italy.

The military men of Europe, including the French, took note of the lesson and before long, the crossbowmen and the cavalry who had for so long done the major fighting in war were replaced by columns of gunners and pikemen called "battles." Up to 25 ranks of arquebusiers were drawn up on a battlefield, taking it in turn to fire their guns. As each rank discharged its load of shot, it withdrew to the back to reload and pre-prime its weapons. Little by little, the ranks moved forward to the front again, where they fired their guns a second time. They then retired to the rear and the whole process began again. The Spaniards became experts at using these "shot and pike" tactics, as they were called, and their effectiveness increased when muskets began to replace the arquebus after about 1500.

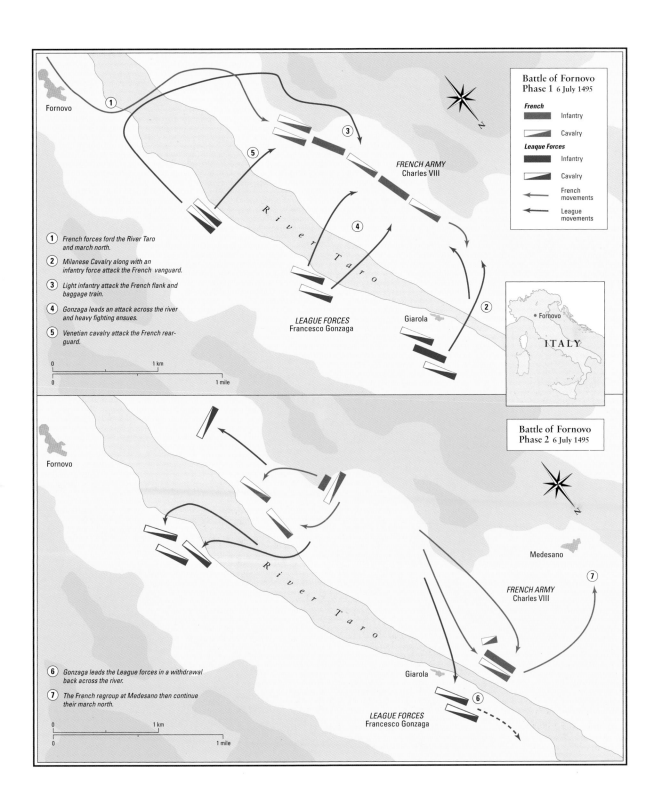

Battle of Fornovo
Phase 1 6 July 1495

French

Infantry

Cavalry

Leaque Forces

Infantry

Cavalry

French movements

League movements

FRENCH ARMY
Charles VIII

River Taro

(1) French forces ford the River Taro and march north.

(2) Milanese Cavalry along with an infantry force attack the French vanguard.

(3) Light infantry attack the French flank and baggage train.

(4) Gonzaga leads an attack across the river and heavy fighting ensues.

(5) Venetian cavalry attack the French rear-guard.

LEAGUE FORCES
Francesco Gonzaga

Giarola

Fornovo

• Fornovo

ITALY

0 ——— 1 km
0 ——————— 1 mile

Battle of Fornovo
Phase 2 6 July 1495

Fornovo

River Taro

Medesano

FRENCH ARMY
Charles VIII

(7)

Giarola

(6)

LEAGUE FORCES
Francesco Gonzaga

(6) Gonzaga leads the League forces in a withdrawal back across the river.

(7) The French regroup at Medesano then continue their march north.

0 ——— 1 km
0 ——————— 1 mile

CROSS VERSUS CRESCENT: THE BYZANTINES AND ISLAM

THE SEQUENCE OF EVENTS CULMINATING IN 1453 WITH THE CAPTURE OF CONSTANTINOPLE, THE BYZANTINE CAPITAL, BY THE OTTOMAN TURKS LED FAR BACK INTO THE HISTORY OF A MIGHTY STRUGGLE BETWEEN CHRISTIANITY AND ISLAM THAT WAS SECOND ONLY TO THE CRUSADES.

Islam, the religion founded in Arabia by Mohammed after c.AD610, meant nemesis for the Byzantine Christian Empire from the start. Byzantine territories were among the first destinations for the Muslim armies that irrupted out of Arabia after Muhamed's death in AD632, determined to spread their faith throughout the world. Persian territories in Mesopotamia, for instance, fell quickly to the extraordinary energy of Islamic arms. Syria was overrun after AD636 and its inhabitants converted to the new faith. Egypt followed eight years later and with that, the Arabs were very close to the Byzantines' doorstep. At this juncture, their impetus flagged and did so long enough for the Byzantine armies to recover Syria and parts of Mesopotamia. But this did not secure the safety of the Empire or its capital, Constantinople. In AD674, the forces of the Umayyad Caliph, the Muslim civil and religious leader based in Damascus, Syria, laid siege to the city but on finding that they could not penetrate its walls, they turned instead to blockading the Bosphorus. By this time, winter was approaching, forcing the Arab army to withdraw to an island 80 miles distant. Effectively, the siege continued, but in AD678, it was raised by the Byzantine navy who utilized their terrible incendiary weapon, Greek fire, to vanquish an Arab fleet in the nearby Sea of Marmara. The Byzantine victory kept the Muslim forces at bay for the next 40 years, until they tried again with a second siege of Constantinople in AD717. This enterprise also failed, succumbing to an exceptionally severe winter in which the ground froze solid and the Arabs, unable to bury their dead, were forced to throw their bodies into the sea.

Nevertheless, the security of the Byzantine Empire was still in doubt, for Muslims from Arabia were

Constantinople's defenders were completely surrounded by Ottoman ships and weapons, that they might have hoped to resist except for one fact: the Ottoman artillery had a far greater range than they imagined, particularly a giant cannon which required a 400-man crew and 60 oxen to drag it into position.

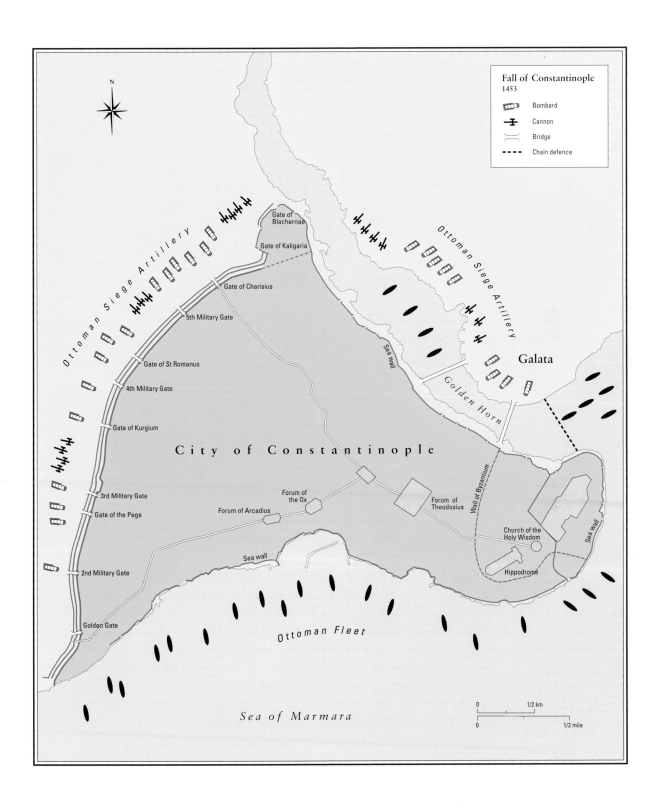

Fall of Constantinople
1453

- Bombard
- Cannon
- Bridge
- Chain defence

Ottoman Siege Artillery

Gate of Blachernae
Gate of Kaligaria
Gate of Charisius
5th Military Gate
Gate of St Romanus
4th Military Gate
Gate of Kurgium
3rd Military Gate
Gate of the Pege
2nd Military Gate
Golden Gate

Ottoman Siege Artillery

Galata

Sea wall

Golden Horn

City of Constantinople

Forum of the Ox
Forum of Arcadius
Forum of Theodosius
Wall of Byzantium
Church of the Holy Wisdom
Sea wall
Hippodrome

Sea wall

Ottoman Fleet

Sea of Marmara

0   1/2 km
0   1/2 mile

not the only threat it faced. The Seljuk Turks, who probably originated in China, were converted to Islam in the 7th and 8th centuries AD and afterward migrated towards Persia, which they reached in the late 10th century. Like the Huns, an earlier Byzantine enemy of Chinese origins, the Turks were ferocious warriors and splendid horsemen and utterly merciless. They captured Baghdad in 1055, destroying the Abassid Caliphate in the process. In 1067, the Turks moved on to Asia Minor where they assaulted Caesarea and Iconium and seized Manzikert (now in eastern Turkey.) For the Byzantines, the Battle of Manzikert, which took place in August 1071, began well enough. The Seljuk horse archers opened proceedings by firing at long range, but the Byzantine cavalry, combined with their own archers, managed to push them back and by late afternoon had captured the Seljuk camp. There was, though, no time to consolidate this success, for nightfall was fast approaching and the Emperor Romanus, in command, decided to withdraw. It was a fatal decision, for the Seljuks took advantage of his move to ambush and overwhelm his army and capture Romanus. Romanus' fate set off a civil war between rival claimants for the Byzantine throne. At the same time, it opened the door to the Seljuks' allies, who swarmed into Anatolia and, by 1081, had seized almost all the Byzantine dominions but for a few fortified seaports along the coast.

The same year, the civil war came to an end when the astute and resourceful Alexius Comnenus declared himself emperor. The Comnenus dynasty ruled for the next four centuries, but all the Empire had to fight for its life against the Seljuks, Normans, Slavs, Franks and Venetians, among others. Weakened and decimated by this plethora of enemies, the Empire was in no condition to resist their last enemy, the Ottoman Turks, who migrated into Anatolia in around 1227.

By the turn of the 14th century, the Byzantines' hold on Anatolia had slipped so far that they had lost control of most of their Anatolian provinces, which now comprised an assortment of Ghazi or Islamic warrior principalities. One of them was ruled by Osman I, who extended his territories westward toward the frontier of the Byzantine Empire. After Osman's death in 1326, the power of the Ottomans, a term derived from his name, spread farther, across the eastern Mediterranean and the Balkans and on into the rest of Europe. By 1396, the Ottomans had acquired almost all the Byzantine territories around Constantinople and the capture of the Byzantine capital seemed imminent. Then, suddenly, in 1402, the Byzantines were given a reprieve when the Turkic-Mongol conqueror Tamerlane invaded Anatolia, seized Ottoman territories in the Balkans, and so forced them onto the defensive. Nearly 50 years passed before the Ottoman Sultan Murad II retrieved the lost lands, completing the task shortly before he died in 1451. By then, Constantinople itself was the sole surviving remnant of the Byzantine Empire. On April 5, 1453, Murad's son and successor Mehmed II laid siege to the Byzantine capital with an army around 200,000 strong. The defenders numbered only 7,000. The Ottomans began by pounding the walls with their heavy artillery, and sealed off the city. Still, though, their efforts to breach the walls were repulsed. But then, on May 22, an eclipse of the Moon occurred and was taken as a prophecy of doom for the defenders of Constantinople. Such prophecies exercised great influence in superstitious times. Even so, the Ottomans were unable to penetrate the walls until, by chance, they discovered that one of the gates was unlocked. With that, the Ottoman Turks surged into Constantinople, running wild through the streets, killing and looting. Those inhabitants able to escape fled the city, which was renamed Istanbul and became the capital of the Ottoman Empire.

As the Ottoman Turks increased their power and their territory, they gradually expanded their grip on the areas surrounding Constantinople and what was left of the Byzantine Empire. It was as if they were strangling the Byzantines and the process went on even after the Fall of Constantinople in 1453.

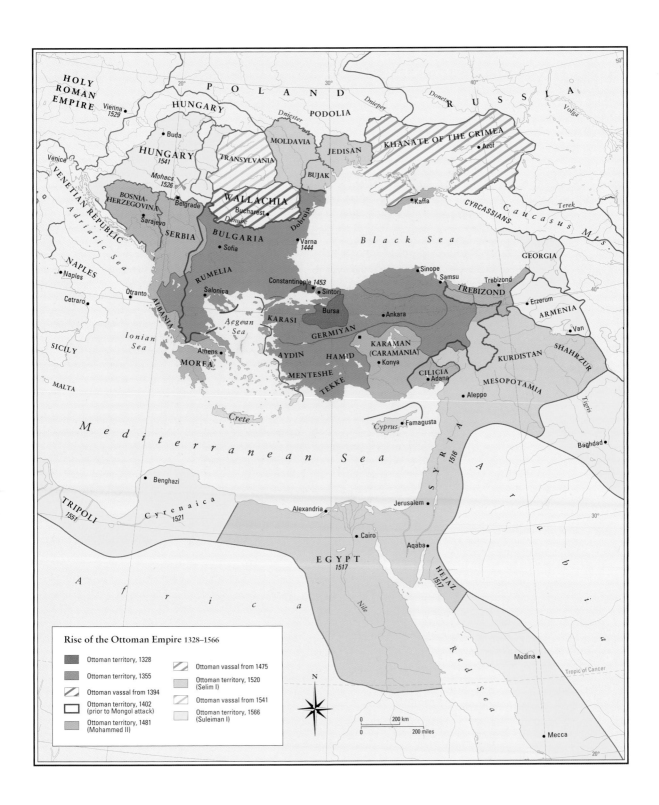

Rise of the Ottoman Empire 1328–1566

- Ottoman territory, 1328
- Ottoman territory, 1355
- Ottoman vassal from 1394
- Ottoman territory, 1402 (prior to Mongol attack)
- Ottoman territory, 1481 (Mohammed II)
- Ottoman vassal from 1475
- Ottoman territory, 1520 (Selim I)
- Ottoman vassal from 1541
- Ottoman territory, 1566 (Suleiman I)

CHAPTER IV — WARFARE IN THE RENAISSANCE: EUROPE 1450-1600

THE RENAISSANCE, WHICH BEGAN AROUND 1450, MAY HAVE SIGNALED REASON AND ENLIGHTENMENT QUITE DIFFERENT FROM THE "BACKWARD" AND SUPERSTITIOUS MIDDLE AGES, BUT IT HAD LITTLE, IF ANY, EFFECT ON WAR WHICH CONTINUED TO BE SPURRED ON BY AGE-OLD HATREDS.

Two of the three major conflicts of the early Renaissance period — the Wars of the Roses in England, in 1455-1485 and the Italian wars of 1494-1559 — originated in dynastic disputes. The Huguenot wars in France, also occurring in the same period, reflected the intolerance created by opposing beliefs, which brought religious war to the European battlefield.

The Wars of the Roses, which began in 1455, were essentially family warfare, in this case between two branches of the Plantagenet ruling family — the House of York and the House of Lancaster. The trigger occurred more than half a century earlier in 1399, when a grandson of King Edward III, Henry Bolingbroke, usurped the throne of England from his cousin, the rightful monarch, King Richard II. Members of the Plantagenet dynasty and the English nobility, many of them related to the royal family, divided their loyalties between the House of York, which claimed descent from the second and fourth sons of Edward III, and the House of Lancaster, which traced its descent from the third son, John of Gaunt, Duke of Lancaster and father of Henry Bolingbroke. The name given to the resultant wars derived from the white rose supposedly chosen as a symbol by the Yorkists and the red rose, chosen by the Lancastrians. Civil conflicts have often been considered particularly vicious and bloody and the Wars of the Roses were no exception. Between the battle of St. Albans in 1455 and the final contest at Bosworth Field 30 years later, the Plantagenets and their nobility virtually decimated themselves; so much so that when the ultimate victor, King Henry VII, another descendant of Edward III, convened his first Parliament, 64 percent of the peers entitled to attend were boys whose fathers had been killed in the fighting. Two kings of England were murdered during the Wars and another, together with a Prince of Wales, heir to the throne, was killed in battle.

European military history often featured royal family warfare. For example, the Valois of France and the Hapsburgs of Spain were regularly at war in the 16th century. A frequent battleground was Italy, where they fought for supremacy at Ravenna, Ceresole, and other battles noted on this map.

SCOTLAND

North Sea

DENMARK

Baltic Sea

D. of Prussia

Ireland

ENGLAND

Lübeck

Hamburg

Stettin

Amsterdam

Utrecht

Münster

In revolt from 1566

Brandenburg

Berlin

KINGDOM OF POLAND

London

Gravelines 1558

Antwerp

Brussels

Berg.

Hessen Kassel

Breslau

Silesia

Calais

Luxemburg

Mainz

Bamberg

Bohemia

Moravia

St Quentin 1557

Rhine Palatinate

Upper Palatinate

Brest

Paris

Württemberg

Bavaria

Augsburg

Vienna

Pressburg

Buda

ATLANTIC OCEAN

Orléans

Lorraine

Munich

Archd. of Austria

Danube

Nantes

VALOIS FRANCE

Basel

Salzburg

Tirol

Mohács

Besançon

Swiss Confederation

Charolais

Bordeaux

Bugey

Franche Comté

Geneva

D. of Savoy

Milan

D. of Milan

REP. OF VENICE

Venice

Carniola

OTTOMAN EMPIRE

K. OF HUNGARY

San Sebastián

Toulouse

Genoa

REP. OF FLORENCE

Adriatic Sea

Marseille

Lucca

see inset

Pamplona

Roussillon

Siena

PAPAL STATES

SPAIN

Cataluña

Saragossa

Barcelona

REP. OF SIENA

Corsica (to Genoa)

Rome

The Garigliano 1503

Madrid

ARAGON

Naples

Cerignola 1503

CASTILLA

Valencia

Palma

Sardinia

KINGDOM OF NAPLES

Murcia

Cartagena

Mediterranean Sea

Palermo

Sicily

Algiers

Bugia

N

OTTOMAN EMPIRE

| 0 | 100 km |
| 0 | 100 miles |

Duelling Dynasties
1494–1559

✗ Habsburg victory

✗ Habsburg defeat

— Boundary of Holy Roman Empire

Habsburg Empire of Charles V

Lands of Philip II of Spain

Lands of the Emperor Ferdinand

Inset:

Milan

Biocca 1522

Novara 1513

Agnadello 1509

Venice

Ceresole 1544

Marignano 1515

Pavia 1525

Genoa

Fornovo 1495

Bologna

Landriano 1529

Ravenna 1512

The Italian Wars comprising eight conflicts fought between 1494 and 1559, began when Charles VIII of France seized Naples in 1494 and declared himself its king. The Spaniards and their Italian allies took umbrage and drove Charles out, only to do it all over again in 1496 after another French monarch, Louis XII, tried to seize Naples. From there, the Italian Wars escalated into a power struggle between France and Spain for control of the Italian city-states. Other contestants who weighed in included the Holy Roman Empire, England, Scotland, Switzerland, and even the Ottoman Turks. The central struggle, though, was a personal one between the Holy Roman Emperor Charles V (King Charles I of Spain) and the King of France, Francis I. At the battle of Pavia in 1525, Charles captured Francis and forced him to renounce his claims in Italy. Francis, it appears, reclaimed them and was obliged to give them up again in 1529. The French finally renounced all claims in Italy in 1559 when the Wars came to an end.

The Huguenot Wars began on 1 March, 1562 with a savage event: a massacre at Vassy led by the Catholic Henri, Prince de Joinville, who set fire to a church, killing some 80 Protestant Huguenots inside and injuring hundreds of others. Ten years after Vassy, an even more bloodstained massacre occurred in Paris. On St. Bartholomew's Day, August 24, Huguenots were hunted down and murdered in the streets, women and children were butchered and their bodies were thrown into Seine.

The Huguenots and Catholics fought three short wars between the massacres. Each of the first two in 1562-1563 and 1567-1568 ended in a nervy truce, but a treaty followed the third, fought between 1568-1570, at the behest of King Charles IX who wanted a peaceful solution.

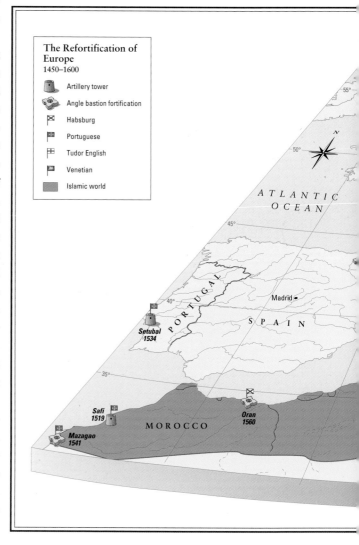

The Refortification of Europe
1450–1600

- Artillery tower
- Angle bastion fortification
- Habsburg
- Portuguese
- Tudor English
- Venetian
- Islamic world

Inevitably, perhaps, the St. Bartholomew Massacre set off another five brief, though indeterminate, wars. Three top-level assassinations took place: Henri, Duc de Guise, the former Prince de Joinville, and his brother Louis, Cardinal de Guise were murdered on successive days in 1588 and in 1589, King Henri III, Charles IX's successor, was also killed.

Henri III's death opened the way to peace. His successor, Henri IV was a Huguenot and had, in fact, narrowly escaped death on St. Bartholomew's day. To bring the hostilities — and the killings — to an end, Henri IV became a Catholic and, as a Catholic king acceptable to his Catholic subjects, promulgated the Edict of Nantes in 1598, granting Huguenots their religious and political freedom.

Guns and gunpowder fundamentally altered the face of battle as it had been known for thousands of years. The introduction of firearms prompted an entirely new brand of fortification designed to resist the immensely increased power and range of weaponry that had entered the business of warfare.

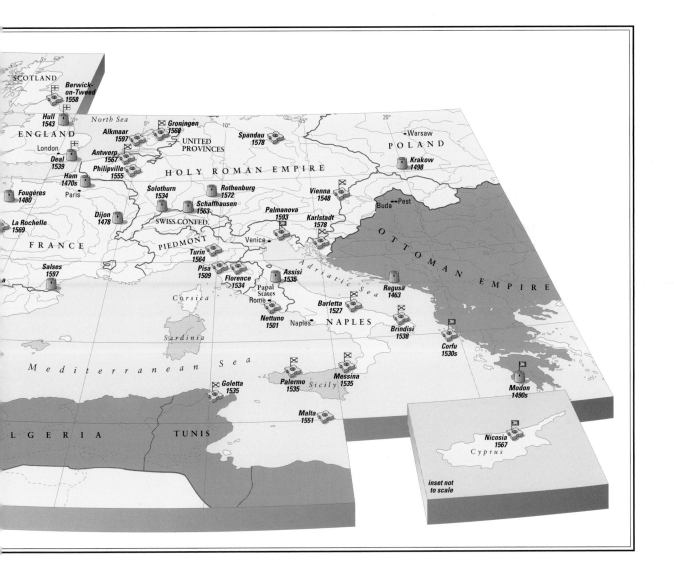

The End of the Knight and the Rise of the Foot Soldier

WHEN THE FOOT SOLDIER WITH A HAND-HELD GUN REPLACED THE MEDIEVAL KNIGHT, IT WAS NOT JUST ONE WARRIOR TAKING THE PLACE OF ANOTHER. GUNS AND GUNPOWDER INTRODUCED NEW TECHNOLOGY AND NEW STRATEGIES TO THE BATTLEFIELD.

In common with all technology, the difference firearms made to the battlefield evolved slowly. The first hand-held gun, the arquebus, was no real danger to the armored knight. If anything, the arquebusiers were in danger from pre-gunpowder weapons, as evidenced by the fact that they needed pikemen to protect them from enemy cavalry and its swords, lances, and other armament. Only when used in considerable numbers could the arquebus hope to put up a decent fight against more long-established weapons. Otherwise, the mounted knight, cloaked head to toe in armor, had little to fear from early firearms. The shot used by the arquebus was made of soft lead which when fired, could not attain sufficient speed to pierce a suit of armor. Even light armor was enough to protect a knight against arquebus shot if, of course, the arquebusier scored a hit in the first place. According to some contemporary accounts, hitting the target was a notable event in the life of an arquebusier, since his weapon was extremely inaccurate. So were the first matchlock muskets, which appeared after about 1500 and replaced the arquebus.

Nevertheless, the musket proved capable of some impressive improvements. By 1615, the matchlock was replaced first by the wheel lock, next, after 1660, by the flintlock. The wheel lock produced a spark to ignite the gunpowder by striking a small piece of iron pyrite against the rough edges of a revolving wheel. The wheel lock was strong and reliable and avoided the hazards of using naked flames to ignite the gunpowder. Unlike the matchlock, the wheel lock musket could be used quickly and at any time. The flintlock musket was even more efficient. A flint fitted into one end of an arm of the "cock" scraped along a steel plate when the trigger was pulled: the resultant shower of sparks ignited a small quantity of priming powder in a pan and this set off the main powder inside the gun barrel.

From there, the design and action of the musket continued to improve until, by the 18th century, it was around 60 times faster than it had been 200 years earlier. Even so, muskets did not need to become that powerful or fast-firing to bring the age of the armored knight to a close. As soon as it became obvious that a musket shot could pierce even as hard a metal as high-tempered steel, armorers began to make their armor thicker. It was possible, of course, to make armor musket-proof, but that also made it so heavy that it slowed down the man wearing it and could make it difficult for him to move. No wonder, then, that medieval armor was discarded — and so rapidly that by 1600, infantry and cavalry were wearing only helmet and either half-armor, which lacked the traditional foot and leg pieces or the cuirasse, comprising breast- and back-plates.

One effect of these changes was to make warfare a great deal faster, and combatants much more nimble. These were important advantages since warfare was so frequent in the 16th and 17th centuries that they contained only ten years of peace. Germany, a constant battleground at that time, lost 30 percent of its population due to war. These centuries saw, too, the rise of permanent armies staffed by professional officers and organized by the state. The first was the Spanish army, which was probably the most successful of the time and operated a comprehensive military system. The basic unit of the Spanish forces was a company of around 200 soldiers. Five companies made up a *colunela* (column) and contained within it pikemen, halberdiers, arquebusiers or musketeers and swordsmen — all the various groups of infantry involved in war at the time. Later on, after about 1530, three *colunelas* were merged to form *atercio* (third) which became known as the Spanish Square. This was a mixed infantry formation comprising around 3,000 swordsmen, arquebusiers, and pikemen which was widely taken up by other armies and dominated European battlefields for over a century.

As time went on, though, firepower assumed greater and greater importance for the Spanish infantry and by 1600, the company added 20 arquebusiers to its ranks. Arquebusiers also replaced swordsmen and the ratio of guns to other, more traditional arms grew until they reached parity. Toward the end of the 16th century, the Dutch military leader Prince Maurice of Nassau introduced the principle of volley fire, which had a significant effect on battlefield formations. Now, armies used linear deployments, a change that maximized the effect of firearms. The infantry was therefore more likely to be involved in hand-to-hand combat, which required greater discipline and courage. Volley fire also required infantrymen to move quickly and in unison, rather like a military *corps de ballet* synchronizing its maneuvers. In order to perfect its moves, the infantry had to undergo stringent training, much of it based on set piece exercises repeated over and over again. There was, though, an important spin-off from this new emphasis on drilling and discipline. The infantry in medieval armies had often been a barely trained lot, once described by the Spanish Duke of Alva as "laborers and lackeys." But the nerve and teamwork demanded by the effective use of firearms forged the infantry into professionals with all the skill and competence the new-style warfare required.

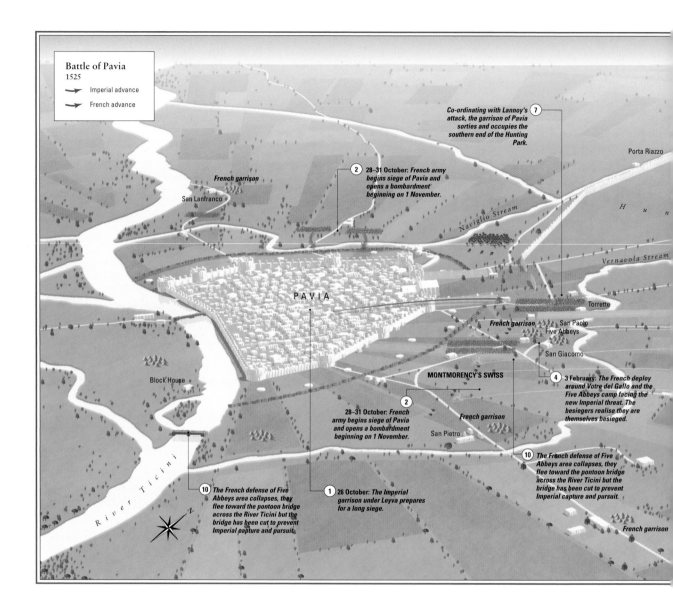

Battle of Pavia
1525

→ Imperial advance

→ French advance

Co-ordinating with Lannoy's attack, the garrison of Pavia sorties and occupies the southern end of the Hunting Park. ⑦

Porta Riazzo

French garrison

San Lanfranco

② 28–31 October: *French army begins siege of Pavia and opens a bombardment beginning on 1 November.*

Naviglio Stream

Vernavola Stream

H u n

Torrette

PAVIA

French garrison

San Paolo
Five Abbeys

San Giacomo

Block House

MONTMORENCY'S SWISS

④ *3 February: The French deploy around Votre del Gallo and the Five Abbeys camp facing the new Imperial threat. The besiegers realise they are themselves besieged.*

② 28–31 October: *French army begins siege of Pavia and opens a bombardment beginning on 1 November.*

French garrison

San Pietro

⑩ *The French defense of Five Abbeys area collapses, they flee toward the pontoon bridge across the River Ticini but the bridge has been cut to prevent Imperial capture and pursuit.*

River Ticini

N

⑩ *The French defense of Five Abbeys area collapses, they flee toward the pontoon bridge across the River Ticini but the bridge has been cut to prevent Imperial capture and pursuit.*

① 26 October: The Imperial garrison under Leyva prepares for a long siege.

French garrison

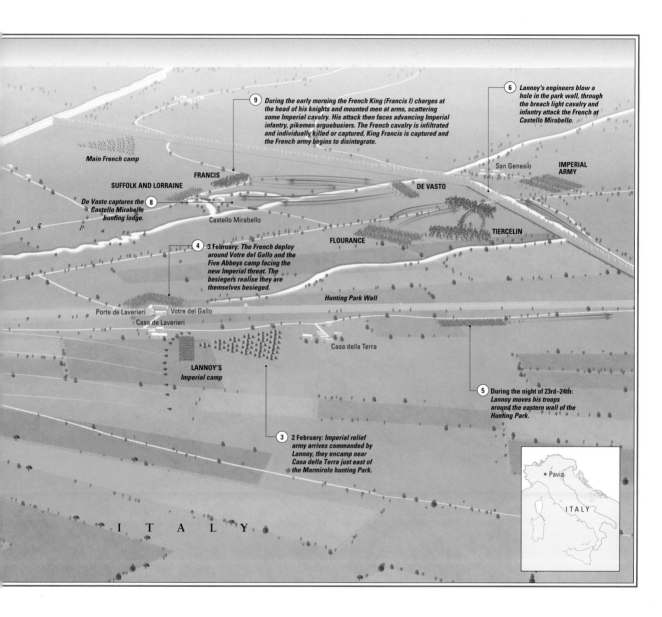

9 During the early morning the French King (Francis I) charges at the head of his knights and mounted men at arms, scattering some Imperial cavalry. His attack then faces advancing Imperial infantry, pikemen arguebusiers. The French cavalry is infiltrated and individually killed or captured, King Francis is captured and the French army begins to disintegrate.

Main French camp

6 Lannoy's engineers blow a hole in the park wall, through the breach light cavalry and infantry attack the French at Castello Mirabello.

San Genesio

IMPERIAL ARMY

FRANCIS

SUFFOLK AND LORRAINE

DE VASTO

8 De Vasto captures the Castello Mirabello hunting lodge.

Castello Mirabello

TIERCELIN

FLOURANCE

4 3 February: The French deploy around Votre del Gallo and the Five Abbeys camp facing the new Imperial threat. The besiegers realise they are themselves besieged.

Hunting Park Wall

Porte de Laverieri   Votre del Gallo

Casa de Laverieri

Casa della Terra

LANNOY'S Imperial camp

5 During the night of 23rd–24th: Lannoy moves his troops around the eastern wall of the Hunting Park.

3 2 February: Imperial relief army arrives commanded by Lannoy, they encamp near Casa della Terra just east of the Marmirolo hunting Park.

I T A L Y

• Pavia

ITALY

The Battle of Pavia, fought on 24 February, 1525, was the decisive confrontation of the Italian War of 1521-1526. Fighting lasted four hours before the Spanish forces divided the French army and inflicted extremely heavy casualties on them. Pavia ensured the supremacy of the Hapsburg royal family in Italy.

The Fall of Islamic Spain

ON JANUARY 2, 1492, 260 YEARS OF RULE BY THE NASRID DYNASTY CAME TO AN END IN SPAIN. THE LAST MUSLIM KING IS SAID TO HAVE WEPT AT HIS DEPARTURE.

The *coup de grace* that terminated Muslim rule in Spain was administered by the Catholic monarchs Ferdinand of Aragon and Isabella of Castile shortly after their marriage in 1479. Their work of completing the Reconquista, the re-conquest of Spain, (see pages 74-77) was greatly aided by internal squabbles within the Nasrid royal house of Granada. In 1482, Abu I-Hassan Ali, the father of King Muhamed XII, was deposed in Muhamed's favor. Two years later, Muhamed attempted to increase his prestige by invading Castile, only to be captured and imprisoned. In 1487, Muhamed was freed, and his kingdom was returned to him, but only after he had agreed that Granada should become a tributary kingdom of Aragon and Castile. Muhamed was also obliged to promise not to interfere with the imminent Christian conquest of Malaga. He had to stand by as Baez, Malaga, and Almeria fell to Christian arms in 1487 and Almunecar and Salobrena in 1489. Finally, by 1491, Granada was the only Muslim kingdom left in the whole of Spain.

Now, Muhamed was expected to surrender Granada to the Catholic monarchs, but he refused. The Christians' response was immediate and robust. In 1491, they laid siege to the city. Before long, the inhabitants of Granada were starving and, in November 1491, Muhamed asked for terms. A settlement was reached on 25 November when the Treaty of Granada was signed on remarkably lenient terms that guaranteed freedom of worship in the city and the protection of Islamic culture. The Treaty came into effect on 2 January,1492, when Muhamed handed King Ferdinand the keys to Granada. Muhamed was treated generously and was granted an estate in Laujar de Andarax, which lay in the mountains of the Sierra Nevada close by the Mediterranean Sea. It was said that as Muhamed and his party rode out of Granada for the last time, he saw the Alhambra, the beautiful palace built by the Nasrids, nestling in the green valley below. He burst into tears, only to be admonished by his mother who told him: "Do not weep like a woman for what you could not defend as a man." Muhamed did not live at his estate for long, but settled in Fez, the traditional northern capital of Morocco, where he died in 1533.

The Christian reconquest of Spain was a very slow process lasting 770 years. The Reconquista, as the Spanish called it, began soon after the Muslim Moorish conquest finished in AD718 and ended in 1492, when Granada, the last city under Moorish rule was handed back to the Spanish King and Queen.

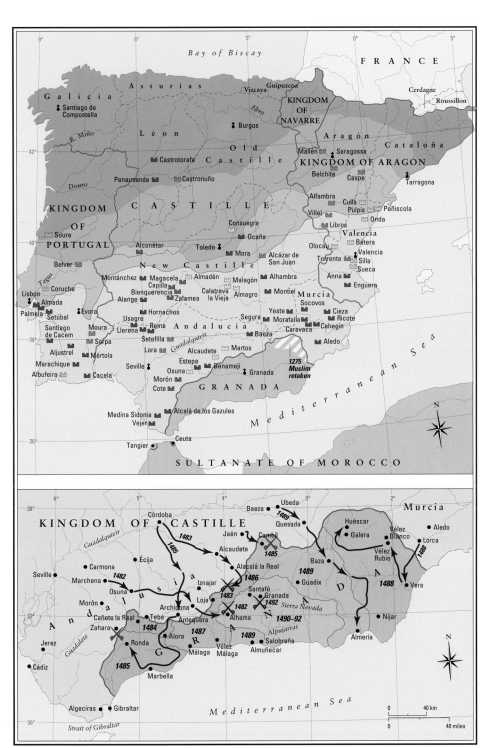

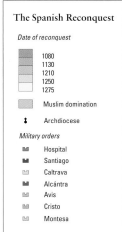

The Spanish Reconquest

Date of reconquest
- 1080
- 1130
- 1210
- 1250
- 1275
- Muslim domination
- Archdiocese

Military orders
- Hospital
- Santiago
- Caltrava
- Alcántra
- Avis
- Cristo
- Montesa

The Fall of Granada
1480–1492
- → Christian advance
- *1489* Date of Christian conquest
- ✗ Christian victory
- ✗ Muslim victory

THE OTTOMAN EMPIRE

THE CAPTURE OF CONSTANTINOPLE IN 1453, WHICH FINALLY DESTROYED THE BYZANTINE EMPIRE, WAS A CATASTROPHE FOR CHRISTIAN EUROPE BUT A TREMENDOUS VICTORY FOR ISLAM. HOWEVER, THE OTTOMAN TURKISH EMPIRE BUILT ON THIS TRIUMPH WAS NOT FINISHED WITH CONQUEST YET.

The Ottoman Empire centered on its capital Istanbul — the renamed Constantinople — was created in less than 150 years after the fall of the Byzantines. It lasted for almost five centuries until it fell, in its turn, in 1923 following defeat in the First World War. From the very humble beginnings of a small emirate in northwestern Asia Minor, the Ottomans rose to dominate the Islamic world and threaten the West. Cavalrymen by preference and tradition, the Turks learnt to incorporate infantry forces (notably the famous Janissaries) engineers and artillerymen into their armies. Their run of success as conquerors was only broken (briefly) by Bayezit's defeat at the hands of Tamburlane near Ankara in 1402. When Constantinople fell in 1453 it became the heart of the empire, from whence flowed victorious fleets and armies.

From the start, this Islamic empire was dominated by the military and first flourished its aggressive powers in 1515 when the army of the Ottoman Sultan Selim I captured the capital of Persia, Tabriz. The next year, Selim underlined this success at Merj-Dabik in Syria, where the Egyptian Mameluke cavalry were thrashed by the Turks' skilful use of artillery and arquebus fire. The Egyptians learned from this shaming experience and the next time they encountered the Ottoman Turks, in the battle of Ridanieh in the Nile Delta in January 1517, they came to the battlefield with artillery of their own. Not that it did them much good — the Ottoman guns had superior range. In an attempt to halt the bombardment, the Mameluke cavalry charged head-on, and though they penetrated the Turkish lines, they were repulsed and thrashed again by a determined counter-attack.

This success was not at all surprising. The Ottoman Turks had been one of the first Middle Eastern states to adopt gunpowder weapons, first introducing firearms into their arsenal some time between 1444 and 1448. At the siege of Constantinople five years later the Ottomans deployed an enormous bronze cannon, known as Mohamed's Great Gun or the Great Turkish Bombard. It was 17 ft. long weighed nearly 19 tons and could fire cannonballs measuring over 2 ft. in diameter. The Great Turkish Bombard was still in action some 350 years later, when ships of the Royal Navy appeared in the Dardanelles during the Anglo-Turkish War of 1807-1809. The British lost 28 sailors killed in the bombardment. The cutting edge of Ottoman expansion lay in the Turcoman nomads and their style of warfare; but the Sultans realized early on that their army needed a greater variety of troops if their state was to be maintained. They never neglected infantry, whether the irregular Azaps or the more famous Janissaries. This elite corps was formed in the mid-14th century, and originally depended on prisoners of war to fill its ranks. In 1438 the devshirme, a levy on Christian boys, was instituted. They were then brought up to be fanatically loyal to the Sultan. A professional force, adept with bow, crossbow, and later, handguns, they wore distinctive, tall white caps.

Turkish expertise with artillery and fire-arms helped account for the impressive speed with which they went on after their triumphs at Merj-Dabik and Ridanieh to forge their extensive empire. During the reign of Selim I which ended in 1520, the Ottoman Empire trebled in size, covering almost one billion acres. The Empire now extended over the Middle East, Egypt and the eastern Mediterranean, and by 1590, stretched even further, along the North African littoral, and into Hungary, Greece, southwest Russia and the Balkan Peninsula.

The Battle of Mohacs between the Ottoman Turks and the Hungarians took place on August 29, 1526 and was a fearful disaster for the Hungarians. They lost their young king, Louis II and suffered monumental casualties: 10,000 infantry and 5,000 cavalry were killed. The survivors of the battle scattered.

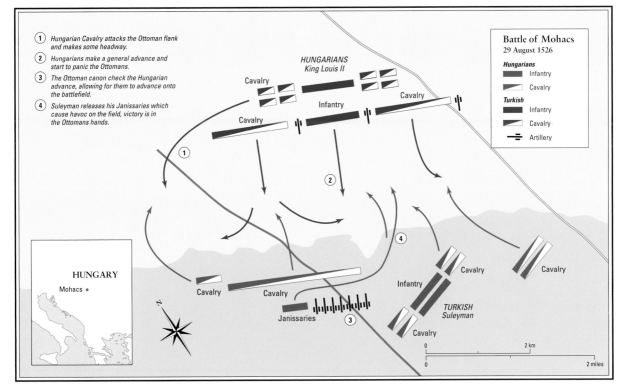

The army that achieved these far-flung conquests was the first standing army in and around Europe since the time of the Romans. Like the Romans, theirs included crack regiments. After the mid-15th century, infantry equipped with guns, the Piyade Topçu, were introduced. Cavalry regiments, the Süvari Topçu were formed and armed with guns, and grenadiers called Kumbaraci were employed to throw explosives, or *khimbara*. There was also a slave army, the Janissaries, who adopted firearms early in the 15th century. By the 16th, their chief weapon was the matchlock musket and they also employed grenades and small, hand-held cannon. The Janissaries, who fought on foot, had their cavalry equivalents in the elite Sipahis whose duties included riding with the Ottoman Sultan during parades and providing him with a mounted bodyguard. Janissaries and Sipahis formed part of a range of special forces which between them performed virtually every duty required of a standing army. There were, for example, irregular infantrymen known as Azabs who built roads and bridges, and provided supplies for the front-line troops. A subdivision of the Azabs known as Bashi-bazouk were the "tough guys" of the army. To ensure they had a suitably brutal approach to their duties, they were recruited from among the criminal class or were homeless men picked off the streets. They were ferocious, cruel, and undisciplined and were especially deadly in close combat. The Akinci were frontline cavalry units who went out on raids and performed reconnaissance in frontier areas and around enemy outposts. The Mehteran comprised what was probably the oldest military marching band in the world: their task was to play marches and other martial music during military campaigns, probably less for entertainment, and more to keep up morale and fighting spirit.

Morale, if not fighting spirit, badly needed boosting after the Ottoman Empire began to stagnate only two centuries after its dramatic inception in 1453. This was partly due to resistance to change among the 17th-century military elite. They were, for example, diffident about advancing technology, such as the replacement of matchlock muskets by the safer and more efficient flintlocks. Another factor was the feebleness of some Sultans, who were virtually in thrall to their families, the Ottoman nobility, and in some cases to their Janissaries and women in their own harems. Meanwhile, European states and their armies were gathering strength and the Ottomans began to lose battles and territory. Hungary was lost after their defeat in the battle for Vienna in 1683. In 1715, Morea, the Pelopponese peninsula in Greece, fell to the

Ottoman Empire
1683–1914

	Territory lost by 1718
	Territory lost by 1812
	Territory lost by 1881
	Territory lost by 1914
	Ottoman Empire, 1914
1811	Date granted autonomy
1830	Date when territory lost

Republic of Venice. By 1828, stagnation had become decline and from there on, the Ottoman Turkish Empire became "the Sick Man of Europe," heading for destruction. The *coup de grace* was administered by the First World War in which the Empire was among the defeated Central Powers. By 1923, the Ottomans had gone. In their place was the secular Republic of Turkey, ruled as its first President by a former army officer, Mustafa Kemal Ataturk.

After the fall of Constantinople, in 1453, the Ottoman Turks expanded their own empire into Europe. However, losses of territory to the French, the British, and other Europeans significantly shrank the Ottoman Empire by 1914.

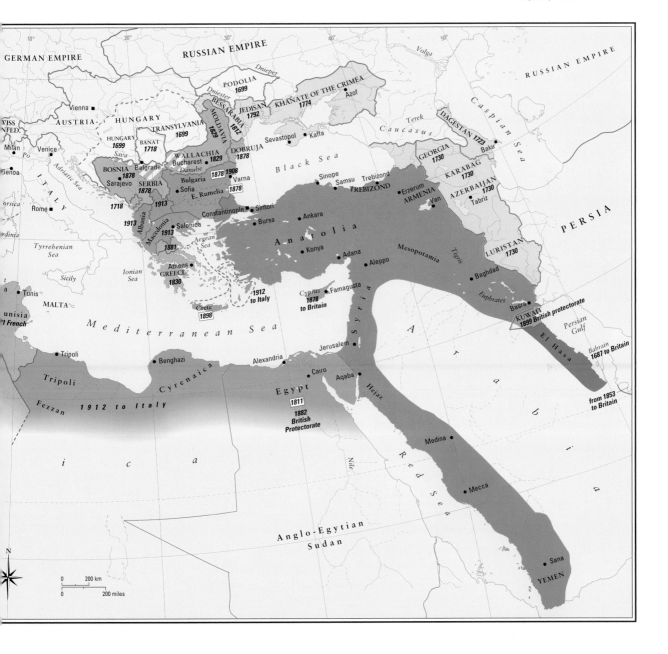

THE AGE OF EUROPEAN ASCENDANCY 1700-1750

IN THE 18TH CENTURY, EUROPE REACHED A PINNACLE OF POWER AND EMINENCE AND WAS FAR MORE ADVANCED IN ITS TECHNOLOGY AND INFLUENCE ABROAD THAN ITS RIVALS IN MANCHU CHINA, MOGUL INDIA, OTTOMAN TURKEY, AND THE SHORT-LIVED EMPIRE IN PERSIA.

Europe's rise to the position of global power and military superiority it attained in the 18th century depended on the disappearance of two economic factors which, till then, had restrained its progress. One was the overwhelmingly agricultural nature of European society, in which most of the food the vast majority of people produced was for their own consumption. This subsistence agriculture was extremely labor-intensive and, since most recruits came from the farms, it was virtually impossible to create large, and therefore more effective, armies. The other restraining factor was the modest industrial capacity of European nations: until the 18th century, mass production on any appreciable scale was unknown, and the supply of goods, including weapons and other munitions, was limited. All this affected the ambitions of five European powers — Britain, France, Spain, Portugal and the Netherlands — which sought to acquire influence and wealth beyond their own home continent. The solution to these problems lay with the agricultural and industrial revolutions, in which mechanization increased production yet at the same time reduced the number of workers that had once been required. For instance, a spinning or weaving machine used in a textile factory could produce as many as ten hand-workers or more, and do it more quickly and more cheaply. Mechanized agriculture, too, produced more food using fewer workers with a resultant increase in population and, for the military, more recruits for larger armies and larger crews of up to 1,000 men for warships. These increases in manpower required a greater supply of weapons and munitions than could be furnished by the old method of hand-crafting weapons. With industrialization, more weapons were produced and, just as important, mass production could ensure that they were standardized. In addition, more food could be produced to feed more men in more locales across a world that was rapidly opening up under the impetus of voyages of discovery, trade, and colonization.

The Industrial Revolution also had a cultural effect that allowed enterprise and innovation to have its head. The expansion of capacity and opportunity opened the way for fresh ideas about how warfare should be improved and conducted. Previously, the military mindset had been cautious and conservative, and strategy and tactics stultified. For example, army commanders might shrink from engaging in battles unless they could be reasonably certain of victory. Others might avoid combat for fear of losing expensively trained soldiers in fruitless fighting. Now, though, commanders were able to envisage larger infantry units which could be trained to move, maneuver, or change direction as one, massing them on the battlefield at will to achieve maximum mobility. As a result, the firepower of muskets or the new rifled guns that were increasingly used during the 18th century was greatly maximized, and so was the effect of shock action during combat.

War at sea underwent a similar revolution once new ideas penetrated the rigid "line ahead" rule that required battleships to follow each other in orderly procession and engage only those enemy vessels that were closest to them. "Line ahead" did not permit fleets to make mass melée attacks on the enemy, which meant passing up easy opportunities to win battles or increasing the risk of losing them. Although the "line ahead" school maintained its grip on naval tactics for some time, this did not prevent a new school of naval officers from trying out more daring tactics. These involved leaving the "line ahead" formation and sailing straight for the enemy ships. They risked being sunk or badly damaged by enemy broadsides but once ships managed to get through the enemy lines, they were able to break up their formations and pick off stragglers with gunfire. The British fired directly at the oak-built enemy hulls to sink or disable their vessels, whereas the French used their guns to bring down their opponents' masts and rigging to immobilize them. The Royal Navy increased its chances of destroying the enemy with more innovative gunnery by adopting the carronade, a short, squat gun that could fire a 32lb (15 kg) ball and, at close range, smashing through enemy hulls before they could bring their longer, more cumbersome 12-,16- or 24-pounders to bear. A further piece of ingenuity was a flintlock device that fired a gun by sending a spark into its touchhole; no gunpowder, no priming, and no slow match, just a dense, startling explosion.

The inventions, innovations, and improvements that arose during the 18th century were not of interest only to the purveyors of continental warfare. This was a time when Europeans exported their warfare across the world as rival nations challenged each other for trade and colonial advantage on a global scale. The Americas and the Caribbean, for example, were the scene of prolonged rivalry and sometimes savage fighting between the British, French, and Dutch. The British and the French fought long and hard for colonial dominance in India. The Spaniards, the first colonizers of America and the ones with the most extensive colonies, battled to stop other Europeans — especially the "heretic" Protestant English — from intruding on their territory. The empires that resulted from the European move overseas — Spanish, British, French, Dutch, Portuguese — not only underpinned Europe's ascendancy but prolonged it far beyond its beginnings into the next two centuries.

SPANISH CONQUESTS IN THE AMERICAS 1492-1600

SPANISH CONQUESTS IN CENTRAL AND SOUTH AMERICA WON THEM THE FIRST SUBSTANTIAL EUROPEAN EMPIRE OVERSEAS. TWO NATIVE EMPIRES — THE AZTEC AND THE INCA — FELL INTO THEIR HANDS. SO DID FABULOUS TREASURE IN THE FORM OF GOLD, SILVER, AND PRECIOUS STONES.

I n 1492, Christopher Columbus set out across the Atlantic to discover a westward sea route to the riches of Asia. What he actually found was something quite unsuspected: a continent previously unknown to Europeans. As Spanish conquistadors would discover in time, this "New World" of America was "new" in many more ways than one. Geographically, it was immense, with loftier mountains, longer rivers, and more extensive forests than could be found in Europe. Its inhabitants differed from Europeans both racially and culturally. Their religions were pagan, whereas the Spaniards and the Portuguese who later colonized Brazil were zealous Christians. But the first difference the Spaniards discovered was by far the most important factor in the future history of the Americas: the native Americans were centuries behind the Europeans in military technology.

Metal weapons were virtually unknown, cannon and firearms looked like terrifying magic, and there were no horses for use in battle or as transport. Just how far warfare in the Americas diverged from the techniques and equipment familiar in Europe was revealed after conquistadors led by Hernan Cortes landed on the east coast of Mexico in 1519. As Cortes' men rode ashore, the awed spectators presumed that horse and rider were all one animal. In a chronicle completed in 1569, the missionary Bernardino de Sahagun recorded the reaction of witnesses who reported a demonstration of Spanish gunnery to their ruler, the Great Speaker of the Aztecs, Moctezuma.

"The great lombard gun expelled the shot which thundered as it went off," they told Moctezuma, who

The European discovery and conquest of the Americas was an unexpected spin-off from efforts made by navigators to reach the riches of China, Japan, and the East by sailing westward across the Atlantic. Until around 1500, European navigators were unaware that they had come upon a previously unknown continent.

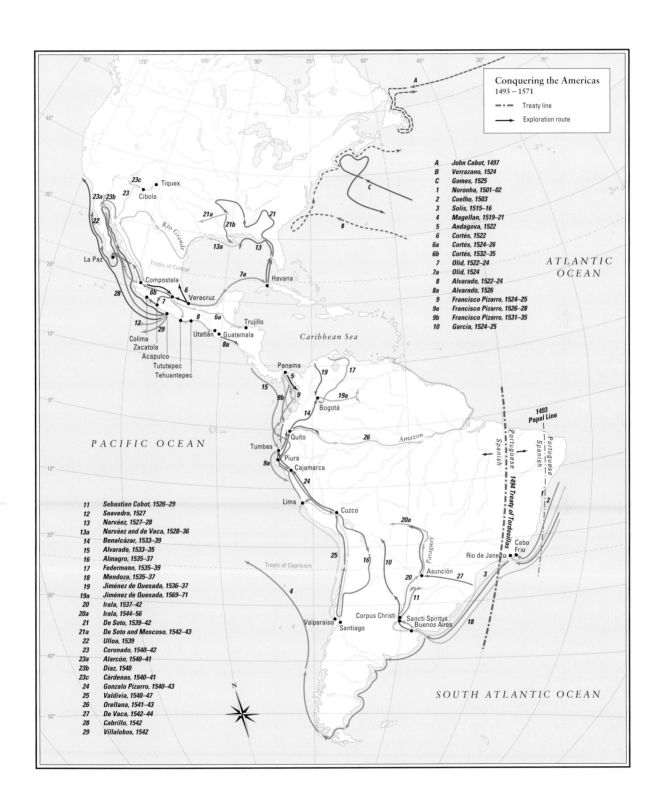

Conquering the Americas
1493 – 1571

— · — Treaty line

——▶ Exploration route

A   John Cabot, 1497
B   Verrazano, 1524
C   Gomes, 1525
1   Noronha, 1501–02
2   Coelho, 1503
3   Solís, 1515–16
4   Magellan, 1519–21
5   Andagova, 1522
6   Cortés, 1522
6a   Cortés, 1524–26
6b   Cortés, 1532–35
7   Olid, 1522–24
7a   Olid, 1524
8   Alvarado, 1522–24
8a   Alvarado, 1526
9   Francisco Pizarro, 1524–25
9a   Francisco Pizarro, 1526–28
9b   Francisco Pizarro, 1531–35
10   García, 1524–25

11   Sebastian Cabot, 1526–29
12   Saavedra, 1527
13   Narváez, 1527–28
13a   Narváez and de Vaca, 1528–36
14   Benalcázar, 1533–39
15   Alvarado, 1533–35
16   Almagro, 1535–37
17   Federmann, 1535–39
18   Mendoza, 1535–37
19   Jiménez de Quesada, 1536–37
19a   Jiménez de Quesada, 1569–71
20   Irala, 1537–42
20a   Irala, 1544–56
21   De Soto, 1539–42
21a   De Soto and Moscoso, 1542–43
22   Ulloa, 1539
23   Coronado, 1540–42
23a   Alarcón, 1540–41
23b   Díaz, 1540
23c   Cárdenas, 1540–41
24   Gonzalo Pizarro, 1540–43
25   Valdivia, 1540–47
26   Orellana, 1541–43
27   De Vaca, 1542–44
28   Cabrillo, 1542
29   Villalobos, 1542

ATLANTIC OCEAN

PACIFIC OCEAN

Caribbean Sea

SOUTH ATLANTIC OCEAN

1493 Papal Line

1494 Treaty of Tordesillas

Spanish   Portuguese

Portuguese   Spanish

Rio Grande

Tropic of Cancer

Tropic of Capricorn

Amazon

Paraguay

Tiquex
Cibola
23c
23a 23b 23
22
La Paz
Compostela
6b
6
28
Veracruz
7
1
12
29
8
6a
Colima
Zacatola
Acapulco
Tututepec
Tehuantepec
Utatlán
Guatemala
8a
Trujillo
Havana
7a
21a
21b
21
13a
13

Panama
5
19
17
15
9b
9
19a
14
Bogotá
Quito
Tumbes
9a
Piura
Cajamarca
24
Lima
Cuzco
26
25
16
10
20a
20
Asunción
27
Rio de Janeiro
Cabo Frio
1
2
3
Valparaíso
Santiago
Corpus Christi
Sancti Spiritus
Buenos Aires
18
11
4

N

awaited their observations in his capital, Tenochtitlan, which lay far inland in the Valley of Mexico. "Something like a stone came out of it in a shower of fire and sparks... and the shot, which struck a mountain, knocked it to pieces, dissolved it. It reduced a tree to sawdust. The tree disappeared as if it had been blown away..." The Aztecs, more properly called the Mexica, were notable conquerors themselves. They had acquired an empire that stretched across Mexico from the Atlantic to the Pacific Oceans. But the report of 1519, combined with other news of Spanish conquests in the Caribbean, gave the Aztecs irrefutable proof that this time they had been outmatched and outgunned.

The Spanish conquests had begun in 1493, after Columbus' second voyage to America. In that year, he established the first permanent Spanish colony in the New World on the island of Hispaniola. The Spaniards who flocked to America in his wake soon invaded and conquered several Caribbean islands — the Bahamas, the Turks and Caicos Islands, Cuba, Jamaica, Puerto Rico. Here, the Tainos and other Arawak inhabitants were enslaved, and worked to death or, like other peoples in what later became Latin America died in droves from European diseases to which they had no resistance. The Tainos fought back as best they could, but their weapons, which included stone-headed arrows and stone and copper maces, were useless against the armed might of the Spaniards.

This does not, of course, mean that the native armies were helpless against the onslaught of the invaders. The Aztecs, for instance, used clubs and spears containing blades and spikes made from obsidian (volcanic rock) which could tear flesh at a touch. The spears were thrown with the aid of an *atlatl*, (spear-thrower), which increased their velocity and power. The Aztec *maquihuitl* was a cross between a sword and a club set with pieces of obsidian which made it so razor-sharp that it could sever a horse's head when used with both hands. The *quauholilli* was a huge stone club that could smash skulls.

Yet, despite the damage that could be done with these weapons, the balance of military power always lay with the Spaniards. The Tainos, Aztecs, and others who encountered the Spaniards had nothing to compare with the superlative Toledo swords, which were given exceptional strength by forging hard steel together with a high soft-steel and carbon content at very high temperatures. There was also a significant difference in morale. The conquistadors were creatures of the Renaissance, with its emphasis on individuality and personal worth and the enterprise fostered by these qualities. By contrast, with a few exceptions, the Tainos, Aztecs, and other inhabitants of America tended to be subject to the dictates of their gods and the orders of their rulers. For example, Hernan Cortes in Mexico and Francisco Pizaro in Peru virtually paralyzed the will to

The systematic, continuous, and documented exploration of the world by sea started with the Portuguese discovery of Madeira in around 1419. The explorations continued for some 360 years until the voyages of the English Captain James Cook crisscrossed the Pacific Ocean between 1768, and his murder in Hawaii in 1779.

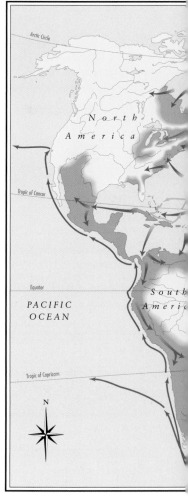

act of their inhabitants by making prisoners of their rulers — Moctezuma in Mexico and the Inca Atahualpa in Peru. Cortes also discovered that capturing the leader of an Aztec army was the best way to panic an opponent's forces into retreat or surrender. This helped explain how an estimated 240,000 Spaniards who came to America in the 16th century overcame American populations numbering millions. More specifically, Hernan Cortes invaded Mexico in 1519 with fewer than 600 men. In Peru, Francisco Pizzaro subdued the Incas with a force only 168-strong. A similar process continued in Central and South America until, by around 1600, Spain owned the first of the overseas empires which in time spread European influence across the world.

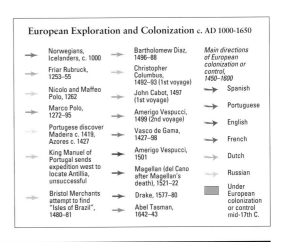

European Exploration and Colonization c. AD 1000-1650

Norwegians, Icelanders, c. 1000	Bartholomew Diaz, 1496–88
Friar Rubruck, 1253–55	Christopher Columbus, 1492–93 (1st voyage)
Nicolo and Maffeo Polo, 1262	John Cabot, 1497 (1st voyage)
Marco Polo, 1272–95	Amerigo Vespucci, 1499 (2nd voyage)
Portugese discover Madeira c. 1419, Azores c. 1427	Vasco de Gama, 1427–98
King Manuel of Portugal sends expedition west to locate Antillia, unsuccessful	Amerigo Vespucci, 1501
	Magellan (del Cano after Magellan's death), 1521–22
Bristol Merchants attempt to find "Isles of Brazil", 1480–81	Drake, 1577–80
	Abel Tasman, 1642–43

Main directions of European colonization or control, 1450–1600

→ Spanish
→ Portuguese
→ English
→ French
→ Dutch
→ Russian

▨ Under European colonization or control mid-17th C.

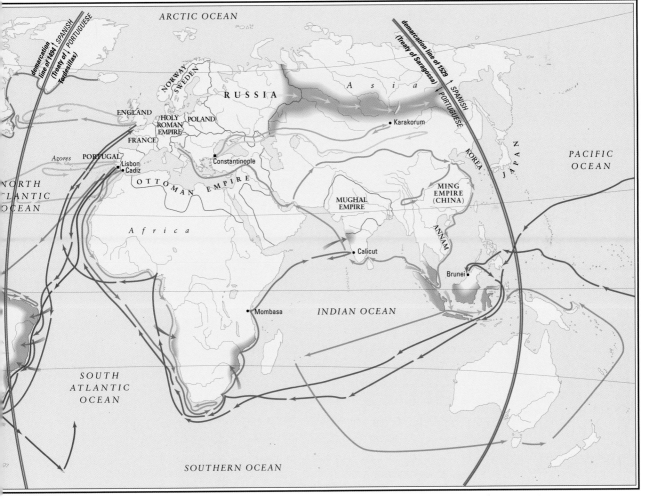

BALANCE OF POWER: FRANCE VERSUS SPAIN 1491-1559

BY 1494, ITALY HAD BEEN AN ASSORTMENT OF INDEPENDENT — AND PERPETUALLY QUARRELLING — STATES FOR MORE THAN A THOUSAND YEARS. THEN, THE FRENCH STEPPED IN WITH A CLAIM TO NAPLES.

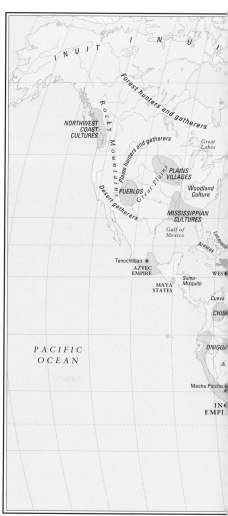

In 1494, the claims of King Charles VIII of France to the throne of Naples, which comprised the southern half of Italy and the island of Sicily, set off a power struggle with Spain that was not resolved for 65 years. Charles VIII, who based his claims on a somewhat distant family connection, provoked immediate opposition from the "Holy League" formed by the Holy Roman Empire, the Pope, Spain, England, Venice, and the Italian city-state of Milan. Despite winning a battle at Fornova in 1495, this formidable combination sent King Charles hastily retreating home to France. The same year, the Spanish invaded Italy and, after losing one battle with the French at Seminara, triumphed in another, the siege of Atella, where they captured the French commander, Gilbert Duc de Montpensier. After that, the French had no option but to withdraw.

During these years, gunpowder was still a new and not entirely familiar factor in war, and successive battles

In 1500, some parts of the world were already beginning to show the results of European exploration and settlement. Among them, the island of Madeira in the north Atlantic had been settled by the Portuguese in around 1425 and another island, Hispaniola in the Caribbean, by the Spaniards in 1493.

between the French and Spanish in Italy continued to demonstrate how armies must adapt to accommodate the new battlefield conditions. One such occurred after the French invaded Italy again in 1502, only to see their cavalry destroyed by Spanish arquebusiers at Cerignola in 1503. This disaster obliged the French to relinquish their claim to Naples. They fared better when hostilities resumed in 1510, but their victory at Ravenna in 1512 was dampened when the Spanish infantry, maintaining tight formation, lived to fight another day by fending off the French cavalry. Obviously, cavalry could no longer expect to be automatically successful against disciplined, highly trained infantry. The next battle, at Novarra, on June 6, 1513 illustrated another lesson when the Spaniards' Swiss infantry were decimated by the French artillery, which inflicted 700 casualties in three minutes. Subsequently, the battle of Pavia in 1525, when the French armored cavalry was again cut down by Spanish arquebusiers, served as another object lesson in the power of infantry firearms.

The World 1500

- ■ Major city
- Ottoman Empire
- England and possessions
- France and possessions
- Union of Kalmar
- Venetian Republic
- Portugal and possessions
- Spain and possessions
- Bahmani Kingdom to 1484
- —— Holy Roman Empire

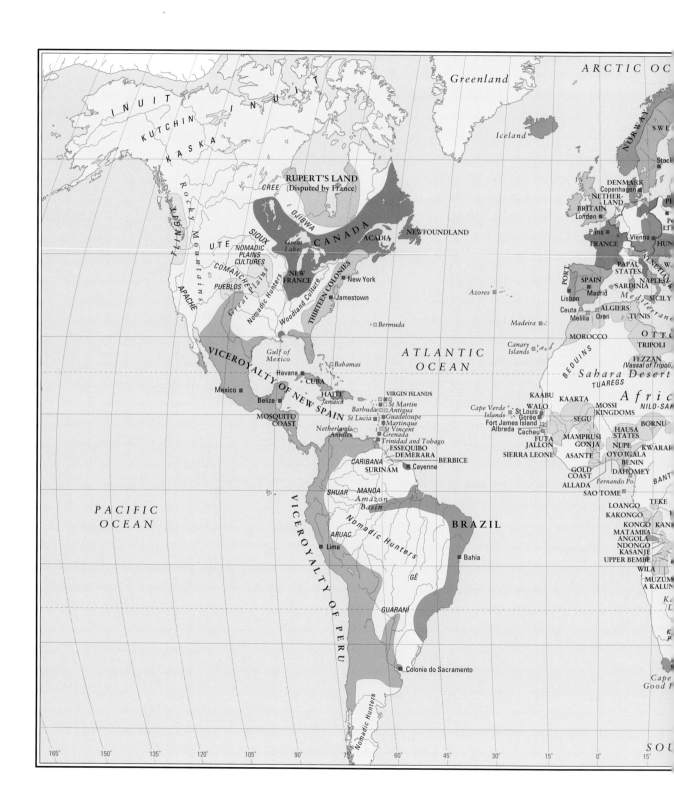

ARCTIC OC

Greenland

Iceland

INUIT

KUTCHIN

KASKA   INUIT

TLINGIT

Rocky Mountains

CREE

RUPERT'S LAND
(Disputed by France)

OJIBWA

CANADA

ACADIA

NEWFOUNDLAND

SIOUX

UTE

NOMADIC
PLAINS
CULTURES

Great
Lakes

NEW
FRANCE

COMANCHE

PUEBLOS

Great Plains

Nomadic Hunters

Woodland Culture

THIRTEEN COLONIES

New York

Jamestown

APACHE

VICEROYALTY OF NEW SPAIN

Gulf of
Mexico

Bermuda

ATLANTIC
OCEAN

Azores

Madeira

Canary
Islands

Bahamas

Havana

CUBA

Mexico

Belize

HAITI
Jamaica

VIRGIN ISLANDS
St Martin
Barbuda   Antigua
St Lucia   Guadeloupe
Martinique
St Vincent
Grenada
Trinidad and Tobago

Cape Verde
Islands

St Louis
Gorée
Fort James Island
Albreda   Cacheu

KAABU   KAARTA

WALO

SEGU

MOSSI
KINGDOMS

MOROCCO

BEDUINS   Sahara Desert
TUAREGS

TRIPOLI

FEZZAN
(Vassal of Tripoli)

OTTO

Afric
NILO-SA

MOSQUITO
COAST

Netherlands
Antilles

ESSEQUIBO
DEMERARA
BERBICE

FUTA
JALLON

SIERRA LEONE

MAMPRUSI
GONJA

ASANTE

GOLD
COAST

ALLADA

HAUSA
STATES

NUPE   KWARAF

OYO IGALA
BENIN

DAHOMEY

SAO TOME

Fernando Po

BORNU

BANT

CARIBANA
SURINAM

Cayenne

SHUAR   MANOA
Amazon
Basin

ARUAC

Lima

Nomadic Hunters

BRAZIL

Bahia

LOANGO
KAKONGO

KONGO   KAN
MATAMBA
ANGOLA
NDONGO
KASANJE
UPPER BEMBE

WILA

MUZUM
A KALUN

TEKE

PACIFIC
OCEAN

VICEROYALTY OF PERU

GÊ

GUARANÍ

Colonia do Sacramento

Nomadic Hunters

SOU

NORWAY

SWE

Stoc

DENMARK
Copenhagen
NETHER-
LAND
BRITAIN
London
Paris
FRANCE

Vienna

PH

LT
H

PORT.
SPAIN

Lisbon   Madrid

Ceuta
Melilla   Oran

ALGIERS
TUNIS

PAPAL
STATES

SARDINIA

Mediterran

NAPLES
SICILY

VENETIAN

Cape
Good

165°   150°   135°   120°   105°   90°   75°   60°   45°   30°   15°   0°   15°

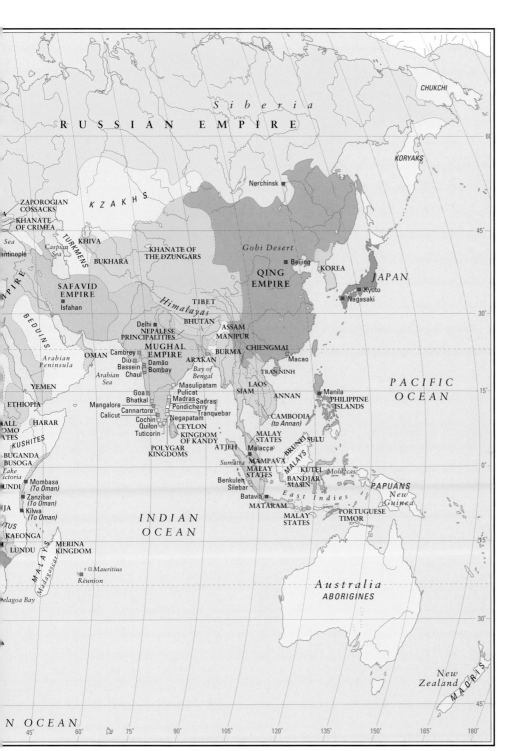

The World 1700

- ■ Major city
- British possessions
- Danish possessions
- French possessions
- Netherlands possessions
- Portuguese possessions
- Spanish possessions
- Swedish possessions
- —— Holy Roman Empire

CHUKCHI

Siberia

RUSSIAN EMPIRE

KORYAKS

ZAPOROGIAN
COSSACKS
KHANATE
OF CRIMEA

KZAKHS

KHIVA

Sea
intinople
Caspian
Sea
TURKMENS
BUKHARA

KHANATE OF
THE DZUNGARS

Gobi Desert

Nerchinsk ■

Beijing ■
KOREA
JAPAN
Kyoto ■
Nagasaki ■

QING
EMPIRE

MPIRE

SAFAVID
EMPIRE
Isfahan ■

Himalayas
TIBET
BHUTAN

Delhi ■
NEPALESE
PRINCIPALITIES

ASSAM
MANIPUR

BEDUINS

OMAN
Cambrey ■
Diu
Bassein
Chaul
Damão
Bombay

MUGHAL
EMPIRE

BURMA
ARAKAN
CHIENGMAI

Arabian
Peninsula

Arabian
Sea

Bay of
Bengal

TRAN NINH

YEMEN

ETHIOPIA

Goa
Bhatkal
Mangalore
Calicut
Cannartore

Masulipatam
Pulicat
Madras Sadras
Pondicherry
Negapatam Tranquebar

LAOS
SIAM
ANNAN

Manila ■
PHILIPPINE
ISLANDS

PACIFIC
OCEAN

Macao ■

ALL
OMO
ATES
HARAR
KUSHITES

Cochin
Quilon
Tuticorin

CEYLON
KINGDOM
OF KANDY

CAMBODIA
(to Annan)

BUGANDA
BUSOGA
Lake
ictoria
UNDI
JA

Mombasa
(To Oman)
Zanzibar
(To Oman)
Kilwa
(To Oman)

POLYGAR
KINGDOMS

ATJEH

MALAY
STATES
Malacca
MALAYS

BRUNEI SULU

KUTEI
BANDJAR
MASIN

Moluccas

PAPUANS
New
Guinea

Sumatra
MAMPAVA
MAEAY
STATES

Benkulen
Silebar

Batavia ■
East Indies

MATARAM

MALAY
STATES

PORTUGUESE
TIMOR

INDIAN
OCEAN

TUS
KAEONGA

LUNDU
MERINA
KINGDOM

MALAYS
Madagascar

□ *Mauritius*
Réunion

Australia
ABORIGINES

elagoa Bay

New
Zealand
MAORIS

N OCEAN

45°   60°   75°   90°   105°   120°   135°   150°   165°   180°

The beginnings of European empires were well established by 1700. The Spaniards were in North and South America, the French in Canada. The Portuguese were in Brazil and along the coasts of Africa. The British had 13 colonies in the east of North America and other possessions in the Caribbean.

The Ottoman Threat

BY THE 16TH CENTURY, THE OTTOMAN EMPIRE WAS AN EVER-PRESENT THREAT TO CHRISTIAN EUROPE. THE THREAT INTENSIFIED DURING THE REIGN OF THE MILITANT SULTAN SULEIMAN I, LEADING TO A FINAL SHOWDOWN AT SEA IN 1571.

The Ottoman Sultan Suleiman I, known in Europe as "The Magnificent" for the legendary splendor of his court, devoted most of his 46-year reign to making war on Christian Europe. In 1521, the year after he succeeded to the Ottoman throne, his army surrounded Nándorfehérvár (present-day Belgrade in Serbia), the greatest fortress in 16th-century Hungary and one of the most important strongholds in southeast Europe. From an island in the River Danube, Suleiman loosed a heavy bombardment on the city, which quickly surrendered. The fall of Belgrade created a wave of fear and panic throughout Europe. Little wonder, for the Ottoman success had dire consequences — the capture of Buda, the royal capital, the conquest of Transylvania, and Hungarian defeat at the battle of Mohacs in 1526, where the 20-year old King Louis II was killed.

As a result, the Ottoman Empire became the strongest power in Europe. Even so, Suleiman was forced to fight to maintain this status, as the Hapsburgs of Austria fought back, retrieving Buda and Hungary and twice holding Vienna against Ottoman onslaughts. But it was Sultan Suleiman who had the last laugh, for in 1541, the Habsburg armies failed in their attempt to lay siege to Buda, which Suleiman had won back in 1529, and afterward lost several of their fortresses to the Ottomans. The war ended in complete disaster for the Austrians. Archduke Ferdinand of Austria had to give up his claims to the crown of Hungary, although he continued to control some Hungarian lands. With his brother, the Holy Roman Emperor, Charles V, who was also King of Spain, Ferdinand was forced against his will to sign a humiliating treaty with Suleiman which imposed on him an annual payment for all of his territories in Hungary.

Next, Suleiman turned his attention to the Knights of St. John, who, in 1530, had been forced by the

After the crusader Knights of St. John settled on the Mediterranean island of Malta in 1522, they defended Rome, the focus of Christian Europe, from Ottoman invasion by attacking Ottoman ships. In 1565, the Ottomans laid siege to Malta, but they were driven away and never tried again.

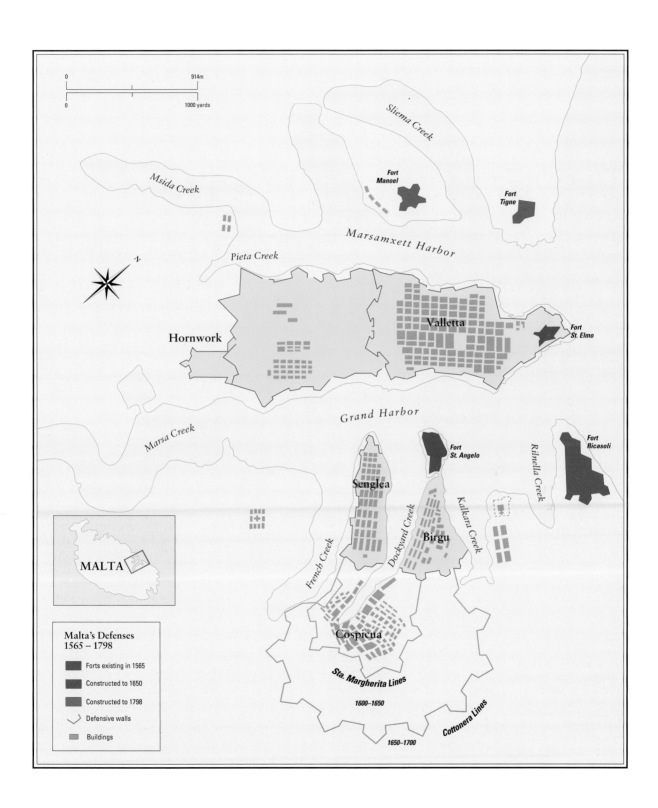

0   914m

0   1000 yards

Sliema Creek

Fort
Manoel

Fort
Tigne

Msida Creek

Marsamxett Harbor

N

Pieta Creek

Hornwork

Valletta

Fort
St. Elmo

Grand Harbor

Marsa Creek

Fort
St. Angelo

Fort
Ricasoli

Senglea

Dockyard Creek

Rinella Creek

Kalkara Creek

Birgu

French Creek

MALTA

Cospicua

Malta's Defenses
1565 – 1798

Forts existing in 1565

Constructed to 1650

Constructed to 1798

Defensive walls

Buildings

Sta. Margherita Lines

1600–1650

Cottonera Lines

1650–1700

Ottoman Sultan to evacuate Rhodes. The Knights had resettled on the Mediterranean island of Malta, where Suleiman attacked them again in 1565, though this time without success. From their massively fortified citadel on Malta, the Knights threw back the assaults of 60,000 Ottomans despite the pounding they received from Suleiman's heavy artillery. Suleiman was forced to withdraw, after losing some 24,000 men. Suleiman died the following year, leaving his son and successor, Selim II, an empire that, despite setbacks, was at the peak of its power.

Selim II continued his father's wars against Christian Europe in 1570 when he attacked the island of Cyprus, which was then ruled by the Republic of Venice. The Ottoman forces soon overcame Nicosia, after storming its fortified walls and, in the summer of 1571, captured Famagusta and executed its garrison. The situation now was so serious that the pope, Pius V, formed a Holy League and declared a "crusade" against the Muslim Ottomans. Fully realizing the danger in which they stood, the Christians of Europe soon raised a special fleet, though most of the ships were contributed by Venice, Spain and Spanish territories in Italy. In October 1571, the Christian fleet of 206 galleys and six galleasses — larger, faster galleys — headed for Lepanto, on the Gulf of Corinth, where the Ottoman fleet of something over 280 ships lay an anchor. The ships of the Christian fleet were manned by nearly 13,000 sailors, and carried close on 28,000 soldiers, including 10,000 superlative Spanish infantrymen. At this time, war at sea was still regarded as a floating version of war of land and it was not uncommon for the soldiers on board to vastly outnumber the sailors. Opposing them was an Ottoman fleet of 222 war galleys, 56 galliots (smaller galleys), and several smaller vessels manned by 13,000 sailors, with 34,000 soldiers also on board. The expected strategy was grappling and boarding, in which the crews attached their ships to the enemy's by means of grappling hooks, after which the soldiers would swarm onto the enemy decks across a temporary bridge and there fight it out with their opponents, hand-to-hand and to the death. However, the invention of gunpowder was soon to have a huge impact on this long-established method of warfare.

The battle of Lepanto, often called "the last crusade," began on October 7, when the Christian galleasses, powered by 32 oars, each requiring the muscle-power of five men, plastered the lighter Ottoman galleys with heavy fire from their gun decks. The galleasses were effectively early men-of-war and the Ottomans mistook them for merchant supply ships, the type of vessel from which they had first been developed. It was a critical error, for in this first encounter alone, the galleasses managed to sink some 70 Ottoman galleys and badly disorganize many others. Meanwhile, a fierce struggle was developing at the center of the battle where both fleets took a great deal of damage. The Christians were holding their own, but suddenly 16 Ottoman galleys swept up in a fast attack on the Christian center and destroyed six of their galleys. Two Spanish ships had to rush to the rescue before the situation was saved.

The fighting went on for five hours, until around four in the afternoon. By then, the Ottoman fleet had lost 210 ships captured or destroyed and the Christians, 30 galleys sunk, and another 30 so badly damaged that they had to be scuttled. The Ottomans lost 15,000 men and 3,500 prisoners, and the Holy League had 7,500 men killed. Lepanto was the first major loss at sea suffered by the Ottoman Turks in a century and although it did not entirely end their attacks, the Holy League's victory undoubtedly saved Europe for Christendom.

"The last crusade," as the naval Battle of Lepanto has been called, was a confrontation against the Ottoman Turks which the Holy League of Christian European powers had to win. Had they not done so, it was feared, with good reason, that Europe would have been open to Islamic conquest.

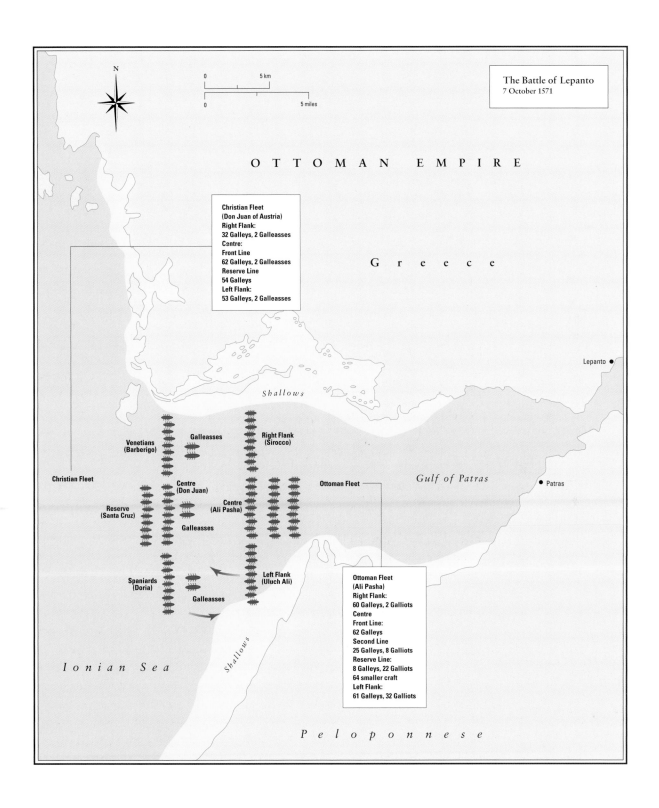

The Battle of Lepanto
7 October 1571

N

0   5 km

0   5 miles

OTTOMAN EMPIRE

Greece

Lepanto ●

Christian Fleet
(Don Juan of Austria)
Right Flank:
32 Galleys, 2 Galleasses
Centre:
Front Line
62 Galleys, 2 Galleasses
Reserve Line
54 Galleys
Left Flank:
53 Galleys, 2 Galleasses

Shallows

Venetians
(Barberigo)

Galleasses

Right Flank
(Sirocco)

Christian Fleet

Centre
(Don Juan)

Centre
(Ali Pasha)

Reserve
(Santa Cruz)

Galleasses

Ottoman Fleet

Gulf of Patras

● Patras

Spaniards
(Doria)

Left Flank
(Uluch Ali)

Galleasses

Ottoman Fleet
(Ali Pasha)
Right Flank:
60 Galleys, 2 Galliots
Centre
Front Line:
62 Galleys
Second Line
25 Galleys, 8 Galliots
Reserve Line:
8 Galleys, 22 Galliots
64 smaller craft
Left Flank:
61 Galleys, 32 Galliots

Ionian Sea

Shallows

Peloponnese

The Spanish Armada 1588

EVER SINCE DAVID FELLED GOLIATH, THE DIMINUTIVE ADVENTURER SUCCESSFULLY CHALLENGING A MIGHTY MAMMOTH HAS HAD UNFAILING APPEAL. IT WAS THIS APPEAL THAT TYPIFIED THE DRAMATIC AND DECISIVE HUMBLING OF THE SPANISH ARMADA BY A MUCH SMALLER ENGLISH FLEET IN 1588.

In the late 16th century, Spain was a superpower, with a gold- and silver-rich empire in America from which she sought to exclude all foreigners. "The enterprise of England," as the purpose of the Armada was termed, was to punish the heretic Protestant English who had dared to raid Spanish colonies in America and seize Spanish treasure ships en route to Europe. On a more practical level, a Spanish invasion of England would unseat Queen Elizabeth I, whose enemies, including King Philip II of Spain, regarded her as illegitimate both as woman and monarch. Since the Pope had not recognized the marriage of her parents, King Henry VIII and his second wife, Anne Boleyn, it followed that Elizabeth had no right to her throne.

For Elizabeth and England, the danger in which they stood was all too real and their material inferiority, all too obvious. The 130 galleons, galleases, merchantmen, carracks, and pinnaces with which King Philip of Spain sought to smash the English fleet was massive in size and armament, and splendid as a show of superiority and strength. In the face of this formidable array, the English initially had ready 64 ships, only 24 of them fighting vessels. In addition, King Philip had a handy springboard for the invasion of England only a few miles across the North Sea, in one of his European possessions, the Spanish Netherlands. It was there that an army under Philip's regent, the Duke of Parma, waited to board the ships of the Armada and sail for England.

On the face of it, the proximity of the Netherlands and the disparity between the Spanish and English fleets suggested an easy victory for Philip. The Spaniards planned to fight a sea battle in traditional fashion, as a floating version of war on land. Philip envisaged his soldiers pouring down musket-fire

The Spanish Armada was known as the "Invincible Armada." This was to prove a shallow boast; and the "enterprise of England" proved a failure.

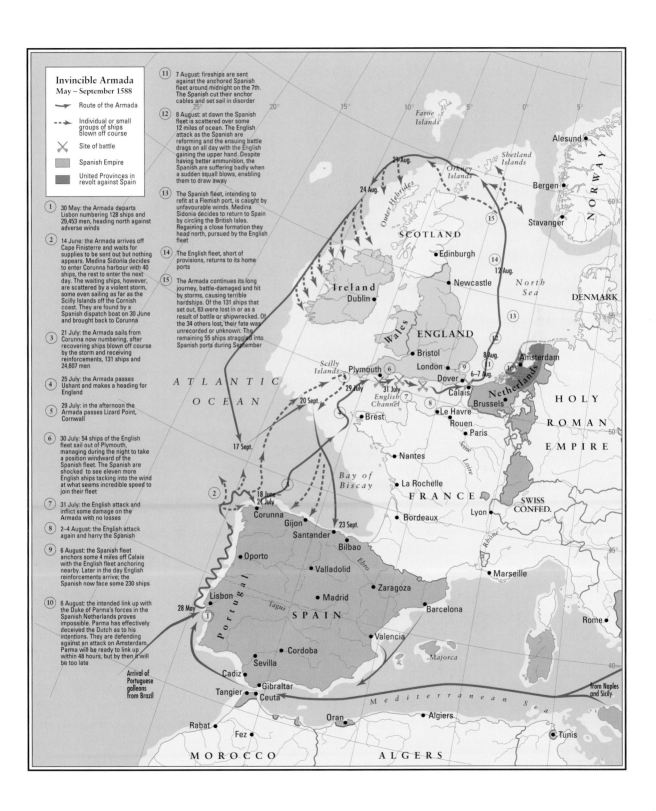

Invincible Armada
May – September 1588

→ Route of the Armada

⇢ Individual or small groups of ships blown off course

✕ Site of battle

▨ Spanish Empire

▨ United Provinces in revolt against Spain

1. 30 May: the Armada departs Lisbon numbering 128 ships and 29,453 men, heading north against adverse winds

2. 14 June: the Armada arrives off Cape Finisterre and waits for supplies to be sent out but nothing appears. Medina Sidonia decides to enter Corunna harbour with 40 ships, the rest to enter the next day. The waiting ships, however, are scattered by a violent storm, some even sailing as far as the Scilly Islands off the Cornish coast. They are found by a Spanish dispatch boat on 30 June and brought back to Corunna

3. 21 July: the Armada sails from Corunna now numbering, after recovering ships blown off course by the storm and receiving reinforcements, 131 ships and 24,607 men

4. 25 July: the Armada passes Ushant and makes a heading for England

5. 29 July: in the afternoon the Armada passes Lizard Point, Cornwall

6. 30 July: 54 ships of the English fleet sail out of Plymouth, managing during the night to take a position windward of the Spanish fleet. The Spanish are shocked to see eleven more English ships tacking into the wind at what seems incredible speed to join their fleet

7. 31 July: the English attack and inflict some damage on the Armada with no losses

8. 2–4 August: the English attack again and harry the Spanish

9. 6 August: the Spanish fleet anchors some 4 miles off Calais with the English fleet anchoring nearby. Later in the day English reinforcements arrive; the Spanish now face some 230 ships

10. 6 August: the intended link up with the Duke of Parma's forces in the Spanish Netherlands proves impossible. Parma has effectively deceived the Dutch as to his intentions. They are defending against an attack on Amsterdam. Parma will be ready to link up within 48 hours, but by then it will be too late

11. 7 August: fireships are sent against the anchored Spanish fleet around midnight on the 7th. The Spanish cut their anchor cables and set sail in disorder

12. 8 August: at dawn the Spanish fleet is scattered over some 12 miles of ocean. The English attack as the Spanish are reforming and the ensuing battle drags on all day with the English gaining the upper hand. Despite having better ammunition, the Spanish are suffering badly when a sudden squall blows, enabling them to draw away

13. The Spanish fleet, intending to refit at a Flemish port, is caught by unfavourable winds. Medina Sidonia decides to return to Spain by circling the British Isles. Regaining a close formation they head north, pursued by the English fleet

14. The English fleet, short of provisions, returns to its home ports

15. The Armada continues its long journey, battle-damaged and hit by storms, causing terrible hardships. Of the 131 ships that set out, 63 were lost in or as a result of battle or shipwrecked. Of the 34 others lost, their fate was unrecorded or unknown. The remaining 55 ships straggled into Spanish ports during September

from platforms high up on the sterns of his galleons, then using them to board the English vessels. However, the English had different ideas. They meant to fight with sleek, easily maneuverable galleons that relied on long-range gun-power to attack the Spaniards from a distance. The English fleet included up to 18 of these revolutionary new galleons as it awaited the Armada, which reached the western end of the English Channel on July 29, 1588.

Philip's orders to the Spanish commander, the Duke of Medina Sidonia, required him to proceed along the Channel in strong, defensive crescent-shaped formation, toward the coast of Flanders where the Duke of Parma's army would rendezvous with the Armada. As the Spanish fleet made its stately progress, the English ships pounced at intervals to snipe away out of range, pin-pricking the Spaniards as a picador does a bull. The bull was rattled, but refused to be provoked. Medina Sidonia was strict in obeying orders not to give battle and keep his formation tight and strong. But on the morning of July 31, the Armada found itself in a tricky position.

During the night, the English ships had sidled out of Plymouth on the coast of Devon on a contrary wind. They worked their way westward and took up a position to windward. From there, the English galleons came close, but not too close, then swung away, bombarding the Spaniards with cannon shot as they did so. Although their tactics unnerved the Spaniards, they were firing at a distance too far away to damage or even delay the Armada. The Spaniards sailed on toward Calais, on the northern coast of France, where the ships anchored off the roads on August 6. However, it was at Calais that the Duke of Medina Sidonia learned that the "enterprise of England" was already a failure. The Duke of Parma's invasion force was trapped in port by English ships on guard at the Downs, the Channel roadstead off Deal in Kent, and Dutch rebel "sea beggars" off Flushing in the Netherlands.

It was the end. There was no alternative but an ignominious return home to Spain. The English fleet was blocking escape westwards along the Channel, and to sail east meant suicide on the dangerous Zeeland Banks off the Netherlands coast. The only way home was northward, through the treacherous North Sea, around the British Isles, and out into the Atlantic. But the Spaniards soon discovered that they would not be allowed to leave the scene of their humiliation unscarred.

At midnight on August 8, the flickering of fire-ships glowed in the dark as eight flaming vessels drifted downwind toward the Armada. These sinister silhouettes moving toward them, outlined against the night sky in roaring fire, snapped the Spaniards' nerves. They slashed their cables and swarmed away in a struggling formless mass. None of the Spanish vessels was even scorched for all the fire-ships missed their targets, and yet the strong, tight formation that English sniping had been unable to break was irretrievably lost.

The English ships which charged the Spanish fleet off Gravelines on August 8 attacked a badly shaken enemy. They positioned themselves far enough away for Spanish grappling irons to fall short, but close enough to thunder murderous broadsides into the Spanish hulls. English round shot tore through the high thick walls of the Spanish ships, spraying the crew with a deadly storm of splinters, and littering the Channel with wreckage. Before long, the Armada was drifting toward shipwreck on the sandbars at Flushing. Then, at long last, timely mercy intervened. The English broke off the action as the wind shifted to the southwest, allowing the Spaniards to struggle off the lee shore and steer for deeper water.

Their way home was now inexorably set. Only 66 ships survived the arduous haul to Spanish home waters. Ships were pounded to a mess of debris on spiky coastal rocks, rushed to disintegration onshore, by mighty Atlantic rollers, or simply sank, as shot-torn timbers yielded to the sea and strained seams split apart. Thousands of Spaniards drowned, succumbed to typhus, dysentery, hunger, exhaustion, melancholy, or died at English and Irish hands as they staggered onto inhospitable shores. Of the 5,000 men who reached Spain in mid-October 1588, two thirds were dead within the month and half their ships never put to sea again.

English losses were few, and none of the English ships were sunk. However after the victory the English were hit with a glut of diseases: typhus, dysentery, and hunger, which killed many sailors and troops (estimated at 6,000–8,000) Controversially, the sick were discharged without pay, and the government's shortfalls left many of the English defenders unpaid for months. The Spanish government on the other hand, was fully supportive of its surviving men.

Although the English fleet was unable to prevent the regrouping of the Armada at the Battle of Gravelines, requiring it to remain on duty even as thousands of its sailors died, the outcome proved that the correct strategy had been adopted. The defeat of the Spanish Armada resulted in a revolution in naval warfare with the wide use of gunnery, which until then had played only a supporting role to ramming and boarding. The battle of Gravelines is regarded by experts in military history as reflecting a lasting shift in the naval balance in favor of the English. This was because it showed the gap in naval technology

and armament between the two nations which continued into the next century. Geoffrey Parker wrote in 1588: "the capital ships of the Elizabethan navy constituted the most powerful battlefleet afloat anywhere in the world." However after its defeat in the Armada campaign the Spanish Navy undertook a massive reform that enabled it to maintain control over its own home waters and ocean routes well into the next century.

The defeat of the Spanish Armada was to boost Elizabeth I's status as rightful claimant to the throne, and was a huge encouragement to the Protestant cause, and commemorative medals were struck to celebrate the Protestant victory.

To the Spanish, Queen Elizabeth I, who ruled England from. 1558 to 1603, was illegitimate and had an unlawful claim to the throne.

THE THIRTY YEARS' WAR: 1618-1648

THE THIRTY YEARS' WAR, ONE OF EUROPE'S MOST BRUTAL WARS, WAS A CONTEST FOR THE SUCCESSION TO THE HOLY ROMAN EMPIRE, A FIGHT BETWEEN PROTESTANTS AND CATHOLICS, AND A DYNASTIC STRUGGLE BETWEEN THREE ROYAL HOUSES.

T he chief battleground in the Thirty Years' War was Germany, but the fighting spilled over from time to time into Spain, France, Italy, and the Netherlands. Sweden, Poland and Denmark became involved and by the time the hostilities were over in 1648, much of the area that had been so bitterly contested was plundered and devastated and thousands of civilians were dead or displaced. Nothing as damaging as this had occurred in Europe since the Mongol invasions of the 13th century.

At the heart of this shattering conflict was the fragmentation of Germany into a collection of some 300 small states, most or all of them in conflict with their putative overlord, the Holy Roman Emperor. These disputes were exacerbated by the rise of Protestantism in the 16th century, which fractured the Christian Church and divided its adherents into warring Catholic and Protestant communities. Their mutual hatred intensified the fighting, which began in Protestant Bohemia in July 1918 and escalated from there, drawing in various rulers who felt themselves in danger from the ambitions of the others. For example, by 1623, it seemed that the Bohemians had been beaten and three years later, the Protestant King Christian IV of Denmark had been sent packing back to his realm by the Catholic armies of the Holy Roman Empire. In both instances, it appeared that the fighting was over. But in 1632, Armand Jean du Plessis, Cardinal-Duc de Richelieu, chief minister to King Louis XIII of France stepped in to reignite the war by encouraging King Gustavus II Adolphus of Sweden to invade northern Germany in order to aid his beleaguered fellow Protestants.

Psychologically, it was a cunning move on Richelieu's part, for the Swedish king was alarmed by signs

Although there was no single cause for the outbreak of the Thirty Years' War in 1618, the struggle between Catholics and Protestants who had broken away from the Church of Rome over the previous century was a significant factor. This conflict was particularly savage.

The Thirty Years' War
1618–29

Imperial campaigns, with dates
→ Tilly
→ Wallenstein
→ Spinola
→ Other Spanish armies

Protestant campaigns, with dates
→ Christian IV of Denmark
→ Mansfield
→ Bethlen Gabor
✕ Battle site
■ Towns captured by Habsburgs, with dates
— Border of Holy Roman Empire
■ Spanish Habsburg territories
■ Austrian Habsburg territories

that the Holy Roman Emperor, the champion of Catholicism, was interested in expanding his power into Sweden's home waters, the Baltic Sea and its adjacent coasts. That was far too close to his kingdom for Gustavus and he allowed himself to be drawn into the hostilities. Gustavus paid for Richelieu's interference with his life, dying in battle at Lützen in Saxony in 1632. The Protestant cause in the Thirty Years' War had lost a brilliant commander, and Sweden a warrior-king.

Richelieu had been using Gustavus as a tool to defuse the ambitions of the Hapsburg dynasty. The Hapsburg network throughout Europe was very extensive. The dynasty had supplied all Holy Roman Emperors since 1452, as well as the rulers of Austria and Spain and had marriage links with Burgundy, Bohemia, and Hungary. After Gustavus' death, Cardinal Richelieu came out into the open and on May 21, 1635 he entered France, declared war on Spain, and allied himself with the Swedes. Richelieu's plan was to capture most of Spanish-controlled Franche-Comté, occupy Lorraine and seize the Valtelline Pass through the Alps, which served as a means of supplying the Spanish garrison in Milan. Spain's response, in 1636, was to invade France. Spanish forces, together with their Bavarian allies, reached as far north as the River Somme and advanced into Compiègne, a mere 43 miles (69 km) from Paris. Just in time, the French raised a large militia of 50,000 men, rushed them into Compiègne, and forced the invaders to withdraw to the Spanish Netherlands. The Spaniards tried again, in 1637 and in 1643, but came to grief at the Battle of Rocroi on May 19, 1643 when their army was virtually annihilated. Meanwhile, the Swedish army invaded Germany, and in 1643 went on to ravage Moravia and Bohemia. An army led by the French Henri de la Tour d'Auvergne, Vicomte de Turenne, and the Swedish Count Carl Gustav Wrangel invaded Bavaria in May 1648 and chased the Bavarian Marshal Peter Melander and his 30,000 men as far as the River Danube. They ravaged the countryside through which they passed, burning and destroying everything in their path.

By the late summer of 1648, the French and Swedes were advancing on Munich, the Bavarian capital, ready to invest the city, when they were halted by Cardinal Jules Mazarin, who had succeeded Richelieu after Richelieu's death in 1642. Mazarin ordered a withdrawal to Swabia in southwest Germany. This unexpected, but timely, intervention was prompted by peace negotiations that would bring the Thirty Years' War to an end. But not before there was one final battle, at Lens near Lille in northern France, on 10 August, 1648. At Lens the French cavalry were led by Louis II de Bourbon. Prince de Condé crushed 18,000 Spanish and Austrian soldiers, despite the fact that they had 38 guns at their disposal. This decisive thrashing brought a halt to Hapsburg attempts to invade France and also ended Spanish military supremacy in Europe.

Although the war between France and Spain continued until 1659, other combatants signed the Peace of Westphalia on October 24, 1648. Among its provisions, the Swedes were given an indemnity and received territories around the Baltic. France, too, received its rewards, in the shape of Alsace and most of Lorraine. A general amnesty was declared and the sovereign rights of German princes and their states were recognized by the Holy Roman Emperor. Within the Empire, Catholics and Protestants were given equality. However, the extensive damage done by the Thirty Years' War was not so easy to repair. The male population of the German states was halved. The Swedes alone destroyed 2,000 castles in Germany, 18,000 villages, and 1,500 towns. It took an estimated 200 years before the ravaged territories and their populations were restored.

Twelve years and more after the Thirty Years' War began, the conflict was starting to change its nature. Now, it was less of a religious war, more of an extension of the long and bitter rivalry between the royal houses of Bourbon and Hapsburg for political supremacy in Europe.

The Thirty Years' War
1640–48

Swedish campaigns, with dates

→ Baner

→ Tortensson

→ Wrangel

→ Other Swedish campaigns

Other campaigns, with dates

→ Austrian

→ French

→ Dutch

→ George Rákóci, Prince of Transylvania

✕ Swedish victory

✕ Swedish defeat

■ Towns captured by Swedes with date

■ Towns captured by French with date

■ Towns captured by Dutch with date

✪ Siege

— Border of Holy Roman Empire

Spanish Habsburg territories

Austrian Habsburg territories

Gustavus Adolphus: The Great Captain

GUSTAVUS II ADOLPHUS, WHO BECAME KING OF SWEDEN IN 1617 AT THE AGE OF 22, WAS A BRILLIANT TACTICIAN AND INNOVATOR WHOSE ADVANCES IN MILITARY SCIENCE MADE SWEDEN THE DOMINANT POWER IN THE BALTIC UNTIL WELL INTO THE 18TH CENTURY.

The integration of infantry, cavalry, and artillery with logistics which Gustavus pioneered during the Thirty Years' War became an object lesson for future military commanders, including Napoleon Bonaparte and Carl von Clausewitz, the Prussian military theorist and historian. In his turn, the Swedish king was influenced by the ideas of Prince Maurice of Nassau, the premier Dutch military strategist, who believed that mobility and firepower on the battlefield was more like to be successful than the shock action on which many 17th century armies relied.

Gustavus made Swedish weaponry lighter to facilitate mobility. Gustavus also boosted the status of the artillery, giving it equal importance with his cavalry and infantry. The King employed horses to give the guns speedier traction than could be managed by men alone and introduced lightweight 4-pounder guns that could fire cartridge rounds of grapeshot. Infantry units now had their own artillery to furnish them with added firepower in battle. A radical change was made when gunners who had been civilians working on contracts were replaced by soldiers who were more available and more susceptible to the discipline and training he imposed on them. The Swedish army also underwent an overhaul when it came to re-ordering its basic elements. Under Gustavus, 72 musketeers and 54 pikemen made up an infantry company and four companies constituted a battalion. There were eight battalions in a regiment and up to four regiments in a brigade. This pattern was soon being emulated by other European armies. The reformed Swedish cavalry did not entirely eliminate the shock action ingredient in warfare. Gustavus dispensed with the caracole system which had been introduced by German Reiter heavy cavalry in the 16th century religious wars in France. In the caracole, cavalry was arranged in deep ranks. After riding

Between 1611 and 1718, Sweden was transformed into an important European power. During this time, it was known as the Swedish Empire *orstormaktstiden* (era of great power). Much of this reputation was due to Sweden's involvement in the Thirty Years' War and its seizure of Russian and Polish-Lithuanian territories.

The Swedish Empire
1600–99

- Swedish territory c. 1600
- By 1617
- By 1629
- By 1645
- By 1648
- By 1658
- Border of Holy Roman Empire
- ✕ Battle site

ARCTIC OCEAN

Kola

Kola Peninsula

White Sea

Kabelvåg

Norwegian Sea

Arctic Circle

0   200 km
0   200 miles

Alstahaug

Lapland

Tornea

Lulea

Uleaborg

SWEDISH EMPIRE

RUSSIAN EMPIRE

Trondheim

Jämtland

Umea

Gulf of Bothnia

Finland

Karelia

Härjedalen

Björneborg

Viborg

Lake Ladoga

Dalarna

Åland

Helsingfors

Gulf of Finland

Ingria

Bergen

Uppland

Reval

Narva

Estonia

Novgorod

Oslo

Uppsala

Stockholm

Oesel

Livonia

Pskov

Norrköping

Kirchholm
17 Sept. 1605

Bohuslånd

Väster-götland

Östergötland

Gotland

Windau

Riga

Velikiye Luki

Göteborg

Jönköping

Småland

Kurland

Libau

Dünaburg

Dvina

Vitebsk

Varberg

Kalmar

Oland

Wallhof
17 January 1626

Halland

Blekinge

Karlskrona

Samogitia

Memel

Baltic Sea

DENMARK

Scania

Vilna

LITHUANIA

North Sea

Fredericia

Copenhagen

Malmo

Bornholm

Minsk

Funen

Zeeland

Königsberg

Danzig

PRUSSIA

Kiel

Rügen

Stralsund

Wolgast

Usedom

Rostock

Wismar

Stettin

KINGDOM OF POLAND

Elbe

Weser

Fehrbellin
28 June 1675

Oder

Berlin

Poznan

Vistula

Warsaw

18–20 July 1656

Bug

Pripyet

Vistula

GERMAN STATES

up to their opponents and coming within range, the first rank fired their pistols. They then retired to the back of the ranks while the second rank took its turn to fire. The idea was that by the time all ranks had fired, the enemy would be so confused that the Reiter could make short work of them with their swords. This left firearms — muskets or pistols — as additional weapons once the enemy was disorganized and the fight had turned into a melée. Gustavus preferred a simpler method in which only three or four ranks of cavalry were deployed and applied shock action with their swords, leaving firearms — muskets or pistols — to serve as supporting weaponry.

The Swedish musketeers were especially admired for their accuracy and their ability to reload three times faster than their contemporaries in other armies. These valuable qualities were the fruit of the first-class training the Swedish army received and the self-confidence instilled by the versatility with various arms which King Gustavus encouraged. Among the Swedes, it was normal for Gustavus' cavalry and infantry to perform maintenance on artillery pieces. Infantry and gunners were trained to ride and handle horses. Similarly, pikemen, whose regular function was to protect musketeers from the cavalry in battle, were themselves trained to use muskets. They might not have been as expert or accurate as professional musketeers, but at least they could keep the guns firing in the heat of battle.

A valuable addition to Swedish firepower on the battlefield was the light field artillery that Gustavus introduced, using smaller, more maneuverable weapons. This element in the Swedish army, the first of its type in military history, solved the problem of cumbersome cannon that were difficult to maneuver. Gustavus' light artillery was arranged in batteries and supported the linear formations adopted by the Swedish forces. The Swedish infantry fought in five or six ranks, rather than the deep traditional squares that could be up to 50 ranks deep. These more flexible formations enabled the Swedes to deploy and reconfigure with great rapidity, a trick that could be very confusing to their opponents.

Swedish morale was of a very high order, mainly because Gustavus eliminated the snobbery present in other armies, where the cavalry was treated as an elite, and looked down on the artillery, which occupied the second social level. In the Swedish army, no one element was favored above another,

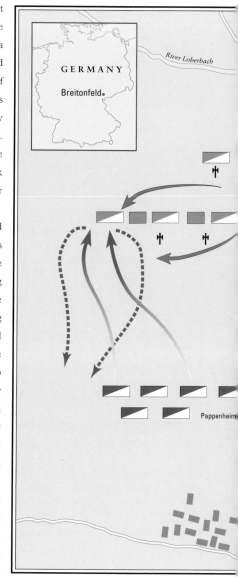

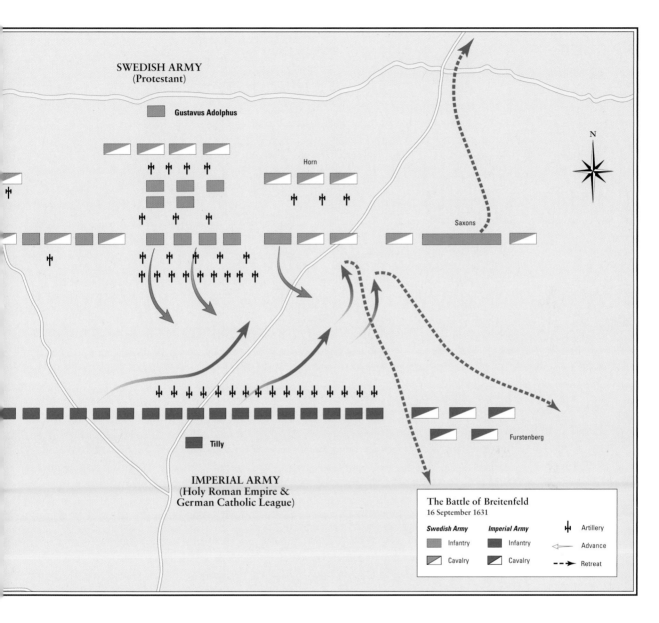

SWEDISH ARMY
(Protestant)

Gustavus Adolphus

Horn

Saxons

N

Tilly

IMPERIAL ARMY
(Holy Roman Empire &
German Catholic League)

Furstenberg

The Battle of Breitenfeld
16 September 1631

Swedish Army	*Imperial Army*	⊹ Artillery
Infantry	Infantry	⟵ Advance
Cavalry	Cavalry	- - ➤ Retreat

which gave all of them a certain pride in their attainments and encouraged mutual amity. Gustavus Adolphus acquired a dazzling reputation in his lifetime and his death at the Battle of Lützen in 1632 was deeply and sincerely mourned. He was considered by Napoleon and Clausewitz to be one of the greatest generals known to military history.

In February 1633, three months after Gustavus' death, the Swedish *Riksdag* (Parliament) voted to make his official name Gustav Adolf den Store, or Gustav Adolf the Great, an appellation never given to any other king of Sweden.

At the Battle of Breitenfeld, near Leipzig, Swedish forces commanded by King Gustavus Adolphus frustrated efforts to break their left flank by the army of the Holy Roman Empire led by John Tserclaes, Count of Tilly. The Swedes broke up Tilly's forces with rapid, accurate gunfire, causing 13,000 casualties.

THE ENGLISH CIVIL WAR: 1642-1649

THE ENGLISH CIVIL WAR WAS FOUGHT TO SETTLE THE QUESTION OF WHETHER IT WAS THE KING OR PARLIAMENT WHO SHOULD GOVERN ENGLAND. FUNDAMENTAL QUESTIONS ABOUT THE POWER OF PARLIAMENT AND THE DIVINE RIGHT OF KINGS WERE DISPUTED ON THE BLOODY BATTLEFIELD.

In 1603, when James I, the first Stuart king of England, arrived in London from his kingdom of Scotland to claim his second crown, he came with the idea that monarchs ruled by Divine Right and that it was not the business of Parliament or any other body of commoners to interfere with his God-given status. James' son and successor in 1625, Charles I, entertained the same belief. However, the Parliament Charles was facing had a clear concept of its own right to claim a share in law-making and a role as advisers to the king. When King and Parliament collided, the inevitable result was civil war.

Hostilities began officially after the King raised the royal battle standard at Nottingham in eastern England on August 22, 1642. For some time, though, the fighting in the civil war was indeterminate and remained so for nearly two years, until both sides sought reinforcements from outside. King Charles made peace with Catholic rebels in Ireland, so releasing for his own cause the army that had been trying to contain them. Parliament recruited the Scots by promising to create a Scots Presbyterian Church in England. Followers of the King became known as Cavaliers, while Parliament's supporters were labeled Roundheads. As things turned out, Parliament made the better deal in recruiting the Scots. This became clear when the Roundhead army met King Charles' Cavaliers at Marston Moor on July 2, 1644 and for the first time since the civil war began, achieved a definite result. The two great individual contestants, both superlative cavalry commanders, were Prince Rupert of the Rhine, Charles' nephew, for the King and Oliver Cromwell for Parliament. At Marston Moor, Cromwell led his Ironsides, as his highly disciplined cavalry was called, in a partly successful assault on the Cavalier cavalry. He did better when he turned the Ironsides to their right, routed the remainder of the royal cavalry, and then weighed in to attack the Cavaliers' center together with the Parliamentary infantry. At Marston Moor, the Cavaliers suffered almost 3,000 killed; the Roundheads nearly 2,000. King Charles' cause was badly damaged, for his strongholds in the north, like York and Newcastle, capitulated to Parliament and Prince Rupert was obliged to escape with some 6,000 Royalist survivors to join the King in the south. Yet despite their success, Cromwell was convinced that that a better trained, more disciplined professional army was required if Parliament was going to get the better of the King. The New Model Army of Great Britain established in 1645 was raised mainly from veterans with strong Puritan religious views who held to the same radical politics that dominated the Puritan Parliament. The Model Army had a complement of 22,000 soldiers; including 11 cavalry regiments of 600 men each and a regiment of 1,000 dragoons. The New Model infantry was paid eight pence a day, the cavalry two shillings, three times as much. The Army's elite forces were its regiments of horse who were armed and

equipped as harquebusiers, the cavalrymen who used the harquebus, a form of carbine that was used in the 17th century for shock action on the battlefield. Like their equivalents in the Swedish army of King Gustavus II Adolphus, who were used by Cromwell as an archetype, New Model troops charged the enemy, sword in hand, and carried two loaded pistols. New Model discipline was distinctly superior to that in the royal army whose cavalry, it seems, never knew when to stop pursuing a fleeing enemy and had a habit of looting the enemy's baggage train. Cromwell, in fact, forbade his harquebusiers to pursue the enemy so that they could regroup after a charge and renew their attacks on the battlefield.

During the English Civil War, Oliver Cromwell and his army of roundheads gained a reputation for their brutal behavior both on and off the battlefield. After defeating the King's forces, Cromwell became Lord Protector of England, Scotland, and Ireland.

Although the Parliamentary cavalry disobeyed that particular order, the New Model Army thoroughly proved itself on 14 June, 1645, when it encountered the Cavalier army at Naseby in Northamptonshire. After Cromwell's army sent the Royalist left fleeing from the battlefield and charged off after them in pursuit, Prince Rupert behaved in his usual flamboyant fashion and joined the chase. Back on the battlefield, the Model Army exploited Rupert's absence to smash the Royalist infantry, which surrendered at once. King Charles, realizing that his cause was lost, fled to Leicester, but three weeks later, he surrendered to the Scots. The King remained a prisoner for some time, as Parliament and the Army disputed what should be done with him. Eventually, on January 20, 1649, King Charles was put on trial at Westminster Hall, London, as "Charles Stewart" who "out of wicked design to erect an unlimited and tyrannical power... traitorously and maliciously levied war against the present Parliament and the people therein represented." Although he refused to plead, maintaining that he did not recognize the right of the court to try him, the King was sentenced to death and on January 30, he was beheaded in front of a large crowd of spectators. Afterwards, Parliament abolished the monarchy and declared England a republic. The war left England, Ireland, and Scotland as one of the few countries in Europe without a monarch.

EUROPEAN IMPERIAL EXPANSION TO 1700

THE EXPLORATION OF THE WORLD BY EUROPEANS WAS ARGUABLY THE GREATEST ADVENTURE OF ALL TIME. ALTHOUGH ITS ULTIMATE OUTCOME — THE FOUNDING AND EXPLOITATION OF EMPIRES — IS NO LONGER SEEN AS GLORIOUS, THE DISCOVERY OF FARAWAY LANDS REQUIRED COURAGE, ENTERPRISE, AND IMAGINATION.

The nation that inaugurated the European exploration of the world was probably the least likely candidate for such a mammoth exercise: Portugal. The Portuguese had never been major players in European affairs, and for much of their history were subject to their mighty neighbor, Spain. What the Portuguese did have, though, was the gift of their geography, sited as they were at the southwestern extremity of Europe, facing the vastness of the Atlantic Ocean. Their other great asset was Prince Henry, third son of King Juan I of Portugal, whose lifelong ambition was to find a sea route to the wealth in silks, satins, precious metals, jewels and other luxuries to be found in Cathay (China), Cipangu (Japan) and the rest of Asia.

Mouthwatering tales of these fabulous riches were contained in a book about his travels to the court of Kublai Khan, Emperor of Cathay, written by the Venetian merchant Marco Polo in around 1320. But there were other tales, terrifying tales of what awaited anyone who dared to venture beyond the safety of European waters. When Prince Henry began his explorations, in 1418, most people believed that the Earth was a flat disk and sailors feared the edge lay along the African coast. If they sailed too close, they believed, they would fall into the Green Sea of Darkness, where demons and sea monsters lurked, waiting to swallow them up. Either that, or they would be burned to ashes in the liquid flame of the Sun's rays. Prince Henry, however, was undaunted and in 1418 and 1419 sent ships out into the Atlantic Ocean to Porto Santo and Madeira. These islands later became the first overseas territories of the Portuguese

For many years, Africa was known as "the Dark Continent" because it was largely unknown and unexplored. In 1830, when the French acquired Algeria, several European countries had possessions in Africa, but they were small and did not open up the vast interior of the continent.

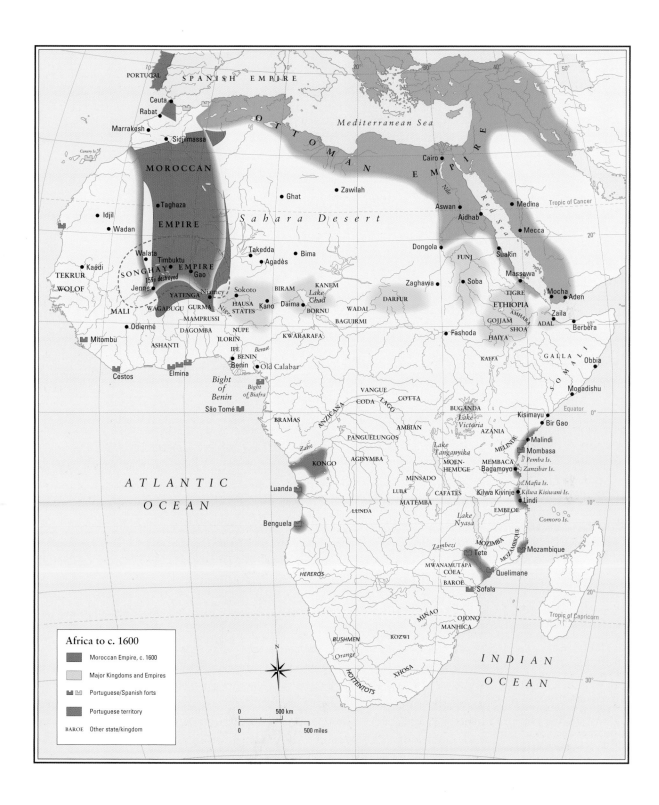

PORTUGAL
SPANISH EMPIRE
Ceuta
Rabat
Marrakesh
Sidjilmassa
Canary Is.
MOROCCAN
EMPIRE
Taghaza
Idjil
Wadan
Sahara Desert
Ghat
Zawilah
Mediterranean Sea
OTTOMAN EMPIRE
Cairo
Aswan
Aïdhab
Nile
Red Sea
Tropic of Cancer
Medina
Mecca
Walata
Timbuktu
SONGHAY EMPIRE
1591 destroyed
Gao
Jenne
Kaédi
TEKRUR
WOLOF
MALI
Takedda
Agadès
Bima
Dongola
FUNJ
Suakin
Massawa
Soba
Zaghawa
TIGRE
Mocha
Aden
YATENGA
Niamey
Sokoto
BIRAM
KANEM
Lake Chad
WADAI
DARFUR
ETHIOPIA
AMHARA
Zaila
ADAL
Berbera
WAGADUGU GURMA
MAMPRUSSI
Odienné
DAGOMBA
NUPE
ILORIN
KWARARAFA
HAUSA STATES
Kano
Daima
BORNU
BAGUIRMI
Fashoda
GOJJAM
SHOA
HAIYA
KAFFA
GALLA
SOMALI
Obbia
Mitombu
ASHANTI
IFE
BENIN
Benin
Old Calabar
Cestos
Elmina
Bight of Benin
Bight of Biafra
São Tomé
BRAMAS
ANZICANA
CODA
COTTA
VANGUE
LAGO
Mogadishu
Equator
BUGANDA
Lake Victoria
Kisimayu
Bir Gao
AZANIA
Malindi
MELINDE
Mombasa
Pemba Is.
AMBIAN
PANGUELUNGOS
AGISYMBA
Lake Tanganyika
MOEN-HEMUGE
MEMBACA
Bagamoyo
Zanzibar Is.
Zaire
KONGO
MINSADO
LUBA
CAFATES
Mafia Is.
Kilwa Kivinje
Kilwa Kisiwani Is.
Lindi
ATLANTIC
OCEAN
Luanda
MATEMBA
LUNDA
EMBEOE
Lake Nyasa
Comoro Is.
Benguela
HEREROS
MOZIMBA
Tete
Mozambique
Zambezi
Quelimane
MWANAMUTAPA
COEA
BAROE
Sofala
MINAO
OJONO
MANHICA
Tropic of Capricorn
BUSHMEN
ROZWI
Orange
HOTTENTOTS
XHOSA
INDIAN
OCEAN

Africa to c. 1600

Moroccan Empire, c. 1600

Major Kingdoms and Empires

Portuguese/Spanish forts

Portuguese territory

BAROE Other state/kingdom

N

0   500 km
0   500 miles

Empire. In subsequent years, Henry sent expedition after expedition down the coast of Africa, each of them designed to push a little farther south.

Although several expeditions returned to Portugal with some excuse or other for failing to reach their destinations, eventually, in 1460, Portuguese navigators crossed the Equator. Nearly 30 years later, in 1488, one of them, Bartholomeu Diaz, rounded the Cape of Good Hope at the southern extremity of Africa and entered the Indian Ocean. Nine years after that, on July 8, 1497, another Portuguese navigator, Vasco da Gama, sailed from Lisbon on the voyage that would complete 77 years of exploration. On November 4, Da Gama reached St. Helena Bay, north of the Cape of Good Hope. He left to sail round the Cape 12 days later. The Portuguese ships had to fight strong headwinds. It was November 22 before they were able to sail on up the east African coast, but they found the Muslim inhabitants very unfriendly. At MalindI, now in Kenya, da Gama had to force the sultan to give him pilots to guide him across the Indian Ocean. The Portuguese sailed from Malindi on April 24, 1498 and on May 20, over ten months after departing Lisbon, Vasco da Gama went ashore at Khozhikode (Calicut) on the west coast of India.

Vasco da Gama's arrival in India ended one of three great voyages of exploration that took place in the 15th and 16th centuries. Six years earlier, in 1492, Christopher Columbus had sailed west, across the Atlantic on the same quest, to find a way to the riches of Asia, and landed on the previously unknown continent of America. The third great voyage, in 1519-1522, was the most all-encompassing: the first circumnavigation of the world by a small fleet of ships led by Ferdinand Magellan, a Portuguese sailing in the service of Spain. Magellan's fleet crossed the Atlantic, then sailed south down the east coast of South America, and turned westward into one of the most turbulent and dangerous waterways on Earth. Now named the Magellan Strait, it led from the Atlantic Ocean into the Pacific. The journey took almost four weeks and a nightmare trans-Pacific voyage lay ahead. Magellan failed to survive it. He was killed on Mactan Island in the Philippines in 1521 while trying to convert the natives to Christianity. Instead, one of his soldiers, Sebastian del Cano, brought Magellan's ship, the Victoria, home to Spain in 1522.

All three voyages were made in very dangerous circumstances. The ships used by Columbus, Vasco da Gama, and Magellan had been built for coast-hugging journeys around Europe and the Mediterranean where landmarks were always in sight, rather than for crossing the open sea out of sight of land where they were subject to mighty ocean rollers and ferocious ocean storms. Navigators were not even able to reckon longitude with absolute certainty. Although the chronometer, a marine clock invented by the English horologist John Harrison, solved the problem, it was not used on-board ship until near the end of the age of exploration. It was 1772 before the English navigator, Captain James Cook took a chronometer on the second of his three voyages which ultimately opened up Australasia and the Pacific.

By that time, the beginnings of empires based on the explorations had long ago been established. The overriding motivation was trade and, in the New World, exploitation of natural advantages such as the unusually fertile soil and extensive forests of North America or the prolific stock of cod and other fish that teemed in the Grand Banks off Newfoundland in Canada. But there were several other incentives. The Spaniards who colonized South and Central America were certainly after gold and other riches, but that was not all they sought. Most of them came from a particularly harsh area of western Spain called Extramadura, meaning "extreme and hard." Extramadura was the sort of place a poor, but ambitious

In the 17th century, North America saw several wars between European colonists and native Americans, and between the Europeans themselves, notably the Spanish and British. The native Americans, armed with bows, arrows, and tomahawks but little else eventually proved to be no match for European guns and other sophisticated weaponry.

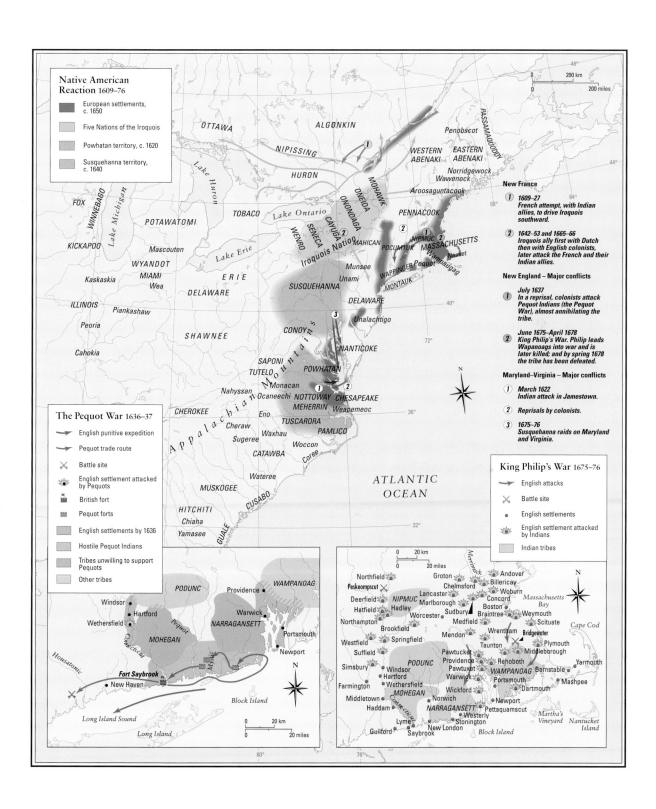

Native American Reaction 1609–76

- European settlements, c. 1650
- Five Nations of the Iroquois
- Powhatan territory, c. 1620
- Susquehanna territory, c. 1640

New France

(1) **1609–27**
French attempt, with Indian allies, to drive Iroquois southward.

(2) **1642–53 and 1665–66**
Iroquois ally first with Dutch then with English colonists, later attack the French and their Indian allies.

New England – Major conflicts

(1) **July 1637**
In a reprisal, colonists attack Pequot Indians (the Pequot War), almost annihilating the tribe.

(2) **June 1675–April 1678**
King Philip's War. Philip leads Wapanoags into war and is later killed; and by spring 1678 the tribe has been defeated.

Maryland–Virginia – Major conflicts

(1) **March 1622**
Indian attack in Jamestown.

(2) **Reprisals by colonists.**

(3) **1675–76**
Susquehanna raids on Maryland and Virginia.

The Pequot War 1636–37

- English punitive expedition
- Pequot trade route
- Battle site
- English settlement attacked by Pequots
- British fort
- Pequot forts
- English settlements by 1636
- Hostile Pequot Indians
- Tribes unwilling to support Pequots
- Other tribes

King Philip's War 1675–76

- English attacks
- Battle site
- English settlements
- English settlement attacked by Indians
- Indian tribes

young man left at the first opportunity, for Spain offered him no realistic hope of advancement.

The New World, by contrast, afforded magnificent chances to acquire land and estates as well as riches and, for the most successful, high-ranking office or noble titles. A further Spanish ambition in America was the chance to convert the heathen to Christianity; which became the quest for hundreds of priests and zealots. Conversely, North America became a haven for religious minorities, mainly Protestants but also some Catholics who sought to leave behind the tribulations of Europe for the fresh air of tolerance they believed they would find in the New World.

Portugal was the first nation to forge a global network of trade. As a small, relatively poor country without the resources, military might, or population of Spain or France, Portugal could not afford to maintain a large spread of colonies overseas but more than made up for it by establishing a series of forts and trading posts — in Africa, on the coasts of Angola and Mozambique or along the coasts and islands of east Asia. Ultimately, they created a link that stretched from Lisbon, through India, Indochina and China to Nagasaki in Japan.

The one really extensive Portuguese colony, Brazil, had a unique commercial attraction — its brazilwood, the source of a bright crimson and purple dye used in the making of cabinets and other luxury furniture. Brazil came Portugal's way by accident in 1500, when the Portuguese navigator Pedro Alvarez Cabral, bound for India, was caught in a storm and drifted into the South America current of the Atlantic. He finally landed on the Brazilian coast. Exploration of the coast told Cabral something Columbus had failed to discern: he believed that the lands he found in 1492 were outlying islands of Asia, but Cabral saw that Brazil lay on a "new" continent that blocked the way to the East.

Brazil, it later transpired, covered 48 percent of South America's land area, with the rest, together with Central America, controlled by Spain. In the 16th century, the two Iberian countries grew rich from the fruits of their American empires, a spectacle regarded with envy by England, France, and the Netherlands. Each of them had a particular bone to chew with Spain. The French, of course, were longstanding rivals and in the mid-16th century, the Protestant Dutch were in revolt against their Spanish rulers. At around the same time, Protestant England was in real danger from the Spaniards who were resolved to unseat the "illegitimate" Tudor Queen Elizabeth I and replace her with a Catholic monarch, an intent which led eventually to the launch of the Spanish Armada.

England had begun to investigate America five years after Columbus' arrival. King Henry VII, the first Tudor monarch, who had once declined to sponsor Columbus, commissioned an Italian navigator, Giovanni Caboto (John Cabot) to search for the westward sea route to Asia which Columbus had not yet discovered. Cabot sailed in 1497 and crossed the Atlantic by a northerly route that avoided the latitudes where Spanish colonists were now active. Cabot reached Newfoundland after a five-week voyage and, like Columbus, presumed that he had reached Asia. In fact, he had probably landed on Cape Breton Island.

Cabot made no attempt to found a settlement on Newfoundland but there were several failed efforts at planting English colonies in North America during the 16th century. Meanwhile, English "sea dogs", including Sir Francis Drake and Sir John Hawkins, took to what the Spaniards labeled "piracy" when they raided Spanish settlements in the New World and captured several Spanish treasure ships as they headed for Europe loaded with gold, silver, jewels, and other luxuries. The enraged Spaniards suspected

Queen Elizabeth of sponsoring their activities, something she never openly admitted.

After Elizabeth's death in 1603, her successor, the Stuart King James I made peace with Spain, so opening the way to the founding of the first permanent English colony on the American mainland, at Jamestown, Virginia. More settlements followed on the Caribbean islands of St. Kitts, Barbados, and Nevis where sugar plantations were established and fortunes were soon made. America was not just a commercial destination though. In 1620, Puritans — the Pilgrim Fathers — began a trend later emulated by many others: they emigrated to Massachusetts to escape religious persecution. Other fugitives from religious harassment later founded Maryland, Rhode Island, Connecticut, and Pennsylvania. Elsewhere, in Canada and west Africa, government charters were granted to companies — the English Hudson's Bay Company and Royal African company, or the Dutch, English, and French East India and West India Companies. Ostensibly, their purpose was to promote trade, or, in the case of west Africa, supply black slaves for the Caribbean plantations. But they also created rivalry and in some areas, open warfare. The result was the same in India where the English, Dutch, and French muscled in on Portuguese interests by setting up trading posts and forts. These rivalries spread, too, to other areas of Asia where European interests collided.

The Dutch, for example, were never major empire-builders — their largest possession was the Dutch East Indies (Indonesia) — but they were capable of doing significant damage to the interests of their rivals. For example, the Dutch drove the Portuguese from their bases in Malacca, Colombo, and Cochin among several other places in Asia and by the mid-17th century had outstripped them in the immensely lucrative spice and silk trades. In the Atlantic, the Dutch West India Company seized the sugar and slave trade from the Portuguese and mounted attacks on Spanish treasure ships. Conversely, the Dutch received some of their own medicine in the New World when the English seized their settlement at New Amsterdam (New York) in 1664, during the second Anglo-Dutch War. They retrieved it in 1673, but were forced to relinquish it again in 1674. This ended the Dutch colonial presence in North America, although they retained some settlements in the Caribbean and in Suriname (also known as Dutch Guiana).

A much more serious and deep-seated rivalry existed between the British and the French. They had been enemies in Europe for centuries, ever since the Normans invaded England from France in 1066. Now, 13 European wars later, they exported their mutual hatred overseas where by the end of the 17th century, the French ruled New France (Canada), Louisiana, and Martinique, and St. Domingue (Haiti) in the Caribbean. In 1674, in India, the French acquired trading rights in Pondicherry and Chandernagore. In 1690, the British gained similar rights in Calcutta, in Bengal. Half a century later, India and New France would become the stage on which Britain and France would confront each other in a final conflict for colonial supremacy, the Seven Years' War.

At the same time, several wars broke out between Europeans and Native Americans, often leading European nations to form alliances to deal with the native threat. The natives however were no match for the Europeans with their superior weaponry, and became unwilling pawns in the Europeans' struggle for lands and power, yet not without fighting back. The Iriquois Imperium, a powerful alliance of six tribes in North East America, waged a terrible war against the French, while Powhaten, angered by continual land seizures by British settlers, led his chiefdom of nearly 30 tribes in a bitter war against the colonists.

Imperial Rivalry: The Seven Years' War

THE SEVEN YEARS' WAR OF 1756 TO 1763 HAS BEEN CALLED THE FIRST WORLD WAR. IT WAS FOUGHT IN EUROPE AND ALSO IN CANADA AND INDIA WHERE IT HAD A DECISIVE EFFECT ON THE IMPERIAL FUTURES OF BRITAIN AND FRANCE.

The Seven Years' War, which began on August 29, 1756 when King Frederick II the Great of Prussia invaded Saxony, was a territorial dispute that eventually involved seven European nations and a coalition of small German states. The territory in dispute was Silesia, which had been seized from Austria by Prussia in 1742. Fourteen years later, the Austrians felt able to retrieve their lost lands after allying themselves with France, Russia, Saxony, and several smaller European states. Ranged against this alliance were Prussia, whose army was the strongest and most tightly trained in the world, and Britain, whose navy was similarly paramount at sea. In Europe, Frederick II, often described as the greatest commander of his time, was initially successful, first capturing Dresden on September 10, 1756, and next thrashing the armies of Saxony and Austria at Lobositz on October 1. The Saxon army was so soundly beaten that its forces were subsequently absorbed into the Prussian army. The Prussian victory was hardly surprising, for Frederick the Great had inherited from his father, Frederick William I, the "Soldier-King," a superlative army that had been through a series of fundamental reforms. Frederick William was virtually obsessed with the Prussian forces and even wore military uniform at his court. Officials who formerly held the highest positions at court, found themselves upstaged by military officers who were given precedence over them by the Soldier-King.

Frederick William instituted a system of relentless drilling for his forces. He also introduced punishments of extreme severity, such as running the gauntlet, in which a soldier had to run between two lines of men each of whom struck him as he passed. The *Stechschritt* (piercing step) popularly termed the "goose step" was also introduced: this was a form of slow march which required each leg

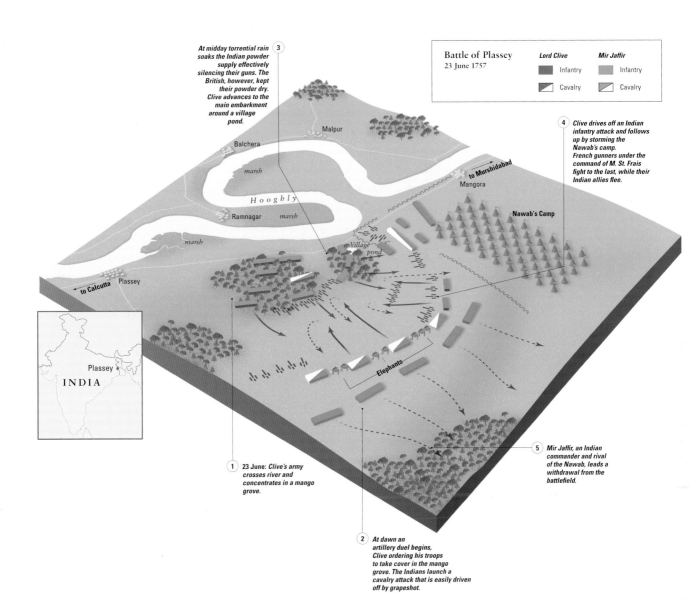

At midday torrential rain soaks the Indian powder supply effectively silencing their guns. The British, however, kept their powder dry. Clive advances to the main embarkment around a village pond. ③

Battle of Plassey
23 June 1757

Lord Clive		Mir Jaffir	
Infantry		Infantry	
Cavalry		Cavalry	

④ Clive drives off an Indian infantry attack and follows up by storming the Nawab's camp. French gunners under the command of M. St. Frais fight to the last, while their Indian allies flee.

Malpur

Balchera

marsh

to Murshidabad

Mangora

H o o g h l y

Nawab's Camp

Ramnagar *marsh*

marsh

Village pond

to Calcutta Plassey

Elephants

Plassey

INDIA

⑤ Mir Jaffir, an Indian commander and rival of the Nawab, leads a withdrawal from the battlefield.

① 23 June: Clive's army crosses river and concentrates in a mango grove.

② At dawn an artillery duel begins, Clive ordering his troops to take cover in the mango grove. The Indians launch a cavalry attack that is easily driven off by grapeshot.

to be extended in turn without bending the knee. The *Stechschritt* required a high degree of muscle control and coordination and was thought to demonstrate great discipline and physical superiority.

Frederick II inherited his father's intense interest in the army and introduced reforms of his own. The most important was the oblique order of battle. Considerable discipline and mobility were required to carry out this strategy in which the infantry went in at speed to carry out a bayonet charge. They were followed by a large contingent of cavalry, which advanced with swords at the ready before their opponents could move in to attack. Although oblique attack could fail at times, it was usually

On June 23, 1757, the Battle of Plassey, fought some 93 miles (150 km) north of Calcutta (Kolkata) in west Bengal, decided whether Britain or France would be the dominant colonial power in India. The answer was Britain, which later made India the "Jewel in the Crown" of the Empire.

irresistible and enabled the Prussians to win several battles, including a brilliant triumph at Rossbach on November 5, 1757. At Rossbach, the Prussians were crucially outnumbered, fielding only 21,000 troops to the 40,000 brought to the battle by the French and Austrians. However, the allied army moved at a much slower pace while Frederick was able to shift his army south, rotate it through ninety degrees, and meet his opponents head on. As the enemy advanced, the Prussians mowed them down with their superior firepower. Frederick settled the battle by first unleashing his cavalry and then his disciplined infantry. The French and Austrians suffered 10,000 casualties, the Prussians only 600.

In other battles, the Prussians frequently found themselves outnumbered but their quality usually overcame their opponents' quantity. The Prussians suffered defeats, most devastatingly at Kunersford at the hands of a Russian-Austrian army in 1759, but they scored many more triumphs. Above all, the Prussians survived and in 1763, when all the combatants in the war were exhausted, Frederick signed a truce at Hubertusberg which allowed Prussia to retain Silesia. Prussian military prestige was greatly increased, while the fighting barely changed the pre-War status quo.

The Seven Years' War, as fought in Canada and India, was much more decisive. Both the British and the French recruited allies from the native Indian tribes. Most of them sided with the French although the powerful Iroquois Nation preferred to back the British and the British colonies in America, who contributed numerous troops to the Mother Country's army. The colonists had good reasons of their own for participating in the War: their fear of being overrun by France or Spain. Fighting was going on in both the French and British territories for some time before the Seven Years' War began in Europe.

In Canada, the struggle had waged on and off since 1690. In India, war broke out in 1744. Two years earlier, Joseph François Dupleix had become governor of the French territories in India. Dupleix was an ambitious man and hoped to create a great French Empire in India. He reckoned, however, without Robert Clive, who arrived in India, aged 18, in 1743 as a factor in the British East India Company offices in Madras (Chennai). Five years later, Clive was still in Madras when it was bombarded by French forces. The British were forced to surrender, but during negotiations between the two sides, Clive escaped to Fort St. David, 20 miles (32 km) south of Madras. Clive was rewarded for his exploit with an ensign's commission in the army of the British East India Company. In 1748, the war between Britain and France came to an end and Clive had to return to his civilian duties. But although he had never received any army training, he possessed natural military skills, which, according to Prime Minister William Pitt the Elder, made him a "heaven-sent general." Clive proved his skills in 1751 when he captured the fort at Arcot, which lay in French-dominated southeastern India, and did so with a minimal force of 200 Europeans and 300 Indian sepoys who had only three artillery pieces between them. Hostilities ceased in 1754. But the peace did not last for long. War broke out again in 1756 by which time Clive was deputy governor of Fort St. David. The final showdown between the British and the French took place the following year, at the battle of Plassey in West Bengal. Clive, commanding a small force of only 3,200 men, faced the 50,000-strong army of the French and their Indian allies.

Furthermore, French forces had 53 heavy guns with which to bombard the mangrove swamp at Plassey, where Clive had taken up his position. Fortunately, heavy monsoon rains came to Clive's aid, soaking the French gunpowder stores and making their guns useless. This enabled Clive and his men to storm out of the mangrove swamp. The Indians fled, terrified and the French soon followed. Clive's

In 1780, after victory in the Seven Years' War, Britain occupied a very large area of Canada to add to its 13 American colonies, while the Spaniards, their principal rivals, extended their colony of New Spain into most of the future mid-west and west of the independent United States.

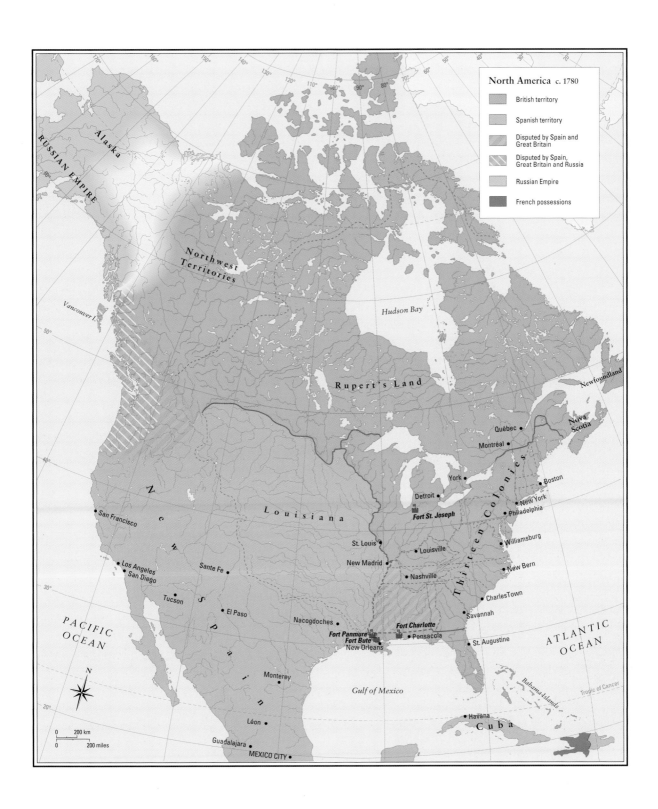

North America c. 1780

British territory

Spanish territory

Disputed by Spain and Great Britain

Disputed by Spain, Great Britain and Russia

Russian Empire

French possessions

triumph gave the British East India Company control of Bengal in eastern India, the richest province in the sub-continent. Robert Clive was rewarded with a noble title as 1st Baron Clive.

After Plassey, French power and influence in India steadily declined. Eventually, the greater part of India came under British rule except for a few outposts held by the French and the Portuguese, and the princely or native states which were governed by their own Indian rulers. British India, also known as the British Raj, was popularly termed the "Jewel in the Crown of the British Empire" until the country became independent in 1947.

As in India, British domination in Canada was secured by a brilliant military victory, the capture of Quebec, capital of New France; which lay along the mighty St. Lawrence River. The French took immense pride in New France which at its greatest extent in 1712 stretched from Newfoundland in the east to the Rocky Mountains in the west and from Hudson's Bay in the north to the Gulf of Mexico in the south. The British equivalent, in importance if not in size, was New England which was located in the northeast of the American colonies, covering the present-day U.S. states of Maine, New Hampshire, Vermont, Massachusetts, Rhode Island, and Connecticut. Both the British and the French had big ambitions to extend their territory, and in particular claim a larger share of the extremely lucrative fur trade. Both also coveted the wealthy fisheries on the Newfoundland Grand Banks.

The initial move by both countries was to claim large areas of territory between the Appalachian Mountains and the Mississippi River, and from the Great Lakes to the Gulf of Mexico. This huge expanse was known as Ohio Country. In 1753, the French began building forts to protect New France — Fort Presque Isle and Fort le Boeuf both in 1753. In 1754, they captured the British Fort Prince George and began the construction of Fort Duquesne.

In the next two years, the War went badly for the British. In 1756, they lost Fort Oswego to the French, who thereby gained control over Lake Ontario. British forces achieved better results in 1758, when they captured the French fortress at Louisbourg which opened up the St. Lawrence River and the route to Canada. Fort Frontenac, which supplied all the French forts in the Ohio River Valley, fell to the British two months later, in August 1758. The following October, the British scored a big diplomatic success when they persuaded Indians in the Ohio River Valley to cease their support for the French in exchange for a promise not to settle lands west of the Allegheny Mountains. As a result, the French war effort was soon being starved of supplies. At Fort Duquesne, the desperate garrison set fire to the Fort, exploded its walls, and retreated to the Allegheny River.

Britain had been rapidly gaining the upper hand in Canada and unlike the French, they had the advantage of supremacy at sea which meant that their army could be easily supplied from Britain. In 1759, two British armies invaded Canada, one from the south and the other westward along the St. Lawrence River, where they put the city of Quebec under siege. Although their artillery bombardments devastated large areas in and around Quebec, the French defenders, commanded by Louis-Joseph de Montcalm-Gozon and Marquis de Saint-Veran, held out for several weeks. The problem for the British commander, Major-General James Wolfe, was that Quebec lay at the top of high cliffs, the Heights of Abraham. Although the Heights were more of a gradual upward slope than its name suggests, they provided the perfect position from which to withstand a siege. The only thing to do was the one thing the French believed impossible: the British would have to climb the Heights.

The Seven Years' War at sea was of particular importance for the British, since ships of the Royal Navy were instrumental in preventing a French invasion of Britain. They also fought in American waters where Admiral George Brydges Rodney, for example, captured the Caribbean islands of St. Lucia, Grenada, and Martinique.

On the night of September 12 1759, some 5,000 British soldiers rowed with muffled oars along the St. Lawrence River. When they reached the Heights of Abraham, they scrambled up and took the French sentries at the top by surprise. After heavy fighting in a battle that lasted the whole day, the British captured Quebec. Both Montcalm and Wolfe were killed.

In 1763, at the end of the Seven Years' War, New France became British territory and France's dream of an empire in Canada, like its empire in India, was gone forever.

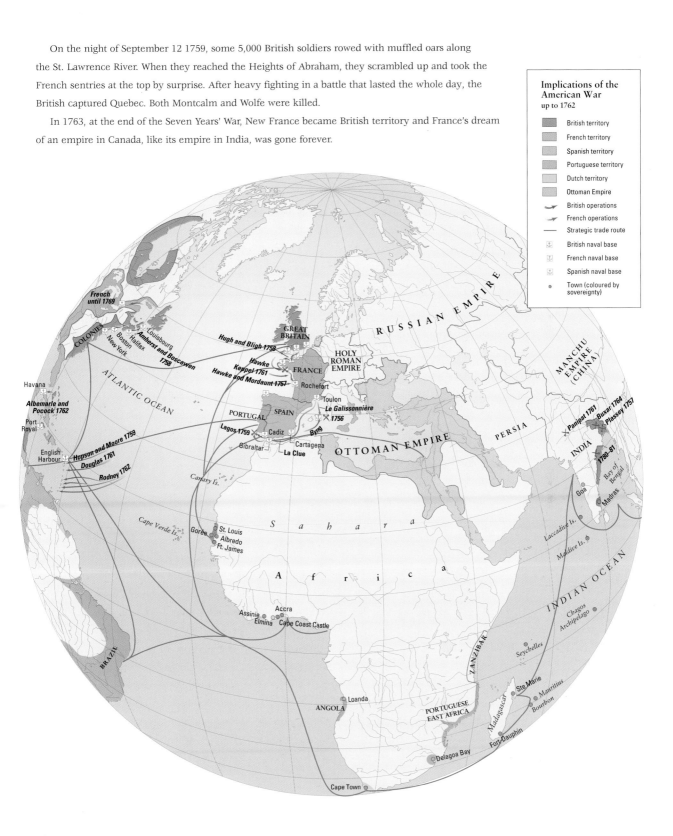

Implications of the American War
up to 1762

- British territory
- French territory
- Spanish territory
- Portuguese territory
- Dutch territory
- Ottoman Empire
- British operations
- French operations
- Strategic trade route
- British naval base
- French naval base
- Spanish naval base
- Town (coloured by sovereignty)

CHAPTER V — THE AMERICAN REVOLUTION 1775-1782: THE AMERICAN REVOLUTION: CAUSES

BY THE 18TH CENTURY, RADICAL NEW IDEAS ABOUT GOVERNMENT, DEMOCRACY, AND HUMAN RIGHTS HAD DEVELOPED AMONG THE 13 BRITISH COLONIES IN NORTH AMERICA. THESE IDEAS WERE IN DIRECT OPPOSITION TO THOSE IN BRITAIN AND ULTIMATELY, THEY LED TO WAR.

An important cause of the American Revolution was the way the government in Britain imposed taxes on the colonists but denied them representation at the British Parliament in London. The aggrieved colonists coined a slogan for this situation — "No taxation without representation!" From the British point of view, these taxes were needed to pay for an army stationed in the colonies for protection against attacks by the French, the Spaniards, and native American Indians. Anger escalated even further in 1765 when the British imposed the first direct tax on the colonists, the Duties in the American Colonies Act, better known as the Stamp Act. This required printed materials to carry a tax stamp. In the same year, the equally controversial Quartering Act was passed in London, requiring the colonists to provide quarters for British troops. There were more violent protests against further taxes on imported sugar, glass, paint, and tea. The furore over the Stamp Act was so great that the British Parliament cancelled it in 1766. But the tax on tea remained and fury over it reached a height at the "Boston Tea Party." On the night of December 16, 1773, members of the anti-British Sons of Liberty disguised themselves as Indians and went on board three British tea ships moored in Boston harbor: they seized the tea cargoes and poured them into the water. The British reaction was fierce. The port of Boston was closed down until the ruined tea had been paid for and military control was imposed in Massachusetts. However, the protests increased. A Continental Congress was formed and organized a ban on trade with Britain. There was also talk of declaring independence. All that was needed now was an incident that would incite revolution, and war.

The Battle of Bunker Hill is shown on this map. The battle was between the British and the Americans. The Americans were eventually forced back to the mainland.

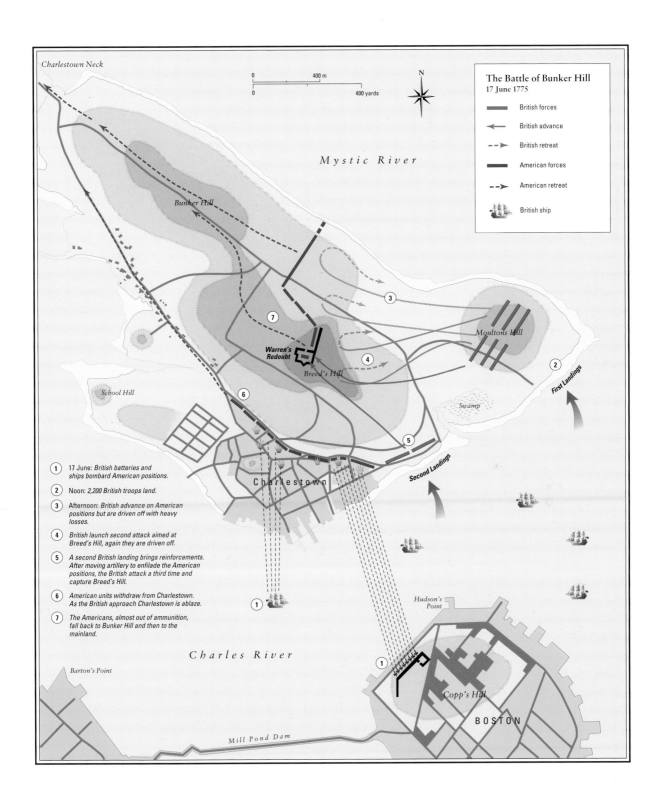

Charlestown Neck

0   400 m
0   400 yards

N

The Battle of Bunker Hill
17 June 1775

—— British forces

←— British advance

--→ British retreat

—— American forces

--→ American retreat

🚢 British ship

Mystic River

Bunker Hill

Moultons Hill

⑦

Warren's Redoubt

③

④

Breed's Hill

②

First Landings

School Hill

⑥

Swamp

⑤

Second Landings

Charlestown

① 17 June: British batteries and ships bombard American positions.

② Noon: 2,200 British troops land.

③ Afternoon: British advance on American positions but are driven off with heavy losses.

④ British launch second attack aimed at Breed's Hill, again they are driven off.

⑤ A second British landing brings reinforcements. After moving artillery to enfilade the American positions, the British attack a third time and capture Breed's Hill.

⑥ American units withdraw from Charlestown. As the British approach Charlestown is ablaze.

⑦ The Americans, almost out of ammunition, fall back to Bunker Hill and then to the mainland.

Hudson's Point

①

①

Charles River

Barton's Point

Copp's Hill

BOSTON

Mill Pond Dam

THE AMERICAN REVOLUTION: THE START OF THE WAR

THE AMERICAN REVOLUTION BECAME THE WAR OF AMERICAN INDEPENDENCE — ON 19 APRIL 1775 WHEN 700 BRITISH SOLDIERS ATTEMPTED TO SEIZE THE ARMS DEPOT IN CONCORD AND WERE CONFRONTED BY A FORCE OF AMERICAN "MINUTEMEN" NUMBERING A TENTH OF THEIR SIZE.

The first shots of the War of Independence were fired at Lexington, when the British went afer munitions, killing eight Minutemen and wounding another ten. After this first, dramatic skirmishing, a call went out from the Massachusetts Provincial Congress for a militia numbering 13,600 men to besiege the British garrison inside Boston. In the event, some 15,000 volunteers arrived from Rhode Island, Connecticut and New Hampshire. On June 15, 1775, they became an official force when the second Continental Congress in Philadelphia recognized them as a Continental Army. At the Battle of Bunker Hill, on the Charlestown Heights above Boston, the British attempted a naval bombardment, an amphibious attack and a charge with fixed bayonets but the battle ended only when the Americans' ammunition ran out. The battle for Boston was far from over, though. On 3 July, 1775, Colonel George Washington took command of the Continental Army and began to build it up into a powerful force of 26,000 men armed with heavy guns brought in from Fort Ticonderoga on Lake Champlain. The threat became so great that on 17 March 1776, General William Howe, in command at Boston, preferred to evacuate the town and withdraw to Halifax, Nova Scotia.

In the Spring of 1776, the American cause was boosted when the French and Spanish, still smarting from their defeat at British hands in the Seven Year' War, authorized supplies of arms to the colonists. The British now resolved to take the offensive and crush the revolution. To this end, General Howe received abundant reinforcements from Britain and orders to proceed from Halifax to New York. Howe arrived there on 2 July, two days before the Americans issued their Declaration of Independence.

George Washington took a desperate risk when his small, weak army attacked the garrison of Hessians at Trenton in the worst possible conditions — a heavy snowstorm. Yet surprise was total, and only 400 of the 1,400 Hessians escaped capture by the Americans. A vast amount of valuable booty was also taken.

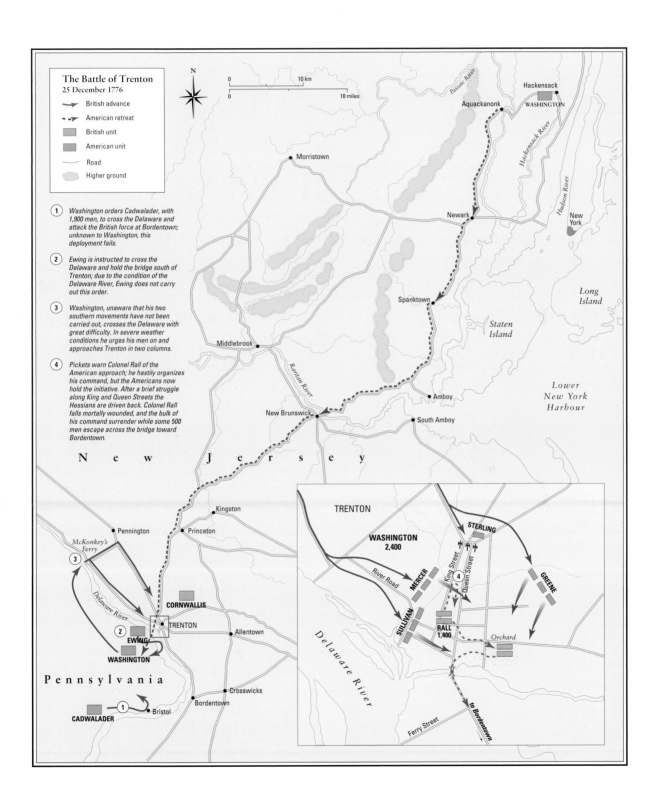

The Battle of Trenton
25 December 1776

British advance
American retreat
British unit
American unit
Road
Higher ground

1. Washington orders Cadwalader, with 1,900 men, to cross the Delaware and attack the British force at Bordentown; unknown to Washington, this deployment fails.

2. Ewing is instructed to cross the Delaware and hold the bridge south of Trenton; due to the condition of the Delaware River, Ewing does not carry out this order.

3. Washington, unaware that his two southern movements have not been carried out, crosses the Delaware with great difficulty. In severe weather conditions he urges his men on and approaches Trenton in two columns.

4. Pickets warn Colonel Rall of the American approach; he hastily organizes his command, but the Americans now hold the initiative. After a brief struggle along King and Queen Streets the Hessians are driven back. Colonel Rall falls mortally wounded, and the bulk of his command surrender while some 500 men escape across the bridge toward Bordentown.

THE WAR OF INDEPENDENCE: EVENTS 1776-1777

THE WAR OF INDEPENDENCE WAS VERY TOUGH FOR THE AMERICANS IN THE YEARS 1776 AND 1777, WITH A FEW SUCCESSES, BUT MANY LOSSES. WHEN THE WAR CAME TO AN END, HOWEVER, IT WAS BECAUSE OF A SERIOUS BRITISH MISTAKE.

In the later stages of the American War of Independence, the fighting spread south, where the battle of Camden was fought in 1780 and the battle of Guilford Court in 1781. In both these battles, General Charles Cornwallis led the British forces and though at great cost, won both of them.

The reinforcements that reached the British General Howe from across the Atlantic meant that the American colonists were vastly outnumbered in New York in the summer of 1776. On 2 July, Howe landed on Staten Island with 32,000 troops, including 9,000 Hessian mercenaries from Germany, whereas Washington had only 13,000 under his command. Holding New York, as instructed by Congress, was a formidable and ultimately hopeless task. Washington deployed half of his army across Flatbush on Long Island while the rest remained on Manhattan. The Battle of Long Island, which ensued on 27 August, was a disaster for the Americans. Some 20,000 British troops drove them onto Brooklyn Heights, killing 200 and capturing another 1,000. Washington did not wait for Howe to advance on the Heights and instead evacuated his forces. On September 12, Washington decided to abandon New York altogether. Washington managed to halt the British at the battle of Harlem Heights on September 16, but his forces were driven off the battlefield at White Plains. At the battle of Princeton, Washington roundly defeated the British and captured a vast amount of military stores. All British garrisons stationed in the west of New Jersey were evacuated since Washington's force now posed a threat to their communications. The next British plan was to seize the Hudson River Valley in order to split the colonies in two. It failed to work out that way, chiefly because there was no coordination between the two forces, one under Howe, the other led by Burgoyne, who had conceived the whole idea. The British scored some success — notably at Ticonderoga which they captured on July 5 — but disaster loomed after the Battle of Bemis Heights on October 7 when Burgoyne's 5,700 troops found themselves surrounded at Saratoga by an American force three times more numerous. Burgoyne had no option but to surrender and allow his troops to be disarmed.

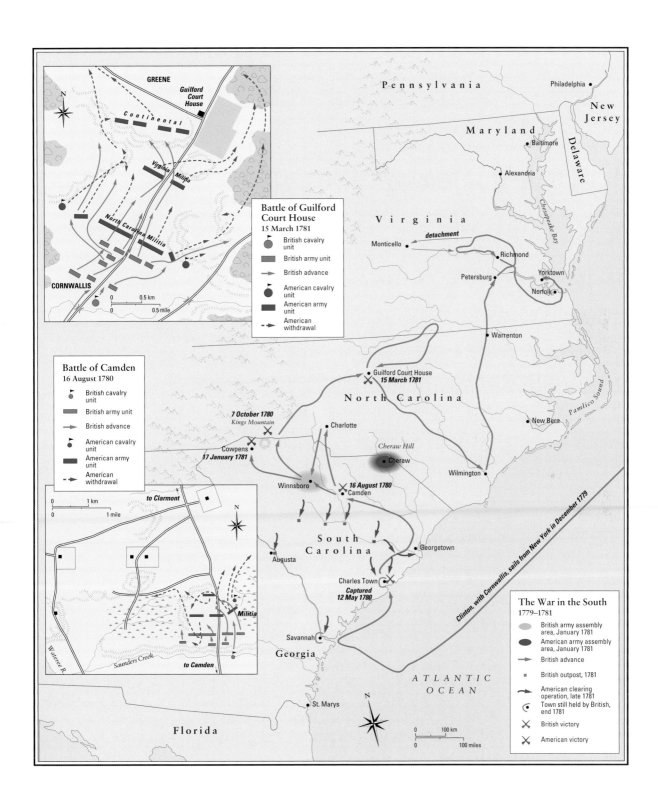

Battle of Guilford Court House
15 March 1781

- ◗ British cavalry unit
- ▬ British army unit
- → British advance
- ● American cavalry unit
- ▬ American army unit
- ⇢ American withdrawal

0 0.5 km
0 0.5 mile

GREENE

Guilford Court House

Continental

Virginia Militia

North Carolina Militia

CORNWALLIS

Battle of Camden
16 August 1780

- ◗ British cavalry unit
- ▬ British army unit
- → British advance
- ◗ American cavalry unit
- ▬ American army unit
- ⇢ American withdrawal

0 1 km
0 1 mile

to Clarmont

to Camden

Militia

Wateree R.

Saunders Creek

Pennsylvania

Philadelphia

New Jersey

Maryland

Delaware

Baltimore

Alexandria

Virginia

detachment

Monticello

Richmond

Yorktown

Petersburg

Norfolk

Chesapeake Bay

Warrenton

Guilford Court House
15 March 1781

North Carolina

Pamlico Sound

New Bern

7 October 1780
Kings Mountain

Charlotte

Cheraw Hill

Cheraw

Wilmington

Cowpens
17 January 1781

Winnsboro

16 August 1780
Camden

South Carolina

Georgetown

Augusta

Charles Town
*Captured
12 May 1780*

Clinton, with Cornwallis, sails from New York in December 1779

Savannah

Georgia

St. Marys

ATLANTIC OCEAN

Florida

The War in the South
1779–1781

- British army assembly area, January 1781
- American army assembly area, January 1781
- → British advance
- ▪ British outpost, 1781
- ⮌ American clearing operation, late 1781
- ⊙ Town still held by British, end 1781
- ✕ British victory
- ✕ American victory

0 100 km
0 100 miles

THE WAR OF INDEPENDENCE: VICTORY!

THE BRITISH GENERAL JOHN BURGOYNE WAS A MAJOR PRIZE FOR THE AMERICANS AND HIS SURRENDER AT SARATOGA IN 1777 WAS THE TURNING POINT IN THE WAR OF INDEPENDENCE. IT LAUNCHED A TRAIN OF EVENTS THAT CULMINATED IN AMERICAN VICTORY.

After the capture of General Burgoyne and his 6,000 troops Washington retired to Valley Forge, Pennsylvania for the winter of 1777-1778. Meanwhile, the British had to rethink their situation. They reorganized their forces, evacuated Ticonderoga and Crown Point in Boston, and abandoned the highlands above the River Hudson. Now, all the British held were New York City, part of Rhode Island, and Philadelphia, and other European countries pledged support. In 1778, the French admiral Charles, Comte D'Estaing arrived off the Georgian port of Savannah and captured two British warships and two supply vessels. In 1779 the Spanish seized Manchac, Natchez, and Baton Rouge in Florida, raided Michigan in 1780, and captured Fort St. Joseph and its British garrison in January 1781. Meanwhile the French began to land with their troops and made some progress in Virginia. On 28 September, Yorktown was invested by a force of 9,500 Americans, 7,800 French regulars, and a battery of powerful field guns. Against this, Cornwallis had only 8,000 men. Cornwallis withdrew his troops to the inner fortifications of Yorktown but the Americans and their French allies stormed in and established more gun batteries. Cornwallis knew a hopeless situation when he saw one, and just how hopeless was emphasized in nearby Chesapeake Bay where the French navy was in command. On 19 October, Cornwallis surrendered. As his troops laid down their arms, their regimental bands played *The World Turned Upside Down*, which for the British, it certainly had. The American victory was later confirmed when the Peace Party, which had never approved of the War, won a vote in the British Parliament not to continue hostilities. Two years later, in the Treaty of Paris signed on 3 September, 1783, Britain officially recognized the independence of its former colonies, and the United States of America came into being.

The battle of Chesapeake on September 5, 1781 (see inset) had a crucial effect on events at Yorktown the following September and October. The victory of the French at Chesapeake prevented much-needed troops and supplies from reaching the British General Cornwallis at Yorktown: he was consequently forced to surrender.

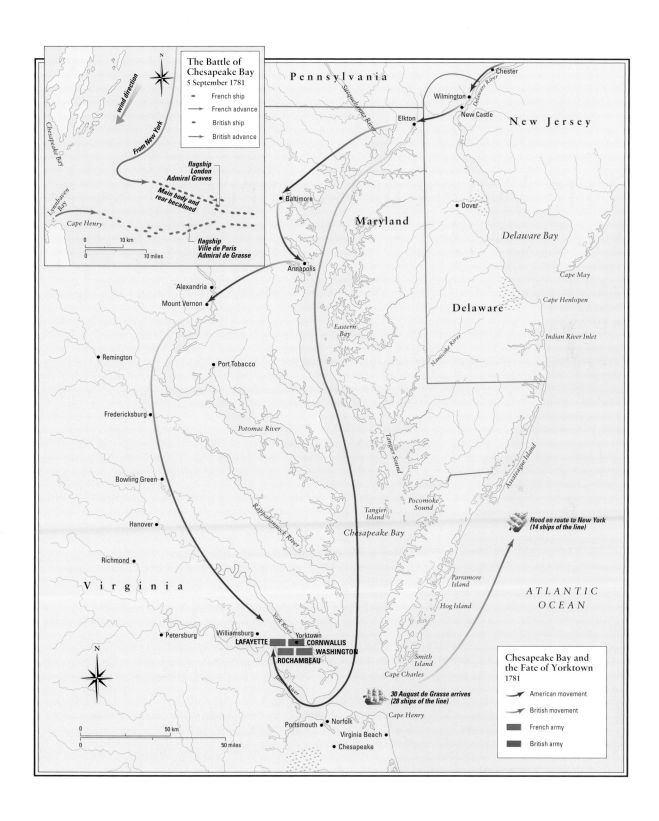

The Battle of Chesapeake Bay
5 September 1781

- ••• French ship
- → French advance
- -•- British ship
- → British advance

wind direction

From New York

flagship
London
Admiral Graves

*Main body and
rear becalmed*

Chesapeake Bay

Lynnhaven Bay

Cape Henry

flagship
Ville de Paris
Admiral de Grasse

0   10 km
0   10 miles

Pennsylvania

Chester

Wilmington

New Castle

Elkton

Delaware River

Susquehanna River

New Jersey

Baltimore

Dover

Maryland

Delaware Bay

Cape May

Cape Henlopen

Annapolis

Eastern
Bay

Delaware

Nanticoke River

Indian River Inlet

Alexandria

Mount Vernon

Remington

Port Tobacco

Fredericksburg

Potomac River

Tangier Sound

Assateague Island

Bowling Green

Rappahannock River

Tangier
Island

Pocomoke
Sound

Hanover

Richmond

Virginia

York River

Chesapeake Bay

Parramore
Island

Hog Island

ATLANTIC
OCEAN

Hood en route to New York
(14 ships of the line)

Petersburg

Williamsburg

Yorktown

LAFAYETTE   **CORNWALLIS**

WASHINGTON

ROCHAMBEAU

James River

N

Smith
Island

Cape Charles

30 August de Grasse arrives
(28 ships of the line)

Portsmouth   • Norfolk

Cape Henry

Virginia Beach

Chesapeake

0   50 km
0   50 miles

**Chesapeake Bay and
the Fate of Yorktown**
1781

- ➤ American movement
- ➤ British movement
- ▬ French army
- ▬ British army

THE UNITED STATES: 1783-1848

WINNING THEIR INDEPENDENCE GAVE AMERICANS THE CHANCE TO FULFILL A LONG-HELD AMBITION — TO EXTEND THEIR TERRITORY BEYOND THE CONFINES OF NEW ENGLAND AND TAKE IT ALL THE WAY TO THE PACIFIC COAST.

One of the many resentments that fueled the American Revolution and War of Independence was British refusal to allow the colonists to settle territory lying to the west of the Cumberland Mountains until the native Indian tribes had been pacified. Geographically, the original 13 colonies were perched in a small northeastern corner of the continent, and pacifying the rest would obviously take an immense amount of time. The mountains formed part of the Appalachians, which stretched for 1,500 miles (2,400 km) down the eastern side of North America, and the colonists' frustrations were increased by the fact that the Cumberland Gap, the way through, had already been discovered in 1750. By 1775, the so-called Wilderness Road, pioneered by the hunter and fur trapper Daniel Boone, was taken through the Gap and thousands of colonists defied the British and used it to settle in Kentucky. By 1784, the population of Kentucky had increased from a mere 100 to 30,000. Although the British had relinquished power by then, they obstructed American ambitions in another way, by giving military support to the Indians. This assistance gave an extra, deadly edge to Indian raids which by the early 19th century were causing fierce fighting in Ohio, Indiana, Michigan, Illinois, and Wisconsin. Other acrimony was caused by British restrictions on American trade with France and the forced recruitment of U.S. citizens into the Royal Navy. Taken together, these animosities led to the Anglo-American War declared on 19 June, 1812. It was fought on several fronts. At sea, British and American warships and privateers attacked each other's merchant shipping. The Atlantic coast of the United States was blockaded by the Royal Navy and damaging raids inland were carried out. More fighting took place along the frontier marked by the shores of the Great Lakes and

The Anglo-American War of 1812-1814 spread widely over United States territory, and extended out into the Atlantic, where the two sides attacked each other's fleets. Fighting took place in the north, by the Great Lakes, and as far south as New Orleans and the Gulf of Mexico.

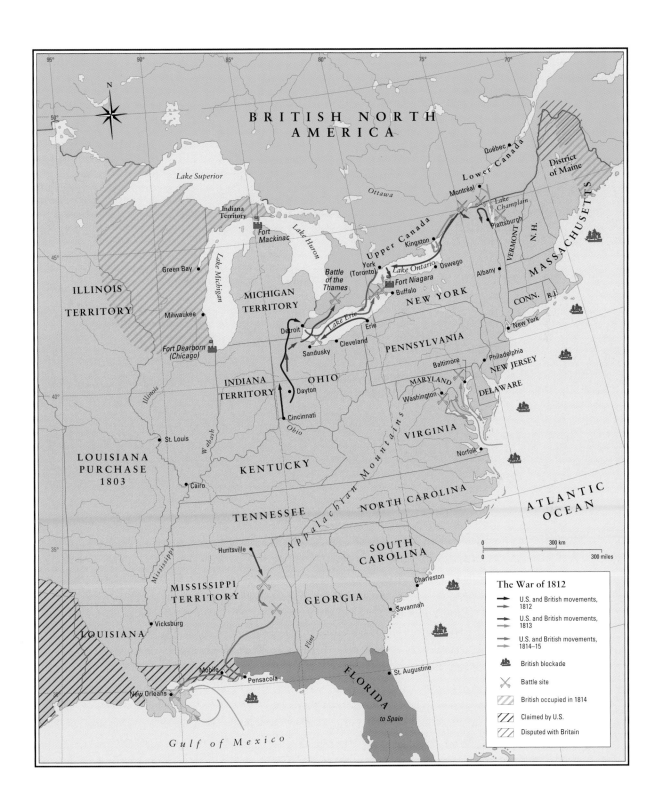

BRITISH NORTH AMERICA

Lake Superior

Québec

Lower Canada

Montréal

District of Maine

Ottawa

Lake Champlain

Plattsburg

N.H.

Indiana Territory

Fort Mackinac

Lake Huron

Upper Canada

Kingston

VERMONT

MASSACHUSETTS

Green Bay

Lake Michigan

MICHIGAN TERRITORY

Battle of the Thames

York (Toronto)

Lake Ontario

Fort Niagara

Oswego

Albany

Buffalo

NEW YORK

CONN.

R.I.

ILLINOIS TERRITORY

Milwaukee

New York

Detroit

Lake Erie

Erie

Fort Dearborn (Chicago)

Sandusky

Cleveland

PENNSYLVANIA

Philadelphia

NEW JERSEY

Baltimore

MARYLAND

DELAWARE

INDIANA TERRITORY

Dayton

OHIO

Washington

Illinois

St. Louis

Cincinnati

Ohio

Wabash

Appalachian Mountains

VIRGINIA

Norfolk

LOUISIANA PURCHASE 1803

Cairo

KENTUCKY

TENNESSEE

NORTH CAROLINA

ATLANTIC OCEAN

Huntsville

SOUTH CAROLINA

Mississippi

MISSISSIPPI TERRITORY

Vicksburg

GEORGIA

Charleston

Savannah

Flint

LOUISIANA

Mobile

Pensacola

FLORIDA

St. Augustine

New Orleans

to Spain

Gulf of Mexico

| 0 | | 300 km |
| 0 | | 300 miles |

The War of 1812

→ U.S. and British movements, 1812

→ U.S. and British movements, 1813

→ U.S. and British movements, 1814–15

⛵ British blockade

✕ Battle site

▨ British occupied in 1814

▨ Claimed by U.S.

▨ Disputed with Britain

St. Lawrence River. In the south, along the Gulf of Mexico, American forces under General Andrew Jackson thrashed the Creek Indians at the battle of Horseshoe Bend and defeated a British army in the battle of New Orleans. However, by the terms of the Treaty of Ghent that ended hostilities on December 24, 1814, little was gained by either side. For example, the British made no concessions over grievances about forced recruitment or trade blockades. However, at least territory seized by the combatants during hostilities — the Americans, for example, occupied Canadian territory near Detroit — were returned to their rightful owners.

The British were not the only rivals to try stunting the expansion of the United States. There was trouble over Texas which declared independence from Mexico after a war in 1835-1836. On 1 March, 1845, the United States annexed Texas but the Mexicans, who had never recognized Texan independence, had warned the U.S. that annexation meant war. Hostilities began on 25 April 1846 before an official declaration of war, when a detachment of 2,000 Mexican cavalry encountered an American patrol north of the Rio Grande. The Mexicans routed the patrol, killing 11 of the 63 Americans. On 3 May, Mexican artillery at Matamoros opened fire on Fort Texas, which lay close to the Rio Grande. The garrison at the Fort replied with a bombardment of their own and the exchange of gunfire went on for almost a week. The Americans were using "flying" or horse artillery mounted on horse-drawn carriages and gun crews that used more horses to ride into battle. This was so effective that the Mexicans became dispirited and sought a better position on the far side of a river bed. It did them no good, for the U.S. cavalry captured their guns and routed them. Eight days later, on May 11, the United States formally declared war on Mexico. Aiming for a short, sharp war, the American military planned to seize northern Mexico and so force the Mexicans to conclude an early peace. While two U.S. armies moved south into Mexico from Texas, a third force of 139 dragoons under Colonel Stephen Kearny headed west to Santa Fé, New Mexico, and from there, on to California. The battles that followed at Palo Alto and Resaca de Palma (Brownsville in southern Texas) inflicted heavy casualties on the Mexican forces. Monterrey in northern Mexico and Los Angeles in California fell into American hands. Despite these American successes, the arid desert terrain of northern Mexico was hazardous fighting country and a course it would be unwise to prolong. At this juncture, General Winfield Scott suggested an ambitious plan with an ambitious purpose: a major amphibious offensive to capture Mexico City, the capital of Mexico, which lay far inland, in the Valley of Mexico. General Scott's armada landed on the shore near Veracruz, on the east Mexican coast on March 9 1847. Scott's army of some 2,000 men spent the next five months fighting their way against strong Mexican opposition through punishing mountain country. The resistance, led by Antonio Lopez de Santa Anna, erstwhile President of Mexico, included five full-scale battles, the last taking place at Chapultepec, on the very threshold of the Mexican capital. Yet it was a futile effort and on 14 September, the Americans reached Mexico City.

The Mexican-American war ended of 2 February, 1848 when the Treaty of Guadeloupe Hidalgo was signed. The Americans had lost 13,780 personnel, while some 25,000 Mexicans were reckoned to have lost their lives. But American gains were extraordinary. They acquired California, Nevada, Utah, Arizona, and parts of Colorado, New Mexico, and Wyoming. Together with Louisiana, purchased from France in 1803 and Florida, ceded to the U.S. by Spain in 1819, Americans were well on the way to

18th-century Americans firmly believed that they had a "manifest destiny" to extend the U.S.A. from the Atlantic to the the Pacific coast. They began fulfilling this destiny shortly after independence but it had its cost and it was the native Americans, the original inhabitants, who paid.

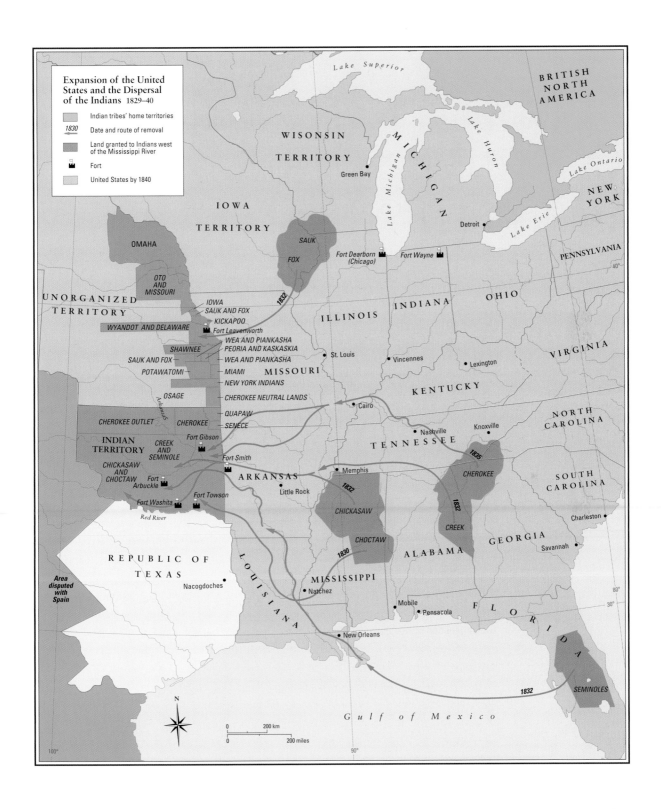

Expansion of the United States and the Dispersal of the Indians 1829–40

- Indian tribes' home territories
- *1830* Date and route of removal
- Land granted to Indians west of the Mississippi River
- Fort
- United States by 1840

CHAPTER VI — FRANCE: REVOLUTION AND EMPIRE 1789-1815: EVENTS 1789-1802

ON JULY 14, 1789 ONE OF THE MOST FORMATIVE — AND TERRIFYING — EVENTS IN EUROPEAN HISTORY OCCURRED IN PARIS: THE FRENCH REVOLUTION. THIS WAS NO ORDINARY UPRISING, BUT ONE THAT AFFECTED THE FUTURE HISTORY OF THE CONTINENT AND STILL REVERBERATES TODAY.

The storming of the Bastille prison in Paris on 14 July, 1789 was the spark that ignited the Revolution and wrought a fundamental change over the political and social face of Europe. At that time, France was ruled by the *ancien régime* (old government) a system of absolute monarchy founded in around the 15th century. This included a massively privileged clergy — the First Estate — and aristocracy — the Second Estate. The Third Estate, comprising 98 percent of the population, was made up of poor peasants and workers and the bourgeoisie — wealthy merchants, traders, and professionals such as lawyers and engineers. Despite the economic gap between them, the poor and the bourgeoisie had grievances in common. They paid very heavy taxes but possessed no political power, most of which was reserved to the King. Louis XVI was desperately short of money, and proposed to raise it by taxing the First and Second Estates who, thus far, had been exempt. The clergy and aristocracy were aghast at the prospect of losing their immunity and objected vigorously. In 1789, in the hope of settling his financial problems, King Louis called a meeting of the French equivalent of parliament, the Estates-General, which comprised representatives of the three Estates. The Estates regarded this as a chance to claim political rights but the Third Estate did not trust the other two and convened on their own. Eventually, the Third Estate forced the King to agree to a new, radical constitution which in effect converted absolute monarchy into a constitutional monarchy.

Meanwhile, bad harvests in 1788 had caused a food shortage that led to protests and riots. In Paris,

The French Revolution of 1789-1795
The Revolution that began in Paris on 14 July, 1789 soon spread through France as towns and cities declared for the revolutionaries. The counter-revolution, confined to a small part of the northwest, was no match for this fervor, despite attacks by foreign armies intent on defeating the Revolution.

mobs attacked buildings, smashed shops, started fires, and shouted fearsome threats against the King. Early on 14 July, 1789, a mob attacked the Bastille, a fortress-prison that had for a long time been a symbol of royal power. It was not long before the violence and unrest spread through France and revolutionary new ideas were being voiced. On August 26, these were enshrined in the Declaration of the Rights of Man and of the Citizen which included freedom of speech, freedom from unjust arrest and imprisonment, freedom from taxation without consent, and freedom of the press. On 21 September 1792, France was declared a republic.

The more extreme revolutionaries who now gained the upper hand resolved to exact revenge on all "enemies of the Revolution," and put King Louis on trial for treason. He was found guilty and on 21 January, 1793 he was publicly beheaded on the guillotine. The following September, the Reign of Terror inaugurated the most bloodthirsty stage of the Revolution in which an estimated 16,000 to

40,000 victims were guillotined. One of them was Queen Marie Antoinette who died on 16 October, 1793.

The Reign of Terror came to an end in 1794, when more moderate revolutionaries, sickened by the bloodletting, guillotined its chief protagonist, Maximilien Robespierre. Yet even before that, horror at what was happening in France had permeated Europe, not least among its rulers whose regimes were scarcely less despotic than Louis XVI's. They became thoroughly alarmed in case their subjects sought to emulate the French. Austria and its Prussian and other allies determined to invade France and restore law and order, however, the French pre-empted them and on 20 April, 1792 issued their own declaration of war.

The Revolutionary concept of a "nation at war" was as radical as Revolutionary politics. As the Convention of August 1793 stated: "All Frenchmen are permanently requisitioned for service in the armies." Under the impetus of this call to arms, the French forces grew massively in size, so much so that numbers had to be reduced for the sake of building up the quality of recruits. Even so, patriotic zeal did not always ensure success against a formidable coalition of enemies who at various times included Austria, Prussia, Spain, Portugal, the Dutch Republic, and even the Ottoman Empire in Turkey.

The War of the First Coalition was under way soon after the declaration of war, when Austria invaded the north and east of France and a Prussian incursion aimed at Paris. The French succeeded in fending off both attacks, but progress was mixed in the years that followed. In 1794, French fortunes changed and they won several battles, re-entering Brussels on 10 July of that year and occupying Antwerp on 27 July. The first few months of 1795 saw one French triumph after another: they occupied the Netherlands, and signed peace with Prussia and Spain: as part of the deal, the Spaniards ceded to France their colony of Santo Domingo in the Caribbean. Several German states — Saxony, Hanover, Hesse Cassel — also withdrew from the War in 1795 until only Austria and Great

The seasoned Austrian commanders who confronted the 27-year old Napoleon Bonaparte when he invaded Italy with his revolutionary army were certain that they would be able to trounce this young upstart. They soon discovered otherwise, as Napoleon used guile, deception, and innovative maneuvers to wrong-foot and defeat them.

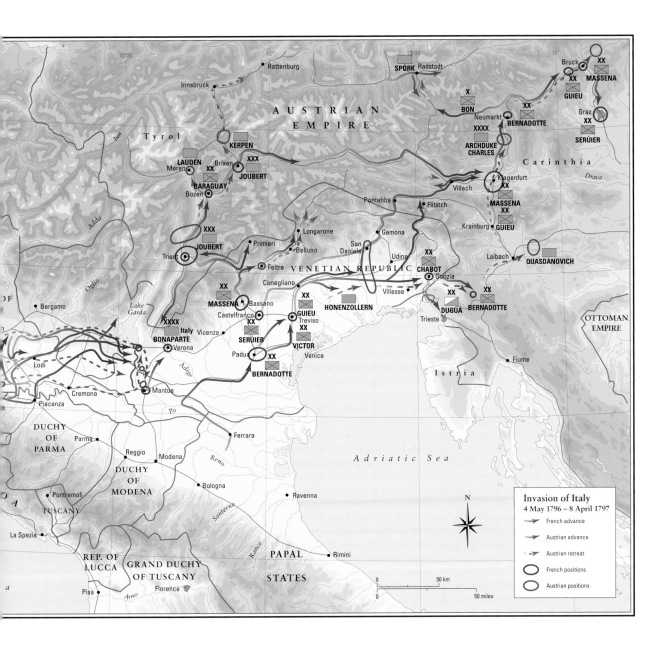

Britain remained in contention.

In mid-1795, a new government, the Directory, took power in France, and was immediately faced with an uprising by *sans-culottes*, a term meaning "without knee breeches" that described the poorer and in some cases wilder, elements of the Third Estate. The force that suppressed the trouble was led by 26-year old Napoleon Bonaparte. Napoleon organized his guns so that they dominated Toulon harbor. A subsequent assault on the town, in which Napoleon participated, obliged the British ships in harbor to withdraw, so terminating the siege.

Napoleon was a rising star of the French Revolutionary armies, even though his army was little more than a ragbag of ill-fed, poorly clothed troops. By mid-May, he had led them to victory in four battles, defeated both the Austrians and the forces of Sardinia-Piedmont, and conquered the whole of Lombardy. From there, Napoleon led his army across the Alps, and by 1797 threatened Vienna. This signaled the collapse of the First Coalition against Revolutionary France. On 17 October, 1797, the Treaty of Campo Formio between France and Austria was signed, giving the French control of Belgium and northern Italy.

On 24 December, 1798, Great Britain and Russia formed the Second Coalition, which was joined by Austria, Portugal, the King of Naples, the Ottoman Turkish Empire and the Vatican. At this time, the Austrians were still active in Italy. So were the French, although without Napoleon, who returned to France in August. By early December 1798, the French General Barthelemy-Catherine Joubert had conquered Piedmont shortly after the Austrian General Karl Mack von Leiberich, leading a Neapolitan army, captured Rome. Leiberich had only two weeks to savor his triumph, for he was driven out of Rome on 15 December by the French General Jean Etienne Championnet. To compound Leiberich's problems, his Neapolitan troops mutinied and he had to run for safety to the French. On 24 January, Championnet overran the Kingdom of Naples. Its monarch, Ferdinand IV, fled and was replaced by the French-backed Parthenopean Republic. This ephemeral republic, which lasted only five months, was the only French success in Italy as the year 1799 went on. Their armies were driven off the battlefield at Magnano on April 5 and Cassano on April 27. On August 15, General Joubert was killed and his army decisively defeated with the loss of 11,000 men at the battle of Novi. Afterward, the 70 year-old Russian Marshal Alexander Suvarov drove the French across the Appenine Mountains. These reverses were so comprehensive that by the end of 1799, almost all the gains Napoleon had made in Italy in 1796 and 1797 had been wiped out. The French had found little more success further north, in Germany. For instance, Austrian forces led by the Archduke Charles smashed through the center of General Joubert's forces in the Battle of Stockach near Lake Constance in southern Germany on 25 March 1799. Joubert lost 3,600 men, and following an enforced withdrawal, he resigned his command. There was better news for the French from Switzerland, where General André Masséna inflicted a severe defeat on a Russian force led by General Aleksander Korsakov at Zurich on 25 September. Korsakov lost some 8,000 men and 100 guns. Meanwhile, General Suvarov was moving through the Alpine passes and reached the St. Gotthard, near the Swiss canton of Ticino, when he learned of Korsakov's defeat. Suvarov struggled back to Ilanz on the upper Rhine but was relieved of his command by an ungrateful Russian Tsar, Paul I. The fate of Korsakov and Suvarov signaled the end of Russian participation in the Second Coalition.

Meanwhile, in France, Napoleon Bonaparte had helped to overthrow the unpopular Directory and replace it with a three-man Consulate: Napoleon was elected First Consul and so became the most powerful man in France. Having settled the political situation at home, Napoleon returned to Italy, determined to retrieve the losses the French had suffered during his absence. Napoleon marched his Army of the Reserve over the St. Bernard Pass into Italy and on June 14, and met the Austrians at the Battle of Marengo, near Alessandria in Piedmont. Napoleon's forces numbered only 18,000 including a

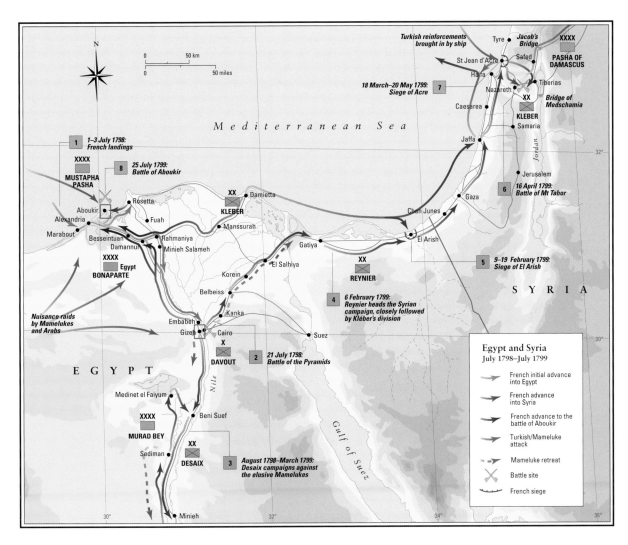

reserve of cavalry, which were scattered over a wide area. Soon, the Austrians, led by General Michael Freiherr von Melashad, enveloped the French right and pushed them back for two miles (3.2km). Somehow, Melas gained the impression that he had won the battle but Napoleon soon defeated the Austrians. The French lost some 4,000 men, the Austrians 9,000. On 3 December, 1800 General Moreau totally crushed them at Hohenlinden. Austria sued for peace and on 9 February, 1801, signed the Treaty of Luneville. Great Britain was now the only member of the Second Coalition still undefeated, but this was a stalemate situation. France might be the dominant land power in Europe but the British were paramount at sea. The two countries had been at war for the past ten years and a certain war-weariness had set in. On 25 March, 1802, Great Britain and France signed the Treaty of Amiens, ending the hostilities. But considering the size and extent of Napoleon's ambitions, it would be merely a brief interlude.

Napoleon's campaigns in Egypt and Syria were meant to protect French trade and obstruct Britain's access to its rich possessions in India. But British sea power and new Ottoman infantry units, the Nizam-i-Cedid, proved too much even for Napoleon. He was forced to withdraw and return to France.

NAPOLEON AND MANEUVER WARFARE

MANEUVER WARFARE, WHICH WAS FREQUENTLY PUT TO BRILLIANT USE BY NAPOLEON BONAPARTE, WAS NOT A NEW IDEA IN HIS TIME. IT WAS AS OLD AS WAR ITSELF AND BASICALLY COMPRISED THE TACTICAL MANIPULATION OF MOVEMENT AND FIREPOWER ON THE BATTLEFIELD.

Maneuver became a dominant military technique in both land and sea warfare in the second half of the 18th century. Its chief protagonists were King Frederick II the Great of Prussia, George Washington, who proved his expertise in this regard in the American War of Independence, Admiral Horatio Nelson, Britain's greatest sea captain, and Napoleon Bonaparte. The most important requirement for maneuver warfare was an immensely disciplined fighting force trained to perfection by constant drilling, with enough flexibility to move as one unit and so take up any position where it could most effectively concentrate shock action combined with massed gunfire. Maneuver has therefore been a feature of armies that are cohesive, tightly trained, and technically more adept and better equipped than forces that relied on attrition, a process that involved wearing down opponents with sustained attacks and hopefully panicking them into headlong flight.

Historically speaking, maneuver has been seen as the successor to attrition, which characterized most armies in the past, but did not completely replace it. Simply killing as many opponents as possible was not the end of attrition. Long after the development of maneuver, attrition retained its destructive uses, which is why it featured in many important wars and battles of the 19th and 20th centuries, such as the large-scale confrontations of the American Civil War of 1861-1865 or the trench warfare and prolonged artillery bombardments of the First World War in Europe, which was fought between 1914 and 1918.

However, maneuver warfare applied a more creative edge to the business of fighting and defeating opponents in war than could be achieved by attrition alone, as maneuver could be used to force an opponent into a position of having to face attritional attacks. This means that in order to destroy opponents, it has been necessary for an army to maneuver its forces so as to concentrate maximum firepower on them. According to Martin van Creveld, one of the world's leading writers on military history and strategy, there are six essentials to maneuver warfare if it is to be successful. The first is application of the so-called OODA loop: OODA stands for observe, orient, decide, act. This represents the sequence of actions required to arrive at a well-informed procedure for battle. Next comes *schwerpunkt* (focal point), that is, striking an opponent in the right place at the right time. Surprise based on deception comes next, and after that a judicious combination of armaments. According to van Creveld, an army has to be flexible in its approach to battle rather than just sticking to rulebook instructions that may not suit a given military situation. Finally, maneuver warfare needs commanders who can assess rapidly changing situations in battle and act accordingly: lower ranks who might otherwise prefer to "wait for orders" also need to understand how to match action with circumstance.

Napoleon Bonaparte had an especially acute understanding of maneuver warfare. He frequently faced numerically superior forces but compensated for this drawback by combining the movements of his cavalry and fast infantry to confuse an enemy and so score victory. A frequent method used by Napoleon was to maneuver his forces so that they trapped and defeated opponents before they had finished moving into position on the battlefield. This, of course, caught them in a state of unreadiness, which was a very favorable time to attack. Napoleon's skill at maneuver warfare had other benefits. For instance, he was able to choose where and when he wanted to attack: this sometimes gave him the chance to pick difficult terrain on which to contest a battle, with the advantage on his army's side, since he had complicated his opponents' ability to respond. Napoleon was also able to dictate the progress of a battle by means of clever maneuvers. For example, at the Battle of Austerlitz on December 2, 1805, he withdrew his forces from a strong position as a means of luring his Austrian and Russian opponents into making a flank attack. Such an attack offered a chance of weakening the center of Napoleon's army — or so he wanted them to think. What actually happened was that once his opponents had fallen for the ruse; Napoleon was able to split the Russians from the Austrians thereby weakening them instead of the other way around. As a result, Austerlitz was one of Napoleon's greatest triumphs. Another of Napoleon's successful methods was his *manoeuvre de derrière* (move to the rear) which meant that he placed his army across his opponent's lines of communication and supply, effectively cutting them off. Communications and supply were life-blood to an army and without them, defeat was virtually inevitable.

Napoleon's reputation as a commander of genius and master of maneuver was made in his twenties, during his campaigns in Italy in 1796 and 1797. Napoleon put into action what later became Martin van Crefeld's third law of maneuver when he found himself confronting the Austrians and Piedmontese outside Alessandria in 1796. He sent a request to the Genoese senate asking for their permission to cross the territory of Genoa, which was neutral in the war. The senate refused, exactly as Napoleon expected: he had also envisaged that the Genoese would inform the Austrians, which they did. In this way, Napoleon deceived the Austrians into believing that he intended to cross the Appenines through the Bochetta Pass, which ran up the mountains from Genoa. As part of the deception, Napoleon sent a decoy force along the Ligurian coast to Voltri. Napoleon had no intention of crossing the Appenines through the Bochetta Pass or of attacking the Austrian army from Voltri. Instead, he took a route that ran between the Bochetta and the Ormea Pass, the other main route through the mountains. Meanwhile, the Austrian forces headed for the Bochetta Pass, intending to attack Voltri, only to find that Napoleon's army had crossed the Appenines unimpeded and dug themselves into a strong defensive position north of Savona. The result was a heavy defeat for the Austrians on April 12, 1796. Before April was out, the Piedmontese had been forced out of the war and signed an armistice with Napoleon at Cherasco. One of its provisions gave Napoleon the right to cross the River Po at Valenza in southwestern Lombardy. The Austrians knew all about this provision and on 7 May, they were watching the river around Valenza while Napoleon crossed the Po at Piacenza. This second deception enabled Napoleon to enter Milan in triumph on 14 May. He was greeted as a savior, freeing the Milanese from the danger of autocratic Austrian rule.

Later on in 1796, at the battle of Castiglione on 5 August, Napoleon again defeated the Austrians, using his "strategic battle plan," which he successfully repeated at Austerlitz in 1805, Friedland in 1806, and Bautzen in 1813. First, Napoleon ordered a frontal assault, a cunning ploy to attract the Austrians' attention while the real attack struck elsewhere. At Castiglione, the Austrian commander, Count Siegmund Graf von Wurmser, had to commit reserves to deal with Napoleon's frontal assault, only to find an envelopment taking place at the rear of his forces as the French attacked along the line of his retreat. Wurmser's natural reaction was to shift troops from the front to the rear, so leaving a gap in his front line. This was precisely what Napoleon had intended all along, to create a weak spot through which he could drive his *masse de rupture*, or breakthrough. This caused panic, which served as the cue for Napoleon's cavalry to attack fleeing soldiers from the rear.

The Battle of Marengo on 14 June, 1800 was close-run thing. The Austrian general, Baron Michael Melas, thought he had won when his army drove Napoleon's into a 2-mile (3.2 km) retreat. Napoleon, undismayed, sent for reinforcements and counterattacked. His cavalry assaulted the Austrian northern flank and won the day.

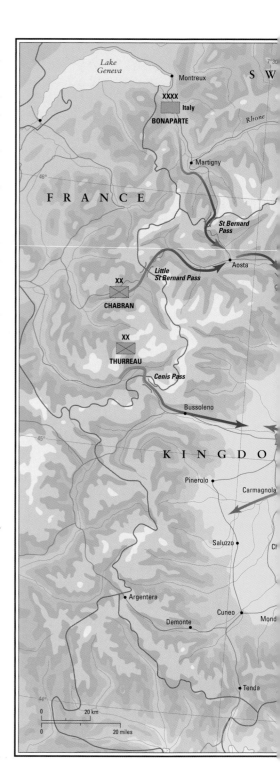

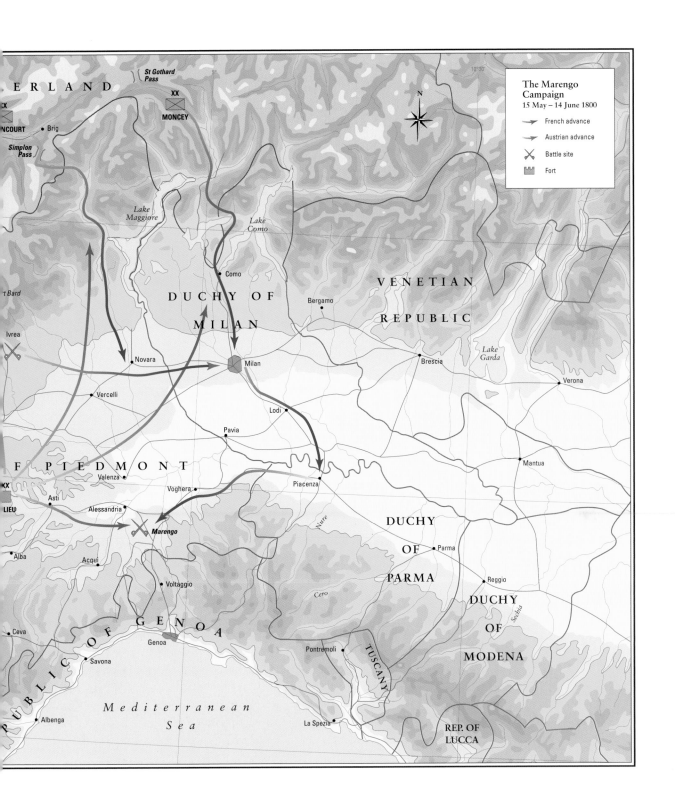

SWITZERLAND

St Gothard
Pass

XX
MONCEY

Simplon
Pass

Brig

NCOURT

t Bard

Ivrea

Lake
Maggiore

Lake
Como

Como

DUCHY OF

MILAN

Milan

Novara

Vercelli

Lodi

Pavia

VENETIAN

REPUBLIC

Bergamo

Brescia

Lake
Garda

Verona

OF   PIEDMONT

Valenza

Voghera

Piacenza

Mantua

Asti

LIEU

Alessandria

Marengo

Nure

DUCHY

Alba

Acqui

OF

Parma

Reggio

Voltaggio

PARMA

DUCHY

Ceva

Cero

Sechia

OF

PUBLIC OF   GENOA

Genoa

MODENA

Savona

Pontremoli

TUSCANY

Albenga

Mediterranean
Sea

La Spezia

REP. OF
LUCCA

**The Marengo
Campaign**
15 May – 14 June 1800

→ French advance

→ Austrian advance

✕ Battle site

⬛ Fort

N

Lessons from Napoleon: On War, Carl von Clausewitz

NAPOLEON DID MUCH TO CHANGE THE NATURE OF WAR, MAGNIFYING ITS SCALE AND INTERPRETING BATTLEFIELD CONDITIONS IN A WAY THAT WAS UNIQUE IN HIS TIME. ONE OF NAPOLEON'S KEENEST AND MOST ASTUTE OBSERVERS WAS A PRUSSIAN OFFICER, CARL VON CLAUSEWITZ.

Napoleon Bonaparte was virtually a lifelong study for Carl von Clausewitz, and the study came about through personal experience of what it was like to oppose him on the battlefield. Napoleon was certainly unlike any other military leader von Clausewitz encountered during his military career of 22 years. The time he spent studying Napoleon's methods, mentality, and achievements, as revealed in a roster of brilliant successes and a few failures, resulted in his book, *Vom Kriege (On War)* which has become the definitive statement on its subject. *On War* is still regarded today as one of the most important treatises on military strategy and a handbook on warfare for armies and their commanders all over the world. Military academies still keep copies of *On War* on their shelves.

Von Clausewitz, who held the rank of Major-General with the Russo-German Legion III Corps in the Prussian army, was introduced to the Napoleon experience at a very young age; he was only 13 when he fought at the Siege of Mainz in 1793 when the Prussian army invaded France near the start of the French Revolutionary Wars. Subsequently, von Clausewitz remained in the Prussian army throughout the wars against France, which lasted from 1806 to 1815, the year of Napoleon's final defeat at Waterloo.

In 1816, von Clausewitz began writing *On War* in 1816 but had not yet completed it when he died in a cholera epidemic in 1831. His wife finished the last two chapters and the book was published in 1832. Von Clausewitz did not confine himself to purely military matters, but took into account ambient factors — politics or social and economic issues — that could influence success or failure in war. War, von Clausewitz concluded, belonged fundamentally to the social realm, strategy to the realm of art, and tactics to the realm of science. Politics was the lynchpin, for "the political object," wrote von Clausewitz, "is the goal, war is the means of reaching it and the means can never be considered in isolation from their purposes." Von Clausewitz' most famous statement on this subject was: "War is not an independent phenomenon, but the continuation of politics by different means."

The focus of it all was, of course, the character, mindset, and skill of the commander and from his knowledge of Napoleon, von Clausewitz drew several important conclusions. "Two qualities are indispensable," he wrote:

First, an intellect that, even in the darkest hour, retains some glimmerings of the inner light which leads to truth, and second, the courage to follow this faint light wherever it may lead. If a commander is filled with high ambition, and if he pursues his aims with audacity and strength of will, he will reach them in spite of all obstacles.

According to von Clausewitz, the use of surprise, always an invaluable element in warfare, owed its "backbone" to a fusion of speed with secrecy. Risk-taking was an inherent part of warfare, for as von Clausewitz believed: "It is better to act quickly and err than to hesitate until the time of action is past." "Never forget," von Clausewitz told his readers "that no military leader has ever become great without audacity... Given the same amount of intelligence, timidity will do a thousand times more damage than audacity." As many of his strategies indicated, Napoleon was not a commander to do everything "by the book" if he suspected the book might be misleading or believed that he knew a better means to achieve an objective. Interpreting the book could, and often did, turn out to be the better way for, as von Clausewitz wrote: "Principles and rules are intended to provide a thinking man with a frame of reference." Having considered this frame of reference, von Clausewitz went on to outline a procedure that was a reflection of the basic strategy Napoleon first employed against the Austrians at Castiglione in 1796 and repeated several times in his later career, most famously at Austerlitz in 1805:

The first and most important rule to observe... is to use our entire forces with the utmost energy. The second rule is to concentrate our power as much as possible against that section where the chief blows are to be delivered and to incur disadvantages elsewhere, so that our chances of success may increase at the decisive point. The third rule is never to waste time. Unless important advantages are to be gained from hesitation, it is necessary to set to work at once. By this speed, a hundred enemy measures are nipped in the bud and public opinion is won most rapidly. Finally, the fourth rule is to follow up our successes with the utmost energy. Only pursuit of the beaten enemy gives the great fruits of victory.

WAR AT SEA 1800-1815

AFTER 1800 THE WAR AT SEA WAS PRIMARILY A STRUGGLE FOR SUPREMACY FOUGHT BETWEEN BRITAIN AND FRANCE. THE CLIMACTIC BATTLE OF TRAFALGAR IN 1805 GAVE BRITAIN THE UPPER HAND, BUT THE WAR CONTINUED AS A SERIES OF RAIDS, SKIRMISHES, AND CONVOY BATTLES AS BOTH SIDES SOUGHT ALLIES TO HELP THEM CONTROL THE TRADE ROUTES.

B y 1800 Britain had reason to believe that it had achieved a mastery of the seas. In 1797 the Spanish fleet had been badly mauled at the Battle of Cape St. Vincent by a British fleet under Admiral Sir John Jervis and Horatio Nelson. Later that year, on 11 October Admiral Adam Duncan had intercepted the main Dutch fleet en route to invade Ireland. Of 11 Dutch ships of the line, nine were captured or sunk.

The following year, the French Mediterranean fleet of 13 ships of the line and four frigates escorted a military convoy carrying the French invasion force to Egypt. Admiral Nelson, with his 13 ships of the line, missed intercepting the convoy, but caught up with the French naval ships in Aboukir Bay near the mouth of the Nile on 1 August. Nelson did not wait to form a plan of battle, but trusted his captains to know his intentions and gave the signal to attack. Four British ships slipped inshore of the anchored French ships while the others attacked from seaward. Caught between two fires, the French fought gallantly but were outgunned. The battle raged late into the night, with the French flagship blowing up when flames reached her magazine. In all two French ships were sunk and nine captured.

Although these actions had knocked out two French allies and destroyed the French Mediterranean fleet, Britain was not yet supreme. On paper the French fleet was still impressive and could be a match for the British. However, in reality the French fleet suffered some significant disadvantages. The most important of these was that the dictator, soon to be Emperor of France, Napoleon Bonaparte was a soldier

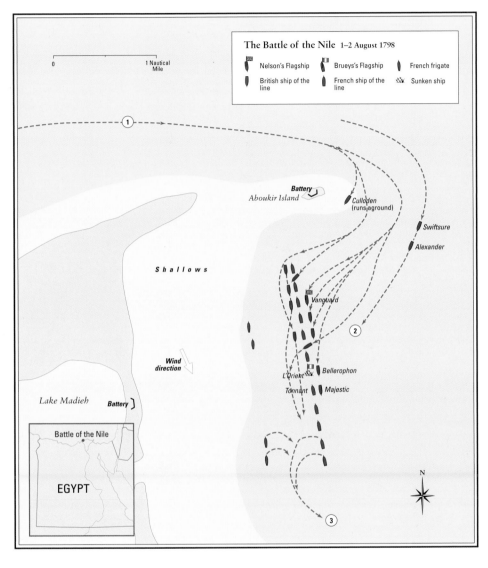

The Battle of the Nile 1–2 August 1798

Nelson's Flagship	Brueys's Flagship	French frigate
British ship of the line	French ship of the line	Sunken ship

1 Nautical Mile

Aboukir Island

Battery

Culloden (runs aground)

Swiftsure

Alexander

Shallows

Vanguard

Wind direction

L'Orient   Bellerophon

Tonnant   Majestic

Lake Madieh   Battery

N

Battle of the Nile

EGYPT

① Nelson's squadron of 11 ships of the line attack with five ships sailing on the landward side of the anchored French fleet. Meanwhile, his six other ships of the line pass along the seaward side of the French ships.

② The British ships, Swiftsure and Alexander, arrive. They engage the centre of the French line. At 10 pm the L'Orient catches fire, explodes and sinks.

③ Three ships, under Admiral Villeneuve, manage to escape. The rest are destroyed or captured by Nelson's squadron.

who neither understood the potential of naval warfare to hurt Britain nor was willing to give the French navy the money and men it needed to fight effectively. As a result the French warships spent most of their time in port where their upkeep was cheapest, but where their officers and men failed to get sea or combat experience.

The naval war took a sudden turn in 1801 when Russia formed an armed coalition with the Baltic powers with which until this date had been neutral. Since Russia was, at this date, friendly to France, Britain was determined to break up the alliance. A fleet commanded by Sir Hyde Parker with Horatio Nelson as his second in command was sent to the Baltic. On 2 April the British fleet sailed into Copenhagen Harbor and opened fire. At one point the British appeared to be losing and Admiral Parker

On August 1-2, 1798, ships of the Royal Navy, commanded by Rear-Admiral Horatio Nelson, Britain's most renowned naval commander, destroyed the French fleet as it lay at anchor near Alexandria. With it went Napoleon's hopes of damaging British trade routes to the East and loosening Britain's hold over India.

ordered his ships to retire. Nelson put the telescope to his blind eye and declared that he could not see the signal, and fought on. By dusk, the entire Danish-Norwegian fleet had been destroyed.

In 1805 Napoleon decided to invade Britain. He gathered a vast army at Boulogne, but the unarmed barges that he prepared to transport his men over the Channel would have been helpless victims under the guns of the British Channel Fleet. He therefore ordered Admiral Pierre de Villeneuve to destroy the British fleet. Villeneuve's plan was to get the assorted French squadrons out of Toulon, Ferrol, Brest, and Rochefort and rendezvous them with the Spanish fleet in the West Indies before sailing for the Channel in overwhelming numbers.

In the event, Villeneuve got only half the French fleet to sea and rendezvoused with the Spanish fleet at Cadiz. On 19 October he put to sea and two days later was met by a British fleet under Nelson. The combined Franco-Spanish fleet numbered 33 ships of the line and seven frigates, while Nelson had 27 ships of the line and four frigates.

Nelson had discussed an attack plan with his captains beforehand so, as at the Nile, he attacked without delay. The British fleet formed into two columns to break through the enemy line of battle and produce a disorganized battle in which the British heavy firepower would have an advantage over the Franco-Spanish maneuvers. The battle began a little before noon and raged until 4.30pm. By that time 20 French and Spanish ships had been captured and the rest badly damaged — only five ever saw action again. The British lost no ships, but had 1,587 killed and wounded. Among the dead was Nelson, shot by a sniper's bullet at the height of the action.

After Trafalgar the British control of the seas was never seriously in question, but the naval war did not end. Frigates and privateers from France and her allies continued to prey on British merchant ships, while the Royal Navy sought to protect them. Some of the most audacious privateers operated out of Calais and Boulogne, capturing merchant ships within sight of the British coast. The Royal Navy also instituted a blockade of France and her allies, stopping all goods that might be of use to the French war effort. This practice of searching neutral merchant ships led to disputes and in 1812 war broke out between Britain and the U.S. The Royal Navy diverted over 80 ships to blockade the U.S. Atlantic coast. There were no large naval actions during the war, but some significant single-ship actions did take place. Perhaps the most significant of these was the victory of the *USS Constitution* of 44 guns over the 48 gun *HMS Guerriere* on 19 August 1812. The Constitution later captured a second British frigate, winning for herself the nickname of "Old Ironsides."

Warships in the 18th century were divided into two basic categories. The larger vessels, "ships-of-the-line" were two-or three-decked craft, essentially floating gun-platforms designed to batter the enemy with their heavy armament. They were classified according to the number of guns they carried, which varied according to nationality and period; but typically "first-raters" would have 110 guns or more, "second-raters" 98, "third-raters" 64-80, and "fourth-raters" from 50 to 64. Naval artillery was generally heavier than that used on land; cannon firing a 32-Ib shot was the standard arm. The cannonade was introduced in the later 18th century, a short-barrelled gun used for close-quarters action, so terribly efficient that it gained the nickname "the smasher." The smaller warships were the frigates of 32-44 guns ("fifth raters"), "sixth-raters" of up to 28 guns, and smaller sloops, brigs, and gunboats.

The most famous ship-of-the-line of the era is the *HMS Victory*, built at Chatham in 1756; a 100-gun

The sea battle of Trafalgar was arguably the most important confrontation of the Napoleonic Wars. Although the British Admiral Horatio Nelson lost his life in the encounter with the French and Spanish fleet near the Strait of Gibraltar, his victory ruined Napoleon's plans to invade Britain.

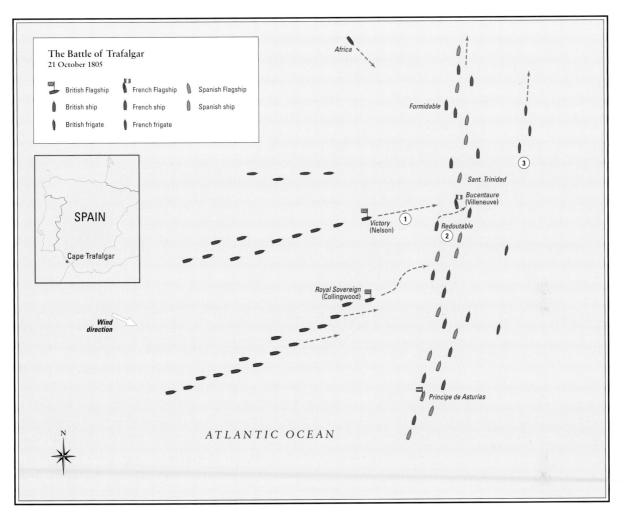

The Battle of Trafalgar
21 October 1805

British Flagship | French Flagship | Spanish Flagship
British ship | French ship | Spanish ship
British frigate | French frigate

SPAIN

Cape Trafalgar

Africa

Formidable

Sant. Trinidad

Bucentaure (Villeneuve)

Victory (Nelson) ①

Redoutable ②

③

Royal Sovereign (Collingwood)

Wind direction

Principe de Asturias

ATLANTIC OCEAN

N

"first-rater" which served as Nelson's flagship at Trafalgar.

Naval tactics were determined by the fact that a ship could only discharge its guns from the sides (producing "broadsides") and thus originated the "line-of-battle" in which opposing fleets would assemble in line astern and batter each other with broadsides. Fights would often be conducted at extremely close-range, and when locked together a boarding party might be sent onto the enemy ship, the crews fighting hand-to-hand. In general, the "line-of-battle" was a sterile formation which precluded exclusive victory. For a decisive action, a revised tactic was necessary, which took advantage of the comparative helplessness of a ship attacked from bow or stern, where its gunnery could not respond. The application of this tactic was perfected by Nelson, who at Trafalgar broke the enemy line in two places, by attacking in two columns, so enabling them to destroy the enemy ships by targeting their gunnery at the enemy's hull.

① *Nelson attacks the French–Spanish fleet from the west. Nelson's column is intended to pierce the enemy line at the position of the enemy flagship. The column, led by Collingwood, then attacks the rear of the enemy fleet.*

② *By midday both British columns pierce the enemy line and close up to fight individual ship-to-ship battles.*
At 1.30 pm the ship Redoutable mortally wounds Admiral Nelson.

③ *The British ships overwhelm their opponents by 4.40 pm. The surviving French and Spanish ships withdraw. Of their 33 ships, 17 are in the hands of the British and one had sunk.*

ITALY: 1799-1800

THE ITALIAN CAMPAIGN OF 1799 TO 1800 WAS ONE OF THE HARDEST
FOUGHT IN NAPOLEON'S CAREER, BRINGING HIM CLOSE TO DEFEAT.
HOWEVER HIS EVENTUAL VICTORY IN THAT BATTLE SECURED
CONTROL OF NORTHERN ITALY FOR FRANCE AND MADE HIS OWN
POSITION AS RULER OF FRANCE UNASSAILABLE.

In 1798 Napoleon Bonaparte left France to invade Egypt, a campaign that would prove to be abortive. Those countries that had lost territory to France in earlier wars decided to take advantage of the absence of the republic's best general by forming a Second Coalition and declaring war on France. Napoleon hurried back to France to organize a military coup that effectively made him dictator. Having failed to make peace, he spent the following year reforming the French army. He sent General Moreau to the Rhine, beyond which an Austrian army was massing. In spring 1800, Napoleon marched over the Alps into northern Italy where the French General Massena was heavily outnumbered by an Austrian army under Baron Melas. Napoleon captured Milan, thus threatening the Austrian supply lines. Late on the afternoon of 13 June Melas, with 31,000 men and 100 cannon, came across Napoleon's army of 28,000 men and 15 cannon near Marengo.

The battle began at dawn next day with a well coordinated assault by Melas. He advanced in three columns, and by 1pm, the French were on the verge of collapse. Sensing that victory was assured, and having been wounded, Melas handed over to his deputy. At 2pm the French general Desaix arrived to aid Napoleon with a fresh force of men and attacked. The Austrian army crumpled under the new attack, though Desaix was killed leading his men. By dusk half the Austrian army had surrendered or become casualties and the rest were fleeing. On 19 June the Austrian army on the Rhine was driven back by Moreau at the Battle of Hochstadt. The diplomatic wrangling took longer than expected, but in February 1801 the Second Coalition broke up and the countries involved made peace with France. Only Britain remained at war.

After his victories in northern Italy in 1796-1797, Napoleon created three republics — the Ligurian Republic, formed on June 14, 1797, the Cisalpine Republic formed on 9 July, 1797, and the Republic of Lucca, where he took over in 1805 and installed his sister, Elisa Bonaparte Bacciochi as "Queen of Etruria."

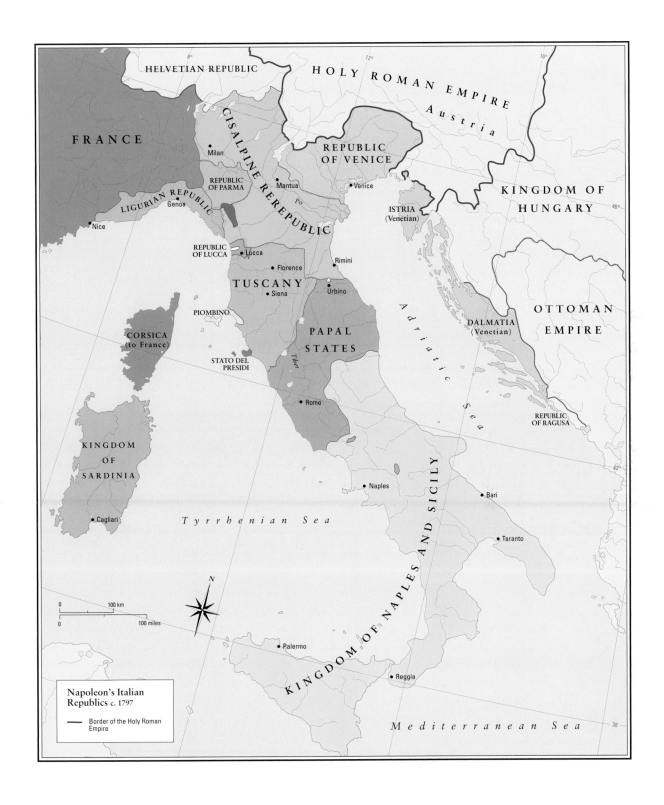

HELVETIAN REPUBLIC

HOLY ROMAN EMPIRE

Austria

FRANCE

CISALPINE REREPUBLIC

• Milan

REPUBLIC
OF PARMA

REPUBLIC
OF VENICE

• Mantua

• Venice

Po

LIGURIAN REPUBLIC

Genoa

• Nice

ISTRIA
(Venetian)

KINGDOM OF
HUNGARY

46°

REPUBLIC
OF LUCCA

• Lucca

• Florence

• Rimini

TUSCANY

• Siena

• Urbino

PIOMBINO

Adriatic Sea

DALMATIA
(Venetian)

OTTOMAN
EMPIRE

CORSICA
(to France)

STATO DEL
PRESIDI

PAPAL
STATES

Tiber

• Rome

REPUBLIC
OF RAGUSA

42°

KINGDOM
OF
SARDINIA

KINGDOM OF NAPLES AND SICILY

• Naples

• Bari

• Cagliari

Tyrrhenian Sea

• Taranto

N

0   100 km

0   100 miles

• Palermo

• Reggia

Napoleon's Italian
Republics c. 1797

—— Border of the Holy Roman
Empire

Mediterranean Sea

38

THE WAR OF THE THIRD COALITION: 1803-06

AGGRESSIVE MOVES BY NAPOLEON IN ITALY AND GERMANY, WHERE LAND WAS ANNEXED OR STATES MADE VASSALS OF FRANCE, ANGERED THE AUSTRIAN GOVERNMENT. AUSTRIA PERSUADED RUSSIA AND A NUMBER OF SMALLER STATES TO DECLARE WAR ON FRANCE, AIDED BY BRITISH SUBSIDIES. ONLY PRUSSIA REMAINED NEUTRAL.

A fter the Battle of Marengo, Napoleon set about a complete reform of the French army. Weapons, uniforms, and other equipment were modernized, while training and tactics were revised. The artillery were given new, heavier guns and trained to fight in massed batteries that could fire several salvoes, then move to a new position to fire again. The cavalry received new training in scouting and harrying that would prove to be vital. The infantry were taught to be aggressive whenever possible. The key reform proved to be the introduction of the corps organization. Each corps was a miniature army in itself, complete with infantry, cavalry, artillery, supply system, and reserve, all under the command of an officer handpicked by Napoleon and given the rank of Marshal. Although the size of a corps would depend on circumstances, they were generally around 20,000 strong. Each corps could act on its own, then join with others to form a larger army when necessary. This gave the French army great flexibility, an advantage Napoleon would use to the full in the War of the Third Coalition. As soon as he heard of the outbreak of war, Napoleon sent the corps marching across the Rhine. By 16 October they had surrounded an isolated Austrian army at Ulm. Cut off from supplies or reinforcement, the Austrians surrendered. The Austrian capital of Vienna was raided by French cavalry, but Napoleon knew the war was not yet won. A Russian army of over 50,000 men under Kutusov was at Braunau, while a second Russian army of over 30,000 men was marching from Russia. An Austrian army of 20,000 men was marching to join Kutusov and more were on the way.

When Napoleon learned that his enemies planned to invade France from across the River Rhine, his army was at Boulogne, preparing an invasion of England. Napoleon abandoned his plans, secretly marched his army westwards and surprised the Austrians by trapping them at Ulm, on the River Danube, forcing them to surrender.

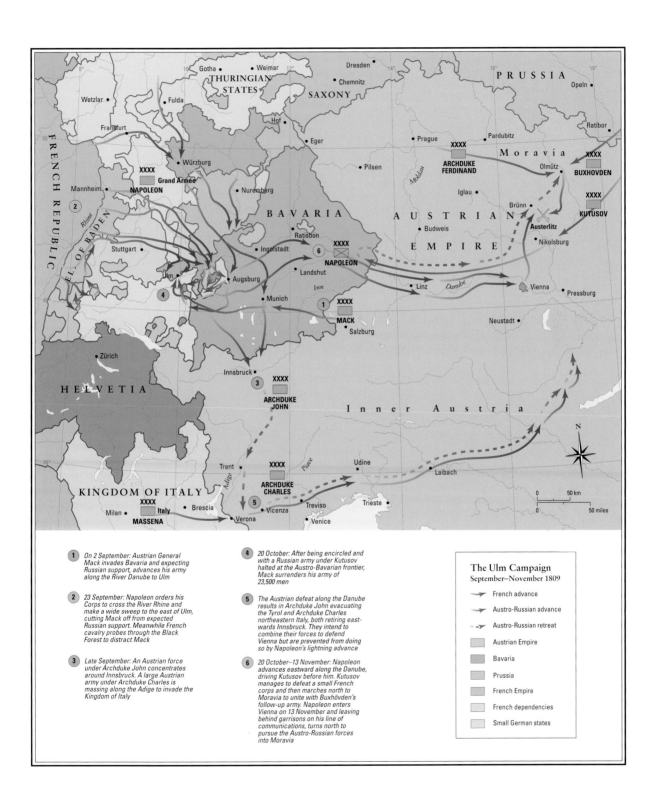

The Ulm Campaign
September–November 1809

→ French advance

→ Austro-Russian advance

⇢ Austro-Russian retreat

▨ Austrian Empire

▨ Bavaria

▨ Prussia

▨ French Empire

▨ French dependencies

▨ Small German states

1 On 2 September: Austrian General Mack invades Bavaria and expecting Russian support, advances his army along the River Danube to Ulm

2 23 September: Napoleon orders his Corps to cross the River Rhine and make a wide sweep to the east of Ulm, cutting Mack off from expected Russian support. Meanwhile French cavalry probes through the Black Forest to distract Mack

3 Late September: An Austrian force under Archduke John concentrates around Innsbruck. A large Austrian army under Archduke Charles is massing along the Adige to invade the Kingdom of Italy

4 20 October: After being encircled and with a Russian army under Kutusov halted at the Austro-Bavarian frontier, Mack surrenders his army of 23,500 men

5 The Austrian defeat along the Danube results in Archduke John evacuating the Tyrol and Archduke Charles northeastern Italy, both retiring eastwards. They intend to combine their forces to defend Vienna but are prevented from doing so by Napoleon's lightning advance

6 20 October–13 November: Napoleon advances eastward along the Danube, driving Kutusov before him. Kutusov manages to defeat a small French corps and then marches north to unite with Buxhövden's follow-up army. Napoleon enters Vienna on 13 November and leaving behind garrisons on his line of communications, turns north to pursue the Austro-Russian forces into Moravia

AUSTERLITZ CAMPAIGN 1805

ALSO KNOWN AS THE BATTLE OF THREE EMPERORS, AUSTERLITZ SAW THE RULERS OF FRANCE, AUSTRIA, AND RUSSIA LEADING THEIR MEN INTO BATTLE. THE CAMPAIGN ENDED WITH TOTAL VICTORY FOR THE FRENCH AND IS OFTEN REGARDED AS NAPOLEON'S MASTERPIECE.

Napoleon's triumph at Austerlitz on 2 December, 1805 has been called his greatest victory and a tactical masterpiece. After almost nine hours of heavy fighting, Napoleon defeated a combined force of Russians and Austrians, commanded by the Russian Tsar Alexander I. This success destroyed the Third Coalition against France.

The Russian commander in Austria, Kutusov, recognized that the newly re-formed French army was likely to win any pitched battle. He decided on a slow withdrawal hoping that the French would run out of supplies. This plan was overruled by the Tsar Alexander who ordered a halt near the village of Austerlitz. Emperor Francis II of Austria joined the army, which by 1 December numbered 60,000 Russians and 25,000 Austrians with 278 cannon. Marching against them was Napoleon with 73,000 men and 139 cannon. Alexander noticed that the French right flank was weak and ordered an attack there in great force, while the center and opposite flank stood on the defensive. This was what Napoleon had wanted. He knew the land on his right flank was marshy and that this would slow and disorder an attack. The battle began at 8am with Russian attacks led by General Buxhowden on the French right flank through dense fog. Napoleon waited until the Russians were committed to the fray, then sent Marshal Soult's corps to assault the thinly held Pratzen Heights in the allied center. As Soult came up the slope the fog lifted and blazing sun illuminated the battlefield. Soult had crushed the Austrian forces on the Pratzen Heights and broke the center of the Austro-Russian army. The allied right flank was forced to withdraw after two hours fighting. At about 2pm Buxhowden realized that he was isolated and got drunk. The Russians began to fall back in disorder, then broke and fled to be pursued by French cavalry. By 4pm the Allies had lost 27,000 killed or captured, while the French had lost only 8,000. Tsar Alexander gathered his shattered army and set off back to Russia, abandoning his allies. Napoleon's peace terms were harsh. Austria had to hand her lands in northern Italy to France. Emperor Francis had to disband the thousand-year old Holy Roman Empire and give up all claims over Germany.

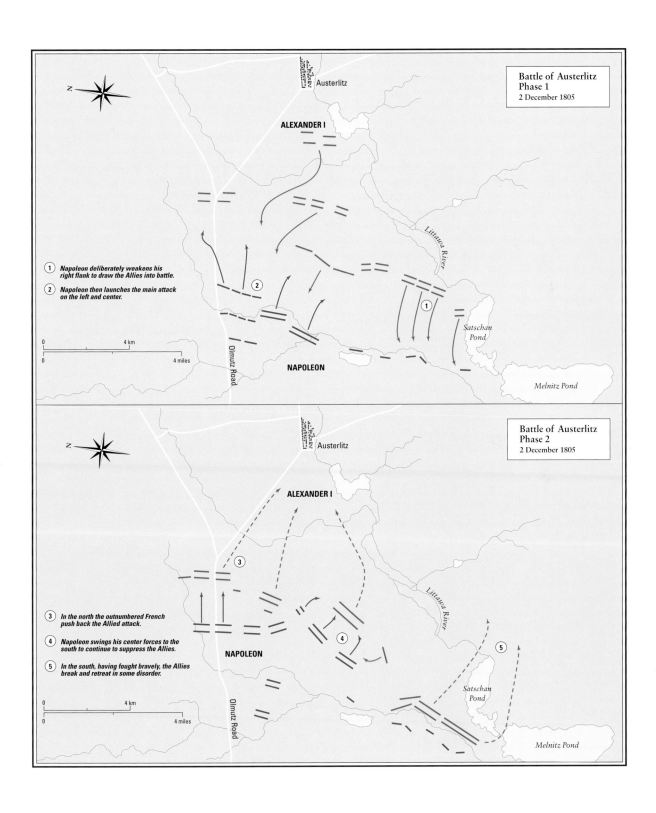

**Battle of Austerlitz
Phase 1**
2 December 1805

Austerlitz

ALEXANDER I

Littawa River

1 Napoleon deliberately weakens his
right flank to draw the Allies into battle.

2 Napoleon then launches the main attack
on the left and center.

2

1

Satschan
Pond

0   4 km
0   4 miles

Olmutz Road

NAPOLEON

Melnitz Pond

**Battle of Austerlitz
Phase 2**
2 December 1805

Austerlitz

ALEXANDER I

Littawa River

3

3 In the north the outnumbered French
push back the Allied attack.

4 Napoleon swings his center forces to the
south to continue to suppress the Allies.

5 In the south, having fought bravely, the Allies
break and retreat in some disorder.

4

5

Satschan
Pond

0   4 km
0   4 miles

NAPOLEON

Olmutz Road

Melnitz Pond

JENA TO EYLAU: 1806-1807

THE NEW FRENCH SYSTEM OF CORPS ORGANIZATION WORKED TO PERFECTION DURING THE WAR AGAINST PRUSSIA IN 1806-07. IT WAS LARGELY THE FLEXIBILITY THAT THE CORPS GAVE TO NAPOLEON'S MANEUVERING THAT ALLOWED HIM TO DEFEAT THE LARGE AND POWERFUL PRUSSIAN FORCES.

King Frederick William of Prussia had remained neutral during the War of the Third Coalition because Napoleon had promised him that a French victory would see the Kingdom of Hannover being ceded to Prussia. In August 1806, however, Frederick William heard that Napoleon had offered Hannover to Britain as part of a proposed peace treaty. The Prussian monarch was furious and declared war. The Prussian army was over 200,000 strong, but was equipped with old-fashioned weapons and used equally outdated tactics. The army commander, Ferdinand of Brunswick, was aged 71 and had failed to study the new style of warfare.

By late September, the Prussians were massed near Amberg, while Napoleon was in northern Bavaria just to the south. Brunswick divided his army into two leading the western force himself while Prince Hohenlohe commanded the eastern column. Napoleon did not realize the Prussians had divided. He led four corps against Hohenlohe's force thinking this was the entire Prussian army. Meanwhile two French corps, those of Davout and Bernadotte, were sent to march around the rear of the Prussians. Napoleon with 56,000 men and 70 cannon met Hohenlohe with 50,000 men and 120 guns at Jena. After a lengthy battle, Hohenlohe's force retreated in disorder pursued by French cavalry. Meanwhile, Davout with his 20,000 men and 40 guns had run into Brunswick with his 54,000 men and 230 cannon at Auerstadt. Davout fought a skilful delaying action, managing to frustrate the Prussian attacks.

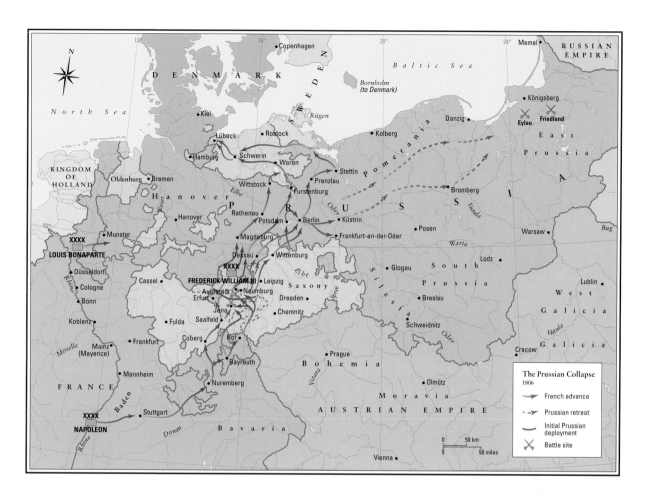

The Prussian Collapse
1806
➤ French advance
⇢ Prussian retreat
— Initial Prussian deployment
✕ Battle site

Brunswick was killed during the fighting and his deputy, Scharnhorst, then pulled back, opting for an orderly fighting withdrawal. The Prussians had lost 40,000 men and 200 cannon, while French losses totaled 11,000 men. Napoleon moved to occupy Berlin, stripping the city of food and horses for his army. He then marched east to confront the Russian army in Poland. The Russian commander, Bennigsen, had marched into Eastern Prussia to meet up with the surviving Prussian forces and it was there that Napoleon met him near the town of Eylau on 7 February. Napoleon had 53,000 men and 200 guns, while Bennigsen had 72,000 men and 400 guns. Nevertheless Napoleon launched an immediate frontal assault. The battle soon degenerated into a static slogging match with high casualties on both sides, but no clear result. Next day Bennigsen retreated, content to have fought Napoleon to a standstill. Bennigsen was finally defeated in June 1807 at Friedland, after which Tsar Alexander made peace with Napoleon.

Frederick of Prussia was undoubtedly one of the greatest commanders of his generation. He had exceptional qualities as a commander, and both the king and his armies became models for much of the remainder of Europe as a result of his outstanding victories.

14 October, 1806 saw double disaster for Prussia. At Jena, shortly after dawn, Napoleon's army struck a 51,000-strong Prussian force that was scattered over a 15-mile (2.4 km) front. By noon, the Prussians were routed. The second disaster occurred at Auerstadt, where the Prussian army disintegrated.

THE PENINSULAR WAR: 1808-1814

WHAT BEGAN AS AN ATTEMPTED COUP D'ETAT LED NAPOLEON INTO A BITTER SIX-YEAR CAMPAIGN THAT COST THE LIVES OF TENS OF THOUSANDS OF MEN, AND DRAINED FRANCE OF MONEY AND MUNITIONS. IT BECAME KNOWN AS "THE SPANISH ULCER".

In the Fall of 1807 Napoleon had sent troops to occupy Lisbon to stop the Royal Navy using that Portuguese port. In the spring of 1808 he demanded that his ally, King Charles IV of Spain, hand over a number of forts to safeguard the supply routes to Lisbon. The Spanish people were tiring of the alliance with France and regarded this as an insult. Riots broke out, forcing Charles to abdicate in favor of his son Ferdinand VII. Napoleon took advantage of the disorder to send troops to oust Ferdinand and install Napoleon's own brother, Joseph, as King of Spain. The Spanish government refused to accept the new king and ordered their army to attack the French. On 19 July 1808 a Spanish army defeated a French army of 18,000 men. The news sparked a general rebellion and persuaded the British to send an army to aid the Spanish. That in turn brought Napoleon himself with a huge army marching into Spain. The Spanish army was quickly defeated and the British forced to evacuate, after which Napoleon marched home with most of his men. Although the Spanish armies had been defeated they had not surrendered.

In April 1809 a new British army arrived in Lisbon led by Arthur Wellesley, better known by his later title of Duke of Wellington. Wellington began by securing Lisbon and fighting a series of inconclusive campaigns in Portugal. Early in 1812, Wellington captured the key border fortresses of Cuidad Rodrigo and Badajoz and then marched into Spain. On 22 July Wellington, with 30,000 British, 17,000 Portuguese, and 3,000 Spanish troops ambushed Marshal Marmont's 50,000 French troops at Salamanca. In less than an hour 15,000 Frenchmen were killed and 7,000 taken prisoner while the rest fled. The Spanish were, meanwhile, waging a destructive guerrilla campaign. They raided

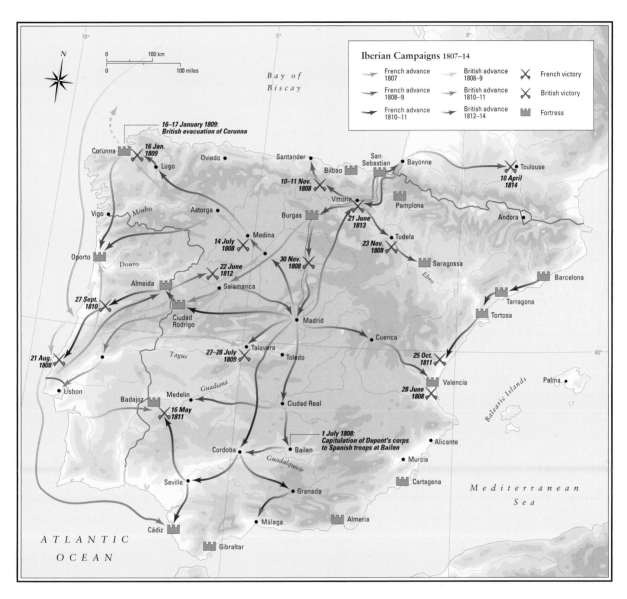

Iberian Campaigns 1807–14

- → French advance 1807
- → French advance 1808–9
- → French advance 1810–11
- → British advance 1808–9
- → British advance 1810–11
- → British advance 1812–14
- ✕ French victory
- ✕ British victory
- ⌂ Fortress

French outposts, ambushed supply convoys, and skirmished with patrols, inflicting serious losses on the French in men and equipment. On 21 June, 1813 Wellington with a combined army of 75,000 British, Portuguese and Spanish troops cornered the main French force of 58,000 under King Joseph and Marshal Jourdan at Vitoria. The French lost 10,000 men in the battle, compared to Wellington's 4,500, and in their haste to escape abandoned all their guns, supplies, and equipment. The Spanish campaign then became a series of small sieges and arduous marches as Wellington eliminated the various French garrisons in Spain. In December 1813 Wellington crossed the Pyrenees into France to lay siege to Toulouse.

Napoleon made a big mistake when he appropriated the throne of Spain on behalf of his brother Joseph. When the Spaniards rose in revolt against this blatant usurpation, the British sent an army to help them fight the French. The Peninsular War that ensued set the stage for Napoleon's final defeat.

THE STRUGGLE WITH AUSTRIA 1809

EVER SINCE DEFEAT AT AUSTERLITZ IN 1805, AUSTRIA HAD BEEN PLOTTING REVENGE AGAINST THE FRENCH. IN 1809 THEY STRUCK, CATCHING NAPOLEON BY SURPRISE AND INFLICTING HEAVY LOSSES ON THE FRENCH. THE CAMPAIGN ENDED IN STALEMATE AND A PEACE TREATY THAT NEITHER SIDE FOUND AGREEABLE.

Stripped of his title of Holy Roman Emperor, Francis II had declared himself to be Emperor Francis I of Austria instead. He spent the next four years laying his plans to gain revenge on France and return Austria to her dominant position in Germany and central Europe. Francis knew that success would depend on the Austrian army, so major reforms were brought in. He appointed his talented brother Archduke Charles to command the army, as his royal blood would force mere noblemen to back down. Charles completely re-equipped the army along French lines with heavier artillery, more cavalry, and infantry trained in assault techniques. He converted nine of the 80 infantry regiments into jaegars, or "hunters," men trained in skirmishing and scouting. The artillery was increased to 760 guns and the army as a whole increased from 200,000 to 340,000. A new drill book emphasized co-operation between cavalry, infantry and artillery. Finally the Austrians copied the British system of raising part-time volunteer regiments for local defense in times of war. These *Landswehr* troops could be used to guard bridges, garrison fortresses, and other duties, but were not considered good enough for major battles. With this new army Austria declared war in March 1809 and invaded France's ally Bavaria with 75,000 men. The French Army of the Rhine under Marshal Berthier was taken by surprise and fell back south of the Danube. The retreat was chaotic and ended with the French army divided into two sections 70 miles (113 km) apart. However, the sudden arrival of Napoleon with reinforcements dissuaded Charles from attacking further. While the Austrians had spent four years improving their army,

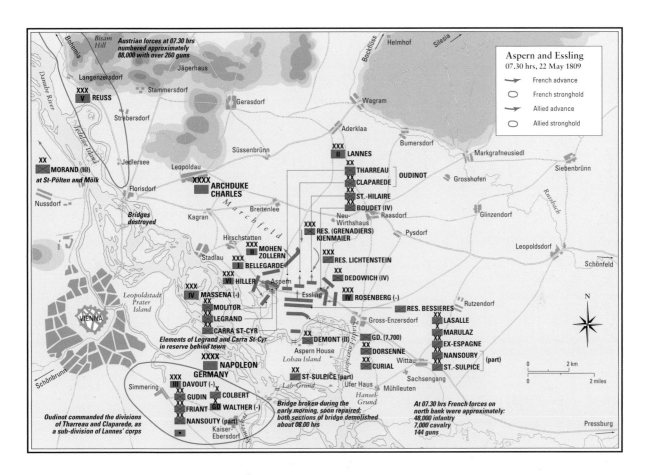

the French had spent four years engaged in arduous campaigning. These years had cost the French army thousands of men, but more seriously the constant fighting had not allowed time for the new recruits to be properly trained, nor could French industry keep up with the demands for new weapons. Napoleon was increasingly forced to rely on foreign allies. Nor could he rely on his men to carry out complex maneuvers in battle, so he had to resort to simple attack plans. Nevertheless, Napoleon mustered 120,000 men to counterattack the Austrians. On 22 April, Napoleon attacked Charles, who had camped his men on hills around the village of Eckmuhl. Napoleon sent a corps led by Davout to get around the Austrian flank, but Charles spotted the move and blocked it. Another flank move by a corp led by Lannes persuaded Charles to retreat. He fell back in good order and his cavalry defeated an assault by the French horsemen. Nevertheless, Charles found himself maneuvered toward Bohemia, exposing Vienna. On 13 May Napoleon captured Vienna, prompting Charles to advance. Napoleon with his main army was on the other side of the Danube. He decided to build pontoon bridges over the river in order to assault the Austrians. The bridges were completed on 20 May and French troops marched over to occupy the villages of Aspern and Essling. Charles was, however, waiting for his time. Having allowed a third of Napoleon's army to cross he sent down the river a number of barges filled with heavy stones that smashed the

The battle of Aspern-Essling on May 21/22, 1809, was a disturbing experience for Napoleon. His attempt at a forced crossing over the River Danube near Vienna was foiled by an Austrian army under the command of Archduke Charles. It was Napoleon's first personal defeat in a decade.

pontoon bridges and isolated the French forces that had crossed. The Austrians attacked on 21 May. After two days of fighting, Napoleon was forced back. This was the first time that Napoleon had ever been defeated in battle and it sent shockwaves through Europe.

Six weeks later Napoleon advanced again. This time he got over the Danube without being interrupted and launched his army, now 154,000 strong, at the 158,000 Austrians that Charles had gathered. On the evening of 5 July the armies met near the village of Wagram, but the main battle did not start until dawn next day. Napoleon pushed forward on the right, but his left was defeated and was falling back. To stabilize the situation he ordered 23 batallions of infantry to attack in a massive column — the largest ever seen — against the Austrian center. The attack worked, but at the loss of 8,000 men, and punched a hole through the Austrian army. Tellingly, the French heavy cavalry then advanced, but were unable to exploit the gap properly as the Austrians brought up their cavalry to stabilize their line. At this point the corps led by Marshal Davout suddenly appeared on a line of hills on the Austrian left. This outflanked the main Austrian line, and put Davout in a position from which he could sweep down on the Austrian rear. Archduke Charles ordered a retreat, managing to disengage and pull back in good order. He took with him 7,000 French prisoners, 21 captured guns, and 12 captured flags. Both sides had lost over 30,000 men. Charles advised his brother to make peace, while he kept his army intact and on the march to persuade Napoleon to agree to more favorable terms than would otherwise have been the case. In itself this was a new strategy. Instead of facing Napoleon in open battle, his enemies were learning to avoid giving him the chance to deliver a knockout blow and instead opted for longer campaigns that would wear down the strength of the French.

The campaign of 1809 was a turning point in the Napoleonic Wars. Before it, Napoleon had never lost a campaign, after it he never won a campaign. France was running out of men, money, and equipment but Napoleon would not recognize these facts and still planned offensive campaigns.

A romantic contemporary portrayal of Napoleon Bonaparte. The Battle of Waterloo was Napoleon's final defeat. In his poem *Ode to Napoleon*, Lord Byron (1788-1824) wrote of Napoleon in exile "… but yesterday A King! … and now thou art a nameless thing: So abject—yet alive!"

Far right: The despots of Europe were mortally afraid of Napoleon Bonaparte and the danger that he would spread the liberal ideas of the French Revolution throughout the continent. By 1810, the Bonapartes had a firm grip on extensive territories and there was plenty more for Napoleon to conquer.

French Empire
1810
Under direct rule by
Napoleon
Under rule by members
of Napoleon's family
Dependent state

0   200 km
0   200 miles

N

*Norwegian
Sea*

NORWAY

S W E D E N

Shetland Is.

Christiana

Stockholm

Gothenburg

Gotland

Baltic Sea

Helsingfors
Reval

St. Petersburg

Novgorod

Riga

Smolensk

Vilna

RUSSIAN
EMPIRE

*North
Sea*

DENMARK
Copenhagen

Åland Is.

Königsberg
East
Prussia

to Sweden

*Helgoland
1807–14 to Br.*

Hamburg
*1807–10
to Fr.*

P R U S S I A

Brandenburg

Berlin

GR. DUCHY
OF WARSAW

Warsaw

*Bialystok
1807 to Russia*

Edinburgh

Dublin

UNITED KINGDOM
OF GREAT BRITAIN
AND IRELAND

Amsterdam
1810 to Fr.

London

Antwerp
Brussels   Cologne

Channel Is.

WESTPHALIA

Erfurt

Frankfurt

Prague

Bohemia

Cracow

Silesia

Galicia

Ternopol

CONFEDERATION
OF THE RHINE

Munich

Vienna

AUSTRIAN

EMPIRE

Bessarabia

Paris

Orléans

Bern
HELVETIA

Geneva
1798–1814 to Fr.

Milan

Styria

Buda ●● Pest

H u n g a r y

Transylvania

Moldavia

FRANCE

Tours

Carinthia

Illyrian Provinces

Banat

Wallachia

Bucharest

Bordeaux

Lyon

Turin

Venice

ITALY

Adriatic Sea

Belgrade

OTTOMAN
EMPIRE

Bulgaria

Toulouse

Marseille

LUCCA
Tuscany
Florence

Papal
States

Rome

Corsica

Sofia

MONTENEGRO

Macedonia

Constantinople

Oporto

PORTUGAL

Madrid

Catalonia
1808–13 to Fr.

Barcelona

Balearic Is.

S P A I N

NAPLES

Naples

SARDINIA

*Corfù
1807–14 to Fr.*

Thessaly

*Aegean
Sea*

Athens

Lisbon

Gibraltar
to Spain

Ceuta
to Spain

Mediterranean   Sea

Palermo

SICILY

Ionian Is.

occupied by Britain

Crete

MOROCCO

Oran

Algiers

ALGERIA

Bona

Tunis

Tunisia

*Malta
1800 to Br.*

ATLANTIC
OCEAN

THE RUSSIAN CAMPAIGN 1812

AFTER MAKING PEACE IN 1807, RUSSIA'S TSAR ALEXANDER HAD BEEN GROWING INCREASINGLY FEARFUL OF NAPOLEON AND HIS AMBITIONS. HE WATCHED THE WAR OF 1809 AND DECIDED TO REFORM HIS ARMY ALONG THE LINES PIONEERED BY AUSTRIA.

Napoleon's *Grand Armée* advanced into Russia on 24 June, 1812 and after crossing the River Nieman reached Kovno the same day. Four days later, Napoleon's forces overran Vilna. Moving on, the *Grand Armée* entered Vitebsk on 29 July and on 17 August, captured Smolensk, losing some 9,000 men in the process.

N apoleon decided to attack Russia before Tsar Alexander could conclude an alliance with Britain and, perhaps, Austria. For the showdown with Russia Napoleon mustered an army of 600,000 men, but 400,000 of these came from allies who were serving more or less under duress and had no real desire to invade Russia. Napoleon knew this and earmarked them for garrison and patrol duty, keeping his 200,000 Frenchmen for the key task of fighting battles. He crossed the border in June. Alexander had about 250,000 men, whom he put under the command of the veteran General Kutusov. Kutusov recognized that his main task was to avoid being defeated, so he opted to withdraw deep in to Russia rather than fight a battle on the borders. He wanted to force Napoleon to leave behind troops to garrison towns and forts, thus weakening his main army. Meanwhile the long supply lines would leave the French short of food and ammunition. Finally, on 7 September, Kutuzov calculated that the French were sufficiently weakened. He stopped to fight at Borodino with 121,000 men. Napoleon could field 130,000 men. The resulting battle was a bloody stalemate that saw the French losing 30,000 men and the Russians 45,000. Realizing he had miscalculated, Kutuzov retreated once more and abandoned Moscow. Napoleon entered the Russian capital in triumph, but it was a hollow victory. He had no food and the Russians stubbornly refused to come to terms. Instead, Napoleon was forced to retreat. The return march became a nightmare as food ran out and the bitter Russian winter closed in — and the Russian army harried the invaders mercilessly. By the time Napoleon regained friendly territory his losses had been enormous. About 350,000 men had died, either in battle or due to disease, while another 100,000 had been taken prisoner. His army had ceased to exist as a major force.

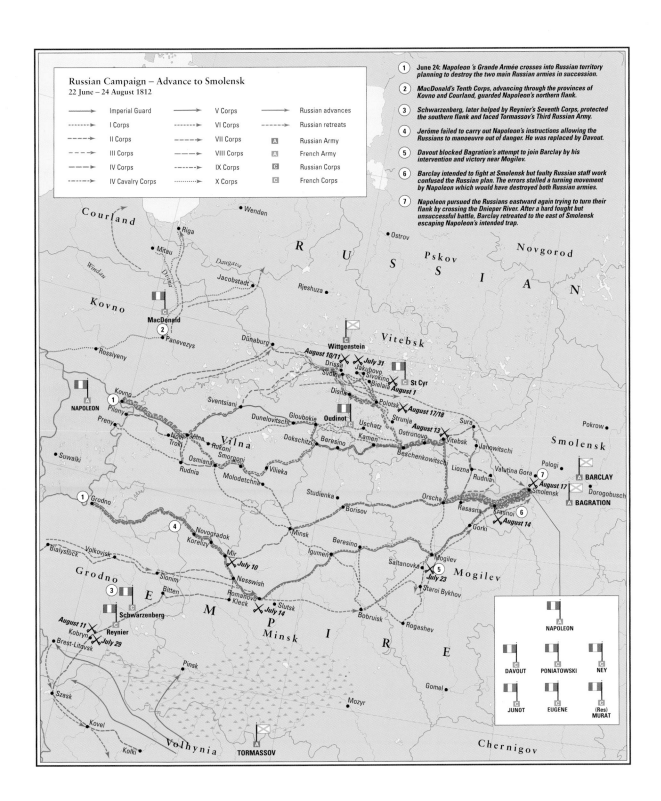

Russian Campaign – Advance to Smolensk
22 June – 24 August 1812

→ Imperial Guard
⇢ I Corps
⇢ II Corps
⇢ III Corps
⇢ IV Corps
⇢ IV Cavalry Corps
→ V Corps
⇢ VI Corps
⇢ VII Corps
⇢ VIII Corps
⇢ IX Corps
⇢ X Corps
→ Russian advances
⇢ Russian retreats
🅰 Russian Army
🅰 French Army
🅒 Russian Corps
🅒 French Corps

1. June 24: Napoleon's Grande Armée crosses into Russian territory planning to destroy the two main Russian armies in succession.

2. MacDonald's Tenth Corps, advancing through the provinces of Kovno and Courland, guarded Napoleon's northern flank.

3. Schwarzenberg, later helped by Reynier's Seventh Corps, protected the southern flank and faced Tormassov's Third Russian Army.

4. Jérôme failed to carry out Napoleon's instructions allowing the Russians to manoeuvre out of danger. He was replaced by Davout.

5. Davout blocked Bagration's attempt to join Barclay by his intervention and victory near Mogilev.

6. Barclay intended to fight at Smolensk but faulty Russian staff work confused the Russian plan. The errors stalled a turning movement by Napoleon which would have destroyed both Russian armies.

7. Napoleon pursued the Russians eastward again trying to turn their flank by crossing the Dnieper River. After a hard fought but unsuccessful battle, Barclay retreated to the east of Smolensk escaping Napoleon's intended trap.

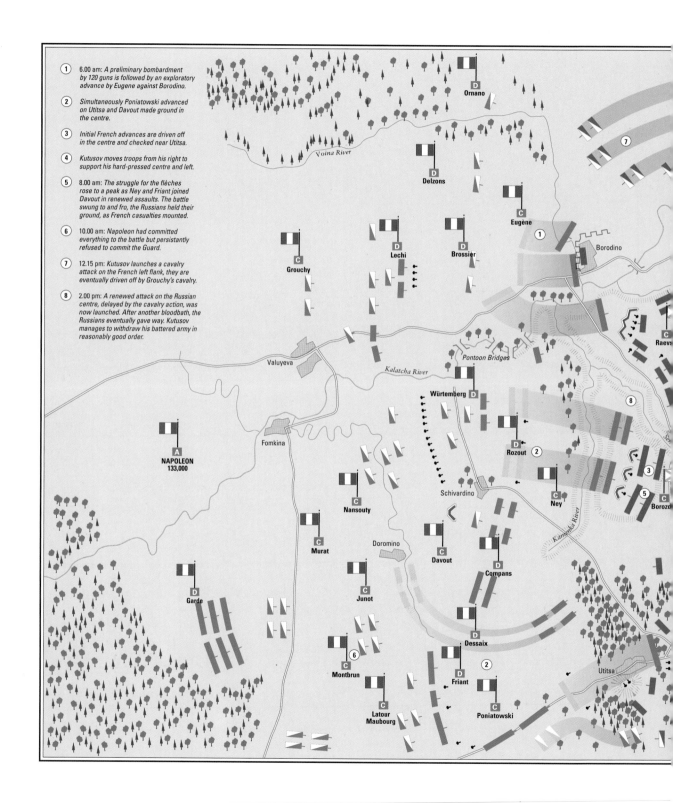

① 6.00 am: A preliminary bombardment by 120 guns is followed by an exploratory advance by Eugene against Borodino.

② Simultaneously Poniatowski advanced on Utitsa and Davout made ground in the centre.

③ Initial French advances are driven off in the centre and checked near Utitsa.

④ Kutusov moves troops from his right to support his hard-pressed centre and left.

⑤ 8.00 am: The struggle for the flèches rose to a peak as Ney and Friant joined Davout in renewed assaults. The battle swung to and fro, the Russians held their ground, as French casualties mounted.

⑥ 10.00 am: Napoleon had committed everything to the battle but persistently refused to commit the Guard.

⑦ 12.15 pm: Kutusov launches a cavalry attack on the French left flank, they are eventually driven off by Grouchy's cavalry.

⑧ 2.00 pm: A renewed attack on the Russian centre, delayed by the cavalry action, was now launched. After another bloodbath, the Russians eventually gave way. Kutusov manages to withdraw his battered army in reasonably good order.

Ornano

Voina River

Delzons

Eugène

Borodino

Raevs

Lechi

Brossier

Grouchy

Valuyeva

Kalatcha River

Pontoon Bridges

Würtemberg

Fomkina

NAPOLEON 133,000

Rozout

Schivardino

Ney

Borozo

Nansouty

Murat

Doromino

Davout

Compans

Kameka River

Garde

Junot

Dessaix

Montbrun

Friant

Poniatowski

Utitsa

Latour Maubourg

The Battle of Borodino
7 September 1812

- French commander
- Russian commander
- **A** Army
- **C** Corps
- **D** Division
- Prepared defensive position
- Artillery
- Infantry unit
- Cavalry unit

Unit movements:
- First position
- Later position
- Direction of movement
- Retreat

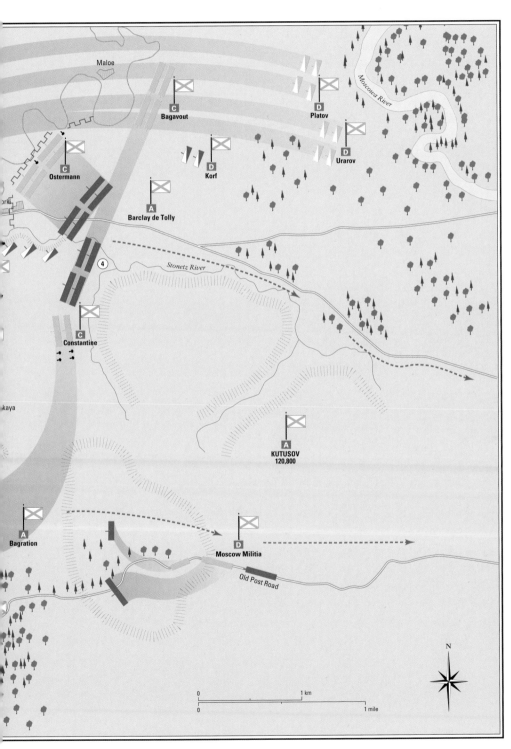

Maloe

Bagavout **C**

Platov **D**

Ostermann **C**

Korf **D**

Urarov **D**

Barclay de Tolly **A**

Stonetz River

④

Constantine **C**

kaya

KUTUSOV
120,800 **A**

Bagration **A**

Moscow Militia **D**

Old Post Road

Moscova River

N

0 ___ 1 km
0 ___ 1 mile

At Borodino, a village 75 miles (320 km) west of Moscow, Napoleon's Grande Armée attacked the Russians under General Mikhail Kutuzov. The fighting was ferocious, making Borodino the bloodiest confrontation of Napoleon's ill-fated Russian invasion. The Russians suffered 40,000 casualties, and withdrew the following day, but the battle itself was a stalemate.

Leipzig to Waterloo: 1813-1815

THE RUSSIAN CAMPAIGN OF 1812 DESTROYED NAPOLEON'S ARMY, BUT HE WAS NOT YET READY TO GIVE IN. THE CAMPAIGNS OF 1813 ARE CONSIDERED TO BE AMONG NAPOLEON'S BEST, BUT HE MET DISASTER IN 1815 AT WATERLOO.

Returning to France in the winter of 1812, Napoleon knew that the Russians would attack the following year. He ordered that the men due to be called up in the summers of 1813 and 1814 should report for duty in February 1813. He stripped the navy of sailors, forming them into 24 infantry battalions, and of guns to be converted into field pieces. By March Napoleon had a new army of 200,000 men ready to march into Germany. The army was, however, poorly trained and desperately short of horses. The Russians were wary of facing Napoleon outside Russia. They advanced only once Prussia had joined them and they had been assured of Austrian neutrality. They entered Germany in April and on 2 May were confronted by Napoleon at Lutzen. The battle ended in stalemate, but the Russians and Prussians withdrew and asked for an armistice. The Russians used the time to gain new allies, including Austria and Sweden, while Napoleon recruited and trained more men.

The war began again in September 1813. The allies had taken the significant step of appointing a supreme commander for all their armies. They chose the Austrian Prince Schwarzenberg. Although a reasonable general, Schwarzenberg's main talent was for getting on with people, which ensured coordination between the various allied armies. His strategy for the coming campaign was simple. Any general who found himself faced by Napoleon in person would retreat, but any general facing another French commander would attack. Throughout the summer of 1813 the allies stuck to Schwarzenberg's plan until by October, Napoleon had concentrated his forces at Leipzig. The allies had no choice but to attack him. On 16 October, Napoleon had 185,000 men. The allies had 160,000 men, but 60,000 Prussians

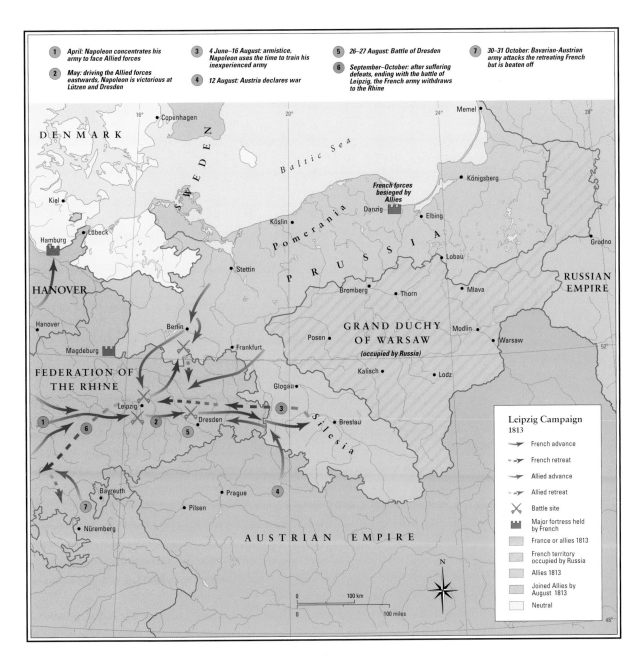

1　April: Napoleon concentrates his army to face Allied forces

2　May: driving the Allied forces eastwards, Napoleon is victorious at Lützen and Dresden

3　4 June–16 August: armistice, Napoleon uses the time to train his inexperienced army

4　12 August: Austria declares war

5　26–27 August: Battle of Dresden

6　September–October: after suffering defeats, ending with the battle of Leipzig, the French army withdraws to the Rhine

7　30–31 October: Bavarian-Austrian army attacks the retreating French but is beaten off

Leipzig Campaign 1813

➤ French advance
➤ French retreat
➤ Allied advance
➤ Allied retreat
✕ Battle site
🏰 Major fortress held by French
　 France or allies 1813
　 French territory occupied by Russia
　 Allies 1813
　 Joined Allies by August 1813
　 Neutral

under Marshal Blucher were marching to join them, as were other contingents adding up to another 50,000 men. The battle raged throughout the 16, 17 and 18 October with neither side gaining much advantage. On 19 October Napoleon accepted defeat and retreated.

The following months were taken up with a series of complex marches and maneuvers that saw little fighting as Napoleon sought to divide his enemies and pounce on any isolated units, while the

In February and March 1813, a new coalition comprising Russia, Prussia, Sweden, and Britain joined together to destroy Napoleon's power in Europe.

allies warily refused to be lured forward and retreated whenever faced by a French army. By the end of February the French army was disintegrating due to exhaustion, sickness, and hunger. On 31 March the Russian army marched into Paris. Napoleon had already abdicated and was on board a ship heading for the U.S. to seek safety. The ship was intercepted by the British navy and Napoleon captured. He was sent into exile on the island of Elba with a bodyguard of 1,000 men.

The allies forced France to accept back the Bourbon dynasty that they had overthrown in the French Revolution 20 years earlier. This was unpopular, so the French welcomed Napoleon when he escaped from Elba and returned to Paris in the spring of 1815, promising to retain the social and political reforms of the revolution.

The allies responded by declaring war on Napoleon, not on France, and mustering their armies to invade France in August. Napoleon struck first in June by marching against the British army of the Duke of Wellington and the Prussian army of Marshal Blucher, both of which were in Belgium. Napoleon had an army of 123,000 well-equipped veterans. Wellington's army of 100,000 included large numbers of new recruits and 43,000 Dutch, who were suspected of favoring Napoleon. Blucher's 115,000 men included 14,000 Saxons who refused to fight and other German contingents of doubtful loyalty. The campaign opened with a brilliant march by Napoleon that isolated 80,000 Prussians at Ligny, where they were defeated on 16 June.

Napoleon then turned on the British. Wellington fell back on the ridge of high ground at Waterloo. This was to be Napoleon's last battle. It also marked the end of the period known as the "Hundred Days," which started in March 1815 when he returned to France from his exile in Elba.

Napoleon attacked on 18 June, but knew that Blucher, with his regrouped Prussians, was marching to aid Wellington, so he tried to batter a way through the British line with a massed assault by 17,000 infantry. The Dutch fled after a brief fight, but Wellington brought up British infantry and cavalry to plug the gap. Napoleon then battered the British line with heavy artillery fire, causing Wellington to pull his men back out of sight behind the ridge. Misinterpreting this as a retreat, Marshal Ney led the massed French cavalry forward in a series of fruitless charges. By 6pm the Prussians were starting to arrive on the French right flank. In a desperate attempt to break Wellington's line, Napoleon sent forward his elite Guard infantry, supported by field artillery. Realizing that the flank of the Guard was not protected by cavalry, Colonel Colborne marched his 52nd Foot to the attack while the French were occupied attacking the British guards to their front. The move shattered the French attack, which fell back in disorder. Seeing the famous French Old Guard in retreat and the Prussians on their flank, the French army collapsed and fled. The Napoleonic wars were finally over.

Napoleon, once master of half of Europe, was forced to end his days on the Atlantic island of St. Helena, an embittered and lonely fate for such a great commander. Yet he left a legacy of military reform which changed the nature of warfare, and was admired even by his opponents. When asked who was the greatest general of his day, Wellington responded: "In this age, in past age, in any age: Napoleon." The Duke of Wellington himself became a national hero in Britain; the defeat of Napoleon being entirely down to his organizational skills and tactical ability, as well as the determination of his troops. His later career saw him hold almost every position in high office, eventually becoming Prime Minister, and he became known on his death as the "Iron Duke."

The Battle of Waterloo marked the end of the "Hundred Days" since Napoleon's escape from confinement on the island of Elba. Napoleon, it seems, was on the brink of victory and might well have won but for the fortuitous last-minute arrival of the Prussians led by General Gebhard Leberecht von Blücher.

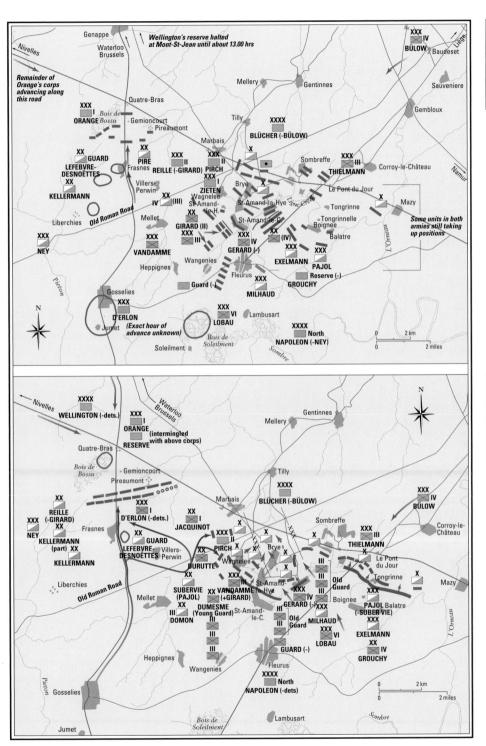

Waterloo Phase 1
About 14.00 hrs, 16 June 1815

→ French advance
→ Allied advance
◯ French concentration

Waterloo Phase 2
21.00 hrs, 16 June 1815

→ French advance
→ Allied advance
⇢ Allied retreat
◯ French concentration
⬭ Allied concentration

CHAPTER VII— THE UNITED STATES 1790-1860: THE RESTLESS GIANT

WHILE THE ATTENTION OF EUROPE WAS FOCUSED ON THE LONG YEARS OF WAR INVOLVING REVOLUTIONARY AND NAPOLEONIC FRANCE, MAJOR DEVELOPMENTS WERE TAKING PLACE ON THE FAR SIDE OF THE ATLANTIC THAT WOULD HAVE PROFOUND AND LASTING LONG-TERM EFFECTS.

In 1790 a census of the newly independent United States of America showed that the country had a population of 3,929,625, of which 697,642 were slaves. This made the country relatively small by the standards of the day, but its potential for growth was enormous. In 1793 the prosperity of the US received a boost with the invention of the cotton gin. This was a machine for removing seeds from cotton far more cheaply and quickly than was possible by hand. The amount of cotton grown, and the money made from the crop, boomed enormously. The Continental Army that had fought the British to win independence for the United States was disbanded as soon as the war ended, any need for armed men being met by the militias of the various states. It was a force of 12,500 militia men who were led by George Washington to put down a rebellion in western Pennsylvania in 1794.

The uprising was led by farmers who objected strongly to a 25 percent tax on whisky, the main Use to which their grain was put. Tax collectors had been beaten up, tarred, and feathered by rioting farmers. However, the farmers dispersed when the militia arrived. Rather more serious was the war against the Northwest Confederation of native tribes including the Shawnee, Delaware, Miami, and Potawatami. The colorful commander "Mad Anthony" Wayne led 3,000 men into the forests to attack the enemy stronghold on the banks of the Maumee River. The Confederation leader, Chief Blue Jacket, had fortified the position with felled trees — so the resulting fight was dubbed the Battle of Fallen Timbers. Wayne won a convincing

victory and in the subsequent peace treaty annexed vast swathes of territory to the United States.

In 1803 the USA doubled in size when President Jefferson purchased the vast Louisiana Territory from France. The land covered almost the entire western drainage basin of the Mississippi River and its various tributaries. About the same time previously thinly populated areas such as Tennessee, Kentucky, and Ohio were formed into states as their populations and prosperity rose and the native tribes were defeated in war.

The USA largely stayed out of the European wars, but in 1812 declared war against Britain after the Royal Navy intercepted American ships heading for Europe. At first, the US suffered humiliating defeats in Canada and saw its capital city of Washington burned. However the tide of war soon changed. The *US Constitution* met *HMS Guerriere* off Canada on 19 August and in a bitter gunfight inflicted so much damage that the British ship first surrendered then had to be abandoned. The *Constitution* went on to sink a second British warship in December, this time off Brazil. Finally, on 8 January, the US army won the Battle of New Orleans despite being heavily outnumbered.

The impressive performance of the new country's armed forces made it a player on the world stage. Thereafter the US government concentrated on the commercial development of its vast territories. The US army was kept busy fighting a series of wars against the native tribes, defeating the Cherokee, Seminole, Winnebago and others. The demand for land was continuous, and westward expansion of the United States put unrelenting pressure on Native Americans.

The Battle of Fallen Timbers, an illustration from *Harper's* magazine, 1896. This decisive battle in 1794, in which the Shawnee tribe were defeated, led to the Treaty of Greenville. The Northwestern Indians were forced into peace as the newly independent USA asserted its power.

THE UNITED STATES 1848-1860

THE MID 19TH CENTURY SAW A REVOLUTION IN THE TECHNOLOGY OF WAR, THOUGH THE ARMIES THAT USED THE NEW WEAPONS TOOK SOME TIME TO CATCH UP WITH THE DEVELOPMENTS. NOWHERE WAS THIS PROCESS CLEARER THAN IN THE USA.

O f the two forms of warfare, land and sea, it was at sea that the most obvious changes were occurring. In the 1830s a revolution began when steam engines were developed that were small enough to fit into a ship yet powerful enough to push it through the seas. These early steamships used paddlewheels mounted on the sides of the ship to transfer the engine power to the water. A steam warship could move even when the wind was not blowing and was able to move directly into the wind without the need to tack from side to side. This gave a steamer a much better chance of getting its guns to bear on the enemy than did a sailing ship. There were, however, disadvantages as well. The most obvious was that the engine and paddlewheels took up so much space that a frigate mounting 46 guns when a sail-only craft, could mount only 16 guns when converted to steam. By the 1850s steam engines powering screws were replacing those with paddles in naval warships. These had the advantage that the engines could be located lower down in the hull and that there were no side paddles to take up large amounts of space that could otherwise house guns.

At this period the US Navy commissioned a number of modern, large warships but due to financial constraints they were left half finished on the slipways, ready to be rushed into service if needed. Instead the US Navy hired civilian steamships to accompany its sail warships on campaign. Some acted as supply craft, but others were tugs that were to tow the warships into action in conditions of calm. The largest of the naval campaigns came in 1858 when a task force was sent to demand an apology and indemnity after Paraguayan forces had fired on a US ship in 1855. Matthew Perry also took a number of steamships to Japan in 1853. At about the same time technological improvements to arms were slowly changing land warfare. The US Army had the advantage of the New England arms industry, led by Samuel Colt.

Between 1784 and 1894, the American Indian Nations made a series of 375 treaties in which they ceded their lands to the Us government. There were, though, other ways of obtaining Indian land. One was the Indian Removal Act of 1830, another the Indian Appropriations Act of 1871.

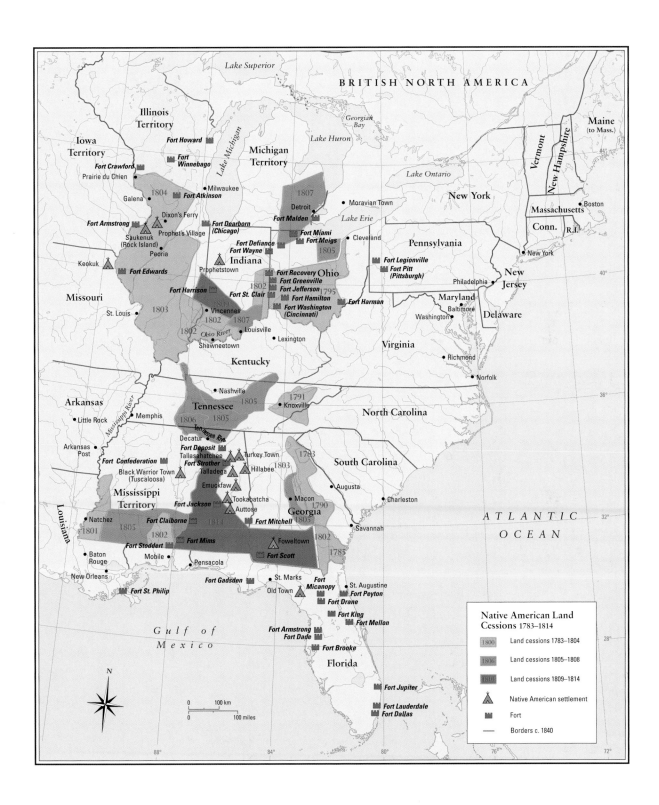

Lake Superior

BRITISH NORTH AMERICA

Illinois
Territory

Georgian
Bay

Lake Huron

Maine
(to Mass.)

Iowa
Territory

Fort Howard

Lake Michigan

Michigan
Territory

Lake Ontario

New York

Fort
Winnebago

Fort Crawford
Prairie du Chien

Vermont

New Hampshire

1804
Fort Atkinson

Milwaukee

1807

Massachusetts
• Boston

Galena

Detroit

New York

Dixon's Ferry

Fort Malden

Lake Erie

Conn.
R.I.

Fort Armstrong

Fort Dearborn
(Chicago)

Fort Miami

• Moravian Town

Pennsylvania

Saukenuk
(Rock Island)

Prophet's Village

Fort Meigs

• Cleveland

New
York

Peoria

Fort Defiance
Fort Wayne

1805

Fort Legionville
Fort Pitt
(Pittsburgh)

• Philadelphia

New
Jersey

Keokuk

Indiana

Prophetstown

Fort Recovery
Fort Greenville

Ohio

Maryland

Fort Edwards

Fort Harrison

1802
Fort St. Clair

Fort Jefferson
Fort Hamilton

1795

Fort Harman

Baltimore

• Washington

Delaware

Missouri

1809
Vincennes

Fort Washington
(Cincinnati)

St. Louis

1803

1802
1807

Virginia

1802
Ohio River

• Louisville

• Richmond

Shawneetown

• Lexington

• Norfolk

Kentucky

Arkansas

• Nashville

1805

1791

Memphis

1806
1805

Knoxville

North Carolina

• Little Rock

Tennessee

Tennessee River

Arkansas
Post

Decatur

Fort Deposit

1783

South Carolina

Fort Confederation

Tallasahatchee
Fort Strother

Turkey Town

1803

Black Warrior Town
(Tuscaloosa)

Talladega

Hillabee

• Augusta

Mississippi
Territory

Emuckfaw

Tookabatcha

Fort Jackson

Auttose

Macon

• Charleston

1790

Georgia

• Natchez

Fort Claiborne

1814

1805

ATLANTIC

1801

1805

Fort Mitchell

1802

OCEAN

Louisiana

1802

Fort Mims

• Baton
Rouge

Fort Stoddert

Mobile

Foweltown

1802

Savannah

32°

Pensacola

Fort Scott

1785

• New Orleans

Fort Gadsden

• St. Marks

Fort
Micanopy

St. Augustine

Fort St. Philip

Old Town

Fort Peyton

Fort Drane

Fort King

Fort Mellon

Gulf   of

Mexico

Fort Armstrong
Fort Dade

28°

Fort Brooke

N

Florida

Fort Jupiter

0   100 km

Fort Lauderdale
Fort Dallas

0   100 miles

**Native American Land
Cessions 1783–1814**

1800	Land cessions 1783–1804
1806	Land cessions 1805–1808
1810	Land cessions 1809–1814
△	Native American settlement
⊞	Fort
—	Borders c. 1840

88°   84°   80°   76°   72°

The revolver developed by Colt in 1835 proved to be a favored sidearm for officers. Ten years later US manufacturers perfected a French idea to produce the modern copper-cased, gas-tight cartridge with a rim at the base. They inserted into this a hollow-based lead bullet that expanded on firing to fit tightly into the grooves of a long-barreled rifle. This resulted in the development of a gun that was more accurate over a longer range and could be fired more often in a given time than previous models. The US Army was slow to re-equip with this new rifle due to the fact that it was relatively unreliable and often jammed.

This reluctance to adopt new weapons was increased by the lack of technologically advanced enemies for the US Army to fight. The main conflict of these years was with the Comanche and associated tribes on the southern plains, particularly northwestern Texas. With the exception of the Battle of Little Robe Creek in 1858 these campaigns were ones of skirmishes, scouting and raids. Lightly armed, mounted units and self-sufficient infantry columns proved ideal for this sort of warfare.

The US Army was aware, however, that it might need to fight a more modern style of warfare and prepared for it. The senior officers generally preferred the theories and ideas of the Swiss Baron Jomini. Jomini studied the wars of Napoleon and concluded that it was essential to gain the initiative early in a campaign by means of swift, decisive attacks, backed up by adequate logistical support. He believed that once an army had an advantage it would be able to keep it so long as it was adequately supplied. The theories of the Prussian general von Clausewitz — that war was inherently unpredictable and a commander had to be ready to adapt his plans in mid-campaign — were largely ignored. Thus it was that the US Army of the mid-19th century was one that laid great stress on the offensive and on properly managed supply lines, but generally had comparatively old-fashioned arms and tactical handbooks.

Photograph, right: Oglaga warriors, from the Pine Ridge Indian Reservation in South Dakota, stage the planning of a raid. The weapons of the Native American tribes were fairly primitive, allowing the US forces an easy victory.

The Americans acquired some new lands in the West by buying it, as in the Gadsden Purchase of 1853 which brought them parts of Arizona and New Mexico. Others were gained by war, as after the Mexican-American War and a long series of battles against the native Americans.

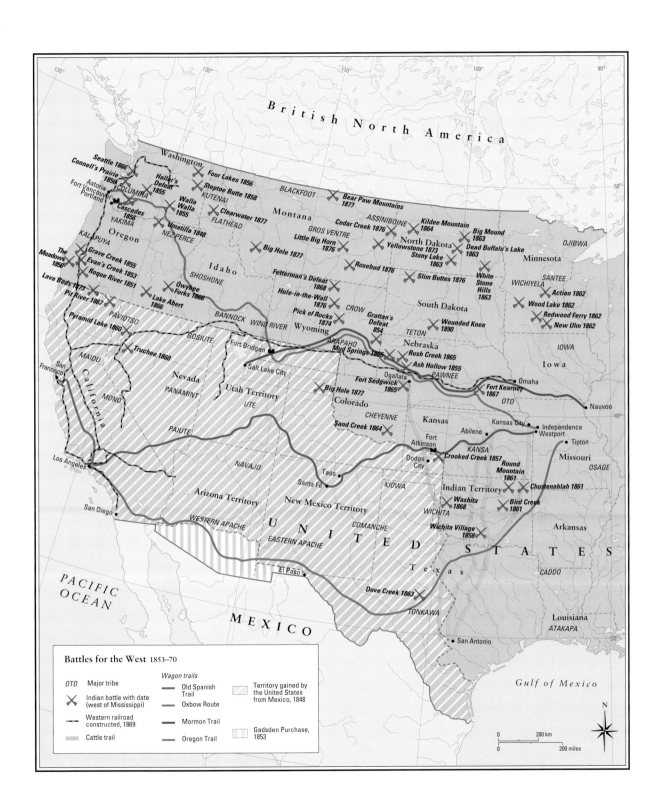

Battles for the West 1853–70

OTO   Major tribe

✗   Indian battle with date (west of Mississippi)

╌╌╌   Western railroad constructed, 1869

▨   Cattle trail

Wagon trails

━━━   Old Spanish Trail

━━━   Oxbow Route

━━━   Mormon Trail

━━━   Oregon Trail

▨   Territory gained by the United States from Mexico, 1848

▨   Gadsden Purchase, 1853

N

0   200 km

0   200 miles

US-MEXICAN WAR 1847-1848

THE WAR OF 1847-48 WAS THE FIRST TIME SINCE THE WAR OF 1812 THAT THE US ARMED FORCES HAD TO FACE AN ENEMY UNIVERSALLY EQUIPPED WITH FIREARMS AND TRAINED IN EUROPEAN STYLE WARFARE, BUT MOST AMERICANS EXPECTED AN EASY VICTORY.

T he war had its origins in the 1836 conflict that brought independence to Texas and was famous for the siege of the Alamo. The Mexican government had never accepted Texan claims to the land between the Rio Grande and Rio Nueces. In 1845 Texas became a state of the USA, so the USA inherited the border dispute. President Polk moved 3,500 regular soldiers under Zachery Taylor up to the Rio Nueces. He also sent John Slidell to Mexico City with an offer to pay $25 million dollars for the disputed land in Texas, plus the Mexican provinces of Alta California and Santa Fe. The Mexicans turned down Slidell's offer in brusque terms, so the envoy returned to Washington in disgust. In Texas, Taylor had built a small fort in the disputed territory. On 25 April 1846 the Mexicans ambushed a patrol of us cavalry in the disputed lands, killing 11 men and capturing the rest. Polk told Congress that the Mexicans had "shed American blood on American soil" and on 13 May war was declared.

Meanwhile, General Mariano Arista led 3,400 Mexicans to attack Taylor's fort, prompting him to march his main force over the Nueces to relieve the surrounded men. The resulting Battle of Palo Alto was dominated by artillery. Taylor used a battery of horse artillery — light guns pulled by fast horses — to hammer the Mexican army, which then fell back into broken country where the horse artillery could not operate. The Mexicans opened fire with their own heavier guns, halting the American advance. Next day Arista retreated over the Rio Grande. Meanwhile, in Alto California, local US settlers had taken matters into their own hands, declaring the province to be independent of Mexico. A force of 60 US soldiers under Captain John Fremont was diverted from Oregon to California to support the American settlers against the local Mexicans. The Americans won the climactic Battle of La Mesa on 9 January, after which the

The Mexicans were big-time losers in the war against the United States fought between 1846 and 1848. They were not only defeated, but lost large areas of territory — for example California, which had been colonized by the Spaniards and, after the end of Spanish rule in 1823 inherited by Mexico.

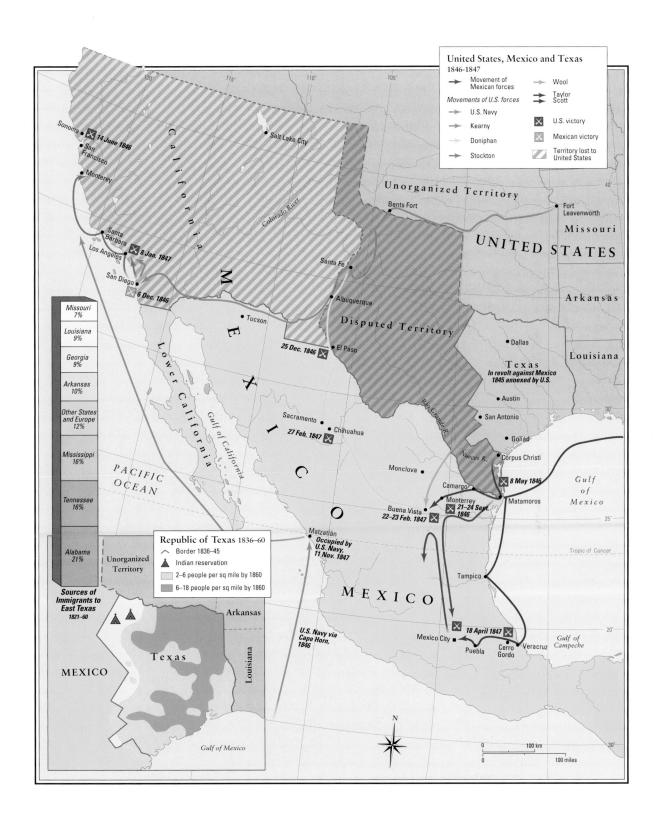

United States, Mexico and Texas
1846-1847

→ Movement of Mexican forces
→ Wool

Movements of U.S. forces
→ U.S. Navy
→ Taylor / Scott
→ Kearny
→ Doniphan
⊠ U.S. victory
→ Stockton
⊠ Mexican victory
▨ Territory lost to United States

Sonoma · ⊠ **14 June 1846**
San Francisco ·
Monterey ·
Santa Barbara ·
Los Angeles · ⊠ **8 Jan. 1847**
San Diego ·
⊠ **6 Dec. 1846**

Salt Lake City ·

Bents Fort ·

Unorganized Territory

Fort Leavenworth ·

UNITED STATES

Missouri

Santa Fe ·
Albuquerque ·

Disputed Territory

Arkansas

Tucson ·

25 Dec. 1846 ⊠ · El Paso

Dallas ·

Louisiana

T e x a s
*In revolt against Mexico
1845 annexed by U.S.*

Austin ·

San Antonio ·

Sacramento ·
27 Feb. 1847 ⊠ · Chihuahua

Goliad ·

Monclova ·
Nueces R.
Corpus Christi ·

Camargo · ⊠ **8 May 1846**

Matamoros ·

Buena Vista · Monterrey · ⊠ **21–24 Sept. 1846**
⊠ **22–23 Feb. 1847**

Gulf of Mexico

Matzatlán
Occupied by U.S. Navy, 11 Nov. 1847

Tropic of Cancer

Tampico ·

M E X I C O

Mexico City ■ ⊠ **18 April 1847** ⊠
Puebla · Cerro Gordo · Veracruz ·

Gulf of Campeche

Missouri 7%
Louisiana 9%
Georgia 9%
Arkansas 10%
Other States and Europe 12%
Mississippi 16%
Tennessee 16%
Alabama 21%

Sources of Immigrants to East Texas 1821–60

Lower California

PACIFIC OCEAN

Gulf of California

M E X I C O

Republic of Texas 1836–60
⌃ Border 1836–45
🛖 Indian reservation
▢ 2–6 people per sq mile by 1860
▨ 6–18 people per sq mile by 1860

Unorganized Territory

Arkansas

U.S. Navy via Cape Horn, 1846

Texas

Louisiana

MEXICO

N

Gulf of Mexico

0 — 100 km
0 — 100 miles

Mexicans retreated from California.

Taylor had meanwhile invaded across the Rio Grande with 2,300 regular troops and a large number of volunteers from Louisiana, Texas, and other southern states. On 21 September he was met by 10,000 Mexicans under Pedro de Ampudia from the fortified town of Monterrey. The resulting battle cost heavy casualties on both sides and ended in an armistice under which Ampudia agreed to retreat on condition that he did so with full honors of war. At this point the former president of Mexico, Santa Anna, was given command of the Mexican army. He promptly launched a military coup to make himself president again, then set out to fight the invaders.

The armies met at Buena Vista on 22 February 1847, a battle which ended in virtual stalemate, though Santa Anna soon retreated. Polk was concerned about Taylor's growing popularity, boosted by newspaper reports of the fighting sent back over telegraph wires by reporters with the army. He therefore sent 12,000 regulars and volunteers under General Winfield Scott to attack the port of Vera Cruz, withholding supplies from Taylor. Scott captured the fortified port after a 12-day siege and began a march on Mexico City. He was met at the pass of Cerro Gordo by Santa Anna with 12,000 men and heavy cannon. Scott first scouted the enemy position, then outflanked it with cavalry and his own cannon. The Mexicans fled, leaving behind 1,000 dead and 3,000 prisoners.

By September Scott was approaching Mexico City, but by this time his army was down to half its original strength. Thousands of men had been lost to yellow fever and dysentery while large numbers of the volunteers had deserted, some joining the Mexicans and others going on looting forays.

Scott's path was blocked at Chapultepec, a former Aztec fortress, by Mexicans in entrenched positions on a steep hill. After a preliminary artillery barrage, the American infantry attacked, along with a force of US Marines. The attack succeeded after intense close quarter fighting and by 6pm the Mexicans were fleeing back into Mexico City pursued by the Americans. Scott hanged dozens of the volunteers who had changed sides. With their capital captured and army defeated, the Mexicans asked for peace

terms. Polk demanded all the territory he had earlier offered to buy for $25 million, but now offered half that. Mexico handed over 500,000 square miles (1.3 million square kilometers) of land, almost two thirds of its territory. The Republican Congressional Committee described the war as "Feculent, reeking Corruption" and "one of the darkest scenes in our history- a war forced upon our and the Mexican people by the high-handed Usurpations of Presbyterian folk in pursuit of territorial aggrandizement."

The Battle of Monterrey took place on 23 September 1846. US forces under the command of Zachary Taylor defeated General Pedro de Ampudia and the Mexican Army.

Latin American Independence 1800-1811

THE SERIES OF WARS THAT LED TO THE INDEPENDENCE OF THE SPANISH AND PORTUGUESE COLONIES IN THE AMERICAS CAUSED MASSIVE LOSS OF LIFE AND WIDESPREAD DESTRUCTION. IT ALSO LED TO YEARS OF POLITICAL INSTABILITY AND ECONOMIC HARDSHIP.

B y 1800 large numbers of Spanish peoples living in the Americas had bitter complaints about the way they were governed. The governors appointed by the monarchs in Europe were often corrupt, inefficient, and rarely interested in the colonies they ran other than as a means to their own promotion. On 5 July 1811 the Spanish colony of Venezuela declared itself to be independent of Spain, prompting an invasion by Spanish troops based in neighboring colonies. This caused the local landowners and aristocracy to abandon the cause of independence, but the poorer people continued the struggle under the leadership of Simon Bolivar. What had begun as a war for independence thus acquired a political dimension as workers fought land-owners. After a long struggle, marred by atrocities on both sides, Bolivar secured Venezuelan independence from Spain at the Battle of Carabobo on 24 June 1821. Meanwhile the people of Colombia, Panama and Ecuador had likewise rebelled, been defeated, rebelled again, and finally gained independence from Spain. Together with Venezuela, these colonies formed the new country of Gran Colombia in 1822. The new state did not last long, fragmenting in 1830, though Panama stayed with Colombia until the 20th century.

In southern South America the wars of independence were led by the local aristocracy. José de San Martin was an officer in the Spanish army when in 1812 he seized Buenos Aires for the rebels. By 1816 Argentina had won its independence. San Martin then raised a volunteer army to cross the Andes and aid the Chileans in their struggle, winning victory by 1818. Paraguay and Uruguay both achieved independence quickly in 1811, largely because the Spanish armies were busy elsewhere. Brazil, meanwhile, had achieved independence peacefully by becoming a kingdom ruled by the brother of the King of Portugal.

Simon Bolivar, known as The Liberator, was a Venezuelan nobleman who facilitated independence movements against the Spanish rulers in South America. In 1821, he became president of the Colombia Republic (Colombia, Venezuela, and Ecuador) and later helped eject the Spaniards from Peru and from Bolivia, which was named after him.

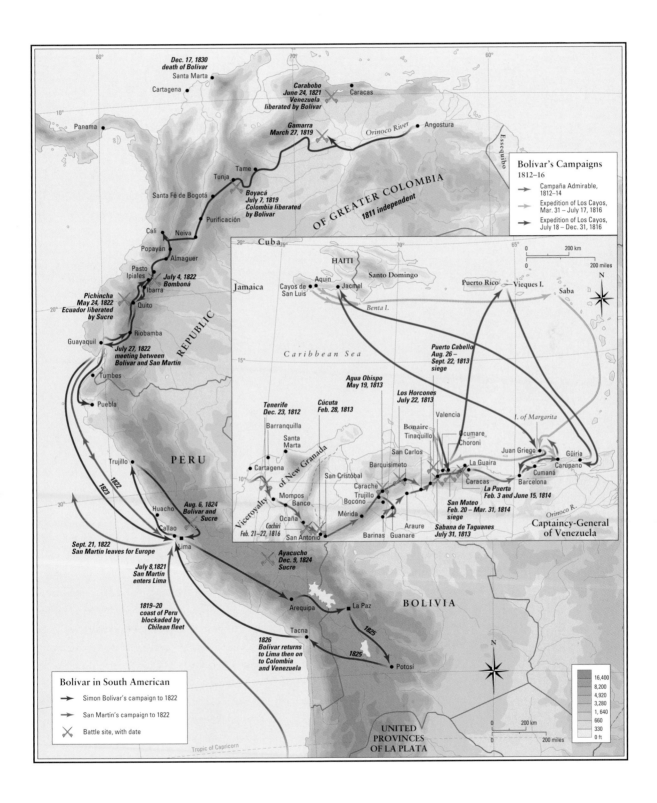

Dec. 17, 1830
death of Bolívar
Santa Marta
Cartagena

Carabobo
June 24, 1821
Venezuela
liberated by Bolívar
Caracas

Panama

Gamarra
March 27, 1819
Orinoco River
Angostura

Tame
Tunja

OF GREATER COLOMBIA

Santa Fé de Bogotá

Boyacá
July 7, 1819
Colombia liberated
by Bolívar

Purificación

1811 independent

Cali
Neiva

Popayán
Almaguer

Pasto
Ipiales
July 4, 1822
Bomboná
Ibarra

REPUBLIC

Pichincha
May 24, 1822
Ecuador liberated
by Sucre
Quito

Riobamba

Guayaquil
July 27, 1822
meeting between
Bolívar and San Martin

Tumbes

Puebla

Bolívar's Campaigns
1812–16
→ Campaña Admirable,
1812–14
→ Expedition of Los Cayos,
Mar. 31 – July 17, 1816
→ Expedition of Los Cayos,
July 18 – Dec. 31, 1816

Cuba
HAITI
Santo Domingo
Puerto Rico   Vieques I.
Saba
Jamaica
Cayos de
San Luis   Aquin   Jacmel
N
Benta I.
Caribbean Sea

Puerto Cabello
Aug. 26 –
Sept. 22, 1813
siege

Agua Obispo
May 19, 1813

Los Horcones
July 22, 1813

Tenerife
Dec. 23, 1812
Cúcuta
Feb. 28, 1813

Valencia

Barranquilla
Santa
Marta

Bonaire
Tinaquillo

Ocumare
Choroni

I. of Margarita

San Carlos

Cartagena   of New Granada
San Cristóbal
Barquisimeto

La Guaira   Juan Griego   Güiria
Cumaná
Carúpano

Viceroyalty

Mompos
Banco

Carache
Trujillo
Bocono

Caracas
La Puerta
Feb. 3 and June 15, 1814
Barcelona

Ocaña

Mérida

San Mateo
Feb. 20 – Mar. 31, 1814
siege

Orinoco R.

Cochiri
Feb. 21–22, 1816

San Antonio
Barinas   Guanare
Araure
Sabana de Taguanes
July 31, 1813

Captaincy-General
of Venezuela

Trujillo
1822
1823

PERU

Huacho
Callao
Lima

Aug. 6, 1824
Bolívar and
Sucre

Sept. 21, 1822
San Martin leaves for Europe

July 8, 1821
San Martin
enters Lima

1819–20
coast of Peru
blockaded by
Chilean fleet

Ayacucho
Dec. 9, 1824
Sucre

Arequipa   La Paz

BOLIVIA

Tacna
1825

1826
Bolívar returns
to Lima then on
to Colombia
and Venezuela

1825
Potosí

N

Bolívar in South American
→ Simon Bolívar's campaign to 1822
→ San Martín's campaign to 1822
✗ Battle site, with date

16,400
8,200
4,920
3,280
1,640
660
330
0 ft

Tropic of Capricorn

UNITED
PROVINCES
OF LA PLATA

200 km
200 miles

CHAPTER VIII — THE INDUSTRIAL AGE: WARS OF THE INDUSTRIAL AGE 1800s

FROM THE 1820S ONWARD THE PACE OF TECHNOLOGICAL ADVANCE IN TERMS OF WEAPONS AND TRANSPORT BEGAN TO HAVE AN INCREASING EFFECT ON WARFARE. PREVIOUSLY MOST OPPONENTS HAD GONE TO WAR WITH ROUGHLY COMPARABLE TYPES OF EQUIPMENT, BUT INCREASINGLY ONE SIDE OR THE OTHER HAD A TECHNICAL EDGE THAT WAS SOMETIMES CRUCIAL.

The industrial revolution produced a mass of technological developments that were soon being applied to the design and manufacture of weapons. Bigger and better weapons that were cheaper and more reliable were continually being developed, though the armies of the world were often slow to appreciate the opportunities being offered to them and even slower to adapt tactics to suit the new weapons. In 1841, the Prussian army adopted a breech-loading gun firing a bullet packed into a cartridge and fired by a firing pin operated by a trigger. In 1870 the French likewise adopted a breech-loading rifle, the "chassepot" and most other armies followed within a few years. All these weapons were single-shot until the 1890s when magazines holding up to six bullets began to be perfected. The rifle thus became a weapon accurate to over 600 yards that could be fired six times a minute. Breech loading artillery did not enter service until the French used them in 1859. The German Krupps works produced a weapon around 1870 that was more accurate and fired a conoidal shell of modern design. In 1884 the more powerful "smokeless" gunpowder greatly increased the range of artillery. All this technical development reached its modern form at the end of the century with the French 75mm field gun. This had a mechanism that absorbed the recoil of the barrel without the gun itself being pushed backward. The machine gun first appeared as the big, heavy and unreliable Gatling gun in the USA

Vintage photograph showing an early machine gun from the Boer War in South Africa.

in 1862. The Gatling, like many early machine guns, was multi-barrelled. As the barrels were rotated, each in succession came level with the magazine, where a cartridge was dropped into its loading-tray. The cartridge was then forced into the chamber by a rammer, was fired and had its spent case extracted as the barrels turned. The French also adopted a machine gun of their own. The Mitrailleuse was developed in the artillery workshop at Meudon, and in 1865 it went into mass production: 215 guns were available by 1 January 1870. The weapon looked like a conventional field-piece, mounted on a wheeled carriage, yet the gun's performance was disappointing, perhaps due to the lack of training of its handlers. Machine guns finally became useful with the innovations of the American Hiram Maxim. The Maxim was the first machine gun that did not depend on the firer operating its mechanism; merely on keeping the trigger pressed. The British adopted the gun in 1891, with many others following suit.

At sea the development of large caliber, breech-loading guns combined with steel armor and screw propulsion came together in HMS Iris, a British warship launched in 1877. It made all other warships obsolete instantly and set the pattern for warship design down to the present day. Armies were also quick to recognize the military potential of the railways for transporting weapons and troops. Railways, and the specialist troops that maintained them, became an indispensible part of mobilisation plans.

CRIMEAN WAR 1854-1856

THE CRIMEAN WAR OF 1854-6 BECAME FAMOUS FOR ITS HEROISM AND CHAOTIC LOGISTICAL FAILURES. IN MANY WAYS IT WAS THE LAST OF THE TRADITIONAL EUROPEAN WARS, FOUGHT FOR LIMITED PURPOSES BETWEEN PROFESSIONAL ARMIES USING OLD-STYLE WEAPONS. WAR WOULD NEVER BE THE SAME AGAIN.

For over a century the Russian Empire had been expanding south at the expense of the decaying Turkish Empire. A new Russian victory in the Battle of Sinope in 1853 threatened to cause a complete Turkish collapse and so destabilize the entire Middle East. France and Britain put together a hurried alliance of states and declared war on Russia. Having stopped the Russian land advance, the allies decided to destroy the main Russian naval base on the Black Sea: Sevastopol. From the start, the Crimean War had an air of black comedy, and was described as "one of the bad jokes of history." An allied army landed on the Crimea in September 1854 and at once ran into problems. Supplies had to be brought across the Mediterranean and the Black Sea to be unloaded at the port of Balaclava, which was too small to cope. The allies won the Battle of the Alma on 20 September, though at great cost. On 20 October the Russians sallied out from Sevastopol in an attempt to capture Balaclava. This battle was to become famous for two incidents. The first was the "Thin Red Line" when a force of red-coated British infantry drawn up in line halted a massed charge of Russian cavalry by disciplined and accurate rifle fire in volleys. The second was the "Charge of the Light Brigade", when 600 British light cavalrymen were unleashed against the wrong target and charged several batteries of well positioned Russian artillery. The cavalry suffered heavy loss, but charged home with perfect discipline. The siege of Sevastopol dragged on through the winter. The allies suffered terribly from disease, hunger and freezing cold while the Russians were snug and warm in their barracks. The British medical services almost collapsed but were saved by an influx of new equipment and a team of nurses led by Florence Nightingale. Sevastopol finally surrendered on 9 September 1855 and peace was agreed in February 1856. The Turkish Empire had been successfully propped up, but Russian ambitions remained undimmed.

The immediate cause of the Crimean War of 1853-1856 was a dispute between France and Russia over access to the Christian holy places in Jerusalem. The real cause was the unwillingness of France and her ally, Britain, to see Russia become more powerful in the Near East.

The Black Sea 1853–54

→ Initial Turkish advances and attacks

→ Initial Russian advances and attacks

→ Allied attacks

Russian Empire

Pro-Russian

Ottoman Empire, allied territory

Pro-Allies territory

Neutral territory

1 July 1853: *Russia advances into Romanian principalities*

2 4 October 1853: *Ottoman Empire declares war and attacks Russian army on the Danube*

3 30 November 1853: *Russian naval squadron attacks Turkish ships at Sinope destroying them completely*

4 January–February 1854: *Greeks invade Ottoman Empire*

5 20 March 1854: *Russians cross the Danube and besiege Silistria*

6 April 1854: *Anglo-French forces occupies Piraeus*

7 10 April 1854: *Anglo-French force lands at Varna to support the Turks*

8 16 April 1854: *Anglo-French force bombards Odessa*

9 April–June 1854: *Austria gathers an army and with Ottoman permission advances into Wallachia to threaten the Russian forces*

10 *Under the combined threat of Austria, Britain, France and the Ottoman Empire, the Russian army withdraws*

11 7 September 1854: *Allied force leaves Varna in 150 ships, with the objective of occupying Sebastopol*

12 13–18 September 1854: *Allied force lands 30 miles north of Sebastopol*

13 20 September 1854 – 9 September 1855: *Allies besiege Sebastopol and fight several major land battles in the vicinity*

14 16 October 1855: *Anglo-French force, including the first use of ironclads, bombards and forces capitulation of the Russian forts at Kinburn*

15 September–November 1855: *Kars is besieged by Russian army, eventually surrendering on 26 November*

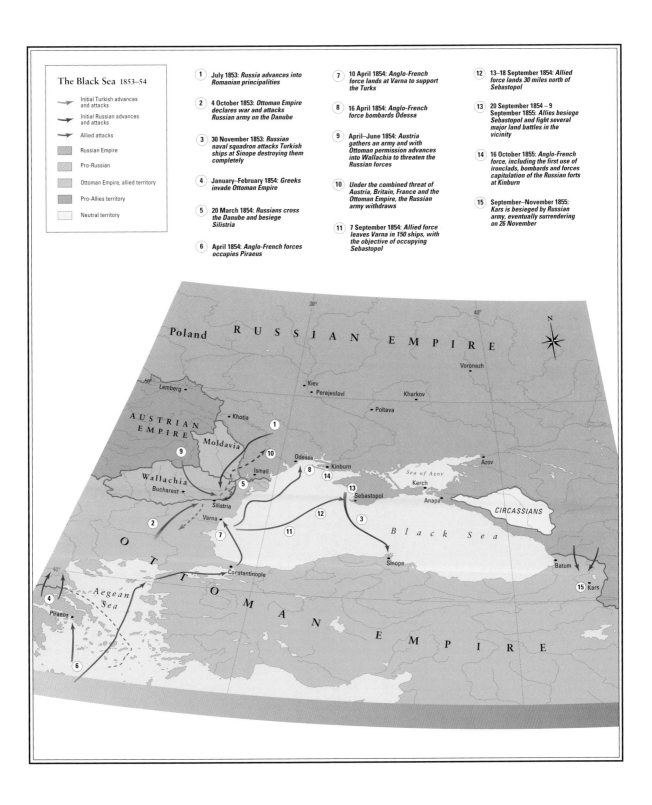

EUROPEAN WARS 1859-1866

AFTER LONG YEARS OF PEACE FOLLOWING THE NAPOLEONIC WARS, EUROPE WAS CONVULSED BY MOVEMENTS FOR NATIONAL UNIFICATION AND FREEDOM THAT FIRST FOUND EXPRESSION AS REVOLUTIONARY UPHEAVALS, THEN FROM 1859 AS WARS BETWEEN STATES FIELDING ARMIES CARRYING INDUSTRIALLY PRODUCED WEAPONS.

I n 1848 rebellions broke out in nearly all the small states of Italy. These aimed to introduce some democracy, to liberalize social and economic conditions and to unite Italian-speaking peoples into one state. The Austrians at this date ruled Trentino, Venetia and Lombardy directly while Austrian puppets – mostly relatives of the Austrian Emperor — ruled in Parma, Romagna, Modena and Tuscany. At first the revolts were successful. The rulers were driven into exile or forced to concede democratic reforms. King Charles Albert of Piedmont, a relatively liberal kingdom in northwestern Italy, sensed Austrian weakness and invaded Lombardy. His advance was halted at the Battle of Custoza where Austrian reinforcements marched over the Alps and defeated the Piedmontese. The defeat of Piedmont took the impetus out of the revolts. Over the course of the next year the autocratic rulers, with Austrian help, reimposed their rule and abrogated any democratic reforms. The events of 1848 had convinced most Italians that any future success for democracy and liberalism would come only under the leadership of Piedmont. However, the new king of Piedmont, Victor Emmanuel II, feared the Austrian armies and refused to co-operate with any of the plans put to him.

In 1859, Emperor Napoleon III of France was looking for a small foreign war in which he could emulate the success of his famous uncle Napoleon I. His agents told him that the Italian states were ripe for another rebellion and that Austria was suffering internal problems. Napoleon III therefore offered to help Piedmont defeat Austria in return for Nice and Savoy. Victor Emmanuel agreed and war

German Unification
1815–71

Prussia, 1815

Border of German Confederation, 1815

Prussia gains by 1867

Border of North German Confederation, 1867

German states joining the Confederation in 1871

Border of German Empire, 1871

German Confederation invades Denmark, 1864

Prussia invades Austria, 1866

Prussia invades France, 1870

Battle site

1 Grand Duchy of Oldenburg
2 Mecklenburg-Strelitz
3 Schaumburg-Lippe
4 Lippe-Detmold
5 Duchy of Brunswick
6 Duchy of Anhalt
7 Thuringian States
8 Waldeck
9 Lichtenberg
10 Principality of Hohenzollern
11 Grand Duchy of Luxembourg

was declared on 26 April 1859. The peoples of Tuscany, Parma and Modena at once rose in rebellion, tying down the Austrian garrisons located in those states and safeguarding the southern flank of the French-Piedmontese advance. Napoleon III then played his trump card. He moved thousands of French soldiers, complete with guns, ammunition and support services across Piedmont by rail. The French therefore arrived much sooner and far fresher than the Austrians had expected. Austrian reinforcements, coming over the Alps by the traditional method of marching, found themselves outmanoeuvred. The local Austrian forces based in Lombardy and Venetia were defeated at Magenta on 4 June. The battle cost the French under MacMahon 4,000 men, but the Austrians under Gyulai suffered more heavily and were thrown back in a hasty retreat first to Milan, and then east toward Verona. The retreating Austrians met their advancing reinforcements at Solferino and hurriedly occupied a strong defensive

In 1815, after the Napoleonic Wars, there was a move towards limited German unification when the number of German states was reduced to 39 and allied in a Confederation led by Austria. The militaristic state of Prussia had other ideas and in 1871, Germany was unified under Prussian leadership.

position on the hills above the town. The Emperor Franz Josef himself had arrived to boost the morale of his men, and the experienced commander Scholick was in operational command. The Austrians had 120,000 men and 451 guns, which were positioned with care on the hills and among the woods.

The advancing allies arrived with 118,000 men and 320 guns. MacMahon surveyed the heights, then decided to assault with his right wing, while holding his left wing back under Niel as the Austrian positions there seemed impregnable. It was 24 June. The French artillery included breech-loading cannon while both sides had infantry armed with rifles. Despite the increases in both range and accuracy of these weapons, the commanders on both sides Used densely packed formations of infantry to launch frontal attacks in Napoleonic style. The fighting went on until dusk, when the French finally succeeded in breaking the Austrian position. Scholick fell back that night to keep his army intact. Casualties were enormous, totaling about 20% on both sides. The carnage was made worse by the fact that neither side had medical services able to cope with such high casualties. The Swiss doctor Henri Dunant was appalled and founded the Red Cross as a consequence. The Austrian retreat proved to be chaotic, but the allies were unable to follow up the victory as there were few railways in Venetia, and the French had not brought enough horses and wagons to supply their army.

The resulting peace treaty gave Lombardy to Piedmont, which went on to annex Parma, Romagna, Modena, Tuscany and some lands belonging to the Pope the following year. In 1866 Austria found itself confronted by Prussia, which wanted to unify Germany under the Prussian king. The architect of the plan was the Prussian nobleman Otto von Bismarck who had persuaded most German states that it was in their economic and cultural self-interest to accept Prussian hegemony. The Prussian commander, Helmuth von Moltke, was convinced he could defeat Austria by using railways to move his armies at speed, and telegraph to communicate even faster.

The Austrians were goaded into declaring war on 21 June 1866, whereupon von Moltke put his plan into action. At first all went well with three widely separated Prussian armies making a well co-ordinated advance into Saxony and Bohemia. Austrian commander General von Benedek had barely got his army of 170,000 men and 600 guns gathered at Sadowa when his cavalry scouts reported that all three Prussian armies were converging on him. Von Benedek took up a strong defensive position and was attacked at dawn on 31 July by two the Prussian forces. As at Solferino, both sides used outdated tactics with infantry in dense formations. The Prussian rifle proved to be more accurate and fast-firing than the Austrian version, so the Austrians suffered heavier casualties, especially when they attempted a cavalry charge to exploit a temporary gap opened in the Prussian lines by artillery fire. At 2pm the third Prussian army arrived and attacked the Austrian right flank. Realising that to stay would invite utter disaster, von Benedek ordered a retreat leaving behind 20,000 casualties, 20,000 prisoners and 178 guns. The Prussians had lost just 10,000 men. As at Solferino, the victors found themselves unable to exploit the victory to the full as their supply system was unable to cope with both the need to evacuate wounded and the need to bring up fresh ammunition and supplies. The Prussian advance was slow, giving the Austrians time to reform and bring up reinforcements.

Rather than risk a second clash, both sides preferred to make peace. Austria agreed to allow Prussia to form a confederation of north German states, but lost no territory herself. These united German states would become profoundly influential in the coming years.

Italy had been a collection of small independent states ever since the break up of the Roman Empire in around 476AD. The move towards Unification — the Risorgimento — began after the defeat of Napoleon and the Congress of Vienna in 1815 and was completed by 1870.

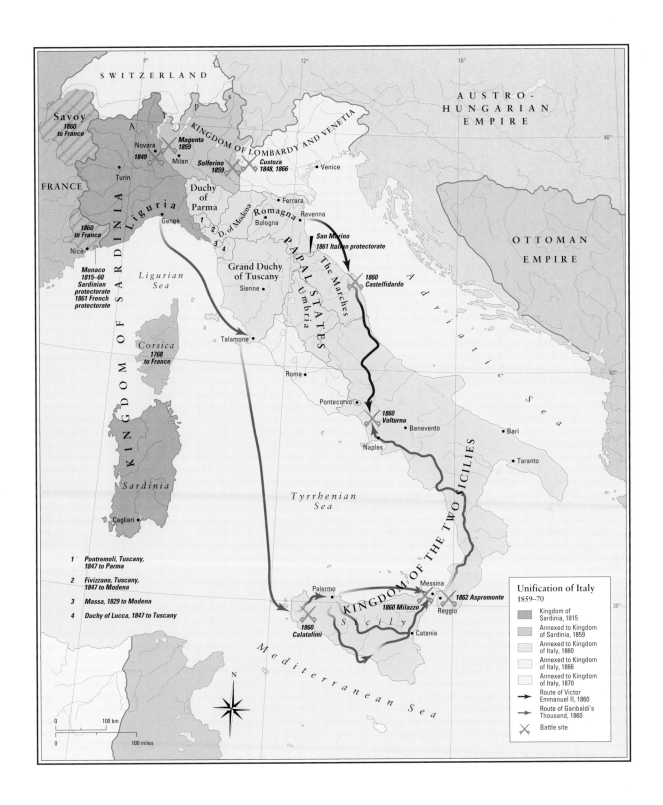

SWITZERLAND

Savoy
1860
to France

FRANCE

KINGDOM OF LOMBARDY AND VENETIA

Magenta
1859

Novara
1849

Milan

Solferino
1859

Custoza
1848, 1866

Venice

AUSTRO-
HUNGARIAN
EMPIRE

Turin

Duchy
of
Parma

Ferrara

1860
to France

Nice

Genoa

1 2
D. of Modena
3 4

Bologna

Romagna

Ravenna

San Marino
1861 Italian protectorate

OTTOMAN
EMPIRE

Monaco
1815–60
Sardinian
protectorate
1861 French
protectorate

Ligurian
Sea

Grand Duchy
of Tuscany

Umbria

The Marches

1860
Castelfidardo

Sienne

Corsica
1768
to France

Talamone

Rome

Sardinia

Pontecorvo

1860
Volturno

Benevento

Bari

Naples

Taranto

Cagliari

Tyrrhenian
Sea

1 Pontremoli, Tuscany,
   1847 to Parma

2 Fivizzano, Tuscany,
   1847 to Modena

3 Massa, 1829 to Modena

4 Duchy of Lucca, 1847 to Tuscany

Palermo

Messina

1862 Aspromonte

1860 Milazzo

Reggio

1860
Calatafimi

Sicily

Catania

Mediterranean Sea

N

0   100 km

0   100 miles

Unification of Italy
1859–70

Kingdom of
Sardinia, 1815

Annexed to Kingdom
of Sardinia, 1859

Annexed to Kingdom
of Italy, 1860

Annexed to Kingdom
of Italy, 1866

Annexed to Kingdom
of Italy, 1870

Route of Victor
Emmanuel II, 1860

Route of Garibaldi's
Thousand, 1860

Battle site

AMERICAN CIVIL WAR 1861-1865

THE WAR BETWEEN THE STATES OF THE USA WAS THE ONLY LARGE-SCALE WAR FOUGHT IN THE CENTURY OF RELATIVE PEACE BETWEEN 1815 AND 1914. IT IS VIEWED AS BEING A TRANSITIONAL WAR WHICH IN SOME WAYS HARKED BACK TO THE NAPOLEONIC ERA, BUT IN OTHERS FORESHADOWED THE WORLD WARS OF THE 20TH CENTURY.

The US Civil War was fought by officers trained at West Point where they had been taught the theories of Jomini, learned tactical deployments based on those of Napoleon, and studied the railway-based campaigns fought in Europe over the previous couple of decades. They had also taken Dunant's views to heart and medical services in the US military were among the best in the world. In the harsh classroom of the battlefield they would realize that none of these had really prepared them for the realities of war in the industrial age.

The reasons for the outbreak of the war were rooted in decades-old disputes about the powers and rights of the federal US government contrasted with those of the individual states. The issue that gave the spark was slavery, supported in the agrarian southern states but opposed in the industrialized northern states. The dispute led several southern states to pass legislation to secede from the USA, the north retaliated by declaring that no state could legally secede. The first shot came from southern artillery batteries firing on Fort Sumter to enforce its surrender. The armed forces of the USA at this date dictated the early phases of the war. The federal government had control of the US Army and US Navy, but was faced by the fact that many of the best officers and men left at once to return to their southern states. Each state had its own militia, but these were of variable quality with widely differing levels of training and equipment. The southern, or Confederate, States began the war with around 120,000 men who were generally of better fighting quality than the 150,000 men fielded by the northern or Unionist States. The Confederates had no navy to speak of, while the Unionists had all 80 ships of the US Navy, albeit that most

The first shots in the Civil War were fired on April 12, 1861 when the Confederates attacked Fort Sumpter and the garrison surrendered. The first all-out battle took place at Manassas on July 21. The Confederate general "Stonewall" Jackson's Valley Campaign was notable among the many confrontations of 1862.

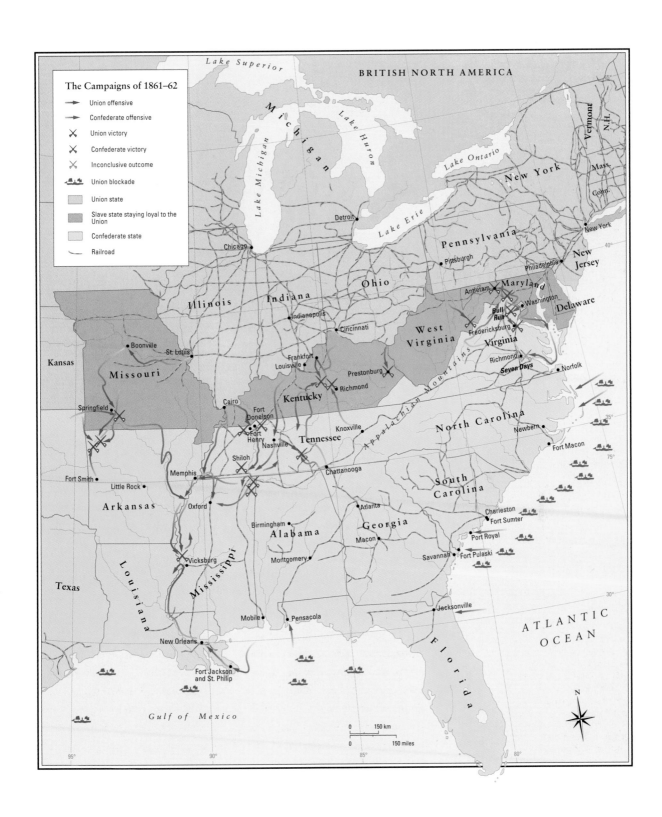

The Campaigns of 1861–62

→ Union offensive
→ Confederate offensive
✕ Union victory
✕ Confederate victory
✕ Inconclusive outcome
⚓ Union blockade
▢ Union state
▢ Slave state staying loyal to the Union
▢ Confederate state
〜 Railroad

A living history event held in modern Maryland. This is a reconstruction of Confederate infantry attacking a Union battle line.

Far right: The Battle of Antietam in Maryland, fought on 17 September, 1862, was the first major confrontation of the Civil War to take place on a northern battlefield. Also known as the battle of Sharpsburg, Antietam was the most costly one-day battle in United States history, with 23,000 casualties.

of them were obsolete and completely under-crewed.

Both sides realized the advantages of railways both to move troops and to keep them supplied. Both sides likewise noted the way Moltke had used telegraph to keep in touch with his scattered armies. When the war opened most troops carried rifles, some of which were breech-loaders, but many militia were still equipped with smoothbore muzzle-loading muskets. The artillery were generally smoothbore muzzle-loaders, though breech-loading rifled guns would gradually replace them as the war dragged on. This gave some infantry a range advantage over guns for the first time. Soon artillery batteries had to be pulled back to shelter behind infantry screens to halt the massive losses to gunners.

Cavalry on both sides rode to war equipped with sabers and carbines — short-barreled versions of infantry rifles. At first the horsemen were used in the traditional roles of scouting on campaign and as shock troops in battle. It was not long before high casualties brought an end to mounted charges against well-formed enemies. Instead cavalry were used as mounted infantry — riding fast to where they were needed and then dismounting to fight on foot. As the war progressed a new use for cavalry was found: raiding. Strong mounted forces would be sent to break through the enemy front, then to ride deep behind his lines to destroy store depots, tear up railway lines, and cause disruption to supply lines. When the war opened in 1861 neither side expected it to last very long. The Unionists hoped a show of force would bring the "rebels" to heel. The Confederates believed that most people in the north were not really bothered about the issues and would rather let the southern states secede than face a protracted struggle.

The first campaign opened in June 1861 when a large, but poorly trained, Unionist army marched south to capture the Confederate capital of Richmond, Virginia. This attack was stopped at First Bull Run with heavy loss. The Confederate President Jefferson Davis ruled out a counteroffensive, hoping the losses would induce Unionist President Abraham Lincoln to agree to peace. It proved a vain hope and the struggle resumed in the spring of 1862 with a renewed Unionist offensive aimed at Richmond. General George McClellan used Unionist naval supremacy to land 100,000 men on the Yorktown Peninsula. The move caught the Confederates off-balance, but General Robert E. Lee responded with his customary speed and skill by hurrying to the scene and attacking McClellan at Chickahominy on 27 June. His attack took the Unionists by surprise and although the Confederate infantry had to advance through heavy artillery fire, they succeeded in smashing a hole in the Unionist center. McClellan pulled back in good order, fighting the whole way in what is known as the Seven Days Battle.

Far to the west at Shiloh in Tennessee a Unionist army of 40,000 men under General Ulysses Grant

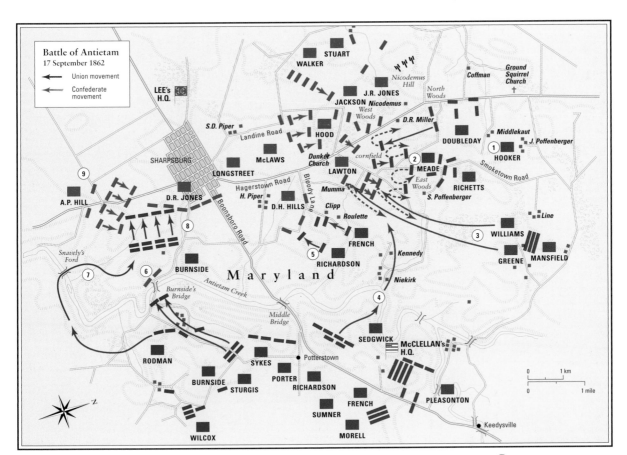

Battle of Antietam
17 September 1862

← Union movement

← Confederate movement

heading for the Mississippi was surprised and assaulted on 6 April by 42,000 Confederates under General Johnston. Grant was defeated and pushed back, but next day received 20,000 reinforcements and attacked. Johnston was killed and his men driven back in confusion. Both generals had pushed their men forward in dense Napoleonic-style formations, which resulted in mass casualties from rifles and artillery with the Confederates losing 11,000 men and the Unionists 14,000. Grant was in no position to exploit his victory, having lost so many men, but by retaining the field he was in a position to move west to cut the Mississippi trade route or to head south to cut the Memphis-Richmond railroad. Either action would cause great damage to the economy of the Confederate states.

Even more financial damage was beginning to be caused by the US Navy, which was cruising the Atlantic seaboard and the Gulf of Mexico. The warships stopped every merchant ship heading to or from the Confederate ports that they could catch. The Confederates were entirely dependent on exports of cotton and other agricultural products to earn money. With only limited arms manufacturing ability the south was likewise reliant on imports from Europe to keep their armies supplied with arms and ammunition. In 1862 the blockade was not entirely effective, and the Confederates had stockpiles of supplies, but as

1. **17 Sept. 6 am:** Hooker's Federal I Corps begins the attack, his left flank fails to make headway under artillery fire from Nicodemus Hill.

2. **7 am:** Hood's Confederates counterattack and halt I Corps' advance.

3. **7:30–9 am:** Mansfield's XII Corps attacks toward the Dunker Church but is driven back by fresh Confederate reinforcements.

4. **10 am:** Sedgwick's division of Summer's II Corps attacks into the West Woods but is driven back with heavy losses.

5. **1 pm:** Richardson's and French's divisions of Summer's II Corps capture Bloody Lane and breach Lee's center.

6. **10 pm–1 pm:** Burnside's IX Corps seize the bridge across Antietam Creek after repeated attempts to cross.

7. **1 pm:** Rodman's division of IX Corps wades through Snavely's Ford and flanks Toombs' Confederates above the bridge.

8. **3 pm:** Burnside launches an assault, pushing Longstreet's Confederates back to the outskirts of Sharpsburg.

9. **4 pm:** A.P. Hill's Confederate division arrives from Harpers Ferry just in time to cripple Burnside's advance with a counterattack against the Federal left flank.

Right: President Jefferson Davis:
By the time he was chosen to
lead the fledgling confederacy,
Davis was widely regarded as the
"foremost man in the South".
Davis' belief in the rightness of
the Southern cause and in states'
rights never wavered.

Opposite: Railroads were the
natural choice to cover the
vast distances involved once
the United States stretched
from coast to coast. By 1860,
the railroad network was
already moving west from the
eastern USA. On 10 May, 1869,
the Golden Spike ceremony
marked the meeting of the
transcontinental railroad at
Promontory, Utah.

Overleaf, right: The battle of
Vicksburg began on May 18, 1863
when the Union army led by
Major General Ulysses S. Grant
besieged the city, trapping the
Confederates under Lieutenant
General John Pemberton inside.
The surrender of Vicksburg on
July 4 divided the Confederacy in
two. Union casualties numbered
10,142, the Confederates' 9,091.

Overleaf, left:
General Nathan Bedford Forrest
Nathan Bedford Forrest, a
plantation owner in the South,
was one of the few participants
in the Civil War to enlist as
a private and end the war
as a general. An extremely
controversial figure, Forrest had
no formal military education,
but devised innovative cavalry
techniques for the
Confederate forces.

time passed this situation was to prove to be a real problem for the Confederates. The southerners were well aware of the issue. Lacking ships in numbers, they put their hopes in innovation. The steam-driven frigate *Merrimack* had its upper-works removed, was entirely encased in iron armor, and armed with six nine-inch, two seven-inch, and two six-inch guns. The ship could not carry fuel or food for a long voyage, but was intended to break the inshore blockade, thus allowing merchant ships to get out to sea, where they stood a chance of evading the US Navy.

On 8 March the *Merrimack* steamed down the James River to attack the Unionist force blockading the river-mouth. It sank a sloop and a frigate, and forced a second frigate ashore without suffering any loss herself. Next day she put out again, but was met by the *Monitor*, a Unionist ship that was likewise covered in iron armor and had a single gun mounted on a traversing turret. For more than three hours the two ships blasted at each other, scoring dozens of hits but inflicting no damage at all. The Merrimack retreated and no further effort to break the blockade was made. Only fast, single ships would be successful in getting through, and they could not carry enough cotton out or guns in to make much difference.

The year 1863 opened much as did 1862, with simultaneous Unionist assaults on Richmond and on the Mississippi. The campaign in the east opened first with 75,000 Unionists under General Hooker marching south. They were met at Chancellorsville by Lee with 53,000 men. Lee used half his men to hold the advance while General Jackson took the rest on a long march around Hooker's right flank. The ruse worked and the Unionists were thrown back, having lost 18,000 casualties and 8,000 prisoners to Lee's 10,000 casualties. Among the Confederate dead was Jackson, perhaps the best general in the entire war. The Unionist forces did better in the west where Grant moved in to lay siege to the Mississippi town of Vicksburg, which controlled all trade along the river. He was in position by 18 May, and although an assault was driven off with heavy loss, Grant had enough men and material to surround the city. Vicksburg had been attacked twice before and beat off both assaults, so defender General Pemberton was confident. Back in the East, the Confederate government began to realize that their war effort was weakening faster than the resolve of the northern states. True, there was a vociferous northern

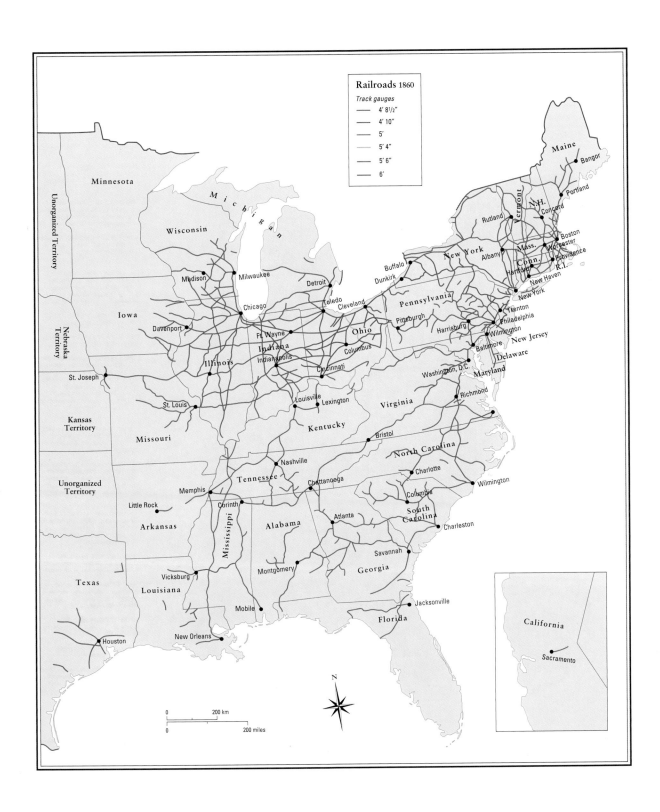

Railroads 1860

Track gauges

— 4' 8½"
— 4' 10"
— 5'
— 5' 4"
— 5' 6"
— 6'

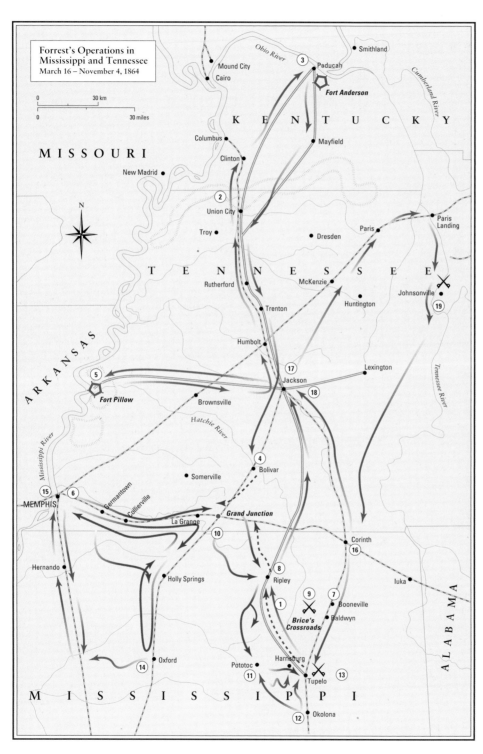

Forrest's Operations in
Mississippi and Tennessee
March 16 – November 4, 1864

① **March 16:** *Forrest rode north for another raid into Tennessee and Kentucky.*

② **March 24:** *Forrest captured at 450-man Union garrison at Union City, Tennessee.*

③ **March 25:** *Forrest reached Paducah and demanded the surrender of Fort Anderson. When the Unionists refused, he attacked but was repulsed and withdrew the next morning.*

④ **March 29:** *Moving rapidly, Forrest reached Bolivar, Tennessee, and drove off a small force of Union cavalry.*

⑤ **April 12:** *Forrest attacked and captured Fort Pillow, where his men slaughtered black troops attempting to surrender.*

⑥ **June 2:** *With orders from Sherman to hunt down Forrest, Major General Samuel D. Sturgis departed Memphis.*

⑦ **June 9:** *Learning of Sturgis's approach, Forrest met with his department commander, Major General Stephen D. Lee, at Booneville to plan a response.*

⑧ **June 9:** *Sturgis's expedition reached Ripley, Mississippi.*

⑨ **June 10:** *Forrest met and defeated Sturgis at Brice's Crossroads.*

⑩ **July 5:** *Sherman dispatched another expedition to hunt down Forrest, this time Major General A. J. Smith with two divisions of infantry and one of cavalry, all from the Sixteenth Corps, and totaling 14,000 men in all. They marched out of La Grange, Tennessee.*

⑪ **July 11:** *Smith's cavalry, commanded by Brigadier General Benjamin H. Grierson, met and drove off a force of Confederate cavalry.*

⑫ **July 13:** *The combined forces of Lee and Forrest, numbering 9,500 men, advanced from Okolona toward Pontotoc. Their advanced forces skirmished with Smith's cavalry.*

⑬ **July 13–14:** *Maneuvering to flank the Confederate position on the Okolona Road, Smith moved east to Harrisburg, near Tupelo. The next morning the Confederates attacked but were repulsed.*

⑭ **August 18:** *Forrest set out on yet another raid, bound this time for Memphis via Hernando, Mississippi.*

⑮ **August 21:** *Forrest and his raiders made an early-morning foray into Memphis before returning quickly the way they had come.*

⑯ **October 19:** *Once again Forrest went raiding, this time setting out from Corinth.*

⑰ **October 22:** *Forrest occupied Jackson, Tennessee.*

⑱ **October 29:** *Using his field artillery from the shore, Forrest captured one gunboat and two transports and began moving them southward, up the Tennessee River, while his troops kept pace on the bank.*

⑲ **November 4:** *Forrest again used his artillery to good advantage, damaging Union transports and supplies at Johnsonville, but he had to abandoned his captured vessels and march back to Corinth overland.*

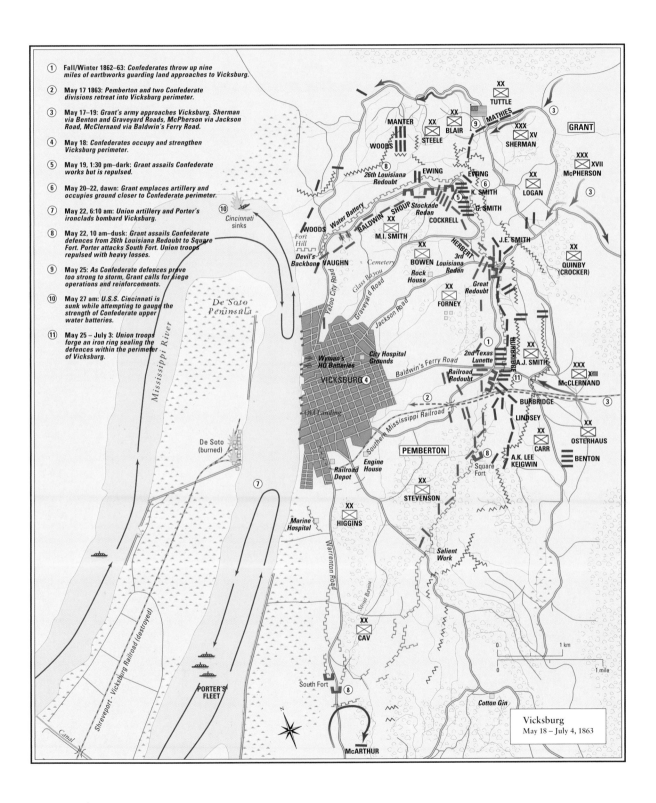

(1) Fall/Winter 1862–63: Confederates throw up nine miles of earthworks guarding land approaches to Vicksburg.

(2) May 17 1863: Pemberton and two Confederate divisions retreat into Vicksburg perimeter.

(3) May 17–19: Grant's army approaches Vicksburg. Sherman via Benton and Graveyard Roads, McPherson via Jackson Road, McClernand via Baldwin's Ferry Road.

(4) May 18: Confederates occupy and strengthen Vicksburg perimeter.

(5) May 19, 1:30 pm–dark: Grant assails Confederate works but is repulsed.

(6) May 20–22, dawn: Grant emplaces artillery and occupies ground closer to Confederate perimeter.

(7) May 22, 6:10 am: Union artillery and Porter's ironclads bombard Vicksburg.

(8) May 22, 10 am–dusk: Grant assails Confederate defences from 26th Louisiana Redoubt to Square Fort. Porter attacks South Fort. Union troops repulsed with heavy losses.

(9) May 25: As Confederate defences prove too strong to storm, Grant calls for siege operations and reinforcements.

(10) May 27 am: U.S.S. Cincinnati is sunk while attempting to gauge the strength of Confederate upper water batteries.

(11) May 25 – July 3: Union troops forge an iron ring sealing the defences within the perimeter of Vicksburg.

Vicksburg
May 18 – July 4, 1863

opposition to the war, but the federal government remained determined to crush the secessionists. Davis decided to invade the north while the south still had the weapons supplies to do so. Lee left his base at Fredericksburg on 3 June. US general Hooker detected the move, but was almost at once replaced with General Meade by Lincoln following a dispute. Meade believed that Lee would aim at Washington so sought to keep his army between the capital and the advancing Confederates.

In fact Lee was intent on a deep penetration of Unionist territory to cause as much alarm and damage as possible. To this end he detached the bulk of his cavalry under JEB Stuart on a wide-ranging raid. This left him without adequate scouts, so he was unsure of Meade's position. When on 30 June a patrol of General Hill's division reported that Unionist forces were at the small town of Gettysburg, Hill marched to investigate. The Unionists had likewise alerted their commander, Buford, who sent in reinforcements

Pickett's Charge, named after Confederate Major-General George Pickett, who took part, occurred on 3 July, 1863, the third day of the battle of Gettysburg. Some 12,500 confederate infantry advanced into heavy rifle and artillery fire in a move to strike at the Union center. Half of them became casualties.

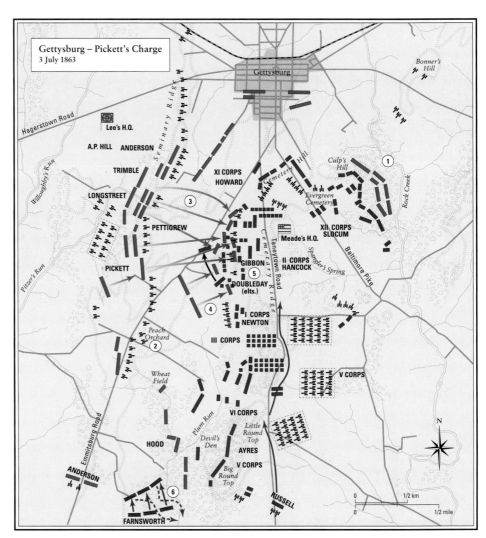

Gettysburg – Pickett's Charge
3 July 1863

1. 3 July, 5:30 am–10 am: *Johnson's division of Ewell's corps launches repeated attacks on Culp's Hill but makes no progress.*

2. 1 pm: *Confederate artillery cannonade begins with 140 cannons, the Federals reply with 80 guns.*

3. 3 pm: *Pickett's, Pettigrew's, and Trimble's Confederate infantry attack toward Seminary Ridge.*

4. 3:30 pm: *Stannard's Federal brigade attacks flank of Pickett's division.*

5. 3:45 pm: *Limit of Confederate infantry attacks.*

6. 5:30 pm: *Farnsworth's cavalry charge against Confederate right is beaten off with heavy losses.*

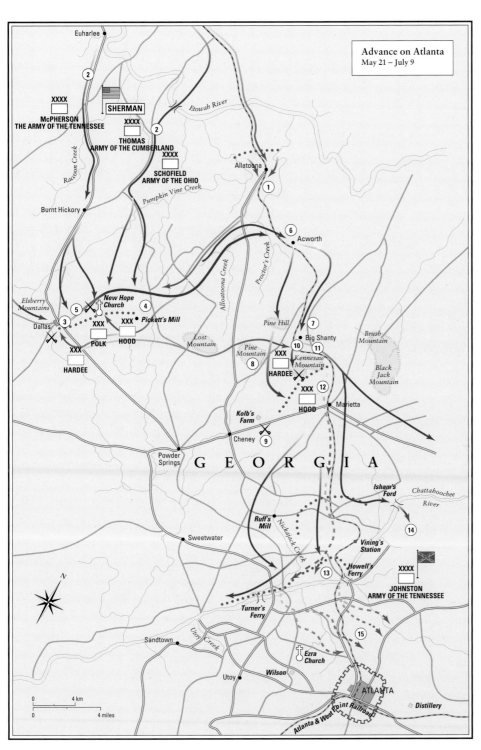

Advance on Atlanta
May 21 – July 9

1. May 20–21: *Johnston's army took up an impregnable position at Allatoona.*

2. May 23–24: *Rather than follow the railroad directly into the teeth of Johnston's defenses, Sherman struck out on roads leading due south, hoping to turn Johnston out of his powerful position.*

3. May 25: *Johnston responded directly and blocked Sherman at Dallas and New Hope Church.*

4. May 27: *Howard's Fourth Corps attempted to turn Johnston's right flank at Pickett's Mill but met with repulse.*

5. May 28: *Acting on the basis of mistaken information, Hardee's corps assaulted the Fifteenth Corps just east of Dallas and suffered a bloody defeat.*

6. May 31–June 6: *Sherman moved back to the east, re-establishing his railroad communications at Acworth.*

7. June 10–19: *Sherman advanced to Big Shanty, then worked his way forward slowly against strong Confederate positions on the surrounding hills.*

8. June 14: *Union artillery fire killed Leonidas Polk atop Pine Mountain.*

9. June 22: *Hood's corps attacked the Twenty-second and Twenty-third Corps at Kolb's Farm and was repulsed with heavy loss.*

10. June 27: *Tiring of flanking manoeuvres, Sherman hurled his troops at the system of Confederate works based on Kennesaw Mountain. Attacks aimed at the subsidiary summit known as Pigeon Hill and at Confederate works farther to the west ended in bloody failure.*

11. June 27–July 2: *Schofield's Twenty-third Corps flanked Johnston out of the Kennesaw Mountain line.*

12. July 3–4: *Johnston took up a line in front of Smyrna but was flanked out of it the next day.*

13. July 5: *Johnston took up another line of entrenchments immediately in front of the Chattahoochee River.*

14. July 8: *The Twenty-third Corps and Sherman's cavalry crossed the Chattahoochee east of Johnston's position.*

15. July 9: *Johnston retreated across the Chattahoochee to the outskirts of Atlanta.*

The Union army led by William Tecumseh Sherman began advancing on Atlanta on May 21 1864, aiming to outflank and snare the Confederates. They avoided the trap and fell back towards Atlanta. Before long, though, the Union army was threatening Atlanta and ultimately besieged the city which surrendered in September.

and in turn passed the news on to Meade. Both armies were therefore converging on Gettysburg thinking that they had in front of them only a small part of the enemy's force. The serious fighting began on 1 July as Confederate forces under Hill drove Buford's men out of the town and back to the ridge behind. Meade arrived on 2 July, as did Lee, so that by dusk there were 88,000 Unionists on the ridge, faced by 75,000 Confederates in the valley below. On 3 July Lee made the fateful decision to launch an infantry attack up the slope to smash the main Unionist army. If he succeeded, he would be free to raid and pillage as he wished; even to capture Washington. The attack was led by the division of General George Pickett, and so became known as Pickett's Charge, although other troops took part. Of the 15,000 men who set out to charge across the open ground in the face of disciplined rifle fire and carefully positioned modern artillery, only 150 reached the crest alive. Meade's men were thrown off the ridge, but a swift counterattack regained the lost ground. At almost the same moment Stuart's cavalry were ambushed and defeated in a separate action. The next day both armies sat motionless, neither side wanting to attack. That night Lee marched off to return south. The great offensive was over. Over the three days of fighting, Lee had lost 27,000 men and Meade 23,000. The South could afford the losses less, and more seriously the failed campaign had not shaken Unionist resolve. Far to the west, Vicksburg surrendered on 4 July. Southern defeat was now only a matter of time.

An innovation by the Confederates by this date was the concept of cavalry units operating entirely separate from the rest of the army. Their task was to ride deep behind enemy lines, attacking any targets that offered themselves, living off the country and relying on speed to evade fights with enemy troops. Some of these raiders were disciplined cavalry units, but many others were little better than brigands using the war as a cover for robbery with violence. Among the latter were two brothers who would later become famous: Frank and Jesse James.

Over the winter, Lincoln appointed Grant to be his commander-in-chief, with Sherman as his deputy. Lee prepared to fight a defensive campaign, hoping to inflict such heavy losses that Lincoln might yet agree to some sort of a compromise peace. Unfortunately, the southern railroads were short of spares and tracks, so Lee's supply system began to break down. The campaigns of 1864 opened in April as Grant led 119,000 men toward Richmond. Lee with 64,000 men was lurking in broken country, called the Wilderness, which Grant considered impassable to troops. Lee proved him wrong and launched a devastating attack on 4 May that smashed Grant's center and cost him over 20,000 men, nearly three times Lee's loss. Grant soon rallied and advanced again, launching a series of costly frontal assaults on Lee's prepared defenses at Spotsylvania on 10 May. After two days of fighting, Grant was forced to withdraw having lost a further 15,000 men to Lee's 4,000.

In the west, Sherman had marched out of Vicksburg to capture the important railroad junction at Chattanooga, almost without a fight. Realizing that the main Confederate forces were with Lee, Sherman took the risk of dispersing his men across a wide front so that they could inflict maximum damage and marched on Atlanta, and from there he continued to the sea. During this "March to the Sea" Sherman deliberately inflicted maximum damage on homes, businesses, civilians, and anything else he could find. It was an exercise in what became known as "frightfulness". Grant had meanwhile brought up fresh reinforcements and supplies and was attacking toward Richmond again. His forces were halted at Petersburg by entrenched Confederate forces. A frontal assault was repulsed amid great slaughter. By

On 15 November, 1864, Union General William Tecumseh Sherman set out from Atlanta, Georgia on his 300-mile (480 km) "march to the sea" with 68,000 men. Heading for Savannah which he reached on 8 December, Sherman adopted a "scorched earth" policy devastating crops and destroying farms, so "making Georgia howl.".

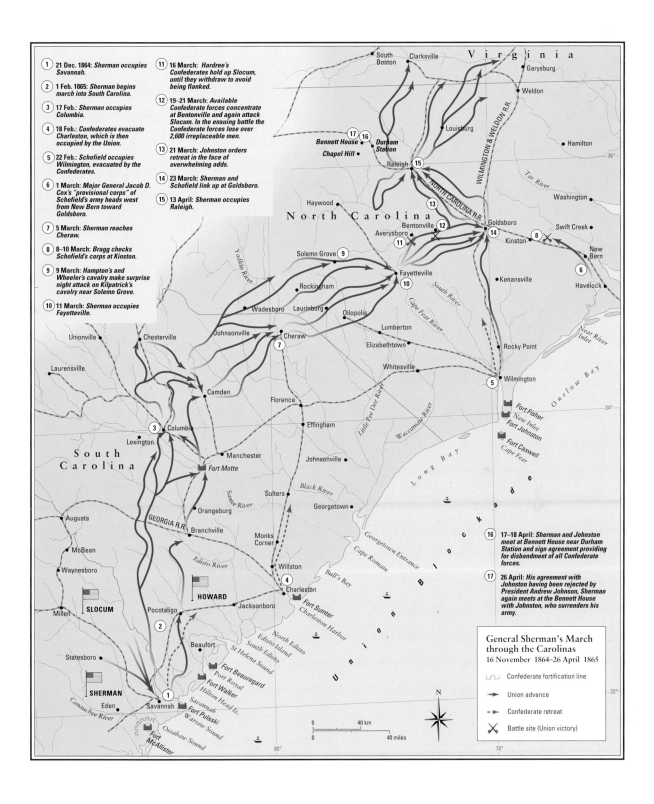

1. **21 Dec. 1864:** *Sherman occupies Savannah.*

2. **1 Feb. 1865:** *Sherman begins march into South Carolina.*

3. **17 Feb.:** *Sherman occupies Columbia.*

4. **18 Feb.:** *Confederates evacuate Charleston, which is then occupied by the Union.*

5. **22 Feb.:** *Schofield occupies Wilmington, evacuated by the Confederates.*

6. **1 March:** *Major General Jacob D. Cox's "provisional corps" of Schofield's army heads west from New Bern toward Goldsboro.*

7. **5 March:** *Sherman reaches Cheraw.*

8. **8–10 March:** *Bragg checks Schofield's corps at Kinston.*

9. **9 March:** *Hampton's and Wheeler's cavalry make surprise night attack on Kilpatrick's cavalry near Solemn Grove.*

10. **11 March:** *Sherman occupies Fayetteville.*

11. **16 March:** *Hardree's Confederates hold up Slocum, until they withdraw to avoid being flanked.*

12. **19–21 March:** *Available Confederate forces concentrate at Bentonville and again attack Slocum. In the ensuing battle the Confederate forces lose over 2,600 irreplaceable men.*

13. **21 March:** *Johnston orders retreat in the face of overwhelming odds.*

14. **23 March:** *Sherman and Schofield link up at Goldsboro.*

15. **13 April:** *Sherman occupies Raleigh.*

16. **17–18 April:** *Sherman and Johnston meet at Bennett House near Durham Station and sign agreement providing for disbandment of all Confederate forces.*

17. **26 April:** *His agreement with Johnston having been rejected by President Andrew Johnson, Sherman again meets at the Bennett House with Johnston, who surrenders his army.*

General Sherman's March through the Carolinas
16 November 1864–26 April 1865

- ⊓⊐ Confederate fortification line
- → Union advance
- –⇢ Confederate retreat
- ✕ Battle site (Union victory)

N

0 40 km
0 40 miles

this time, however, Lee had only 30,000 men with him and had heard of the terrible actions of Sherman. He pulled back and marched to Appomattox to await orders from his political superiors. Grant arrived first, and Lee surrendered his army on 9 April. The war continued until 26 May when the Confederate government accepted the inevitable and surrendered.

The US Civil War left a trail of bitterness and resentment behind it. The Unionists insisted that the Confederacy had to accept not only reincorporation into the Union but also a host of Federal laws that effectively destroyed the agricultural economy of the defeated states. This foreshadowed the concept of "total war" to come with unconditional surrender as the only outcome acceptable to the victors.

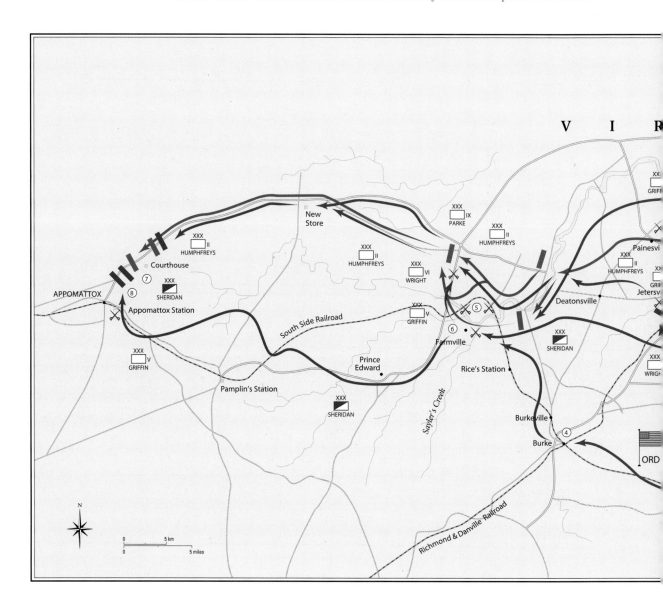

The Appomattox campaign
was a series of battles fought
between 3 April and 9 April 1865
in Virginia which resulted in the
surrender of the Confederate
army of Northern Virginia and
the end of the American
Civil War. The campaign was an
example of clever maneuver and
relentless pursuit. The surrender
of Lee was a blow from
which the South were
unable to recover.

① April 3: Confederate forces moved west on various routes, fleeing Richmond and Petersburg.

② April 4–5: Lee's army concentrated around Amelia Court House, pausing to gather much-needed supplies.

③ April 5: The Army of the Potomac reached Jetersville, cutting off Lee's avenue of flight to the south.

④ April 5: Ord's Army of the James reached Burke.

⑤ April 6: At Sayler's Creek Union troops caught and cut off part of Lee's rear guard, taking six thousand prisoners.

⑥ April 7: The Confederate rear guard succeeded in beating off a Union attack and crossing the Appomattox

⑦ April 8: Lee's army reached Appomattox Court House.

⑧ April 9: Lee surrendered to Grant.

APPOMATTOX APRIL 3–9 1865

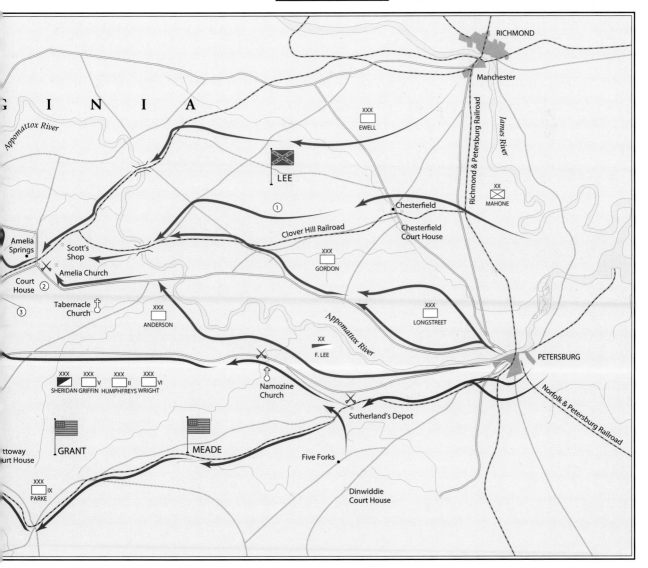

Franco-Prussian War 1870-1871

IT WAS THE FRANCO-PRUSSIAN WAR THAT FINALLY ESTABLISHED THE GERMAN ARMED FORCES AS BEING THE FINEST IN EUROPE, PERHAPS THE WORLD. IT WAS NOT GERMAN WEAPONS OR MEN THAT PROVED DECISIVE, HOWEVER, BUT THE NEW CONCEPT OF A GENERAL STAFF, WHICH OTHER NATIONS WERE QUICK TO EMULATE.

After the Austro-Prussian War of 1866, the Prussian commander Helmuth von Moltke engaged in detailed study of what had worked and what had gone wrong. He decided that the key problem had been at the detailed level of logistics. Put simply, men and supplies had been ordered to follow routes that were unsuitable, either because of narrow bridges, or poor road surfaces or single-track railroads. He therefore formed a General Staff in Berlin divided into three seperate divisions: Operational, Administrative, and Supply. The staff was to be responsible for deciding how many men or supplies could be moved along any particular railroad or road in a given period of time, and then of drawing up detailed movement orders to make maximum effective use of the transport network. By contrast to this detailed work, Moltke believed that his generals should be given a free hand to implement as they saw fit his broadly defined objectives.

The system worked perfectly when France declared war on Prussia and her German allies on 15 July 1870. Within two weeks, the Prussians had 475,000 men on the border complete with heavy artillery and full supply wagons. The French had by this date managed to mobilize only 224,000 men, most of whom were still in barracks without their supply transport having arrived. The Prussians attacked, inflicting a series of defeats on the outnumbered and outmaneuvered French at Saarbrücken, Spichern, Mars-le-Tour, Gravelotte and Metz. The French were staring defeat in the face. The final battle at Sedan on 1 September saw the last French army crushed and Emperor Napoleon III taken prisoner. Moltke, who commanded

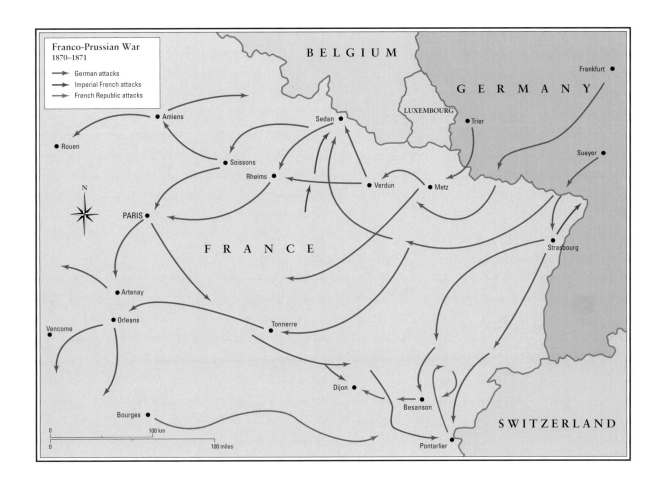

150, 000 men under the Crown Prince of Prussia, intended to relieve the French army, trapped at Metz, of the Rhine. MacMahon left Chalons in an effort to join Bazaine, who was expected to break out of Metz. The French advance was beset by contrary orders and poor logistics, and on 31 August MacMahon took up a defensive position at Sedan, hoping to resume his march after a day's rest. Moltke had set off in search of MacMahon with the Third army on his southern flank and the Army of the Meuse to its north. His cavalry did not find MacMahon until 26 August, and on 30 August an isolated French corps was beaten at Beaumont. Moltke then ordered his army commanders to pin the French against the Belgian frontier, the Army of the Meuse moving up from the east and the Third Army from the south; he aimed at a battle of encirclement, trapping the whole French army. The Germans succeeded in surrounding the French, who were forced to capitulate. The French then declared a republic and hastily fortified Paris. Although the war dragged on, Sedan was its decisive battle. The resulting siege lasted until 15 February, 1871 when France finally surrendered, and conquering Prussia occupied France. Prussia gained not only a free hand to unify Germany under the King of Prussia, including those German states that did not favor the move, but also annexed the long-disputed border territories of Alsace and Lorraine.

In 1870, the French sought to retrieve territory lost to Prussia during the Napoleonic Wars. However, in the Franco-Prussian War that followed, the superior Prussian army thrashed the French and as a final insult, proclaimed the unification of Germany under Prussian leadership at the Palace of Versailles, near Paris.

THE BOER WARS 1899-1902

THE HEAVY CASUALTIES SUFFERED BY MOST COMBATANTS IN THE LATER 19TH CENTURY SHOWED THE POWER OF MODERN WEAPONS. THE BOER WAR DEMONSTRATED WHAT NEW TACTICS COULD DO TO MINIMIZE THOSE LOSSES WHILE STILL DELIVERING MILITARY VICTORY ON THE BATTLEFIELD.

Vintage photograph showing soldiers and cannon of the Royal Artillery off to the front at the time of the Boer War in South Africa.

The first Boer War broke out in 1881 when the Boers, European settlers of Dutch descent, rose to throw off British rule. They succeeded and established a number of separate republics in the interior of South Africa. These new states had essentially pastoral and agricultural economies, and allowed only Boers to vote or hold public office. When huge deposits of gold and diamonds were discovered in the Boer republics, the Boers had neither the expertise nor the interest to mine themselves. Instead they brought in outsiders to do the mining, contenting themselves with taxing the profits. However, most incomers were British who resented the fact that they had no rights under the Boer governments, while the British government wanted to reassert direct rule. The tensions led to the outbreak of war on 11 October, 1899.

The Boers advanced quickly to lay siege to the towns of Mafeking, Kimberley, and Ladysmith. Both sides dug into elaborate trench systems to avoid the murderous rifle and artillery fire that were deployed in the battles. It was quickly

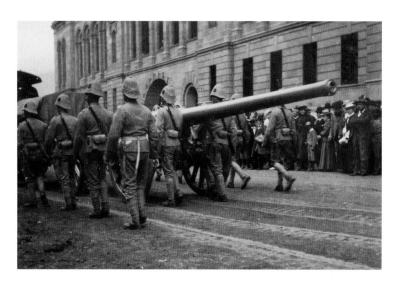

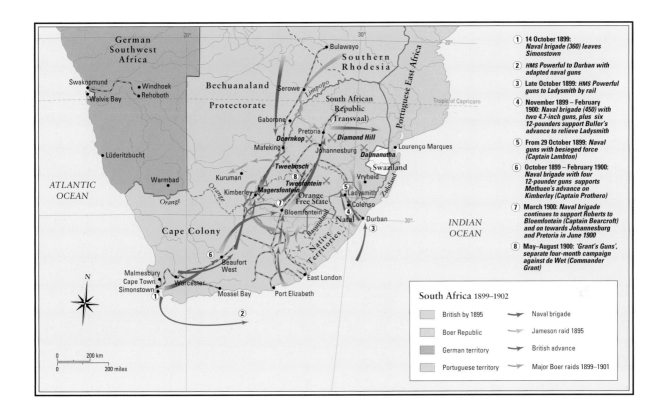

1. **14 October 1899:** *Naval brigade (360) leaves Simonstown*

2. *HMS Powerful to Durban with adapted naval guns*

3. **Late October 1899:** *HMS Powerful guns to Ladysmith by rail*

4. **November 1899 – February 1900:** *Naval brigade (450) with two 4.7-inch guns, plus six 12-pounders support Buller's advance to relieve Ladysmith*

5. **From 29 October 1899:** *Naval guns with besieged force (Captain Lambton)*

6. **October 1899 – February 1900:** *Naval brigade with four 12-pounder guns supports Methuen's advance on Kimberley (Captain Prothero)*

7. **March 1900:** *Naval brigade continues to support Roberts to Bloemfontein (Captain Bearcroft) and on towards Johannesburg and Pretoria in June 1900*

8. **May–August 1900:** *'Grant's Guns', separate four-month campaign against de Wet (Commander Grant)*

South Africa 1899–1902

British by 1895	→ Naval brigade
Boer Republic	→ Jameson raid 1895
German territory	→ British advance
Portuguese territory	→ Major Boer raids 1899–1901

apparent that the trenches, with interlocking fire, were invulnerable to infantry assault so the sieges soon became contests of endurance and dwindling supplies. In the open field, the Boers operated as "commandos," small and self-contained mounted units armed with highly accurate breech-loading rifles with clips of up to six bullets. The Boers fought lying down, not needing to stand to reload their rifles, or from hastily dug "foxholes." They therefore suffered fewer casualties than the British; who were still trained to fight standing up in formed units. The two styles of fighting were most starkly displayed at Spion Kop on 23 January 1900, when a British brigade lost a third of its men when caught in the open by Boer riflemen who hardly lost a man. Thereafter the British began to adopt the scattered formations and dull uniform colors of the Boers.

Later in 1900 a new British command arrived in the form of Anglo-Indian Lord Frederick Roberts — known to his adoring men as "Bobs" — and logistics expert Horatio Kitchener. The supply system was thoroughly reformed to allow British troops to operate anywhere in large numbers, while tactics and strategy were altered to isolate, trap, and eliminate the fast-moving commandos one by one. The Boer capital of Pretoria fell on 13 June, but a guerrilla war dragged on until May 1902.

The Boer Wars were significant in that they proved to be a major turning point in British history, due chiefly to the world's reaction to anti-insurgency tactics used by Britain. Britain, in order to gain allies, was forced to change its foreign policy.

The Boer War of 1899-1902 arose chiefly out of the reluctance of the Boers, who were of Dutch ancestry, to live under British rule. Previous British "colonial" wars had featured battles against tribesmen, primitively equipped: the Boers, however, were expert riflemen and knew how to fight on horseback.

WARS OF THE TECHNOLOGICAL AGE

THE 20TH CENTURY HAS BEEN DOMINATED BY WARS FOUGHT ON A SCALE NEVER BEFORE THOUGHT POSSIBLE. THE ABILITY OF INDUSTRIALIZED SOCIETIES TO MANUFACTURE INCREASINGLY EFFECTIVE AND DESTRUCTIVE WEAPONRY WHILE MOBILIZING ARMIES OF MILLIONS OF MEN HAS MADE WAR MORE COSTLY AND DESTRUCTIVE THAN EVER BEFORE.

In 1631 the German city of Magdeburg was captured by storm after a lengthy siege by an army of Croats and Walloons. The victorious troops went on a rampage, carrying out an orgy of rape and murder that left tens of thousands of civilians dead. The event shocked Europe. Thereafter a firm distinction was drawn between civilians and combatants and rules drawn up that governed when and how surrenders could be effected, along with how prisoners should be treated. There was a host of other, largely informal conventions that governed the conduct of war between European states.

Several wars in the later 19th century — notably the Franco-Prussian, Austro-Prussian and Franco-Austrian conflicts — were over quickly. The nation able to mobilize quickest won. However, the US Civil War had been more drawn out and had been effectively decided by the greater wealth and manpower of the Unionist states. Future wars would be won by the country able to stay for the long haul. Not only did factories need to be converted to produce arms, but the entire national economy had to be turned over to supporting the war effort. As the 19th century progressed, however, the custom of observing the informal rules of war came under pressure. The increasing industrialization of warfare meant that the factories producing guns and ammunition became legitimate targets for destruction, as did the roads and railroads that carried those supplies to armed forces.

The size of armies was also growing at an unprecedented rate. Using flags, drums and trumpets a commander could exert effective control over an army in the field numbering up to around 100,000 men. Any force much larger than that would cover too much ground for such communication systems to work. However, Napoleon's corps system allowed a central commander to control much larger forces via subordinate marshals. Soon after that the introduction of telegraph and later telephone systems speeded up command control systems greatly. After 1850 it became usual for countries to conscript all young men for military training and service, and for all men to remain liable to be called up for some years thereafter. This move meant that countries could field very large armies of adequately trained men at very short notice. By 1900 most European countries were able to mobilize armies of millions of men within a matter or weeks. Conscription also made all men actual or potential soldiers. It blurred the previously firm lines between soldier and civilian in a way that Europe had not seen since the siege of Magdeburg over 250 years earlier. Troops became far more likely to treat civilians as legitimate targets of war than had their fathers or grandfathers. This attitude would reach its peak in the bombing of cities during World War II, but was already to be seen in World War I.

The increasing range and greater killing power of weapons had a profound effect on how battles were fought. In 1800 the average infantryman had a musket with a killing range of about 100 yards. By 1900 the same man would be armed with a rifle able to hit and kill a man at a range of a mile. Artillery experienced an even greater increase in range and destructive ability. When bomber aircraft entered the scene in World War I, the area of danger on a battlefield was no longer about 300 yards deep, but extended for several miles. This made it effectively impossible for a fighting man to seek safety by running away, and allowed a victorious army to slaughter retreating troops more effectively than before.

Given the huge sacrifices being expected of nations at war, the old concept of limited objectives was abandoned. In the 18th centuries wars had been fought for control of provinces and strips of land, but in the 20th century wars became conflicts to the bitter end with unconditional surrender an increasingly common war aim. In World War I the governments of both Germany and Austria-Hungary knew that defeat would mean the end of those states as they then stood. The Allies had made it a precondition of any peace deal that the ethnic minorities in both empires should be given free votes on whether or not they wanted to achieve independence – though this stipulation was not extended to the Russian Empire which was fighting on the Allied side. Despite this, both the German Kaiser and the Austrian Emperor chose to accept personal abdication and the oblivion of their empires rather than see enemy armies fighting across their territory.

World War II was different. Instead of wars between rival dynastic rulers espousing different methods of government, the war of 1939 was fought between dictatorships rooted in deeply held political ideologies that could comprehend neither compromise with the enemy nor any future after defeat. Unlike Kaiser Wilhelm in 1918, Hitler preferred to see Germany laid waste by the enemy military rather than either to seek a compromise peace or to accept surrender. As a result the death toll – especially among civilians – was much higher. Combined with the ability of new war industries to produce increasingly destructive weaponry and with the ability of modern transport and communication technology to move and co-ordinate armies millions of men strong, this made warfare far more costly, bloody, and destructive than ever before. Wars of the Technological Age had arrived with a vengeance.

ATTEMPTS AT ARMAMENTS CONTROL

IN THE 19TH CENTURY THE GOVERNMENTS OF NATION STATES BEGAN TO CONSIDER ATTEMPTING TO LIMIT THE TYPES OR NUMBERS OF WEAPONS TO BE USED IN TIMES OF WAR.

The European alliances that helped precipitate the First World War in 1914 — the Allied states and the Central Powers — appear on this map, with their overseas possessions. The preponderance of Allied States is deceptive, for the Central Powers, particularly Germany, were well prepared for war and the long, hard slog ahead.

A t all periods of history there had been sporadic attempts to impose limits on warfare, usually under the authority of religion. In 1868 the Russians called a conference aimed at writing down and codifying the existing informal rules of war. The meeting resulted in the St. Petersburg Declaration, which generally achieved its stated aim. There was also an arms limitation clause, the first time such a thing had been attempted. This stated that projectiles of under 14 oz (400 g) could not be flammable, explosive, or expanding. The ban applied only to wars between the nations that signed the declaration, most of which were European or American. This had the unfortunate effect, however, that weapons banned between "civilized" states were allowed to be used on "uncivilized" peoples. A key problem that was recognized even at the time was how to enforce the agreement. There was no mechanism by which anyone could go to inspect

The World
August – November 1914

Allied States and territories

Central Powers and territories

Neutral States at November 1914

the military arsenals of a country as these were usually stored in conditions of great secrecy. Nor was it clear how a country should be punished if it were found to break the agreement.

In 1899 the Hague Convention reaffirmed the St. Petersburg Declaration, but added new agreements. The first was a vague promise to submit international disputes to arbitration whenever possible. More definite were the provisions that banned the dropping of explosive devices from balloons and the use of poison gas or other noxious chemicals. In 1907 a second Hague Conference was called, principally to include naval warfare. Generally the earlier agreement was reaffirmed and new provisions introduced. These covered the laying of underwater mines, the uses of submarines, the distinction between a merchant ship and a warship, and the status of neutral states caught up in a war. The ban on dropping bombs from balloons was not extended to airplanes and the ban on poison gas was lifted.

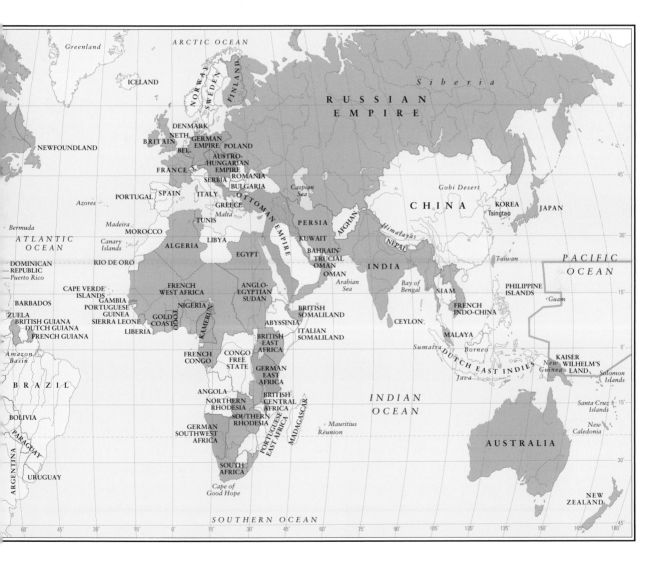

CHAPTER IX — WORLD WAR I 1914-1918: WORLD WAR I: EUROPE 1914

THE OUTBREAK OF THE FIRST WORLD WAR CAUGHT NEARLY EVERYONE BY SURPRISE. SIMILARLY MOST PEOPLE WERE EXPECTING THE WAR TO BE SHORT, FOLLOWING THE PATTERN ESTABLISHED OVER THE PAST 40 YEARS, AS PROPERLY ORGANIZED OFFENSIVES WERE CONSIDERED TO BE UNSTOPPABLE.

European alliances helped cause the First World War. When Austria-Hungary declared war on Serbia after a Serbian assassin murdered the heir to the Austrian throne, Russia, Serbia's ally, declared war on Austria. Germany, Austria's ally, declared war on Russia, and Russia's allies, Britain and France, declared war on Germany.

From 1871 onward the great European powers had been at peace, but tensions had been growing steadily. These centered around the growing industrial prosperity and military might of France and Germany as the agrarian Russian and Austrian Empires slipped into decline. The spark that ignited war came when the heir to the Austrian throne, Archduke Franz Ferdinand was murdered in 1914 by a terrorist who wanted Serb lands within the Austrian Empire to join Serbia. The Austrians chose to believe the Serb government was behind the plot and declared war on 28 July 1914. Russia mobilized to support Serbia, prompting Germany to declare war on Russia on 1 August, and then on Russia's ally France on 3 August 1914. When German troops marched into neutral Belgium to bypass French border fortifications, Britain declared war to protect her ally Belgium. Japan, an ally of Britain, then declared war on Germany and quickly conquered numerous German colonies. The German war plan called for France to be knocked out within six weeks by a sweeping flank march to capture Paris, after which the Germans would move against Russia. The huge German attack was slowed by the unexpected arrival of the British army at Mons, then halted by the French on 4 September 1914. To stop the French counterattack, the Germans dug into a series of field works protected by machine guns and artillery. The French and British responded in kind and by November there was a continuous line of trenches from the Swiss border to the Channel 400 miles (643 km) to the north. On the Eastern Front, the Germans halted a badly organized Russian advance at the Battle of Tannenberg on 26-30 August, killing 30,000 and capturing 90,000. The subsequent German counterattack was in turn halted at Warsaw, in part due to the fact that most German supply transport was on the Western Front.

Alliances on the Eve of War
July 1914

- Austro-German Alliance, 1879–1918
- Triple Alliance, 1882–1915
- Franco-Russian Alliance, 1894–1917
- Triple Entente, 1907–1917
- Varying independence and nationalist movements sponsored by Russia, 1879–1914
- Sympathetic to 'Central Powers'
- Sympathetic to 'Entente Powers'
- Neutrality guaranteed by United Kingdom
- Neutral

0   200 km
0   200 miles

Arctic Circle

Norwegian Sea

N

Finland

● Helsingfors   ■ St Petersburg

Christiana ●

Stockholm ■

North Sea

Baltic Sea

DENMARK
Copenhagen ■

RUSSIAN EMPIRE

Glasgow ● ● Edinburgh

UNITED KINGDOM

Liverpool ● ● Hull

Hamburg ■

▶ Berlin

Poland

Birmingham ●

Amsterdam ■

GERMAN EMPIRE

Lemberg ●

Bristol ●

NETHERLANDS

Prague ● ● Cracow

London ●

Calais ●

Brussels ●
BELGIUM   L

Rhine

● Frankfurt

▶ Paris

ATLANTIC OCEAN

● Orléans

Vienna ● ▶

● Budapest

AUSTRO-HUNGARIAN EMPIRE

FRANCE

Bern ●
SWITZERLAND

Danube

ROMANIA

Lyon ●

● Milan

Trieste ●
Venice ●

● Bucharest

Black Sea

● Bordeaux

Genoa ●

● Belgrade

SERBIA

BULGARIA

MONTE-NEGRO

● Sofia

Marseille ●

Adriatic Sea

ANDORRA

I T A L Y

ALBANIA

Constantinople ■

OTTOMAN EMPIRE

Corsica

● Barcelona

Rome ▶

● Madrid

SPAIN

Naples ●

GREECE

Aegean Sea

Balearic Is.

Sardinia

Smyrna ●

Lisbon ■

PORTUGAL

● Alicante

Cádiz ● ● Almería

Tangier ● Gibraltar
to Great Britain

M e d i t e r r a n e a n

Sicily

Athens ■

Italian occupied

Morocco
to France

A l g e r i a
to France

Tunis
to France

S e a

Crete

WORLD WAR I: 1915

THE YEAR 1915 WAS ONE OF INCREASING FRUSTRATION AND MOUNTING CASUALTIES AS COMMANDERS ON BOTH SIDES FOUND THEIR OFFENSIVE PLANS BLOCKED BY THE POWER OF THE DEFENSE. INCREASINGLY DESPERATE ATTEMPTS TO BREAK THE STALEMATE ALL ENDED IN FAILURE.

T he trench networks on the Western Front were expected to be merely temporary winter defenses. March 1915 saw a British offensive at Neuve Chapelle under Sir John French. The infantry broke through the German line, but were stopped by a hurriedly organized defensive position when their own artillery ran out of shells. In April 1915 the Germans unleashed poison gas on the British at Ypres and surprised themselves by breaking through the British line. The Germans had no reserves to push forward. On 9 May 1915 the French attacked at Artois on a six-mile (ten km) front. Again the front line was captured with heavy loss, but the French were stopped by a second line of German defenses three miles (five km) behind the first. The fighting on the Western Front culminated at Artois-Loos in September. The Allies launched a coordinated series of assaults on the German trenches, breaking through the first and second lines but suffering such horrific losses that no troops were left to burst through and exploit the successes. The Western Front stagnated into trenches for a second winter. On the Eastern Front a joint German-Austrian assault at Gorlice in late April smashed the Russian 3rd Army. Pushing forward with combined infantry-artillery-cavalry tactics, the Germans advanced at high speed to conquer thousands of square miles of productive farmland, inflict a million casualties on the Russians, and take a million prisoners. The advance halted only when the Austro-German troops ran out of supplies. At sea, the British navy achieved complete mastery of the high seas by January of 1915, having destroyed the German Pacific Fleet at the Battle of the Falkland. Isolated German warships continued to be a nuisance to merchant ships, but losses were comparatively small. In April 1915 an attempt by the British navy to break through the Dardenelles, capture Constantinople, and knock Turkey out of the war ended in failure at the hands of the Turkish heavy artillery.

Not long after the start of the First World War, the opposing armies had begun to dig themselves into lines of defensive trenches. This was because modern weapons were ten times more destructive than they had been a century earlier and battles could no longer be fought on open battlefields.

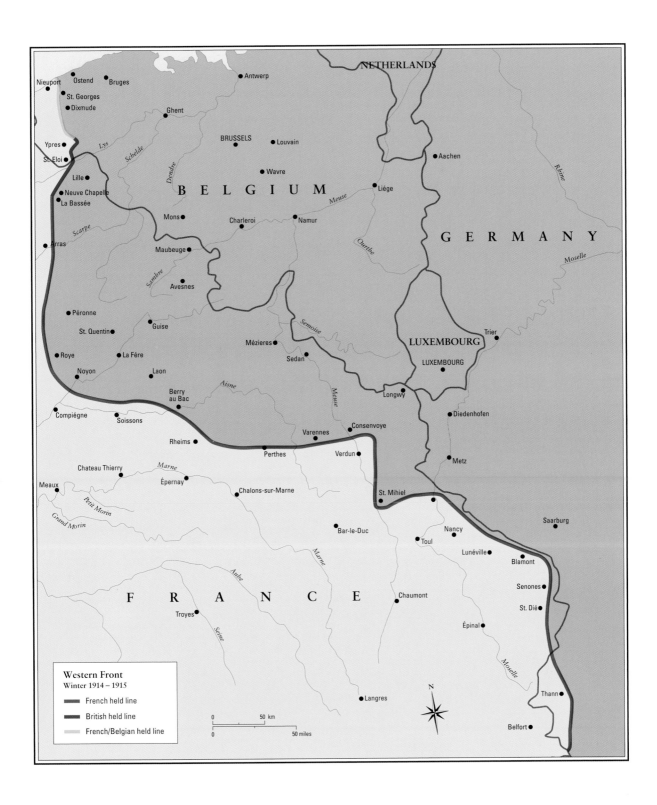

WORLD WAR I: 1916

OVER THE COURSE OF THE WINTER OF 1916 THE SENIOR COMMANDERS IN ALL ARMIES REFLECTED ON THEIR EXPERIENCES TO PREPARE THEM TO GAIN VICTORY. THEY CAME TO RADICALLY DIFFERENT CONCLUSIONS WITH THE RESULT THAT THE STALEMATE OF 1915 WAS REPEATED — AT HORRIFIC COST IN LIFE — INTO 1916.

The failures to break through the trench defenses on the Western Front were due to the overwhelming strength of defensive positions made up of trenches and strong-points manned by infantry equipped with accurate rifles and machine guns with heavy artillery in support. With no way to outflank these positions, increasingly constructed in depth, the commanders had launched frontal assaults that had cost thousands of lives, but had come close to success. The lessons the German commanders drew was that well organized and well supplied defense in depth was invulnerable. The Allies, however, drew the lesson that an overwhelming assault would break the enemy line if it was adequately supported by artillery, was followed up immediately by strong reserves and if the commanders were prepared to accept high casualties in the first attacking wave.

As early as the first campaign of the war, it was apparent that artillery was becoming the decisive weapon of land warfare. In the Russo-Japanese War only ten percent of the total casualties had been caused by artillery fire but, between 1914 and 1918, this would increase to an estimated 70 percent of total casualties. Nevertheless, sufficient numbers of defenders still often survived a bombardment to break up an infantry attack.

The next assault on the Western front in 1916 was the Battle of Verdun. The Germans struck first. On 21 February 1916 German commander-in-chief von Falkenhayn attacked Verdun with his 5th Army. His aim was to seek a battle of attrition in the Verdun salient. The French fortress of Verdun had never been captured and von Falkenheyn calculated that the French would defend to the last man. A massive artillery bombardment smashed the forward French defenses, allowing the Germans to capture Fort Douaumont and Fort Vaux. Falkenhayn then sat back to smash with artillery and machine guns the

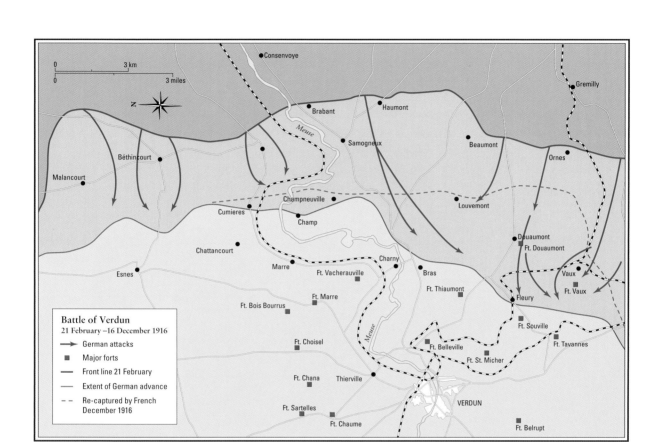

Battle of Verdun
21 February –16 December 1916

→ German attacks

■ Major forts

— Front line 21 February

— Extent of German advance

-- Re-captured by French
December 1916

inevitable French counterattacks. The French would lose half a million men at Verdun. In November 1916 a counterattack planned by General Nivelle won back the lost forts.

The terrible French losses at Verdun prompted British commander, Douglas Haig, to launch his long planned attack on 1 July 1916. The assault was to be launched in the Somme Valley and would be preceded by a heavy artillery bombardment lasting six days. The first wave of infantry attackers were to seize the shattered German trenches, the second wave would establish a corridor through the rear German defenses, then the cavalry would ride through to raid supply lines, capture enemy headquarters and generally create mayhem so that infantry reserves could advance at little cost.

On 1 July 1916 the infantry attack began at dawn on a 15-mile (24 km) front carried out by 18 British divisions with 16 French divisions in support. The artillery had not damaged the defenses as much as expected and the advancing infantry were caught in a murderous cross-fire of machine guns and artillery fire. Although the first wave failed to take its objectives, the second wave was sent forward according to plan. Only then did failure become obvious and the cavalry were halted. On the first day 20,000 British were killed and 40,000 wounded. Renewed infantry attacks continued for six weeks, but little was gained except 418,000 British casualties, 195,000 French, and 650,000 German. On the Eastern Front the year opened with the utter defeat of Serbia by Austria, the survivors of the Serb army marching through

The battle of Verdun was the longest and most costly battle of the First World War and ended after ten months with no clear victory for either the French or the German side. Some 40 million artillery shells were fired, around 250,000 men died, and another 500,000 were wounded.

The Battle of Jutland was fought between the British and German fleets in the Skaggerak, part of the North Sea in their only major encounter in the First World War. The battle proved indecisive, but it deterred the German High Seas Fleet from venturing out to fight again.

Albania to be evacuated by the British navy. On 4 June 1916 the Russian commander Brusilov launched an offensive against the Austrians at Kovel designed to force the Austrians to pull men out of Italy where they had just defeated the Italians at Trentino. Brusilov's assault was supposed to be only a diversion to keep the enemy occupied until the main Russian attack took place farther north under Evert. The attack succeeded brilliantly, but Evert refused to attack, allowing the Germans to move troops by rail to halt Brusilov's drive. Brusilov's offensive prompted Romania to join the Allies, as a result of which Germany swiftly conquered the kingdom and seized its strategic oil wells.

At sea, the British blockade of Germany and Austria was beginning to have an effect. The war industries of the two empires were starting to run short of some raw materials. The German High Seas Fleet had been probing British reactions for some time. On 30 May 1916 the fleet steamed out into the North Sea in an attempt to ambush and destroy the British battle cruisers.

The resulting Battle of Jutland saw the main war fleets clash off southern Sweden. Faced with the superiority of the Royal Navy, the German strategy was to isolate and destroy a portion of the British Grand Fleet. Thus, whereas Admiral Jellicoe of Britain intended to maneuver the Grand Fleet so as to allow its heavy guns to bear on the German High Seas Fleet in any naval engagement, his German opposite number, Vice-Admiral Scheer, had no intention of becoming involved in a gunnery duel. The conflicting intentions were to contribute to the inconclusive nature of the only great naval battle of the war. Britain numbered 151 ships, while Germany had 103. Rear-Admiral Hipper's battlecruisers were designated as bait to draw Vice-Admiral Beatty's battlecruisers on to the main High Seas Fleet before Jellicoe could come to Beatty's support. The first clash between the battlecruisers took place at 1548 hours on 31 May 1916 off Jutland, Beatty losing the ships *Indefatigable* and *Queen Mary* and suffering damage to the Lion. However, upon sighting the main High Seas Fleet, Beatty turned back toward Jellicoe at 1726 hours and almost succeeded in luring Scheer in turn. Scheer promptly executed a "battle turnaway" in the process of which another battlecruiser, *Invincible*, was sunk. The two fleets again clashed in fading light at 1915 hours upon which Scheer covered his retirement by a massed torpedo attack which forced Jellicoe to turn away. Overall, Britain lost 14 ships and Germany 11. Having sunk 14 ships including the three battlecruisers for the loss of 11 of their own ships including the battlecruiser, Lutzow, the Germans could claim a tactical success; but the strategic advantage still lay with the Royal Navy.

The maneuvers that followed were complex and confusing. They ended with the Germans narrowly avoiding blundering into the heart of the British fleet, but managing to escape back to port. The British had lost substantially more ships in the encounter, but are generally believed to have won as the German fleet never again put to sea to risk a major battle. The British blockade remained intact. In Mesopotamia, the British army under siege at Kut surrendered to the Turks on 29 April 1916. It took until December 1916 to organize a fresh invasion force from India, which landed in Mesopotamia to begin yet another advance up the valley. Meanwhile, the tribes of Arabia had risen in revolt against the Turks, led by Sherif Husain Ibn Ali of Mecca. The British sent a junior intelligence officer, T.E. Lawrence, to assess the situation. He persuaded the British to send the Arabs large quantities of arms, while advising Husain to concentrate on attacking Turkish supply lines, not the Turkish army itself. Lawrence's writings which include *The Seven Pillars of Wisdom*, have been read around the world. Lawrence became the subject of the major film, *Lawrence of Arabia*.

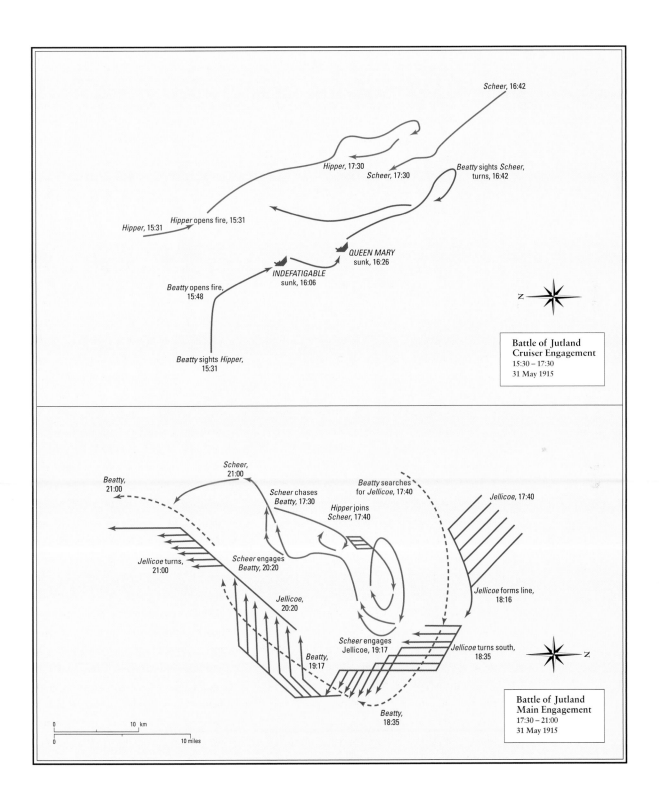

Scheer, 16:42

Hipper, 17:30

Scheer, 17:30

Beatty sights Scheer,
turns, 16:42

Hipper opens fire, 15:31

Hipper, 15:31

QUEEN MARY
sunk, 16:26

INDEFATIGABLE
sunk, 16:06

Beatty opens fire,
15:48

Beatty sights Hipper,
15:31

N

Battle of Jutland
Cruiser Engagement
15:30 – 17:30
31 May 1915

Scheer,
21:00

Beatty,
21:00

Scheer chases
Beatty, 17:30

Beatty searches
for Jellicoe, 17:40

Jellicoe, 17:40

Hipper joins
Scheer, 17:40

Jellicoe turns,
21:00

Scheer engages
Beatty, 20:20

Jellicoe forms line,
18:16

Jellicoe,
20:20

Scheer engages
Jellicoe, 19:17

Jellicoe turns south,
18:35

Beatty,
19:17

N

Beatty,
18:35

Battle of Jutland
Main Engagement
17:30 – 21:00
31 May 1915

0   10 km

0   10 miles

WORLD WAR I: 1917

BY 1917 WAR WEARINESS WAS SETTING IN. ALL COMBATANT NATIONS HAD SUFFERED HEAVY LOSSES, AND YET NO END TO THE WAR WAS IN SIGHT. THERE WERE NO INDICATIONS THAT VICTORY WAS ABOUT TO BE ACHIEVED, AND STILL THE BLOODBATH CONTINUED.

The year began with conflicting actions by Germany. On 12 December 1916 the German Chancellor, Theobald Hollweg, had issued a "Peace Note" declaring that Germany was willing to negotiate with her enemies. US President Wilson decided to act as neutral arbiter and invited all the belligerents to state their war aims in the hope that a compromise peace was possible, but neither side was willing to compromise at all and the initiative failed. In March 1917 came news of the Zimmerman Telegram, a message sent by the German government to Mexico offering to reward Mexico with Texas, California and other areas lost to the USA after the US-Mexican War if Mexico would declare war on the USA. On 2 April 1917 the US declared war on Germany. Having recaptured the German gains at Verdun, French general Robert Nivelle thought that he had perfected a method for attacking trenches. Nivelle's plan was to launch a massive surprise attack to overwhelm the German front line, followed by leapfrog attacks to break through the rear. To make surprise even more certain, the British launched a diversionary attack at Arras on 9 April 1917. The assault was designed to give every impression of being a major offensive, but was in fact planned to capture the strategic Vimy Ridge. Once that was captured, the attack ended. Nivelle's attack was launched with a million soldiers on 16 April 1917, and failed dismally. Within 48 hours 200,000 men were killed or wounded for no advance worth recording. The French army cracked. A total of 54 divisions mutinied and refused to obey orders; two even set out to march on Paris to start a revolution but backed off when faced by loyal regiments.

On 7 June 1917 the British began the Third Battle of Ypres, often pronounced "Wipers" by the British. Massive mines filled with explosives were set off under the German front line on Messines Ridge. The ridge was captured at once, but assaults on other high ground were halted by unseasonably heavy

Unlike its prelude, the Battle of Messines, which achieved its objective of capturing a defensive ridge southeast of Ypres, the third Battle of Ypres failed to win control of the village of Passchendaele for the Allied forces. They were unsuccessful in cracking the German defenses, despite several massive attacks.

rains turning the Flanders plains to liquid mud. On 30 October 1917 a new attack toward the village of Passchendaele finally captured the high ground, but at terrible cost. In Italy, a relatively quiet year exploded into violence on 24 October 1917 with a joint German-Austrian offensive at Caporetto which smashed the Italian army. The victorious generals contented themselves with securing high ground that could be easily defended for the German troops were needed elsewhere.

On the Eastern Front the year began with mutinies among the Russian army. Tsar Nicholas II abdicated on 15 March 1917. The new republican government tried to continue the war, but the revolutionary fervor was too strong. In November the Communist Party, led by Lenin, staged a coup that overthrew the government. Lenin at once opened peace negotiations with Germany. Russia was out of the war. On the Turkish front, Lawrence

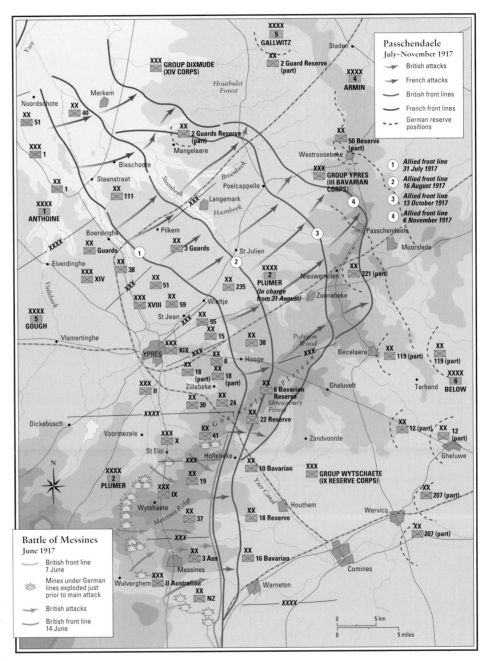

was having great success in Arabia; capturing the port off Aqaba to open up a direct route for British arms and supplies to reach the Arab rebels. At the same time a British army was advancing from Egypt along the coast and by October had reached Jerusalem. In Mesopotamia the newly arrived British-Indian army refused to be lured inland and instead fought and defeated the Turks within reach of the sea. Only then did the advance on Baghdad begin.

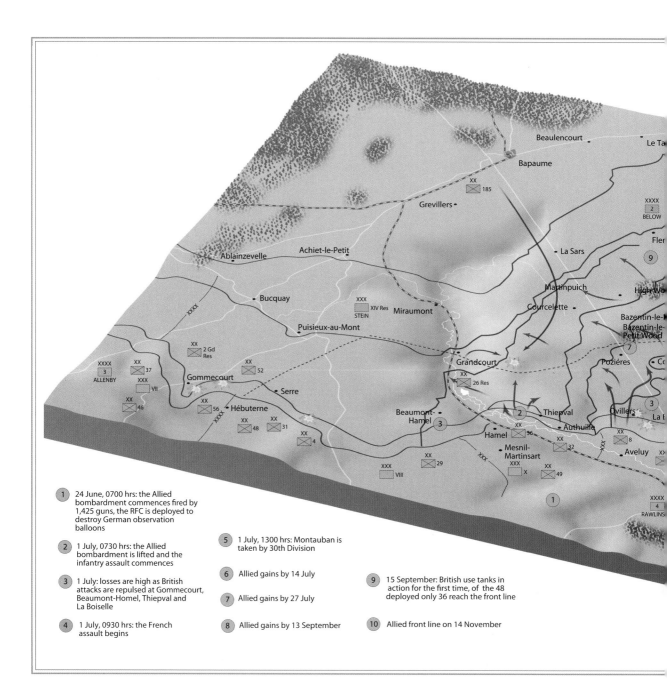

1. 24 June, 0700 hrs: the Allied bombardment commences fired by 1,425 guns, the RFC is deployed to destroy German observation balloons

2. 1 July, 0730 hrs: the Allied bombardment is lifted and the infantry assault commences

3. 1 July: losses are high as British attacks are repulsed at Gommecourt, Beaumont-Homel, Thiepval and La Boiselle

4. 1 July, 0930 hrs: the French assault begins

5. 1 July, 1300 hrs: Montauban is taken by 30th Division

6. Allied gains by 14 July

7. Allied gains by 27 July

8. Allied gains by 13 September

9. 15 September: British use tanks in action for the first time, of the 48 deployed only 36 reach the front line

10. Allied front line on 14 November

To win a quick victory, the French General Robert Nivelle planned simultaneous Anglo-French attacks on German-held territory. The plan failed. The preliminary bombardment was ineffective and the French had too few howitzers. By the time Nivelle's offensive ended on May 9, the French had lost 187,000 men.

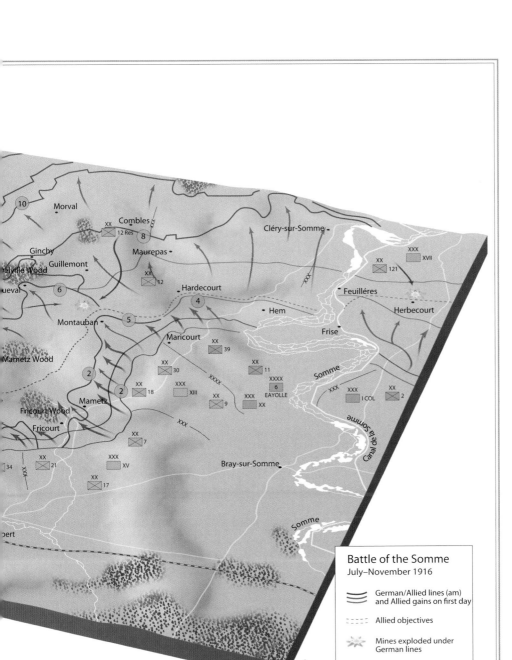

10
Morval
XX
12 Res
Combles
8
Cléry-sur-Somme
XXX XVII
Ginchy
Guillemont
Maurepas
XX
12
Hardecourt
4
Hem
Feuilléres
XX
121
Delville Wood
6
5
Montauban
Maricourt
XX
39
Herbecourt
Frise
Somme
Mametz Wood
2
XX
30
XX
11
XXXX
6
EAYOLLE
XXX
I COL
XX
2
2
XX
18
XXX
XIII
XX
9
XXX
XX
Mametz
Fricourt Wood
Fricourt
XX
7
Somme
Canal de la Somme
34
XX
21
XXX
XV
Bray-sur-Somme
XX
17
Somme
bert
Somme

Battle of the Somme
July–November 1916

≋ German/Allied lines (am) and Allied gains on first day

⊏⊐⊏⊐ Allied objectives

✳ Mines exploded under German lines

WORLD WAR I: 1918

THE WAR WEARINESS THAT HAD EMERGED IN 1917 DEVELOPED IN 1918 INTO UTTER EXHAUSTION. THE COMBATANT NATIONS WERE BEING DRAINED OF MEN AND MONEY ON A COLOSSAL SCALE. SO MANY MEN WERE FIGHTING WITH SUCH EXPENSIVE WEAPONS ON SUCH WIDE FRONTS THAT THE EFFORT SIMPLY COULD NOT BE MAINTAINED.

Among the more expensive items being demanded by the war were the new weapons that had emerged only in the 20th century. Three of these — heavy field artillery, machine guns, and concrete emplacements — could be argued to be developments of weapons already in use the previous century. Two, however, were completely new: the aircraft and the tank. Between them they would revolutionize warfare. By 1918 the ability of the aircraft to co-operate with ground forces to good effect was appreciated and most of the big battles of the year had a distinctive air element. Specialized bombers carried out raids on railroads, supply dumps, and troop concentrations behind enemy lines, while fighters — then called scouts — protected the bombers, attacked enemy bombers and shot up ground targets. It was the Germans who first grouped bombers and fighters into separate squadrons and trained pilots accordingly.

The tank grew out of the British military tractor of 1907. This was a machine running on caterpillar tracks and armored against enemy small arms fire that was used to tow artillery, carry supplies across open ground, and collect wounded. The early tanks were cumbersome, slow, and vulnerable to artillery fire. They were designed to advance to the enemy trench line and knock out machine gun positions, so that the infantry could rush forward to capture the trenches. They first entered conflict in large numbers at the Battle of Cambrai in 1917 and achieved a spectacular breakthrough, though the cavalry that poured through the gap were soon halted by artillery and machine guns in reserve positions. The British therefore developed new tank models — called "whippets" — designed to move faster and farther so that they could accompany the cavalry into enemy rear areas. The Germans and French, meanwhile, were copying the idea with trench-attack models of their own. The first battles on the Western Front in which

The Germans launched "Michel", their last series of offensives of the War on 21 March, 1918 with a 6,000-gun bombardment and a gas attack. More offensives followed, but the German troops were starving and eventually tired, making them vulnerable to the final Allied assaults that began in July 1918.

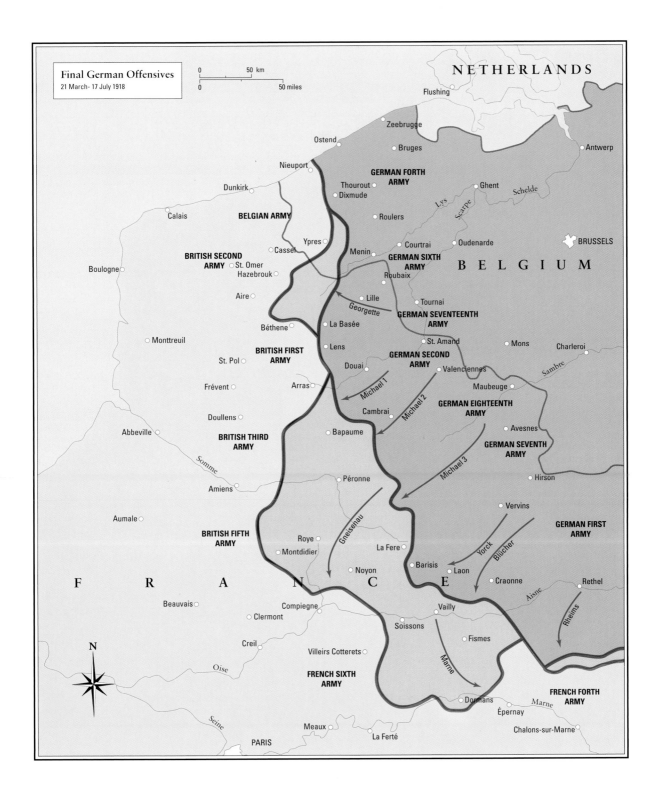

Final German Offensives
21 March- 17 July 1918

0 ___ 50 km
0 ___ 50 miles

NETHERLANDS

Flushing

Zeebrugge

Ostend   Bruges   Antwerp

Nieuport

GERMAN FORTH
ARMY

Dunkirk   Thourout   Ghent   Schelde
                 Dixmude

Calais   BELGIAN ARMY   Roulers   Lys   Scarpe

Boulogne   Ypres   Courtrai   Oudenarde   BRUSSELS

BRITISH SECOND   Cassel   Menin   GERMAN SIXTH
ARMY   St. Omer   ARMY   BELGIUM
         Hazebrouk   Roubaix

Aire   Lille   GERMAN SEVENTEENTH
                 Georgette   ARMY
Béthene   La Basée   Tournai
                              St. Amand   Mons   Charleroi

Monttreuil   Lens   GERMAN SECOND
St. Pol   BRITISH FIRST   ARMY   Sambre
            ARMY   Douai   Valenciennes
Frévent   Maubeuge
            Arras   Michael 1
                     Michael 2   GERMAN EIGHTEENTH
Doullens   Cambrai   ARMY   Avesnes

Abbeville   BRITISH THIRD   Bapaume   GERMAN SEVENTH
              ARMY   ARMY

                              Michael 3
                 Somme   Hirson

Amiens   Péronne   Vervins

Aumale   GERMAN FIRST
                                              ARMY
         BRITISH FIFTH   Roye
         ARMY   Montdidier   La Fere   Yorck   Blücher
                              Gneisenau   Barisis   Laon
                     Noyon   Craonne   Rethel
F R A   N   C   E   Aisne
                 Compiegne   Vailly   Rheims
Beauvais   Soissons
         Clermont   Fismes

         Creil
                 Villeirs Cotterets   Marne
N   Oise   FRENCH SIXTH
                         ARMY
                                   Dormans   Marne   FRENCH FORTH
                                        Épernay   ARMY
         Seine   Meaux   La Ferté   Chalons-sur-Marne
PARIS

the new weapons were used went well. Shifting the forces that had been fighting the Russians to form the assault forces, Germany was able to mount major offensives in the west. The top German commanders, Hindenburg and Ludendorff, recognized that they needed to defeat Britain and France by August 1918. If they failed, the men and resources of the USA would have arrived on the Western Front and Germany

Opposite page: The American advance during the Meuse-Argonne offensive of 1918 began on 25 September. Ten American divisions advanced to capture Montfauon on 27 September and Cunel and Romagne by 13 October. By 5 November they reached Sedan. The Germans were shocked into withdrawal. Six days later, the war ended.

On 4 June, four armies commanded by the great Russian General Alexei Brusoliv attacked the Austrians across the border with Galicia. The Russians penetrated deep into Austrian territory and captured 13,000 prisoners. But this successful start failed to continue. Faced by the Germans as well as the Austrians, the Russian effort faded out by September 1916. The Russians suffered staggering losses in the process.

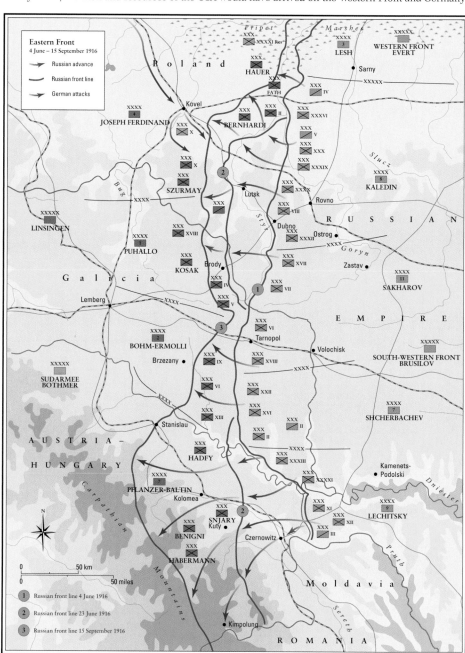

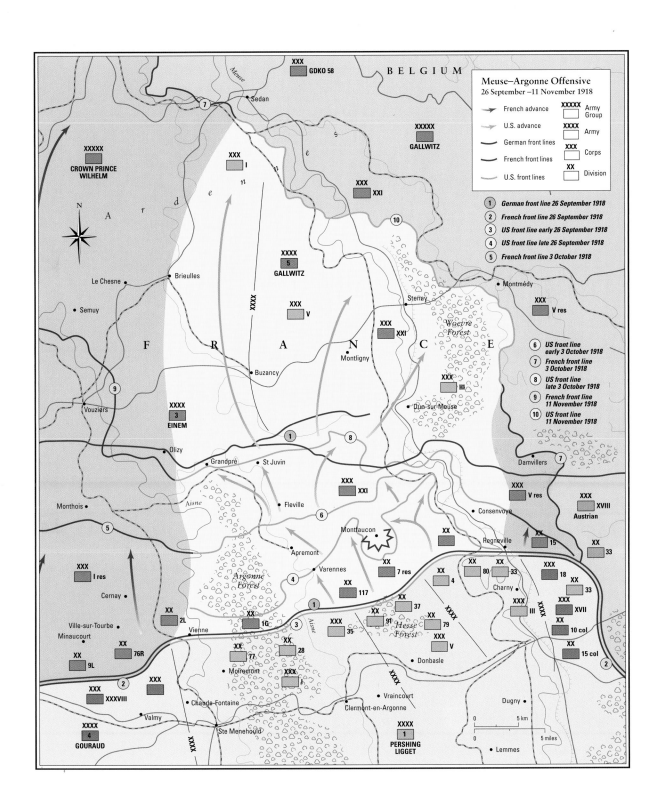

Meuse–Argonne Offensive
26 September –11 November 1918

→ French advance
→ U.S. advance
— German front lines
— French front lines
— U.S. front lines

XXXXX Army Group
XXXX Army
XXX Corps
XX Division

① German front line 26 September 1918
② French front line 26 September 1918
③ US front line early 26 September 1918
④ US front line late 26 September 1918
⑤ French front line 3 October 1918
⑥ US front line early 3 October 1918
⑦ French front line 3 October 1918
⑧ US front line late 3 October 1918
⑨ French front line 11 November 1918
⑩ US front line 11 November 1918

would be outmatched.

The German assault began before dawn on 21 March 1918 when 6,000 artillery opened up to pound key defense points in the British lines around St Quentin. At dawn tanks lumbered forward to overrun the front line trenches while specialist storm-trooper infantry units — equipped with grenades and light machine guns — pushed ahead to attack and disrupt the rear trenches and support defenses. Simultaneously bomber aircraft flew in to pound supply lines and reinforcements while the main infantry attack followed up to overtake the tanks and storm-troopers. On 24 March 1918 the Germans broke through the final defense line. Infantry and cavalry poured forwards to sweep across the landscape, chase the British soldiers, and loot the villages. But the great breakthrough failed to win the war. The German supply lines up to the trench system were a superb blend of rail and road transport. But getting supplies over the captured trenches and through the devastated lands beyond meant horse-drawn wagons able to cope with the terrain. There were simply not enough of them, and within a week the German advance came to a halt due to lack of ammunition and food. The Germans launched two more massive attacks that spring, at Armentiéres and the Aisne. Both achieved stunning gains at first, but they too were eventually halted.

The Allies had been awaiting the arrival of the Americans and launched only modest counterattacks during the early summer. The main offensive opened on 8 August at Amiens with a US division leading the way. The attack was spearheaded by the biggest tank assault of the war and for the first time it was planned and directed by tank officers. The German defenses were broken within hours, after which whippet tanks and cavalry burst through to create mayhem in the German rear areas. Six German divisions collapsed. In September 1918 the Germans halted on the prepared defenses of the Hindenburg Line. The Allied high command gave the task of piercing the line to a joint US-French assault in the Meuse-Argonne sector. General Pershing prepared his US 1st Army well, instructing them on all the latest tactics and calling up tanks and aircraft from his allies. The attack went in as fog blanketed the battlefield, obscuring the American troops from German artillery and machine guns. Working smoothly with their Allies, the Americans broke through each defensive line in turn, stepping aside to allow reserves through to assault the next line. By dusk it was over, the German defenses had crumbled. Hindenburg and Ludendorff realized that the war was lost. Fearing Britain and France would want to impose harsh terms, the offer of an armistice was sent to President Wilson of the USA on 3 October 1918. Consulting his allies, Wilson refused the terms offered and suggested his own. The war went on. In Mesopotamia and Palestine the advance of the British and Arab forces had been steady all year. Baghdad fell in March, Jericho in September 1918, and Damascus in October. On 31 October 1918 the Turks called for an immediate armistice and stopped fighting. In Italy the front had been quiet throughout the year, but a joint Italian-British attack with 57 divisions smashed the Austrian front line and pushed on over the key Piave River. Austrian Emperor Karl recognized that defeat was imminent. On 27 October 1918 he sent a note to the German Kaiser saying that he was about to surrender, which he did on 4 November. In the west the Allied advance toward the Rhine was grinding mercilessly onward. With his allies gone, Kaiser Wilhelm sacked Ludendorff and replaced him with Gröner. Four days later the German navy mutinied, demanding peace. On 9 November 1918 rioting broke out in Berlin. Wilhelm abdicated rather than surrender — a task left to the civilian government to carry out on 11 November 1918. The war was over.

The Germans launched several offensives late in 1918, hoping for a quick victory before the Americans could fully deploy their forces. But with serious unrest in Germany and mutiny threatening in the armed forces, they had no chance, and by October 1918, they were forced to ask for an armistice.

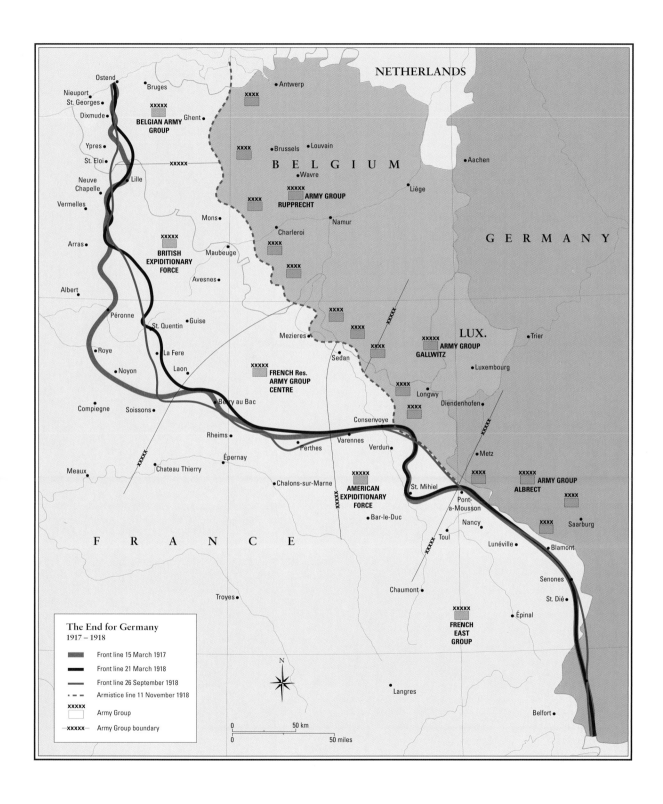

NETHERLANDS

Ostend
Nieuport
St. Georges
Dixmude
• Bruges
• Antwerp
xxxx
**BELGIAN ARMY
GROUP**
Ghent •
Ypres •
St. Eloi •
• Brussels • Louvain
xxxx
B E L G I U M
• Aachen
Neuve
Chapelle •
Lille •
• Wavre
• Liége
Vermelles •
xxxxx
**ARMY GROUP
RUPPRECHT**
xxxx
Mons •
• Charleroi
• Namur
G E R M A N Y
Arras •
xxxxx
**BRITISH
EXPIDITIONARY
FORCE**
Maubeuge •
xxxx
Albert •
Avesnes •
xxxx
Péronne •
• Guise
St. Quentin •
Mezieres •
xxxx
xxxx
LUX.
xxxxx
**ARMY GROUP
GALLWITZ**
• Trier
Roye •
La Fere •
xxxx
Sedan •
xxxxx
**FRENCH Res.
ARMY GROUP
CENTRE**
xxxx
Longwy •
• Luxembourg
• Noyon
Laon •
• Berry au Bac
xxxx
Diendenhofen •
Compiegne •
Soissons •
Conservoye •
Rheims •
Varennes •
Verdun •
• Metz
Meaux •
Perthes •
• Épernay
xxxx
St. Mihiel •
• Chateau Thierry
xxxxx
**AMERICAN
EXPIDITIONARY
FORCE**
Pont-
a-Mousson •
xxxxx
**ARMY GROUP
ALBRECT**
xxxx
• Chalons-sur-Marne
F   R   A   N   C   E
• Bar-le-Duc
Nancy •
xxxx
Saarburg
• Toul
Lunéville •
• Blamont
Troyes •
Chaumont •
Senones •
St. Dié •
xxxxx
**FRENCH
EAST
GROUP**
• Épinal
• Langres
Belfort •

The End for Germany
1917 – 1918

▬ Front line 15 March 1917
▬ Front line 21 March 1918
▬ Front line 26 September 1918
┅ Armistice line 11 November 1918
xxxxx □ Army Group
—xxxxx— Army Group boundary

N

0   50 km
0   50 miles

World War I: Armistice Treaty 1918

THE ARMISTICE TREATY AGREED IN THE FALL OF 1918 BROUGHT AN END TO THE WAR, BUT NOT TO THE VIOLENCE. CHAOS ERUPTED IN THE DEFEATED EMPIRES AS BANKRUPTCY, FAMINE, AND UNREST LED TO REBELLIONS, REVOLUTIONS, AND CIVIL WAR.

I n Germany, the abdication of the Kaiser was followed by the declaration of a republic by the members of the Reichstag, the German parliament. Street fighting between political factions then broke out and an attempt at a revolution by Communist forces was made. The recently defeated German army appeared on the streets to enforce order while a national assembly of politicians met at Weimar to draw up a new constitution in 1919. In 1923 the new Nazi Party attempted a coup in Munich to seize the Bavarian state, but the rebellion was put down and the Nazi leader, Adolf Hitler, thrown into prison. Thereafter Germany seemed to stabilize, though political street violence never ceased.

The Austrian Empire, meanwhile, was collapsing. The Empire was made up of many different nationalities held together only by a shared loyalty to the Hapsburg monarchy. That loyalty was shaken first by the death of the popular Emperor Franz Joseph in 1916 then shattered by the military defeat and the hardships that followed. By December 1918 the various nationalities were busy transforming their local governments into fully independent states. The Romanian areas were simply taken over by Romania, as the Italian areas passed to Italy. The Polish areas joined with Polish areas of what had been Germany and Russia to build a new Polish state, while the Czechs, Slovaks, Serbs, Slovenes, and others set up their own states.

The anarchy was worst in Russia. The Communist coup of November 1917 had been an urban Russian revolution with little support in rural areas or non-Russian parts of the empire. By mid-1918 several areas had declared themselves independent of Moscow, rural areas were refusing to obey new laws, and several armies of pro-Tsarist troops were on the march. The fighting would last until 1921 and cost 13 million lives through war, famine, and disease. Finland, Estonia, Latvia, Lithuania, and Poland achieved independence, but elsewhere the Communists were triumphant.

Disastrous military defeats and the weakness and military ineptitude of the autocratic Tsar, Nicholas II, combined in 1917 to promote two Russian revolutions, first by the moderate Mensheviks, then by the more extremist Bolsheviks. In 1918, the Bolsheviks murdered the Tsar and his family and set up a Communist republic.

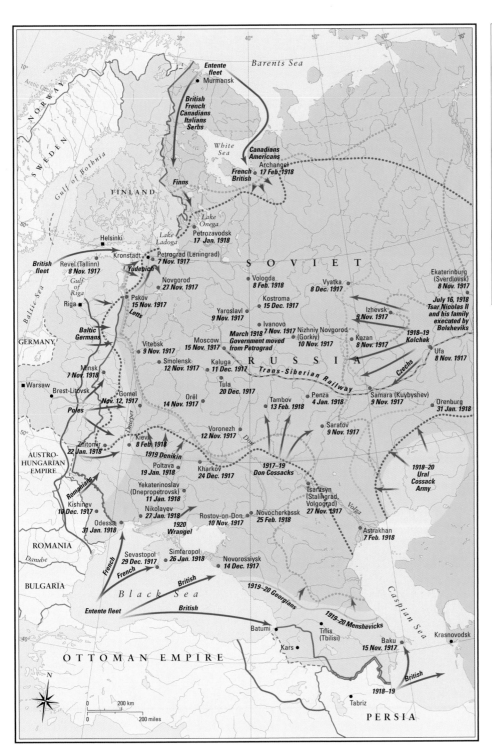

The Russian Revolution
1917-1921

Territory of the Russian Empire, 1914

Russian front, March 1917

Line set by Treaty of Brest-Litovsk, March 1918

White Russian armies

Non-Russian anti-Bolshevik forces

Town taken over by Bolsheviks, Nov. 1917–Feb. 1918 (date given in new calendar)

Boundary of areas controlled by Bolsheviks

August 1918

Eastern front, April 1919

October 1919

Controlled by the Soviet Union, May 1920

Soviet boundary, March 1921

Barents Sea

NORWAY

Arctic Circle

SWEDEN

Gulf of Bothnia

Entente fleet
Murmansk

British French Canadians Italians Serbs

White Sea

Canadians Americans
Archangel 17 Feb. 1918

French British

FINLAND

Finns

SOVIET

Lake Onega
Lake Ladoga

Petrozavodsk 17 Jan. 1918

Helsinki

Kronstadt

British fleet

Revel (Tallinn) 8 Nov. 1917

Yudenich

Petrograd (Leningrad) 7 Nov. 1917

Ekaterinburg (Sverdlovsk) 8 Nov. 1917

Gulf of Riga

Pskov 15 Nov. 1917

Letts

Novgorod 27 Nov. 1917

Vologda 8 Feb. 1918

Vyatka 8 Dec. 1917

July 16, 1918 Tsar Nicolas II and his family executed by Bolsheviks

Riga

Baltic Sea

Baltic Germans

Kostroma 15 Dec. 1917

Izhevsk 9 Nov. 1917

1918–19 Kolchak

GERMANY

Vitebsk 9 Nov. 1917

Yaroslavl 9 Nov. 1917

Ivanovo 7 Nov. 1917

Nizhniy Novgorod (Gorkiy) 10 Nov. 1917

Kazan 8 Nov. 1917

Ufa 8 Nov. 1917

Minsk 7 Nov. 1918

Moscow 15 Nov. 1917

March 1918 Government moved from Petrograd

Smolensk 12 Nov. 1917

RUSSIA

Warsaw

Brest-Litovsk

Kaluga 11 Dec. 1917

Trans-Siberian Railway

Czechs

Gomel Nov. 12, 1917

Orël 14 Nov. 1917

Tula 20 Dec. 1917

Samara (Kuybyshev) 9 Nov. 1917

Orenburg 31 Jan. 1918

Poles

Dnieper

Tambov 13 Feb. 1918

Penza 4 Jan. 1918

AUSTRO-HUNGARIAN EMPIRE

Zhitomir 22 Jan. 1918

Kiev 8 Feb. 1918

1919 Denikin

Voronezh 12 Nov. 1917

Don

Saratov 9 Nov. 1917

1918–20 Ural Cossack Army

Poltava 19 Jan. 1918

Kharkov 24 Dec. 1917

1917–19 Don Cossacks

Kishinev 10 Dec. 1917

Yekaterinoslav (Dnepropetrovsk) 11 Jan. 1918

Tsaritsyn (Stalingrad, Volgograd) 27 Nov. 1917

Romanians

Nikolayev 27 Jan. 1918

Rostov-on-Don 10 Nov. 1917

Novocherkassk 25 Feb. 1918

Volga

ROMANIA

Odessa 31 Jan. 1918

1920 Wrangel

Astrakhan 7 Feb. 1918

Danube

Sevastopol 29 Dec. 1917

French

Simferopol 26 Jan. 1918

Novorossiysk 14 Dec. 1917

French

BULGARIA

Black Sea

British

1919–20 Georgians

Caspian Sea

Entente fleet

British

British

1919–20 Mensheviks

Batumi

Tiflis (Tbilisi)

Baku 15 Nov. 1917

Krasnovodsk

OTTOMAN EMPIRE

Kars

N

British

1918–19

0 ___ 200 km

0 ___ 200 miles

Tabriz

PERSIA

Aftermath of War 1918-1939

THE YEARS BETWEEN THE TWO WORLD WARS OF THE 20TH CENTURY ARE GENERALLY CONSIDERED TO BE ONES OF PEACE, ALBEIT WITH TENSIONS RISING THAT WOULD ULTIMATELY EXPLODE INTO THE SECOND WORLD WAR. HOWEVER, SEVERAL SMALLER WARS BROKE OUT AROUND THE WORLD.

I n 1919 the League of Nations was established to find a peaceful solution to any future conflict. Based in Geneva, the League was joined by all the victors of the First World War, except the USA, and most neutral countries. Germany and the USSR joined later. Although it managed to solve disputes between smaller states in the 1920s, it failed to constrain aggression by larger states in the 1930s. Early in 1912 Chinese rebel army officers and provincial governors had seized power and announced that the six-year old emperor, Puyi, had abdicated in favor of a republic. The new regime proved to be just as ineffectual as that it replaced. The provinces of Tibet and Mongolia declared themselves independent while several provincial governors acted as independent warlords. In 1926 a new force, the Kuomintang led by Chiang Kai-shek announced that it wanted to see a strong, united China. Gathering mass support from peasants and city dwellers in central China, Chiang seized the central government and by 1930 had imposed his rule on most of China.

In 1931 a dangerous new element entered the turbulent Chinese scene. Japan had long been a major investor in Chinese industry, with Japanese-owned enterprises being concentrated in the north around Tientsin and Lu Shan, which lay close to Korea, held by Japan since 1910. Worried by the instability of warlord activity, the Japanese invaded Manchuria in 1931, later expanding into the neighboring province of Jehol. Two years later the Japanese brought Puyi out of retirement and declared him to be Emperor of Manchuria, though real power remained with the Japanese. In 1936 the Japanese invaded China in force

Ultra-conservative, right-wing activity was common in Europe during the 1930s, even in countries not ruled by fascist dictatorships or subject to repressive governments. The Fascist regimes were headed by Adolf Hitler in Nazi Germany, Benito Mussolini in Fascist Italy and, after 1939, by Francisco Franco in Spain.

The Fascist States c. 1937

- Democratic countries
- Repressive or conservative countries
- Fascist countries
- Communist dictatorship
- Right-wing activity

0   200 km
0   200 miles

N

Arctic Circle

Norwegian Sea

Faeroe Islands
to Denmark

FINLAND

■ Helsinki   • Leningrad

Oslo   ■ Tallinn

■ Stockholm   ESTONIA

Baltic Sea   ■ Riga

N O R W A Y   S W E D E N   LATVIA

North Sea   DENMARK   LITHUANIA   ■ Kaunas
Copenhagen ■   Danzig   Königsberg
    free city under   ■ Kaunas
    League of Nations   East

Glasgow ●   ● Edinburgh   Prussia   U.S.S.R.

UNITED KINGDOM   ■ Hamburg

● Dublin   ■ Berlin   ■ Warsaw   ■ Brest Litovsk
Liverpool ●
IRELAND   ● Birmingham   P O L A N D

London ■   GERMANY   ● Cracow   ● Lvov
    Amsterdam ■
    NETHERLANDS
● Calais   Brussels ■   ● Frankfurt   CZECHOSLOVAKIA
    BELGIUM   SAAR   ● Prague
    Rhine   **autonomous under**
    ● Paris   **League of Nations**   Vienna ●
A T L A N T I C   Budapest ●
O C E A N   ● Orléans   AUSTRIA   HUNGARY   R O M A N I A
    Bern ● SWITZ.
    F R A N C E   Lyon ●   ● Milan   Trieste ●   ● Bucharest
    Belgrade ■   *Danube*
    ● Bordeaux   ● Genoa   Venice ●
    YUGOSLAVIA   BULGARIA
    Marseille ●   ● Sofia   *Black Sea*
ANDORRA   I T A L Y   *Adriatic Sea*

PORTUGAL   ● Barcelona   Rome ●   ALBANIA   Istanbul ■

Lisbon ■   ● Madrid   Naples ●   *Aegean Sea*   TURKEY
S P A I N   GREECE   ● Izmir
    Balearic Is.   Athens ●
● Alicante   **Italian occupied**

Cádiz ■   ● Almería
Gibraltar
Tangier   **to Great Britain**
international zone   M e d i t e r r a n e a n   S e a

Morocco   A l g e r i a   Tunisia

to   F r a n c e   Libya
    to Italy

and by 1939 had occupied all important coastal cities and great swathes of northern China.

Other troubles were on a smaller scale, but were not less violent or significant. In the Middle East the former provinces of the Turkish Empire were transferred to the League of Nations, but administrated by either Britain or France. In 1920 a serious rebellion broke out in Iraq, which led the British to appoint Prince Faisal to be King of Iraq though he had only limited powers until 1932. In 1922 a similar uprising in Egypt caused the British to grant effective self-government, though a large British army remained to guard the crucial Suez Canal. The situation in Palestine was more complicated as the British had earlier agreed to support Jewish settlement in the area, and this was opposed by the native Palestinians. Riots, rebellions, and assassinations continued in Palestine throughout the 1920s and 1930s.

In North Africa in 1911 the French faced rebellions in Morocco and Algeria from inland tribes who resented rule by the coastal peoples almost as much as they did French economic dominance. The French chose not to compromise, but instead opted for a large-scale military occupation that was successful, but costly. In Libya the Italians faced similar, but less intense, unrest.

After the economic crash of 1929, many areas began to suffer poverty and hardship on a scale not met before. The Indian subcontinent was especially badly hit. In those areas ruled by Britain there was widespread unrest between 1930 and 1934 that led to a growing political movement demanding independence. Most of the states still ruled by local dynasties remained quiet. In Europe social and economic problems led to a number of dictatorships being established. The first of these dictators was Benito Mussolini, who took power in Italy in 1922, though he cloaked his rule in legal clothes under King Victor Emmanuel III who remained head of state. Mussolini pushed through an industrialization policy and went a long way to stamping out the endemic corruption of the Italian government. He later annexed Albania and Ethiopia to Italian rule. In Hungary in 1920 Admiral Horthy allowed some limited local democracy while claiming to rule on behalf of the absent Hapsburg emperors. In 1926 power in Poland was seized by former president Jozef Pilsudski, who ruled until his death in 1935.

In Spain during the 1930s a brutal civil war ended with General Francisco Franco leading a military dictatorship. Army garrisons in Spanish Morocco, led by General Franco, revolted against the left-wing government in Spain. Within a few months Germany and Italy had sent air and ground forces to help Franco, while the Russians did the same for the Republicans. This enabled all three countries to test their latest weapons in combat and the war became a technical laboratory. Amid the inevitable atrocities that civil war brings, the German bombing of the Basque town of Guernica on 25 April, 1937 was the most prominent, and confirmed people's worst fears of what a major European war would be like. Though the Republicans, aided by foreign volunteers (the International Brigades) managed to hold Madrid throughout most of the war, Franco's Nationalists gradually brought the whole country under their control. Britain and France adopted a non-interventionist policy, and attempted a naval blockade, but Germany and Italy were uncooperative and continued to supply arms.

Events were to prove that the most dangerous of the various European dictators was Adolf Hitler who was elected to power in Germany in 1933 only to spend the next three years consolidating his power into one of absolute dictatorship. An Austrian-born German politician, he was the leader of the National Socialist German Worker's Party, which became popularly known as the Nazi Party. He gained support by promoting nationalism, anti-semitism, and anti-Communism.

After 1912, when the Chinese emperor was deposed and replaced by a republic, Japan attempted to obtain commercial and diplomatic privileges in China. In 1931, the Japanese invaded and occupied the Chinese region of Manchuria where they set up the puppet state of Manchukuo. A full-scale war followed in 1937.

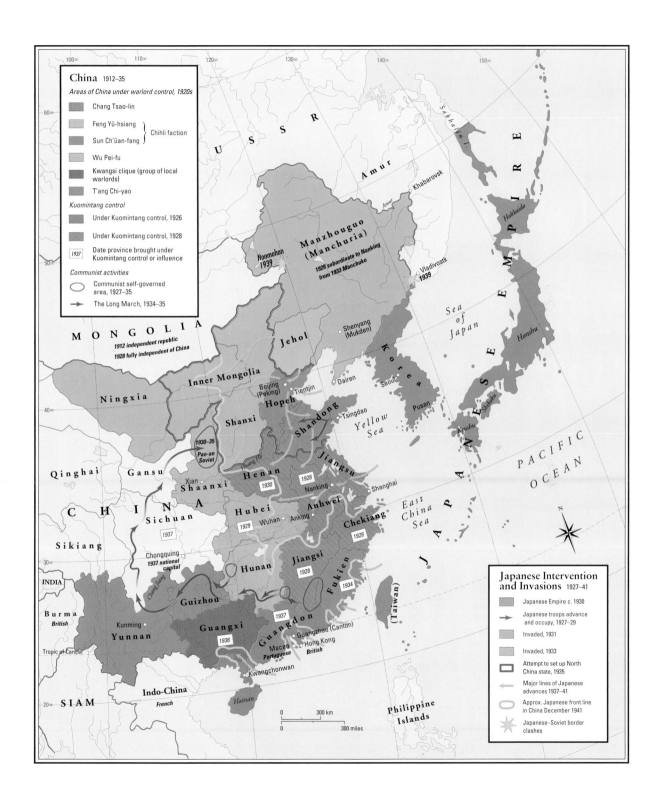

China 1912–35

Areas of China under warlord control, 1920s

Chang Tsao-lin

Feng Yü-hsiang }
Sun Ch'üan-fang } Chihli faction

Wu Pei-fu

Kwangsi clique (group of local warlords)

T'ang Chi-yao

Kuomintang control

Under Kuomintang control, 1926

Under Kuomintang control, 1928

1937 Date province brought under Kuomintang control or influence

Communist activities

Communist self-governed area, 1927–35

The Long March, 1934–35

Japanese Intervention and Invasions 1927–41

Japanese Empire c. 1930

Japanese troops advance and occupy, 1927–29

Invaded, 1931

Invaded, 1933

Attempt to set up North China state, 1935

Major lines of Japanese advances 1937–41

Approx. Japanese front line in China December 1941

Japanese–Soviet border clashes

THE SHADOW OF WAR 1935-1938

FROM 1935 ONWARD INTERNATIONAL TENSIONS BEGAN TO RISE ALARMINGLY. BY 1938 IT SEEMED THAT A RENEWED CONFLICT WAS ALL BUT INEVITABLE.

In 1933 the Nazi Party under its leader Adolf Hitler had been elected to power in Germany promising to solve the economic distress of the Great Depression and to restore German national pride, so badly battered by defeat in the First World War. Hitler began by introducing social welfare systems and policies to aid German industry. The resulting prosperity and national unity was mobilized to support the rebuilding of the German military — although this was banned by the Treaty of Versailles that had ended the First World War. Hitler quickly threw off the remaining shackles of Versailles with a wide-ranging rearmament program. The German navy was given legitimacy through the 1935 Anglo-German Naval Agreement. While this limited Germany's surface fleet to a third of that of the Royal Navy, she was significantly allowed parity in submarines on the basis that convoying ASDIC (Sonar) and agreements on restricting submarine warfare (1936 London Protocol) had much reduced the threat of this weapon. The German army underwent a massive expansion, while the Luftwaffe grew from nothing to one of Europe's largest air forces in the space of just a few years.

By the mid-1930s growing tension in Europe, largely created by Hitler, forced Britain and France into a degree of rearmament. France pinned her faith on fixed defenses on her border with Germany, the Maginot Line, believing that this was sufficient to deter aggression. Britain, on the other hand, put priority on maintaining her naval supremacy and in strenghtening the RAF in order to match Hitler's Luftwaffe. The army was a poor third, with the main effort going into anti-aircraft guns, but much progress was made in replacing the horse by the petrol engine. Yet while Germany mechanized from the front, Britain motorized from the rear. As for the Soviet Union,

Hitler's Annexations
1936–39

	Germany after 1919
	Troops into demilitarized Rhineland March 1936
	Auschluss (union with Austria), March 1938
	Occupation of Sudetenland October 1938
	Original Czechoslovakian border
	Formerly Czechoslovakia occupied March 1939
	Moravian and Slovak territory to Poland October 1938
	Memel territory to Germany March 1939

the impressive progress that the Red Army had made in developing concepts of war came to naught. Stalin had broken up the tank formations and removed the best brains in the armed forces.

In 1936 Hitler sent the German army into the Rhineland, the area of Germany that bordered France. The Versailles Treaty had forbidden such a move, but France made no moves to stop the occupation. Hitler grew bolder. In March 1938 the German army marched into Austria to be greeted by cheering crowds. The Austrians voted to join Germany soon afterward. Hitler turned to the Sudetenland. This area of the former Austrian Empire had been given to Czechoslovakia at the Treaty of Versailles, despite the fact that the population of the area was overwhelmingly German. Hitler mobilized the German army in August 1936 and marched it up to the border. The Czechoslovak army was likewise mobilized and moved into position to defend the border.

In September 1936 Prime Ministers Chamberlain of Britain and Deladier of France traveled to Munich to discuss the crisis with Hitler. The Czechoslovaks were not invited. The French and British knew that their armed forces were in no state to fight Germany, so they agreed to German occupation of the disputed territories. Britain and France both speeded up their existing programs of rearmament, but did nothing to interfere when Hitler annexed half of what remained of Czechoslovakia in March 1939. Hitler then began complaining about the status of German-speaking areas within Poland. Chamberlain and Deladier both declared that this time they would not permit any German annexations. War loomed.

Between 1936 and 1939, the Nazi German Führer Adolf Hitler tested the willingness of Britain and France to let him get away with annexing territory in Europe. The fact that he succeeded every time encouraged Hitler to believe that his opponents were weak and could be easily overcome in war.

CHAPTER X — WORLD WAR II 1939-1945: WORLD WAR II: 1939

THE WAR THAT BROKE OUT IN 1939 WOULD PROVE TO BE THE BLOODIEST, MOST DESTRUCTIVE, AND MOST COSTLY IN HISTORY. TENS OF MILLIONS WERE KILLED, VAST AREAS LAID WASTE, AND GREAT SWATHES OF THE WORLD PLUNGED UNDER THE RULE OF BRUTAL DICTATORSHIPS THAT WOULD LAST FOR DECADES.

Throughout much of 1939 the dictator of Germany, Adolf Hitler, had been complaining vociferously about the treatment of the German-speaking population of Poland. In particular he demanded that the city of Danzig, now Gdansk, and surrounding areas with German populations should be returned to Germany. Fearing that they were soon to be invaded, the Poles signed an alliance with Britain and France and put their army onto a war footing. With over 40 divisions, 475 tanks, and 315 aircraft the Poles had one of the largest armies in Europe. The men were trained to operate on the open plains and poor roads of Poland. The plan devised by the Allies was for the Poles to keep the German army occupied for the 20 days that it was estimated it would take for the French to mobilize and invade Germany from the west.

On 1 September 1939 the German army advanced over the Polish border. The Germans used a new type of tactic that they called *Blitzkrieg* or "lightning war." They used their tanks, or panzers, massed together in large numbers to punch through the enemy front line. If the panzers encountered strong resistance they used radios to call up precision bombers to destroy the enemy position. The panzers would then race ahead, accompanied by field artillery and infantry riding in lorries, to attack supply lines, overrun reinforcements, and spread chaos. Meanwhile, the infantry would march up to secure the ground that had been captured and overcome any enemy units that had escaped the panzers. The Polish commander, General Smigly-Ridz, had played into the German plans by placing most of his men close to the border. Once the panzers had smashed through these thin defenses there were few Polish forces in reserve to stop them driving wherever they wanted. By 20 September 1939 most of the Polish army had

The forces of Nazi Germany began their blitzkrieg (lightning war) assault on Poland on 1 September, 1939 from the west while Russian forces invaded from the east. The Polish defenders were helpless before the power of the fast, brutal *blitzkrieg* and by the end of September, they were crushed.

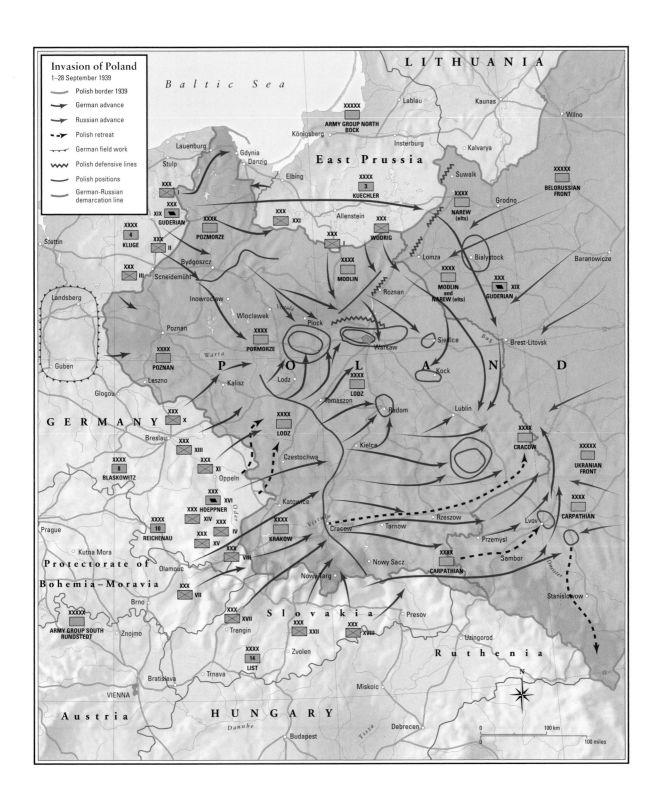

Invasion of Poland
1–28 September 1939

- Polish border 1939
- German advance
- Russian advance
- Polish retreat
- German field work
- Polish defensive lines
- Polish positions
- German-Russian demarcation line

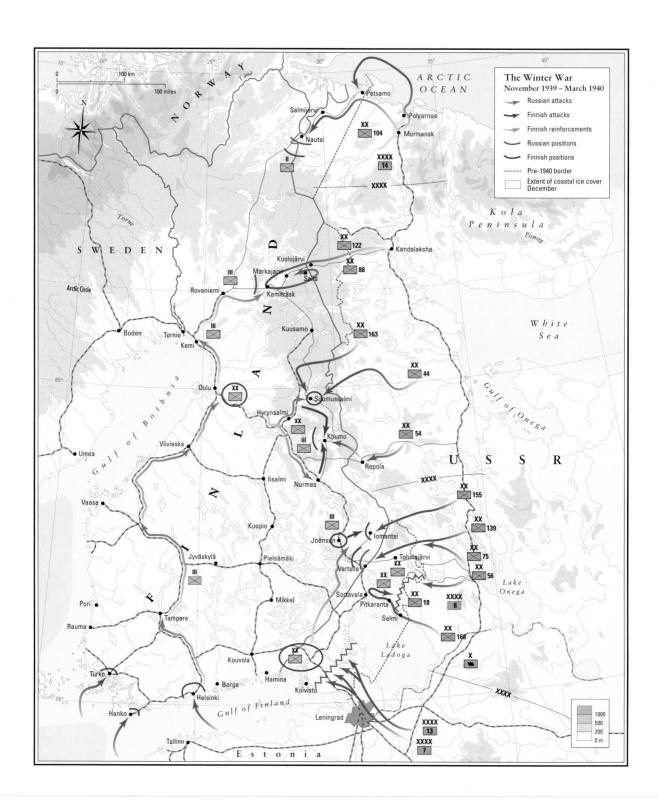

The Winter War
November 1939 – March 1940

→ Russian attacks
→ Finnish attacks
→ Finnish reinforcements
— Russian positions
— Finnish positions
---- Pre-1940 border
▢ Extent of coastal ice cover December

been defeated and the Germans attacked Warsaw. The city fell on 27 September 1939 and although a few fortresses fought on, the war was effectively over. The Polish collapse had been hastened when Russian troops invaded from the East to grab provinces of the old Russian Empire that had been lost to Poland after the First World War.

In the West, Britain and France had declared war on Germany on 3 September 1939. More than 3 million French troops were mobilized and marched to the border. A few patrols were sent out and some small local attacks were made, but Poland had capitulated before the French were ready to launch a major attack. In any case, the British and French high command both expected the war to be fought from static defense lines as had the First World War. The French had built the massive Maginot Line of interlocking bunkers and fortresses along the border with Germany and were confident it was impregnable. They preferred to wait until the Germans had dissipated their strength assaulting the Maginot Line and then launch a counterattack to take them all the way to Berlin. Both sides settled down to wait for the other to make a move. At sea, the German pocket battleship *Admiral Graf Spee* was busy attacking and sinking British merchant ships in the Indian and Atlantic Oceans. On 13 December 1939 she encountered three British cruisers off the River Plate and was badly damaged. Her captain, Langsdorff, later scuttled her rather than face a reinforced British force in battle.

This photograph shows a parade in Berlin, in which Hitler leads a motorcade from the Reichstag. This was ceremony on a huge scale, designed to hypnotize, and intimidate, both the German people and foreigners.

Far left: By 1939, the Russians, alarmed at the growing power of Nazi Germany, sought to protect themselves by building naval bases in neighboring countries. Finland, which had once been part of Tsarist Russia, refused and the so-called Winter War ensued. The Russians, whose forces vastly outnumbered the Finns, were the victors.

Meanwhile, Soviet dictator Josef Stalin had not been content with taking part of Poland. On 30 November the Russian army invaded Finland, which until 1917 had been part of Tsarist Russia. The Finnish army was small, but well trained and equipped for war in the northern forests and commanded by experienced officers. The Russian army, conversely, had been starved of new equipment by Stalin who feared a military coup and had had most of its officers executed in the past few years for similar reasons. The first Russian invasion was not just halted, but thrown back in utter confusion. Stalin then called up massive reinforcements to swamp the defenders. On 14 February 1939 the Finns began to retreat, still inflicting horrific losses on the Soviets. On 21 March 1939 the Russians captured the town of Viipuri and offered the Finns a peace deal which would see Russia annex Viipuri, Petsamo, and surrounding lands, plus the naval base of Hango. The Finns agreed and the "Winter War" ended.

WORLD WAR II: 1940

WITH POLAND OUT OF THE WAR, THE FOCUS FOR MILITARY ACTION SHIFTED TO THE WEST. THE RESULTING CAMPAIGN WAS TO BE A MAGNIFICENT DEMONSTRATION OF GERMAN *BLITZKRIEG* TACTICS. THE FRENCH WOULD NOT FIGHT WELL, AND BRITAIN WOULD THEN BE LEFT ALONE TO FACE THE MIGHT OF GERMANY.

Although in early 1940 the British and French were confident that any direct German attack would be halted by the defenses of the Maginot Line, they were aware of a serious flaw to this plan. Although the defenses guarded the Franco-German border they were incomplete along the Franco-Belgian border. In 1914 the Germans had invaded France by way of Belgium and they might do so again. To guard against this the Allies drew up Plan D. This called for the British army and the best units of the French army to march into Belgium as soon as the German army moved. They would dig in on the strong defensive line from Antwerp to Dinant and halt the Germans there. Preparing for a long war, the British wanted to impose a naval blockade of Germany. However, ships carrying Swedish iron ore from Narvik could slip down the Norwegian coast inside Norwegian neutral waters. The British debated whether to mine Norwegian waters, occupy Narvik, or try to catch the ships as they crossed the sea to Germany. German dictator Hitler also worried about his iron supplies. He decided to safeguard them by occupying Denmark and Norway. The invasion began at dawn on 9 April 1940. Tiny Denmark was overrun and surrendered before breakfast. King Haakon of Norway opted to fight. The key cities of Norway were captured quickly, but the army fell back into the mountains. They held out until 5 May 1940 when a lack of supplies forced their surrender. At Narvik the Norwegians, aided by a Franco-British force, held out until 8 June 1940. At sea the British and Norwegian navies fought fierce battles with the German navy, with high losses on both sides.

On 10 May 1940 the main German attack was launched against France. The first attacks were made on the Netherlands and Belgium. This prompted the Allies to begin Plan D, but it was only a diversion.

The Maginot Line, built during the 1930s to prevent another German invasion of France, had a fatal flaw: there was a gap along the Belgian frontier and in 1940, this was exploited by the forces of Nazi Germany to invade western Europe through the Ardennes forests of Belgium, Luxembourg, and France.

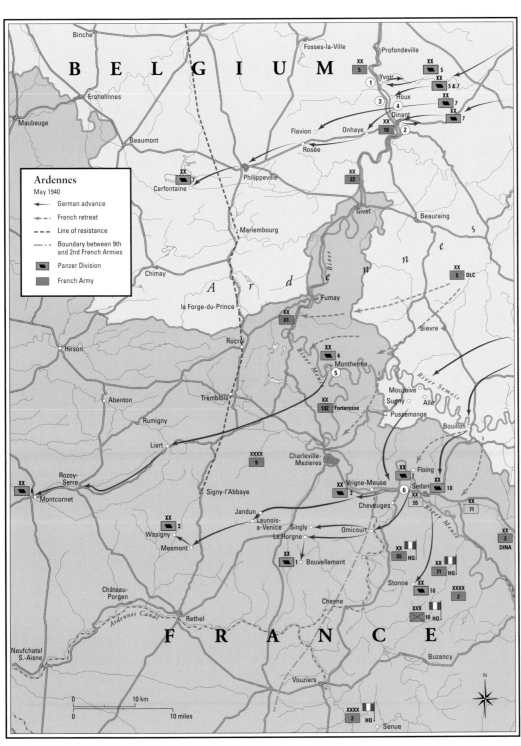

Ardennes

May 1940

→ German advance

⇠-- French retreat

--- Line of resistance

-·- Boundary between 9th and 2nd French Armies

▰ Panzer Division

▰ French Army

① 12 May: Yvoir Bridge blown up as German armored cars attempt to cross

② 12 May: Bridge at Dinant blown as German tanks approach

③ 13 May: Weir near Houx crossed by German Infantry

④ 13 May 4.45 am: 7th Panzer Division commanded by Rommel crossed the River Meuse

⑤ 13 May: Meuse crossed by 6th Panzer Division

⑥ 13/14 May: 1st, 2nd and 10th Panzer Divisions cross the Meuse

The troops in this photograph failed to be rescued from Dunkirk, and faced a future as German prisoners of war.

The German blitzkrieg which began on 10 May, 1940, tore through the Netherlands, Belgium, and France with irresistible speed and power. The Dutch capitulated on 14 May, the Belgians on 28 May. France signed an armistice on 22 June, while the collaborationist Vichy government took over the south of the country.

The main German attack was being made by massed panzer divisions farther south through the Ardennes hills. French defenses here were weak because it was thought that the twisting roads of the Ardennes could not cope with the thousands of trucks needed to supply a major offensive. The Germans had surveyed the roads and knew better. Their main worry was that they needed to get across the wide, deep Meuse River before the French realized what was happening and brought up men to defend the crossing. The panzers reached the Meuse on 12 May 1940 to find it only lightly defended. At 11pm the first German infantry got over the river using a weir, more infantry followed by boat to establish a bridgehead, and behind them engineers hurriedly built a bridge. The crossing was completed by 6am on 14 May 1940 and the first panzers stormed over. Led by the talented panzer general, Heinz Guderian, and supported by a second leading tank commander, Erwin Rommel, the German panzers headed west at high speed. Now behind the Allied front lines, the panzers met only slight resistance from reserve units and hurriedly assembled reinforcements. They reached the sea at Abbeville on 19 May 1940. The entire British and Belgian armies, plus much of the French army, was surrounded with their backs to the sea. Recognizing the danger, British General Gort ordered his men to fall back on the port of Dunkirk and asked the Royal Navy to evacuate his men. The epic defense of Dunkirk in the face of repeated German attacks allowed most of the surrounded troops to get away, though they left behind most of their equipment.

The French meanwhile drew up a new defensive line along the Somme. The Germans attacked on 5 June to find the French defenders had already virtually lost the will to fight. Once again the panzers burst through to wreak havoc behind the French lines and once again the French army collapsed. British units still in France raced for the nearest port to be evacuated, taking with them some Polish and Czech regiments. On 14 June the French government abandoned Paris and headed for Bordeaux. There the Prime Minister Reynaud resigned to be replaced by the 84-year-old General Pétain, who surrendered to

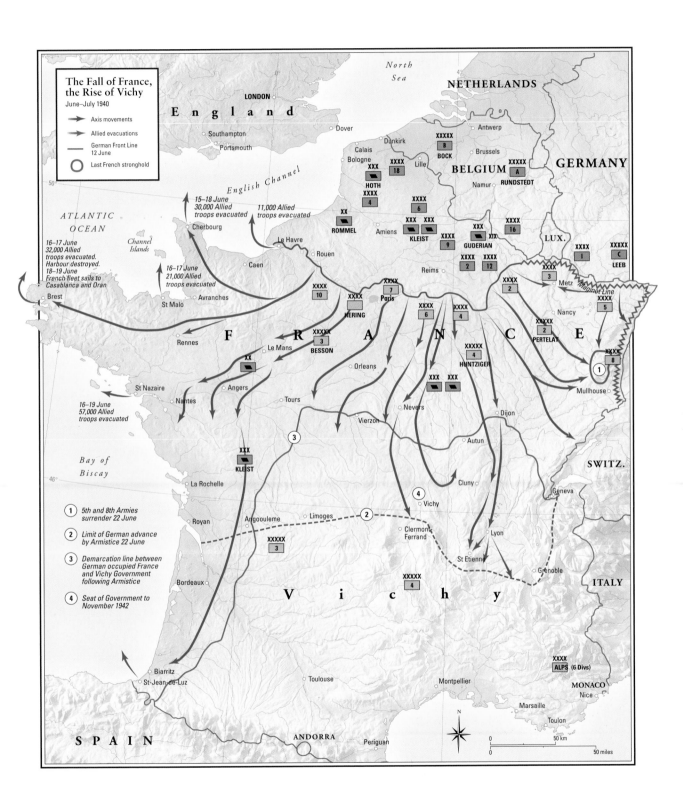

The Fall of France,
the Rise of Vichy
June–July 1940

→ Axis movements

→ Allied evacuations

— German Front Line
12 June

◯ Last French stronghold

North
Sea

NETHERLANDS

LONDON

England

Southampton

Portsmouth

Dover

Antwerp

Calais
Bologne

Dunkirk

Brussels

Lille

BELGIUM

Namur

GERMANY

XXXXX
B
BOCK

XXX
18

XXXX
A
RUNDSTEDT

XXX
HOTH

XXXX
4

English Channel

ATLANTIC
OCEAN

Channel
Islands

Cherbourg

Le Havre

Rouen

Caen

Amiens

Reims

XX
ROMMEL

XXXX
6

XXX   XXX
KLEIST

XXXX
9

LUX.

XXX
GUDERIAN

XIX

XXXX
16

XXXX
1

XXXXX
C
LEEB

16–17 June
32,000 Allied
troops evacuated.
Harbour destroyed.
18–19 June
French fleet sails to
Casablanca and Oran

15–18 June
30,000 Allied
troops evacuated

11,000 Allied
troops evacuated

Brest

16–17 June
21,000 Allied
troops evacuated

St Malo

Avranches

XXXX
10

Rennes

Le Mans

BESSON
XXXXX
3

XXXX
NEHRING

XXXX
2

XXXX
12

XXXX
7
Paris

XXXX
6

XXXX
4

XXXX
3

XXXX
2

Maginot Line

Metz

Nancy

XXXXX
2
PERTELAT

XXXX
5

XXXX
8

1

Mullhouse

F   R   A   N   C   E

XX

St Nazaire

Nantes

Angers

Orleans

Tours

Vierzon

Nevers

XXXXX
4
HUNTZIGER

XXX   XXX

Dijon

Autun

SWITZ.

Bay of
Biscay

16–19 June
57,000 Allied
troops evacuated

XXX
KLEIST

La Rochelle

Royan

3

Angouleme

Limoges

2

Cluny

Lyon

Grenoble

Geneva

St Etienne

Vichy

Clermont
Ferrand

4

ITALY

1   5th and 8th Armies
surrender 22 June

2   Limit of German advance
by Armistice 22 June

3   Demarcation line between
German occupied France
and Vichy Government
following Armistice

4   Seat of Government to
November 1942

Bordeaux

V   i   c   h   y

XXXXX
3

XXXXX
4

XXXX
ALPS (6 Divs)

Biarritz

St-Jean-de-Luz

Toulouse

Montpellier

MONACO
Nice

Marsaille

Toulon

SPAIN

ANDORRA

Periguan

N

0   50 km

0   50 miles

Germany on 22 June 1940.

As the Allies were being defeated, Italian dictator Mussolini decided to try to regain areas lost to France in 1866. He declared war on 10 June and invaded the disputed territory. In the peace treaty that Hitler forced on Petain, Mussolini was rewarded with most of what he wanted, while Germany took the Alsace and Lorraine. North and western France were to be occupied by the Germans until the British were defeated, but the rest of France was left untouched. Pétain thought he had got a good deal.

The German generals were keen to invade Britain as quickly as possible, but the German navy was wary of the powerful British fleet. Hitler declared that he did not really want to conquer Britain. He made a speech offering peace terms, but these were rejected. Hitler ordered that Britain was to be invaded and conquered, but by this time the British had had time to plant mines on the beaches, build fortifications on the roads heading inland, and partially re-equip their army. The German generals recognized that they would need to land panzers in force to be certain of victory. That required a substantial number of transport ships, which the German navy could not promise to protect unless the German air force, the Luftwaffe, could stop British bombers from attacking. In turn that meant that the Luftwaffe had to destroy the British Royal Air Force. So began the fight for control of the air over the English Channel, better known as the Battle of Britain. Hermann Göring's Luftwaffe had about 2,700 aircraft, of which half were modern fighters. The RAF had just 600 fighters. However, the British did have the advantage of radar to warn them of when German formations were heading for Britain. Added to this the RAF was fighting over its own ground, allowing fighters to refuel and rearm quickly, while the Germans had to fly back to France first.

On 8 August the Luftwaffe began attacks on coastal towns, hoping to lure the RAF into costly combats. On 24 August 1940 the Luftwaffe switched to attacking RAF bases and British losses rose alarmingly. Radar stations were knocked out and fighter bases were badly damaged, and even abandoned. British fighters, and pilots, were being lost faster than they could be replaced. Fighter chief Sir Hugh Dowding began to fear he was losing the battle. However, German losses were even higher, and British bombers were launching raids across the Channel to bomb German troops and the ships being gathered for the invasion. Hitler set the invasion date for 24 September, while Göring switched his attacks away from RAF bases in the mistaken belief that they could not be repaired quickly. Instead the Luftwaffe bombed London heavily and repeatedly with lighter attacks on other cities. On 17 September 1940 Hitler held a top-level military conference at which the naval chiefs convinced him that the RAF had not yet been destroyed. The invasion of Britain was postponed until further notice. Göring was told to continue to bomb British cities in the hope that this alone would induce Prime Minister Churchill to agree to negotiate peace. The Blitz that followed saw many British cities bombed heavily. The worst single attack was on Coventry on 14 November when a large force of bombers got through British defenses on the night of a full moon. The entire city center was flattened and hundreds were killed. It was London that came off worst, with week after week of relentless night bombing laying waste to large areas of the city center. By the end of 1940 a total of 23,000 British civilians had been killed, and 40,000 injured by bombing.

Meanwhile the British refusal to surrender had meant that British and Italian armed forces faced each other in the North African desert where Italian-owned Libya bordered on Egypt, where a large British army was based.

The Battle of Britain saved Britain from invasion by Nazi Germany. Although the Royal Air Force had fewer planes than the German Luftwaffe, they had the advantage of fighting over home territory. German pilots could spend only some 25 minutes over British targets before returning to their airfields in northern Europe.

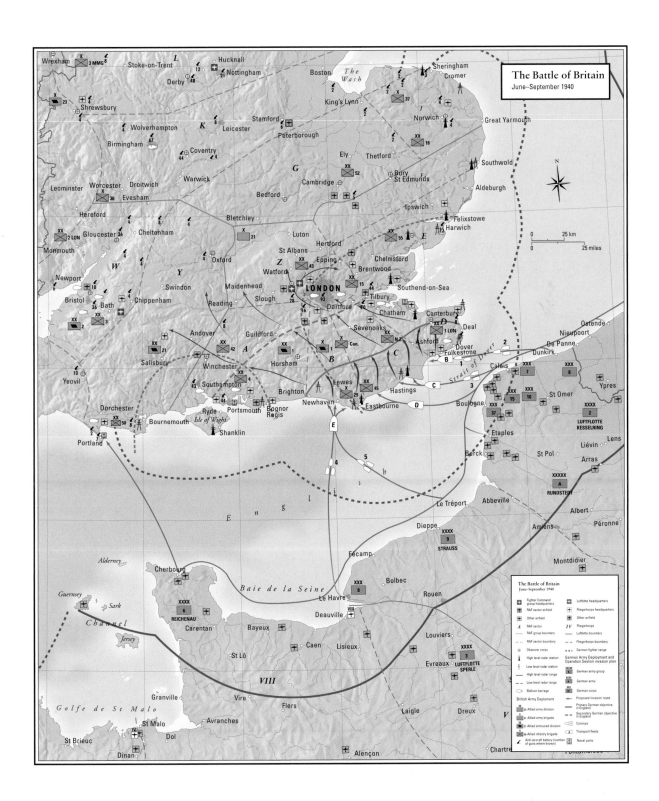

The Battle of Britain
June–September 1940

Africa in the Second World War
1939 - mid 1942

→ German and Italian advance from 1942

→ Allied movements

Colonial possessions

British

French

Portuguese

Spanish

Italian

Belgium

Anglo-Egyptian Sudan

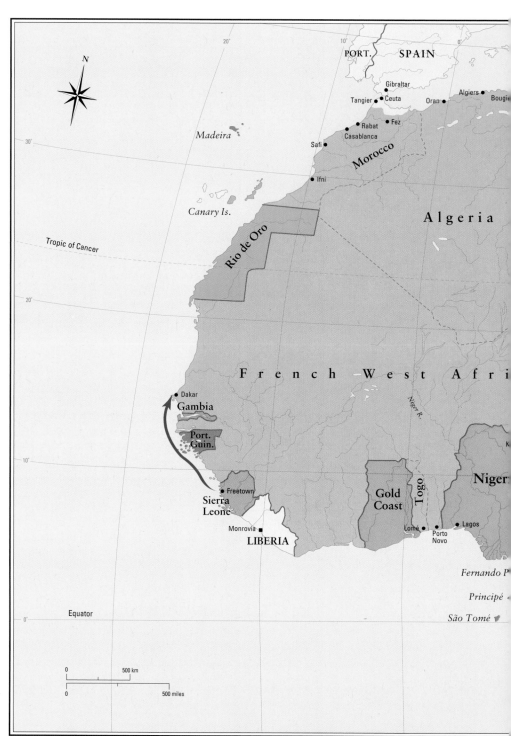

After Nazi Germany overran most of northern Europe by 1940, North Africa was the only place where the British forces could confront them in battle. Their main purpose was to prevent the Germans and Italians from capturing the Suez Canal, the vital "short" route to British Empire territories in Asia. In North Africa, the British first fought against the Italians in 1940-1941(the Italians did not enter the war until 1940). The Germans first fought in North Africa (i.e. the Afrika Korps headed by General Rommel) in March 1941).

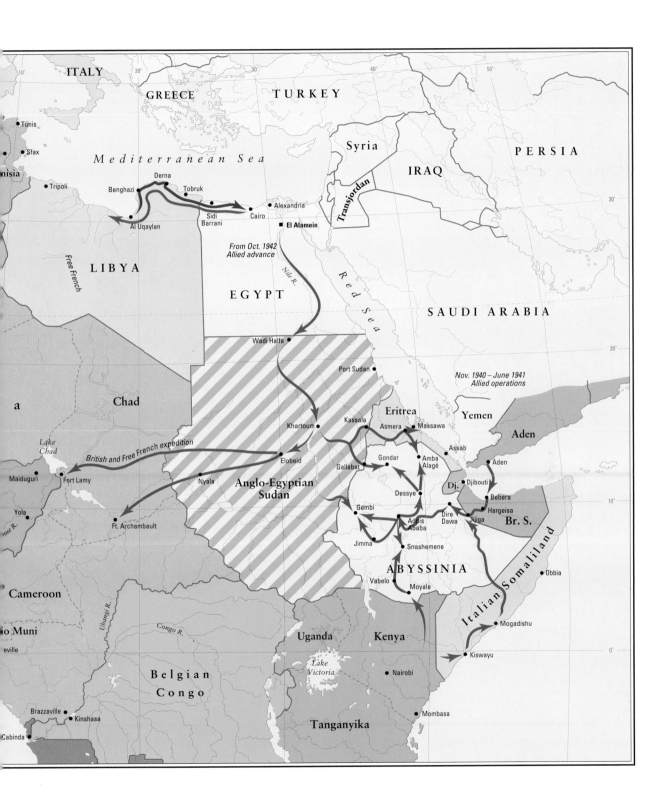

WORLD WAR II: 1941

THE YEAR 1941 WOULD PROVE TO BE THE MOST DRAMATIC OF THE WAR AS THE USA, USSR, AND JAPAN ALL ENTERED THE CONFLICT IN SENSATIONAL FASHION.

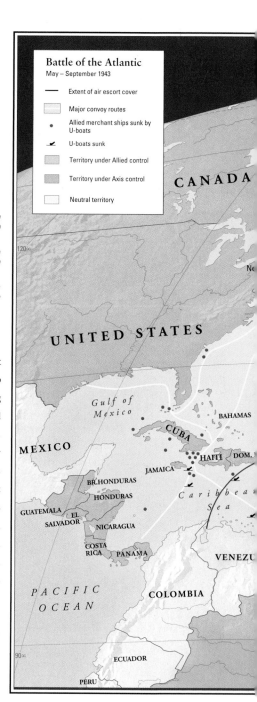

Battle of the Atlantic
May – September 1943

— Extent of air escort cover

Major convoy routes

• Allied merchant ships sunk by U-boats

U-boats sunk

Territory under Allied control

Territory under Axis control

Neutral territory

British Prime Minister Winston Churchill called the Battle of the Atlantic the most vital battle of the whole war. The British depended heavily on supplies brought in from the Americas, for without them, Churchill reasoned, Britain was likely to be starved into submission by the forces of Nazi Germany.

The skies over Britain were filled each night by German bombers coming to bomb cities, and by British fighters climbing up to drive them off. The Channel, however, had stopped any German invasion so a stalemate set in. In the Mediterranean, however, things were very different. On 27 March 1941 the main Italian battle fleet was attacked by the British Mediterranean fleet in the battle of Cape Matapan and lost five cruisers and two destroyers. Other naval skirmishes would take place over the coming year, but the British generally kept naval superiority. In North Africa a joint British-Indian-Australian attack drove the Italians back hundreds of miles from the Egyptian border to El Agheila. On 31 March 1941 the newly arrived German Afrika Korps counter attacked under their commander Erwin Rommel and harried the British all the way back to Egypt. The key port of Tobruk was held by an Australian garrison that managed to hold out against

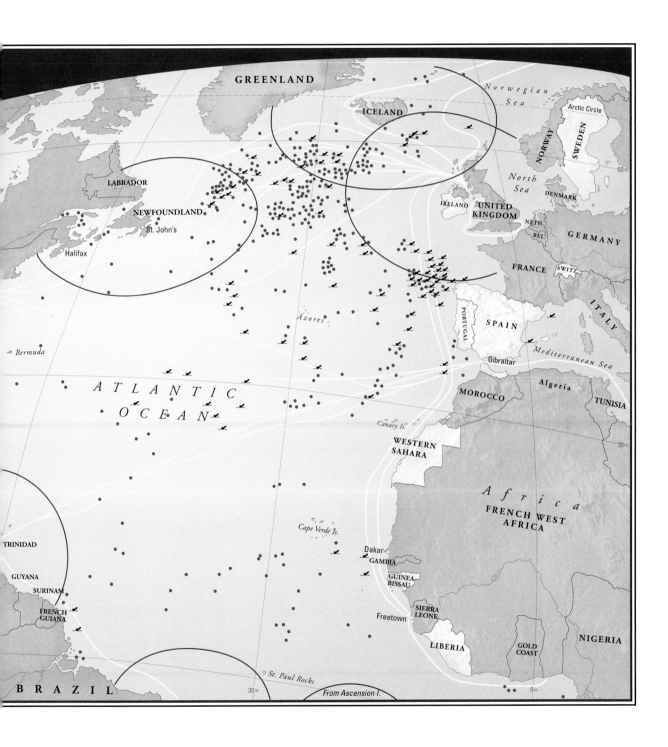

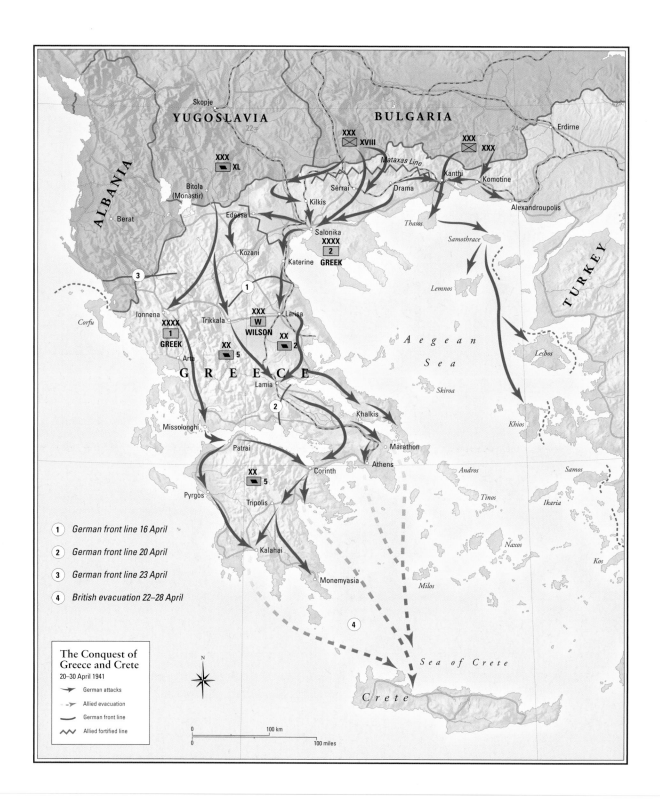

ALBANIA

YUGOSLAVIA

BULGARIA

Skopje

Erdirne

XXX XVIII

XXX XXX

Mataxas Line

XXX XL

Bitola (Monastir)

Berat

Sérrai

Drama

Xanthi

Komotine

Kilkis

Edessa

Alexandroupolis

Thasos

Kozani

Salonika
XXXX 2 GREEK

Samothrace

Katerine

3

Lemnos

Ionnena

Corfu

Trikkala

Larisa

XXX W WILSON

Aegean Sea

XXXX 1 GREEK

1

XX 5

XX 2

Lesbos

Arta

GREECE

Lamia

Skiroa

2

Khios

Missolonghi

Khalkis

Marathon

Patrai

Corinth

Athens

Andros

Samos

Pyrgòs

XX 5

Tripolis

Tinos

Ikaria

Kos

Kalahai

Naxos

Monemyasia

Milos

4

Sea of Crete

1 German front line 16 April

2 German front line 20 April

3 German front line 23 April

4 British evacuation 22–28 April

Crete

The Conquest of Greece and Crete

20–30 April 1941

➤ German attacks

⇢ Allied evacuation

— German front line

⌁ Allied fortified line

N

0   100 km

0   100 miles

determined German attacks. Rommel was thus denied the ability to bring up supplies by sea, but had to rely on the poor desert roads. On 19 November 1941 British General Auchinleck attacked Rommel and after a confused tank battle that cost the British heavily, the Germans and Italians fell rapidly back to El Agheila where Rommel knew that reinforcements and fresh supplies were waiting. In East Africa the British invaded Italian Abyssinia from Kenya and the Sudan in February 1941. The capital city of Addis Ababa was captured on 6 April but the talented Italian General Aosta fell back into the mountains to begin a guerrilla campaign that dragged on until November.

Italy had declared war on Greece in October 1940, but there was little fighting until January 1941 when the Greeks threw back a major Italian attack near Ionnena. Mussolini called for German help, and Hitler asked the Yugoslav government to allow German troops to drive through their country to reach the battlefield. The Yugoslavs refused. On 6 April the German and Italian armies invaded Yugoslavia, conquering the kingdom in just 12 days. The *Blitzkrieg* rolled on to Greece which was forced to capitulate on 23 April. Crete was captured by paratroop attack on 1 June 1941.

Hitler then pulled his men back. He had secured the mainland of Europe and was not bothered about British outposts in North Africa. He had already decided to attack Russia. The reasons why Hitler turned on his ally Russia have been much debated. He certainly wanted to secure his oil supply from Romania from attack and feared Russian ambitions in the Baltic. Just as certainly Hitler desired to expand Germany still further. Perhaps the obvious weaknesses of the Soviet army revealed in the Finnish War convinced him that Germany could win without undue trouble. Whatever the reason, Germany invaded Russia on 22 June along with allied troops from Romania, Hungary, and Finland. More than 3.5 million men, 3,600 tanks and 2,800 aircraft surged east against the Russian forces of 3 million men, 15,000 tanks, and

Opposite page: In 1941, the Germans came to the rescue of their Italian allies, who made such a mess of their invasion of Greece on 28 October, 1940 that the Greeks seemed likely to drive them out. The German invaded Greece on 6 April, 1941 and the Greeks surrendered 17 days later.

On 20 May, 1941, the Germans mounted a mammoth air attack on Crete by dropping some 30,000 airborne troops on the island's three main airfields. Despite spirited resistance, the British defenders were overwhelmed and had to be rescued by ships of the Royal Navy. The casualties on both sides were immense.

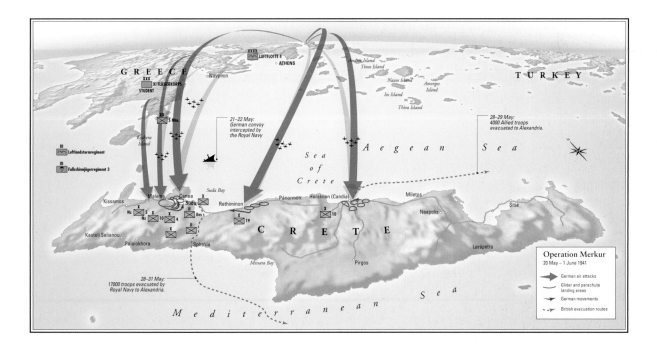

8,000 aircraft. At every point the German tactics of blitzkrieg were stunningly successful. The Russian front collapsed into a mass of disorganized, fragmented units as the panzers surged past them and the infantry hurried up behind to mop up the shattered remnants. Entire Russian armies were encircled and captured: 300,000 men surrendered at Bialystock, 500,000 at Vyasma, and 600,000 at Kiev.

On 21 August 1941 Hitler turned his panzers south to capture the Ukrainian wheat-fields, the coal of the Donetz Basin, and the industrial cities near the Black Sea. In the north a more conventional campaign by infantry and artillery surrounded, but failed to capture, the great city of Leningrad. Despite these glittering victories the German generals were worried by November. They had expected to face about 200 Russian divisions and had planned accordingly. They had already defeated at least that many, and yet 160 Soviet divisions still remained in front of them. Nor had the enemy front disintegrated entirely. Every time the front line was smashed and annihilated a new line of defenses was found behind it. Just as frustrating was the fact that Hitler was refusing to allow the panzers to race ahead of the infantry as they had in France; instead they were ordered to slow down to allow the foot soldiers to catch up. The year ended with the German army deep inside Russia but as yet with no end to the war in sight.

Canadian troops also got their first taste of combat in 1941. Approximately one million Canadians served in the armed forces during World War II and the majority of them who wore military uniforms saw action in Italy, Holland and France. Smaller numbers of Canuck soldiers found themselves in North Africa, Southeast Asia and the Aleutian Islands. Although their contributions were not the most visible or pivotal, they were important and nonetheless impressive for a nation which at that time had a population of 11 million people. In December 1941, Candian ground troops were ordered to Hong Kong to try and repel an invasion by Japanese forces. The Royal Rifles and Winnipeg Grenadiers were the units assigned to the island. After eighteen days of fighting the Canadians, who had run out of food and ammunition, surrendered near their position at Wong Nei Chong Gap. The survivors were taken to POW camps. For Canadians, the war had kicked into high gear.

Canada contributed to the war effort in other respects. Between the fall of France in June 1940 and the German invasion of the USSR in June 1941, Canada supplied Britain with much needed food, weapons, and war materials by naval convoys and airlifts, as well as pilots and planes who fought in the Battle of Britain and the Blitz. If the planned German invasion of Britain had taken place in 1941, units of I Canadian Corps were ready to be deployed between the English Channel and London.

Although only entering in 1941, Canadian troops were to make a significant contribution throughout the war. From 1939 through to the end of the war in Europe in May 1945, the Royal Canadian Navy and the Canadian Merchant Navy played an especially vital role in the Second Battle of the Atlantic. Canada was the primary location of the British Commonwealth Air Training Plan, still the largest air force training program in history; over 167,000 Commonwealth air force personnel, including more than 50,000 pilots, trained at airbases in Canada from 1940 to 1945. More than half of the BCAT graduates were Canadians who went on to serve with the Royal Canadian Air Force (RCAF)and Royal Air Force (RAF). One out of the six RAF Bomber Command groups flying in Europe was Canadian.

At the time, Canada had one of the largest automobile manufacturing industries in the world. During the war, this industry was put to good use, with Canada producing the most trucks and ammunitions of all the allies apart from the United States.

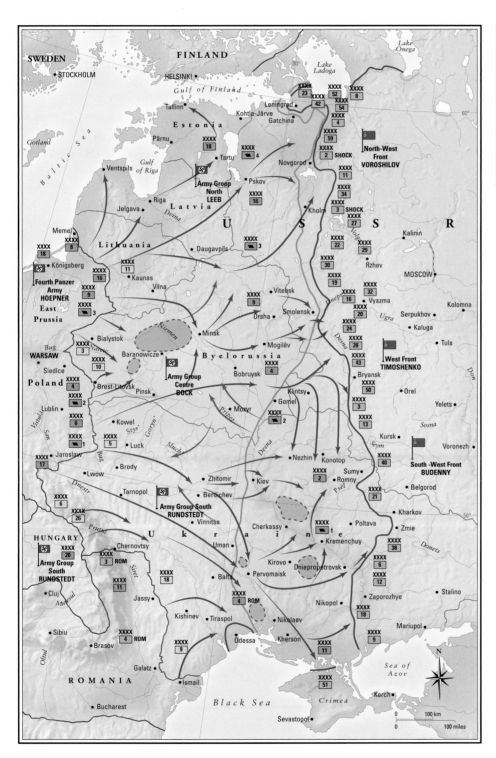

Operation Barbarossa
22 June – early October 1941

- ⟶ German attack
- Soviet positions 22 June
- Soviet units encircled
- ⟶ Soviet counter attacks
- German front line, end of August
- German front line, early October
- Soviet positions early October

When the forces of Nazi Germany invaded Russia on 22 June, 1941, they expected their *Blitzkrieg* tactics would bring about a speedy victory. However, Russia was far too vast for *Blitzkrieg* to work, its climate was far too severe and the Russians were far too obdurate to give in easily.

WORLD WAR II: 1941 PEARL HARBOR

THE JAPANESE ATTACK ON PEARL HARBOR STUNNED THE WORLD — AND BROUGHT THE USA INTO THE SECOND WORLD WAR. THE ATTACK WAS MADE WITHOUT WARNING AND WITHOUT A DECLARATION OF WAR, A FACT WHICH ENSURED A DEVASTATING JAPANESE VICTORY BUT MEANT ALSO THAT THE USA WOULD FIGHT HARD TO ACHIEVE REVENGE.

Following the defeat of France by Germany, the Japanese had insisted that they be allowed to station troops in French colonies in Indo-China. Under pressure from Germany, France had agreed. Although there was no formal alliance between Italy, Germany, and Japan they became known collectively as the Axis Powers. US President Roosevelt viewed the move with deep suspicion. He was already opposed to the Japanese invasion of China and feared that this presaged a greater expansion still. He introduced an immediate trade embargo, along with the British, and persuaded the Dutch government-in-exile in Britain to suspend exports of oil from the East Indies to Japan. Without oil from the East Indies and rubber from British Malaya the Japanese army would quickly grind to a halt. The Japanese decided to invade both territories to secure the supplies, but worried about the US reaction. If the US declared war, the Japanese would be severely overstretched, particularly at sea. The only way to avoid overstretch was to destroy the US Pacific Fleet at the outbreak of war. Thus it was decided to assault the main US naval base at Pearl Harbor without warning.

The planning of the attack was given to Admiral Yamamoto, even though he thought that making war with America was a grave mistake. Many of the military commanders thought it impossible to attack a fleet at anchor, especially with torpedoes which would simply lodge into the mud of a relatively shallow harbor. Yet the Japanese trained their pilots extensively on the attack and modified their torpedoes with wooden fins to prevent them going below a certain depth. Planned by Admiral Yamamoto, the attack was to be made by aircraft launched from aircraft carriers. A convenient storm front was used to mask the approach of the Japanese fleet from the American base until the moment that the aircraft were flown off just after dawn on 7 December 1941. Among the 350 Japanese aircraft were conventional fighters and

Ford Island in the middle of Pearl Harbor, was the site of the U.S. Naval Station and was very heavily bombed by the Japanese on 7 December, 1941. Battleship Row was located along its shores, and nine U.S. ships including the *Arizona* were berthed there at the time.

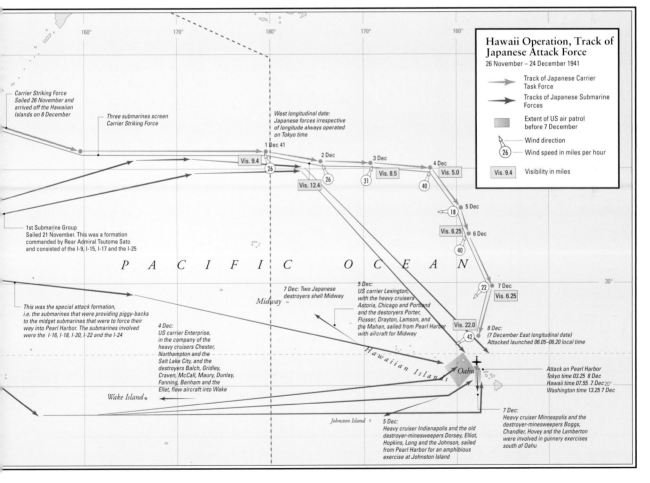

For its attack on the U.S. Pacific fleet at Pearl Harbor on 7 December, 1941, the Japanese carrier fleet sailed across the Pacific in secret. But they failed in one important regard: the American carriers were elsewhere during the attack.

bombers, plus torpedo bombers equipped with specially designed torpedoes that would run just below the surface in the shallow waters of Pearl Harbor.

After intense training the fleet left for Hawaii, taking a northern route so as not to be easily detected by the U.S. Navy. Accompanying the six carriers were two battleships, numerous escort vessels, and eight support ships. There would also be a force of midget submarines that would infiltrate the harbor and cause as much damage as possible, once launched from its larger parent submarine. The submarine force arrived before the task force. Having time to reconnoiter ships entering and leaving the harbor, it was in a position to attack ships at anchor or in the immediate area, should the air attack fail. Even though the American intelligence expected an attack at some point from the Japanese, they expected it would occur in the Phillipines. Pearl Harbor was taken entirely by surprise.

The first wave of the attack began at 7.55am. Resistance was negligible as the Americans were caught by surprise. There was to be no respite for the servicemen at Pearl Harbor: as soon as the first wave left the second wave of attack planes arrived. However, the defenders were by now starting to get themselves in order and were throwing up a ferocious amount of anti-aircraft fire and, with the smoke from the fires started in the first attack, the Japanese could not cause as much damage as the initial assault. By the time the second attack wave arrived at 8.40am; some American fighters were in the air and anti-aircraft gunners were active. The Japanese lost a total of 29 aircraft and five midget submarines that had launched an abortive attack. The US lost four battleships and 11 other warships, with many more damaged, plus 247 aircraft and 2,330 men. By pure luck the American aircraft carriers were at sea when the attack took place and survived. The USS Arizona was destroyed when a bomb penetrated the magazine and blasted the ship to pieces.

Although this was a massive blow to the American psyche, the country was united in defeating a deceitful and vicious enemy, something Yamamoto had always feared: instead of weakening the beast they had only succeeded in making it angry. Nagumo had also missed the opportunity to destroy the U.S carrier fleet, which was much more important than sinking six outmoded battleships. However, with the US fleet out of action, the Japanese went ahead with their plans. On 8 December Japanese forces landed in Malaya and two days later sank the main British naval force in the Pacific. The conquest of Malaya would be completed by 15 February 1942. Also on 8 December, Japanese troops began landing on the Philippines. Dogged resistance by US troops and the Filipino army led by General Douglas MacArthur continued until 6 May. MacArthur had been ordered to leave by Roosevelt who knew he was too valuable to lose. As he left MacArthur vowed "I will return".

The invasion of the Dutch East Indies began on 20 December and soon became a series of amphibious operations. On 27 February 1942 the Dutch Admiral Doorman steamed his joint Dutch-British-US task force to intercept the Japanese invasion fleet heading for Java. He managed to sink two transports and one destroyer, but at the cost of four cruisers and four destroyers. The surviving Allied warships fled to Australia. The East Indies were secured by the Japanese by 8 March.

The conflict between the Japanese and the Americans escalated into what is known as the Pacific War. This affected the Pacific islands and East Asia. It began as a conflict between China and Japan, but with the bombing oif Pearl Harbor became part of the wider world war.

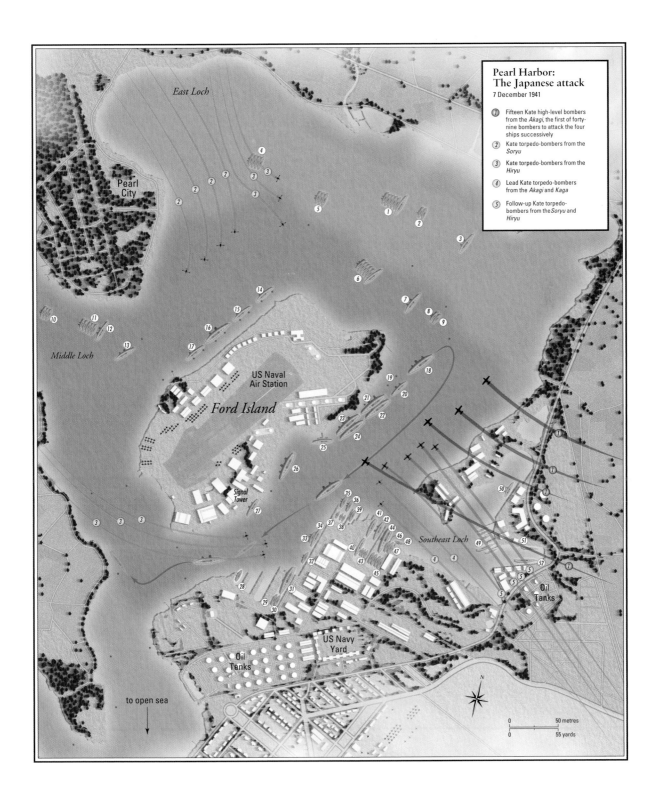

**Pearl Harbor:
The Japanese attack**
7 December 1941

① Fifteen Kate high-level bombers from the *Akagi*, the first of forty-nine bombers to attack the four ships successively

② Kate torpedo-bombers from the *Soryu*

③ Kate torpedo-bombers from the *Hiryu*

④ Lead Kate torpedo-bombers from the *Akagi* and *Kaga*

⑤ Follow-up Kate torpedo-bombers from the *Soryu* and *Hiryu*

East Loch

Pearl City

Middle Loch

US Naval Air Station

Ford Island

Signal Tower

Southeast Loch

US Navy Yard

Oil Tanks

Oil Tanks

to open sea

N

0 — 50 metres
0 — 55 yards

WORLD WAR II: 1942

THE YEAR 1942 SAW THE ALLIED FORTUNES AT THEIR LOWEST EBB. EVERYWHERE THE GERMANS, ITALIANS, AND JAPANESE SEEMED TO BE TRIUMPHANT. AND YET EVEN AS THEY REACHED THEIR GREATEST VICTORIES, THE AXIS POWERS WERE SOWING THE SEEDS OF THEIR OWN DESTRUCTION.

J apan had not yet finished the conquest of her primary targets when, on 20 January 1942, her armies marched into the British colony of Burma. The attack was launched from Siam (now Thailand), a rather reluctant ally of Japan. The Indian army units in Burma began a fighting withdrawal up the Irrawaddy Valley and over the mountains into India, finally halting at Imphal in May. Transport in much of Burma relied upon trained elephants, nearly all of which were hidden in the jungles by Colonel J.H. Williams, who thus found fame as "Elephant Bill."

The Japanese fleet was meanwhile very busy. In March 1942 Admiral Nagumo steamed into the Bay of Bengal with five carriers, four battleships, and attendant cruisers and destroyers. He bombed several cities in India and Ceylon, sank a British carrier and two cruisers, then returned to the Pacific. In May 1942 a Japanese fleet was escorting an invasion task force to Port Moresby, New Guinea, when it was detected by a US fleet in the Coral Sea. The resulting battle was the first to be fought primarily by aircraft flown off carriers and in which the ships never came within sight of an enemy. It ended with the Japanese having lost two carriers, to the US loss of one carrier, a destroyer, and a tanker.

The Japanese were aware that they needed to destroy the three remaining American carriers if they were to control the Pacific. Admiral Yamamoto drew up a plan to ambush the ships off Midway Island in June. The plan was complicated and relied on both surprise and the Americans making mistakes. Due to US Intelligence having partially broken the Japanese radio codes neither happened. Admiral Spruance was waiting and ready. The Battle of Midway began soon after dawn and ended in complete defeat for Yamamoto, who lost all four of the carriers in his attack force, having sunk only one American carrier and one destroyer. The disaster was in part due to the Japanese lack of self-sealing petrol tanks and open

Japan's attack on the U.S. Pacific fleet in Pearl Harbor was intended to destroy American power and enable the Japanese South East Asia Co-Prosperity Sphere to dominate the Pacific. Pearl Harbor shocked the Americans but they soon recovered and by June 1942 the war had turned against Japan.

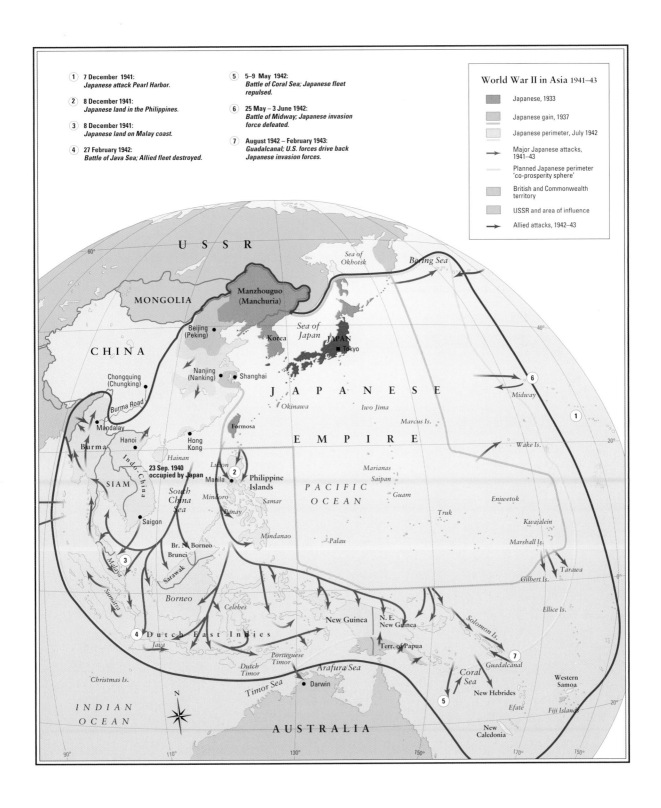

① **7 December 1941:**
Japanese attack Pearl Harbor.

② **8 December 1941:**
Japanese land in the Philippines.

③ **8 December 1941:**
Japanese land on Malay coast.

④ **27 February 1942:**
Battle of Java Sea; Allied fleet destroyed.

⑤ **5–9 May 1942:**
Battle of Coral Sea; Japanese fleet repulsed.

⑥ **25 May – 3 June 1942:**
Battle of Midway; Japanese invasion force defeated.

⑦ **August 1942 – February 1943:**
Guadalcanal; U.S. forces drive back Japanese invasion forces.

World War II in Asia 1941–43

- Japanese, 1933
- Japanese gain, 1937
- Japanese perimeter, July 1942
- Major Japanese attacks, 1941–43
- Planned Japanese perimeter 'co-prosperity sphere'
- British and Commonwealth territory
- USSR and area of influence
- Allied attacks, 1942–43

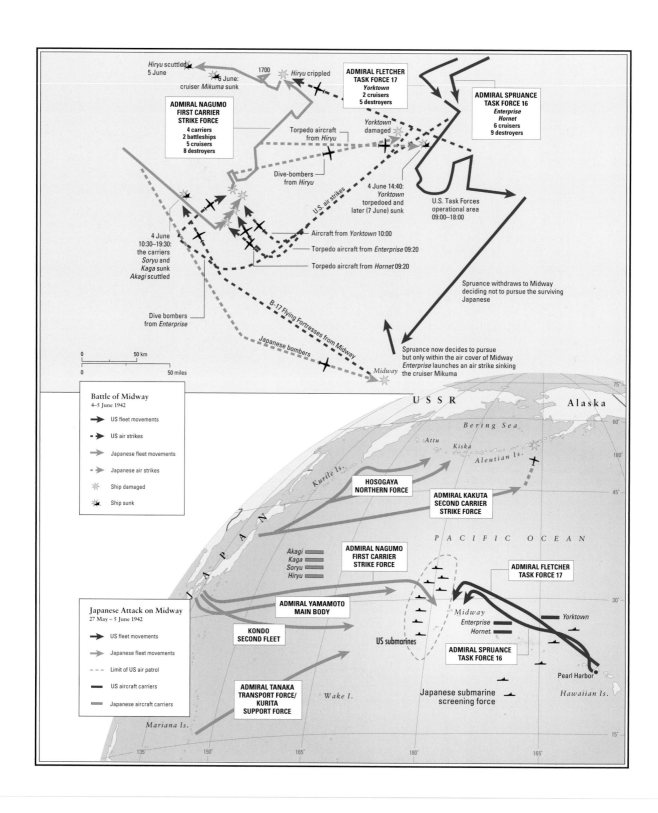

Hiryu scuttled
5 June

6 June:
cruiser *Mikuma* sunk

1700 *Hiryu* crippled

**ADMIRAL FLETCHER
TASK FORCE 17**
Yorktown
2 cruisers
5 destroyers

**ADMIRAL SPRUANCE
TASK FORCE 16**
Enterprise
Hornet
6 cruisers
9 destroyers

**ADMIRAL NAGUMO
FIRST CARRIER
STRIKE FORCE**
4 carriers
2 battleships
5 cruisers
8 destroyers

Torpedo aircraft
from *Hiryu*

Yorktown
damaged

Dive-bombers
from *Hiryu*

U.S. air strikes

4 June 14:40:
Yorktown
torpedoed and
later (7 June) sunk

U.S. Task Forces
operational area
09:00–18:00

4 June
10:30–19:30:
the carriers
Soryu and
Kaga sunk
Akagi scuttled

Aircraft from *Yorktown* 10:00

Torpedo aircraft from *Enterprise* 09:20

Torpedo aircraft from *Hornet* 09:20

Spruance withdraws to Midway
deciding not to pursue the surviving
Japanese

Dive bombers
from *Enterprise*

B-17 Flying Fortresses from Midway

Japanese bombers

Midway

Spruance now decides to pursue
but only within the air cover of Midway
Enterprise launches an air strike sinking
the cruiser Mikuma

0 ——— 50 km
0 ——— 50 miles

Battle of Midway
4–5 June 1942

➤ US fleet movements

▪▪➤ US air strikes

➤ Japanese fleet movements

--➤ Japanese air strikes

✳ Ship damaged

✳ Ship sunk

U S S R   Alaska

Bering Sea

Attu   Kiska   Aleutian Is.

**HOSOGAYA
NORTHERN FORCE**

**ADMIRAL KAKUTA
SECOND CARRIER
STRIKE FORCE**

P A C I F I C   O C E A N

Akagi
Kaga
Soryu
Hiryu

**ADMIRAL NAGUMO
FIRST CARRIER
STRIKE FORCE**

**ADMIRAL FLETCHER
TASK FORCE 17**

J A P A N

**ADMIRAL YAMAMOTO
MAIN BODY**

Midway   *Yorktown*

Enterprise
Hornet

**KONDO
SECOND FLEET**

US submarines

**ADMIRAL SPRUANCE
TASK FORCE 16**

Pearl Harbor

Japanese Attack on Midway
27 May – 5 June 1942

➤ US fleet movements

➤ Japanese fleet movements

-- Limit of US air patrol

▬ US aircraft carriers

▬ Japanese aircraft carriers

**ADMIRAL TANAKA
TRANSPORT FORCE/
KURITA
SUPPORT FORCE**

Wake I.

Japanese submarine
screening force

Hawaiian Is.

Mariana Is.

135°   150°   165°   180°   165°

hangar decks. Once one bomb had penetrated a carrier and started a fire it was almost impossible to stop the ship burning to wreckage. Despite the disaster, the Japanese continued to consolidate their victories in the Pacific, being halted only on Guadalcanal by determined resistance by US Marines and on New Guinea by equally tough Australian defenses.

In North Africa, a new Italian-German offensive led by Rommel surged forward in January and pushed the British far back into Egypt, halting at El Alamein which was dangerously close to Alexandria and Suez. However, Rommel had used up most of his reserves and supplies in the advance. An attack by new British commander Bernard Montgomery in late October finally broke Rommel's Afrika Korps. On 8 November an American force landed in the French colonies of northwest Africa. Although Rommel fought a skillful retreat, the remnants of the Afrika Korps was forced to surrender in May 1942.

The largest battles of the year were fought on the Eastern Front. Keen to capture the Caucasus oil fields, Hitler ordered that the main offensive should be launched southeast over the Donets River to secure the area between the Black Sea, Caspian Sea, the Turkish border, and the Volga River. As the previous year, the German assault began well and vast swathes of territory were captured and massive losses imposed on the Russians. However, the excellent Soviet T34 tank was now in action in large numbers and went a long way to reducing German superiority in armor. One notable failure came in June when the great city of Stalingrad was surrounded, but not captured. Hitler became obsessed by the city, believing that capturing it would entail a massive blow to Stalin's personal prestige. More and more reinforcements

were poured into Stalingrad when they could have been better used elsewhere.

In Western Europe the bombing operations on Germany of the RAF and USAAF were gathering momentum. As yet the damage they inflicted was relatively slight, but the raids did force the Germans to keep fighters and anti-aircraft guns at home that would have been useful in Russia. A raid on the northern coast of France in August 1942, code named Operation Jubilee, was spearheaded by Winston Churchill's new chief of Combined Operations, Louis Mountbatten. The main

In June 1942, at the battle of Midway Island fought by American and Japanese carrier aircraft out of sight of their fleets, the strategic initiative in the Pacific War turned permanently against the Japanese. Their most crucial loss was the destruction of four aircraft carriers — two-thirds of their carrier fleet.

Japanese soldiers were masters of jungle warfare. Here, they march along a jungle trail in Burma.

The Caucasus
June – November 1942

→ German attacks
--→ German retreat
⌒ German front line
--→ Russian retreat
⚒ Oilfield

Kursk

XXXX
2

XXXX
40

Don

Voronezh

XXXXX
VORONEZH FRONT
GALIKOV

Saratov

XXXX
6

Svoboda

Belgorod

①

②

Pavlovsk

Khoper

XXXXX
SOUTHWEST FRONT
VATUTIN

Medvelitsa

Kamishin

XXXXX

XXXXX
DON FRONT
ROKOSSOVSKY

K a z a k h s t a n

XXXX
2
HUNGARIAN
(elts)

XXXX
1 Guards

XXXX
5

XXXX
21

Kharkov

XXXXX
B
WEICHS

XXXX
65

XXXX
24

XXXX
66

XXXXX

Izyum

U K R A I N E

Donets

XXXX
8
ITALIAN

XXXX
3
ROMANIAN

Stalingrad

XXXXX
STALINGRAD FRONT
YEREMENKO

Baskunchak

Lugansk

XXXX
6
PAULUS

XXXX
62

XXXX
64

Volga

XXXXX
SOUTH
BOCK

XXXX
4
HOTH

Don

XXXX
57

XXXX
51

Mariopol

Rostov

Novo Cherhassk

XXXX
4
ROMANIAN

③

XXXX
28

Astrakhan

Yejsk

XXXXX

Elista

S e a
o f
A s o v

XXXX
17
RUOFF

XXXXX
A
LIST

Ulan Erge

XXXXX

Kerch

XXXX
11 (-)

Krapotkin

XXXXX
NORTH CAUCASUS FRONT
BUDENNY

Taman

Kuban

C a s p i a n

Krasnovar

Armavir

Kuma

Stavropol

XXXX
1
KLEIST

S e a

Novorossiisk

XXXX
47

XXXX
56

Maikop

Kisliar

Tuapse

Georgiyevsk

Grozny

Sochi

XXXX
12

③

Piatigorsk

Mozdok

XXXX
44

Terek

German front lines:

① June 1942

XXXX
18

Nalchik

XXXX
9

Makhach Kala

② 23 July 1942

Sukhum

Ordzhonikidze

③ November 1942

B l a c k   S e a

XXXX
37

C a u c a s u s

M o u n t a i n s

N

Kutais

XXXXX
TRANS-CAUCASUS FRONT
TYULENEV

0   100 km
0   100 miles
40

Poti

Tiflis

Batumi

G E O R G I A

XXXX

45

AZERBAIJAN

TURKEY

goals were to test amphibious equipment and to seize and hold a major port on the English Channel. Also, Allied losses in North Africa were severe so everyone was hoping for a much needed victory.

In the spring of 1942 it was decided to settle the issue by actually trying to capture a French port intact. The port chosen was Dieppe and the pretext for the attack was a desire to destroy the German naval facilities there. The date set for the Dieppe Raid was 19 August 1942. The troops ordered to take part were largely Canadian, chosen for their famously aggressive spirit in battle. The raid was planned meticulously. There was to be a strong naval escort to protect the landing craft across the Channel. The RAF had a complex plan that enabled them to concentrate huge numbers of fighters over Dieppe throughout the day and so gain and secure temporary control of the air. Bombers would launch diversionary raids on other towns to confuse the Germans.

The landing force itself was to be backed by naval guns and by tanks brought ashore in landing craft. Smaller groups of commandoes, led by Lord Lovat, would assault the cliffs around Dieppe to capture and destroy large guns that dominated the town. The main force would land on the beaches, assault the town and capture port. The German facilities would then be demolished and the landing forced evacuated.

In the event the raid went badly. The RAF performed well, as did Lovat's raiders. However, the naval gunners found it much more difficult to identify and hit the German positions around Dieppe than had been expected. Even worse, the beach was more steeply shelving than expected, while the deep banks of shingle near the seawall were unable to support the weight of a tank, so all the tanks foundered and stalled. That left the Canadian infantry with the difficult task of taking a town without armored support and with inaccurate artillery support. Despite this the assault was carried out with determination and skill. The key objectives were eventually taken, but the town itself was not secured. The South Saskatchewan Regiment and the Cameron Highlanders had achieved a small degree of surprise at Pourville on the western flank, but things changed once they crossed the Scie River. Before long German reinforcements began arriving and they successfully interfered with the planned evacuation. Of the 6,000 men who landed, only 2,330 got back to the waiting landing craft in one piece. The rest were killed, wounded or captured. 600 men went in but only 125 made it back. The total number of deaths came to 900, and 1,200 more were taken prisoner. Although the losses had been extremely heavy, the Dieppe Raid showed what could, and what could not, be achieved. The lessons learned proved to be invaluable for the planning of D-Day in 1944. The raid on Dieppe ended in complete failure, but did teach the Allied planners important lessons about launching amphibious landings against determined resistance. Two Canadians were recognized with the Victoria Cross for actions at Dieppe; Lieutenant Colonel "Cec" Merritt of the South Saskatchewan Regiment and Honorary Captain John Foote of the Royal Hamilton Light Infantry.

The Atlantic U-boat campaign reached its peak in late 1942. The opening years of the war had been dominated by damaging voyages by German surface warships, but the sinking of the Bismarck in 1941 had persuaded Hitler to concentrate on U-boats instead. Admiral Donitz had 200 of these submarines with which to attack Allied shipping, allowing him to keep as many as 75 U-boats in the Atlantic at any one time. The submarines were organized into "wolf packs" that could close in on a convoy to attack from all sides. In 1942 almost half the Allied ships on convoy protection duty were Canadian. The U-boats proved to be audacious, sinking the Canadian destroyer *Charlottetown* in the St Lawrence River.

In the summer of 1942, the situation looked very grim for the Russians in the Caucasus where the Red Army's resistance in the Crimea ended on 1 July. But in November, the Red Army encircled the Germans at Stalingrad and began a long, bloody struggle in which they eventually prevailed.

WORLD WAR II: 1943

THE TIDE OF WAR DEFINITELY BEGAN TO TURN ON ALL FRONTS IN 1943. AS AMERICAN INDUSTRIAL PRODUCTION CAME INCREASINGLY ON STREAM THE RATES TURNED AGAINST THE AXIS.

Since the outbreak of war the British had been fighting a long, arduous campaign to keep open the routes of merchant convoys bringing much-needed war material to Britain, and carrying exports out to pay for them. In May 1941 the German battleship *Bismarck*, the most powerful ship afloat, had been sunk in the Atlantic, but more of a long-term threat were the German U-boats, or submarines, which cruised the Atlantic attacking any target they found. Under their talented commander Admiral Dönitz the U-boat captains developed sophisticated "wolf pack" tactics for locating and attacking convoys. In 1942 the U-boats sank 1,664 ships, and 1943 opened with even higher monthly totals than 1942. During that year, however, long-range aircraft equipped with depth charges and increasingly large numbers of US escort ships enabled the British to inflict such heavy losses

Cartwheel was the code name for the Allied operation to capture the Solomon Islands, New Guinea, New Britain, and New Ireland from the Japanese. All objectives were achieved by the end of 1943 and it was decided to move on toward the Philippine Islands and tackle the Japanese there.

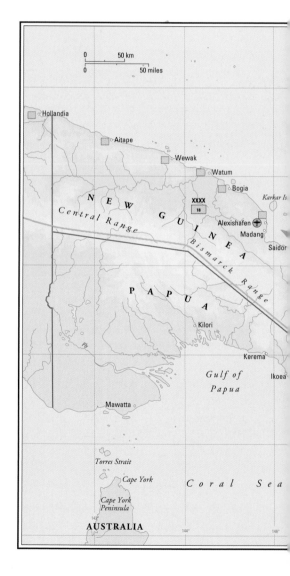

on the Germans that Dönitz called off the campaign in June.

On the Eastern Front a massive Soviet counterattack had surrounded the German 6th Army in Stalingrad in November 1942. On 2 February von Paulus surrendered his 6th Army. The Germans had lost 200,000 dead and 91,000 prisoners. The Russians followed up with a counterattack that drove the Germans out of the Caucasus and back to the Ukraine. To the north a Russian attack launched in January succeeded in breaking through German lines to reach the city of Leningrad, which had been surrounded since November 1941. The route through to the city and losses among supply convoys were heavy until the Germans pulled back in December of 1943. During the siege an estimated 900,000 Russian civilians had died and losses among the armies on both sides had been heavy.

Hitler ordered his own counterattack and gathered the largest panzer force of the war to assault

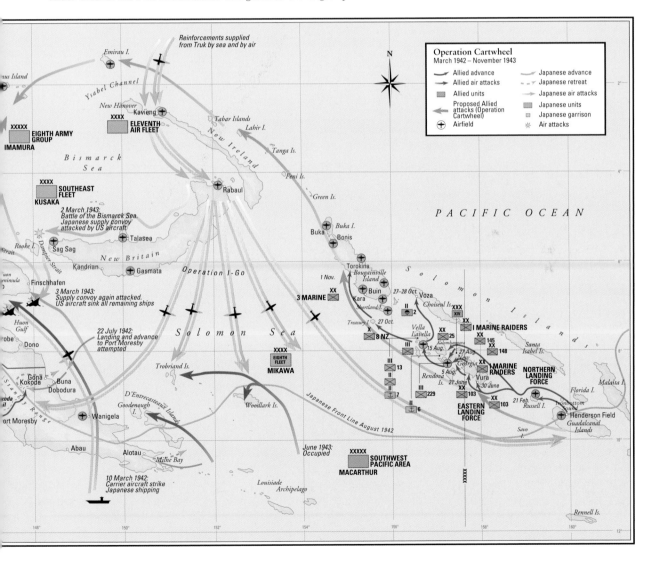

Russian positions at Kursk, exposing the southern flank of Moscow. Russian commander Zhukov correctly guessed where the attack would come and prepared well. He built massive static defenses in depth and prepared his own massive armored force to launch a counterattack once the Germans were halted. The battle began on 5 July 1943 and went exactly according to Zhukov's plan. The Germans lost 70,000 men, 2,900 panzers, 200 guns, and 1,400 aircraft. The Germans began a retreat that would take them all the way to Berlin.

With the German army now totally exhausted, Hitler's sights moved to the southern Russian steppe and the vast oilfields and wide agricultural lands that would fuel his country's war machine. He decided to strike toward Stalingrad. The capture of the city would be a massive propaganda coup for the Germans

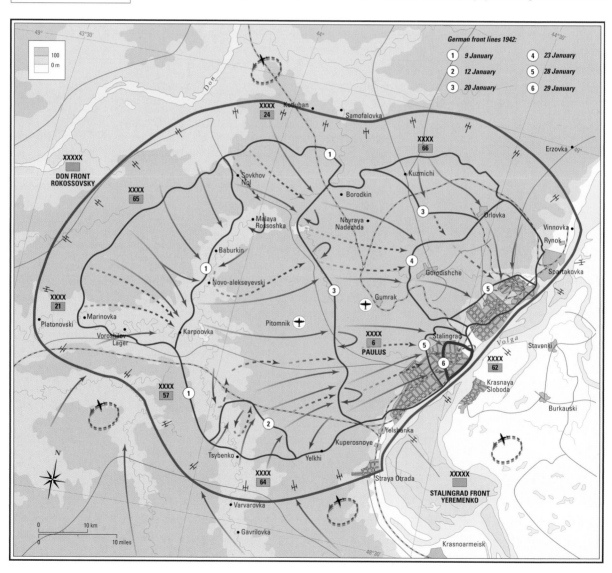

The Battle for Stalingrad
September 1942–February 1943

➤ Soviet attacks
➤ German counter-attacks
⇢ German retreats
— German front lines
— Limit of Soviet artillery
⇉ Soviet air support

German front lines 1942:
1 9 January
2 12 January
3 20 January
4 23 January
5 28 January
6 29 January

as well as denying Russia its link to the Caspian Sea and the Caucasus oilfields. Although German air strikes decimated the city, Stalin ordered that no civilians were to leave, in order to continue production of firearms and tanks, and to boost the morale of the troops defending them. The Battle for Stalingrad was horrific in scale and magnitude. The Germans were eventually pushed to the banks of the River Volga, and forced to surrender on 2 February 1943. A total of 91,000 starving troops marched into captivity, most destined to die in the harsh conditions of Soviet labor camps. It is estimated that the Germans and their allies suffered close to 850,000 casualties and the Russians 1,128,000, making it the highest number of casualties in a single battle in human history.

In the Mediterranean the victorious Allies moved from North Africa to capture Sicily in July 1943 and in September 1943 launched an invasion of mainland Italy. The move prompted the Italian government to vote Mussolini out of office and replace him with Marshal Badoglio who surrendered to the Allies on 8 September. German troops were already in Italy, and reinforcements were rushed in under Marshal Kesselring, who halted the Allied advance south of Rome along the Gustav Line of defenses in October.

The air offensive against Germany flown by British and US bombers operating out of Britain increased greatly in strength during 1943. The famous Dambuster Raid by the RAF in May destroyed two key dams in the industrial Ruhr area. Of more long-term importance were the night raids launched on industrial cities by the RAF. These destroyed factories, transport links and workers' houses, but due to navigational problems were generally effective only in western Germany. US daylight raids were more accurate, but the USAAF 8th Air Force was as yet small and untried, so the bombers tended to go for specific targets in occupied France, Belgium and the Netherlands where accuracy was needed to minimize civilian casualties. One major raid deep into Germany was the attack on the ball bearing factories at Schwienfurt carried out on 17 August 1943. Losses were very heavy, with 36 bombers shot down and 81 damaged out of 230 that took part.

In the Pacific the victory at Midway had given the US dominance at sea, but the Japanese navy remained a potent force. For most of the year the US concentrated on building up their strength and on a prolonged submarine offensive against Japanese merchant shipping.

In August 1943 Operation Cartwheel was launched to recapture the Solomon Islands and Bismarck Archipelago. Progress proved to be painfully slow in the face of Japanese jungle tactics and by the end of the year the operation was not even half completed. In November the US Marines assaulted and captured Tarawa and Makin in the Gilbert Islands, but suffered heavy losses. In Burma the British launched a few small-scale attacks but these were beaten off by the Japanese.

Operation Lightfoot was the codename for the British Eighth Army's defeat of the German Afrika Korps, commanded by General Erwin Rommel, at El Alamein on 23 October, 1942. After an intense artillery barrage, the British infantry would breach the Afrika Korps' lines, allowing the British tanks and armor to pass through.

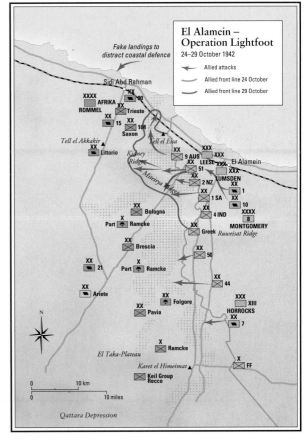

Strategic Bombing
1943

☐ Main Headquarters
☐ Group Headquarters
○ Bomber Command airfields
● US 8th Air Force airfields
✴ RAF-bombed target
✴ USAAF-bombed target
✴ RAF and USAAF target
— Fighter Division boundary
[4] Fighter Division
⊚ German radar station
● German night fighter station
∞ Searchlight batteries
▦ Anti-aircraft batteries

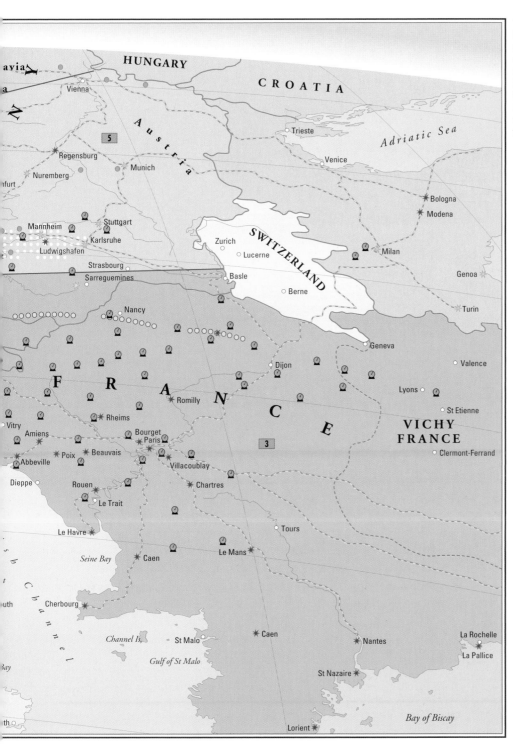

"Strategic bombing" described bombing operations by the Allied air forces on German factories, military installations, and other industrial targets. At first, half the bombers were lost in the raids, but this situation improved after 1943 when the P-51 Mustang fighters escorted and protected them to the target and back.

HUNGARY

CROATIA

Vienna

Austria

5

Trieste

Adriatic Sea

Regensburg

Venice

Nuremberg

Munich

Bologna

Modena

Mannheim

Stuttgart

SWITZERLAND

Karlsruhe

Zurich

Ludwigshafen

Lucerne

Milan

Strasbourg

Basle

Genoa

Sarreguemines

Berne

Turin

Nancy

Geneva

Valence

Dijon

FRANCE

Lyons

Romilly

St Etienne

Rheims

VICHY
FRANCE

Vitry

Amiens

Bourget

3

Paris

Clermont-Ferrand

Poix

Beauvais

Abbeville

Villacoublay

Dieppe

Rouen

Chartres

Le Trait

Le Havre

Tours

Caen

Le Mans

Seine Bay

Cherbourg

Channel Is.

St Malo

Caen

Nantes

La Rochelle

Gulf of St Malo

La Pallice

St Nazaire

Bay of Biscay

Lorient

WORLD WAR II: 1944

WITH THE AXIS FORCES EVERYWHERE IN RETREAT, THE ISSUES OF STRATEGY FOR THE ALLIES BECAME MORE A MATTER OF HOW BEST TO DEFEAT THE ENEMY, HOW TO ALLOCATE RESOURCES, AND WHAT PLANS SHOULD BE PUT IN PLACE FOR THE WORLD AFTER THE EVENTUAL VICTORY.

Until 1944 the Allies had been effectively fighting three different wars. In the Pacific, the US and British imperial troops had first held the Japanese onslaught and then made modest gains. In Western Europe the British and Americans, with some units from occupied countries, had been fighting actively in the Mediterranean and at sea while planning for an opportunity to invade mainland Europe through France. The western Allies had decided to give priority in terms of men and supplies to the campaign against Germany and her allies. Russia was, meanwhile, fighting a largely quite separate war on the Eastern Front. There the Soviets faced the combined forces of Germany, Romania, Finland, and Hungary. Bulgaria had remained neutral but surrounded by German allies had been forced to make many concessions to the Axis. Stalin had since 1942 been demanding that the western Allies do more against Germany without offering much in return. Churchill was deeply suspicious of Stalin's ambitions, though Roosevelt was more inclined to accept Stalin's statements.

The first large scale actions of 1944 took place on the Eastern Front where the Russians launched an attack in the southern Ukraine that captured Kirovgrad and encircled substantial German forces that managed to fight their way out only with heavy loss. The next major offensive, Operation Bagration, saw the Russians attack on the northern sector through Belorussia. On 23 June 1944 1.4 million Russians supported by 31,000 guns, 5,200 tanks and 500 aircraft surged forward. By late July the Soviets had effectively destroyed the German Army Group Center as a fighting force, inflicting casualties of over 60%. The advance had carried the Soviets into pre-war Estonia, Latvia, Lithuania, and Poland. All of Russia had been liberated from the Germans. In the autumn the Soviets launched an offensive into the Balkans that carried them through Romania into Hungary and Yugoslavia. As the Russians

Operation Bagration, named after a Russian general of the Napoleonic Wars, was called "the most calamitous defeat of all the German armed forces in the Second World War". Fought in Belorussia on June 22, 1944, Bagration destroyed the German Army Group Center and liberated most of German-occupied Russia.

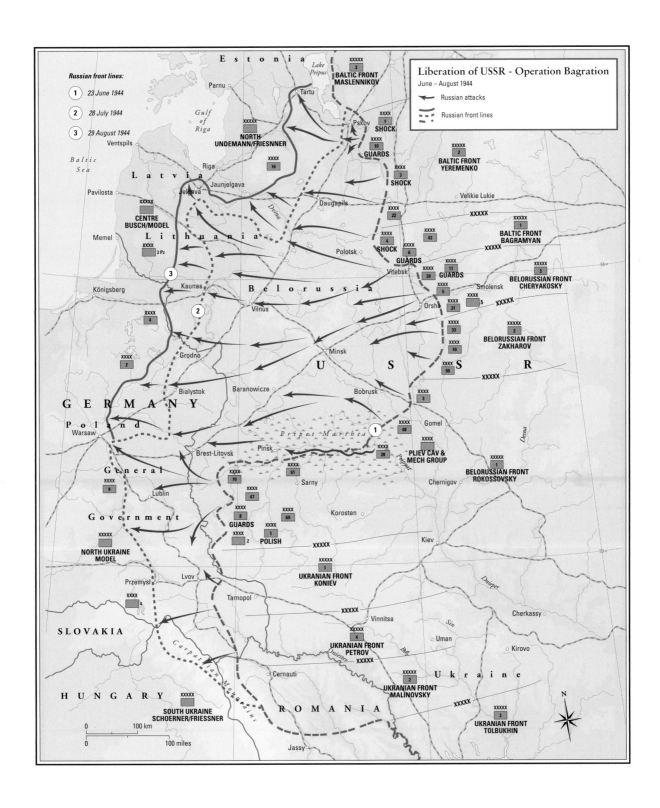

Liberation of USSR - Operation Bagration
June – August 1944

→ Russian attacks

⌐⌐⌐⌐ Russian front lines

Russian front lines:

① 23 June 1944

② 28 July 1944

③ 29 August 1944

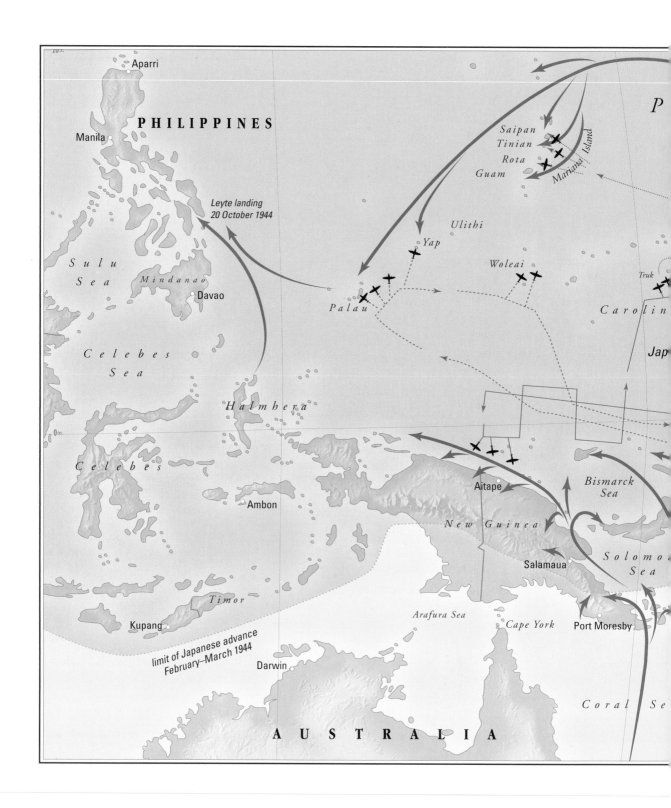

Aparri

PHILIPPINES

Manila

P

Saipan
Tinian
Rota
Guam

Mariana Island

Leyte landing
20 October 1944

Ulithi

Yap

Woleai

S u l u
S e a

Mindanao

Davao

Palau

Truk

C a r o l i n

C e l e b e s
S e a

Jap

H a l m h e r a

0°

C e l e b e s

Aitape

Bismarck
Sea

New Guinea

Solomo
Sea

Ambon

Salamaua

Timor

Arafura Sea

Cape York

Port Moresby

Kupang

limit of Japanese advance
February–March 1944

Darwin

C o r a l   S e

A U S T R A L I A

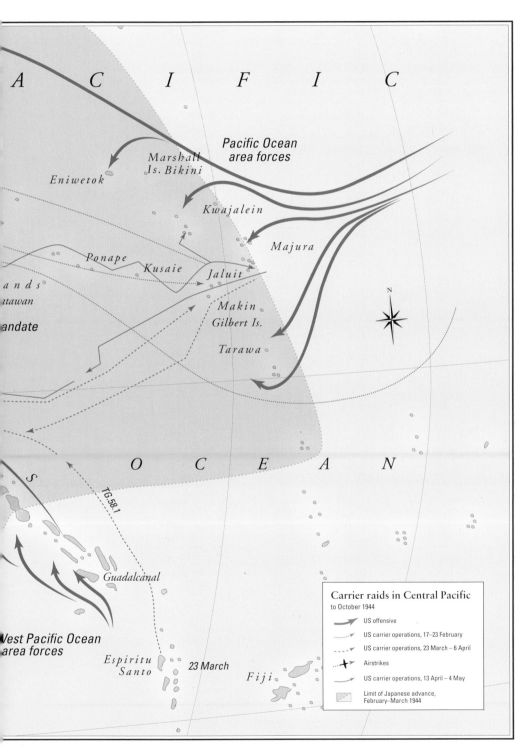

P A C I F I C

*Pacific Ocean
area forces*

Eniwetok

*Marshall
Is. Bikini*

Kwajalein

Majura

Ponape

Kusaie

Jaluit

*Makin
Gilbert Is.*

Tarawa

*ands
atawan*

andate

N

TG.58.1

O C E A N

S

Guadalcanal

*Vest Pacific Ocean
area forces*

*Espiritu
Santo*

23 March

Fiji

Carrier raids in Central Pacific
to October 1944

→ US offensive

....▸ US carrier operations, 17–23 February

-- ▸ US carrier operations, 23 March – 6 April

✈ Airstrikes

~~ US carrier operations, 13 April – 4 May

▨ Limit of Japanese advance,
February–March 1944

During the Pacific war, the aircraft carrier replaced the battleship as the most important vessel in naval warfare. Launching attack aircraft from the decks of the carriers sited off Japanese-held islands was the only feasible way for the Americans to destroy enemy defenses before sending in invasion forces.

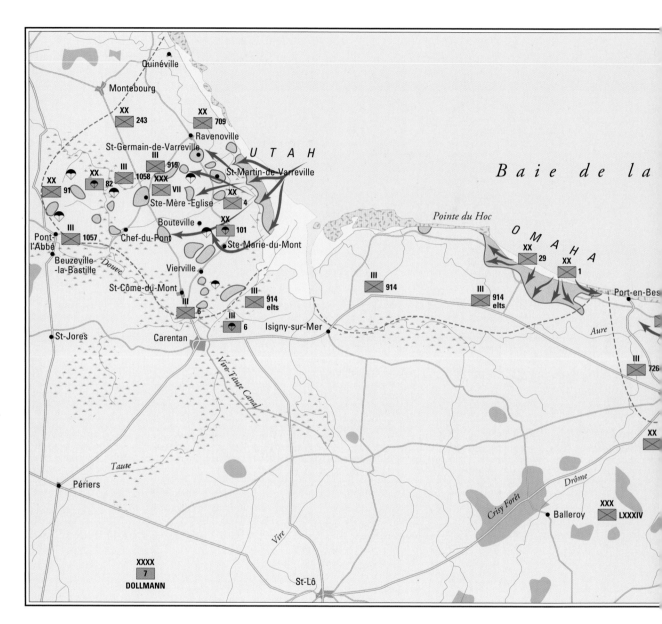

On 6 June, 1944, the first day of
the Normandy invasion, 5,000
vessels were involved in landing
troops on the beaches: around
154,000 Americans, and 83,115
British and Canadians, 23,000 of
them arriving by parachute and
glider. In addition, the Allied air
forces carried out some 11,000
sorties against German targets.

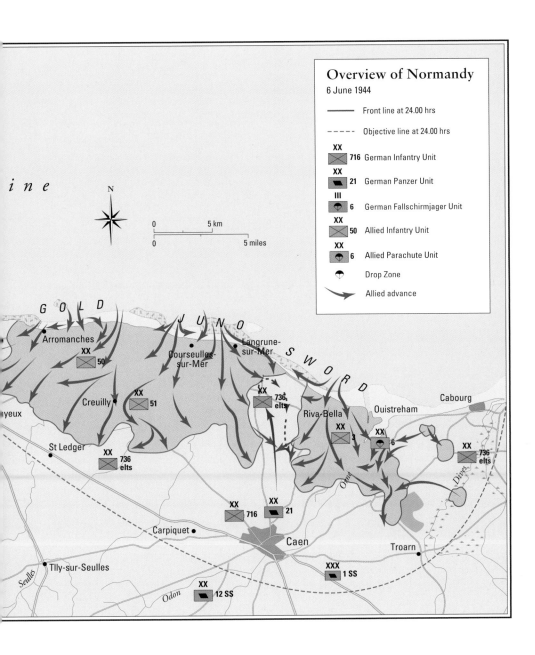

Overview of Normandy
6 June 1944

—————— Front line at 24.00 hrs

- - - - - - - Objective line at 24.00 hrs

716 German Infantry Unit

21 German Panzer Unit

6 German Fallschirmjäger Unit

50 Allied Infantry Unit

6 Allied Parachute Unit

Drop Zone

Allied advance

approached neutral Bulgaria, the Bulgarians declared war on Germany. But the Russians declared war on Bulgaria and invaded, overrunning the country and installing a Communist government. Churchill's suspicions were being borne out.

The dogged Japanese resistance in the Pacific had persuaded the Allies that they needed a new strategy. They developed the process of "island hopping". Instead of attacking every Japanese occupied island, the Americans would assault only those that they needed as air or naval bases. Strict blockades would then be imposed on the isolated Japanese garrisons left behind to starve them of supplies and ensure they were unable to break out. Bypassing the Bonin and Caroline Islands and most of the smaller Marshall and Gilbert Islands, the Americans next went for Saipan, Guam and Tinian in the Marianas. These islands were needed as they could be used as airbases from which the new long-range B29 bomber could reach Japan. Saipan was attacked first on 15 June, the first Marines ashore taking huge casualties. The island was secured by mid July 1944. Guam and Tinian were attacked in July and taken by the end of August. In June 1944 the Japanese fleet steamed to attack American ships in the Marianas. The two fleets met at the Battle of the Philippine Sea on 15 June 1944. The heavy losses among Japanese carrier pilots earlier in the war was now revealed in the poor tactics and flying skills of their hastily trained replacements. The Japanese lost 370 aircraft and three carriers while the Americans lost just 50 aircraft. In Western Europe the Allied bombing offensive was having a major impact on German war industries. The output of military equipment, especially tanks and aircraft, was being seriously affected, hampering the armed forces on the battlefield. The main focus for the western Allies was, however, on the invasion of France. This took place on 6 June 1944 in an assault officially known as Operation Overlord, but more widely known as D-Day. A complex deception persuaded the Germans that the attack would be made around Calais, though the German General Rommel correctly believed the landings would be made in Normandy.

The first troops into Europe were paratroops who seized key bridges and road junctions around 2am. Gilder troops came in around 4am to support the paratroops. At dawn

Considering the island nature of the "battlefield", it was inevitable that aircraft carriers and their aircraft, together with other planes operating from captured airfields, should predominate in the war in the Pacific. The decisive factor was the American island-hopping campaign which brought them within reach of Japan by June 1945.

Overleaf: The Philippine landings began on October 20, 1944, when the U.S. Sixth Army went ashore on Leyte island. Against this and subsequent landings, together with an attack on Manila, the Philippines capital, Japanese resistance was fanatical. By the end of April 1945 however, the Americans had prevailed.

World War II in Asia
1943–45

Japanese perimeter, March 1944

Japanese perimeter, Aug. 1945

Major allied attacks, late 1943–Aug. 1945

Long-range bomber attack on Japan

1. June 1942 – July 1943
Operation Cartwheel. Allied forces
advance.

2. November 1943 – September 1944
U.S. drive through central Pacific.

3. February – June, 1944
Unsuccessful Japanese invasion of India.

4. 19–21 October 1944
Battle of the Philippine Sea. U.S. Task
Force 58 destroys Japanese Mobile Fleet.

5. 20 October 1944
U.S. forces land in Philippines.

6. 24 November 1944
20th Air Force begins air attack
on Japan from Island bases.

7. November 1944.
British offensive into Burma.

8. 19 February – 26 March 1945
U.S. captures Iwo Jima
1 April – June 1945
U.S. land and capture Okinawa.

9. April – June 1945
Chinese offensives.

10. 9 August 1945
Soviet offensive begins.

11. 6 August and 9 August 1945
U.S. nuclear attacks on Japan.

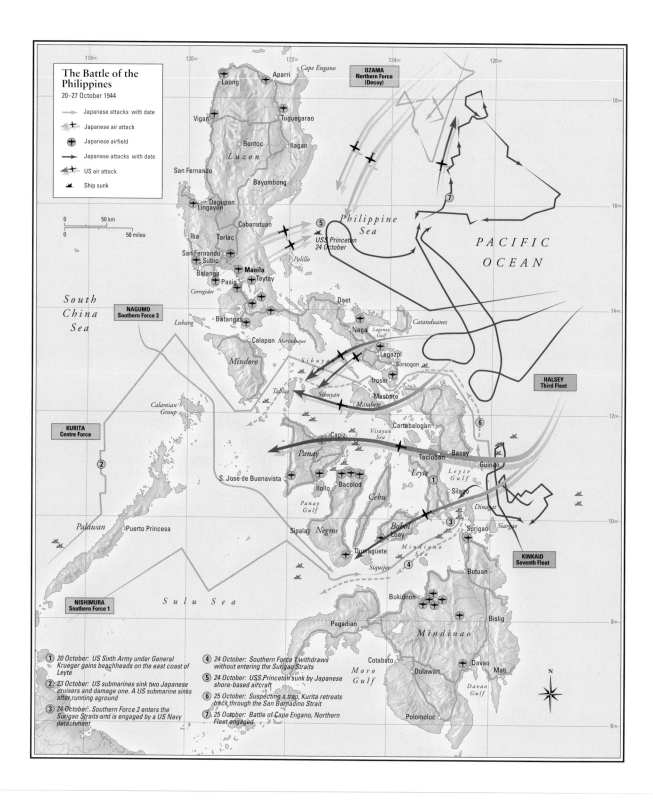

The Battle of the Philippines
20–27 October 1944

→ Japanese attacks with date
✈ Japanese air attack
⊕ Japanese airfield
→ Japanese attacks with date
✈ US air attack
⚓ Ship sunk

0 ____ 50 km
0 ____ 50 miles

OZAMA
Northern Force
(Decoy)

Cape Engano

Laong
Aparri
Vigan
Tuguegarao
Bontoc
Ilagan
Luzon
San Fernando
Bayombong
Dagupan
Lingayen
Cabanatuan

Philippine Sea

⑤ USS Princeton
24 October

PACIFIC
OCEAN

Iba
Tarlac
San Fernando
Subic
Balanga
Manila
Pasig
Taytay
Corregidor
Polillo

⑦

Daet

South China Sea

NAGUMO
Southern Force 3

Lubang
Batangas
Calapan
Marinduque
Naga
Lagonay Gulf
Catanduanes

Mindoro
Sibuyan
Legazpi
Sorsogon
Tablas
Sibuyan
Irosin
Masbate
Masabate

HALSEY
Third Fleet

Calamian Group

KURITA
Centre Force

②

Cartabalogan
Capiz
Visayan Sea
Basey
Panay
Tacloban
Leyte
Guinan
⑥
S. Jose de Buenavista
Ilollo
Bacolod
Cebu
① *Leyte Gulf*
Silago

Palawan
Puerto Princesa

Panay Gulf
Sipalay
Negros
Bohol
Loay
Mindinao Sea
Dinagat
③
Surigao
Siargao

KINKAID
Seventh Fleet

NISHIMURA
Southern Force 1

Sulu Sea
Dumaguete
Siquijor
④
Butuan

Bukidnon

Pagadian
Bislig

Mindinao

Cotabato
Moro Gulf
Dulawan
Davao
Mati

Polomoloc
Davao Gulf

N

① 20 October: US Sixth Army under General Krueger gains beachheads on the east coast of Leyte

② 23 October: US submarines sink two Japanese cruisers and damage one. A US submarine sinks after running aground

③ 24 October: Southern Force 2 enters the Surigao Straits and is engaged by a US Navy detachment

④ 24 October: Southern Force 1 withdraws without entering the Surigao Straits

⑤ 24 October: USS Princeton sunk by Japanese shore-based aircraft

⑥ 25 October: Suspecting a trap, Kurita retreats back through the San Bernadino Strait

⑦ 25 October: Battle of Cape Engano, Northern Fleet engaged

warships moved in to shell German beach defenses while bombers hit the areas immediately behind the beaches. The troops began to go ashore at 6.30am in the face of determined German resistance.

In the east, near Caen, the British and Canadians were quickly off the beaches and heading inland in numbers, but at noon the 21st Panzer Division suddenly attacked and broke through to the sea. Amongst the troops were the First Candian army. The Royal Candian Air Force and the Royal Canadian Navy had played a significant part in bombing key targets to prepare for the D-Day landings. The resulting battle

The Battle of the Bulge in the Ardennes Forest saw the Germans' last attack of the War in December 1944. Initially, they scored some success against their American opponents, but they could not sustain their assaults.

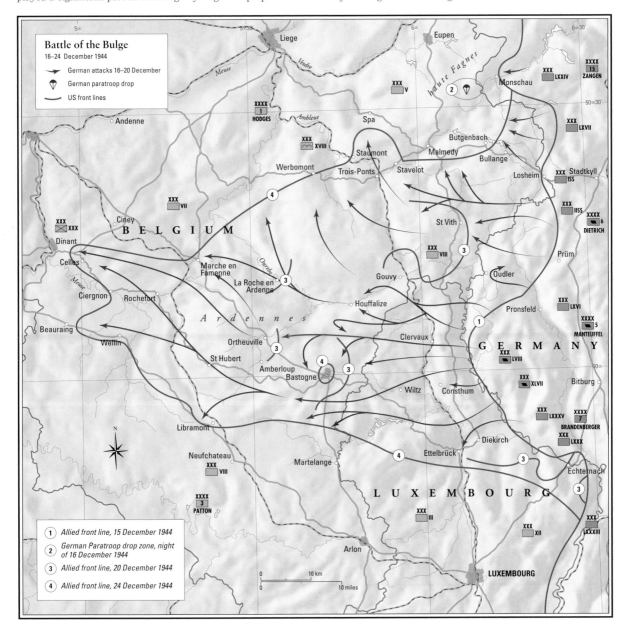

Battle of the Bulge
16–24 December 1944

→ German attacks 16–20 December

⊽ German paratroop drop

— US front lines

① Allied front line, 15 December 1944
② German Paratroop drop zone, night of 16 December 1944
③ Allied front line, 20 December 1944
④ Allied front line, 24 December 1944

slowed down the advance and stopped the invaders from capturing their twin objectives of Caen and Bayeux. In the west the Americans established a firm beach-head, but also failed to get as far inland as they had hoped. In the center on the beach code-named Omaha German defenses were almost intact, and American casualties were correspondingly very high.

Allied progress inland through Normandy was slow as the Germans continued to feed in reinforcements to man the cleverly designed defenses. By 24 July 1944 the Allies were still not so far inland as they had planned to be by 20 June 1944. Then the Americans broke through the German defenses at Avranches and the US 3rd Army under General Patton stormed forward. Patton's advance was rapid, and once his armor was rampaging through the German rear areas the enemy line collapsed allowing a general advance on all fronts. Early in August Franco-American forces landed in southern France and after some

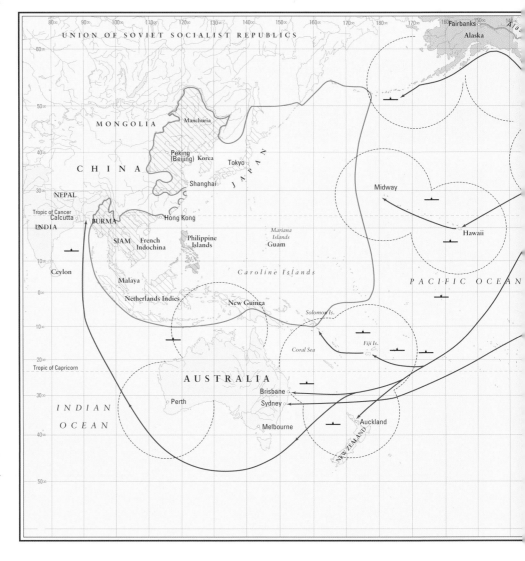

Even before they entered the War in 1941, the Americans were supplying Britain with arms, ammunition and food to boost the British war effort. As the War progressed, a giant network of supply routes grew up to supply the Allied campaigns in North Africa, the Pacific and, ultimately, in Europe.

fighting were advancing quickly up the Rhone valley. On 18 August the Paris police force rebelled against the Germans and thousands of citizens poured on to the streets to man barricades. The Americans tactfully stood back while a division of the Free French headed for Paris to take the German surrender. Meanwhile the Allied advance swept on finding virtually no German resistance. The advance finally came to an end in eastern France and central Belgium due to a lack of fuel. That gave the Germans time to organize a defense and dig in. Hitler gathered together all his reserves and threw them at the Americans in southern Belgium on 15 December 1944. Taken completely by surprise, the Americans fell back in disorder which was made worse by English-speaking German troops pretending to be military policemen who issued false orders to American units. The heroic defense of the key road junction of Bastogne by a mixed American force under General McAuliffe severely disrupted the German advance.

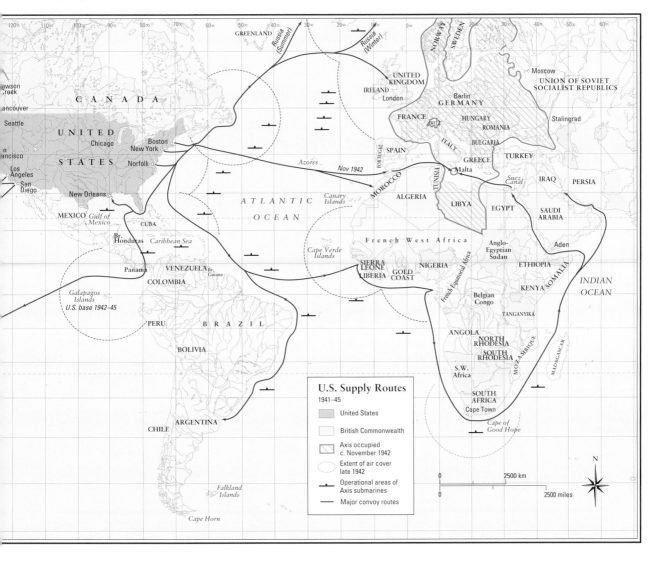

WORLD WAR II: 1945

BY THE START OF 1945 IT WAS CLEAR TO ALL THAT THE AXIS POWERS FACED DEFEAT. THE ONLY QUESTIONS THAT REMAINED INVOLVED HOW THAT DEFEAT COULD BE BROUGHT ABOUT AND AT WHAT COST TO THE VICTORIOUS ALLIES. MUCH HINGED ON THE ABILITY AND WILL OF THE AXIS TO CONTINUE THE FIGHT.

With hindsight the most important questions of the war in early 1945 were why Germany and Japan kept on fighting. Both nations were clearly doomed to defeat, a fact that was known to their government leaders. In 1918, Germany, Austria, and Turkey had surrendered rather than face the wrath of enemy armies invading their territories. The peace treaties imposed in 1919 were harsh by any standards, but the destruction of war fought to the bitter end would have been far worse. In 1945 Germany made the opposite choice, opting for bloody destruction rather than humiliating surrender. The reason for this was Adolf Hitler. When he had launched the German invasion of Russia in 1941, Hitler had been quite clear that this was to be a war of annihilation between rival and incompatible civilizations. The final plan in the event of victory was for the Russians to be reduced to the status of a slave people while German settlers were brought in to own and inhabit lands forcibly cleared of inhabitants. During the invasion members of the Communist Party were routinely shot out of hand, prisoners sent off to work as slave labor in factories, and Jews rounded up to be machine-gunned.

The extent to which the German army was aware of these activities has long been the subject of debate, but certainly the higher levels of the Nazi Party and those carrying out their orders knew all that was going on. From 1943 onward the killing of Jews, Gypsies, and other unwanted ethnic groups was put on an industrial scale with dedicated extermination camps established in the east. Hitler and most senior Nazis knew that in the event of surrender the Allies would have little mercy. Many of them would expect to be executed, the rest to receive lengthy prison sentences. In the circumstances it must have seemed better to fight on and hope something would come up.

In the Spring of 1945, Allied forces were advancing into Germany from the west and the east. On 30 April, Führer Adolf Hitler committed suicide in his bunker in Berlin, two days before the Russians captured the German capital. Five days after that, on 7 May, Nazi Germany surrendered.

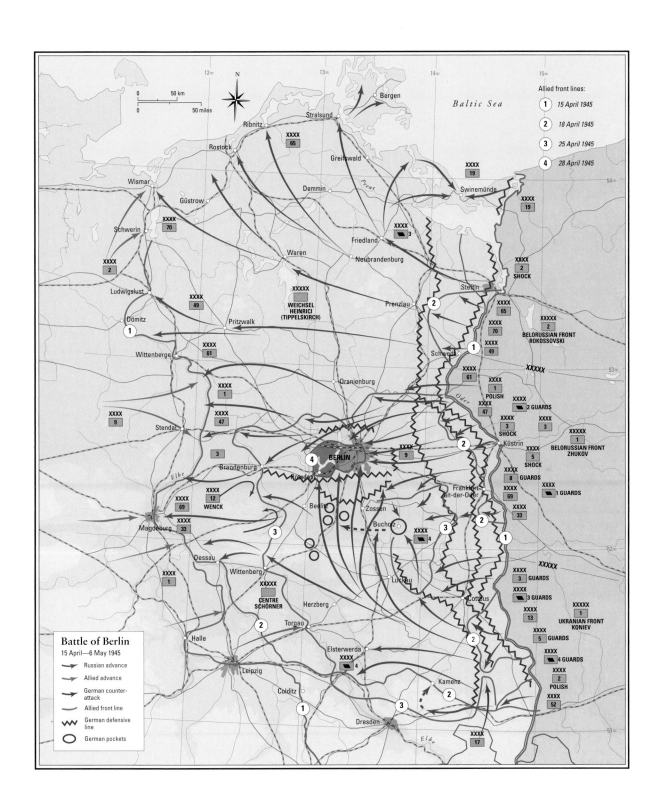

Allied front lines:
1 *15 April 1945*
2 *18 April 1945*
3 *25 April 1945*
4 *28 April 1945*

Battle of Berlin
15 April—6 May 1945

→ Russian advance
→ Allied advance
→ German counter-attack
— Allied front line
⋀⋀ German defensive line
○ German pockets

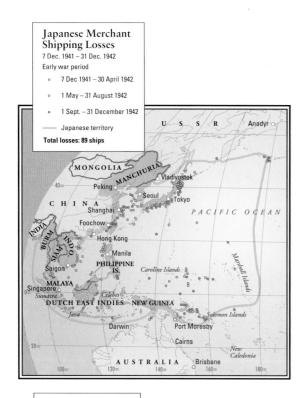

Japanese Merchant Shipping Losses
7 Dec. 1941 – 31 Dec. 1942
Early war period
- 7 Dec 1941 – 30 April 1942
- 1 May – 31 August 1942
- 1 Sept. – 31 December 1942
— Japanese territory
Total losses: 89 ships

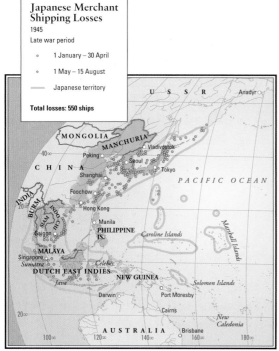

Japanese Merchant Shipping Losses
1945
Late war period
- 1 January – 30 April
- 1 May – 15 August
— Japanese territory
Total losses: 550 ships

Meanwhile the Nazi Party had such a tight grip on Germany that anyone below the level of Hitler having the authority to surrender was unthinkable. The wives and children of senior army officers were rounded up by the Gestapo secret police. If the officer surrendered his forces, his family was shot. And the Nazi propaganda machine remained ferociously efficient at maintaining morale among ordinary Germans. Not until just weeks before the end did the average civilian accept that defeat was inevitable. So it was that the German armies faced their final campaigns determined to fight. In the West, the failure of the Market Garden campaign had convinced General Eisenhower that he should advance on a broad front rather than risk a narrow thrust as was suggested by most of his subordinate generals. The advance over the Rhine began on 24 March 1945 as the British-Canadian forces under Montgomery crossed the river at Wesel. Patton's 3rd US Army had jumped the gun by crossing in the south ahead of schedule.

At first German resistance was fierce and progress slow, but on 28 March 1945 the German front gave way. Field Marshal Model pulled his Army Group B back into the heavily populated and easily defended Ruhr region, allowing the Allied armies to sweep past him and head east. As armored columns swept on, followed by infantry in lorries, they came across numerous German soldiers who threw their hands up in surrender as soon as they were met. It soon became clear that many German units were hurrying west with the sole aim of surrendering to the Americans or British — anything rather than face the Russian onslaught.

The Soviet advance had begun earlier, on 12 January 1945, on a broad front stretching from Presov in Slovakia to Lablau on the Baltic. The advance lasted six weeks before it ground to a halt on the Oder River. Stalin ordered a re-organization for the final assault on Berlin. He gave the northern sector to Zhukov and the southern to Koniev, his two best generals. Whichever force got to Berlin first, Stalin said, would have the honor of taking the enemy capital. He demanded that the city be taken before 1 May, the great Communist festival.

The drive to Berlin began on 15 April 1945. For three days little progress was made, then the German line broke in two places and the Russians surged forward. By 28 April 1945 Berlin was surrounded. Inside the city were 200,000 armed men from a mixed variety of units with limited heavy weaponry. The Russians had more than a million men, with full complements of tanks and guns. The result

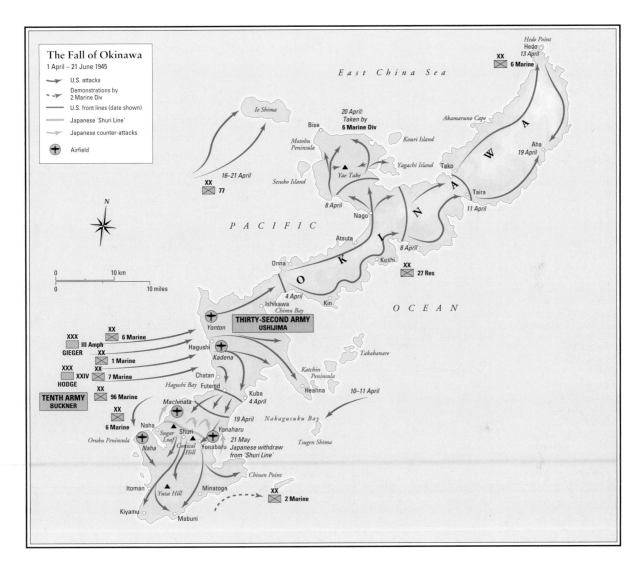

The Fall of Okinawa
1 April – 21 June 1945

→ U.S. attacks
Demonstrations by
2 Marine Div
— U.S. front lines (date shown)
Japanese 'Shuri Line'
Japanese counter-attacks
⊕ Airfield

was never in doubt, but Stalin's demand for a quick result forced Zhukov and Koniev to adopt costly tactics of frontal assault that cost many thousands of lives. On 30 April 1945 Hitler committed suicide as the Russian troops were just 100 yd (90 m) from his command bunker. So chaotic was the situation that the general commanding the troops did not hear until 2 May 1945, whereupon he surrendered. On 8 May 1945 Admiral Dönitz, who was appointed leader by Hitler in his will, surrendered to the Allies, choosing to do so to American General Eisenhower, not to the Russians.

In the Pacific, the Japanese government recognized that they could not win. The destruction of their merchant fleet by US submarines had starved their weapons factories of raw materials while the increasingly heavy US bombing of Japan was causing mass civilian casualties and the destruction of entire cities. The block to peace here was the Anglo-American demand for unconditional surrender. To

On 1 April, 1945 some 16,000 U.S. combat troops invaded the island of Okinawa. Japanese resistance was always fanatical, but Okinawa, 330 miles (530 km) from Japan, was defended with extra fervor. The Japanese lost over 135,000 killed in the fight for Okinawa which ended with their surrender on 21 June.

the Japanese government this would have been a total betrayal of their loyal fighting men who were willing to die for the national cause. The government also feared that the demand was a cover for the Allied desire to unseat the Japanese emperor and end some two thousand years of rule by the divine dynasty. Such a thing was unthinkable.

In Burma the Anglo-Indian advance had begun in December 1944 after the defeat of a Japanese invasion of India at Kohima. By mid February 1945 the Allies were over the jungle-covered mountains of the border area and into the broad Irrawaddy valley. Aided by American and Chinese troops, the advance continued south capturing Meiktila on 5 March 1945 and Mandalay two weeks later. On 2 May 1945 an amphibious force was landed near the mouth of the Irrawaddy and Japanese resistance collapsed. Rangoon was captured on 5 May and the disorganized Japanese survivors fled east over the mountains toward Siam.

The American liberation of the Philippines had begun in October 1944 with landings on smaller islands, but the invasion of the main island of Luzon took place in January 1945. US General MacArthur

As the American "island-hopping" campaign drew nearer to Japan, it became easier for U.S. aircraft to deliver more frequent bombing raids on Japanese cities from airfields on the captured islands. The seizure of Okinawa, for example, allowed for five raids over a period of less than seven weeks.

Far Right: By March 1945, Japanese forces opposing the Americans in the Philippine islands were close to defeat. Fighting ended on Iwo Jima and on 1 April, U.S. forces landed on Okinawa. The Japanese kamikaze suicide campaign began soon afterwards, but could not prevent the capture of Okinawa on 22 June.

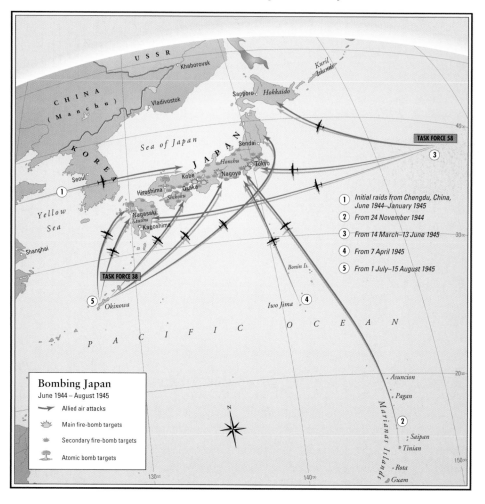

Bombing Japan
June 1944 – August 1945

Allied air attacks

Main fire-bomb targets

Secondary fire-bomb targets

Atomic bomb targets

1 Initial raids from Chengdu, China, June 1944–January 1945
2 From 24 November 1944
3 From 14 March–13 June 1945
4 From 7 April 1945
5 From 1 July–15 August 1945

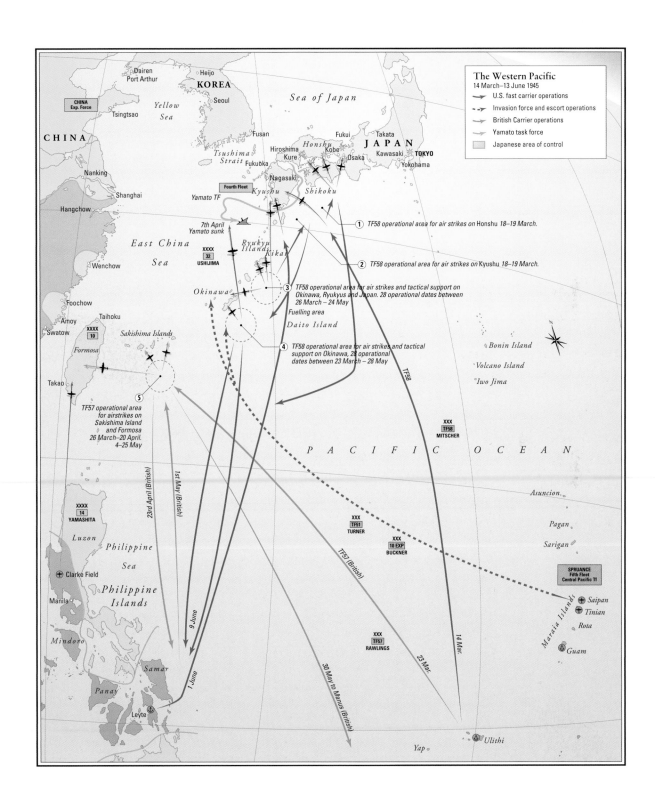

The Western Pacific
14 March–13 June 1945

→ U.S. fast carrier operations
⇢ Invasion force and escort operations
→ British Carrier operations
→ Yamato task force
▢ Japanese area of control

① TF58 operational area for air strikes on Honshu *18–19 March.*

② TF58 operational area for air strikes on Kyushu *18–19 March.*

③ TF58 operational area for air strikes and tactical support on Okinawa, Ryukyus and Japan. 28 operational dates between 26 March – 24 May

④ TF58 operational area for air strikes and tactical support on Okinawa, 28 operational dates between 23 March – 28 May

⑤ TF57 operational area for airstrikes on Sakishima Island and Formosa 26 March–20 April. 4–25 May

had finally fulfilled his promise to return. The fighting in the Philippines proved to be every bit as savage as elsewhere with the Japanese fighting to the death. Manila was captured only after savage street fighting which saw the Japanese garrison exterminated and 100,000 civilians killed. Once the main cities were liberated and the strategic airfields captured, the Japanese forces holding out in the mountains were left alone. Many of them were still holding out in August.

Meanwhile, the island-hopping campaign had attacked its next target of Iwo Jima on 19 February 1945. The island was needed as it had an airfield that could be used by fighters escorting bombers to attack Japan. The five-mile long island was held by 22,000 men under General Kuribayashi dug into a network of bunkers. The attack by US Marines was preceded by a massive naval barrage, but even so it took until 26 March 1945 to secure the island, by which time the Marines had suffered 6,800 casualties.

The next island was the much larger Okinawa which the Americans wanted to act as a forward base for the invasion of Japan that was being planned for 1946. After prolonged bombing of the defenses, 50,000 US troops landed on 1 May 1945. As usual, the 100,000 defenders fought to the death. By this time, however, the Japanese were lacking heavy weapons and the Americans were learning how to deal with the defensive bunkers. Only 8,000 Americans were killed and 35,000 wounded by the time resistance ended on 2 July 1945.

On 20 June Emperor Hirohito of Japan had informed his government that they had to make peace. Prince Konoye was sent to Moscow to ask Stalin to find out if the Allies would accept an armistice pending discussions about a peace treaty. Stalin brushed off Konoye, but passed the message on. Churchill thought it worth asking what terms the Japanese had in mind, but US President Truman did not. Stalin, meanwhile, had his eye on grabbing territory from Japan and wanted to delay peace until he could declare war. On 28 July 1945 an urgent message from Tokyo reached Stalin offering to surrender on the sole condition the imperial dynasty continued. No answer came from Stalin or Truman. On 8 August 1945 Russia declared war on Japan. A vast Russian army swept into Manchuria and northern China, while amphibious forces landed on the Pacific islands that Stalin wanted to secure for Russia. Already, however, the war was effectively over.

On 6 August an atomic bomb was dropped on the Japanese city of Hiroshima, instantly killing around 80,000 people and laying waste the city. The bomb was nicknamed "Little Boy". This was the first occasion that the newly-developed atom bomb was used in warfare, the aim being to force the unconditional surrender of Japan and so avoid the need for a costly Allied ground invasion of the Japanese home islands.

When the first atom bomb, dropped on Hiroshima on 6 August, 1945 failed to produce a Japanese surrender, another bomb, "Fat Man" containing 14.1 lb (6.3 kg) of plutonium was dropped on Nagasaki. Some 75,000 people died immediately and an area 1.6 miles (4.1 km) square was destroyed. The Japanese surrendered on 14 August.

Three days later Nagasaki was wiped out by a second atomic bomb. Although one of the largest sea ports in Southern Japan, Nagasaki had never been subjected to large-scale bombing; this changed on 9 August 1945 when an atomic bomb was dropped on the city. The bomb had originally been intended for Kokura but a cloudbank had moved in, obscuring the target—a stroke of bad luck for Nagasaki. It is estimated that 70,000 people were killed instantly and up to 60,000 were injured. Several thousand more died as a result of radiation poisoning. On 14 August 1945 Hirohito told his government to surrender immediately and unconditionally rather than risk a third bombing. The decision was announced on radio later that day. The Japanese signed the Instrument of Surrender, effectively ending the Pacific War.

Hiroshima had inaugurated a totally new age in warfare.

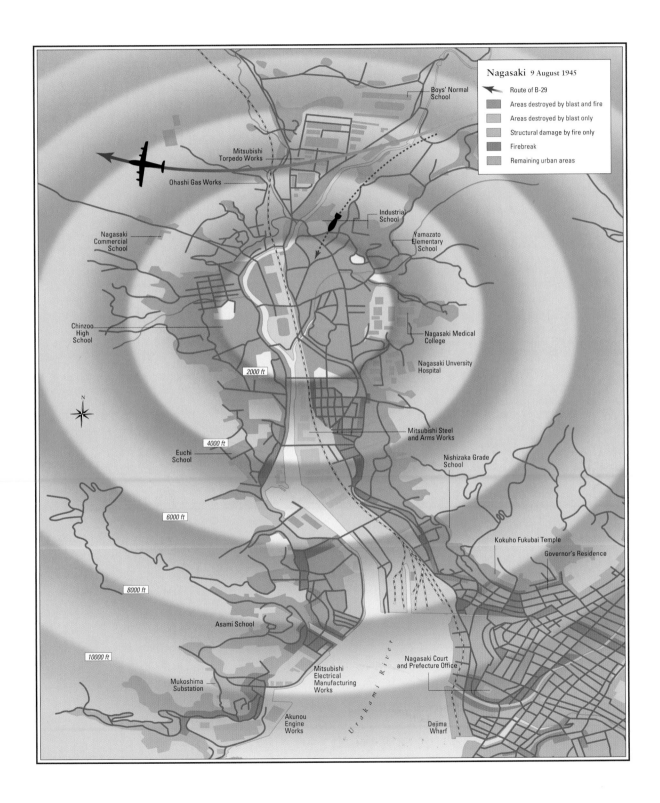

Nagasaki 9 August 1945

➤ Route of B-29

Areas destroyed by blast and fire

Areas destroyed by blast only

Structural damage by fire only

Firebreak

Remaining urban areas

Boys' Normal School

Mitsubishi Torpedo Works

Ohashi Gas Works

Industrial School

Nagasaki Commercial School

Yamazato Elementary School

Chinzoo High School

Nagasaki Medical College

Nagasaki Unversity Hospital

2000 ft

4000 ft

Euchi School

Mitsubishi Steel and Arms Works

Nishizaka Grade School

6000 ft

Kokuho Fukubai Temple

Governor's Residence

8000 ft

Asami School

Urakami River

Nagasaki Court and Prefecture Office

10000 ft

Mukoshima Substation

Mitsubishi Electrical Manufacturing Works

Akunou Engine Works

Dejima Wharf

CHAPTER XI — COMMUNISM AND THE COLD WAR 1945-1975: NUCLEAR AGE 1938-1945

THE OBLITERATION OF TWO JAPANESE CITIES BY ATOMIC BOMBS NOT ONLY SHOCKED JAPAN INTO PROMPT SURRENDER, BUT AMAZED AND STARTLED THE WORLD. THAT SUCH POWERFUL WEAPONS COULD EXIST WAS SIMPLY BEYOND THE IMAGINATION OF MOST PEOPLE.

I n 1938 German scientists Hahn and Strassman proved theoretically that radioactive uranium could be pushed into a violent chain reaction releasing enormous amounts of energy. In 1942 the British and Americans put together a team of scientists under Robert Oppenheimer to build such a bomb. The effort consumed huge amounts of money and manpower, and was carried out in conditions of absolute secrecy deep in the New Mexico desert. Communist spies in both Britain and Russia got to hear of the project, and informed Stalin who gave orders that the Soviet secret service had to put every effort into getting the plans for an atomic bomb. On 13 July 1945 the atomic bomb was successfully tested, prompting a heated debate in US government circles as to whether or not it should be used. President Truman decided that it should be used on Japan to enforce an instant surrender in order to save the lives of the tens of thousands of Allied servicemen who would be killed during a conventional invasion.

The possession of the atomic bomb gave the USA a great advantage in international relations. But this was cancelled out when the Soviets tested their first bomb in 1949. That caused the USA to restart their stalled programme to develop a nuclear fusion weapon, usually called a hydrogen bomb, which was many times more powerful than a fission atomic bomb. The first such weapon was tested in 1952 — utterly destroying the remote Pacific island on which it was set off. The Russians soon had their first hydrogen bomb as well.

All these weapons relied on being dropped from aircraft, and thus had only limited chances of getting through to an enemy city. In 1957 both the USA and Russia produced missiles able to carry a nuclear warhead from one continent to another. Both states now had the ability to cause massive

A B-29 "superfortress" named "Enola Gay" flown by Colonel Paul Tibbets, USAAF, was the aircraft employed to deliver the first nuclear weapon. It was dropped on the city of Hiroshima on 6 August, 1945. A similar aircraft was used for the second raid on Nagasaki.

damage to the other.

While 1939-45 was by no means the first total war — indeed, there are numerous instances of these throughout history — it directly affected people in many more parts of the world than ever before. National resources and populations were, Giulio Douhert said, "sucked into the maw of war" to a greatly increased extent. Conscription of the civil population for war work was widespread. Strategic bombing placed the civilian increasingly in the firing line. Women became more directly involved, whether in the Resistance movements of Axis-occupied Europe, tracking enemy aircraft by radar, or, in the Russian case, actual fighting. With increased totality came increased ruthlessness in the way in which war was waged. The Holocaust and the Japanese treatment of prisoners of war are but two examples.

The development too, of increasingly destructive weapons added to this totality, and none more so than the atomic bomb. While it finally brought the Second World War to an end, it opened the door to an ever more awesome concept of future war. Even though Hiroshima and Nagasaki might have finally proved the pre-war prophets right, they would have taken little comfort from it.

Hiroshima, devastated by the first atomic bomb. The shock effect and destructive power of one single weapon had a huge impact on a stunned world.

EUROPE'S IMPERIAL ECLIPSE

BY 1945 THE EUROPEAN COUNTRIES THAT OWNED VAST EMPIRES WERE ECONOMICALLY EXHAUSTED. THE COLONIES THAT FOR SO MANY YEARS HAD BEEN SOURCES OF INCOME WERE, IN A GROWING NUMBER OF CASES, COSTING MORE TO KEEP THAN THEY PRODUCED IN TAXES. CHANGE WAS CLEARLY ON THE WAY.

Many colonies that had a majority or substantial minority of white settlers had gained effective independence long before the Second World War. Canada, Australia and New Zealand were all self-governing dominions that had the same monarch as did Britain, but few real constitutional ties. Some forms of limited self-government had been ceded to other colonies in the expectation that this process would lead to independence in due course. The process was furthest advanced in British India, where there was also a growing political movement calling for immediate independence. When peace came a mass movement led by Mahatma Gandhi persuaded the British to grant independence by 1947.

India was split in two, with predominantly Hindu areas being designated India and predominantly Muslim areas becoming Pakistan. Inter-communal rioting between religious factions cost thousands of lives, but generally the transition went well. There was serious fighting only in the northern state of Kashmir. A ceasefire line was agreed in 1949, but neither India nor Pakistan still claim all of Kashmir.

In Africa a number of uprisings against European rule were staged in the 1950s. In many cases, these were essentially tribal rebellions — as was the Kikuyu-led Mau Mau uprising in Kenya from 1952 to 1959. Most of these were put down, but did prompt the eventual independence of the colony in question by 1970.

In Algeria a very large French minority had been in residence for generations and did not wish to break their ties with France. Guerrilla war broke out in Algeria in 1954, prompting some French settlers to begin a terrorist campaign. In 1962 Algeria won independence and most of the ethnic French population moved to France. The Portuguese colonies of Angola and Mozambique erupted into violence in 1961.

The Algerian War of Independence, which began in 1954, was especially vicious, since French settlers put up ferocious opposition under their slogan "Algérie française!" (Algeria is French!). Terrorism against civilians, torture used by both sides and guerrilla warfare were all employed before Algeria at last gained its freedom in 1962.

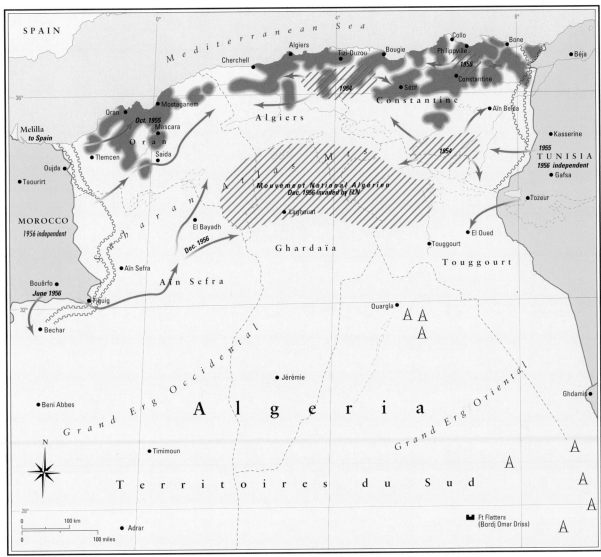

The Portuguese attempted to keep the colonies by military means, but the rebels turned to the Soviet Union for help. The Russians willingly pushed in weapons and instructors and by 1975 both colonies were independent under pro-Soviet communist regimes.

The British colony of Rhodesia had a large white population and, in 1961, declared itself independent with democracy limited to the whites. A long civil war ensued that ended in 1979 with multi-ethnic elections that led to the effective dictatorship of Marxist Robert Mugabe. By 1980 virtually every European colony had been granted independence. In many cases the states have been plagued by civil wars and repeated coups, largely due to inter-tribal violence as the boundaries drawn by colonial convenience did not match those of tribal or ethnic populations.

Algerian War of Independence 1954–62

▬ Areas of French settlement

Oran French administrative and military districts

〰〰〰 French–built frontier defense lines

→ Front de Libération National (FLN) lines of supply and lines of advance

▨ FLN major areas of activity

A Oil fields

SUPERPOWERS: US AND USSR PLAN FOR GLOBAL WAR

THE MASS DESTRUCTION OF THE SECOND WORLD WAR LEFT TWO
COUNTRIES IN THE WORLD THAT WERE VASTLY WEALTHIER, MORE
POPULOUS, AND BETTER ARMED THAN ANY OTHER. THE USA AND
THE SOVIET UNION WERE SOON CONSUMED BY MUTUAL DISTRUST
AND BEGAN TO PLAN FOR WAR WITH EACH OTHER.

The Soviet Union had suffered enormously during the Second World War. Around 10 million men had been killed in the fighting, and a further 18 million civilians had died from starvation, disease, and massacre — around 16% of the pre-war population. Russia's dictator Stalin had wanted to execute every senior German officer, but backed off in the face of Anglo-American peace opposition. Instead, Stalin decided to ensure that Germany could never again mount such an invasion. He used the might of the Red Army to strip Germany of all industrial machinery, which was shipped to Russia. The eastern parts of Germany were transferred to either Poland or Russia and the population evicted at gunpoint — as were ethnic German minorities in other countries. The Red Army was also used to reconfigure Eastern Europe. Latvia, Estonia and Lithuania were annexed by the Soviet Union, while Communist governments were imposed on Bulgaria, Romania, Yugoslavia, Albania, Hungary, Czechoslovakia, East Germany and Poland. Greece escaped only because a small British army was in Athens. The USA and Britain viewed these developments with alarm and began arming themselves in case Stalin ordered the Red Army into Western Europe. This caused Stalin to fear that they might be about to invade Russia to destroy the Communist system, so he stepped up Soviet armaments. The resulting mutual suspicion became known as the Cold War. For the most part the two superpowers engaged in commercial rivalry, propped up puppet rulers in small states, or sought to undermine each other with spies and unrest. However, both sides prepared for real war.

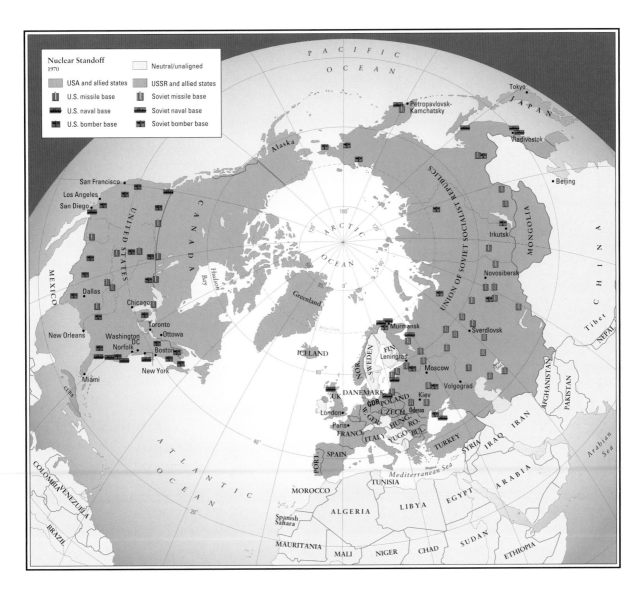

Russia formed the Warsaw Pact, a military alliance of the Communist states in Europe pledged to support each other in war. The USA led the North Atlantic Treaty Alliance (NATO), a group of non-Communist states that was opposed to Russia. Some states in Europe remained neutral, among them Switzerland, Finland, and Austria. By 1961 NATO could field 450 intercontinental missiles, 2,260 bombers, 16,000 tanks, 8 million men, 292 submarines, 76 carriers and battleships, 66 cruisers, and 1,107 other warships. The Warsaw Pact had 75 intercontinental missiles, 1,600 bombers, 38,000 tanks, 8 million men, 507 submarines, 30 cruisers, and 189 other warships. In the event of war, both sides stated that they would resort to launching nuclear weapons against the other rather than submit to total defeat. This policy was called deterrence and was intended to stop the other side from attacking in the first place.

After the Second World War ended, the Cold War began. This involved a standoff between the "superpowers" the United States and the Soviet Union, with each of them using the threat posed by their nuclear weaponry to rival the other. The Cold War continued until the Soviet Union collapsed in 1991.

GLOBAL REACH: THE SUPER NAVY

A KEY TASK OF NAVIES THROUGHOUT HISTORY HAS BEEN THEIR ABILITY TO CARRY THE MILITARY POWER OF THEIR COUNTRY TO FAR DISTANT PARTS OF THE WORLD. WITH THE ONSET OF THE COLD WAR, BOTH SIDES TURNED TO THEIR NAVIES TO DEMONSTRATE THEIR POWER TO SMALLER COUNTRIES.

I n 1945 the disparity between Soviet sea power and that of the USA and allies was vast. Russia had fought a land war against Germany, while both the USA and Britain had fought a major naval war against Japan. When peace came, the western powers both undertook a massive program of decommissioning warships, between them getting rid of over 3,000 naval craft. Russia, by contrast, began a process of building up her navy. The rise in the Soviet navy first alarmed the western powers a couple of years later when Soviet "trawlers" packed with sophisticated monitoring equipment began following NATO warships at sea. For the following 30 years the rival navies engaged in cat and mouse games of mounting exercises, monitoring each other, attempting to evade monitoring, and constant technological advance.

In 1973 Iceland unilaterally increased its territorial waters and used naval ships to arrest foreign fishing boats. The British navy moved in to protect the fishermen and a non-shooting "cod war" developed. The ultimate expression of sea power came in the Falklands War of 1982. On 2 April 1973 a seaborne Argentinian invasion force overwhelmed the resident 61 Royal Marines and seized the islands that Argentina had claimed for years. On 5 April 1973 the first British naval ships left Portsmouth, heading south. The job of the task force was to land an armed force on the islands able to recapture them.

After several tough battles the Argentinians surrendered on 14 June. It had been a triumph for a naval force projecting the power of its nation across thousands of miles of sea.

The Strategic Defense Initiative — nicknamed Star Wars after a 1977 space movie — was proposed by U.S. President Ronald Reagan on 23 March, 1983. SDI was meant to replace the threat of mutually assured destruction (MAD) as national defense with protection from attack by nuclear ballistic missiles.

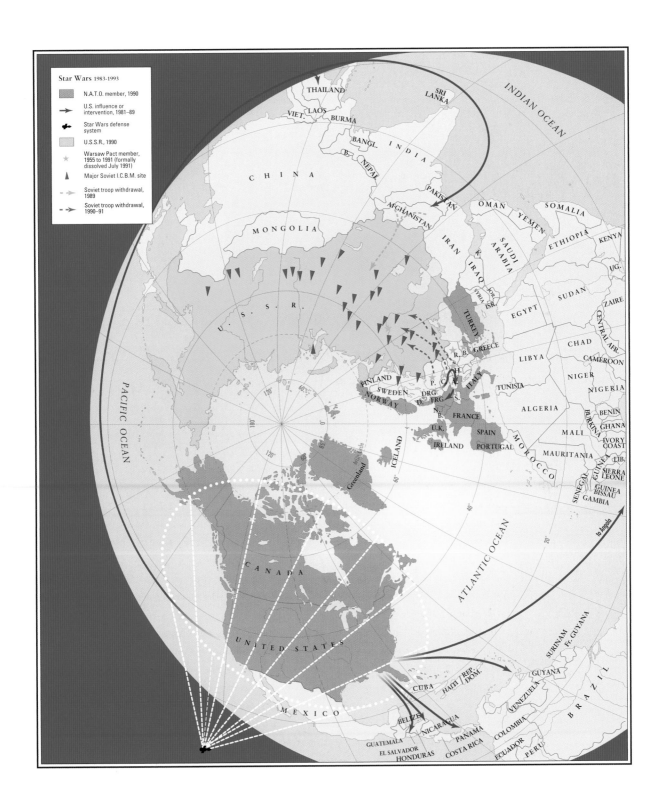

Star Wars 1983-1993

- N.A.T.O. member, 1990
- U.S. influence or intervention, 1981–89
- Star Wars defense system
- U.S.S.R., 1990
- Warsaw Pact member, 1955 to 1991 (formally dissolved July 1991)
- Major Soviet I.C.B.M. site
- Soviet troop withdrawal, 1989
- Soviet troop withdrawal, 1990–91

KOREAN WAR 1950-1953

THE KOREAN WAR WAS THE FIRST "HOT" CONFLICT WITHIN THE WIDER COLD WAR. IT WAS FOUGHT AT FIRST BETWEEN THE KOREANS, BUT LATER OTHER STATES BECAME INVOLVED AS THE CONFLICT THREATENED TO SPREAD. ALTHOUGH FIGHTING ENDED IN 1953 A FORMAL PEACE WAS TO PROVE ELUSIVE.

When the Soviets invaded China in 1945 to retake areas occupied by the Japanese they pushed on to occupy Korea. In the following peace treaties it was agreed that Korea would be first occupied by Soviet forces to the north of the 38th Parallel and US forces to the south. It was expected that they occupying powers would co-operate in setting up an independent Korea. In the event, the Soviets established a Communist state in the north and the Americans a free market state in the south.

In 1949 the occupying forces withdrew, but the government of North Korea at once began to infiltrate guerrillas into the south in the hope of agitating a Communist coup. When this failed, the North Korean Army invaded South Korea on 25 June 1950 with seven divisions. The units had been equipped with modern Russian weaponry and had been fully trained by Soviet advisors. Surprise was total and the South Korean capital of Seoul fell within three days. South Korean troops fell back to fortify the port of Inchon, which was bypassed by the North Koreans as they raced south. In contrast to the troops of the north, the South Korean army had not undergone disciplined training in combat, and quickly gave way.

The conflict was fought with weapons and tactics broadly similar to those prevailing in the closing months of the Second World War. There were, however, some clear differences. In the air, jet aircraft were present in large numbers, especially among fighters, and piston-engined aircraft were increasingly relegated to support roles. The arrival of the Soviet MiG 15, often with Soviet pilots, from mid-1950 outclassed their enemies until the F86 Sabre was introduced by the USAF. The United Nations viewed this as unprovoked aggression and gave authority to the US to put together a force to intervene. The first few US troops to arrive went into action at Osan and halted the North Korean advance. However the South

Overleaf: The Korean War began on June 25, 1950 when communist North Korea invaded South Korea. The North Koreans advanced down to Pusan in the south of South Korea before an American-led United Nations force drove them back to their own territory. An armistice was signed on July 27, 1953.

Korean unit on the American flank fell back and the US troops retreated with heavy loss. Increasing numbers of US and British troops and equipment were being landed at the southern port of Pusan where, on 7 July 1950 General Douglas MacArthur arrived to take command.

MacArthur was able to call on American heavy bombers based in Japan, lighter aircraft flying off a British and an American carrier off Pusan, and gunfire from US, British and Australian warships. The North Koreans arrived in front of the defenses on 5 August. MacArthur at once unleashed his air power to destroy the roads and bridges on which the North Koreans relied for supply while artillery and naval guns pummeled the enemy's forward positions. Under the circumstances the North Koreans found it impossible to break the defenses. The action was notable for a tactical innovation by the US Navy that was to have far-reaching importance. The loss of aircrew from carrier aircraft that were shot down had been bad for morale and a drain on manpower during the Second World War. By 1951 the US Navy had perfected a rescue system that involved light helicopters taking off from the carriers to locate a crash site and land to rescue the downed crew. The helicopters carried stretchers lashed to their skids to enable them to bring back the dead and badly wounded. It would not be long before all US armed forces operated similar medical rescue helicopters and other countries followed suit.

In September 1951, MacArthur moved the 1st US Marines and 7th Infantry Division to Inchon where they broke out to assault the North Korean supply lines. This action forced the Communists to retreat back to North Korea by 26 September 1951, chased by the UN forces. By mid-November 1951 the UN forces had occupied most of North Korea and in places were on the Chinese border at the Yalu River. On 1 November the first of over 120,000 Chinese troops streamed over the border in secret to support their fellow Communists — though the Chinese government refused to acknowledge any involvement. The Chinese lacked heavy weaponry, and instead adopted a style of infantry assault not dissimilar to that used by the Germans in 1918. Small numbers of infantry were first infiltrated through enemy lines to get into good firing positions on the flanks or rear of the unit to be attacked. A mass frontal assault was then staged, whereupon the infiltrated men opened fire to confuse and distract the enemy while they were overwhelmed from the front. The UN forces were thrown back in disarray and in the northeast the first US Marines were cut off near Chosin. Struggling back through bitterly cold weather and difficult mountainous terrain, the Marines finally fought their way to the port of Hungnam where a US naval task force was waiting for them. Determined bombing from the air had slowed the Chinese advance, giving the Marines time to destroy the port facilities with a series of enormous demolition explosions before embarking and heading south to join the rest of the UN forces in retreat.

Seoul fell again in January 1951 and the UN forces fell back toward Taejon before organizing a defensive line. It was during this retreat that the famous Daido Ko naval action took place. Three Canadian, two Australian and one US destroyers were sent up the Daido Ko inlet to provide naval gunnery to cover the withdrawal from Pyongyang. The British carrier *Theseus* provided air cover from beyond the horizon. The North Koreans had mined the inlet and thought it unusable. The UN destroyers thus achieved total surprise when, having negotiated the minefield they emerged from a snowstorm to begin shelling. On 22 April 1951 a fresh massed attack by the Chinese was made on the western side of the peninsula, but by this time the UN forces had the measure of the Chinese "human wave" style of attack and managed to halt the attack and inflict very heavy casualties.

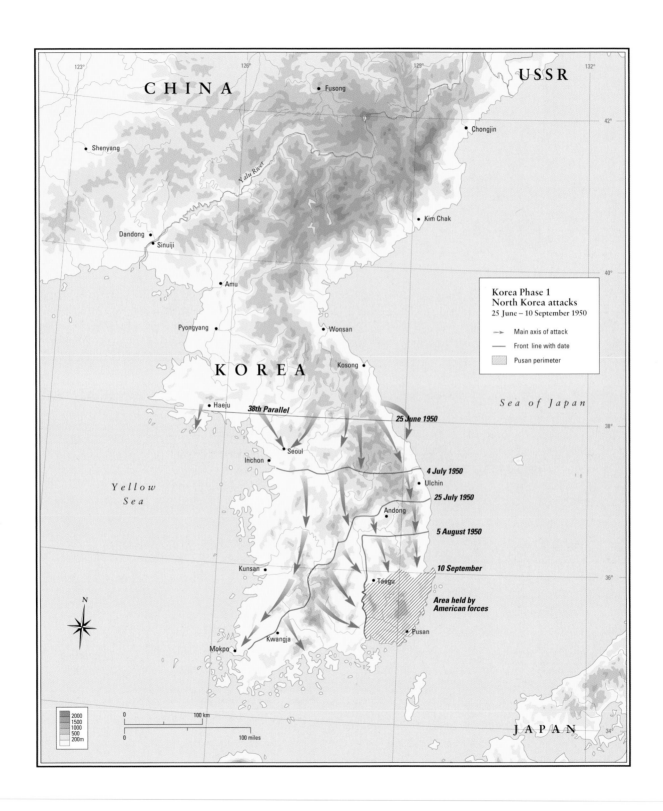

CHINA

Fusong

USSR

Chongjin

Shenyang

Yalu River

Dandong

Sinuiji

Kim Chak

Amu

Pyongyang

Wonsan

KOREA

Kosong

Haeju

38th Parallel

Sea of Japan

Korea Phase 1
North Korea attacks
25 June – 10 September 1950

→ Main axis of attack

— Front line with date

▨ Pusan perimeter

25 June 1950

Seoul

Inchon

4 July 1950

Ulchin

25 July 1950

Andong

5 August 1950

Yellow
Sea

Kunsan

10 September

Taegu

Area held by
American forces

Pusan

N

Mokpo

Kwangja

2000
1500
1000
500
200m

0   100 km

0   100 miles

JAPAN

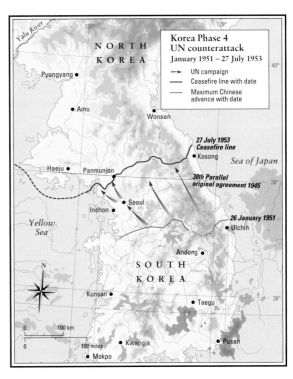

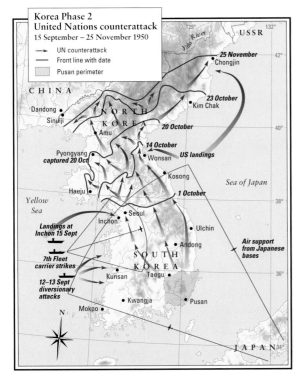

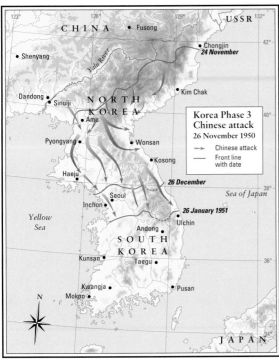

Korea Phase 1

The Korean War began on 25 June 1950, when communist North Korea invaded South Korea. Within weeks the KPA had occupied all of South Korea except for a small area around Pusan in the southeast, where the USA had assembled a predominantly American multinational force under the banner of the United Nations (UN).

Korea Phase 2:

On 25 September 1950 the UN commander-in-chief, General Douglas MacArthur, mounted an amphibious landing at Inchon, high up the west coast of South Korea, which combined with a successful breakout from Pusan to drive the remnants of the KPA back into the North and bring the UN forces within striking distance of the Yalu.

Korea Phase 3:

On 26 November 1950 the Chinese mounted their counter-attack, driving the UN troops back across the 38th parallel as quickly as they had advanced into the North.

Korea Phase 4:

The Chinese attack was not a success. After suffering heavy losses they were driven back to the border by UN counter-attacks in the spring of 1951. The war settled down into two years of attrition. By mid-1953, with the South Korean army strong enough to defend the country, an armistice was signed on 27 July 1953.

VIETNAM (INDO CHINA) WAR 1945-1975

THE SERIES OF WARS FOUGHT IN INDO-CHINA OVER MORE THAN 30 YEARS AFTER THE END OF THE SECOND WORLD WAR WERE OFTEN CONFUSED, BOTH AT THE TIME AND WITH HINDSIGHT, BY POLITICAL CONSIDERATIONS AND VESTED INTERESTS. EVEN NOW, UNPICKING THE TRUTH IS NOT EASY.

Following the defeat of the Japanese in 1945, the pre-war colonial rulers returned to Indo-China: the British in Malaya, the French in Laos, Cambodia, and Vietnam. They found that Chinese agents had been busy spreading Communist ideology and that local peoples desired independent rule. Not only that but the defeats suffered by the colonial powers in 1941 and 1942 had utterly destroyed their reputation for military invincibility that had largely kept them in power. No longer were the subject peoples willing to accept their position.

In Malaya, the Malayan Communist Party (MCP) launched a series of strikes and assassinations, backed up by a guerrilla war fought from the jungles. The British responded by establishing a sophisticated intelligence system and launching a highly effective "hearts and minds" campaign that ensured the bulk of the Malayan population remained on their side. They were helped by the fact that the leadership of the MCP was exclusively Chinese and that the native Malays resented this fact. By 1954 the MCP had been defeated and Malaya later became independent of Britain as a stable constitutional monarchy.

The French granted self-government to Laos and Cambodia under their native royal families in the later 1940s. Both kingdoms seemed to be set on a path toward a stable and prosperous future, but would be disrupted and transformed by conflict overspill from Vietnam. In Vietnam the French were faced by the Indo-Chinese Communist Party led by Ho Chi Minh and its armed wing, the Vietminh under Vo Giap. Inspired by the success of Mao in China, Ho Chi Minh believed that a persistent, unending but low intensity guerrilla war waged by his committed Communist followers would gradually wear down

The Vietnam War was fought in neighboring Laos and Cambodia as well as Vietnam. There were four main combatants — the Viet Cong communist guerrillas, the North Vietnamese and South Vietnamese armies and the United States which tried but, by 1975, failed, to prevent a north Vietnamese takeover of the South.

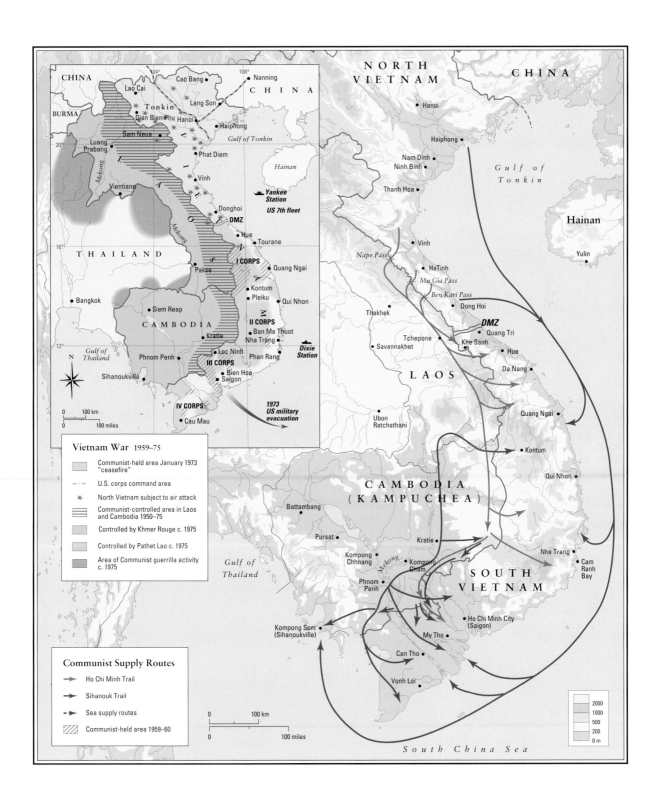

CHINA
Lao Cai
Cao Bang
Nanning
Lang Son
CHINA
Tonkin
Dien Bien Phu Hanoi
BURMA
Haiphong
Gulf of Tonkin
Sam Neua
Luang Prabang
Phat Diem
Vinh
Vientiane
Hainan
Yankee Station
US 7th fleet
Donghoi
DMZ
THAILAND
Hue
Tourane
I CORPS
Pakse
Quang Ngai
Kontum
Pleiku
Bangkok
Qui Nhon
Siem Reap
II CORPS
CAMBODIA
Ban Me Thuot
Kratie
Nha Trang
Dixie Station
Gulf of Thailand
Phnom Penh
Loc Ninh
III CORPS
Phan Rang
Sihanoukville
Bien Hoa
Saigon
IV CORPS
1973 US military evacuation
Cau Mau

Vietnam War 1959–75

- Communist-held area January 1973 "ceasefire"
- U.S. corps command area
- ✳ North Vietnam subject to air attack
- Communist-controlled area in Laos and Cambodia 1950–75
- Controlled by Khmer Rouge c. 1975
- Controlled by Pathet Lao c. 1975
- Area of Communist guerrilla activity c. 1975

0 100 km
0 100 miles

Communist Supply Routes

- ➤ Ho Chi Minh Trail
- ➤ Sihanouk Trail
- ➤ Sea supply routes
- Communist-held area 1959–60

0 100 km
0 100 miles

NORTH VIETNAM
Hanoi
CHINA
Haiphong
Nam Dinh
Ninh Binh
Gulf of Tonkin
Thanh Hoa
Hainan
Vinh
Yulin
Nape Pass
HaTinh
Mu Gia Pass
Ben Kari Pass
Dong Hoi
Thakhek
DMZ
Quang Tri
Savannakhet
Tchepone
Khe Sanh
Hue
Da Nang
LAOS
Quang Ngai
Ubon Ratchathani
Kontum
Qui Nhon
CAMBODIA (KAMPUCHEA)
Battambang
Pursat
Kratie
Nha Trang
Kompong Chhnang
Mekong
Kompong Cham
SOUTH VIETNAM
Cam Ranh Bay
Gulf of Thailand
Phnom Penh
Kompong Som (Sihanoukville)
Ho Chi Minh City (Saigon)
My Tho
Can Tho
Vonh Loi
South China Sea

2000
1000
500
200
0 m

the better armed, but less committed French. His strategy paid off. The Communists had by 1951 gained control of the countryside and the support of the population in northern Vietnam. In November 1953 the French commander, Navarre, tried to regain both the initiative and the control of the rural areas by a daring strategy. He pushed a heavily armed column of 14,000 men deep into the countryside to Dien Bien Phu where they constructed a series of inter-locking defenses from which they could patrol and control the surrounding region. The force was to be supplied by aircraft. Giap saw the opportunity to defeat a major French force and recognized the supply lines as the French weak spot. He flooded the area with 72,000 men backed by 200 guns and mortars. Although the Viet Minh suffered heavy casualties, their intense fire made the two French airstrips un-useable, forcing Navarre to rely on parachute drops. These often fell off target, allowing the Viet Minh to grab the food and ammunition, and in any case simply could not bring in the quantity needed by the 14,000 Frenchmen. By May 1954, 2,300 Frenchmen were dead, 5,000 wounded, sick, or otherwise unfit for duty, and those still fighting were out of ammunition. They surrendered. Two months later, the French opted to give the Vietminh control of North Vietnam, while establishing South Vietnam as a democratic republic. Minh sent agents south to spread Communist propaganda. In 1959 Giap calculated it was time to start a guerrilla war in the south and mobilized the Viet Cong, a mix of activists from the North and volunteers from the South. Using the strategies and tactics used against the French, Giap began to undermine support for the South Vietnamese government.

At the time, the USA had a policy of "containment", that is not allowing Communists to take over any new countries. From 1961 US troops were active in South Vietnam to support the local army, and there followed a steady increase in American involvement. A turning point came in June 1964 when General William Westmoreland was appointed to command US troops in South Vietnam. Westmoreland had studied both the campaigns of the French in Vietnam and those of the British in Malaya. He decided that he would need to work at several levels: intelligence would need to be paramount, the civilian population would need to be kept on side and the Viet Minh would need to be defeated in the field. Westmoreland did what he could to turn public opinion in Vietnam, but was continually undermined by the incompetence of the South Vietnamese government. He also sought a military solution to the war and brought in many innovative tactics. Amongst these was using heavy tanks to spearhead assaults on Viet Cong positions. The tanks crushed paths through the densest jungle and fired canisters of thousands of pellets to strip camouflaging foliage from enemy bunkers, making them vulnerable to infantry assault. He launched seek and destroy missions to locate, pin down and annihilate Viet Cong units. Often this involved sending out a weak patrol in the hope it would be ambushed, whereupon massive forces would be flown in by helicopter to ambush the ambushers.

In 1965 the US forces began bombing targets in North Vietnam and quickly escalated in scale. The main targets were military bases and armaments factories, but inevitably some bombs went astray and civilians were killed. However, Westmoreland's pleas for bombing of Viet Cong supply lines were refused as these ran through Laos and Cambodia. The US commanders in Vietnam also suffered from the policy of rotating US personnel so that few units were in Vietnam for very long. The decision was taken for domestic political reasons as no politician wanted men from his area to spend years in combat while those from other districts enjoyed peaceful garrison duty in Europe or elsewhere. This policy meant that at any given moment most US troops were inexperienced in combat and in dealing with the Vietnamese.

The Tet offensive of 1968 was meant to destroy military and civilian command and control centers in South Vietnam and oust its government. The Christmas Bombing of 1972 was intended by the U.S.A. to teach the North Vietnamese a lesson for baulking at peace talks. Neither attack achieved its aim.

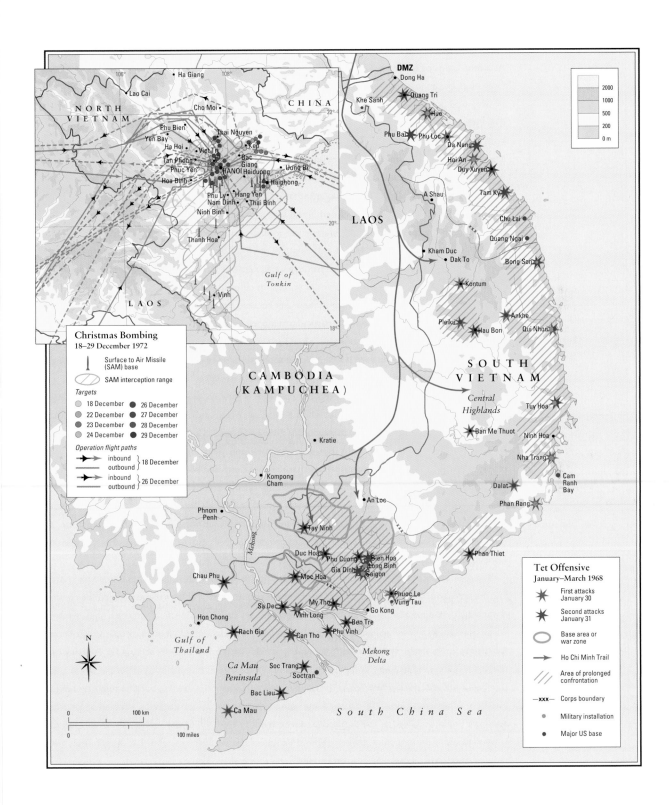

Christmas Bombing
18–29 December 1972

⫯ Surface to Air Missile
(SAM) base

⬭ SAM interception range

Targets
○ 18 December   ● 26 December
○ 22 December   ● 27 December
● 23 December   ● 28 December
○ 24 December   ● 29 December

Operation flight paths
→ inbound ⎱ 18 December
— outbound ⎰
→ inbound ⎱ 26 December
— outbound ⎰

Tet Offensive
January–March 1968

✷ First attacks
January 30

✸ Second attacks
January 31

⬭ Base area or
war zone

→ Ho Chi Minh Trail

⫽ Area of prolonged
confrontation

—xxx— Corps boundary

● Military installation

● Major US base

CHAPTER XII — MODERN CONFLICTS 1975-PRESENT:
ARAB-ISRAELI WARS: 1922-PRESENT

SYMPATHY AMONG MANY WESTERN NATIONS FOR JEWISH DESIRES FOR A HOMELAND LED TO THE ESTABLISHMENT OF THE STATE OF ISRAEL, SOMETHING THAT HAS NEVER BEEN FULLY ACCEPTED BY SEVERAL ARAB STATES.

The Six Day war which began on 5 June, 1967, took place in three sectors: the Sinai Desert, and the Jordanian and Syrian fronts. Although the Israelis were vastly outnumbered, the speed and decisiveness of their attacks crumbled the Arab war effort and won victory in less than a week.

From 1922 onward Jewish immigration to Palestine, the ancient homeland of the Jews, began. It increased after Nazi persecution of the Jews began in the 1930s and became a flood at the end of the Second World War. The British authorities tried to restrain violence between the incoming Jews and the native Arabs, largely without success. From 1944 Jewish terrorists began a campaign against the British and the Arabs, which gradually escalated into effective civil war by 1947. The United Nations voted to create a Jewish state, named Israel, in the hope that dividing the communities into separate political states would bring peace. In fact it led to an intensification of the civil war in Palestine and an invasion by the armies of Egypt, Lebanon, Syria, and Jordan to support the Palestinian Arabs. In the north the fighting settled down to attritional combats from defensive positions, but in the south mobile Israeli units defeated the Egyptians at Beersheba and Eilat. In January 1949 a cease-fire was declared with Israel now established, but still under threat.

On 29 October 1949 the Israelis invaded Egypt and by 5 October 1949 had conquered most of the Sinai with armored columns. This action proved to have been carried out with the collusion of the British and French who had wanted to wrest the Suez Canal from Egypt. International pressure forced all three to pull back from their gains, so that Egypt regained the canal and the Sinai. By 1967 the Egyptians and Syrians had gained Soviet support in terms of military equipment and training as well as civil engineering projects. Israel, meanwhile, had gained support from the USA in both economic and technological forms. To some extent, therefore, the local disputes between Arabs and Israelis had become part of the wider Cold War between Communist and democratic systems.

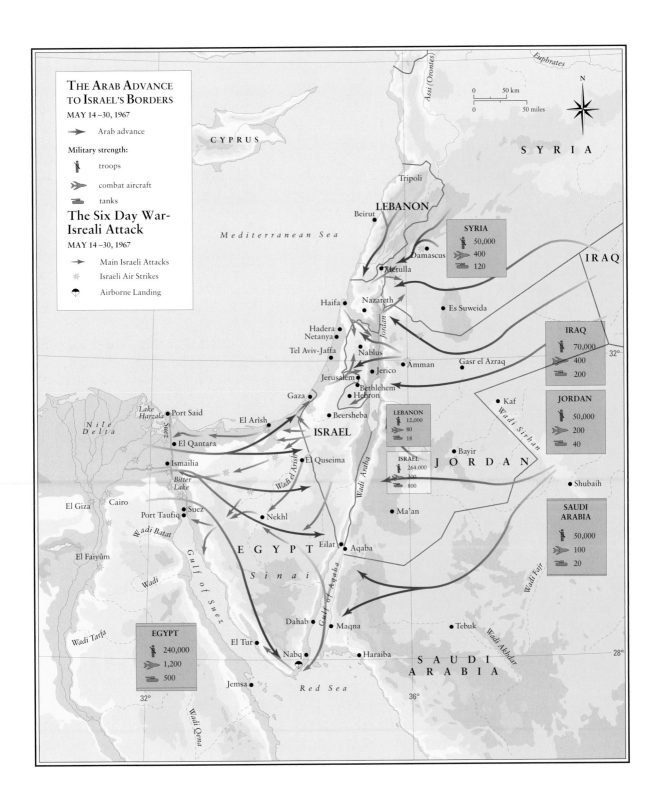

**THE ARAB ADVANCE
TO ISRAEL'S BORDERS**

MAY 14–30, 1967

➤ Arab advance

Military strength:

🧍 troops

✈ combat aircraft

🛡 tanks

**The Six Day War-
Isreali Attack**

MAY 14–30, 1967

➤ Main Israeli Attacks

✳ Israeli Air Strikes

⛴ Airborne Landing

CYPRUS

Mediterranean Sea

Tripoli

LEBANON

Beirut

Damascus

Metulla

SYRIA

SYRIA	
🧍	50,000
✈	400
🛡	120

IRAQ

Haifa   Nazareth

Es Suweida

Hadera
Netanya

Jordan

Tel Aviv-Jaffa   Nablus

Amman   Gasr el Azraq

IRAQ	
🧍	70,000
✈	400
🛡	200

32°

Jerusalem   Jerico

Bethlehem

Gaza   Hebron

JORDAN	
🧍	50,000
✈	200
🛡	40

Lake
Harzala   Port Said

El Arísh   Beersheba

ISRAEL

Kaf

Wadi Sirhan

*Nile
Delta*

LEBANON	
🧍	12,000
✈	80
🛡	18

Suez

El Qantara   El Quseima

ISRAEL	
🧍	264,000
✈	300
🛡	800

JORDAN

Ismailia   Bayir

*Bitter
Lake*

El Giza   Cairo

Wadi Araba

Ma'an   Shubaih

Port Taufiq   Suez

Nekhl

| SAUDI
ARABIA | |
🧍	50,000
✈	100
🛡	20

Wadi Batat

EGYPT   Eilat   Aqaba

El Faiyûm

Sinai

Gulf of Aqaba

Wadi

Gulf of Suez

Wadi Fajr

28°

Wadi Tarfa

Dahab   Tebuk

Wadi Akhdar

EGYPT	
🧍	240,000
✈	1,200
🛡	500

El Tur   Maqna

Nabq   Haraiba

SAUDI
ARABIA

Jemsa   *Red Sea*

32°   36°

Wadi Qena

0   50 km
0   50 miles

N

Throughout the early months of 1967, Egypt, Syria, and Jordan carried out a series of training maneuvers and moved units closer to the Israeli border. Believing that they were about to be attacked, the Israelis launched a pre-emptive strike of their own. The war began before dawn on 5 June when the Israeli air force took off and headed out over the Mediterranean at low height to avoid being detected by radar. They flew far out to sea before turning south to enter Egypt from the north. The Egyptian air bases were plastered with bombs, knocking most of them out of action and destroying 360 aircraft on the ground. Simultaneously, Israeli armored columns attacked Egyptian tank units in the Sinai. Fighting was at first fierce, but once past the front-line units, the Israeli tanks destroyed supplies and disrupted the Egyptian command system, inflicting a total defeat. Back from Egypt, the Israeli air force overwhelmed the Jordanian army, allowing ground troops to take Jerusalem, Jericho, Hebron, and Ramallah. In the north a combined assault quickly captured the Golan Heights on the Syrian border and drove off attempts by the Syrians to win them back. The war was over within 80 hours and so became known as the Six Day War. For the following six years both sides built up their armed forces, aware that a new conflict was likely. By 1972 cross-border raids and guerrilla activity had begun to build up. On 6 October Syrian artillery opened up a massive barrage, which was followed by two armored thrusts by over a thousand tanks. The attack was timed to coincide with the important Jewish religious holiday of Yom Kippur, and thus the following conflict was dubbed the Yom Kippur War. The northern Syrian column was composed of 500 tanks with motorized infantry support. As it headed for Kuneitra, the column as met by the 100 tanks of Israel's 7th Armored Brigade operating around a complex of concrete strongpoints. The attack ground to a halt as the Syrians tried to batter through the defenses. The southern column of 600 tanks and infantry support overran the weaker Israeli defenses in the southern Golan region and surged forward, heading for the Israeli operational HQ at Naffekh. By the following morning Naffekh was surrounded and advanced Syrian units were approaching the Yaakov Bridge over the River Jordan.

Meanwhile the Egyptians had attacked over the Suez Canal with infantry in boats supported by heavy artillery. Working frantically, Egyptian engineers had completed 11 pontoon bridges by mid-afternoon and tanks and artillery began streaming across the canal. Israeli aircraft trying to bomb the bridges were shot down. The following day Israeli armored units came up and attacked, but were met by well-trained Egyptian gunners using modern Soviet anti-tank weapons. More than 200 Israeli tanks were destroyed that day and another 100 the next day. On 8 October 1972 the Egyptians attempted to break out of their bridgehead, but the Israelis were now more cautious and managed to slow the Egyptian advance to a crawl. By 10 October 1872 the Israelis had recovered from their surprise and had mobilized reserves. In the north an armored counterattack was supported by Israeli jets dropping bombs and napalm on the Syrian tanks. The sudden assault threw the Syrian forces back over the Golan Heights, to be pursued by the Israelis. On 16 October the Israelis were at Sassa, only 24 miles (39 km) from Damascus. They were attacked there by fresh Syrian units, supported by tanks from Jordan and Iraq. The fighting swirled around the open ground at high speed, but by dusk the Israelis had won a narrow victory. The fighting in Syria slowed as the Israelis were wary of advancing farther. In Sinai, Israeli counterattacks defeated the Egyptians in a great tank battle on 14 October 1972, but suffered heavy losses in a renewed tank battle four days later. On 19 October elements of the Israeli army got over the Suez Canal to cut the supply lines of the Egyptian troops east of the canal. On 25 October a UN sponsored ceasefire ended the fighting.

Overleaf: The Soviet Union invaded Aghanistan with 100,000 men, looking to prop up its failing Communist government. They met ferocious resistance from the Mujahedeen guerrillas. In 1989, after suffering 15,000 casualties, the Russians gave up and pulled out of Afghanistan.

Opposite page: The Yom Kippur War of 1973, which broke out on Yom ha-kippurim, the Jewish Day of Atonement — was the fourth in a series of wars between Israel and the Muslim Arab states that began in 1948, when the State of Israel was originally established by a vote in the United Nations.

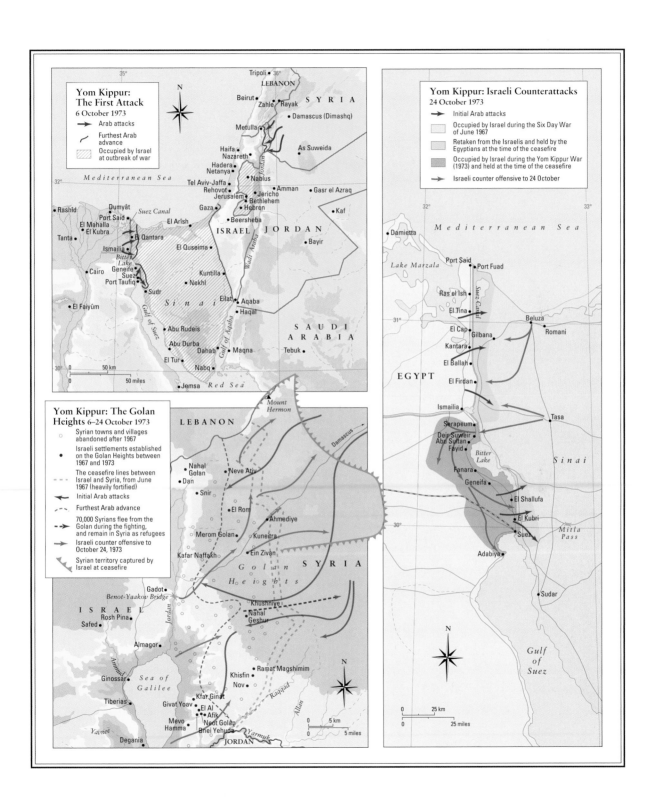

Yom Kippur: The First Attack
6 October 1973
→ Arab attacks
╲ Furthest Arab advance
▨ Occupied by Israel at outbreak of war

Yom Kippur: Israeli Counterattacks
24 October 1973
→ Initial Arab attacks
☐ Occupied by Israel during the Six Day War of June 1967
▨ Retaken from the Israelis and held by the Egyptians at the time of the ceasefire
▨ Occupied by Israel during the Yom Kippur War (1973) and held at the time of the ceasefire
→ Israeli counter offensive to 24 October

Yom Kippur: The Golan Heights 6–24 October 1973
○ Syrian towns and villages abandoned after 1967
● Israeli settlements established on the Golan Heights between 1967 and 1973
--- The ceasefire lines between Israel and Syria, from June 1967 (heavily fortified)
← Initial Arab attacks
╴╴ Furthest Arab advance
⇢ 70,000 Syrians flee from the Golan during the fighting, and remain in Syria as refugees
→ Israeli counter offensive to October 24, 1973
⇨ Syrian territory captured by Israel at ceasefire

After their defeat in the Yom Kippur War the Arab nations accepted that they were unlikely to defeat Israel in a conventional war. Although their governments have kept up anti-Israeli rhetoric there has been no renewal of open war. In 1979 Egypt and Israel signed a formal peace treaty that saw Sinai returned to Egypt. The long years of fighting left many thousands of Palestinian Arabs living in refugee camps outside Israel. A number of guerrilla groups were formed there which, after the Yom Kippur War, turned to terrorism as a method to

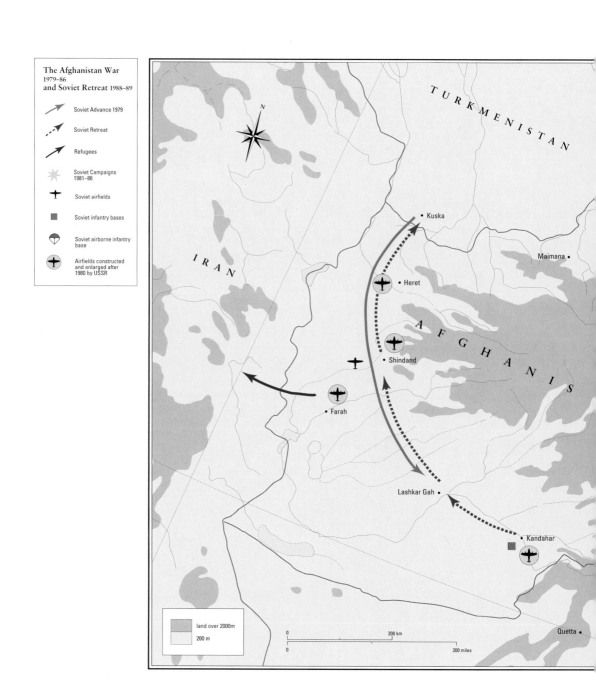

The Afghanistan War
1979–86
and Soviet Retreat 1988–89

Soviet Advance 1979

Soviet Retreat

Refugees

Soviet Campaigns
1981–86

Soviet airfields

Soviet infantry bases

Soviet airborne infantry
base

Airfields constructed
and enlarged after
1980 by USSR

land over 2000m

200 m

0   200 km
0   200 miles

destabilize Israel. In Lebanon the presence of armed militias and terrorist groups led to a collapse of government authority and intermittent civil war. Some factions used bases in Lebanon to launch attacks on Israel. In 1982 Israel invaded Lebanon, advancing rapidly to Beirut. The Israelis took the opportunity to destroy all weapons and bases used by the armed factions before withdrawing in 1985. Syria then stepped in to try to enforce peace on the warring parties within Lebanon.

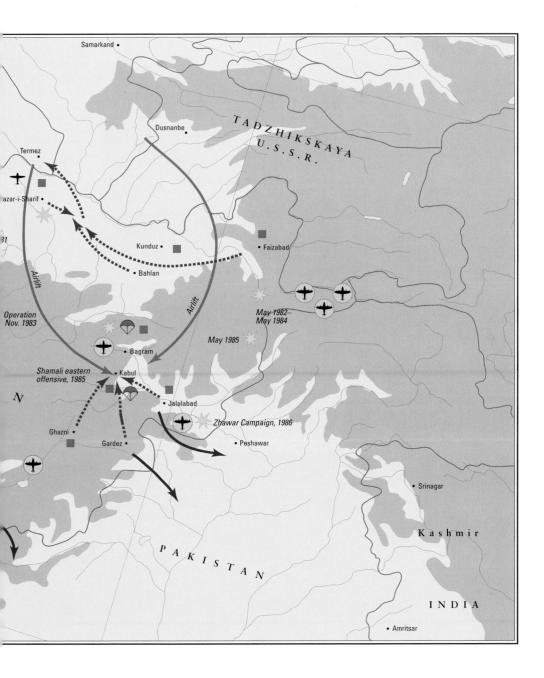

THE BALANCE OF POWER: 1980

BY 1980 THE COLD WAR HAD BEEN UNDERWAY FOR 35 YEARS AND HAD COME TO DOMINATE DIPLOMACY AND INTERNATIONAL RELATIONS ACROSS THE WORLD. THE COLD WAR HAD SEEN WAR SCARES, RISING TENSION, INCREASED DÉTENTE, AND A HOST OF OTHER FEATURES, BUT BY 1980 UNDERLYING FACTORS WERE FORESHADOWING THE END OF THE CONFLICT.

By the early 1970s, both the Soviet Union and the USA had large numbers of nuclear weapons mounted on intercontinental ballistic missiles able to reach any point in the territory of the other. Effectively either the USA or the USSR could utterly destroy each other, wiping out hundreds of millions of people, and possibly making most, if not all, of the planet uninhabitable. This status was known as Mutually Assured Destruction (MAD) and was considered to be such an appalling prospect that neither side would risk going to war for fear of the consequences. In efforts to ease the situation, the USA and USSR held a series of Strategic Arms Limitations Talks (SALT) aimed at reducing the size and cost of the nuclear arsenals. These led to the treaties of SALT 1 and SALT 2 which resulted in a modest decrease in nuclear weapons. However, other nuclear-armed nations such as China, France, and Britain were not covered by SALT and both Russia and the USA remained suspicious of each other.

By 1976 this spirit of détente seemed to be drawing to a close. Under Leonid Brezhnev the Soviet Union became less tolerant of internal criticism and ensured that its Communist satellite states launched a similar crackdown on human rights. At the same time Brezhnev seemed to pursue a more tolerant line abroad. Then, in 1979, the Soviet Union sent an army into Afghanistan to support a Communist faction in its bid to establish a Soviet-style dictatorship. This raised fears in the west that the Soviets were about to embark on a fresh round of Communist expansion. Already much of Asia and Africa was divided into countries favoring either the USA, China, or the USSR. Things seemed about to get worse. Coincidentally the Soviet invasion of Afghanistan came just prior to the election of two new leaders in the west, US

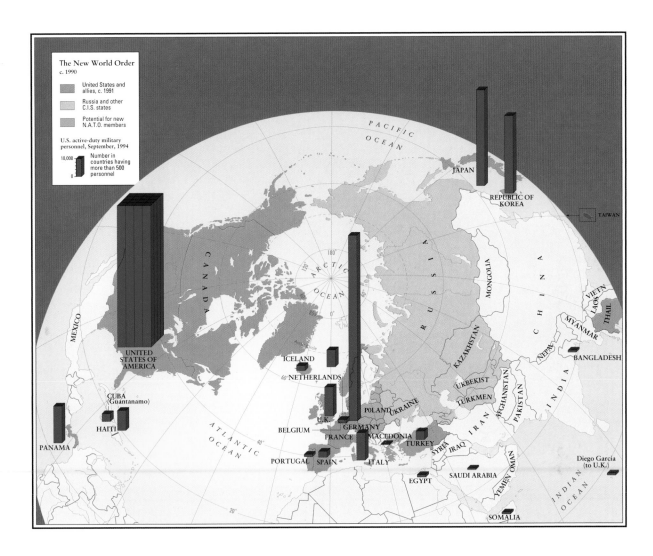

The New World Order
c. 1990

United States and allies, c. 1991

Russia and other C.I.S. states

Potential for new N.A.T.O. members

U.S. active-duty military personnel, September, 1994

10,000 — Number in countries having more than 500 personnel
0 —

President Ronald Reagan and British Prime Minister Margaret Thatcher. Both were determined to face down the new Soviet threat and would prove to be firm in their resolve.

One of the most disturbing aspects of the arms-reduction process was the revelation of the scale of chemical weapon stockpiles in Europe, and the difficulties involved in disposing of them. NATO's strategy to dispose of its chemical weapons stocks involved transporting 100,000 artillery shells containing some 7,000 tons of nerve agent to Johnston Atoll in the Pacific, where they were burnt in special incinerators. The agreements on chemical and conventional weapons were prefigured by the December 1987 treaty committing the United States and the USSR to eliminate all nucleur missiles with ranges of between 311 miles (500 km) and 3,417 miles (5,500 km).

Over the years there have been several treaties and agreements limiting the use of nuclear weapons, including a proposed nuclear test ban.

After the communist Soviet Union collapsed in 1991, the map of Europe was fundamentally changed. The former Russian satellite countries in eastern Europe, together with states within the Soviet Union, became independent and some of them were potential candidates for membership of NATO (as the map shows) and also of the EEC.

THE GULF WAR: 1990-1991

THE RISING TENSIONS OF THE COLD WAR WERE SHATTERED IN
UNEXPECTED FASHION BY THE GULF WAR OF 1990-91. THIS WAS
TRIGGERED BY THE IRAQI INVASION OF KUWAIT, WHICH TOOK MANY
GOVERNMENTS BY SURPRISE. THE WAR PROVED TO BE SHORT BUT
BRUTAL, AND LEFT TENSIONS AND RESENTMENTS IN THE REGION
THAT MANY BLAME FOR THE OUTBREAK OF THE IRAQ WAR OF 2003.

The neighboring oil-rich Arab states of Iraq and Kuwait had a complex history of tensions and friendships dating back to the time when both were part of the Turkish Empire. Iraq had a vague claim to part or all of Kuwait based on Turkish provincial boundaries, but by the 1980s nobody took such claims seriously. Iraqi dictator Saddam Hussein, however, revived the claims when he found himself unable to pay his debts to the Kuwaiti ruling dynasty. On 2 August 1990 the large Iraqi army drove into Kuwait, conquering the small country in hours. The international response was swift. On 6 August the UN Security Council imposed tough sanctions on Iraq.

Two days later Saudi Arabia requested help defending itself from a feared Iraqi invasion, and US troops moved into the desert kingdom. Soon after two powerful US naval battle-groups appeared off the Kuwaiti coast. There then followed a long period of diplomatic activity as US President George Bush sought to build a broad coalition of countries willing to join or support military action against Iraq. He was especially keen to gain support from Arab countries so that Iraq could not portray a US campaign as an attack on Islam.

On 15 January 1991 a UN deadline set for Iraqi withdrawal passed. On the next day an intense aerial bombardment of Iraq began by the US and allies. Among the key weapons used by the US were the stealth bombers which were virtually invisible to radar and cruise missiles able to hit a predetermined target with pinpoint precision. The principle targets were military and government bases, but transport

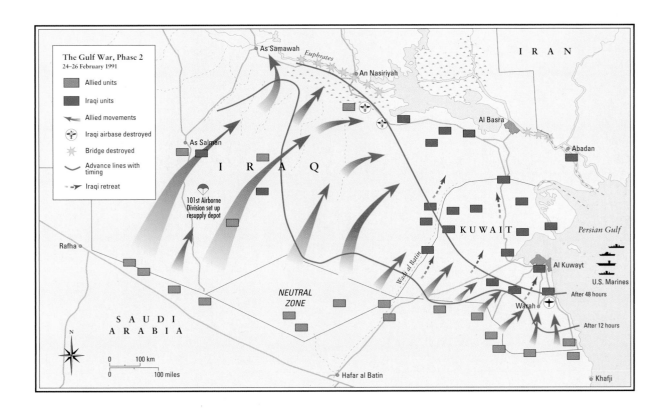

The Gulf War, Phase 2
24–26 February 1991

Allied units

Iraqi units

Allied movements

Iraqi airbase destroyed

Bridge destroyed

Advance lines with timing

Iraqi retreat

101st Airborne Division set up resupply depot

As Samawah

Euphrates

An Nasiriyah

IRAN

Al Basra

Abadan

As Salman

I R A Q

KUWAIT

Persian Gulf

Rafha

U.S. Marines

Al Kuwayt

After 48 hours

Warah

After 12 hours

NEUTRAL ZONE

Wadi al Batin

SAUDI ARABIA

0   100 km
0   100 miles

N

Hafar al Batin

Khafji

links and power stations were also attacked. In all 75 aircraft were lost to Iraqi anti-aircraft fire. Iraq also fired missiles at Israel, but damage was slight. US commander Norman Schwarzkopf decided by mid-February that the air attack had achieved its main goals and ordered the ground assault to begin on 24 February. The attack was to be in two parts. First units from various coalition nations would attack Kuwait from Saudi Arabia to fix the Iraqi forces in Kuwait.

Meanwhile, a large-scale armored assault by US M1 Abrams and British Challenger tanks would sweep deep into Iraq to the west of Kuwait. The armor would then turn east to reach the coast north of Kuwait and thus trap the main Iraqi army. It was considered that most Iraq units were of limited ability, but the elite Republican Guards with Soviet T-72 tanks were well trained and were thought to be tougher adversaries. In the event the armored advance developed faster and more successfully than had been planned. Indeed, there were some instances of friendly fire as units got ahead of schedule. In Kuwait the regular Iraq army began to collapse as soon as it was attacked. Many soldiers fled, stealing Kuwaiti cars, buses, and lorries to drive up the coastal highway to Iraq. The Republican Guards fought, but proved to be less effective than feared.

The campaign soon became a series of running fights and mass surrenders. The fighting had largely ended by 28 February 1991, when President Bush ordered Schwarzkopf to cease the pursuit of the Iraqi army. The coalition forces had lost almost 400 killed; Iraqi losses were never firmly established but seem to have been around 30,000.

Operation Desert Storm, the U.S.-led assault launched by a 30-nation coalition on 17 January, 1991, was designed to liberate Iraqi-occupied Kuwait. After 38 days of punishing air attacks, a ground assault cleared Iraqi forces out of Kuwait within four days. A ceasefire followed on 28 February.

Collapse of Soviet Power 1991

IN 1980 THE SOVIET UNION HAD APPEARED TO BE AT THE HEIGHT OF ITS POWER. IT HAD THE LARGEST AND MOST POWERFUL ARMED FORCES IN THE WORLD, IT WAS THE CENTER OF A MILITARY ALLIANCE THAT WAS EVEN MORE FEARSOME, AND CONTROLLED DOZENS OF CLIENT STATES AROUND THE WORLD. AND YET, LESS THAN 12 YEARS LATER, IT CEASED TO EXIST.

Under Leonid Brezhnev the Soviet Union had begun to suffer serious economic decline. Born before the revolution and coming to political power under Stalin, Brezhnev and his successors Yuri Andropov and Konstantin Chernenko could imagine no way forward except orthodox Communism. After Chernenko's death in 1985, power passed to Mikhail Gorbachev, who was aged only 54 and had entered politics after Stalin's death. He recognized the economic problems and sought to deal with them by restructuring, termed "perestroika," the command economy while keeping the basic features of a Communist society. In 1987 Gorbachev sought to reinvigorate the Communist Party by allowing multi-candidate elections for key posts for the first time — though other political parties remained banned. This move, "glasnost" led to the rise of politicians in many provinces who wanted their states to be independent of the Soviet Union. In 1990 Latvia, Lithuania, and Estonia declared themselves to be independent, and it was clear that other parts of the Soviet Union were about to declare their own independence.

Meanwhile a group of old-style Communists had been plotting a return to repression and Stalinist rule. On 19 August 1991 Soviet Vice President Gennadi Yanayev, Prime Minister Valentin Pavlov, Defense Minister Dmitriy Yazov, and KGB chief Vladimir Kryuchkov announced that they were forming a State Emergency Committee. Soldiers were sent to arrest Gorbachev, who was on vacation, to close down newspapers and radio stations and to seize key government buildings across the Soviet Union. The

New European States Emerge 1991–93

- Reunited, 1990
- New state, 1991
- New state, 1992
- New state, 1993
- Area not under control of the new government
- ■ Capital of new state
- Russian Federation
- Border of USSR to 1991
- Ex-Soviet satellite states

1 Serbian backed "Independent Krajina"

2 Serbian and Croatian populations seize control of their own ethnic areas

3 Russian majority form Transnistrian Republic

4 Gagauzian separatist movement

5 Abkhazian separatist movement

6 South Ossetian separatist movement

7 Chechenian separatist movement

8 Armenian population struggle to control Nagorno-Karabakh and adjacent territory to the south

President of the Russian Republic, the largest in the Soviet Union, was Boris Yeltsin who responded by declaring his support for Gorbachev and calling on all loyal citizens to join him at his office building, nicknamed the White House. Yeltsin and his staff got to the White House before the coup's troops and were quickly joined by thousands of Muscovites. When troops in armored vehicles began arriving, Yeltsin feared they were from the Emergency Committee, but they turned out to be units answering his call for support. When the coup supporters did finally arrive, they refused to attack fellow Russians.

On 21 August 1991 the coup collapsed. Gorbachev was released, but he emerged only to find that the Soviet Union he had sought to reform and preserve had been destroyed. Yeltsin, the hero of the hour, was interested only in Russia and the other republics were quick to begin acting as independent states. In November the Communist Party was banned in Russia and on 8 December the heads of government of the various republics within the Soviet Union met to agree to the formal dissolution of the Soviet Union — which finally ceased to exist four days later.

Gorbachev's contribution to the end of the Cold War earned him the Nobel Peace Prize in 1990. In 2001, he established the Social Democratic Party of Russia and in 2007 the Union of Social-Democrats. In September 2008 Gorbachev and Alexander Lebedev, a prominent Russian billionaire, announced they would form the Independent Democratic Party of Russia together. This has been Gorbachev's third attempt to establish a party of political significance in Russian politics. Despite the collapse of the Soviet Union, Russia is still a major superpower.

The collapse of the Soviet Union in 1991 drastically changed the face of Europe. Former Soviet satellites — Poland, Bulgaria, Hungary, Romania — became independent. Yugoslavia broke up into its constituent parts — violently. More peacefully, Czechoslovakia became two states, Slovakia and the Czech Republic. Germany, divided since the Second World War, reunited.

IRAQ WAR: 2003-PRESENT

THE INVASION OF IRAQ BY A BROAD COALITION OF COUNTRIES PROVED TO BE ONE OF THE MOST CONTROVERSIAL IN MODERN HISTORY. THE MILITARY CAMPAIGN PROVED TO BE ONE OF THE MOST SUCCESSFUL OF RECENT DECADES, BUT THE POLITICAL REPERCUSSIONS WERE ACRIMONIOUS AND LONG-LASTING.

From 2001 onward the US government of President George W. Bush and the British government of Prime Minister Tony Blair began issuing statements and making allegations about the regime of Iraqi President Saddam Hussein. It was alleged that Hussein showed a brutal disregard for the human rights of ethnic minorities in Iraq and that his dictatorial regime had murdered numerous internal critics. More controversial were claims that Hussein possessed weapons of mass destruction and was giving large-scale support to Islamist terrorist groups, including Al Qaeda. The United Nations had passed numerous resolutions calling on the Iraqi regime to co-operate with UN teams seeking to verify whether or not Iraq had weapons of mass destruction, but Hussein did not fully comply.

Declaring that the Iraqi regime was a serious and imminent threat to regional and global security, the Americans and British put together a coalition of 40 countries and prepared to invade. The invasion was launched from Kuwait on 20 March 2003 under the command of US General Tommy Franks. The advance took the form of a conventional armored thrust, supported by artillery and infantry moving in motorized transport. The resistance from the main Iraqi army proved to be slight, and that from the elite Republican Guards was not much better. On 9 April the capital city of Baghdad fell to coalition forces, and spontaneous anti-Hussein demonstrations broke out.

Hussein himself was nowhere to be found. He was eventually captured on 13 December, long after his sons and most leading members of his government had been killed or captured. He was later executed. Meanwhile, several local militias had sprung up, arming themselves with looted weapons and seeking to enforce their rule on different cities and areas. Dealing with these ethnic or religious factions would prove to be a major on-going task for the occupying troops. By this time it had become clear that Iraq

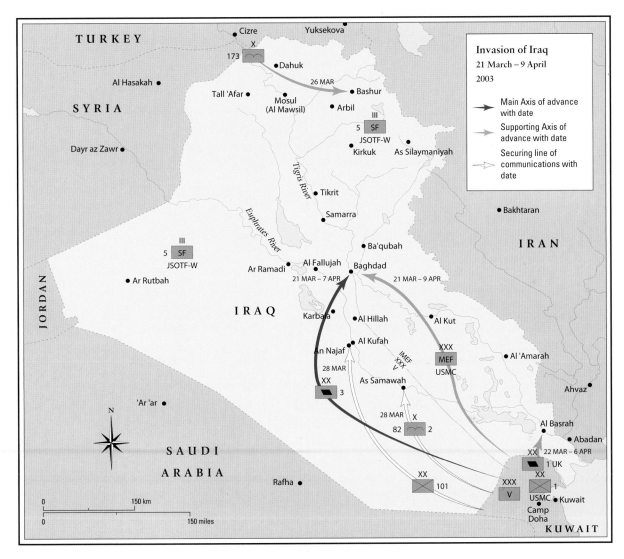

The invasion of Iraq on March 20, 2003 followed mounting tension over the refusal of the Iraqi ruler, Saddam Hussein, to co-operate with United Nations weapons inspectors. The initial invasion phase was carried out by the United States, Australia, and Britain with a small 194-man contingent from Poland.

had possessed no weapons of mass destruction and no evidence of support for Islamist terrorists had been found. This included fears that Al Quaeda were operating there. These revelations caused several countries to withdraw from the coalition and pull their military forces out of Iraq. There were also widespread political disputes in Britain and the US with anti-war groups vociferously stating that the war had been illegal. The controversy is considered to have had a role in the decline in popularity of the Republican Party in the USA.

The US-Iraq Status of Forces Agreement was approved by the Iraqi government in late 2008. This agreement states that U.S. combat forces will withdraw from Iraq cities by 30 June, 2009, and that all U.S. forces will have completely withdrawn by 31 December, 2011. It is hoped that by this time the insurgency will have been significantly curbed to allow this move.

WAR ON TERROR: 2001-PRESENT

THE WAR ON TERROR WAS DECLARED IN 2001 AND IS A CONTINUING CAMPAIGN AGAINST ISLAMIST TERRORISTS BEING WAGED BY VARIOUS WESTERN STATES.

On 11 September 2001 a team of terrorists belonging to the Al Qaeda terrorist organization led by Saudi religious extremists Osama bin Laden carried out a series of attacks on the USA. Hijacked jet airliners were deliberately flown into the twin towers of the World Trade Center in New York and the Pentagon in Washington DC. Another aircraft, apparently heading for the White House, crashed as passengers on board tried to overpower the hijackers. American public opinion responded with shocked outrage, as did that in most other countries. Stunning as the attacks of 9/11 had been, however, they were only the most dramatic in a number of terrorist attacks that had been launched by Islamist extremists on western targets in previous years.

On 20 September US President George W. Bush made a speech to US Congress in which he stated, "Our war on terror begins with Al Qaeda, but it does not end there. It will not end until every terrorist group of global reach has been found, stopped, and defeated." The War on Terror is generally believed to have started at this point. A number of military operations have since taken place. The first of these was a campaign against the Taliban regime of Afghanistan, known to be a major supporter of Al-Qaeda. A campaign of air bombing was followed up by a land campaign which ousted the Taliban from power in Afghanistan. That country is still the scene of fighting between US and British troops and local factions.

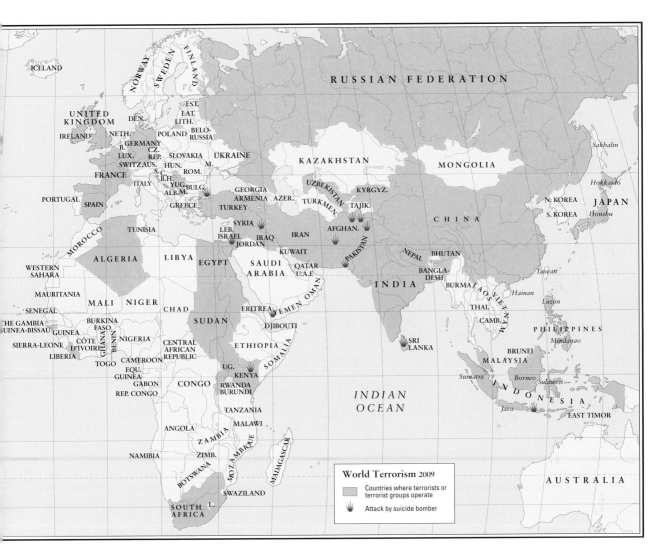

In 2007 the US gave military aid to the Lebanese government to help it put down a rising by the Fatah-al-Islam religious movement. The US has also given military aid to the Pakistani government to help it counter religious extremist groups active along the Afghan border.

The terrorists have struck back with a number of attacks. London was hit by a number of bombs in July 2005 that killed 57 people. Western tourists on Bali were targeted by a series of bombs that hit bars and clubs, killing over 200 people in 2002. There have been increasing criticisms of the War on Terror. It has been alleged that the Islamist terrorist movement is not a single entity but a number of entirely separate bodies. Some have questioned whether large-scale military efforts are appropriate, arguing that intelligence-led police actions might be more effective, and there have been concerns voiced that laws passed in some countries aimed at terrorists are in fact curtailing the rights of law-abiding citizens.

In the 21st century, wholesale nuclear destruction has been replaced by global terrorism as the greatest military danger the world faces. Small groups promoting sectional interests, some religious, others political, have proved able to terrorize whole communities and even countries, seize hostages, kill them at will, and hold governments to ransom.

BIBLIOGRAPHY

Archer, Christon *World History of Warfare*
University of Nebraska Press, 2008

Arrian, J.R. Hamilton and de Selincourt, Aubrey
The Campaigns of Alexander Penguin Books, 1976

Arnold, Thomas *The Renaissance at War* HarperCollins, 2006

Badsey, Stephen *The Franco-Prussian War 1870-1871*
Osprey Publishing, 2003

Barker, Phil *Alexander the Great's Campaigns* P.Stephens
Publishers, 1979

Black, Jeremy *Warfare in the Eighteenth Century*
HarperCollins, 2006

Carey, Brian Todd et al *Warfare in the Ancient World*
Leo Cooper Ltd., 2005

Cawthorne, Nigel *Vietnam: A War Lost and Won* Arcturus, 2008

Farwell, Byron *The Great Boer War* Pen & Sword Military, 2009

Ferrill, Arthur *The Origins of War: From the Stone Age to Alexander
the Great* Westview Press 1997

Fletcher, Ian *The Crimean War: A Clash of Empires*
Spellmount Publishers Ltd, 2004

Fuller, J.F.C. *The Generalship of Alexander the Great* Da Capo
Press Inc. 2004

Gilbert, Martin *The Second World War* Phoenix, 2009

Griffith, Paddy *The Viking Art of War* Greenhill Books 1998

Guilaine, Jean and Zammit, Jean *The Origins of War: Violence in
Prehistory* Blackwell 2005

Guthrie, William P. *Battles of the Thirty Years' War 1618-1635*
Greenwood Press, 2001

Hale, John Rigby *War and Society in Renaissance Europe 1450-1620*
McGill-Queen's University Press 1998

Hart, Peter *The Somme* Phoenix, 2006

Hastings, Sir Max *The Korean War* Pan Books, 2000

Johnson, Paul *Napoleon* Phoenix, 2003

Keegan, John *A History of Warfare* Vintage, 1994

Knight, Roger *The Pursuit of Victory: The Life and Achievement of
Horatio Nelson* Penguin, 2006

Lengel, Edward G. *To Conquer Hell: The Meuse-Argonne, 1918*
Henry Holt & Company, 2008

Lowry, Richard S. *The Gulf War Chronicles: A Military History of
the First War with Iraq* Universe Star, 2008

Martin, Deborah *Troubled Times: Violence and Warfare in the Past*
Routledge, 1998

McPherson, James M. *The American Civil War* Osprey Publishing,
2003

Meed, Douglas *The Mexican War 1846-1848* Osprey Publishing,
2002

Nardo, Don *Science, Technology and Warfare of Ancient
Mesopotamia* Lucent Library of Historical Eras, 2008

Parker, Geoffrey *The Cambridge Illustrated History of Warfare*
Cambridge University Press, 2008

Platt Thomas, Benjamen *Abraham Lincoln: A Biography* Southern
Illinois University Press, 2008

Riley-Smith, Jonathan *The Oxford Illustrated History of the
Crusades* Oxford University Press 2002

Rothenberg, Gunther E. *Napoleonic Wars* Weidenfeld & Nicolson,
2001

Sage, Michael *Warfare in Ancient Greece: A Sourcebook* Routledge,
1996

Seward, Desmond *The Hundred Years' War 1337-1453* Penguin
Books, 1999

Smith, Digby *The Greenhill Napoleonic Wars Data Book: Actions
and Losses in Personnel, Colours, Standards and Artilllery 1792-1815*
Greenhill Books, 1998

Snow, W.P., *Lee and His Generals: Profiles of Robert E.Lee and
Seventeen Other Generals of the Confederacy*
Gramercy Books, 1997

Spalinger, Anthony J. *War in Ancient Egypt: The New Kingdom*
Blackwell 2005

Spector, Ronald *Eagle Against The Sun: The American War With
Japan* Phoenix, 2001

Stevenson, David *1914-1918: The History of the First World War*
Penguin, 2005

Strachan, Hew *The Oxford Illustrated History of the First World
War* Oxford Paperbacks, 2000

Turnbull, Stephen *The Art of Renaissance Warfare from the Fall of
Constantinople to the Thirty Years' War* Greenhill Books, 2006

Tyerman, Christopher *God's War: A New History of the Crusades*
Bel Kap Press of Harvard University Press, 2009

Warry, John Gibson *Warfare in the Classical World* University of
Oklahoma Press, 1995

Weir, William *Fifty Weapons that Changed Warfare* New Page
Books, 2005

Wilson, Peter H *The Thirty Years' War: Europe's Tragedy'*
Cambridge Bel Kap Press of Harvard University Press, 2009

Wint, Guy *The Penguin History of the Second World War*
Penguin, 1999

INDEX

ACKNOWLEDGMENTS

For Cartographica Press
Maps: Jeanne Radford, Alexander Swanston, Malcolm Swanston, and Jonathan Young

The publishers would like to thank the following picture libraries for their kind permission to use their pictures and illustrations:

Istock: 31, 85, 128, 245, 251, 275

TELL US WHAT YOU THINK!

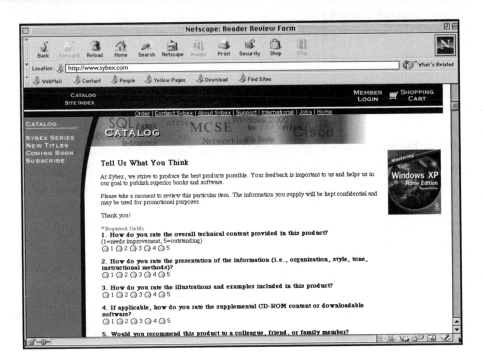

Your feedback is critical to our efforts to provide you with the best books and software on the market. Tell us what you think about the products you've purchased. It's simple:

1. Go to the Sybex website.
2. Find your book by typing the ISBN or title into the Search field.
3. Click on the book title when it appears.
4. Click **Submit a Review.**
5. Fill out the questionnaire and comments.
6. Click **Submit.**

With your feedback, we can continue to publish the highest quality computer books and software products that today's busy IT professionals deserve.

www.sybex.com

SYBEX Inc. • 1151 Marina Village Parkway, Alameda, CA 94501 • 510-523-8233

Exam Objectives (#1Z0-040)

SYBEX

OBJECTIVE	PAGE
Automatic Storage Management	
Describe Automatic Storage Management	5
Set up initialization parameter files for ASM and database instances	5
Execute SQL commands with ASM file names	5
Start up and shut down ASM instances	5
Administer ASM disk groups	5
Use RMAN to migrate your database to ASM	5
Maintain Software	
Understand the supported upgrade paths to Oracle Database 10g	1
Use new utility to perform pre-upgrade validation checks	1
Use simplified upgrade process that automatically determines components to be upgraded	1
Start up the database using a new mode when upgrading	1
Security	
Apply a column level VPD policy	8
Apply static and non-static policies	8
Share VPD policy functions	8
Use the unified audit trails	8
Use fine-grained auditing for DML statements	8
Miscellaneous New Features	
Provide greater flexibility by enabling resumable timeout at the instance level	8
Use regular expression support in SQL and PL/SQL for string searching, matching and replacing	8
Use additional linguistic comparison and sorting methods in SQL	8
Aggregate more meaningful statistics across a multitier environment	8
Use SQL to flush the buffer cache	8

Exam objectives are subject to change at any time without prior notice and at Oracle's sole discretion. Please visit Oracle's web site (education.oracle.com) for the most current listing of exam objectives.

SYBEX

Exam objectives are subject to change at any time without prior notice and at Oracle's sole discretion. Please visit Oracle's web site (education.oracle.com) for the most current listing of exam objectives.

SYBEX

SYBEX

OCP:
Oracle 10*g* New Features
for Administrators
Study Guide

OCP:
Oracle 10*g* New Features for Administrators
Study Guide

Bob Bryla

Biju Thomas

San Francisco • London

SYBEX

Associate Publisher: Neil Edde
Acquisitions and Developmental Editor: Jeff Kellum
Production Editor: Erica Yee
Technical Editors: Joe Johnson, Bob Wahl
Copy Editor: Kim Wimpsett
Compositor: Happenstance Type-O-Rama
Graphic Illustrator: Jeff Wilson, Happenstance Type-O-Rama
CD Coordinator: Dan Mummert
CD Technician: Kevin Ly
Proofreaders: Amy Rasmussen, Nancy Riddiough
Indexer: Nancy Guenther
Book Designer: Bill Gibson
Cover design: Archer Design
Cover photograph: Photodisc and Victor Arre

Library of Congress Card Number: 2004109303

ISBN: 0-7821-4355-5

Acknowledgments

I would like to thank all the folks at Sybex who made this a most enjoyable and rewarding experience, including Erica Yee and Jeff Kellum, who reinforced my attention to detail. Thanks go to Biju for not letting me write too many of these chapters myself (again). Thanks also to Kim Wimpsett, who filled in the gaps from my college writing courses, and to Joe Johnson and Bob Wahl for their insightful comments and suggestions.

This book wouldn't be possible without the love and support from my family throughout the long nights and weekends when I still managed to find time to give the kids a bath and read books before bedtime. I loved every minute of it.

Thanks also to my professional colleagues, both past and present, who provided me with inspiration, support, and guidance and who pushed me a little further to take a little risk now and then, starting with that math teacher in high school, whose name eludes me at the moment, who introduced me to computers on a DEC PDP-8 with a teletype and a paper tape reader.
—Bob Bryla

I would like to thank the wonderful people at Sybex for their high-quality work. Thank you, Jeff (development editor), for supporting me, making valuable comments, and ensuring the chapters have the smooth flow and transition. I thank Erica Yee (production editor) for making sure every piece of the book ties together. I thank each one of the professionals at Sybex involved in the publication of this book for their hard work.

I thank Kim Wimpsett (copy editor) for her patience with my writing. Thank you, Kim; your edits removed the confusion from several sentences and made a difference to the chapters. I thank Joe Johnson and Bob Wahl for their technical review and invaluable comments. Bob (Bryla), thank you for doing the initial study and laying the groundwork for the book.

I owe for the support and encouragement from my colleagues at work. Thank you, Paul, Wendy, Charles, and Balbir.

Finally, all of this was possible because of the love and support from my beloved wife, Shiji. Thank you, Shiji, for occupying Joshua while I sat in front of the computer. Thank you, Joshua, for leaving me alone and playing with "Thomas" when I said that "Appa is working."
—Biju Thomas

Contents at a Glance

Contents

Introduction

The information technology (IT) industry has high demand for professionals, and Oracle certifications are the hottest credential in the database world. You have made the right decision to pursue an upgrade to your certification, because keeping your Oracle certification current will give you a distinct advantage in this highly competitive market.

Most readers should already be familiar with Oracle and do not need an introduction to the Oracle database world. For those who aren't familiar with the company, Oracle, founded in 1977, sold the first commercial relational database and is now the world's leading database company and second-largest independent software company, with revenues of more than $10 billion, serving more than 145 countries.

Oracle databases are the de facto standard for large Internet sites, and Oracle advertisers are boastful but honest when they proclaim that "the Internet runs on Oracle." Almost all big Internet sites run Oracle databases. Oracle's penetration of the database market runs deep and is not limited to dot-com implementations. Enterprise resource planning (ERP) application suites, data warehouses, and custom applications at many companies rely on Oracle. The demand for database administrator (DBA) resources remains higher than others during weak economic times.

This book is intended to help you upgrade from an Oracle 9*i* Certified Professional to an Oracle 10*g* Certified Professional (OCP), clearing the way to pursue an Oracle Certified Master (OCM) certification. Using this book and a practice database, you can learn the new features of the Oracle 10*g* Database (Oracle 10*g*) and pass the 1Z0-040 Oracle Database 10*g*: New Features for Administrators exam.

Why Become an Oracle Certified Professional?

The number-one reason to become an OCP or maintain an OCP certification is to gain more visibility and greater access to the industry's most challenging opportunities. Oracle certification is the best way to demonstrate your knowledge and skills in Oracle database systems.

Certification is proof of your knowledge and shows that you have the skills required to support Oracle core products. The Oracle certification program can help a company identify proven performers who have demonstrated their skills and who can support the company's investment in Oracle technology. It demonstrates that you have a solid understanding of your job role and the Oracle products used in that role.

OCPs are among the best paid in the IT industry. Salary surveys consistently show the OCP certification to yield higher salaries than other certifications, including Microsoft, Novell, and Cisco.

So, if you have an Oracle 9*i* OCP certification, you have a solid practical background as a DBA, and you're ready to upgrade your certification to Oracle 10*g*, this book is for you!

Oracle Certifications

Oracle certifications follow a track that is oriented toward a job role. The certifications consist of database administration, application developer, and web application server administrator tracks. Within each track, Oracle has a multitiered certification program.

In addition to this multitiered approach, Oracle provides upgrade paths from previous versions of Oracle as well as special accreditations that you can attach to your certification.

The material in this book will address only the upgrade from the Oracle 9*i* to the Oracle 10*g* database administration track and the exam 1Z0-040 Oracle Database 10*g*: New Features for Administrators. Other Sybex books at http://www.sybex.com can help students new to the DBA world prepare for the OCA exam 1Z0-042 Oracle Database 10*g*: Administration I and for the OCP exam 1Z0-043 Oracle Database 10*g*: Administration II.

 See the Oracle website at http://www.oracle.com/education/certification for the latest information on all of Oracle's certification paths along with Oracle's training resources.

The role of the DBA has become a key to success in today's highly complex database systems. The best DBAs work behind the scenes but are in the spotlight when critical issues arise. They plan, create, maintain, and ensure that the database is available for the business. They are always watching the database for performance issues and to prevent unscheduled downtime. The DBA's job requires broad understanding of the architecture of Oracle database and requires expertise in solving problems.

Since this book focuses on the DBA track, the following sections present a closer look at the different tiers of this track.

Oracle Database 10*g* Administrator Certified Associate

The Oracle 10*g* Administrator Certified Associate certification is a streamlined, entry-level certification for the database administration track and is required to advance toward the more senior certification tiers. This certification requires you pass the following exam that demonstrates your knowledge of Oracle basics:

- 1Z0-042 Oracle Database 10*g*: Administration I

Oracle Database 10*g* Administrator Certified Professional

The OCP tier of the database administration track challenges you to demonstrate your continuing experience and knowledge of Oracle technologies. The Oracle 10*g* Administrator Certified Professional certification requires achievement of the Administrator Certified Associate certification, as well as passing the following exam:

- 1Z0-043 Oracle Database 10*g*: Administration II

In addition, the OCP candidate must take one instructor-led in-class course from the following list:

- Oracle Database 10*g*: Administration Workshop I
- Oracle Database 10*g*: Administration Workshop II
- Oracle Database 10*g*: Introduction to SQL
- Oracle Database 10*g*: New Features for Administrators
- Oracle Database 10*g*: Program with PL/SQL

If you already have your OCP 9*i* or earlier and have elected to take the upgrade path, you do not need to take a class to achieve your OCP for Oracle 10*g*.

 You should verify this list against the Oracle education website (www.oracle .com/education), as this list may change without any notice.

Oracle Database 10g Certified Master

Oracle Database 10*g* Administration Certified Master is the highest level of certification that Oracle offers. To become a certified master, you must first achieve Certified Professional status, then complete two advanced instructor-led classes at an Oracle education facility, and finally pass a hands-on, two-day exam at Oracle Education. The classes and practicum exam are offered only at an Oracle education facility and may require travel.

 More details on the required coursework will be available in late 2004.

Oracle 10g Upgrade Paths

Existing OCPs can upgrade their certification in a number of ways: A single exam can upgrade an Oracle 8*i* DBA directly to Oracle Database 10*g* certification in addition to the certification upgrade from Oracle 9*i* to Oracle Database 10*g* covered in this book. Also, Oracle 7.3 and Oracle 8 DBAs can upgrade to an Oracle 9*i* certification with a single exam.

Oracle Database 10g Administrator Special Accreditations

New to the Oracle certification program are the Oracle Database 10g Administrator Special Accreditation programs. These accreditations formally recognize the specialized knowledge of OCPs, in particular database administration areas such as high availability, security, and 10*g* Grid Control. OCPs who pass one of these special accreditation exams will receive a certificate that formally recognizes their specialized competency. The first Oracle Database 10g Special Accreditation will be the High Availability Special Accreditation, available in 2004.

Oracle Database 10*g* DBA Assessment

Oracle also provides an optional (and free) prerequisite to all the proctored exams, which is the following online exam:

- 1Z0-041 Oracle Database 10*g*: DBA Assessment

This exam evaluates your proficiency with basic administration and management of Oracle Database 10*g*, and upon passing this online exam you receive a certificate of completion from Oracle University. Although anyone can take this exam, it is designed for those new to Oracle and is an excellent measurement of how familiar you are with the new Oracle 10*g* database.

Oracle Exam Requirements

The Oracle Database 10*g*: New Features for Administrators exam covers a number of core subject areas. As with many typical multiple-choice exams, you can follow a number of tips to maximize your score on the exam.

Skills Required for the Oracle Database 10*g*: New Features for Administrators Exam

To pass the Oracle 9*i* to Oracle 10*g* certification upgrade exam, you need to master the following subject areas in Oracle 10*g*:

- Installation
- Server configuration
- Data loading and unloading
- Automatic management
- Manageability infrastructure
- Application tuning
- Support for analytical applications
- System resource management
- Automating tasks with the Scheduler
- Space management
- Improved VLDB support
- Backup and recovery enhancements
- Flashback any error
- General storage enhancement
- Automatic storage enhancement
- Software maintenance
- Security
- Miscellaneous new features

Tips for Taking the OCP Exam

Use the following tips to help you prepare for and pass the exam:

- The OCP upgrade exam contains about 55–80 questions to be completed in 90 minutes. Answer the questions you know first so that you do not run out of time.

- Many questions on the exam have answer choices that at first glance look identical. Read the questions carefully. Do not just jump to conclusions. Make sure you clearly understand what each question asks.

- Some questions are based on scenarios. Some of the scenarios contain nonessential information and exhibits. You need to be able to identify what's important and what's not important.

- Do not leave any questions unanswered. There is no negative scoring; always answer a question rather than leave it blank. After selecting an answer, you can mark a difficult question or one that you're unsure of and come back to it later.

- When answering questions you are not sure about, use a process of elimination to get rid of the obviously incorrect answers first. Doing this greatly improves your odds if you need to make an educated guess.

- If you are not sure of your answer, mark it for review and then look for other questions that may help you eliminate any incorrect answers. At the end of the test, you can review the questions you marked earlier.

You should be familiar with the exam objectives, which are included in the front of this book as a perforated tear-out card. You can also find them at www.oracle.com/education/certification/objectives/index.html?40.html. In addition, if you would like information about recommended classes and passing scores, visit www.oracle.com/education/certification/index .html?dba_upgrade.html.

Where Do You Take the New Features Exam?

The 1Z0-040 Oracle Database 10*g*: New Features for Administrators exam is available at any of the more than 900 Sylvan Prometric Authorized Testing Centers around the world. For the location of a testing center near you, call 1-800-891-3926. Outside the United States and Canada, contact your local Sylvan Prometric Registration Center.

To register for a proctored OCP exam at a Sylvan Prometric test center, follow these steps:

1. Determine the number of the exam you want to take. For the New Features exam, it is 1Z0-040.

2. Register with Sylvan Prometric online at http://www.prometric.com or in North America by calling 1-800-891-EXAM (800-891-3926). At this point, you will be asked to pay for the exam. At the time of this writing, the exams are $125 each and must be taken within one year of payment.

3. When you schedule the exam, you'll get instructions regarding all appointment and cancellation procedures, the ID requirements, and information about the testing location.

You can schedule exams up to six weeks in advance or as soon as one working day before the day you want to take it. If you need to cancel or reschedule your exam appointment, contact Sylvan Prometric at least 24 hours or one business day in advance.

What Does This Book Cover?

This book covers everything you need to pass the Oracle 10g New Features for Administrators exam. Each chapter begins with a list of exam objectives.

Chapter 1   In this chapter, we discuss the new Oracle 10g installation procedures, either for an upgrade from a previous installation or for a new installation.

Chapter 2   This chapter explains the Oracle 10g Job Scheduler, the new Data Pump export and import features, and enhancements to external tables.

Chapter 3   In this chapter, we discuss the various automated management features of Oracle 10g, such as the new statistics collection methods, the Automatic Workload Repository (AWR), and the Resource Manager enhancements.

Chapter 4   In this chapter, you will learn about the storage and space management enhancements, including the SYSAUX tablespace and bigfile tablespaces.

Chapter 5   This chapter explains the automated space management enhancements in Oracle 10g, including how to set up and manage an Automatic Storage Management (ASM) instance with ASM disk groups. In addition, this chapter covers proactive space management features and new segment space management features.

Chapter 6   In this chapter, we discuss performance enhancements, especially in the areas of statistics collection, SQL statement tuning, and Automatic Shared Memory Management (ASMM).

Chapter 7   This chapter explains the new database availability features in Oracle 10g. In addition to a number of Recovery Management (RMAN) enhancements, several new types of human error correction methods are covered: Flashback Database, Flashback Drop, Flashback Versions Query, Flashback Transaction Query, and Flashback Table.

Chapter 8   Here, we discuss security enhancements related to Virtual Private Databases (VPDs), as well as a number of miscellaneous enhancements in data warehouse and analytical application environments.

Each chapter ends with a list of exam essentials, which summarize the chapter, with a slant on the topics you need to be familiar with for the exam. The chapters conclude with 20 review questions specifically designed to help you retain the knowledge presented. To really hone your skills, read and answer each question carefully.

How to Use This Book

This book provides a solid foundation for the serious effort of preparing for the Oracle 10g OCP upgrade exam. To best benefit from this book, use the following study method:

1. Take the assessment test immediately following this introduction. (The answers are at the end of the test.) Carefully read the explanations for any questions you get wrong, and note in which chapters the material is covered. This information should help you plan your study strategy.

2. Study each chapter carefully, making sure you fully understand the information and the test objectives listed at the beginning of each chapter. Pay close attention to any chapter related to questions you missed in the assessment test.

3. Complete all hands-on exercises in the chapter, referring to the chapter so that you understand the reason for each step you take. If you do not have an Oracle database available, be sure to study the examples carefully. Answer the review questions related to that chapter. (The answers appear at the end of each chapter, after the "Review Questions" section.)

4. Note the questions that confuse or trick you, and study those sections of the book again.

5. Take the two bonus exams included on the accompanying CD. This will give you a complete overview of what you can expect to see on the real test.

6. Remember to use the products on the CD included with this book. The electronic flashcards and the Sybex Test Engine exam preparation software have been specifically designed to help you study for and pass your exam.

To learn all the material covered in this book, you will need to apply yourself regularly and with discipline. Try to set aside the same time period every day to study, and select a comfortable and quiet place to do so. If you work hard, you will be surprised at how quickly you learn this material. All the best!

What's on the CD?

We have worked hard to provide some really great tools to help you with your certification process. All the following tools should be loaded on your workstation when you're studying for the test.

The Sybex Test Engine Preparation Software

This test-preparation software helps you to pass the 1Z0-040 Oracle Database 10g: New Features for Administrators exam. In this test, you will find all the questions from the book, plus two additional bonus exams that appear exclusively on the CD. You can take the assessment test, test yourself by chapter, or take the practice exams. The test engine installs on both a Windows platform and Linux platform.

Here is a sample screen from the Sybex Test Engine:

Chapter Review: Chapter 3

☐ Mark	Time Left: 1 hr 15 min(s)	Question: 10 of 20

Identify two statements that are true regarding the procedures of DBMS_STATS.

☐ **A.** Every time you collect statistics on a table, schema, or database using DBMS_STATS, the previous version of statistics is stored in the AWR.

☑ **B.** The retention period of optimizer statistics in the AWR is determined by the DBMS_WORKLOAD_REPOSITORY.MODIFY_SNAPSHOT_SETTINGS (RETENTION=> nn) procedure.

☑ **C.** When you lock statistics on a table, the schema level statistics collection skips the table.

☐ **D.** Restoring statistics from the AWR is based on the time stamp when the statistics were collected.

Answer: AC
The retention period of the statistics history kept in the AWR is 31 days by default, which can be modified by using the DBMS_STATS.ALTER_STATS_HISTORY_RETENTION procedure. The statistics from the AWR are restored using the time stamp as an argument to restore statistics as of that time stamp (not when the statistics are collected).

Your Answer: BC

(<) (>) (Show Answer)   (Finish) 🏠 (?)

Electronic Flashcards for PC and Palm Devices

After you read the *OCP: Oracle 10g New Features for Administrators Study Guide*, read the review questions at the end of each chapter, and study the practice exams included in the book and on the CD. You can also test yourself with the flashcards included on the CD.

The flashcards are designed to test your understanding of the fundamental concepts covered in the exam. Here is what the Sybex flashcard interface looks like:

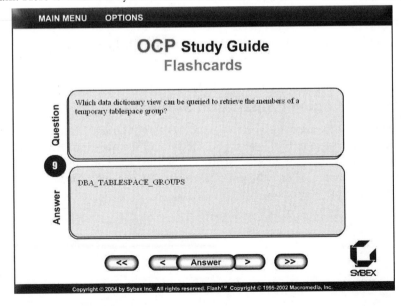

OCP: Oracle 10g New Features for Administrators Study Guide in PDF

Many people like the convenience of being able to carry their study guide on a CD, which is why we included this book in PDF. This will be extremely helpful to readers who fly or commute on a bus or train and don't want to carry a book, as well as to readers who find it more comfortable reading from their computer. We've also included a copy of Adobe Acrobat Reader on the CD.

How to Contact the Authors

To contact Bob Bryla, you can e-mail him at rjbryla@centurytel.net.

To contact Biju Thomas, you can e-mail him at biju@bijoos.com or visit his website for DBAs at http://www.bijoos.com/oracle.

About the Authors

Bob Bryla is an Oracle 8, 8*i*, 9*i*, and 10*g* Certified Professional with more than 15 years of experience in database design, database application development, training, and database administration. He is an Internet database analyst and Oracle DBA at Lands' End, Inc., in Dodgeville, Wisconsin.

Biju Thomas is an Oracle 7.3, Oracle 8, Oracle 8*i*, Oracle 9*i*, and Oracle 10*g* Certified Professional with more than 11 years of Oracle database management and application development experience. He is a senior database administrator for Delinea Corporation and resides in Fort Worth, Texas. He maintains a website for DBAs at http://www.bijoos.com/oracle.

Assessment Test

1. When manually upgrading an Oracle 9*i* database to Oracle 10*g*, which shutdown option must be used in Oracle 9*i* before starting the database in Oracle 10*g* for upgrade?

   A. SHUTDOWN UPGRADE

   B. SHUTDOWN MIGRATE

   C. SHUTDOWN IMMEDIATE

   D. SHUTDOWN ABORT

2. When installing the Oracle 10*g* database software Enterprise Edition with the Enterprise Manager (EM) Database Control, how many CDs are required?

   A. 2

   B. 1

   C. 3

   D. 4

3. Identify the statement that is true regarding the COMPATIBLE parameter in Oracle 10*g*.

   A. For upgrading a database to Oracle 10*g*, you must have the COMPATIBLE parameter set to 9.2.0 or higher.

   B. After upgrading the database to Oracle 10*g* and starting the database with COMPATIBLE= 10.1.0, you can restart the database using COMPATIBLE=9.2.0 if you did not like the optimizer plans generated by the Oracle 10*g* database.

   C. When upgrading an Oracle 8*i* database to Oracle 10*g*, the COMPATIBLE parameter must be set to 8.1.7.

   D. If you do not explicitly set the COMPATIBLE parameter in the initialization parameter file while upgrading to Oracle 10*g*, you can downgrade the database to Oracle 9*i*.

4. Which Data Pump parameters can be used to unload or export data from SCOTT.EMP table where the rows belong to DEPT=10? (Choose three that apply.)

   A. EXCLUDE

   B. INCLUDE

   C. QUERY

   D. CONTENT

   E. ROWS

5. Using calendaring expressions to schedule a job, how would you specify the Wednesday two weeks prior to the last Wednesday of every month?

    A. FREQ=MONTHLY; BYDAY=-2WED

    B. FREQ=WEEKLY; BYWEEK=-2

    C. FREQ=MONTHLY; BYWEEK=-2WED

    D. FREQ=WEEKLY; BYDAY=-2WED

6. Identify the statement that best describes the behavior of AWR snapshots.

    A. Snapshots are created every 60 minutes, and the interval cannot be changed.

    B. Snapshots are created every 60 minutes, and the interval can be changed by setting an initialization parameter.

    C. Snapshots intervals must be 30-minute increments.

    D. The DBMS_WORKLOAD_REPOSITORY.MODIFY_SNAPSHOT_SETTINGS procedure can be used to set the interval of snapshots.

7. Which two parameter settings enable Automatic Shared Memory Management in Oracle 10g?

    A. SGA_MAX_SIZE

    B. SGA_TARGET

    C. TIMED_STATISTICS

    D. STATISTICS_LEVEL

    E. OPTIMIZER_MODE

8. Identify the attribute that is not valid when setting DBMS_RESOURCE_MANAGER.SET_CONSUMER_GROUP_MAPPING.

    A. SERVICE_MODULE

    B. MODULE_NAME_ACTION

    C. CLIENT_PROGRAM_ACTION

    D. CLIENT_MACHINE

    E. SERVICE_NAME

9. A bigfile tablespace can consist of how many datafiles?

    A. One

    B. Only one, and there can be only one bigfile tablespace per database

    C. Limited only by the DB_FILES initialization parameter

    D. Two—one for tables, and one for indexes

10. Which tablespaces are required in an installation of Oracle 10*g*? (Choose all that apply.)

    A. USERS

    B. UNDO

    C. SYSTEM

    D. SYSAUX

    E. TEMP

    F. All of the above

11. Which types of files can be copied using the COPY_FILE and PUT_FILE procedures? (Choose all that apply.)

    A. Tablespace datafiles

    B. A 4TB binary LOB

    C. Files that do not need character set conversion

    D. Binary files that are a multiple of 1,024 bytes

12. Which of the following statements is not true about temporary tablespace groups?

    A. A temporary tablespace may belong to no temporary tablespace groups.

    B. A temporary tablespace group can have no members.

    C. A temporary tablespace may belong to one and only one temporary tablespace group.

    D. Users can be assigned a temporary tablespace or to a temporary tablespace group.

13. Given the index HR.IDX_PK_EMP on the table HR.EMPLOYEES and following ALTER INDEX command

    ALTER INDEX HR.IDX_PK_EMP COALESCE;

    which of the following commands also accomplishes this task? (Choose the best answer.)

    A. ALTER TABLE HR.EMPLOYEES SHRINK SPACE CASCADE;

    B. ALTER TABLE HR.EMPLOYEES SHRINK SPACE;

    C. ALTER TABLE HR.EMPLOYEES SHRINK SPACE COMPACT;

    D. ALTER INDEX HR.IDX_PK_EMP REBUILD;

14. Which type of queue is supported by sorted hash clusters?

    A. DEQUE

    B. LIFO

    C. FIFO

    D. A queue represented by a two-way linked list

15. Automatic Storage Management disk group mirroring is done at which level?

    A. Tablespace level

    B. Extent level

    C. Segment level

    D. Datafile level

16. Which of the following statements is not true about segment shrink operations?

   A. The compaction phase of segment shrink is done online.

   B. During the compaction phase, the entire segment is locked but only for a very short period of time.

   C. When the second phase of segment shrink occurs, the HWM is adjusted.

   D. User DML can block the progress of the compaction phase until the DML is committed or rolled back.

   E. Using the COMPACT keyword, the movement of the HWM can occur later during nonpeak hours by running the command without the COMPACT keyword.

17. What value for OPTIMZER_MODE will allow you to minimize resource costs for executing queries and return all rows?

   A. ALL_ROWS

   B. CHOOSE

   C. RULE

   D. FIRST_ROWS

18. Which of the following are not default components of the cost optimizer model? (Choose two.)

   A. CPU usage

   B. Memory usage

   C. Session waits

   D. I/O usage

19. Which of the following RMAN commands will create a full backup of the database in compressed backupset format?

   A. BACKUP AS COMPRESSED BACKUPSET DATABASE;

   B. BACKUP DATABASE AS COMPRESSED BACKUPSET;

   C. BACKUP FULL DATABASE;

   D. BACKUP AS COMPRESSED IMAGE DATABASE;

20. Which type of file is not backed up in the flash recovery area? Choose two.

   A. The control file

   B. RMAN files

   C. Online redo log files

   D. Datafile copies

   E. Archived log files

   F. Control file autobackups

   G. Password files

21. The Flashback Table functionality provides all of the following advantages except for which option?

    A. A Flashback Table operation is performed in place while the database is online.

    B. Restoring a table that was dropped.

    C. All dependent objects are restored as a single transaction along with the target table.

    D. Flashback Table can often be used instead of point-in-time recovery of the database or a tablespace.

22. Which of the following initialization parameters ensures that all database files will use OMF to name the files at the operating system level? Choose two.

    A. DB_CREATE_FILE_DEST

    B. DB_RECOVERY_FILE_DEST_SIZE

    C. DB_RECOVERY_FILE_DEST

    D. DB_CREATE_ONLINE_LOG_DEST_*n*

23. Which statement is not true regarding the enhancements to the MERGE statement in Oracle 10*g*?

    A. The ON clause is optional, which lets you perform unconditional inserts.

    B. You can provide the DELETE in the WHEN MATCHED clause to delete rows.

    C. You can add an optional WHERE clause to the WHEN MATCHED and WHEN NOT MATCHED clauses.

    D. You may omit the WHEN MATCHED or WHEN NOT MATCHED clauses.

24. Choose the policy type that is default in Oracle 10*g* when creating a security policy.

    A. Static

    B. Dynamic

    C. Shared static

    D. Context sensitive

25. Which attribute enables Oracle 10*g* to perform end-to-end application tracing in a multitier environment?

    A. Service name

    B. Module name

    C. Action name

    D. Client identifier

Answers to Assessment Test

1. C. For database upgrade, the database must have a clean shutdown. SHUTDOWN IMMEDIATE, NORMAL, or TRANSACTIONAL can be used for a clean shutdown. SHUTDOWN ABORT should never be used. SHUTDOWN MIGRATE and SHUTDOWN UPGRADE are not valid options. For more information about startup and shutdown options when upgrading a database, refer to Chapter 1.

2. B. Oracle 10*g* facilitates installing the most common database features—the EM Database Control, database templates, and sample schema—from one CD. The companion CD includes JPublisher, Java libraries, and Legato Single Server. For more information on the components that can be installed from each CD, read Chapter 1.

3. A. The minimum value for the COMPATIBLE parameter in an Oracle 10*g* database is 9.2.0. For upgrade, this must be the minimum value. Once the database is started using COMPATIBLE=10.1.0, you cannot start the database with COMPATIBLE=9.2.0 because of the irreversible datafile compatibility. If you do not set the COMPATIBLE value, the default is 10.0.0; hence, you cannot start the database in Oracle 9*i* for downgrade. To learn more about the steps involved in the database upgrade to Oracle 10*g* and the restrictions on the COMPATIBLE parameter, read Chapter 1.

4. B, C, D. The parameters should be INCLUDE=SCOTT.EMP, CONTENT=ALL, and QUERY='WHERE DEPT=10'. ROWS is not a supported Data Pump parameter. INCLUDE and EXCLUDE parameters are mutually exclusive. To learn about Oracle Data Pump, read Chapter 2.

5. A. FREQ=MONTLY specifies the repeat interval is every month. BYDAY=-2WED specifies the second-to-last Wednesday. To learn more about calendaring expressions and the components of the scheduler, refer to Chapter 2.

6. D. The MMON process takes the AWR snapshots are taken by every hour, and you can change the interval using the MODIFY_SNAPSHOT_SETTINGS procedure. The minimum value for the interval is 10 minutes, but the increments need not be 30 minutes. For more information on the AWR and the manageability infrastructure, read Chapter 3.

7. B, D. To enable Automatic Shared Memory Management, the STATISTICS_LEVEL parameter should not be BASIC and the SGA_TARGET should be a nonzero value. The default for STATISTICS_LEVEL is TYPICAL. To learn more about the automatic features of Oracle 10*g*, read Chapter 3.

8. C. The SET_CONSUMER_GROUP_MAPPING procedure is used to set the consumer group when logged into a session. CLIENT_PROGRAM is the valid attribute, and CLIENT_PROGRAM_ACTION is not. For more information on resource manager enhancements in Oracle 10*g*, read Chapter 3.

9. A. The correspondence between bigfile tablespaces and their datafiles is 1:1, and every tablespace in the database can be a bigfile tablespace. Also, a database can contain both bigfile and smallfile tablespaces. Chapter 4 discusses bigfile tablespaces.

10. C, D.   Only the SYSTEM and SYSAUX tablespaces are required for an installation of Oracle 10*g*. However, it is strongly recommended that default tablespaces for both permanent and temporary segments such as USERS and TEMP be created to prevent contention in the SYSTEM tablespace. The UNDO tablespace supports automatic undo management and is also recommended but is not required. Chapter 4 discusses the new SYSAUX tablespace in detail.

11. A, C, D.   Copying files with the procedures PUT_FILE and COPY_FILE in the DBMS_FILE_ TRANSFER package can transfer only binary files with an upper limit of 2TB and must be a multiple of 512 bytes; also, only files that do not need character set conversion can be copied with COPY_FILE and PUT_FILE. To learn about copying database and other binary files with Oracle directories and the DBMS_FILE_TRANSFER package, refer to Chapter 4.

12. B.   A temporary tablespace group cannot exist without any members; dropping the last temporary tablespace from the group drops the group itself. The syntax for adding a user to a temporary tablespace is identical to the syntax for adding a user to a temporary tablespace group. To learn more about temporary tablespace groups, see Chapter 4.

13. A.   Using the CASCADE keyword in any segment shrink operation will shrink the free space in any dependent objects such as indexes. Chapter 5 discusses segment shrink functionality.

14. C.   Sorted hash clusters are similar to standard hash clusters except that they store data sorted by nonprimary key columns and make access by applications that use the rows in a first in, first out (FIFO) manner very efficient; no sorting is required. Chapter 5 covers how sorted hash clusters are created and used.

15. B.   Disk group mirroring for ASM is done at the extent level. To learn about Automatic Storage Management mirroring, see Chapter 5.

16. B.   During the compaction phase, locks are held only on individual rows, causing some minor serialization with concurrent DML operations. For more information about segment shrink, see Chapter 5.

17. A.   ALL_ROWS, the default for OPTIMIZER_MODE, maximizes throughput and minimizes the resources needed to complete the entire statement. CHOOSE and RULE are no longer valid. FIRST_ ROWS (along with FIRST_ROWS_*n*) optimizes resources to improve response time for the initial rows returned from the query. Chapter 6 discusses changes to initialization parameters related to the optimizer.

18. B, C.   As of Oracle 9*i*, CPU usage can be factored into the cost model to accommodate CPU-only or CPU-intensive operations. As of Oracle 10*g*, CPU+I/O is the default. Chapter 6 discusses enhancements to the Oracle query optimizer.

19. A.   The BACKUP AS COMPRESSED BACKUPSET DATABASE command will create a compressed backupset backup. All other choices are syntactically incorrect. You may omit the AS COMPRESSED BACKUPSET clause if the default backup type for DISK is set to COMPRESSED BACKUPSET. Chapter 7 discusses creating and maintaining compressed backups.

20. C, G.   Online redo log files are used for recovery after an instance failure and should not be backed up under any backup scenario. Chapter 7 details using the flash recovery area. Password files are not backed up to the flash recovery area.

21. B.   Flashback Drop restores a table that was dropped. To learn about Flashback Table and all the other flashback options, see Chapter 7.

22. A, D.   Both DB_CREATE_FILE_DEST and DB_CREATE_ONLINE_LOG_DEST_n enable the DBA to use OMF for file naming in the database area. The parameters DB_RECOVERY_FILE_DEST_SIZE and DB_RECOVERY_FILE_DEST do not directly enable OMF, but files can be created in the flash recovery area using OMF. To learn more about using OMF with the flash recovery area, see Chapter 7.

23. A.   The MERGE statement allows you to perform unconditional inserts by using a constant predicate for the ON clause, for example, ON (1=0). To learn more about MERGE statement and other SQL enhancements, read Chapter 8.

24. B.   Dynamic was the only policy type available in Oracle 9*i*. Though other policy types are available in Oracle 10*g*, the dynamic policy type is the default. Learn more about security enhancements in Chapter 8.

25. D.   The client identifier uniquely identifies a client and is carried through all tiers to the database server. To read more about end-to-end application tracing and other Oracle 10*g* enhancements, read Chapter 8.

Chapter

1

Installing and Upgrading to Oracle 10*g*

ORACLE DATABASE 10*g* NEW FEATURES FOR ADMINISTRATORS EXAM OBJECTIVES COVERED IN THIS CHAPTER:

✓ **Installation**

- ▪ Describe installation new features support
- ▪ Describe installation performance enhancements

✓ **Server Configuration**

- ▪ Simplify instance configuration using a subset of initialization parameters
- ▪ Use policy-based database configuration framework
- ▪ Use DBCA to clone database
- ▪ View database usage statistics through EM

✓ **Maintain Software**

- ▪ Understand the supported upgrade paths to Oracle Database 10*g*
- ▪ Use new utility to perform pre-upgrade validation checks
- ▪ Use simplified upgrade process that automatically determines components to be upgraded
- ▪ Start up the database using a new mode when upgrading

 Exam objectives are subject to change at any time without prior notice and at Oracle's sole discretion. Please visit Oracle's Training and Certification website (http://www.oracle.com/education/certification/) for the most current exam objectives listing.

With the release of Oracle Database 10*g* (Oracle 10*g*), DBAs have a database that is simple to set up, more robust, and self-managing. Oracle 10*g* is full of new features, most of which the DBAs long awaited and many of which are designed with the DBA in mind. Though this book is not intended to review and explain all the new features of Oracle 10*g*, we will explain all the features relevant to the OCP New Features for Administrators exam.

According to the International Oracle Users Group (IOUG), DBAs spend more than 50 percent of their time managing the database, which includes tuning, managing space, managing storage, and performing backup and recovery. Oracle 10*g* has put a lot of focus on the managing database area so that you can spend your time on proactive and strategic planning. Oracle 10*g* is a self-managing database. Automatic management of the database includes storage management, SQL management and tuning, resource management, space management, and backup recovery management.

The *g* in Oracle 10*g* stands for *grid*. Grid computing is designed to reduce costs, make the most efficient use of all resources, and easily adapt to the ever-growing needs of the business. Oracle's grid architecture combines all the available resources (network, servers, and disk) into a large pool of resources (the grid); users can subscribe to these resources based on their requirements. Grid computing uses sophisticated workload management that makes it possible for applications to share resources across many servers. Data processing capacity can be added or removed on demand, and resources within a location can be dynamically provisioned. According to Larry Ellison, grid computing for end users is like subscribing to the electric (utility) company. You consume what you need. When you consume more, more resources are made available. The subscriber does not know where the generator is or how the electric grid is wired.

In Oracle 10*g*, you can clone a database and the Oracle software installation (the Oracle installation home directory) to a location on the same server or to a remote server. The Enterprise Manager comes with several out-of the box policy verifications that can alert you to the database security and configuration issues. In this chapter, we will discuss the installation features, configuration enhancements, and upgrade options available for Oracle 10*g*.

Installing Oracle 10*g*

With Oracle 10*g*, the emphasis is on self-managing and keeping things simple. Oracle has removed many redundant and obvious choices from the installation. As a DBA, you need to enter only minimal (that is, absolutely required) information to install an Oracle database.

For a clean and trouble-free install, you must install the software to an empty directory. Do not install in the same directory where you have a previous version of Oracle software installed. For

all platforms, read the platform-specific installation document to make sure you have minimum required hardware and OS versions. On Unix platforms, you need to adjust the kernel parameters.

You can find the installation documentation—Oracle Database Quick Installation Guide—at http://www.oracle.com/technology/documentation/database10g.html.

In the following sections, we will discuss using the Oracle Universal Installer (OUI) to install Oracle 10*g* software, what new features of Oracle 10*g* the OUI supports, what installation checks the OUI performs, and enhancements made to the installation process.

Using the Oracle Universal Installer

As in the previous releases of Oracle, Oracle 10*g* uses the OUI to install the software. With the OUI, the Oracle 10*g* installation process is simple. The most common Oracle 10*g* installation can be performed with just one CD. The OUI performs the necessary preinstall checks to make sure the operating system is certified and properly configured, the necessary patches are applied, and enough resources are available. If any problems are detected, it even recommends corrective action.

On the Windows platform, the OUI is invoked automatically when you insert the CD. To manually invoke the OUI, simply double-click the `setup.exe` icon from the root directory of the CD. On Unix platforms, you invoke the OUI by executing the `runInstaller` script. In the Oracle 10*g* database CD, `runInstaller` is in the root directory. If you're using the DVD, this script is under the `db` folder.

The OUI in Oracle 10*g* does a lot more checking for necessary resources before the installation begins. Figure 1.1 shows the OUI checking the necessary system requirements.

FIGURE 1.1   The OUI verifying install requirements

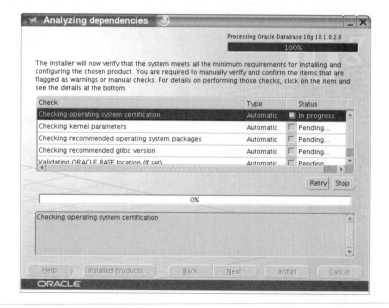

On Linux (and Unix) platforms, you invoke the OUI by using the script runInstaller; you may use the -ignoreSysPrereqs option to continue with Oracle 10g install, even if the flavor of Linux is not certified by Oracle. If you do not use this flag, runInstaller will fail. You do not have to use this flag on Red Hat 2.1, Red Hat 3, and United Linux 1.0.

In the next section, we will discuss the preinstall checks performed by the OUI before installing the Oracle 10g software, the software components you can install, and the options for creating a database along with the software install.

Checking Preinstall Requirements

The OUI automatically performs the following verifications (some steps are specific to the Linux/Unix platform):

- Checks for certified version of operating system software. For example, only the SuSE SLES-7, Red Hat Advanced Server 2.1, and United Linux 1.0 platforms are supported under Linux, and only Solaris 2.8 or higher is supported for Sun platforms. (Always verify current certifications at http://technet.oracle.com.)

- Checks to make sure 32-bit Oracle 10g software components are not installed to an Oracle home directory with 64-bit Oracle 10g software and vice versa.

- Verifies that all the required operating system patches are installed.

- Checks for all the required kernel parameters.

- Checks if the DISPLAY variable and X Server permissions are set.

- Verifies sufficient swap space and temporary space are available.

- Verifies that the Oracle home directory where the software being installed is either empty or has the supported version of software components. Previous versions of Oracle were allowed to install software to an Oracle home directory with a different software version, but Oracle 10g does not allow this. It warns you if the software directory is not empty.

Choosing the Components to Install

The Select Installation Type screen lets you choose the components of the database to install. The components are preconfigured into two major categories: Enterprise Edition and Standard Edition. You should choose the right component based on the requirement and license agreement.

Enterprise Edition includes all the database components, which may be essential for mission-critical applications. Standard Edition does not have certain features enabled, such as the data compression, materialized view query rewrite, transportable tablespaces, and so on.

Windows platforms have an additional installation option: Personal Edition. This is similar to the Enterprise Edition and meant for single-user applications. Real Application Clusters (RAC) is not included in the Personal Edition.

You can also choose a custom installation type, where you can pick and choose the components to install.

Introducing Starter Database Options

The OUI, along with the software installation, can create an Oracle 10g database for you. If you're not creating a database along with the software install, you can specify that by choosing the Do Not Create a Starter Database option in the Select Database Configuration screen (see Figure 1.2).

FIGURE 1.2   The OUI: Select Database Configuration screen

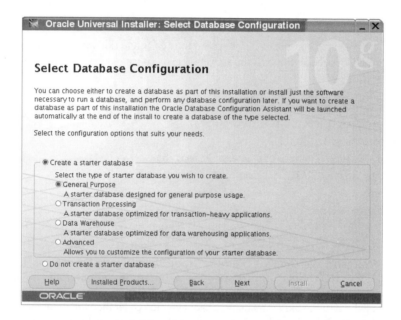

The next screen you see will depend on which option you select in the Select Database Configuration screen. If you choose Do Not Create a Starter Database, the OUI shows the installation summary and proceeds with the software installation. If you choose General Purpose, Transaction Processing, or Data Warehouse as the type of the database, the OUI will get minimal information such as database management, file storage, backup location, and password for default accounts. After the software is installed, OUI will invoke the *Database Configuration Assistant (DBCA)* tool in noninteractive mode to create the database. The DBCA is a GUI tool to create a new database, configure an existing database, delete a database or clone a database.

The DBCA is discussed in detail later in the section "DBCA Enhancements."

If you choose Advanced as the database type, the OUI will install the software and at the end of installation invoke the DBCA utility interactively to get more information on the database options.

You can install sample *schemas* using the DBCA when creating the database. Sample schemas are schema objects with sample data in them. The following are the five schemas in the sample schema installation:

- HR
- IX
- OE
- PM
- SH

Most of the examples and sample code provided in the Oracle documentation are based on these sample schemas. Oracle will install the EXAMPLE tablespace using the following transportable tablespace method:

```
imp transport_tablespace=y
file=/orahome/product/10.1.0/assistants/dbca/
       ➥templates/example.dmp
log=/ora1/admin/ORA10GP/create/tts_example_imp.log
datafiles=/ora5/oradata/ORA10GP/example01.dbf
tablespaces=EXAMPLE
tts_owners=hr,oe,pm,ix,sh
```

You can install Oracle 8, Oracle 8*i*, Oracle 9*i*, and Oracle 10*g* databases in multiple (separate) Oracle home directories on the same computer and have Oracle 8 (8.0.6), Oracle 8*i* (8.1.7), Oracle 9*i* (9.2), and Oracle 10*g* clients connecting to any or all the databases. When using a client version older than the database release, all features specific to the release of the database may not be available to the client.

Examining the OUI Support for New Features

Oracle 10*g* is feature rich with Automatic Storage Management (ASM), Flashback database, Enterprise Manager Database Control, RAC control, and so on. The OUI includes screens to set up these options if you decide to create a starter database.

These screens will display only if you install a preconfigured database. For a custom install, or for using advanced database options, you obtain this information through the DBCA interface.

We will look at these options and how to install them in the following sections.

The specifics of these features will be discussed throughout the book.

Introducing Database Management Options

You can manage Oracle databases using the web-based tool *Oracle Enterprise Manger (EM)*. EM is a GUI tool to manage the Oracle environment, which includes database, host server, listener, HTTP server, and web applications. In the Select Database Management Option screen (see Figure 1.3), you can choose to manage all databases at a centralized location or manage a single database using the EM.

FIGURE 1.3   The Select Database Management Option screen

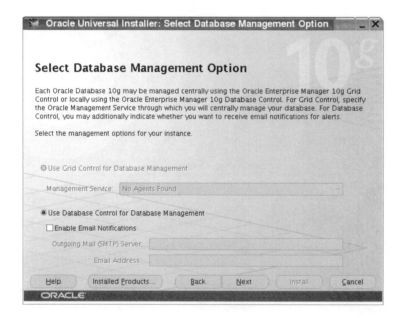

EM is installed by default if you install a preconfigured database (if you choose a custom install, you have the option not to install it). The options available are as follows:

Use the Grid Control for database management   Choose this option if you want to manage more than one database using a single EM interface. To deploy EM centrally, at least one Oracle Management Repository, at least one Oracle Management Service, and Oracle Management Agent must be installed on every server that you want to manage. EM 10g Grid Control is installed from a separate CD.

Use the Database Control for database management   This option is selected by default if an *Oracle Management Agent* is not installed on the computer. Oracle Management Agent is responsible for monitoring all targets on the host, for communicating that information to the middle-tier Management Service, and for managing and maintaining the host and its targets. However, even if a Oracle Management Agent is installed, you can still choose to configure the Database Control to manage the database. Using this option, you can also specify an e-mail address where you want to receive the database alerts.

Introducing Database File Storage Options

The OUI gives the option to specify the type of storage you want for the database using the Specify Database File Storage Option screen, as shown in Figure 1.4.

FIGURE 1.4   The Specify Database File Storage Option screen

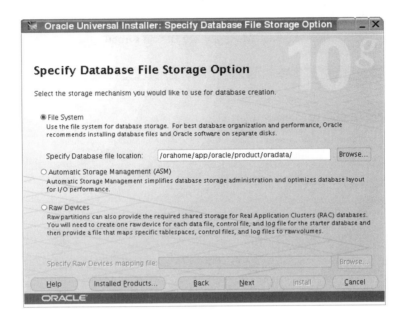

Oracle 10g supports the following three types of storage for its data:

File system   Oracle database files are created under the directory you specify in this option. This method is the most commonly used and the easiest to set up. Oracle recommends creating the database files in a different file system that stores the Oracle software or operating system files. The file system could be a disk physically attached to the computer, a RAID/Logical Volume Manager configuration, or an NFS-mounted file system. Once File System is chosen, the next screen will accept the location of the data files.

Automatic Storage Management (ASM)   Choose this option if you would like the data files to be stored in ASM disks. *Automatic Storage Management (ASM)* is a new feature in Oracle 10g. ASM manages the disk for database use and tunes I/O automatically. To use ASM, one or more ASM disk groups must exist. A disk group is a set of disk devices that ASM manages as a single unit. ASM spreads data evenly across all the devices in the disk group to optimize performance and utilization. When you choose ASM, Oracle checks if an ASM instance is running on the machine; if not, it will create one for you.

Raw devices   If you choose this option, Oracle data files will be stored on disk directly, bypassing the operating system layer. Raw devices are disk partitions or logical volumes that have not been formatted with a file system. When using raw devices for database file storage, Oracle writes data directly to the partition or volume, bypassing the operating system's file system layer.

Introducing Backup and Recovery Options

You may enable automated database backup using the Specify Backup and Recovery Options screen (see Figure 1.5). Oracle uses Recovery Manager (RMAN) to back up the files and can set up a job to perform the backups.

You can choose the following options from this screen:

Do Not Enable Automated Backups   Choose this option if you do not want the OUI to set up backups. All databases should be backed up, so if you choose this option, make sure you define other methods to back up the database for data protection.

Enable Automated Backups   Choose this option to set up backup job to run automatically every day. The backups can be written to a file system area or to ASM storage. The default disk quota configured for the flash recovery area is 2GB. The default job execution time is 2 a.m.

For ASM disk groups, the required disk space depends on the redundancy level of the disk group you choose. Normal redundancy is two-way mirroring, and high redundancy is three-way mirroring.

FIGURE 1.5   The Specify Backup and Recovery Options screen

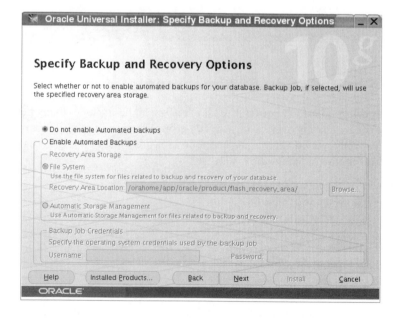

Introducing Database Schema Password Options

Using the Specify Database Schema Passwords screen (see Figure 1.6), you can provide separate passwords for each administrative user, such as SYS, SYSTEM, SYSMAN, and DBSNMP, or provide one password for all.

FIGURE 1.6   The Specify Database Schema Passwords screen

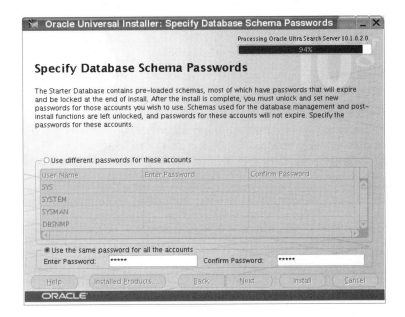

Introducing Installation Enhancements

In addition to the new installation features, the Oracle 10g installer includes many performance and management enhancements over 9i. Oracle 10g groups the products into separate CDs so that you need to use only one CD at a time. The following are some of the CDs that ship with Oracle 10g; all these are included in one DVD:

- Oracle Database 10g
- Oracle Database 10g Companion CD
- Oracle Database 10g Client
- Oracle Cluster Ready Services
- Oracle Database Documentation Library

Oracle Enterprise Manager 10g Grid Control is shipped separately in one DVD or three CDs.

The installation completes in about 20 minutes and requires only one CD. The EM Webstage and Apache, which were installed with Oracle 9*i*, are no longer installed with the Oracle 10*g* database.

Oracle 10*g* has a simplified software install and database creation; the disk requirement for software is now less. The following are some of the install enhancements:

Simplified install The Oracle 10*g* installer can install the software and create a database with default settings from one screen. This simplifies the install actions required and is really useful for a new user. Figure 1.7 shows the install screen from a Windows platform. The Advanced Installation option lets you choose location, type of software installation, and other options.

FIGURE 1.7   The Welcome to the Oracle Database 10g Installation screen

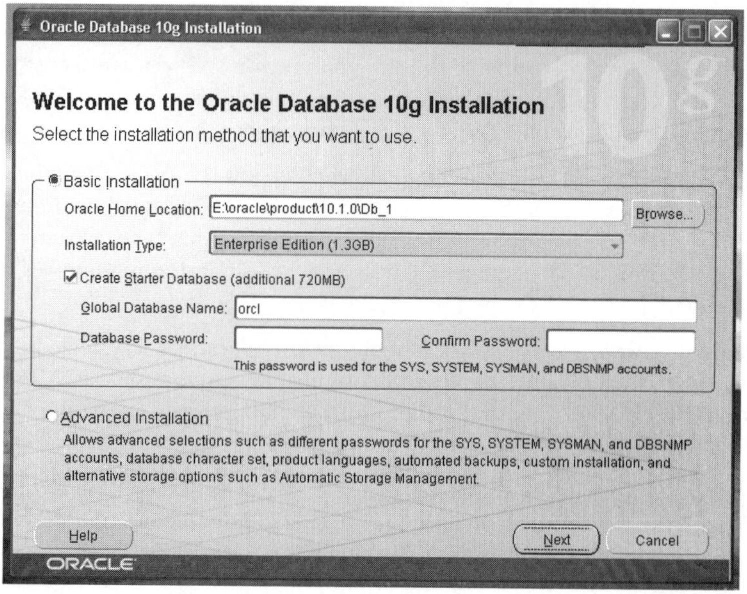

Memory and disk Oracle 10*g* requires a minimum of 512MB for an instance with the Database Control and a minimum of 256MB for an instance without the Database Control. The OUI automatically checks the disk space requirements. The minimum is 1GB swap space (or twice the RAM), between 500MB and 2.5GB of disk space depending on the options, and about 1200MB for the preconfigured database.

Administrative passwords In Oracle 9*i* Release 2, you were required to enter the passwords for SYS and SYSTEM twice—once during installation and once after the database creation. In Oracle 10*g*, this information is required only once during installation.

Clean removal The Oracle 10*g* OUI removes the Oracle software cleanly, meaning no files are left in the Oracle home directory; files outside the Oracle home directory related to the install are also removed. Software removal also shuts down any databases that are currently using the Oracle home directory.

The silent install of Oracle using a reponse file in Unix is truly silent; you have no need to set up a DISPLAY variable. The response file records only the values used in dialog boxes needing user inputs.

Though most of the features used by the Oracle database can be installed from one CD, you may want to install a few products from the Oracle Database 10g Companion CD. The Oracle 10g Companion CD includes the following two main product options:

Oracle 10g products   These products must be installed to an existing Oracle 10g home directory:

Oracle database examples   Database examples are product demonstrations to learn the product features. These mostly use the sample schema data to demonstrate features.

JPublisher   JPublisher is a Java utility that generates Java classes to represent the user-defined database entities in a Java program. JPublisher enables you to specify and customize the mapping of SQL object types, object reference types, and collection types (VARRAYs or nested tables) to Java classes in a strongly typed paradigm.

Legato Single Server Version   Legato Single Server Version (LSSV) is a backup and recovery application that is developed by Legato Systems Inc. LSSV software includes a media management layer. Oracle RMAN requires this layer when using tape storage for database backups and restoration. LSSV manages the backup schedule and communicates with Oracle Recovery Manager (RMAN) to copy the Oracle data to tape.

Natively compiled Java libraries   The CD includes JAccelerator and Oracle interMedia Image Accelerator, which contain the natively compiled Java libraries (NCOMPs) for Oracle JVM and Oracle interMedia. These libraries improve the performance of the Oracle JVM and Oracle interMedia.

Oracle text-supplied Knowledge Bases   An Oracle Text Knowledge Base is a hierarchical tree of concepts used for indexing themes, performing ABOUT queries, and deriving themes for document services.

Oracle 10g companion products   These products must not be installed to the Oracle 10g database Oracle home directory; they must be installed to a separate Oracle home directory.

Oracle HTTP server   *Oracle 10g HTTP Server (OHS)* is based on the Apache web server 1.3.28 and is designed to take advantage of the latest optimizations and security features. OHS includes SSL session renegotiation and death detection and the restart of failed processes.

Oracle HTML DB   *HTML DB* is new in Oracle 10g. HTML DB is a Rapid Application Development (RAD) tool for the Oracle database, and it has many built-in themes and features. Using only a web browser, developers can build web applications faster. Before installing HTML DB, an Oracle 10g database must be configured and should be able to connect using SQLNet. Also, OHS and HTML DB must be installed in the same Oracle home directory. Figure 1.8 shows the HTML configuration screen of the OUI.

FIGURE 1.8   HTML DB configuration options

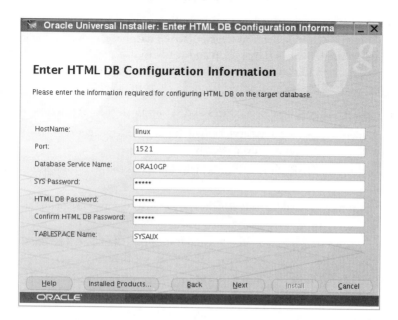

    In earlier releases of Oracle, the client software was part of the database install CD. In Oracle 10*g*, the client is installed from the Oracle Database 10*g* CD when installing the database software. To install the Oracle client software alone, you need to use the Oracle Database 10*g* Client CD.

Configuring Oracle 10*g*

Oracle 10*g* provides several configuration enhancements over 9*i*. Most of the tasks are completed automatically, thus reducing manual intervention and errors. The architectural enhancements include a new SYSAUX tablespace to store all auxiliary metadata (discussed in Chapter 4, "General Storage Enhancements"), store workload information, and collect statistics to optimize performance. In addition, the DBCA is enhanced in Oracle 10*g* to include all these architectural changes.

You invoke the DBCA on Unix platforms using the dbca executable. On Windows, choose Database Configuration Assistant from the Configuration and Migration Tools folder.

In the following sections, we will discuss the enhancements to DBCA, how you can set up the database using simplified initialization parameters, and how to verify the database feature and high-watermark usage.

Examining DBCA Enhancements

The DBCA is a GUI tool for database creation and configuration changes. The DBCA can create a stand-alone database, a Real Application Cluster (RAC) database, or a standby database. A database created using the DBCA is fully set up and ready to use.

When creating a database, the DBCA can configure the following new features of Oracle 10g:

- Automatically create the SYSAUX tablespace to store auxiliary metadata information.

- Implement backup and recovery procedures and set up flash recovery area.

- Create management repository and services. The Enterprise Manager repository, jobs, and event subsystems are configured automatically.

- Automatically register LDAP (if available), which eliminates the need for manual LDAP.ORA configuration.

- Simplify the creation of a seed database, which is powerful and makes use of all the Oracle 10g features.

- Make the database ready for management using Enterprise Manager. The database can be centrally managed using EM Grid control. DBCA can set this up.

- Configure ASM storage options, and if an ASM instance is not already installed, create an ASM instance.

- Specify initialization parameters as typical, where you need to provide only minimal information. Choosing Custom enables you to configure parameters.

- Create sample schemas.

- Create a database as a clone of an existing database. The DBCA can clone the database entirely or just the structure.

In addition, when a database is deleted using the DBCA, the DBCA deletes all the files associated with the database and, on Windows, also removes the services.

You can also change many options using the DBCA utility at a later time, if you decide to do so. Choose the Configure Database option from the main screen of the DBCA.

Using the DBCA to Clone a Database

The DBCA can create a database, configure database options, delete a database, or manage templates. These are the four options you see when you start the DBCA. Managing the templates clones the database. Figure 1.9 shows the Template Management screen of the DBCA.

DBCA templates are XML files that contain information required to create a database—new databases or clones of existing databases. The information in the templates includes database options, initialization parameters, and storage attributes (for data files, tablespaces, control files, and redo logs).

FIGURE 1.9   The DBCA: Template Management screen

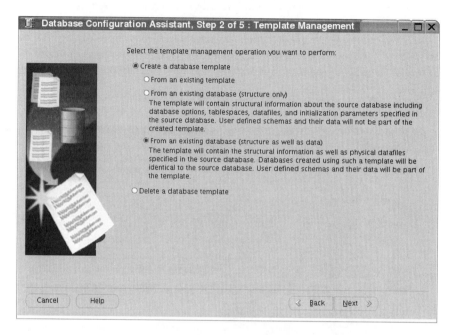

Cloning a database using templates saves time in database creation, because copying an already created seed database's files to the correct locations takes less time than creating them as new. Templates are stored in the $ORACLE_HOME/assistants/dbca/templates directory. Templates are easy to share and can be copied from one machine to another.

Two types of templates exist: seed and nonseed. *Seed templates* have the extension .dbc and include the data files of an existing database. When creating a database using DBCA, if you choose seed template, the database creation is faster because the physical files and schema of the database have already been created. Your database starts as a copy of the seed database, rather than having to be built. DBCA copies the data files to the location you specify and creates a control file and opens the database with RESETLOGS option.

A nonseed template has the extension .dbt and does not include data files. If you choose a nonseed template while creating the database, the database creation assistant builds a fresh database and runs all the scripts on the database. Nonseed database templates have more flexibility in customizing database creation.

For seed database templates, you can change only the following:

- Name of the database
- Destination of the data files
- Number of control files
- Number of redo log groups
- Initialization parameters

Templates can be created from an existing template or an existing database. Cloning of database is performed when you create a template using the From an Existing Database (Structure As Well As Data) option, as shown in Figure 1.9.

Choose the database you want to clone. The database file locations can be maintained or the files can be converted to an OFA structure. See Figure 1.10, which shows this option. When you click Finish, the confirmation window pops up and the template creation is started.

FIGURE 1.10   Location of database related files

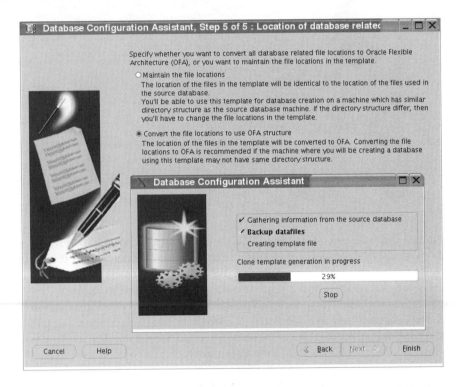

DBCA will shut down the database and start in the mount state to create the template. If the database is already shut down, the DBCA will start it in mount state. At mount state, the data files are copied to the XML file template. When the template creation is completed, two files will exist for seed database templates: the template with a `.dbc` extension and another file with a `.dfb` extension that contains all the database files. The template files are by default stored under the `$ORACLE_HOME/assistants/dbca/templates` directory.

Copy these two files to another host or to a different Oracle home directory if you want to clone the database at a different host or location. To clone the database, start the DBCA, and choose the Create Database option. You will see that the new template you just created is listed along with other Oracle supplied templates. To summarize, the following are the steps needed in cloning a database using DBCA.

1.   Start DBCA and choose Manage Templates.

2. Choose the From an Existing Database (Structure As Well As Data) option.

3. Choose the database to be cloned.

4. If the database is cloned on a different server, copy the .dbc and .dfb file to the remote server.

5. Start DBCA on the destination server and choose the Create Database option.

6. Choose the template you just copied.

Oracle supplies four templates: General Purpose, Transaction Processing, Data Warehouse, and Custom Database. Except for Custom Database, the other three are seed templates (they include data files).

Once you have created the template to clone the database, you can remove it from the templates using the Manage Template screen of the DBCA.

Simplifying Instance Configuration

In Oracle 10g, the instance parameters (also known as *initialization parameters*) are categorized into two groups: basic and advanced. You can achieve most of the database setup and simple tuning with the basic parameters. The following are the basic parameters:

CLUSTER_DATABASE

COMPATIBLE

CONTROL_FILES

DB_BLOCK_SIZE

DB_CREATE_FILE_DEST

DB_CREATE_ONLINE_LOG_DEST_n

DB_DOMAIN

DB_NAME

DB_RECOVERY_FILE_DEST

DB_RECOVERY_FILE_DEST_SIZE

DB_UNIQUE_NAME

INSTANCE_NUMBER

JOB_QUEUE_PROCESSES

LOG_ARCHIVE_DEST_n

LOG_ARCHIVE_DEST_STATE_n

NLS_LANGUAGE

NLS_TERRITORY

OPEN_CURSORS

PGA_AGGREGATE_TARGET

PROCESSES

REMOTE_LISTENER

REMOTE_LOGIN_PASSWORDFILE

ROLLBACK_SEGMENTS

SESSIONS

SGA_TARGET

SHARED_SERVERS

STAR_TRANSFORMATION_ENABLED

UNDO_MANAGEMENT

UNDO_TABLESPACE

> Oracle recommends you set up the database using these basic parameters and use the advanced parameters on an as-needed basis.

You can view/modify the initialization parameters used for the database through the EM Database Control page. A check mark in the Basic column indicates the parameter is basic. A blank in the Dynamic column indicates the parameter is static, meaning you are required to restart a database for the changes to take effect.

> The COMPATIBLE parameter in Oracle 10g is irreversible; once you set it, you cannot change its value to one that is less than a previous value. To lower the value, you need to perform a point-in-time recovery of the database.

Using the Enterprise Manager

Oracle Enterprise Manager (EM) in Oracle 10g is completely revamped, includes many new features, and is very DBA friendly. Unlike the Java-based Oracle 9i EM, the HTML-based 10g EM can be accessed from any computer on the network using a web browser and can be used to manage all databases in your enterprise. EM can have two types of installations: Database Control and Grid Control.

The Oracle Management Repository stores host configurations and database configurations that are collected by the Oracle Management Agent on the hosts. The set of all host configurations and database configurations stored in a Management Repository is known as the *enterprise configuration*.

When you are using Enterprise Manager Database Control, the enterprise configuration includes the host configuration for a single host and the database configuration for the databases installed on that host. When you are using Enterprise Manager Grid Control, the enterprise configuration includes all the host configurations collected and all the database configurations collected by the Oracle management agent on each host.

Every 12 hours, the Oracle Management Agent on the host communicates the database configuration information over HTTPS to the Oracle Management Service, which loads the information to the Oracle Management Repository. The database configuration information you see on the EM is the information from the Oracle Management Repository. The database configuration information collected by the EM includes the following:

- Database and instance names
- Whether the database is running in ARCHIVELOG mode
- Initialization parameter and System Global Area values
- Information on tablespaces and rollback segments
- Attributes of data files, control files, and redo logs
- License and high-availability information

The Oracle Management Agent sends the host configuration information to the Management Repository every 24 hours. The host configuration information collected by the EM includes the following:

- Hardware information

- Operating system information, including patches

- Installed Oracle software, its patch level, and all product information

- Oracle patches installed by the OPatch utility

- Operating system–registered software

The EM Database Control is installed by default when you create a database using the DBCA utility (refer to Figure 1.3). By default, the Database control can be accessed from any web browser using port 5500 of your host. Figure 1.11 shows Enterprise Manager Database Control main page.

FIGURE 1.11   Enterprise Manager Database Control

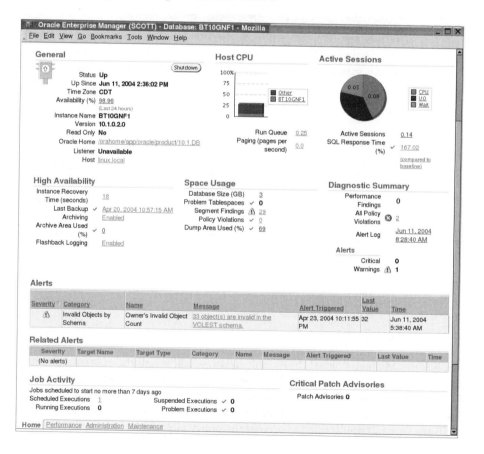

Many organizations have rules to manage the IT infrastructure, which translate into policies for the database administrator. In the next section, we will discuss the policies defined and monitored by EM. We will also discuss how you can use Enterprise Manager to clone Oracle home directories.

Configuring a Database Policy

Oracle 10g Enterprise Manager includes several out-of-the-box policies that are based on the best practices followed in the industry. The policies are categorized into configuration, security, and storage. The policy rules are given different priorities, such as High, Medium, and Informational. Enterprise Manager compares each host and database in the enterprise with the policy rules and identifies the policy violations for each host and database. The main page of the Database Control shows the number of policy violations for the database. When you click the Policy Violations count, all policy violations display, as shown in Figure 1.12.

FIGURE 1.12   Policy violations

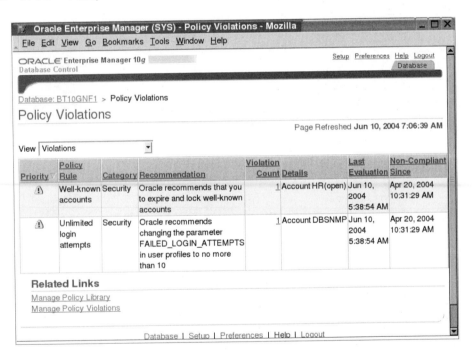

Click the Manage Policy Library link, and you will see all the policies defined for the enterprise. On this page, you can view the priority, category, and description of each policy rule. The Target Type column tells you which infrastructure component the policy is evaluated against; examples are Host, Database, Listener, HTTP Server, and so on. You can disable certain policies if they are not applicable to you or if the policy violation is to be ignored. The Disabled By

column shows the user who disabled the policy rule. Figure 1.13 shows the Manage Policy Library screen.

FIGURE 1.13   Manage Policy Library

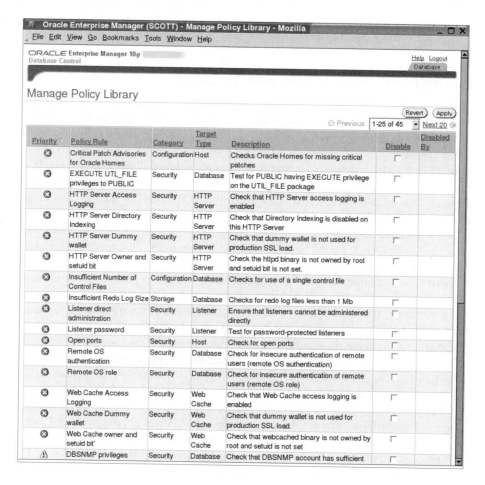

Priority ▽	Policy Rule	Category	Target Type	Description	Disable	Disabled By
⊗	Critical Patch Advisories for Oracle Homes	Configuration	Host	Checks Oracle Homes for missing critical patches	☐	
⊗	EXECUTE UTL_FILE privileges to PUBLIC	Security	Database	Test for PUBLIC having EXECUTE privilege on the UTIL_FILE package	☐	
⊗	HTTP Server Access Logging	Security	HTTP Server	Check that HTTP Server access logging is enabled	☐	
⊗	HTTP Server Directory Indexing	Security	HTTP Server	Check that Directory Indexing is disabled on this HTTP Server	☐	
⊗	HTTP Server Dummy wallet	Security	HTTP Server	Check that dummy wallet is not used for production SSL load.	☐	
⊗	HTTP Server Owner and setuid bit	Security	HTTP Server	Check the httpd binary is not owned by root and setuid bit is not set.	☐	
⊗	Insufficient Number of Control Files	Configuration	Database	Checks for use of a single control file	☐	
⊗	Insufficient Redo Log Size	Storage	Database	Checks for redo log files less than 1 Mb	☐	
⊗	Listener direct administration	Security	Listener	Ensure that listeners cannot be administered directly	☐	
⊗	Listener password	Security	Listener	Test for password-protected listeners	☐	
⊗	Open ports	Security	Host	Check for open ports	☐	
⊗	Remote OS authentication	Security	Database	Check for insecure authentication of remote users (remote OS authentication)	☐	
⊗	Remote OS role	Security	Database	Check for insecure authentication of remote users (remote OS role)	☐	
⊗	Web Cache Access Logging	Security	Web Cache	Check that Web Cache access logging is enabled	☐	
⊗	Web Cache Dummy wallet	Security	Web Cache	Check that dummy wallet is not used for production SSL load.	☐	
⊗	Web Cache owner and setuid bit'	Security	Web Cache	Check that webcached binary is not owned by root and setuid is not set	☐	
⚠	DBSNMP privileges	Security	Database	Check that DBSNMP account has sufficient	☐	

WARNING   When you disable a particular rule, you also delete any violations from the Management Repository that were previously detected for the rule.

Enterprise Manager considers Oracle-critical patches that are not applied to appropriate Oracle software installations (ORACLE_HOME) as policy violations. From the main page of the Database Control, you can see if any such critical patches are to be applied. Enterprise Manager logs into Oracle's support site (Metalink) with the credentials provided by you to check for the critical patch availability. By default this patch search job is set to run once daily.

The jobs Enterprise Manager uses to verify the policy violations and to check for critical patches are maintained by the job system inside Enterprise Manager. You can create, edit, and manage jobs by clicking the Jobs link on the Database Control main page. For more information about Enterprise Manager jobs, click the Help link found on the top-right corner of the page.

Cloning the Oracle Home and Database

You can use the EM to clone Oracle software installations on the same server or different servers. This ensures that all patches and settings in the source and destination are the same. Cloning is faster than installing new software and applying the patches; also it is less error prone.

EM cloning uses the Enterprise Manager job system, which allows you to clone an Oracle home directory to multiple hosts and multiple Oracle home directories in a single cloning job. Enterprise Manager clones only the Oracle home directories that are clonable. An Oracle home directory is clonable when it was installed from an OUI that has built-in cloning support (for example, the Oracle 10g OUI).

From the Database Control main page, navigate to the Maintenance tab. Under Deployments, click the Clone Oracle Home link. Choose the Oracle home directory that you need to clone. In the six steps to set up a cloning job, you specify the source, destination, and when to clone.

Enterprise Manager can also clone a database. The Clone Database link is available under the Deployments The Clone Database tool clones a database instance to an existing Oracle home directory. If you want to create a new Oracle home directory to clone the instance to, use the Clone Oracle Home tool to create a new Oracle home directory and then use the Clone Database tool to clone the instance to that home directory.

Figure 1.14 shows the Review screen of the Clone Database operation. You must follow five steps to set up the clone job. In step 3, you can specify destination file locations. The clone job can be executed immediately or can be set for a future time.

Cloning a database has several advantages. It saves time compared to creating a new database and populating it. The database can be cloned while it is up; the clone tool uses the RMAN to perform the cloning and then applies the archive logs to make it consistent. Note that DBCA cloning does not use RMAN, it copies the template and data files to XML files. EM Clone Database uses RMAN and performs the following operations:

- Backs up each database file and stores it in a working directory
- Transfers each backup file from source to the destination host
- Restores each backup file to the existing destination Oracle home directory
- Recovers the cloned database with saved archived logs
- Opens the cloned database with RESETLOGS

If the source database is in ARCHIVELOG mode, the source database is kept up and running while the cloning operation is performed.

FIGURE 1.14   Clone Database: Review

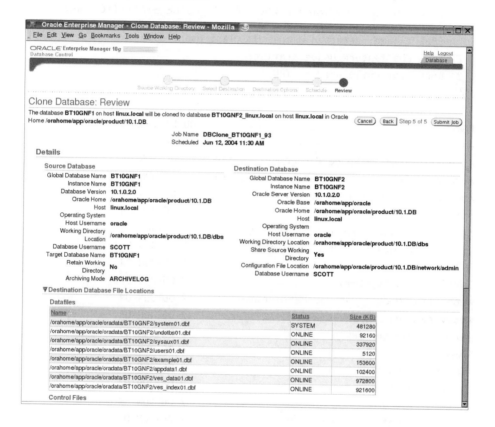

Viewing Database Usage

Oracle 10g keeps track of how the database is being used. The information is collected by the MMON process and is recorded in the Automatic Workload Repository (AWR). AWR is a new feature of Oracle 10g database and is discussed in Chapter 3, " Automating Management." AWR collects the following two types of database usage metrics:

- Database feature usage
- High watermark (HWM) of database attributes

Introducing Database Feature Usage

Database Feature usage of EM shows the usage statistics of various database features such as audit options, data mining, flashback database, MTTR advisor, and so on. You can determine what feature of the database is used how often. You can query the usage information using the DBA_FEATURE_USAGE_STATISTICS view. The NAME column identifies the feature, and the DESCRIPTION column provides a description on what/how the feature is monitored.

Here is a sample query from the DBA_FEATURE_USAGE_STATISTICS view:

```
SQL> SELECT name, detected_usages DU, last_usage_date
  2  FROM dba_feature_usage_statistics
  3  WHERE currently_used = 'TRUE'
SQL> /


NAME                                          DU LAST_USAG
--------------------------------------------- -- ---------
Automatic Segment Space Management (system)    7 06-JUN-04
Automatic Segment Space Management (user)      7 06-JUN-04
Automatic SQL Execution Memory                 7 06-JUN-04
Automatic Undo Management                       7 06-JUN-04
Locally Managed Tablespaces (system)           7 06-JUN-04
Locally Managed Tablespaces (user)             7 06-JUN-04
MTTR Advisor                                   6 06-JUN-04
Partitioning (system)                          7 06-JUN-04
Protection Mode - Maximum Performance          7 06-JUN-04
Recovery Area                                  7 06-JUN-04
Recovery Manager (RMAN)                        6 06-JUN-04
RMAN - Disk Backup                             6 06-JUN-04
SQL Access Advisor                             3 06-JUN-04
Streams (system)                               7 06-JUN-04
Streams (user)                                 7 06-JUN-04
Virtual Private Database (VPD)                  7 06-JUN-04

16 rows selected.

SQL>
```

You may use EM to get the database feature usage. From the EM Database Control page, navigate to the Administration tab, then navigate to Configuration Management, and next click Database Usage Statistics. Click the Feature Usage tab. Figure 1.15 shows the EM screen on the Database Usage Statistics.

FIGURE 1.15   The Database Usage Statistics screen

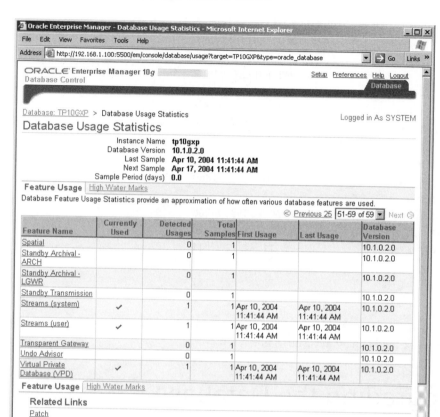

Introducing the HWM of Database Attributes

The Oracle 10g database keeps the usage statistics of various database attributes at its highest usage point. Information includes the size of the largest segment, the number of tables, the number of indexes, the maximum number of partitions per table/index, and the maximum concurrent sessions. You can query the information using the DBA_HIGH_WATER_MARK_STATISTICS view. The NAME column shows the name of the statistic, and the DESCRIPTION column provides a short explanation.

If the high-water statistics and database feature usage statistics are not populated, you can perform execute dbms_stats.gather_database_stats to collect the statistics.

Here is a sample query from the DBA_HIGH_WATER_MARK_STATISTICS view:

```
SQL> SELECT name, highwater, last_value
  2    FROM dba_high_water_mark_statistics;

NAME                     HIGHWATER  LAST_VALUE
--------------------     ---------- ----------
USER_TABLES                    764         764
SEGMENT_SIZE             158334976   158334976
PART_TABLES                      0           0
PART_INDEXES                     0           0
USER_INDEXES                  1400        1400
SESSIONS                         3           3
DB_SIZE                 1553203200  1553203200
DATAFILES                       10          10
TABLESPACES                     11          11
CPU_COUNT                        1           1
QUERY_LENGTH                    87          87
SERVICES                         4           4
```

You may use the EM to get the high-watermark information. In the Database Usage Statistics page, click the High Water Marks link.

Upgrading the Database

You can upgrade your database from one release to a higher release to use the new features and to be in a supported database version. Oracle typically announces the "de-support" date for a database version several months ahead so that you can plan and test the database migration.

Follow the database upgrade process when you're ready to transform your pre–Oracle 10g database to Oracle 10g. Before upgrading the production database, make sure you upgrade the test database and thoroughly check all the application features.

Oracle 10g has several upgrade options.

- Direct upgrade to Oracle 10g using *Database Upgrade Utility (DBUA)*. The DBUA is a GUI tool to upgrade an existing database to Oracle 10g. Using the DBUA is Oracle's preferred method.

- Direct upgrade to Oracle 10g by running scripts (this is a manual upgrade).

- Export/import utilities to copy data to a new Oracle 10g database.

- Copy data to a new Oracle 10g database using SQL tools.

Upgrading a database to Oracle 10*g* typically involves these tasks:

- Identify the supported upgrade options for the database.
- Decide on the method to be used to upgrade the database.
- Verify if the database is ready for direct upgrade.
- Upgrade the database.

In the following sections, we will discuss the supported releases for direct upgrade to Oracle 10*g*, the preupgrade checks provided by Oracle for a smooth trouble-free upgrade, and how to upgrade an Oracle database to Oracle 10*g* using the DBUA (GUI and command line) and using scripts.

 Before upgrading the database to Oracle 10g, check with the application vendor to verify that the application is certified on Oracle 10g database and/or if the vendor has an upgraded application that works with Oracle 10g.

Introducing Upgrade-Supported Releases

Oracle 10*g* supports the direct upgrade of database from the following releases:

- Oracle 8 Release 8.0.6
- Oracle 8*i* Release 8.1.7
- Oracle 9*i* Release 1 – 9.0.1
- Oracle 9*i* Release 2 – 9.2.0

For all other database releases, you must upgrade the database to an upgrade-supported release using the methods suggested in that release before using the direct upgrade method. You have some restrictions, though. To upgrade any database prior to release 8.0.6, you must upgrade the database to 8.0.6 first and then use the DBUA utility (or manual upgrade) to upgrade to Oracle 10*g*. To upgrade an 8.1.5 or 8.1.6 database to Oracle 10*g*, you must first upgrade the database to Oracle 8*i* 8.1.7. To upgrade a 7.3.4 database, first upgrade to 9.2.0 and then to Oracle 10*g*.

The upgrade path you choose and the steps involved depend on the release of the database you are upgrading. For smaller databases in non-upgrade-supported releases (older than 8.0.6, or 8.1.5, or 8.1.6), it may be faster to perform an export/import rather than going through two upgrade processes.

Upgrading a database using the export/import method has the following advantages and disadvantages:

- How long the upgrade process takes depends on the size of the database.
- A new database for Oracle 10*g* needs to be created, which makes the current database a backup archive. Therefore, you need to double the amount of disk space required.
- The import process can defragment data that would improve performance. It also gives you an opportunity to create tablespaces using the new features of Oracle 10*g* database.

When installing Oracle 10*g* software, the OUI provides an option to invoke the DBUA if it finds any existing Oracle database in /var/opt/oracle/oratab, in /etc/oratab, or in the Windows Registry. The DBUA also can be invoked as a stand-alone tool.

After upgrading a database, its Oracle home directory changes to the new Oracle 10*g* home directory. DBUA automatically updates the oratab file with the right Oracle home directory. You must use the new Oracle home directory to start and stop the database.

Validating the Database Before Upgrade

Oracle 10*g* provides a utility script—utlu101i.sql—to perform preupgrade validation on the database to be upgraded. The DBUA automatically runs this tool (and takes corrective action) as part of the upgrade process. You can find the SQL script in the administration scripts directory ($ORACLE_HOME/rdbms/admin).

The utlu101i.sql script needs to be run as SYSDBA before you plan on performing a manual upgrade. It is preferred to copy this script to a temporary folder and run it after spooling the output to a file. You must run this script on the database to be upgraded. The script performs the following tasks:

- Checks database compatibility (the COMPATIBLE parameter must be set to 9.2.0 before upgrade)
- Verifies the redo log file size is at least 4MB
- Estimates time for upgrade
- Looks for obsolete, renamed, and special parameters
- Applies new values for certain upgrade parameters
- Finds all the components installed
- Finds the default tablespace for each database component schema
- Finds tablespace size estimates
- If the SYSAUX tablespace already exists, warns the user the properties may not be right and displays the required properties of the SYSAUX tablespace SYSAUX tablespace is covered in depth in Chapter 4.
- Checks the installed database options
- Checks the database character set and national character set are supported in Oracle 10*g*.

If the database version is not one that supports a direct upgrade, an error displays and the script terminates.

The following output shows the result of executing the `utlu101i.sql` script on an Oracle *9i* Release 2 database under Linux; the installation home for `ora0109` database is `/orahome/app/oracle/product/9.2.0`:

```
linux:oracle>pwd
/home/oracle/temp
linux:oracle>echo $ORACLE_HOME
/orahome/app/oracle/product/9.2.0
linux:oracle>echo $ORACLE_SID
ora0109
linux:oracle>sqlplus '/ as sysdba'

SQL*Plus: Release 9.2.0.1.0 - Production on Fri Mar 19Copyright (c) 1982, 2002,
Oracle Corporation.
All rights reserved.
Connected to:
Oracle9i Enterprise Edition Release 9.2.0.1.0 - Production
With the Partitioning and Oracle Data Mining options
JServer Release 9.2.0.1.0 - Production

sys@ORA0109> spool ora0109upgcheck.lst
sys@ORA0109> @utlu101i.sql
Oracle Database 10.1 Upgrade Information Tool.
***********************************************************
Database:
---------
--> name: ORA0109
--> version: 9.2.0.1.0
--> compatibility: 9.2.0.0.0
.
***********************************************************
Logfiles: [make adjustments in the current environment]
---------------------------------------------------
-- The existing log files are adequate.
   No changes are required.
.
***********************************************************
Tablespaces: [make adjustments in the current environment]
----------------------------------------------------------
--> SYSTEM tablespace is adequate for the upgrade.
.... owner: SYS
.... minimum required size: 501 MB
--> DRSYS tablespace is adequate for the upgrade.
```

```
.... owner: CTXSYS
.... minimum required size: 10 MB
--> ODM tablespace is adequate for the upgrade.
.... owner: ODM
.... minimum required size: 9 MB
--> XDB tablespace is adequate for the upgrade.
.... owner: XDB
.... minimum required size: 48 MB
.
*****************************************************************Options: [present in
existing database]
------------------------------------
--> Partitioning
--> Spatial
--> Oracle Data Mining
WARNING: Listed option(s) must be installed with
         Oracle Database 10.1
.
*****************************************************************Update Parameters:
[Update Oracle Database 10.1 init.ora or spfile]
-----------------------------------------------------WARNING: --> "shared_
pool_size" needs to be increased to
   at least "150944944"
WARNING: --> "pga_aggregate_target" needs to be increased
   to at least "25165824"
--> "large_pool_size" is already at "16777216" calculated
   new value is"16777216"
--> "java_pool_size" is already at "83886080" calculated
 new value is "83886080"
.
*****************************************************************Deprecated Parameters:
[Update Oracle Database 10.1 init.ora or spfile]
----------------------------------------------------------- No deprecated
parameters found. No changes required.
.
*****************************************************************Obsolete Parameters:
[Update Oracle Database 10.1 init.ora or spfile]
-----------------------------------------------------------> "hash_join_enabled"
.
*****************************************************************Components: [The
following database components will be
upgraded or installed]
```

```
--------------------------------------------------------> Oracle Catalog
Views           [upgrade]  VALID
--> Oracle Packages and Types     [upgrade]   VALID
--> JServer JAVA Virtual Machine [upgrade]   VALID
...The 'JServer JAVA Virtual Machine' JAccelerator(NCOMP)
...is required to be installed from the 10g Companion CD.
...
--> Oracle XDK for Java          [upgrade]   VALID
--> Oracle Java Packages         [upgrade]   VALID
--> Oracle XML Database          [upgrade]   VALID
--> Oracle Workspace Manager     [upgrade]   VALID
--> Oracle Data Mining           [upgrade]
--> Oracle interMedia            [upgrade]
...The 'Oracle interMedia Image Accelerator' is
...required to be installed from the 10g Companion CD.
...
--> Spatial                      [upgrade]
--> Oracle Text                  [upgrade]   VALID
--> Oracle Ultra Search          [upgrade]   VALID
--> Oracle Label Security        [upgrade]   VALID
  .
*************************************************************SYSAUX Tablespace:
[Create tablespace in Oracle
Database 10.1 environment]
-------------------------------------------------------> New "SYSAUX"
tablespace
.... minimum required size for database upgrade: 500 MB
Please create the new SYSAUX Tablespace AFTER the Oracle
 Database  10.1 server is started and BEFORE you invoke
the upgrade script.
  .
*************************************************************Oracle Database 10g:
Changes in Default Behavior
-------------------------------------------------
This page describes some of the changes in the behavior
of Oracle Database 10g from that of previous releases.
In some cases the default values of some parameters have
changed.  In other cases new behaviors/requirements have
been introduced that may affect current scripts or
applications. More detailed information is in the
documentation.
```

SQL OPTIMIZER
The Cost Based Optimizer (CBO) is now enabled by default.
* Rule-based optimization is not supported in 10g (setting
OPTIMIZER_MODE to RULE or CHOOSE is not supported). See Chapter
12, "Introduction to the Optimizer," in Oracle Database
Performance Tuning Guide.
* Collection of optimizer statistics is now performed by
default, automatically for all schemas (including SYS),
for pre-existing databases upgraded to 10g, and for newly
created 10g databases.
Gathering optimizer statistics on stale objects is
scheduled by default to occur daily during the maintenance
window. See Chapter 15, "Managing Optimizer Statistics"
in Oracle Performance Tuning Guide.
* See the Oracle Database Upgrade Guide for changes in
behavior for the COMPUTE STATISTICS clause of
CREATE INDEX, and for behavior changes in
SKIP_UNUSABLE_INDEXES.

UPGRADE/DOWNGRADE
* After upgrading to 10g, the minimum supported release
to downgrade to is Oracle 9i R2 release 9.2.0.3 (or later)
and the minimum value for COMPATIBLE is 9.2.0. The only
supported downgrade path is for those users who have kept
COMPATIBLE=9.2.0 and have an installed 9i R2 (release
9.2.0.3 or later) executable. Users upgrading to 10g from
prior releases (such as Oracle 8, Oracle 8i or 9iR1)
cannot downgrade to 9i R2 unless they first install 9i R2.
When upgrading to10g, by default the database will remain
at 9i R2 file format compatibility, so the on disk
structures that 10g writes are compatible with 9i R2
structures; this makes it possible to downgrade to
9i R2. Once file format compatibility has been explicitly
advanced to 10g (using COMPATIBLE=10.x.x), it is no longer
possible to downgrade.
See the Oracle Database Upgrade Guide.
* A SYSAUX tablespace is created upon upgrade to 10g.
The SYSAUX tablespace serves as an auxiliary tablespace
to the SYSTEM tablespace. Because it is the default

tablespace for many Oracle features and products that
previously required their own tablespaces, it reduces
the number of tablespaces required by Oracle that you,
as a DBA, must maintain.

MANAGEABILITY
* Database performance statistics are now collected by the
Automatic Workload Repository (AWR) database component,
automatically upon upgrade to 10g and also for newly
created 10g databases. This data is stored in the SYSAUX
tablespace, and is used by the database for automatic
generation of performance recommendations. See Chapter 5,
"Automatic Performance Statistics" in the Oracle Database
Performance Tuning Guide.
* If you currently use Statspack for performance data
gathering, see section 1. of the Statspack readme
(spdoc.txt in the RDBMS ADMIN directory) for directions
on using Statspack in 10g to avoid conflict with the AWR.

MEMORY
* Automatic PGA Memory Management is now enabled by
default (unless PGA_AGGREGATE_TARGET is explicitly set
to 0 or WORKAREA_SIZE_POLICY is explicitly set to MANUAL).
PGA_AGGREGATE_TARGET is defaulted to 20% of the SGA size,
Unless explicitly set. Oracle recommends tuning the value
of PGA_AGGREGATE_TARGET after upgrading. See Chapter 14
of the Oracle Database Performance Tuning Guide.
* Previously, the number of SQL cursors cached by PL/SQL
was determined by OPEN_CURSORS. In 10g, the number of
cursors cached is determined by SESSION_CACHED_CURSORS.
See the Oracle Database Reference manual.
* SHARED_POOL_SIZE must increase to include the space
needed for shared pool overhead.
* The default value of DB_BLOCK_SIZE is operating system
specific, but is typically 8KB (was typically 2KB in
previous releases).

TRANSACTION/SPACE
* Dropped objects are now moved to the recycle bin, where

the space is only reused when it is needed. This allows
'undropping' a table using the FLASHBACK DROP feature.
See Chapter 14 of the Oracle Database Administrator's
Guide.
* Auto tuning undo retention is on by default. For more
information, see Chapter 10, "Managing the Undo
Tablespace," in the Oracle Database Administrator's Guide.

CREATE DATABASE
* In addition to the SYSTEM tablespace, a SYSAUX
tablespace is always created at database creation, and
upon upgrade to 10g. The SYSAUX tablespace serves as an
auxiliary tablespace to the SYSTEM tablespace. Because it
is the default tablespace for many Oracle features and
products that previously required their own tablespaces,
it reduces the number of tablespaces required by
Oracle that you, as a DBA, must maintain. See Chapter 2,
"Creating a Database," in the Oracle Database
Administrator's Guide.
* In 10g, by default all new databases are created with
10g file format compatibility. This means you can
immediately use all the 10g features. Once a database
uses 10g compatible file formats, it is not possible to
downgrade this database to prior releases. Minimum and
default logfile sizes are larger. Minimum is now 4 MB,
default is 50MB, unless you are using Oracle Managed
Files (OMF) when it is 100 MB.

PL/SQL procedure successfully completed.

sys@ORA0109> spool off

   We showed the result in its entirety because of the useful tips that follow the checks and
warnings. Please read them. We copied the utlu101i.sql script from the Oracle 10g $ORACLE_
HOME/rdbms/admin directory to the /home/oracle/temp directory.

Before upgrading the database, make sure you have a good backup. You have
the option to back up the database while using the DBUA.

Performing the Upgrade

You can perform a direct upgrade of an Oracle database to Oracle 10*g* by using Oracle's GUI interface, the DBUA, or by running scripts using the command-line SQL*Plus. Oracle 10*g* has a simplified upgrade procedure. In the earlier releases, you were supposed to run different scripts based on the database options. In Oracle 10*g*, the components to be upgraded are determined automatically and are executed in the correct dependency order. Oracle 10*g* has one script upgrade, which upgrades all the database components.

Oracle uses the DBMS_REGISTRY package to determine the objects to be upgraded. In Oracle 10*g*, the database and all the components have been integrated into the cmpdbmig.sql script. The cmpdbmig.sql script determines which components are in the database by performing specific callouts to the component REGISTRY.

The versions of Oracle prior to Oracle 9*i* Release 2 do not have a component REGISTRY. When upgrading from the older versions of Oracle, the upgrade automatically creates and populates the component REGISTRY. You can query the components using the DBA_REGISTRY view.

The following components are identified automatically by the upgrade process and are upgraded or installed (if a required component):

- Oracle Database Catalog Views
- Oracle Database Packages and Types
- JServer Java Virtual Machine
- Oracle Database Java Packages
- Oracle XDK
- Oracle Real Application Clusters
- Oracle Workspace Manager
- Oracle interMedia
- Oracle XML Database
- OLAP Analytic Workspace
- Oracle OLAP API
- OLAP Catalog
- Oracle Text
- Spatial
- Oracle Data Mining
- Oracle Label Security
- Messaging Gateway

The next section describes the direct database upgrade performed by using the DBUA.

Using the DBUA

The DBUA will be invoked by the OUI if you choose the Upgrade Database option when first installing the Oracle 10g software. On Unix platforms, you can invoke the DBUA by using the command dbua. On Windows platforms, you can invoke the DBUA by choosing Start ➤ Program Files ➤ Oracle Configuration and Migration Tools ➤ Database Upgrade Assistant.

The upgrade process is automated by DBUA, including the preupgrade steps. The following are some of the DBUA features and their advantages:

- Proceeds with upgrade only if the selected database release is supported for direct upgrade.
- Runs the preupgrade validation and identifies the options to be upgraded. It performs the necessary adjustments.
- Checks for disk space and tablespace requirements.
- Updates obsolete initialization parameters.
- Includes an option to back up the database prior to upgrade.
- Shows upgrade progress and writes detailed traces and log files.
- Disables archiving of the database during upgrade.
- Includes an option to configure the database with the EM.
- Includes an option to recompile invalid objects after upgrade; on multiCPU systems, the recompilation happens in parallel.
- Shows summary page prior to upgrade and after the upgrade.
- Includes an HTML report of upgrade summary.
- Able to upgrade all nodes of a database in RAC.
- Supports silent mode upgrade with a single command line.

To upgrade the database with the DBUA, follow these steps:

1. Choose the database to be upgraded from the list. You can choose only one database for upgrade at one time, and the database must be running.

2. The SYSAUX tablespace will be created in the database. Specify the file location and size of this tablespace. The minimum recommended size is 500MB. You cannot change other properties of the SYSAUX tablespace.

3. Choose if you would like to recompile all the invalid objects at the end of upgrade. During the upgrade, it is common that many of the objects will become invalid. By selecting this option, the DBUA runs the utlrp.sql script. If there are multiple CPUs on the server, an additional screen displays to change the degree of parallelism during recompile. This can speed up the recompilation time.

4. Choose the option to back up the database. If the backup is performed by the DBUA, it writes the backup files to a directory on the server, uncompressed. The DBUA also creates

a script to restore the database. The script is named <*dbname*>BACK.BAT on Windows and <*dbname*>back.sh on Unix.

5. Chose the option to configure the database with the EM and schedule daily backups.

6. Specify a location and size of the flash recovery area. This screen displays only if you choose to back up the database using the EM in the previous screen.

7. Specify passwords for the EM administrative accounts: SYSMAN and DBSNMP.

8. The summary of the upgrade displays (see Figure 1.16). Verify all the information, especially the database name, Oracle home directories (source and target), and version. The summary page also shows the components to be upgraded, the parameter changes, and the estimated upgrade time (excluding recompiling objects). The upgrade starts as soon as you click the Finish button. No one should connect to the database until the upgrade is completed.

Figure 1.17 shows the DBUA Progress screen. You can stop the upgrade at any time, but you may have to restore the database from the backup.

FIGURE 1.16   The DBUA: Summary screen

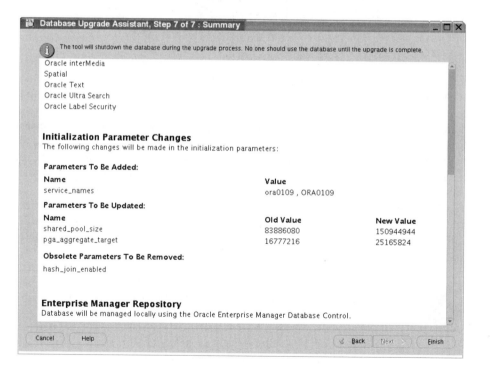

FIGURE 1.17   The DBUA: Progress screen

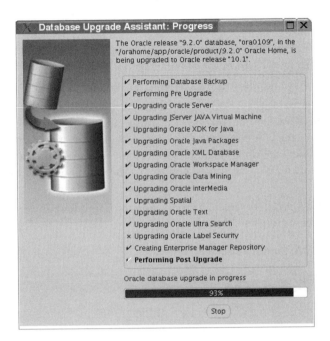

After the upgrade is completed, the upgrade results display on the DBUA Upgrade Results screen (see Figure 1.18). You are also given the option to change passwords and to restore the database. All the user accounts created by the upgrade process are locked for security reasons. Click the Configure Database Parameters button to assign new password and to unlock the accounts. If the DBUA is used to back up the database, restoring will put back the original database and the parameters. If you used other tools to back up the database, the DBUA restores only the original database settings (parameters) without the data files.

DBUA removes the database entry from the `listener.ora` file of the old database and adds it to the `listener.ora` file of the new database. Both listeners are reloaded automatically. If you have only the Oracle 10g listener, the Oracle home value is adjusted to reflect the upgrade.

Oracle 10g collects optimizer statistics for all the dictionary tables that lack statistics during upgrade. You can minimize the database upgrade downtime if you collect statistics on tables owned by SYS, SYSTEM, DBSNMP, and OUTLN and all other system schema using exec `dbms_stats.gather_schema_stats('<schema>'`, `method_opt => 'FOR ALL COLUMNS SIZE AUTO'`, `cascade => TRUE)` prior to the upgrade.

FIGURE 1.18   The DBUA: Upgrade Results screen

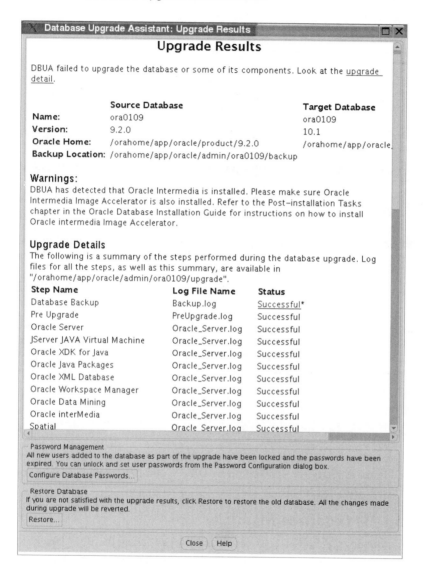

Using the DBUA Command Line

You can invoke the DBUA in command-line mode. You can specify several parameters with the command line dbua. The command line is invoked if you specify any parameter with the command dbua. dbua –h shows the help information.

Table 1.1 lists the command-line **dbua** parameters and their purpose.

TABLE 1.1   DBUA Command-Line Parameters

Parameter	Purpose
-dbName	Name of the database to be upgraded. This is the only mandatory argument.
-silent	Performs the upgrade in silent mode.
-disableUpgradeScriptLogging	Use this parameter to disable logging during upgrading.
-backupLocation	Name of the directory where the database should be backed up before upgrading.
-postUpgradeScripts	Comma-separated names of files that need to run after the upgrade. Specify full path along with file names.
-initParam	Specify comma-separated values of parameters to start up the database for upgrade.
-emConfiguration	Specify how you want the database to be managed: database configuration or grid configuration. Use dbua -h to see the other -emConfiguration arguments such as passwords.

For example,

```
dbua -silent -dbName ORA9
```

will upgrade the ORA9 database to Oracle 10g, detailed logging information will be written to log files, the database will not be backed up by DBUA, and the database will be configured to use the Enterprise Manager locally.

Upgrading the Database Manually

You can manually upgrade the database by running scripts using the SQL*Plus utility. Though manual upgrade provides you with more control, the process is error prone, involves more work, and could take more time.

To manually upgrade the database, follow these steps:

1. Connect to the database to be upgraded and run utlu101i.sql to determine the preupgrade tasks to be completed.

2. Resize the redo log files if they are smaller than 4 MB.

3. Adjust the size of the tablespaces where the dictionary objects are stored.

4. Perform a cold backup of the database.

5. Shut down the database (do not perform a SHUTDOWN ABORT; perform only SHUTDOWN IMMEDIATE or SHUTDOWN NORMAL). On Windows you will have to do NET STOP, ORADIM - DELETE from the old Oracle home directory and ORADIM -NEW from the new Oracle 10*g* home directory.

6. Copy the parameter file (initDB.ora or spfileDB.ora) and password file from the old Oracle home directory to the Oracle 10*g* Oracle home directory. The default location for parameter file is $ORACLE_HOME/dbs on Unix platforms and ORACLE_HOME\database on Windows. Adjust the following parameters:

   - Adjust the COMPATIBLE parameter; the minimum value required is 9.2.0 for the upgrade. If you set this to 10.0, you will never be able to downgrade the database to 9*i*.

   - Update the initialization parameters. You must remove obsolete parameters.

   - Set the DB_DOMAIN parameter properly.

   - Make sure memory parameters have at least the minimum size required for upgrade: SHARED_POOL_SIZE (96MB for 32-bit platforms, 144MB for 64-bit), PGA_AGGREGATE_ TARGET (24MB), JAVA_POOL_SIZE (48MB), and LARGE_POOL_SIZE (8MB). Use the sizes recommended by the preinstall verification utility.

7. Make sure all the environment variables are set to correctly reference the Oracle 10*g* Oracle home. On Unix, verify ORACLE_HOME, PATH, ORA_NLS33, and LD_LIBRARY_PATH.

8. Use SQL*Plus, and connect to the database using the SYSDBA privilege. Start the instance by using the STARTUP UPGRADE mode.

9. Create the SYSAUX tablespace with the following attributes:

   - online

   - permanent

   - read write

   - extent management local

   - segment space management auto

   The syntax could be as follows:

```
CREATE TALESPACE sysaux
DATAFILE '/ora01/oradata/OR0109/sysaux.dbf' SIZE 500M
EXTENT MANAGEMENT LOCAL
SEGMENT SPACE MANAGEMENT AUTO;
```

10. Run the upgrade script from the $ORACLE_HOME/rdbms/admin directory. Based on the version of the old database, the name of the upgrade script varies. The following lists the old release and the upgrade script name:

Database Version	Script to Run
8.0.6	u0800060.sql
8.1.7	u0801070.sql
9.0.1	u0900010.sql
9.2.0	u0902000.sql

For example, to upgrade an Oracle 8.1.7 database to Oracle 10g, you must run u0801070.sql.

```
SQL> spool ora8i7upg.log
SQL> @?/rdbms/admin/u0801070.sql
SQL> spool off
```

If you get any errors during the upgrade script execution, reexecute the script after fixing the error. The postupgrade status utility—utlu101s.sql—gives the name of specific script to run to fix the failed component.

11. Run the utlu101s.sql utility with the TEXT option. It queries the DBA_SERVER_REGISTRY to determine upgrade status and provides information about invalid or incorrect component upgrades. It also provides names of scripts to rerun to fix the errors.

Here is an example (output truncated to fit in single line):

```
sys@ORA0109> @?/rdbms/admin/utlu101s.sql TEXT


PL/SQL procedure successfully completed.


Oracle Database 10.1 Upgrade Status Tool 19-MAR-2004
  --> Oracle Database Catalog Views      Normal successful
  --> Oracle Database Packages and Types Normal successful
  --> JServer JAVA Virtual Machine       Normal successful
  --> Oracle XDK                         Normal successful
  --> Oracle Database Java Packages      Normal successful
  --> Oracle XML Database                Normal successful
  --> Oracle Workspace Manager           Normal successful
  --> Oracle Data Mining                 Normal successful
  --> Oracle interMedia                  Normal successful
  --> Spatial                            Normal successful
```

```
--> Oracle Text                      Normal successful
--> Oracle Ultra Search              Normal successful
--> Oracle Label Security            Problem detected
WARNING:----> required option not installed
----> component not upgraded

PL/SQL procedure successfully completed.


sys@ORA0109>
```

12. Shut down and restart the instance to reinitialize the system parameters for normal operation. The restart also performs Oracle 10g database initialization for JServer Java Virtual Machine and other components. Perform a clean shutdown (SHUTDOWN IMMEDIATE); starting the instance flushes all caches, clears buffers, and performs other housekeeping activities. This is an important step to ensure the integrity and consistency of the upgraded database.

13. Run the utlrp.sql script to recompile all invalid objects.

14. Update the listener.ora file with the new database information.

15. Back up the database.

On Unix environments, to connect to the database as SYSDBA, the single quotes are no longer required in Oracle 10g. In the prior releases you had to specify sqlplus '/ as sysdba' whereas in Oracle 10g sqlplus / as sysdba will work.

Using the *STARTUP UPGRADE* Option

To upgrade the database to Oracle 10g, you must start the instance with the STARTUP UPGRADE option (introduced in Oracle 9i Release 2). If you try to start the database in any other mode, you will get an error. This mode automatically handles certain system parameter values for the upgrade. Also, this option suppresses the ORA-00942 error for the DROP TABLE statements in the upgrade script. So when reviewing for errors, you will see only genuine errors in the log file. For successful upgrade, you should not see any ORA- or PLS- errors in the log file. Here is an example of logging into the database using SQL*Plus with the SYSDBA privilege and starting up using the STARTUP UPGRADE method:

```
linux:oracle>sqlplus / as sysdba
SQL*Plus: Release 10.1.0.2.0 - Production on Fri Jun 11 Copyright (c) 1982,
2004, Oracle.  All rights reserved.
Connected to an idle instance.
```

```
SQL> startup upgrade
ORACLE instance started.

Total System Global Area   197132288 bytes
Fixed Size                    778076 bytes
Variable Size              162537636 bytes
Database Buffers            33554432 bytes
Redo Buffers                  262144 bytes
Database mounted.
Database opened.
SQL>
```

Downgrading Your Database

Sometimes it may be necessary to downgrade a database to its previous release because of issues with an application in the new database. Though the safe method is to restore from the backup taken prior to the upgrade, Oracle provides an option to downgrade the database to Oracle 9*i* Release 2. After upgrading the database to Oracle 10g release 1, the only supported downgrade option is downgrading to Oracle 9*i* Release 2. If you have set the COMPATIBLE parameter to 10.0 or higher, you will not be able to downgrade the database.

To downgrade the database, follow these steps:

1. Run d0902000.sql script from the Oracle 10g Oracle home directory after starting the instance using the STARTUP DOWNGRADE option.

2. Shut down the database, and start it from the Oracle 9*i* Release 2 home directory after adjusting the system parameters.

3. Connect to the database as SYSDBA, and start using the STARTUP MIGRATE option. Run catrelod.sql to reinstall the Oracle 9*i* Release 2 dictionary objects.

4. Perform a SHUTDOWN IMMEDIATE, and start the database in normal mode.

 **Real World Scenario**

Upgrading Oracle 8*i* Database to Oracle 10g

We have an Oracle 8.1.7 database that is couple of terabytes big. Since the database is still in 8.1.7 and its support ends by the end of 2004, we have to upgrade the database to a higher release. We chose to upgrade to 10g, skipping 9*i* to avoid another major upgrade and the time spent on testing. Since the application is homegrown, we have to perform thorough testing.

The only practical upgrade option for this database to upgrade to Oracle 10*g* is to use the direct method. The other option—export/import—would require several days and is prone to errors when dealing with a database of this size.

Since we have decided on the upgrade path, the first step is to run the `utlu101i.sql` script to see what items should be fixed in the database for a successful upgrade. The following is the advice from the preupgrade check utility where changes need to be made:

```
Database:
---------
--> name: DBNAME
--> version: 8.1.7.4.0
--> compatibility: 8.1.7
WARNING: Database compatibility must be set to 9.2.0 prior to
 upgrade.
 .
 ****************************************************************
Options: [present in existing database]
--------------------------------------
--> Partitioning
WARNING: Listed option(s) must be installed with Oracle
 Database 10.1
 .
 ****************************************************************
Update Parameters: [Update Oracle Database 10.1 init.ora or
spfile]
----------------------------------------------------------WARNING: -->
"shared_pool_size" needs to be increased to at
          least "440688496"
WARNING: --> "pga_aggregate_target" is not currently defined
          and needs a value of at least "25165824"
--> "large_pool_size" is already at "104857600" calculated
          new value is "104857600"
WARNING: --> "java_pool_size" needs to be increased to at
          least "50331648"
 ****************************************************************
Obsolete Parameters: [Update Oracle Database 10.1 init.ora or
spfile]
---------------------------------------------------------->
"db_block_lru_latches"
--> "max_rollback_segments"
--> "job_queue_interval"
--> "optimizer_max_permutations"
--> "fast_start_io_target"
--> "max_enabled_roles"
```

```
--> "log_archive_start"
.
.
*******************************************************Components: [The fol-
lowing database components will be
 upgraded or installed]
----------------------------------------------------------> Oracle Catalog
Views          [upgrade]
--> Oracle Packages and Types    [upgrade]
--> JServer JAVA Virtual Machine [upgrade]
...The 'JServer JAVA Virtual Machine' JAccelerator (NCOMP)
...is required to be installed from the 10g Companion CD.
...
--> Oracle XDK for Java          [upgrade]
--> Oracle Java Packages         [install]
.
.
**************************************************************
```

The first warning is the compatibility, which we can fix only during the upgrade. In fact, we let the DBUA fix all the parameter changes required in the upgraded Oracle 10*g* database. Since the tablespace sizes are adequate, the item we need to be working on is to install the JServer Java Virtual Machine from the companion CD.

We performed a backup and initiated the DBUA utility to upgrade the database after installing the JServer JVM component. This upgrade was tested successfully in the test database. Now the developers and users are testing the application. Our testing typically takes three months, so we hope we will be upgrading the production database to Oracle 10*g* soon.

Summary

The Oracle Universal Installer (OUI) is enhanced to include the entire new Oracle 10g database feature install. You perform the installation of the Oracle database software and the most common components from one CD. The companion CD includes HTTP Server and HTML DB along with other database products. The Oracle client is shipped in a separate CD.

For creating preconfigured database during software install, the OUI invokes the DBCA in a noninteractive mode. For custom databases, the DBCA is invoked interactively. The OUI and the DBCA include several options to capture user input for all the new features of the Oracle 10g database. You can also configure the database management using the Database Control (local) or Grid Control (centralized management).

The OUI and the DBCA have screens to capture the installation options for the new Oracle 10*g* features. The database data files can be using file system, raw devices, or ASM storage. Also, you can set up database management locally or using central management.

You can use the DBCA to clone a database. You do this by creating a template with structure and data. Enterprise Manager has several new features and has a new look in Oracle 10*g*. EM comes with several out-of-the-box policy rules for monitoring the enterprise. You can see the policy violations from the Database Control main page.

Oracle 10*g* keeps track of the database feature usage and database high-watermark usage. You can query the information from the data dictionary or using EM. The COMPATIBLE database parameter is irreversible in Oracle 10*g*; it cannot be set to a value less than a previous value. The minimum value is 9.2.0.

Upgrading a database to Oracle 10*g* is simplified by using the DBUA. DBUA does the pre-install tasks, backs up the database, adjusts parameters, upgrades the database, does the post-upgrade status, and recompiles all the invalid objects. Directly upgrading the database is possible from the 9.2.0, 9.0.1, 8.1.7, and 8.0.6 databases. For other releases, you must first upgrade to an intermediate release and then upgrade to Oracle 10*g* or use other methods of the upgrade such as export/import.

Manually upgrading the database is made simple by using the one-script upgrade method. The database identifies all the components to be upgraded and performs the upgrade. The postupgrade status utility gives the status of all the components of the database and, if any component is invalid, provides the name of the script to run to fix the component.

The SYSAUX tablespace is mandatory in all Oracle 10*g* databases. The DBUA creates this as part of the upgrade. If you are performing a manual upgrade, you must create this tablespace. You must start the database in the STARTUP UPGRADE mode to begin the database upgrade.

Once the database is upgraded to Oracle 10*g*, it can be downgraded only to Oracle 9*i* Release 2. If the COMPATIBLE parameter was set to 10.0 or higher, a database downgrade is not possible.

Exam Essentials

Understand the new features of Oracle 10*g* database supported by the Oracle Universal Installer. Be familiar with the performance enhancements and preinstallation checks.

Understand the features of the Database Configuration Assistant. Learn to install the sample schema, when and how the DBCA is invoked by the OUI, and how to invoke the DBCA in stand-alone mode.

Familiarize with the Database Control main pages Know where to get the database feature usage and high-watermark usage.

Understand the policy violations pages Know the major links and their purpose on the Database Control Administration, Maintenance and Performance pages.

Learn which versions of Oracle can be upgraded directly to Oracle 10g, and learn the upgrade path for other versions.   Oracle supports direct upgrade of the database to the Oracle 10g from 8.0.6, 8.1.7, 9.0.1, and 9.2.0 versions. For other database versions, you need to first upgrade to one of these releases before upgrading to Oracle 10g.

Remember the scripts to perform preupgrade check and postupgrade validation.   Know the script to run on pre–Oracle 10g databases to check what needs be done before upgrade. Understand the results of the postupgrade utility script. Remember the script names.

Understand the advantages of using the Database Upgrade Assistant to upgrade a database rather than performing a manual upgrade.   Using the DBUA automates the upgrade process. The DBUA can back up the database, perform the preupgrade checks and make changes, and upgrade the database with detailed log files.

Familiarize yourself with the steps involved in upgrading a database to Oracle 10g manually. Learn the scripts to perform the database checks (preupgrade and postupgrade), and learn the script to perform the upgrade based on the version of the database.

Understand cloning a database using DBCA   Know the steps involved in cloning a database using DBCA and how to create templates.

Review Questions

1. On most platforms, to install Oracle 9*i* software, you needed three installation CDs. How many CDs are required for Oracle 10*g* installation?

   A. 4

   B. 3

   C. 2

   D. 1

2. Of the following options, which is not true when installing Oracle 10*g*?

   A. The operating system must be certified.

   B. A product key must be entered and activated.

   C. 512MB RAM is required for each database instance with Database Control

   D. Enough swap space available

3. Which component can be installed from the Oracle 10*g* database installation CD?

   A. Legato Single Server Version

   B. Database examples

   C. Oracle Enterprise Manager Database Control

   D. Oracle Database Client

4. When using the DBCA GUI tool to create a database, which feature is supported?

   A. Databases that use ASM storage

   B. Databases that need to be controlled using the Enterprise Manager Central Management Control

   C. Real Application Cluster database

   D. All of the above

5. Identify the statement that is true regarding cloning a database using DBCA.

   A. When cloning a database, the source database must not be started.

   B. When cloning a database, the source database must be started.

   C. Cloning using the DBCA creates a copy of the database data files under templates and can be used for creating any number of cloned databases at any time.

   D. When cloning a database to more than one destination, the source database must remain in the mount state until all cloning operations are completed.

6. When upgrading a database to Oracle 10g, which of the following options are true?

  A. Any version of Oracle 8, Oracle 8i, or Oracle 9i database can be upgraded to Oracle 10g using the DBUA.

  B. Only the versions 8.0.6, 8.1.7, 9.0.1, and 9.2.0 can be upgraded to Oracle 10g.

  C. Once upgraded to Oracle 10g, the database can be downgraded only to Oracle 9i 9.2.0.

  D. The upgraded database can be downgraded to its original version by using the DBUA if no Oracle 10g–related feature is implemented in the database.

7. Which option in the database is used to monitor the database feature usage?

  A. Automatic Workload Repository

  B. Enterprise Manager Database Control

  C. Database monitoring feature

  D. The SYSAUX tablespace

8. Which is the best option to upgrade an Oracle 8i, 8.1.7 database to Oracle 10g?

  A. Use the export utility from Oracle 8i and import utility from Oracle 10g.

  B. Perform a direct upgrade using DBUA.

  C. Upgrade to Oracle 9i 9.2.0 using the Oracle 9i DBUA and then upgrade the database to Oracle 10g using the Oracle 10g DBUA.

  D. Run u0801070.sql script on an Oracle 8i instance and then start the instance in Oracle 10g.

9. When upgrading a database using the DBUA to Oracle 10g, which activity is not performed by the DBUA?

  A. Perform preupgrade steps.

  B. Create the SYSAUX tablespace.

  C. Change the listener.ora file to enter new Oracle home directory information.

  D. Back up the database after upgradDisable archiving during upgrade.

  E. Lock new user accounts created.

  F. Adjust initialization parameter values.

  G. Remove deprecated initialization parameters.

  H. Recompile invalid objects.

10. When performing a manual upgrade to Oracle 10g, in what order are the following steps performed? (Note: Some steps may be missing.)

  1 Run utlu101s.sql.

  2 Run utlu101i.sql.

  3 Run utlrp.sql.

  4 Create the SYSAUX tablespace.

5   Start the database using the STARTUP UPGRADE option.

   A. 1, 2, 3, 4, 5.

   B. 2, 5, 4, 1, 3.

   C. 5, 4, 2, 1, 3.

   D. 5, 2, 4, 1, 3.

11. When using the DBCA to create a database, which types of file storage cannot be chosen for the database?

   A. Raw device

   B. ASM storage

   C. File system

   D. Oracle Managed Files (OMF)

   E. None of the above

12. Which of the following actions are performed by the preupgrade utility utlu101i.sql?

   A. Resize redo log files to 4MB if they are smaller.

   B. Create the SYSAUX tablespace.

   C. Resize the SYSTEM tablespace.

   D. Suggest the size for the PGA_AGGREGATE_TARGET parameter.

13. Which two options are not true with the STARTUP UPGRADE mode instance startup?

   A. Prepares the database for upgrade; no need to run any special script.

   B. Suppresses spurious and unnecessary error messages, especially the ORA-00942.

   C. Handles certain system startup parameters that could interfere with the upgrade.

   D. This option is more of a documentation purpose when the database is started for upgrade; its functionality is no different from the default STARTUP option.

14. When you click the Restore button on the Upgrade Results page, which options must be true to perform a complete restore?

   A. The database upgraded from 9.2.0 to Oracle 10g.

   B. The database must be backed up using the DBUA.

   C. The COMPATIBLE parameter value must be 9.2.0.

   D. You must have backed up the database prior to upgrading.

15. Which product option installed from the Oracle 10g Companion CD must be installed in an Oracle home directory with database software installation?

   A. JPublisher

   B. HTML DB

   C. HTTP Server

   D. None

16. Which of the following database options must be upgraded after upgrading the database to Oracle 10*g*?

    A. JServer Java Virtual Machine

    B. Oracle Real Application Clusters

    C. Oracle XML Database

    D. All of the above

    E. None of the above

17. When creating a database to Oracle 10*g*, what is the minimum size for the redo log files?

    A. 40KB

    B. 4MB

    C. 50MB

    D. 100MB

18. Which component is used by Oracle to identify the options that need to be upgraded while upgrading a database to Oracle 10*g*?

    A. V$OPTION

    B. V$LICENSE

    C. DBMS_REGISTRY

    D. DBMS_OPTIONS

19. When you choose to create a Transaction Processing database while installing Oracle software, which of the following statements is most appropriate?

    A. The OUI will invoke the DBCA in an interactive mode, where you enter more information about the database and data files.

    B. The OUI will not invoke the DBCA; the OUI collects all the information to create the database and creates the database.

    C. The OUI will invoke DBCA in a noninteractive mode to create the database.

    D. Irrespective of the type of database, the OUI always invokes DBCA in noninteractive mode.

20. Before manually upgrading an Oracle 8*i* 8.1.7 database, which of the following would be the appropriate value of COMPATIBLE parameter? (Choose two.)

    A. 8.1.7.

    B. 9.2.0.

    C. Any value between 8.1.7 and 10.1.0.

    D. Leave the COMPATIBLE parameter's default value.

Answers to Review Questions

1. D. Oracle has made several enhancements to Oracle 10*g* installation. Oracle 10*g* can be installed with just one CD. You can also install a preconfigured database or a custom database with the software install. Oracle achieved this by removing all duplicate files and having only one database template. The Oracle database examples are installed from the companion CD.

2. B. You do not need to provide or activate any product key to install the Oracle1Oracle 10*g* software.

3. C. The EM Database Control is installed by default for Enterprise Edition or Standard Edition; for custom install you can optionally not install this. Legato and database examples are installed from the companion CD. (Remember, database examples are not the same as sample schema; sample schema can be installed along with the database creation.) Beginning with Oracle 10*g*, the client software can be installed only from database client installation media.

4. D. The DBCA supports RAC, ASM, backup and recovery options, administrative passwords, and so on. The DBCA supports all the new features of Oracle 10*g* database including database management control using Enterprise Manager. You can also use the DBCA to clone an existing database.

5. C. Database cloning using DBCA is accomplished by creating a template with structure and data option. Once the template is created, it can be used to create any number of similar (cloned) databases. The source database will be in the mount state when creating the template. The state of the source database does not matter when creating the clones using the template.

6. C. The Oracle 10*g* database provides the provision to downgrade the database to Oracle 9*i* Release 2, provided the COMPATIBLE parameter is still set to 9.2.0. Not all versions of the database can be upgraded to Oracle 10*g* using the DBUA; only 8.0.6, 8.1.7, 9.0.1, and 9.2.0 databases can be directly upgraded to Oracle 10*g*. The DBUA supports only direct upgrade. Any version of Oracle database can be upgraded to Oracle 10*g* either using the direct upgrade method, first upgrading to a version supported by direct upgrade, or by using export/import method.

7. A. The AWR is used to monitor the database feature usage. The MMON process collects information on database feature usage (can be queried from DBA_FEATURE_USAGE_STATISTICS view) and database high-watermark statistics (can be queried from DBA_HIGH_WATER_MARK_STATISTICS view).

8. B. Oracle 10*g* supports direct upgrade from 8.0.6, 8.1.7, 9.0.1, and 9.2.0 databases.

9. D. The DBUA has an option to back up the database prior to upgrade. It's up to you to back up the database after the upgrade is completed.

10. B. The first step is to run the preupgrade information utility utlu101i.sql. Fix all the discrepancies listed in this result, and shut down the database. Start the Oracle 10*g* instance after adjusting any initialization parameters using STARTUP UPGRADE. Create the SYSAUX tablespace and then run the upgrade script based on the release of the database from which you're upgrading. After the upgrade, verify the status of upgrade using utlu101s.sql. Shut down and start up the database, and recompile any invalid objects using utlrp.sql script.

11. E.   DBCA in Oracle 10g provides provisions to create the database with any of the storage options. OMF is a subcategory of file system storage.

12. D.   The preupgrade information utility—`utlu101i.sql`—does not make any database changes; it advises you on what parameters need to be changed and tablespaces that need more space for a successful database upgrade. This utility is run on the database environment that needs the upgrade. When upgrading the database manually, you must perform all the suggestion by the `utlu101i.sql` before performing the upgrade. If you're using DBUA to upgrade, it will take care of all these changes.

13. A, D.   `STARTUP UPGRADE` is the only way you can bring up an instance of Oracle 10g database prior to upgrading a database. You still need to upgrade the database using the upgrade scripts after creating the SYSAUX tablespace. Though the `STARTUP UPGRADE` option prepares the database for upgrade, you still need to run the database upgrade script based on the release of the database. This option suppresses ORA-00942 error messages and disables certain startup parameters.

14. B.   DBUA performs a restore from the backup it created prior to upgrade, and it restores the database files and configuration files from the backup location. If the backup is performed by you, the DBUA only restores the database settings—data files are not restored.

15. A.   JPublisher, was well as Legato Single Server Version, Java libraries, and other products, must be installed in the same Oracle home directory as the database software. HTTP Server must be installed in a separate Oracle home directory, and HTML DB must be installed in the same Oracle home directory as HTTP Server.

16. E.   Oracle 10g has a very simplified upgrade process, which determines all the components of the database to be upgraded and automatically upgrades them. Oracle uses `DBMS_REGISTRY` to identify the components to be upgraded.

17. B.   The minimum size of redo log file in Oracle 10g is 4MB. When creating a new database, the default is 50MB. If you're using OMF, the default is 100MB.

18. C.   Oracle uses `DBMS_REGISTRY` to keep the status of components loaded to the database. You can query `DBA_REGISTRY` to see all the components and their status. It also provides the schema owner of the component and the script to run if a component is invalid.

19. C.   When installing database software, you are given choice to create four types of databases: General Purpose, Data Warehouse, Transaction Processing, and Advanced. If you choose Advanced, the OUI invokes the DBCA in an interactive mode, where more information about the database is obtained by the DBCA. For the other three choices, OUI invokes DBCA in noninteractive mode to create the database; OUI gets the necessary information for database creation.

20. B, D.   The minimum `COMPATIBLE` value for Oracle 10g database is 9.2.0. You can set this value to 9.2.0 or 10.0.0 prior to upgrading the database (that is, prior to starting the instance in Oracle 10g). The default value of `COMPATIBLE` parameter in 10g is 10.0.0.

Chapter

2

Moving Data and Managing the Scheduler

ORACLE DATABASE 10*g* NEW FEATURES FOR ADMINISTRATORS EXAM OBJECTIVES OFFERED IN THIS CHAPTER:

✓ **Load and Unload Data**

- Transport tablespaces across different platforms
- Explain Data Pump architecture
- Monitor a Data Pump job
- Use Data Pump export and import
- Create external tables for data population
- Define your external table properties

✓ **Automating Tasks with the Scheduler**

- Simplify management tasks by using the Scheduler
- Create a job, program, schedule and window
- Reuse scheduler components for similar tasks
- View information about job executions and job instances

Exam objectives are subject to change at any time without prior notice and at Oracle's sole discretion. Please visit Oracle's training and certification website (http://www.oracle.com/education/certification/) for the most current exam objectives listing.

Oracle Database 10g (Oracle 10g) has several enhancements and new utilities to move data across Oracle databases. The major enhancement is the introduction of Data Pump, a new server-based utility, to unload and load data. Data Pump can move data as well as metadata. Data Pump is an enhanced version of the old export/import utilities. The Enterprise Edition of Oracle includes parallelism for Data Pump.

External table was introduced in Oracle 9i mainly to help load jobs for data warehouse-like environments. In Oracle 10g, you can populate data to an external table, which is unloading data to a file (proprietary format—direct path API).

In Oracle 10g, the transportable tablespace feature supports across platforms. This, with the multiple block size introduced in Oracle 9i, will help a great deal in moving data between OLTP systems and data warehouses. The job scheduling features have a new set of programs that enable you to manage jobs, schedules, and programs. You can schedule regular database maintenance, application logic, and backups through the database. The new package DBMS_SCHEDULER is available in Oracle 10g to schedule and manage jobs.

In this chapter you will learn more about all these new features.

Introducing Data Pump

Moving data across databases is an integral part of enterprise architecture. You need to move data from a production database to test databases for realistic testing, move data from OLTP databases to data warehouse databases, send data from one location to another for troubleshooting, and at times recover or restore data using these methods. Oracle 10g introduces new utilities to make the data movement operation simple and fast.

Data Pump is a new feature of Oracle 10g database that provides fast parallel bulk data and metadata movement between Oracle databases. Data Pump is fully integrated with the Oracle database and is installed automatically during database creation or database upgrade. Data Pump is available in Oracle the Enterprise, Standard, and Personal Editions, but the parallel capability is only available in the Enterprise Edition.

With the direct path method and parallel execution, Data Pump loads/unloads are several times faster than the traditional export/import methods. Data Pump also supports restarting jobs, monitoring progress, and adjusting the degree of parallelism on the fly.

Data Pump is an excellent choice for large export and import jobs. When compared to the exp/imp utilities, the startup time is longer for Data Pump, because it has to set up the jobs, queues, and master table. Also, at the end of the export operation the master table data is written to the dump file set, and at the beginning of the import job the master table is located and loaded in the schema of the user.

Data Pump is a major step forward for Oracle in loading and unloading data as well as copying data from one database to another.

In the following sections, we will discuss the architecture of Data Pump and the new Data Pump export and import utilities.

Introducing the Architecture of Data Pump

In Oracle 10g Data Pump, the database does all the work. This is a major deviation from the earlier architecture of export/import utilities, which ran as clients and did the major part of the work. The dump files for export/import were stored at the client whereas the Data Pump files are stored at the server. Figure 2.1 shows the Data Pump architecture. Data Pump consists of the following components:

Data Pump API   DBMS_DATAPUMP is the PL/SQL API for Data Pump, which is the engine. Data Pump jobs are created and monitored using this API.

Metadata API   The DBMS_METADATA API provides the database object definition to the Data Pump processes.

Client tools   The Data Pump client tools expdp and impdp use the procedures provided by the DBMS_DATAPUMP package. These tools make calls to the Data Pump API to initiate and monitor Data Pump operations.

Data movement APIs   Data Pump uses the direct path API (DPAPI) to move data. Certain circumstances do not allow the use of DPAPI; in such cases, the Oracle external table with ORACLE_DATADUMP access driver API is used.

FIGURE 2.1   Data Pump architecture

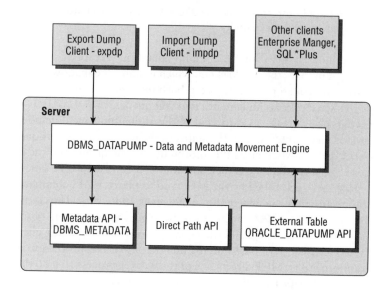

Oracle Data Pump jobs, once started, are performed by various processes on the database server. The following are the processes involved in the Data Pump operation:

Client process This process is initiated by the client utility: expdp, impdp, or other clients to make calls to the Data Pump API. Since the Data Pump is completely integrated to the database, once the Data Pump job is initiated, this process is not necessary for the progress of the job.

Shadow process When a client logs into the Oracle database, a foreground process is created (a standard feature of Oracle). This shadow process services the client data dump API requests. This process creates the master table and creates Advanced Queuing (AQ) queues used for communication. Once the client process is ended, the shadow process also goes away.

Master control process (MCP) *Master control process* controls the execution of the Data Pump job; there is one MCP per job. MCP divides the Data Pump job into various metadata and data load or unload jobs and hands them over to the worker processes. The MCP has a process name of the format *ORACLE_SID_*DMnn*_PROCESS_ID*. It maintains the job state, job description, restart, and file information in the master table.

Worker process The MCP creates the worker processes based on the value of the PARALLEL parameter. The worker process performs the tasks requested by MCP, mainly loading or unloading data and metadata. The worker processes have the format *ORACLE_SID_*DWnn_ *PROCESS_ID*. The worker processes maintain the current status in the master table that can be used to restart a failed job.

Parallel Query (PQ) processes The worker processes can initiate parallel query processes if external table is used as the data access method for loading or unloading. These are standard parallel query slaves of the parallel execution architecture.

Oracle Data Pump cannot be used to load data into a database from data exported using the exp utility.

Let's consider the example of an export Data Pump operation and see all the activities and processes involved. User A invokes the expdp client, which initiates the shadow process. The client calls the DBMS_DATAPUMP.OPEN procedure to establish the kind of export to be performed. The OPEN call starts the MCP process and creates two AQ queues.

The first queue is the status queue, used to send status of the job, which includes logging information and errors. Clients interested in the status of the job can query this queue. This is strictly a unidirectional queue—MCP posts the information to the queue, and the clients consume the information. The second queue is the command and control queue, which is used to control the worker processes established by the MCP and to perform API commands and file requests. This is a bidirectional queue where the MCP listens and writes. The commands are sent to this queue by the DBMS_DATAPUMP methods or by using the parameters of expdp client.

Once all the components (parameters and filters) of the job are defined, the client (expdp) invokes DBMS_DATAPUMP.START_JOB. Based on the number of parallel processes requested, MCP starts the worker processes. MCP directs one of the worker processes to do the metadata extraction using the DBMS_METADATA API.

During the operation, a master table is maintained in the schema of the user who initiated the Data Pump export. The master table has the same name as the name of the Data Pump job. This table maintains one row per object with status information. In the event of a failure, Data Pump uses the information in this table to restart the job. The master table is the heart of every Data Pump operation; it maintains all the information about the job. Data Pump uses the master table to restart a failed or suspended job. The master table is dropped (by default) when the Data Pump job finishes successfully.

The master table is written to the dump file set as the last step of the export dump operation and is removed from the user's schema. For the import dump operation, the master table is loaded from the dump file set to the user's schema as the first step and is used to sequence the objects being imported.

While the export job is underway, the original client who invoked the export job can detach from the job without aborting the job. This is especially useful when performing long-running data export jobs. Users can attach the job any time using the DBMS_DATAPUMP methods and query the status or change the parallelism of the job.

Since the master table is created in the Data Pump user's schema as a table, if there is an existing table in the schema with the Data Pump job name, the job fails. The user must have appropriate privileges to create the table and must have appropriate tablespace quotas.

Introducing Data Access Methods

Data Pump chooses the most appropriate data access method. Two methods are supported: direct path access and external table access.

Direct path export has been supported since Oracle 7.3 and therefore will not be discussed here.

External tables were introduced in Oracle 9*i*, and Oracle 10*g* supports writing to external tables. Data Pump provides an external table access driver (ORACLE_DATAPUMP) that can be used to read and write files. The format of the file is the same as the direct path methods; hence, this makes it possible to load data that is unloaded in another method. Data Pump uses the direct load API whenever possible. The following are the exceptions when the direct load API cannot be used and the external tables method will be used instead:

- Tables with fine-grained access control enabled in INSERT and SELECT operations.
- A domain index exists for a LOB column.
- A global index on multipartition table exists during a single-partition load.
- Tables in a cluster or if the table has an active trigger during import.
- Table contains BFILE columns.
- A referential integrity constraint is present during import.

- Table contains a VARRAY column with an embedded opaque type.
- Loading and unloading very large tables and partitions, where the PARALLEL SQL clause can be used to advantage.
- Loading tables that are partitioned different at load time and unload time.

Exploring the Advantages of Data Pump

Prior to Oracle 10g, the only export/import utility available with Oracle databases was the exp/imp tools. The Data Pump has the following advantages over the traditional expand imp tools:

- Data access methods are decided automatically. For circumstances where direct path cannot be used, the external method is used.
- Can perform export in parallel. It can also write to multiple files on different disks. (Specify parameters PARALLEL=2 and the two directory names with file specification DUMPFILE= DDIR1:/file1.dmp,DDIR2:/file2.dmp.)
- Has the ability to attach and detach from a job gives the DBA opportunity to monitor job progress remotely and make adjustments to the job as needed.
- Has the ability to restart a failed job from where it failed.
- Has more options to filter metadata objects. The INCLUDE and EXCLUDE options of the expdp and impdp utilities—which are described in the following section—make it possible to extract metadata with several possible combinations.

 See the section "Using Data and Metadata Filters" later in this chapter for more information.

- Has the option to filter data rows during import.
- The ESTIMATE_ONLY option can be used to estimate disk space requirements before actually performing the job.
- Data can be exported from a remote database and imported to a remote database using a database link.
- Its job status can be queried from the database directly or by using the Enterprise Manager.
- Jobs can be allocated resources dynamically based on the workload.
- Explicit database version can be specified, so only supported object types are exported.
- Its operations can be performed from one database to another without writing to a dump file, using the network method.
- During import, you can change target file names, schema, and tablespaces.

Using Data Pump Clients

Oracle 10*g* comes with the expdp utility to invoke Data Pump for export and impdp for import. The expdp utility can unload data and metadata to a set of operating system files called *dump files*. The impdp utility loads data and metadata stored in an export dump file to a target database. The expdp and impdp utilities accept parameters that are then passed to the DBMS_DATAPUMP program. The command-line executable name for Data Pump Export is expdp, and for Data Pump Import is impdp on Windows as well as Unix platforms.

For a user to invoke expdp/impdp, you as the DBA need to set up a directory where the dump files will be stored, and the user must have appropriate privileges to perform Data Pump export/import.

In the next section, we will discuss setting up the export dump location.

Setting Up a Dump Location

Since the Data Pump is server based, directory objects must be created in the database where the Data Pump files will be stored. The user executing Data Pump must have been granted permissions on the directory. READ permission is required to perform import, and WRITE permission is required to perform export and to create log files or SQL files.

The following code creates a directory in the database and also grants privileges on the directory to the user SCOTT:

```
SQL> CREATE DIRECTORY dumplocation
     AS '/oradata/dumpfiles';

Directory created.

SQL> GRANT READ, WRITE ON DIRECTORY dumplocation TO scott;

Grant succeeded.

SQL>
```

Note that the user (who owns the software installation and database files) must have READ and WRITE operating system privileges on the directory. The user SCOTT does not need any operating system privileges on the directory for Data Pump to succeed.

A default directory can be created for Data Pump operations in the database. Once this directory is created, privileged users (with the EXP_FULL_DATABASE or IMP_FULL_DATABASE privilege) do not need to specify a directory object name when performing the Data Pump operation. The name of the default directory must be DATA_PUMP_DIR. Also, the privileged users do not need to have explicit READ or WRITE permissions on DATA_PUMP_DIR.

Here is an example of creating the default DATA_PUMP_DIR:

```
SQL> create directory DATA_PUMP_DIR
     AS '/oradata/defaultdatadumps';
```

```
Directory created.
```

```
SQL>
```

Data Pump may write three types of files to the operating system directory defined in the database.

> Remember, absolute paths are not supported; Data Pump can write only to a directory defined by a directory database object.

The file types are as follows:

Dump files   These contain data and metadata information.

Log files   These record the standard output to a file and contain job progress and status information.

SQL files   These files contain the SQL statements extracted from the dump files using the impdp utility. Data Dump Import can extract the metadata information from a dump file and write them to a SQL script, which can be used to create database objects without using the Data Pump import utility.

You can specify the location of the files to the Data Pump clients using the following three methods (given in the order of precedence):

- Prefix the file name with the directory name separated by a colon, as shown in this example:

  `DUMPFILE=dumplocation:myfile.dmp`

- Use the DIRECTORY parameter.

- Define the DATA_DUMP_DIR directory in the database for privileged users.

Performing an export and import using the expdp and impdp tools can have different modes based on your requirement. The next section will discuss this.

Specifying Export and Import Modes

Export and import using the Data Pump clients can be performed in five different modes to unload or load different portions of the database. When performing the dump file import, specifying the mode is optional; when no mode is specified, the entire dump file is loaded with the mode automatically set to the one used for export. Table 2.1 describes the modes.

TABLE 2.1   Export and Import Modes

Mode	Export	Import
Database. Performed by specifying the FULL=Y parameter.	Export user requires the EXP_FULL_DATABASE role.	Import user requires the IMP_FULL_DATABASE role.
Tablespace. Performed by specifying the TABLESPACES parameter.	Data and metadata for only objects contained in the specified tablespaces are unloaded. Export user requires the EXP_FULL_DATABASE role.	All objects contained in the specified tablespaces are loaded. Import user requires IMP_FULL_DATABASE privilege. The source dump file can be exported in database, tablespace, schema, or table mode.
Schema. Performed by specifying the SCHEMAS parameter. This is the default mode.	Only objects belonging to specified schema are unloaded.

The EXP_FULL_DATABASE role is required to specify list of schema. | All objects belonging to the specified schema are loaded. The source can be a database or schema mode export. The IMP_FULL_DATABASE role is required to specify list of schema. |
| Table. Performed by specifying the TABLES parameter. | Only the specified table, its partitions, and its dependent objects are unloaded. Export user must have SELECT privilege on the tables. | Only the specified table, its partitions, and its dependent objects are loaded. Requires the IMP_FULL_DATABASE role to specify tables belonging to a different user. |
| Transport tablespace. Performed by specifying the TRANSPORT_TABLESPACES parameter. | Only metadata for tables and their dependent objects within the specified set of tablespaces are unloaded. Use this mode to transport tablespaces from one database to another. | Metadata from a transport tablespace export is loaded. |

In the next sections we will discuss using the expdp (Data Pump export utility) and impdp (Data Pump import utility).

Using *expdp*

The *expdp* utility performs Data Pump exports. Any user can export objects or complete schema owned by the user without any additional privileges. Nonprivileged users must have WRITE permission on the directory object and must specify the DIRECTORY parameter or specify the directory object name along with the dump filename.

Here is an example to perform an export by the user SCOTT (since Scott is not a privileged user, he must specify the DIRECTORY object name as in the first part of the example).

```
linux:oracle>expdp scott/tiger

Export: Release 10.1.0.2.0 - Production on Tuesday,
20 April,   2004 18:03

Copyright (c) 2003, Oracle.  All rights reserved.

Connected to: Oracle Database 10g Enterprise Edition
     Release 10.1.0.2.0   - Production
With the Partitioning, OLAP and Data Mining options
ORA-39002: invalid operation
ORA-39070: Unable to open the log file.
ORA-39145: directory object parameter must be specified
          and non-null


linux:oracle>
linux:oracle>expdp directory=dumplocation

Export: Release 10.1.0.2.0 - Production on Tuesday,
 20 April, 2004  14:48

Copyright (c) 2003, Oracle.  All rights reserved.

Username: scott/tiger

Connected to: Oracle Database 10g Enterprise
Edition Release  10.1.0.2.0 - Production
```

```
With the Partitioning, OLAP and Data Mining options
FLASHBACK automatically enabled to preserve database
integrity.
Starting "SCOTT"."SYS_EXPORT_SCHEMA_01":  scott/********
  directory=dumplocation
Estimate in progress using BLOCKS method...
Processing object type SCHEMA_EXPORT/TABLE/TABLE_DATA
Total estimation using BLOCKS method: 192 KB
Processing object type
  SCHEMA_EXPORT/SE_PRE_SCHEMA_PROCOBJACT/PROCACT_SCHEMA
Processing object type SCHEMA_EXPORT/TABLE/TABLE
Processing object type SCHEMA_EXPORT/TABLE/INDEX/INDEX
Processing object type
            SCHEMA_EXPORT/TABLE/CONSTRAINT/CONSTRAINT
Processing object type
  SCHEMA_EXPORT/TABLE/INDEX/STATISTICS/INDEX_STATISTICS
Processing object type
          SCHEMA_EXPORT/TABLE/STATISTICS/TABLE_STATISTIC
Processing object type SCHEMA_EXPORT/TABLE/COMMENT
Processing object type
            SCHEMA_EXPORT/TABLE/CONSTRAINT/REF_CONSTRAINT
. . exported "SCOTT"."DEPT"          5.656 KB
    4 rows
. . exported "SCOTT"."EMP"           7.820 KB
    14 rows
. . exported "SCOTT"."SALGRADE"      5.585 KB
    5 rows
. . exported "SCOTT"."BONUS"            0 KB
    0 rows
Master table "SCOTT"."SYS_EXPORT_SCHEMA_01" successfully
    loaded/unloaded
**********************************************************
Dump file set for SCOTT.SYS_EXPORT_SCHEMA_01 is:
  /oradata/dumpfiles/expdat.dmp
Job "SCOTT"."SYS_EXPORT_SCHEMA_01" successfully
  completed at 14:49
linux:oracle>
```

Since we did not specify any other parameters, the **expdp** used default values for the filenames (`expdat.dmp`, `export.log`), did schema-level export (login schema), calculated job estimation using blocks method, used a default job name (SYS_EXPORT_SCHEMA_01), and exported both data and metadata.

The next section discusses parameters.

This output looks similar to the exp utility. Though most of the parameters of exp and **expdp** are similar, they both are different products. We will compare these two products in the next section. While comparing, we will examine the new parameters available for **expdp**.

Comparing *exp* and *expdp*

The exp utility is still available in Oracle 10*g*; expdp is an advanced version of exp. Many parameters are common to both utilities. Table 2.2 lists the parameters that are common to both exp and **expdp**, and their behavior is same.

TABLE 2.2   *exp* and *expdp* Common Parameters

Parameter Name	Purpose
FILESIZE	Specifies maximum size for each dump file. Default is 0 (unlimited). The size can be specified in bytes (the default), kilobytes, megabytes, and gigabytes.
FLASHBACK_SCN	Specifies the System Change Number (SCN). Export will be performed with data that is consistent as of this SCN.
FLASHBACK_TIME	The SCN that closely matches the specified time is found and export is performed with data that is consistent of that time.
FULL	When Y is specified, does a complete database export.
HELP	Displays a help screen with the parameters and their purpose.
PARFILE	Specifies name of a file with parameter values.
QUERY	When specified, a WHERE clause is added to the table export to filter data.

TABLE 2.2   *exp* and *expdp* Common Parameters *(continued)*

Parameter Name	Purpose
TABLES	Lists the table names for table mode export.
TABLESPACES	Lists the tablespaces to be exported in tablespace mode.
TRANSPORT_TABLESPACES	When Y is specified, transportable tablespace mode export is performed.

WARNING

FLASHBACK_SCN and FLASHBACK_TIME are mutually exclusive parameters.

A few parameters have a new name in the expdp, but their behavior is similar to their counterpart in exp. Table 2.3 lists such parameters.

TABLE 2.3   Comparing *exp* and *expdp* Parameters

Exp Parameter	Expdp Parameter	Purpose
FEEDBACK	STATUS	Displays detailed status of current operation. The integer for STATUS specifies the frequency in seconds; for FEEDBACK, it is the number of rows exported.
FILE	DUMPFILE	Specifies the name of the file to store the export information. DUMPFILE can accept multiple filenames or substitution variable %U. The %U will be expanded to 01 through 99 during export.
LOG	LOGFILE	Specifies the name of the file to save the log information.
OWNER	SCHEMAS	Specifies the name of the users/schema to export.
TTS_FULL_CHECK	TRANSPORT_FULL_CHECK	When Y is specified, checks for dependencies for those objects in the transportable set and those outside the transportable set.

Several parameters are specific to the **expdp** utility command line. Table 2.4 lists such parameters.

TABLE 2.4   *expdp* Command-Line parameters

Parameter	Purpose
ATTACH	Attaches a client session to an existing Data Pump job and automatically places you in the interactive command mode.
CONTENT	Specifies what to export. The default is ALL. DATA_ONLY unloads only table row data. METADATA_ONLY unloads only database object definitions.
DIRECTORY	Specifies the name of the database directory object. The dump file will be written to this location on the server. Privileged users can use DATA_DUMP_DIR without specifying this parameter.
ESTIMATE	Specifies the method (BLOCKS or STATISTICS) to estimate how much disk space each table in the export job will consume. Estimate does not include metadata!
ESTIMATE_ONLY	Estimates the space required for the export but does not perform the export job. You should not specify the DUMPFILE parameter with ESTIMATE_ONLY=Y.
EXCLUDE	Lists the metadata object types to be excluded from the export. For more information, see the "Data and Metadata Filters" section.
INCLUDE	List the metadata object types to be included in the export. See the "Using Data and Metadata Filters" section.
JOB_NAME	Specifies a name for the export job. The default is SYS_operation_mode_NN. The master table will be created in the schema of the user with the job name.
KEEP_MASTER	Specify Y not to drop the master table after the export job completes. This could be useful for debugging or reporting.
NETWORK_LINK	Specifies name of a database link to perform network export. The local database that runs the expdp, contacts the remote database through the db link to retrieve data, and writes the data to the dump file.
NOLOGFILE	Specify Y if you do not want to create a log file.
PARALLEL	Specifies the maximum number of threads for the export job.
VERSION	Specifies version of database. Database objects that are incompatible with the specified version will not be exported.

The DUMPFILE parameter can specify more than one file. The filenames can be comma separated, or you can use the %U substitution variable. If you specify %U in the DUMPFILE file-name, the number of files initially created is based on the value of the PARALLEL parameter. Preexisting files that match the name of the files generated are not overwritten; an error is flagged. The FILESIZE parameter determines the size of each file. Table 2.5 shows some examples.

TABLE 2.5   File Name and File Size Examples

Parameter Examples	File Characteristics
DUMPFILE=exp%U.dmp FILESIZE=200M	Initially, the exp01.dmp file will be created; once the file is 200MB, the next file, called exp02.dmp, will be created.
DUMPFILE=exp%U_%U.dmp PARALLEL=3	Initially three files will be created—exp01_01.dmp, exp02_02.dmp, and exp03_03.dmp. Notice that every occurrence of the substitution variable is incremented each time. Since there is no FILESIZE parameter, no more files will be created.
DUMPFILE=DMPDIR1:exp%U.dmp, DMPDIR2:exp%U.dmp FILESIZE=100M	The dump files are stored in directories defined by DMPDIR1 and DMPDIR2. This method is especially useful if you do not have enough space in one directory to perform the complete export job.

You can specify all the parameters in a file and specify the filename with the PARFILE parameter. The only exception is the PARFILE parameter inside the parameter file. Recursive PARFILE is not supported.

In the next section, we will discuss the impdp utility, which does the import from a dump file created using expdp.

Using *impdp*

The impdp utility can read and apply the dump file created by the expdp utility. The directory permission and privileges for using impdp are similar to that of expdp.

Let's try importing the export dump file created using the following parameters of the expdp:

```
expdp dumpfile=quotes.dmp logfile=quotes.log
    schemas=quotes
```

For the import, you do not specify any other parameters except the dump filename. The user QUOTES does not exist in the target database, and will be created as part of the import.

Here is an example:

```
linux:oracle>impdp dumpfile=quotes.dmp

Import: Release 10.1.0.2.0 - Production on Wednesday,
 21 April, 2004  7:09

Copyright (c) 2003, Oracle.  All rights reserved.

Username: bill/billthedba

Connected to: Oracle Database 10g Enterprise Edition
   Release 10.1.0.2.0 - Production
With the Partitioning, OLAP and Data Mining options
Master table "BILL"."SYS_IMPORT_FULL_01"
   successfully loaded/unloaded
Starting "BILL"."SYS_IMPORT_FULL_01":
   bill/******** dumpfile=quotes.dmp
Processing object type SCHEMA_EXPORT/USER
Processing object type SCHEMA_EXPORT/SYSTEM_GRANT
Processing object type SCHEMA_EXPORT/ROLE_GRANT
Processing object type SCHEMA_EXPORT/DEFAULT_ROLE
Processing object type SCHEMA_EXPORT/TABLESPACE_QUOTA
Processing object type
   SCHEMA_EXPORT/SE_PRE_SCHEMA_PROCOBJACT/PROCACT_SCHEMA
Processing object type SCHEMA_EXPORT/TABLE/TABLE
Processing object type SCHEMA_EXPORT/TABLE/TABLE_DATA
. . imported "QUOTES"."SEC_FILINGS"
                            124.3 KB     382 rows
. . imported "QUOTES"."ALERT"
                            5.531 KB       6 rows
. . imported "QUOTES"."ANALYST"
                            7.671 KB      36 rows
. . imported "QUOTES"."CAN_QUOTE"
                            7.117 KB       1 rows
. . imported "QUOTES"."CHART"
                            7.242 KB      67 rows
. . imported "QUOTES"."EVENT"
                            12.34 KB      49 rows
. . imported "QUOTES"."NEWS_RELEASE"
                            11.96 KB      49 rows
```

```
. . imported "QUOTES"."EARNINGS_ESTIMATE"
                                 9.812 KB        11 rows
. . imported "QUOTES"."QUOTE"
                                 7.117 KB         1 rows
. . imported "QUOTES"."SYNC_CONTROL"
                                  5.75 KB         9 rows
. . imported "QUOTES"."URLS"
                                 5.375 KB         2 rows
. . imported "QUOTES"."ITEM"
                                    0 KB          0 rows
. . imported "QUOTES"."ITEM_INDEX"
                                    0 KB          0 rows
Processing object type SCHEMA_EXPORT/TABLE/INDEX/INDEX
Processing object type
                SCHEMA_EXPORT/TABLE/CONSTRAINT/CONSTRAINT
Processing object type
SCHEMA_EXPORT/TABLE/INDEX/STATISTICS/INDEX_STATISTICS
Processing object type
SCHEMA_EXPORT/TABLE/STATISTICS/TABLE_STATISTICS
Processing object type SCHEMA_EXPORT/TABLE/COMMENT
Processing object type SCHEMA_EXPORT/FUNCTION/FUNCTION
Processing object type
                SCHEMA_EXPORT/FUNCTION/ALTER_FUNCTION
Job "BILL"."SYS_IMPORT_FULL_01" successfully
   completed at 07:09
linux:oracle>
```

Many parameters in impdp are similar to the imp utility. We will discuss and compare the parameters in next section.

Comparing *imp* and *impdmp*

impdp is advanced and has several new features when compared to the imp utility. Many parameters are common to both imp and impdp, with the same behavior, as described in Table 2.6.

TABLE 2.6   *imp* and *impdp* Common Parameters

Parameter	Purpose
FULL	Specify Y for full database import.
HELP	Shows a help screen with all the parameters.
PARFILE	Names the file that has all the parameters to be used for the import.

TABLE 2.6   *imp* and *impdp* Common Parameters *(continued)*

Parameter	Purpose
QUERY	Restricts the rows imported based on the condition specified in this parameter.
SKIP_UNUSABLE_INDEXES	If set to Y, does not load the tables with unusable indexes, and the job continues without error.
TABLES	Lists the tables to be imported.
TABLESPACES	Loads Objects that belong to the specified tablespaces.
TRANSPORT_TABLESPACES	Specifies the tablespaces that are imported using the transport tablespace method.

A few parameters have a new name in the impdp utility, but their behavior is similar to their counterpart in imp. Table 2.7 describes such parameters.

TABLE 2.7   Comparing *imp* and *impdp* Parameters

Imp Parameter	Impdp Parameter	Purpose
DATAFILES	TRANSPORT_DATAFILES	Specifies the list of datafiles to be imported using the transport tablespace method.
DESTROY	REUSE_DATAFILES	When creating tablespace during full import, specifies whether to overwrite existing datafiles.
FEEDBACK	STATUS	Displays detailed status of current operation.
FILE	DUMPFILE	Names the export dump file to import.
FROMUSER	SCHEMAS and REMAP_ SCHEMAS	SCHEMAS can be used to import a schema, where the source and target are the same. REMAP_SCHEMA can be used to import to a different target schema. For more information, see the section "Using Import Transformations."
IGNORE	TABLE_EXISTS_ACTION	IGNORE can ignore the create error and continue with import. The TABLE_EXISTS_ACTION has more options: SKIP, APPEND, TRUNCATE, or REPLACE.

TABLE 2.7   Comparing *imp* and *impdp* Parameters *(continued)*

Imp Parameter	Impdp Parameter	Purpose
INDEXFILE SHOW	SQLFILE	Writes the metadata SQL statements to a file specified in this parameter. The SQL is not executed and the target system remains unchanged.
LOG	LOGFILE	Lists the filename where the status of the import will be written.
TOUSER	REMAP_SCHEMA	Specifies a username to import the objects into. See the section "Using Import Transformations" for more information.

Several parameters are specific to the impdp utility command line. Table 2.8 describes such parameters.

TABLE 2.8   *impdp* Command-line Parameters

Parameter	Purpose
FLASHBACK_SCN	Performs import operation that is consistent with the SCN specified from the source database. Valid only when the NETWORK_LINK parameter is used.
FLASHBACK_TIME	Similar to FLASHBACK_SCN, but Oracle finds the SCN close to the time specified.
NETWORK_LINK	Performs import directly from a source database using database link name specified in the parameter.
REMAP_DATAFILE	Changes name of the source datafile to a different name in the target. See the "Using Import Transformations" section for more information.
REMAP_SCHEMA	Loads objects to a different target schema name. See the "Using Import Transformations" section for more information.
REMAP_TABLESPACE	Changes name of the source tablespace to a different name in the target. See the "Using Import Transformations" section for more information.
TRANSFORM	Enables to change certain attributes of object creation DDL. See the "Using Import Transformations" section for more information.

You can use the CONTENT, INCLUDE, and EXCLUDE parameters in the impdp utility to filter the metadata objects. Their behavior is the same as in the expdp utility. The "Using Data and Metadata Filters" section will discuss this in detail.

In the next section, we will discuss methods to use a different target for tablespaces, schema, and datafiles.

When using the schema-level import with the SCHEMAS parameter, if the schema does not exist in the target database, the import operation creates it with same attributes from the source. The schema created by the import operation will need to have the password reset.

Using Import Transformations

While performing the import, you can specify a different target name for datafiles, tablespaces, or schema. These transformations are possible because the object metadata is stored in the dump file as XML. You use the REMAP_ parameters to specify this. When any of the three REMAP_ parameters are used, Data Pump makes transformations to the metadata DDL during import. The IMP_FULL_DATABASE role is required to use these parameters. You may use these parameters multiple times, if there is more than one transformation to be made, but the same source cannot be repeated more than once.

The REMAP_ parameters are as follows:

REMAP_DATAFILES   Using this parameter, you can specify a different name for the datafile. The filename referenced could be in a CREATE TABLESPACE, CREATE LIBRARY, or CREATE DIRECTORY statement. REMAP_DATAFILES is especially useful when performing a full database import, when the tablespaces are being created by the impdp, and when the source directories do not exist in the target database server or the source and target platforms are different (VMS, Windows, Unix). The syntax is as follows:

```
REMAP_DATAFILE=source_datafile:target_datafile
```

The following example shows the parameters used to perform a full import on a Unix system from an export taken from Windows system.

```
impdp directory=mydumpdir dumpfile=winexp.dmp
    remap_datafile='D:/ORADATA/MYDB/userdata01.dbf': ➥
'/orad01/oradata/mydb/userdata01.dbf'
```

REMAP_SCHEMA   Using this parameter, you can load all the objects belonging to the source schema to a target schema. Multiple source schemas can map to the same target schema. If the target schema specified does not exist, the import operation creates the schema and performs the load. The syntax is as follows:

```
REMAP_SCHEMA=source_schema:target_schema
```

The following example shows copying objects from the SCOTT schema of the source database to the BILL schema in the target database. If the BILL schema does not exist, it will be created.

```
impdp directory=mydumpdir dumpfile=scott.dmp
    remap_schema=SCOTT:BILL
```

REMAP_TABLESPACE   Using this parameter, you can create the objects that belong to a tablespace in the source to another in the target. The syntax is as follows:

```
REMAP_TABLESPACE=source_tablespace:target_tablespace
```

The following example shows copying objects from the SCOTT schema of the source database to the BILL schema in the target database. The objects owned by SCOTT are stored in the SCOTT_DATA tablespace, we want to import these objects to the BILL_DATA tablespace.

```
impdp directory=mydumpdir dumpfile=scott.dmp
    remap_schema=SCOTT:BILL
    remap_tablespace=SCOTT_DATA:BILL_DATA
```

TRANSFORM   Using the TRANSFORM parameter, you can specify that the storage clause should not be generated in the DDL for import. This is useful if the storage characteristics of the source and target databases are different. TRANSFORM has the following syntax:

```
TRANSFORM=name:boolean_value[:object_type]
```

The name of the transform can be either SEGMENT_ATTRIBUTES or STORAGE. STORAGE removes the STORAGE clause from the CREATE statement DDL whereas SEGMENT_ATTRIBUTES removes physical attributes, tablespaces, logging, and storage attributes. The boolean_value can be Y or N; the default is Y. The type of object is optional; the valid values are TABLE and INDEX.

For example, if you want to ignore the storage characteristics during the import, and use the defaults for the tablespace, you may do:

```
impdp dumpfile=scott.dmp  transform=storage:N:table ➡
exclude=indexes
```

The next example will remove all the segment attributes, and the import will use the user's default tablespace and its default storage characteristics.

```
impdp dumpfile=scott.dmp  transform=segment_attributes:N
```

In the next section, we will discuss how data can be copied from one database to another without using a dump file.

 **Real World Scenario**

Using Network Mode to Refresh Test Data from Production

We periodically refresh the test database with production data. Since we have to preserve all the grants on the test schema, we perform the following steps in an Oracle 8*i* database to perform the data refresh:

- Disable all foreign keys.

- Disable all primary keys.

- Drop indexes so that the import goes faster.

- Truncate tables.

- Export data from the production database.

- Import data to the test database using the following parameters.

```
COMMIT=Y
BUFFERS=10485760
FROMUSER=SCHEMAPROD
TOUSER=SCHEMATEST
IGNORE=Y
GRANTS=N
```

After upgrading the test and production databases to Oracle 10*g*, we perform the import in just one step using the following impdp parameters:

```
SCHEMAS=SCHEMAPROD
NETWORK_LINK=TEST_SCHEMA
REMAP_SCHEMA=SCHEMAPROD:SCHEMATEST
TABLE_EXISTS_ACTION=REPLACE
EXCLUDE=OBJECT_GRANT
```

Specifying Network Mode Import

The NETWORK_LINK enables the network mode import using a database link. The database link must be created before the export is started. The export is performed on the source database based on the various parameters; the data and metadata are passed to the source database using the database link and loaded. To get a consistent export from the source database, you can use the FLASHBACK_SCN or FLASHBACK_TIME parameter.

Using FLASHBACK_SCN, FLASHBACK_TIME, ESTIMATE, or TRANSPORT_TABLESPACES requires you also specify the NETWORK_LINK parameter.

The following is an example of copying the SCOTT schema in the source (remote) database to LARRY in the target (local) database. Scott's objects are stored in the USERS tablespace; in the target we will create Larry's objects in the EXAMPLE tablespace. The database link name is NEW_DB.

```
impdp schemas=scott network_link=new_db
➥remap_schema=scott:larry
➥remap_tablespace=users:example
```

WARNING   The network mode import is different from using SQL*Net to perform the import: impdp username/*password@database*.

Using Data and Metadata Filters

Data Pump provides fine-grained object selection to filter the metadata objects during exporting and importing. You can specify the EXCLUDE and INCLUDE parameters with expdp and impdp clients to filter metadata objects. You can use the CONTENT parameter to specify whether you need to export/import just data, just metadata, or both. You can use the QUERY parameter to filter data rows.

The EXCLUDE and INCLUDE parameters are mutually exclusive. Also, when you specify either parameter, you cannot specify the CONTENT parameter with DATA_ONLY value. The QUERY, EXCLUDE and INCLUDE parameters have the following syntax:

```
QUERY=[schema.][table_name:]"query clause"
EXCLUDE=object_type[:"object names"]
INCLUDE=object_type[:"object names"]]
```

Table 2.9 shows examples of data and metadata filter usage. Though the explanation says *unloaded*, it is applicable to loading also.

TABLE 2.9   Data Pump Filter Examples

Parameter Examples	Accomplishes
schemas=traing content=metadata_only	Unloads the metadata information for all objects owned by the TRAING schema. No data row will be unloaded.
content=data_only schemas=traing query=traing.student:"where ee_ dept = 'IST'"	No metadata will be unloaded; only data rows will be unloaded. All data rows will be unloaded for all tables owned by TRAING, except STUDENT table, where only the rows that belong to the IST department is unloaded.

TABLE 2.9 Data Pump Filter Examples *(continued)*

Parameter Examples	Accomplishes
content=data_only tables=traing.student query="where ee_dept = 'IST'"	Only rows in the STUDENT table that belong to the IST department are unloaded.
schemas=traing exclude=view,package,procedure, function,grant,trigger exclude=index:"like 'S%'"	Table rows will be unloaded. Metadata definition for view, trigger, procedure, function, grants, packages, and indexes that begin with S are not unloaded.
Content=data_only schemas=hr include=table:"in ('EMPLOYEES','DEPARTMENTS')" query="where DEPARTMENT_ID = 10"	Only rows belonging to department 10 are unloaded from the EMPLOYEES and DEPARTMENTS tables.

You can obtain the parameter values for INCLUDE and EXCLUDE by querying the OBJECT_PATH column from the following data dictionary views:

- DATABASE_EXPORT_OBJECTS for full database export parameters
- SCHEMA_EXPORT_OBJECTS for schema-level export parameters
- TABLE_EXPORT_OBJECTS for table-level export parameters

The following query shows the values that can be used with INCLUDE/EXCLUDE parameters when performing a schema level export that is related to packages:

```
SQL> select object_path, comments
  2  from schema_export_objects
  3  where object_path like '%PACKAGE%'
SQL> /

OBJECT_PATH        COMMENTS
------------------ -----------------------------------
ALTER_PACKAGE_SPEC Recompile package specifications in
                   the selected   schemas
PACKAGE            Packages (both specification and body)
                   in  selected schemas and their
                   dependent grants and audits
```

| PACKAGE_BODY | Package bodies in the selected schemas |
| PACKAGE_SPEC | Package specifications in the selected schemas |

SQL>

Data Pump has the ability to monitor the jobs and make adjustments to the jobs. You can monitor and modify the jobs initiated by impdp and expdp by using the same clients. In the next section, we will discuss managing the jobs by using expdp and impdp.

Managing Data Pump Jobs

The Data Pump clients expdp and impdp provide an interactive command interface. Since each export and import operation has a job name, you can attach to that job from any computer and monitor the job or make adjustments to the job. Table 2.10 lists the parameters that can be used interactively.

TABLE 2.10   Data Pump Interactive Commands

Parameter	Purpose
ADD_FILE	Adds another file or a file set to the DUMPFILE set.
CONTINUE_CLIENT	Changes mode from interactive client to logging mode.
EXIT_CLIENT	Leaves the client session and discontinues logging but leaves the current job running.
KILL_JOB	Detaches all currently attached client sessions and terminates the job.
PARALLEL	Increases or decreases the number of threads.
START_JOB	Starts (or restarts) a job that is not currently running. The SKIP_CURRENT option can skip the recent failed DDL statement that caused the job to stop.
STOP_JOB	Stops the current job; the job can be restarted later.
STATUS	Displays detailed status of the job; the refresh interval can be specified in seconds. The detailed status is displayed to the output screen but not written to the log file.

The data dictionary view DBA_DATAPUMP_JOBS shows the active job information along with its current state, the number of threads, and the number of client sessions attached. You can join this view with DBA_DATAPUMP_SESSIONS to get the SADDR column of the sessions attached and can join the SADDR column with V$SESSION to get more information. The V$SESSION_LONGOPS view also has info onthe progress of the job. Use the SID and SERIAL# columns from V$SESSION to query V$SESSION_LONGOPS.

The following example should help you understand the parameters more clearly. We have an export dump job to be performed. The DBA starts the job with the following parameters in a parameter file:

```
DIRECTORY=DUMPLOCATION
DUMPFILE=volest.dmp
LOGFILE=volest.exp.log
SCHEMAS=volest
JOB_NAME=VOLEST_EXP_TEST
```

A table with name VOLEST_EXP_TEST is created in the DBA's schema. This is the master control table. Querying the DBA_DATAPUMP_JOBS view will show the status of the jobs running.

```
SQL> SELECT job_name, state
  2  FROM dba_datapump_jobs;

JOB_NAME                        STATE
------------------------------- ----------------
VOLEST_EXP_TEST                 EXECUTING

SQL>
```

By pressing **Ctrl+C**, you can stop the logging screen, and you can enter the interactive mode. The DBA finds that the job is halfway through and is consuming resources on the server, so the DBA will suspend the job and restart it later when the server is less busy.

```
Export> stop_job
Are you sure you wish to stop this job ([y]/n): y
oracle@linux>
```

From home the DBA logs in to see the status of the job, and the job is in suspended mode. Now, the DBA wants to use the more processing power available in the server. So the first step is to attach to the job, like so:

```
oracle@linux:> expdp bill/thedba attach=VOLEST_EXP_TEST
```

```
Export: Release 10.1.0.2.0 - Production on
Friday, 23 April, 2004
Copyright (c) 2003, Oracle.  All rights reserved.
Connected to: Oracle Database 10g Enterprise
Edition Release 10.1.0.2.0 - Production
With the Partitioning, OLAP and Data Mining options

Job: VOLEST_EXP_TEST
  Owner: BILL
  Operation: EXPORT
  Creator Privs: FALSE
  GUID: D8C25554B641EF14E030007F0200562C
  Start Time: Friday, 23 April, 2004 15:16
  Mode: SCHEMA
  Instance: BT10GNF1
  Max Parallelism: 1
  EXPORT Job Parameters:
  Parameter Name        Parameter Value:
      CLIENT_COMMAND          bill/**** parfile=volest.par
      DATA_ACCESS_METHOD      AUTOMATIC
      ESTIMATE                BLOCKS
      INCLUDE_METADATA        1
      LOG_FILE_DIRECTORY      DUMPLOCATION
      LOG_FILE_NAME           volest.exp.log
      TABLE_CONSISTENCY       0
      USER_METADATA           1
  State: IDLING
  Bytes Processed: 730,622,512
  Percent Done: 69
  Current Parallelism: 1
  Job Error Count: 0
  Dump File: /oradata/dumpfiles/volest.dmp
    bytes written: 733,958,144

Worker 1 Status:
  State: UNDEFINED
```

```
Export> parallel=4

Export> status=60

Job: VOLEST_EXP_TEST
  Operation: EXPORT
  Mode: SCHEMA
  State: IDLING
  Bytes Processed: 730,622,512
  Percent Done: 69
  Current Parallelism: 4
  Job Error Count: 0
  Dump File: /oradata/dumpfiles/volest.dmp
    bytes written: 733,958,144

Worker 1 Status:
  State: UNDEFINED

Export> start_job

Export> continue_client
```

After attaching to the job, we increased the threads to four from one (`parallel=4`), set up to display detailed status to the screen every minute (`status=60`), restarted the job (`start_job`), and let the output display on the screen (`continue_client`).

Real World Scenario

Using Fine-Grained Object Selection

The fine-grained object selection in Oracle 10*g* for export came as a real boon for us. We perform daily exports on the OLTP database excluding certain large (maybe we should say *huge*) tables. In Oracle 8*i* and Oracle 9*i*, we had to re-create one of the dictionary views to exclude certain multimillion row transaction tables. Now in Oracle 10*g*, we simply use the EXCLUDE= TABLESPACE:"`like '%LARGE%'`", which excludes all the objects created in the %LARGE% tablespaces.

Multiple clients (sessions) can attach to a job.

You can also use the Oracle Enterprise Manager (EM) Grid Control or the Database Control to perform the Data Pump export and import. The OEM can also do the job monitoring. The next section will discuss how to use the Data Pump wizard in the EM.

Using the Data Pump Wizard

You can use the EM Database Control to export and import data using Data Pump. From the Database Control home page, click the Maintenance tab. Under Utilities, you will see the following three links:

- Export To Files
- Import From File
- Import From Database

The export and import supports Database, Schema, and Table modes. The wizard accepts input for each option and shows the final review screen where you can see the actual DBMS_ DATAPUMP calls. Figure 2.2 shows a screen where you would specify the export options.

While performing the import, options are available to transform the schema, tablespace, or datafiles. The jobs can be executed immediately or can be scheduled for a later time.

The following is a sample of the DBMS_DATAPUMP calls prepared by the EM wizard for a schema import (this PL/SQL block is available on the Review screen of the export/import):

```
declare
h1    NUMBER;
 begin
  begin
     h1 := dbms_datapump.open (
           operation => 'IMPORT',
           job_mode => 'FULL',
           job_name => 'IMPORT000028',
           version => 'COMPATIBLE');
  end;
  begin
    dbms_datapump.set_parallel(handle => h1,
                  degree => 1);
```

```
    end;
    begin
       dbms_datapump.add_file(handle => h1,
                       filename => 'IMPORT.LOG',
                       directory => 'DATA_PUMP_DIR',
                       filetype => 3);
    end;
    begin
       dbms_datapump.set_parameter(handle => h1,
                       name => 'KEEP_MASTER',
                       value => 0);
    end;
    begin
       dbms_datapump.add_file(handle => h1,
                       filename => 'volest.dmp',
                       directory => 'DUMPLOCATION',
                       filetype => 1);
    end;
    begin
       dbms_datapump.set_parameter(handle => h1,
                       name => 'DATA_ACCESS_METHOD',
                       value => 'AUTOMATIC');
    end;
    begin
       dbms_datapump.set_parameter(handle => h1,
                       name => 'INCLUDE_METADATA',
                       value => 1);
    end;
    begin
       dbms_datapump.set_parameter(handle => h1,
                       name => 'REUSE_DATAFILES',
                       value => 0);
    end;
    begin
       dbms_datapump.set_parameter(handle => h1,
                       name => 'SKIP_UNUSABLE_INDEXES',
                       value => 0);
    end;
    begin
```

```
    dbms_datapump.start_job(handle => h1,
                    skip_current => 0,
                    abort_step => 0);
end;
begin
    dbms_datapump.detach(handle => h1);
end;
end;
/
```

FIGURE 2.2   EM export options

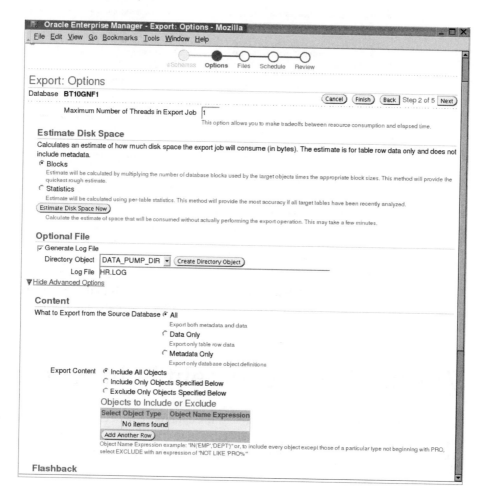

Once the Data Pump job is submitted, you can view its progress by clicking the View Job button. A summary of job will be displayed, as shown in Figure 2.3.

FIGURE 2.3   Import job run status

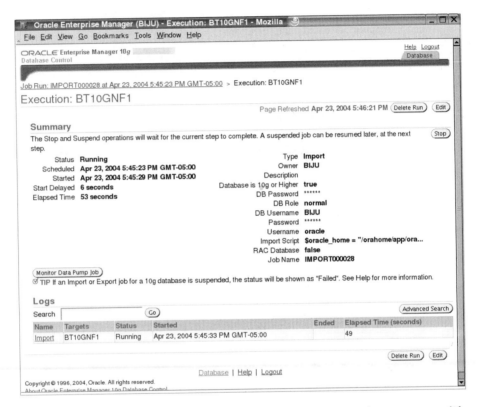

The Monitor Data Pump Job button will take you to the details of the job. You can modify the parallelism or kill/stop the job. You may also use impdp client to monitor this job after attaching to the job.

Making Data Movement Enhancements

Apart from Data Pump, Oracle has improved the data movement capabilities of two other major components of Oracle 10*g*. Transportable tablespaces support cross-platform movement, and external tables support writing from the database (unloading). We will discuss these enhancements in the next two sections.

Using Cross-Platform Transportable Tablespaces

Oracle 8*i* introduced the transportable tablespace feature. Oracle 8*i* and Oracle 9*i* supported the transportable tablespaces feature when the Oracle databases were running on the same architecture and operating system. Oracle 10*g* supports moving datafiles across different platforms.

Each operating system supports either big- or little-Endian format to store numerical values. On platforms with big-Endian format, values are stored with the most significant bytes first in memory. On platforms with little-Endian format, values are stored with least significant bytes first.

When doing cross-platform transportable tablespaces, you can copy the datafiles directly if their Endian formats are the same. If the Endian formats are different, you must use RMAN to convert the datafiles before importing them to the target database. The V$TRANSPORATABLE_PLATFORM view shows Endian format for each platform.

```
SQL> select platform_id, platform_name, endian_format
  2  from    v$transportable_platform
  3  order by platform_name
SQL> /


PLATFORM_ID PLATFORM_NAME                           ENDIAN
----------- ------------------------------------    ----------
          6 AIX-Based Systems (64-bit)              Big
         16 Apple Mac OS                            Big
         15 HP Open VMS                             Little
          5 HP Tru64 UNIX                           Little
          3 HP-UX (64-bit)                          Big
          4 HP-UX IA (64-bit)                       Big
          9 IBM zSeries Based Linux                 Big
         13 Linux 64-bit for AMD                    Little
         10 Linux IA (32-bit)                       Little
         11 Linux IA (64-bit)                       Little
         12 Microsoft Windows 64-bit for AMD        Little
          7 Microsoft Windows IA (32-bit)           Little
          8 Microsoft Windows IA (64-bit)           Little
          1 Solaris[tm] OE (32-bit)                 Big
          2 Solaris[tm] OE (64-bit)                 Big

15 rows selected.

SQL>
```

The V$DATABASE includes two new columns, PLATFORM_ID and PLATFORM_NAME.

With cross-platform tablespaces, data can be easily distributed across multiple platforms. Usually in data warehouse environments, the data marts are on smaller platforms, and the data warehouse is on a larger platform. It also allows database to be migrated from one platform to another by building the database and transporting application data tablespaces.

In the following sections, we will review the limitations of cross-platform transportable tablespaces and discuss the steps involved in using cross-platform transportable tablespaces.

Introducing the Limitations of Cross-Platform Transportable Tablespaces

For the cross-platform tablespace to work, you need to have the COMPATIBLE parameter set to 10.0.0 or higher on both databases. All the datafiles must be platform aware. When you first open the database with COMPATIBLE set to 10.0 or higher, all online read-write datafiles are made platform aware. So before transporting read-only tablespaces to another database, make sure to make the tablespaces read-write once at least with the COMPATIBLE parameter set to 10.0 or higher (applicable only to databases that are upgraded from earlier releases with read-only tablespaces).

The databases must use the same database character set and national character set. Character set conversion is not possible in transportable tablespaces.

A limitation exists on the CLOB datatype columns created prior to Oracle 10g (applicable only if the database was upgraded from an earlier release). RMAN does not convert the CLOB data; the application must take care of the conversion if any is required. Prior to Oracle 10g, CLOB datatype was represented as UCS2, which is Endian-dependent, and in Oracle 10g CLOB is represented as AL16UTF16, which is Endian-independent. The big-Endian UCS2 is same as AL16UTF16, so no conversion is needed.

Introducing the Steps for Transporting Tablespaces Across Platforms

The steps involved in transporting tablespaces to another database within the same platform and across platforms are similar if the Endian formats of the platforms are the same. These are the steps involved:

1. Determine if the platforms use the same Endian format by querying the V$TRANSPORTABLE_PLATFORM in the source and target databases:

```
SQL> select a.platform_id, a.platform_name,
            endian_format
  2  from   v$transportable_platform a, v$database b
  3* where  a.platform_id = b.platform_id
SQL> /

PLATFORM_ID PLATFORM_NAME                    ENDIAN_FOR
----------- ------------------------------   ----------
         10 Linux IA (32-bit)                Little

SQL>
```

2. Ensure the tablespaces to be transported are self-contained. Use the DBMS_TTS.TRANSPORT_ SET_CHECK procedure to determine this. For example:

```
SQL> EXEC DBMS_TTS.TRANSPORT_SET_CHECK( -
            'SALES_DATA,SALES_INDEX',TRUE);
```

3. Make the tablespaces to be transported read-only in the source database.

```
SQL> ALTER TABLESPACE SALES_DATA READ ONLY;
SQL> ALTER TABLESPACE SALES_INDEX READ ONLY;
```

4. Use the expdp utility to unload the metadata information for the tablespaces to be transported.

```
$ expdp system DUMPFILE=sales_tts.dmp
  LOGFILE=sales_tts.log
  DIRECTORY=dumplocation TRANSPORT_FULL_CHECK=Y
  TRANSPORT_TABLESPACES=SALES_DATA,SALES_INDEX
```

5. In step 1, if we have determined that the Endian formats are same for the platforms, you can skip this step and proceed to step 6. If the Endian formats are different, the datafiles need to be converted using RMAN.

    To convert the datafiles from the little-Endian format (Linux) to the big-Endian format (Sun Solaris), do the following:

```
$ rman target /
RMAN> CONVERT TABLESPACE 'sales_data, sales_index'
2> TO PLATFORM 'Solaris[tm] OE (64-bit)'
3> DB_FILE_NAME_CONVERT =
4> '/oradata/BT10GNF1/sales_data01.dbf',
5> '/tmp/sales_data01_sun.dbf',
6> '/oradata/BT10GNF1/sales_index01.dbf',
7> '/tmp/sales_index01_sun.dbf';
```

    If you decide to convert the datafiles at the target platform, you can do so—just replace line 2 with FROM_PLATFORM 'Linux IA (32-bit)'.

6. Use operating system utilities to copy the converted datafiles and the metadata dump file to the target server. Use the impdp utility on the target to import the metadata and plug-in the tablespaces. The target user must already exist in the target database, if not, you can make the objects owned by an existing user using the REMAP_SCHEMA parameter, as shown here:

```
$impdp system DUMPFILE=sales_tts.dmp
  LOGFILE=sales_tts_imp.log DIRECTORY=data_dump_dir
  TRANSPORT_DATAFILES='/oradata/SL10H/sales_data01.dbf',
  '/oradata/SL10H/sales_index01.dbf'
```

7. Make the new tablespaces read-write in the target database, like so:

```
SQL> ALTER TABLESPACE SALES_DATA READ WRITE;
SQL> ALTER TABLESPACE SALES_INDEX READ WRITE;
```

Writing and Projecting External Tables

Oracle 9*i* introduced external tables and were read-only from the Oracle database. In Oracle 10*g*, you can write to external tables. The external table enhancements in Oracle 10*g* also include the parallel populate operation and projected column feature. DML statements or index creation is still not permitted on external tables.

In Oracle9*i*, ORACLE_LOADER was the only access driver available for external tables. Oracle 10*g* has a new access driver called the ORACLE_DATAPUMP. Only tables created with ORACLE_DATAPUMP can be written to. The external tables that use ORACLE_LOADER access driver are still read-only— they read ASCII flat files from the operating system. Only the external tables created with ORACLE_DATAPUMP access driver can be written to. The resulting file is in proprietary format (Oracle native external representation, DPAPI), which only the Oracle Data Pump can read. You may use this file to load to another Oracle database.

You may wonder how this is beneficial. Why don't you use the Oracle Data Pump clients to generate the file? Well, though Oracle Data Pump client utilities (expdp and impdp) can handle a certain level of filtering, join operations with another table is not possible. Using the external table ORACLE_DATAPUMP access driver, you can unload data that is derived from complex queries. This is useful in loading data marts from data warehouse or similar applications.

In the following sections, we will discuss using the external tables for data loading and unloading.

Loading Using External Tables

The ORACLE_LOADER access driver loads data to an Oracle database from a flat file using the external table method. You can specify the PARALLEL clause when creating the table; ORACLE_ LOADER access driver divides the large flat file into chunks that can be processed separately. Loading data in the context of external table means reading data from external table (flat file) and loading to a table in the database using a INSERT statement.

Let's create an external table using the ORACLE_LOADER access driver; the user already has privilege to read and write the directory WORK_DIR. The source datafile is employee.dat, which has fixed column data (name, title, salary). The following code shows the contents of the employee.dat file, creates the external table using the ORACLE_LOADER driver, and queries the external table:

```
linux:oracle>cat employee.dat
SMITH    CLERK      800
SCOTT    ANALYST    3000
ADAMS    CLERK      1100
MILLER   CLERK      1300
linux:oracle>
SQL> CREATE TABLE employees (
  2    ename   VARCHAR2 (10),
  3    title   VARCHAR2 (10),
  4    salary  NUMBER (8))
```

```
 5  ORGANIZATION EXTERNAL (
 6  TYPE ORACLE_LOADER
 7  DEFAULT DIRECTORY WORK_DIR
 8  ACCESS PARAMETERS
    (RECORDS DELIMITED BY NEWLINE FIELDS (
 9  ename CHAR(10),
10  title CHAR(10),
11  salary CHAR(8)))
12  LOCATION ('employee.dat'))
13  PARALLEL
SQL> /

Table created.

SQL> SELECT * FROM employees;

ENAME       TITLE       SALARY
----------  ----------  ----------
SMITH       CLERK            800
SCOTT       ANALYST         3000
ADAMS       CLERK           1100
MILLER      CLERK           1300

SQL>
```

You can use the data from this external table to load other tables using INSERT statements. The characteristics shown in the example work the same on an Oracle 9*i* database; the code is provided here for completeness of the loading and unloading discussion.

 Only the SELECT statement is allowed on external tables; no INSERT/UPDATE/DELETE operation is permitted on external tables.

Unloading Using External Tables

The ORACLE_DATAPUMP access driver unloads data from an Oracle database to a flat file (DPAPI format) using the external table method. The external table must be created using the CREATE TABLE ... AS SELECT ... (CTAS) method. You can specify the PARALLEL clause when creating the table; ORACLE_DATAPUMP access driver unloads data into multiple flat files at the same time. One parallel execution server will write to only one file at a time. Unloading data in the context of external table means creating an external table (flat file) using CTAS method.

During the unload (or populate) operation, the data goes from the subquery to the SQL engine for the data to be processed and is extracted in the DPAPI format to write to the flat file. The external table to unload data can be created only using the CTAS method with the ORACLE_DATAPUMP access driver. The unload operation does not include the metadata for the tables. You can use the VERSION clause when unloading the data to make sure it loads correctly on the target database.

Let's demonstrate unloading data using the ORACLE_DATAPUMP access driver. We will join the EMPLOYEES and DEPARTMENTS tables of the HR schema to unload data. User SCOTT has write privilege on the directory WORK_DIR and has SELECT privilege on the tables in the subquery. The following statement creates the table in the database as well as creates two files—empl_comm1.dmp and empl_comm2.dmp—in the operating system.

```
SQL> CREATE TABLE empl_commission
  2  ORGANIZATION EXTERNAL (TYPE ORACLE_DATAPUMP
  3  DEFAULT DIRECTORY work_dir
  4  LOCATION ('empl_comm1.dmp','empl_comm2.dmp'))
  5  PARALLEL 2
  6  AS
  7  SELECT employee_id,
  8         first_name || ' ' || last_name employee_name,
  9         department_name,
 10         TO_CHAR(hire_date,'DD-MM-YYYY') hire_date,
 11         salary * NVL(commission_pct, 0.5) commission
 12  FROM hr.employees
 13       JOIN hr.departments
 14       USING (department_id)
 15  ORDER BY first_name || ' ' || last_name
SQL> /

Table created.

SQL> SELECT department_name, sum(commission) total_comm
  2  FROM    empl_commission
  3  GROUP BY department_name;

DEPARTMENT_NAME                 TOTAL_COMM
------------------------------- ----------
Accounting                           10150
Finance                              25800
Human Resources                       3250
Marketing                             9500
Purchasing                           12450
```

Sales	72640
Shipping	78200
Administration	2200
Executive	29000
IT	14400
Public Relations	5000

11 rows selected.

SQL>

Now you can copy the dump files to another Oracle 10g database and load it using the Data Pump utility or create an external table on these dump files and load from it. Let's create an external table using these dump files and query it:

```
SQL> CREATE TABLE new_empl_commission (
  2   employee_id  NUMBER (6),
  3   employee_name VARCHAR2 (40),
  4   department_name VARCHAR2 (30),
  5   hire_date VARCHAR2 (10),
  6   commission NUMBER)
  7   ORGANIZATION EXTERNAL (TYPE ORACLE_DATAPUMP
  8   DEFAULT DIRECTORY work_dir
  9   ACCESS PARAMETERS (
 10   LOGFILE 'new_empl_commission.log')
 11   LOCATION ('empl_comm1.dmp', 'expl_comm2.dmp'));

Table created.

SQL> SELECT department_name, sum(commission) total_comm
  2   FROM   new_empl_commission
  3   GROUP BY department_name;
```

DEPARTMENT_NAME	TOTAL_COMM
Accounting	10150
Administration	2200
Executive	29000
Finance	25800
Human Resources	3250
IT	14400
Marketing	9500

```
Public Relations                    5000
Purchasing                          12450
Sales                               72640
Shipping                            78200

11 rows selected.

SQL>
```

When dealing with external table files that contain rows of data that may be rejected, the projected column feature gets a consistent result set. The next section will discuss projected columns.

The data dictionary views DBA_EXTERNAL_TABLES and DBA_EXTERNAL_LOCATIONS can be queried to view the characteristics, location, and filenames of external tables.

Using Projected Columns

Since external tables are based on flat files, they could contain unclean or malformed data that may get rejected. For this reason, Oracle 10g processes all the columns of the external table even if they are not used in the SELECT statement every time you access the external table. If you know that the data is safe, you can improve performance by making Oracle process only the columns in the SELECT statement. You accomplish this by using the following:

```
ALTER TABLE external_table_name
PROJECT COLUMN REFERENCED;
```

PROJECT COLUMN ALL is the default for the external table.

Let's demonstrate using an example. Refer to the table EMPLOYEES created under the section "Loading Using External Tables." You are going to create a bad row in the employees.dat file (non-numeric value in the salary column for SCOTT). The REJECT LIMIT (number of bad rows allowed) is by default 0; you have to change it first to do this demonstration.

```
linux:oracle>cat employee.dat
SMITH     CLERK     800
SCOTT     ANALYST   3AAA
ADAMS     CLERK     1100
MILLER    CLERK     1300
linux:oracle>
SQL> ALTER TABLE employees REJECT LIMIT UNLIMITED;

Table altered.
```

```
SQL> SELECT COUNT(ename) FROM employees;

COUNT(ENAME)
------------
           3

SQL> SELECT COUNT(salary) FROM employees;

COUNT(SALARY)
-------------
           3

SQL> ALTER TABLE employees PROJECT COLUMN REFERENCED;

Table altered.

SQL> SELECT COUNT(ename) FROM employees;

COUNT(ENAME)
------------
           4

SQL> SELECT COUNT(salary) FROM employees;

COUNT(SALARY)
-------------
           3

SQL>
```

The PROPERTY column in DBA_EXTERNAL_TABLES shows you the projected column status of the table. The default is ALL in Oracle 10g; in Oracle 9i the only behavior available was REFERENCED.

Managing the Scheduler

Oracle 10g includes a very sophisticated scheduling mechanism to automate routine tasks. The scheduler offers you the ability to manage the Oracle database environment by breaking the tasks into manageable components. It is a collection of procedures and functions in the DBMS_ SCHEDULER package. The earlier versions of Oracle included the DBMS_JOB program to schedule jobs; this utility is still available in Oracle 10g.

The main differences between DBMS_JOB and DBMS_SCHEDULER are

- DBMS_JOB can execute only stored programs or anonymous PL/SQL blocks. The new DBMS_SCHEDULER can execute stored programs, anonymous blocks and OS executables.
- There is only one component in DBMS_JOB, the job. The DBMS_SCHEDULER has several components that enhance the scheduling capabilities and works with the resource manager.
- The job or schedule intervals can be defined in a more complex and in natural language using DBMS_SCHEDULER. DBMS_JOB accepts only SQL date expressions.
- DBMS_SCHEDULER has a more detailed job run status and failure information that can be queried from the data dictionary.

You can manage the scheduler using the DBMS_SCHEDULER package programs or by using the Oracle Enterprise Manger. We will discuss both in this chapter.

The scheduler helps DBAs and developers to control when, where, and what various tasks take place. A typical example of using the scheduler is to automate database maintenance jobs such as performing database backups, loading data warehouse data, calculating statistics, refreshing materialized views, checking for audit violations, creating month-end reports, and so on.

In the following sections we discuss the concepts and components of the scheduler.

Understanding Scheduler Concepts

The scheduler is a set of programs in the DBMS_SCHEDULER package. They are callable from any PL/SQL program or by using the EM Database Control. The following are the basic components of the scheduler:

Program   A *program* determines what task needs to be performed. The program is a collection of metadata information about the name of the program, its type, and its arguments. The program type could be an anonymous PL/SQL block, stored procedure, or operating system executable. You create programs in the scheduler using the DBMS_SCHEDULER.CREATE_PROGRAM procedure.

Schedule   A *schedule* specifies when and how often a task (job) will be executed. You can schedule jobs to run immediately or at a later time. For jobs that repeat, you can also specify the frequency and end date. You create schedules in the scheduler using the DBMS_SCHEDULER.CREATE_SCHEDULE procedure.

Job   *Job* specifies the program that needs to be executed and the schedule. A program and schedule can be shared in the database. Each user can have a job created using the program and schedule. A job instance represents a specific run of the job. You create jobs in the scheduler using the DBMS_SCHEDULER.CREATE_JOB procedure.

The scheduler also includes the following advanced components that can be used to prioritize jobs and to ensure resources are allocated appropriately:

Job class   A *job class* defines a group of jobs that share the same characteristics and have common resource usage requirements. A job can belong to only one job class. A job class can be associated with a resource consumer group. The resource consumer group determines the resources that are allocated to the jobs in the job class. Within each job class, you can prioritize the jobs.

Window and window group   A *window* can activate different resource plans at different times. The window represents an interval with a well-defined start and end time. A *window group* is a list of windows. A window or window group is also a valid schedule for a job; this ensures that a job runs only when a particular resource plan is active.

Each component of the scheduler is considered as a database object. You can manage privileges on these objects as you would on a table or procedure. When you try to drop an object or alter an object that does not exist in the scheduler, a PL/SQL exception is raised. If you try to enable or disable an object that is already enabled or disabled, no error is generated.

Creating Basic Scheduler Components

You should use the DBMS_SCHEDULER program to create the scheduler components using any PL/SQL interface. You can also create the components using the EM interface. From the database home page of EM, click the Administration tab to manage the components of the scheduler.

In the following sections, we will discuss how to create programs, jobs, and schedules.

Creating Programs

As stated earlier, a program is a collection of metadata about what is run by the scheduler. The CREATE JOB privilege is required for creating a job in the user's schema; CREATE ANY JOB privilege lets the user create the program in any schema. For another user to execute the programs created by you, you have to grant the EXECUTE privilege on the program to that user. The DBMS_SCHEDULER.CREATE_PROGRAM procedure has the following arguments:

PROGRAM_NAME   Specifies the name of the program; must be unique in the SQL namespace. This parameter does not have a default value.

PROGRAM_TYPE   Specifies the type of the program. Three types of programs exist: plsql_block, stored_procedure, and executable. This parameter does not have a default value.

PROGRAM_ACTION   Specifies the PL/SQL code, name of the PL/SQL procedure, or name of the external executable including the full path name. This parameter does not have a default value.

NUMBER_OF_ARGUMENTS   Specifies the number of arguments for an executable or stored procedure. The default is 0 (no arguments).

ENABLED   Specifies if the program should be created and enabled. A program must be enabled before it can be used. The default is FALSE.

COMMENTS   Specifies a comment for the program. The default is NULL.

Let's create a program using the scheduler. The task is to run a shell script executable. Here is the code to do this:

```
SQL> BEGIN
  2   DBMS_SCHEDULER.CREATE_PROGRAM(
  3   program_name=>'SCOTT.CHECK_ALERT_LOG_ERRORS',
  4   program_action=>'/dba_script/cron/check_alert.sh',
  5   program_type=>'EXECUTABLE',
  6   comments=>'Email DBA if errors in the alert file',
  7   enabled=>TRUE);
  8   END;
  9   /

PL/SQL procedure successfully completed.

SQL>
```

Here is another example where the program runs a stored procedure that takes two arguments:

```
SQL> BEGIN
  2   DBMS_SCHEDULER.CREATE_PROGRAM(
  3   program_name=>'SCP_PURGE_LOG_TABLE',
  4   program_action=>'SCOTT.PURGE_LOG_TABLE',
  5   program_type=>'STORED_PROCEDURE',
  6   number_of_arguments=>2,
  7   comments=>'Purge the Log tables');
  8   END;
SQL> /

PL/SQL procedure successfully completed.

SQL>
```

The arguments to the program are defined using the DBMS_SCHEDULER.DEFINE_PROGRAM_ARGUMENT procedure. You can define the arguments to a program irrespective of whether the program is enabled or disabled. The following are the parameters in the DEFINE_PROGRAM_ARGUMENT procedure:

PROGRAM_NAME   Specifies the name of the program; the program must exist before you can define argument. This parameter does not have a default value.

ARGUMENT_NAME   Specifies the name of the argument; this parameter is optional and defaults to NULL

ARGUMENT_POSITION   Specifies the position of the argument when it is passed to the program. The valid values are from 1 to the *number_of_arguments* defined in the program specification. This parameter does not have a default value.

ARGUMENT_TYPE   Specifies the datatype of the argument. This parameter does not have a default value.

DEFAULT_VALUE   Specifies any default values to be used. This parameter does not have a default value.

OUT_ARGUMENT   This must be set to FALSE; the parameter is reserved for future use. The default is FALSE.

Let's now define the arguments to the program defined earlier:

```
SQL> BEGIN
  2  DBMS_SCHEDULER.DEFINE_PROGRAM_ARGUMENT(
  3  program_name=>'SCOTT.SCP_PURGE_LOG_TABLE',
  4  argument_name=>'SCHEMA_NAME',
  5  argument_position=>1,
  6  argument_type=>'VARCHAR2',
  7  default_value=>'SCOTT',
  8  out_argument=>FALSE);
  9
 10  DBMS_SCHEDULER.DEFINE_PROGRAM_ARGUMENT(
 11  program_name=>'SCOTT.SCP_PURGE_LOG_TABLE',
 12  argument_position=>2,
 13  argument_type=>'VARCHAR2');
 14  END;
SQL> /

PL/SQL procedure successfully completed.

SQL>
```

Figure 2.4 shows the EM screen to create a program. You can also define the arguments to the program in the same screen.

Creating Schedules

As mentioned earlier, schedules define when a task needs to be run. The CREATE JOB privilege is required to create a schedule. The CREATE ANY JOB privilege lets you create the schedule in any schema in the database. You use the DBMS_SCHEDULER.CREATE_SCHEDULE procedure to create schedules.

FIGURE 2.4   EM Create Program screen

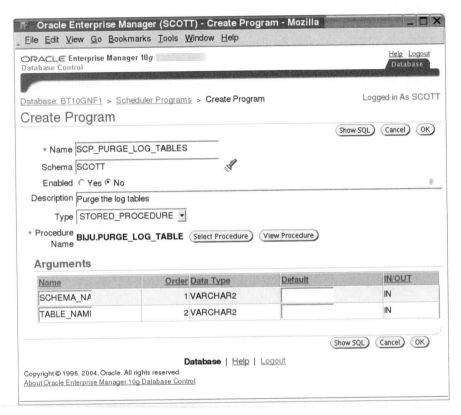

The following are the parameters to the CREATE_SCHEDULE procedure:

SCHEDULE_NAME   Specifies name of the schedule. The name has to be unique in the SQL namespace. This parameter does not have a default value.

START_DATE   Specifies the first date when the schedule becomes active. For repeating schedules, start_date determines the first instance of the schedule. The default value is NULL.

REPEAT_INTERVAL   Specifies in calendar expression how often the job should repeat (see the section "Specifying Calendaring Expressions" for more information). SQL expressions such as 'TRUNC(SYSDATE)+28/24' are not valid when defining named schedules. This parameter does not have a default value.

END_DATE   Specifies the date after which the schedule becomes inactive. The end_date must be after the start_date. The default value is NULL.

COMMENTS   Specifies and optional comments to the schedule. The default value is NULL.

The following example creates a schedule with the name SCS_TUES_AM in SCOTT's schema. The schedule runs every Tuesday at 8 a.m. with no end date and is valid from April 27.

```
SQL> BEGIN
  2  SYS.DBMS_SCHEDULER.CREATE_SCHEDULE(
  3  repeat_interval => 'FREQ=WEEKLY;BYDAY=TUE;BYHOUR=8;➡
BYMINUTE=0;BYSECOND=0',
  4  start_date => to_timestamp_tz(➡
'2004-04-27 US/Central', 'YYYY-MM-DD TZR'),
  5  comments => 'Tuesday AM Schedule',
  6  schedule_name => '"SCOTT"."SCS_TUES_AM"');
  7  END;
SQL> /

PL/SQL procedure successfully completed.

SQL>
```

Figure 2.5 shows the screen to create a schedule using the EM. The Repeat drop-down selection determines the columns and parameters for the interval. The Repeat drop-down list does not have seconds as an option for repeat interval, though the scheduler supports it.

You specify the start and end times to a schedule using the TIMESTAMP datatype. The precision is only up to a second.

Creating Jobs

As noted earlier, a job is a combination of the schedule and program. A job can use named schedules and named programs or define the schedule and program as part of the job definition. The job definition can be in any of the following combinations:

- Using a named program (a program defined using the CREATE_PROGRAM) and a named schedule (a schedule defined using CREATE_SCHEDULE)

- Using a named program and an inline schedule (a schedule defined as part of the job)

- Using an inline program (a program defined as part of the job) and named schedule

The DBMS_SCHEDULER.CREATE_JOB procedure has the following parameters:

JOB_NAME   Specifies the name of the job. This parameter does not have a default value.

PROGRAM_NAME   Specifies the name of the program to run. This parameter does not have a default value.

SCHEDULE_NAME   Specifies the name of the schedule to use. This parameter does not have a default value.

FIGURE 2.5 EM Create Schedule screen

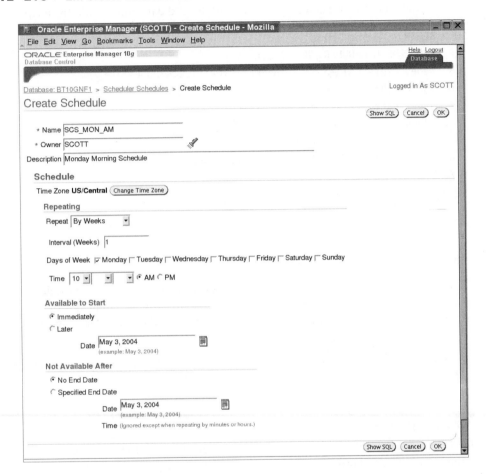

JOB_CLASS Specifies to which class the job belongs. If not specified, the job is assigned to the DEFAULT_JOB_CLASS job class.

ENABLED Specifies if the job is enabled. The default is FALSE. You have to enable a job before it can be used.

AUTO_DROP Specifies if the job should be automatically removed when its status is changed to COMPLETED. The default is TRUE, which means for one-time jobs, the job definition will be dropped as soon as the job completes; for repeating jobs, the definition will be removed when the end date of the schedule reached.

COMMENTS Specifies a description of the job. This parameter does not have a default value.

You can use the following parameters to replace the PROGRAM_NAME parameter (defining inline program):

JOB_TYPE   Specifies type of the job, equivalent to PROGRAM_TYPE. Valid values are plsql_block, stored_procedure, and executable.

JOB_ACTION   Specifies what needs to be executed; equivalent to PROGRAM_ACTION.

NUMBER_OF_ARGUMENTS   Specifies the number of arguments to a stored procedure or executable. The default is 0.

You can use the following parameters to replace the SCHEDULE_NAME parameter (defining inline schedule):

START_DATE   Specifies the date when the job becomes active. This parameter has a default value of NULL.

REPEAT_INTERVAL   Specifies the frequency of the repeating jobs. You can specify this using the calendaring expressions or using PL/SQL expressions. If no repeat interval is specified, the job runs only once on the specified start date.

END_DATE   Specifies the date when the job becomes inactive. Let's create a job that runs every week at 8 a.m. Though the calendaring expressions are easy and more readable, this example uses a SQL expression for the repeat interval (to demonstrate that it can be used when defining job schedule). The job does not use a named program or a named schedule. The schedule and program are defined with the job.

```
SQL> BEGIN
  2  SYS.DBMS_SCHEDULER.CREATE_JOB(
  3  job_name => 'SCOTT.SCJ_WEEKLY_DATA_CHECK',
  4  job_type => 'EXECUTABLE',
  5  job_action => '/scripts/app/weekly_data_check.sh',
  6  repeat_interval => 'TRUNC(SYSDATE)+176/24',
  7  start_date => TRUNC(SYSDATE)+8,
  8  comments => 'Check if data from Vendor loaded right',
  9  auto_drop => FALSE,
 10  enabled => TRUE);
 11  END;
SQL> /

PL/SQL procedure successfully completed.

SQL>
```

If you have a saved program and a saved schedule, the create job statement would be as follows:

```
SQL> BEGIN
  2   SYS.DBMS_SCHEDULER.CREATE_JOB(
  3   job_name => 'SCOTT.SCJ_TUE_PURGE',
  4   program_name => 'SCOTT.SCP_PURGE_LOG_TABLES',
  5   schedule_name => 'SCOTT.SCS_TUES_AM',
  6   comments => 'Purge Activity Logs on Tuesday',
  7   auto_drop => FALSE,
  8   enabled => TRUE);
  9   END;
SQL> /

PL/SQL procedure successfully completed.

SQL>
```

If multiple jobs need to be run at the same time, using saved schedules helps manage them better. If you want to change the time of the schedule, you need to change repeat_interval or end_date only once for the saved schedule, instead of changing each job. When a schedule is modified, each job using the schedule is automatically updated to use the new schedule.

Use the DBMS_SCHEDULER.SET_JOB_ARGUMENT_VALUE procedure to set parameter values for a job (similar to setting parameter values to a program). You can specify the parameter name using argument_name (only for saved programs) or argument_position.

Here is an example of setting up a job using a stored procedure that accepts two parameters, with a named schedule:

```
SQL> BEGIN
  2   SYS.DBMS_SCHEDULER.CREATE_JOB(
  3   job_name => 'SCOTT.SCJ_PURGE_DAILY_ACTIVTY',
  4   job_type => 'STORED_PROCEDURE',
  5   job_action => 'SCOTT.PURGE_LOG_TABLE',
  6   schedule_name => 'SCOTT.SCS_TUES_AM',
  7   comments => 'Named schedule inline procedure with
                    arguments',
  8   number_of_arguments => 2,
  9   enabled => FALSE);
 10   SYS.DBMS_SCHEDULER.SET_JOB_ARGUMENT_VALUE(
 11   job_name => 'SCOTT.SCJ_PURGE_DAILY_ACTIVTY',
 12   argument_position => 1,
 13   argument_value => 'HR');
 14   SYS.DBMS_SCHEDULER.SET_JOB_ARGUMENT_VALUE(
 15   job_name => 'SCOTT.SCJ_PURGE_DAILY_ACTIVTY',
```

```
 16    argument_position => 2,
 17    argument_value => 'DAILY_ACTIVITY');
 18    END;
SQL> /

PL/SQL procedure successfully completed.

SQL>
```

A job instance is a specific run of a job. For nonrepeating jobs, there will be only one instance. For jobs that repeat, there will be multiple instances.

Oracle *calendaring expressions* are used for the repeat interval of saved schedule; the repeat interval on a job could use either a calendaring expression or a SQL expression. In the next section, we will discuss how to use the calendaring expressions.

Specifying Calendaring Expressions

`repeat_interval` specifies how often a job or schedule repeats, using the calendaring expressions of Oracle. The calendaring expression has the following three parts:

- Frequency
- Interval
- Specifier

You specify the components using the keywords FREQ=, INTERVAL=, and *specifier_name=*. Semicolons separate each part and the components.

Frequency is the only mandatory part in the calendaring expression. You can specify frequency using any of the following types of recurrence:

```
YEARLY
MONTHLY
WEEKLY
DAILY
HOURLY
MINUTELY
SECONDLY
```

Interval is specified as a numeric integer; valid values are between 1 and 99.

The specifier provides detailed information about when the job should be run. Using *specifier_name*, you can determine which hours the job should be run or on what days the job should be run. The following are the available specifiers:

BYMONTH   Specifies which month the job should be run. You can specify the month as 1 through 12 or JAN through DEC.

BYWEEKNO   Specifies the week numbers of the year (follows ISO-8601 standard). The week number can be between 1 and 53. BYWEEKNO is valid only for FREQ=YEARLY.

BYYEARDAY Specifies the day of the year as a number. Must be careful with leap years when specifying BYYEARDAY. Valid values are between 1 and 366. You can specify negative numbers, which will evaluate to the same day irrespective of leap year. The number –17 will evaluate to December 15 always.

BYMONTHDAY Specifies day of the month (1 through 31). Negative values can be used. The number –1 means the last day of the month.

BYDAY Specifies the day of the week as a three-character abbreviation (MON, TUE, and so on).

BYHOUR Specifies the hour of the day. Values can range from 0 through 23.

BYMINUTE Specifies the minute of the hour. Values are from 0 through 59.

BYSECOND Specifies the second on the minute. Values are from 0 through 59.

Table 2.11 shows examples of using calendaring expressions.

Using the calendaring expressions, you can schedule jobs for every possible combination of run dates. You may use the DBMS_SCHEDULER.EVALUATE_CALENDAR_STRING procedure to verify the calendar syntax without running a real job.

TABLE 2.11 Calendaring Expression Examples

Calendaring Expression	Result
FREQ=HOURLY;INTERVAL=4	Every 4 hours
FREQ=DAILY;INTERVAL=10;BYHOUR=8;BYMINUTE=0;BYSECOND=0	Every 10 days at 8 a.m.
FREQ=WEEKLY;INTERVAL=3;BYDAY=WED,SAT;BYHOUR=6;BYMINUTE=30	Every third Wednesday and Saturday at 6:30 a.m.
FREQ=MONTHLY;INTERVAL=2;BYMONTHDAY=-1,15;BYHOUR=17	Every other month, on the 15th and the last day of the month at 5 p.m.
FREQ=YEARLY;BYYEARDAY=-276	Every March 31st
FREQ=YEALY;BYMONTH=MAR;BYMONTHDAY=31	Every March 31st
FREQ=YEARLY;BYWEEKNO=1;BYDAY=SAT	First Saturday of the year
FREQ=MONTHLY;BYDAY=-2FRI	Second-to-last Friday of every month
FREQ=HOURLY;BYMONTHDAY=1,-1	Every hour on the first and last day of the month

Using the Scheduler

The scheduler objects (schedules, programs, jobs) are all treated as individual database objects, and they follow the same rules for privileges and naming other database objects. In the following sections, we will discuss the programs available for setting the scheduler environment and to administer the scheduler components.

To create a job, schedule, or program, you need the CREATE JOB privilege. To create a job, schedule, or program in another schema, you need the CREATE ANY JOB privilege. For a user to use a scheduler component created by you, the user must have the EXECUTE privilege on the object or the EXECUTE ANY PROGRAM privilege. When a named schedule is created, all users in the database (PUBLIC) have access to the schedule. The following are the privileges on individual scheduler objects:

```
EXECUTE ON program>
ALTER ON job, program or schedule
ALL ON job, program or schedule
```

The object privileges are granted using the regular SQL syntax of GRANT and REVOKE statements.

In the next section we will discuss enabling/disabling the job components and administering the scheduler components.

Administering Scheduler Components

You can modify and drop programs, schedules, and jobs once they are created. To modify or drop a component, you must be the owner of the component, have explicit ALTER/ALL privilege on the component, or have CREATE ANY JOB privilege.

You can enable a job or program using the DBMS_SCHEDULER.ENABLE procedure. You can disable a job or program using the DBMS_SCHEDULER.DISABLE procedure. ENABLE and DISABLE procedures have only one parameter, the program or job name.

The following example disables the SCJ_TUE_PURGE job and enables the SCP_PURGE_LOG_TABLES program:

```
SQL> BEGIN
  2    SYS.DBMS_SCHEDULER.DISABLE('SCOTT.SCJ_TUE_PURGE');
  3    SYS.DBMS_SCHEDULER.ENABLE
                       ('SCOTT.SCP_PURGE_LOG_TABLES');
  4    END;
SQL> /

PL/SQL procedure successfully completed.

SQL>
```

The ENABLE and DISABLE procedures can accept multiple jobs or programs as a comma-delimited list. Here is an example:

```
SQL> EXEC SYS,DBMS_SCHEDULER.ENABLE(  -
    'SCOTT.SCP_XR, HR.SCP_PAYROLL, VOLEST.SCJ_WEEKLY');
```

Let's discuss the administrative options available in each type of component.

Managing Jobs

Once a job is created and is enabled, you can run it using the DBMS_SCHEDULER.RUN_JOB procedure. The procedure accepts the job name as the parameter. If you want to run the job in the background, specify FALSE as the second parameter.

Many occurrences of the job can be running at the same time, if you run the job in the current session (second parameter TRUE). Here is an example to run the job SCJ_TUE_PURGE in the background:

```
SQL> EXEC DBMS_SCHEDULER.RUN_JOB('SCOTT.SCJ_TUE_PURGE',FALSE);
```

If a job is running currently and you want to stop it, use the DBMS_SCHEDULER.STOP_JOB procedure. *job_name* and force are the parameters to this procedure. If you set force to TRUE, the job slave process is terminated when the scheduler cannot stop the job gracefully using an interrupt mechanism. To force stop a job, you need the MANAGE SCHEDULER system privilege, which is not applicable to jobs of type EXECUTABLE. To stop multiple jobs, you can specify a comma-delimited list of jobs as the job name. Here is an example to stop the currently running SCJ_TUE_PURGE job. The second example shows force stopping the job.:

```
SQL> EXEC DBMS_SCHEDULER.STOP_JOB('SCOTT.SCJ_TUE_PURGE');
SQL> EXEC DBMS_SCHEDULER.STOP_JOB('SCOTT.SCJ_TUE_PURGE', TRUE);
```

To drop a job from the scheduler, use DBMS_SCHEDULER.DROP_JOB procedure. The job name can be a list of jobs and job classes. To drop a job that is currently running, specify TRUE as the second parameter (force). When the job is dropped, it arguments are also dropped. The following example drops two jobs:

```
SQL> EXEC DBMS_SCHEDULER.DROP_JOB('SCOTT.SCJ_DAILY1, -
    SCOTT.SCJ_DAILY2');
```

You can clear the values for job arguments using the DBMS_SCHEDULER.RESET_JOB_ARGUMENT_VALUE procedure. This procedure accepts two parameters: job_name and argument_position or argument_name. If the corresponding saved program does not have a default value, the job will be disabled. The following two examples show resetting argument value using positional notation and using argument name (SCHEMA_NAME).

```
SQL> EXEC DBMS_SCHEDULER.RESET_JOB_ARGUMENT_VALUE ( -
>        'SCOTT.SCJ_PURGE_DAILY_ACTIVTY', 1);
SQL> EXEC DBMS_SCHEDULER.RESET_JOB_ARGUMENT_VALUE ( -
>        'SCOTT.SCJ_PURGE_DAILY_ACTIVTY', SCHEMA_NAME);
```

You can use the DBMS_SCHEDULER.COPY_JOB procedure to copy all the attributes of an existing job to a new job. There are two parameters: old_job and new_job.

Figure 2.6 shows the EM screen to manage jobs. The jobs are listed under three tabs: Scheduled, Running, and Disabled. You can also view the run history. Using this screen, you can create, view, edit, drop, and copy jobs.

FIGURE 2.6   EM Scheduler Jobs screen

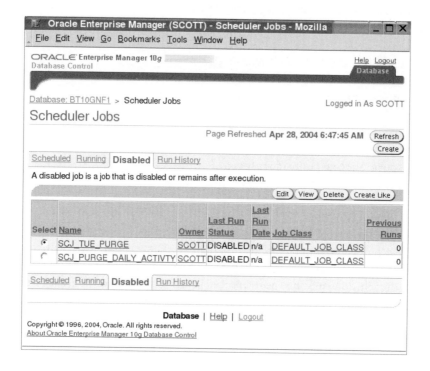

Managing Programs

You have seen enabling and disabling programs using the DBMS_SCHEDULER.ENABLE and DBMS_SCHEDULER.DISABLE procedures earlier. You can drop a saved program using the DBMS_SCHEDLER.DROP_PROGRAM procedure. This procedure accepts two parameters: program_name and force. The default for force is FALSE, which means you can drop a program only if no jobs reference the program. If it is set to TRUE, the jobs referencing the program are disabled before dropping the program. If a job is running when the program is dropped, the job continues with no issues. The program_name parameter can accept a list of comma-delimited program names.

Here is an example:

```
SQL> EXEC DBMS_SCHEDULER.DROP_PROGRAM ( -
'SCOTT.SCP_PURGE_LOG, SCOTT.SCP_TRUNC_DAILY');
```

You can use the DBMS_SCHEDULER.DROP_PROGRAM_ARGUMENT procedure to drop the arguments to a saved program. This overloaded procedure accepts two parameters: program_name and argument_ position or argument_name. The following example shows dropping the arguments from the saved program SCP_PURGE_LOG_TABLE:

```
SQL> BEGIN
  2   DBMS_SCHEDULER.DROP_PROGRAM_ARGUMENT(
  3   program_name=>'SCOTT.SCP_PURGE_LOG_TABLE',
  4   argument_name=>'SCHEMA_NAME');
  5
  6   DBMS_SCHEDULER.DROP_PROGRAM_ARGUMENT(
  7   program_name=>'SCOTT.SCP_PURGE_LOG_TABLE',
  8   argument_position=>2);
  9   END;
SQL> /

PL/SQL procedure successfully completed.

SQL>
```

Managing Schedules

You can use the DBMS_SCHEDULER.DROP_SCHEDULE procedure to drop a schedule. This procedure accepts two parameters: schedule_name and force. If the value of force is set to FALSE (the default), the schedule must not be referenced in any jobs. If set to TRUE, the referenced jobs are disabled before dropping the schedule. The schedule_name can be a list of schedules separated by comma.

Here is an example:

```
SQL> EXEC DBMS_SCHEDULER.DROP_SCHEDULE( -
          'ST.SCS_WED, ST.SCS_THU');
```

Setting Scheduler Attributes

The scheduler has procedures to set global values for the scheduler and to set values for individual scheduler object attributes. You can set three scheduler attributes at a global level using DBMS_SCHEDULER.SET_SCHEDULER_ATTRIBUTE to affect all the scheduler components. They are as follows:

DEFAULT_TIMEZONE   The default time zone specified as the time zone name (U.S./Pacific) or using an offset (–8:00).

LOG_HISTORY   The number of days log information should be kept. Its default is 30.

MAX_JOB_SLAVE_PROCESSES   Specifies the maximum number of slave processes. The default is NULL, and the range is 1–999.

Here is an example of setting these attributes:

```
SQL> BEGIN
  2   DBMS_SCHEDULER.SET_SCHEDULER_ATTRIBUTE
  3     ('DEFAULT_TIMEZONE','US/Central');
  4   DBMS_SCHEDULER.SET_SCHEDULER_ATTRIBUTE
  5     ('LOG_HISTORY','45');
  6   DBMS_SCHEDULER.SET_SCHEDULER_ATTRIBUTE
  7     ('MAX_JOB_SLAVE_PROCESSES','6');
  8   END;
SQL> /

PL/SQL procedure successfully completed.

SQL>
```

You can retrieve the arguments values of the scheduler using the DBMS_SCHEDULER.GET_ SCHEDULER_ATTRIBUTE procedure. Pass the attribute as the first parameter, and get the value using the second parameter.

You can change the arguments of individual scheduler components using the DBMS_ SCHEDULER.SET_ATTRIBUTE procedure. You can change all the attributes using this procedure except the component name. The procedure has three attributes: name, attribute, and value. Since the procedure is overloaded, it can accept values to many different datatypes. Table 2.12 shows a few of the common attributes that can be changed for each component.

TABLE 2.12 *DBMS_SCHEDULER.SET_ATTRIBUTE* Values

Component	Attribute	Possible Values
Job	LOGGING_LEVEL	DBMS_SCHEDULER.LOGGING_OFF, DBMS_SCHEDULER.LOGGING_RUNS (default), and DBMS_SCHEDULER.LOGGING_FULL.
Job	RESTARTABLE	TRUE (default) and FALSE.
Job	MAX_FAILURES	1 to 1,000,000. The default is NULL.
Job	JOB_WEIGHT	1 to 100. The default is 1.
Job	JOB_PRIORITY	1 to 5; 1 is the first to be picked up.

T A B L E 2 . 1 2   *DBMS_SCHEDULER.SET_ATTRIBUTE* Values *(continued)*

Component	Attribute	Possible Values
Job	SCHEDULE_LIMIT	1 to 99 minutes.
Job	PROGRAM_NAME	Name of the program.
Job	JOB_ACTION	PL/SQL block, executable name, or stored procedure name.
Job	JOB_TYPE	PLSQL_BLOCK, STORED_PROCEDURE, and EXECUTABLE.
Job, program	NUMBER_OF_ARGUMENTS	Number of arguments.
Job	SCHEDULE_NAME	Name of schedule.
Job, schedule	REPEAT_INTERVAL	PL/SQL expression or calendar expression.
Job, schedule	START_DATE	A specific date.
Job, schedule	END_DATE	A specific date.
Job,	JOB_CLASS	A specific job class.
Job, program, schedule	COMMENTS	A specific comment.
Job	AUTO_DROP	TRUE and FALSE
Program	PROGRAM_ACTION	PL/SQL block, executable name, or stored procedure name.
Program	PROGRAM_TYPE	PLSQL_BLOCK, STORED_PROCEDURE, and EXECUTABLE
Job	STOP_ON_WINDOW_CLOSE	If the job uses a window for schedule, specifying TRUE will stop the job when closing the window.
Job	JOB_PRIORITY	Specifies the priority of the job among other jobs in the same job class. Values can be 1 through 5; 1 is the first to be picked up.

Here is an example of setting the attributes to a job:

```
SQL> BEGIN
  2  SYS.DBMS_SCHEDULER.DISABLE(
          'SCOTT.SCJ_WEEKLY_DATA_CHECK' );
  3  SYS.DBMS_SCHEDULER.SET_ATTRIBUTE(
  4  name => 'SCOTT.SCJ_WEEKLY_DATA_CHECK',
  5  attribute => 'job_priority', value => 1);
  6  SYS.DBMS_SCHEDULER.SET_ATTRIBUTE(
  7  name => 'SCOTT.SCJ_WEEKLY_DATA_CHECK',
  8  attribute => 'max_failures', value => 5);
  9  SYS.DBMS_SCHEDULER.SET_ATTRIBUTE(
 10  name => 'SCOTT.SCJ_WEEKLY_DATA_CHECK',
 11  attribute => 'restartable', value => TRUE);
 12  SYS.DBMS_SCHEDULER.ENABLE(
          'SCOTT.SCJ_WEEKLY_DATA_CHECK' );
 13  END;
SQL> /

PL/SQL procedure successfully completed.

SQL>
```

Notice that in the previous example the job is disabled and then enabled after setting the attributes. This is not mandatory; the scheduler automatically disables the job before changing any attribute value and enables it after the attribute is set. If there is an error in setting the attribute, the job will remain disabled.

You can use the DBMS_SCHEDULER.SET_ATTRIBUTE_NULL procedure to set an attribute value to NULL (to unset an attribute). The following example removes comments from a job:

```
SQL> EXEC SYS.DBMS_SCHEDULER.SET_ATTRIBUTE_NULL( -
> name => 'SCOTT.SCJ_WEEKLY_DATA_CHECK',  -
> attribute => 'comments');

PL/SQL procedure successfully completed.

SQL>
```

So far we discussed only the basic scheduler components: programs, schedules, and jobs. In the next section, we will discuss the advanced components: job classes, windows, and window groups.

Managing Advanced Scheduler Components

Oracle provides advanced scheduler components to manage jobs efficiently. Job classes group individual jobs with common characteristics. You can prioritize jobs within a job class. Windows provide the ability to activate different resource plans at different times. (Resource plans are defined and managed using Resource Manager.) Only one window can be active at any given time, but they are allowed to overlap. A window group is a named collection of windows.

In the following section, we will discuss using these components of the scheduler. The MANAGE_SCHEDULER privilege is required to create a job class, a window, and window groups.

Using Job Classes

You create job classes using the DBMS_SCHEDULER.CREATE_JOB_CLASS procedure. Job classes always belong to the SYS schema. Every database has a job class named DEFAULT_JOB_CLASS. When creating jobs, if no job class is specified, they belong to DEFAULT_JOB_CLASS. The following are the parameters to the CREATE_JOB_CLASS procedure:

JOB_CLASS_NAME   Specifies the name of the job class. SYS owns all the job classes; if a schema name is specified, it must be SYS. There is no default for this parameter.

RESOURCE_CONSUMER_GROUP   Specifies the name of the resource consumer group. If a resource group is not specified or if the resource group is dropped, the job class will belong to the DEFAULT_CONSUMER_GROUP. The default value for this parameter is NULL.

SERVICE   Specifies the name of the service to which the job class belongs. This parameter can be left out and is relevant to Real Application Clusters (RAC) environments. The default value for this parameter is NULL.

LOGGING_LEVEL   Specifies how much information is logged when jobs are run. The possible values are DBMS_SCHEDULER.LOGGING_OFF (no logging), DBMS_SCHEDULER.LOGGING_RUNS (information of all job runs in the class), and DBMS_SCHEDULER.LOGGING_FULL (information on runs and operations on jobs such as enable, disable, alter, and so on). The default value for this parameter is NULL.

LOG_HISTORY   Specifies the number of days to retain log files. The default is specified using the DBMS_SCHEDULER.SET_SCHEDULER_ATTRIBUTE. The default value for this parameter is NULL.

COMMENTS   Specifies a description of the job class. The default value for this parameter is NULL.

The following code creates a job class named FRIDAY_MIRR_BKUP_JOBS that uses the SYS_GROUP consumer group:

```
SQL> BEGIN
  2    SYS.DBMS_SCHEDULER.CREATE_JOB_CLASS(
  3    job_class_name => 'FRIDAY_MIRR_BKUP_JOBS',
  4    logging_level => DBMS_SCHEDULER.LOGGING_FULL,
```

```
 5  log_history => 21,
 6  resource_consumer_group => 'SYS_GROUP',
 7  comments => 'Jobs that backup files from mirror');
 8  END;
 9  /
```

PL/SQL procedure successfully completed.

SQL>

When creating new jobs, you can use the JOB_CLASS parameter to specify the job class where the job belongs. To change the job class in a job, use the SET_ATTRIBUTE procedure. The following code shows assigning the SALES_DB_BKUP job to the FRIDAY_MIRR_BKUP_JOBS job class:

```
SQL> BEGIN
  2  SYS.DBMS_SCHEDULER.SET_ATTRIBUTE(
  3  name => 'SCOTT.SALES_DB_BKUP',
  4  attribute => 'job_class',
  5  value => 'FRIDAY_MIRR_BKUP_JOBS');
  6* END;
SQL> /
```

PL/SQL procedure successfully completed.

SQL>

For other users to use the job class, they must have the EXECUTE privilege on the job class:

```
SQL> GRANT execute ON sys.friday_mirr_bkup_jobs TO anna;
```

Grant succeeded.

SQL>

Though log information is needed for reviewing what happened, over time the logs can accumulate. The LOG_HISTORY defines the number of days the log information is kept. You can also use the DBMS_SCHEDULER.PURGE_LOG procedure to clear the log files. The PURGE_LOG procedure can take zero to three parameters. If no parameters are specified, all the log files will be deleted.

The three parameters are as follows:

- **log_history** This specifies how much history (in days) to keep. The valid range is 0–999. If set to 0, no history is kept.

- *which_log* This specifies which type of log. The possible values for *which_log* are JOB_LOG (delete only job logs), WINDOW_LOG (delete only window logs), and the default JOB_AND_WINDOW_LOG (delete all logs).

- *job_name* This specifies which job-specific entries must be purged from the job log. Specify the *job_name* if you want to delete only the logs that belong to a specific job (or list of job names separated by comma).

Here is an example that deletes all the log files:

```
SQL> EXEC DBMS_SCHEDULER.PURGE_LOG();
```

The following example deletes job logs that are older than seven days:

```
SQL> BEGIN
  2   DBMS_SCHEDULER.PURGE_LOG (
  3   log_history=> 7,
  4   which_log=>'JOB_LOG');
  5   END;
SQL> /

PL/SQL procedure successfully completed.

SQL>
```

As with the other components of the scheduler, the job class can be modified using the SET_ATTRIBUTE procedure. You can drop job classes using the DBMS_SCHEDULER.DROP_JOB_CLASS procedure. The job_class_name and force procedures are the parameters to this procedure. The job_class_name can be a list of job classes, delimited by comma. The following example drops the FRIDAY_MIRR_BKUP_JOBS job class.

```
SQL> BEGIN
  2   SYS.DBMS_SCHEDULER.DROP_JOB_CLASS(
  3   job_class_name => 'FRIDAY_MIRR_BKUP_JOBS',
  4   force          => TRUE );
  5   END;
  6   /

PL/SQL procedure successfully completed.

SQL>
```

Using Windows and Window Groups

A window represents a well-defined interval of time for which specific resource parameters are specified. Windows activate different resource plans at different times. In the previous section, you saw how to assign the resource consumer group names to prioritize jobs when creating job classes. Resource plans specify the resource consumer group that belongs to the plan and has directives for how resources have to be allocated among the groups. A systemwide resource plan can be associated with a window to mange the overall resource usage for jobs. The schedule, duration, and resource plan are defined in a window.

You can create a window using the DBMS_SCHEDULER.CREATE_WINDOW procedure. The SYS schema always owns the window. The procedure has the following parameters:

WINDOW_NAME   Specifies a unique name for the window. There is no default value for this parameter.

RESOURCE_PLAN   Specifies the name of the resource plan. Only one resource plan can be associated with a window. There is no default value for this parameter.

SCHEDULE_NAME   Specifies the name of the schedule associated with the window. There is no default value for this parameter.

DURATION   Specifies how long the window will be open. You specify the duration in INTERVAL DAY TO SECOND with ranges from 1 minute to 99 days.

WINDOW_PRIORITY   Specifies which window will be open when windows overlap. The possible values are HIGH and LOW. The default is LOW.

COMMENTS   Specifies notes for the window. There is no default value for this parameter.

If the SCHEDULE_NAME is not specified, you must specify START_DATE, REPEAT_INTERVAL, and END_DATE. The following example creates a window that uses the resource plan meant for online users. The window starts every day at 8 a.m. for 9 hours (until 5 p.m.). This window has high priority.

```
SQL> BEGIN
  2   DBMS_SCHEDULER.CREATE_WINDOW(
  3   window_name=>'BUSINESS_HOURS',
  4   resource_plan=>'ONLINE_PLAN',
  5   start_date=>systimestamp at time zone 'US/Central',
  6   duration=>numtodsinterval(9, 'hour'),
  7   repeat_interval=>'FREQ=DAILY;BYHOUR=8',
  8   window_priority=>'HIGH',
  9   comments=>'Resources for Online users');
 10* END;
SQL> /

PL/SQL procedure successfully completed.

SQL>
```

Figure 2.7 shows creating a window using the EM. The screen has options for you to view existing resource plans or to create a new resource plan that should be used with the window. The interval can be specified using the Repeat drop down list.

At any given time, only one window can be active. If there are overlapping windows, the window with the highest priority gets preference. If there are two windows with the same priority, the window that started earlier remains active. At the end of the running window, if two or more windows with the same priority exist, the database switches to the window that has the highest percentage of its duration left.

Because of overlapping windows, there is possibility that a window will not be active at all. The job that uses this window as its schedule will not be executed.

When switching from a low-priority to a high-priority window, the jobs currently running in the LOW priority window continue to run unless the job has the attribute STOP_ON_WINDOW_ CLOSE explicitly set to TRUE.

FIGURE 2.7   EM Create Window screen

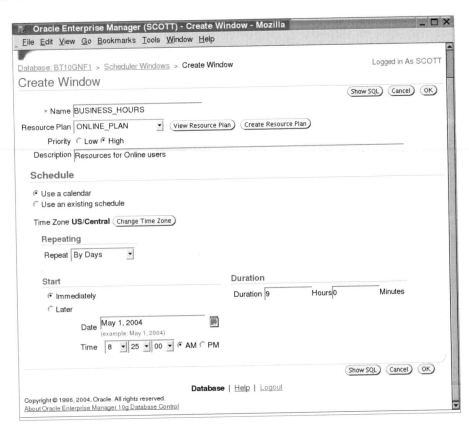

> You can use the ALTER SYSTEM SET RESOURCE_MANAGER_PLAN *plan name* FORCE to prevent the scheduler window from switching resource plans if you see a need for a specific plan to be effective (maybe when the president of the company is using the database).

A window group is a named collection of windows, created in the SYS schema. You create a window group using the DBMS_SCHEDULER.CREATE_WINDOW_GROUP procedure.

GROUP_NAME Specifies the name of the window group. There is no default value for this parameter.

WINDOW_LIST Specifies the list of windows that should be part of the window group. The default value for this parameter is NULL.

COMMENTS Specifies a comment that can be added to the window group. The default value for this parameter is NULL.

To create a window group, you need to specify a name for the window group and a list of windows. Here is an example:

```
SQL> BEGIN
  2   DBMS_SCHEDULER.CREATE_WINDOW_GROUP(
  3   group_name=>'ALL_MAINTENANCE',
  4   window_list=>'WEEKEND_WINDOW, SYSTEM_MAINT,
     TABLE_MAINT');
  5   END;
SQL> /

PL/SQL procedure successfully completed.

SQL>
```

You can use the DBMS_SCHEDULER.ADD_WINDOW_GROUP_MEMBERS procedure to add more windows to the window group. The group_name and window_list parameters are used with this procedure.

Lets discuss the scheduler programs available for administering windows and window groups in the next two sections.

Administering Windows

A window is open if it is in effect. You can use the DBMS_SCHEDULER.OPEN_WINDOW procedure to open a window. If the FORCE parameter is used, any higher-priority window that is already open will be closed. The new window will be active for the duration specified in the window, which can be overridden by using the DURATION parameter in the OPEN_WINDOW procedure.

Forcefully opening a window does not change the schedule of the window (when it should be opened automatically). Here is an example of force opening a window for two hours:

```
EXEC DBMS_SCHEDULER.OPEN_WINDOW ( -
window_name=> 'CRITICAL_UPDATE', -
duration=> '2 0:00:00', -
force=> TRUE);
```

Similarly, you can close a window using the DBMS_SCHEDULER.CLOSE_WINDOW procedure. The WINDOW_NAME parameter is the only parameter to this procedure. Running jobs with the attribute STOP_ON_WINDOW_CLOSE will be closed when closing a window.

To drop a window, use the DBMS_SCHEDULER.DROP_WINDOW procedure. If the FORCE parameter is set to TRUE, the window will be dropped even it is open, and the jobs that use the window will be disabled. The WINDOW_NAME can be a list of comma-delimited window names.

You can enable and disable windows using the ENABLE and DISABLE procedures of DBMS_ SCHEDULER.

> Windows—as well as window groups—are created with access to PUBLIC; therefore, no privileges are needed to access window or window groups.

Managing Window Groups

Use the DBMS_SCHEDULER.REMOVE_WINDOW_GROUP_MEMBERS procedure to delete windows from a window group. The group_name and window_list parameters are used with this procedure.

As with other components, window groups can be enabled and disabled using ENABLE and DISABLE procedures.

Setting Scheduler Administrator Privileges

Though we have discussed the privileges required to create and manage each component of the scheduler in their respective sections, in this section we will discuss the administrative privileges associated with scheduler. The following are the privileges and roles:

ANY privileges   The CREATE ANY JOB system privilege is required to create a job, schedule, or program in a schema other than yours. The EXECUTE ANY PROGRAM system privilege gives the user the ability to use the programs belonging to another user. The EXECUTE ANY CLASS system privilege gives the user ability to assign a job to any job class (submit a job with higher privileges).

MANAGE_SCHEDULER privilege   The MANAGE_SCHEDULER system privilege is required to create and manage job classes, window, and window groups. This privilege gives the user ability to stop any job and start and stop windows prematurely.

SCHEDULER_ADMIN role   The SCHEDULER_ADMIN role has CREATE JOB, CREATE ANY JOB, EXECUTE ANY PROGRAM, EXECUTE ANY CLASS, and MANAGE SCHEDULER privileges. These privileges are granted to this role with the WITH GRANT OPTION. The DBA role has SCHEDULER_ADMIN role by default.

Querying the Data Dictionary

Several data dictionary views hold information about the scheduler components and their status. Table 2.13 lists the dictionary views pertaining to the scheduler.

TABLE 2.13   Scheduler Related Dictionary Views

View Name	Description
DBA_SCHEDULER_GLOBAL_ATTRIBUTE ALL_SCHEDULER_GLOBAL_ATTRIBUTE	Displays information about the global attributes for the scheduler
DBA_SCHEDULER_JOBS ALL_SCHEDULER_JOBS USER_SCHEDULER_JOBS	Displays information about the scheduler jobs
DBA_SCHEDULER_JOB_ARGS ALL_SCHEDULER_JOB_ARGS USER_SCHEDULER_JOB_ARGS	Displays information about the arguments of the scheduler job
DBA_SCHEDULER_JOB_CLASSES ALL_SCHEDULER_JOB_CLASSES	Displays information about the scheduler job classes
DBA_SCHEDULER_JOB_LOG ALL_SCHEDULER_JOB_LOG	Displays log information of the scheduler jobs
DBA_SCHEDULER_JOB_RUN_DETAILS ALL_SCHEDULER_JOB_RUN_DETAILS USER_SCHEDULER_JOB_RUN_DETAILS	Displays log run details for the scheduler jobs (contains each instance of the job)
DBA_SCHEDULER_PROGRAMS ALL_SCHEDULER_PROGRAMS USER_SCHEDULER_PROGRAMS	Displays information about the scheduler programs
DBA_SCHEDULER_PROGRAM_ARGS ALL_SCHEDULER_PROGRAM_ARGS USER_SCHEDULER_PROGRAM_ARGS	Displays information about the arguments of the scheduler programs
DBA_SCHEDULER_RUNNING_JOBS ALL_SCHEDULER_RUNNING_JOBS USER_SCHEDULER_RUNNING_JOBS	Displays information about the scheduler jobs that are currently running
DBA_SCHEDULER_SCHEDULES ALL_SCHEDULER_SCHEDULES USER_SCHEDULER_SCHEDULES	Displays information about the scheduler schedules

TABLE 2.13   Scheduler Related Dictionary Views *(continued)*

View Name	Description
DBA_SCHEDULER_WINDOWS ALL_SCHEDULER_WINDOWS	Displays information about the scheduler windows
DBA_SCHEDULER_WINDOW_DETAILS ALL_SCHEDULER_WINDOW_DETAILS	Displays log details for scheduler windows
DBA_SCHEDULER_WINDOW_GROUPS ALL_SCHEDULER_WINDOW_GROUPS	Displays information about the scheduler window groups
DBA_SCHEDULER_WINDOW_LOG ALL_SCHEDULER_WINDOW_LOG	Displays log information for the scheduler windows
DBA_SCHEDULER_WINGROUP_MEMBERS ALL_SCHEDULER_WINGROUP_MEMBERS	Displays the members of the scheduler's window groups

The following are examples of queries using these views. Job execution details are available in DBA_SCHEDULER_JOB_RUN_DETAILS view, one row for each instance of the job:

```
SQL> SELECT job_name, status, error#,
  2         actual_start_date, run_duration
  3  FROM   dba_scheduler_job_run_details
  4  WHERE  owner = 'SCOTT';
```

To view under which resource group a job is currently running, use the following:

```
SQL> SELECT session_id, slave_process_id,
  2         resource_consumer_group,
  3         elapsed_time, cpu_used
  4  FROM   dba_scheduler_running_jobs
  5  WHERE  job_name = 'SCJ_ADD_PARTITION';
```

To view general information about the jobs owned by current user, use the following:

```
SQL> SELECT program_name, job_type, schedule_name, state,
  2         last_run_duration, stop_on_window_close
  3  FROM   user_scheduler_jobs;
```

To view the job management activities performed on the jobs owned by SCOTT, use the following:

```
SQL> SELECT job_name, operation, status, user_name
  2  FROM    dba_scheduler_job_log
  3  WHERE   operation != 'RUN'
  4  and     owner = 'SCOTT';
```

To view the global attributes defined, use the following:

```
SQL> SELECT attribute_name, value
  2  FROM    dba_scheduler_global_attribute;
```

To view information about all the schedules in the database, use the following:

```
SQL> SELECT owner, schedule_name, start_date,
  2         repeat_interval, end_date
  3  FROM    dba_scheduler_schedules;
```

To view the members of window groups, use the following:

```
SQL> SELECT window_group_name, window_name
  2  from dba_scheduler_wingroup_members;
```

To view the argument values for a job, use the following:

```
SQL> SELECT argument_name, argument_position, value
  2  FROM    all_scheduler_job_args
  3  WHERE   owner = 'ANN'
  4  AND     job_name = 'PARTITION_EXCHANGE';
```

Summary

In this chapter, we discussed Oracle Data Pump, enhancements to external tables, and the Oracle scheduler. Data Pump is a high-speed infrastructure for data and metadata movement. The new client utilities expdp and impdp unload and load data and metadata.

The Data Pump architecture includes the data and metadata movement engine DBMS_DATAPUMP, a direct path API that supports a stream interface, the metadata API DBMS_METADATA, an external tables API, and the client utilities. Though the Data Pump utilities expdp and impdp are similar to exp and imp, they are different products.

Data Pump export can perform in different modes based on the requirement. It can be a full database export or at a table level. The EXP_FULL_DATABASE privilege is required to perform a schema export (other than the users) as well as a full or tablespace export. The import can be performed from the export dump file without specifying a mode.

Data Pump export and import take place on the server. You can attach to a job from any computer and monitor its progress or make resource adjustments. In the interactive mode, you can add a file to export a dump file set, kill a job, stop a job, change parallelism, and enable detailed status logging.

Data Pump export and import supports fine-grained object selection using the CONTENT, INCLUDE, and EXCLUDE parameters. Using a database link, you can perform network export and network import. Also, using a database link you can perform an import from another database directly without using a dump file.

External tables in Oracle 10g can be populated using the ORACLE_DATAPUMP access driver. The external tables are populated and created by using the CREATE TABLE ... AS SELECT ... method. Population can be performed in parallel, and each file in the dump file set can reside in different locations. The ability to define the projected column feature helps performance.

In Oracle 10g, the transportable tablespace feature is improved to transport tablespaces across platforms. If the Endian format of the platform is different, you must use RMAN to convert the datafiles.

The Oracle scheduler—DBMS_SCHEDULER—is an advanced version of its predecessor DBMS_JOB. The scheduler components are job, program, schedule, job class, window, and window group. Jobs, schedule, and programs are created in the schema of the user whereas job class, window, and window groups are created in the SYS schema.

The SCHEDULER_ADMIN role and MANAGE SCHEDULER system privilege give administrative rights on the scheduler components. In this chapter, you learned to create, drop, and modify all the scheduler components. A job can have a named schedule and a named program. Job classes help prioritize jobs using the resource consumer groups. Windows manage the resource plan for the database. Window group is a collection of windows. Windows and window groups reside in the SYS schema and everyone has access to window and window groups.

In this chapter you also learned to query the data dictionary to view information on the Data Pump jobs, external table properties, and scheduler components and execution details.

Exam Essentials

Understand the enhancements to cross-platform tablespaces.   Know the dictionary view name to check the Endian format of the source and destination database. Learn how to convert a datafile using RMAN to copy to an operating system platform with different Endian format.

Know the architecture of Data Pump.   Understand the components involved in the Data Pump architecture. Review the benefits of Data Pump.

Understand how to use the Data Pump components.   Be familiar with the methods to attach to a running job, stop a job, kill a job, and change its characteristics. Know the data and metadata filtering options available. Know the dictionary views to monitor the Data Pump job. Understand the methods available to remap and transform database objects.

Learn the external table enhancements.   Know the access driver used to unload data (or populate an external table). Understand the projected column feature.

Know the components of the scheduler.   Understand the purpose of each scheduler component. Learn the privileges required to create each component.

Know how to use the scheduler.   Learn to specify calendaring expressions for schedule and jobs. Know how to prioritize jobs. Know to change the characteristics (attributes) of scheduler components.

Review Questions

1. Which two PL/SQL packages are used by the Oracle Data Pump?

   A. UTL_DATAPUMP

   B. DBMS_METADATA

   C. DBMS_DATAPUMP

   D. UTL_FILE

   E. DBMS_SQL

2. Which of the following options that list the benefits of Oracle Data Pump are not true? (Choose two.)

   A. Data Pump supports fine-grained object selection using the EXCLUDE, INCLUDE, and CONTENT options.

   B. Ability to specify the target version of the database so that the objects exported is compatible. This is useful in moving data from Oracle 10g to Oracle 9i.

   C. Ability to specify the maximum number of threads to unload data.

   D. The DBA can choose to perform the export using direct path or external tables.

   E. The Data Pump job can be monitored from another computer on the network.

3. The Data Pump job maintains a master control table with information about Data Pump. Which of the following statements are true?

   A. The master table is the heart of Data Pump operation and is maintained in the SYS schema.

   B. The master table contains one row for the operation that keeps track of the object being worked so that the job can be restarted in the event of failure.

   C. During the export, the master table is written to the dump file set at the beginning of export operation.

   D. The Data Pump job runs in the schema of the job creator with that user's rights and privileges.

   E. All of the above.

4. When using the expdp and impdp clients, the parameters LOGFILE, DUMPFILE, and SQLFILE need a directory object, where the files will be written to or read from. Which of the following are nonsupported methods of specifying the directory?

   A. Specify the DIRECTORY parameter.

   B. Specify the file name parameters with directory:file_name

   C. Use the initialization parameter DATA_PUMP_DIR.

   D. None of the above (all of the above are supported).

5. Which command-line parameter of expdp and impdp clients connects you to an existing job?

    A. CONNECT_CLIENT

    B. CONTINUE_CLIENT

    C. APPEND

    D. ATTACH

6. Which option unloads the data and metadata of the SCOTT user, except the tables that begin with TEMP? The dump file also should have the DDL to create the user.

    A. CONTENT=BOTH TABLES=(not like 'TEMP%') SCHEMAS=SCOTT

    B. SCHEMAS=SCOTT EXCLUDE=TABLE:"LIKE 'TEMP%'"

    C. INCLUDE=METADATA EXCLUDE=TABLES:"NOT LIKE 'TEMP%'" SCHEMAS=SCOTT

    D. TABLES="NOT LIKE 'TEMP%'" SCHEMAS=SCOTT

7. Which parameter is not a valid one for using the impdp client?

    A. REMAP_TABLE

    B. REMAP_SCHEMA

    C. REMAP_TABLESPACE

    D. REMAP_DATAFILE

8. When performing Data Pump import using impdp, which of the following options is not a valid value to the TABLE_EXISTS_ACTION parameter?

    A. SKIP

    B. APPEND

    C. TRUNCATE

    D. RECREATE

9. When do you use the FLASHBACK_TIME parameter in the impdp utility?

    A. To load data from the dump file that was modified after a certain time.

    B. To discard data from the dump file that was modified after a certain time.

    C. Used when the NETWORK_LINK parameter is used.

    D. FLASHBACK_TIME is valid only with expdp, not with impdp.

10. Choose two statements that are true regarding external tables.

    A. The PROJECT COLUMN REFERENCED clause of ALTER TABLE for external tables improves the performance of data loads to the external table.

    B. You can use INSERT statements to populate external tables.

    C. You can have the external table populated in Oracle and use the file to load to another database.

    D. Oracle uses the ORACLE_LOADER access driver to populate external tables.

    E. The PROPERTY column of the DBA_EXTERNAL_TABLES view shows the projected column setting.

11. You have a Unix script to be executed on the FINANCE database every four hours. What components must be created in the database to schedule this using the DBMS_DATAPUMP subprograms?

   A. Program, schedule, job

   B. Schedule, job

   C. Job

   D. Job, window

   E. Program, schedule

12. Which privilege is the least powerful that is required to create a program under your schema?

   A. CREATE PROGRAM

   B. CREATE JOB

   C. MANAGE SCHEDULER

   D. EXECUTE ANY PROGRAM

13. When specifying the frequency for schedules using Oracle calendaring expressions, which one of the following is not a valid expression?

   A. YEARLY

   B. QUARTERLY

   C. MONTHLY

   D. WEEKLY

   E. SECONDLY

14. How do you prioritize jobs in the scheduler?

   A. Using the CREATE_JOB procedure

   B. Using the CREATE_JOB_CLASS procedure

   C. Using the SET_ATTRIBUTE procedure

   D. Using the SET_SCHEDULER_ATTRIBUTE procedure

15. The following are valid calendaring expressions:

   1 FREQ=YEARLY; BYYEARDAY=-4; BYHOUR=20
   2 FREQ=MONTHLY; BYMONTH=12; BYMONTHDAY=28; BYHOUR=20
   3 FREQ=MONTHLY; BYYEARDAY=-4; BYHOUR=20
   4 FREQ=YEARLY; BYMONTH=DEC; BYMONTHDAY=28; BYHOUR=20

   Choose from the following options the expressions that specify to run a schedule every Dec. 28 at 8 p.m.?

   A. Items 1, 2, and 4

   B. Items 1 and 4

   C. Items 2 and 3

   D. Items 1, 2, 3, and 4

16. Which data dictionary view can be used to know the latest change made to a job owned by you?

   A. USER_SCHEDULER_JOBS

   B. USER_SCHEDULER_JOB_LOG

   C. USER_JOBS

   D. USER_SCHEDULER_JOB_RUN_DETAILS

17. To which component is the resource manager resource plan associated with?

   A. Window

   B. Job class

   C. Job

   D. Window and Job class

18. What happens when creating a job if you do not specify the job class?

   A. The JOB_CLASS column of USER_SCHEDULER_JOBS will be NULL.

   B. An error occurs; you must specify a job class.

   C. The job is assigned to a default job class defined by the SET_SCHEDULER_ATTRIBUTE.

   D. None of the above.

19. What should be the value for PROGRAM_TYPE when defining an anonymous PL/SQL block?

   A. ANONYMOUS_BLOCK

   B. STORED_PROCEDURE

   C. PLSQL_PROCEDURE

   D. PLSQL_BLOCK

   E. EXECUTABLE

20. When you create a window, in which schema does it get created? (Choose the most appropriate answer.)

   A. Irrespective of whom creates the window, the window will be always created in the SYS schema.

   B. In the schema of the user who creates the window.

   C. The schema specified with the window name.

   D. You must be logged in with SYSDBA privilege, so it always gets created in the SYS schema.

Answers to Review Questions

1. **B, C.** The DBMS_METADATA package provides the database object definitions to the export worker process in the proper order of their creation. The DBMS_DATAPUMP package has the API for high-speed export and import for bulk data and metadata loading and unloading.

2. **B, D.** Oracle Data Pump is known to versions Oracle 10g and higher. Oracle 9i does not support Data Pump. Though Data Pump can perform data access using the direct path or external table method, Data Pump makes the decision automatically; DBA cannot specify the data access method. Data Pump also supports network mode to import directly from the source database and can estimate the space requirements for dump file.

3. **D.** The master table is the heart of the Data Pump operation and is maintained in the schema of the job creator. It bears the name of the job, contains one row for each object and each operation, and keeps status. Using this information helps to restart a failed job or to suspend and resume a job. The master table is written to the dump file as the last step of the export and is loaded to the schema of the user as the first step of the import.

4. **C.** If a directory object is created with the name DATA_PUMP_DIR, the privileged users can use this location as the default location for Data Pump files. Privileged users are users with EXP_FULL_DATABASE or IMP_FULL_DATABASE roles. Using %U in the filename generates multiple files for parallel unloads with each parallel process writing to one file.

5. **D.** The ATTACH parameter lets you attach or connect to an existing Data Pump job and places you in the interactive mode. The ATTACH without any parameters attaches to the currently running job, if there is only one job from the user. Otherwise, you must specify the job name when using the ATTACH parameter.

6. **B.** If the CONTENT parameter is not specified, both data and metadata will be unloaded. The valid values for CONTENT are METADATA_ONLY, DATA_ONLY, and ALL. If Scott is performing the export, SCHEMAS=SCOTT is optional.

7. **A.** REMAP_DATAFILE changes the name of the source datafile to the target datafile name in all DDL statements where the source datafile is referenced. REMAP_SCHEMA loads all objects from the source schema into the destination schema. When using REMAP_TABLESPACE, all objects selected for import with persistent data in the source tablespace are remapped to create in the destination tablespace. Since the Dump File is in XML format, the Data Pump can make these transformations easily.

8. **D.** REPLACE is the valid value; it drops the existing table and creates the table using the definition from the dump file. SKIP leaves the table untouched. APPEND inserts rows to the existing table. TRUNCATE leaves the structure but removes all existing rows before inserting rows.

9. C. You can specify FLASHBACK_TIME or FLASHBACK_SCN parameters only when performing a network import, where the source is a database.

10. C, E. The PROJECT COLUMN REFERENCED clause helps the queries on external tables, where only a few columns are queried. The default is ALL; set it to REFERENCED if you know the datafile where the external table is referenced is clean. Only using the CREATE TABLE ... AS SELECT ... with ORACLE_DATAPUMP as the access loader can populate external tables.

11. C. Though named programs and named schedules can be used when creating a job, they are not a must. The job can define what need to be executed and when.

12. B. The CREATE JOB privilege is required to create a job, program, or schedule in your schema. CREATE PROGRAM is not a valid privilege. MANAGE SCHEDULER system privilege gives you the ability to administer scheduler components. EXECUTE ANY PROGRAM privilege gives you the ability to execute a program that belongs to another schema. CREATE ANY JOB gives you privilege to create program, schedule, or job in any schema.

13. B. QUARTERLY is not a valid expression. To perform a job quarterly, you need to specify the frequency as MONTHLY and INTERVAL as 3.

14. C. Using the JOB_PRIORITY as the argument to the SET_ATTRIBUTE procedure, you can specify the priority of job from 1 through 5 within the job class.

15. D. All the four calendaring expressions execute a schedule every Dec. 28 at 8 p.m. "BYYEARDAY=-4" or "BYMONTH=DEC; BYMONTHDAY=28" specifies the date and month for the interval Though all four are correct, the most meaningful and easy to understand would be item 1 or 4.

16. B. The LOG_DATE and OPERATION columns of the USER_SCHEDULER_JOB_LOG view show the time and activity on the job.

17. A. A systemwide resource plan can be associated with a window. A resource consumer group is associated with the job class.

18. D. When a job class is not specified while creating a job, the job belongs to the DEFAULT_JOB_CLASS. This job class is the default for the scheduler, which cannot be changed using SET_SCHEDULER_ATTRIBUTE.

19. D. Specify PLSQL_BLOCK for anonymous PL/SQL blocks, EXECUTABLE for any external program, and STORED_PROCEDURE for all stored programs in the database. ANONYMOUS_BLOCK and PLSQL_PROCEDURE are not valid values for PROGRAM_TYPE.

20. A. Job classes, windows, and window groups are always created in the SYS schema. Any user with the MANAGE SCHEDULER privilege can create windows.

Chapter

3

Automating Management

ORACLE DATABASE 10*g* NEW FEATURES FOR ADMINISTRATORS EXAM OBJECTIVES OFFERED IN THIS CHAPTER:

✓ **Automatic Management**

- Use Automatic Database Diagnostic Monitor
- Use Automatic Shared Memory Management
- Use Automatic Optimizer Statistics Collection
- Use Automatic Undo Retention Tuning

✓ **Manageability Infrastructure**

- Monitor and maintain the AWR
- Use the Active Session History (ASH)
- Monitor and manage server-generated alerts
- Explain the automated tasks feature
- Describe the advisory framework

✓ **System Resource Management**

- Automatically switch a session back to the original consumer group at the end of the top call
- Set idle time-outs for consumer groups
- Create mappings for the automatic assignment of sessions to consumer groups

 Exam objectives are subject to change at any time without prior notice and at Oracle's sole discretion. Please visit Oracle's training and certification website (http://www.oracle.com/education/certification/) for the most current exam objectives listing.

Oracle Database 10g (Oracle 10g) has implemented several steps to relieve you from routine monitoring and administrative activities and to help you concentrate on the enterprise architecture. The self-managing features of Oracle 10g capture information on key performance metrics and keep them in a repository. You can review the findings of Oracle 10g automatic collections and take appropriate action. The database even has options to fix the problems automatically.

The Oracle 10g Common Manageability Infrastructure (CMI) includes several components to manage and tune the database. In this chapter, we will discuss the components of CMI.

The Automatic Workload Repository (AWR) collects and maintains the statistics for tuning and problem detection. The Automatic Database Diagnostic Monitor (ADDM) is a self-diagnostic engine built in the Oracle 10g database engine that uses the WR information. Using the AWR information, Oracle 10g can alert you to potential issues based on the threshold metrics defined.

Oracle 10g also automatically manages the components of the Shared Global Area (SGA), which helps achieve the maximum memory utilization. For the optimizer to generate optimal execution plans, it needs to have statistics on the objects involved in the query. In Oracle 9i, the DBA was responsible for making sure the statistics are current. The Automatic Optimizer Statistics Collection feature is automated, and the DBA no longer needs to worry about stale statistics (exceptions exist, however).

Using the statistics collected by the Oracle database, Oracle 10g automatically tunes the undo retention and checkpoints. The Resource Manager has many enhancements, such as returning a session back to its original consumer group and defining a maximum idle time. In Oracle 10g, you can flush the buffer cache in addition to flushing the shared pool.

We will discuss all these new features in this chapter.

Collecting Performance Statistics

Oracle introduced the STATSPACK program in Oracle 8i. This program collected and stored database performance statistics in the database. Oracle 10g has improved the Automatic Optimizer Statistics Collection feature to collect more sophisticated information about the operating system and database by introducing a new set of programs called the *Automatic Workload Repository (AWR)*. The AWR takes a snapshot of the database in specified intervals (the default is one hour) and stores it in the SYSAUX tablespace.

In Oracle 10*g*, the statistical and performance information is collected automatically with minimal or no DBA intervention. Also, you do not need to worry about what to capture and where to save the statistics that were gathered.

The AWR is the central element of the *Common Manageability Infrastructure* (CMI). The CMI is a sophisticated self-management infrastructure that allows the database to learn about itself, use this information to adapt to the workload of the database, and correct any potential problems. Figure 3.1 shows the components of CMI architecture, which will be discussed in the following sections.

FIGURE 3.1   The CMI architecture

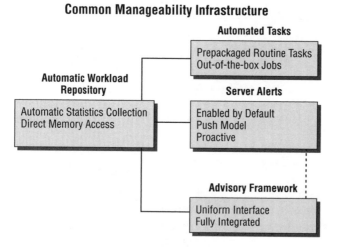

The Automatic Workload Repository may not contain detailed information on currently active sessions since it is populated on set intervals. The Active Sessions History (ASH) samples the V$SESSION view every second for active sessions and records the information, which can be used for current diagnosis. The ASH and AWR together provide detailed diagnostic information. We will discuss these in the following sections.

Using the Automatic Workload Repository

The AWR contains performance statistics and workload information on the database. The information is captured every hour and preserved for seven days by default. Historical information is important to diagnose a performance problem that has already happened. Normally when you know about the performance issue, the session would have already disconnected from

the database. Another reason to have historical statistics is for trend analysis. You must set the proper retention period policy based on the business requirements. Remember, the more days or frequent snapshots, the more disk space you need.

AWR is enabled only when the STATISTICS_LEVEL initialization parameter is set to TYPICAL (the default) or ALL. A value BASIC turns off all AWR statistics and metrics collection and disables all self-tuning capabilities of the database. The V$STATISTICS_LEVEL view shows the statistic component, description, and at what level of the STATISTICS_LEVEL parameter the component is enabled. Here is an example:

```
SQL> SELECT statistics_name, activation_level
  2  FROM   v$statistics_level
SQL> /


STATISTICS_NAME                          ACTIVAT
---------------------------------------- -------
Buffer Cache Advice                      TYPICAL
MTTR Advice                              TYPICAL
Timed Statistics                         TYPICAL
Timed OS Statistics                      ALL
Segment Level Statistics                 TYPICAL
PGA Advice                               TYPICAL
Plan Execution Statistics                ALL
Shared Pool Advice                       TYPICAL
Modification Monitoring                  TYPICAL
Longops Statistics                       TYPICAL
Bind Data Capture                        TYPICAL
Ultrafast Latch Statistics               TYPICAL
Threshold-based Alerts                   TYPICAL
Global Cache Statistics                  TYPICAL
Cache Stats Monitor                      TYPICAL
Active Session History                   TYPICAL
Undo Advisor, Alerts and Fast Ramp up    TYPICAL


17 rows selected.


SQL>
```

The AWR data is used by many components within the database (such as ADDM, discussed later in the section "Using the Automatic Database Diagnostic Monitor") and by external clients (such as SQL*Plus or the Enterprise Manager).

AWR consists of two main components.

In-memory statistics collection area   These are statistics collected and saved in the memory (the SGA). You can access these statistics using fixed views. The size of the SGA area allocated for AWR statistics is fixed and depends on the operating system and number of CPUs but is never more than five percent of the shared pool size. The in-memory statistics collection area is a circular buffer, where the old data is overwritten after flushing to disk.

AWR   Snapshots of the memory statistics are captured at specific intervals (the default is one hour or whenever the in-memory area becomes full) and stored in the disk. AWR is the persistent statistical data used for historical analysis. Data is owned by the SYS schema and can be accessed using data dictionary views. The MMON (which stands for *manageability monitor*) process is responsible for filtering and transferring the memory statistics to the disk every hour. When the buffer is full, the MMNL (which stands for *manageability monitor light*) process is responsible to flush the information to the repository.

For more information, see the section "Working with Active Session History."

AWR collects the following types of data:

- Time model statistics that show the amount of time spent by each activity
- Object statistics that determine access and usage of database segments (database feature usage)
- Selected statistics from V$SYSSTAT and V$SESSTAT (wait classes)
- SQL statements that are producing high load on the system
- ASH, which represents the history of recent sessions activity sampled from V$SESSION every second
- Operating system statistics

We will explain the AWR in more detail in the section "Working with the Automatic Workload Repository."

In the next section we will discuss the contents of ASH.

Working with Active Session History

The *ASH* contains recent information on active sessions sampled every second. The AWR takes snapshots of the database every hour, so the information in the AWR could be almost an hour old and will not help in diagnosing issues that are current on the database. Typically, to resolve issues currently on the database, detailed information pertaining to the last 5 or 10 minutes is

critical. Because recording session activity is expensive, ASH samples V$SESSION every second and records the events for which the sessions are waiting.

ASH is designed as a rolling buffer in memory; old information is overwritten after saving it to the AWR. You can query ASH information using the V$ACTIVE_SESSION_HISTORY view. The view contains one row for each active session per sample and returns the latest session's sample rows first. Most of the columns of this view are present in V$SESSION view. They include the following:

- SQL identifier of SQL statement

- Object number, file number, and block number

- Wait event identifier and parameters

- User identifier, session identifier, and serial number

- Client identifier and name of operating system program

For instance, to diagnose the performance problems for SID 12, you can use the following query:

```
SELECT session_state, event, current_obj#
FROM   v$active_session_history
WHERE  session_id  = 12;
```

History of the V$ACTIVE_SESSION_HISTORY view resides in the DBA_HIST_ACTIVE_SESS_HISTORY view. This view does not contain all the information but instead contains sampled information.

Working with Automatic Workload Repository

The AWR is a collection of persistent system performance statistics owned by the SYS schema. Over time, you should purge the statistics, and sometimes you may want to get a snapshot of the system for performance diagnosing outside the regular interval. Oracle 10g provides several programs in a package named DBMS_WORKLOAD_REPOSITORY. Using these programs, you can manage the snapshots and perform baselines. We will discuss the programs in the following sections.

Creating Snapshots

The DBMS_WORKLOAD_REPOSITORY.CREATE_SNAPSHOT procedure creates a snapshot at a time other than the one generated automatically. It can accept the optional parameter flush_level, with default value of TYPICAL. Here is an example of creating a snapshot:

```
SQL> EXEC sys.dbms_workload_repository.create_snapshot();

PL/SQL procedure successfully completed.
```

```
SQL> SELECT sys.dbms_workload_repository.create_snapshot()
  2  FROM    dual;


SYS.DBMS_WORKLOAD_REPOSITORY.CREATE_SNAPSHOT()
----------------------------------------------
                                           453

SQL>
```

The CREATE_SNAPSHOT is also a function. The return value will be the snapshot ID.

The DBA_HIST_SNAPSHOT dictionary view shows the snapshot information. It includes the database startup time along with snapshot details. Here is an example:

```
SQL> SELECT snap_id id, begin_interval_time,
  2         end_interval_time
  3  FROM    dba_hist_snapshot
  4  WHERE   snap_id > 450
SQL> /


 ID BEGIN_INTERVAL_TIME        END_INTERVAL_TIME
--- -------------------------- --------------------------
451 13-MAY-04 09.00.43.893 AM  13-MAY-04 10.00.08.258 AM
452 13-MAY-04 10.00.08.258 AM  13-MAY-04 10.31.37.335 AM
453 13-MAY-04 10.31.37.335 AM  13-MAY-04 10.32.06.113 AM

SQL>
```

The code output shows 3 snapshot ids. 451 and 452 were taken with an hour difference, but 453 is taken after 31 minutes of 452, which was taken manually.

Dropping Snapshots

You can drop snapshots by using the DBMS_WORKLOAD_REPOSITORY.DROP_SNAPHOT_RANGE procedure. The parameters to this procedure are low and high snapshot IDs. A third optional parameter can be the database ID, which defaults to the local database. The following example drops the snapshots from 200 to 250:

```
SQL> EXEC dbms_workload_repository.drop_snapshot_range -
>    (200,250);
```

When dropping the snapshots, the ASH history (DBA_HIST_ACTIVE_SESS_HISTORY) that belongs to the time period is also dropped from the AWR.

WARNING Though the snapshot creation of the AWR is similar to the snapshot creation of STATSPACK, the AWR does not directly support the statspack information. You also have no way to migrate the statspack data to the AWR.

Creating Baselines

AWR baselines are performance data that you can use for comparison when a problem occurs. You can have many baselines defined for different times of the database. The DBMS_WORKLOAD_ REPOSITORY.CREATE_BASELINE procedure creates a baseline. It can accept four parameters:

- Start snapshot ID
- End snapshot ID
- Name for the baseline
- An optional database ID

The following example shows a query on the DBA_HIST_SNAPSHOT whose output is used to create an online baseline called ONLINE PEAK based on the workload between 8 a.m. and 6 p.m.; the example also shows querying the DBA_HIST_BASELINE dictionary view to see the baselines created:

```
SQL> SELECT snap_id, begin_interval_time
  2  FROM   dba_hist_snapshot
  3  WHERE  begin_interval_time between
  4         TO_TIMESTAMP('12-MAY-04 08.00.00 AM') and
  5         TO_TIMESTAMP('12-MAY-04 06.00.00 PM')
SQL> /

   SNAP_ID BEGIN_INTERVAL_TIME
---------- ------------------------
       426 12-MAY-04 08.00.09.836 AM
       427 12-MAY-04 09.00.35.691 AM
       428 12-MAY-04 10.01.01.591 AM
       429 12-MAY-04 11.00.25.928 AM
       430 12-MAY-04 12.00.51.854 PM
       431 12-MAY-04 01.00.16.196 PM
       432 12-MAY-04 02.00.42.015 PM
       433 12-MAY-04 03.00.06.369 PM
       434 12-MAY-04 04.00.32.365 PM
       435 12-MAY-04 05.00.58.567 PM
```

```
10 rows selected.

SQL> BEGIN
  2   dbms_workload_repository.create_baseline (
  3    start_snap_id => 426,
  4    end_snap_id => 435,
  5    baseline_name => 'ONLINE PEAK');
  6   END;
  7  /

PL/SQL procedure successfully completed.

SQL>
SQL> SELECT baseline_name, start_snap_time, end_snap_time
  2  FROM   dba_hist_baseline;

BASELINE_NA  START_SNAP_TIME         END_SNAP_TIME
-----------  ----------------------  ---------------------
ONLINE PEAK  12-MAY-04 09.00.35 AM   12-MAY-04 06.00.23 PM

SQL>
```

Similar to the CREATE_SNAPSHOT function, CREATE_BASELINE also can be called as a function, which returns the baseline ID.

The snapshots belonging to a baseline are retained until the baseline is dropped.

Dropping Baselines

You can drop baseline using the DBMS_WORKLOAD_REPOSITORY.DROP_BASELINE procedure. You must specify the baseline name as a parameter. This procedure also has optional CASCADE and DBID parameters.

The default for CASCADE is FALSE, which means the snapshots related to the baseline are not dropped when the baseline is dropped. Here is an example of dropping a baseline:

```
SQL> EXEC dbms_workload_repository.drop_baseline -
>         ('ONLINE PEAK');
```

Changing Snapshot Settings

You can change the interval of the snapshot generation and how long the snapshots are retained using the DBMS_WORKLOAD_REPOSITORY.MODIFY_SNAPSHOT_SETTINGS procedure. This determines the snapshot capture and purging policy.

The RETENTION parameter specifies the new retention period in minutes. The specified value must be in the range of 1,440 minutes (1 day) to 52,560,000 minutes (100 years). If you specify zero, the maximum value of 100 years will be used; if you specify NULL, the retention will not be changed. The MMON process is responsible for purging the WR data.

The INTERVAL parameter specifies the new snapshot interval in minutes. The specified value must be between 10 minutes and 5,256,000 (1 year). If you specify zero, the maximum value of 1 year will be used; if you specify NULL, the interval will not be changed.

You can view the current settings from the DBA_HIST_WR_CONTROL dictionary view. The following example shows changing the retention period to 15 days and the interval to 30 minutes:

```
SQL> SELECT * from dba_hist_wr_control;

      DBID SNAP_INTERVAL              RETENTION
---------- ------------------------- ------------------
2449818325 +00000 01:00:00.0         +00007 00:00:00.0


SQL> BEGIN
  2   dbms_workload_repository.modify_snapshot_settings (
  3    retention => 21600,
  4    interval => 30);
  5  END;
SQL> /

PL/SQL procedure successfully completed.

SQL> SELECT * from dba_hist_wr_control;

      DBID SNAP_INTERVAL              RETENTION
---------- ------------------------- ------------------2449818325 +00000
00:30:00.0         +00015 00:00:00.0

SQL>
```

You can access the AWR using the Enterprise Manager (EM) Database Control, from its Administration tab. Click the Automatic Workload Repository from the Workload section. You can change the WR settings, you can define the baselines, and you can view detailed information of snapshots using the EM Database Control.

Figure 3.2 shows the Automatic Workload Repository screen.

FIGURE 3.2   The Automatic Workload Repository screen

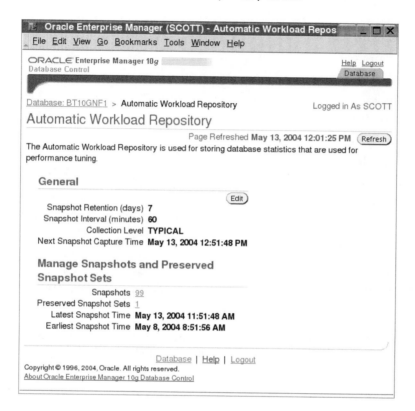

 If AWR detects that SYSAUX tablespace is out of space, it automatically reuses space occupied by the oldest set of snapshots by deleting them. An alert is also sent to the DBA to indicate that the SYSAUX is out of space.

Viewing AWR Reports

You can view AWR reports using the `awrrpt.sql` and `awrrpti.sql` scripts located in the `$ORACLE_HOME/rdbms/admin` directory. The `awrrpt.sql` script displays statistics for a range of snapshot IDs. The report can be saved as text file or HTML file. The `awrrpti.sql` script is similar to `awrrpt.sql`; the only difference is you can specify the database ID and instance ID as parameters. The report contains the following categories of information:

- Report summary
- Wait events statistics
- SQL statistics

- Instance activity statistics
- I/O statistics
- Buffer pool statistics
- Advisory statistics
- Wait statistics
- Undo statistics
- Latch statistics
- Segment statistics
- Dictionary cache statistics
- Library cache statistics
- SGA statistics
- Resource limit statistics
- `init.ora` parameters

You need the SELECT ANY DICTIONARY privilege to run the AWR reports.

The `awrinfo.sql` script displays general information on AWR such as snapshot information and ASH usage information. The report includes the following:

- AWR snapshots information
- SYSAUX tablespace usage
- Size estimates for AWR snapshots
- Space usage by AWR components
- Space usage by non-AWR components
- AWR control settings: interval and retention
- AWR contents: row counts for each snapshots
- ASH histogram
- ASH details
- ASH sessions

The data dictionary view DBA_HIST_DATABASE_INSTANCE shows the database instances in the Automatic Workload Repository. Each instance startup will have one row.

Base Statistics and Metrics

Base statistics represent the raw data collected by the Oracle server. For example, the number of physical reads since instance startup is a base statistic. A *metric* is a secondary statistic derived from base statistics. Metrics track the rate of changes in the database. For example, the average SQL response time for the last 30 minutes is a metric. The AWR has several metrics information. The V$ views without the _HISTORY extension show the most current information, the V$ views with the _HISTORY extension show all the information in the database, and DBA_HIST_ views show persistent information captured with the snapshots. Table 3.1 lists the data dictionary views with metric information.

TABLE 3.1   Data Dictionary Views with Metric Information

Most Current	Instance	Persistent
V$METRICGROUP	V$METRIC_HISTORY	DBA_HIST_METRIC_NAME
V$METRICNAMEV	$SYSMETRIC_HISTORY	DBA_HIST_SYSMETRIC_HISTORY
V$METRIC	V$SYSMETRIC_SUMMARY	DBA_HIST_SYSMETRIC_SUMMARY
V$SYSMETRIC	V$FILEMETRIC_HISTORY	DBA_HIST_SESSMETRIC_HISTORY
V$SESSMETRIC	V$WAITCLASSMETRIC_HISTORY	DBA_HIST_FILEMETRIC_HISTORY
V$FILEMETRIC	V$SERVICEMETRIC_HISTORY	
V$EVENTMETRIC		
V$WAITCLASSMETRIC		
V$SERVICEMETRIC		

To look at the database as a whole, the common metric you can use for comparison is time. Oracle 10*g* uses the time model statistics to identify quantitative effects on the database operations. You can view the time model statistics using the V$SYS_TIME_MODEL and V$SESS_TIME_MODEL dictionary views. The time reported is the total elapsed or CPU time in microseconds. Here is a sample query from V$SYS_TIME_MODEL:

```
SQL> SELECT stat_name, value
  2  FROM   v$sys_time_model;
```

```
STAT_NAME                                            VALUE
-------------------------------------------  ----------
DB time                                          8529656260
DB CPU                                           3346929994
background elapsed time                          1.5619E+10
background cpu time                               612558894
sequence load elapsed time                           419315
parse time elapsed                                245993518
hard parse elapsed time                           201029366
sql execute elapsed time                         7524056827
connection management call elapsed time            12167988
failed parse elapsed time                            150737
failed parse (out of shared memory) elapsed time          0
hard parse (sharing criteria) elapsed time          4925958
hard parse (bind mismatch) elapsed time             1702307
PL/SQL execution elapsed time                    1777438570
inbound PL/SQL rpc elapsed time                           0
PL/SQL compilation elapsed time                    43689860
Java execution elapsed time                         6424790

17 rows selected.

SQL>
```

The MMON process is responsible for updating the metric data from the corresponding base statistics. The metrics are kept in memory for one hour.

Diagnosing Performance Statistics

The AWR has all the information on the activities and waits on the Oracle 10g database. The database also includes tools for diagnosing these base statistics and metrics and provides you with proactive information. The *ADDM* is the primary client for the AWR information. ADDM can be considered as an expert residing in the Oracle 10g database.

In addition to providing suggestions for fixing problems, Oracle 10g can automatically fix certain problems. In the following sections, we will discuss the ADDM and other components available in the database that assist the DBA in achieving the best performance from the database.

Using the Automatic Database Diagnostic Monitor

The ADDM, part of the overall advisory architecture of Oracle 10g, is a self-diagnostic engine built into the database server. The ADDM is automatically invoked by the Oracle 10g database and performs analysis to determine any issues in the database. The ADDM recommends solutions to the issues it identifies.

ADDM analysis is performed every time an AWR snapshot is taken. The MMON process triggers ADDM analysis each time a snapshot is taken to do an analysis of the period corresponding to the last two snapshots. This approach proactively monitors the database and detects bottlenecks before they become significant problems. It is also possible to invoke the ADDM manually to analyze across any two snapshots. Along with areas that have problems identified, ADDM also reports areas of the system that have no problems. This allows you to quickly see that there is little to be gained by performing actions in those areas.

The results of the ADDM analysis are also stored in the AWR and are accessible through the dictionary views and the EM Database Control. Analysis is performed from the top down, identifying symptoms first and then refining them to reach the root cause.

The goal of analysis is to reduce a single throughput metric called the DBtime. DBtime is the cumulative time spent by the database server in processing user requests, which includes wait time and CPU time. You can view this metric from the time model dictionary views. By reducing DBtime, the database is able to support more user requests using the same resources; in other words, the database can perform the same workload in less time.

Since the ADDM is integrated into the database server, running the analysis has a minor impact on the database. It normally takes less than three seconds to complete the analysis. The ADDM analysis results are represented as findings, and each finding belongs to one of three categories: problem (root cause), symptom, or information.

ADDM results can be viewed using the EM Database Control, the next section discusses this.

Viewing ADDM Results Using EM

The ADDM results are best viewed using the EM Database Control. From the Database home page, under Diagnostic Summary, click the Performance Findings link to go to the ADDM page. Figure 3.3 shows the ADDM main page of the EM Database Control.

On the ADDM page, you can see the details of findings. Here you can click View Report to see the ADDM report as a text file and save it to disk. Click the finding, and you will be taken to another screen with more details on the finding, the recommended solution, and the finding's impact. Depending on the type of recommendation, it is possible that the ADDM recommends invoking another adviser such as the SQL Tuning Advisor or the Segment Tuning Advisor.

Figure 3.4 shows the Performance Finding Details screen. The screen shows the performance findings, the recommendation for the performance problem and why ADDM arrived at the solution.

FIGURE 3.3 The ADDM page

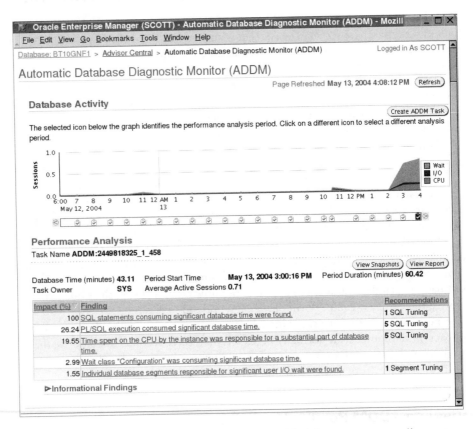

From the ADDM page, you can click the Create ADDM Task button to manually create snapshots.

Querying the ADDM Dictionary

You can query the ADDM findings using the `DBA_ADVISOR_FINDINGS` database dictionary view. The following query shows the number of findings of ADDM for the last 24 hours by category:

```
SQL> SELECT type, count(*)
  2  FROM   dba_advisor_findings
  3  NATURAL JOIN dba_advisor_tasks
  4  WHERE  created between sysdate -1 and sysdate
  5  GROUP BY type
SQL> /
```

```
TYPE           COUNT(*)
-----------    ----------
INFORMATION        26
PROBLEM            15
SYMPTOM            10

SQL>
```

You can invoke the ADDM report using SQL*Plus by running the $ORACLE_ HOME/rdbms/admin/addmrpt.sql script. The output is saved as a text file. The addmrpti.sql is another SQL*Plus script that prompts for dbid and instance_ number to run ADDM analysis on a pair of AWR snapshots and display the textual ADDM report of the analysis.

FIGURE 3.4   The Performance Finding Details page

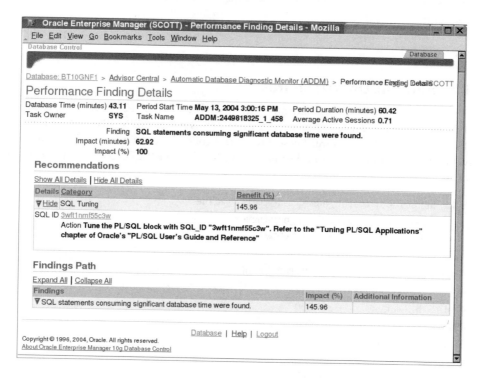

The DBA_ADVISOR_RECOMMENDATIONS view shows the result of the completed diagnostic task with recommendations for the problems identified in each run. You should look at the recommendations in the order they're listed in the RANK column. The BENEFIT column gives the resulting affect to the system if the recommendation is carried out. Here is an example query:

```
SQL> SELECT distinct message
  2  FROM   dba_advisor_recommendations
  3  JOIN   dba_advisor_findings
  4  USING  (finding_id, task_id)
  5  WHERE  rank = 0
SQL> /


MESSAGE
--------------------------------------------------------
Individual database segments responsible for significant
user I/O wait were found.
The buffer cache was undersized causing significant
additional read I/O.


SQL>
```

Changing ADDM Attributes

The ADDM is enabled automatically only when the STATISTICS_LEVEL parameter is set to TYPICAL or ALL. You can adjust some attributes using the DBMS_ADVISOR.SET_DEFAULT_TASK_PARAMETER procedure. These parameters control the advisory results. You can query the values of the parameters from the DBA_ADVISOR_DEF_PARAMETERS dictionary view. Here is an example:

```
SQL> SELECT parameter_name, parameter_value
  2  FROM   dba_advisor_def_parameters
  3  WHERE  advisor_name = 'ADDM';

PARAMETER_NAME        PARAMETER_VALUE
--------------------  --------------------
ANALYSIS_TYPE         PERIOD
DBIO_EXPECTED         10000
DB_ELAPSED_TIME       0
DB_ID                 0
HISTORY_TABLE         UNUSED
SCOPE_TYPE            UNUSED
SCOPE_VALUE           UNUSED
```

```
7 rows selected.
```

```
SQL>
```

For example, if you determine you have a slow hard disk and the typical I/O speed is around 16 milliseconds, you can change the parameter using the following:

```
SQL> EXEC dbms_advisor.set_default_task_parameter ( -
'ADDM', 'DBIO_EXPECTED', 16000);
```

```
PL/SQL procedure successfully completed.
```

```
SQL>
```

Using Server-Generated Alerts

Server-generated alerts are part of the Oracle 10*g* CMI. It is the capability of the Oracle 10*g* database to automatically detect alarming situations and suggest some remedial actions. Server-generated alerts are used when problems cannot be resolved automatically by the database and require your intervention.

The database's monitoring activities take place during normal database operation, which ensures that the database is aware of the problem as soon as it arises. With the introduction of the MMON process, internal components can schedule regular monitoring actions. You can have alerts triggered because of threshold levels or simply because an event has occurred. Threshold-based alerts can be triggered at the warning level and/or critical level. The value for these levels can be user-defined.

The Oracle 10*g* database keeps a history of the metrics in the AWR, which is used by the self-tuning components. In the previous releases of Oracle, the EM maintained the performance metrics of the database (after they are set up and enabled). The server-generated metrics and alerts are more efficient because the metric computation and threshold validation are performed by MMON process, which can access the SGA directly.

When the Oracle 10*g* database discovers an alert condition, it creates an alert with the following information and queues it to the predefined alert queue ALERT_QUE owned by SYS:

- The identity of the database entity on which the alert is produced
- A description of the problem
- A remedial or corrective action
- An optional name of an advisor for detailed advice
- The level of severity

Third-party tools and SQL*Plus may use PL/SQL API to read the alert queue. The EM Database Control is the primary subscriber of the alert queue. Depending on the setup in the EM

Database Control, the administrators are notified by e-mail or pager. The alerts are always displayed on the EM Database Control home page. Figure 3.5 shows the server-generated alerts architecture of Oracle 10g.

FIGURE 3.5   Server-generated alerts architecture

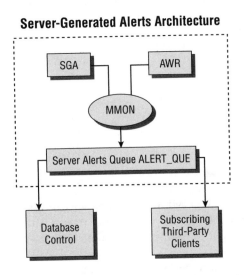

Threshold alerts, also known as *stateful alerts*, are automatically cleared when the alert condition clears. The alerts appear in the DBA_OUTSTANDING_ALERTS view and are moved to DBA_ALERT_HISTORY with a resolution of CLEARED when the alert condition is automatically cleared.

The nonthreshold alerts, also known as *event-based alerts* or *stateless alerts*, go directly to DBA_ALERT_HISTORY. "Snapshot too old" errors or "resumable session suspended" errors are examples of stateless alerts. Clearing a stateless alert is applicable only when using the EM Database Control, because the EM stores the stateless alerts in its own repository.

The V$ALERT_TYPES dictionary view shows information about each alert reason type. Here is an example:

```
SQL> SELECT DISTINCT type, group_name, object_type
  2  FROM   v$alert_types
SQL> /

TYPE       GROUP_NAME          OBJECT_TYPE
---------  ------------------  --------------------
Stateful   Performance         EVENT_CLASS
Stateful   Performance         FILE
Stateful   Performance         SERVICE
Stateful   Performance         SESSION
Stateful   Performance         SYSTEM
```

```
Stateful   Space           DATA OBJECT
Stateful   Space           QUOTA
Stateful   Space           RECOVERY AREA
Stateful   Space           ROLLBACK SEGMENT
Stateful   Space           SYSTEM
Stateful   Space           TABLESPACE
Stateless  Configuration   EVENT_CLASS
Stateless  Configuration   FILE
Stateless  Configuration   SERVICE
Stateless  Configuration   SESSION
Stateless  Configuration   SYSTEM
Stateless  Configuration   TABLESPACE
Stateless  Performance     SYSTEM
Stateless  Space           ROLLBACK SEGMENT
Stateless  Space           SYSTEM
Stateless  Space           TABLESPACE

21 rows selected.

SQL>
```

Figure 3.6 shows the All Metrics screen of the EM Database Control, where the status of each metric displays. Navigate to this screen from the EM Database Control home pages using the All Metrics link at the bottom of the page.

The figure shows the metrics in groups and when the metric was last collected. You can expand the metric to see each component, for example in the figure the Alert Log is expanded to show all the components.

The server-generated alert history is purged according to the snapshot purging policy.

The following are out-of-the-box server-generated alerts, set up in the database by default:

- "Tablespace space usage" (warning 85 percent, critical 97 percent)
- "Snapshot too old" error
- "Recovery area low on free space"
- "Resumable session suspended"

The alerts avoid false peak values. For an alert to be triggered, the observation period and number of consecutive occurrences must be satisfied.

FIGURE 3.6   The All Metrics page

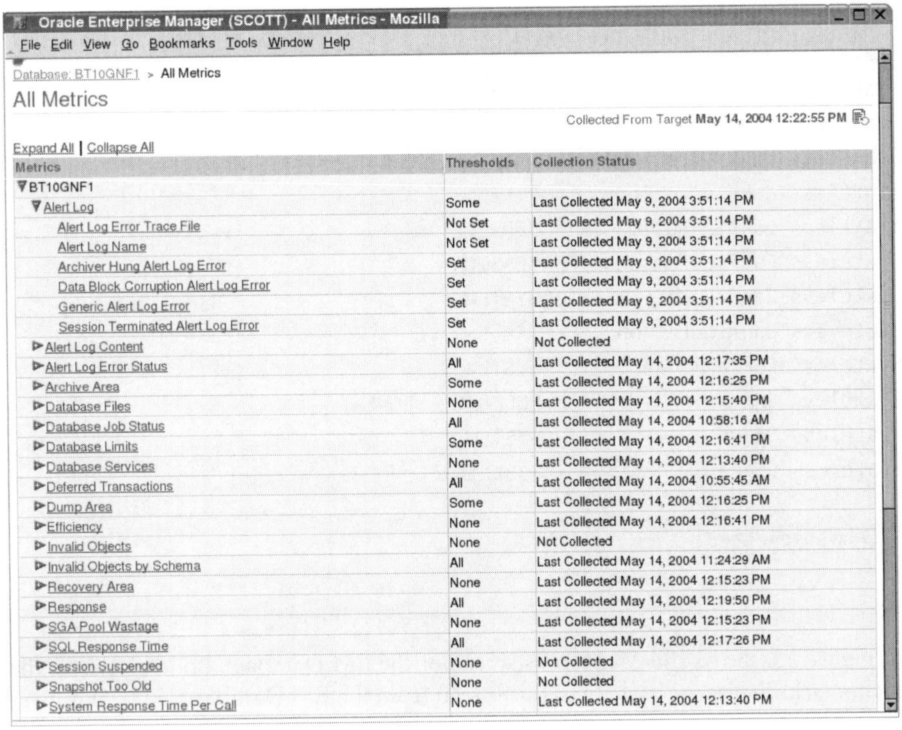

Setting Alert Thresholds

You can change alert thresholds using the EM Database Control or using PL/SQL. To edit the thresholds using the EM Database Control, from the home page click the Manage Metrics link at the bottom of the page. The Manage Metrics page shows the current thresholds for each metric. Click the Edit Threshold button to make changes to the thresholds. Figure 3.7 shows the screen to edit thresholds using the EM Database Control. In the screen, the Metric and Comparison Operator are predefined. You can set the Warning Threshold and Critical Threshold. If the Select button is enabled for a threshold, you can use the Specify Multiple Threshold button to specify more than one threshold. For example, in Archive Area Used you can specify different threshold levels for each archive log destination.

Using the EM Database Control for setting the threshold has two advantages that are not available when using PL/SQL. The EM Database Control has the ability to specify response action when thresholds are violated. The response action can be a script or stored procedure. It can also specify thresholds based on baselines.

FIGURE 3.7   The Edit Thresholds page

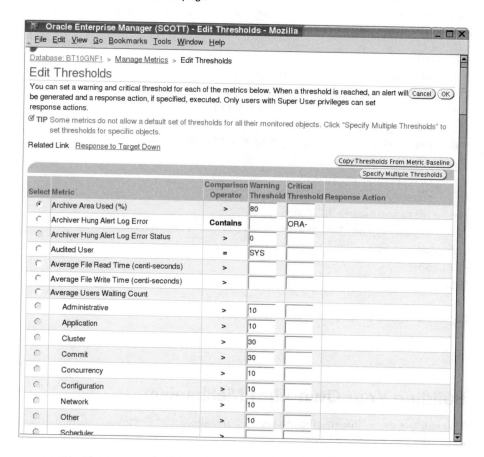

You can set the thresholds using the PL/SQL package DBMS_SERVER_ALERT. You can use the SET_THRESHOLD procedure to define a threshold and the GET_THRESHOLD procedure to retrieve the current threshold value for the metric. Both procedures use metrics_id as a parameter, which can be found from the V$METRICNAME view. There are more than 180 metrics defined.

DBMS_SERVER_ALERT has the metric names defined internally and can be used instead of the metric ID. The object types and relational operators are also defined as constants in the DBMS_SERVER_ALERT package, which can be used in the SET_THRESHOLD procedure.

The DBA_THRESHOLDS dictionary view shows the threshold settings. The V$ALERT_TYPE shows information on each alert reason type. The V$METRIC and V$METRIC_HISTORY contain system-level metric values in memory.

The following example shows using the DBMS_SERVER_ALERT constants to define a threshold for the number of users blocked by a session. Here we set an alert for the number of blocked users in the database and define 2 as the warning level and 4 as the critical level.

```
SQL> BEGIN
  2   DBMS_SERVER_ALERT.SET_THRESHOLD (
  3    metrics_id=>DBMS_SERVER_ALERT.BLOCKED_USERS,
  4    warning_operator=>DBMS_SERVER_ALERT.OPERATOR_GE,
  5    warning_value=>2,
  6    critical_operator=>DBMS_SERVER_ALERT.OPERATOR_GE,
  7    critical_value=>4,
  8    observation_period=>2,
  9    consecutive_occurrences=>4,
 10    instance_name=>'BT10GNF1',
 11    object_type=>DBMS_SERVER_ALERT.OBJECT_TYPE_SESSION,
 12    object_name=>NULL);
 13  END;
SQL> /

PL/SQL procedure successfully completed.

SQL>
```

Building Your Own Alert Mechanism

You can use the following steps to set up a threshold and alert mechanism if you do not want to use the EM Database Control:

1. Query V$METRICNAME to identify the metrics in which you are interested.

2. Set warning and critical thresholds using the DBMS_SERVER_ALERT.SET_THRESHOLD procedure.

3. Subscribe to the ALERT_QUE AQ using the DBMS_AQADM.ADD_SUBSCRIBER procedure.

4. Create an agent for the subscribing user of the alerts using the DBMS_AQADM.CREATE_AQ_AGENT procedure.

5. Associate the user with the AQ agent using the DBMS_AQADM.ENABLE_DB_ACCESS procedure.

6. Grant the DEQUEUE privilege using the DBMS_AQADM.GRANT_QUEUE_PRIVILEGE procedure.

7. Optionally register for the alert *enqueue* notification using the DBMS_AQ.REGISTER procedure.

8. Configure e-mail using the DBMS_AQELM.SET* procedures.

9. Dequeue the alert using the DBMS_AQ.DEQUEUE procedure.

10. After the message has been dequeued, use DBMS_SERVER_ALERT.EXPAND_MESSAGE to expand the text of the message.

Automating Database Management

Oracle 10*g* has automated several of the components to manage automatically or provide automatic tuning advice. In the following sections, we will discuss the management enhancements made to the Oracle 10*g* database that help you be more proactive.

Using Automatic Shared Memory Management (ASMM)

Automatic Shared Memory Management (ASMM) is another self-management enhancement in Oracle 10*g*. This functionality automates the management of shared memory structures used by the database and relieves you from configuring each component. This feature simplifies the SGA administration by introducing a dynamic, flexible, and automatic memory management scheme.

In previous releases of Oracle, you had to manually configure the shared pool size, Java pool size, large pool size, and database buffer cache. It was often a challenge to optimally configure these components because sizing them too small could cause memory errors and sizing them too large could lead to waste of memory. In Oracle 10*g*, you need to specify only the SGA_TARGET parameter, which specifies the total size of the SGA. Individual components of the SGA are automatically allocated by the database based on the workload and history information. So during the normal online operations, the buffer cache and Java pool may be bigger. During the batch window, the database can automatically increase the large pool and reduce the buffer cache.

The new parameter SGA_TARGET is the size of total SGA, which includes the automatically sized components, manually sized components, and any internal allocations during instance startup.

Let us discuss how we can enable and disable Automatic Shared Memory Management in the next section.

Enabling Automatic Shared Memory Management

ASMM is enabled when the STATISTICS_LEVEL parameter is set to TYPICAL or ALL and the SGA_TARGET parameter is set to a nonzero value. When enabled, ASMM distributes memory appropriately for the following memory areas:

- Database buffer cache (default pool): DB_CACHE_SIZE
- Shared pool: SHARED_POOL_SIZE
- Large pool: LARGE_POOL_SIZE
- Java pool: JAVA_POOL_SIZE

The following areas should be manually configured and are not affected by ASMM:

- Log buffer: LOG_BUFFER
- Other buffer caches: DB_KEEP_CACHE_SIZE, DB_RECYCLE_CACHE_SIZE, DB_nK_CACHE_SIZE
- Streams pool: STREAMS_POOL_SIZE
- Fixed-SGA area and internal allocations

The memory allocated for the manually configured areas are included in the SGA_TARGET size. For example, if SGA_TARGET is 400MB, LOG_BUFFER is set to 1MB, and DB_KEEP_CACHE_SIZE is set to 50MB, then the memory available for automatically configured components is 349MB.

The SGA_TARGET parameter is dynamic and can be resized using the ALTER SYSTEM statement. The value of SGA_TARGET cannot be higher than the SGA_MAX_SIZE parameter, which is not dynamically changeable. Reducing the size of SGA_TARGET affects only the autotuned components of the SGA. SGA_TARGET can be reduced until one of the autotuned components reaches its minimum size (a user-specified or Oracle-determined minimum).

You can also enable/disable ASMM using the EM Database Control. From the Administration tab, select Memory Parameters under the Instance heading. When you click the Enable button, enter the value for SGA_TARGET. To change the SGA_MAX_SIZE parameter (which requires a cycle of the database), you need to be logged in as SYSDBA. Figure 3.8 shows the Memory Parameters screen of the EM Database Control.

You can query the current sizes of the SGA components using the V$SGA_DYNAMIC_COMPONENTS dictionary view, like so:

```
SQL> SELECT component, current_size
  2  FROM   v$sga_dynamic_components;
```

COMPONENT	CURRENT_SIZE
shared pool	100663296
large pool	4194304
java pool	50331648
streams pool	0
DEFAULT buffer cache	37748736
KEEP buffer cache	0
RECYCLE buffer cache	0
DEFAULT 2K buffer cache	0
DEFAULT 4K buffer cache	0
DEFAULT 8K buffer cache	0
DEFAULT 16K buffer cache	0
DEFAULT 32K buffer cache	0

```
OSM Buffer Cache                        0

13 rows selected.

SQL>
```

When SGA_TARGET is set to a nonzero value, the autotuned SGA parameters will have default values of zero. If you specify a value for the autotuned SGA parameters, the value will be treated as the lower limit of that component.

FIGURE 3.8 The Memory Parameters page

Oracle Enterprise Manager (SCOTT) - Memory Parameters - Mozilla

File Edit View Go Bookmarks Tools Window Help

Database: BT10GNF1 > Memory Parameters

⚠ You are not logged on with SYSDBA privilege. Only controls for dynamic parameters are editable

Memory Parameters

Page Refreshed **May 13, 2004 5:54:39 PM** (Refresh)

SGA | PGA

The System Global Area (SGA) is a group of shared memory structures that contains data and control information for one Oracle database system. The SGA is allocated in memory when an Oracle database instance is started.

Automatic Shared Memory Management **Disabled** (Enable)

Shared Pool	96	MB ▼	(Advice)
Buffer Cache	32	MB ▼	(Advice)
Large Pool	8	MB ▼	
Java Pool	48	MB ▼	

Other (MB) **1**

Total SGA (MB) **185**

SGA

- Shared Pool(51.8%)
- Buffer Cache(17.3%)
- Large Pool(4.3%)
- Java Pool(25.9%)
- Other(0.7%)

1% 26% 52% 4% 17%

Maximum SGA Size

The Maximum SGA Size specifies how much memory is allocated when the database starts up. If you specify the Maximum SGA Size, you can later dynamically change SGA component sizes (provided the total SGA size does not exceed the Maximum SGA Size).

Maximum SGA Size (MB) 188

SGA | PGA

☞ **TIP** * indicates controls, if changed, must restart database to invoke.

(Show SQL) (Revert) (Apply)

Setting SGA_TARGET to zero will disable ASMM. The autotuned components will have values of their current sizes, and these values are written to the SPFILE to use for the next instance startup.

Resizing the autotuned SGA parameters is possible even if ASMM is enabled. For autotuned parameters, manual resizing will result in immediate component resizing if the current value is smaller than the new value. If the new value is smaller, the component is not resized, but a new minimum size is set.

For manually configured SGA parameters, resizing will immediately take effect to the precise new value. If the size of a component is increased, one or more of the autotuned components will be reduced. If the size of a manually configured component is reduced, the memory that is released is given to the automatically sized components.

The following views provide information on the dynamic SGA resize operations:

V$SGA_CURRENT_RESIZE_OPS   SGA resize operations that are currently in progress

V$SGA_RESIZE_OPS   Information about the last 400 completed SGA resize operations

V$SGA_DYNAMIC_COMPONENTS   Information about the dynamic components of the SGA

V$SGA_DYNAMIC_FREE_MEMORY   Information about the amount of SGA memory available for future dynamic SGA resize operations

The Memory Manager Process

Oracle 10g comes with the new MMAN process (which stands for *memory manager*) to manage the automatic shared memory. MMAN serves as the SGA memory broker and coordinates the sizing of the memory components. It keeps track of the sizes of the components and pending resize operations.

The MMAN process observes the system and workload to determine the ideal distribution of memory. MMAN performs this check every few minutes so that memory can always be present where needed. Based on the workload, ASMM does the following:

- It captures statistics periodically in the background.
- It uses different memory advisors.
- It performs what-if analysis to determine optimal distribution of memory.
- It moves memory to where it is needed.
- When SPFILE is used, component sizes are used from the last shutdown.

Tuning Automatic Undo Retention

Oracle 9i introduced automatic undo management. Oracle 10g goes one step further and calculates the optimum value for the UNDO_RETENTION parameter. The default for this parameter is 900 seconds. If UNDO_RETENTION is set to zero or if no value is specified, Oracle 10g automatically tunes the undo retention for the current undo tablespace using 900 as the minimum value. If you set UNDO_RETENTION to a value other than zero, Oracle 10g autotunes the undo retention using the specified value as the minimum.

🌐 Real World Scenario

Tuning Memory in OLTP DSS Systems

One of our critical databases is big in disk storage size and SGA size. For better performance of online applications, we had a huge portion of SGA allocated for buffer cache. Since the tables used by nightly batch jobs were huge and were heavy users of parallel query, we had a big large pool size also. After upgrading the database to Oracle 10*g*, the first thing we did on the database was enable ASSM. Querying V$SGA_RESIZE_OPS, we could see that the buffer and that the large pool was increased automatically a little after the batch window started.

Automatic tuning is performed by collecting database usage statistics, such as the undo generation rate, and estimating undo capacity needed for successfully completing queries. Automatic undo retention tuning is enabled by the architecture (meaning you cannot disable it). Undo retention is tuned for longest-running query, and query duration information is collected every 30 seconds.

The Undo Advisor is a new feature in Oracle 10*g*: the database automatically analyzes the undo usage to advise the undo tablespace size to support the longest-running query when using automatic undo.

Figure 3.9 shows the Undo Advisor screen of the EM Database Control. You can specify the required undo retention minutes, the Undo Advisor uses the metrics collected to determine the undo tablespace size. The graph shows the undo retention minutes and the space required in the tablespace.

> You can also invoke the Undo Advisor from PL/SQL using the DBMS_ADVISOR package, which is discussed later in the chapter.

Oracle 10*g* also simplifies the undo configuration by removing several undo-related parameters of previous releases. The parameters are as follows:

- MAX_ROLLBACK_SEGMENTS
- UNDO_SUPPRESS_ERRORS
- ROW_LOCKING
- SERIALIZABLE
- TRANSACTION_AUDITING

Oracle 10*g* automatically tunes the UNDO_RETENTION parameter to avoid the "snapshot too old" error. But when heavy DML operations are performed on the database, UNDO_RETENTION is not guaranteed. Oracle 10*g* introduces a RETENTION GUARANTEE clause to guarantee the undo retention. This means that the database will make certain that undo will always be available for the specified undo retention period. You can use the RETENTION GUARANTEE clause when creating the undo tablespace (CREATE UNDO TABLESPACE or CREATE DATABASE) or later using the ALTER TABLESPACE statement. To turn the retention guarantee off, use the RETENTION NOGUARANTEE clause. You can view the current retention from the DBA_TABLESPACES view.

FIGURE 3.9   The Undo Advisor

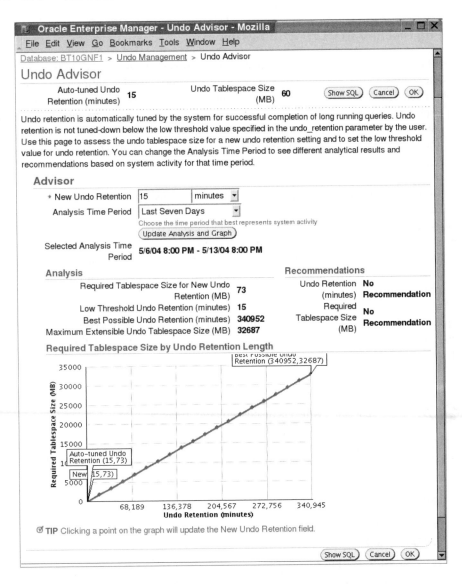

The following example code demonstrates the undo guarantee setting:

```
SQL> SELECT tablespace_name, contents, retention
  2  FROM   dba_tablespaces;


TABLESPACE_NAME CONTENTS  RETENTION
--------------- --------- -----------
```

```
SYSTEM          PERMANENT NOT APPLY
UNDOTBS1        UNDO      NOGUARANTEE
SYSAUX          PERMANENT NOT APPLY
TEMP            TEMPORARY NOT APPLY
EXAMPLE         PERMANENT NOT APPLY
APPDATA         PERMANENT NOT APPLY


SQL> ALTER TABLESPACE undotbs1 RETENTION GUARANTEE;

Tablespace altered.

SQL> SELECT tablespace_name, contents, retention
  2  FROM   dba_tablespaces
  3  WHERE  contents = 'UNDO';


TABLESPACE_NAME CONTENTS  RETENTION
--------------- --------- -----------
UNDOTBS1        UNDO      GUARANTEE

SQL>
```

Tuning the Automatic Checkpoint

The Mean Time to Recovery Advisor (the MTTR Advisor) performs automatic checkpoint tuning. Oracle 9*i* introduced the FAST_START_MTTR_TARGET parameter to specify the expected crash recovery time. Though Oracle 9*i* Release 2 introduced the MTTR Advisor, it was not easy to set the right target for MTTR_FAST_START_TARGET. You always had a trade-off between the small recovery time and runtime physical I/Os.

By default, Oracle 10*g* supports the automatic checkpoint tuning by making the best effort to write out dirty buffers without impacting the throughput, thus achieving reasonable crash-recovery time. With automatic checkpoint tuning, you do not need to set up any checkpoint-related parameters.

Setting the FAST_START_MTTR_TARGET parameter to a nonzero value or not setting this parameter enables automatic checkpoint tuning. If you explicitly set this parameter to zero, you disable automatic checkpoint tuning. The STATISTICS_LEVEL parameter must be set to TYPICAL or ALL.

After the database runs a typical workload for some time, the V$MTTR_TARGET_ADVICE dictionary view shows advisory information and an estimate of the number of additional I/O operations that would occur under different FAST_START_MTTR_TARGET values.

A new column OPTIMAL_LOGFILE_SIZE is now available in V$INSTANCE_RECOVERY. This column shows the redo log file size in megabytes, which is considered optimal based on the current FAST_START_MTTR_TARGET setting. The online redo log files must be at least set to the size recommended.

Chapter 5, "Automated Storage Management," discusses the Redo Logfile Size Advisor.

Collecting Automatic Optimizer Statistics

For the query optimizer to generate optimal query execution plans, the statistics on the objects must be valid. The optimizer statistics collection has improved with each version of the Oracle database. Oracle 8*i* introduced the DBMS_STATS package. The DBA determined when to gather statistics and how to gather statistics. Oracle 9*i* introduced the monitoring feature; the database determined how to gather statistics (the monitoring option must be manually enabled), but you determined when to gather statistics. You used the GATHER AUTO option to update the statistics for the objects when the current statistics were considered stale.

In Oracle 10*g*, the optimizer statistics collection is fully automated. You don't need to worry about statistics gathering at all, and table monitoring is enabled by default.

The automatic table monitoring is enabled when the STATISTICS_LEVEL parameter is set to TYPICAL (default) or ALL. The [NO]MONITORING clause of ALTER TABLE and CREATE TABLE are obsolete in Oracle 10*g*. The clause is still valid, but Oracle 10*g* ignores it.

How Statistics Are Maintained Current

When an Oracle 10*g* database is created or a database is upgraded to Oracle 10g, a job by the name of GATHER_STATS_JOB is created. The job is managed by the scheduler and runs when the MAINTENANCE_WINDOW_GROUP window group is opened. The MAINTENANCE_WINDOW_GROUP window group, which has the WEEKEND_WINDOW window and the WEEKNIGHT_WINDOW window, are also created at the database creation time. By default WEEKNIGHT_WINDOW opens Monday through Friday at 10 p.m. for 8 hours. By default WEEKEND_WINDOW opens Saturday at 0000 hours and continues for 48 hours.

The GATHER_STATS_JOB job is scheduled to run only when you create the database using the DBCA utility or you upgrade the database using DBUA utility. Otherwise, the job is created but is not scheduled to run.

The GATHER_STATS_JOB executes the DBMS_STATS.GATHER_DATABASE_STATS_JOB_PROC procedure, which is internal to Oracle 10*g* but is similar to the DBMS_STATS.GATHER_DATABASE_STATS procedure. It collects statistics on database objects when the object has no previously gathered statistics or when the existing statistics are stale because the underlying object has more than 10 percent of the rows modified. The DBMS_STATS.GATHER_DATABASE_STATS_JOB_PROC procedure prioritizes the database objects that require statistics so that the objects that need the statistics most are processed first, before the maintenance window closes. Unlike the DBMS_STATS.GATHER_DATABASE_STATS_JOB_PROC procedure, the GATHER_STATS_JOB continues until finished even if it exceeds the allocated time for the maintenance window.

You can adjust the automatic statistics-gathering job to start at a different time by changing the window properties using the EM Database Control or the procedures discussed in Chapter 2, "Moving Data and Managing the Scheduler." You can also disable the automatic statistics gathering using the DBMS_SCHEDULER.DISABLE ('GATHER_STATS_JOB') procedure. Disabling the GATHER_STATS_JOB is not recommended unless you have other methods to keep the statistics current.

You must gather statistics manually for the following situations:

- When a table is loaded using bulk operation
- When using external tables
- To collect system statistics
- To collect statistics on fixed objects (dynamic performance dictionary tables)

For Automatic Optimizer Statistics Collection to work, the STATISTICS_LEVEL parameter must not be set to BASIC. Since GATHER_STATS_JOB updates statistics only for stale objects, with STATISTICS_LEVEL set to BASIC, there will be no tracking mechanism.

Collecting Statistics on Dictionary Objects

Unlike previous versions of Oracle, for the best performance Oracle 10g requires statistics on all dictionary objects and the operating system. DBMS_STATS includes programs to collect dictionary statistics and fixed table statistics.

It is best to analyze the dictionary using the GATHER AUTO option. That way only objects that need statistics are analyzed. Executing any of the following three DBMS_STATS programs can collect statistics on dictionary objects:

DBMS_STATS.GATHER_DATABASE_STATS (GATHER_SYS=>TRUE, OPTIONS=> 'GATHER AUTO');   The default for GATHER_SYS parameter is FALSE. If you set it to TRUE, the statistics on the objects owned by the SYS schema are analyzed along with the other objects of the database.

DBMS_STATS.GATHER_SCHEMA_STATS ('SYS', OPTIONS=>'GATHER AUTO');   Use this option to gather the schema statistics by specifying the SYS schema name.

DBMS_STATS.GATHER_DICTIONARY_STATS (OPTIONS=>'GATHER AUTO');   This option collects statistics on the SYS, SYSTEM, and any other schema that owns the server components.

You would need the new privilege ANALYZE ANY DICTIONARY to collect dictionary statistics. OPTIONS=>'GATHER AUTO' is specified in all the three methods to show a best practice; it is not required to use this option.

None of the previous options gather statistics on the fixed memory tables. It is necessary to collect statistics on the fixed dictionary objects only once, preferably during normal workload. The DBMS_STATS.GATHER_FIXED_OBJECTS_STATS procedure collects statistics on fixed dictionary objects. Since the fixed tables do not have I/O cost because the rows reside in memory, the optimizer takes into account only the CPU cost of reading rows.

When deriving an execution plan for a query, the optimizer considers the I/O and CPU resources required for the query. Collecting system statistics enables the optimizer to estimate the CPU and I/O costs more accurately. Use the DBMS_STATS.GATHER_SYSTEM_STATS procedure to gather the system statistics (available in Oracle9i). When this procedure is invoked, the system statistics are gathered over a period of time. The first argument to this procedure is GATHERING_MODE, which defaults to NOWORKLOAD, which means the database is idle and is good time to capture the average read seek time and transfer speed for the I/O system. Workload can be used to specify if the database is performing normal operations or is doing specific tasks. For workload specific statistics, you can use the START and STOP values for this parameter. If system statistics should be collected for a specific time, specify INTERVAL as the value for GATHERING_ MODE. You must specify the time in minutes using the INTERVAL parameter when INTERVAL is specified as GATHERING_MODE.

The following code collects statistics when there is no workload; run this typically after creating the database and all tablespaces:

```
SQL> EXEC DBMS_STATS.GATHER_SYSTEM_STATS ('NOWORKLOAD');
```

To collect statistics when there is specific workload, use the following code at the beginning of the work:

```
SQL> EXEC DBMS_STATS.GATHER_SYSTEM_STATS ('START');
```

When the work is finished, run the procedure with STOP as the parameter.

 The Automatic Optimizer Statistics Collection job collects statistics on the dictionary objects automatically. It does not collect statistics for external tables, system statistics, and fixed tables.

Managing Statistics

Due to application design sometimes it may be necessary to lock statistics on tables. If a table is populated by a job and is being used in the job subsequently, it would be a good idea to collect stats on the table when the table is populated and lock the statistics on the table. When working with Oracle8i and Oracle9i, how many times you would have wished that you saved the statistics before you analyzed the table, which the new analyze changed the execution plan completely. Oracle 10g provides answers to all these - you can lock statistics, maintain statistics history and restore statistics. In the following sections, we will discuss these significant enhancements made to the DBMS_STATS program in Oracle 10g.

Locking Statistics

Statistics on a table or schema can be locked. Once locked, gathering statistics will not update the statistics on those tables or schema. Locking table statistics is useful for tables that are populated only during certain operations. You can also lock statistics on a table without statistics (after deleting the statistics) to prevent automatic statistics collection so that dynamic sampling will be used during query execution.

The DBMS_STATS.LOCK_TABLE_STATS procedure locks table statistics. You need to provide the owner name and table name as parameters. When statistics on a table are locked, all its dependents' statistics are also locked (for example, column statistics, histograms, and index statistics).When table statistics are locked, using the SET_*, DELTE_*, IMPORT_*, or GATHER_* procedures of DBMS_STATS with the locked table as a parameter will generate an error, but gathering schema statistics will skip modifying the statistics of a table if it is locked.

Use the DBMS_STATS.UNLOCK_TABLE_STATS procedure to unlock table statistics. Similar to the LOCK_TABLE_STATS procedure, you need to provide the owner and table name as parameters.

The DBMS_STATS.LOCK_SCHEMA_STATS procedure locks all the table statistics of a schema. DBMS_STATS.UNLOCK_SCHEMA_STATS unlocks the schema statistics.

The STATTYPE_LOCKED column of the DBA_TAB_STATISTICS dictionary view will be marked as ALL when the statistics are locked. The following code shows examples of using the lock statistics programs of DBMS_STATS:

```
SQL> EXEC dbms_stats.lock_table_stats -
        ('TRAING','ENROLLMENT');

PL/SQL procedure successfully completed.

SQL> EXEC dbms_stats.lock_schema_stats('HR');

PL/SQL procedure successfully completed.

SQL> EXEC dbms_stats.gather_table_stats
        ('TRAING','ENROLLMENT');

ERROR at line 1:
ORA-20005: object statistics are locked (stattype = ALL)
ORA-06512: at "SYS.DBMS_STATS", line 11568
ORA-06512: at "SYS.DBMS_STATS", line 11587
ORA-06512: at line 1

SQL> EXEC dbms_stats.gather_schema_stats('TRAING');
```

```
PL/SQL procedure successfully completed.

SQL> EXEC dbms_stats.gather_schema_stats('HR');

PL/SQL procedure successfully completed.

SQL> SELECT owner, table_name
  2  FROM   dba_tab_statistics
  3  WHERE  stattype_locked = 'ALL'
SQL> /

OWNER       TABLE_NAME
----------  ------------------------------
HR          REGIONS
HR          COUNTRIES
HR          LOCATIONS
HR          DEPARTMENTS
HR          JOBS
HR          EMPLOYEES
HR          JOB_HISTORY
TRAING      ENROLLMENT

8 rows selected.

SQL>
```

Using the FORCE=>TRUE argument for the DELETE_*, IMPORT_*, RESTORE_*, and SET_* procedures of DBMS_STATS will override the statistics even if they are locked.

Managing History

Whenever statistics are modified using the DBMS_STATS programs, old versions of the statistics are saved automatically for future restoration. This is a useful feature when new statistics adversely affect the query's performance. The GATHER_*, IMPORT_*, and SET_* procedures of DBMS_STATS write the current statistics to the AWR before updating the new statistics.

The DBA_OPTSTAT_OPERATIONS dictionary view shows the start and end time of all database-level and schema-level statistics update operations. The DBA_TAB_STATS_HISTORY view shows the statistics updated at a table level.

The following sample query shows the times when the statistics for the enrollment table was updated:

```
SQL> SELECT stats_update_time
  2  FROM    dba_tab_stats_history
  3  WHERE   owner = 'TRAING'
  4  AND     TABLE_NAME = 'ENROLLMENT';

STATS_UPDATE_TIME
-----------------------------------
20-APR-04 11.45.49.898795 AM -05:00
14-MAY-04 06.20.41.034775 AM -05:00

SQL>
```

The old statistics are purged from the AWR at regular intervals; the default is 31 days. You can change the retention days using the DBMS_STATS.ALTER_STATS_HISTORY_RETENTION procedure. The DBMS_STATS.GET_STATS_HISTORY_RETENTION function gives the current setting for history retention. The DBMS_STATS.GET_STATS_HISTORY_AVAILABILITY function gives the oldest time stamp for which statistics history is available. You can also manually purge the statistics using the DBMS_STATS.PURGE_STATS procedure.

The following are examples of using these programs:

```
SQL> SELECT DBMS_STATS.GET_STATS_HISTORY_RETENTION
  2  FROM    dual;

GET_STATS_HISTORY_RETENTION
---------------------------
                         31

SQL> SELECT DBMS_STATS.GET_STATS_HISTORY_AVAILABILITY
  2  FROM    dual;

GET_STATS_HISTORY_AVAILABILITY
--------------------------------------
12-APR-04 10.07.31.886403000 PM -05:00

SQL> EXEC DBMS_STATS.ALTER_STATS_HISTORY_RETENTION (15);

PL/SQL procedure successfully completed.
```

```
SQL> EXEC DBMS_STATS.PURGE_STATS -
          (TO_TIMESTAMP('010504','DDMMYY'));

PL/SQL procedure successfully completed.

SQL> SELECT DBMS_STATS.GET_STATS_HISTORY_AVAILABILITY
  2  FROM   dual;

GET_STATS_HISTORY_AVAILABILITY
--------------------------------------
01-MAY-04 12.00.00.000000000 AM -05:00

SQL> SELECT DBMS_STATS.GET_STATS_HISTORY_RETENTION
  2  FROM   dual;

GET_STATS_HISTORY_RETENTION
--------------------------
                        15

SQL>
```

The following procedures are available in DBMS_STATS to restore various types of statistics:

- RESTORE_DATABASE_STATS
- RESTORE_DICTIONARY_STATS
- RESTORE_FIXED_OBJECTS_STATS
- RESTORE_SCHEMA_STATS
- RESTORE_SYSTEM_STATS
- RESTORE_TABLE_STATS

All the RESTORE_* procedures use a time stamp as an argument to restore the statistics as of that time stamp.

When statistics are gathered using ANALYZE statements, old versions are not stored in the AWR and are not available for restore.

In Oracle 10g index statistics collection occurs by default during index creation and rebuilding (except when statistics are locked). The COMPUTE STATISTICS clause of CREATE INDEX and ALTER INDEX is now obsolete.

Identifying the Advisory Framework

The advisory framework is another component of the CMI. The advisory framework consists of various server components that provide diagnosis and recommendations on database resource utilization and performance. In this chapter we have already discussed the ADDM, the ultimate advisor for Oracle 10*g*. Figure 3.10 shows the components of the advisory framework.

FIGURE 3.10   Advisory framework

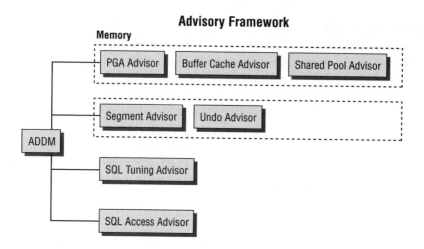

The advisory framework provides a uniform interface for all advisors. It also provides seamless integration between the advisors, because all advisors have a common data source and results storage using the AWR.

The components of the advisory framework are as follows:

ADDM   ADDM does a top-down instance analysis, identifies problems, and provides recommendations. It also gives recommendations to use the other more detailed advisors of the advisory framework.

SQL Tuning Advisor   The SQL Tuning Advisor provides expert tuning advice for badly performing SQL statements. The SQL Tuning Advisor uses the Automatic Tuning Optimizer to tune the SQL statements.

Chapter 6, "Performance and Application Tuning," discusses the SQL Tuning Advisor.

SQL Access Advisor   The SQL Access Advisor can automatically analyze the schema for a given workload and recommend indexes and materialized views to create, retain, or drop as appropriate for the workload.

Chapter 6 also discusses the SQL Access Advisor.

Segment Advisor The Segment Advisor makes recommendations on space-related issues such as wasted-space reclamation and growth trend analysis.

Undo Advisor The Undo Advisor suggests parameter values for the best undo retention and advises on additional space needed to support flashback for a specific time.

PGA Advisor The Program Global Area (PGA) Advisor tunes PGA memory allocated to the server processes. It recommends optimal value for the `PGA_AGGREGATE_TARGET` parameter.

Memory Advisor The Memory Advisor determines the optimum size for the buffer cache and the optimal shared pool size by tracking its use by the library cache. The Memory Advisor statistics provide information on predicting how changes in the size of the shared pool can affect how long objects are kept in the shared pool.

You can invoke the advisors from the EM Database Control using the Advisor Central link on the Database home page. Figure 3.11 shows the Advisor Central page of the EM Database Control. Notice that the EM does not support all the advisors. You can view the advisor recommendations and make changes using the EM Database Control.

FIGURE 3.11 The Advisor Central page

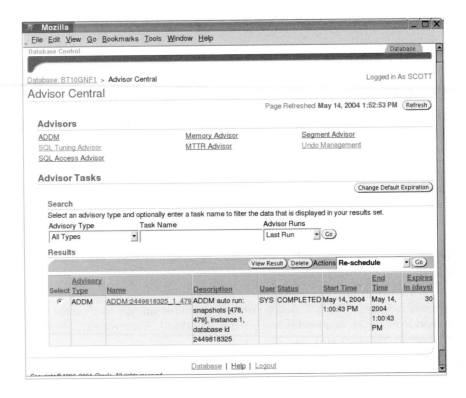

In the next section we will discuss using the DBMS_ADVISOR PL/SQL package to analyze and report advisor findings.

Using *DBMS_ADVISOR*

The DBMS_ADVISOR package, new to Oracle 10g, provides the PL/SQL application programming interface (API) to manage all the advisors. The ADVISOR privilege is required to use the procedures in the DBMS_ADVISOR package. The data dictionary view DBA_ADVISOR_DEFINITIONS contains the unique advisor names that can be used in the DBMS_ADVISOR package to get tuning advice.

```
SQL> SELECT * FROM dba_advisor_definitions;

ADVISOR_ID ADVISOR_NAME                          PROPERTY
---------- ----------------------------------- ----------
         1 ADDM                                         1
         2 SQL Access Advisor                          15
         3 Undo Advisor                                 1
         4 SQL Tuning Advisor                           3
         5 Segment Advisor                              3
         6 SQL Workload Manager                         0
         7 Tune MView                                  31

7 rows selected.

SQL>
```

Table 3.2 lists the commonly used procedures of the DBMS_ADVISOR package that are available to all advisors. Certain procedures are applicable only to specific advisors; for example, the TUNE_MVIEW is applicable only to the SQL Access Advisor.

TABLE 3.2   *DBMS_ADVISOR* Programs

Procedure Name	Purpose
CREATE_TASK	Creates a new advisor task in the repository.
DELETE_TASK	Deletes the specified advisor task.
EXECUTE_TASK	Executes a specified task. The execution is a synchronous operation; control will not be returned to the caller until the operation is completed or an interrupt was detected.
CANCEL_TASK	Cancels a currently executing task.

TABLE 3.2   *DBMS_ADVISOR* Programs *(continued)*

Procedure Name	Purpose
INTERRUPT_TASK	Stops the currently executing task, with normal exit.
RESUME_TASK	Resumes an interrupted task.
RESET_TASK	Resets a task to its original state.
CREATE_OBJECT	Defines objects, normally input data for advisors. For the Segment Advisor, defined at the segment or tablespace level.
UPDATE_TASK_ATTRIBUTES	Changes various attributes of a task.
SET_TASK_PARAMETER	Modifies a user parameter within a task. A task can be modified only when it is in its initial state.
MARK_RECOMMENDATION	Accepts, rejects, or ignores a recommendation.
GET_TASK_SCRIPT	Creates a SQL*Plus-compatible SQL script of all the recommendations that are accepted from a specified task. The output is a CLOB buffer.
GET_TASK_REPORT	Creates and returns an XML report for the specified task. The type can be text, HTML, or XML.
CREATE_FILE	Creates an external file from a PL/SQL CLOB variable, used for creating scripts and reports.
QUICK_TUNE	Analyzes and generates recommendations for a single SQL statement.

Using the procedures of the DBMS_ADVISOR package, a typical tuning advisor session may comprise the following steps:

1. Create an advisor task using the DBMS_ADVISOR.CREATE_TASK procedure. The advisor task is a data area in the advisor repository that manages the tuning efforts. An existing task can be a template for another task.

2. Use the DBMS_ADVISOR.SET_TASK_PARAMETERS procedure to set up appropriate parameters to control the advisor's behavior. Typical parameters are TARGET_OBJECTS, TIME_WINDOW, and TIME_LIMIT.

3. Perform analysis using the DBMS_ADVISOR.EXECUTE_TASK procedure. You can interrupt the analysis process anytime to review the results up to that point. You can then resume the interrupted analysis for more recommendations, or you can adjust the task parameters and then resume execution.

4. Review the results using the DBMS_ADVISOR.GET_TASK_REPORT procedure. You can also view the results using dictionary views.

> The $ORACLE_HOME/rdbms/admin/addmrpti.sql script is a good example of DBMS_ADVISOR usage.

The following example shows analyzing ADDM manually using the DBMS_ADVISOR procedures (the snapshots range 450 to 460 is used for the analysis; inline comments are provided to explain each step):

```
declare
 taskid number;
 taskname varchar2(100);
BEGIN

 -- create a new task, task name is system generated
 dbms_advisor.create_task('ADDM', taskid, taskname);

 -- set the snapshots to analyze
 dbms_advisor.set_task_parameter(taskname,
             'START_SNAPSHOT', 450);
 dbms_advisor.set_task_parameter(taskname,
             'END_SNAPSHOT', 460);

 -- perform analysis
 dbms_advisor.execute_task(taskname);

 -- buffer the report and save to file
 -- WORK_DIR is a directory already created in the db
 dbms_advisor.create_file(
    dbms_advisor.get_task_report(taskname, 'TEXT', 'ALL'),
                    'WORK_DIR', 'addmrpt.txt');
end;
/
```

One section of the report mentioned the following:

```
FINDING 7: 2% impact (104 seconds)
----------------------------------
Individual database segments responsible for significant
user I/O wait were found.

    RECOMMENDATION 1: Segment Tuning, 2% benefit
                    (104 seconds)
      ACTION: Run "Segment Advisor" on
                        TABLE "VOLEST.DAILY_ESTIMATES"
        with object id 53122.
        RELEVANT OBJECT: database object with id 53122
      ACTION: Investigate application logic involving I/O
        on TABLE  "VOLEST.DAILY_ESTIMATES" with
        object id 53122.
        RELEVANT OBJECT: database object with id 53122
      RATIONALE: The SQL statement with SQL_ID
        "3wft1nmf55c3w" spent  significant time
        waiting for User I/O on the hot object.
        RELEVANT OBJECT: SQL statement with SQL_ID
        3wft1nmf55c3w
        BEGIN
        SYS.KUPW$WORKER.MAIN('SYS_IMPORT_FULL_01',
                        'SCOTT');
      END;


    SYMPTOMS THAT LED TO THE FINDING:
      Wait class "User I/O" was consuming significant
      database time. (5.2% impact [269 seconds])
```

~~~~~~

Though it is clear that the I/O wait was caused by the Import operation, for the sake of demonstration, we will invoke the Segment Advisor for more advice. The following code analyzes the DAILY_ESTIMATES table using the Segment Advisor. The Segment Advisor determines if an object is a good candidate for shrink operation. Here also inline comments are provided for each step.

Here is the code:

```
declare

  objectid number;
  taskid   number;
  taskname varchar2(100) := 'SEGADV001';

  BEGIN
   -- Create task, task name is passed in
   dbms_advisor.create_task(
     advisor_name=>    'Segment Advisor',
     task_id=>         taskid,
     task_name=>       taskname);

   -- Define the object where analysis to be made
   dbms_advisor.create_object (
       task_name=>      taskname,
       object_type=>    'TABLE',
       attr1=>          'VOLEST',
       attr2=>          'DAILY_ESTIMATES',
       attr3=>          'NULL',
       attr4=>          'NULL',
       attr5=>          'NULL',
       object_id=>      objectid);

   -- Define the level of analysis
   dbms_advisor.set_task_parameter (
       task_name=>      taskname,
       parameter=>      'RECOMMEND_ALL',
       value=>          'TRUE');

   -- Execute task
   dbms_advisor.execute_task(taskname);

end;
/
```

View the result from the dictionary using the following query:

```
SQL> SELECT message, more_info
  2  FROM    dba_advisor_findings
  3  WHERE   task_name = 'SEGADV001';
```

```
MESSAGE
MORE_INFO
-------------------------------------------------------
The object has less than 1% free space, it is not worth
shrinking.
Allocated Space:545259520: Used Space:543181080:
Reclaimable Space :0:


SQL>
```

 NOTE   The previous example of using ADDM and the Segment Advisor is readily available in the Database Control. You do not need to write any code but just need to click, click, click....

Advisor Dictionary Views

Many advisor-related data dictionary views exist. For each DBA_ADVISOR view listed here, a corresponding USER_ and ALL_ dictionary view exists. The views are as follows:

DBA_ADVISOR_ACTIONS   Displays information about the actions associated with all recommendations in the database.

DBA_ADVISOR_COMMANDS   Displays information about the commands used by all advisors for specifying recommendation actions.

DBA_ADVISOR_DEFINITIONS   Displays properties of all the advisors in the database; contains one row for each task.

DBA_ADVISOR_FINDINGS   Displays the findings discovered by all advisors.

DBA_ADVISOR_JOURNAL   Displays journal entries for all tasks in the database.

DBA_ADVISOR_LOG   Displays information about the current state of all tasks in the database.

DBA_ADVISOR_OBJECTS   Displays information about the objects currently referenced by all the advisors.

DBA_ADVISOR_PARAMETERS   Displays the parameters and their current values for all tasks.

DBA_ADVISOR_RATIONALE   Displays information about the rationales for all recommendations.

DBA_ADVISOR_RECOMMENDATIONS   Displays the results of an analysis. A recommendation can have multiple actions associated with it.

DBA_ADVISOR_SQLA_*   Displays recommendation and workload information on SQL Access Advisor findings.

DBA_ADVISOR_SQLW_* Displays the workload parameters, templates, objects that are used by the SQL Access Advisor.

DBA_ADVISOR_TASKS Displays information about the tasks in the database; contains one row for each task.

DBA_ADVISOR_TEMPLATES Displays information about all templates.

DBA_ADVISOR_USAGE Displays the usage information for each type of advisor.

Automating Tasks

Automatic routine administration tasks are another component of the CMI. By analyzing the information stored in the AWR, the database can identify the need to perform routine maintenance tasks, such as updating optimizer statistics. The automated tasks infrastructure enables the database to perform such operations. It uses the scheduler to run such tasks in a predefined window.

Please review Chapter 2 to read about the job scheduling features.

Automated Optimizer Statistics Collection is an example of automated task. It is created automatically at the Oracle 10*g* database creation time and runs every day during the maintenance window.

Chapter 1 reviewed another example of an automated task, when we discussed the *Database Configuration Assistant* (DBCA). If you enable automatic backups, the database will setup a job to perform the backup every day at 2 a.m.

Resource Manager Enhancements

The Database Resource Manager gives the Oracle database more control over resource management. The DBMS_RESOURCE_MANAGER and DBMS_RESOURCE_MANAGER_PRIVS packages administer resource management. Oracle 8*i* introduced the Database Resource Manager.

You can administer the Resource Manager using the EM Database Control. From the database home page, click the Administration tab; under Resource Manager you will see several links to manage the components of the Resource Manager.

Oracle 10*g* introduced new features into the Resource Manager to effectively manage resources. The key features include switching a session back to its original consumer group, setting resource directives to limit the amount of session idle time, and establishing priorities to consumer groups using the adaptive mapping feature. In the following sections, we will discuss the enhancements made to the Resource Manager.

Automatic Session Switchback

Oracle 9*i* allowed automatic switching of users from one resource group to another if a user's session executed longer than the specified amount of time defined in the user's resource group. Once the switching was done, the session remained in the switched group for the remainder of the life of the session.

In Oracle 10g, you can specify that at the end of a switched resource group call the session be returned to its original resource group. You do this by introducing a new parameter, SWITCH_TIME_IN_CALL, for the DBMS_RESOURCE_MANAGER.CREATE_PLAN_DIRECTIVE procedure and the NEW_SWITCH_TIME_IN_CALL parameter for the DBMS_RESOURCE_MANAGER.UPDATE_PLAN_DIRECTIVE procedure. These parameters accept the time in seconds.

If you use the SWITCH_TIME parameter, the behavior will be as it was in Oracle 9*i* where the session will be switched to the new resource group and remain in that group until the session ends. The SWITCH_TIME and SWITCH_TIME_IN_CALL parameters are mutually exclusive, and they specify the time in seconds that a session can execute before an action is taken. The default for both parameters is NULL.

Whether you use SWITCH_TIME or SWITCH_TIME_IN_CALL, the SWITCH_GROUP parameter specifies the resource group to which the session will be switched if the switch criteria are met.

The SWITCH_TIME_IN_CALL parameter is primarily beneficial for three-tier applications where the middle tier is implementing session pooling. In this situation, the middle tier uses the same session for different calls from different users (the boundary of work is a call). The new parameter will help in not penalizing the users for the calls made by a prior user. The SWITCH_TIME parameter is primarily beneficial for the client-server architecture.

The following is an example of creating a new resource plan directive with automatic switching to the OTHER_GROUPS resource group from ONLINE_GROUP when the session uses 100 percent of the CPU for five minutes. Once the call is completed, the session will be switched back to ONLINE_GROUP. Here is the example:

```
SQL> BEGIN
  2   DBMS_RESOURCE_MANAGER.CREATE_PENDING_AREA();
  3   DBMS_RESOURCE_MANAGER.CREATE_CONSUMER_GROUP (
  4   CONSUMER_GROUP      => 'ONLINE_GROUP',
  5   COMMENT             => 'New Group for online users');
  6   DBMS_RESOURCE_MANAGER.CREATE_PLAN_DIRECTIVE(
  7   PLAN                => 'ONLINE_PLAN',
  8   GROUP_OR_SUBPLAN    => 'ONLINE_GROUP',
  9   CPU_P1              => 100,
 10   CPU_P2              => 0,
 11   SWITCH_GROUP        => 'OTHER_GROUPS',
 12   SWITCH_TIME_IN_CALL=> 300,
 13   COMMENT             => 'Automatic Switch Example');
 14   DBMS_RESOURCE_MANAGER.SUBMIT_PENDING_AREA();
 15   END;
 16   /
```

```
PL/SQL procedure successfully completed.

SQL>
```

Setting Idle Timeout

Oracle 10*g* has two new settings to limit the idle time for a session. You can specify the amount of time a session can be idle, as well as specify if the session is idle and blocking other sessions. This new option of limiting the idle time by blocking other session features is useful for online applications, where users update certain transactions and go out for lunch, for example, thus blocking a bunch of other users.

The MAX_IDLE_TIME parameter defines the maximum amount of time in seconds a session can be inactive or idle. The default is NULL (unlimited). When the session exceeds the limit, the PMON process will terminate the session and clean up its state.

The MAX_IDLE_BLOCKER_TIME parameter defines the maximum amount of time in seconds a session can be idle and block the acquisition of resources for another user. The default is NULL (unlimited).

The following example updates the ONLINE_GROUP to set the idle time to one hour and the idle blocking time to five minutes:

```
SQL> BEGIN
  2    DBMS_RESOURCE_MANAGER.CREATE_PENDING_AREA();
  3    DBMS_RESOURCE_MANAGER.UPDATE_PLAN_DIRECTIVE(
  4    PLAN                        => 'ONLINE_PLAN',
  5    GROUP_OR_SUBPLAN            => 'ONLINE_GROUP',
  6    NEW_MAX_IDLE_TIME          => 3600,
  7    NEW_MAX_IDLE_BLOCKER_TIME => 300);
  8    DBMS_RESOURCE_MANAGER.SUBMIT_PENDING_AREA();
  9    END;
SQL> /

PL/SQL procedure successfully completed.

SQL>
```

Creating a Mapping

A new procedure for DBMS_RESOURCE_MANAGER maps users to an initial resource group based on certain attributes of the user when connecting to the database (known as the Adaptive Consumer Group Mapping feature). The SET_CONSUMER_GROUP_MAPPING procedure can add,

delete, or modify entities that map sessions to resource consumer groups based on the session's login and runtime attributes.

The ATTRIBUTE, VALUE, and CONSUMER_GROUP are parameters to the SET_CONSUMER_GROUP_MAPPING procedure. The following example shows how to assign the user B2T to ONLINE_GROUP based on the Oracle login username and how to assign a user to LOW_GROUP when the client program used is TOAD.EXE:

```
SQL> BEGIN
  2  DBMS_RESOURCE_MANAGER.CLEAR_PENDING_AREA();
  3  DBMS_RESOURCE_MANAGER.CREATE_PENDING_AREA();
  4  DBMS_RESOURCE_MANAGER.SET_CONSUMER_GROUP_MAPPING (
  5    DBMS_RESOURCE_MANAGER.ORACLE_USER,
                              'B2T', 'ONLINE_GROUP');
  6  DBMS_RESOURCE_MANAGER.SET_CONSUMER_GROUP_MAPPING (
  7    DBMS_RESOURCE_MANAGER.CLIENT_PROGRAM,
                              'TOAD.EXE', 'LOW_GROUP');
  8  DBMS_RESOURCE_MANAGER.SUBMIT_PENDING_AREA();
  9  END;
SQL> /

PL/SQL procedure successfully completed.

SQL>
```

The SET_INITIAL_CONSUMER_GROUP procedure has been deprecated in Oracle 10g. You should use the SET_CONSUMER_GROUP_MAPPING procedure instead.

The valid ATTRIBUTE constants are as follows:

- CLIENT_MACHINE: The login attribute specifies the name of the machine from which a client is making connection to the database.

- CLIENT_OS_USER: This login attribute specifies OS username of the client that is logging in to the database.

- CLIENT_PROGRAM: This login attribute specifies the name of the client program used to login to the database.

- MODULE_NAME: This runtime attribute specifies the module name in the application that is currently executing. Module name is set by the DBMS_APPLICATION_INFO.SET_MODULE_NAME procedure.

- MODULE_NAME_ACTION: This runtime attribute specifies the current module and action being performed by the user. The attribute is specified by the module name, followed by a period (.), followed by the action name.

- ORACLE_USER: This login attribute specifies standard Oracle user name.
- SERVICE_MODULE: This runtime attribute specifies a combination service and module names in this form *service_name.module_name*
- SERVICE_MODULE_ACTION: This runtime attribute specifies a combination of service, module name and action name, in this form *service_name.module_name.action_name*
- SERVICE_NAME: This login attribute specifies the service name used by the client to establish a connection to the database.

If more than one attribute satisfies a session, then the default attribute precedence set in the database determines the resource consumer group. For example, say that it is defined that when CLIENT_OS_USER is BILL, use DSS_GROUP; and when the ORACLE_USER is LARRY, use ONLINE_GROUP. Then, if Larry uses Bill's machine to log into the database using his own ID, you have ambiguity. The default attribute priorities are set so that the Oracle user name takes precedence over the client operating system user name.

To change the default attribute priorities, use the SET_CONSUMER_GROUP_MAPPING_PRI procedure. The following example shows all the parameters of this procedure and how to set the priority. The priorities are defined using an integer of value 1 through 10; 1 is the highest, and 10 is the lowest. EXPLICIT is the priority of the explicit mapping. Here is the example:

```
SQL> BEGIN
  2   DBMS_RESOURCE_MANAGER.CLEAR_PENDING_AREA();
  3   DBMS_RESOURCE_MANAGER.CREATE_PENDING_AREA();
  4   DBMS_RESOURCE_MANAGER.SET_CONSUMER_GROUP_MAPPING_PRI
  5   (EXPLICIT            => 1,
  6   ORACLE_USER          => 2,
  7   SERVICE_NAME         => 3,
  8   CLIENT_OS_USER       => 4,
  9   CLIENT_PROGRAM       => 5,
 10   CLIENT_MACHINE       => 6,
 11   MODULE_NAME          => 7,
 12   MODULE_NAME_ACTION   => 8,
 13   SERVICE_MODULE       => 9,
 14   SERVICE_MODULE_ACTION=> 10);
 15   DBMS_RESOURCE_MANAGER.SUBMIT_PENDING_AREA();
 16   END;
SQL> /

PL/SQL procedure successfully completed.

SQL>
```

The MODULE_NAME and MODULE_NAME_ACTION attributes are useful for middle-tier applications that use the same username for all clients but set their module and actions consistently for different operations performed by the users. The modules and actions characterize the type of work performed, which the Resource Manager can use to determine the resource management policy.

You can set up the Resource Manager mappings and priorities using the EM Database Control. From the Administration tab of the EM Database Control home page, click the Resource Consumer Group Mappings link under Resource Manager. Figure 3.12 shows the screen where you can define the mappings. You can click the Priorities tab to define priorities. The figure also shows a portion of the Priorities screen in the inset.

FIGURE 3.12   The Resource Consumer Group Mapping screen

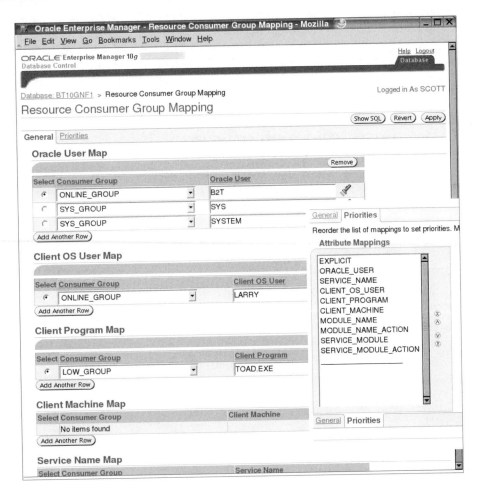

Changes to Resource Allocation Method

In Oracle 9*i*, the only CPU allocation method allowed when creating a resource plan was EMPHASIS, which was also the only method available. In Oracle 10*g*, a new method—RATIO— is available. The default method is still EMPHASIS, which is used for multilevel plans that use percentages to specify how the CPU is distributed among consumer groups. In Oracle 10*g*, you can specify an additional CPU allocation policy, called the RATIO policy, for single-level plans to partition CPU resources by using ratios.

Specify RATIO as the value for the CPU_MTH parameter of the CREATE_PLAN procedure to define ratio-based CPU allocation.

You specify a resource allocation method for the distribution of CPU among sessions in the consumer group using the CPU_MTH parameter of the CREATE_CONSUMER_GROUP procedure. The default and only value available for CPU_MTH in Oracle 9*i* was ROUND-ROBIN. In Oracle 10*g*, the default is ROUND ROBIN, but you can also specify RUN-TO-COMPLETION. RUN-TO-COMPLETION specifies that sessions with the largest active time be scheduled ahead of other sessions. ROUND-ROBIN scheduling ensures that sessions are fairly executed.

Summary

In this chapter, you learned about the components of the Common Management Infrastructure (CMI) and the automatic management of the database. The Automatic Workload Repository (AWR) is the central element of the management infrastructure. It provides services to internal Oracle database components to collect, maintain, process, and use performance statistics for problem detection and self-tuning purposes. The AWR has two main areas: the in-memory statistics collection area stored in the SGA and the Workload Repository stored in the SYSAUX tablespace. The in-memory statistics is transferred to the disk by the MMON process.

The Active Sessions History (ASH) represents the history of recent sessions activity, to analyze the system performance at the current time. ASH samples the active sessions at one-second intervals and records the events for which these sessions are waiting.

The initialization parameter STATISTICS_LEVEL controls the level of statistics capture. BASIC turns off statistics collection, TYPICAL is the default and collects most statistics needed for monitoring the database, and ALL collects all the possible statistics that can be used for manual diagnosis.

Server-generated alerts allow Oracle 10*g* to automatically detect alarming situations in the database and suggest remedial actions. Oracle 10*g* discovers alert conditions using the threshold specified. The alerts can be threshold based or events based. The DBMS_SERVER_ALERTS package is the PL/SQL API to set thresholds.

The automated tasks component of the CMI schedules automatic jobs using the scheduler. The Automatic Optimizer Statistics Collection feature on the database is one such automatic job. The predefined job GATHER_STATS_JOB is scheduled to run during the MAINTENANCE_WINDOW_GROUP window group.

The DBMS_STATS package includes new features to lock statistics on a table or schema. The new DBA_OPTSTAT_OPERATIONS view shows start and end times of all DBMS_STATS operations executed at the schema or database level. The history of statistic collection is kept in the AWR, and DBMS_STATS has procedures to restore the statistics as of a previous date if needed.

The advisory framework is another component of the CMI. Advisors provide useful feedback about resource utilization and performance of a component. The Automatic Database Diagnostic Monitor (ADDM) is the advisor for the database instance. It can invoke other advisors such as the SQL Tuning Advisor, the Segment Advisor, or Memory Advisors. The DBMS_ADVISOR PL/SQL package contains constants and all procedure declarations for all advisor modules.

ADDM is a server-based performance expert in the database that is automatically used for proactive and effective tuning. ADDM is scheduled to run every hour by the MMON process and detect problems. The ADDM findings display on the EM Database Control home page.

The Automatic Shared Memory Management (ASMM) feature enables the database to automatically determine the size of each of the SGA components, within the limits of the total SGA size. DB_CACHE_SIZE, SHARED_POOL_SIZE, LARGE_POOL_SIZE, and JAVA_POOL_SIZE are managed automatically.

The Automatic Undo Retention Tuning feature of the database automatically determines the optimal undo retention time depending on the size of the undo tablespace. Oracle 10g can dynamically adjust to the change in undo requirements depending on undo activity. With this feature, you have no need to manually set the undo retention period.

You also learned about the Resource Manager enhancements in this chapter. At the end of every top call, a session can be returned to its original consumer group. The session can be terminated if it is idle for a certain time period or if the session is idle and blocking other users resources. Using the Adaptive Consumer Group Mapping feature, you can establish priorities and assign consumer groups.

Exam Essentials

Understand the Automatic Database Diagnostics Monitor.   Know how the ADDM uses a top-down approach to drill down to the root cause of problems. Learn to change the ADDM attributes.

Learn Automatic Shared Memory Management.   Know the components of SGA that are managed by ASSM. Understand the benefits of ASSM. Learn the behavior of the autotuned SGA parameters and manually tuned SGA parameters when they are resized.

Learn how Automatic Optimizer Statistics Collection works.   Understand the window group, windows, the job name, and the internal procedure used to collect statistics. Learn how statistics can be locked and forcefully overwritten using the FORCE option. Learn how previous versions of statistics are kept in the AWR and how they can be restored.

Understand the automatic tuning capabilities of the database.   Know how the Automatic Undo Retention Tuning and Automatic Checkpoint Tuning features work.

Know how the Automatic Workload Repository operates.   Understand the purpose of the MMON process. Know where to look for the ASH. Learn to change the retention policies and snapshot intervals of AWR.

Understand server-generated alerts.   Know the architecture of server-generated alerts and the types of alerts. Remember an alert is generated only when the observation period and consecutive occurrences are satisfied. Learn to set alert thresholds and how to query the information about them.

Know the enhancements to the Resource Manager.   Learn to set idle timeouts. Know how sessions can be switched back to their original resource consumer group at the end of a call. Understand how to use the mapping feature and set priorities.

Review Questions

1. To enable the Automatic Workload Repository performance statistic collection at a minimal scale, the STATISTICS_LEVEL parameter must be set to what?

   A. TYPICAL

   B. NONE

   C. ALL

   D. BASIC

2. Which process is responsible for analyzing the AWR information for the ADDM?

   A. PMON

   B. MMON

   C. ADDM

   D. SNPn

3. Which data dictionary view would you query to find out the stateless (event-based or nonthreshold) server alerts?

   A. DBA_ALERT_LOG

   B. DBA_OUTSTANDING_ALERTS

   C. DBA_ALERT_HISTORY

   D. DBA_ADVISOR_FINDINGS

4. Which of the following is not an out-of-the-box server-generated alert?

   A. "Tablespace space usage"

   B. "Recovery area low on free space"

   C. "Resumable session suspended"

   D. "Tables missing optimizer statistics"

   E. "Snapshot too old"

5. Which parameters enable the Automatic Shared Memory Management feature? (Choose two.)

   A. SGA_SIZE

   B. SGA_TARGET

   C. AUTO_SGA

   D. STATISTICS_LEVEL

6. Which component of the SGA is not automatically configured when Automatic Shared Memory Management is enabled?

   A. Java pool

   B. Buffer cache

   C. Log buffer

   D. Large pool

7. Which process is responsible for allocating the various components of the SGA when Automatic Shared Memory Management is used?

   A. PMON

   B. SMON

   C. MMON

   D. MMAN

8. How is automatic undo retention tuning enabled?

   A. Set the UNDO_RETENTION parameter to zero.

   B. Set the UNDO_MANAGEMENT parameter to AUTO.

   C. Configure it using the DBMS_ADVISOR package.

   D. Set the UNDO_RETENTION parameter to nonzero value.

9. Identify the statement that is not true regarding the Automatic Optimizer Statistics Collection feature in Oracle 10*g*.

   A. After creating an Oracle 10*g* database, the DBA does not have to perform any special activity to keep the optimizer statistics current.

   B. After upgrading an Oracle database to Oracle 10*g*, the DBA does not have to perform any special activity to keep the optimizer statistics current.

   C. The statistics are kept current by periodically (automatic) executing the DBMS_STATS.GATHER_DATABASE_STATS procedure with the GATHER AUTO option.

   D. For the automatic statistic collection to work properly, the STATISTICS_LEVEL must be set to TYPICAL or ALL.

10. Identify two statements that are true regarding the procedures of DBMS_STATS.

   A. Every time you collect statistics on a table, schema, or database using DBMS_STATS, the previous version of statistics is stored in the AWR.

   B. The retention period of optimizer statistics stored in the AWR is determined by the DBMS_WORKLOAD_REPOSITORY.MODIFY_SNAPSHOT_SETTINGS (RETENTION=> *nn)* procedure.

   C. When you lock statistics on a table, the schema level statistics collection skips the table.

   D. Restoring statistics from the AWR is based on the time stamp when the statistics were collected.

11. The following are a few of the steps involved in getting the tuning advice from AWR snapshots using the DBMS_ADVISOR PL/SQL API.
1 Use the DBMS_ADVISOR.SET_TASK_PARAMETERS procedure.
2 Use the DBMS_ADVISOR.CREATE_TASK procedure.
3 Use the DBMS_ADVISOR.GET_TASK_REPORT procedure.
4 Use the DBMS_ADVISOR.EXECUTE_TASK procedure.

In which order should be these steps executed?

A. 1, 3, 4, 2

B. 1, 2, 3, 4

C. 2, 1, 4, 3

D. 2, 1, 3, 4

12. Choose the most appropriate statement regarding collecting optimizer statistics:

A. The DBMS_STATS package and the ANALYZE statement have same behavior.

B. When statistics are collected using the ANALYZE statement, previous version of statistics is saved in the Workload Repository.

C. When statistics are collected using the DBMS_STATISTICS package, the previous version of statistics is saved in the Workload Repository.

D. When gathering statistics using the DBMS_STATS package, you must specify the SAVE_VERSION parameter to save the old statistics to the Workload Repository.

13. Which parameter of the DBMS_RESOURCE_MANAGER.CREATE_PLAN_DIRECTIVE procedure ensures that at the end of the switched resource group call, the session is returned back to its original resource group?

A. SWITCH_TIME_IN_CALL

B. SWITCH_TIME

C. SWITCH_GROUP

D. SWITCH_BACK_AT_CALL_END

14. In the DBMS_RESOURCE_MANAGER.CREATE_PLAN_DIRECTIVE procedure, the MAX_IDLE_TIME parameter is used to define what?

A. The maximum amount of time a session is inactive and is blocking another session. The session will be switched to switch group defined when the amount of time is met.

B. The total amount of time a session is inactive or idle cumulative since the session startup. The session will be terminated when the criteria is met.

C. The maximum amount of time a session is idle. The session will be switched to switch group defined when the amount of time is met.

D. The maximum amount of time a session is idle. The session will be terminated when the criteria is met.

15. Identify two statements that are not true regarding AWR.

   A. The snapshot data is not purged from the AWR for the snapshots that are part of a baseline.

   B. The automatic capturing of AWR snapshots is disabled by dropping or disabling the corresponding job using DBMS_SCHEDULER.

   C. To get AWR report in HTML format, you must use the EM Database Control.

   D. No data migration from STATSPACK to AWR is supported.

16. The alerts generated by the database server are delivered to the DBA using which method?

   A. Writing the alert to the database alert log file

   B. Sending e-mail to the DBA using the e-mail address specified when creating the database

   C. Using a trigger on the DBA_OUTSTANDING_ALERTS view

   D. Using DBMS_AQ procedures

17. When is the ADDM analysis performed?

   A. Every time an AWR snapshot is taken

   B. Whenever an AWR snapshot is taken automatically by the MMON process

   C. Whenever an AWR snapshot is taken using the CREATE_SNAPSHOT procedure

   D. Every hour or at specified interval irrespective on AWR snapshots

18. Identify a true statement from the following regarding Automatic Shared Memory Management.

   A. ASMM is enabled by default.

   B. ASMM is disabled by setting SGA_TARGET to zero.

   C. SGA_TARGET cannot be altered dynamically using ALTER SYSTEM.

   D. When SGA_TARGET is specified as a nonzero value, all the SGA parameters related to the autotuned components must be set to zero.

   E. The MMON process is responsible for coordinating the sizing of the memory components.

19. The FORCE=>TRUE option of the DBMS_STATS.DELETE_TABLE_STATS procedure is used for what?

   A. To delete statistics from the table, even if the table is read only.

   B. To delete statistics from the table and to clear out all the SQL statements referring to the table from the shared pool.

   C. To delete statistics from the table, even if the statistics on the table are locked.

   D. The value of FORCE must be TRUE always, as this parameter is reserved for a future enhancement.

20. Which of the following is true about Automatic Checkpoint Tuning?

   A. You do not need to specify the LOG_CHECKPOINT_INTERVAL or LOG_CHECKPOINT_TIMEOUT parameter.

   B. You do not need to specify the FAST_START_MTTR_TARGET parameter.

   C. You do not need to specify the LOG_BUFFER parameter.

   D. All of the above are true.

Answers to Review Questions

1. **A.** The valid values for STATISTICS_LEVEL parameter are BASIC, TYPICAL, and ALL. BASIC disables the AWR and other statistics collection, TYPICAL collects statistics needed for day-to-day monitoring, and ALL collects statistics for manual diagnosis.

2. **B.** The new process MMON is responsible for writing the ASH information to the Automatic Workload Repository and also analyzing the statistics each time an AWR snapshot is taken.

3. **C.** The stateless alerts are always written to DBA_ALERT_HISTORY. DBA_OUTSTANDING_ALERTS will have the alerts for threshold or stateful alerts. When the status of such alerts is CLEARED, they will be moved to DBA_ALERT_HISTORY.

4. **D.** In Oracle 10g, the optimizer statistics for tables, including the dictionary, are collected automatically unless the STATISTICS_LEVEL parameter is set to BASIC. The tables have the MONITORING feature enabled by default. So, no need exists for such an alert to look for missing optimizer statistics.

5. **B, D.** Setting the SGA_TARGET and leaving the STATISTICS_LEVEL to its default (TYPICAL) enables ASMM. SGA_TARGET specifies the total size of the SGA, including the manually config-ured areas. SGA_TARGET cannot be higher than SGA_MAX_SIZE.

6. **C.** The log buffer should be configured using the LOG_BUFFER parameter. Setting SGA_TARGET automatically manages SHARED_POOL_SIZE, JAVA_POOL_SIZE, LARGE_POOL_SIZE, and BUFFER_CACHE.

7. **D.** The memory manager process (MMAN) is responsible for managing the components of SGA when the Automatic Shared Memory Management feature is used. It serves as a memory broker, coordinates the sizing of the memory components, and keeps track of the component's sizes.

8. **B.** By keeping UNDO_MANAGEMENT set to AUTO (this is the default when creating a new database), the Automatic Undo Retention Tuning feature is enabled in Oracle 10g. If you set a value for the UNDO_RETENTION parameter, Oracle 10g uses that value as the minimum. If no value or zero is set for UNDO_RETENTION, Oracle 10g uses 900 seconds as the default minimum.

9. **C.** The DBMS_STATS.GATHER_DATABASE_STATS_JOB_PROC internal procedure collects the missing statistics and update statistics in the database. This procedure prioritizes the database objects that require statistics so that the objects that need the statistics most are processed first, before the maintenance window closes.

10. **A, C.** The retention period of the statistics history kept in the AWR is 31 days by default, which can be modified by using the DBMS_STATS.ALTER_STATS_HISTORY_RETENTION procedure. The statistics from the AWR are restored using the time stamp as an argument to restore statistics as of that time stamp (not when the statistics are collected).

11. **C.** To get tuning advice using the advisory framework DBMS_ADVISOR package, you should create the task first, set appropriate parameters for the task (specify the start snapshot and end snapshot), perform analysis, and optionally get a report or query from the DBA_ADVISOR_FINDINGS view.

12. C.   Oracle10g saves the statistics to the workload repository before setting new statistics values using the DBMS_STATS package. Statistics are not preserved when using the ANALYZE statement.

13. A.   The SWITCH_TIME and SWITCH_TIME_IN_CALL parameters are mutually exclusive, and they specify the time in seconds that a session can execute before an action is taken. The default for both parameters is NULL. The SWITCH_TIME_IN_CALL parameter specifies that the session should be returned to the original consumer group at the end of the call, where as when using the SWITCH_TIME, the session remains in the switched consumer group. Whether you use SWITCH_TIME or SWITCH_TIME_IN_CALL, the SWITCH_GROUP parameter specifies the resource group to which the session will be switched if the switch criteria are met.

14. D.   The MAX_IDLE_TIME parameter defines the maximum amount of time in seconds a session can be inactive or idle. When the session exceeds the limit, the PMON process will terminate the session and clean up its state. The MAX_IDLE_BLOCKER_TIME parameter defines the maximum amount of time in seconds a session can be idle and block the acquisition of resources for another user.

15. B, C.   You can disable the automatic capturing of AWR snapshots by setting the INTERVAL parameter to zero in the DBMS_WORKLOAD_REPOSITORY.MODIFY_SNAPSHOT_SETTINGS procedure. You can produce AWR reports in HTML format using SQL*Plus by specifying the report type as HTML or text. The snapshots that are older than the retention period defined are not purged when they are part of a baseline. Though STATSPACK is still available in Oracle 10g, no integration exists between the data collected by STATSPACK and AWR.

16. D.   The alerts generated by the server are queued to the AQ mechanism of the database, a predefined persistent queue ALERT_QUE. You may write your own subscribing programs. You can use the EM Database Control to enable paging and e-mail to the DBA. You may also query DBA_OUTSTANDING_ALERTS to view the alerts that are not resolved. A message about the alert is written to the alert log file only if the alert cannot be written to the ALERT_QUE.

17. A.   ADDM is run by the MMON process every time an AWR snapshot is performed—automatic or manual. Each time a snapshot is taken, ADDM is triggered to do an analysis of the period corresponding to the last two snapshots. You may run the addmrpti.sql script to analyze the data between two different snapshot IDs.

18. B.   The default value for SGA_TARGET is zero, which means ASMM is not enabled by default. SGA_TARGET can be increased or decreased dynamically within the limits of the SGA_MAX_SIZE parameter. When ASMM is used and a value for the automatically tuned component is also specified, the value would be considered as the minimum required size for the component. The memory manager process (MMAN) is the SGA memory broker and is responsible for the sizing of the SGA components.

19. C.   You can use the FORCE=>TRUE option with the DELETE_*_STATS, IMPORT_*_STATS, RESTORE_*_STATS, and SET_*_STATS procedures of the DBMS_STATS package to overwrite the statistics even if they are locked.

20. A.   Automatic Checkpoint Tuning is enabled if you specify a value for the FAST_START_MTTR_TARGET or if you do not specify any value for this parameter. Automatic Checkpoint Tuning is disabled when FAST_START_MTTR_TARGET is set to zero explicitly. You do not need to specify any of the checkpoint-related parameters when the FAST_START_MTTR_TARGET parameter is set.

Chapter

4

General Storage Management

ORACLE DATABASE 10*g* NEW FEATURES FOR ADMINISTRATORS EXAM OBJECTIVES OFFERED IN THIS CHAPTER:

✓ **Improved VLDB Support**

- Create and maintain bigfile tablespaces
- Create temporary tablespace groups
- Assign temporary tablespace groups to users
- Skip unuseable indexes
- Specify storage characteristics for index partitions in the table partition DML commands
- Create hash-partitioned global indexes
- Maintain hash-partitioned global indexes

✓ **General Storage Enhancement**

- Create the SYSAUX tablespace
- Relocate SYSAUX occupants
- Rename tablespaces
- Create a default permanent tablespace
- Copy files using the Database Server

Exam objectives are subject to change at any time without prior notice and at Oracle's sole discretion. Please visit Oracle's training and certification website (http://www.oracle.com/education/certification/) for the most current exam objectives listing.

Oracle Database 10*g* (Oracle 10*g*) provides a number of general enhancements to help the DBA manage the disk space in the database. These general enhancements fall into two broad categories: tablespace management and index management. In both cases, the Oracle Enterprise Manager (EM) Database Control provides wizards and a graphical interface for these enhancements, making it easy to leverage these enhancements in short order.

At the tablespace level, there is a new required tablespace and new ways to create tablespaces; temporary tablespaces can be grouped together to provide adequate temporary space for multiple concurrent sessions for a single user. In addition, several new tablespace features reduce the number of manual steps a DBA needs to perform functions such as renaming a tablespace, transporting a tablespace with the same name, or copying tablespace images between databases.

Partitioning methods are also enhanced in Oracle 10*g*. EM Database Control automates many of the partitioning tasks; partitioning capabilities have been expanded for Index Organized Tables (IOTs).

Index maintenance and usability has been enhanced. By default, unusable indexes because of partition maintenance no longer generate fatal ORA- errors. Hash partitioning is a new index type available for global indexes, improving the performance of inserts in an OLTP environment.

In this chapter, we will review many new and enhanced tablespace-related features, such as how to create and maintain one of the new tablespaces in Oracle 10*g*, the SYSAUX tablespace. We'll show you how to specify the default permanent tablespace in the database to ensure that user objects are not created in the SYSTEM tablespace. Temporary tablespaces have a number of enhancements including how a group of temporary tablespaces can be combined into a tablespace group. Last, but not least, we'll show you how to create a bigfile tablespace, both increasing the maximum size of the database as well as simplifying maintenance tasks on a tablespace. At the end of the chapter we'll review the new index-related enhancements: skipping unusable indexes, more flexible index storage specifications, and hash-partitioned global indexes.

Managing Tablespaces

The release of Oracle 10*g* brings a number of features that enhance the performance, availability, and maintainability of the database. The new SYSAUX tablespace offloads noncritical application metadata from the SYSTEM tablespace, reducing or eliminating hotspots in the SYSTEM tablespace, in addition to consolidating the metadata from several other tablespaces.

Bigfile tablespaces not only expand the maximum size of the database, but because a bigfile tablespace contains only one datafile, it also moves the maintenance point from the physical

datafile level to the logical database level. This increases the maintainability of the tablespace. Arriving along with bigfile tablespaces is a new ROWID format, along with the stored procedures and packages to support the new ROWIDs.

To increase the throughput of queries and other operations, the DBA can create tablespace groups for temporary tablespaces. Temporary tablespace groups are used anywhere that a temporary tablespace is used.

Other general enhancements to tablespace management include renaming tablespaces, creating a default permanent tablespace, and performing datafile and other binary file copy operations between directories on the same database server or between different servers on the network.

The *SYSAUX* Tablespace

The SYSAUX *tablespace*, a companion tablespace to the SYSTEM tablespace, helps to improve the availability of the database by offloading some application data from applications that used the SYSTEM tablespace or other separate tablespaces before Oracle 10g. As a result, some of the I/O bottlenecks frequently associated with the SYSTEM tablespace have been reduced or eliminated.

The SYSAUX tablespace is required and has the same storage characteristics as the SYSTEM tablespace.

- ONLINE
- PERMANENT
- READ WRITE
- EXTENT MANAGEMENT LOCAL
- SEGMENT SPACE MANAGEMENT AUTO

To put it another way, the SYSAUX tablespace cannot ever be OFFLINE, cannot be a temporary tablespace, cannot be READ ONLY, and cannot be dictionary managed (and therefore eliminate some of the benefits of reducing SYSTEM tablespace overhead). Also, its segment extent sizes cannot be manually defined and maintained.

The SYSAUX tablespace reduces the overall number of tablespaces in the database in addition to reducing the space requirements of the SYSTEM tablespace. For example, in previous versions of Oracle, the Enterprise Manager Repository metadata was stored in the tablespace OEM_REPOSITORY. Using the SYSAUX tablespace helps reduce the total number of tablespaces that the DBA must maintain and monitor. The applications that use the SYSAUX tablespace are not permanently tied to that tablespace; as you will see later in this section, you can move some of the SYSAUX occupants into their own tablespace if circumstances require it, such as when a space problem exists in the SYSAUX tablespace.

In a Real Application Clusters (RAC) environment using raw devices, the SYSAUX tablespace can ease tablespace management, as each tablespace in this environment requires a separate raw device.

When a new database is created, the SYSAUX tablespace is created along with the SYSTEM tablespace, the undo tablespace, and the temporary tablespace in the CREATE DATABASE command,

but a development or test database require only the SYSTEM and SYSAUX tablespaces. A database upgraded from a previous version of Oracle requires that a SYSAUX tablespace be created during the database upgrade procedure.

In the following sections, we'll show you how to create a SYSAUX tablespace, either as part of a new database or for an upgraded database; we'll also show you how to review the contents of the SYSAUX tablespace. Finally, we'll show you how to move a SYSAUX occupant to another tablespace, and back again if necessary.

Creating the *SYSAUX* Tablespace

The SYSAUX tablespace is created in one of two scenarios: as part of a new database or as part of an upgrade from a previous version of Oracle. In both cases, you have two ways to create the tablespace, with a GUI-based Oracle tool or from the SQL*Plus command line.

Creating *SYSAUX* As Part of a Database Upgrade

For a database upgrade to Oracle 10*g*, the Database Upgrade Assistant (DBUA) requires you to create a SYSAUX tablespace but allows you to specify the datafile name as well as whether the datafile will be automatically extensible using the AUTOEXTEND parameter. From the SQL*Plus command line, creating the SYSAUX tablespace is part of a several-step procedure. If there is a tablespace in the previous database version named SYSAUX, it must be dropped or renamed before upgrading the database. First, start up the database in MIGRATE mode.

```
SQL> STARTUP MIGRATE;
```

Next, create the SYSAUX tablespace with the required attributes.

```
SQL> CREATE TABLESPACE SYSAUX
  2        DATAFILE '/U05/ORADATA/ORD/SYSAUX.DBF' SIZE 200M
  3        AUTOEXTEND ON
  4        EXTENT MANAGEMENT LOCAL
  5        SEGMENT SPACE MANAGEMENT AUTO;
```

Finally, to complete the database upgrade and convert all data dictionary objects to the latest version, run the script corresponding to the previous version of the database; in this case, you are upgrading from an Oracle 9*i* Release 2 database:

```
SQL> @u0902000.sql
```

After the script has run successfully, you can shut down the database and start it up normally.

You can find a complete discussion of database upgrade issues and procedures in the *Oracle Database Upgrade Guide 10*g *Release 1.*

Creating *SYSAUX* As Part of a New Database

For a new database installation, the Database Configuration Assistant (DBCA) will automatically include a SYSAUX tablespace as one of the tablespaces created during the installation, and it will allow you to adjust the storage parameters just as the DBUA does. If you are creating a database from the command line, you can include the definition of the SYSAUX tablespace:

```
SQL> CREATE DATABASE
  2      DATAFILE '/u01/oradata/ord/system01.dbf' SIZE 250M
  3      SYSAUX DATAFILE '/u02/oradata/ord/sysaux01.dbf'
  4        SIZE 350M
  5      DEFAULT TEMPORARY TABLESPACE
  6       TEMP TEMPFILE '/u03/oradata/ord/temp01.dbf'
  7        SIZE 100M
  8      UNDO TABLESPACE UNDO1
  9        DATAFILE '/u04/oradata/ord/undo01.dbf'
 10        SIZE 100M;
```

If the SYSAUX tablespace definition is omitted in the CREATE DATABASE command, it is automatically created in the default tablespace location for the database, either $ORACLE_HOME/dbs on Unix or %ORACLE_HOME%\database on Windows.

Oracle recommends using the DBUA to upgrade a database from a previous version and the DBCA to create a new database.

Contents of the *SYSAUX* Tablespace

The dynamic performance view V$SYSAUX_OCCUPANTS provides not only the list of applications that use the SYSAUX tablespace but also the amount of space used by each application and the name of the schema that owns each application. The query that follows shows the contents of the SYSAUX tablespace:

```
SQL> select occupant_name, schema_name,
  2            space_usage_kbytes from v$sysaux_occupants;
```

OCCUPANT_NAME	SCHEMA_NAME	SPACE_USAGE_KBYTES
LOGMNR	SYSTEM	7488
LOGSTDBY	SYSTEM	0
STREAMS	SYS	192
AO	SYS	960
XSOQHIST	SYS	960

SM/AWR	SYS	68352
SM/ADVISOR	SYS	7360
SM/OPTSTAT	SYS	21120
SM/OTHER	SYS	3328
STATSPACK	PERFSTAT	0
ODM	DMSYS	5504
SDO	MDSYS	6080
WM	WMSYS	6656
ORDIM	ORDSYS	512
ORDIM/PLUGINS	ORDPLUGINS	0
ORDIM/SQLMM	SI_INFORMTN_SCHEMA	0
EM	SYSMAN	61632
TEXT	CTXSYS	4736
ULTRASEARCH	WKSYS	7296
JOB_SCHEDULER	SYS	256

```
20 rows selected.
```

The SPACE_USAGE_KBYTES column may indicate that an application needs to be moved to its own tablespace.

 We will show you how to relocate an application from the SYSAUX tablespace in the next section.

The EM Database Control displays the contents and space usage of the SYSAUX tablespace in a more visual format, as you can see in Figure 4.1.

Relocating *SYSAUX* Occupants

In some environments, it may be necessary to move some of the occupants out of the SYSAUX tablespace.

In this example, while the LogMiner application metadata does not appear to be taking up a lot of space right now, you expect the usage to be heavy over the next six months; therefore you decide to create a dedicated tablespace for LogMiner.

```
SQL> create smallfile tablespace LOGMNR_REP
  2     datafile '/u06/oradata/ord/logmnr_rep01.dbf'
  3         size 10g
  4     autoextend on next 5g;
Tablespace created.
```

FIGURE 4.1 Viewing SYSAUX with the EM

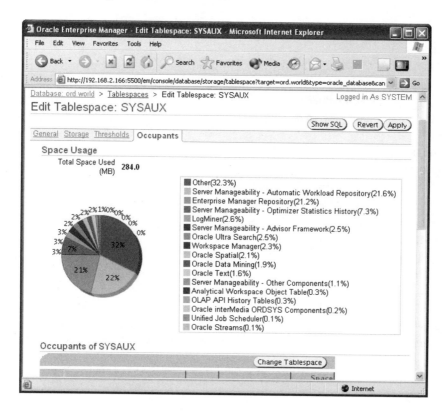

Next, find the name of the procedure you can use to move the LogMiner Repository data out of the SYSAUX tablespace. Once again, query the dynamic performance view V$SYSAUX_ OCCUPANTS:

```
SQL> select occupant_name, move_procedure from
  2       v$sysaux_occupants;

OCCUPANT_NAME   MOVE_PROCEDURE
--------------- ----------------------------------------

LOGMNR          SYS.DBMS_LOGMNR_D.SET_TABLESPACE
LOGSTDBY        SYS.DBMS_LOGSTDBY.SET_TABLESPACE
STREAMS
AO              DBMS_AW.MOVE_AWMETA
XSOQHIST        DBMS_XSOQ.OlapiMoveProc
```

```
SM/AWR
SM/ADVISOR
SM/OPTSTAT
SM/OTHER
STATSPACK
ODM              MOVE_ODM
SDO              MDSYS.MOVE_SDO
WM               DBMS_WM.move_proc
ORDIM
ORDIM/PLUGINS
ORDIM/SQLMM
EM               emd_maintenance.move_em_tblspc
TEXT             DRI_MOVE_CTXSYS
ULTRASEARCH      MOVE_WK
JOB_SCHEDULER

20 rows selected.
```

 SYSAUX occupants without a value for MOVE_PROCEDURE in the view V$SYSAUX_
OCCUPANTS cannot be moved out of the SYSAUX tablespace.

For LogMiner, use the procedure SYS.DBMS_LOGMNR_D.SET_TABLESPACE:

```
SQL> begin
  2     SYS.DBMS_LOGMNR_D.SET_TABLESPACE('logmnr_rep');
  3   end;

PL/SQL procedure successfully completed.
```

Checking V$SYSAUX_OCCUPANTS again, notice that LogMiner is still a resident.

```
SQL> select occupant_name, space_usage_kbytes
  2     from v$sysaux_occupants
  3   where occupant_name = 'LOGMNR';

OCCUPANT_NAME    MOVE_PROCEDURE
---------------  -------------------------------------
LOGMNR           SYS.DBMS_LOGMNR_D.SET_TABLESPACE

1 row selected.
```

This is because you still need a row in V$SYSAUX_OCCUPANTS to indicate how you can move the application back into the SYSAUX tablespace at some future date. However, looking at the pie chart in EM Database Control, notice that the space usage for LogMiner, formerly using 2.6 percent of the SYSAUX tablespace, is no longer in the pie chart (see Figure 4.2).

FIGURE 4.2   SYSAUX occupants after a move operation

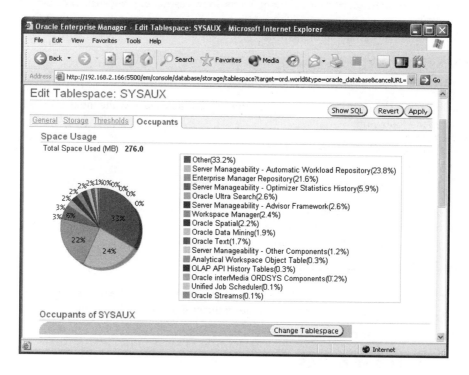

The V$SYSAUX_OCCUPANTS view confirms this.

```
SQL> select occupant_name, space_usage_kbytes
  2    from v$sysaux_occupants
  3  where occupant_name = 'LOGMNR';

OCCUPANT_NAME   SPACE_USAGE_KBYTES
--------------- ------------------
LOGMNR                           0

1 row selected.
```

🌐 Real World Scenario

SYSAUX: Dos and Don'ts

While the SYSAUX tablespace is similar in nature to any other locally managed tablespace with automatic segment space management, it has a few restrictions because of its close ties with the SYSTEM tablespace. Like any other tablespace, you can add datafiles to the SYSAUX tablespace if it is a smallfile tablespace:

```
SQL> ALTER TABLESPACE SYSAUX ADD
  2    DATAFILE '/u08/ordata/ord/sysaux02.dbf' SIZE 250M;
```

But you cannot perform a few actions on the SYSAUX tablespace while the database is open, such as the following:

```
SQL> ALTER TABLESPACE SYSAUX OFFLINE;
SQL> DROP TABLESPACE SYSAUX;
SQL> ALTER TABLESPACE SYSAUX RENAME TO SYSAUX00;
```

These operations may be required, however, if the database is in RESTRICTED mode during a maintenance or repair operation. If the SYSAUX tablespace is a bigfile tablespace—discussed in the following section—then the following command is valid:

```
SQL> ALTER TABLESPACE SYSAUX AUTOEXTEND ON;
```

Since a bigfile tablespace consists of one and only one datafile, the only option you have to expand the size of the tablespace is to extend the size of the single datafile.

Bigfile Tablespaces

One of the most significant changes to tablespace management in Oracle 10*g* is the introduction of *bigfile tablespaces*. A bigfile tablespace is a tablespace containing a single datafile that can be as large as 128 terabytes (TB), depending on the block size of the tablespace. In conjunction with setting the initialization parameter DB_FILES to the maximum value of 65,635, the total size of the database can be more than 8 exabytes (EB); in contrast, a database with smallfile tablespaces can only be 8 petabytes (PB) in size. In Table 1.1, you can see the maximum tablespace size for a bigfile tablespace given the block size.

In contrast, a *smallfile tablespace* is the name given to the type of tablespace available in previous releases of Oracle; it can still be created in Oracle 10*g*.

You can calculate the maximum amount of space (M) in a single Oracle database as the maximum number of datafiles (D) multiplied by the maximum number of blocks per datafile (F) multiplied by the tablespace block size (B): M = D * F * B. Therefore, the maximum database size, given the maximum block size and the maximum number of datafiles, is 65,535 datafiles * 4,294,967,296 blocks per datafile * 32,768 block size = 9,223,231,299,366,420,480 = 8EB.

TABLE 4.1   Maximum Tablespace Sizes

Tablespace Block Size	Maximum Tablespace Size
2K	8TB
4K	16TB
8K	32TB
16K	64TB
32K	128TB

In addition to expanding the size of the tablespace itself, the implementation of bigfile tablespaces means you never need to add datafiles to a tablespace. A bigfile tablespace has one and only one datafile. This simplifies the maintenance of a bigfile tablespace; operations that formerly were performed at the datafile level are now performed at the logical tablespace level. In conjunction with Oracle Managed Files (OMF) or Automatic Storage Management (ASM), you may never need to know the name of the tablespace's underlying datafile name.

We'll present several aspects of bigfile tablespaces so you can leverage their advantages in your terabyte database. First, we'll show you how to create and maintain a bigfile tablespace using new keywords in the CREATE TABLESPACE command. We'll also show you how the format of ROWIDs changes when you use a bigfile tablespace. Finally, we'll go over the related changes to initialization parameters, data dictionary tables, and utilities for bigfile tablespaces.

Creating and Maintaining Bigfile Tablespaces

Bigfile tablespaces must be created as locally managed with automatic segment space management. While the default allocation policy for bigfile tablespaces is AUTOALLOCATE, you should consider changing the default to UNIFORM with a large extent size for situations where you know how big the table will be to start out with and how it will grow in the future. As with smallfile tablespaces, using AUTOALLOCATE is best for tablespaces whose table usage and growth patterns are indeterminate.

Creating a bigfile tablespace is identical to creating a traditional smallfile tablespace, with the addition of the BIGFILE keyword and the capability to specify the size of the tablespace in gigabytes (G) or terabytes (T).

```
SQL> create bigfile tablespace big_users
  2      datafile '/u09/oradata/ord/big_users.dbf'
  3      size 10g autoextend on;
```

By default, tablespaces are created as smallfile tablespaces; you can specify the default tablespace type when the database is created or at any time with the ALTER DATABASE command.

```
SQL> alter database set default bigfile tablespace;
```

When a bigfile tablespace is running out of room, you can change the size of the underlying datafile by resizing the tablespace to the desired size, like so:

```
SQL> alter tablespace big_users resize 20g;
```

Alternatively, you can turn on AUTOEXTEND so that the file will grow automatically depending on the value of the NEXT parameter when the tablespace was created, like so:

```
SQL> alter tablespace big_users autoextend on;
```

Managing *ROWID*s with Bigfile Tablespaces

Bigfile tablespaces have a slightly different format for extended ROWIDs of table rows. First, let's review the format for ROWIDs in previous versions of Oracle and for smallfile tablespaces in Oracle 10*g*.

The format for a smallfile ROWID consists of four parts: OOOOOO, FFF, BBBBBB, and RRR. Table 4.2 explains each part of the ROWID.

TABLE 4.2 Smallfile *ROWID* Piece Definitions

Smallfile ROWID **Piece**	**Definition**
OOOOOO	Data object numberidentifying the database segment (table, index, materialized view)
FFF	Relative datafile number within the tablespace of the datafile that contains the row
BBBBBB	The data block containing the row, relative to the data file
RRR	Slot number, or row number, of the row inside a block

A bigfile tablespace has only one datafile, so the relative data file number is always 1024 and therefore is not needed as part of the ROWID; instead, it is used to expand the block number to allow for a larger number of blocks in a data file and, as a result, a tablespace. The concatenation of the relative data file number (FFF) and the data block number (BBBBBB) results in a new construct called an *encoded block number*. Table 4.3 summarizes the pieces of a bigfile ROWID, which consists of three parts—OOOOOO, LLLLLLLLL, and RRR.

Because of the changes to the ROWID format, and the two different types of tablespaces that can exist in a database, some of the parameters have changed for procedures in the DBMS_ROWID package.

TABLE 4.3   Bigfile ROWID Piece Definitions

Bigfile ROWID Piece	Definition
OOOOOO	Data Object Number identifying the database segment (table, index, view)
LLLLLLLLL	Encoded block number, relative to the tablespace and unique within the tablespace
RRR	Slot number, or row number, of the row inside a block

WARNING   In previous releases, DBMS_ROWID was not the only way to extract a ROWID from a table; in a bigfile tablespace, DBMS_ROWID is required to extract the correct ROWID.

The procedures within the DBMS_ROWID package operate much as before, except for a new parameter, TS_TYPE_IN, which identifies the type of tablespace to which a particular row belongs. The value of TS_TYPE_IN is either BIGFILE or SMALLFILE.

In the following example, you will extract the block number for a particular set of rows in a copy of the HR.EMPLOYEES table, which was recently moved to a bigfile tablespace:

```
SQL> select rowid,
  2      dbms_rowid.rowid_block_number(rowid,'BIGFILE')
  3         bigblock,
  4      employee_id, last_name from big_emp
  5   where employee_id < 110;


ROWID              BIGBLOCK EMPLOYEE_ID LAST_NAME
------------------ ---------- ----------- --------------
AAAMnfAAAAAAAAUAAA        20         100 King
AAAMnfAAAAAAAAUAAB        20         101 Kochhar
AAAMnfAAAAAAAAUAAC        20         102 De Haan
AAAMnfAAAAAAAAUAAD        20         103 Hunold
AAAMnfAAAAAAAAUAAE        20         104 Ernst
AAAMnfAAAAAAAAUAAF        20         105 Austin
AAAMnfAAAAAAAAUAAG        20         106 Pataballa
AAAMnfAAAAAAAAUAAH        20         107 Lorentz
AAAMnfAAAAAAAAUAAI        20         108 Greenberg
AAAMnfAAAAAAAAUAAJ        20         109 Faviet

10 rows selected.
```

Miscellaneous Bigfile Considerations

A number of other changes to initialization parameters and the data dictionary are related to bigfile tablespaces. We will cover these changes, along with some changes to DBVERIFY (one of Oracle's external utilities), in the next few sections.

Initialization Parameter Changes for Bigfile Tablespaces

No new initialization parameters or changes to existing parameters exist because of bigfile tablespaces; however, the values for two existing initialization parameters may be reduced because a bigfile tablespace needs only one datafile. These two parameters are as follows:

DB_FILES   This is the maximum number of data files that can be opened for this database. If there are less data files to maintain, memory requirements are reduced in the System Global Area (SGA).

MAXDATAFILES   When creating a new database or creating a new control file, this parameter specifies the size of the control file section allocated to maintain information about data files. Using bigfile tablespaces, the size of the control file is smaller.

Data Dictionary Changes for Bigfile Tablespaces

The data dictionary view DATABASE_PROPERTIES, which contains a number of other characteristics of the database, such as the database's NLS settings and the name of the default permanent and temporary tablespaces, has a property called DEFAULT_TBS_TYPE. This property indicates the default tablespace type for the database. Here is an example:

```
SQL> select property_name, property_value, description
  2      from database_properties
  3          where property_name = 'DEFAULT_TBS_TYPE';


PROPERTY_NAME      PROPERTY_VALUE   DESCRIPTION
-----------------  ---------------  ----------------------
DEFAULT_TBS_TYPE   BIGFILE          Default tablespace type


1 row selected.
```

The data dictionary views USER_TABLESPACES and DBA_TABLESPACES, which show information about tablespaces in the database, both have a new column called BIGFILE. The value of the column is YES if the corresponding tablespace is a bigfile tablespace. The same column exists in the dynamic performance view V$TABLESPACE.

Using *DBVERIFY* with Bigfile Tablespaces

The DBVERIFY utility, available since Oracle 7.3, checks the integrity of an offline database; the files can be datafiles, online redo log files, or archived redo log files. DBVERIFY has been enhanced to analyze the datafile for a bigfile tablespace. In previous versions, several instances of DBVERIFY could simultaneously analyze individual datafiles. However, since a bigfile tablespace consists of a single datafile, you need a new way to analyze the datafile using multiple processes.

The DBVERIFY utility, initiated by the dbv command on all platforms, has two new parameters: START and END, representing the first and last block of the file to analyze. As a result, you must know how many blocks are in the datafile; you can use the dynamic performance view V$DATAFILE to obtain this information.

```
SQL> select file#, blocks, name from v$datafile;

    FILE#     BLOCKS NAME
---------- ---------- ------------------------------------
        1      58880 /u05/oradata/ord/system01.dbf
        2       3840 /u05/oradata/ord/undotbs01.dbf
        3      38400 /u05/oradata/ord/sysaux01.dbf
        4       1280 /u05/oradata/ord/users01.dbf
        5      19200 /u05/oradata/ord/example01.dbf
        6       1280 /u09/oradata/ord/oe_trans01.dbf
        7        640 /u05/oradata/ord/users02.dbf
        8       1280 /u06/oradata/ord/logmnr_rep01.dbf
        9       1280 /u09/oradata/ord/big_users.dbf

9 rows selected.
```

Suppose you want to analyze datafile #9, the datafile for the bigfile tablespace BIG_USERS. At the Unix command prompt, you can analyze the file with three parallel processes, operating on three different sections of the datafile.

```
$ dbv file=/u09/oradata/ord/big_users.dbf
                        start=1 end=500 &
[1] 11472
$ dbv file=/u09/oradata/ord/big_users.dbf
                        start=501 end=1000 &
[2] 11506
$ dbv file=/u09/oradata/ord/big_users.dbf
                        start=1001 &
[3] 11509
```

Note that if you do not specify the end= keyword in dbv, it is assumed that you will be analyzing the datafile all the way to the end of the datafile. All three instances of dbv run simultaneously. The output from all three commands would look similar to the following:

```
DBVERIFY: Release 10.1.0.2.0 - Production on ➡
Sun Mar 28 15:50:42 2004

Copyright (c) 1982, 2004, Oracle.  All rights reserved.
```

```
DBVERIFY - Verification starting : ➡
FILE = /u09/oradata/ord/big_users.dbf

DBVERIFY - Verification complete

Total Pages Examined         : 280
Total Pages Processed (Data) : 0
Total Pages Failing   (Data) : 0
Total Pages Processed (Index): 0
Total Pages Failing   (Index): 0
Total Pages Processed (Other): 0
Total Pages Processed (Seg)  : 0
Total Pages Failing   (Seg)  : 0
Total Pages Empty            : 280
Total Pages Marked Corrupt   : 0
Total Pages Influx           : 0
```

Temporary Tablespace Groups

In a nutshell, a *temporary tablespace group* is a shortcut or a synonym for a list of temporary tablespaces. A temporary tablespace group can have only temporary tablespaces as members.

A temporary tablespace group consists of at least one temporary tablespace; a temporary tablespace group cannot be empty. After the last member of a temporary tablespace group has been dropped, the temporary tablespace group no longer exists. The temporary tablespace group is created when the first temporary tablespace is added to the group.

Wherever a temporary tablespace can be referenced, a temporary tablespace group can be referenced as well. Therefore, because a temporary tablespace and a temporary tablespace group share the same namespace, a temporary tablespace cannot have the same name as a temporary tablespace group.

Temporary tablespaces allow a single user with multiple sessions to potentially use a different temporary tablespace in each session. Here is an example of how it works: The user SCOTT is assigned the temporary tablespace group TEMPGRP consisting of temporary tablespaces TEMP1, TEMP2, and TEMP3. The user SCOTT in session #1 may use the actual temporary tablespace TEMP1, and the user SCOTT in session #2 may use the actual temporary tablespace TEMP3. Not only does this prevent large tablespace operations from running out of temporary space, it also allows parallel operations within a single session to potentially use more than one actual temporary tablespace, even though in all the previous scenarios, SCOTT was assigned the TEMPGRP temporary tablespace group. Logically, the same temporary tablespace was used in every session.

In the following sections, we will show you how to create and drop temporary tablespace groups, as well as assigning these groups to users. In addition, we will show the data dictionary views used with temporary tablespaces.

Creating and Dropping Temporary Tablespace Groups

You can use EM Database Control to create temporary tablespace groups, as demonstrated in Figure 4.3.

FIGURE 4.3 Creating temporary tablespace groups using EM Database Control

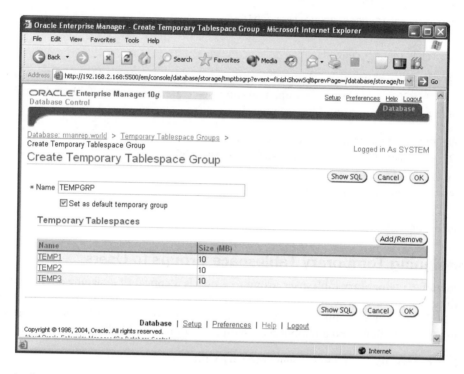

The equivalent command-line version looks like this:

```
alter tablespace temp1 tablespace group tempgrp;
alter tablespace temp2 tablespace group tempgrp;
alter tablespace temp3 tablespace group tempgrp;
alter database default temporary tablespace tempgrp;
```

Note that along with creating a new temporary tablespace group, you are making the group the default temporary tablespace for the database. You cannot drop the tablespace group unless you change the default temporary tablespace first. You can, however, drop one of the members of the group.

```
SQL> alter tablespace temp3 tablespace group '';

Tablespace altered.
```

When you create a temporary tablespace, you can immediately add it to an existing group, or create a new group with one member as in the following example:

```
SQL> create temporary tablespace temp6
  2       tempfile '/u08/oradata/ord/temp6.dbf'
  3       size 10m
  4       tablespace group tempgrp2;


    Tablespace created.
```

If the group TEMPGRP2 did not exist before creating the TEMP6 tablespace, it is created, otherwise TEMP6 is added to the group. You can also create a temporary tablespace and explicitly assign it to no group using this command:

```
SQL> create temporary tablespace temp7
  2       tempfile '/u08/oradata/ord/temp7.dbf'
  3       size 10m
  4       tablespace group '';

Tablespace created.
```

Assigning Temporary Tablespace Groups to Users

Assigning a temporary tablespace group to a user is identical to assigning a temporary tablespace to a user. The assignment can take place either when the user is created or afterward.

In the following example, you will create a new user OLIVERT with a default permanent tablespace of USERS and a temporary tablespace group of TEMPGRP:

```
SQL> create user olivert identified by wist
  2     default tablespace users
  3     temporary tablespace tempgrp;

User created.
```

Note that if you did not specify a temporary tablespace for OLIVERT, the user would still be assigned TEMPGRP as the temporary tablespace, since it is the default for the database.

Suppose you also want to change the temporary tablespace for SCOTT, so you run the following command:

```
SQL> alter user scott temporary tablespace tempgrp;
```

Tablespace Groups Data Dictionary Views

The views ALL_USERS, USER_USERS, and DBA_USERS still have the column TEMPORARY_ TABLESPACE, as in previous versions of Oracle. This column, however, will now contain either the name of the temporary tablespace assigned to the user or the name of a temporary tablespace group.

The new view DBA_TABLESPACE_GROUPS shows the members of each temporary tablespace group.

```
SQL> select group_name, tablespace_name ➥
from dba_tablespace_groups;

GROUP_NAME                        TABLESPACE_NAME
------------------------------    -------------------------
TEMPGRP                           TEMP1
TEMPGRP                           TEMP2
TEMPGRP                           TEMP3

3 rows selected.
```

Other Tablespace Enhancements

A number of other tablespace enhancements can ease your administrative efforts, especially when tablespaces are transported between databases. In addition, you can specify a default permanent tablespace; in previous releases of Oracle, the SYSTEM tablespace was assigned as the user's permanent tablespace if a tablespace was not explicitly assigned when the user was created. You will look at each of these enhancements in the following sections.

Renaming Tablespaces

As transportable tablespaces become more common, so does the potential for naming conflicts. For instance, in previous versions of Oracle, if the target database already had a tablespace called USERS and you wanted to plug in a tablespace named USERS from a different database, the only option available was to create a new tablespace in the source or target database, copy the objects to the new tablespace, and drop the original tablespace.

Oracle 10g allows you to rename either one of the tablespaces before unplugging from one database and plugging into another. In the following example, we are renaming the tablespace BIG_USERS to USERS2:

```
SQL> alter tablespace big_users rename to users2;
Tablespace altered.
```

If you are not using OMF to automatically name datafiles, do not rely on naming conventions for datafiles; after a tablespace renaming operation, the name of the datafile may no longer reflect the name of the tablespace containing the datafile.

After the tablespace is renamed, all references to the tablespace name are updated in the data dictionary, control file, and the online datafile headers for the tablespace's datafiles. If you are using an SPFILE to maintain your initialization parameters, all references to the renamed tablespace are updated. If you are still using a text-based initialization parameter file, a message is recorded in the alert log that reminds you to update the initialization file manually.

Of course, a few restrictions exist for tablespace renaming. The SYSTEM and SYSAUX tablespaces cannot be renamed. If any datafile in the tablespace is offline, or if the entire tablespace is offline, the tablespace cannot be renamed. While you can rename a tablespace that is READ ONLY, the datafile headers are not updated until the tablespace is READ WRITE.

Creating a Default Permanent Tablespace

In previous releases of Oracle, the SYSTEM tablespace was designated as the default permanent tablespace if no permanent tablespace was specified in the CREATE USER command. Since you want to reduce the contention as much as possible on the SYSTEM tablespace, it is a bad idea to store user objects in the SYSTEM tablespace. You could specify a default temporary tablespace in Oracle 9*i*, but now in Oracle 10*g* you can specify a *default permanent tablespace*.

You can define the default permanent tablespace in the CREATE DATABASE command or later using ALTER DATABASE.

In the following example, we are changing the default permanent tablespace to the USERS2 tablespace:

```
SQL> alter database default tablespace users2;
Database altered.
```

Similar to how temporary tablespaces are assigned, all users who are not specifically assigned a default permanent tablespace will now use the USERS2 tablespace for permanent objects. The data dictionary view DATABASE_PROPERTIES reflects this new assignment.

```
SQL> select property_name, property_value, description
  2      from database_properties
  3        where property_name =
  4            'DEFAULT_PERMANENT_TABLESPACE';
```

PROPERTY_NAME	PROPERTY_VALUE	DESCRIPTION
DEFAULT_PERMANENT_TABLESPACE	USERS2	Name of default permanent tablespace

```
1 row selected.
```

Using the DBCA to create a database, the USERS tablespace is automatically designated as the default permanent tablespace.

The default permanent tablespace does not apply to system users, such as SYS, SYSTEM, and OUTLN; their default tablespace is still SYSTEM. In addition, a tablespace that has been designated as the default permanent tablespace cannot be dropped until a new tablespace has been designated as the default permanent tablespace.

Copying Tablespaces Using the Database Server

As an added convenience to you, and to make application development more seamless by reducing the number of interfaces required to accomplish a given task, Oracle 10g now supports copying binary files between directories on the same server or between a remote server and a local server. The package DBMS_FILE_TRANSFER contains three procedures to accomplish these features. Table 4.4 lists the procedures available in DBMS_FILE_TRANSFER.

TABLE 4.4   *DBMS_FILE_TRANSFER* Procedures

Procedure	Description
COPY_FILE	Reads a local file and creates a copy of the file on the local file system; this is the same file system containing the database files.
PUT_FILE	Reads a local file, authenticates with a remote database using a database link, and creates a copy of the file in the remote file system.
GET_FILE	Authenticates with a remote database using a database link to copy a file on the remote file system to the local file system.

While the package DBMS_FILE_TRANSFER is primarily intended to copy Data Pump dump sets and tablespace files between databases, it can be used for any type of file as long as it is a binary file, the file size is a multiple of 512 bytes, and it is no larger than 2TB.

In the next few sections, we will describe how each of the DBMS_FILE_TRANSFER procedures work.

COPY_FILE

The COPY_FILE procedure takes four arguments, as listed in Table 4.5.

The user executing the COPY_FILE procedure must have read permissions in the source directory and write permissions in the destination directory.

In the following example, your goal is to move the datafiles for the EXAMPLE tablespace to a different file system on the server. To accomplish this, you will create two new directories, take the tablespace offline, copy the datafile to the destination directory, change the name of the underlying datafile in the control file, and bring the tablespace back online. To clean up after yourself, you will use UTL_FILE.FREMOVE to remove the original copy of the file.

TABLE 4.5 *COPY_FILE* Parameters

Parameter	Description
source_directory_object	The Oracle directory object from which the binary file will be copied on the local file system.
source_file_name	The name of the file in the local file system in the Oracle directory specified by the first argument.
destination_directory_object	The Oracle directory object into which the binary file will be copied.
destination_file_name	The name of the file in the destination directory; this may or may not be the same as source_file_name, but this file must not already exist in the destination directory.

Here is what you would do to accomplish this:

```
SQL> alter tablespace example offline;
Tablespace altered.

SQL> create directory src_dir as '/u05/oradata/ord';
Directory created.

SQL> create directory tgt_dir as '/u09/oradata/ord';
Directory created.

SQL> begin
  2      dbms_file_transfer.copy_file(
  3          source_directory_object => 'SRC_DIR',
  4          source_file_name => 'example01.dbf',
  5          destination_directory_object => 'TGT_DIR',
  6          destination_file_name => 'example01.dbf');
  7  end;
PL/SQL procedure successfully completed.

SQL> alter database rename file
  2      '/u05/oradata/ord/example01.dbf' to
  3      '/u09/oradata/ord/example01.dbf';
Database altered.

SQL> alter tablespace example online;
```

```
Tablespace altered.

SQL> begin
  2      utl_file.fremove (
  3          location    => 'SRC_DIR',
  4          filename    => 'example01.dbf');
  5  end;
PL/SQL procedure successfully completed.

SQL> ! ls -l /u09/oradata/ord/example*.*
-rw-r-----   1 oracle   oinstall 209723392
         Jul 13 19:07 /u09/oradata/ord/example01.dbf

SQL> select d.name
  2      from v$datafile d join v$tablespace t using(ts#)
  3      where t.name = 'EXAMPLE';

NAME
----------------------------------------
/u09/oradata/ord/example01.dbf
/u06/oradata/example02.dbf

2 rows selected.
```

Notice the two steps at the end of the example: you should verify that the datafile has been actually copied, as well as verifying the copy by using V$DATAFILE.

As with all of the DBMS_FILE_TRANSFER procedures, you can monitor the progress of the file copy by querying the V$SESSION_LONGOPS dynamic performance view.

PUT_FILE

The PUT_FILE procedure is similar to the COPY_FILE procedure, except that the file is transferred to a file system outside the database file system, in other words, a file system on a different server. The PUT_FILE procedure takes five arguments, as listed in Table 4.6.

TABLE 4.6   *PUT_FILE* Parameters

Parameter	Description
source_directory_object	The Oracle directory object from which the binary file will be copied on the local file system.
source_file_name	The name of the file in the local file system in the Oracle directory specified by the first argument.

TABLE 4.6 *PUT_FILE* Parameters *(continued)*

Parameter	Description
destination_directory_object	The name of the Oracle directory object in the remote file system into which the binary file will be copied. This directory object must resolve to a valid pathname in the target database's file system.
destination_file_name	The name of the file in the destination directory; this may or may not be the same as source_file_name, but this file must not already exist in the destination directory.
destination_database	The name of a database link to the remote database through which the file is copied to the remote file system.

The user executing the PUT_FILE procedure must have read permissions in the source directory, and the connected user defined in the database link must have write permissions in the destination directory. Also, the destination file name must not already exist.

GET_FILE

The GET_FILE procedure performs the copy in the opposite direction as PUT_FILE; it copies the file from the remote file system to the local file system. The GET_FILE procedure takes five arguments, as listed in Table 4.7.

TABLE 4.7 *GET_FILE* Parameters

Parameter	Description
source_directory_object	The Oracle directory object from which the binary file will be copied on the remote file system.
source_file_name	The name of the file in the remote file system in the Oracle directory specified by the first argument.
source_database	The name of a database link to the remote database from which the file is copied to the remote file system.
destination_directory_object	The name of the Oracle directory object in the local file system into which the binary file will be copied. This directory object must resolve to a valid pathname in the local database's file system.
destination_file_name	The name of the file in the destination directory of the local file system; this may or may not be the same as source_file_name, but this file must not already exist in the destination directory.

The parameters are the same as for PUT_FILE, just in a different order, reflecting the different direction of the file copy.

Making Partitioning Enhancements

Partitioned tables, available since Oracle 8, have been incrementally enhanced in every version of Oracle including the current version. As with most other database features, partition maintenance is enhanced by the web-based EM Database Control, with wizards and other tips to help you perform the partitioning tasks quickly and accurately.

In addition, IOTs have been enhanced to allow a number of new partitioning options, including list-partitioned IOTs and more robust global index maintenance for partitioned IOTs. We will discuss both of these enhancements in further detail in the next couple of sections.

Partition Maintenance Using EM Database Control

Creating and maintaining partitioned tables using EM Database Control saves you both time and the potential for errors when working with table and index partitions. In Figure 4.4, you can start the process of creating the ORD_ITEM table to support a new order entry system. On this screen, you specify the table name, the schema where it will reside, and the tablespace. You also specify the names, types, and sizes of the columns.

FIGURE 4.4   Creating a table using EM Database Control

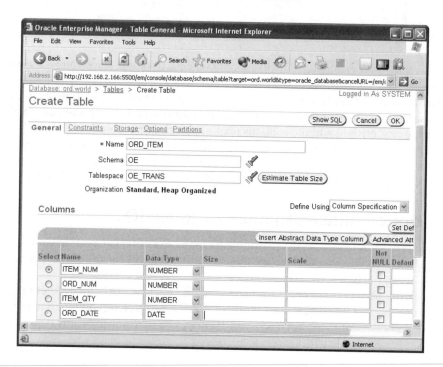

Once you have the columns defined, you can define the constraints, storage requirements, and other options, including a partitioning scheme. From the screen shown in Figure 4.4, click the Partitions tab to specify the partitioning method for this table, as shown in Figure 4.5.

FIGURE 4.5 Partitioning methods using EM Database Control

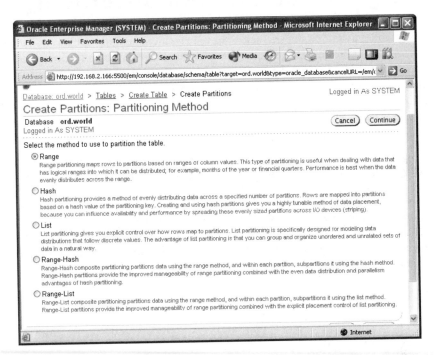

In this particular example, you will choose range partitioning, since you will use the ORD_ DATE column to put the rows into a specific partition.

Once a partition table has been created, it is easy to maintain the partitioned table using EM Database Control. In Figure 4.6 you can see all the partitions for the table SH.COSTS along with the partitioning method and the columns used to partition the table.

To edit the characteristics of a partition, or even to truncate a partition, select the partition and click Advanced Options. Figure 4.7 shows an example of how you can edit some of the advanced storage options for the COSTS_Q2_1998 partition of the SH.COSTS table.

Partitioned Index Organized Tables (IOTs)

In previous releases of Oracle, the partitioning capabilities of IOTs lagged behind the partitioning capabilities of the other table types. Oracle 10g has remedied many of these deficiencies, as you will see in the following paragraphs.

List-partitioned IOTs are now fully supported. In Oracle 9i, IOTs used either range or hash partitioning, but not list partitioning. Furthermore, the partitioning columns had to be a subset of the primary key columns. In Oracle 10g, IOTs can be partitioned by any column.

FIGURE 4.6   Partition maintenance using EM Database Control

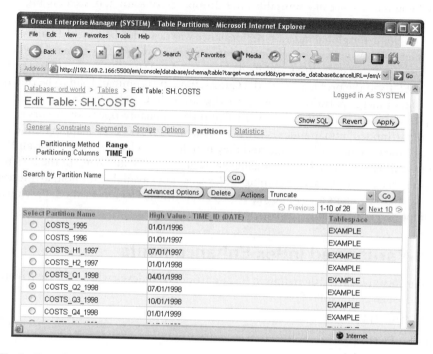

FIGURE 4.7   Advanced partition options using EM Database Control

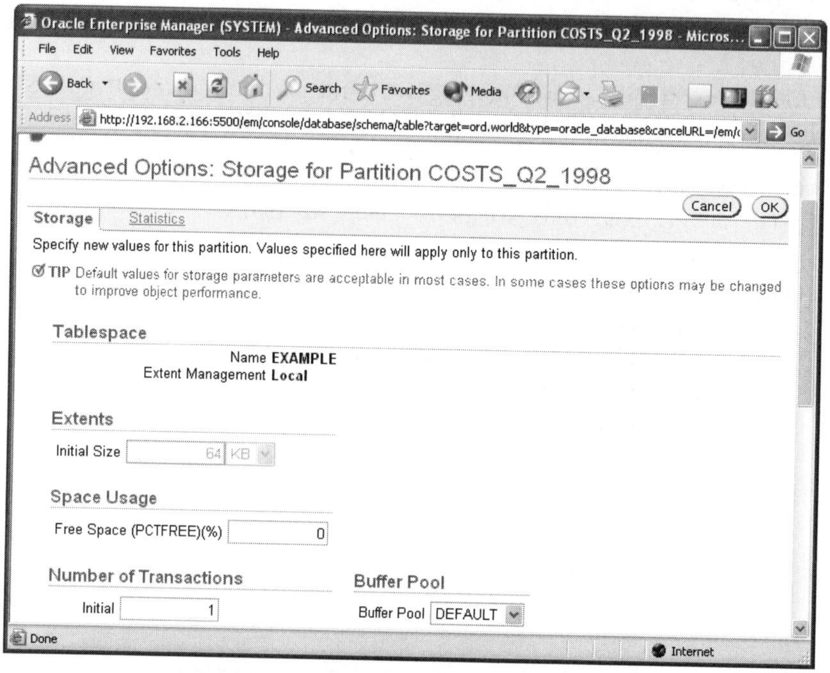

In previous versions, global indexes were not maintained for most IOT maintenance operations. Global indexes became unusable after dropping, truncating, or exchanging a partition. While other partition maintenance operations such as moving, splitting, or merging partitions did not invalidate the global indexes, performance was degraded because the Guess-Data Block Access (Guess-DBA) values became inaccurate over time, requiring a primary key lookup to locate the actual row in the IOT. While the command ALTER INDEX ... UPDATE BLOCK REFERENCES fixed the problems with the Guess-DBAs, this command had to be run after every move, split, or merge partition maintenance operation. In Oracle 10g, the block references are kept up-to-date automatically when any partition maintenance operation occurs.

Local partitioned bitmap indexes are now available for IOTs if a mapping table is created. Mapping tables are heap organized, and they map local-to-physical ROWIDs for an IOT. The mapping table is partitioned with the same name and physical attributes of the IOT partitions. In previous versions of Oracle, mapping tables were only available for nonpartitioned IOTs.

Finally, LOB columns are supported for IOTs partitioned by any method. Previously, LOBs were supported only in range-partitioned IOTs.

Local-Partitioned Index Enhancements

Improvements in Oracle 10g maintain local-partitioned indexes when you use partition DDL commands such as the following:

- ADD PARTITION
- SPLIT PARTITION
- MERGE PARTITION
- MOVE PARTITION

In addition, the associated indexes no longer have to be stored in the same tablespace as the table.

In the following example, we are merging two of the partitions in the SH.COSTS table, maintaining the local indexes, and relocating the index into the USERS2 tablespace:

```
SQL> alter table sh.costs
  2      merge partitions costs_h1_1997, costs_h2_1997
  3          into partition costs_1997
  4      update indexes (
  5          sh.costs_prod_bix
  6              (partition costs_1997 tablespace users2),
  7          sh.costs_time_bix
  8              (partition costs_1997 tablespace users2));

Table altered.
```

Looking at the data dictionary view DBA_IND_PARTITIONS, you can see that the index partition is still valid.

```
SQL> select index_name, partition_name,
  2      tablespace_name, status
  3  from dba_ind_partitions
  4  where index_name = 'COSTS_PROD_BIX';
```

INDEX_NAME	PARTITION_NAME	TABLESPACE_NAME	STATUS
COSTS_PROD_BIX	COSTS_1995	EXAMPLE	USABLE
COSTS_PROD_BIX	COSTS_1996	EXAMPLE	USABLE
COSTS_PROD_BIX	**COSTS_1997**	**USERS2**	**USABLE**
COSTS_PROD_BIX	COSTS_Q1_1998	EXAMPLE	USABLE
. . .			
COSTS_PROD_BIX	COSTS_Q4_2003	EXAMPLE	USABLE

```
27 rows selected.
```

As with most every other enhancement in Oracle 10*g*, this operation is also available via EM Database Control, as you can see in Figure 4.8.

FIGURE 4.8   Merging partitions using EM Database Control

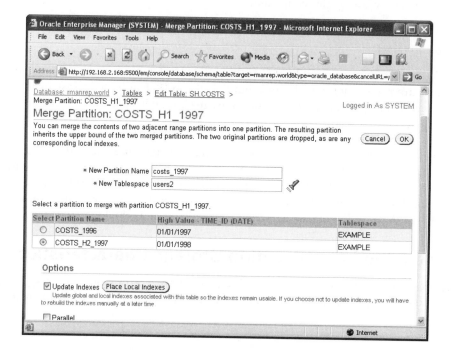

Leveraging Index Enhancements

The enhancements to indexes in Oracle 10g improve both the availability and the performance of global indexes. Invalid global partition indexes can be skipped instead of generating an ORA-message; new clauses in the index maintenance commands can prevent the global indexes from becoming invalid in the first place.

In the following sections, we will also discuss how hash-partitioned global indexes can improve query processing times by increasing the number of parallel processes that can access each partition in a hash-partitioned index. In addition, a hash-partitioned global index can further reduce hotspots in global indexes by spreading the creation of new index leaf nodes among all partitions in the index.

Bitmap indexes have also been improved in Oracle 10g, with major improvements in performance because of reduced fragmentation of bitmap indexes in environments with heavy DML activity.

Skipping Unusable Indexes

In previous versions of Oracle, when an index partition became unusable because of partition maintenance commands such as ADD PARTITION, SPLIT PARTITION, MERGE PARTITION, or MOVE PARTITION, any SQL SELECT statements that attempted to use the unusable index returned an ORA-01502 "index 'schema.indexname' or partition of such index is in unusable state" error message. At the session level, the user was able to direct the optimizer to skip the unusable index by issuing this command:

```
SQL> alter session set skip_unusable_indexes = true;
Session altered.
```

This parameter was also modifiable at the system level, but it was not dynamic. In Oracle 10g, this parameter is not only dynamic but defaults to TRUE at both the system level and the session level. The optimizer automatically skips any unusable indexes when constructing a query plan.

While setting SKIP_UNUSABLE_INDEXES can avoid ORA-01502 errors, and the query still runs, the optimizer may choose a suboptimal execution plan since one of the indexes is not available. To monitor the database for unusable indexes, you should monitor the data dictionary view DBA_IND_PARTITIONS for invalid indexes; in addition, the alert log records an event when a local index partition becomes invalid. In addition, a user can reanalyze the query with EXPLAIN PLAN to see if an index is suddenly unavailable and rebuild the relevant indexes.

Maintaining Index Partition Storage Characteristics

Range-partitioned global indexes are no longer the only type of global indexes available in Oracle 10g. *Hash-partitioned global indexes* add new DDL options for partition maintenance,

along with increased availability and performance, by eliminating index hotspots in heavy OLTP environments. Both ADD PARTITION and COALESCE PARTITION are available for both range-partitioned and hash-partitioned global indexes.

Range-partitioned global indexes can cause a performance issue during INSERT operations whose inserted rows contain a primary key generated from an Oracle sequence; this creates a hotspot in a small number of index leaf blocks in one of the index partitions. While using a reverse-key global index alleviates this problem somewhat using range partitioning, the problem is alleviated in only one index partition. Using hash-partitioned global indexes, the index entries are spread out not only to different leaf nodes within an index partition but also to different partitions.

In the next few sections, we'll review the typical maintenance activities you'd perform on any index: creating and maintaining hash-partitioned global indexes. We'll also show how you can leverage the parallel processing advantages of hash-partitioned global indexes.

Creating Hash-Partitioned Global Indexes

Creating a hash-partitioned index is just as easy as creating a range-partitioned index; in fact, you have two different ways to create the index. In the CREATE INDEX command, you can specify the name of each partition individually with the associated tablespace, or you can specify the number of partitions and the list of the partitions. A couple of examples will demonstrate the two different syntax options.

In the first example, we will create a global hash-partitioned index on the HIRE_DATE column of the HR.EMPLOYEES table, naming each partition and associating the partition with a tablespace to store the index partition.

```
SQL> create index emp_id_ix2 on hr.employees(hire_date)
  2        global partition by hash(hire_date)
  3        (partition p1 tablespace idx_1,
  4         partition p2 tablespace idx_2,
  5         partition p3 tablespace idx_3,
  6         partition p4 tablespace idx_4,
  7         partition p5 tablespace idx_5);

Index created.
```

Alternatively, you can create the index more easily if you do not need to assign partition names.

```
SQL> create index emp_id_ix2 on hr.employees(hire_date)
  2        global partition by hash(hire_date)
  3        partitions 5
  4        store in (idx_1, idx_2, idx_3, idx_4, idx_5);

Index created.
```

The data dictionary table DBA_IND_PARTITIONS reveals how Oracle automatically assigns names to the partitions using the second format.

```
SQL> select index_name, partition_name,
  2        tablespace_name, status
  3  from dba_ind_partitions
  4  where index_name = 'EMP_ID_IX2';
```

INDEX_NAME	PARTITION_NAME	TABLESPACE_NAME	STATUS
EMP_ID_IX2	SYS_P185	IDX_1	USABLE
EMP_ID_IX2	SYS_P186	IDX_2	USABLE
EMP_ID_IX2	SYS_P187	IDX_3	USABLE
EMP_ID_IX2	SYS_P188	IDX_4	USABLE
EMP_ID_IX2	SYS_P189	IDX_5	USABLE

```
5 rows selected.
```

Using EM Database Control, creating hash-partitioned indexes is even easier. Figure 4.9 shows how you can create a hash-partitioned global index using the first method.

When you click on the Show SQL button, you can see the SQL command that will be executed to create the new index as follows:

```
CREATE INDEX "SYS"."EMP_ID_IX2" ON "HR"."EMPLOYEES" ("HIRE_DATE")
TABLESPACE "USERS" PCTFREE 10 INITRANS 2 MAXTRANS 255
STORAGE ( FREELISTS 1 FREELIST GROUPS 1
          BUFFER_POOL DEFAULT) NOLOGGING
GLOBAL PARTITION BY HASH ("HIRE_DATE")
(PARTITION "EMP_ID_IX2_P1" TABLESPACE "IDX_1",
 PARTITION "EMP_ID_IX2_P2" TABLESPACE "IDX_2",
 PARTITION "EMP_ID_IX2_P3" TABLESPACE "IDX_3",
 PARTITION "EMP_ID_IX2_P4" TABLESPACE "IDX_4",
 PARTITION "EMP_ID_IX2_P5" TABLESPACE "IDX_5")
```

Maintaining Hash-Partitioned Global Indexes

As with other types of partitions, you can use ADD PARTITION to create additional partitions to a hash-partitioned global index, or you can remove partitions by using COALESCE PARTITION.

Following the example from the previous section, suppose you have a global hash-partitioned index on the HIRE_DATE column with five partitions defined. Oracle recommends that the number of partitions be a power of two to more evenly spread the index entries among the partitions;

as a result, you will want to either drop the partitions back down to four (2^2) or increase it to eight (2^3). In the first attempt, we will try to optimize the performance of the index by using the COALESCE PARTITION option to redistribute the contents of one of the partitions to the remaining partitions and drop the partition.

```
SQL> alter index emp_id_ix2 coalesce partition;

Index altered.
```

FIGURE 4.9 Using EM Database Control to create global indexes

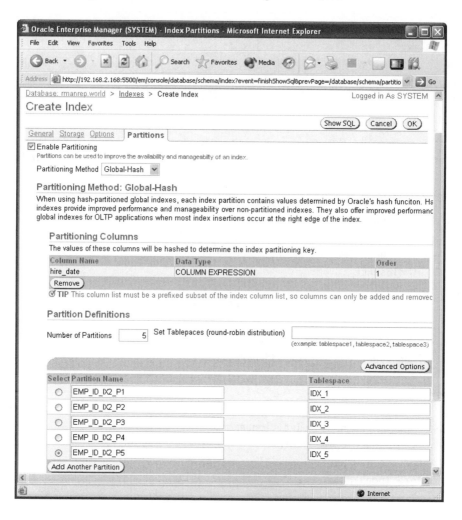

Oracle chooses which index partition is the best candidate, redistributes its contents to the remaining partitions, and drops the partition. Looking at the DBA_IND_PARTITIONS data dictionary view, you see that the index now has only four partitions

```
SQL> select index_name, partition_name,
  2      tablespace_name, status
  3  from dba_ind_partitions
  4  where index_name = 'EMP_ID_IX2';


INDEX_NAME     PARTITION_NAME      TABLESPACE_NAME   STATUS
-------------  ------------------  ----------------  --------
EMP_ID_IX2     P1                  IDX_1             USABLE
EMP_ID_IX2     P2                  IDX_2             USABLE
EMP_ID_IX2     P3                  IDX_3             USABLE
EMP_ID_IX2     P4                  IDX_4             USABLE

4 rows selected.
```

After a few weeks, the performance of the index does not meet your service-level agreements, so you decide that it would be better to have eight partitions instead of four; therefore, you use the ADD PARTITION command four times.

```
SQL> alter index emp_id_ix2 add partition p5
  2      tablespace idx_5;
Index altered.
SQL> alter index emp_id_ix2 add partition p6
  2      tablespace idx_6;
Index altered.
SQL> alter index emp_id_ix2 add partition p7
  2      tablespace idx_7;
Index altered.
SQL> alter index emp_id_ix2 add partition p8
  2      tablespace idx_8;
Index altered.

SQL> select index_name, partition_name,
  2      tablespace_name, status
  3  from dba_ind_partitions
  4  where index_name = 'EMP_ID_IX2';
```

INDEX_NAME	PARTITION_NAME	TABLESPACE_NAME	STATUS
EMP_ID_IX2	P1	IDX_1	USABLE
EMP_ID_IX2	P2	IDX_2	USABLE
EMP_ID_IX2	P3	IDX_3	USABLE
EMP_ID_IX2	P4	IDX_4	USABLE
EMP_ID_IX2	P5	IDX_5	USABLE
EMP_ID_IX2	P6	IDX_6	USABLE
EMP_ID_IX2	P7	IDX_7	USABLE
EMP_ID_IX2	P8	IDX_8	USABLE

8 rows selected.

In both cases, Oracle automatically redistributes and balances the index entries to maximize performance. Looking at the data dictionary view DBA_IND_PARTITIONS, you can see by the leaf block count that the index entries have been evenly distributed to all eight of the partitions:

```
SQL> select index_name, partition_name, leaf_blocks
  2      from dba_ind_partitions
  3   where index_name = 'EMP_ID_IX3';
```

INDEX_NAME	PARTITION_NAME	LEAF_BLOCKS
EMP_ID_IX3	EMP_ID_IX3_P1	2
EMP_ID_IX3	EMP_ID_IX3_P2	2
EMP_ID_IX3	EMP_ID_IX3_P3	2
EMP_ID_IX3	EMP_ID_IX3_P4	2
EMP_ID_IX3	EMP_ID_IX3_P5	2
EMP_ID_IX3	EMP_ID_IX3_P6	2
EMP_ID_IX3	EMP_ID_IX3_P7	2
EMP_ID_IX3	EMP_ID_IX3_P8	2

8 rows selected.

As expected, a few operations available for range-partitioned indexes are not available for hash-partitioned global indexes, such as SPLIT INDEX PARTITION and MERGE INDEX PARTITION. Hash-partitioned indexes can be rebuilt but only on a partition-by-partition basis. The only modification you can make with ALTER INDEX MODIFY PARTITION is to manually mark the partition UNUSABLE.

Using Hash-Partitioned Global Indexes

Paradoxically, hash-partitioned indexes have another distinct advantage over range-partitioned indexes when performing parallel long-running queries with range predicates: While some of the partitions can be pruned given the range specified, the degree of parallelism is limited to the number of partitions in the index. For example, even if you specify a SELECT query with a degree of eight for a table with a global range-partitioned index containing only four partitions, the degree of parallelism is limited to four. With hash-partitioned global indexes, however, multiple parallel processes can access each pruned partition in the global index.

Using the earlier global partition example with eight index partitions, run the following query:

```
SQL> select /* parallel_index(emp,emp_id_ix2,16) */
  2      employee_id, email from employees emp
  3      where hire_date between '1-jan-1990' and '31-dec-2004';
```

Up to two parallel query processes will be assigned to each of the eight partitions in the EMP_ID_IX2 index.

Bitmap Index Storage Enhancements

Under certain DML situations, the performance of bitmap indexes may deteriorate over time, requiring a rebuild of the index. Improvements in Oracle 10*g* to the internal structure of bitmap indexes reduce the impact of frequent single-row DML operations against the table containing the bitmap index.

To take advantage of any of these improvements, the COMPATIBLE parameter must be set to 10.0.0.0 or greater. Some bitmap indexes that performed poorly before adjusting the COMPATIBLE parameter should be rebuilt; bitmap indexes that performed adequately before upgrading the COMPATIBLE parameter will enjoy some of the benefits of the new bitmap structure. Any new indexes created after the COMPATIBLE parameter is raised to 10.0.0.0 will take advantage of all improvements.

Ideally, all bitmap indexes created with lower COMPATIBLE values should eventually be rebuilt to take advantage of the new bitmap index functionality.

Summary

In this chapter we covered all the general storage enhancements in Oracle 10*g*. We started with the new SYSAUX tablespace: how it is created, either during a database upgrade or as part of a new database. We reviewed what applications use the SYSAUX tablespace and how the SYSAUX tablespace improves the performance of the database by taking some of the contention away from the SYSTEM tablespace. We showed you how to move some of the applications out of SYSAUX and into another tablespace when the SYSAUX tablespace itself gets too big. Finally, we provided some tips on how to manage the SYSAUX tablespace and some of its restrictions: While you can add datafiles to the SYSAUX tablespace, you cannot take it offline, you cannot rename it, and you cannot drop it.

Real World Scenario

Bitmap Index Performance

On one of our production Oracle servers, we maintain several databases containing the Enterprise Data Warehouse plus several data marts. Because of the inherent benefits of bitmap indexes in data warehouse environments, where typically there are few updates and many indexed columns in a star schema, most every column used in a join with low cardinality had a bitmap index. An earlier analysis revealed that, for some tables, using a tradition B-tree index would take almost as much disk space as the tables themselves!

A few weeks after the successful implementation of one of the data marts, some of the analysts started to complain that their queries were starting to run slowly, sometimes taking twice as long as they did a month earlier. However, the amount of data did not double in the last month, so some analysis was warranted.

As it turns out, one of the developers changed the load scripts so that some of the tables were being updated from the OLTP system in real time, instead of being updated at night in a batch run. As a result, the continual updates increased the size of the bitmap index dramatically and reduced the efficiency of the queries using the bitmap index.

Until the daily updates were turned off, we rebuilt the index nightly to address the performance issue. With the enhancements to bitmap index maintenance in Oracle 10*g*, we will be setting the COMPATIBLE parameter to 10.0.0.0, rebuilding the bitmap indexes in our data warehouse once, and we can reconsider turning the daily updates back on without affecting query performance.

Bigfile tablespaces provide a number of benefits to a busy DBA. Because a bigfile tablespace consists of only one datafile, the management of bigfile tablespaces moves from the datafile level to the tablespace level; in fact, many operations once reserved for datafiles can now be performed on bigfile tablespaces. Furthermore, we discussed how the ROWID format changes for bigfile tablespaces, along with the changes to the initialization parameters and data dictionary. Finally, we showed how several instances of the DBVERIFY utility can run in parallel to analyze different sections of a bigfile datafile.

Temporary tablespace groups improve the concurrency and performance of multiple sessions logged in with the same account, reducing the possibility that temporary sort operations may run out of temporary space. We reviewed how temporary tablespace groups are created and assigned to users; we also reviewed the data dictionary view related to temporary tablespace groups: DBA_TABLESPACE_GROUPS.

Various other tablespace enhancements can help save you time and potentially reduce the possibility of human error. Renaming tablespaces can save some of the extra steps required in previous versions of Oracle when the source and the target database have tablespaces with the same name. Specifying a default permanent tablespace is another enhancement to Oracle 10*g* that can prevent permanent objects from being created in the SYSTEM tablespace, further enhancing the reliability and response time for objects that must reside in the SYSTEM tablespace.

Finally, we reviewed one of the new packages available in Oracle 10*g*: DBMS_FILE_TRANSFER. The procedures COPY_FILE, PUT_FILE, and GET_FILE can copy binary files, usually tablespace datafiles and Data Pump files, between directories on the same server or between local and remote servers using a database link.

Partitioning support has been enhanced dramatically, for both tables and indexes. The partitioning capabilities of Index Organized Tables (IOTs) have been expanded to include list partitioning; in addition, local bitmap indexes are available for IOTs if a mapping table is created. LOB columns can be stored in IOTs partitioned by any method.

Index enhancements in Oracle 10*g* increase the availability of the database in a number of ways. The initialization parameter SKIP_UNUSABLE_INDEXES is now a dynamic parameter and performs the same function as in previous releases: to direct the optimizer to skip unusable index partitions and avoid ORA-01502 errors. Hash-partitioned global indexes go beyond the capabilities of range-partitioned global indexes by expanding the number of parallel query processes that can access an index partition in a SELECT query. Bitmap indexes are enhanced to prevent performance degradation because of frequent single-row DML statements against a table with a bitmap index.

Exam Essentials

Understand the purpose and usage of the SYSAUX tablespace. Be able to create a SYSAUX tablespace for both a new database and an upgrade to a database at a previous version of Oracle. Identify the contents of the SYSAUX tablespace, and be able to identify the procedure needed to move the contents of a particular application out of the SYSAUX tablespace.

Describe how bigfile tablespaces are created, maintained, and used. Know how to create a bigfile tablespace, and understand the differences in ROWID format between a smallfile and a bigfile tablespace. Be able to use DBVERIFY to check the validity of a bigfile datafile using parallel operating system processes.

Understand the concept of temporary tablespace groups and their performance and availability benefits. Describe how temporary tablespace groups are created, dropped, and assigned to users.

Enumerate the miscellaneous tablespace enhancements in Oracle 10*g*. Be able to rename a tablespace and define a default permanent tablespace.

Describe the new packages and procedures for tablespace maintenance. Understand how to use the DBMS_FILE_TRANSFER package to copy files between directories on the local server and between servers.

Understand the index enhancements in Oracle 10*g*. Be able to specify that unusable indexes should be skipped instead of generating an error message.

List the new data dictionary and dynamic performance views related to storage management.
Identify the new columns in data dictionary views related to bigfile tablespaces, new rows in
DATABASE_PROPERTIES, and new views identifying the members of temporary tablespace
groups.

Be able to take advantage of partitioning enhancements for both IOTs and partitioned indexes.
Create and maintain hash-partitioned indexes using both EM Database Control and SQL*Plus,
as well as constructing parallel queries to take advantage of hash-partitioned global indexes.

Review Questions

1. Which of the following ALTER commands is supported for hash-partitioned indexes?

   A. ALTER INDEX REBUILD

   B. ALTER INDEX MODIFY PARTITION

   C. ALTER TABLE SPLIT INDEX PARTITION

   D. ALTER TABLE MERGE INDEX PARTITIONS

   E. None of the above

2. Which of the following recommended practices should a DBA implement to take advantage of bitmap index storage enhancements? (Choose all that apply.)

   A. Rebuilding all bitmap indexes manually after adjusting the COMPATIBLE parameter

   B. Raising the COMPATIBLE parameter to at least 10.0.0.0

   C. Considering rebuilding bitmap indexes when large volumes of single-row DML operations occur on a table

   D. Rebuilding bitmap indexes that exhibit a slowdown after adjusting the COMPATIBLE parameter

   E. Raising the COMPATIBLE parameter to at least 9.2.0.0

3. What is the maximum number of bytes that can be stored in a bigfile tablespace with a database block size of 16KB?

   A. 8 exabytes

   B. 8,000,000 terabytes

   C. 8 petabytes

   D. 64 terabytes

4. Which of the following commands creates a temporary tablespace group TMPGRP1 and adds a temporary tablespace named TMPMEMB1? (Choose two.)

   A. CREATE TEMPORARY TABLESPACE GROUP TMPGRP1 MEMBERS (TMPMEMB1);

   B. ALTER TEMPORARY TABLESPACE GROUP TMPGRP1
      ADD TEMPORARY TABLESPACE TMPMEMB1
      TEMPFILE 'tmpmem1.dbf ' SIZE 100M;

   C. ALTER TABLESPACE TMPMEMB1 TABLESPACE GROUP TMPGRP1;

   D. CREATE TEMPORARY TABLESPACE TMPMEMB1
      TEMPFILE 'tmpmem1.dbf' SIZE 100M
      TABLESPACE GROUP TMPGRP1;

   E. None of the above

5. With a non-SYSTEM default permanent tablespace, which users still have SYSTEM as their default permanent tablespace? (Choose all that apply.)

   A. SYSMAN

   B. SYS

   C. OUTLN

   D. SYSTEM

   E. DBSNMP

   F. SCOTT

6. Which of the following statement(s) are not true about default permanent tablespaces?

   A. The default permanent tablespace cannot be dropped until another tablespace is defined as the default permanent tablespace.

   B. EM Database Control can be used to change the default permanent tablespace.

   C. The Database Configuration Assistant defines the USERS tablespace as the default permanent tablespace.

   D. In the CREATE DATABASE command, you use the DEFAULT PERMANENT TABLESPACE to assign the default permanent tablespace for users that are not otherwise assigned a default tablespace.

   E. The data dictionary view DATABASE_PROPERTIES can be used to retrieve the name of the default permanent tablespace.

7. Which of the following applications can be moved out of the SYSAUX tablespace?

   A. Automatic Workload Repository

   B. Oracle Streams

   C. StatsPack

   D. Job Scheduler

   E. LogMiner

8. Which data dictionary or dynamic performance view(s) indicates whether a tablespace is a big-file or smallfile tablespace? (Choose all that apply.)

   A. V$TABLESPACE

   B. V$DATABASE

   C. V$DATAFILE

   D. DBA_TABLESPACES

   E. DATABASE_PROPERTIES

9.   Which of the following is not true about the initialization parameter SKIP_UNUSABLE_INDEXES?

   A.   SKIP_UNUSABLE_INDEXES is a dynamic parameter.

   B.   Even if set to TRUE, a user may still get ORA-01502 messages if UPDATE INDEXES was not specified in partition maintenance.

   C.   The default value is TRUE at the session and system level.

   D.   Even if set to TRUE, the optimizer may choose a suboptimal execution plan.

   E.   The data dictionary view DBA_IND_PARTITIONS can be monitored to see if a local index partition has become invalid.

10.   Identify the new partitioning method available for global indexes.

   A.   Range partitioned

   B.   Range-hash partitioned

   C.   Hash partitioned

   D.   List-hash partitioned

11.   Identify the main differences between the procedures COPY_FILE and PUT_FILE in the DBMS_FILE_TRANSFER package. (Choose all that apply.)

   A.   COPY_FILE copies a file to a destination on the same server, and PUT_FILE copies a file to a remote server.

   B.   PUT_FILE copies a file to a destination on the same server, and COPY_FILE copies a file to a remote server.

   C.   PUT_FILE can copy only binary files; COPY_FILE can copy binary and Unicode files.

   D.   The PUT_FILE procedure requires a destination server name.

12.   Which of the following operations is not supported for hash-partitioned global indexes?

   A.   DROP INDEX IX_ORD;

   B.   ALTER INDEX IX_ORD REBUILD;

   C.   ALTER INDEX IX_ORD UNUSABLE;

   D.   ALTER INDEX IX_ORD MODIFY PARTITION IX_ORD_P1 UNUSABLE;

   E.   ALTER INDEX IX_ORD REBUILD PARTITION IX_ORD_P2;

13. Given the commands

```
CREATE TEMPORARY TABLESPACE PRDTTS1
TEMPFILE 'prdtts1.dbf' SIZE 100M
TABLESPACE GROUP PRDTMP;

CREATE TEMPORARY TABLESPACE PRDTTS2
TEMPFILE 'prdtts2.dbf' SIZE 100M
TABLESPACE GROUP PRDTMP;
```

which command does not assign the temporary tablespace group PRDTMP to a user?

A. CREATE USER KELLYM IDENTIFIED BY TJPO
    DEFAULT TABLESPACE USERS
    TEMPORARY TABLESPACE PRDTMP;

B. ALTER USER KELLYM TEMPORARY TABLESPACE GROUP PRDTMP;

C. ALTER DATABASE DEFAULT TEMPORARY TABLESPACE PRDTMP;

D. CREATE USER KELLYM IDENTIFIED BY TJPO
    TEMPORARY TABLESPACE PRDTMP;

14. Given a hash-partitioned global index IX_ORD on the table ORD, with four partitions, and the following SELECT statement:

```
SELECT /*+ PARALLEL_INDEX(ORD,IX_ORD,12) */
  ORDER_ID, ORDER_DATE FROM ORD
  WHERE ORDER_ID BETWEEN 110000 AND 190000;
```

which of the following is true about the number of processes used to execute the query?

A. Only one process is spawned since the index is hash-partitioned, and the WHERE clause uses a range.

B. After pruning the partitions down to those having the range of order IDs in the WHERE clause, the 12 processes are divided equally among the remaining partitions.

C. If the number of remaining partitions after pruning is fewer than 12, then not all 12 query processes are spawned; a maximum of one query process per partition is allowed for hash-partitioned global indexes.

D. The number of parallel query processes can only be a power of two, therefore, as many as 16 processes may be spawned.

15. Which of the following are true about renaming tablespaces? (Choose all that apply.)

    A. Tablespaces that are READ ONLY cannot be renamed and must be changed to READ WRITE before renaming.

    B. When a tablespace is renamed, all references to the tablespace name in the data dictionary, control file, online datafile headers, and initialization parameter files are updated.

    C. You cannot rename the SYSTEM or SYSAUX tablespaces.

    D. The tablespace must be online to be renamed.

    E. Temporary tablespaces, undo tablespaces, and permanent tablespaces can be renamed.

16. Which of the following is a benefit of hash-partitioned global indexes?

    A. Contention for the same index leaf blocks is reduced in an OLTP environment.

    B. Indexes are smaller in a DSS environment because hash partitioning compresses duplicate entries for dimension keys in a star schema.

    C. Hash-partitioned global indexes do not become invalid when partition maintenance occurs on the table partitions.

    D. The application developer no longer needs to use a reverse-key index to optimize the updates to the index.

17. Identify the way(s) a DBA can find out if a suboptimal execution plan is being used for a query because a local partitioned index has become invalid and the SKIP_UNUSABLE_INDEXES parameter is set to TRUE. (Choose all that apply.)

    A. Monitoring the data dictionary view DBA_IND_PARTITIONS for invalid indexes

    B. Monitoring the alert log

    C. Using EXPLAIN PLAN to preview the execution plan used for all queries

    D. Monitoring user trace files

    E. All of the above

18. Under which of the following conditions is the tablespace SYSAUX created? (Choose all that apply.)

    A. When the database is created

    B. When you need to use features such as Ultra Search or the EM Repository

    C. When the SYSTEM tablespace can no longer autoextend

    D. When the database is upgraded from a previous version of Oracle

    E. You do not need the SYSAUX tablespace; it is optional

19. Which of the following operations are allowed on the SYSAUX tablespace?

   A. Transporting the SYSAUX tablespace to another database

   B. Renaming the SYSAUX tablespace

   C. Adding a datafile to the SYSAUX tablespace

   D. Dropping the SYSAUX tablespace

   E. Changing the SYSAUX tablespace from SEGMENT SPACE AUTO to SEGMENT SPACE MANUAL

20. Which of the following methods can be used to verify the bigfile tablespace bfile.dbf with the DBVERIFY utility and enable parallel processing?

   A. ```
$ dbv FILE=bfile.dbf START=1 END=25000 &
$ dbv FILE=bfile.dbf START=25000 END=50000 &
$ dbv FILE=bfile.dbf START=50001 &
```

   **B.** `$ dbv FILE=bfile.dbf PARALLEL=3`

   **C.** Parallel processing is automatically enabled for DBVERIFY depending on the value of PARALLEL_MAX_SERVERS.

   **D.** Since a bigfile tablespace has only one datafile, parallel processing cannot be enabled.

   **E.** Parallel processing is automatically enabled for offline datafiles only.

   **F.** ```
$ dbverify FILE=bfile.dbf START=1 END=25000 &
$ dbverify FILE=bfile.dbf START=25000
  END=50000 &
$ dbverify FILE=bfile.dbf START=50001 &
```

Answers to Review Questions

1. B. None of the choices contain an ALTER command that is allowed for hash-partitioned indexes, except for the ALTER INDEX MODIFY PARTITION command with the UNUSABLE option—in other words, marking a partition of a hash-partitioned index as unusable.

2. B, D. Not all bitmap indexes need to be rebuilt after the COMPATIBLE parameter is adjusted, unless they still exhibit a slowdown or get worse. The COMPATIBLE parameter should be set to 10.0.0.0 to take advantage of all enhancements.

3. D. Bigfile tablespaces increase the maximum size of a tablespace to 128TB with a block size of 32KB; therefore, with a block size of 16KB, a bigfile tablespace can be 64TB.

4. C, D. A temporary tablespace group is created when the first temporary tablespace member is added and is deleted when the last member is removed from the group. If a temporary tablespace already exists, it can be added to an existing group with the ALTER TABLESPACE command.

5. B, C, D. Only the system users SYS, SYSTEM, and OUTLN still use the SYSTEM tablespace as their default permanent tablespace.

6. D. In the CREATE DATABASE command, you can only specify DEFAULT TABLESPACE; the PERMANENT keyword is not required nor allowed in the command.

7. E. Of the available answers, only LogMiner can be relocated out of the SYSAUX tablespace.

8. A, D. Both V$TABLESPACE and DBA_TABLESPACES contain a new column called BIGFILE to indicate if the tablespace is a bigfile tablespace. V$DATABASE has no tablespace-specific information; V$DATAFILE contains only information relevant to the datafiles of the tablespace; and DATABASE_PROPERTIES has a row indicating the default tablespace type for the database.

9. B. By setting SKIP_UNUSABLE_INDEXES to TRUE either at the system level or the session level, the optimizer may choose a suboptimal execution plan, but the query will not return an ORA-01502 error message.

10. C. Oracle 10g now supports hash-partitioned global indexes; each partition contains values derived from an internal hash function based on the partitioning key or keys and the number of partitions defined for the global index. Range partitioned global indexes are not new to Oracle 10g. There is no such partitioning method known as global list-hash partitioning.

11. A, D. COPY_FILE copies files on the same server; PUT_FILE copies files to a remote server. Both procedures can copy only binary files. Since PUT_FILE copies to a remote server, it requires a destination server name, unlike COPY_FILE, which copies to a destination on the same server.

12. B. For hash-partitioned indexes, each individual index must be rebuilt individually. Other operations not supported for hash-partitioned indexes are ALTER TABLE SPLIT INDEX PARTITION and ALTER INDEX MODIFY PARTITION.

13. B.   Logically, a temporary tablespace group is equivalent to an individual temporary tablespace. If a user is not assigned a default temporary tablespace, they are assigned the database's default temporary tablespace.

14. B.   With range-partitioned indexes, partition pruning occurs, but only one parallel query process is spawned per partition whereas multiple query processes may be spawned for each pruned partition in a hash-partitioned global index.

15. C, D, E.   Tablespaces that are READ ONLY can be renamed, but the datafile header is not changed. References to the tablespace are updated in an SPFILE if necessary, but a text-based initialization parameter file is not changed.

16. A.   Hash partitioning spreads the activity to more leaf blocks and therefore reduces the contention for a given leaf block in an OLTP environment.

17. A, B.   The DBA can monitor the view DBA_IND_PARTITIONS to see if index partitions become invalid; in addition, the alert log will contain messages when an index has been marked unusable. While EXPLAIN PLAN may alert a user that the index is not being chosen to run the query, it is impractical for the DBA to run the EXPLAIN PLAN command for all user queries. User trace files will not contain messages regarding invalid indexes.

18. A, D.   The SYSAUX tablespace is required for all new Oracle 10g database installations, as well as upgrading a previous version of Oracle to Oracle 10g. The SYSAUX table must exist, even if the applications that use the SYSAUX table are not installed.

19. C.   A datafile can be added to the SYSAUX tablespace, just as any other tablespace, as long as it is a smallfile tablespace. All the other operations listed are not allowed on the SYSAUX tablespace.

20. A.   The DBVERIFY utility, invoked as dbv on every platform, can be spawned multiple times, with each instance of DBVERIFY accessing a different portion of the datafile. No PARALLEL clause exists for DBVERIFY. Since the DBVERIFY utility is an external utility, it does not use database initialization parameters such as PARALLEL_MAX_SERVERS.

Chapter 5

Automated Storage Management

ORACLE DATABASE 10*g* NEW FEATURES FOR ADMINISTRATORS EXAM OBJECTIVES OFFERED IN THIS CHAPTER:

✓ **Space Management**

- Reduce space related error conditions through proactively managing tablespace usage
- Reclaim wasted space from tables and indexes using the segment shrink functionality
- Use the Segment Advisor
- Use the Undo Advisor
- Use sorted hash clusters

✓ **General Storage Enhancement**

- Use the Redo Logfile Size Advisor

✓ **Automatic Storage Management**

- Describe Automatic Storage Management
- Set up initialization parameter files for ASM and database instances
- Execute SQL commands with ASM file names
- Start up and shut down ASM instances
- Administer ASM disk groups
- Use RMAN to migrate your database to ASM

Exam objectives are subject to change at any time without prior notice and at Oracle's sole discretion. Please visit Oracle's training and certification website (http://www.oracle.com/education/certification/) for the most current exam objectives listing.

Oracle Database 10*g* (Oracle 10*g*) provides a number of automated enhancements to help you manage the disk space in the database.

Proactive tablespace monitoring uses the `DBMS_SERVER_ALERT` PL/SQL package to set up thresholds at which you are notified of a potential space issue; ideally, this happens long before a user calls you because they cannot create a table because of lack of space in a tablespace.

To make table access more space efficient and reduce the amount of I/O needed to access a table, Oracle provides segment shrink functionality to compress a table whose data blocks are sparsely populated. The Segment Advisor notifies you of segments, either table or index segments, that would benefit from a segment shrink operation.

Other automated advisors introduced in Oracle 10*g* include the Undo Advisor and the Redo Logfile Size Advisor. The Undo Advisor collects statistics on an ongoing basis to help you size the undo tablespace so that DML transactions can complete successfully while at the same time allowing `SELECT` statements to complete successfully without receiving the all-too-familiar "Snapshot too old" error.

One of the biggest automated storage enhancements introduced in Oracle 10*g* is Automatic Storage Management (ASM). ASM is a cluster file system that can be used either with stand-alone Oracle instances or with Oracle Real Application Clusters (RAC) to provide a vertically integrated subsystem encapsulating a file system, a volume manager, and a fault-tolerant environment specifically designed for Oracle databases. It works in concert with other Oracle features such as Oracle Managed Files (OMF) to not only make disk space management easier but also to enhance the performance of the database by automatically spreading the I/O load across all available hardware devices.

In all of these cases, the Oracle Enterprise Manager (EM) Database Control provides wizards and a graphical interface for these enhancements, making it easy to leverage these enhancements when the command-line syntax is unfamiliar or difficult to remember.

In this chapter, we will review how to set up server alerts, both with the PL/SQL interface and the EM Database Control. We will also show how to identify segments that can benefit from space reclamation using the Segment Advisor and how to shrink these segments with segment shrink operations. We will present a few other enhancements such as sorted hash clusters. Finally, we will provide an in-depth look at ASM along with some comprehensive examples of how it can be used to both ease administrative effort and enhance I/O performance.

Enhancing Space Management

The space management enhancements in Oracle 10*g* fall into the following four general categories:

- Tablespace management
- Segment optimization
- Undo tablespace sizing
- Redo logfile sizing

Oracle 10*g* introduces the package DBMS_SERVER_ALERT to set thresholds at which you'll be notified when the space usage exceeds one of the thresholds. Segment optimization includes the Segment Advisor and segment shrink functionality; segments that inefficiently utilize space are detected with the Segment Advisor and compacted with segment shrink. Finally, the Automatic Workload Repository accumulates information about undo and redo usage to allow the Undo Advisor and the Redo Logfile Size Advisor to provide optimal sizing information for the undo tablespace and redo log files, respectively.

Proactive Tablespace Monitoring

Oracle Database 10*g* manages the disk space in two ways: reactively and proactively. Through database alerts, you are notified of tablespace disk space usage at two different levels: at a warning level and at a critical level. By default, the warning level is 85 percent, and the critical level is 97 percent. While these levels are by definition reactive, they can arguably be considered proactive in that you will have an opportunity to increase the amount of space in the tablespace before it runs out of space.

In a truly proactive manner, Oracle Database 10*g* collects statistics on space usage in the *Automatic Workload Repository (AWR)* at 30-minute intervals to assist you with tablespace and segment growth trend analysis and capacity planning. The AWR collects vital statistics and workload information, including CPU usage, user sessions, I/O usage, and many other metrics at 30-minute intervals and stores them in the SYSAUX tablespace for later analysis.

In the following sections, we will go into some of the details of how Oracle monitors tablespace usage. In addition, we will show you how you can view and modify the alert thresholds, both for an individual tablespace as well as for the database default, via the EM Database Control interface as well as via the PL/SQL package DBMS_SERVER_ALERT. We will also touch upon a special case of tablespace monitoring: undo tablespace monitoring.

Space Usage Monitoring

If a tablespace does not have specific percentage thresholds defined, the database default of 85 percent for the warning level and 97 percent for the critical level apply. You can also change these default thresholds, as you will see in the next couple of sections.

The background process *MMON* checks for tablespace space problems every 10 minutes; alerts are triggered both when a threshold is exceeded and once again when the space usage for a tablespace falls back below the threshold. For example, assume that the default thresholds of 85 percent and 97 percent are in effect. Within a five-minute period, the USERS tablespace reaches 86 percent full, and MMON generates an alert. Fifteen minutes later, the USERS tablespace passes the 97 percent mark and finally reaches 99 percent full, and MMON signals a second alert, this time a critical alert. You allocate a new datafile to the USERS tablespace to bring the overall space usage to 92 percent. The next time MMON checks for space problems in the USERS tablespace, the space usage has fallen back below the 97 percent threshold, and a third alert is sent to denote that the critical alert has been cleared.

For Oracle databases that have been upgraded from a previous version to Oracle 10*g*, all tablespace alerts are off by default.

Alerts are not necessary under a few conditions. For example, tablespaces that are read-only or are offline do not need thresholds defined, as their contents will not increase or decrease while they are read-only or offline.

Some tablespaces are defined as autoextensible; this presents a challenge to tablespace threshold monitoring because even though the space usage of the datafile at a particular point in time may be at a warning or critical level, the datafile will automatically autoextend when it runs out of space. To avoid generating false alerts, thresholds on these tablespaces are computed in one of two ways: based on the maximum size specified when the tablespace was created or the maximum operating system file size, whichever is smaller.

Dictionary-managed tablespaces do not support server-generated alerts, which is yet another good reason to convert tablespaces from a previous version of Oracle to locally managed and to create all new tablespaces as locally managed.

Editing Thresholds with the Enterprise Manager Database Control

You can edit space usage thresholds for tablespaces in one of two ways via the EM Database Control, one from an overall threshold perspective and the other from an individual tablespace perspective.

To access the thresholds from a database-wide point of view, click the Manage Metrics link at the bottom of the EM Database Control database Home tab, and you'll see all possible database alerts listed as in Figure 5.1.

Clicking the Edit Thresholds button brings up the Edit Thresholds screen, where you can change one or more of these thresholds, as you can see in Figure 5.2.

As the tip on the screen indicates, some metrics allow different thresholds for different objects of the same type, such as tablespaces. For instance, if you select the Tablespace Space Used (%) metric (see Figure 5.3) and then click the Specify Multiple Thresholds on the Edit Thresholds screen, you arrive at the Specify Multiple Thresholds: Tablespace Space Used (%) screen, as shown in Figure 5.4.

FIGURE 5.1   All database thresholds

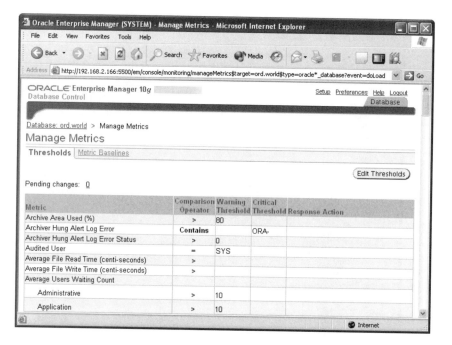

FIGURE 5.2   Editing thresholds

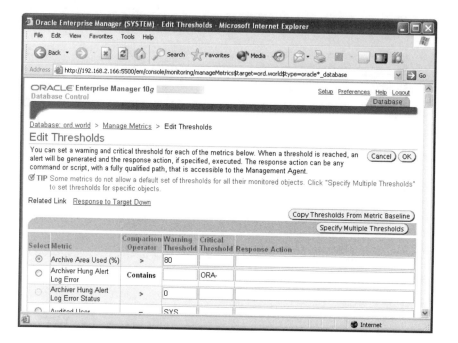

FIGURE 5.3   Selecting the Tablespace Space Used (%) metric

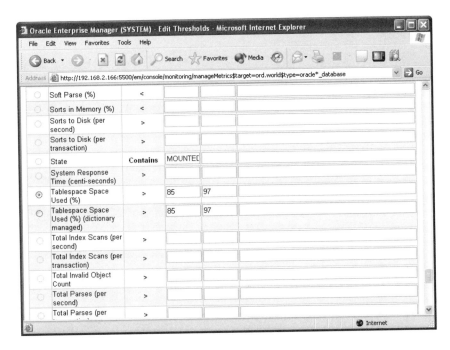

FIGURE 5.4   Altering specific tablespace thresholds

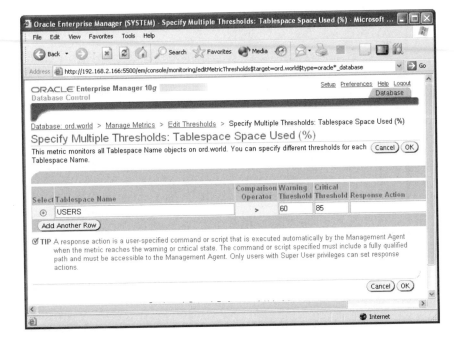

Because the USERS tablespace tends to grow quickly, notice in Figure 5.4 you set the thresholds for the tablespace at 60 percent and 85 percent, a bit lower than the default, so that you will have more time to allocate the space for the USERS tablespace when the alert is generated. Also, note that this screen has a place for a response action: it can range from a script containing a SQL command to automatically freeing up the space in the tablespace or adding a new datafile to the tablespace.

You can also edit the thresholds for a tablespace by clicking the Tablespaces link from the Administration tab on the EM Database Control database Administration page. Clicking the link for the USERS tablespace, you see the general characteristics of the tablespace in Figure 5.5.

Clicking the Thresholds link brings you to the Edit Tablespace: USERS screen (see Figure 5.6). Here, you can see the current space usage for the USERS tablespace and change the thresholds for the warning and critical levels. As with the previous example, the thresholds for the USERS tablespace were changed to 60 percent and 85 percent.

On this same screen, you have the option to change the database-wide defaults by clicking the Modify Database Defaults button, which opens the Modify Database Defaults screen (see Figure 5.7). Using this screen, you can edit the database's default thresholds or disable them completely.

FIGURE 5.5   Tablespace general characteristics

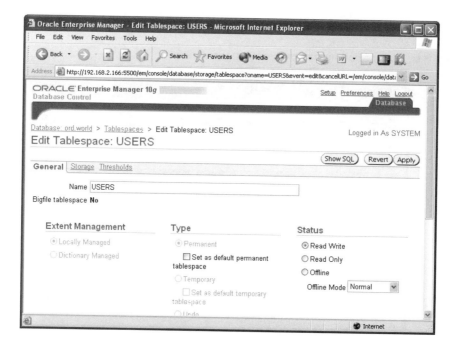

FIGURE 5.6 Editing tablespace thresholds

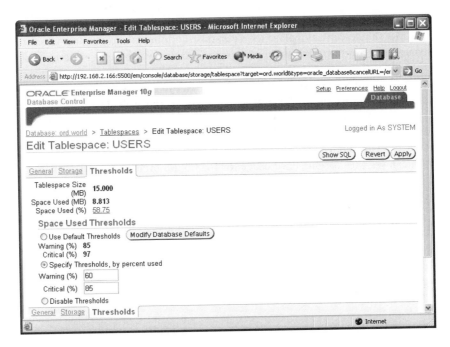

FIGURE 5.7 Editing database default thresholds

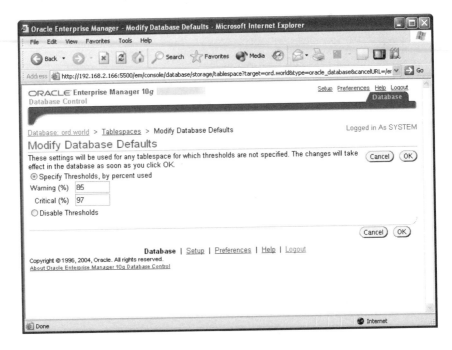

Referring to the Edit Tablespace: USERS screen (shown earlier in Figure 5.6), you want to apply your changes for the USERS tablespace thresholds. But before you do, you want to look at the SQL commands that will be executed by clicking the Show SQL button. As with most EM Database Control screens, you can brush up on the command-line syntax while enjoying the ease of use of a GUI. Figure 5.8 shows the command that will be run when you click the Apply button.

Referring to Figure 5.6, note that the USERS tablespace is already at 58.75 percent full. Let's see what happens when you add a few more segments to the USERS tablespace.

```
SQL> create table oe.customers_archive
  2       tablespace users
  3       as select * from oe.customers;
Table created.
```

The thresholds screen for the USERS tablespace in Figure 5.9 shows that you have not only exceeded the warning level but also the critical level.

Within 10 minutes, the MMON process will notify you of the critical tablespace problem in one of three ways: via the EM Database Control Home tab, via an e-mail message sent to the e-mail address configured when the database was created, or using the script in the Response Action column, if one was specified, shown in Figure 5.4 when the tablespace thresholds were modified.

FIGURE 5.8   Showing SQL for tablespace thresholds

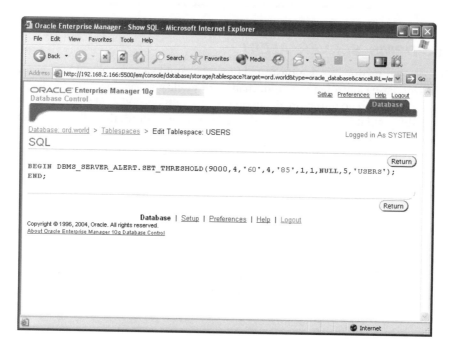

FIGURE 5.9   Viewing current tablespace usage

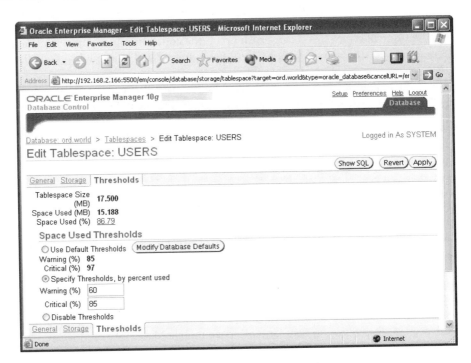

Using *DBMS_SERVER_ALERT*

In the previous section, we demonstrated how you could view the actual SQL commands that the EM Database Control uses to add, change, or modify space usage thresholds. In the following sections, we will go into more detail on how the DBMS_SERVER_ALERT package works. The DBMS_SERVER_ALERT package contains a number of procedures that allows you to set, view, and modify a variety of alert conditions.

For managing space usage alerts, as with every other type of alert, the three procedures available are as follows:

- SET_THRESHOLD
- GET_THRESHOLD
- EXPAND_MESSAGE

SET_THRESHOLD

As the name implies, the SET_THRESHOLD procedure sets the threshold for a particular alert type. Table 5.1 describes the parameters for SET_THRESHOLD.

TABLE 5.1   *SET_THRESHOLD* Parameters

Parameter Name	Description
METRICS_ID	The name of the metric, using an internally defined constant
WARNING_OPERATOR	The comparison operator for comparing the current value with the warning threshold value
WARNING_VALUE	The warning threshold or NULL if no warning threshold exists
CRITICAL_OPERATOR	The comparison operator for comparing the current value with the warning threshold value
CRITICAL_VALUE	The critical threshold or NULL if no critical threshold exists
OBSERVATION_PERIOD	The timer period at which the metrics are computed against the threshold; the valid range is 1 to 60 minutes
CONSECUTIVE_OCCURRENCES	How many times the threshold needs to be exceeded before the alert is issued
INSTANCE_NAME	The name of the instance for which the threshold applies; this value is NULL for all instances in a RAC database and is NULL for database-wide alerts
OBJECT_TYPE	The type of object—for example, a tablespace, session, or service—using a set of internally defined constants
OBJECT_NAME	The name of the object, such as the tablespace name

For monitoring tablespace space usage, only one metric object type is available: the TABLESPACE_PCT_FULL metric. The operators for exceeding a threshold are either OPERATOR_ GE or OPERATOR_GT. OPERATOR_GE indicates that the current value of the metric is compared to the WARNING_VALUE or CRITICAL_VALUE using the greater than or equal to operator (>=); similarly, OPERATOR_GT indicates that the current value of the metric is compared to the WARNING_VALUE or the CRITICAL_VALUE using the greater than operator (>). The object type is always OBJECT_TYPE_TABLESPACE.

Because the USERS2 tablespace in the database is an infrequently used tablespace and not part of the production environment, you want to raise the alert thresholds for space usage to reduce the total number of alerts you receive every day. In the following example, we are changing the warning threshold to 90 percent and the critical threshold to 99 percent. These thresholds

will be compared to the percentage of space used in the USERS2 tablespace every minute, causing an alert the first time the threshold is exceeded for the tablespace USERS2.

```
SQL> execute
  2    dbms_server_alert.set_threshold(
  3    dbms_server_alert.tablespace_pct_full,
  4    dbms_server_alert.operator_ge, 90,
  5    dbms_server_alert.operator_ge, 99,
  6    1, 1, null,
  7    dbms_server_alert.object_type_tablespace,'USERS2');
PL/SQL procedure successfully completed.
```

The new threshold goes into effect immediately. The next time MMON runs, an alert will be generated if the space usage on the USERS2 tablespace is at 90 percent or higher.

GET_THRESHOLD

Similarly, GET_THRESHOLD retrieves the values of a defined alert. Table 5.2 describes the parameters for GET_THRESHOLD.

TABLE 5.2 *GET_THRESHOLD* Parameters

Parameter Name	Description
METRICS_ID	The name of the metric, using an internally defined constant
WARNING_OPERATOR	The comparison operator for comparing the current value with the warning threshold value
WARNING_VALUE	The warning threshold or NULL if no warning threshold exists
CRITICAL_OPERATOR	The comparison operator for comparing the current value with the warning threshold value
CRITICAL_VALUE	The critical threshold or NULL if no critical threshold exists
OBSERVATION_PERIOD	The timer period at which the metrics are computed against the threshold; the valid range is 1 to 60 minutes
CONSECUTIVE_OCCURRENCES	How many times the threshold needs to be exceeded before the alert is issued
INSTANCE_NAME	The name of the instance for which the threshold applies; this value is NULL for all instances in a RAC database

TABLE 5.2   *GET_THRESHOLD* Parameters *(continued)*

Parameter Name	Description
OBJECT_TYPE	The type of object—for example, a tablespace, session, or service—using a set of internally defined constants
OBJECT_NAME	The name of the object, such as the tablespace name

Not surprisingly, the parameters for GET_THRESHOLD are identical to SET_THRESHOLD, except that the values of WARNING_OPERATOR through CONSECUTIVE_OCCURENCES are OUT parameters instead of IN. In the following example, you will retrieve the threshold values you set for the USERS tablespace earlier in this chapter:

```
SQL> begin
  2     dbms_server_alert.get_threshold(
  3      dbms_server_alert.tablespace_pct_full,
  4      :warn_oper, :warn_value, :crit_oper, :crit_value,
  5      :obs_per, :cons_oc, null,
  6      dbms_server_alert.object_type_tablespace, 'USERS');
  7   end;
  8  /

PL/SQL procedure successfully completed.

SQL> print warn_value

WARN_VALUE
--------------------------------
60

SQL> print crit_value

CRIT_VALUE
--------------------------------
85
```

Setting the last parameter to NULL instead of the tablespace name will retrieve the database-wide default values instead of the values for a particular tablespace.

EXPAND_MESSAGE

The EXPAND_MESSAGE procedure is very straightforward, translating a numeric message number to a text format. Table 5.3 describes the parameters for EXPAND_MESSAGE.

TABLE 5.3 *EXPAND_MESSAGE* Parameters

Parameter Name	Description
USER_LANGUAGE	The current session's language
MESSAGE_ID	The alert message ID number
ARGUMENT_1	The first argument returned in the alert message
ARGUMENT_2	The second argument returned in the alert message
ARGUMENT_3	The third argument returned in the alert message
ARGUMENT_4	The fourth argument returned in the alert message
ARGUMENT_5	The fifth argument returned in the alert message

If additional values are returned along with the alert code number, they are specified using ARGUMENT_1 through ARGUMENT_5 and are substituted into the alert message as needed. For server alert message number 6, you can retrieve the text of the message as follows:

```
SQL> select dbms_server_alert.expand_message
  2      (null,6,null,null,null,null,null) alert_msg
  3  from dual;


ALERT_MSG
-----------------------------------
Read and write contention on database
blocks was consuming significant
database time. However, no single
object was the predominant cause for
this contention.
```

Rarely will you have to call EXPAND_MESSAGE; it is primarily used for third-party applications that read alert messages from the alert queue. The EM Database Control automatically retrieves the text of all alert messages.

Undo Tablespace Monitoring

Undo tablespaces are monitored just like any other tablespace: if a specific set of space thresholds is not defined, the database default values are used; otherwise a specific set of thresholds can be assigned.

Running out of space in an undo tablespace, however, may also trigger an "ORA-01555: Snapshot too old" error. Long-running queries that need a read-consistent view of one or more tables can be at odds with ongoing transactions that need undo space. Unless the undo tablespace is defined with the RETENTION GUARANTEE parameter, ongoing DML can use undo space that may be needed for long-running queries. As a result, a "Snapshot too old" error is returned to the user executing the query, and an alert is generated. This alert is also known as a *long query warning alert.*

 This alert may be triggered independently of the space available in the undo
NOTE tablespace if the UNDO_RETENTION initialization parameter is set too low.

Regardless of how often the "Snapshot too old" error occurs, the alert is generated at most once per a 24-hour period. Increasing the size of the undo tablespace or changing the value of UNDO_RETENTION does not reset the 24-hour timer: For example, an alert is generated at 10 a.m. and you add undo space at 11 a.m. The undo tablespace is still too small, and users are still receiving "Snapshot too old" errors at 2 p.m. You will not receive a long query warning alert until 10 a.m. the next day, but chances are you will get a phone call before then!

Segment Management

Oracle 10*g* provides a number of new ways to manage segments in the database. To use disk space more efficiently and to reduce the I/O required to access a segment, segment shrink functionality will compact the space within a segment and optionally move the high watermark (HWM), freeing up space for other segments.

The Segment Advisor, one of many advisors in Oracle 10*g*, can analyze one segment or all the segments within a tablespace and determine if a segment is a good candidate for a segment shrink operation.

Finally, sorted hash clusters is a new way to manage a segment, expanding upon the space efficiency of hash clusters by adding the capability to maintain the sort order of hash table entries, reducing the need for additional sorts and disk space in a query that retrieves rows from a sorted hash cluster in a first-in, first-out (FIFO) manner.

Segment Shrink

If rows were added only to tables, then segment shrink would not be needed; however, deletes and updates to a table, and ultimately the index, leave many blocks with fewer or no rows. While this space can be used by future inserts or updates, you have no guarantee that the space will be reused, if ever. In addition, since the HWM only stays the same or gets larger, full table scans must read every block whether or not it is empty.

In the following sections, we will discuss the benefits of segment shrink; we will also cover a few of the restrictions regarding the types of segments you can shrink and where the segments must reside. Finally, we will provide some practical examples of how segment shrink works, both using the command line and the EM Database Control.

Overview of Segment Shrink

Segment shrink compresses the data blocks in a table or index and optionally moves the HWM down, making the unused space available for other segments in the tablespace. In addition to making full table scans more efficient, a shrunken segment makes even single I/Os for individual data blocks more efficient, since more rows are retrieved for each I/O. Indexes that are shrunk are also more efficient for the same reason: during an index range scan operation, more index entries are read for each I/O, reducing overall I/O for the query.

While chained rows may be eliminated by performing a segment shrink operation, it is not guaranteed that all chained rows will be repaired because not all blocks may be accessed in a segment shrink operation.

Figure 5.10 shows a sparsely populated table segment before and after a shrink operation.

FIGURE 5.10 Segment before and after shrink

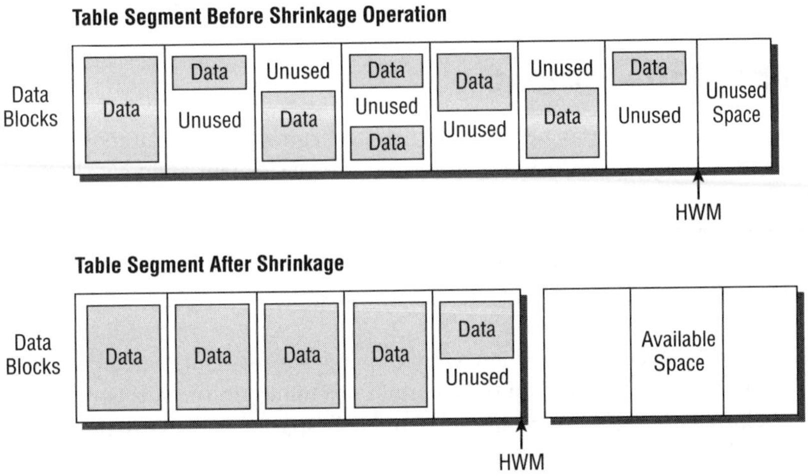

Table Segment Before Shrinkage Operation

Data Blocks | Data | Data | Unused | Data | Data | Unused | Data | Unused Space
Unused | Data | Unused | Data | Data | Unused | Data | Unused

HWM

Table Segment After Shrinkage

Data Blocks | Data | Data | Data | Data | Data / Unused | Available Space

HWM

Before Oracle 10*g*, the HWM could be moved down only if the segment was moved or truncated. While online table redefinition or Create Table As Select (CTAS) operations can provide similar results to segment shrink, those methods must temporarily provide double the amount of space occupied by the table. Segment shrink is online and in place, requiring a negligible amount of extra space and remaining available during the entire operation except for a brief period when the HWM is moved.

Segment Shrink Restrictions and Considerations

Segment shrink operations have one major restriction: Segments managed with freelists cannot be shrunk; in other words, the tablespace containing the segment must be defined with automatic segment space management.

The most common types of segments can be shrunk:

- Heap-organized and index-organized tables

- Indexes

- Partitions and subpartitions

- Materialized views and materialized view logs

Other segment types or segment with specific characteristics cannot be shrunk:

- Clustered tables

- Tables with LONG columns

- Tables with on-commit or ROWID-based materialized views

- LOB segments

- IOT mapping tables or overflow segments

- Tables with function-based indexes

During a segment shrink operation, the ROWID may change for a row when it moves between blocks. Therefore, segments that rely on ROWIDs being constant, such as an application that maintains ROWIDs as pointers in another table, cannot be shrunk. In any case, ROW MOVEMENT must be enabled for table segments that are candidates for shrink operations.

All indexes are maintained and useable both during and after the shrink operation.

Performing Segment Shrink

To perform segment shrink, you can use either SQL commands or the EM Database Control. If you have hundreds of segments to shrink, a series of batch jobs with SQL commands submitted overnight is most likely the best way to perform the operation. For only one or two shrink operations on an occasional basis, the EM Database Control is probably the fastest and easiest to use.

SQL COMMANDS AND SEGMENT SHRINK

As mentioned previously, segment shrink operations may change the ROWID of one or more rows of a table segment. Therefore, row movement on the segment must be enabled before the segment can be shrunk. In the following example, you'll enable row movement for the HR.EMPLOYEES table:

```
SQL> alter table hr.employees enable row movement;
Table altered.
```

The ROW MOVEMENT capability appeared in Oracle 8*i* to allow rows to move between partitions of a partitioned table.

Shrinking the space in a segment is performed as an extension to the ALTER TABLE or ALTER INDEX command, with the SHRINK SPACE clause, as shown here:

```
SQL> alter table hr.employees shrink space;
Table altered.
```

In this example, the table HR.EMPLOYEES is shrunk, and the HWM is moved in the same operation.

Although the table is available for use by all users while the shrink operation is in progress, the I/O throughput may be decreased. Therefore, it may be advantageous to split the operation into two commands using the COMPACT clause to compress the rows without moving the HWM, as shown here:

```
SQL> alter table hr.employees shrink space compact;
Table altered.
```

At a later time, when the database is not as busy, you can complete the rest of the operation by omitting the COMPACT clause.

```
SQL> alter table hr.employees shrink space;
Table altered.
```

Any fragmentation that has occurred in the meantime is addressed, and the HWM is moved. Whether the operation is performed all at once or in two steps, only a small number of rows are locked at any given time. Conversely, a user DML command may lock one or more rows and temporarily prevent segment shrink from completing compaction of the rows. When the HWM is moved, the entire table is locked for a brief amount of time.

Another potential benefit of splitting the operation into two parts is based on PL/SQL code that may have cursors open while the segment is being accessed: with the COMPACT option, all cursors defined on the segment remain valid; without the COMPACT option, all cursors on the segment are invalidated.

Another option available with the ALTER TABLE . . . SHRINK SPACE command is the CASCADE keyword. When CASCADE is specified, all dependent objects, such as indexes, are also shrunk. In the following example, you'll use the CASCADE example to shrink all the indexes defined on the HR.EMPLOYEES table:

```
SQL> alter table hr.employees shrink space cascade;
Table altered.
```

Without the CASCADE keyword, you would have to identify all the indexes defined on the table and execute a series of commands instead of just one command.

```
SQL> select index_name from dba_indexes where
  2      table_name = 'EMPLOYEES' and owner = 'HR';
```

```
INDEX_NAME
------------------------------
EMP_EMAIL_UK
EMP_EMP_ID_PK
EMP_DEPARTMENT_IX
EMP_JOB_IX
EMP_MANAGER_IX
EMP_NAME_IX

6 rows selected.

SQL> alter index hr.emp_email_uk shrink space;
Index altered.

SQL> alter index hr.emp_emp_id_pk shrink space;
Index altered.

SQL> alter index hr.emp_department_ix shrink space;
Index altered.

SQL> alter index hr.emp_job_ix shrink space;
Index altered.

SQL> alter index hr.emp_manager_ix shrink space;
Index altered.

SQL> alter index hr.emp_name_ix shrink space;
Index altered.
```

THE EM DATABASE CONTROL AND SEGMENT SHRINK

Performing segment shrink with the EM Database Control is even easier. From the Administration tab on the EM Database Control database Home tab, click the Tables link under the Schema heading. Search for the tables you want to shrink, and select the Shrink Segment action, as shown in Figure 5.11.

The EM Database Control screen gives you all the options that are available on the command line, including the COMPACT and the CASCADE options (see Figure 5.12).

Another benefit to using the EM Database Control is that the segment shrink operation will be submitted as a job and run in the background, allowing you to immediately perform other tasks with the EM Database Control.

FIGURE 5.11 Selecting tables for segment shrink

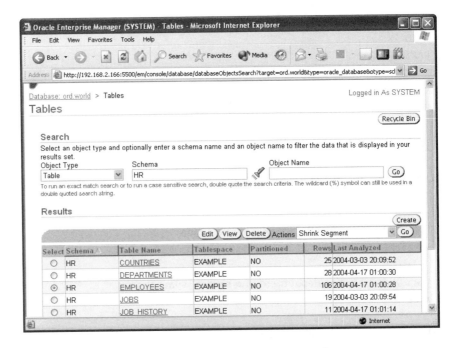

FIGURE 5.12 The EM Database Control segment shrink options

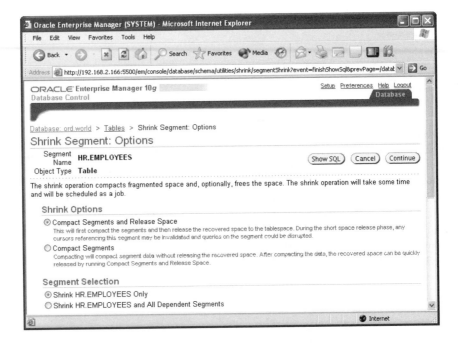

Segment Advisor

Oracle's *Segment Advisor* provides several types of functionality to manage the space occupied by database segments, such as tables and indexes. This functionality is available through both the EM Database Control and PL/SQL procedures.

The Segment Advisor can provide advice regarding a particular table, schema, or tablespace that contains segments that are good candidates for shrink operations; in addition, using the data collected within the AWR, the Growth Trend Report can help predict how much space a segment will occupy based on previous growth patterns. Finally, Segment Resource Estimation can help make preliminary sizing estimates for a table given the column datatypes and the estimated number of rows in the table.

EM Database Control and Segment Advisor

As with nearly all Oracle Database 10*g* features, the EM Database Control provides an intuitive graphical interface to make the most common segment analysis tasks easy to perform. In addition to the ability to perform a complete analysis on all segments within a tablespace, the EM Database Control can use data in the AWR to use segment growth patterns to predict future space usage needs. Plus, the EM Database Control provides a segment resource estimation tool to help size a table's space usage needs even before it is created.

SEGMENT ADVISOR

To use the Segment Advisor, select the Advisor Central link under any tab. Click Segment Advisor, which brings you to the Segment Advisor (see Figure 5.13).

FIGURE 5.13   Segment Advisor

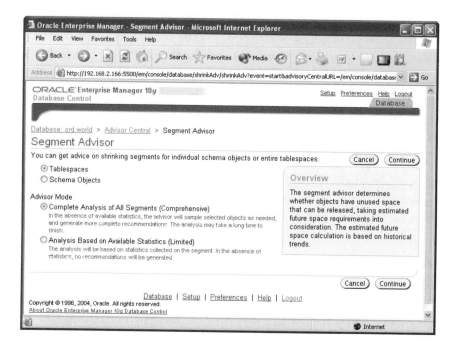

Click Continue, which brings you to the Segment Advisor: Tablespaces screen, where you select the tablespaces to be analyzed (see Figure 5.14). In this example, the USERS tablespace is added to the list.

FIGURE 5.14   Selecting tablespaces for the Segment Advisor

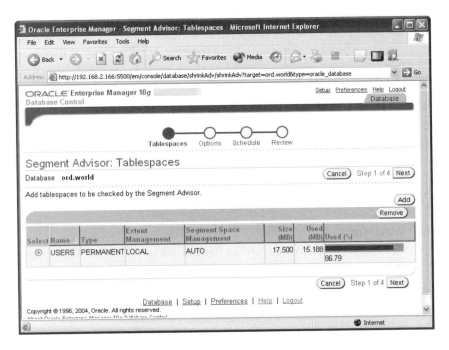

Clicking Next, you can specify how long to run the analysis on the Segment Advisor: Options screen (see Figure 5.15). Since the USERS tablespace is relatively small, you will not specify a time limit; but for much larger tablespaces, you may want to prevent I/O contention, even during a nonpeak time interval, and settle for a limited analysis. In Figure 5.15, the results of the analysis are to be retained for 30 days.

Clicking Next will open the Segment Advisor: Schedule screen (see Figure 5.16). Here, you can set up the task name and the scheduling options; in this example, the job will run immediately.

In the last screen of the Segment Advisor—Segment Advisor: Review—you have one more chance to review the analysis options and to review the SQL commands that will be submitted to perform the analysis. Figure 5.17 shows the summary.

FIGURE 5.15   Segment Advisor options

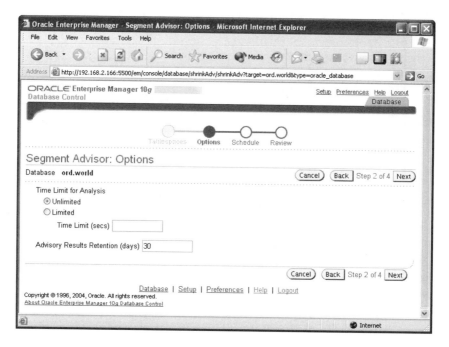

FIGURE 5.16   Task scheduling options

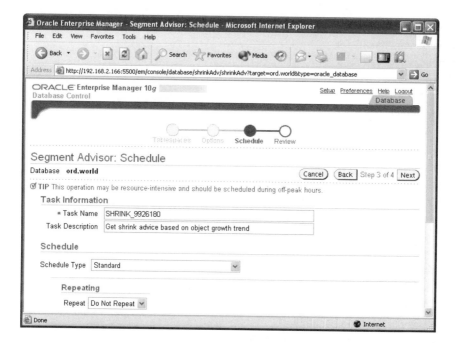

FIGURE 5.17 Segment Advisor task summary

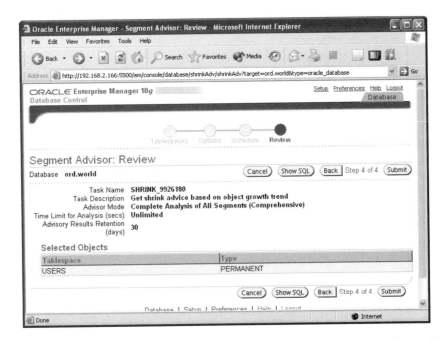

Clicking the Show SQL button, you can review the anonymous PL/SQL procedures that will perform the tasks just configured.

```
DECLARE
taskname varchar2(100);
taskdesc varchar2(128);
task_id number;
object_id number;
advMode varchar2(25);
timeLimit varchar2(25);
numDaysToRetain varchar2(25);
objectName varchar2(100);
objectType varchar2(100);
BEGIN
taskname := 'SHRINK_9926180';
taskdesc :='Get shrink advice based on object
      growth trend';
advMode :='COMPREHENSIVE';
numDaysToRetain :='30';
dbms_advisor.create_task('Segment Advisor',?,
      taskname,taskdesc,NULL);
dbms_advisor.create_object(taskname, 'TABLESPACE',
```

```
        'USERS', ' ', ' ', NULL, object_id);

dbms_advisor.set_task_parameter(taskname,
        'MODE', advMode);
dbms_advisor.set_task_parameter(taskname,
        'RECOMMEND_ALL', 'TRUE');
dbms_advisor.set_task_parameter(taskname,
        'DAYS_TO_EXPIRE',  numDaysToRetain);

END;

DECLARE
taskname varchar2(100);
BEGIN
taskname := 'SHRINK_9926180';
dbms_advisor.reset_task(taskname);
dbms_advisor.execute_task(taskname);
END;
```

Clicking Submit submits the SQL commands to be run. A few moments later, click the Refresh button on the Advisor Central screen. In Figure 5.18, notice that the Segment Advisor task has completed.

FIGURE 5.18   Advisor Central Task Completion

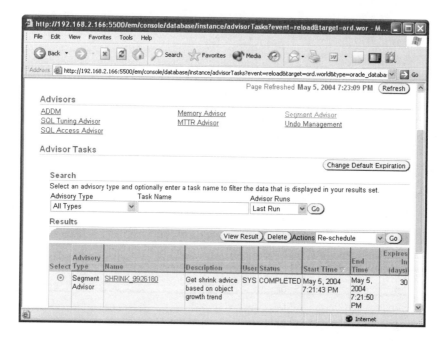

Click the link containing the job name of the task you just ran—in this case, SHRINK_ 9926180—to see that there are no segments in the USERS tablespace that can benefit from a shrink operation early in the evening (see Figure 5.19).

Emphasizing the dynamic nature of space management in any database, you may run the analysis again and find that there is now a table that can benefit from a shrink operation: the HR.EMPLOYEES_HIST table. You can shrink the HR.EMPLOYEES_HIST table by selecting one of the recommendations on the bottom of the results screen for task name SHRINK_6871100 in Figure 5.20. These options are identical to those used in Figures 5.11 and 5.12, except that you can perform a shrink operation on more than one table at a time.

GROWTH TREND REPORT

The *Growth Trend Report*, based on the AWR data collected at 30-minute intervals or when space-related server-generated alerts are triggered, helps to predict future growth trends for selected segments. Given the predicted growth pattern, you know when space will need to be added to support segment growth.

To access the Growth Trend Report, start at the Administration tab, and click the Tables link under the Schema heading. In Figure 5.21, you want to predict the growth of the HR.EMPLOYEES_HIST table.

Clicking the table name, select the Segments tab and enter a future date to see when more space should be allocated to the segment. In the example, enter **5/16/04** and click the Refresh button. Figure 5.22 shows the results of the analysis.

FIGURE 5.19   Segment Advisor recommendations at 7:21 p.m.

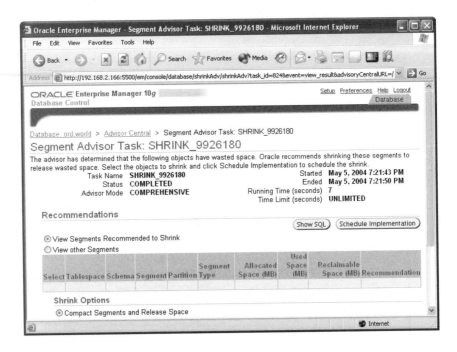

FIGURE 5.20 Segment Advisor recommendations at 11:12 p.m.

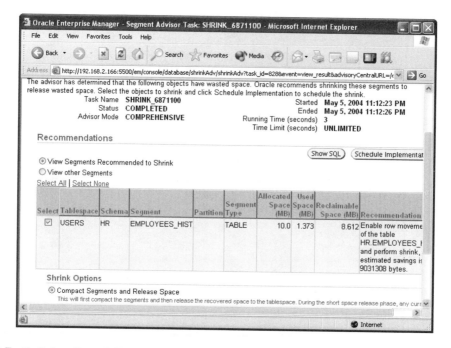

FIGURE 5.21 Growth Trend Report segment selection

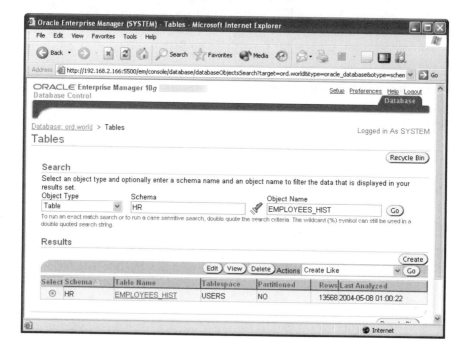

FIGURE 5.22 Growth Trend Report segment analysis

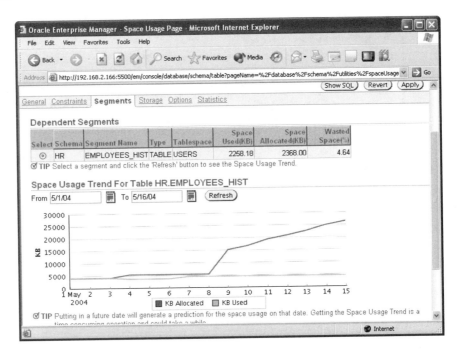

This report was run on May 8, 2004, and although the overall usage is predicted to be relatively flat, the Segment Advisor has predicted that amount of space allocated for the segment will rise dramatically within the next week.

As with the Segment Advisor, the Growth Trend Report is supported only for locally managed tablespaces.

SEGMENT RESOURCE ESTIMATION

The *Segment Resource Estimation* tool gives you a good estimate of how much disk space a new segment will require. While it is not directly a part of the Segment Advisor, it is a point-in-time analysis tool to give you sizing advice so you can estimate space usage for a new segment given the columns, datatypes, sizes, and PCTFREE for the segment.

To use Segment Resource Estimation, start at the Administration tab from the EM Database Control home page, and click the Tables link. Instead of searching for an existing table, click the Create link. In Figure 5.23, a table called HR.EMPLOYEE_REVIEW with three columns is created.

Clicking the Estimate Table Size link, enter an estimated row count of **5000** for the first year, and click the Estimated Table Size link again. In Figure 5.24, see that 5,000 rows of the table will occupy just more than 13MB, with the allocated space at 14MB.

FIGURE 5.23   EM Database Control: Create Table

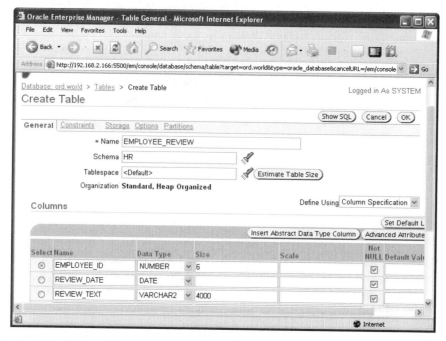

FIGURE 5.24   Estimating table size

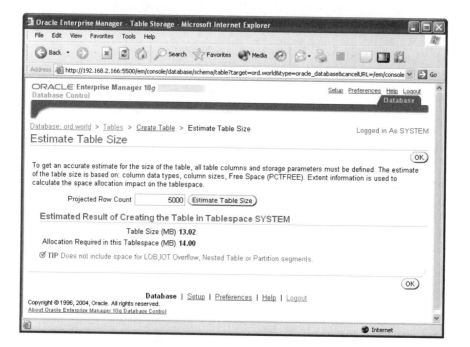

Segment Advisor within *PL/SQL*

Although the Segment Advisor is easy to use from the EM Database Control, sometimes you may want to perform some of these operations from within a PL/SQL procedure. You may want to automate the advisors in a nightly batch job, for example.

To access Segment Advisor functionality within PL/SQL, use the package DBMS_ADVISOR. Since DBMS_ADVISOR is used with the AWR for all advisors within the Oracle 10*g* advisory framework, not all procedures within DBMS_ADVISOR are applicable to all advisors, and the parameters for a particular procedure will also vary depending on the advisor. For the Segment Advisor, you typically use the following procedures:

- CREATE_TASK
- CREATE_OBJECT
- SET_TASK_PARAMETER
- EXECUTE_TASK
- DELETE_TASK
- CANCEL_TASK

We will explain each of these procedures in the following sections, as well as provide two examples of analyzing a table using the Segment Advisor and implementing Segment Advisor recommendations.

CREATE_TASK

As the name implies, CREATE_TASK creates a new advisor task. For the Segment Advisor, the procedure requires the text string Segment Advisor, a variable to contain the assigned task number, a task name, and a description. Here is an example:

```
dbms_advisor.create_task
        ('Segment Advisor', :task_id, task_name,
            'Free space in OE.CUSTOMERS', NULL);
```

After the task is created, the assigned task number is stored in the SQL*Plus variable task_id. The unique task name is automatically generated if you leave task_name null; otherwise Oracle will use the task name specified. In both cases, the task name must be unique among all tasks created by a particular user. Assigning a task name or description can help identify the results when querying the advisor-related data dictionary views.

CREATE_OBJECT

The CREATE_OBJECT procedure specifies an object to be analyzed within the task. For the Segment Advisor, the object to be analyzed is typically a table or index; for other advisors, such as the SQL Access Advisor, the object to be analyzed is a SQL statement. To create a task object that will analyze the OE.CUSTOMERS table, use the following:

```
dbms_advisor.create_object
        (task_name, 'TABLE', 'OE', 'CUSTOMERS',
            NULL, NULL, object_id);
```

The PL/SQL variable `object_id` is assigned a unique identifier for this object. The NULL parameters are not needed for advisor objects within the Segment Advisor.

SET_TASK_PARAMETER

The SET_TASK_PARAMETER procedure allows you to specify any additional parameters needed to run the analysis for the database objects specified with CREATE_OBJECT. In the case of the Segment Advisor, you have a Boolean parameter called RECOMMEND_ALL that you set to TRUE for the analysis on the table.

```
dbms_advisor.set_task_parameter
     (task_name, 'RECOMMEND_ALL', 'TRUE');
```

When set to TRUE, the parameter RECOMMEND_ALL provides recommendations for all objects specified by the user, not just the objects eligible for segment shrink. Objects not eligible for segment shrink include objects such as tables that don't have ROW MOVEMENT enabled or tables that reside in tablespaces that do not have automatic segment space management enabled.

EXECUTE_TASK

Once all the tasks are created and their parameters specified, EXECUTE_TASK performs the analysis. The only parameter specified is the task name generated in a previous step in your code by the CREATE_TASK procedure.

```
dbms_advisor.execute_task(task_name);
```

To view the status of the executing task, especially for a long-running task such as a full tablespace analysis, the data dictionary view DBA_ADVISOR_LOG contains the task name, the start and stop time, the current status, and estimated percent complete for the task.

DELETE_TASK

The DELETE_TASK procedure removes a single Advisor task from the AWR, even if the task has not been executed yet.

```
dbms_advisor.delete_task(task_name);
```

CANCEL_TASK

CANCEL_TASK will terminate a currently executing task. Because all Advisor procedures are synchronous, the CANCEL_TASK procedure must be called from a different session for the same user account.

```
dbms_advisor.cancel_task(task_name);
```

In the next section, we will put all these procedures together in two anonymous PL/SQL blocks.

ANALYZING A TABLE USING SEGMENT ADVISOR

The code examples that follow call these procedures to determine if the table OE.CUSTOMERS needs to be shrunk.

The last change to the table OE.CUSTOMERS added a field called CUST_COMMENTS to contain any suggestions, complaints, or information about the customer.

```
SQL> alter table oe.customers
          add (cust_comments varchar2(2000));
Table altered.
```

After a number of months using this new field, you realize that the comments should be broken out by date and decide to create a new table to hold a time stamp and a comment for that particular date and time. After the new table is implemented and the comments moved to the new table, drop the column from the OE.CUSTOMERS table.

```
SQL> alter table oe.customers drop (cust_comments);
Table altered.
```

You realize that this table may be a good candidate for segment shrink and decide to use a PL/SQL procedure to analyze the table.

```
-- SQL*Plus variable to contain the task ID
variable task_id number

-- PL/SQL block follows
declare
    task_name  varchar2(100);
    task_descr varchar2(100);
    object_id  number;
begin
    task_name := ''; -- unique name generated
                     -- by create_task
    task_descr := 'Free space in OE.CUSTOMERS';
    dbms_advisor.create_task
        ('Segment Advisor', :task_id, task_name,
          task_descr, NULL);
    dbms_advisor.create_object
        (task_name, 'TABLE', 'OE', 'CUSTOMERS',
            NULL, NULL, object_id);
    dbms_advisor.set_task_parameter
        (task_name, 'RECOMMEND_ALL', 'TRUE');
    dbms_advisor.execute_task(task_name);
end;

PL/SQL procedure successfully completed.
```

Using the SQL*Plus PRINT command, you will identify the task ID number to use in your data dictionary queries.

```
SQL> print task_id

    TASK_ID
----------
        680
```

Using this task number, you can query the data dictionary view DBA_ADVISOR_FINDINGS to see the recommendations:

```
SQL> select owner, task_id, task_name, type,
  2          message, more_info from dba_advisor_findings
  3          where task_id = 680;

OWNER         TASK_ID TASK_NAME    TYPE
---------- ---------- ------------ -----------
SYS               680 TASK_680     INFORMATION

MESSAGE
----------------------------------------------------------
Enable row movement of the table OE.CUSTOMERS and perform
shrink, estimated savings is 775878 bytes.

MORE_INFO
----------------------------------------------------------
Allocated Space:983040: Used Space:205110:
Reclaimable Space :775878:


1 row selected.
```

Note that the Segment Advisor reminds you to enable row movement for the table; it is a required prerequisite before a shrink can be performed. The space in each block occupied by the CUST_COMMENTS column is unused, and by compacting this table you can reclaim almost 80 percent of the allocated space.

IMPLEMENTING SEGMENT ADVISOR RECOMMENDATIONS

To shrink the table OE.CUSTOMERS, you need to enable row movement.

```
SQL> alter table oe.customers enable row movement;
Table altered.
```

Because you have no applications or triggers that depend on the ROWIDs of this table, you will leave row movement enabled.

Next, perform the shrink operation; the data dictionary view DBA_ADVISOR_ACTIONS provides the SQL for the shrink operation.

```
SQL> select task_id, task_name, command, attr1 from
  2        dba_advisor_actions where task_id = 680;

  TASK_ID TASK_NAME    COMMAND
---------- ------------ ---------------
      680 TASK_680     SHRINK SPACE


ATTR1
----------------------------------------------------------
alter table "OE"."CUSTOMERS" shrink space

1 row selected.

SQL> alter table "OE"."CUSTOMERS" shrink space;
Table altered.
```

The shrink operation requires a negligible amount of disk space, and the table is available to other users during the shrink operation except for a short period of time at the end of the shrink operation to move the HWM. Because this table is relatively large, you may consider performing this operation in two steps, the first time with the COMPACT option to free the space and the second time without the COMPACT option to move the HWM.

Finally, remove this task from the AWR, as you have no need to retain this information once the segment has been shrunk.

```
SQL> execute dbms_advisor.delete_task('TASK_680');

PL/SQL procedure successfully completed.
```

Sorted Hash Clusters

Sorted hash clusters extend the functionality of hash clusters that have been available since Oracle 8*i* by maintaining a sort order for rows that are retrieved by the same cluster key. In heap-organized tables and traditional hash clusters, the order in which rows are returned is not under user control and depends on internal algorithms and the relative physical location of data blocks on disk. For each hash cluster key, Oracle maintains a list of rows sorted by one or more sort columns.

Maintaining the sort order of rows upon insert incurs minimal overhead but provides a tangible benefit when the data is updated or queried: CPU time and private memory requirements are reduced because no additional sorts are required, as long as the ORDER BY clause references the sort key columns or the sort key columns prefix; in fact, the ORDER BY clause is not required

if you are only retrieving rows for a single hash cluster key and want to order the rows by the sort key columns. This processing implies another valuable benefit of sorted hash clusters in that it supports FIFO processing: the sort order within each cluster key guarantees that rows are returned in the same order in which they were inserted.

 For queries with an ORDER BY using nonprefixed sort key columns, you can use a traditional index to maintain the performance of queries on the table in the cluster.

A couple of examples will help demonstrate the value of sorted hash clusters. In the sample order entry system, you want to make sure to process the customer orders for a given customer in the order in which the orders were received without the extra overhead of sorting on the time stamp of the order.

The first step is to create a single table sorted hash cluster, as follows:

```
create cluster order_cluster
    (customer_number        number,
     order_timestamp        timestamp sort)
hashkeys 10000000
single table hash is customer_number
size 500;
```

You expect at most 10 million unique customer numbers, and the average size of the row in your cluster will be 500 bytes. The next step is to create the order table itself.

```
create table orders
    (cust_number        number,
     order_date         timestamp,
     order_number       number,
     spec_instr         varchar2(1000))
cluster order_cluster(cust_number, order_date);
```

Note that the names of the cluster keys do not have to match as long as the relative positions match and the datatypes are compatible.

Next, add a few orders with the following INSERT statements. Depending on when the orders were submitted and the locations where the orders are placed, the orders may not necessarily be inserted in chronological order:

```
insert into orders values(3045,
    timestamp'2004-05-05 15:04:14',
    405584,'Reorder from last month');
insert into orders values(1958,
    timestamp'2004-05-05 15:05:01',
    348857,'New customer');
insert into orders values(3045,
    timestamp'2004-05-04  9:26:59',
```

```
     938477,'GGT Promotion');
insert into orders values(3045,
     timestamp'2004-05-07 12:33:23',
     703749,'');
insert into orders values(3045,
     timestamp'2004-05-02 19:47:09',
     389233,'Needs order in time for Mothers Day');
```

However, because you are storing the orders in a sorted hash cluster, they are automatically maintained in the order of the sort key columns for each customer without specifying an ORDER BY clause:

```
SQL> select cust_number,
  2      to_char(order_date,'yyyy-mm-dd hh:mi pm')
  3                order_date,
  4      order_number, spec_instr
  5  from orders where cust_number = 3045;


CUST_NUMBER ORDER_DATE           ORDER_NUMBER SPEC_INSTR
----------- -------------------- ------------ ------------
       3045 2004-05-02 07:47 pm        389233 Needs order i
                                              n time for Mo
                                              thers Day

       3045 2004-05-04 09:26 am        938477 GGT Promotion
       3045 2004-05-05 03:04 pm        405584 Reorder from
                                              last month

       3045 2004-05-07 12:33 pm        703749


4 rows selected.


Execution Plan
----------------------------------------------------------
   0      SELECT STATEMENT Optimizer=ALL_ROWS
              (Cost=0 Card=4 Bytes=2164)
   1    0   TABLE ACCESS (HASH) OF 'ORDERS'
                  (CLUSTER (HASH))
```

Even though you had no ORDER BY clause, all rows selected using a specific customer number (in this case, customer number 3045) will automatically return the rows ordered by the sort keys because the sorted hash cluster maintains the order within the customer number cluster key.

To make sure that the new access path is used, you must ensure that the cost-based optimizer is enabled and statistics are gathered for the table. An EXPLAIN PLAN of any query on a sorted hash cluster will show an access method of TABLE ACCESS HASH without a sort operation. Also, any queries must use an equality predicate; if the previous query was instead written as follows, then an ORDER BY clause would be necessary to keep the rows in the desired sequence:

```
SQL> select cust_number,
  2        to_char(order_date,'yyyy-mm-dd hh:mi pm')
  3              order_date,
  4        order_number, spec_instr
  5  from orders where cust_number >= 3045;
```

CUST_NUMBER	ORDER_DATE	ORDER_NUMBER	SPEC_INSTR
3045	2004-05-05 03:04 pm	405584	Reorder from last month
3045	2004-05-04 09:26 am	938477	GGT Promotion
3045	2004-05-07 12:33 pm	703749	
3045	2004-05-02 07:47 pm	389233	Needs order i n time for Mo thers Day

```
4 rows selected.
```

Similarly, if you accessed the table using a reference to only the SPEC_INSTR column in the WHERE clause, a sort would be necessary to return the rows in the desired order.

To make further improvements in performance, you may consider creating a multitable hash cluster to hold both the orders and the order items, but for now the improvements in processing orders alone will help you avoid new hardware acquisitions for a few months.

Miscellaneous Space Management Features

Two other automated space management features fall into the advisor category: the Undo Advisor and the Redo Logfile Size Advisor. In both cases, Oracle collects statistics on a continuous basis to help you size the undo tablespace and the size of the online redo logs to enhance both performance and availability.

Undo Advisor

The EM Database Control *Undo Advisor* helps you determine how large of an undo tablespace is necessary given adjustments to the undo retention setting.

In Figure 5.25, the Undo Advisor screen shows the autotuned undo retention of 753 minutes and an undo tablespace size of 94MB. If you don't expect your undo usage to increase or you don't expect to need to retain undo information longer than 753 minutes, you can drop the size of the undo tablespace if it is significantly more than 94MB.

FIGURE 5.25   Autotuned undo retention settings

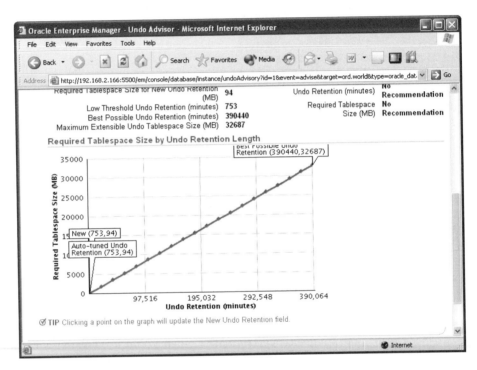

On the other hand, if you expect to need undo information for longer than 753 minutes, you can see the impact of this increase by either entering a new value for undo retention and refreshing the page or by clicking a point on the graph corresponding to the estimated undo retention. Figure 5.26 shows the results of increasing the undo retention to 103,204 minutes.

To support an undo retention setting of 103,204 minutes given the current undo usage, the undo tablespace will have to be increased in size to 8,625MB, or 8.625GB.

Redo Logfile Size Advisor

The *Redo Logfile Size Advisor* provides an automatic method for sizing redo log files. In general, redo logs should be sized large enough so that checkpoints do not occur too frequently; if the logs switch more often than every 20 minutes, performance of the database may be affected. On the other hand, redo logs that are too big may impact disk space usage without a measurable benefit.

FIGURE 5.26   Specifying new undo retention settings

![Oracle Enterprise Manager - Undo Advisor screenshot showing analysis and recommendations for undo retention settings with a graph of Required Tablespace Size by Undo Retention Length]

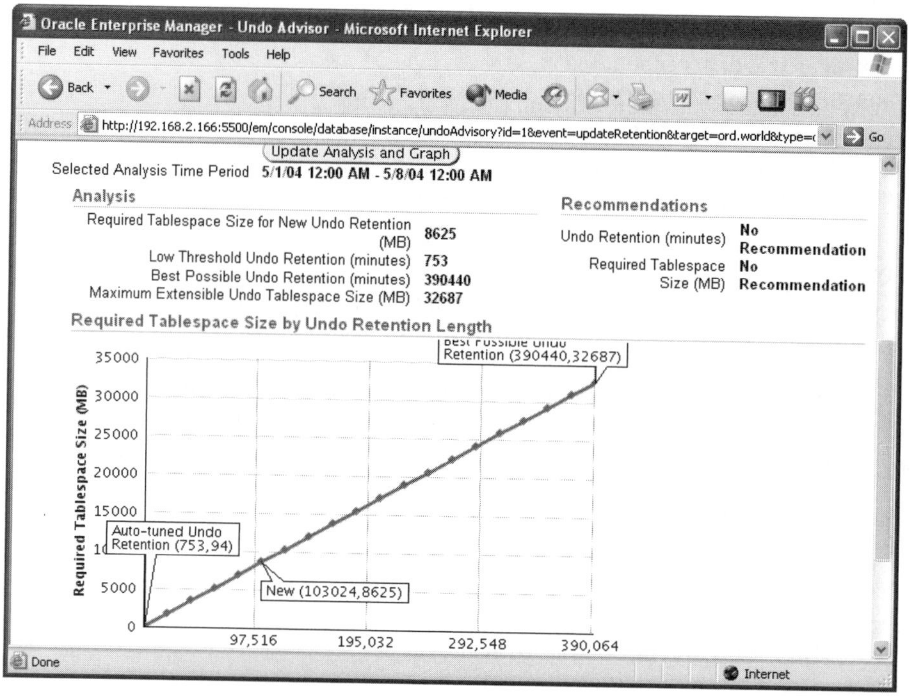

In addition to the amount of redo generated, the other factor that directly affects the proper sizing of the redo logs is the initialization parameter FAST_START_MTTR_TARGET. A parameter available since Oracle 9*i*, FAST_START_MTTR_TARGET indicates the time, in seconds, that instance recovery should take after a crash or instance failure. For the Redo Logfile Size Advisor to provide a value for the optimal log file size, this parameter must be nonzero. As one of Oracle's automated advisors, statistics for optimizing the redo log file size are collected automatically and continually.

The initialization parameters FAST_START_IO_TARGET and LOG_CHECKPOINT_INTERVAL can still be specified to control instance recovery, but setting either of these parameters disables FAST_START_MTTR_TARGET.

In the sample order database, the redo log files are sized as follows:

```
SQL> select member from v$logfile;

MEMBER
----------------------------------------
```

```
/u07/oradata/ord/redo03.log
/u07/oradata/ord/redo02.log
/u07/oradata/ord/redo01.log
/u08/oradata/ord/redo01.log
/u08/oradata/ord/redo02.log
/u08/oradata/ord/redo03.log

6 rows selected.

SQL> !ls -l /u07/oradata/ord/redo03.log
-rw-r-----    1 oracle   oinstall 10486272 Apr 20 14:01
                       /u07/oradata/ord/redo03.log
```

The redo log files are sized at 10MB each, the default size for redo log files when the database was created. The parameter FAST_START_MTTR_TARGET is set for 30 seconds; in other words, you don't want instance recovery to take more than 30 seconds after a crash or instance failure.

```
SQL> show parameter fast_start_mttr_target

NAME                             TYPE          VALUE
-------------------------------- ----------- ---------------
fast_start_mttr_target           integer       30
SQL>
```

You have two ways to retrieve the optimal log file size calculated by the Redo Logfile Size Advisor: using a new column in the view V$INSTANCE_RECOVERY or using the EM Database Control. The view V$INSTANCE_RECOVERY contains a new column, OPTIMAL_LOGFILE_SIZE, which recommends a minimum size for the redo logfiles.

```
SQL> select optimal_logfile_size from v$instance_recovery;
OPTIMAL_LOGFILE_SIZE
--------------------
                  49


1 row selected.
```

Given the current log file size of 10MB, you should probably increase the log file size to at least 49MB to reduce the number of log file switches.

Using the EM Database Control, you can retrieve the same information via a graphical interface. In Figure 5.27, review the Redo Log Groups screen containing the number and size of each redo log file.

In the drop-down list on the right, select Sizing Advice, and click Go. Figure 5.28 shows the recommendation for the redo log file size, which coincidentally corresponds with the information obtained from the view V$INSTANCE_RECOVERY.

FIGURE 5.27   Redo Log Groups screen

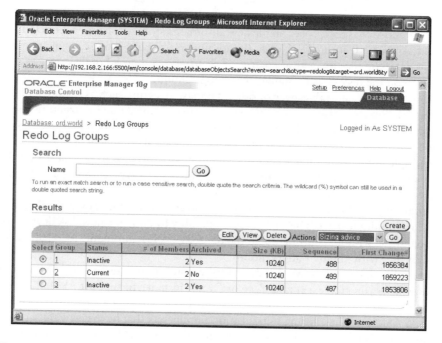

FIGURE 5.28   Redo log group sizing advice

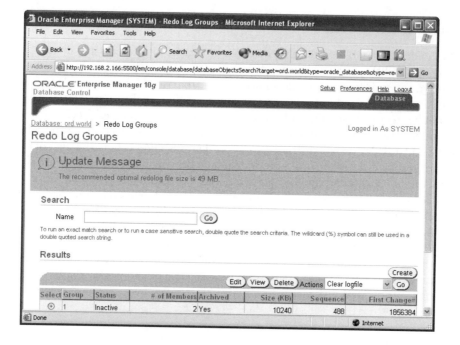

Automatic Storage Management

While this entire chapter focuses on the new automated storage features in Oracle 10g, the most automated storage feature, *ASM*, eases the administrative burden of managing potentially thousands of database files by instead creating *disk groups*, composed of disk devices and the files that reside on the disk devices managed as a logical unit.

When creating a new tablespace or other database structure such as a control file or redo log file, you can specify a disk group as the storage area for the database structure instead of an operating system file. ASM takes the ease of use of OMF and combines it with mirroring and striping features to provide a robust file system and logical volume manager that can even support multiple nodes in an Oracle RAC. ASM eliminates the need to purchase a third-party logical volume manager. To provide further benefits beyond a typical third-party logical volume manager, ASM stripes files, not logical volumes.

In addition, ASM not only enhances performance by automatically spreading database objects over multiple devices but increases availability by allowing new disk devices to be added to the database without shutting down the database; ASM automatically rebalances the distribution of files with minimal intervention.

In the following sections, we will delve further into the architecture of ASM. In addition, we will show how you create a special type of Oracle instance to support ASM as well as how to start up and shut down an ASM instance. We will review the new initialization parameters related to ASM and the existing initialization parameters that have new values to support an ASM instance. Finally, we will use some raw disk devices on a development Unix server to demonstrate how disk groups are created and maintained.

ASM Architecture

ASM divides the datafiles and other database structures into extents and divides the extents among all the disks in the disk group to enhance both performance and reliability. Instead of mirroring entire disk volumes, ASM mirrors the database objects to provide the flexibility to mirror or stripe the database objects differently depending on their type. Optionally, the objects may not be striped at all if the underlying disk hardware is already RAID enabled, for example.

Automatic rebalancing is another key feature of ASM. When you need an increase in disk space, you can add disk devices to a disk group, and ASM moves a proportional number of files from one or more existing disks to the new disks to maintain the overall I/O balance across all disks. This happens in the background while the database objects contained in the disk files are still online and available to users. If the impact to the I/O subsystem is high during a rebalance operation, the speed at which the rebalance occurs can be reduced using an initialization parameter.

As mentioned earlier in the chapter, ASM supports virtually all Oracle object types as well as RAC, eliminating the need to use any other logical volume manager or cluster file system. Figure 5.29 shows an example of a database that contains tablespaces consisting of files both from a traditional file system and from an ASM disk group and another database that allocates all datafiles from an ASM disk group.

FIGURE 5.29 Tablespaces using ASM and traditional datafiles

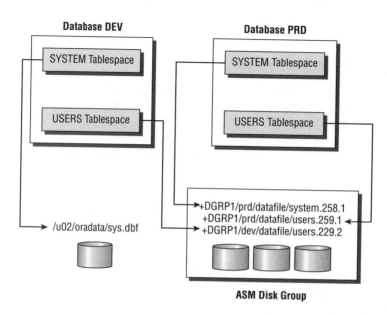

Note that the example in Figure 5.29 shows that more than one database may allocate files from the same ASM disk group. An ASM file is always spread over all ASM disks in the ASM group; an ASM disk belongs to only one ASM disk group.

 ASM disks are partitioned in units of 1MB each.

ASM requires a special type of Oracle instance to provide the interface between a traditional Oracle instance and the file system; the ASM software components are shipped with the database and are always available as a selection when choosing the storage type for the SYSTEM, SYSAUX, and other default tablespaces when the database is created.

 We'll show how an ASM instance is created in the next section.

Using ASM does not, however, preclude you from mixing ASM disk groups with manual Oracle datafile management techniques, but the ease of use and performance of ASM makes a strong case for eventually converting all your storage to ASM disk groups.

Two new background processes support ASM instances: *RBAL* and *ORBn*. RBAL coordinates the disk activity for disk groups, and ORBn, where *n* can be from 0 to 9, performs the actual extent movement between disks in the disk groups.

For databases that use ASM disks, two new background processes also exist: OSMB and RBAL. OSMB performs the communication between the database and the ASM instance, and RBAL performs the open and close of the disks in the disk group on behalf of the database.

Creating an ASM Instance

ASM requires a dedicated instance to manage the disk groups. An ASM instance generally has a smaller memory footprint in the range of 60MB to 100MB and is automatically configured when ASM is specified as the database's file storage option when installing the Oracle software and an existing ASM instance does not already exist (see Figure 5.30).

As an example, suppose your Linux server has a number of raw disk devices with the capacities listed in Table 5.4.

You will use these raw devices to create, alter, and delete ASM disk groups throughout the rest of this chapter.

Configure the first disk group within the Oracle Universal Installer (OUI), as shown in Figure 5.31.

The name of the first disk group is DATA1, and you will be using /dev/raw/raw1 and /dev/raw/raw2 to create the normal redundancy disk group. After the database is created, both the regular instance and the ASM instance are started.

FIGURE 5.30 Specifying ASM for database file storage

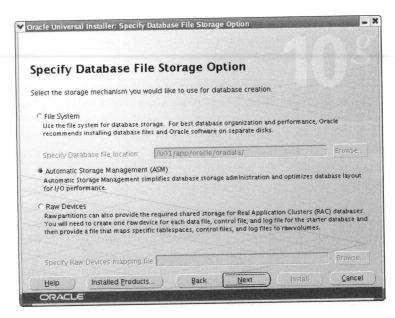

TABLE 5.4   Sample Raw Devices and Capacities

Device Name	Capacity
/dev/raw/raw1	8GB
/dev/raw/raw2	8GB
/dev/raw/raw3	6GB
/dev/raw/raw4	6GB
/dev/raw/raw5	6GB
/dev/raw/raw6	6GB

An ASM instance has a few other unique characteristics. While it does have an initialization parameter file and a password file, it has no data dictionary, and therefore all connections to an ASM instance are via SYS and SYSTEM using operating system authentication only. Disk group commands such as CREATE DISKGROUP, ALTER DISKGROUP, and DROP DISKGROUP are valid only from an ASM instance. Finally, an ASM instance is always in a NOMOUNT state, since it does not have a control file.

FIGURE 5.31   Specifying disk group member disks

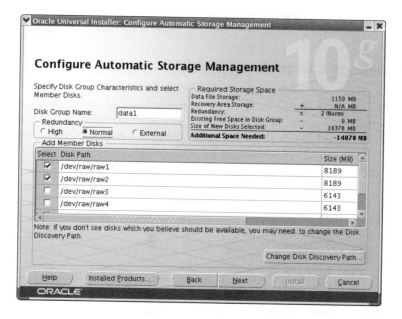

ASM Instance Characteristics

ASM instances cannot be accessed using the variety of methods available with a traditional database. In the following sections, we will talk about the privileges available to you that connect with SYSDBA and SYSOPER privileges. We will also distinguish an ASM instance by the new and expanded initialization parameters available only for an ASM instance. Finally, we will present the procedures for starting and stopping an ASM instance along with the dependencies between ASM instances and the database instances they serve.

Accessing an ASM Instance

As mentioned earlier in the chapter, an ASM instance does not have a data dictionary, so access to the instance is restricted to users who can authenticate with the operating system—in other words, connecting as SYSDBA or SYSOPER by an operating system user that is in the dba group.

Users who connect to an ASM instance as SYSDBA can perform all ASM operations, such as creating and deleting disk groups as well as adding and removing disks from disk groups.

The SYSOPER users have a much more limited set of commands available in an ASM instance. In general, the commands available to SYSOPER commands give only enough privileges to perform routine operations for an already configured and stable ASM instance. The list that follows contains the operations available as SYSOPER:

- Starting up and shutting down an ASM instance
- Mounting or dismounting a disk group
- Altering a disk group's disk status to ONLINE or OFFLINE
- Rebalancing a disk group
- Performing an integrity check of a disk group
- Accessing V$ASM_* dynamic performance views

ASM Initialization Parameters

A number of initialization parameters either are specific to ASM instances or have new values within an ASM instance. An SPFILE is highly recommended over an initialization parameter file for an ASM instance: for example, parameters such as ASM_DISKGROUPS will automatically be maintained when a disk group is added or dropped, potentially freeing you from ever having to manually change this value.

We will discuss the various parameters in the following sections.

INSTANCE_TYPE

For an ASM instance, the INSTANCE_TYPE parameter has a value of ASM. The default, for a traditional Oracle instance, is RDBMS.

DB_UNIQUE_NAME

The default value for the DB_UNIQUE_NAME parameter is +ASM and is the unique name for a group of ASM instances within a cluster or on a single node; the default value needs to be modified only if you're trying to run multiple ASM instances on a single node.

ASM_POWER_LIMIT

To ensure that rebalancing operations do not interfere with ongoing user I/O, the ASM_POWER_ LIMIT parameter controls how fast rebalance operations occur. The values range from 1 to 11, with 11 being the highest possible value; the default value is 1 (low I/O overhead). Since this is a dynamic parameter, you may set this to a low value during the day and set it higher overnight whenever a disk rebalancing operation must occur.

ASM_DISKSTRING

The ASM_DISKSTRING parameter specifies one or more strings, which are operating system dependent, to limit the disk devices that can be used to create disk groups. If this value is NULL, all disks visible to the ASM instance are potential candidates for creating disk groups.

Here is the value for the development server:

```
SQL> show parameter asm_diskstring

NAME                    TYPE        VALUE
----------------------- ----------- -------------------
asm_diskstring          string      /dev/raw/*
```

When creating disk groups, the only disks available on this server are raw disks.

ASM_DISKGROUPS

The ASM_DISKGROUPS parameter specifies a list containing the names of the disk groups to be automatically mounted by the ASM instance at startup or by the ALTER DISKGROUP ALL MOUNT command. Even if this list is empty at instance startup, any existing disk group can be manually mounted.

LARGE_POOL_SIZE

The LARGE_POOL_SIZE parameter is useful for both regular and ASM instances; however, this pool is used differently for an ASM instance. All internal ASM packages are executed from this pool, so this parameter should be set to at least 8MB.

ASM Instance Startup and Shutdown

An ASM instance is started much like a database instance, except that the STARTUP command defaults to STARTUP MOUNT. Since there is no control file, database, or data dictionary to mount, the ASM disk groups are mounted instead of a database. STARTUP NOMOUNT starts up the instance but does not mount any ASM disks. In addition, you can specify STARTUP RESTRICT to temporarily prevent database instances from connecting to the ASM instance to mount disk groups.

Performing a SHUTDOWN command on an ASM instance performs the same SHUTDOWN command on any database instances using the ASM instance; before the ASM instance finishes a shutdown, it waits for all dependent databases to shut down. The only exception to this is if you use the SHUTDOWN ABORT command on the ASM instance, the ASM instance does not pass the ABORT command to the dependent databases; however, all dependent databases immediately perform a SHUTDOWN ABORT because there is no longer an ASM instance available to manage the database's storage.

For multiple ASM instances sharing disk groups, such as in a RAC environment, the failure of an ASM instance does not cause the database instances to fail. Instead, another ASM instance performs a recovery operation for the failed instance.

ASM Dynamic Performance Views

A few new dynamic performance views are associated with ASM instances. The contents of these views varies depending on whether they are displaying data for an ASM instance or a standard, non-ASM (RDBMS) instance. Table 5.5 contains the common ASM-related dynamic performance views.

 We'll provide further explanation where appropriate later in this chapter for some of these views.

TABLE 5.5 ASM Dynamic Performance Views

View Name	Contents In ASM Instance	Contents In RDBMS Instance
V$ASM_DISK	One row for each disk discovered by an ASM instance, whether used by a disk group or not.	One row for each disk in use by the instance.
V$ASM_DISKGROUP	One row for each disk group containing general characteristics of the disk group.	One row for each disk group in use whether mounted or not.
V$ASM_FILE	One row for each file in every mounted disk group.	Not used.
V$ASM_OPERATION	One row for each executing long running operation in the ASM instance.	Not used.
V$ASM_TEMPLATE	One row for each template in each mounted disk group in the ASM instance.	One row for each template for each mounted disk group.
V$ASM_CLIENT	One row for each database using disk groups managed by the ASM instance.	One row for the ASM instance if any ASM files are open.
V$ASM_ALIAS	One row for every alias in every mounted disk group.	Not used.

ASM Filenames

All ASM files are OMF, so the details of the actual filename within the disk group is not needed for most administrative functions. When an object in an ASM disk group is dropped, the file is automatically deleted. Certain commands will expose the actual filenames, such as ALTER DATABASE BACKUP CONTROLFILE TO TRACE, as well as some data dictionary views. For example, the data dictionary view V$DATAFILE shows the actual filenames within each disk group.

```
SQL> select file#, name, blocks from v$datafile;

   FILE# NAME                                       BLOCKS
------- ------------------------------------- ---------
       1 +DATA1/rac0/datafile/system.256.1          57600
       2 +DATA1/rac0/datafile/undotbs1.258.1         3840
       3 +DATA1/rac0/datafile/sysaux.257.1          44800
       4 +DATA1/rac0/datafile/users.259.1             640
       5 +DATA1/rac0/datafile/example.269.1         19200
       6 +DATA2/rac0/datafile/users3.256.1          12800

6 rows selected.
```

ASM filenames can be one of six different formats. In the sections that follow, we'll give an overview of the different formats and the context where they can be used: either as a reference to an existing file, during a single-file creation operation, or during a multiple-file creation operation.

Fully Qualified Names

Fully qualified ASM filenames are used only when referencing an existing file. A fully qualified ASM filename has the format

+*group*/*dbname*/*file type*/*tag.file.incarnation*

where *group* is the disk group name, *dbname* is the database to which the file belongs, *file type* is the Oracle file type, *tag* is the type-specific information about the specific file type, and the *file.incarnation* pair ensures uniqueness. An example of an ASM file for the USERS3 tablespace is as follows:

+DATA2/rac0/datafile/users3.256.1

The disk group name is +DATA2, the database name is rac0, it's a datafile for the USERS3 tablespace, and the file number/incarnation pair 256.1 ensures uniqueness if you decide to create another ASM datafile for the USERS3 tablespace.

Numeric Names

Numeric names are used only when referencing an existing ASM file. It allows you to refer to an existing ASM file by only the disk group name and the file number/incarnation pair. The numeric name for the ASM file in the previous section is as follows:

```
+DATA2.256.1
```

Alias Names

You can use an alias either when referencing an existing object or when creating a single ASM file. Using the ALTER DISKGROUP ADD ALIAS command, you can create a more user-friendly name for an existing or a new ASM file; they are distinguishable from regular ASM filenames because they do not end in a dotted pair of numbers (the file number/incarnation pair). In the following example, we create a directory object to the **data2** diskgroup, then we use the ALTER DISKGROUP ADD ALIAS command to create a more user-friendly alias in the newly created directory object to point to a fully qualified datafile name.

```
SQL> alter diskgroup data2
  2     add directory '+data2/redempt';

Diskgroup altered.
SQL> alter diskgroup data2
  2     add alias '+data2/redempt/users.dbf'
  3     for '+data2/rac0/datafile/users3.256.1';

Diskgroup altered.

SQL>
```

Alias with Template Names

You can use an alias with a template only when creating a new ASM file. Templates provide a shorthand way of specifying a file type and a tag when creating a new ASM file.

 The "ASM File Types and Templates" section covers default ASM templates.

An example of an alias using a template for a new tablespace in the +DATA2 disk group is as follows:

```
SQL> create tablespace users4 datafile
  2     '+data2/uspare(datafile)';
Tablespace created.
```

Incomplete Names

You can use an incomplete filename format either for single file or for multiple file creation operations. You specify only the disk group name, and you use a default template depending on the type of file, as shown here:

```
SQL> create tablespace users5 datafile '+data1';
Tablespace created.
```

Incomplete Names with Template

As with incomplete ASM filenames, you can use an incomplete filename with a template for single-file or multiple-file creation operations. Regardless of the actual file type, the template name determines the characteristics of the file.

Even though you are creating a tablespace, the characteristics of a `tempfile` are used instead as the attributes for the datafile, as shown here:

```
SQL> create tablespace users6 datafile '+data1(tempfile)';
Tablespace created.
```

ASM File Types and Templates

ASM supports all types of files used by the database except for files such as operating system executables. Table 5.6 contains the complete list of ASM file types; *File Type* and *Tag* are those presented previously for ASM filenaming conventions.

TABLE 5.6   ASM File Types

Oracle File Type	File Type	Tag	Default Template
Control files	controlfile	cf (control file) or bcf (backup control file)	CONTROLFILE
Datafiles	datafile	*tablespace name.file#*	DATAFILE
Online logs	online_log	log_*thread#*	ONLINELOG
Archive logs	archive_log	parameter	ARCHIVELOG
Temp files	temp	*tablespace name.file#*	TEMPFILE
RMAN datafile backup piece	backupset	Client specified	BACKUPSET

TABLE 5.6   ASM File Types *(continued)*

Oracle File Type	File Type	Tag	Default Template
RMAN incremental backup piece	backupset	Client specified	BACKUPSET
RMAN archivelog backup piece	backupset	Client specified	BACKUPSET
RMAN datafile copy	datafile	*tablespace name.file#*	DATAFILE
Initialization parameters	init	spfile	PARAMETERFILE
Broker config	drc	drc	DATAGUARDCONFIG
Flashback logs	rlog	*thread#_log#*	FLASHBACK
Change tracking bitmap	ctb	bitmap	CHANGETRACKING
Auto backup	autobackup	Client specified	AUTOBACKUP
Data Pump dumpset	dumpset	dump	DUMPSET
Cross-platform datafiles			XTRANSPORT

Table 5.7 presents the default ASM file templates referenced in the Default Template column of Table 5.6.

TABLE 5.7   ASM File Templates

System Template	External Redundancy	Normal Redundancy	High Redundancy	Striping
CONTROLFILE	Unprotected	Two-way mirroring	Three-way mirroring	Fine
DATAFILE	Unprotected	Two-way mirroring	Three-way mirroring	Coarse
ONLINELOG	Unprotected	Two-way mirroring	Three-way mirroring	Fine
ARCHIVELOG	Unprotected	Two-way mirroring	Three-way mirroring	Coarse

TABLE 5.7 ASM File Templates *(continued)*

System Template	External Redundancy	Normal Redundancy	High Redundancy	Striping
TEMPFILE	Unprotected	Two-way mirroring	Three-way mirroring	Coarse
BACKUPSET	Unprotected	Two-way mirroring	Three-way mirroring	Coarse
XTRANSPORT	Unprotected	Two-way mirroring	Three-way mirroring	Coarse
PARAMETERFILE	Unprotected	Two-way mirroring	Three-way mirroring	Coarse
DATAGUARDCONFIG	Unprotected	Two-way mirroring	Three-way mirroring	Coarse
FLASHBACK	Unprotected	Two-way mirroring	Three-way mirroring	Fine
CHANGETRACKING	Unprotected	Two-way mirroring	Three-way mirroring	Coarse
AUTOBACKUP	Unprotected	Two-way mirroring	Three-way mirroring	Coarse
DUMPSET	Unprotected	Two-way mirroring	Three-way mirroring	Coarse

The mirroring options in the High Redundancy column of Table 5.7 are discussed in the next section under Disk Group Architecture.

When a new disk group is created, a set of ASM file templates copied from the default templates in Table 5.4 is saved with the disk group; as a result, individual template characteristics can be changed and apply only to the disk group where they reside. In other words, the DATAFILE system template in disk group +DATA1 may have the default coarse striping, but the DATAFILE template in disk group +DATA2 may have fine striping. You can create your own templates in each disk group as needed.

When an ASM datafile is created with the DATAFILE template, by default the datafile is 100MB, the datafile is autoextensible, and the maximum size is unlimited.

Administering ASM Disk Groups

Using ASM disk groups benefits you in a number of ways: I/O performance is improved, availability is increased, and the ease with which you can add a disk to a disk group or add an entirely new disk group enables you to manage many more databases in the same amount of time. Understanding the components of a disk group as well as correctly configuring a disk group is an important goal for a successful DBA.

In the following sections we will delve more deeply into the details of the structure of a disk group. Also, we will review the different types of administrative tasks related to disk groups and show how disks are assigned to failure groups, how disk groups are mirrored, and how disk groups are created, dropped, and altered. We will also briefly review the EM Database Control interface to ASM.

Disk Group Architecture

As defined earlier in this chapter, a *disk group* is a collection of physical disks managed as a unit. Every ASM disk, as part of a disk group, has an ASM disk name that is either assigned by the DBA or automatically assigned when it is assigned to the disk group.

Files in a disk group are striped on the disks using either coarse striping or fine striping. *Coarse striping* spreads files in units of 1MB each across all disks. Coarse striping is appropriate for a system with a high degree of concurrent small I/O requests, such as an OLTP environment. Alternatively, *fine striping* spreads files in units of 128KB and is appropriate for traditional data warehouse environments or OLTP systems with low concurrency and maximizes response time for individual I/O requests.

Failure Groups and Disk Group Mirroring

Before defining the type of mirroring within a disk group, you must group disks into failure groups. A *failure group* is one or more disks within a disk group that share a common resource, such as a disk controller, whose failure would cause the entire set of disks to be unavailable to the group. In most cases, an ASM instance does not know the hardware and software dependencies for a given disk. Therefore, unless you specifically assign a disk to a failure group, each disk in a disk group is assigned to its own failure group.

Once the failure groups have been defined, you can define the mirroring for the disk group; the number of failure groups available within a disk group can restrict the type of mirroring available for the disk group. The following three types of mirroring are available:

External redundancy *External redundancy* requires only one failure group and assumes that the disk is not critical to the ongoing operation of the database or that the disk is managed externally with high-availability hardware such as a RAID controller.

Normal redundancy *Normal redundancy* provides two-way mirroring and requires at least two failure groups within a disk group. The failure of one of the disks in a failure group does not cause any downtime for the disk group or any data loss other than a slight performance hit for queries against objects in the disk group.

High redundancy *High redundancy* provides three-way mirroring and requires at least three failure groups within a disk group. The failure of disks in two out of the three failure groups is for the most part transparent to the database users as in normal redundancy mirroring.

Mirroring is managed at a very low level; extents, not disks, are mirrored. In addition, each disk will have a mixture of both primary and mirrored (secondary and tertiary) extents on each disk. While there is a slight overhead incurred for managing mirroring at the extent level, it provides the advantage of spreading the load from the failed disk to all other disks instead of a single disk.

Disk Group Dynamic Rebalancing

Whenever the configuration of a disk group changes, whether it is adding or removing a failure group or a disk within a failure group, *dynamic rebalancing* occurs automatically to proportionally reallocate data from other members of the disk group to the new member of the disk group. This rebalance occurs while the database is online and available to users; any impact to ongoing database I/O can be controlled by adjusting the value of the initialization parameter ASM_POWER_LIMIT to a lower value.

Not only does dynamic rebalancing free you from the tedious and often error-prone task of identifying hot spots in a disk group, it also provides an automatic way to migrate an entire database from a set of slower disks to a set of faster disks while the entire database remains online during the entire operation. The faster disks are added as two or more new failure groups in an existing disk group and the automatic rebalance occurs. The failure groups containing the slower disks are dropped, leaving a disk group with only fast disks. To make this operation even faster, both the ADD and DROP operations can be initiated within the same ALTER DISKGROUP command.

Creating and Deleting Disk Groups

Sometimes you may want to create a new disk group with high redundancy to hold tablespaces for a new gift card redemption application. Using the view V$ASM_DISK, you can view all disks discovered using the initialization parameter ASM_DISKSTRING along with the status of the disk—in other words, whether it is assigned to an existing disk group or it is unassigned. Here is how you do that:

```
SQL> select group_number, disk_number, name,
  2        failgroup, create_date, path from v$asm_disk;


GROUP_ DISK_
NUMBER NUMBER NAME        FAILGROUP  CREATE_DA PATH

------ ------ ---------- ---------- --------- ---------
    0     0                                    /dev/raw/
                                               raw6
    0     1                                    /dev/raw/
                                               raw5
    0     2                                    /dev/raw/
                                               raw4
    0     3                                    /dev/raw/
                                               raw3
```

```
1        1 DATA1_0001 DATA1_0001 18-APR-04 /dev/raw/
                                                    raw2
1        0 DATA1_0000 DATA1_0000 18-APR-04 /dev/raw/
                                                    raw1

6 rows selected.

SQL>
```

Out of the six disks available for ASM, only two of them are assigned to a single disk group, each in their own failure group. You can obtain the disk group name from the view V$ASM_DISKGROUP.

```
SQL> select group_number, name, type, total_mb, free_mb
  2    from v$asm_diskgroup;

GROUP_NUMBER NAME          TYPE    TOTAL_MB   FREE_MB
------------ ------------- ------ ---------- ----------
           1 DATA1         NORMAL      16378      14024

SQL>
```

Note that if you had a number of ASM disks and disk groups, you could have joined the two views on the GROUP_NUMBER column and filtered the query result by GROUP_NUMBER. Also, you see from V$ASM_DISKGROUP that the disk group DATA1 is a NORMAL REDUNDANCY group consisting of two disks.

Your first step is to create the disk group.

```
SQL> create diskgroup data2 high redundancy
  2    failgroup fg1 disk '/dev/raw/raw3' name d2a
  3    failgroup fg2 disk '/dev/raw/raw4' name d2b
  4    failgroup fg3 disk '/dev/raw/raw5' name d2c
  5    failgroup fg4 disk '/dev/raw/raw6' name d2d;

Diskgroup created.

SQL>
```

Looking at the dynamic performance views, you see the new disk group available in V$ASM_DISKGROUP and the failure groups in V$ASM_DISK.

```
SQL> select group_number, name, type, total_mb, free_mb
  2    from v$asm_diskgroup;
```

```
GROUP_NUMBER NAME          TYPE    TOTAL_MB   FREE_MB
------------ ------------  ------  ---------- ----------
           1 DATA1         NORMAL     16378      14024
           2 DATA2         HIGH       24572      24420

SQL> select group_number, disk_number, name,
  2        failgroup, create_date, path from v$asm_disk;

GROUP_ DISK_
NUMBER NUMBER NAME        FAILGROUP  CREATE_DA PATH
------ ------ ----------  ---------- --------- ---------
     2      3 D2D         FG4        11-MAY-04 /dev/raw/
                                               raw6
     2      2 D2C         FG3        11-MAY-04 /dev/raw/
                                               raw5
     2      1 D2B         FG2        11-MAY-04 /dev/raw/
                                               raw4
     2      0 D2A         FG1        11-MAY-04 /dev/raw/
                                               raw3
     1      1 DATA1_0001 DATA1_0001 18-APR-04 /dev/raw/
                                               raw2
     1      0 DATA1_0000 DATA1_0000 18-APR-04 /dev/raw/
                                               raw1

6 rows selected.

SQL>
```

However, if disk space is tight, you do not need four members; for a high-redundancy disk group, only three failure groups are necessary, so the disk group is dropped and re-created with only three members.

```
SQL> drop diskgroup data2;

Diskgroup dropped.
```

If the disk group had any database objects other than disk group metadata, you would have to specify INCLUDING CONTENTS in the DROP DISKGROUP command. This is an extra safeguard to make sure that disk groups with database objects are not accidentally dropped. Here is how you do that:

```
SQL> create diskgroup data2 high redundancy
  2     failgroup fg1 disk '/dev/raw/raw3' name d2a
```

```
 3    failgroup fg2 disk '/dev/raw/raw4' name d2b
 4    failgroup fg3 disk '/dev/raw/raw5' name d2c;

Diskgroup created.

SQL> select group_number, disk_number, name,
 2          failgroup, create_date, path from v$asm_disk;
```

GROUP_ NUMBER	DISK_ NUMBER	NAME	FAILGROUP	CREATE_DA	PATH
0	3			11-MAY-04	/dev/raw/ raw6
2	2	D2C	FG3	11-MAY-04	/dev/raw/ raw5
2	1	D2B	FG2	11-MAY-04	/dev/raw/ raw4
2	0	D2A	FG1	11-MAY-04	/dev/raw/ raw3
1	1	DATA1_0001	DATA1_0001	18-APR-04	/dev/raw/ raw2
1	0	DATA1_0000	DATA1_0000	18-APR-04	/dev/raw/ raw1

```
6 rows selected.

SQL>
```

Now that the configuration of the new disk group has been completed, you can create a tablespace in the new disk group from the database instance.

```
SQL> create tablespace users3 datafile '+DATA2';
Tablespace created.
```

Since ASM files are OMF, no other datafile characteristics need to be specified when creating the tablespace.

Altering Disk Groups

You can add and drop disks from a disk group; also, you can alter most characteristics of a disk group without re-creating the disk group or impacting user transactions on objects in the disk group.

When a disk is added to a disk group, a rebalance operation is performed in the background after the new disk is formatted for use in the disk group. As mentioned earlier in this chapter, the initialization parameter ASM_POWER_LIMIT controls the speed of the rebalance.

Continuing with the example in the previous section, suppose you decide to improve the I/O characteristics of the disk group DATA1 by adding the last available raw disk to the disk group as follows:

```
SQL> alter diskgroup data1
  2     add failgroup d1fg3 disk '/dev/raw/raw6' name d1c;


Diskgroup altered.
```

The command returns immediately, and the format and rebalance continues in the background. You then check the status of the rebalance operation by checking V$ASM_OPERATION.

```
SQL> select group_number, operation, state, power, actual,
  2     sofar, est_work, est_rate, est_minutes
  3  from v$asm_operation;
```

GROUP_ NUMBER	OPERA	STAT	POWER	ACTUA	SOFAR	EST_WORK	EST_RATE	EST_ MIN
1	REBAL	RUN	1	1	3	964	60	16

This output shows that with a POWER setting of 1, the ASM operation is expected to take approximately 16 minutes more to complete. Since the estimate is a bit higher than you expected, you decide to allocate more resources to the rebalance operation and change the power limit for this particular rebalance operation.

```
SQL> alter diskgroup data1 rebalance power 8;


Diskgroup altered.
```

Checking the status of the rebalance operation confirms that the estimated time for completion in the column EST_MINUTES has been reduced to 4 minutes instead of 16.

```
SQL> select group_number, operation, state, power, actual,
  2     sofar, est_work, est_rate, est_minutes
  3  from v$asm_operation;
```

GROUP_ NUMBER	OPERA	STAT	POWER	ACTUA	SOFAR	EST_WORK	EST_RATE	EST_ MIN
1	REBAL	RUN	8	8	16	605	118	4

About four minutes later, you check the status once more.

```
SQL> /
```

```
no rows selected
```

Finally, you can confirm the new disk configuration from the V$ASM_DISK and V$ASM_DISKGROUP views.

```
SQL> select group_number, disk_number, name,
  2    failgroup, create_date, path from v$asm_disk;
```

GROUP_ NUMBER	DISK_ NUMBER	NAME	FAILGROUP	CREATE_DA	PATH
1	2	D1C	D1FG3	11-MAY-04	/dev/raw/ raw6
2	2	D2C	FG3	11-MAY-04	/dev/raw/ raw5
2	1	D2B	FG2	11-MAY-04	/dev/raw/ raw4
2	0	D2A	FG1	11-MAY-04	/dev/raw/ raw3
1	1	DATA1_0001	DATA1_0001	18-APR-04	/dev/raw/ raw2
1	0	DATA1_0000	DATA1_0000	18-APR-04	/dev/raw/ raw1

```
6 rows selected.
```

```
SQL> select group_number, name, type, total_mb, free_mb
  2      from v$asm_diskgroup;
```

GROUP_NUMBER	NAME	TYPE	TOTAL_MB	FREE_MB
1	DATA1	NORMAL	22521	20116
2	DATA2	HIGH	18429	18279

```
SQL>
```

Note that the disk group is still normal redundancy, even though it has three failure groups. However, the I/O performance of SELECT statements against objects in the disk group is improved because of additional copies of extents available in the disk group.

🌐 **Real World Scenario**

Mixing Disk Types within Disk Groups

For our shop floor scheduling and trouble ticket system, we wanted to improve the response time for technicians who checked the status of a repair job, as the application issuing the queries against the database were taking up to 10 seconds during the first shift. To help alleviate the problem, we noticed that we had two spare disk drives in the server running the Oracle 10*g* instance and put the disks to good use by using them in another failure group for the existing disk group.

After only a few minutes of testing, the performance of the queries got worse instead of better in many cases. Upon further investigation, we discovered why the extra disk drives in the server were not used for the database: They were older, slower disks, and as a rule of thumb a disk group should not mix disk drives of different performance levels. Depending on which disk the database object's extents are mapped to, the I/O response time will vary dramatically and may actually be slower than using only the faster disks.

One situation exists where this configuration is temporarily an acceptable configuration: when converting a disk group from slower disks to faster disks. As the faster disks are added, the disk group rebalances, and once the rebalance operation is complete, the slower disks can be dropped from the disk group.

Other disk group ALTER commands are as follows:

ALTER DISKGROUP ... DROP DISK   This removes a disk from a failure group within a disk group and performs an automatic rebalance.

ALTER DISKGROUP ... DROP ... ADD   This drops a disk from a failure group and adds another disk in the same command.

ALTER DISKGROUP ... MOUNT   This makes a disk group available to all instances.

ALTER DISKGROUP ... DISMOUNT   This makes a disk group unavailable to all instances.

ALTER DISKGROUP ... CHECK ALL   This verifies the internal consistency of the disk group.

Using the EM Database Control with ASM Disk Groups

You can also use the EM Database Control to administer disk groups. For a database that uses ASM disk groups, the link Disk Groups under the Administration tab brings you to a login screen for the ASM instance, as shown in Figure 5.32. Remember that authentication for an ASM instance uses operating system authentication only.

After authentication with the ASM instance, you can perform the same operations that you performed earlier in this chapter at the command line: mounting and dismounting disk groups, adding disk groups, adding or deleting disk group members, and so forth. Figure 5.33 shows the ASM administration screen, and Figure 5.34 shows the statistics and options for the disk group DATA1.

FIGURE 5.32   ASM instance authentication

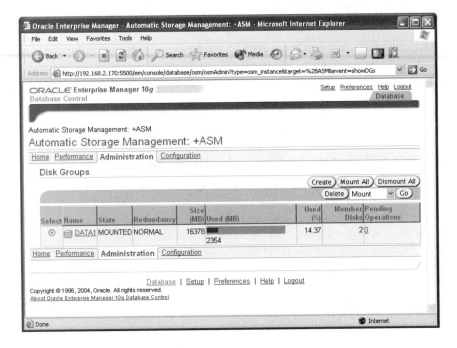

FIGURE 5.33   ASM administration screen

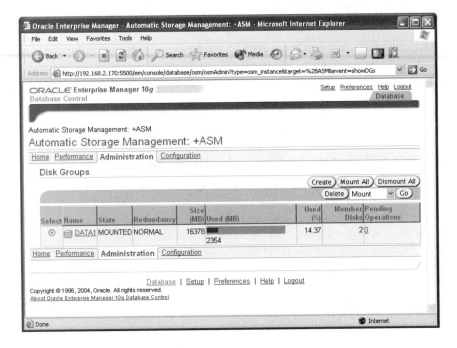

FIGURE 5.34   Disk group maintenance screen

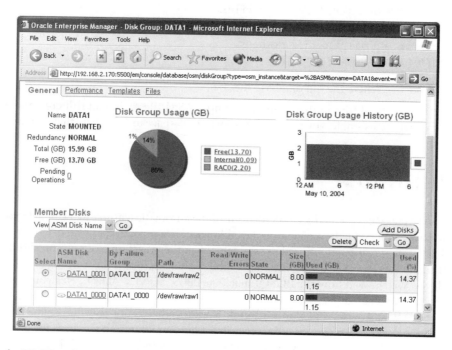

Other the EM Database Control ASM-related screens show things such as I/O response time for the disk group, the templates defined for the disk group, and the initialization parameters in effect for this ASM instance.

Database Migration to ASM

Because ASM files cannot be accessed via the operating system, you must use the Recovery Manager (RMAN) to move database objects from a non-ASM disk location to an ASM disk group. Follow these steps to move these objects:

1. Note the filenames of the control files and the online redo log files.
2. Shut down the database NORMAL, IMMEDIATE, or TRANSACTIONAL.
3. Back up the database.
4. Edit the SPFILE to use OMF for all file destinations.
5. Edit the SPFILE to remove the CONTROL_FILES parameter.
6. Run the following RMAN script, substituting your specific filenames as needed:
```
STARTUP NOMOUNT;
RESTORE CONTROLFILE FROM '<controlfile location>';
ALTER DATABASE MOUNT;
BACKUP AS COPY DATABASE FORMAT
    '+<disk group destination>';
```

```
SWITCH DATABASE TO COPY;
SQL "ALTER DATABASE RENAME <logfile1>
         TO '+<disk group destination>' ";
# repeat for all log file members
ALTER DATABASE OPEN RESETLOGS;
```

7. Delete or archive the old database files.

Even though all files in this example are now ASM files, you can still create a non-ASM tablespace if, for example, you want to transport a tablespace to a database that does not use ASM.

Summary

In this chapter we presented an in-depth tour of the automatic features that can help you manage tablespaces along with the segments in the tablespaces in a proactive, instead of a reactive, manner.

Tablespaces can be monitored proactively when they reach one of two thresholds, and an alert can be generated to notify you that a tablespace has crossed the warning or critical threshold level. We showed how the PL/SQL package DBMS_SERVER_ALERT gives you a way to programmatically change these thresholds.

The Segment Advisor and segment shrink work together to not only find segments that have unused space but also to compact the space in a segment and free up the space for other database objects. Sorted hash clusters provides you not only with another way to use disk space efficiently but also to optimize the performance of applications that use data in a first-in, first-out (FIFO) fashion.

Going beyond tablespaces and segments to all Oracle file types, we showed you how Automatic Storage Management (ASM) can reduce or eliminate the headaches involved in managing the disk space for all Oracle file types, including online and archived logs, RMAN backupsets, flashback logs, and even initialization parameter files (SPFILEs).

We reviewed the concepts related to a special type of instance called an ASM instance along with the initialization parameters specific to an ASM instance. In addition, we presented the dynamic performance views that allow you to view the components of an ASM disk group as well as to monitor the online rebalancing operations that occur when disks are added or removed from a disk group. Starting and stopping an ASM instance is similar to a traditional database instance, with the added dependencies of database instances that use the disk groups managed by an ASM instance and therefore will not be available to users if the ASM instance is not available to service disk group requests.

ASM filenames have a number of different formats and are used differently depending on whether existing ASM files or new ASM files are being referenced. ASM templates are used in conjunction with ASM filenames to ease the administration of ASM files.

Near the end of the chapter, we reviewed ASM disk group architecture, showing how failure groups can provide redundancy and performance benefits while at the same time eliminating the need for a third-party logical volume manager. Dynamic disk group rebalancing automatically tunes I/O performance when a disk is added or deleted from a disk group or a disk in a disk group fails. While we focused on the SQL commands necessary to manage disk groups, we also presented the EM Database Control interface for performing these same operations.

Exam Essentials

Be able to monitor space usage in a tablespace.   Respond to space warning and critical alerts by adding disk space or removing objects. Adjust the space thresholds using either DBMS_SERVER_ALERT or the EM Database Control interface.

Understand how the Segment Advisor and segment shrink work together to optimize space usage and performance.   Use the Segment Advisor to analyze one segment or an entire tablespace, and then use segment shrink functionality to compress one or more segments and optionally move the HWM.

Describe how sorted hash clusters are created and used.   Identify the types of applications that can benefit from hash clusters whose elements are maintained in a sorted list for each value of the cluster key.

Identify the purpose of the Undo Advisor and Redo Logfile Size Advisor within the Oracle advisory framework.   Be able to optimize the UNDO_RETENTION parameter as well as the size of the undo tablespace by using Undo Advisor. Use Redo Logfile Size Advisor to maximize performance by optimizing the time between log file switches.

Enumerate the benefits and characteristics of Automatic Storage Management.   Understand how ASM can relieve you of manually optimizing I/O across all files in the tablespace by using ASM disk groups. Show how ASM operations can be performed online with minimal impact to ongoing database transactions.

Be able to create an ASM instance and configure its initialization parameters.   Understand the new initialization parameters INSTANCE_TYPE, ASM_POWER_LIMIT, ASM_DISKSTRING, and ASM_DISKGROUPS. Configure DB_UNIQUE_NAME and LARGE_POOL_SIZE for an ASM instance. Start up and shut down an ASM instance noting the dependencies with database instances that are using the ASM instance's disk groups.

Understand how ASM filenames are constructed and used when creating Oracle objects.   Differentiate how different ASM file formats are used depending on whether the file is an existing ASM file, whether a new ASM file is being created, or multiple ASM files are being created. Understand the different system templates for creating ASM files and how the characteristics are applied to the ASM files.

Be able to create, drop, and alter ASM disk groups.   Define multiple failure groups for new disk groups and how the number of failure groups is different for two-way and three-way mirroring. Show how disk rebalancing can be controlled or rolled back.

Identify the steps involved in converting non-ASM files to ASM files using RMAN.   Migrate a database to ASM disk groups by shutting down the database, editing the SPFILE, running an RMAN script for each file to be converted, and opening the database with RESETLOGS.

Review Questions

1. Which data dictionary view provides the recommended action, as a SQL statement, from the Segment Advisor?

   A. DBA_ADVISOR_FINDINGS

   B. DBA_ADVISOR_RECOMMENDATIONS

   C. DBA_ADVISOR_ACTIONS

   D. DBA_ADVISOR_RATIONALE

2. Which of the following is not true about sorted hash clusters?

   A. The new access path is used regardless of the type of predicate in the WHERE clause.

   B. You are allowed to create indexes on sorted hash clusters.

   C. The cost-based optimizer must be used to take advantage of the new access path.

   D. Additional sorts are not necessary if you access the cluster by one of the lists of hash key columns.

   E. More than one table can be stored in a sorted hash cluster.

3. Consider the following scenario: The user SCOTT runs a query at 8:25 a.m. that receives an "ORA-01555: Snapshot too old" error after running for 15 minutes. An alert is sent to the DBA that the undo tablespace is incorrectly sized. At 10:15 a.m. the DBA checks the initialization parameter UNDO_RETENTION, and its value is 3600; the parameter is sized correctly. The DBA doubles the size of the undo tablespace by adding a second datafile. At 1:15 p.m. the user SCOTT runs the same query and once again receives an "ORA-01555: Snapshot too old" error. What happens next? (Choose the best answer.)

   A. The DBA receives another alert indicating that the undo tablespace is still undersized.

   B. The user SCOTT calls the DBA to report that the query is still failing.

   C. The second datafile autoextends so that future queries will have enough undo to complete when there is concurrent DML activity.

   D. Resumable Space Allocation suspends the query until the DBA adds another datafile to the undo tablespace and then the query runs to completion.

4. The background process _____ checks for tablespace threshold violation or clearance every _____ minutes.

   A. MMON, 10

   B. SMON, 10

   C. TMON, 30

   D. PMON, 15

   E. MMON, 30

5. Which of the following initialization parameters influences the recommended redo logfile size provided by the Redo Logfile Size Advisor?

    A. LOG_CHECKPOINT_INTERVAL

    B. OPTIMAL_LOGFILE_SIZE

    C. FAST_START_IO_TARGET

    D. FAST_START_MTTR_TARGET

    E. None of the above

6. Which of the following is not a benefit of segment shrink?

    A. Full table scans will take less time.

    B. Better index access because of a smaller B*Tree.

    C. Space is freed up for other database objects.

    D. All chained rows are fixed.

    E. Space below the HWM is released and the HWM moved down.

7. Which of the following ASM file templates are not striped as Fine?

    A. FLASHBACK

    B. ARCHIVELOG

    C. CONTROLFILE

    D. ONLINELOG

8. You want to migrate your database to ASM, so you've done a clean shutdown, made a closed backup of the entire database, noted the location of your control files and online redo log files, and changed your SPFILE to use OMF. The last step is running an RMAN script to do the conversion. Using the following steps, which is the correct order or the RMAN commands?

```
1    STARTUP NOMOUNT
2    ALTER DATABASE OPEN RESETLOGS
3    SQL "ALTER DATABASE RENAME 'logfile1 path' TO '+dgrp4'"    # plus all
     other log files
4    SWITCH DATABASE TO COPY
5    BACKUP AS COPY DATABASE FORMAT '+dgrp4'
6    ALTER DATABASE MOUNT
7    RESTORE CONTROLFILE FROM 'controlfile_location'
```

    A. 2, 5, 3, 1, 7, 6, 4

    B. 1, 7, 6, 5, 4, 3, 2

    C. 5, 1, 2, 7, 4, 6, 3

    D. 7, 3, 1, 5, 6, 2, 4

9. The EM Database Control Segment Resource Estimation feature uses all the following characteristics of the proposed table except for which one?

    A. Column datatypes

    B. PCTUSED

    C. PCTFREE

    D. Column sizes

    E. Estimated number of rows

10. To reference existing ASM files, you need to use a fully qualified ASM filename. Your development database has a disk group named DG2A, the database name is DEV19, and the ASM file you want to reference is a datafile for the USERS02 tablespace. Which of the following is a valid ASM filename for this ASM file?

    A. dev19/+DG2A/datafile/users02.701.2

    B. +DG2A/dev19/datafile/users02.701.2

    C. +DG2A/dev19/users02/datafile.701.2

    D. +DG2A.701.2

    E. +DG2A/datafile/dev19.users.02.701.2

11. Which of the following is not a benefit of sorted hash clusters? (Choose the best answer.)

    A. Rows within a given cluster key value are sorted by the sort key(s).

    B. The ORDER BY clause is not required to retrieve rows in ascending or descending order of the sort key(s).

    C. Cluster key values are hashed.

    D. Rows selected by a cluster key value using an equality operator are returned in ascending or descending order.

12. On the development database rac0 there are six raw devices /dev/raw/raw1 through /dev/raw/raw6. /dev/raw/raw1 and /dev/raw/raw2 are 8GB each, and the rest are 6GB each. An existing disk group +DATA1, of NORMAL REDUNDANCY, uses /dev/raw/raw1 and /dev/raw/raw2. Which series of the following commands will drop one of the failgroups for +DATA1, create a new disk group +DATA2 using two of the remaining four raw devices, and then cancel the drop operation from +DATA1?

    A.
    ```
    ALTER DISKGROUP DATA1 DROP DISK DATA1_0001;
    CREATE DISKGROUP DATA2 NORMAL REDUNDANCY
        FAILGROUP DATA1A DISK '/dev/raw/raw3'
        FAILGROUP DATA1B DISK '/dev/raw/raw4';
    ALTER DISKGROUP DATA1 UNDROP DISKS;
    ```

B. ALTER DISKGROUP DATA1 DROP DISK DATA1_0001;
   CREATE DISKGROUP DATA2 HIGH REDUNDANCY
     FAILGROUP DATA1A DISK '/dev/raw/raw3'
     FAILGROUP DATA1B DISK '/dev/raw/raw4';
   ALTER DISKGROUP DATA1 UNDROP DISKS;

C. ALTER DISKGROUP DATA1 DROP DISK DATA1_0001;
   CREATE DISKGROUP DATA2 NORMAL REDUNDANCY
     FAILGROUP DATA1A DISK '/dev/raw/raw3'
     FAILGROUP DATA1B DISK '/dev/raw/raw4';
   ALTER DISKGROUP DATA1 UNDROP DATA1_0001;

D. ALTER DISKGROUP DATA1 DROP DISK DATA1_0001
   ADD DISKGROUP DATA2 NORMAL REDUNDANCY
     FAILGROUP DATA1A DISK '/dev/raw/raw3'
     FAILGROUP DATA1B DISK '/dev/raw/raw4';
   ALTER DISKGROUP DATA1 UNDROP DISKS;

13. In the following scenario, the DBA wants to reclaim a lot of wasted space in the HR.EMPLOYEES table by using the segment shrink functionality. Which of the following is the correct order of the steps?

```
1  ALTER TABLE HR.EMPLOYEES SHRINK SPACE;
2  ALTER TABLE HR.EMPLOYEES DISABLE ROW MOVEMENT;
3  ALTER TABLE HR.EMPLOYEES ENABLE ROW MOVEMENT;
4  ALTER TABLE HR.EMPLOYEES SHRINK SPACE COMPACT;
5  ALTER TABLE HR.EMPLOYEES SHRINK SPACE CASCADE;
```

A. 3, 4, 1, 5, 2

B. 4, 1, 3, 2, 5

C. 5, 2, 1, 3, 4

D. 4, 1, 2, 3, 5

14. Which of the following calls to DBMS_SERVER_ALERT.SET_THRESHOLD will set the thresholds for the UNDOTBS1 tablespace to 60 percent and 90 percent? (Choose the best answer.)

A. dbms_server_alert.set_threshold(
   dbms_server_alert.tablespace_pct_full,
   dbms_server_alert.operator_ge, 60,
   dbms_server_alert.operator_ge, 90,
   1, 1, null,
   dbms_server_alert.object_type_tablespace,
   null);

B. dbms_server_alert.set_threshold(
    dbms_server_alert.tablespace_pct_full,
    dbms_server_alert.operator_le, 60,
    dbms_server_alert.operator_le, 90,
    1, 1, null,
    dbms_server_alert.object_type_datafile,
    'UNDOTBS1');

C. dbms_server_alert.set_threshold(
    dbms_server_alert.tablespace_full,
    dbms_server_alert.operator_ge, 60,
    dbms_server_alert.operator_ge, 90,
    1, 1, null,
    dbms_server_alert.object_type_tablespace,
    'UNDOTBS1');

D. dbms_server_alert.set_threshold(
    dbms_server_alert.tablespace_pct_full,
    dbms_server_alert.operator_ge, 60,
    dbms_server_alert.operator_ge, 90,
    1, 1, null,
    dbms_server_alert.object_type_tablespace,
    'UNDOTBS1');

15. Which of the following statements is not true about segment shrink operations? (Choose the best answer.)

    A. Tables with ROWID-based materialized views are maintained.

    B. Segment shrink is only allowed on segments whose space is automatically managed.

    C. Heap-organized and index-organized tables can be shrunk.

    D. ROW MOVEMENT must be enabled for heap-organized segments.

    E. Chained rows may be repaired during a segment shrink operation.

    F. Triggers are not fired during a segment shrink operation.

16. Which of the following is not a feature of the Segment Advisor within the EM Database Control?

    A. Growth trend analysis

    B. Segment resource estimation

    C. Finding candidates for segment shrink

    D. Finding table segments with chained rows

17. Choose the set of the following initialization parameters that is valid and recommended for an ASM instance.

A. INSTANCE_TYPE=RDBMS
ASM_POWER_LIMIT=2
LARGE_POOL_SIZE=8MB
DB_UNIQUE_NAME=+ASM
ASM_DISKGROUPS=DATA1,DATA2

B. INSTANCE_TYPE=ASM
ASM_POWER_LIMIT=2
LARGE_POOL_SIZE=8MB
DB_UNIQUE_NAME=+ASM
ASM_DISKGROUPS=DATA1,DATA2

C. INSTANCE_TYPE=ASM
ASM_POWER_LIMIT=15
LARGE_POOL_SIZE=8MB
DB_UNIQUE_NAME=+ASM
ASM_DISKGROUPS=DATA1,DATA2

D. INSTANCE_TYPE=ASM
ASM_POWER_LIMIT=2
LARGE_POOL_SIZE=4MB
DB_UNIQUE_NAME=+ASM
ASM_DISKGROUPS=DATA1,DATA2

18. Which of the following scenarios concerning ASM instance shutdown is correct?

A. When an ASM instance is shut down with NORMAL, IMMEDIATE or TRANSACTIONAL, the same shutdown command is passed to the dependent instances and the ASM instance waits for all dependent instances to shut down before it shuts down.

B. When an ASM instance shuts down with NORMAL, an alert is sent to all dependent instances, notifying the DBA to shut down the dependent instances manually before the ASM instance shuts down.

C. When an ASM instance shuts down with the TRANSACTIONAL option, all dependent instances shut down with either NORMAL, IMMEDIATE or TRANSACTIONAL, depending on the dependent database's default.

D. When an ASM instance is shut down with NORMAL, IMMEDIATE or TRANSACTIONAL, the same shutdown command is passed to the dependent instances and the ASM instance does not wait for all dependent instances to shut down before it shuts down.

E. When an ASM instance shuts down with the IMMEDIATE option, the ASM instance shuts down immediately and all dependent instances shut down with ABORT.

19. Which of the following conditions will trigger an additional sort on a sorted hash cluster? (Choose two.)

   A. The ORDER BY clause specifies nonsort columns that are not indexed.

   B. An ORDER BY clause is used in the query although the sort may still fit in memory.

   C. The cost-based optimizer is in effect.

   D. The ORDER BY clause is omitted, and the WHERE clause does not reference the cluster key.

   E. The ORDER BY clause specifies trailing sort columns.

20. Which of the following is not true about segment shrink operations in tablespaces with automatic segment space management?

   A. Clustered tables cannot be shrunk.

   B. LOB segments can be shrunk.

   C. IOT mapping tables and overflow segments cannot be shrunk.

   D. Tables with function-based indexes cannot be shrunk.

   E. ROW MOVEMENT must be enabled for heap-based segments.

Answers to Review Questions

1. C. The data dictionary view DBA_ADVISOR_ACTIONS contains the SQL statement(s) that the Segment Advisor supplies to implement its recommendation for segment maintenance. DBA_ADVISOR_FINDINGS contains the results of the analysis, but no SQL. DBA_ADVISOR_RECOMMENDATIONS presents one or more findings and the benefits for performing the recommendation. DBA_ADVISOR_RATIONALE provides a more detailed set of reasons why the recommendation should be implemented, along with the impact of not performing the recommendation.

2. A. The new access path in a sorted hash cluster is used only if an equality predicate is used.

3. B. Even if the size of the undo tablespace is adjusted after an undo space problem, only one alert is sent for each 24-hour period. Therefore, the only way that the problem will be resolved promptly is for SCOTT to call the DBA, as the DBA will not receive another alert until the next day when another query fails.

4. A. The new background process MMON checks for threshold violations every 10 minutes. An alert is triggered when the threshold is reached or is cleared.

5. D. FAST_START_MTTR_TARGET specifies the desired time, in seconds, for instance recovery after a crash or an instance failure. Therefore, the Redo Logfile Size Advisor uses this value to determine the optimal logfile size. OPTIMAL_LOGFILE_SIZE is not an initialization parameter but a column in the view V$INSTANCE_RECOVERY. The initialization parameters FAST_START_IO_TARGET specifies recovery at the I/O level, and LOG_CHECKPOINT_INTERVAL specifies the frequency of checkpoints in terms of redo logfile blocks used.

6. D. While some chained rows may be fixed with segment shrink functionality, it is not guaranteed that all chained rows will be fixed since not all blocks may be read in a segment shrink operation.

7. B. Files such as ARCHIVELOG files use coarse-grained striping. Fine striping stripes the files every 128KB while coarse striping stripes the files every 1MB. All file types with the exception of FLASHBACK, CONTROLFILE, and ONLINELOG are striped coarse.

8. B. After the RMAN script is run, and the database is up and running successfully, you may delete the old database files.

9. B. Only PCTFREE is used in the calculation, as it is the amount of space to leave free in the block for updates to existing rows. PCTUSED is not needed unless the segment space management is not AUTO. In addition, extent sizes calculated by this feature helps assess the impact on the tablespace where this segment will be stored.

10. B. A fully qualified existing ASM filename has the format +*group*/*dbname*/*filetype*/*tag*.*file*.*incarnation*. In this case, *filetype* is datafile, and *tag* is the tablespace name to which it belongs, or users02.

11. C. While cluster key values in a sorted hash cluster are hashed, this is also true of regular hash clusters and therefore is not a benefit unique to sorted hash clusters.

12. A. Note that the UNDROP operation will cancel a drop operation in progress but cannot reverse a drop operation that has already completed. For HIGH REDUNDANCY, at least three failure groups must be specified. While you can combine a drop and add operation into one command, the command can reference only one disk group.

13. A. While the segment shrink operation could combine steps A and D, the impact to the users may be lessened by performing two smaller operations instead of one large one.

14. D. The call to DBMS_SERVER_ALERT.SET_THRESHOLD must specify the metric TABLESPACE_PCT_FULL, the two thresholds, an object type of tablespace, and the tablespace name itself. Specifying NULL for the tablespace name will set the threshold for all tablespaces, not just the UNDOTBS1 tablespace.

15. A. Because the ROWIDs are changed with a segment shrink operation, tables with ROWID-based materialized views cannot be shrunk unless the materialized views are dropped and re-created after the segment shrink operation.

16. D. The Segment Advisor is not used to find tables with chained rows, but instead is used for finding segments that are good candidates for segment shrink or may be growing too fast.

17. B. The INSTANCE_TYPE for an ASM instance is ASM; otherwise, it is RDBMS whether it uses ASM or not. The ASM_POWER_LIMIT command controls the speed of a disk group rebalance, but its maximum value is 11. For an ASM instance, the minimum recommended value for LARGE_POOL_SIZE is 8MB.

18. A. When an ASM instance shuts down with NORMAL, IMMEDIATE or TRANSACTIONAL, the same shutdown option is passed to all dependent instances and the ASM instance waits for the dependent instances to shut down before shutting itself down. If an ASM instance shuts down with ABORT, it immediately shuts down, the dependent instances lose their connection to the ASM instance and as a result shut down with ABORT either before or after the ASM instance shuts down completely.

19. A, E. If a query on a sorted hash cluster retrieves rows and an ORDER BY clause specifies either nonsort columns or a suffix of the sort columns, additional sorting is required, assuming that indexes are not defined on the columns in the ORDER BY clause.

20. B. For segments in tablespaces with automatic segment space management, LOB segments cannot be shrunk. In addition, tables with LONG columns, on-commit materialized views, and ROWID-based materialized view cannot be shrunk. In all cases, shrink operations cannot be performed on segments managed by freelists.

Chapter
6

Performance and Application Tuning

ORACLE DATABASE 10*g* NEW FEATURES FOR ADMINISTRATORS EXAM OBJECTIVES OFFERED IN THIS CHAPTER:

✓ **Application Tuning**

- Use the new optimizer statistics
- Use the SQL Tuning Advisor
- Use the SQL Access Advisor
- Use the performance pages of Database Control

 Exam objectives are subject to change at any time without prior notice and at Oracle's sole discretion. Please visit Oracle's training and certification website (http://www.oracle.com/education/certification/) for the most current exam objectives listing.

Oracle Database 10*g* (Oracle 10*g*) provides a number of new features and tools to make tuning a database more automated and less error prone. The retirement of the rule-based optimizer model along with the automated statistics-gathering features can significantly improve the overall performance of queries. In addition, DML activities can be automatically monitored for all tables in the database to help the Automatic Database Diagnostic Monitor (ADDM) identify which objects need new statistics generated.

The SQL Tuning Advisor uses an enhanced mode to take a heavily used and resource-intensive SQL statement and perform a number of analyses to generate an optimal execution plan that can be far superior to the execution plan generated by the traditional cost-based optimizer algorithm. The SQL Tuning Advisor will also use the information from the ADDM to compensate for stale or missing statistics until the statistics can be recomputed.

The SQL Access Advisor, run by itself or from a recommendation by the SQL Tuning Advisor, is used typically in a data warehouse environment to recommend changes to an indexing or materialized view strategy, taking into account storage and maintenance trade-offs.

In this chapter, we'll present the new automatic statistics-gathering features of Oracle 10*g* and the corresponding data dictionary views. We will talk about the desupport of the rule-based optimizer and what is replacing it in Oracle 10*g*. Next, we will give you a tour of the SQL Tuning Advisor and how it can automate many of the labor-intensive tuning tasks required in previous versions of Oracle. For a DSS environment, we will review how the SQL Access Advisor can recommend changes to a database's indexing and materialized view strategy to maximize throughput and optimize storage requirements. Finally, we will take you on a tour of some key performance pages in the Enterprise Manager (EM) Database Control and show how you can drill down and identify potential problem areas in a GUI environment.

Managing Optimizer Statistics

The optimizer statistics-gathering function in Oracle 10*g* has been enhanced to become more automated. If the database is created using the Database Creation Assistant (DBCA), a batch job is automatically created and started at database creation to collect statistics on database objects with missing or stale statistics.

To account for CPU-intensive or CPU-only operations, the optimizer now takes into account both CPU time and I/O load when creating an execution plan; in addition, the optimizer can use dynamic sampling to generate additional statistics at runtime to further fine-tune the execution plan. To further enhance the performance of CPU-bound queries on fixed tables and data dictionary tables, the DBMS_STATS package has been enhanced to gather statistics on these tables.

Monitoring tables for DML activity has been simplified by using a single initialization parameter to control the collection of statistics instead of collecting statistics on individual tables.

Given the comprehensive support for statistics collection, the rule-based optimizer has been desupported. In the following sections, we'll review the new initialization parameter values available to control the behavior of the cost-based optimizer.

Gathering Automatic Statistics

When a new database is created, the job GATHER_STATS_JOB is automatically created and scheduled. This job gathers statistics on a regular basis for database objects whose statistics are either missing or stale. It calls the procedure DBMS_STATS.GATHER_DATABASE_STATS_JOB_PROC, which operates similarly to the procedure DBMS_STATS.GATHER_DATABASE_STATS with the GATHER AUTO option available in previous releases of Oracle.

The GATHER_DATABASE_STATS_JOB_PROC procedure provides additional benefits beyond automating the collection process: it processes objects that most need updated statistics first.

In Figure 6.1, the EM Database Control Scheduler Jobs page (reachable from the EM Database Control Administration tab via the Jobs link under Scheduler) shows the GATHER_STATS_JOB and the program it runs: SYS.GATHER_STATS_PROG.

FIGURE 6.1   EM Database Control job editing

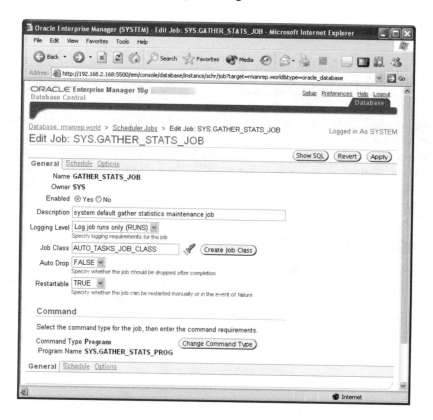

This program in turn calls the procedure DBMS_STATS.GATHER_DATABASE_STATS_JOB_ PROC as you can see on the Edit Program screen in Figure 6.2.

FIGURE 6.2 EM Database Control program editing

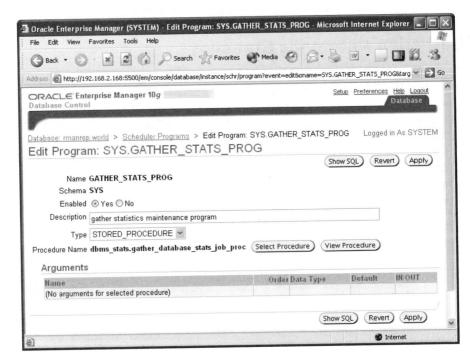

On the job editing schedule page, shown in Figure 6.3, you can see the two maintenance windows for running this job.

Within the specified maintenance windows, the GATHER_STATS_JOB procedure may not have time to update all missing and stale object statistics. As a result, the prioritization process performed by GATHER_DATABASE_STATS_JOB_PROC ensures that at a minimum the objects needing statistics the most are analyzed.

Leveraging Enhanced Query Optimization

Oracle's enhanced cost model now takes into account CPU-intensive or CPU-only operations, in contrast to versions of Oracle before Oracle 9*i* that only considered I/O costs. In Oracle 10*g*, the default cost model considers both CPU and I/O. Also, the table PLAN_TABLE has a new column, TIME, that estimates the elapsed time, in seconds, for the query as estimated by the new cost model.

FIGURE 6.3   EM Database Control job window editing

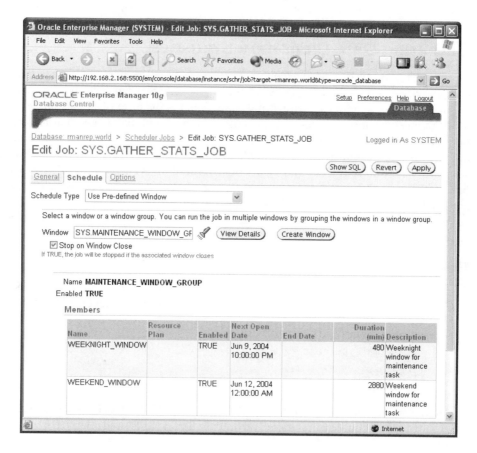

The new initialization parameter OPTIMIZER_DYNAMIC_SAMPLING controls how the enhanced query optimizer can deal more effectively with objects at runtime that have no statistics, have stale statistics, or are very volatile. Setting OPTIMIZER_DYNAMIC_SAMPLING to a number other than zero determines how much *dynamic sampling* will occur when the execution plan is generated. Dynamic sampling is a method of statistics collection, controlled by the initialization parameter OPTIMZER_DYNAMIC_SAMPLING, that produces compile-time statistics for query objects that have stale or missing statistics. The range of this parameter is from 0 to 10, with a default value of 2. For queries against very volatile objects, it is wise to not explicitly compute statistics and let dynamic sampling drive the generation of the execution plan.

Another initialization parameter that is changed as part of the enhanced query optimizer is PGA_AGGREGATE_TARGET. Automatic PGA memory management is enabled by default unless

PGA_AGGREGATE_TARGET is set to 0 or the parameter WORKAREA_SIZE_POLICY is set to MANUAL. By default, PGA_AGGREGATE_TARGET is 20 percent of the SGA size.

Gathering Data Dictionary Statistics

As of Oracle 10*g*, it is beneficial to collect statistics on data dictionary tables, both fixed and real tables. A *fixed table* is a table that exists in memory only that typically contains information about instance or memory structures and is presented in the form of a table. Since fixed tables reside in memory only, they have no I/O cost associated with them; now that the cost-based optimizer takes into account CPU cost, a more robust execution plan can be generated when taking into account statistics on fixed tables. In contrast, a real table is stored in a datafile, persists between instance restarts and incurs I/O overhead unless it is specifically cached in memory. Gathering statistics on real data dictionary tables provides the same benefit as statistics gathered on user or application tables: better execution plans.

In this section we'll show you how to gather statistics on both real and fixed tables, as well as review the other changes to the DBMS_STATS package.

Getting Statistics on Real Data Dictionary Tables

To collect statistics on data dictionary tables, use the procedure DBMS_STATS.GATHER_SCHEMA_STATS or DBMS_STATS.GATHER_DATABASE_STATS with the parameter GATHER_SYS set to TRUE.

```
SQL> exec dbms_stats.gather_database_stats( -
  2         estimate_percent => 5, -
  3         gather_sys => true);
PL/SQL procedure successfully completed.
```

Alternatively, a new procedure called DBMS_STATS.GATHER_DICTIONARY_STATS is convenient shorthand for gathering statistics on only the SYS, SYSTEM, and other RDBMS component tables.

```
SQL> exec dbms_stats.gather_dictionary_stats;
PL/SQL procedure successfully completed.
```

Either the SYSDBA privilege or the new system privilege ANALYZE ANY DICTIONARY is required to analyze data dictionary or fixed tables.

Getting Statistics on Fixed Data Dictionary Tables

If you use DBMS_STATS.GATHER_DATABASE_STATS, you can set the parameter GATHER_FIXED, which defaults to FALSE, to TRUE to gather statistics for fixed tables in addition to any other statistics collected.

If the need arises to collect statistics on an individual fixed table, you can use the DBMS_STATS package as with any traditional table.

```
SQL> exec dbms_stats.gather_table_stats( -
  2        ownname => 'SYS', -
  3        tabname => 'x$le');
PL/SQL procedure successfully completed.
```

Only fixed table statistics can be gathered with the procedure GATHER_FIXED_OBJECT_STATS.

```
SQL> exec dbms_stats.gather_fixed_object_stats;
PL/SQL procedure successfully completed.
```

Gathering statistics on fixed tables is typically required only once during a typical system workload; in other words, unless a new application has been installed, a monthly data warehouse load has been performed, or the database software has been patched or upgraded, it is not necessary to regather fixed table statistics.

Exploring Other Changes to *DBMS_STATS*

In addition to the new procedures in DBMS_STATS, new values for the parameters GRANULARITY and DEGREE are available in all the GATHER_*_STATS procedures.

The new values for GRANULARITY are AUTO (the default value) and GLOBAL AND PARTITION. Using AUTO will determine the granularity value based on the partitioning and subpartitioning type: If the subpartition type is LIST, the global, partition, and subpartition statistics are generated; otherwise, only global and partition statistics are generated. Using GLOBAL AND PARTITION gathers only global and partition statistics even if subpartitions exist.

DEGREE can now have a value of AUTO_DEGREE. Depending on the number of CPUs and the size of the object, Oracle sets DEGREE to either 1 or DEFAULT_DEGREE. The default value of DEGREE is NULL, which directs the DBMS_STATS procedures to use the default value specified for DEGREE when the table or index was created or altered.

The default values for these parameters should be sufficient in most cases.

Monitoring DML Tables

In previous versions of Oracle, you would use the command ALTER TABLE … MONITORING to capture the amount of DML activity against one or more tables and subsequently use DBMS_STATS to gather statistics on these tables under the assumption that the statistics have become stale.

Starting with Oracle 10g, you can no longer monitor individual tables and must use the initialization parameter STATISTICS_LEVEL. The values for STATISTICS_LEVEL are as follows:

- BASIC
- TYPICAL
- ALL

A value of BASIC disables monitoring, and as a result the Automatic Workload Repository (AWR) snapshots are disabled in addition to the ADDM. Using BASIC may be advisable only in a DSS environment where the queries rarely vary day to day, the system has been thoroughly tuned already, the size of the database changes infrequently, the database is static, and the fastest possible execution speed of all queries is the top priority.

Using a value of TYPICAL will collect most statistics required for database self-management and delivers the best overall performance; specifying ALL collects additional statistics such as timed operating system statistics and plan execution statistics, but incurs a significant amount of overhead above and beyond the TYPICAL level that may have a noticeable impact on user transactions.

Understanding Rule-Based Optimizer Desupport

While the rule-based optimizer (RBO) still exists in Oracle 10*g*, it is no longer supported. The RBO has no changes in Oracle 10*g*, and no bug fixes will be provided for the RBO. As a result, the values CHOOSE and RULE are no longer valid for the OPTIMIZER_MODE initialization parameter. In addition, the CHOOSE and RULE optimizer hints are no longer supported. The only valid values for OPTIMIZER_MODE are as follows:

FIRST_ROWS   A value of FIRST_ROWS directs the optimizer to use costs and internal algorithms to deliver the first few rows quickly.

FIRST_ROWS_n   FIRST_ROWS_*n*, where *n* can be 1, 10, 100, or 1000, uses a cost-based approach to deliver the first *n* rows as quickly as possible.

ALL_ROWS   ALL_ROWS is the default value for OPTIMIZER_MODE. The optimizer picks an execution plan to provide the best throughput to return all results of the query, minimizing the total resources needed to run the query.

Understanding the SQL Tuning Advisor

Oracle 10*g*'s Automatic SQL Tuning feature of the query optimizer replaces manual tuning and, as a result, automates the entire tuning process. You access the Automatic SQL Tuning feature via the *SQL Tuning Advisor*. The SQL Tuning Advisor has two modes: *normal mode* and *tuning mode*.

Normal mode is much like the query optimizer in previous versions of Oracle. The SQL statement is compiled, and an execution plan is generated, usually generating a good plan for most SQL statements given the very narrow time constraints in normal mode, usually a fraction of a second.

Tuning mode is used only for previously identified high-load SQL, since its analysis is measured in minutes rather than fractions of a second. The output from tuning mode goes beyond an execution plan to a series of recommended actions and rationales that should produce a better execution plan for future executions of the SQL statement. In tuning mode, the Oracle query optimizer is called the *Automatic Tuning Optimizer* (ATO).

In the following sections, we will provide details on how each tuning mode works: its components, how to use it, how to use one of its subcomponents directly, and how to access this functionality via the EM Database Control.

Introducing the SQL Tuning Advisor

Before you can tune a high-load SQL statement, you must be able to identify which SQL statements are causing the high load on the system. In previous versions of Oracle, this process alone was labor intensive or required third-party tools. In Oracle 10*g*, the ADDM automates the process of identifying the high-load SQL from the SQL workload. In Figure 6.4, ADDM has identified a number of high-load SQL statements from the selected five-minute interval.

FIGURE 6.4   EM Database Control High-load SQL

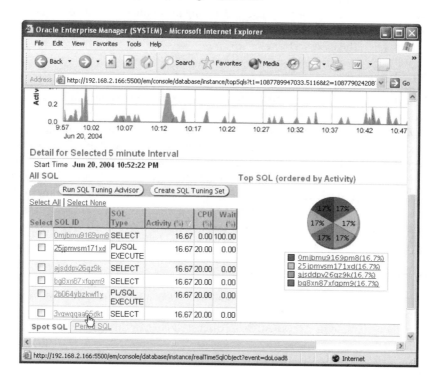

For more information on ADDM, see Chapter 3, "Automating Management."

The SQL Tuning Advisor receives one or more SQL statements as input, and considering a number of factors, including CPU, I/O, and temporary space usage, provides advice on how to improve the execution plan along with expected benefits. The SQL Tuning Advisor performs four specific types of analysis:

- Statistics analysis
- SQL profiling
- Access path analysis
- SQL structure analysis

Statistics Analysis

The ATO verifies if the objects in the query have up-to-date statistics. If not, it recommends gathering statistics; in the mean time, it provides information to take the place of statistics until new statistics are gathered, such as dynamic sampling techniques controlled by the initialization parameter `OPTIMIZER_DYNAMIC_SAMPLING`. The information gathered is stored in a SQL profile, discussed in the next section.

SQL Profiling

The SQL profiling step uses other methods to verify its analysis in the statistics analysis phase and creates customized optimizer settings for the SQL query being analyzed, such as `ALL_ROWS` or `FIRST_ROWS_n`. Verification methods include past executions of the SQL statement or even partially executing the SQL statement. It recommends creating a *SQL profile* to store this information for future use by the query optimizer when it is running in normal mode. A SQL profile is a collection of additional information about a SQL query that is collected during the automatic tuning of a SQL statement that can be used to improve the execution plan for future executions of the SQL statement. The creation and use of the profile is completely transparent to the user running the same SQL statement in the future; the user may, however, notice that the query runs faster than the last time!

Access Path Analysis

ATO's *access path analysis* may indicate that a new index can dramatically improve the query's performance; part of ATO's recommendations may include one or more new indexes on each table in the query. The SQL Access Advisor, discussed later in this chapter, performs a similar

---

Real World Scenario

Longevity of a SQL profile

Information in a SQL profile does not necessarily become obsolete after a day or two; it stays flexible even in the face of added or deleted indexes or growth of tables. We had just saved a SQL profile for an order-entry table earlier in the week, so we were concerned when the analysts were complaining about slower queries later in the week. It turned out that three different things happened that we were not aware of nor paid attention to: first, the domain codes for the order types were modified to include new overseas locations. This made the statistics for the table stale, and the statistics collection window was not large enough to capture new statistics for the order entry table yet; other, worse-performing tables were being analyzed ahead of the order table. In addition, the ADDM put one of the SQL statements near the top of the high-load SQL list, but those queries were always high on the list to begin with, and we did not notice it moving up in the list. We were also behind on standardizing the interface for performing queries against the order tables and the data warehouse tables, so any one particular SQL statement was most likely different from the rest.

The lesson to be learned here is fourfold. First, stay on the distribution list for changes to business rules that will most likely affect the performance of your database so you can be proactive instead of reactive. Second, pay attention to the alerts generated by the ADDM before the users start calling. Third, even though the statistics collection may be automated, you still have to have the maintenance window large enough to analyze your largest and most volatile tables on a frequent basis. Fourth, and probably something that has been true since the Oracle database first cached SQL statements, limit the ad-hoc SQL on a production system to avoid memory problems and improve the chances that the SQL a user is executing is already in the cache.

---

analysis. In fact, since the access path analysis does not look beyond one SQL statement, one of the recommendations may be to run the SQL Access Advisor to perform further analysis along with the rest of the SQL workload.

SQL Structure Analysis

ATO's SQL structure analysis tries to find potential coding errors in a SQL statement or SQL constructs that may produce bad plans. Its recommendations include alternate coding methods for the SQL statement. For example, the SQL structure analysis may recommend a NOT IN instead of a NOT EXISTS, or it may recommend a UNION ALL if it determines that a UNION (and therefore an additional sort) may not be necessary. In addition, mismatched datatypes

in the predicates, which can potentially eliminate the use of an index, are flagged by the analysis. Other potential design mistakes such as using a Cartesian product are also identified. However, the final determination as to whether these recommendations will be implemented is up to the end user: for example, in rare cases a Cartesian product is a valid construct in a SQL statement.

Using SQL Tuning Advisor

The SQL Tuning Advisor uses a number of different sources for the SQL statements to be analyzed.

- High-load SQL identified by the ADDM
- SQL statements that are still in the cursor cache
- SQL statements from the AWR
- A user-defined set of SQL statements

Note that the user-defined set of SQL statements may never have been executed: the SQL Tuning Advisor is a great way to analyze your SQL long before it goes into production.

If the SQL statements come from the cursor cache, AWR, or a custom workload, they can be filtered or sorted before going to the Tuning Advisor.

For a custom workload consisting of more than one SQL statement, you can use a *SQL Tuning Set (STS)*. An STS is a convenient way to maintain a set of SQL statements along with its execution information, such as the schema name under which the SQL was executed, the values of the bind variables, average elapsed time to execute, and how many times the statement has been executed. An STS may be stacked: a new STS can consist of other SQL statements and STSs.

In the following sections, we will show you how to use the SQL Tuning Advisor with both the EM Database Control and via the DBMS_SQLTUNE package. In addition, we'll present the new initialization parameter that controls the behavior of the SQL Tuning Advisor.

SQL Tuning and the EM Database Control

Identifying top SQL statements within the EM Database Control and tuning these SQL statements with the SQL Tuning Advisor is very straightforward using the EM Database Control's web-based interface. Clicking the Top SQL link under the Performance tab on the database home page, you can identify which SQL statements are using the most resources.

In the following example, one of the application developers has created an employee history table named HR.EMPLOYEES_HISTORY that contains employees who have either changed

departments or left the company. One of the top SQL statements that accesses this new table is as follows:

```
select eh.last_name, d.department_name
    from hr.employees_history eh, hr.departments d
    where job_id like 'ST_%' or job_id like 'AC_%';
```

The Top SQL page of the EM Database Control identifies this query as using a lot of resources compared to the rest of the SQL load. On the SQL Details page shown in Figure 6.5 you can see the SQL statement itself along with the execution plan used.

FIGURE 6.5   EM Database Control SQL Details page

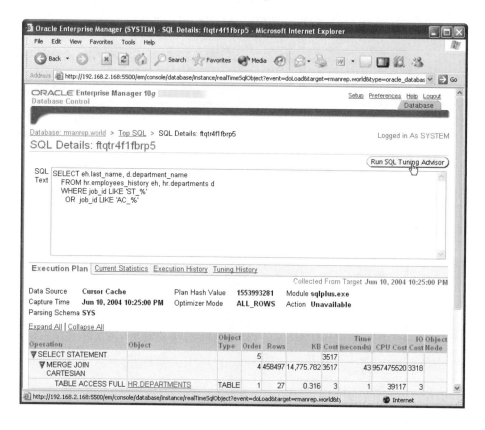

You suspect that improvements could be made to this query, so you click the Run SQL Tuning Advisor link and schedule a job to perform the analysis on the Schedule Advisor page, shown in Figure 6.6.

Clicking the OK button submits the job. On the Recommendations page shown in Figure 6.7, you see that there are three findings: one of the tables does not have any statistics, there are no indexes on one of the tables, and the query itself has a Cartesian join, which is almost always a query design error.

To implement one of these recommendations, you can select the recommendation and click the Implement link. For example, if you select Index and click Implement, you can schedule a job to implement the creation of the index. Before you submit the job, you can view the SQL that will be used to implement the recommendation, as you can see in Figure 6.8.

FIGURE 6.6 EM Database Control Schedule Advisor page

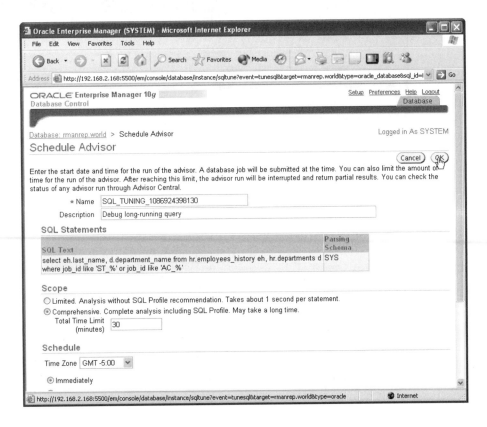

FIGURE 6.7 EM Database Control Recommendations page

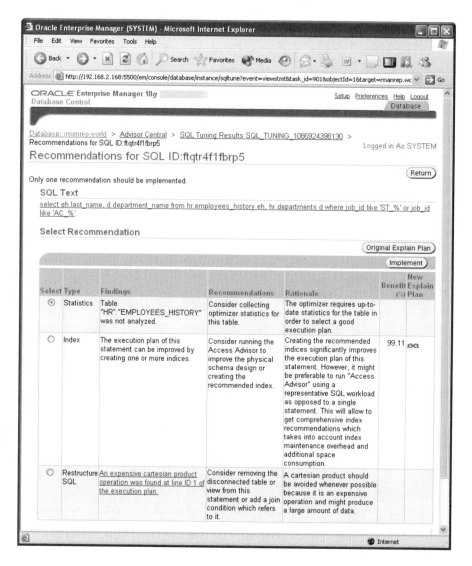

FIGURE 6.8   EM Database Control Indexing Recommendation SQL

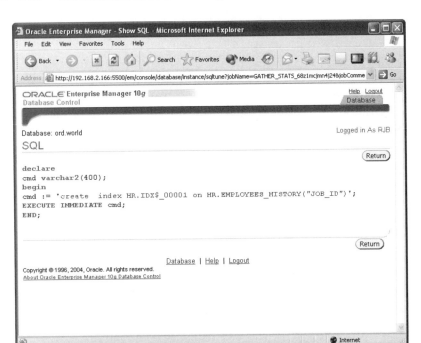

SQL Tuning and the *DBMS_SQLTUNE* Package

While the EM Database Control interface makes it easy to access the SQL Tuning Advisor, sometimes either the command-line interface or a PL/SQL application must be used to perform tuning tasks. For example, a third-party application that provides an ad-hoc query tool and a PL/SQL debugging module may also integrate an interface into the SQL Tuning Advisor to provide a single interface to an application developer. The package DBMS_SQLTUNE provides access to the SQL Tuning Advisor.

The packages in DBMS_SQLTUNE fall into the following three general categories:

SQL tuning task management   This involves creating or dropping a tuning task, running a tuning task, or displaying a SQL Tuning Advisor recommendation.

SQL profile management   This involves accepting and saving a profile, dropping a profile, or changing a profile's attributes.

STS management   This involves creating or dropping an STS, adding SQL statements to an STS, or displaying the SQL statements in an STS.

A typical session using the SQL Tuning Advisor would use DBMS_SQLTUNE procedures and functions as follows:

1.   Create a tuning task with CREATE_TUNING_TASK.

2. Execute the tuning task using EXECUTE_TUNING_TASK.

3. Review the results of the tuning task by calling the function REPORT_TUNING_TASK.

4. Accept the SQL profile generated by the tuning task using ACCEPT_SQL_PROFILE.

At a minimum, the ADVISOR privilege is required to use DBMS_SQLTUNE to create and execute tuning tasks. This is the same privilege required to use the other advisors built upon Oracle's advisory framework, which includes the Segment Advisor, Undo Advisor, Redo Logfile Size Advisor, and so forth. The CREATE ANY SQL PROFILE privilege is required to create and save a SQL profile.

SQL Tuning Initialization Parameters

The new initialization parameter SQLTUNE_CATEGORY defines the category to use when applying a SQL profile to a SQL statement. The default value is DEFAULT. Similarly, when a SQL profile is saved, the default category assigned to the profile is DEFAULT.

Creating other categories may be useful in a development environment. To test a new SQL profile, you may assign the category TEST when saving the profile. When you connect to the database and change the value of SQLTUNE_CATEGORY to TEST at the session level using ALTER SESSION SET SQLTUNE_CATEGORY=TEST, only those profiles saved with the TEST category will apply to the session and you can test the new profile; conversely, other user sessions will continue to use the SQL profiles assigned to the DEFAULT category, unaffected by your work with the new profiles.

 The combination of the category name and the SQL text uniquely identifies a SQL profile. As a result, identical SQL statements can exist in multiple profiles as long as each profile is in a different category.

When the testing is complete, you can change the category for the profile to DEFAULT, and it will automatically apply to all sessions that use the DEFAULT category. For example, executing the following PL/SQL procedure changes the category of the SQL profile SYS_SQLPROF_3887495559238 from TEST to DEFAULT:

```
SQL> exec dbms_sqltune.alter_sql_profile( -
  2      name => 'SYS_SQLPROF_3887495559238', -
  3      attribute_name => 'CATEGORY' -
  4      value => 'DEFAULT');
PL/SQL procedure successfully completed.
```

Here is a complete list of the attributes for a SQL profile that can be changed with the ATTRIBUTE_NAME parameter:

- STATUS: Can be either ENABLED or DISABLED to enable or disable the profile

- NAME: Can change the name of the profile; this must be a valid Oracle identifier and unique within the database

- DESCRIPTION: Can be any string up to 500 characters

- CATEGORY: Can be set to any category name; this must be a valid Oracle identifier and must be unique when combined with the SQL text

Understanding the SQL Access Advisor

The SQL Access Advisor, another component of the Oracle advisory framework and the DBMS_ ADVISOR package, helps you determine which indexes, materialized views, and materialized view logs will help the performance of a single query, an entire workload, or a derived workload based on a specified schema. The SQL Access Advisor provides the most benefits in a data warehouse or decision support environment, where the activity is primarily SELECT statements.

In the following sections, we will provide an overview of the SQL Access Advisor and the types of recommendations it can provide; in addition, we will present some examples of the SQL Access Advisor using the EM Database Control.

Introducing the SQL Access Advisor

The SQL Access Advisor provides a number of benefits. It uses rules from the optimizer itself, making it highly likely that any recommended changes to the workload will improve the execution plan. It's also an intuitive, GUI- and wizard-based application that automatically generates scripts to implement its recommendations.

Input to the SQL Access Advisor can come from one or all of the following sources:

- Current SQL statements from V$SQL (the SQL cache)
- A user-specified list of SQL statements
- The name of a schema; in a data warehouse environment, this is typically a dimensional model in a single schema
- STSs previously saved in the workload repository

Given the workload, the SQL Access Advisor performs an analysis that includes all the following tasks:

- Considers whether only indexes, only materialized views, or a combination of both would provide the most benefit
- Balances storage and maintenance costs against the performance gains when recommending new indexes or materialized views
- Generates DROP recommendations to drop an unused index or materialized view if a full workload is specified
- Optimizes materialized views to leverage query rewrite and fast refresh where possible
- Recommends materialized view logs to facilitate fast refresh
- Recommends combining multiple indexes into a single index where appropriate

You can specify that a workload is either a *full workload* or a *partial workload*. A full workload is typically the entire set of SQL statements run as part of an application or throughout a business day. A partial workload may be one SQL statement or a group of problematic SQL statements. When running the SQL Access Advisor, it is important to specify whether the

workload is full or partial. If the workload is partial, the SQL Access Advisor will not recommend dropping indexes, changing the index type, or dropping a materialized view, as dropping an index may dramatically affect the performance of a query that was not included in the partial workload.

When the SQL Access Advisor is analyzing a partial workload, it is operating in *limited mode*. In contrast, when analyzing a full workload, the SQL Access Advisor is operating in *comprehensive mode*.

Using the SQL Access Advisor

To run the SQL Access Advisor wizard via the EM Database Control, click the Performance tab from the database home page and then the Advisor Central link at the bottom of page. From the Advisor Central page, click the SQL Access Advisor link. The SQL Access Advisor wizard launches, bringing you to the SQL Access Advisor Workload Source page shown in Figure 6.9.

FIGURE 6.9   SQL Access Advisor's Workload Source page

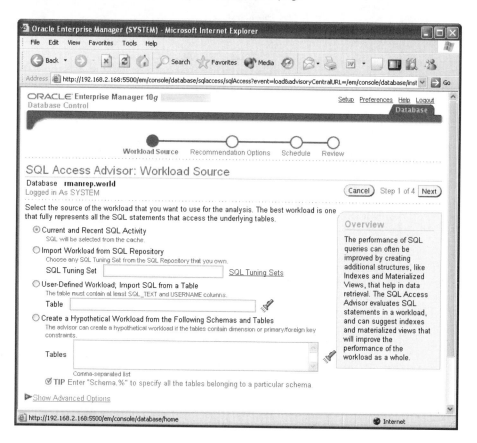

To use the SQL Access Advisor, consider an example. You will use recent SQL activity from the SQL cache to perform your analysis and then click Next. On the SQL Access Advisor Recommendations Options page shown in Figure 6.10, you will want to perform a quick analysis of the recent SQL statements, since you do not want to wait until your nightly maintenance window to perform the analysis; a comprehensive analysis during peak processing times may impact the overall throughput of the database. As a result, you are going to see if new indexes or statistics collection can benefit the highest-cost SQL statements run recently.

FIGURE 6.10 SQL Access Advisor Recommendation Options page

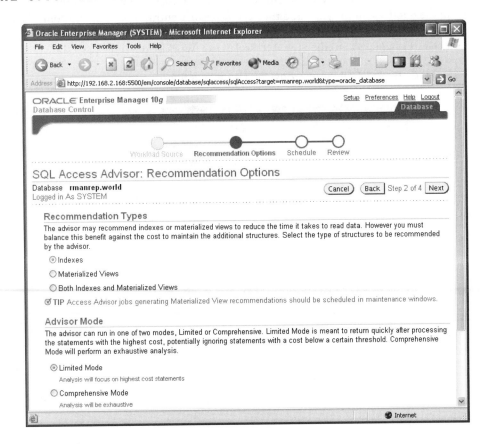

Since you want to see the results immediately, you specify that the analysis job should be started immediately on the SQL Access Advisor Schedule page, shown in Figure 6.11. On the page you can also provide a name and a description for the task to make it easy to identify the task output later.

In the last step of the SQL Access Advisor wizard, the Review page shown in Figure 6.12, you have one more opportunity to review the parameters of the job before you submit it.

A few moments later, from the Advisor Central page shown in Figure 6.13, you can see that the job you submitted has completed.

Clicking the link containing the name of the job you just submitted brings you to the Advisor Central's Recommendation Summary page; clicking one of the recommendation links brings you to one of the individual recommendation pages, as shown in Figure 6.14.

FIGURE 6.11   SQL Access Advisor Schedule page

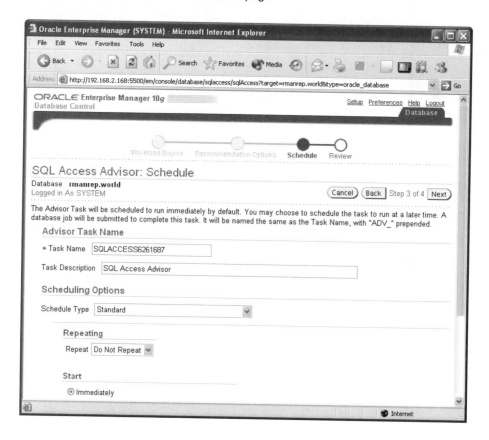

FIGURE 6.12 SQL Access Advisor Review page

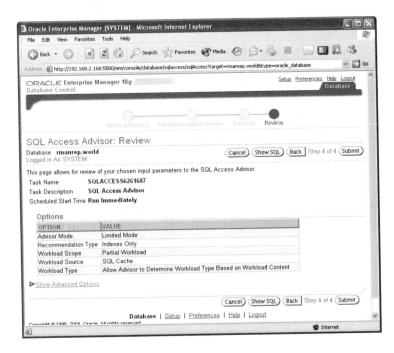

FIGURE 6.13 Advisor Central's completed jobs

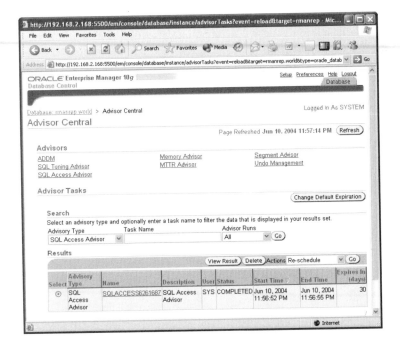

FIGURE 6.14   A SQL Access Advisor recommended action

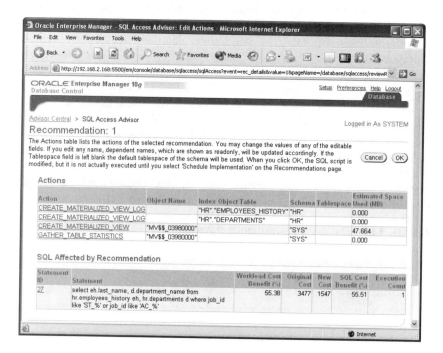

Not surprisingly, one of the recommendations provided by the SQL Access Advisor is the same as one of the recommendations from the SQL Tuning Advisor: collect statistics on the HR.EMPLOYEES_HISTORY table. As you can also see from the recommendation, implementing all the recommendations will reduce the execution cost by more than half but will require an additional 47.664MB of disk space to store the recommended materialized view.

Accessing the Database Control Performance Pages

Under the SQL Tuning Advisor and the SQL Access Advisor, you focused specifically on the SQL statements that have a high impact on the database throughput. From a much broader perspective, the EM Database Control also gives you an overall look at both the host system and the instance, potentially advising you of conditions outside the instance that may impact performance. The three major tuning areas exposed by the EM Database Control performance pages are as follows:

- CPU usage
- Top SQL statements that affect the instance
- Top sessions that affect the instance

Notice the database page shown in Figure 6.15. You can see that about half the CPU capacity is being used, with the Oracle instance being responsible for just more than 10 percent of the load on the server.

Clicking the Performance tab gives you a more detailed look at both the host performance and database session wait classes, as you can see on the Performance tab shown in Figure 6.16.

The wait events are divided into classes, such as User I/O, Network Usage, and CPU Used. In Figure 6.16, the Configuration wait class seems to have spiked the most along with most other wait classes starting at around 12:40 a.m. Clicking the Configuration link or on the corresponding portion of the graph allows you to drill down further into the sessions and SQL wait statistics. On the Active Sessions Waiting: Configuration page, shown in Figure 6.17, you can drill down either by session or by top SQL.

While waits are inevitable in any instance, you should be looking out for any SQL or sessions with a disproportionate percentage of waits compared to other SQL or sessions.

FIGURE 6.15   Database performance statistics

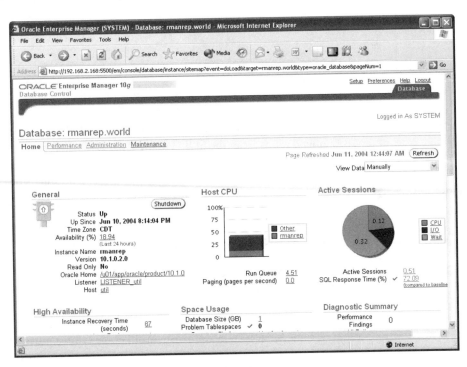

FIGURE 6.16   Database Performance tab

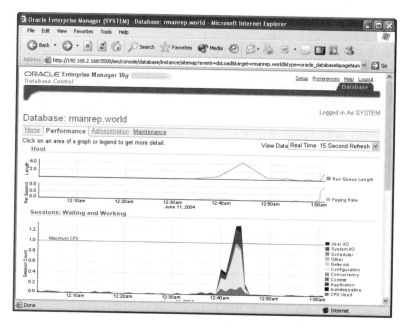

FIGURE 6.17   Active Sessions Waiting: Configuration page

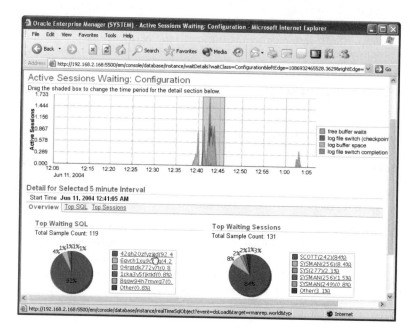

Summary

In this chapter, we presented a number of new automated methods for statistics collection in Oracle 10g. Not only do these collection methods save time for the busy DBA, they also make execution plans more efficient; even when statistics have not been explicitly collected for a table, dynamic sampling will collect statistics on the fly during SQL statement compile time.

Now that the Oracle optimizer's cost model considers both CPU and I/O costs as the default, it is important to collect statistics on both data dictionary tables and fixed tables. In addition, the deprecation of Oracle's rule-based optimizer brings with it a number of changes to the optimizer-related initialization parameters.

The SQL Tuning Advisor, one of many wizards in Oracle 10g, is an in-depth analysis tool for high-load SQL statements. The SQL Tuning Advisor will perform a number of tasks in tuning mode once high-load SQL statements have been identified by the ADDM: It provides advice on how to optimize the execution plan, estimates on the benefits for the advice, and even the SQL scripts required to implement the advice. In addition, it creates a SQL profile so that subsequent executions of the high-load SQL will be more efficient.

The SQL Access Advisor performs a more specific analysis of one SQL statement, a workload, or a schema, recommending what indexes, materialized views, and materialized view logs can be added or dropped to improve performance of queries, especially in a data warehouse environment. The SQL Access Advisor presents not only the execution benefits of its recommendations but also any additional costs such as storage and maintenance costs of new indexes or materialized views.

Near the end of the chapter, we reviewed the performance pages within the EM Database Control, showing how easy it is to identify performance problems in the database and drilling down to the session or SQL statement contributing to the performance problem.

Exam Essentials

Be able to enumerate the new features of the cost-based optimizer model. Identify the initialization parameters used to control dynamic sampling and the behavior of the cost-based model: OPTIMIZER_DYNAMIC_SAMPLING, STATISTICS_LEVEL, ALL_ROWS, and FIRST_ROWS_*n*.

List the new PL/SQL packages and scheduler jobs. Be able to use the DBMS_STATS package to gather statistics on data dictionary and fixed tables.

Understand the purpose of the SQL Tuning Advisor and how it works. Explain the two different modes for Automatic SQL Tuning using the SQL Tuning Advisor—normal mode and tuning mode—and the circumstances where each mode is appropriate. Describe the four types of analysis performed by the SQL Tuning Advisor in tuning mode: statistics analysis, SQL profiling, access path analysis, and SQL structure analysis.

Enumerate the procedures within DBMS_SQLTUNE.   Identify the purpose of each procedure within DBMS_SQLTUNE and how they are used as an alternative to the EM Database Control interface for accessing SQL Tuning Advisor.

Identify the purpose of the SQL Access Advisor.   Differentiate the types of environments in which the SQL Access Advisor is most beneficial and list the types of analyses and recommendations it performs. Describe the differences in the types of recommendations produced by the SQL Access Advisor in full mode and partial mode. Be able to use the EM Database Control wizard to produce a set of recommendations from the SQL Access Advisor wizard.

Be able to effectively use the performance pages of the EM Database Control.   Identify the purposes of each graph within the performance pages and how they relate to both Oracle processes and the host machine. Be able to drill down within the Active Sessions graph to identify the sessions and SQL statements responsible for each wait class.

Review Questions

1. Which value of the initialization parameter STATISTICS_LEVEL provides the best overall performance?

   A. ALL

   B. NONE

   C. TYPICAL

   D. BASIC

2. In which of the following steps would the Automatic Tuning Advisor (ATO) recommend changes to a query containing predicates with mismatched datatypes or functions?

   A. SQL structure analysis.

   B. Statistics analysis.

   C. Access path analysis.

   D. SQL profiling.

   E. None of the above; this recommendation would come out of the SQL Access Advisor.

3. The initialization parameter SQLTUNE_CATEGORY provides what functionality for the SQL Tuning Advisor?

   A. SQLTUNE_CATEGORY specifies the source for SQL statements used by the SQL Advisor.

   B. SQLTUNE_CATEGORY specifies the default category name for the SQL profile that is used by default when a session first connects.

   C. SQLTUNE_CATEGORY specifies whether CPU or I/O should have precedence when tuning a SQL statement.

   D. There is no such initialization parameter.

4. The predefined job _____ gathers statistics for objects in the database using the procedure _____.

   A. GATHER_STATS_JOB, DBMS_STATS.GATHER_DATABASE_STATS_JOB_PROC

   B. GATHER_STATS, DBMS_STATS.GATHER_DATABASE_STATS_JOB_PROC

   C. GATHER_STATS_JOB, DBMS_STATS.GATHER_DATABASE_STATS

   D. GATHER_STATS_JOB, DBMS_STATS.GATHER_AUTO

5. Database users can launch the SQL Tuning Advisor from the EM Database Control provided they have which of the following system privileges?

   A. DBA

   B. SYSDBA

   C. SQL_ADVISOR

   D. ADVISOR

   E. ADMINISTER SQL TUNING SET

6. Choose the correct statement regarding the SQL Access Advisor.

   A. The SQL Access Advisor takes an actual workload as input and recommends changes to SQL statements from the workload.

   B. The SQL Access Advisor takes a hypothetical workload from a schema and generates missing statistics.

   C. The SQL Access Advisor generates materialized views on the fly for high-load SQL statements identified by ADDM.

   D. The SQL Access Advisor takes an actual workload as input and recommends a new index on a table.

   E. The SQL Access Advisor takes an individual SQL statement, generates the most efficient execution plan possible, and saves it in a SQL profile.

7. The performance pages of the EM Database Control provide tuning information about all except which of the following areas?

   A. Top sessions

   B. High DML activity

   C. Top SQL statements

   D. CPU and wait classes

8. Which of the following steps is not performed by the enhanced query optimizer in tuning mode?

   A. Check objects in the query for stale or missing statistics.

   B. Identify SQL statements that tend to have bad execution plans and recommend alternatives.

   C. Determine if a new index can improve access to each table in the query.

   D. An initial execution plan is generated only for high-load SQL statements.

   E. Collect information from previous executions of the SQL statement and build a SQL profile.

9. Automatic SQL Tuning can be accessed through a command-line interface in addition to the EM Database Control. Identify the PL/SQL package used to access Automatic SQL Tuning.

   A. DBMS_MONITOR

   B. DBMS_SQLTUNE

   C. DBMS_SQL_ADVISOR

   D. DBMS_ADVISOR

   E. DBMS_SQL

10. The SQL Access Advisor can provide all except which of the following as output from its analysis?

    A. Considers storage and maintenance costs if new objects are recommended

    B. Generates drop recommendations even for a partial workload

    C. Recommends combining multiple indexes into one index

    D. Recommends materialized view logs where possible for fast refresh

11. Which of the following procedures will gather statistics on dictionary objects? (Choose all that apply.)

    A. DBMS_STATS.GATHER_FIXED_OBJECTS_STATS

    B. DBMS_STATS.GATHER_SCHEMA_STATS with the GATHER_SYS argument set to TRUE

    C. DBMS_STATS.GATHER_DATABASE_STATS with the GATHER_SYS argument set to TRUE

    D. DBMS_STATS.GATHER_DICTIONARY_STATS

12. The SQL Tuning Advisor uses one or more SQL statements as input. Which of the following is not a source of SQL statements for the SQL Tuning Advisor?

    A. SQL statements that were in the cursor cache during the previous seven days

    B. High-load SQL statements identified by ADDM

    C. A user's custom workload

    D. SQL statements captured by the AWR

13. Which of the following columns is new to the table PLAN_TABLE?

    A. CPU

    B. TIME

    C. IO

    D. SPACE

14. Statistics cannot be gathered for which of the following types of tables?

   A. Fixed tables

   B. Real tables in the Data Dictionary

   C. Real tables in non-SYSTEM user schemas

   D. None of the above, statistics can be gathered on all tables, in any schema, regardless of whether they are fixed or real.

15. If the initialization parameter STATISTICS_LEVEL is set to BASIC, what is the monitoring level for DML operations on tables?

   A. Table DML changes are not monitored

   B. The monitoring level is the same as using the command ALTER TABLE . . . MONITORING

   C. The monitoring level is the same as using the command ALTER TABLE . . . NOMONITORING

   D. BASIC is not a valid value for this parameter, only NONE, TYPICAL and ALL are allowed values

16. Which of the following values are no longer supported for the OPTIMIZER_MODE initialization parameter?

   A. CHOOSE and RULE

   B. COST and RULE

   C. FIRST_ROWS and ALL_ROWS

   D. FIRST_ROWS and FIRST_ROWS_*n*

17. Which of the following SQL statements is not a good candidate for the SQL Tuning Advisor?

   A. Transactions that have SQL statements with multiple large sorts

   B. SQL statements with heavy I/O requirements

   C. A user's ad-hoc query against the data warehouse

   D. A statement that consumes a relatively high amount of CPU time every day of the week

18. Which of the following statements about a SQL profile is not true?

   A. A SQL profile is stored persistently in the data dictionary

   B. A SQL profile can be accepted or rejected

   C. A SQL profile is used in conjunction with existing statistics to generate a good execution plan

   D. A SQL profile is used in tuning mode to produce a good execution plan

19. During the SQL Structure Analysis phase of the SQL Tuning Advisor, which of the following is not recommended by the ATO? Choose two.

A. Substituting a UNION ALL for a UNION

B. A recommendation to create an index

C. Using NOT IN instead of EXISTS

D. Data type mismatches between predicates and indexed columns

E. A recommendation to create a materialized view

20. Which of the following values is not valid for the ATTRIBUTE_NAME parameter of the procedure DBMS_SQLTUNE.ALTER_SQL_PROFILE?

A. STATUS

B. CATEGORY

C. VALUE

D. DESCRIPTION

E. NAME

Answers to Review Questions

1. C. A value of TYPICAL for STATISTICS_LEVEL collects all major statistics required for database self-management. Specifying ALL collects all statistics for TYPICAL in addition to timed operating system statistics and plan execution statistics; however, ALL adds a significant amount of overhead and may impact overall database throughput. When you specify BASIC, most statistics collections are turned off, limiting the functionality of the AWR and ADDM. The value NONE is not valid for STATISTICS_LEVEL.

2. A. Using a function or mismatched datatypes in a predicate can prevent the use of an index. SQL structure analysis will also recommend things such as using UNION ALL instead of UNION or point out Cartesian joins or other possible design mistakes.

3. B. When a SQL profile is created, you assign a category to it. When a session connects to the database, all SQL profiles with a category name that matches the value of SQLTUNE_CATEGORY automatically apply to the session. SQLTUNE_CATEGORY is a dynamic parameter that is modifiable both at the session level and for the instance.

4. A. The new procedure DBMS_STATS.GATHER_DATABASE_STATS_JOB_PROC runs in the predefined job GATHER_STATS_JOB to collect statistics on the objects that need updated statistics the most before the maintenance window closes. There is no such predefined job GATHER_STATS, and while DBMS_STATS.GATHER_DATABASE_STATS operates similarly to DBMS_STATS.GATHER_DATABASE_STATS_JOB_PROC with the GATHER AUTO option, it is not called from GATHER_STATS_JOB.

5. D. The ADVISOR system privilege is required to create a tuning task. DBA is a role and contains more privileges than necessary to use the SQL Tuning Advisor. The system privilege SYSDBA is also not required. SQL_ADVISOR is not a system privilege, and the ADMINISTER SQL TUNING SET privilege is only required to create and maintain SQL tuning sets.

6. D. The SQL Access Advisor either takes an actual workload or derives a workload from a schema and recommends indexes, materialized views, and materialized view logs to speed the execution path for queries in the workload.

7. B. While high DML activity can contribute to sessions using high CPU and I/O, it is not specifically measured and reported by the EM Database Control.

8. D. While an initial execution plan is generated for both normal mode and tuning mode, it is not limited to high-load SQL statements.

9. B. DBMS_SQLTUNE contains a number of packages used to create, drop, and execute tuning tasks, in addition to managing SQL profiles and SQL tuning sets.

10. B. The SQL Access Advisor will not generate drop recommendations for partial workloads.

11. A, B, C, D.   Several of the procedures in DBMS_STATS will gather statistics on all or some of the objects in the data dictionary, which can include statistics on fixed tables.

12. A.   The SQL Tuning Advisor cannot access SQL statements that are no longer in the cursor cache, only those that are currently in the cursor cache, unless they were captured by AWR or identified by ADDM.

13. B.   The table PLAN_TABLE has only one new column, TIME.

14. D.   Statistics can be gathered on any table in any schema, fixed or real. In addition to gathering statistics on fixed tables using the GATHER_FIXED argument of GATHER_DATABASE_STATS, statistics on individual fixed tables can be gathered by using the existing procedures within DBMS_STATS with a fixed table name as an argument.

15. A.   When STATISTICS_LEVEL is set to BASIC, table monitoring for DML changes is disabled. MONITORING and NOMONITORING are still part of the ALTER TABLE syntax, but they are ignored because monitoring is no longer allowed only at the object level. NONE is not a valid value for the STATISTICS_LEVEL parameter.

16. A.   CHOOSE and RULE are no longer supported; the only valid values for OPTIMZER_MODE are ALL_ROWS, FIRST_ROWS, and FIRST_ROWS_*n*, where n is 1, 10, 100, or 1000.

17. C.   The SQL Tuning Advisor is not useful for an occasional ad-hoc query from a user; it is most suited for frequently executed queries that have high CPU, I/O or temporary space requirements.

18. D.   A SQL profile is used in normal mode to produce a good execution plan; the profile is created in tuning mode.

19. B, E.   Recommendations to create an index comes from the ATO's Access Path Analysis or the SQL Access Advisor; recommendations for new materialized views comes from the SQL Access Advisor

20. C.   VALUE is not a valid value for ATTRIBUTE_NAME, however, it is another one of the parameter names for DBMS_SQLTUNE.ALTER_SQL_PROFILE.

Chapter

7

Backup, Recovery, and High Availability

ORACLE DATABASE 10*g* NEW FEATURES FOR ADMINISTRATORS EXAM OBJECTIVES OFFERED IN THIS CHAPTER:

✓ **Backup and Recovery Enhancements**

- Simplify file management for all recovery-related files
- Reduce restore time by applying incremental backups to data file image copies
- Simplify recovery after opening the database with the RESETLOGS option
- Speed backup times by creating faster incremental backups
- Minimize load requirements by specifying limits in backup time windows
- Save storage space through writing compressed backup sets

✓ **Flashback Any Error**

- Configure and use Flashback Database
- Recover dropped tables with the Flashback Drop feature
- Retrieve row history information with the Flashback Versions Query feature
- Audit or recover FROM transactions with the Flashback Transaction Query feature
- Recover tables to a point in time with the Flashback Table feature

 Exam objectives are subject to change at any time without prior notice and at Oracle's sole discretion. Please visit Oracle's training and certification website (http://www.oracle.com/education/certification/) for the most current exam objectives listing.

Oracle Database 10*g* (Oracle 10*g*) provides the flash recovery area where you can store not only the traditional components found in a backup strategy such as control files, archived log files, and Recovery Manager (RMAN) datafile copies but also a number of other file components such as flashback logs. The flash recovery area simplifies backup operations, and it increases the availability of the database because many backup and recovery operations using the flash recovery area can be performed when the database is open and available to users.

With each release of Oracle since Oracle 8, RMAN has gotten a number of dramatic enhancements, and Oracle 10*g* is no exception. The RMAN command syntax has been significantly standardized, making command-line syntax easier to use. RMAN provides another way to reduce the recovery time for a tablespace or the entire database: incrementally updated backups. You can apply any RMAN incremental backup to an image copy of a datafile to significantly reduce the amount of time needed to recover the datafile in case of a media failure.

RMAN also provides a number of other enhancements, making it easier to back up part of the database or the entire database. You can create image copies for the entire database with just one command instead of one command for each tablespace. Also, RMAN provides the functionality to provide a hot-swappable capability to the files in the flash recovery area, improving upon the manual techniques required in previous releases of Oracle. Finally, RMAN supports binary compression of backup sets to not only save disk space in the flash recovery area but also to potentially reduce the amount of time needed to perform the backup.

Leveraging the flash recovery area, Oracle 10*g* has a number of flashback features that can recover from nearly every logical error that you as a DBA or a user may encounter. Improving on Flashback Query from previous Oracle releases, Oracle 10*g* adds Flashback Versions Query to see all versions of rows between two times and adds Flashback Transaction Query to see all changes made by an individual transaction.

Other flashback features make recovery operations simpler and faster than in previous releases of Oracle. Flashback Database moves the database back to a previous point in time using a new type of log saved in the flash recovery area appropriately called *flashback logs*. At the table level, Flashback Table can recover a table to a previous point in time along with its dependent objects; in addition, a dropped table can easily be recovered by leveraging the new recycle bin capabilities available in each tablespace. At the row level, the Flashback Query features mentioned previously can also provide the SQL commands necessary to undo only selected portions of the table.

In this chapter, we will thoroughly review the capabilities of the flash recovery area and show how to monitor and maintain it to maximize recovery capabilities while minimizing the impact to its availability. In addition, we will cover the new features available in RMAN along with a number of miscellaneous enhancements available for backing up and recovering the database at the SQL command level. Finally, we will review the entire flashback architecture and show you how it can recover from virtually any type of logical error, from the database level all the way down to one row erroneously deleted in one table.

Leveraging the Flash Recovery Area

As the price of disk space drops, the difference in its price compared to tape is offset by the advantages of using disk as the primary backup medium: Even a slow disk can be accessed randomly a magnitude faster than a tape drive. This rapid access means that any database recovery operation will take only minutes instead of hours.

Using disk space as the primary medium for all database recovery operations is the key component of Oracle 10*g*'s flash recovery area. The *flash recovery area* is a single, unified storage area for all recovery-related files and recovery activities in an Oracle database.

The flash recovery area can be a single directory, an entire file system, or an Automatic Storage Management (ASM) disk group. To further optimize the use of disk space for recovery operations, a flash recovery area can be shared by more than one database.

In the following sections, we will cover all major aspects of a flash recovery area: what can and should be kept in the flash recovery area and how to set up a flash recovery using initialization parameters and SQL commands. Also, as with other aspects of Oracle 10*g*, we will show how you can manage most parts of the flash recovery area using the Enterprise Manager (EM) Database Control. We will also explain how to manage the flash recovery area efficiently, including how to back up the flash recovery area itself. Finally, we will review the data dictionary views related to the flash recovery area and present a few best practices for the flash recovery area in conjunction with Oracle Managed Files (OMF).

Flash Recovery Area Occupants

All the files needed to recover a database from a media failure or a logical error are contained in the flash recovery area. The files that can reside in the flash recovery area are as follows:

Control files A copy of the control file is created in the flash recovery area when the database is created. This copy of the control file can be used as one of the mirrored copies of the control file to ensure that at least one copy of the control file is available after a media failure.

Archived log files When the flash recovery area is configured, the initialization parameter LOG_ARCHIVE_DEST_10 is automatically set to the flash recovery area location. The corresponding ARC*n* processes create archived log files in the flash recovery area and any other defined LOG_ARCHIVE_DEST_*n* locations.

Flashback logs If Flashback Database is enabled, then its flashback logs are stored in the flash recovery area.

You can find more information about configuring and using flashback logs with Flashback Database later in this chapter in the section entitled "Flashback Database"

Control file and SPFILE autobackups The flash recovery area holds control file and SPFILE autobackups generated by RMAN, if RMAN is configured for control file autobackup. When RMAN backs up datafile #1, the control file is automatically included in the RMAN backup.

Data file copies   For RMAN BACKUP AS COPY image files, the default destination is the flash recovery area.

 You can find more information on RMAN image copy enhancements later in this chapter in the section entitled "Recovery with Incrementally Updated Backups."

RMAN backup sets   By default, RMAN uses the flash recovery area for both backup sets and image copies. In addition, RMAN puts restored archive log files from tape into the flash recovery area in preparation for a recovery operation.

Flash Recovery Area and SQL Commands

You must define two initialization parameters to set up the flash recovery area: DB_RECOVERY_FILE_DEST_SIZE and DB_RECOVERY_FILE_DEST. Since these are both dynamic parameters, the instance need not be shut down and restarted for the flash recovery area to be usable.

DB_RECOVERY_FILE_DEST_SIZE, which must be defined before DB_RECOVERY_FILE_DEST, defines the size of the flash recovery area. To maximize the benefits of the flash recovery area, it should be large enough to hold a copy of all datafiles, all incremental backups, online redo logs, archived redo logs not yet backed up to tape, control files, and control file autobackups. At a bare minimum, you should have enough space to hold the archived log files not yet copied to tape.

Here is an example of configuring DB_RECOVERY_FILE_DEST_SIZE:

```
SQL> alter system
  2   set db_recovery_file_dest_size = 8g scope=both;
```

The size of the flash recovery area will be 8GB, and since we used the SCOPE=BOTH parameter in the ALTER SYSTEM command, the initialization parameter will take effect immediately and will stay in effect even after a database restart.

 All instances in a Real Application Clusters (RAC) database must have the same values for DB_RECOVERY_FILE_DEST_SIZE and DB_RECOVERY_FILE_DEST.

The parameter DB_RECOVERY_FILE_DEST specifies the physical location where all flash recovery files are stored. The ASM disk group or file system must have at least as much space as the amount specified with DB_RECOVERY_FILE_DEST_SIZE, and it can have significantly more; DB_RECOVERY_FILE_DEST_SIZE, however, can be increased on the fly if more space is needed and the file system where the flash recovery area resides has the space available.

In the following example, we use the directory fra in the ASM disk group +DATA2 for the flash recovery area, like so:

```
SQL> alter system
  2   set db_recovery_file_dest = '+DATA2/fra' scope=both;
```

Clearing the value of DB_RECOVERY_FILE_DEST disables the flash recovery area; the parameter DB_RECOVERY_FILE_DEST_SIZE cannot be cleared until the DB_RECOVERY_FILE_DEST parameter has been cleared first.

Flash Recovery Area and the EM Database Control

You can create and maintain the flash recovery area using the EM Database Control. After selecting the Maintenance tab, click the Configure Recovery Settings link, and you will see the Configure Recovery Settings page shown in Figure 7.1.

In the Flash Recovery Area section of the page, you see that the flash recovery area has been configured for this database in the file system /OraFlash, with a maximum size of 15000MB (15GB). Just more than 3GB of space is currently used in the flash recovery area. Flashback logging has not yet been enabled for this database.

We will present Flashback Database and how it uses flashback logs later in this chapter in the section entitled "Flashback Database."

FIGURE 7.1   Configure Recovery Settings page

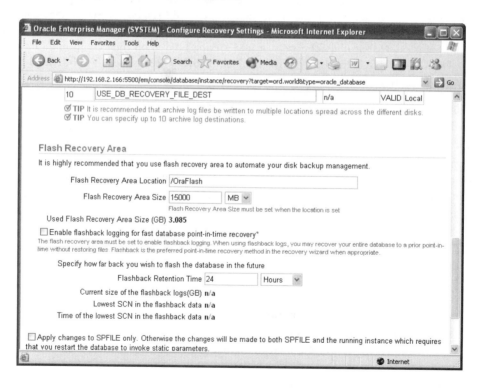

Flash Recovery Area Management

Because the space in the flash recovery area is limited by the initialization parameter DB_RECOVERY_FILE_DEST_SIZE, the Oracle database keeps track of which files are no longer needed on disk so that they can be deleted when there is not enough free space for new files. Each time a file is deleted from the flash recovery area, a message is written to the alert log.

A message is written to the alert log in other circumstances. If no files can be deleted, and the recovery area used space is at 85 percent, a warning message is issued. When the space used is at 97 percent, a critical warning is issued. These warnings are recorded in the alert log file, are viewable in the data dictionary view DBA_OUTSTANDING_ALERTS, and are available to you on the main page of the EM Database Control

When you receive these alerts, you have a number of options. If your retention policy can be adjusted to keep fewer copies of datafiles or reduce the number of days in the recovery window, this can help alleviate the space problems in the flash recovery area. Assuming that your retention policy is sound, you should instead add more disk space or back up some of the files in the flash recovery area to another device such as a tape device, as you will see in the next section.

Flash Recovery Directory Structure

The flash recovery area directory structure is used by RMAN in a very organized fashion with separate directories for each file type, such as archived logs, backupsets, image copies, control file autobackups, and so forth. In addition, each subdirectory is further divided by a datestamp, making it easy to locate backupsets or image copies based on their creation date.

In this example, you can see how the flash recovery area is cleanly subdivided by instance name (ORD), date, and backup type:

```
SQL> show parameter db_recovery_file_dest

NAME                            TYPE         VALUE
------------------------------- -----------  ------------------
db_recovery_file_dest           string       /OraFlash
db_recovery_file_dest_size      big integer  15000M


SQL> ! find /OraFlash -print
/OraFlash
/OraFlash/ORD
/OraFlash/ORD/archivelog
/OraFlash/ORD/archivelog/2004_03_22
/OraFlash/ORD/archivelog/2004_03_29
/OraFlash/ORD/archivelog/2004_03_29/
             o1_mf_1_374_06j6k8rv_.arc
...
/OraFlash/ORD/archivelog/2004_03_29/
             o1_mf_1_388_06kzq6kh_.arc
```

```
/OraFlash/ORD/archivelog/2004_03_30
/OraFlash/ORD/archivelog/2004_03_30/
                o1_mf_1_389_061387rz_.arc
/OraFlash/ORD/archivelog/2004_03_30/
                o1_mf_1_390_06139gg0_.arc
...
/OraFlash/ORD/archivelog/2004_05_03/
                o1_mf_1_803_09g5chc7_.arc
/OraFlash/ORD/archivelog/2004_05_04
/OraFlash/ORD/archivelog/2004_05_04/
                o1_mf_1_804_09g95191_.arc
/OraFlash/ORD/archivelog/2004_05_04/
                o1_mf_1_805_09gdd6fz_.arc
...
/OraFlash/ORD/archivelog/2004_05_04/
                o1_mf_1_806_09gdfqmz_.arc
/OraFlash/ORD/archivelog/2004_05_04/
                o1_mf_1_807_09gdh5j6_.arc
/OraFlash/ORD/archivelog/2004_05_20/
                o1_mf_1_1192_0btrwov1_.arc
/OraFlash/ORD/archivelog/2004_07_28/
                o1_mf_1_1605_0jjczwjb_.arc
/OraFlash/ORD/archivelog/2004_07_28/
                o1_mf_1_1608_0jjpybv1_.arc
/OraFlash/ORD/backupset
/OraFlash/ORD/backupset/2004_03_29
/OraFlash/ORD/backupset/2004_03_29/
                o1_mf_nnnd1_TAG20040329T085843_06jgf8m3_.bkp
/OraFlash/ORD/backupset/2004_03_29/
                o1_mf_nnnd1_TAG20040329T164957_06kb0r82_.bkp
/OraFlash/ORD/backupset/2004_03_28
...
/OraFlash/ORD/backupset/2004_03_28/
                o1_mf_ncnnf_TAG20040328T133408_06gb5m45_.bkp
/OraFlash/ORD/backupset/2004_03_28/
                o1_mf_nnnd0_TAG20040328T133534_06gb8872_.bkp
/OraFlash/ORD/backupset/2004_04_15
/OraFlash/ORD/autobackup
/OraFlash/ORD/autobackup/2004_03_29/
                o1_mf_s_522078814_06jzoyoz_.bkp
...
```

```
/OraFlash/ORD/autobackup/2004_03_28/
               o1_mf_s_521989816_06g8ryqb_.bkp
/OraFlash/ORD/autobackup/2004_03_28/
               o1_mf_s_522020993_06h771yb_.bkp
/OraFlash/ORD/datafile

SQL>
```

Backing Up the Flash Recovery Area

A new RMAN command makes it easy to back up recovery files in the flash recovery area once a tape drive destination is configured, as in the following example:

```
RMAN> configure channel device type sbt parms '. . .';

RMAN> backup device type sbt recovery files;
```

The BACKUP RECOVERY FILES command in this example backs up all recovery files on disk that have not previously been backed up to tape, including full and incremental backup sets, control file autobackups, archived redo logs, and datafile copies.

The EM Database Control provides identical functionality when scheduling a backup and specifying a customized backup strategy in the Schedule Backup: Strategy page shown in Figure 7.2.

Flash Recovery Area Data Dictionary Views

To support the flash recovery area, you can use one new dynamic performance view and two new columns in several existing dynamic performance views.

The new dynamic performance view V$RECOVERY_FILE_DEST provides information about the flash recovery area, such as the location of the flash recovery area, how much disk space is allocated to the flash recovery area, how much space is currently allocated in the flash recovery area, how many files are in the flash recovery area, and how much space can be freed in the flash recovery area if there is space pressure on the flash recovery area.

The query that follows displays the contents of the V$RECOVERY_FILE_DEST view:

```
SQL> select name, space_limit max_size,
  2       space_used used, space_reclaimable obsolete,
  3       number_of_files num_files
  4  from v$recovery_file_dest;


NAME           MAX_SIZE         USED   OBSOLETE   NUM_FILES
------------- ---------- ---------- ---------- ----------
/OraFlash     1.5729E+10 3392246272  181256192        272

1 row selected.
```

FIGURE 7.2   Schedule Backup: Strategy page, with the Customized option

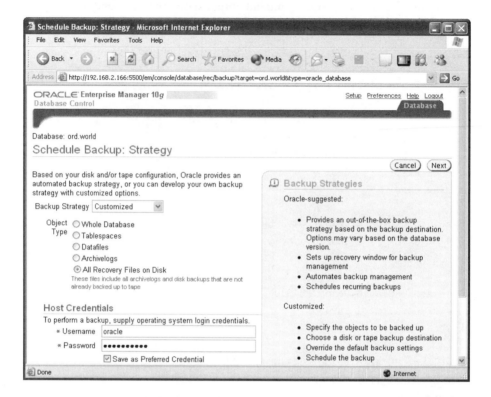

The size of the recovery area is still 15GB, unchanged from our previous query using the EM Database Control. Approximately 3.4GB of the flash recovery area is in use, and if space is running low, about 181MB of disk space can be freed. Currently 272 files are in the flash recovery area.

While using the EM Database Control is convenient and a time-saver in many cases, sometimes you need to query the dynamic performance views directly. The two columns in the preceding query—SPACE_RECLAIMABLE (OBSOLETE) and NUMBER_OF_FILES (NUM_FILES)—are not exposed via the EM Database Control interface.

In addition to the new dynamic performance view V$RECOVERY_FILE_DEST, two new columns appear in existing dynamic performance views: IS_RECOVERY_DEST_FILE and BYTES.

The column IS_RECOVERY_DEST_FILE appears in the following dynamic performance views:

- V$CONTROLFILE

- V$LOGFILE

- V$ARCHIVED_LOG

- V$DATAFILE_COPY

- V$BACKUP_PIECE

The value of the column is YES if the file was created in the flash recovery area; otherwise the value is NO. The following SQL command output shows the name and status for archived redo log files created in the last three hours:

```
SQL> select name, completion_time, is_recovery_dest_file
  2    from v$archived_log
  3   where completion_time > sysdate-0.125;


NAME                       COMPLETIO IS_
-------------------------- --------- ---
/OraFlash/ORD/archivelog/ 04-JUL-04 YES
2004_07_04/o1_mf_1_1891_0
gkg9x52_.arc

/OraFlash/ORD/archivelog/ 04-JUL-04 YES
2004_07_04/o1_mf_1_1892_0
gkgqq60_.arc

/OraFlash/ORD/archivelog/ 04-JUL-04 YES
2004_07_04/o1_mf_1_1893_0
gkj2bcw_.arc

/OraFlash/ORD/archivelog/ 04-JUL-04 YES
2004_07_04/o1_mf_1_1894_0
gkmlpcp_.arc

/OraFlash/ORD/archivelog/ 04-JUL-04 YES
2004_07_04/o1_mf_1_1895_0
gkqzfoz_.arc


5 rows selected.
```

In this database, all the archived redo logs are created in the flash recovery area.

The other new column is the BYTES column in the view V$BACKUP_PIECE. This column indicates the size, in bytes, of the file in the flash recovery area. Here is an example:

```
SQL> select recid, handle, bytes from v$backup_piece
  2    where recid = 25;


    RECID HANDLE                                       BYTES
---------- ------------------------------------ ----------
       25 /u10/oradata/ord/0tfh79h4_1_1          179591168


1 row selected.
```

Flash Recovery Area Best Practices

While Oracle Managed Files (OMF) has been available since Oracle 9*i*, it was recommended only for testing and development databases or production databases with logical volume managers that supported large, dynamically extensible files with RAID support.

Now that Oracle 10*g* supports OMF with ASM and the flash recovery area, OMF is a viable and useful option for many more database environments. Setting the initialization parameters DB_CREATE_FILE_DEST and DB_CREATE_ONLINE_LOG_DEST_*n* to a location in an ASM disk group lets Oracle manage the file naming for all database files while ASM manages the performance and redundancy capabilities required in a production database environment.

Setting the initialization parameters DB_RECOVERY_FILE_DEST_SIZE and DB_RECOVERY_FILE_DEST puts all recovery-related files in one place, simplifying administration. OMF is automatically used for file naming when a flash recovery area is defined.

Performing Incremental and Incrementally Updated Backups

Two new features of RMAN further reduce the time it takes to both back up and restore your database. Incrementally updated backups apply RMAN incremental backups to an existing image copy, potentially reducing recovery time in the event of media failure. Conversely, RMAN's fast incremental backup capability uses a tracking file to identify only the blocks that need to be backed up in an incremental backup scenario, potentially reducing the amount of time it takes to create the incremental backup in the first place.

Recovery with Incrementally Updated Backups

An RMAN *incrementally updated backup* recovers a copy of a datafile by applying an RMAN incremental backup to an existing RMAN image copy. The updated image copy is identical to an image copy made at the same system change number (SCN) as the incremental backup that was applied to the image copy. For example, assume that you make an image copy of datafile #1 (part of the SYSTEM tablespace) on Sunday at SCN 1052340 and then perform one or more incremental backups through Wednesday at SCN 2283487. Next, you perform an incrementally updated backup after the last incremental backup: The image copy of datafile #1 is identical to an image copy of datafile #1 made at SCN 2283487. Incrementally updated backups save time in recovery situations because fewer archived log files need to be applied in a media failure scenario.

In the following example, you have at least one image copy of the SYSTEM tablespace's datafiles, and you perform an incremental RMAN backup:

```
[oracle@oltp oracle]$ rman target /

Recovery Manager: Release 10.1.0.2.0 - Production
```

```
Copyright (c) 1995, 2004, Oracle.  All rights reserved.

connected to target database: ORD (DBID=1387044942)

RMAN> backup incremental level 1 tablespace system;

Starting backup at 05-JUL-04
using target database controlfile
          instead of recovery catalog
allocated channel: ORA_DISK_1
channel ORA_DISK_1: sid=254 devtype=DISK
channel ORA_DISK_1: starting compressed incremental
    level 1 datafile backupset
channel ORA_DISK_1: specifying datafile(s) in backupset
input datafile fno=00001
          name=/u05/oradata/ord/system01.dbf
channel ORA_DISK_1: starting piece 1 at 05-JUL-04
channel ORA_DISK_1: finished piece 1 at 05-JUL-04
piece
  handle=/OraFlash/ORD/backupset/2004_07_05/
    o1_mf_nnnd1_TAG20040705T084706_0glpyyjy_.bkp
          comment=NONE
channel ORA_DISK_1: backup set complete,
          elapsed time: 00:01:36
Finished backup at 05-JUL-04

Starting Control File and SPFILE Autobackup at 05-JUL-04
piece handle=/OraFlash/ORD/autobackup/2004_07_05/
    o1_mf_s_530700523_0glq1zo2_.bkp comment=NONE
Finished Control File and SPFILE Autobackup at 05-JUL-04

RMAN>
```

Since you have not performed an image copy in a while, you decide to update the existing image copy of the database with the recent incremental backups, including the one you just made.

```
RMAN> recover copy of datafile 1;

Starting recover at 05-JUL-04
using channel ORA_DISK_1
channel ORA_DISK_1: starting incremental
        datafile backupset restore
```

```
channel ORA_DISK_1: specifying datafile copies to recover
recovering datafilecopy fno=00001
   name=/OraFlash/ORD/datafile/o1_mf_system_0ggyw94d_.dbf
channel ORA_DISK_1: restored backup piece 1
piece handle=/OraFlash/ORD/backupset/2004_07_05/
      o1_mf_nnnd1_TAG20040705T084706_0glpyyjy_.bkp
         tag=TAG20040705T084706
channel ORA_DISK_1: restore complete
Finished recover at 05-JUL-04

Starting Control File and SPFILE Autobackup at 05-JUL-04
piece handle=/OraFlash/ORD/autobackup/2004_07_05/
      o1_mf_s_530702222_0glrq0n9_.bkp comment=NONE
Finished Control File and SPFILE Autobackup at 05-JUL-04
```

RMAN>

The image copy of datafile #1, /OraFlash/ORD/datafile/o1_mf_system_0ggyw94d_ .dbf, is now updated with all incremental backups and can reduce the amount of time it takes to perform a recovery of the SYSTEM tablespace since any archived redo log files created before the incremental recovery do not need to be applied. If multiple image copies of the SYSTEM tablespace's datafiles exist, only the latest version of the image copy is updated with the incremental backup.

It is easy to set up automated incrementally updated backups using the Oracle-suggested strategy in the EM Database Control. On the Schedule Backup: Strategy page, shown in Figure 7.3, you select the Oracle-suggested backup strategy and specify Disk as the only backup medium.

Oracle's suggested strategy starts with a full database copy as the first backup, with incremental backups and incrementally updated backups daily.

Fast Incremental Backups

Fast incremental backups optimize an RMAN incremental backup by quickly identifying those data blocks that have changed since the previous backup. Fast incremental backups require the use of a *change-tracking file* to track the physical location of all database changes. During an incremental backup, RMAN uses the change tracking file to quickly identify only the blocks that have changed, avoiding the time-consuming task of reading the entire datafile to determine which blocks have changed. The slight overhead of maintaining the tracking file is easily offset by the time savings whenever an incremental backup occurs, especially in databases that are not heavily updated, although most online transaction processing system (OLTP) databases can benefit from fast incremental backups.

Disk space is another consideration when using fast incremental backups: The size of the change-tracking file is proportional to the size of the database and the number of nodes in a RAC environment. A new background process, *CTWR (Change Tracking Writer)*, is also required when using fast incremental backups.

FIGURE 7.3   Schedule Backup: Strategy page, with the Oracle-Suggested option selected

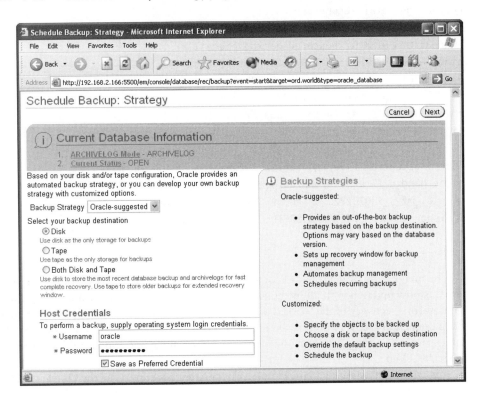

Enabling block change tracking is straightforward using OMF and an **ALTER DATABASE** command, as in this example:

```
SQL> alter database enable block change tracking;
Database altered.
```

Because we used OMF, the block change-tracking file was automatically named and placed in the directory specified by the **DB_CREATE_FILE_DEST** initialization parameter.

```
SQL> show parameter db_create_file_dest

NAME                        TYPE          VALUE
------------------------    -----------   ----------------
db_create_file_dest         string        /u04/oradata

SQL> ! ls -l /u04/oradata/ORD/changetracking
total 11348
-rw-r-----    1 oracle    oinstall 11600384 Jul  5 10:05
```

```
o1_mf_Oglvc2gb_.chg
```

SQL>

If you are not using OMF, then you will have to add the USING FILE clause to the ALTER DATABASE command when enabling block change tracking, as in this example:

```
SQL> alter database
  2    enable block change tracking using file
  3    '/u04/oradata/ord/changetracking/chg01.dbf';
Database altered.
```

> Oracle recommends placing the block change-tracking file on the same disk as the database files; this is automatic if you are using OMF.

ALTER DATABASE DISABLE BLOCK CHANGE TRACKING turns off support for fast incremental backups. Enabling and disabling via the EM Database Control is also straightforward, as you can see in Figure 7.4, the Configure Backup Settings page.

FIGURE 7.4   Configure Backup Settings page: Performing fast incremental backups

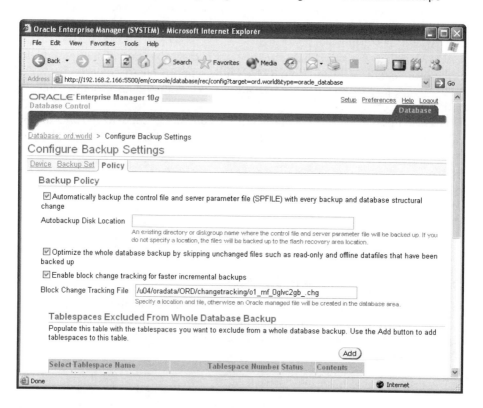

On the EM Database Control page in Figure 7.4, you can see the block change-tracking file you created in the SQL ALTER DATABASE command.

The dynamic performance view V$BLOCK_CHANGE_TRACKING shows where the block change-tracking file is stored, whether it is enabled, and how large it is, as you can see in the following query:

```
SQL> select * from v$block_change_tracking;

STATUS      FILENAME                        BYTES
----------  --------------------------  ----------
ENABLED     /u04/oradata/ORD/changetra   11599872
            cking/o1_mf_0glvc2gb_.chg


1 row selected.
```

Using Miscellaneous Backup Features

A number of other enhancements have been made to both RMAN and traditional backup commands to make the syntax more consistent as well as to make certain operations less error prone and easier to perform.

RMAN enhancements include an easier way to create backups of multiple tablespaces as well as the entire database; in addition, RMAN now supports binary compression of backup sets to reduce the disk space required for backups, as well as providing a compression scheme that is optimized for Oracle datafiles.

For backups outside RMAN, the new ALTER DATABASE...BEGIN/END BACKUP command provides shorthand for placing individual tablespaces into BACKUP mode while skipping read-only or missing datafiles for any tablespace in the database.

RMAN Command Changes

Other enhancements to RMAN include the ability to drop a database, including the backup files; automatic channel failover; enhanced RMAN scripts; and controlling the resources used by RMAN during backup and recovery operations by using the new duration and throttling options.

Dropping a Database in RMAN

Although you can drop a database from the SQL*Plus command line and the Database Configuration Assistant (DBCA), dropping the database from RMAN has the additional benefit of dropping all backup copies and archived log files for the database if you include the INCLUDING BACKUPS clause, as shown here:

```
RMAN> drop database including backups;
```

If you drop the database from DBCA or SQL*Plus, or you omit the INCLUDING BACKUPS clause in RMAN, you can still remove the database files manually. To remove the database information from the repository catalog when you drop a database from DBCA or SQL*Plus, use the RMAN UNREGISTER DATABASE command. If you are only using the control file for your RMAN metadata, this command is not necessary.

Automatic Channel Failover

If you are using multiple channels during an RMAN backup to either tape or disk and one of the channels fails, the backup job continues on the remaining channels. Any errors including channel errors are reported in the dynamic performance view V$RMAN_OUTPUT after the backup job is complete.

Enhanced Scripting Capabilities

Scripting capabilities have been enhanced in RMAN. Text scripts can be converted to stored scripts, and vice versa; in addition, *global script* capabilities allow all databases that connect to the same catalog database to share scripts, reducing script maintenance efforts.

Duration, Throttling, and Partial Backup Options

To reduce the impact to ongoing transactions in the database while RMAN backups are running, new duration, throttling, and partial backup options are available in RMAN BACKUP commands. The options are as follows:

BACKUP...DURATION   By specifying a maximum duration or time frame for a backup operation, you can minimize the impact of the backup operation in a 24/7 environment. The new DURATION option, which replaces RATE and READRATE in previous versions of RMAN, throttles the I/O requirements of the backup operation. To spread out the backup of the USERS tablespace over a maximum of two hours, use the following command:

```
RMAN> backup tablespace users duration 2:00;
```

By default, the backup will complete as fast as possible within the two-hour time frame; see MINIMIZE LOAD and MINIMIZE TIME.

BACKUP...DURATION...PARTIAL   Adding PARTIAL to the BACKUP command prevents an error message from being issued by RMAN in case the backup does not finish the operation in the specified amount of time. Any complete backup sets are available for recovery operations, and any partial or incomplete backup operations will have to be restarted.

BACKUP...DURATION...MINIMIZE LOAD   The MINIMIZE LOAD clause, used with disk backups only, automatically adjusts the throughput of the backup operation to complete the backup in the estimated completion time specified by DURATION.

BACKUP...DURATION...MINIMIZE TIME   MINIMIZE TIME, the default when using DURATION, will complete the backup in the shortest possible time.

In the following example you will back up the USERS tablespace over a two hour period, minimizing the impact to the rest of the database:

```
RMAN> backup duration 2:00 minimize load
2> tablespace users;

Starting backup at 29-JUL-04
using channel ORA_DISK_1
channel ORA_DISK_1: starting compressed
     full datafile backupset
channel ORA_DISK_1: specifying datafile(s) in backupset
input datafile fno=00004 name=/u05/oradata/ord/users01.dbf
input datafile fno=00007 name=/u05/oradata/ord/users02.dbf
channel ORA_DISK_1: starting piece 1 at 29-JUL-04
channel ORA_DISK_1: finished piece 1 at 29-JUL-04
piece handle=/OraFlash/ORD/backupset/2004_07_29/
     o1_mf_nnndf_TAG20040729T223445_0jmjgpmj_.bkp
     comment=NONE
channel ORA_DISK_1: backup set complete,
     elapsed time: 01:59:55
channel ORA_DISK_1: throttle time: 1:59:37
Finished backup at 29-JUL-04

Starting Control File and SPFILE Autobackup at 29-JUL-04
piece handle=/OraFlash/ORD/autobackup/2004_07_29/
     o1_mf_s_532823802_0jmjld7d_.bkp comment=NONE
Finished Control File and SPFILE Autobackup at 29-JUL-04

RMAN>
```

As the backup proceeds, RMAN may speed up or slow down the operation based on its estimate of the number of blocks to back up and the current throughput of the backup operation to hit the duration target as closely as possible.

Online Backup Mode

For environments that are not yet using RMAN for backup and recovery operations, the BEGIN BACKUP and END BACKUP clauses have been added to the ALTER DATABASE command.

Entire Database Backup

To put every tablespace into online backup mode, you can use the following command:

```
SQL> alter database begin backup;
```

You no longer have a need to place each tablespace into backup mode individually unless you want to back up only one tablespace at a time for performance reasons. The only requirements for this mode are that the database must be in ARCHIVELOG mode and the database must be mounted and open.

Once the entire database is in online backup mode, the database cannot be shut down normally, tablespaces cannot be placed in read-only mode, and tablespaces cannot be taken offline.

File Status and *BEGIN BACKUP*

When the entire database is in online backup mode with BEGIN BACKUP, no error messages are generated if any datafiles are missing, offline or read-only. However, error messages are still issued if an individual tablespace is placed into online backup mode and any of its datafiles are missing, offline, or read-only.

In the following example, the USERS2 tablespace is READ ONLY when the database is placed into BEGIN BACKUP mode:

```
SQL> alter tablespace users2 begin backup;
Database altered.

alter tablespace users2 begin backup
*
ERROR at line 1:
ORA-01642: begin backup not needed for read only tablespace 'USERS2'
```

File Status and *END BACKUP*

As with BEGIN BACKUP, taking the entire database out of online backup mode with END BACKUP will not generate an error message if any datafiles are read-only, missing, or offline. However, a warning message is generated for any offline datafiles.

Backing Up Different Object Types with RMAN

Enhancements to RMAN commands make your job even easier either by reducing the number of commands needed to perform a backup or by expanding the number of options available for backing up each type of object, whether it is a tablespace, a datafile, an archived log file, or the entire database.

Creating Image Copies

In previous versions of RMAN, the COPY command made image copies of datafiles. This command is deprecated in Oracle 10g's version of RMAN for the BACKUP AS COPY command, which can copy an entire database, multiple tablespaces, datafiles, archived log files, or datafile copies in a single command. For disk devices, the default backup type is COPY; for tape devices, the default backup type is still BACKUPSET.

In the following example, you use the BACKUP AS COPY command to make an image copy of both the SYSTEM and SYSAUX tablespaces to the flash recovery area:

```
RMAN> backup as copy tablespace system, sysaux;

Starting backup at 05-JUL-04
using channel ORA_DISK_1
channel ORA_DISK_1: starting datafile copy
input datafile fno=00001
     name=/u05/oradata/ord/system01.dbf
output filename=/OraFlash/ORD/datafile/
     o1_mf_system_0gm4w4fz_.dbf tag=TAG20040705T124433
     recid=31 stamp=530714993
channel ORA_DISK_1: datafile copy complete,
     elapsed time: 00:05:19
channel ORA_DISK_1: starting datafile copy
input datafile fno=00003
     name=/u05/oradata/ord/sysaux01.dbf
output filename=/OraFlash/ORD/datafile/
     o1_mf_sysaux_0gm563sn_.dbf tag=TAG20040705T124433
     recid=32 stamp=530715257
channel ORA_DISK_1: datafile copy complete,
     elapsed time: 00:04:26
Finished backup at 05-JUL-04

Starting Control File and SPFILE Autobackup at 05-JUL-04
piece handle=/OraFlash/ORD/autobackup/2004_07_05/
     o1_mf_s_530715260_0gm5gmfm_.bkp comment=NONE
Finished Control File and SPFILE Autobackup at 05-JUL-04

RMAN>
```

Notice that RMAN automatically determines which datafiles belong to each tablespace and performs the image copy for each. In addition, the image copies generated by RMAN can be used directly in a recovery operation without using RMAN to extract a datafile from a previous backup set.

Using the EM Database Control, it's easy to change from backup sets to image copies on the Configure Backup Settings page, as you can see in Figure 7.5.

Full Database Backup

You can back up the entire database with the following command:

RMAN> backup database;

Depending on the default backup type, either backup sets will be created for all datafiles in the database or, as in the previous example, image copies.

You may want to back up a previous backup to tape, rather than create a direct backup to tape, so as not to impact a database that is up and running. In RMAN, you can use the following command to back up a previous copy of the entire database to the default tape device:

RMAN> backup copy of database;

Note the syntax differences between this and the BACKUP AS COPY DATABASE command: BACKUP AS COPY creates a direct image copy of the database, and BACKUP COPY OF creates a copy of the backup itself.

FIGURE 7.5   Configure Backup Settings page, with the Image Copy option selected

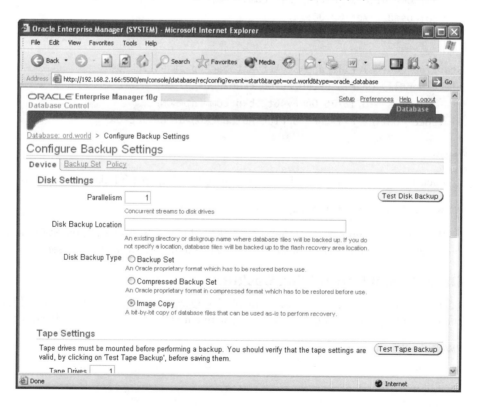

Individual Tablespace Backup

As you saw earlier in this chapter, RMAN makes it easy to make image copies of all datafiles within one or more tablespaces. As with most RMAN BACKUP commands, you can specify either AS COPY or AS BACKUPSET. If the default backup type is COPY, you can still take advantage of the convenient tablespace syntax, as in the following example:

```
RMAN> backup as backupset tablespace idx_8;

Starting backup at 05-JUL-04
using channel ORA_DISK_1
channel ORA_DISK_1: starting full datafile backupset
channel ORA_DISK_1: specifying datafile(s) in backupset
input datafile fno=00017 name=/u08/oradata/ord/idx08.dbf
channel ORA_DISK_1: starting piece 1 at 05-JUL-04
channel ORA_DISK_1: finished piece 1 at 05-JUL-04
piece handle=/OraFlash/ORD/backupset/2004_07_05/
     o1_mf_nnndf_TAG20040705T131930_0gm6x1z1_.bkp
     comment=NONE
channel ORA_DISK_1: backup set complete,
     elapsed time: 00:00:15
Finished backup at 05-JUL-04

Starting Control File and SPFILE Autobackup at 05-JUL-04
piece handle=/OraFlash/ORD/autobackup/2004_07_05/
     o1_mf_s_530716786_0gm6y46t_.bkp comment=NONE
Finished Control File and SPFILE Autobackup at 05-JUL-04

RMAN>
```

Backing up a tablespace backup is similar to backing up a full database backup to tape.

```
RMAN> backup copy of tablespace idx_8;
```

If the BACKUP command includes datafile #1, which is always part of the SYSTEM tablespace, then RMAN will add a copy of the control file and SPFILE in the backup set.

Datafile and Control File Backup

Backing up individual datafiles and control files operates similarly to backing up tablespaces. In the following example, you are explicitly backing up the control file to the flash recovery area:

```
RMAN> backup current controlfile;
```

The backup made by the previous command is identical to the backup made by the following command in SQL*Plus:

```
SQL> alter database backup controlfile to '/u04/oradata/ord/ctl.bk';
```

Compressed Backups

RMAN has been enhanced to provide *binary compression* for backup sets, reducing the amount of disk space required to make a backup. In many cases, the additional overhead required to compress the backup set is offset by the reduced I/O load when writing the backup set to disk. In addition, the binary compression algorithm used by RMAN is optimized for use with Oracle datafiles, making it a better alternative than using operating system file system or tape device compression schemes.

You can specify compression for a specific RMAN backup, or you can set it as the default for all RMAN backup sets. To specify compression in an RMAN command, add the COMPRESSED keyword. Here is an example of using the COMPRESSED keyword on a backup of the USERS2 tablespace:

```
RMAN> backup as compressed backupset
2>          tablespace users2;

Starting backup at 29-JUL-04
using target database controlfile instead of
     recovery catalog
allocated channel: ORA_DISK_1
channel ORA_DISK_1: sid=242 devtype=DISK
channel ORA_DISK_1: starting compressed
     full datafile backupset
channel ORA_DISK_1: specifying datafile(s) in backupset
input datafile fno=00009 name=/u09/oradata/ord/big_users.dbf
channel ORA_DISK_1: starting piece 1 at 29-JUL-04
channel ORA_DISK_1: finished piece 1 at 29-JUL-04
piece handle=/OraFlash/ORD/backupset/2004_07_29/
     o1_mf_nnndf_TAG20040729T230940_0jmlj8rh_.bkp
     comment=NONE
channel ORA_DISK_1: backup set complete,
     elapsed time: 00:00:16
Finished backup at 29-JUL-04

Starting Control File and SPFILE Autobackup at 29-JUL-04
```

```
piece handle=/OraFlash/ORD/autobackup/2004_07_29/
     o1_mf_s_532825797_0jmljq92_.bkp comment=NONE
Finished Control File and SPFILE Autobackup at 29-JUL-04

RMAN> quit

Recovery Manager complete.
```

Note that the backup time for this backup is less than half than the uncompressed version of the backup, with the added bonus of a smaller backup set; In the example below, you compare the size of the backupset to the size of the tablespace you just backed up:

```
$ ls -l /OraFlash/ORD/backupset/2004_07_29
-rw-r-----    1 oracle   oinstall   1818624 Jul 29 23:09
                 o1_mf_nnndf_TAG20040729T230940_0jmlj8rh_.bkp

$ ls -l /u05/oradata/ord/users02.dbf
-rw-r-----    1 oracle   oinstall   5251072 Jul 29 23:05
                 /u05/oradata/ord/users02.dbf
$
```

The compression of the USERS2 tablespace is well over 60 percent.

 RMAN image copies cannot be compressed.

It's also easy to make compression the default for disk or tape using the CONFIGURE command.

```
RMAN> configure device type disk
2>        backup type to compressed backupset;

old RMAN configuration parameters:
CONFIGURE DEVICE TYPE DISK BACKUP TYPE TO
     BACKUPSET PARALLELISM 1;
new RMAN configuration parameters:
CONFIGURE DEVICE TYPE DISK BACKUP TYPE TO
     COMPRESSED BACKUPSET PARALLELISM 1;
new RMAN configuration parameters are successfully stored
released channel: ORA_DISK_1

RMAN>
```

Using the EM Database Control, it's easy to specify compression for all disk backups, as you can see in Figure 7.6, the Configure Backup Settings screen.

FIGURE 7.6   Configure Backup Settings page, with Compression Backup Set option selected

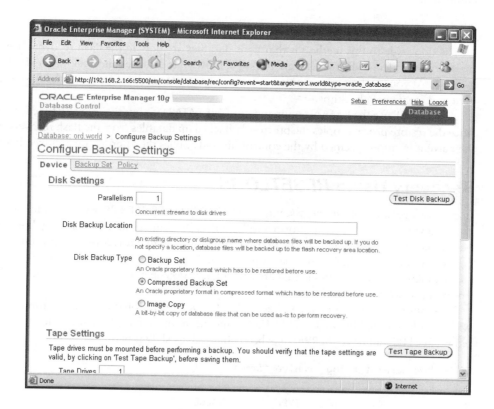

Introducing Miscellaneous Recovery Features

In the following sections, we will cover a couple of miscellaneous enhancements to both RMAN and SQL that make backups even more versatile in a recovery situation. RMAN now supports a fast way to recover an entire database by using the backup datafiles in the flash recovery area as the primary datafiles, dramatically reducing the amount of time it takes to bring the database back online compared to other recovery methods. The new RESETLOGS recovery option allows you to retain the use of archived log files created before the RESETLOGS command was issued.

Fast Recovery Using *SWITCH DATABASE*

The new RMAN command `SWITCH DATABASE` is the fastest way to recover a database using backup copies of the database: No files are copied, and no files need to be renamed. It takes one command.

```
RMAN> switch database to copy;
```

The downside to this method is that your datafiles are now in the flash recovery area. This may cause problems when you create backups: Now your datafiles and backups are in the same location. At your earliest opportunity, you should migrate the datafiles out of the flash recovery area and create new backups.

You can still use the RMAN command `RESTORE DATABASE`, but the recovery time is increased since the restore process copies the previously backed up datafiles from the flash recovery area to the current location specified by the control file and applies the appropriate archived log files.

Recovery Using *RESETLOGS*

In previous versions of Oracle, issuing the `ALTER DATABASE OPEN RESETLOGS` command required you to immediately perform a full database backup. In addition, any backups created before the `RESETLOGS` operation were not usable for subsequent recovery operations.

As of Oracle 10g, the RMAN backups created before the `RESETLOGS` operation are still usable. Incremental backups created after the `RESETLOGS` operation can be applied to full backups of a previous database incarnation.

To ensure that log files created after the `RESETLOGS` operation do not have naming conflicts with log files created before the `RESETLOGS` operation, the default format for the initialization parameter `LOG_ARCHIVE_FORMAT` has been changed, as shown here:

```
SQL> show parameter log_archive_format

NAME                           TYPE        VALUE
------------------------------ ----------- -----------------
log_archive_format             string      %t_%s_%r.dbf
```

The parameter %r represents the `RESETLOGS` identifier and changes every time a `RESETLOGS` operation occurs, ensuring that no filename collisions exist in the flash recovery area or an archived log file destination.

Flashing Back Any Logical Error

Oracle 10g supports a number of features that both users and DBAs alike can use to *flashback*, or recover, from many different types of logical errors that can occur in a database, including

a row erroneously deleted from a table, a table that was accidentally dropped, and database-wide logical corruption because the nightly batch job ran twice.

Flashback Query, available in Oracle 9*i*, has been enhanced to include two new types of queries: Flashback Versions Query and Flashback Transaction Query. Flashback Versions Query allows a user or the DBA to see all versions of a table's row between two times, and with Flashback Transaction Query you can see all transactions that changed a row between two times.

Flashback Database provides an easy way to move the entire database back to a point of time in the past if widespread corruption is found in the database and if restoring individual tables or specific rows in tables would be too time-consuming.

Flashback Table brings a table and all its dependent objects back to a point in time if only a small number of tables have been corrupted; Flashback Drop restores a table to its previous state if it has been erroneously or inadvertently dropped.

While all these features are referred to as *flashback features*, they are implemented in a number of ways. Flashback Query relies on undo information in the undo tablespace, and Flashback Versions and Transaction Query rely on online and archived redo log files. Flashback Drop uses a new construct available in each tablespace called the *recycle bin*. Finally, Flashback Database uses a new type of log file that is saved in the flash recovery area called, appropriately enough, *flashback logs*.

Flashback Database

Flashback Database allows you to quickly revert the entire database to its state as of a previous point in time. Rather than restoring an older copy of each datafile and performing incomplete recovery, the starting point is the present and recent changes are backed out of the database. For databases that get larger and larger, traditional point-in-time recovery techniques become prohibitive in terms of the amount of time it takes to restore datafiles; using Flashback Database can take significantly less time since only the most recent changes need to be backed out. Figure 7.7 shows how Flashback Database saves time: after a user error, the time-consuming file restoration step has been eliminated.

Whenever Flashback Database is enabled, the new background process RVWR is started in order to write data from the *flashback buffer* in the System Global Area (SGA) to flashback logs in the flash recovery area. For large production databases, the value of the LOG_BUFFER parameter should be at least 8MB to ensure that 16MB is allocated to the flashback buffer; 16MB is the maximum size of the flashback buffer (one granule).

In the following sections, we will show you the SQL commands or the EM Database Control web pages used to configure flashback database and flashback logs in the flash recovery area. We will present the new data dictionary views that can help you identify how much space in the flash recovery area will be needed to satisfy your retention target; in addition, you will see how to use both SQL commands and the EM Database Control to perform the actual flashback command. Finally, we will show you how to exclude tablespaces from generating flashback logs, as well as a few caveats for using flashback database.

FIGURE 7.7   Flashback Database Eliminates Restore Time

Incomplete Recovery Scenario:

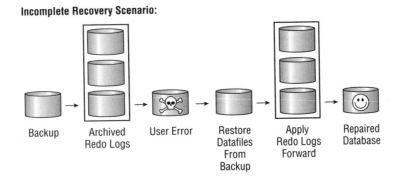

| Backup | Archived Redo Logs | User Error | Restore Datafiles From Backup | Apply Redo Logs Forward | Repaired Database |

Flashback Database Scenario:

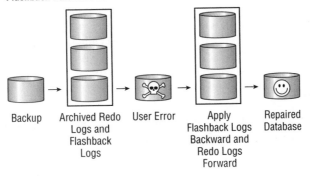

| Backup | Archived Redo Logs and Flashback Logs | User Error | Apply Flashback Logs Backward and Redo Logs Forward | Repaired Database |

Configuring Flashback Database Using SQL

Flashback data is stored in the flash recovery area. The number of flashback logs to keep in the flash recovery area is measured in minutes using the initialization parameter DB_FLASHBACK_RETENTION_TARGET. You enable Flashback Database with an ALTER DATABASE command. Here are the SQL commands to set the parameter and enable Flashback Database:

```
SQL> shutdown immediate;
Database closed.
Database dismounted.
ORACLE instance shut down.

SQL> startup mount exclusive
ORACLE instance started.
```

```
Total System Global Area   197132288 bytes
Fixed Size                    778076 bytes
Variable Size              162537636 bytes
Database Buffers            33554432 bytes
Redo Buffers                  262144 bytes
Database mounted.


SQL> alter system set
  2      db_flashback_retention_target=60
  3      scope=both;

System altered.

SQL> alter database flashback on;

Database altered.

SQL> alter database open;

Database altered.

SQL>
```

In this example, you shut down the database and restart the database in MOUNT EXCLUSIVE mode; you must be in MOUNT EXCLUSIVE and ARCHIVELOG mode to disable Flashback Database. The initialization parameter DB_FLASHBACK_RETENTION_TARGET is set to 60 minutes. Finally, the database is opened. Any changes to the database are recorded in both the redo log files and the flashback logs.

To ensure that Flashback Database is enabled, you can check the dynamic performance view V$DATABASE, as in the following example:

```
SQL> select flashback_on from v$database;

FLA
---
YES


1 row selected.
```

Disabling Flashback Database with ALTER DATABASE FLASHBACK OFF automatically deletes all flashback logs in the flash recovery area.

Flash Back Using SQL or RMAN Commands

In the previous example, you configured Flashback Database to keep enough flashback logs in the flash recovery area to support a database flashback up to 60 minutes into the past. In the following example, you discover that several order-entry database tables in the database were accidentally overwritten with rows from the previous night's batch run; the users indicate that the batch job ran about 15 minutes ago. You decide to use Flashback Database to flash the database back 30 minutes to a state before the critical order entry tables were corrupted. You run the following SQL command:

```
SQL> flashback database to timestamp(sysdate-(1/48));
flashback database to timestamp(sysdate-(1/48))
*
ERROR at line 1:
ORA-38757: Database must be mounted EXCLUSIVE and not
     open to FLASHBACK.

SQL> shutdown immediate;
Database closed.
Database dismounted.
ORACLE instance shut down.
SQL> startup mount exclusive;
ORACLE instance started.

Total System Global Area  197132288 bytes
Fixed Size                   778076 bytes
Variable Size             162537636 bytes
Database Buffers           33554432 bytes
Redo Buffers                 262144 bytes
Database mounted.
SQL> flashback database to timestamp(sysdate-(1/48));

Flashback complete.

SQL> alter database open;
alter database open
*
ERROR at line 1:
ORA-01589: must use RESETLOGS or NORESETLOGS option
     for database open

SQL> alter database open resetlogs;
```

```
Database altered.
```

SQL>

Note from this example that the database must be in MOUNT EXCLUSIVE mode to execute the flashback operation; in addition, once the flashback operation is complete, the database must be opened with RESETLOGS as if a traditional incomplete recovery had been performed; Flashback Database is essentially another form of incomplete recovery.

In addition to using a TIMESTAMP value for the FLASHBACK DATABASE command, you can use an SCN in the SQL version; using RMAN, you can flash back to a time stamp, SCN, or log sequence number (SEQUENCE) and thread number (THREAD).

Configuring and Using Flashback Database with the EM Database Control

Using the EM Database Control, you can enable Flashback Database on the Configure Recovery Settings page accessible from the Maintenance tab, as shown in Figure 7.8.

FIGURE 7.8   Configure Recovery Settings page: Enabling Flashback Database

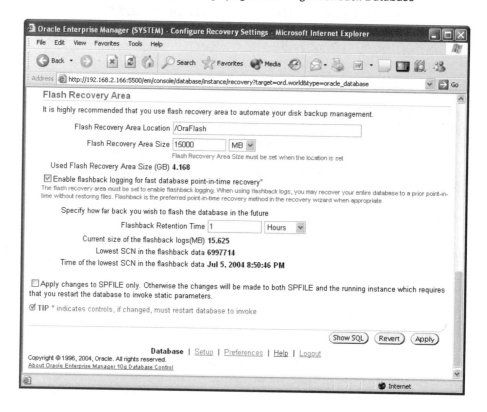

Flashing back the database using the EM Database Control is almost as easy as configuring Flashback Database using the EM Database Control. Using the wizards on the Perform Recovery pages, you step through the same commands as if you typed the SQL or RMAN commands: you shut down the database, specify a whole database point-in-time recovery, and generate an RMAN script to flashback the database and re-open the database with RESETLOGS.

Monitoring Flashback Database

Two new dynamic performance views help you monitor the retention target you set with the DB_FLASHBACK_RETENTION_TARGET initialization parameter: V$FLASHBACK_DATABASE_LOG and V$FLASHBACK_DATABASE_STAT.

V$FLASHBACK_DATABASE_LOG

V$FLASHBACK_DATABASE_LOG helps you monitor the estimated and actual size of the flashback logs in the flash recovery, as you can see in the following query:

```
SQL> select retention_target, flashback_size,
  2      estimated_flashback_size
  3  from v$flashback_database_log;


RETENTION_TARGET FLASHBACK_SIZE ESTIMATED_FLASHBACK_SIZE
---------------- -------------- ------------------------
              60       28442624                 23486464


1 row selected.
```

The FLASHBACK_SIZE column indicates that you have more than 16MB of flashback logs; the ESTIMATED_FLASHBACK_SIZE column provides an estimate of how much space will be needed in the flash recovery area for flashback logs. In this example, if your flash recovery area is running low on space and does not have at least another 16MB of free space for flashback logs, you should consider either adding more space to the flash recovery area or reducing the value of RETENTION_TARGET.

V$FLASHBACK_DATABASE_STAT

The dynamic performance view V$FLASHBACK_DATABASE_STAT monitors the overhead of logging flashback data in the flashback logs. It contains at most 24 rows, with one row for each of the last 24 hours. In the following example, you query the newest row in the table, representing the flashback generation for the last hour:

```
SQL> select to_char(end_time,'yyyy-mm-dd hh:miAM')
  2      end_timestamp,
  3      flashback_data, db_data, redo_data
  4      from v$flashback_database_stat where rownum=1;
```

```
END_TIMESTAMP          FLASHBACK_DATA    DB_DATA   REDO_DATA
------------------     --------------    ---------- ----------
2004-07-05 10:50PM          23625728     77225984   13787136
```

1 row selected.

The FLASHBACK_DATA column represents the number of bytes of flashback data written during the last one-hour period, the DB_DATA column is the number of bytes of data blocks read and written, and the REDO_DATA column is the number of bytes of redo data written.

Excluding Tablespaces from Flashback Database

By default, flashback data is generated from all tablespaces. Sometimes you may not want to generate flashback data: for example, you may have a training tablespace with high DML activity whose contents are frequently initialized from a database export file. In this case, you can disable flashback generation at the tablespace level with an ALTER TABLESPACE command, as in the following example:

```
SQL> alter tablespace example flashback off;
```

If you need to flashback the database at any point in time, the EXAMPLE tablespace must be taken offline and recovered using other methods, if necessary. The column FLASHBACK_ON in the dynamic performance view V$TABLESPACE indicates whether flashback is enabled for each tablespace.

Flashback Database Considerations

You cannot use Flashback Database in a number of situations and must use other incomplete recovery methods.

You cannot use Flashback Database to recover dropped datafiles that were dropped after your target recovery time. In addition, you cannot flashback a datafile that was shrunk after the target recovery time.

If the control file was restored or re-created after the target recovery time, or the database was opened with RESETLOGS after the target recovery time, an incomplete recovery method such as applying archived redo log files to backup datafiles must be used instead.

Flashback Drop

Another one of Oracle 10g's flashback features, *Flashback Drop*, lets you restore a dropped table without using point-in-time recovery, as required in previous versions of Oracle. While point-in-time recovery could effectively restore a table and its contents to a point in time before it was dropped, it was potentially time-consuming and had the side effect of losing work from other transactions that occurred within the same tablespace after the table was dropped.

In the following sections, we will talk about the new logical structure available in each tablespace; the recycle bin; and how you can query the recycle bin, retrieve dropped objects from the recycle bin, and purge the recycle bin.

Recycle Bin Concepts

The *recycle bin* is a logical structure within each tablespace that holds dropped tables and objects related to the tables, such as indexes. The space associated with the dropped table is not immediately available but shows up in the data dictionary view DBA_FREE_SPACE. When space pressure occurs in the tablespace, objects in the recycle bin are deleted in a first-in first-out (FIFO) fashion, maximizing the amount of time that the most recently dropped object remains in the recycle bin.

 The recycle bin is implemented as a data dictionary table.

The dropped object still belongs to the owner and still counts against the quota for the owner in the tablespace; in fact, the table itself is still directly accessible from the recycle bin, as you will see in subsequent examples.

Retrieving Dropped Tables from the Recycle Bin

Retrieving a dropped table from the recycle bin is performed from the SQL command line by using the FLASHBACK TABLE...TO BEFORE DROP command. In the following example, the user GARY retrieves the table ORDER_ITEMS from the recycle bin after discovering that the table was inadvertently dropped:

```
SQL> select order_id, line_item_id, product_id
  2  from order_items
  3  where rownum < 5;
from order_items
     *
ERROR at line 2:
ORA-00942: table or view does not exist


SQL> flashback table order_items to before drop;

Flashback complete.

SQL> select order_id, line_item_id, product_id
  2  from order_items
  3  where rownum < 5;
```

```
 ORDER_ID LINE_ITEM_ID PRODUCT_ID
---------- ------------ ----------
      2355            1       2289
      2356            1       2264
      2357            1       2211
      2358            1       1781
```

SQL>

If the table ORDER_ITEMS was re-created after it was dropped, GARY would add the RENAME TO clause in the FLASHBACK TABLE command to give the restored table a new name, as in the following example:

```
SQL> drop table order_items;

Table dropped.

SQL> flashback table order_items to before drop
  2         rename to order_items_old_version;

Flashback complete.

SQL> select order_id, line_item_id, product_id
  2  from order_items_old_version
  3  where rownum < 5;

 ORDER_ID LINE_ITEM_ID PRODUCT_ID
---------- ------------ ----------
      2355            1       2289
      2356            1       2264
      2357            1       2211
      2358            1       1781
```

SQL>

If the table to be retrieved from the recycle bin was dropped more than once, and you want to retrieve an incarnation of the table before the most recent one, you can use the name of the table in the recycle bin; you will see how to find out the recycle bin name in the next section.

Using the EM Database Control, you can retrieve a dropped table from the recycle bin on the Perform Recovery: Dropped Objects Selection page, as you can see in Figure 7.9.

FIGURE 7.9 Perform Recovery: Dropped Objects Selection page

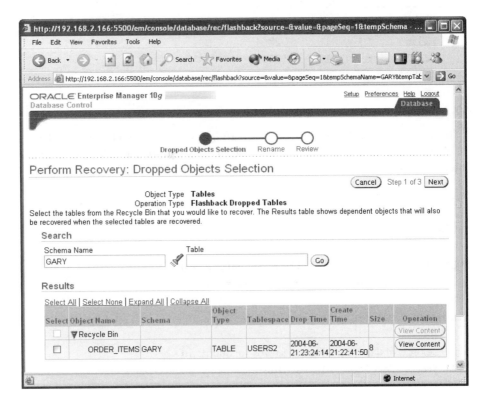

The user GARY has one table, ORDER_ITEMS, in the recycle bin that was dropped on June 21, 2004. Subsequent pages in this wizard allow you to rename the restored tables if a naming conflict exists with an existing object.

Querying the Recycle Bin

The contents of the recycle bin are available from a user's schema by querying the view USER_ RECYCLEBIN or just RECYCLEBIN. As with most other data dictionary views, DBA_RECYCLEBIN shows objects that have been dropped by all users, along with an OWNER column. The important columns in DBA_RECYCLEBIN are as follows:

OWNER The schema owner of the object.

ORIGINAL_NAME The name of the object before it was dropped.

OBJECT_NAME The system-generated name of the object after it was dropped.

TYPE The object type (for example, TABLE or INDEX).

TS_NAME The tablespace to which the dropped object belongs.

CREATETIME Time stamp at which the original object was created.

DROPTIME   Time stamp at which the object was dropped.

DROPSCN   SCN at which the object was dropped.

CAN_UNDROP   The object is available for retrieval from the recycle bin; in other words, it has not been purged explicitly or because of space pressure in the tablespace.

RELATED   The object identifier of the dropped object.

SPACE   The amount of space, in blocks, that the dropped object occupies.

Within SQL*Plus, you can use SHOW RECYCLEBIN. The user GARY queries his dropped objects in the recycle bin using the SHOW RECYCLEBIN command, as in the following example:

```
SQL> show recyclebin
ORIGINAL NAME   RECYCLEBIN NAME     OBJECT TYPE   DROP TIME
-------------   ------------------  -----------   ----------

ORDER_ITEMS     BIN$3Wxk60gIDFbgMK  TABLE         2004-06-21
                jApgIiFQ==$0                       :23:24:14
SQL>
```

If GARY needs to access the contents of the purged ORDER_ITEMS table before it is undropped, he can refer to it in a SQL statement using the recycle bin name, as in the following example:

```
SQL> select order_id, line_item_id, product_id
  2  from "BIN$3Wxk60gIDFbgMKjApgIiFQ==$0"
  3  where rownum < 5;

  ORDER_ID LINE_ITEM_ID PRODUCT_ID
---------- ------------ ----------
      2355            1       2289
      2356            1       2264
      2357            1       2211
      2358            1       1781

SQL>
```

As we mentioned earlier, when a table is dropped its dependent objects, such as indexes, triggers, and constraints, are also placed into the recycle bin. The dependent objects have cryptic names in the recycle bin just as the table does; when the table is recovered, the dependent objects are recovered as well, but they keep their cryptic names. Therefore, it is advisable to query the recycle bin and DBA_CONSTRAINTS before flashing back a dropped table and renaming the dependent objects manually after flashing back.

Only SELECT statements are allowed against tables that reside in the recycle bin.

Using the EM Database Control, GARY can access the dropped table's contents on the View Data for Table page, as you can see in Figure 7.10. This page is accessible from the Perform Recovery page in Figure 7.9.

FIGURE 7.10   View Data for Table page

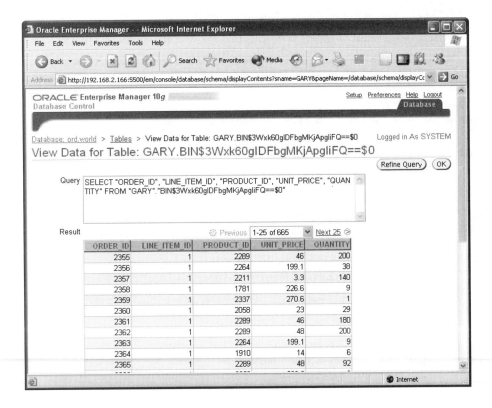

Recycle Bin Space Reclamation

As long as a tablespace has no space pressure, dropped objects are available indefinitely for recovery. Dropped objects are removed automatically under certain circumstances or can be removed manually by a user or by the DBA.

Automatic Space Reclamation

Automatic space reclamation occurs when the tablespace has space pressure: Either there is no free space outside of the space occupied by the objects in the recycle bin or a user's dropped objects in the recycle bin are exhausting the user's quota in a particular tablespace. Free space is allocated for new objects occurs in the following order:

1. Free space in the tablespace that is not occupied by dropped objects

2. Free space that corresponds to dropped objects (remember that once an object is dropped, its space is recorded in DBA_FREE_SPACE as being available)

3. Free space allocated by autoextending a tablespace, if one or more datafiles in the tablespace are autoextensible

Manual Space Reclamation

You can free the space occupied by dropped objects manually using several variations of the PURGE command. You can purge individual tables or indexes, you can purge users' dropped tables from a tablespace, or you can purge the entire recycle bin.

The PURGE TABLE and PURGE INDEX commands permanently remove tables and indexes from the recycle bin. Purging a table will automatically purge the dependent objects in the recycle bin as well.

If you use PURGE TABLESPACE, all objects in a specified tablespace are permanently removed from the recycle bin as are any dependent objects residing in other tablespaces. In the following example, you can remove all of GARY's objects from the recycle bin for the USERS2 tablespace:

```
SQL> purge tablespace users2 user gary;
Tablespace purged.
```

Any other objects in the recycle bin on USERS2 not owned by GARY remain in the recycle bin.

PURGE RECYCLEBIN, functionally equivalent to PURGE USER_RECYCLEBIN, purges all objects that belong to the user executing the PURGE command. If you have the DBA role or the SYSDBA privilege, PURGE DBA_RECYCLEBIN removes all objects from the recycle bin in all tablespaces.

If more than one copy of a table or an index is in the recycle bin, the PURGE command using the object's original name removes the oldest copy from the recycle bin first in a FIFO fashion. In other words, using the original object name, you must execute the PURGE command as many times as there are copies of the object in the recycle bin.

Bypassing the Recycle Bin

In situations where you want to bypass the recycle bin, you can add the PURGE keyword to the DROP TABLE command, as in the following example:

```
SQL> drop table order_items purge;
Table dropped.
```

When you use the command DROP TABLESPACE...INCLUDING CONTENTS, the dropped objects in the tablespace are not placed in the recycle bin; since each tablespace has its own logical recycle bin, dropping the tablespace drops its associated recycle bin and any objects currently in the recycle bin.

DROP USER...CASCADE operates similarly to dropping a tablespace with INCLUDING CONTENTS. The user and all of the objects owned by the user are dropped; any objects in the recycle bin belonging to the dropped user are purged.

Recycle Bin Considerations and Limitations

The recycle bin has a few limitations: Only non-SYSTEM locally managed tablespaces can have a recycle bin. However, dependent objects in a dictionary managed tablespace are protected if the dropped object is in a locally managed tablespace.

In addition, tables using Fine Grained Auditing (FGA) or Virtual Private Database (VPD) policies defined on them cannot reside in a recycle bin, regardless of the type of tablespace in which they reside.

A table's dependent objects are saved in the recycle bin when the table is dropped, except for the following objects:

- Bitmap join indexes
- Referential integrity constraints (foreign key constraints)
- Materialized view logs

Finally, indexes are protected only if the table is dropped first; explicitly dropping an index does not place the index into the recycle bin by itself.

Flashback Query

Flashback Query has been enhanced to include two new types: Flashback Versions Query and Flashback Transaction Query. Flashback Versions Query, as the name implies, retrieves all versions of all rows in a table between two time stamps or SCNs; Flashback Transaction Query provides a different point of view by retrieving all rows affected by a particular transaction.

In the following sections, you'll see how each of these new flashback options can make recoverability more transparent, impacting availability less and putting more recovery tools in the hands of the end user. You will also see how you can use both Flashback Versions Query and Flashback Transaction Query together in a recovery scenario.

Flashback Versions Query

Flashback Versions Query provides an easy way to show all versions of all rows in a table between two SCNs or time stamps, whether the rows were inserted, deleted, or updated. Even if a row was deleted and reinserted several times, all of these changes are available with Flashback Versions Query.

The syntax of the Flashback Query command is as follows:

```
SELECT [pseudo_columns]...FROM table_name
   VERSION BETWEEN
     {SCN | TIMESTAMP {expr | MINVALUE} AND
                     {expr | MAXVALUE}}
   [AS OF {SCN|TIMESTAMP expr}]
WHERE [pseudo_column | column] . . .
```

Real World Scenario

User Education and New Features

Whenever our data center installs a new version of Oracle, a number of our users embrace all the new features as time-savers whereas most users just want their queries to run the same way they did in previous versions. Oracle 10*g* was no exception: after a very smooth upgrade from Oracle 9*i*, we would get an occasional phone call from one of our "bleeding-edge" users asking how to use Flashback Transaction Query or the new MERGE options.

Other users, however, were complaining that the new recycle bin functionality was not working: They had to re-create the indexes every time they retrieved a table from the recycle bin with the FLASHBACK TABLE...TO BEFORE DROP command. Knowing that the recycle bin holds all dependent objects in addition to the dropped table, we were puzzled. We stepped through one of the user's scripts and noticed that they were dropping the index explicitly before dropping the table. As a result, the index was not being placed in the recycle bin.

The moral to this story is that you need to evaluate the new features to make sure that they will not impact existing processes and cause more problems than they solve; in addition, you need to educate the users about how to use the new features effectively for each new release. A small investment in training up front saves you headaches down the road.

If you don't know the oldest SCN or time stamp of the oldest available flashback data, you can use MINVALUE; similarly, MAXVALUE represents the most recent SCN or time stamp. Using the AS OF clause leverages the flashback features introduced in Oracle 9*i* to run this query from the perspective of a point of time in the past.

The pseudo-columns available with this syntax are as follows:

VERSIONS_STARTSCN   The SCN at which this version of the row was created

VERSIONS_STARTTIME   The time stamp at which this version of the row was created

VERSIONS_ENDSCN   The SCN at which this row no longer existed (either changed or deleted)

VERSIONS_ENDTIME   The time stamp at which this row no longer existed (either changed or deleted)

VERSIONS_XID   The transaction ID of the transaction that created this version of the rows

VERSIONS_OPERATION   The operation done by this transaction: I=Insert, D=Delete, U=Update

The pseudo-columns VERSIONS_STARTSCN and VERSIONS_STARTTIME are NULL if the SCN or time stamp is outside the range specified or outside the undo retention period; VERSIONS_ENDSCN and VERSIONS_ENDTIME are NULL if the version of the row is still intact as of the query time or if it has been deleted.

In the following example, you are investigating the reason why the salary of employee number 124 has doubled. The HR Department said it noticed it sometime earlier this morning, so you use midnight as your starting point for the Flashback Versions Query, as in the following example:

```
SQL> select versions_startscn startscn,
  2    versions_endscn endscn,
  3    versions_xid xid, versions_operation oper,
  4    employee_id empid, last_name name, salary sal
  5  from hr.employees
  6    versions between timestamp trunc(systimestamp)
  7      and systimestamp
  8  where employee_id = 124;
```

STARTSCN	ENDSCN	XID	O	EMPID	NAME	SAL
7119027		01002900 23160000	U	124	Mourgos	11600
7117480	7119027	04000900 BE1D0000	U	124	Mourgos	11600
	7117480			124	Mourgos	5800

```
3 rows selected.
```

Between midnight and the time you ran this query, two update operations in two separate transactions made changes to the row for employee ID 124, one of which doubled the salary. You will use the transaction ID (VERSIONS_XID) in the next section to reveal the SQL statements necessary to undo the changes to this row.

As with most every feature of Oracle 10g, you can use the EM Database Control to execute a Flashback Versions Query and browse changed rows, as you can see in Figure 7.11, on the Perform Recovery: Choose SCN page.

Flashback Versions Query has a few limitations. It cannot be used to query external tables, temporary tables, or fixed tables. In addition, you cannot use Flashback Versions Query to query a view, although a view definition can have a Flashback Versions Query as part of its definition. Finally, you cannot retrieve rows in a Flashback Versions Query if the SCN or time stamp range includes structural changes to the table being flashed back.

Flashback Versions Query works on index-organized tables (IOTs) as well, however, an UPDATE operation on an IOT may be translated into pairs of INSERT and UPDATE operations on the IOT.

FIGURE 7.11   Perform Recovery: Choose SCN page

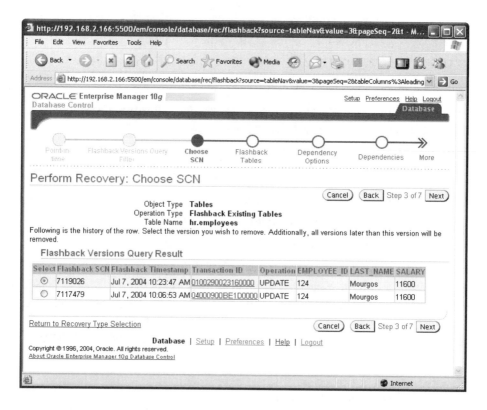

Flashback Transaction Query

Flashback Transaction Query, in contrast, drills down into the history of table changes based on a transaction ID. Using Flashback Versions Query, you found out which transaction changed the salary information, but you don't know who made the change. Flashback Transaction Query provides this additional level of detail.

In contrast to referencing the actual table in Flashback Versions Query, Flashback Transaction Query uses the data dictionary view FLASHBACK_TRANSACTION_QUERY to retrieve transaction information for all tables involved in a transaction. This view provides the SQL statements that you can use to undo the changes made by a particular transaction. In previous versions of Oracle, LogMiner provided some of the same information; however, Flashback Transaction Query data is indexed for faster access to undo data.

The columns available in the view FLASHBACK_TRANSACTION_QUERY are as follows:

XID   The transaction ID number

START_SCN   The SCN for the first DML in the transaction

START_TIMESTAMP   The time stamp of the first DML in the transaction

COMMIT_SCN   The SCN when the transaction was committed

COMMIT_TIMESTAMP   The time stamp when the transaction was committed

LOGON_USER   The user who owned the transaction

UNDO_CHANGE#   The undo SCN

OPERATION   The DML operation performed: DELETE, INSERT, UPDATE, BEGIN, or UNKNOWN

TABLE_NAME   The table changed by DML

TABLE_OWNER   The owner of table changed by DML

ROW_ID   The row modified by DML

UNDO_SQL   The SQL statement to undo the DML operation

To use this view, you need to have the SELECT ANY TRANSACTION system privilege. Note also that COMMIT_SCN and COMMIT_TIMESTAMP are NULL for an active transaction.

In the following example, you use the transaction identifier from the Flashback Versions Query in the previous section to find out more about the salary information changes to employee number 124:

```
SQL> select start_scn, commit_scn, logon_user,
  2      operation, table_name, undo_sql
  3  from flashback_transaction_query
  4  where xid = hextoraw('04000900BE1D0000');


START_SCN COMMIT_SCN LOGON_USER OPERATION   TABLE_NAME
--------- ---------- ---------- ---------- ---------------
UNDO_SQL
------------------------------------------------------------

  7117445    7117480 RJB          UPDATE      EMPLOYEES
  7117445    7117480 RJB          BEGIN

update "HR"."EMPLOYEES" set "SALARY" = '5800' where ROWID
='AAAMAeAAFAAAABUAA1';


2 rows selected.
```

The output from this query shows that the user RJB made the change to the salary information along with the SQL command necessary to reverse the update. To correct the problem with the salary information, you can cut and paste the query provided in the UNDO_SQL column into SQL*Plus, as follows:

```
SQL> update "HR"."EMPLOYEES" set "SALARY" = '5800'
  2      where ROWID ='AAAMAeAAFAAAABUAA1';
1 row updated.

SQL> commit;
Commit complete.
```

For any given transaction, you may choose to execute some or all of the SQL commands provided in the UNDO_SQL column, depending on the user requirements.

If you need to track transactions for chained rows and cluster tables, you may need to enable supplemental log data collection with the following command:

```
SQL> alter database add supplemental log data;
```

Flashback Table

Flashback Table allows you to recover one or more tables to a specific point in time without having to use more time-consuming recovery operations such as point-in-time recovery that may also affect the availability of the rest of the database. Flashback Table happens in place by rolling back only the changes made to the table or tables and their dependent objects, such as indexes. Note that Flashback Table is different from Flashback Drop: Flashback Table undoes recent transactions to an existing table whereas Flashback Drop recovers a dropped table; Flashback Table uses data in the undo tablespace whereas Flashback Drop uses the recycle bin.

The FLASHBACK TABLE command brings one or more tables back to a point in time before any number of logical corruptions have occurred on the tables. To be able to flashback a table, you must enable row movement for the table; because DML operations are used to bring the table back to its former state, the ROWIDs in the table change. As a result, Flashback Table is not a viable option for applications that depend on the table's ROWIDs to remain constant.

In the following example, you find out that someone in the HR Department has accidentally deleted all the employees in department 60, the IT Department, along with the row for IT in the DEPARTMENTS table. Because this happened less than 15 minutes ago, you are sure that there is enough undo information to support a Flashback Table operation; otherwise, you would have to use point-in-time recovery to bring back all the IT employees.

Before performing the Flashback Table operation, you first enable row movement in the two affected tables, as in the following example:

```
SQL> alter table hr.employees enable row movement;
Table altered.

SQL> alter table hr.departments enable row movement;
Table altered.
```

Before running the FLASHBACK TABLE command, you confirm that the row in DEPARTMENTS for the IT Department is still missing using this query:

```
SQL> select * from hr.departments where
  2      department_name = 'IT';


no rows selected
```

Next, you flash back the table to 15 minutes ago, specifying both tables in the same command, as follows:

```
SQL> flashback table hr.employees, hr.departments
  2      to timestamp systimestamp - interval '15' minute;


Flashback complete.
```

Finally, you check to see if the IT Department is truly back in the table:

```
SQL> select * from hr.departments where
  2      department_name = 'IT';


DEPARTMENT_ID DEPARTMENT_NAME     MANAGER_ID LOCATION_ID
------------- ------------------- ---------- -----------
           60 IT                         103        1400

SQL>
```

If you either flashback too far or not far enough, you can simply rerun the FLASHBACK TABLE command with a different time stamp or SCN, as long as the undo data is still available.

While the rest of the database is unaffected by a Flashback Table operation, the FLASHBACK TABLE command acquires exclusive DML locks on the tables involved in the flashback. This is usually not an availability issue, since the same users who would normally use the table are waiting for the flashback operation to complete anyway!

Note also that integrity constraints are not violated when one or more tables are flashed back; this is why you would typically group together tables related by integrity constraints or parent-child relationships in the FLASHBACK TABLE command.

Finally, a couple more things are worth mentioning about Flashback Table. As with Flashback Versions Query and Flashback Transaction Query, Flashback Table operations cannot be used if the flashback operation crosses a table structure change or a table shrink operation.

Guaranteed Undo Retention

Because most of the flashback features rely on undo information in the undo tablespace, you may want to guarantee that undo information is retained for just this purpose: The UNDO_ RETENTION initialization parameter is not a guarantee. As a result, you can create or alter an undo tablespace with the RETENTION GUARANTEE clause to ensure that unexpired undo data is preserved even if it means current transactions that need to generate undo may fail. In the following example, you change the retention guarantee for the tablespace UNDOTBS1:

```
SQL> alter tablespace undotbs1 retention guarantee;
Tablespace altered.
```

SCN and Time Mapping Enhancements

With most flashback features, you can specify either an SCN or a time stamp as one of the arguments to the flashback command. Because SCNs are used as the internal mechanism for representing database time, a mapping must occur between time stamps and SCNs. In previous releases of Oracle, this was accurate only to the nearest five minutes. As of Oracle 10g, the granularity has been reduced to three seconds to improve the accuracy of flashback operations that specify a time stamp.

In addition, you can retain this mapping information for longer than the previous value of five days by setting the initialization parameter UNDO_RETENTION to a larger value.

Two new built-in functions support conversion between SCNs and time stamps: SCN_TO_ TIMESTAMP and TIMESTAMP_TO_SCN. In the following example, you want to find out the SCN corresponding to the current time:

```
SQL> select timestamp_to_scn(systimestamp) from dual;

TIMESTAMP_TO_SCN(SYSTIMESTAMP)
------------------------------
                       7126585
```

Not coincidentally, this SCN is very close to the current timestamp recorded in V$DATABASE.

```
SQL> select current_scn from v$database;

CURRENT_SCN
-----------
    7126590
```

Flashback Privileges

Various system and object privileges are required to use each flashback feature. In Table 7.1, you can see the privileges required for each of the flashback features.

TABLE 7.1   Required Flashback Privileges

Flashback Feature	Required Privileges
Flashback Database	SYSDBA database connection
Flashback Table	FLASHBACK TABLE system privilege and the appropriate object privileges
Flashback Versions Query	FLASHBACK TABLE system privilege and the appropriate object privileges
Flashback Transaction Query	SELECT ANY TRANSACTION system privilege
Flashback Drop	Object privileges for objects in the recycle bin before they were dropped

Summary

In this chapter, we presented an in-depth tour of both the flash recovery area and the new flashback features in Oracle 10*g*.

The flash recovery area helps reduce the amount of time spent managing and restoring RMAN backups; you can back up every type of critical file in the Oracle database to the flash recovery area. The flash recovery area is easy to set up and maintain: only two initialization parameters control the size and location of the flash recovery area: DB_RECOVERY_FILE_DEST_SIZE and DB_RECOVERY_FILE_DEST.

Making extensive use of the flash recovery area, RMAN adds a number of new features in Oracle 10*g*, improving both disk space usage and backup time. Incremental backups can be applied to existing datafile image copies to reduce recovery time; backup time is reduced using the block change-tracking feature to more quickly identify blocks that have changed for an incremental backup instead of reading every block of each datafile. RMAN can also specify a duration for backup, either limiting the amount of time that a backup will occur or spreading a backup over a longer period of time to reduce the impact on the rest of the database. RMAN's support for compressed backups can potentially reduce backup time, I/O usage, network bandwidth, and disk space with a minimal amount of CPU overhead.

Oracle 10*g* introduces a number of new flashback features, giving both DBAs and end users alike an easy way to recover from a number of logical errors. Flashback Database brings the entire database back to a point in time in the past; for logical errors that are isolated to a small number of tables, Flashback Drop and Flashback Table provide recovery from dropped or corrupted tables

with minimal impact on the database and less intervention by the DBA, who now may not need to perform as many point-in-time recovery operations. For logical corruptions at the row level, Flashback Versions Query can retrieve all changes for a particular set of rows during a specified time frame; Flashback Transaction Query provides the user with a way to identify all changes to database tables within a given transaction, along with the SQL statements needed to undo those changes.

Other miscellaneous changes to the granularity of time stamp–to-SCN mapping make recovery operations more precise; changing the undo retention capabilities of the undo tablespace can ensure that undo data is available for these new flashback features in environments where the flashback features are more critical than transactions that may need undo space for long-running transactions.

Exam Essentials

Configure and manage the flash recovery area. Be able to identify and set the values of the initialization parameters that control the location and size of the flash recovery area. Manage the space in the recovery area by monitoring system alerts. Back up the flash recovery area to tape.

Optimize backup operations. Use new RMAN features to apply incremental backups to existing image copies, potentially reducing recovery time. Create incremental backups using a block change-tracking file, reducing backup time. Use compressed backups to reduce disk space requirements.

Understand new RESETLOGS options. Be able to retain archived redo logs created before a RESETLOGS operation and understand how the new log file format supports multiple database incarnations.

Be able to use Flashback Database effectively. Understand the requirements for using Flashback Database and when this method is preferable to other recovery methods. Configure and enable flashback logs to support Flashback Database.

Identify the characteristics and usage of the recycle bin. Describe how the recycle bin is constructed, how objects are placed in the recycle bin and recovered from the recycle bin, and the retention period for objects in the recycle bin.

Enumerate the key features of Flashback Version Query. Understand which rows are retrieved from Flashback Version Query and describe the pseudo-columns available with the VERSIONS keyword.

Use Flashback Transaction Query to undo changes. In combination with Flashback Version Query, use the transaction ID to review changes across all tables for the transaction and use the SQL provided with Flashback Transaction Query to undo some or all of the changes made during a transaction.

Understand new features that support flashback operations. Identify the new and existing system and object privileges necessary to use each flashback feature. Identify the new built-in functions used to convert SCNs to time stamps, and vice versa. Be able to discuss the granularity and retention improvements for SCN to time stamp mappings.

Review Questions

1. Oracle 10*g* supports fast incremental backups. Which of the following is not true about the incremental backup's change-tracking file?

   A. The size if the tracking file is proportional to the size of the database.

   B. If a block tracking file exists, it is no longer necessary for each datafile to be read in its entirety during an incremental backup.

   C. A change-tracking file is created by default when the database is created.

   D. The block tracking file must be at least 10MB in size.

   E. RMAN uses the block change-tracking file to determine which blocks to back up during an incremental backup.

2. Which dynamic performance view or data dictionary view has a column that indicates whether the database is configured for Flashback Database?

   A. V$DATABASE

   B. V$INSTANCE

   C. V$FLASHBACK_DATABASE_STAT

   D. DATABASE_PROPERTIES

3. Which two initialization parameters define the flash recovery area?

   A. DB_RECOVERY_FILE_DEST and DB_RECOVERY_FILE_SIZE

   B. DB_RECOVERY_FILE_DEST_SIZE and DB_RECOVERY_FILE_DEST

   C. LOG_ARCHIVE_DEST_10 and FLASH_RECOVERY_DEST

   D. DB_RECOVERY_FILE_DIR_SIZE and DB_RECOVERY_FILE_DIR

4. Which of the following is true about space associated with a dropped table?

   A. The space from the dropped table is reflected in the DBA_FREE_SPACE table, but the space is still counted against the table owner's quota.

   B. The space from the dropped table is reflected in the DBA_FREE_SPACE table, and the table owner's quota is reduced accordingly.

   C. The space from the dropped table is not reflected in the DBA_FREE_SPACE view until the PURGE TABLE command is issued.

   D. The space from the dropped table is not reflected in the DBA_FREE_SPACE view until the PURGE USER_RECYCLEBIN command is issued.

5. You have just run the following RMAN commands:
    RMAN> `configure controlfile autobackup off;`
    RMAN> `backup datafile 1;`
    What are the results?

    A. The first datafile of the SYSTEM tablespace is backed up as an image copy without the control file.

    B. The SYSTEM tablespace is backed up as an image copy along with the control file.

    C. The tablespace containing datafile #1 is backed up without the control file.

    D. The first datafile of the SYSTEM tablespace is backed up along with the control file.

    E. None of the above.

6. Which of the following methods does not show the contents of the recycle bin for a user with DBA privileges?

    A. Query the view USER_RECYCLEBIN.

    B. Use the command SHOW RECYCLEBIN.

    C. Query the view DBA_RECYCLEBIN.

    D. Query the view RECYCLEBIN.

    E. You can use all of the above methods to query the contents of the recycle bin.

7. Which of the following statements is not true about space reclamation and a tablespace's recycle bin?

    A. Free space outside of the recycle bin is used first for new space requests.

    B. If there are objects in the recycle bin, the datafile is autoextended before the contents of the recycle bin are reused.

    C. Recycle bin objects are purged from the recycle bin in a FIFO method when free space outside of the recycle bin is not available.

    D. More free space is available in the tablespace when a PURGE command is issued; however, those objects can no longer be recovered using Flashback Drop.

8. As of Oracle 10g, the RMAN COPY command has been deprecated. Which RMAN command should you use instead to back up all the datafiles in the database?

    A. BACKUP AS BACKUPSET DATABASE;

    B. BACKUP AS COPY (TABLESPACE SYSTEM, SYSAUX, USERS, UNDOTBS);

    C. BACKUP AS COPY ALL;

    D. BACKUP AS COPY DATABASE;

9. The user SCOTT drops and re-creates the EMPLOYEES table four times. How many times must SCOTT issue the PURGE command to free up the space occupied by the dropped copies of the EMPLOYEES table?

   A. Once, if SCOTT specifies the table's original name.

   B. Four.

   C. SCOTT can use only PURGE RECYCLEBIN to remove the dropped tables from the recycle bin.

   D. Once, after all the dependent objects in the recycle bin are dropped first.

10. Which of the following backup file types are not backed up when the RMAN BACKUP RECOVERY AREA command is issued?

   A. Full backup sets

   B. Flashback logs

   C. Incremental backup sets

   D. Datafile copies

   E. Archive logs

11. Choose the following statement that is true regarding Flashback Versions Query.

   A. All rows that existed between the two SCNs or time stamps specified in the VERSIONS clause are returned, including rows that have been deleted and reinserted and rows that have not yet been committed.

   B. All rows that existed between the two SCNs or time stamps specified in the VERSIONS clause are returned, not including rows that have been deleted and reinserted or uncommitted.

   C. All rows that existed between the two SCNs or time stamps specified in the VERSIONS clause are returned, including rows that have been deleted and reinserted, but not uncommitted rows.

   D. All rows that existed between the two SCNs or time stamps specified in the VERSIONS clause are returned, including both rows that have been deleted and reinserted and uncommitted rows in a current transaction.

12. You recently performed an RMAN image copy backup of the USERS tablespace consisting of datafiles #4 and #7. Next, you run the following command in RMAN:
```
RMAN> recover copy of datafile 7;
```
What are the results of this command?

A. Only the latest image copy of datafile #7 is updated with the contents of all incremental backup files created since the image copy was created.

B. If the most recent copy of datafile #7 is damaged or missing, it is re-created from an earlier image copy and the subsequent incremental backups; otherwise this command has no effect.

C. All image copies of datafile #7 are updated with the contents of all incremental backup files created since the image copy was created.

D. Both datafile #4 and datafile #7 are merged into a single image copy and updated with recent incremental backups.

E. Datafile #7 in the database area is recovered if a media error has occurred; otherwise this command has no effect.

13. Which of the following columns is not in the FLASHBACK_TRANSACTION_QUERY view?

A. REDO_SQL

B. START_SCN

C. UNDO_SQL

D. TABLE_OWNER

E. COMMIT_TIMESTAMP

14. What happens when you execute the following RMAN command?
```
RMAN> backup copy of database;
```

A. It creates a backup of all datafiles to the flash recovery area as image copies by default.

B. A copy of all datafiles, control files, archived log files, and SPFILE are copied to the flash recovery area as image copies by default.

C. A copy of all datafiles, control files, archived log files, and SPFILE are copied to the flash recovery area as backup sets by default.

D. It creates a backup of previous image copies of all datafiles and control files in the database—in other words, a backup of a previous backup.

15. Identify the two columns of V$RECOVERY_FILE_DEST that are not accessible via the EM Database Control.

    A. SPACE_RECLAIMABLE, SPACE_LIMIT

    B. SPACE_RECLAIMABLE, NUMBER_OF_FILES

    C. SPACE_LIMIT, SPACE_USED

    D. SPACE_USED, NUMBER_OF_FILES

16. To ensure that undo data is retained in an undo tablespace for flashback features even if operations that need to generate undo may fail, what clause should be specified in the CREATE UNDO TABLESPACE or ALTER UNDO TABLESPACE?

    A. FLASHBACK OFF

    B. GUARANTEE RETENTION

    C. RETENTION GUARANTEE

    D. UNDO_RETENTION

17. Each row in the dynamic performance view V$FLASHBACK_DATABASE_STAT represents what time interval?

    A. 24 hours

    B. One hour

    C. One minute

    D. 30 minutes

18. Which of the following is not true about a table recovered from the recycle bin using the FLASHBACK TABLE...TO BEFORE DROP command?

    A. All recovered indexes, triggers, and constraints associated with the table are no longer valid and must be re-created before they can be used.

    B. If you recover a table that has been dropped several times, only the most recent version of the dropped table is restored unless you specify the name of the table in the recycle bin.

    C. If the recovered table has the same name as an existing table, you must use the RENAME TO clause or recover the table to another schema.

    D. Assuming that a new table with the same name has not yet been created, recovering a table from the recycle bin using either the original name or the recycle bin name achieves the same result.

19. You place all database files in online backup mode with the following command:
ALTER DATABASE BEGIN BACKUP;
Which of the following is not a requirement when you use this command?

   A. You must use RMAN to perform the backup.

   B. The database must be mounted and open.

   C. The database must be in ARCHIVELOG mode.

   D. A tablespace cannot be placed into read-only mode when this command is issued.

20. Choose the statement that is not true about space management in the flash recovery area.

   A. A warning is issued when the flash recovery area is 85 percent full, and a critical warning is issued when the flash recovery area is 97 percent full.

   B. When the flash recovery reaches 100 percent capacity, only files backed up to tape or another disk are considered for deletion to free up space for new backup files.

   C. When files are written to the flash recovery area, a message is written to the alert log.

   D. Obsolete files are automatically removed from the flash recovery area when the flash recovery area reaches 100 percent capacity.

   E. When files are deleted from the flash recovery area, a message is written to the alert log.

Answers to Review Questions

1. C. Change tracking is not enabled by default. When enabled, however, it incurs a slight amount of overhead whenever a block in any datafile is updated. This is offset by the time saved during incremental backup operations.

2. A. The dynamic performance view V$DATABASE contains a new column FLASHBACK_ON that indicates whether Flashback Database is enabled.

3. B. DB_RECOVERY_FILE_DEST_SIZE specifies the maximum size of the flash recovery area, and DB_RECOVERY_FILE_DEST specifies the location of the flash recovery area. DB_RECOVERY_FILE_SIZE, FLASH_RECOVERY_DEST, DB_RECOVERY_FILE_DIR_SIZE, and DB_RECOVERY_FILE_DIR are not valid initialization parameters. LOG_ARCHIVE_DEST_10 points to the flash recovery area by default but does not define the flash recovery area.

4. A. While the space from a dropped table shows up as additional free space in DBA_FREE_SPACE, the space is still counted against the user's quota until the PURGE USER_RECYCLEBIN or PURGE TABLE command is issued.

5. D. The command CONFIGURE CONTROLFILE AUTOBACKUP OFF disables the automatic backup of the control file unless the backup includes any datafiles of the SYSTEM tablespace.

6. E. In addition to the previous methods, the EM Database Control can display the current contents of the recycle bin.

7. B. The objects in the recycle bin are dropped to satisfy space requests before any of the tablespace's datafiles are autoextended.

8. D. The BACKUP AS COPY DATABASE command will copy all datafiles in one command. BACKUP AS BACKUPSET DATABASE will back up the entire database but not in image copy format. BACKUP AS COPY ALL is not a valid RMAN command. BACKUP AS COPY using individual tablespaces will back up only the datafiles for the specific tablespaces in the database and does not include the archived logs, SPFILE, or control files.

9. B. The PURGE command can be issued four times to remove the four copies of the EMPLOYEES table. Alternatively, SCOTT can issue the PURGE RECYCLEBIN command to remove all dropped tables from the recycle bin.

10. B. The RMAN BACKUP RECOVERY AREA command backs up all flash recovery files created in the flash recovery area that have not yet been backed up to tape, which includes full and incremental backup sets, control file autobackups, archive logs, and datafile copies; flashback logs, incremental bitmaps, current control file, and online redo log files are not backed up.

11. C. Flashback Versions Query returns only rows that have been committed between two SCNs or time stamps. In addition, rows that have been deleted, reinserted, and committed are also returned.

12. A. The RECOVER COPY OF DATAFILE command applies incremental RMAN backups to an image copy of the datafile and potentially reduces the amount of time needed for media recovery of the datafile because fewer archive log files are necessary to bring the datafile up to the latest SCN in the case of a media failure.

13. A. There is no such column REDO_SQL in FLASHBACK_TRANSACTION_QUERY.

14. D. The BACKUP COPY OF DATABASE is usually used to create a copy of a backup already in the RMAN backup destination to another device type, such as tape. The copy can either be another image copy or be a backup set.

15. B. To view the values for SPACE_RECLAIMABLE and NUMBER_OF_FILES, you must use the dynamic performance view V$RECOVERY_FILE_DEST.

16. C. Turning off flashback generation for a tablespace has no effect on undo retention. GUARANTEE RETENTION is syntactically incorrect. UNDO_RETENTION is an initialization parameter, not an undo tablespace property.

17. B. The dynamic performance view V$FLASHBACK_DATABASE_STAT contains statistics that monitor the overhead of logging flashback data in the Flashback Database logs at 1-hour intervals for a total of 24 hours.

18. A. The indexes, triggers, and constraints keep their recycle bin names when the related table is restored, but they are still valid and usable. It is highly recommended, however, that the related structures be re-created or renamed with the original names.

19. A. The ALTER DATABASE BEGIN BACKUP command is only used when you are not using RMAN to ensure a consistent backup.

20. B. Obsolete files are also considered for deletion when the flash recovery area reaches 100 percent capacity, even if they have not yet been backed up to tape or another disk device.

Chapter

8

Security and SQL Enhancements

ORACLE DATABASE 10*g* NEW FEATURES FOR ADMINISTRATORS EXAM OBJECTIVES OFFERED IN THIS CHAPTER:

✓ **Support for Analytical Applications**

- Write MERGE statements with the new conditions and extensions
- Use partitioned outer join syntax for densification
- Use interrow calculations to enhance SQL for analytical capabilities
- Use new fast refresh capabilities for Materialized Join Views

✓ **Security**

- Apply a column level VPD policy
- Apply static and non-static policies
- Share VPD policy functions
- Use the unified audit trails
- Use fine-grained auditing for DML statements

✓ **Miscellaneous New Features**

- Provide greater flexibility by enabling resumable timeout at the instance level
- Use regular expression support in SQL and PL/SQL for string searching, matching and replacing
- Use additional linguistic comparison and sorting methods in SQL
- Aggregate more meaningful statistics across a multitier environment
- Use SQL to flush the buffer cache

Exam objectives are subject to change at any time without prior notice and at Oracle's sole discretion. Please visit Oracle's training and certification website (http://www.oracle.com/education/certification/) for the most current exam objectives listing.

In the last seven chapters, you learned about all the major enhancements to Oracle Database 10g (Oracle 10g). In this chapter we will cover the miscellaneous enhancements and behavior changes to Oracle 10g. SQL and PL/SQL are two areas where every new release always contains enhancements.

One of the significant Oracle 10g SQL enhancements is the ability to do spreadsheet-like array computations in SQL statements. It lets you view rows as a multidimensional array, which allows you to do calculations on individual cells or range of cells. We will review this and other SQL enhancements in this chapter. We will also discuss the enhancements made to the Virtual Private Database (VPD) and other miscellaneous database enhancements.

Securing Data

Oracle 10g includes new features designed to secure data more effectively within the database. The VPD can now enforce column-level privacy. Oracle 10g introduces static and context-sensitive VPD policies that can improve performance.

The auditing of the database operations also has improvements. Fine-grained auditing (FGA), introduced in Oracle 9i, supports Data Manipulation Language (DML) statements in Oracle 10g. The following sections discuss the security enhancements of Oracle 10g.

Leveraging Virtual Private Database

The VPD is an option that comes with the Enterprise Edition of the Oracle 10g. VPD was introduced in Oracle 8i, which enables row-level security. The database privileges are granted on the object level. If a user has SELECT privilege on the table, he can see all the rows in the table. VPD can restrict the rows seen by the user based on a policy defined in the database. The policy determines the predicate to be applied to the WHERE clause based on the login ID of the user. The DBMS_RLS package manages the row-level security in the database.

When a user directly or indirectly accesses a table, view, or synonym associated with a VPD security policy, the Oracle database server automatically modifies the user's SQL statement to filter the rows. The modification is based on the WHERE clause returned by a function, which implements the security policy. The modification to the SQL is dynamic and is transparent to the user.

The following are the new features for VPD in Oracle 10g:

- Column-level privacy and column masking
- Static, context-sensitive, and shared policies
- Support for parallel queries

User SYS is always exempt from all VPD policies. Users with the EXEMPT ACCESS POLICY system privilege also are exempt from VPD policies.

In the following sections we will discuss the enhancements made to VPD in Oracle 10g.

Column-Level VPD

Column-level VPD policies give more fine-grained access controls on data. Security policies are applied only when certain columns are accessed in the user's query. You accomplish this by introducing a new parameter SEC_RELEVANT_COLS to the DBMS_RLS.ADD_POLICY procedure. The new parameter is optional; if you omit this parameter, the policy behaves as in Oracle 9i, where the policy is applied to all columns.

Column-level privacy enforces row-level access control only when a statement accesses security relevant columns.

Let's learn more about the column-level VPD using an example. The employee table has four columns with the following information (the employee table is a subset of employees table in the HR sample schema):

```
SQL> SELECT * FROM employee;
```

FIRST_NAME	HIRE_DATE	SALARY	DEPARTMENT_ID
NEENA	21-SEP-89	17000	90
LEX	13-JAN-93	17000	90
ALEXANDER	03-JAN-90	9000	60
BRUCE	21-MAY-91	6000	60
DAVID	25-JUN-97	4800	60
DANIEL	16-AUG-94	9000	80
JOHN	28-SEP-97	8200	100
ISMAEL	30-SEP-97	7700	80
ALEXANDER	18-MAY-95	3100	30
SIGAL	24-JUL-97	2800	80
HR	15-NOV-98	2600	50
KAREN	10-AUG-99	2500	30
KIMBERLY	24-MAY-99	7000	50

```
13 rows selected.

SQL>
```

Now, create a policy function that restricts the sensitive information. Here we allow the user to see only his/her own record.

```
SQL> CREATE OR REPLACE FUNCTION EMPLOYEE_PF
  2  (owner VARCHAR2, objname VARCHAR2)
  3  RETURN VARCHAR2
  4  IS
  5  where_clause  VARCHAR2 (2000);
  6  BEGIN
  7  where_clause :=
     'first_name=SYS_CONTEXT(''USERENV'',
                            ''SESSION_USER'')';
  8  RETURN where_clause;
  9  END;
SQL> /

Function created.

SQL>
```

Create a VPD policy using the DBMS_RLS.ADD_POLICY; restrict the salary information on the employee table using the function we just created.

```
SQL> BEGIN
  2  SYS.DBMS_RLS.ADD_POLICY (
  3  object_schema       => 'HR',
  4  object_name         => 'EMPLOYEE',
  5  policy_name         => 'FILTER_EMP',
  6  function_schema     => 'HR',
  7  policy_function     => 'EMPLOYEE_PF',
  8  sec_relevant_cols => 'SALARY');
  9  END;
SQL> /

PL/SQL procedure successfully completed.

SQL>
```

Let's assume user DAVID is trying to access the employee information. The following are a couple of sample queries. You can see that when user DAVID is accessing the salary information, only his record displays; when he is not interested in salary, all information displays.

```
SQL> show user
USER is "DAVID"
SQL> SELECT first_name, salary, department_id
  2  FROM   hr.employee;

FIRST_NAME               SALARY DEPARTMENT_ID
-------------------- ---------- -------------
DAVID                      4800            60


SQL> SELECT first_name, hire_date, department_id
  2  FROM   hr.employee;

FIRST_NAME           HIRE_DATE DEPARTMENT_ID
-------------------- --------- -------------
NEENA                21-SEP-89            90
LEX                  13-JAN-93            90
ALEXANDER            03-JAN-90            60
BRUCE                21-MAY-91            60
DAVID                25-JUN-97            60
DANIEL               16-AUG-94            80
JOHN                 28-SEP-97           100
ISMAEL               30-SEP-97            80
ALEXANDER            18-MAY-95            30
SIGAL                24-JUL-97            80
HR                   15-NOV-98            50
KAREN                10-AUG-99            30
KIMBERLY             24-MAY-99            50

13 rows selected.

SQL>
```

What you see in the previous example is the default behavior of column-level VPD. In the default behavior, the number of rows returned by the query are restricted. Rows with sensitive information are not shown to the user.

Another way of configuring is known as *column-masking behavior*. In column-masking behavior, the sensitive information is NULL, but the rest of the information displays. You accomplish column-masking behavior using DBMS_RLS.ALL_ROWS as an option to the ADD_POLICY

procedure. Let's re-create the policy definition to mask the salary information and hire date rather than restricting the rows.

```
SQL> EXEC dbms_rls.drop_policy('HR','EMPLOYEE',
                               'FILTER_EMP');

PL/SQL procedure successfully completed.

SQL>
SQL> BEGIN
  2  SYS.DBMS_RLS.ADD_POLICY (
  3  object_schema       => 'HR',
  4  object_name         => 'EMPLOYEE',
  5  policy_name         => 'FILTER_EMP',
  6  function_schema     => 'HR',
  7  policy_function     => 'EMPLOYEE_PF',
  8  sec_relevant_cols   => 'SALARY, HIRE_DATE',
  9  sec_relevant_cols_opt => DBMS_RLS.ALL_ROWS);
 10* END;
SQL> /

PL/SQL procedure successfully completed.

SQL>
```

Now, when user DAVID queries the employee information, he sees all the rows, but the salary and hire date information displays for only his own record, as shown here:

```
SQL> SELECT first_name, hire_date, salary
  2  FROM   hr.employee
SQL> /

FIRST_NAME           HIRE_DATE    SALARY
-------------------- ---------- ----------
NEENA
LEX
ALEXANDER
BRUCE
DAVID                25-JUN-97       4800
DANIEL
JOHN
ISMAEL
```

```
ALEXANDER
SIGAL
HR
KAREN
KIMBERLY

13 rows selected.

SQL>
```

The column-masking behavior applies only to SELECT statements.

VPD Policy Types

The execution of policy functions can consume a lot of system resources; therefore, minimizing the number of times a policy function is executed can improve performance. In Oracle 9*i* and Oracle 8*i*, the policies were dynamic, which means the database executed the policy function for each DML statement. Oracle 10*g* introduces static and context-sensitive policies.

In Oracle 10*g*, you can define five different types of policies.

- Dynamic (default, pre–Oracle 10*g* behavior)

- Static

- Shared-static

- Context-sensitive

- Shared context-sensitive

When defining a policy using the DBMS_RLS.ADD_POLICY procedure, you can specify the type of the policy using the POLICY_TYPE parameter.

We will discuss each of these policy types in the following sections.

Dynamic

This is the default policy type. Policies of this type are created by taking the default of not specifying a policy type or by specifying DBMS_RLS.DYNAMIC as the value to the parameter POLICY_TYPE. The server assumes the policy predicate will be affected by the system and so executes the policy function each time a DML statement is parsed or executed.

Dynamic policy type was the only policy type available in Oracle9i and its behavior in Oracle 10g is not changed.

Static

For static policy types, specify `DBMS_RLS.STATIC` as the value to the parameter `POLICY_TYPE`. For static policy types, the predicate is assumed to be the same regardless of the runtime environment. Static policy functions are executed once and are cached in the Shared Global Area (SGA). This makes the static policies very fast since the database does not have to execute the policy function for each query. Statements accessing the same object do not re-execute the policy function, though each execution could produce different set of results based on attributes such as `SYS_CONTEXT` and `SYSDATE`.

Shared-Static

When a function is used in multiple policies, it is called a shared policy. Shared policies eliminate the need to create one policy function for each object when the business policy is the same for multiple objects. Each policy has its own name, but the policy function used is the same.

For a shared-static policy type, specify `DBMS_RLS.SHARED_STATIC` as the value to the parameter `POLICY_TYPE`. The behavior is same as `STATIC` except that the server first looks for a cached predicate generated by the same policy function of the same policy type.

Context-Sensitive

For content-sensitive policy types, specify `DBMS_RLS.CONTEXT_SENSITIVE` as the value to the parameter `POLICY_TYPE`. Context-sensitive policy functions are reevaluated by the database if it detects a context change since the last use of the cursor. The policy function is evaluated for each session when the statement is first parsed or if there is a related application context change. The resulting policy predicate is cached in the user's session memory.

The policy predicate can change when certain context attributes are changed within the user's session. So a context-sensitive policy assumes that the policy predicate may change after statement parsing for a session, and such change can occur only if there are some session context changes. Therefore, the database evaluates the policy function at statement execution time if it detects context changes since the last use of the cursor. The policy predicate is cached in the session memory.

Here is an example of context-sensitive policy. Assume that you want to add the predicate `WHERE department_id =` *deptno* for all the managers accessing the employee table and for regular users, you want to add `WHERE employee_id =` *empno*. When the user's session is initiated, you could identify the context whether the user is a manager or regular user and determine the values for *deptno* and *empno*. The policy to apply will be determined based on the context of the user.

Shared Context-Sensitive

For shared context-sensitive policy types, specify `DBMS_RLS.SHARED_CONTEXT_SENSITIVE` as the value to the parameter `POLICY_TYPE`. This type is similar to the context-sensitive, except that the function is shared. When a context-sensitive policy shares its policy function, the caching behavior is similar except that the server first looks for a cached policy predicate generated by the same policy function for the same policy type within the same database session.

Other VPD Enhancements

In Oracle 10*g*, the parameter STATEMENT_TYPES in the procedure DBMS_RLS.ADD_POLICY can accept a new type named INDEX. In Oracle 9*i*, the valid values were SELECT, INSERT, UPDATE, or DELETE. The default in Oracle 10*g* is to apply all these types except INDEX. The INDEX type was introduced to enforce security policies on index maintenance operations. Users need full table access to create table indexes.

A user who has privilege to maintain an index can see all the row data even if the user does not have full table access when using a query. The INDEX type in Oracle 10*g* was introduced to prevent users from reading secured data when creating function-based indexes, which would otherwise allow a knowledgeable user to write out values using the index function that the VPD features are supposed to obscure. The INDEX type will ensure that the security policy is applied when creating the index.

Another enhancement made to Oracle 10*g* in the ADD_POLICY procedure is the LONG_PREDICATE parameter. This new parameter has a default value of FALSE, which means the policy function can return up to 4,000 bytes of the predicate value. When this parameter is set to TRUE, the policy function can return a predicate text string up to 32KB.

Auditing Enhancements

Auditing in the Oracle database is the monitoring and recording of selected user actions in the database. Oracle 10*g* has the following types of auditing:

Mandatory auditing   The database always records certain actions. Examples are database startup and shutdowns, which are recorded in the alert log file. Connections to the database using the SYSOPER or SYSDBA privilege are also recorded in the operating system audit file usually located at $ORACLE_HOME/rdbms/audit (you can change this destination by setting the AUDIT_FILE_DEST parameter). This provides accountability for users with administrative privileges.

Standard auditing   Setting the AUDIT_TRAIL initialization parameter enables auditing on the database. Once auditing is enabled, you can specify the objects and type of actions to be audited. For example, AUDIT UPDATE ON HR.EMPLOYEES statement enables auditing for any updates that are performed on the HR.EMPLOYEES table. The audit information is written to the SYS.AUD$ table and can be queried from DBA_AUDIT_OBJECT dictionary view.

Fine-grained auditing (FGA)   *FGA* enables auditing based on data content. FGA uses policies that you add to an object. An audit policy can have sophisticated means to decide whether the database should create an audit record based on the query, the condition, and the data the statement accesses. In Oracle 10*g*, you have the option of auditing only those statements that reference a particular column.

The following sections describe the enhancements in Oracle 10*g* in auditing.

DML Support for Fine-Grained Auditing

FGA was introduced in Oracle 9*i*; it supported only SELECT statements. In Oracle 10*g*, FGA supports INSERT, UPDATE, and DELETE statements. The DBMS_FGA.ADD_POLICY procedure now has a new parameter named STATEMENT_TYPES to specify the type of action to audit.

You set up FGA using the DBMS_FGA.ADD_POLICY procedure. Let's set up an audit on the employee table that we used in the previous section. We will audit the SELECT and UPDATE statements on this table that go against the salary column with rows that have a salary of more than $10,000. You can define the FGA policy as follows:

```
SQL> BEGIN
  2   DBMS_FGA.ADD_POLICY(
  3   policy_name          => 'AUD_EMPLOYEE_SAL',
  4   object_schema        => 'HR',
  5   object_name          => 'EMPLOYEE',
  6   audit_column         => 'SALARY',
  7   audit_condition      => 'SALARY >= 10000',
  8   statement_types      => 'SELECT, UPDATE');
  9   END;
SQL> /

PL/SQL procedure successfully completed.

SQL>
```

 Note that we disabled the FILTER_EMP VPD policy for this demonstration using the DBMS_RLS.ENABLE_POLICY('HR', 'EMPLOYEE', 'FILTER_EMP', FALSE) procedure.

User DAVID is now updating and selecting rows from the employee table that meet our audit condition.

```
SQL> show user
USER is "DAVID"
SQL> UPDATE hr.employee
  2   SET     salary = 20000
  3   WHERE   first_name = 'NEENA';

1 row updated.

SQL> SELECT first_name
  2   FROM    hr.employee
  3*  WHERE   salary > 15000
SQL> /
```

```
FIRST_NAME
--------------------
NEENA
LEX

SQL>
```

Let's now query the FGA audit log to see the audit information.

```
SQL> SELECT dbuid, lsqltext FROM sys.fga_log$;

DAVID
UPDATE hr.employee
SET    salary = 20000
WHERE  first_name = 'NEENA'

DAVID
SELECT first_name
FROM   hr.employee
WHERE  salary > 15000

SQL>
```

The database inserted the audit record into the FGA_LOG$ table using an autonomous transaction. Even if you roll back the update statement, the update action will still be logged in this table. The FGA_LOG$ table contains other relevant information such as table name, policy name, transaction ID, session and machine information, and so on. Sometimes it may be too much overhead to write the SQL and bind variable information to the FGA_LOG$ table. When defining the policy, you may turn off the extended logging by setting the AUDIT_TRAIL parameter to DBMS_FGA.DB. The DBMS_FGA.DB_EXTENDED is the default for AUDIT_TRAIL and thus populates the LSQLTEXT and LSQLBIND columns of the SYS.FGA_LOG$. AUDIT_TRAIL parameter; this is demonstrated in the next example of DBMS_FGA.ADD_POLICY.

In Oracle 10g, you can define a FGA policy with more than one relevant column for the AUDIT_COLUMNS parameter. The default for AUDIT_COLUMNS is NULL, which audits if any column is accessed. When specifying more than one column in the AUDIT_COLUMNS parameter, the statement is audited if any one of the columns is present in the SQL statement.

Sometimes it may make sense only to audit access on a combination of columns. For example, the following query is fairly harmless:

```
SELECT MAX(salary) FROM hr.employee;
```

The query does not identify the employee; it just checks for the maximum salary. Maybe you wanted to audit queries that are a combination of the salary and employee name. To change the default behavior or to specify the behavior, you can specify the values DBMS_FGA.ANY_COLUMNS

or DBMS_FGA.ALL_COLUMNS for the AUDIT_COLUMN_OPTS parameter in the DBMS_FGA.ADD_POLICY procedure. Here is an example of auditing if only all the columns listed in the AUDIT_COLUMNS parameter are accessed in the SQL:

```
SQL> BEGIN
  2   DBMS_FGA.ADD_POLICY(
  3   policy_name        => 'AUD_EMPLOYEE_SAL_FN',
  4   object_schema      => 'HR',
  5   object_name        => 'EMPLOYEE',
  6   audit_column       => 'SALARY, FIRST_NAME',
  7   statement_types    => 'SELECT, UPDATE',
  8   audit_column_opts  => DBMS_FGA.ALL_COLUMNS,
  9   audit_trail        => DBMS_FGA.DB);
 10   END;
SQL> /

PL/SQL procedure successfully completed.

SQL>
```

Let's now perform a query on the employee table and see the entry from the FGA_LOG$ table.

```
SQL> SHOW USER
USER is "SCOTT"
SQL> SELECT salary FROM hr.employee
  2   WHERE  first_name = 'SIGAL';

    SALARY
---------
      2800

SQL>
SQL> SELECT oshst, dbuid, obj$name
  2   FROM    sys.fga_log$
  3   WHERE   policyname = 'AUD_EMPLOYEE_SAL_FN';

OSHST            DBUID          OBJ$NAME
---------------- -------------- --------------------
linux            SCOTT          EMPLOYEE

SQL>
```

When the AUDIT_CONDITION is omitted or specified as NULL (default), it is evaluated as TRUE. In Oracle 9*i*, this parameter was mandatory, and we used to specify 1=1 to satisfy the condition.

When FGA policy is defined for DML statements, the statement is audited if the data rows (new and old) being manipulated meet the policy predicate criteria. For DELETE statements, specifying relevant columns is ignored, because all columns are accessed for deleting a row. The FGA supports the MERGE statements by auditing the underlying INSERT or UPDATE operation that is performed by the MERGE statement.

Uniform Audit Trail

Oracle 10g tracks the same columns for standard and fine-grained auditing. The database audit trail is a single table in the SYS schema named the AUD$, which is stored in the SYSTEM tablespace. The FGA audit trail is also a single table in the SYS schema named FGA_LOG$, which is stored in the SYSTEM tablespace. Oracle provides many predefined views that show the relevant information based on the type of audit. These views are shown in Table 8.1.

TABLE 8.1   DBA Dictionaries with Audit Information

View Name	Description
DBA_AUDIT_TRAIL	Displays all audit trail entries for standard auditing
DBA_AUDIT_EXISTS	Displays audit trail entries produced by AUDIT EXISTS and AUDIT NOT EXISTS
DBA_AUDIT_OBJECT	Displays audit trail records for all objects in the database (DML and DDL audit)
DBA_AUDIT_SESSION	Displays audit trail entries for session connects and disconnects (AUDIT SESSION)
DBA_AUDIT_STATEMENT	Displays audit trail records for GRANT, REVOKE, AUDIT, NOAUDIT, and ALTER SYSTEM statements
DBA_OBJ_AUDIT_OPTIONS	Describes the auditing options in the database for the objects audited
DBA_FGA_AUDIT_TRAIL	Displays all audit trail entries for fine-grained auditing
DBA_AUDIT_POLICIES	Displays the fine-grained audit policies defined in the database

TABLE 8.1 DBA Dictionaries with Audit Information *(continued)*

View Name	Description
DBA_AUDIT_POLICY_COLUMNS	Displays the policy name and column name for the policies in the database.
DBA_COMMON_AUDIT_TRAIL	Displays audit records for both standard and fine-grained auditing

The exact SQL statement executed by the user and the bind variables used with the SQL are collected in the audit trail when the initialization parameter AUDIT_TRAIL is set to DB_EXTENDED. The DB or TRUE value will not populate the SQLTEXT and SQLBIND columns of the AUD$ table.

> In the previous section you learned how to populate the similar columns LSQLTEXT and LSQLBIND of the FGA_LOG$ table.

Many new columns have been added to the DBA_AUDIT_TRAIL and DBA_FGA_AUDIT_TRAIL views to allow them to store additional audit information and to have uniform consistent information in both views.. The following are the new columns added to the DBA_AUDIT_TRAIL view:

EXTENDED_TIMESTAMP Time stamp of when the audit trail entry was created, in UTC (Coordinated Universal Time) time.

PROXY_SESSIONID Proxy session serial number if the session was logged in through a proxy mechanism.

GLOBAL_UID Global user identifier for the user, if the user has logged in as an enterprise user. The USERNAME column shows the user's identity in the database, and the GLOBAL_UID column shows the same user's global identity (when using an LDAP-compliant directory).

INSTANCE_NUMBER Instance number as specified by the INSTANCE_NUMBER initialization parameter (applicable only to Real Application Clusters [RAC]).

OS_PROCESS Operating system process identifier of the Oracle process.

TRANSACTIONID Transaction identifier of the transaction in which the object is accessed. This helps to group audit records of a single transaction.

SCN System change number of the SQL. Added to complement the FGA audit trail.

SQL_BIND Bind variable data of the query. The SQLBIND column of the AUD$ table is the CLOB data type, and it is converted using TO_NCHAR in this column.

SQL_TEXT SQL text of the query. The SQLTEXT column of the AUD$ table is the CLOB data type, and it is converted using TO_NCHAR in this column.

The following are the new columns added to the DBA_FGA_AUDIT_TRAIL view (many of the columns now complement the DBA_AUDIT_TRAIL):

STATEMENT_TYPE   Statement type of the SQL: SELECT, INSERT, UPDATE or DELETE.

EXTENDED_TIMESTAMP   Time stamp of the SQL in UTC time.

PROXY_SESSIONID   Proxy session serial number, if user logged in through proxy mechanism.

GLOBAL_UID   Global user identifier if the user logged in as an enterprise user. The DB_USER column shows the user's identity in the database, and the GLOBAL_UID column shows the same user's global identity.

INSTANCE_NUMBER   Instance number as specified by the INSTANCE_NUMBER initialization parameter (applicable only to RAC).

OS_PROCESS   Operating system process identifier of the Oracle process.

TRANSACTIONID   Transaction identifier of the transaction in which the object is accessed.

STATEMENTID   Numeric ID for each statement run.

ENTRYID   Numeric ID for each audit trail entry in the session. The combination of STATEMENTID and ENTRYID makes each entry unique.

A new view DBA_COMMON_AUDIT_TRAIL is available in Oracle 10g. It combines the information in the AUD$ and FGA_AUD$ tables (or the DBA_AUDIT_TRAL and DBA_FGA_AUDIT_TRAL views). The AUDIT_TYPE column identifies the audit trail type. This view is very useful to get all the audit information in a query instead of performing a UNION between DBA_AUDIT_TRAIL and DBA_FGA_AUDIT_TRAIL.

The following example enables standard auditing on the hr.employee table for any updates to the employee table. Remember we still have the AUD_EMPLOYEE_SAL_FN fine-grained policy defined to audit SELECT and UPDATE on first_name and salary columns of this table.

```
SQL> AUDIT UPDATE ON hr.employee;

Audit succeeded.

SQL> SHOW USER
USER is "HR"
SQL> UPDATE hr.employee
  2  SET    hire_date = '30-JAN-90'
  3  WHERE  hire_date = '03-JAN-90';

1 row updated.

SQL>
SQL> SHOW USER
USER is "SCOTT"
```

```
SQL> UPDATE hr.employee
  2  SET     salary = 3000
  3  WHERE   first_name = 'SIGAL';

1 row updated.

SQL>
```

Let us now query the DBA_AUDIT_TRAIL, DBA_FGA_AUDIT_TRAIL and DBA_COMMON_AUDIT_TRAIL views to see the audit records in each view for the employee table. Notice that the update done by HR is not showing in the DBA_FGA_AUDIT_TRAIL because the columns updated were not part of the fine-grained auditing. The SCN column is displayed for each record to compare the results. There is a lot more information available in these views, due to space limitation we are showing only few columns.

```
SQL> SELECT username, timestamp, action_name, scn
  2  FROM    dba_audit_trail
  3  WHERE   owner = 'HR'
  4  AND     obj_name = 'EMPLOYEE';

USERNAME        TIMESTAMP ACTION_NAME                SCN
-------------   --------- -----------------   -----------

HR              23-AUG-04 SESSION REC            4196929
SCOTT           23-AUG-04 SESSION REC            4197496

SQL>
SQL> SELECT db_user, timestamp, policy_name, scn
  2  FROM    dba_fga_audit_trail
  3  WHERE   object_schema = 'HR'
  4  AND     object_name = 'EMPLOYEE';

DB_USER     TIMESTAMP POLICY_NAME                  SCN
----------  --------- ------------------------  ----------
DAVID       15-JUN-04 AUD_EMPLOYEE_SAL          2916018
DAVID       15-JUN-04 AUD_EMPLOYEE_SAL          2916049
SCOTT       23-AUG-04 AUD_EMPLOYEE_SAL_FN       4196894
SCOTT       23-AUG-04 AUD_EMPLOYEE_SAL_HD       4196894
SCOTT       23-AUG-04 AUD_EMPLOYEE_SAL          4196894
HR          23-AUG-04 AUD_EMPLOYEE_SAL_FN       4197448
HR          23-AUG-04 AUD_EMPLOYEE_SAL          4197448
SCOTT       23-AUG-04 AUD_EMPLOYEE_SAL_FN       4197496
SCOTT       23-AUG-04 AUD_EMPLOYEE_SAL          4197496

SQL>
```

```
SQL> SELECT audit_type, db_user, policy_name, scn
  2  FROM   dba_common_audit_trail
  3  WHERE  object_schema = 'HR'
  4  AND    object_name = 'EMPLOYEE';
```

AUDIT_TYPE	DB_USER	POLICY_NAME	SCN
Standard Audit	HR		4196929
Standard Audit	SCOTT		4197496
Fine Grained Audit	DAVID	AUD_EMPLOYEE_SAL	2916018
Fine Grained Audit	DAVID	AUD_EMPLOYEE_SAL	2916049
Fine Grained Audit	SCOTT	AUD_EMPLOYEE_SAL_FN	4196894
Fine Grained Audit	SCOTT	AUD_EMPLOYEE_SAL_HD	4196894
Fine Grained Audit	SCOTT	AUD_EMPLOYEE_SAL	4196894
Fine Grained Audit	HR	AUD_EMPLOYEE_SAL_FN	4197448
Fine Grained Audit	HR	AUD_EMPLOYEE_SAL	4197448
Fine Grained Audit	SCOTT	AUD_EMPLOYEE_SAL_FN	4197496
Fine Grained Audit	SCOTT	AUD_EMPLOYEE_SAL	4197496

In the next section we will discuss the major enhancements to SQL in Oracle 10*g*.

Introducing SQL New Features

Every new release of the Oracle database comes with a lot of SQL enhancements, and Oracle 10*g* is no exception. We covered many of the new SQL syntax in earlier chapters; for example, the new SQL statements used to manage Automatic Storage Management (ASM) disks or the syntax in ALTER SYSTEM to flush the buffer cache. In the following sections we will discuss some of the new features in Oracle 10*g* SQL that relate to data manipulation and application development, including the following:

- The MERGE command allows conditional extensions and the DELETE clause.

- You can convert dense data to sparse data using Partition Outer Join.

- You can perform inter-row calculations using the MODEL clause.

- It supports regular expressions.

- New data types introduced to support floating-point numbers.

- You can perform case- and accent-insensitive searches.

- You can use the quote operator.

MERGE Improvements

Oracle 9*i* introduced the MERGE command as an "Upsert" statement, where you can perform inserts and updates to a table in a single SQL statement. MERGE selects rows from one or more

sources for updating or inserting into one or more tables. The conditions specify whether to insert or update the target table. The MERGE statement has the following major improvements in Oracle 10*g*:

- The UPDATE or INSERT clause is optional.

- You can do a conditional UPDATE for a MERGE.

- You can perform a conditional INSERT using the WHERE clause.

- It has a new ON constant filter predicate to insert all rows to the target without joining source and target tables.

- An optional DELETE clause can remove rows while performing updates.

Since MERGE performs INSERT, UPDATE, and DELETE actions on the target table, you must have the appropriate privilege on the target table to perform the operation. Let's discuss the enhancements in detail with examples. Each example in this section uses the PRODUCTS and NEWPRODUCTS tables, which have the following sample data:

```
SQL> SELECT * FROM products;

PRODUCT_ID PRODUCT_NAME         CATEGORY
---------- -------------------- ----------
      1501 VIVITAR 35MM         ELECTRNCS
      1502 OLYMPUS IS50         ELECTRNCS
      1600 PLAY GYM             TOYS
      1601 LAMAZE               TOYS
      1666 HARRY POTTER         DVD

SQL> SELECT * FROM newproducts;

PRODUCT_ID PRODUCT_NAME         CATEGORY
---------- -------------------- ----------
      1502 OLYMPUS CAMERA       ELECTRNCS
      1601 LAMAZE               TOYS
      1666 HARRY POTTER         TOYS
      1700 WAIT INTERFACE       BOOKS

SQL>
```

After demonstrating each example in the following sections, the changes are rolled back. Before each example, the contents of products and newproducts table look as above.

Omitting *UPDATE* or *INSERT* Clause

In Oracle 9*i*, the MERGE statement required that you specify both INSERT and UPDATE clauses. In Oracle 10g, you can omit either the INSERT or UPDATE clause. The following example updates the PRODUCTS table with information from the NEWPRODUCTS table if the PRODUCT_ID matches:

```
SQL> MERGE INTO products p
  2  USING newproducts np
  3  ON (p.product_id = np.product_id)
  4  WHEN MATCHED THEN
  5  UPDATE
  6  SET  p.product_name = np.product_name,
  7       p.category     = np.category;


3 rows merged.

SQL> SELECT * FROM products;

PRODUCT_ID PRODUCT_NAME            CATEGORY
---------- --------------------    ----------
      1501 VIVITAR 35MM            ELECTRNCS
      1502 OLYMPUS CAMERA          ELECTRNCS
      1600 PLAY GYM                TOYS
      1601 LAMAZE                  TOYS
      1666 HARRY POTTER            TOYS
SQL>
SQL> ROLLBACK;


Rollback complete.

SQL>
```

In the example, the rows affected by the MERGE statement are product ids 1502, 1601 and 1666. Their product name and category are updated with the values from **newproducts** table.

The following example omits the UPDATE clause, and it inserts into the PRODUCTS table when a PRODUCT_ID is new in the NEWPRODUCTS table; no action is taken when the PRODUCT_ID matches. You can see from the example, product id 1700 is added to the **products** table.

```
SQL> MERGE INTO products p
  2  USING newproducts np
  3  ON (p.product_id = np.product_id)
  4  WHEN NOT MATCHED THEN
  5  INSERT
```

```
  6   VALUES (np.product_id, np.product_name,
  7           np.category);
```

1 row merged.

```
SQL> SELECT * FROM products;

        1501 VIVITAR 35MM        ELECTRNCS
        1502 OLYMPUS IS50        ELECTRNCS
        1600 PLAY GYM            TOYS
        1601 LAMAZE              TOYS
        1666 HARRY POTTER        DVD
        1700 WAIT INTERFACE      BOOKS
```

Conditional Updates and Inserts

You can add an optional WHERE clause to the UPDATE or INSERT clause of the MERGE statement to skip an update or insert operation for certain rows. The following example updates the PRODUCTS table with information from the NEWPRODUCTS table only when the CATEGORY matches:

```
SQL> MERGE INTO products p
  2   USING newproducts np
  3   ON (p.product_id = np.product_id)
  4   WHEN MATCHED THEN
  5   UPDATE
  6   SET p.product_name = np.product_name
  7   WHERE p.category = np.category;

2 rows merged.

SQL> SELECT * FROM products;

PRODUCT_ID PRODUCT_NAME         CATEGORY
---------- -------------------- ----------
        1501 VIVITAR 35MM        ELECTRNCS
        1502 OLYMPUS CAMERA      ELECTRNCS
        1600 PLAY GYM            TOYS
        1601 LAMAZE              TOYS
        1666 HARRY POTTER        DVD

SQL>

SQL> rollback;
```

In the example, product ids 1502, 1601 and 1666 match the ON condition but the category for 1666 does not match. So the MERGE statement updates only two rows.

The next example demonstrates using the WHERE clause in the UPDATE and INSERT clauses of the MERGE statement:

```
SQL> MERGE INTO products p
  2  USING newproducts np
  3  ON (p.product_id = np.product_id)
  4  WHEN MATCHED THEN
  5  UPDATE
  6  SET p.product_name = np.product_name,
  7      p.category    = np.category
  8  WHERE p.category = 'DVD'
  9  WHEN NOT MATCHED THEN
 10  INSERT
 11  VALUES (np.product_id, np.product_name, np.category)
 12  WHERE  np.category != 'BOOKS'
SQL> /

1 row merged.

SQL> SELECT * FROM products;

PRODUCT_ID PRODUCT_NAME         CATEGORY
---------- -------------------- ----------
      1501 VIVITAR 35MM         ELECTRNCS
      1502 OLYMPUS IS50         ELECTRNCS
      1600 PLAY GYM             TOYS
      1601 LAMAZE               TOYS
      1666 HARRY POTTER         TOYS

SQL>
```

Notice that the INSERT did not insert any rows to PRODUCTS because of the WHERE condition. The only row that satisfied the WHEN NOT MATCHED condition did not satisfy the WHERE clause of the INSERT. The MERGE updated product ID 1666.

Unconditional Inserts

You can insert rows from the source table to the target table without joining the source and target. This is useful when you want to insert all rows from the source to the target. Oracle 10g supports the constant filter predicate in the ON clause condition. An example of constant filter

is ON (1=0). The following example inserts rows from the source to the PRODUCTS table without checking its existence in the PRODUCTS table:

```
SQL> MERGE INTO products p
  2  USING newproducts np
  3  ON (1=0)
  4  WHEN NOT MATCHED THEN
  5  INSERT
  6  VALUES (np.product_id, np.product_name, np.category)
  7  WHERE  np.category = 'BOOKS'
SQL> /

1 row merged.

SQL> SELECT * FROM products;

PRODUCT_ID PRODUCT_NAME          CATEGORY
---------- --------------------  ----------
      1501 VIVITAR 35MM          ELECTRNCS
      1502 OLYMPUS IS50          ELECTRNCS
      1600 PLAY GYM              TOYS
      1601 LAMAZE                TOYS
      1666 HARRY POTTER          DVD
      1700 WAIT INTERFACE        BOOKS

6 rows selected.

SQL>
```

In the example, notice that the row with product id 1700 is added because it is the only row that satisfies the WHERE np.category = 'BOOKS' condition in the newproducts table.

New *DELETE* Clause

MERGE in Oracle 10*g* provides the option to cleanse rows while performing data operations. You can include the DELETE clause along with WHEN MATCHED THEN UPDATE clause. The DELETE clause must have a WHERE condition to remove rows that match certain conditions. Rows that match the DELETE WHERE condition but do not match the ON condition are not deleted from the table.

The following example demonstrates the DELETE clause. Here we merge the rows from NEWPRODUCTS into PRODUCTS and delete any rows from PRODUCTS whose category is ELECTRNCS. The contents of PRODUCTS and NEWPRODUCTS are listed again to help understand the result.

```
SQL> SELECT * FROM products;

PRODUCT_ID PRODUCT_NAME          CATEGORY
---------- --------------------  ----------
      1501 VIVITAR 35MM          ELECTRNCS
      1502 OLYMPUS IS50          ELECTRNCS
      1600 PLAY GYM              TOYS
      1601 LAMAZE                TOYS
      1666 HARRY POTTER          DVD

SQL> SELECT * FROM newproducts;

PRODUCT_ID PRODUCT_NAME          CATEGORY
---------- --------------------  ----------
      1502 OLYMPUS CAMERA        ELECTRNCS
      1601 LAMAZE                TOYS
      1666 HARRY POTTER          TOYS
      1700 WAIT INTERFACE        BOOKS

SQL> MERGE INTO products p
  2  USING newproducts np
  3  ON (p.product_id = np.product_id)
  4  WHEN MATCHED THEN
  5  UPDATE
  6  SET p.product_name = np.product_name,
  7      p.category     = np.category
  8  DELETE WHERE (p.category = 'ELECTRNCS')
  9  WHEN NOT MATCHED THEN
 10  INSERT
 11  VALUES (np.product_id, np.product_name, np.category)
SQL> /

4 rows merged.

SQL> SELECT * FROM products;

PRODUCT_ID PRODUCT_NAME          CATEGORY
---------- --------------------  ----------
      1501 VIVITAR 35MM          ELECTRNCS
      1600 PLAY GYM              TOYS
      1601 LAMAZE                TOYS
      1666 HARRY POTTER          TOYS
      1700 WAIT INTERFACE        BOOKS

SQL>
```

The product ID 1502 was deleted from PRODUCTS because it matched the ON condition and the DELETE WHERE condition. The product ID 1501 matched the DELETE WHERE condition but did not match the ON condition, so it was not deleted. The product ID 1700 did not match the ON condition, so it was inserted into the PRODUCTS table. The product IDs 1601 and 1666 matched the ON condition but did not match the DELETE condition, so they were updated with the new values from the NEWPRODUCTS table.

The MERGE statement in Oracle 10g is more flexible and can accomplish several tasks in one step. Let's now move onto the next new feature: partitioned outer joins.

Partitioned Outer Join

A *partitioned outer join*, also known as a *group outer join*, is an excellent method to convert sparse data into a dense form. In data warehouse schemas that use dimension and fact tables, time-specific data is normally stored in a sparse form in the database; if no value exists for specific time period, no row exists in the fact table. Time series calculations are easier when dense data fill a consistent number of rows for each period.

You can use the partitioned outer join syntax to fill the gaps in time series by extending the conventional outer join syntax to apply the outer join to each partition defined in the query. It is similar to a regular outer join except the outer join is applied to each partition. The Oracle database logically partitions the rows in your query based on the expression you specify in the PARTITION BY clause. The result of a partitioned outer join is a UNION of the outer joins of each of the groups in the logically partitioned table with the table on the other side of the join.

The PARTTION BY...RIGHT OUTER JOIN has the following syntax:

```
SELECT select_expression
FROM   table_reference
PARTITION BY (expr [, expr ]... )
RIGHT OUTER JOIN table_reference
```

The LEFT OUTER JOIN...PARTTION BY has the following syntax:

```
SELECT select_expression
FROM   table_reference
LEFT OUTER JOIN table_reference
PARTITION BY {expr [,expr ]...)
```

To demonstrate the partitioned outer join, let's consider the following data. The DB_DOWNTIME table records instances when a database is not available.

```
SQL> SELECT * FROM db_downtime;
```

DBNAME	DOWN_STARTTIME	DOWN_ENDTIME
DALP01	07-JUN-2004 11:47:38	07-JUN-2004 12:47:38
DALP01	06-JUN-2004 11:48:02	06-JUN-2004 13:48:02
DALP01	16-JUN-2004 11:48:17	16-JUN-2004 13:18:17

```
FTWP01   06-JUN-2004 11:48:26 06-JUN-2004 13:18:26
FTWP01   15-JUN-2004 11:48:39 15-JUN-2004 16:48:39

SQL>
```

The following example densifies the missing data of downtime minutes in the last 15 days for each date and each database using the new PARTITION BY...OUTER JOIN syntax.

```
SQL> SELECT pdate, dbname,
  2          NVL((down_endtime-down_starttime)*24*60,0)
             as downminutes
  3   FROM   db_downtime dbd
  4   PARTITION BY (dbname)
  5   RIGHT OUTER JOIN (
  6   SELECT TRUNC(sysdate)-15+rownum pdate
  7   FROM all_objects
  8   WHERE rownum <= 15) alldates
  9   ON trunc(dbd.down_starttime) = alldates.pdate
 10   ORDER BY 1
SQL> /
```

PDATE	DBNAME	DOWNMINUTES
02-JUN-2004 00:00:00	DALP01	0
02-JUN-2004 00:00:00	FTWP01	0
03-JUN-2004 00:00:00	DALP01	0
03-JUN-2004 00:00:00	FTWP01	0
04-JUN-2004 00:00:00	DALP01	0
04-JUN-2004 00:00:00	FTWP01	0
05-JUN-2004 00:00:00	DALP01	0
05-JUN-2004 00:00:00	FTWP01	0
06-JUN-2004 00:00:00	DALP01	120
06-JUN-2004 00:00:00	FTWP01	90
07-JUN-2004 00:00:00	DALP01	60
07-JUN-2004 00:00:00	FTWP01	0
<< output truncated >>		
15-JUN-2004 00:00:00	DALP01	0
15-JUN-2004 00:00:00	FTWP01	300
16-JUN-2004 00:00:00	DALP01	90
16-JUN-2004 00:00:00	FTWP01	0

```
30 rows selected.

SQL>
```

In the example notice that there are no records for many dates between 2-JUN-2004 and 15-JUN-2004 in the db_downtime table. The query using the partition outer join method densifies the result with all missing dates. The down minutes for the records generated are NULL, but using a NVL function, we interpreted the NULL values as zero. Since we do not have a table with all the dates of the month, we used the ALL_OBJECTS view and ROWNUM to generate the continuous dates.

Once you have the dense data available, you can use it to perform analytical calculations or to plot charts.

The partitioned outer join supports only RIGHT OUTER JOIN and LEFT OUTER JOIN. It does not support FULL OUTER JOIN. The new syntax has been accepted by ANSI and ISO to be included in the SQL standard.

Using Partitioned Outer Joins with Analytic Functions

A partitioned outer join will return rows with NULL values in some queries, but you may want those rows to hold the most recent non-NULL value in the series. That is, you may want to have NULLs replaced with the first non-NULL value you see as you scan upward in a column.

Let's consider an example. The DB_TABSIZE table tracks the size of the table each month, and if the size does not change, no information is entered in the table. The table has the following data:

```
SQL> SELECT * FROM db_tabsize;


OWNER      TABNAME              STATDATE   TABSIZE
---------- -------------------- ---------- ----------
BILL       SALES                01-JAN-04     262144
BILL       SALES                01-MAR-04     524288
BILL       SALES                01-MAY-04    1048576
BILL       SALES                01-JUN-04    2097152
BILL       INVENTORY            01-JAN-04     262144
BILL       INVENTORY            01-MAR-04     524288
BILL       INVENTORY            01-APR-04   10485760
BILL       INVENTORY            01-JUN-04   20971520

SQL>
SQL> SELECT * FROM months;

MONTHDATE
```

```
---------
01-JAN-04
01-FEB-04
01-MAR-04
01-APR-04
01-MAY-04
01-JUN-04

SQL>
```

Here you see that if an event does not exist, then no row exists for the table for that month. The table SALES has no row for February and April, and the table INVENTORY has no row for February and May because their sizes remained the same. Let's try to make this data dense using the partition outer join.

```
SQL> SELECT owner, tabname, monthdate, tabsize
  2  FROM   db_tabsize
  3  PARTITION BY (owner, tabname)
  4  RIGHT OUTER JOIN months
  5  ON (db_tabsize.statdate = months.monthdate)
SQL> /
```

OWNER	TABNAME	MONTHDATE	TABSIZE
BILL	INVENTORY	01-JAN-04	262144
BILL	INVENTORY	01-FEB-04	
BILL	INVENTORY	01-MAR-04	524288
BILL	INVENTORY	01-APR-04	10485760
BILL	INVENTORY	01-MAY-04	
BILL	INVENTORY	01-JUN-04	20971520
BILL	SALES	01-JAN-04	262144
BILL	SALES	01-FEB-04	
BILL	SALES	01-MAR-04	524288
BILL	SALES	01-APR-04	
BILL	SALES	01-MAY-04	1048576
BILL	SALES	01-JUN-04	2097152

```
12 rows selected.

SQL>
```

But this is not the data we want. When we make the time dimension dense, we want to see a size value for each month. When using the partition outer join, we see a NULL, which is not the size value. We want the size of the table SALES in April to be displayed as being the same as it was in March. You can accomplish this by using the new keyword IGNORE NULLS introduced in the FIRST_VALUE and LAST_VALUE analytic functions in Oracle 10*g*.

```
SQL> SELECT owner, tabname, monthdate,
  2             LAST_VALUE(tabsize IGNORE NULLS)
  3             OVER (PARTITION BY owner, tabname
  4                      ORDER BY monthdate) tabsize
  5  FROM    (
  6  SELECT owner, tabname, monthdate, tabsize
  7  FROM db_tabsize
  8  PARTITION BY (owner, tabname)
  9  RIGHT OUTER JOIN months
 10  ON (db_tabsize.statdate = months.monthdate))
 11  ORDER BY owner, tabname, monthdate
SQL> /
```

OWNER	TABNAME	MONTHDATE	TABSIZE
BILL	INVENTORY	01-JAN-04	262144
BILL	INVENTORY	01-FEB-04	262144
BILL	INVENTORY	01-MAR-04	524288
BILL	INVENTORY	01-APR-04	10485760
BILL	INVENTORY	01-MAY-04	10485760
BILL	INVENTORY	01-JUN-04	20971520
BILL	SALES	01-JAN-04	262144
BILL	SALES	01-FEB-04	262144
BILL	SALES	01-MAR-04	524288
BILL	SALES	01-APR-04	524288
BILL	SALES	01-MAY-04	1048576
BILL	SALES	01-JUN-04	2097152

```
12 rows selected.

SQL>
```

As you can see, the PARTITION...OUTER JOIN syntax is useful in doing analytic calculations. Combining the partition outer join with several analytic functions and using it with hierarchical cubes can yield results faster in Oracle 10*g*. The dense data makes it simple to use analytic functions such as LAG or LEAD, which perform better when a row exists for each combination of dimensions. The performance of the partitioned outer join syntax is several times faster and improves the overall calculation performance.

Spreadsheet Computations Using the *MODEL* Clause

The SQL MODEL *clause* is a significant new feature of the Oracle 10*g* database in the business intelligence area. This clause will help accountants who like to take data out of Oracle and put it into a spreadsheet to perform analytic functions. The purpose of the SQL MODEL clause is to give SQL statements the ability to create a multidimensional array from the results of a normal SELECT statement and then perform several interdependent inter-row and inter-array calculations on this SQL spreadsheet. You can use the results of the MODEL clause to update the base tables using the INSERT, UPDATE, and MERGE statements.

The MODEL clause defines a multidimensional array by mapping the columns of a query into three groups: partitions, dimensions, and measures. *Partitions* define logical blocks of the result set and are viewed as an independent array. *Dimensions* identify each measure cell within a partition. These columns are identifying characteristics such as date and product name. *Measures* are the actual data cells. They are analogous to the measures of a fact table in a star schema. Measures typically contain numeric values such as sales units or revenue. You can access each cell within its partition by specifying its full combination of dimensions. Table 8.2 demonstrates these components.

TABLE 8.2   Sample Data to Demonstrate MODEL Clause

Partition	Dimension	Dimension	Measure
Country	Company	Year	Revenue
C1	ABC	2002	450
C1	ABC	2001	455
C2	ABC	2002	500
C2	ABC	2001	550
C1	XYZ	2002	67
C1	XYZ	2001	78

TABLE 8.2   Sample Data to Demonstrate MODEL Clause *(continued)*

Partition	Dimension	Dimension	Measure
C2	XYZ	2002	85
C2	XYZ	2001	80

The MODEL clause of the SELECT statement has several options. The MODEL clause is processed after all the other clauses of the SELECT statement but before the ORDER BY clause. The core syntax of the MODEL clause is as follows:

```
<prior clauses of SELECT statement>
MODEL   [RETURN [UPDATED | ALL] ROWS]
[reference models]
[PARTITION BY (<cols>)]
DIMENSION BY (<cols>)
MEASURES (<cols>) [IGNORE NAV] | [KEEP NAV]
[RULES
[UPSERT | UPDATE]
[AUTOMATIC ORDER | SEQUENTIAL ORDER]
[ITERATE (n) [UNTIL <condition>] ]
( <cell_assignment> = <expression> ... )
```

The previous syntax is the most simplified version.

NOTE   Refer to *Oracle 10g SQL Reference Manual* for the complete syntax of the SELECT statement MODEL clause.

We will demonstrate the use of MODEL clause using examples. For simplicity let's consider you have the previous data in a single table.

```
SQL> SELECT * FROM revenues;

COUNTRY  COMPANY      YEAR     REVENUE
-------- --------  ---------- ----------
C1       ABC          2002       450
C1       ABC          2001       455
C2       ABC          2002       500
C2       ABC          2001       550
C1       XYZ          2002        67
```

```
C1      XYZ         2001        78
C2      XYZ         2002        85
C2      XYZ         2001        80

SQL>
```

The revenue data for years 2001 and 2002 are available; we can use the MODEL clause to project the 2003 revenues using 2001 and 2002 data. Let's say the 2003 projection is going to be the total revenue of 2001 and 2002 for company XYZ and 20 percent higher than 2002 for company ABC. The MODEL clause would be as follows:

```
SQL> SELECT country, company, year, revenue
  2  FROM    revenues
  3  MODEL
  4  PARTITION BY (country)
  5  DIMENSION BY (company, year)
  6  MEASURES (revenue)
  7  RULES (
  8    revenue['ABC',2003] = revenue['ABC',2002]*1.2,
  9    revenue['XYZ',2003] = revenue['XYZ',2001] +
 10                           revenue['XYZ',2002])
 11  ORDER BY country, company, year
SQL> /


COUNTRY   COMPANY      YEAR      REVENUE
--------  --------  ----------  ----------
C1        ABC          2001        455
C1        ABC          2002        450
C1        ABC          2003        540
C1        XYZ          2001        78
C1        XYZ          2002        67
C1        XYZ          2003        145
C2        ABC          2001        550
C2        ABC          2002        500
C2        ABC          2003        600
C2        XYZ          2001        80
C2        XYZ          2002        85
C2        XYZ          2003        165

12 rows selected.

SQL>
```

> The MODEL clause is the last query clause, executed after the WHERE and GROUP BY clauses but before the ORDER BY clause.

The result shows the new rows generated by the MODEL clause as well as the existing rows. If you're interested only in the new rows created by the query, use the RETURN UPDATED ROWS clause, as in the following example:

```
SQL> SELECT country, company, year, revenue
  2  FROM    revenues
  3  MODEL RETURN UPDATED ROWS
  4  PARTITION BY (country)
  5  DIMENSION BY (company, year)
  6  MEASURES (revenue)
  7  RULES (
  8    revenue['ABC',2003] = revenue['ABC',2002]*1.2,
  9    revenue['XYZ',2003] = revenue['XYZ',2001] +
 10                          revenue['XYZ',2002])
 11  ORDER BY country, company, year
SQL> /
```

COUNTRY	COMPANY	YEAR	REVENUE
C1	ABC	2003	540
C1	XYZ	2003	145
C2	ABC	2003	600
C2	XYZ	2003	165

```
SQL>
```

A full discussion of all these options is outside the scope of the OCP exam and this book, but a brief example of cell addressing is discussed in the next section for demonstration purposes.

> The MODEL clause does not update existing data in tables, and it does not insert new data into tables. To change values in a table, you must supply the MODEL results to an INSERT, UPDATE, or MERGE statement.

Addressing Cells and Values

Understanding cell reference is important to get the most out of the MODEL clause. By default the rules in the MODEL clause have "Upsert" semantics. If the cell that is indicated by the left side on

the rule exists, it is updated; otherwise a new row containing that cell is generated. Again, the base table is not updated or inserted with new values, they are shown as a result of the operation. You must use appropriate INSERT or UPDATE statements to perform the update or insert to the base table. A reference to a cell must qualify all dimensions listed in the DIMENSION BY clause. You can use either positional reference or symbolic reference. Cell references are discussed in the following sections.

Positional Cell Reference

In positional reference, each value provided in the brackets matches the dimension in the equivalent position of the DIMENSION BY clause. The following is an example of a query that uses positional cell reference to match the appropriate dimension based on its position in the expression: The DIMENSION BY clause determines the position assigned to each dimension. In this example, the first position is the company, and the second position is the year. The revenue for company ABC year 2001 is updated to 1000 when showing the result. Notice that the value for revenue for this record in the base table is 455.

```
SQL> SELECT country, company, year, revenue
  2  FROM    revenues
  3  WHERE   country = 'C1'
  4  MODEL RETURN UPDATED ROWS
  5  PARTITION BY (country)
  6  DIMENSION BY (company, year)
  7  MEASURES (revenue)
  8  RULES (
  9    revenue['ABC',2001] = 1000)
SQL> /
```

COUNTRY	COMPANY	YEAR	REVENUE
C1	ABC	2001	1000

```
SQL>
```

Symbolic Cell Reference

With symbolic cell reference, a single dimension value is qualified by a SQL Boolean condition. You can use conditions such as <, >, IN, and BETWEEN. You need to include as many conditions inside the brackets as there are dimensions in the DIMENSIONS BY clause. Symbolic references are solely for updating existing cells, and they cannot create new cells. The following SQL is an

example of symbolic reference. Here we reference all the rows that belong to company ABC and are above year 2000 using the symbolic reference. For such rows, we update the revenue to 100.

```
SQL> SELECT country, company, year, revenue
  2  FROM    revenues
  3  WHERE   country = 'C1'
  4  MODEL RETURN UPDATED ROWS
  5  PARTITION BY (country)
  6  DIMENSION BY (company, year)
  7  MEASURES (revenue)
  8  RULES (
  9    revenue[company='ABC',year>2000] = 100)
SQL> /


COUNTRY  COMPANY      YEAR   REVENUE
-------- --------  ----------  ----------
C1        ABC        2002        100
C1        ABC        2001        100

SQL>
```

Using Current Value Function

The current value function (CV()) is a powerful tool used on the right side of formulas to copy left-side specifications that refer to multiple cells. This allows for compact and flexible multicell formulas. You can consider the current value function as a SQL join condition that is compact and readable.

In the following example, we add 20 percent to the revenue of XYZ Company in country C2 and make that the revenue of company ABC. The CV(year) function returns the year dimension value of the cell currently referenced on the left side.

```
SQL> SELECT country, company, year, revenue
  2  FROM    revenues
  3  WHERE   country = 'C2'
  4  MODEL RETURN UPDATED ROWS
  5  PARTITION BY (country)
  6  DIMENSION BY (company, year)
  7  MEASURES (revenue)
  8  RULES (
  9    revenue['ABC', year BETWEEN 2001 and 2002] =
 10    revenue['XYZ', CV(year)] * 1.2)
SQL> /
```

COUNTRY	COMPANY	YEAR	REVENUE
C2	ABC	2002	102
C2	ABC	2001	96

SQL>

The current value function takes the dimension key as the argument. It is also possible to use CV function without any arguments, as in CV( ), which causes positional referencing.

Miscellaneous *MODEL* Clause Options

The MODEL clause includes several options and subclasses that make the MODEL clause a powerful tool for analytical applications. In the following sections we will discuss a few of the important options.

FOR Loop

The FOR construct can be useful in applying a single formula to generate multiple cells. In the following example, the cells for year 2005 are generated for the company C2 using a FOR construct:

```
SQL> SELECT country, company, year, revenue
  2  FROM    revenues
  3  WHERE   country = 'C2'
  4  MODEL RETURN UPDATED ROWS
  5  PARTITION BY (country)
  6  DIMENSION BY (company, year)
  7  MEASURES (revenue)
  8  RULES (
  9     revenue [FOR company IN ('ABC','XYZ'), 2004 ]
 10             = 2 * revenue [CV(company), 2002])
SQL> /
```

COUNTRY	COMPANY	YEAR	REVENUE
C2	XYZ	2004	170
C2	ABC	2004	1000

SQL>

Rules Ordering

By default, rules are evaluated in the order they appear in the MODEL clause (the default is SEQUENTIAL ORDER). The AUTOMATIC ORDER clause evaluates the dependencies in the RULES and processes them in the order the values are evaluated. The following two queries demonstrate

the order and the difference in results. Notice that in the first SQL example, the second rule is executed before the first rule. In the second SQL example, the values are NULL, because revenue ['XYZ',2004] is evaluated to NULL.

```
SQL> SELECT country, company, year, revenue
  2  FROM    revenues
  3  MODEL RETURN UPDATED ROWS
  4  PARTITION BY (country)
  5  DIMENSION BY (company, year)
  6  MEASURES (revenue)
  7  RULES AUTOMATIC ORDER (
  8      revenue ['ABC', 2004] =
         revenue ['ABC', 2002] + revenue ['XYZ',2004],
  9      revenue ['XYZ', 2004] =
         revenue ['ABC', 2001] + revenue ['XYZ',2001])
SQL> /
```

COUNTRY	COMPANY	YEAR	REVENUE
C2	XYZ	2004	630
C2	ABC	2004	1130
C1	XYZ	2004	533
C1	ABC	2004	983

```
SQL>
SQL> SELECT country, company, year, revenue
  2  FROM    revenues
  3  MODEL RETURN UPDATED ROWS
  4  PARTITION BY (country)
  5  DIMENSION BY (company, year)
  6  MEASURES (revenue)
  7  RULES SEQUENTIAL ORDER (
  8      revenue ['ABC', 2004] =
         revenue ['ABC', 2002] + revenue ['XYZ',2004],
  9      revenue ['XYZ', 2004] =
         revenue ['ABC', 2001] + revenue ['XYZ',2001])
SQL> /
```

COUNTRY	COMPANY	YEAR	REVENUE
C2	ABC	2004	

C2	XYZ	2004	630
C1	ABC	2004	
C1	XYZ	2004	533

SQL>

Ignoring *NULLs*

You can use the IGNORE NAV option to ignore NULL and substitute a value for the NULL value. When a NULL is involved in calculations, the dependent results are NULL. The IGNORE NAV options will prevent NULL values from propagating through a set of related calculations. When you use the IGNORE NAV option, Oracle assigns the following values for NULL values:

- Zero for numeric data types

- 01-JAN-2000 for date and time stamp data types

- An empty string for character data types

- NULL for all other data types

Let's apply the IGNORE NAV clause to the previous example and see the results. Notice how the revenue values for ABC company are now displayed as 500, instead of NULL as before.

```
SQL> SELECT country, company, year, revenue
  2  FROM    revenues
  3  MODEL IGNORE NAV RETURN UPDATED ROWS
  4  PARTITION BY (country)
  5  DIMENSION BY (company, year)
  6  MEASURES (revenue)
  7  RULES SEQUENTIAL ORDER (
  8     revenue ['ABC', 2004] =
        revenue ['ABC', 2002] + revenue ['XYZ',2004],
  9     revenue ['XYZ', 2004] =
        revenue ['ABC', 2001] + revenue ['XYZ',2001])
SQL> /
```

COUNTRY	COMPANY	YEAR	REVENUE
C2	ABC	2004	500
C2	XYZ	2004	630
C1	ABC	2004	450
C1	XYZ	2004	533

SQL>

Reference Models

In a single MODEL clause, you can reference multiple multidimensional arrays. The multidimensional array that has existing cells updated and new cells added is called the *main model*. Along with the main model, you can define one or more multidimensional arrays called the *reference models*. The reference models are read-only and are used as lookup tables.

Reference models are similar to the main SQL model where you have a query block with DIMENSION BY and MEASURES clauses. The reference model cannot have a PARTITION clause. A MODEL clause can have more than one reference model, but each reference model must have a different name.

The following example uses the conversion rate of currency as a reference model and uses it in the MODEL clause to show base revenue and converted revenue:

```
SQL> SELECT * FROM conversion_rate;

COUNTRY        C_RATE
---------- ----------
C1              1.75
C2                 5


SQL> SELECT country, year, locrevenue, convrevenue
  2  FROM    revenues
  3  GROUP BY country, year
  4  MODEL RETURN UPDATED ROWS
  5  REFERENCE conv_rate_model ON (
  6    SELECT country, c_rate AS cr
  7    FROM    conversion_rate)
  8  DIMENSION BY (country)
  9  MEASURES (cr)
 10  MAIN main_model
 11  DIMENSION BY (country, year)
 12  MEASURES (SUM(revenue) revenue,
             0 locrevenue, 0 convrevenue)
 13  RULES (
 14    locrevenue ['C1', 2004] =
 15        revenue ['C1', 2002] + revenue ['C1',2001],
 16    convrevenue ['C1', 2004] =
 17        (revenue ['C1', 2002] + revenue ['C1',2001]) *
 18                        conv_rate_model.cr['C1'],
 19    locrevenue ['C2', 2004] =
 20        revenue ['C2', 2002] + revenue ['C2',2001],
 21    convrevenue ['C2', 2004] =
 22        (revenue ['C2', 2002] + revenue ['C2',2001]) *
```

```
 23                              conv_rate_model.cr['C2']
 24          )
SQL> /
```

COUNTRY	YEAR	LOCREVENUE	CONVREVENUE
C2	2004	1215	6075
C1	2004	1050	1837.5

```
SQL>
```

Cyclic References and Iterations

Using the ITERATE option of the MODEL clause, you can evaluate formulas iteratively a specified number of times. The number of iterations is specified as an argument to the ITERATE clause. Optionally, you can specify a termination condition to stop formula evaluation before reaching the maximum iteration. This condition is specified in the UNTIL option of the ITERATE clause and is checked at the end of each iteration.

In the next section we will discuss another major SQL improvement, the regular expression support for string searching.

Regular Expressions

Regular expressions are a powerful, efficient text-processing feature for searching and manipulating complex patterns. Regular expressions can be as simple as a search command in a text editor or as powerful as a text-processing language.

In Oracle 10g, both SQL and PL/SQL support regular expressions. Regular expression implementation in Oracle 10g complies with the POSIX standard for pattern matching and Unicode regular expression guidelines.

Regular expressions in Oracle are especially useful to validate data such as phone numbers, ZIP codes, e-mail addresses, and so on. They are also useful in searching for Hypertext Markup Language (HTML) tags, dates or e-mail addresses.

The following four functions support regular expressions:

- REGEXP_LIKE
- REGEXP_INSTR
- REGEXP_REPLACE
- REGEXP_SUBSTR

REGEXP_LIKE

REGEXP_LIKE is used in SQL as a Boolean operator, similar to the LIKE operator. You must use REGEXP_LIKE in SQL in the WHERE or HAVING clause, again similar to the LIKE operator. You can use the REGEXP_LIKE function as a function that returns Boolean result in PL/SQL.

The syntax of REGEXP_LIKE is as follows:

```
REGEXP_LIKE ( source_string, pattern [, match_parameter] )
```

The *source_string* is the search value, which can be a string literal or a character column (CHAR, VARCHAR2, NCHAR, NVARCHAR2, CLOB, or NCLOB). The *pattern* is the regular expression you're trying to match in the *source_string*. The *match_parameter* changes the default matching behavior. The match_parameter can be one or more of the following values:

- i specifies case-insensitive matching.
- c specifies case-sensitive matching.
- n allows the period (.) to match a new line character.
- m treats the source string as multiple lines, where ^ and $ are identified as the start and end of the line.

WARNING   If the data type of the regular expression is different from the data type of the search string, the regular expression is implicitly converted to the data type of the search string.

The following example queries the EMPLOYEES table in the HR sample schema to find the first names of employees whose first names start with a vowel, whose second character is an L, and whose first name is at least six characters long. The ^ represents the beginning of line and we check for a vowel immediately following the ^. The i option is used to ignore the case while comparing. The :alpha: checks that the character is an alphabet, the "6," is interpreted as at least 6 characters.

```
SQL> SELECT first_name, last_name
  2  FROM    employees
  3  WHERE   REGEXP_LIKE (first_name, '^[aeiou]l','i')
  4  AND     REGEXP_LIKE (first_name, '[[:alpha:]]{6,}')
SQL> /


FIRST_NAME           LAST_NAME
-------------------- -------------------------
Elizabeth            Bates
Alexis               Bull
Alberto              Errazuriz
Alexander            Hunold
Alyssa               Hutton
Alexander            Khoo
Oliver               Tuvault
```

7 rows selected.

SQL>

This second example looks for employees with a space in their last names. It also makes sure at least one character appears before and after the space, as we do not want to take into account the leading or trailing spaces if there are any. `[[:alpha:]]` matches any alphabet, `.+` matches one or more characters, and `.*` matches zero or more characters. The `{ }` specifies the width of the matching string, which is 1, and means 1 or more.

```
SQL> SELECT first_name, last_name
  2  FROM    employees
  3  WHERE   REGEXP_LIKE
       (last_name, '[[:alpha:]]{1,} [[:alpha:]]{1,}')
SQL> /

FIRST_NAME           LAST_NAME
-------------------- ------------------------
Lex                  De Haan

SQL> SELECT first_name, last_name
  2  FROM    employees
  3  WHERE   REGEXP_LIKE (last_name, '.+ .+')
SQL> /

FIRST_NAME           LAST_NAME
-------------------- ------------------------
Lex                  De Haan

SQL> SELECT first_name, last_name
  2  FROM    employees
  3  WHERE   REGEXP_LIKE (last_name, '.*[[:space:]].*')
SQL> /

FIRST_NAME           LAST_NAME
-------------------- ------------------------
Elizabeth              Bates
Lex                  De Haan

SQL>
```

NOTE Discussing all the metacharacters of regular expression pattern matching requires a book by itself. Please refer to *Oracle Regular Expressions Pocket Reference* and *Mastering Regular Expressions, Second Edition* to learn more about pattern matching and regular expressions.

REGEXP_INSTR

The REGEXP_INSTR function is similar to the INSTR function, but it extends the INSTR functionality by searching the string for a regular expression pattern. The function returns the position where the match is found. The syntax of REGEXP_INSTR is as follows:

```
REGEXP_INSTR (source_string, pattern
             [,position [,occurrence
             [,return_option [,match_parameter ] ] ] ])
```

The following example shows the position of the second occurrence (*occurrence* = 2) of a vowel (*pattern* = [aeiou]) in the first name of employees, with case-insensitive (*match_parameter* = i) searching from the first character (*position* = 1). The *return_option* of 0 is the default, which returns the position of the first character of the occurrence; 1 returns the position of the character following the occurrence.

```
SQL> SELECT first_name, REGEXP_INSTR(first_name,
  2                    '[aeiou]', 1, 2, 0, 'i') reginstr
  3  FROM    employees
  4  WHERE   last_name like 'S%'
SQL> /

FIRST_NAME             REGINSTR
-------------------- ----------
Nandita                      5
Ismael                       4
John                         0
Sarath                       4
Lindsey                      6
William                      5
Stephen                      6
Martha                       6
Patrick                      5

9 rows selected.

SQL>
```

REGEXP_REPLACE

REGEXP_REPLACE searches for a regular expression pattern and replaces it with a replacement string. It extends the functionality of the REPLACE function. The syntax of REGEXP_REPLACE is as follows:

```
REGEXP_REPLACE (source_string, pattern
        [,position [,occurrence [,match_parameter ] ] ])
```

The following two examples demonstrate the REGEXP_REPLACE function. The first example adds a space after each character, and the second example changes the "last name, first name" format to "first name, last name" format.

```
SQL> SELECT REGEXP_REPLACE
            ('United States', '(.)', '\1 ') repl
  2  FROM    dual
SQL> /


REPL
-------------------------
U n i t e d   S t a t e s

SQL>
SQL> SELECT REGEXP_REPLACE
        ('Ellison, Larry', '(.+), (.*)', '\2 \1') name
  2 FROM    dual
SQL> /


NAME
------------
Larry Ellison

SQL>
```

REGEXP_SUBSTR

REGEXP_SUBSTR searches for a regular expression pattern within a given string and returns the matched substring. This function extends the functionality of the SUBSTR function. The syntax of REGEXP_SUBSTR is similar to REGEXP_REPLACE.

```
REGEXP_SUBSTR (source_string, pattern
        [,position [,occurrence [,match_parameter ] ] ])
```

The following example extracts the domain name from an e-mail address:

```
SQL> SELECT REGEXP_SUBSTR ('xyz@sybex.com', '@.*') dname
  2  FROM    dual
SQL> /

DNAME
----------
@sybex.com

SQL>
```

Data Type Enhancements

In the earlier releases of Oracle, the maximum size for LOB columns (CLOB, BLOB, and NCLOB data types) was 4GB. In Oracle 10*g*, the maximum size has been increased to (4GB −1byte)*DB_BLOCK_SIZE. Since the DB_BLOCK_SIZE can vary from 2KB to 32KB, the LOB size could range between 8TB to 128TB.

All procedures in the DBMS_LOB package support the terabyte-sized LOBs. A new function—DBMS_LOB.GET_STORAGE_LIMIT—returns the storage limit for the database. All the Oracle call interface (OCI) APIs also support the new larger LOB size.

In the following sections we will discuss the implicit LOB conversion and the new floating-point data types introduced in Oracle 10g.

Implicit LOB Conversion

Explicit conversion between CLOB and NCLOB data types were available in Oracle 9*i* using the TO_CLOB and TO_NCLOB functions. Oracle 10*g* introduces implicit conversion for SQL IN and OUT bind variables for queries and DML operations and well as for PL/SQL function and procedure parameter passing. The following example demonstrates this conversion.

Note that in the SELECT and INSERT statements CLOB value is selected and inserted with NCLOB, and vice versa, to show the implicit conversion.

```
SQL> CREATE TABLE clob_conversion (
  2  clob_col    CLOB,
  3  nclob_col   NCLOB);

Table created.
```

```
SQL> DECLARE
  2    clob_var  CLOB;
  3    nclob_var NCLOB;
  4  BEGIN
  5    clob_var := 'Clob Value';
  6    nclob_var:= clob_var;
  7    INSERT INTO clob_conversion
  8       VALUES (nclob_var, clob_var);
  9    SELECT nclob_col, clob_col
 10    INTO   clob_var, nclob_var
 11    FROM   clob_conversion;
 12  END;
SQL> /

PL/SQL procedure successfully completed.

SQL>
```

In Oracle 9*i*, accessing the :NEW attribute value for a LOB inside a before row INSERT or UPDATE trigger failed. In Oracle 10*g*, this shortcoming has been corrected, and the behavior of the database trigger on a table with a LOB is like any other data type.

Native Floating-Point Data Types

Oracle 10*g* supports two new numeric data types: BINARY_FLOAT and BINARY_DOUBLE. The BINARY_FLOAT is single precision 32-bit, and BINARY_DOUBLE is double precision 64-bit. These data types are based on the IEEE 754 standard for binary floating-point arithmetic and are more efficient than the NUMBER data type. These floating-point data types are widely accepted by the majority of numerical computation users. They also work well with Extensible Markup Language (XML) and Java. While the NUMBER data type is implemented in the Oracle software, floating-point arithmetic operations are the standard numeric format on most hardware platforms.

SQL and PL/SQL offer full support for BINARY_FLOAT and BINARY_DOUBLE data types. BINARY_FLOAT data types require 5 bytes of storage, and BINARY_DOUBLE data types require 9 bytes; the NUMBER data type can take anywhere between 1 and 22 bytes. The new data types support numbers that are much larger and much smaller than the numbers supported by the NUMBER data type.

The following example shows using the BINARY_FLOAT and BINARY_DOUBLE data types when creating a table and when using DML statements:

```
SQL> CREATE TABLE binary_example (
  2  bf  BINARY_FLOAT,
  3  bd  BINARY_DOUBLE);
```

```
Table created.

SQL> DESCRIBE binary_example
 Name                       Null?    Type
 ----------------------- -------- ---------------
 BF                                 BINARY_FLOAT
 BD                                 BINARY_DOUBLE


SQL> INSERT INTO binary_example VALUES (3.0f, 4.0d);

1 row created.

SQL> INSERT INTO binary_example VALUES (5, 9);

1 row created.

SQL> SELECT * FROM binary_example;

        BF          BD
---------- ----------
   3.0E+000   4.0E+000
   5.0E+000   9.0E+000


SQL>
```

New syntax has been added to SQL to support literal values representing floating-point numbers. As shown in the previous example, floating-point literals can use f or d as the suffix. Untagged numeric literals are parsed as NUMBER.

Arithmetic Operations

Arithmetic operations on BINARY_FLOAT and BINARY_DOUBLE data types produce a numeric value or a special value. The special values can be zero (0), positive infinity (+INF), negative infinity (-INF), and not-a-number (NaN). Predefined constants are available in SQL and PL/SQL to represent the special values. The constants are as follows:

- BINARY_FLOAT_NAN
- BINARY_FLOAT_INFINITY
- DOUBLE_FLOAT_NAN
- DOUBLE_FLOAT_INFINITY

The following new functions were introduced in Oracle 10g to support the new data types:

TO_BINARY_FLOAT   Converts a BINARY_DOUBLE, NUMBER, VARCHAR2, or CHAR value to BINARY_FLOAT value

TO_BINARY_DOUBLE   Converts a BINARY_FLOAT, NUMBER, VARCHAR2, or CHAR value to BINARY_DOUBLE value

IS [NOT] NAN   Determines whether a floating-point value is NaN

IS [NOT] INFINITE   Determines whether a floating-point value is infinite

NANVL   Translates NaN to a specified value

NaN is considered as the largest value, and -INF is considered the smallest value in the floating-point arithmetic.

Case- and Accent-Insensitive Queries

Oracle 10g supports case-insensitive and accent-insensitive queries and sorts. This is supported through the NLS_SORT parameter, affixing _AI for accent-insensitive sorts and _CI for case-insensitive sorts. You can change the value of NLS_SORT at the session level. If the NLS_SORT value is BINARY, the collating sequence for the sort is based on the numeric value of characters and thus requires less system overhead.

You can also change the NLS_SORT value using the NLSSORT function in the ORDER BY clause of the query, instead of changing it at the session level.

The following are some examples of sorting behavior:

```
SQL> SELECT name FROM emp1
  2  ORDER BY name;


NAME
--------------------
SteVen
Stephen
Steven


SQL> SELECT name FROM emp1
  2  ORDER BY NLSSORT(name, 'NLS_SORT=BINARY_CI');


NAME
--------------------
Stephen
Steven
SteVen


SQL> ALTER SESSION SET NLS_SORT=FRENCH_M_CI
```

```
SQL> /

Session altered.

SQL> SELECT name FROM empl
  2  ORDER BY name
SQL> /

NAME
--------------------
Stephen
Steven
SteVen

SQL>
```

 WARNING   Setting the NLS_SORT to anything other than BINARY causes a sort to use a full table scan, regardless of the path chosen by the optimizer.

The following SQL clauses support the NLS_SORT setting:

- WHERE
- ORDER BY
- START WITH
- HAVING
- IN and NOT IN
- BETWEEN
- CASE...WHEN

Quote Operator

In the pre-Oracle 10g releases, to have a single quotation mark in the string, you had to specify two quotation marks. In Oracle 10g, you can specify your own delimiter using the quote operator q, thus eliminating the confusion in strings with quotation marks. The delimiter chosen by you can be the CHAR or NCHAR literal or any of the [], {}, (), or <> pairs.

The following example shows the pre–Oracle 10g method and then contrasts that with a query using the new quote operator:

```
SQL> SELECT 'Don''t look at John''s bike' EX
  2  FROM dual;
```

```
EX
-----------------------
Don't look at John's bike

SQL> SELECT q'!Don't look at John's bike!' EX
  2  FROM dual;

EX
-----------------------
Don't look at John's bike

SQL> SELECT q'!Look at John's bike! Wow!' EX
  2* FROM dual
SQL> /

EX
-----------------------
Look at John's bike! Wow

SQL>
```

The ! is used as a delimiter and is qualified with the quote operator q. Notice that the string is enclosed in '! and !'. You could have a ! inside the string as in the third example, which is considered part of the string

Introducing Miscellaneous Database Enhancements

In the following sections we will cover the database enhancements introduced in Oracle 10g that were not covered in earlier chapters. There are many major and minor enhancements to the Oracle 10g database. All the major enhancements have been discussed in the earlier chapters. Here we discuss the enhancements that are relevant to the OCP exam. In Oracle10g, you can flush the data buffer cache, enable resumable space allocation at the database level, consider list partitioning for partition change tracking, connect to the database without any configuration files, and there are more enhancements worth knowing. We discuss these enhancements in these sections.

MAXTRANS Ignored

Prior to Oracle 10g, MAXTRANS specified the maximum number of concurrent update transactions for a data block belonging to the table, index, or cluster segment. In Oracle 10g, this parameter

is ignored when specified with the physical storage attributes. In Oracle 10*g*, objects are pre-configured for maximum concurrency, which means that the database allows up to 255 concurrent update transactions for any data block, depending on the available space in the block.

Flushing the Buffer Cache

In the previous releases of Oracle, you were able to flush the shared pool using the ALTER SYSTEM FLUSH SHARED_POOL statement. In Oracle 10*g*, you can also flush the buffer cache portion of the SGA using the ALTER SYSTEM FLUSH BUFFER_CACHE statement.

Flushing the buffer cache is not intended for production databases during normal operation. The intent of flushing the database buffer cache is to provide for an identical starting point for comparison of rewritten SQL statements. Once you execute the ALTER SYSTEM FLUSH BUFFER_CACHE statement, you will have 100 percent cache miss for the next SQL statement.

The benefit of this feature is to allow a consistent testing environment. In prior releases, you had to shut down and restart the instance every time to start with a clean buffer cache.

Resumable Space Allocation

Oracle 9*i* introduced resumable space allocation to suspend a session when an out-of-space condition occurred in the database. The resumable space allocation feature must be turned on in the session level using the ALTER SESSION ENABLE RESUMABLE statement. In Oracle 10*g*, a new parameter RESUMABLE_TIMEOUT was introduced, where the resumable space allocation feature can be turned on at the database level.

The RESUMABLE_TIMEOUT parameter specifies the time in seconds for a session to be suspended when an out-of-space condition occurs. The default for this parameter is 0, which means the resumable timeout is not enabled. The parameter is modifiable using ALTER SESSION or ALTER SYSTEM, as in the following example:

```
SQL> ALTER SYSTEM SET
  2  RESUMABLE_TIMEOUT = 3600 SCOPE=BOTH
SQL> /

System altered.

SQL> ALTER SESSION DISABLE RESUMABLE;

Session altered.

SQL>
```

When a session is suspended, an error is reported in the alert log file, and the Resumable Session Suspended alert is triggered. If a trigger is defined for the AFTER SUSPEND event, it is also fired. You can obtain information on the suspended session by querying the DBA_RESUMABLE view.

Materialized View Enhancements

Oracle 10*g* incorporates several enhancements to materialized views. In this section we will discuss the following:

- Partition change tracking (PCT) materialized views for fast refresh
- Refresh using trusted constraints to provide reliable data
- Fast refreshing of the materialized join view without aggregation
- Detecting if the refresh of the materialized view is dependent on the refresh of other materialized views
- Tuning materialized views using the DBMS_ADVISOR.TUNE_MVIEW procedure

Partition Change Tracking Materialized Views

PCT is the ability to identify which rows in a materialized view are affected by DML activity on the partition of detail tables that comprise that materialized view. PCT was introduced in Oracle 9*i*, but it supported only the RANGE and RANGE-HASH partitioning schemes. In Oracle 10*g*, PCT supports the LIST partitioning scheme.

In Oracle 10*g*, at materialized view creation time, LIST-partitioned detail tables are recognized as a qualified PCT partition scheme; hence, relevant PCT information is recorded in the materialized view metadata.

Another enhancement related to PCT is that Oracle 10*g* now supports ROWID as a PCT column. In the previous releases, table partition keys and partition markers (PMARKER) were considered as PCT columns at the materialized view creation time and were used by the PCT refresh to identify a table partition. In Oracle 10*g*, you can use a PCT-based refresh if the materialized view contains a join dependent expression of one of its detail tables. A join dependent expression is an expression consisting of columns from tables directly or indirectly joined through equijoins to the partitioned detail table on the partitioning key.

In Oracle 9*i*, the PCT refresh always executes a DELETE statement to remove rows from the materialized view. In Oracle 10*g*, you make the refresh operation efficient by using the TRUNCATE PARTITION to remove rows from the materialized when it is partitioned like the PCT detail table. You can use the TRUNCATE PARTITION PCT refresh method when these conditions are true:

- The partition method of both the detail table and the materialized view are RANGE, and the partition method is the same in the detail table and the materialized view.
- The materialized view is partitioned on its single PCT key column.
- A one-to-one relationship exists between detail table partitions and materialized view partitions.

The PCT refresh using TRUNCATE PARTITION is nonatomic, meaning the TRUNCATE PARTITION is a DDL statement and cannot be rolled back. So the PCT refresh cannot be done in a single transaction.

The DBMS_MVIEW.REFRESH procedure can accept a new value P for the refresh methods to force a refresh of a materialized view using the PCT refresh method. This is in addition to the values C (complete), F (fast), and ? (force).

Refresh Using Trusted Constraints

Primary key/foreign key relationships created using the RELY option or reliance on dimension hierarchies may result in inconsistent results when refreshing a materialized view, because these constraints are not enforced by the Oracle 10g database. These can cause unreliable query rewrites.

You can now specify whether query rewrites can occur in cases where these unenforced trusted constraints are being used. When creating the materialized view, you can specify either the USING ENFORCED CONSTRAINTS or USING TRUSTED CONSTRAINTS clause. You can also modify these clauses using the ALTER MATERIALIZED VIEW statement.

A TRUSTED materialized view can use unenforced relationships for a refresh. An ENFORCED materialized view can be refreshed using only validated relationships that are known to return correct data. The DBA_MVIEWS data dictionary view contains a new column, UNKNOWN_TRUSTED_FD. If this column is set to Y, it indicates that the materialized view is in an unknown state because trusted functional dependencies were used for the refresh. You can use such materialized views for rewrite in TRUSTED or STALE_TOLERATED modes only.

Materialized Join View Fast Refresh Enhancements

Oracle 9i supported fast refreshes for materialized join views that contained joins with aggregations. Oracle 10g supports fast refresh for materialized join views (MJV) with no aggregation for the following cases:

- If the MJV has multiple instances of a table in the FROM clause, ROWID columns for each instance must be included in the SELECT clause of the materialized view definition.

- The associated materialized view log also contains the ROWID column.

- The Oracle server must be able to do complete view merging for any inline or named views in the FROM clause of the MJV. Also, the merged MJV must meet the requirements for a fast refresh. Materialized view logs must be present on all base tables of any merged view.

- If the MJV has remote tables in the FROM clause, all tables in the FROM clause must be located on that same site.

- The COMPATIBLE parameter must be set to 10.0.1 or higher.

Dependent Materialized View Refreshes

In Oracle 10g, you can create materialized views with the BUILD DEFERRED option if some materialized views depend on the result of another materialized view. Oracle 10g detects the dependencies and refreshes the materialized views in the proper order.

Once the materialized views are created with the BUILD DEFERRED option, they are not populated with data until a DBMS_MVIEW.REFRESH or DBMS_MVIEW.REFRESH_DEPENDENT procedure is executed. When these refresh procedures are executed, Oracle determines the hierarchical relationships between the views and refreshes them based on those relationships.

Tuning Materialized Views

The Oracle *9i* database introduced the DBMS_MVIEW.EXPLAIN_MVIEW procedure to determine if a materialized view is fast refreshable or eligible for a query rewrite. Oracle 10g introduces a new procedure, DBMS_ADVISOR.TUNE_MVIEW, to identify and advise any materialized view log problems and provide an optimized way of defining queries to enable fast refreshes and general query rewrites.

You can query the results of the advisor findings from the DBA_TUNE_MVIEW dictionary view.

The following example demonstrates a tuning task. It shows that to enable fast refresh, you cannot use TRUNC(TIME_ID, 'MON') in the SELECT clause and also shows the syntax required creating the materialized view logs:

```
SQL> DECLARE
  2    taskname varchar2 (20) := 'tunemviewtask';
  3  BEGIN
  4  DBMS_ADVISOR.TUNE_MVIEW (taskname,
  5  'CREATE MATERIALIZED VIEW monthly_prod_sales
  6  REFRESH FAST WITH ROWID ENABLE QUERY REWRITE
  7  AS
  8  SELECT TRUNC(TIME_ID,''MON'') smonth,
           PROD_ID, SUM(AMOUNT_SOLD)
  9  FROM   sales
 10  group by TRUNC(TIME_ID,''MON'') , PROD_ID');
 11  END;
SQL> /

PL/SQL procedure successfully completed.

SQL>
SQL> SELECT statement
  2  FROM   dba_tune_mview
  3  WHERE  task_name = 'tunemviewtask'
  4  ORDER BY script_type, action_id
SQL> /

STATEMENT
----------------------------------------------------------
CREATE MATERIALIZED VIEW LOG ON "SH"."SALES" WITH ROWID
, SEQUENCE ("PROD_ID","TIME_ID","AMOUNT_SOLD")
```

```
INCLUDING NEW VALUES

ALTER MATERIALIZED VIEW LOG FORCE ON "SH"."SALES" ADD
ROWID, SEQUENCE ("PROD_ID","TIME_ID","AMOUNT_SOLD")
INCLUDING NEW VALUES

CREATE MATERIALIZED VIEW SH.MONTHLY_PROD_SALES   REFRES
H FAST WITH ROWID ENABLE QUERY REWRITE AS SELECT SH.SAL
ES.TIME_ID C1, SH.SALES.PROD_ID C2, SUM("SH"."SALES"."A
MOUNT_SOLD") M1, COUNT("SH"."SALES"."AMOUNT_SOLD") M2,
COUNT(*) M3 FROM SH.SALES GROUP BY SH.SALES.TIME_ID, SH
.SALES.PROD_ID

DROP MATERIALIZED VIEW SH.MONTHLY_PROD_SALES

SQL>
```

 You need the ADVISOR privilege to execute the DBMS_ADVISOR.TUNE_MVIEW procedure.

Other MV Enhancements

Oracle 10*g* includes a new hint, REWRITE_OR_ERROR, that you can use in the queries that must be rewritten. If for some reason the query is not rewritten, an error (ORA-30393) is returned. This is useful when you know that if the SQL is not rewritten using the materialized view, it would take a long time to execute. You can use the DBMS_MVIEW.EXPLAIN_REWRITE procedure to identify why the rewrite failed.

In Oracle 9*i*, you performed the partition maintenance operations on the materialized view container tables using the ALTER TABLE statement. In Oracle 10*g*, you can perform the partition maintenance operations on materialized views using the ALTER MATERIALIZED VIEW statement. The ALTER MATERIALIZED VIEW statement supports the following:

- Truncate partition
- Drop partition
- Exchange partition with table

The execution plan using materialized views in Oracle 10*g* shows the keywords MATERIALIZED VIEW instead of TABLE in the PLAN_TABLE and V$SQL_PLAN views. The execution plans also show the difference between the materialized view used directly and the optimizers using the materialized view for the query rewrite. For query rewrite plans, the keywords MATERIALIZED VIEW REWRITE would display in the explain plan.

Database Connectivity Improvements

Oracle 10*g* introduces improvements to database connectivity. Now you can connect to a database without configuration files. The configuration of the shared server is also made simple in this release. Let's discuss these in the following sections.

Connecting without Configuration Files

Using an Oracle 10*g* client, you can connect to a database without a `tnsnames.ora` file or a `sqlnet.ora` file. You can specify the host, port, and Session identifier (SID) name directly in the connect string to connect to the database. This will work only for TCP/IP networks. If the listener is using the standard 1521 port, you do not need to specify the port number. You can connect to the Oracle 8*i* or 9*i* database using an Oracle 10*g* client with this method. The syntax of the new connect method is as follows:

```
CONNECT username/password@[//]host[:port][/service_name]]
```

In the following example, we connect to an Oracle 8*i* database using the hostname and SID syntax (since the listener is using port 1521, the port number is not provided as part of the connect string):

```
$ sqlplus /nolog
SQL*Plus: Release 10.1.0.2.0 - Production on Mon Jul 12
Copyright (c) 1982, 2004, Oracle.  All rights reserved.
SQL> connect dbastats/dbastats@//ftw1hp/FTWP000D
Connected.
SQL> select * from v$version;
BANNER
-----------------------------------------------------------------
Oracle8i Enterprise Edition Release 8.1.7.4.0
         - 64bit Production
PL/SQL Release 8.1.7.4.0 - Production
CORE    8.1.7.0.0       Production
TNS for HPUX: Version 8.1.7.4.0 - Production
NLSRTL Version 3.4.1.0.0 - Production
SQL>
```

The hostname is mandatory. If the host lookup fails, an error is returned. The default for `service_name` is whatever the host is set to be. Advanced features such as load balancing or connect time failover are not available with this method.

Simplified Shared-Server Configuration

In prior versions of Oracle, at least one dispatcher was required to be configured to use Oracle's *shared-server* (multithreaded server) feature. Oracle 10*g* is shared-server aware by default, and

a value greater than zero for **SHARED_SERVERS** parameter will enable the feature. The SHARED_ SERVERS parameter is dynamic and hence can be enabled or disabled using the ALTER SYSTEM statement. The following code demonstrates changing the value of SHARED_SERVERS for the current instance and making the change permanent by changing the `spfile` also (SCOPE=BOTH changes the memory and initialization file).

```
SQL> ALTER SYSTEM SET SHARED_SERVERS=4 SCOPE=BOTH;

System altered.

SQL>
```

In Oracle 10*g*, one TCP protocol dispatcher starts up automatically, making the instance shared-server aware regardless of the parameter settings. In the shared-server architecture, the listener assigns each new client session to one of the available dispatchers. As the user makes a request, the dispatcher sends the request to a shared server. It is possible that different shared servers could handle the requests from one session.

Several Multi-threaded server (MTS) parameters have been deprecated in Oracle 10*g* and replaced by new parameters. Table 8.3 shows these parameters. Notice that the new parameters were introduced in Oracle 9*i*, but the MTS parameters are obsolete in Oracle 10*g*. All the new parameters are dynamic.

TABLE 8.3 Shared-Server Configuration Parameters

Obsolete Parameter	Replaced by Parameter
MTS_SERVERS	SHARED_SERVERS
MTS_MAX_SERVERS	MAX_SHARED_SERVERS
MTS_DISPATCHERS	DISPATCHERS
MTS_MAX_DISPATCHERS	MAX_DISPATCHERS
MTS_CIRCUITS	CIRCUITS
MTS_SESSIONS	SHARED_SERVER_SESSIONS
MTS_SERVICE	SERVICE_NAMES
MTS_LISTENER_ADDRESS	LOCAL_LISTENER
MTS_MULTIPLE_LISTENERS	LOCAL_LISTENER

A new view V$DISPATCHER_CONFIG is available in Oracle 10*g* that gives information on the existing dispatchers. You can join the CONFIG_INDX column of this view with V$DISPATCHER to see detailed information on the dispatcher. Here is an example:

```
SQL> SELECT dispatchers, connections, pool,
  2        listener
  3  FROM   v$dispatcher_config
SQL> /

DISPATCHERS CONNECTIONS POOL LISTENER
----------- ----------- ---- ----------------------------
          1         972 OFF  (ADDRESS=(PROTOCOL=TCP)(HOST=
                             linux)(PORT=1521))


SQL>
```

LogMiner Enhancements

In Oracle 10*g*, if the LogMiner is used against the same database that generated the redo log files, LogMiner can automatically determine the redo log files required for mining based on the start time or start SCN you provide. LogMiner adds the redo log files from the mining database by default. You have no need to explicitly map the time frame to redo log files when the CONTINUOUS_MINE option is used with the STARTTIME or STARTSCN. Here is an example:

```
SQL> BEGIN
  2  DBMS_LOGMNR.START_LOGMNR (options=>
     DBMS_LOGMNR.CONTINUOUS_MINE, starttime =>
     to_date('12-JUL-04 10:00','DD-MON-YY HH24:MI'));
  3  END;
SQL> /

PL/SQL procedure successfully completed.


SQL>
```

Transaction Rollback Monitoring

Oracle 10*g* provides methods to monitor the transaction rollback and the transactions recovered by SMON. In the previous releases, the parallel transaction recovery could be monitored using V$FAST_START_SERVERS and V$FAST_START_TRANSACTIONS views.

In Oracle 10*g*, in addition to viewing normal transaction rollback and transaction recovery by SMON in real time, you can view historical information about transaction recovery and transaction rollback. Using the historical transaction recovery, you can calculate the average rollback duration. When you have the current state of recovery, determining how much has been done and how much more work remains is possible. The V$FAST_START_TRANSACTIONS view contains progress information on the transaction recovery. The STATE column will have the value RECOVERING for transactions that are being recovered; the value will be RECOVERED for the recovered transactions. You can run the following query immediately after the instance startup to see the progress of transaction recovery:

```
SELECT usn, pid, state, undoblocksdone,
       undoblockstotal, cputime
FROM   v$fast_start_transactions;
```

You can join the V$FAST_START_TRANSACTIONS view to the V$FAST_START_ SERVERS view, using the XID column common to both views, to see information on all the servers working on the transaction recovery.

Tracing Enhancements

Tracing in Oracle 10*g* has been enhanced to include end-to-end application tracing and to better trace the information from shared-server connections where you have than one session to trace. *Statistics aggregation* was introduced in Oracle 9*i* Release 2, but it has been enhanced to monitor performance on individual clients and services. We will discuss end-to-end application tracing and statistics aggregation in the following sections.

End-to-End Application Tracing

End-to-End application tracing enables you to diagnose performance problems in multitier environments where a request from a user is sent to the database by the middle tier using many sessions. End-to-end application tracing uses a client identifier to uniquely trace a specific client through all tiers to the database server. Once the tracing information is written to files, the files can be consolidated using the trcsess utility and analyzed using the tkprof utility.

Prior to Oracle 10*g* no easy way existed to keep track of a client process across different database sessions. The CLIENT_IDENTIFIER attribute, which is carried across on all tiers and sessions uniquely, identifies the client session. The client identifier is visible in the new CLIENT_ IDENTIFIER column of the V$SESSION view. You can also use the following query to obtain the client identifier for the current session:

```
SELECT SYS_CONTEXT('USERENV','CLIENT_IDENTIFIER')
FROM   dual;
```

Oracle provides a graphical screen to enable and disable application tracing. We will discuss using the EM for end-to-end application tracing in the next section.

Using EM for End-to-End Application Tracing

The Enterprise Manager (EM) is the primary tool for enabling and disabling end-to-end application tracing. From the Database Central home page, click the Performance link. From the Performance page, click the Top Consumers link. Figure 8.1 shows the Overview tab of the Top Consumers screen.

From the Overview tab, you can navigate to the Top Services, Top Modules, Top Actions, Top Clients, and Top Sessions tabs. In each of these tab you have buttons to enable and disable tracing. Figure 8.2 shows the Top Sessions tab. Notice the Enable SQL Trace and Disable SQL Trace buttons along with other session management buttons.

The tracing will be in effect until the session disconnects or you turn off tracing by using the Disable SQL Trace button. The trace files are written to the directory specified in the USER_DUMP_DEST parameter.

FIGURE 8.1   Top Consumers screen, Overview tab

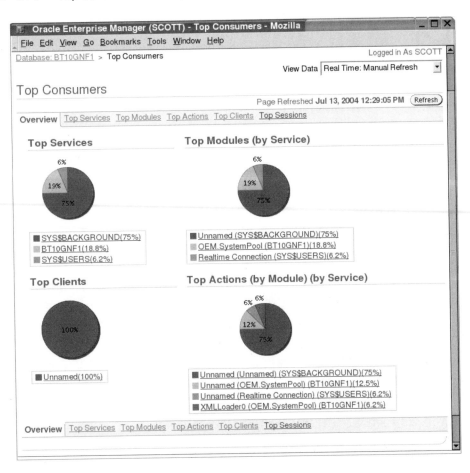

FIGURE 8.2   Top Sessions tab

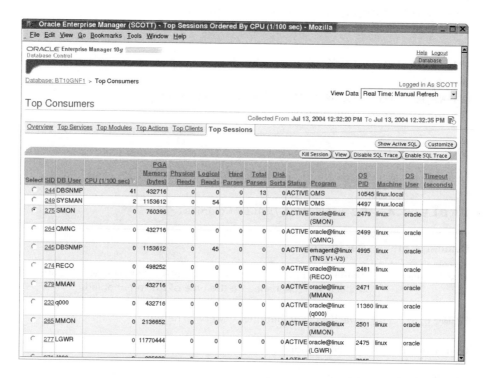

Trace Using *DBMS_MONITOR*

You can use the DBMS_MONITOR package to enable tracing at a global (database) level or at a session level. You can enable the trace using a specified client identifier or a hierarchical combination of the service name, module name, and action name. The DBMS_MONITOR.CLIENT_ID_TRACE_ENABLE parameter enables tracing, and DBMS_MONITOR.CLIENT_ID_TRACE_DISABLE disables a trace that uses the client identifier. You can also monitor WAITS and BINDS using these procedures. In earlier versions of Oracle, the DBMS_SUPPORT.START_TRACE_IN_SESSION procedure gave this ability to trace WAITS and BINDS (event 10046 trace) on a specific session.

The following code shows how to enable tracing and how to query the information on enabled traces from the DBA_ENABLED_TRACES view:

```
SQL> exec dbms_monitor.client_id_trace_enable -
          ('HR', WAITS=>TRUE, BINDS=>TRUE);

PL/SQL procedure successfully completed.
```

```
SQL>
SQL> SELECT trace_type, waits, binds, primary_id
  2  FROM   dba_enabled_traces;

TRACE_TYPE  WAITS BINDS PRIMARY_ID
----------- ----- ----- ------------------------
CLIENT_ID   TRUE  FALSE SCOTT@linux.local@Mozilla
CLIENT_ID   TRUE  TRUE  HR

SQL>
```

Table 8.4 shows the columns in DBA_ENABLED_TRACES.

TABLE 8.4   *DBA_ENABLED_TRACES* Columns

Column Name	Description
TRACE_TYPE	Values are CLIENT_ID, SESSION, SERVICE, SERIVCE_MODULE, and SERVICE_ MODULE_ACTION, based on the type of tracing enabled.
PRIMARY_ID	Specific client identifier or service name.
QUALIFIER_ID1	Specific module name.
QUALIFIER_ID2	Specific action name.
WAITS	TRUE if waits are traced (default is TRUE for the tracing procedures).
BINDS	TRUE if bind variables are traced (default is FALSE for the tracing procedures).
INSTANCE_NAME	Instance name where tracing is enabled (used for RAC).

Different procedures are available in the DBMS_MONITOR package to enable and disable tracing. Table 8.5 shows the tracing procedures in the DBMS_MONITOR package.

TABLE 8.5   *DBMS_MONITOR* Tracing Procedures

Procedure Name	Purpose	Parameters
CLIENT_ID_TRACE_ENABLE	Enable tracing based on client identifier.	Client_id, waits, binds
CLIENT_ID_TRACE_DISABLE	Disable client identifier tracing.	Client_id

TABLE 8.5 *DBMS_MONITOR* Tracing Procedures *(continued)*

Procedure Name	Purpose	Parameters
SESSION_TRACE_ENABLE	Enable tracing based on SID and SERIAL# of V$SESSION.	session_id, serial_num, waits, binds
SESSION_TRACE_DISABLE	Disable session tracing.	session_id, serial_num
SERV_MOD_ACT_TRACE_ENABLE	Enable tracing for a given combination of service name, module, and action.	service_name, module_name, action_name, waits, binds, instance_name
SERV_MOD_ACT_TRACE_DISABLE	Disable service, module, and action tracing.	service_name, module_name, action_name, instance_name

Using the *trcsess* Utility

In shared-server environments, you could end up with several trace files when tracing is enabled. You can use the new **trcsess** utility to combine all the relevant trace files based on the session or client identifier or the service name, module name, and action name hierarchy combination. You can format the output file from the **trcsess** utility using the **tkprof** utility.

Typing **trcsess** without any argument shows the parameters that can be used to pass into this utility, as follows:

```
$ trcsess
Session Trace Usage error: Wrong parameters passed.
trcsess [output=<output file name >]
   [session=<session ID>]
   [clientid=<clientid>]
   [service=<service name>]
   [action=<action name>]    [module=<module name>] <trace file names>
output=<output file name> output destination
      default being standard output.
session=<session Id> session to be traced.
   Session id is a combination of session Index &
   session serial number e.g. 8.13.
clientid=<clientid> clientid to be traced.
service=<service name> service to be traced.
action=<action name> action to be traced.
module=<module name> module to be traced.
<trace_file_names> Space separated list of trace
   files with wild card '*' supported.
```

The following example shows how to combine the trace files generated by the module name SQL*Plus and analyze them using tkprof:

```
$ trcsess output=b.trc module='SQL*Plus' *.trc
$ tkprof b.trc b.out sys=no
```

Statistics Aggregation

Statistics aggregation is useful in identifying performance issues. By default statistics are gathered at the SQL level, session level, and instance level. New procedures in the Oracle 10g DBMS_ MONITOR package enable statistics aggregation at the client identifier or at the service name or service, module, and action name hierarchical combination levels.

These additional dimensions make statistics accumulation for multitier architectures using connection pooling or shared-server configuration more meaningful. You can enable and disable statistics aggregation using the Enterprise Manager or using the DBMS_MONITOR package.

Using the EM for Statistics Aggregation

You'll see buttons to enable statistics aggregation on the tabs on the Top Consumers screen. We reviewed this screen previously (please refer to Figure 8.1). The Enable Aggregation and Disable Aggregation buttons are available in the Top Modules, Top Actions, and Top Clients tabs. Figure 8.3 shows the Top Actions tab.

FIGURE 8.3   Top Actions tab

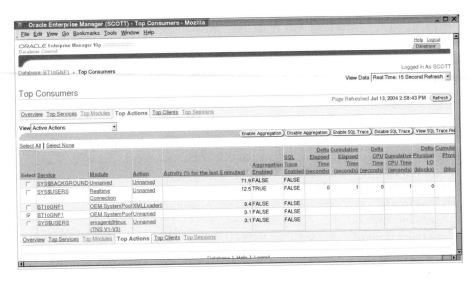

Using *DMBS_MONITOR* for Statistics Aggregation

Similar to various procedures available for tracing the sessions, procedures are available in DBMS_MONITOR to gather aggregate statistics. Statistics gathering is global for the database and persistent across instance starts and restarts. Table 8.6 lists the procedures available for statistics aggregation.

TABLE 8.6   Procedures for Statistics Aggregation

Procedure Name	Description	Parameters
CLIENT_ID_STAT_ENABLE	Enables statistics gathering for a given client identifier	client_id
CLIENT_ID_STAT_DISABLE	Disables statistics gathering for client identifier	client_id
SERV_MOD_ACT_STAT_ENABLE	Enables statistics gathering for a given combination of service name, module, and action name	service_name,module_name,action_name
SERV_MOD_ACT_STAT_DISABLE	Disables statistics gathering for service name, module, and action hierarchical combination	service_name, module_name, action_name

You can view the statistics aggregations gathered from the data dictionary using the views listed in Table 8.7.

TABLE 8.7   Querying Statistics Aggregation Values

View Name	Description
DBA_ENABLED_AGGREGATIONS	Shows global statistics for the currently enabled statistics
V$CLIENT_STATS	Shows statistics for a client identifier
V$SERVICE_STATS	Shows statistics for a specified service
V$SERV_MOD_ACT_STATS	Shows statistics for a combination of specified service, module, and action
V$SVCMETRIC	Shows statistics for elapsed time of database calls and for CPU

The following is a query from the DBA_ENABLED_AGGREGATIONS view: There are two aggregations enabled in the database. The first is using the client identifier and the second is using the service, module, action. PRIMARY_ID is the qualifier - either the client id or service name.

```
SQL> SELECT aggregation_type, primary_id
  2  FROM   dba_enabled_aggregations;


AGGREGATION_TYPE        PRIMARY_ID
--------------------    ------------------------
CLIENT_ID               SCOTT@linux.local@Mozilla
                        /5.0 (X11; U; Linux i686;
                        en-US; rv:1.


SERVICE_MODULE_ACTION SYS$USERS

SQL>
```

Summary

We covered several new features and enhancements of Oracle 10g in this chapter. Virtual Private Database (VPD) is enhanced to include column-level VPD in order to enforce row-level access control based on the access on certain columns. The statements are rewritten by VPD only when they access relevant secure columns. You use the new parameter SEC_RELEVANT_COLS in DBMS_RLS.ADD_POLICY to enforce column-level VPD.

Another enhancement to VPD is the introduction of different policy types. In Oracle 9i only the dynamic policy type was available; Oracle 10g introduces these additional types: static, shared static, context-sensitive, and shared context-sensitive. When a static policy is applied, VPD always enforces the same predicate regardless of user. The database executes the policy function only once for static policies. A context-sensitive policy is evaluated at statement execution time for context changes and executes the policy function if a context change is detected.

Auditing in Oracle 10g has been enhanced to have uniform audit trails for database auditing and fine-grained auditing. The DBA_COMMON_AUDIT_TRAIL view combines the standard and fine-grained audit log records. Also, Oracle 10g supports fine-grained auditing for DML statements such as INSERT, UPDATE, DELETE, and MERGE.

The MERGE statement has several improvements. In Oracle 10g, MERGE allows conditional updates and inserts by using a WHERE clause in the UPDATE and INSERT clauses. The UPDATE clause is enhanced to include an optional DELETE clause to delete rows that meet certain criteria.

Partitioned outer join is a feature in Oracle 10g that overcomes the problem of sparse data when performing certain SQL analytical functions. Partitioned outer joins extend the conventional

outer join syntax by applying the outer join to each logical partition defined in the query. The result of a partitioned outer join is a union of the outer joins of each of the groups in the logically partitioned table with the table on the other side of the join.

The MODEL clause is another significant enhancement in Oracle 10*g* for spreadsheet-like array computations. The MODEL clause allows symbolic cell addressing, and it does not update existing data in the tables. In Oracle 10*g*, you can perform regular expression searches using the REGEXP_LIKE function. Oracle's implementation of regular expression complies with the POSIX standard for pattern matching and Unicode regular expression guidelines. The other functions available for regular expression manipulation are REGEXP_SUBSTR, REGEXP_INSTR, and REGEXP_REPLACE.

Oracle 10*g* supports terabyte-sized LOB data types. BINARY_FLOAT and BINARY_DOUBLE are two new data types introduced in Oracle 10*g* for floating-point arithmetic. Case- and accent-insensitive queries are possible by setting the NLS_SORT parameter with the _CI or _AI suffix. You can use the quote operator q to define your own delimiter in SQL strings.

When creating tables, indexes, and clusters, the physical storage attribute MAXTRANS defaults to the maximum value of 255 based on the space available in the block. Oracle 10*g* does not error out if you specify this clause; it just ignores it. You can enable the resumable timeout for sessions at the database level by setting the RESUMABLE_TIMEOUT parameter to a nonzero value.

Oracle 10*g* made several enhancements to materialized views. The materialized join views now support fast refreshes for self-joins, views that can be flattened, and data access from tables in remote databases. The partition change tracking also supports the LIST partitioning scheme. In Oracle 10*g*, you can make the refresh operation efficient by using TRUNCATE PARTITION to remove rows from the materialized when the materialized view is partitioned like the PCT detail table.

In Oracle 10*g*, you can specify whether query rewrites can occur in cases where unenforced trusted constraints are being used. A TRUSTED materialized view can use unenforced relationships for refreshes. An ENFORCED materialized view can be refreshed only using validated relationships that are know to return correct data. You can tune materialized views using the DBMS_ADVISOR.TUNE_MVIEW procedure.

The new syntax *username/password@//hostname:port/service_name* is available in Oracle 10*g* to connect to databases without network configuration files such as tnsnames.ora and sqlnet.ora. The Oracle 10*g* database by default is shared-server aware, and setting SHARED_SERVERS parameter to a nonzero value enables shared-server connectivity to the database.

You have no need to specify each redo log filename when using LogMiner in the same database to which the redo log files belong. You can use the CONTINUOUS_MINE option with the STARTSCN or STARTTIME parameter to mine redo logs.

The V$FAST_START_TRANSACTIONS view contains progress information on the transaction recovery. You can find the numbers of undo blocks recovered and remaining to recover from this dynamic view.

With the introduction of CLIENT_IDENTIFIER, end-to-end application tracing is possible. The DBMS_MONITOR package has procedures to enable detailed level traces and to collect statistics aggregation. You can use the EM to enable and disable tracing and aggregation.

Exam Essentials

Know the enhancements in the Virtual Private Database.   Learn how to use column-level VPD to enforce row-level access control based on accessed security columns. Know how to create static, context-sensitive, and shared policies and when they should be used.

Understand the new features introduced in auditing.   Describe the types of auditing options available in the database. Enumerate the benefits of uniform audit trail for standard auditing and fine-grained auditing. Fine-grained auditing supports DML statement auditing and supports auditing on more than the relevant column.

Identify the SQL enhancements for business intelligence applications.   The MERGE command allows conditional updates and inserts, and an optional DELETE clause was introduced. Know how to convert dense data to a sparse form using the partitioned outer join syntax. Learn the options available with the new MODEL clause for spreadsheet-like array computations.

Describe the enhancements to materialized views.   Understand the situations when a materialized join view is fast refreshable. Know the query rewrite enhancements. Tune materialized views using the DBMS_ADVISOR.TUNE_MVIEW procedure. Identify when partition change tracking will be supported for fast refreshes.

Understand the initialization parameter improvements.   Know the parameter used to set a resumable timeout at the database level. Identify the new shared-server parameters.

Know the functions that are available for regular expressions support.   Be able to identify the REGEXP_ functions and their purposes.

Understand the usage of quote operator and case-insensitive sorts.   Know how to enable accent-insensitive and case-insensitive sorts. Be able to use the quote operator. Be able to monitor the transaction rollback progress.

Learn how to enable statistics and tracing at a global level.   Know the pages of the EM to gather tracing and statistics aggregation. Identify the procedures in DBMS_MONITOR to enable tracing and statistics aggregation. Understand the dimensions of statistic aggregation.

Review Questions

1. Column-level privacy enforces row-level access control only when a statement accesses security relevant columns. Which procedure is used to set up column-level VPD in Oracle 10*g*?

   A. DBMS_VPD.ADD_POLICY

   B. DBMS_RLS.ADD_POLICY

   C. DBMS_POLICY.ADD_RLS

   D. DBMS_POLICY.ADD_VPD

2. In fine-grained auditing, which one of the following is not a valid statement type?

   A. DELETE

   B. INSERT

   C. UPDATE

   D. MERGE

   E. INDEX

   F. SELECT

3. Which policy type in fine-grained auditing reevaluates the policy function at statement execution for context changes since the last use of the cursor and looks for a cached predicate generated by the same policy function of the same policy type in the same session?

   A. STATIC

   B. DYNAMIC

   C. CONTEXT_SENSITIVE

   D. SHARED_STATIC

   E. SHARED_CONTEXT_SENSITIVE

4. Which table or view contains audit trail from standard database auditing and fine-grained auditing?

   A. AUD$

   B. FGA_LOG$

   C. DBA_AUDIT_TRAIL

   D. DBA_COMMON_AUDIT_TRAIL

5. In the MERGE statement, you can optionally use the DELETE clause when which of the following is true?

   A. In the WHEN MATCHED section

   B. In the WHEN NOT MATCHED section

   C. In both the WHEN MATCHED and WHEN NOT MATCHED sections

   D. By itself, without an INSERT or UPDATE clause

6. Which clause in Oracle 10*g* makes the sparse data dense?

   A. MODEL

   B. PARTITION BY

   C. PARTITION BY...OUTER JOIN

   D. PARTITIONED OUTER JOIN

7. The MODEL clause enables spreadsheet-like array computations using SQL. Choose the three groups that define the multidimensional array.

   A. Facts

   B. Measures

   C. Partitions

   D. Blocks

   E. Dimensions

8. Which procedure can obtain the materialized views definition that is eligible for a fast refresh?

   A. DBMS_MVIEW.EXPLAIN_MVIEW

   B. DBMS_MVIEW.EXPLAIN_REWRITE

   C. DBMS_MVIEW.TUNE_MVIEW

   D. DBMS_ADVISOR.TUNE_MVIEW

   E. DBMS_ADVISOR.EXPLAIN_MVIEW

9. Which physical attribute is ignored by the Oracle database when creating a table?

   A. INITRANS

   B. MAXTRANS

   C. PCTFREE

   D. PCTUSED

   E. STORAGE

10. Which four methods enable resumable space allocation?

   A. ALTER SYSTEM ENABLE RESUMABLE

   B. ALTER SESSION ENABLE RESUMABLE

   C. ALTER SYSTEM SET RESUMABLE_TIMEOUT = 72000

   D. ALTER SYSTEM SET RESUMABLE_TIMEOUT = 72000 SCOPE=BOTH

   E. ALTER SESSION SET RESUMABLE_TIMEOUT = 72000

11. Which is the new syntax available to connect to a database using the Oracle 10*g* client?

   A. *username/password@hostname*:*port*:*service_name*

   B. *username/password@//hostname*:*port*:*service_name*

   C. *username/password@//hostname/port/service_name*

   D. *username/password@//hostname*:*port/service_name*

12. What is the maximum supported size for a LOB column?

   A. 128GB

   B. 4GB

   C. 128TB

   D. Unlimited

13. Which function is best suitable to find if the phone numbers in a table follow the *nnn-nnn-nnnn* format, where *n* is a digit?

   A. SUBSTR

   B. REGEXP_SUBSTR

   C. LIKE

   D. REGEXP_LIKE

14. Which parameter would you set to enable case-insensitive sorts?

   A. NLS_SORT

   B. NLS_LANGUAGE

   C. NLS_SORT_CI

   D. NLS_COMP

15. Which option in the DBMS_LOGMNR.START_LOGMNR procedure automatically adds redo log files for mining if the redo log files belong to the same database where mining is done?

   A. DBMS_LOGMNR.AUTO_ADD_REDO

   B. DBMS_LOGMNR.CONTINUOUS_MINE

   C. DBMS_LOGMNR.STARTTIME

   D. DBMS_LOGMNR.STARTSCN

16. Which data dictionary view contains information on the progress of the rollback transactions the Oracle server (SMON) is recovering?

   A. V$FAST_START_SERVERS

   B. V$FAST_START_TRANSACTIONS

   C. V$FAST_START_ROLLBACK

   D. V$WAITSTAT

17. Oracle 10g is shared-server aware by default. Which parameter replaces the MTS_SESSIONS parameter in Oracle 10g?

   A. The SESSIONS parameter.

   B. The SHARED_SESSIONS parameter.

   C. The SHARED_SERVER_SESSIONS parameter.

   D. Oracle 10g has no equivalent parameter, because the database is shared-server aware by default.

18. Which data dictionary view contains information on the traces enabled in the database?

   A. V$SESSION

   B. V$TRACE

   C. V$SESSION_TRACE

   D. DBA_ENABLED_TRACES

19. Choose three dimensions where statistics aggregation can be enabled using the DBMS_MONITOR package.

   A. Session

   B. Client Identifier

   C. Service name

   D. Service name, module name, action name

   E. Instance name

20. Which one of the following is a valid use of the quote operator to assign John's book to a variable in PL/SQL?

A. VS := quoteJohn's Bookendquote

B. VS := bq'John's Book'eq

C. VS := q'[John's Book]'

D. VS := q'[John's Book]'q

Answers to Review Questions

1. B. The DBMS_RLS (row level security) package is used for fine-grained auditing. The ADD_POLICY procedure has a new parameter, SEC_RELEVANT_COLUMNS, that specifies the column names to be secured.

2. D. MERGE is not a valid statement type in DBMS_RLS.ADD_POLICY. MERGE is enforced by the underlying INSERT and UPDATE statement types. By default the policy applies to SELECT, INSERT, UPDATE, and DELETE. Default does not apply to INDEX.

3. E. For shared policy types, Oracle server looks for cached predicate generated by the same policy function. For STATIC policies, VPD always enforces the same predicate for access control regardless of the user. STATIC policies are executed once, and the predicate result is cached in the SGA. For CONTEXT_SENSITIVE policies, VPD reevaluates the policy function at statement execution time for context changes and executes the policy function if it detects any context changes.

4. D. In Oracle 10g, you have uniform audit trail, which means the same type of information is available for standard and fine-grained audit trails. The standard audit trail information is available in AUD$ and DBA_AUDIT_TRAIL. The fine-grained audit trail information is available in FGA_LOG$ and DBA_FGA_AUDIT_TRAIL. DBA_COMMON_AUDIT_TRAIL has information on both standard and fine-grained auditing.

5. A. Oracle 10g introduced the DELETE clause in the WHEN MATCHED THEN UPDATE section of the MERGE statement. The DELETE clause can optionally delete rows that match the ON condition and the WHERE condition.

6. C. The partitioned outer join clause makes sparse data dense. It is used to replace missing values, mostly along the time dimension. The Oracle database logically partitions the rows in the query based on the expression in the PARTITION BY clause.

7. B, C, E. Partitions, measures, and dimensions are the three groups. Partitions define logical blocks of the result set. Measures typically contain numerical data and are analogous to the measures of a fact table in a star schema. Dimensions identify each measure cell within a partition.

8. D. The DBMS_ADVISOR.TUNE_MVIEW procedure shows how to restate the materialized view in a way that is more advantageous for fast refreshes and query rewrites. It also shows how to fix materialized view logs and to enable query rewrites. Using the DBMS_MVIEW.EXPLAIN_MVIEW procedure, you can determine if a materialized view is fast refreshable and what types of query write you can perform. You can then use the DBMS_MVIEW.EXPLAIN_REWRITE procedure to learn why a query failed to rewrite or which MV will be used to rewrite.

9. B. In Oracle 10g, objects are preconfigured for maximum concurrency, and the system allows for up to 255 concurrent update transactions per block, depending on the available space.

10. B, C, D, E. The RESUMABLE_TIMEOUT parameter can be set at the instance level to enable resumable timeout. The parameter is dynamic and can be modified using ALTER SYSTEM and ALTER SESSION. The ALTER SESSION ENABLE RESUMABLE syntax used in Oracle 9i is still supported in Oracle 10g.

11. D. The new syntax does not rely on configuration files such as tnsnames.ora. The hostname is the only mandatory part after @. The default port is 1521, and the default *service_name* is whatever the host is. The new connect identifier can be used only on platforms that support TCP/IP.

12. C. For the database with 32KB block size, the maximum size for a LOB column is 128TB. For a 2KB block size database, the maximum LOB size is 8TB. You can use the function DBMS_LOB.GET_STORAGE_LIMIT to find the storage limit for the database.

13. D. Oracle 10g supports regular expressions using the functions REGEXP_LIKE, REGEXP_SUBSTR, REGEXP_INSTR, and REGEXP_REPLACE. Regular expressions are best suited for pattern matching.

14. A. The NLS_SORT parameter specifies the linguistic sort name. Adding the suffix _CI to the linguistic sort name enables case-insensitive sorts. For accent-insensitive sorts, add suffix _AI as in, NLS_SORT= JPAPANESE_CI or NLS_SORT=BINARY_AI.

15. B. You use the DBMS_LOGMNR.CONTINUOUS_MINE option with the STARTIME or STARTSCN parameter to add redo log files automatically for mining.

16. B. The V$FAST_START_TRANSACTIONS view has information about the transactions the Oracle server is recovering and recovered.

17. C. The MTS_SESSIONS parameter is replaced by the SHARED_SERVER_SESSIONS parameter in Oracle 10g. The dynamic parameter SHARED_SERVERS can be adjusted to enable and disable the shared-server architecture.

18. D. You can determine the DBA_ENABLED_TRACES view to determine the traces enabled. It also shows the trace type and whether waits and binds are being included in the trace file.

19. B, C, D. Statistics aggregation is provided by default at the session, instance, and SQL levels. Additional statistics aggregation can be enabled by using the DBMS_MONITOR.CLIENT_ID_STAT_ENABLE and DBMS_MONITOR.SERV_MOD_ACT_STAT_ENABLE procedures.

20. C. The quote operator eliminates the need for additional quotation strings in character literals by choosing your own quotation mark delimiter. The quotation mark delimiter is defined using the quote operator q followed by single quote.

Appendix A

SQL*Plus Enhancements

This appendix discusses the enhancements made to SQL*Plus in Oracle Database 10*g* (Oracle 10*g*). For more information on these features, please refer to the Oracle documentation *SQL*Plus User's Guide and Reference* Release 10.1. The Oracle documentation is available at `http://technet.oracle.com`.

The following are the major enhancements to SQL*Plus:

- The DESCRIBE command validates invalid objects.

- The SQL*Plus profile files have changed in behavior.

- White spaces allowed in file names.

- The SPOOL command had changed.

- It includes new predefined variables.

- It includes a new SHOW command option.

- The process of invoking SQL*Plus has changed.

Enhancements to the *DESCRIBE* Command

The DESCRIBE command lists the column definitions for tables, views, types, and synonyms or the specifications for functions, procedures, and packages.

In Oracle 9*i* and previous releases, if you describe an object that is invalid in the database, the DESCRIBE command fails with an error. In Oracle 10*g*, DESCRIBE will try to validate the object first, and if the object is still invalid after validation, it gives the "Invalid object for describe" error. If the validation is successful, the DESCRIBE command will be successful.

Changes to Profile File Calls

The glogin.sql and login.sql files are the profile files used to customize your SQL*Plus environment when you log into the database. The glogin.sql file is the site profile file (located in the $ORACLE_HOME/sqlplus/admin directory), which enables you to set up the SQL*Plus environment defaults for all users of SQL*Plus. The login.sql file is the user profile and is executed after the glogin.sql file. SQL*Plus searches for login.sql in the directories specified by the SQLPATH environment variable.

If Oracle 10g, the glogin.sql and login.sql scripts are executed after each successful CONNECT command. In earlier releases, they were executed only when SQL*Plus was started.

Supporting Whitespace in Filenames

Oracle 10g supports whitespace in filenames and paths. The START, @, @@, RUN, SPOOL, SAVE, and EDIT commands recognize the whitespace in the file/pathnames. To reference files or paths containing whitespace, enclose the name in double quotes as in the following example (shows both UNIX and Windows path references):

```
SQL> SPOOL "/Oracle Reports/monthly report.txt"
SQL> SAVE "C:\My Documents\montly report.txt"
```

Changes to the *SPOOL* Command

The SPOOL command stores query results in a file. In Oracle 10g, the SPOOL command includes the APPEND extension to add the contents of the buffer to the end of a file. The following are examples of using the SPOOL command:

```
SQL>  SPOOL example.txt
SQL>  SELECT * FROM employees;
SQL>  SPOOL OFF
SQL>  SPOOL example.txt APPEND
SQL>  SELECT * FROM departments;
SQL>  SPOOL OFF
```

Similar to APPEND, you can use CREATE or REPLACE to create or replace the file. The default behavior is REPLACE.

Introducing New Predefined Variables

Oracle 10g SQL*Plus includes three new predefined variables. They are _DATE, _PRIVILEGE, and _USER. Table A.1 lists all the predefined variables of SQL*Plus.

TABLE A.1 SQL*Plus Predefined Variables

Variable Name	Description
_CLIENT_IDENTIFIER	Connection identifier used to connect to the database
_DATE	Current date
_EDITOR	Default editor name used by the EDIT command
_O_VERSION	Current version of the Oracle database
_O_RELEASE	Full release number of the Oracle database
_PRIVILEGE	Privilege level of the current connection
_SQLPLUS_RELEASE	Full release number of the SQL*Plus tool
_USER	Username used to connect to the database

The following are some examples of using the predefined variables in the SET SQLPROMPT command and using the DEFINE command to list the current value:

```
SQL> set SQLPROMPT "_DATE SQL>"
18-JUL-04 SQL>
18-JUL-04 SQL>set SQLPROMPT "_DATE _USER SQL> "
18-JUL-04 SCOTT SQL>
18-JUL-04 SCOTT SQL> connect HR/HR
Connected.
18-JUL-04 HR SQL>
18-JUL-04 HR SQL> DEFINE _USER
DEFINE _USER            = "HR" (CHAR)
18-JUL-04 HR SQL> DEFINE _DATE
DEFINE _DATE            = "18-JUL-04" (CHAR)
18-JUL-04 HR SQL> DEFINE _PRIVILEGE
DEFINE _PRIVILEGE       = "" (CHAR)
18-JUL-04 HR SQL>
```

Changes to the *SHOW* Command

The SHOW command displays the value of a SQL*Plus environment variable. In Oracle 10*g* you can use the SHOW RECYCLEBIN command to display the objects in the Recycle Bin that can be reverted with the FLASHBACK BEFORE DROP command. Here is an example of using the SHOW RECYCLEBIN command:

```
SQL> DROP TABLE EMPL;

Table dropped.

SQL> SHOW RECYCLEBIN
ORIGINAL NAME     RECYCLEBIN NAME
OBJECT TYPE   DROP TIME
--------------- ------------------------------
EMPL              BIN$34f+0SUClbTgMAB/AgBZ6w==$0
TABLE         2004-07-18:20:21:58
SQL>
```

You can follow the SHOW RECYCLEBIN command with the original name of the table to see details of a specific table, as in the following example:

```
SQL> SHOW RECYCLEBIN empl
```

 The default for the PAGESIZE system variable has changed to 14 from 24 in Oracle 10*g*.

Invoking SQL*Plus

In earlier releases, you had to enclose / as SYSDBA or *user* AS SYSDBA in quotes when the connect information was provided with sqlplus. In Oracle 10*g*, you do not need to enclose the connect information in quotes. For example:

```
linux:oracle>sqlplus scott as sysdba

SQL*Plus: Release 10.1.0.2.0 - Production on Sun Jul 18 20:27:19 2004

Copyright (c) 1982, 2004, Oracle.  All rights reserved.
```

```
Enter password:

Connected to:
Oracle Database 10g Enterprise Edition Release 10.1.0.2.0 - Production
With the Partitioning, OLAP and Data Mining options

SQL>
```

You can set the SQL*Plus compatibility when calling SQL*Plus using the -c option. This allows you to set the SQLPLUSCOMPATIBILITY variable before executing the glogin.sql or login.sql profile file. Here is an example:

```
linux:oracle>sqlplus -c 9.2 / as sysdba

SQL*Plus: Release 10.1.0.2.0 - Production on Sun Jul 18 20:32:04 2004

Copyright (c) 1982, 2004, Oracle.  All rights reserved.

Connected to:
Oracle Database 10g Enterprise Edition Release 10.1.0.2.0 - Production
With the Partitioning, OLAP and Data Mining options

SQL> SHOW SQLPLUSCOMPATIBILITY
sqlpluscompatibility 9.2.0
SQL> SET SQLPLUSCOMPATIBILITY 10.1
SQL> SHOW SQLPLUSCOMPATIBILITY
sqlpluscompatibility 10.1.0
SQL>
```

Appendix B

New and Obsolete Initialization Parameters

This appendix gives the new initialization parameters introduced in Oracle 10*g* and the obsolete parameters. For more information on the new parameters, please refer to the *Oracle Database Reference 10g* Release 1 documentation.

New Parameters

The following are the new initialization parameters in Oracle 10g:

asm_diskgroups   Specifies a list of names of disk groups to be mounted by an Automatic Storage Management instance at instance startup or when an `ALTER DISKGROUP ALL MOUNT` statement is issued.

asm_diskstring   Specifies an operating system–dependent value used by ASM to limit the set of disks considered for discovery.

asm_power_limit   Specifies the maximum power of an ASM instance for disk rebalancing.

create_stored_outlines   Determines whether Oracle automatically creates and stores an outline for each query submitted during the session.

db_flashback_retention_target   Specifies the upper limit in minutes on how far back in time the database may be flashed back.

db_recovery_file_dest   Specifies the default location for the flash recovery area.

db_recovery_file_dest_size   Specifies in bytes the hard limit on the total space used by target database recovery files created in the flash recovery area.

db_unique_name   Specifies a globally unique name for the database.

ddl_wait_for_locks   Specifies whether DDL statements wait and complete instead of timing out if the statement is not able to acquire all the required locks.

fileio_network_adapters   Specifies a list of network adapters that can be used to access the disk storage.

gcs_server_processes   Specifies the initial number of server processes in the Global Cache Service to serve the interinstance traffic among RAC instances.

instance_type   Specifies whether an instance is a database instance or an ASM instance.

ldap_directory_access   Specifies whether Oracle refers to Oracle Internet Directory for user authentication information.

log_archive_config   Enables or disables the sending of redo logs to remote destinations and the receipt of remote redo logs.

log_archive_local_first   Specifies when the archiver processes (ARCn) transmit redo data to remote standby database destinations.

plsql_code_type   Specifies the compilation mode (INTERPRETED or NATIVE) for PL/SQL library units.

plsql_debug   Specifies whether PL/SQL library units will be compiled for debugging.

plsql_optimize_level   Specifies the optimization level that will be used to compile PL/SQL library units. The higher the setting of this parameter, the more effort the compiler makes to optimize PL/SQL library units.

plsql_warnings   Enables or disables the reporting of warning messages by the PL/SQL compiler and specifies which warning messages to show as errors.

resumable_timeout   Enables or disables resumable statements and specifies resumable timeouts at the system level.

sga_target   Specifies the total size for all SGA components. This parameter enables Automatic Shared Memory Management.

skip_unusable_indexes   Enables or disables the use and reporting of tables with unusable indexes or index partitions.

smtp_out_server   Specifies the SMTP host and port to which UTL_MAIL delivers outbound e-mail.

sqltune_category   Specifies the category name for use by sessions to qualify the lookup of SQL profiles during SQL compilation.

streams_pool_size   Specifies in bytes the size of stream pool, from which memory is allocated for streams.

Obsolete Parameters

The following initialization parameters are available in Oracle 9*i* Release 2 but are obsolete in Oracle 10*g*:

dblink_encrypt_login   Specifies whether attempts to connect to other Oracle databases through database links should use encrypted passwords.

hash_join_enabled   Specifies whether the optimizer should consider using a hash join as a join method.

log_parallelism   Specifies the level of concurrency for redo allocation within Oracle.

max_rollback_segments   Specifies the maximum number of rollback segments that can be kept online. In Oracle 10*g*, always uses the default value.

mts_circuits   In Oracle 10*g*, use CIRCUITS instead. All the MTS related new parameters are discussed in Chapter 8.

mts_dispatchers   In Oracle 10*g*, use DISPATCHERS instead.

mts_listener_address   In Oracle 10*g*, use LOCAL_LISTENER instead.

mts_max_dispatchers   In Oracle 10*g*, use MAX_DISPATCHERS instead.

mts_max_servers   In Oracle 10*g*, use MAX_SHARED_SERVERS instead.

mts_multiple_listeners   In Oracle 10*g*, use LOCAL_LISTENER instead.

mts_servers   In Oracle 10*g*, use SHARED_SERVERS instead.

mts_service   In Oracle 10*g*, use SERVICE_NAMES instead.

mts_sessions   In Oracle 10*g*, use SHARED_SERVER_SESSIONS instead.

optimizer_max_permutations   Restricts the number of permutations the optimizer will consider in queries with joins. In Oracle 10*g*, this parameter is hidden.

oracle_trace_collection_name   Specifies the Oracle Trace collection name for the instance.

oracle_trace_collection_path   Specifies the directory where the trace collection definition (.cdf) and data collection (.dat) files are located.

oracle_trace_collection_size   Specifies in bytes the maximum size of the Oracle Trace collection file (.dat).

oracle_trace_enable   Enables or disables the Oracle Trace collection.

oracle_trace_facility_name   Specifies the event set that Oracle Trace collects.

oracle_trace_facility_path   Specifies the directory where the Oracle Trace facility definition (.cdf) files are located.

partition_view_enabled   Specifies whether the optimizer uses partition views.

plsql_native_c_compiler   Specifies a full directory name of a C compiler that is used to compile the generated C file into an object file.

plsql_native_linker   Specifies the full directory of a linker such as ld in Unix.

plsql_native_make_file_name   Specifies the full directory name of a make file.

plsql_native_make_utility   Specifies the full directory name of a make utility such as make in Unix.

row_locking   Specifies whether row locks are acquired during UPDATE operations.

transaction_auditing   Determines whether to record user information, operating system information, and client information in the redo logs. In Oracle 10g, the behavior is similar to a TRUE value.

undo_suppress_errors   Enables users to suppress errors while executing manual undo management mode operations. In Oracle 10g, the behavior is similar to a TRUE value.

Deprecated Parameters

You can query the deprecated parameters in Oracle 10g from the **V$PARAMETER** view. The following query provides the name and description of deprecated parameters:

```
SQL> SELECT UPPER(name) parameter_name, description
  2  FROM v$parameter
  3  WHERE isdeprecated = 'TRUE'
SQL> /

PARAMETER_NAME
DESCRIPTION
-------------------------------------------------
LOCK_NAME_SPACE
lock name space used for generating lock names for
 standby/clone database

BUFFER_POOL_KEEP
Number of database blocks/latches in keep buffer pool

BUFFER_POOL_RECYCLE
Number of database blocks/latches in recycle buffer pool

LOG_ARCHIVE_START
start archival process on SGA initialization

PARALLEL_SERVER
if TRUE startup in parallel server mode

PARALLEL_SERVER_INSTANCES
number of instances to use for sizing OPS SGA structures
```

FAST_START_IO_TARGET
Upper bound on recovery reads

MAX_ENABLED_ROLES
max number of roles a user can have enabled

GLOBAL_CONTEXT_POOL_SIZE
Global Application Context Pool Size in Bytes

PLSQL_COMPILER_FLAGS
PL/SQL compiler flags

PARALLEL_AUTOMATIC_TUNING
enable intelligent defaults for parallel execution
 parameters

DRS_START
start DG Broker monitor (DMON process)

12 rows selected.

SQL>

Appendix C

PL/SQL Enhancements and New Packages

This appendix provides information on the enhancements to PL/SQL in Oracle 10*g* and the new system packages. In this appendix we will discuss the following:

- Changes to the PL/SQL compiler
- List of enhancements in PL/SQL
- New system packages introduced in Oracle 10*g*

Enhancements to the PL/SQL Compiler

Oracle 10g has a completely redesigned PL/SQL compiler that features code optimization. The new compiler includes all the modern and current industry techniques that provide an immediate improvement in the quality of the code generated, thus improving the execution performance of PL/SQL programs. The new compiler increases the performance of PL/SQL code almost two times faster than the Oracle 8*i* PL/SQL compiler where code is not SQL intensive.

PL/SQL compilation is controlled by the following three parameters, which are dynamic and can be set using ALTER SESSION or ALTER SYSTEM:

PLSQL_DEBUG   Specifies whether PL/SQL library units will be compiled for debugging. The default is FALSE.

PLSQL_OPTIMIZE_LEVEL   Specifies the optimization level that will be used to compile PL/SQL library units. The higher the setting of this parameter, the more effort the compiler makes to optimize PL/SQL library units. The valid values are 1 or 2, and the default is 2.

PLSQL_CODE_TYPE   Specifies if the code is NATIVE or INTERPRETED. INTERPRETED is the default, but NATIVE compilation runs faster.

The parameter PLSQL_COMPILER_FLAGS is deprecated in Oracle 10*g*.

To change a compiled PL/SQL program object from interpreted to native-type code, you need to first set the parameter PLSQL_CODE_TYPE to NATIVE and recompile the program. Oracle provides two scripts that can be used to convert all users' PL/SQL programs to native compilation (dbmsupgnv.sql) or to convert them to interpreted compilation (dbmsupgin.sql).

You can query the PL/SQL compilation settings from DBA_PLSQL_OBJECT_SETTINGS, ALL_PLSQL_OBJECT_SETTINGS, or USER_PLSQL_OBJECT_SETTINGS. The DBA_PLSQL_OBJECT_SETTINGS setting has the following information:

```
SQL> DESCRIBE DBA_PLSQL_OBJECT_SETTINGS
 Name                     Null?     Type
 ------------------       --------  ----------------
 OWNER                    NOT NULL  VARCHAR2(30)
 NAME                     NOT NULL  VARCHAR2(30)
 TYPE                               VARCHAR2(12)
 PLSQL_OPTIMIZE_LEVEL               NUMBER
 PLSQL_CODE_TYPE                    VARCHAR2(4000)
 PLSQL_DEBUG                        VARCHAR2(4000)
 PLSQL_WARNINGS                     VARCHAR2(4000)
 NLS_LENGTH_SEMANTICS               VARCHAR2(4000)

SQL>
```

Enhancements to PL/SQL

The following is a summary of enhancements made to PL/SQL in Oracle 10*g*. For more information on these features, please refer to the Oracle documentation, *PL/SQL User's Guide and Reference 10g* Release 1.

- The bulk bind operations have been enhanced to improve performance. It is also possible to use sparse collection and index arrays in bulk operations. Two new bulk bind operations for sparse array syntax were introduced (INDICES OF and VALUES OF).

- Compiler warnings were introduced to improve productivity and to avoid common coding pitfalls. You can enable and disable this feature using the PLSQL_WARNINGS parameter (the default is DISABLE:ALL). You can see the warnings after compilation using the SHOW ERROR command or querying from the DBA_ERRORS or USER_ERRORS view. You can use the new package DBMS_WARNINGS to change the PLSQL_WARNINGS parameter in a more granular basis.

- When the synonym name is changed from one table to another, Oracle 10*g* does not invalidate the dependent objects when certain conditions on columns, privileges, partitions, and so on, are met. This minimizes the downtime during code upgrades or schema changes.

- Oracle 10*g* provide web services for PL/SQL and Java stored procedure calls, SQL queries, and SQL DML.

- PL/SQL supports the new SQL enhancements. Some of the enhancements are the new datatypes BINARY_FLOAT and BINARY_DOUBLE, the new quote operator q, regular expressions, the implicit conversion of CLOB and NCLOB, flashback query functions, and so on.

New Packages in PL/SQL

The following are the new system packages introduced in Oracle 10g:

DBMS_ADVANCED_REWRITE   Contains interfaces for advanced query rewrites to create, drop, and maintain functional equivalence declarations.

DBMS_ADVISOR   Contains programs for the Server Manageability suite of advisors.

DBMS_CRYPTO   Provides an interface to encrypt and decrypt stored data.

DBMS_DATAPUMP   Contains programs for data and metadata movement.

DBMS_DIMENSION   Contains programs for verifying dimension relationships and displaying dimension definitions.

DBMS_FILE_TRANSFER   Provides procedures to copy a binary file within a database or to transfer a binary file between databases.

DBMS_FREQUENT_ITEMSET   Enables frequent item set counting.

DBMS_LDAP   Provides access to data from LDAP servers.

DBMS_LDAP_UTIL   Contains Oracle LDAP utility functions.

DBMS_MONITOR   Contains programs for controlling additional tracing and statistics gathering.

DBMS_SCHEDULER   Provides a collection of scheduling functions and procedures.

DBMS_SERVER_ALERT   Contains programs to set and get the threshold values for server-generated alerts.

DBMS_SERVICE   Contains programs to create, delete, activate, and deactivate services for a single instance.

DBMS_SQLTUNE   Provides interface to tune SQL statements.

DBMS_STAT_FUNCS   Provides statistical functions.

DBMS_STREAMS_AUTH   Provides interfaces for granting and revoking privileges to/from stream administrators.

DBMS_STREAMS_MESSAGING   Provides interfaces to enqueue messages into, and dequeue messages from, a SYS.AnyData queue.

DBMS_STREAMS_TABLESPACE_ADM   Contains administrative interfaces for copying tablespaces between databases and moving tablespace from one database to another. This package uses transportable tablespaces, Data Pump, and DBMS_FILE_TRANSFER.

DBMS_WARNING   Provides a way to manipulate the behavior of PL/SQL warning messages to control what kinds of warnings are suppressed, displayed, or treated as errors.

DBMS_WORKLOAD_REPOSITORY   Contains programs to manage the Workload Repository.

DBMS_XMLSTORE   Provides the ability to store XML data in relational tables.

UTL_COMPRES   Contains a set of data compression utilities for RAW, BLOB, or BFILE datatypes. The LZ_COMPRESS and LZ_UNCOMPRESS functions use the Lempel-Ziv compression algorithm.

UTL_DBWS   Provides database web services.

UTL_I18N   Provides a set of services that help developers build multilingual applications.

UTL_LMS   Retrieves and formats error messages in different languages.

UTL_MAIL   Provides utilities for managing e-mail. This is a noteworthy utility in Oracle 10*g*, which performs a send e-mail operation in one PL/SQL call. It requires the SMTP_OUT_SERVER initialization parameter defined with the correct SMTP host and port to deliver outbound e-mail. This package is not installed by default; you need to run the utlmail.sql and utlmail.plb scripts from the $ORACLE_HOME/rdbms/admin directory to create the UTL_MAIL ackage.

Glossary

A

access path analysis The component of the Automatic Tuning Optimizer that identifies whether a new index will significantly improve the execution plan for one or more tables in a query.

ATO *See* Automatic Tuning Optimizer.

Automatic Database Diagnostic Monitor (ADDM) Automatic Database Diagnostic Monitor (ADDM) lets the Oracle Database diagnose its own performance and determine how identified problems could be resolved. ADDM runs automatically after each AWR statistics capture, making the performance diagnostic data readily available.

Active Session History (ASH) Active session history provides sampled session activity in the instance. Active sessions are sampled every second and are stored in a circular buffer in SGA. Using the Active Session History enables you to examine and perform detailed analysis on both current data in the V$ACTIVE_SESSION_HISTORY view and historical data in the DBA_HIST_ACTIVE_SESS_HISTORY view.

Automatic Shared Memory Management (ASMM) Automatic Shared Memory Management simplifies the configuration of the SGA. Each component of the SGA is adjusted based on the requirement to maximize memory utilization. To use Automatic Shared Memory Management, set the SGA_TARGET initialization parameter to a nonzero value and set the STATISTICS_LEVEL initialization parameter to TYPICAL or ALL.

Automatic Storage Management (ASM) A cluster file system that can be used with either stand-alone Oracle instances or with Oracle RAC to provide a vertically integrated subsystem encapsulating a file system, a volume manager, and a fault-tolerant environment specifically designed for Oracle databases. ASM is a new feature introduced in Oracle 10*g* that manages the disk for database use and tunes I/O automatically. ASM spreads data evenly across all the devices in the disk group to optimize performance and utilization.

Automatic Tuning Optimizer (ATO) A component of the Oracle optimizer that is called by the SQL Tuning Advisor to perform several specific types of analyses in tuning mode to optimize the execution plan of a query.

Automatic Workload Repository (AWR) Automatic Workload Repository (AWR) is a built-in repository in every Oracle Database. At regular intervals (default 1 hour) the MMON process makes a snapshot of all vital statistics of the database and workload information and stores them in AWR.

B

BACKUP AS COPY A new RMAN command option to back up the database, tablespaces, or individual datafiles as an image copy. Replaces the COPY command in previous versions of RMAN.

Baselines   Basic performance data collected from the database when the database is operating normally.

bigfile tablespace   A tablespace consisting of only one datafile with a new ROWID format and a larger address space allowing for a maximum size of 128TB. Bigfile tablespaces move the maintenance point up from the datafile to the tablespace.

binary compression   Compression algorithm available for backup sets in RMAN to save disk space with minimal CPU overhead. Unlike operating system or tape controller compression, RMAN's binary compression is optimized for Oracle datafiles.

BINARY_DOUBLE   BINARY_DOUBLE is a new native numeric data type in Oracle 10g with 64-bit precision. It's based on the IEEE 754 standard for binary floating-point arithmetic.

BINARY_FLOAT   BINARY_FLOAT is a new native numeric data type in Oracle 10g with 32-bit precision. It's based on the IEEE 754 standard for binary floating-point arithmetic.

C

calendaring expressions   Specify the frequency of schedules or jobs. It uses each calendar component.

change-tracking file   A binary database file, usually stored with the other database datafiles, that maintains a list of changed blocks in the database since the last backup. This file reduces the amount of time RMAN requires to perform an incremental backup.

coarse striping   An ASM striping method for higher-latency objects that uses a stripe size of 1MB.

Common Manageability Infrastructure (CMI)   Components of the database that manage and tune the Oracle 10g database. The components are Automatic Workload Repository, automated tasks feature, sever generated alerts and advisory framework.

comprehensive mode   A mode within the SQL Access Advisor that performs its analysis under the assumption that an entire workload, in contrast to a partial workload or a single SQL statement, is being analyzed.

CTWR   A new background process that maintains the change-tracking file for RMAN incremental backups.

D

Data Pump   A new feature of Oracle 10g that provides fast parallel bulk data and metadata movement between Oracle databases. Data Pump is fully integrated with the Oracle database and is installed automatically during database creation or database upgrade.

Database Configuration Assistant (DBCA)   The Database Configuration Assistant (DBCA) is a GUI tool to create a database, configure an existing database, and delete a database. DBCA can also clone an existing database.

DATABASE_PROPERTIES   A data dictionary view containing one row for various characteristics of the database, such as NLS parameters, the names of the default permanent and temporary tablespaces, and the default type of tablespace created with CREATE TABLESPACE.

Database Upgrade Utility (DBUA)   The Database Upgrade Utility (DBUA) is a GUI tool to upgrade an existing database to Oracle 10*g*. DBUA does all the necessary checking prior to the upgrade and performs the upgrade with minimal intervention.

DBMS_FILE_TRANSFER   A system package that is used for copying binary files between directories on the same server or between directories on different servers, without leaving the PL/SQL environment.

DBMS_SERVER_ALERT   A PL/SQL package to configure and retrieve warning and critical threshold levels for tablespace space usage and other database resources.

Dbtime   A unit of measure in which database performance is measured. DBtime is the cumulative time spent by the database server in processing user requests, which includes wait time and CPU time.

default permanent tablespace   The tablespace assigned to a user to store permanent objects when a permanent tablespace is not explicitly assigned to the user.

disk group   A group of disks treated as a unit in an ASM instance for both redundancy and performance.

dynamic rebalancing   An ASM feature that automatically reallocates extents within an ASM file when a disk in an ASM disk group is added, deleted, or fails.

dynamic sampling   A method of statistics collection, controlled by the initialization parameter OPTIMZER_DYNAMIC_SAMPLING, that produces compile-time statistics for query objects that have stale or missing statistics.

E

expdp   Oracle Data Pump client utility to export data.

encoded block number   A new component of a ROWID in a bigfile tablespace, combining the relative datafile number and data block number from the smallfile ROWID format to form a block number with a much larger address space.

End-to-end application tracing   Tracing sessions from its start at the client to its end at the server. Oracle 10g allows tracing client sessions using the client identifier across multiple sessions when a middle-tier or shared-server configuration is involved.

external redundancy   For an ASM disk group with only one failure group, relying on the external disk hardware subsystem to provide mirroring.

External Table   A type of oracle database table, where the actual data is stored in external files (operating system files). The definition of the table reside in the database dictionary.

F

failure group   Disks as part of an ASM disk group that share a common resource whose failure will cause the entire set of disks to be unavailable to the disk group.

fast incremental backups   An RMAN backup type that uses the change-tracking file to perform an incremental backup more quickly by reading only those blocks from the database datafiles that have changed.

Fine-grained auditing   Auditing user actions at the row level—row-level security. Data changes and queries can be audited at the row level in addition to the object level auditing.

fine striping   An ASM striping method for low-latency objects that uses a stripe size of 128KB.

fixed table   A table that exists in memory only that typically contains information about instance or memory structures and is presented in the form of a table. These tables often begin with X$, are not documented for general use, and are the basis for many of the V$ dynamic performance views.

flash recovery area   A single, unified storage area for all recovery-related files and recovery activities in an Oracle database. Configured with the initialization parameters DB_RECOVERY_FILE_DEST_SIZE and DB_RECOVERY_FILE_DEST.

flashback buffer   Whenever Flashback Database is enabled, this new memory area within the SGA stores changes to data blocks to facilitate Flashback Database. The RVWR process writes the blocks in the flashback buffer to flashback logs in the flash recovery area.

Flashback Database   A flashback feature that allows you to quickly revert the entire database to its state as of a previous point in time.

Flashback Drop   A flashback feature that retrieves a table after it has been dropped without using other more complicated recovery techniques.

Flashback Table   A flashback feature that allows you to recover one or more existing tables to a specific point in time. Flashback Table is done in place by rolling back only the changes made to the table or tables and their dependent objects, such as indexes.

Flashback Transaction Query A recovery technique that retrieves all changes within the database for a specified time period and for a particular transaction number. Uses the data dictionary view FLASHBACK_TRANSACTION_QUERY.

Flashback Versions Query A recovery technique that shows all versions of all rows in a table between two SCNs or time stamps, whether the rows were inserted, deleted, or updated.

full workload An option within the SQL Access Advisor to specify that a workload is the full set of SQL statements run as part of an application or throughout a business day.

G

GET_THRESHOLD A procedure within the package DBMS_SERVER_ALERT to retrieve the threshold levels for a tablespace or other database resource.

Growth Trend Report A report available within the EM Database Control that uses AWR data to show segment growth in the past and predict segment growth in the future.

global script A new type of RMAN script that can be shared between databases.

H

hash-partitioned global indexes Global indexes that use an internal hashing algorithm to assign index entries to partitions in a partitioned global index. Hash-partitioned global indexes increase the performance of parallel queries by allowing multiple parallel processes per partition in a parallel SELECT query.

high redundancy For an ASM disk group, a level of redundancy that requires at least three failure groups in the disk group.

HTML DB HTML DB is a Rapid Application Development (RAD) tool for the Oracle database and has many built-in themes and features. Using only a web browser, developers can build web applications faster.

I

impdp Oracle Data Pump client utility to import data.

incrementally updated backup The process of updating an existing image copy of a datafile with incremental backups to reduce the number of archived redo log files, and therefore the amount of time, needed to recover a datafile.

J

job   Specifies what program needs to be executed and the schedule of when.

job class   Defines a group of jobs that share the same characteristics and have common resource usage requirements. A job can belong to only one job class.

L

limited mode   A mode within SQL Access Advisor that performs its analysis under the assumption that a subset of the entire workload, such as a single SQL statement, is being analyzed.

long query warning alert   An alert generated when a user receives a "Snapshot too old" error. This alert is generated at most once per 24-hour period.

M

master control process (MCP)   Controls the execution of the Data Pump job; there is one MCP per job. MCP divides the Data Pump job into various metadata and data load or unload jobs and hands them over to the worker processes.

MMAN   MMAN is the Memory Manager process responsible for Automatic Shared Memory Management.

MMON   A new Oracle background process that checks for tablespace space problems every 10 minutes; alerts are triggered both when a threshold is exceeded and once again when the space usage for a tablespace falls back below the threshold.

MODEL clause   A new clause available in the SELECT statement to perform spreadsheet-like array computations.

N

normal mode   A mode of the SQL Tuning Advisor that performs much like the optimizer in previous versions of Oracle to provide a reasonable execution plan within limited time constraints.

normal redundancy   For an ASM disk group, a level of redundancy that requires at least two failure groups in the disk group.

O

OPTIMIZER_DYNAMIC_SAMPLING   A new initialization parameter that controls the level of runtime statistics collection for objects that have stale or missing statistics.

Oracle 10g HTTP Server (OHS)   The Oracle 10g HTTP Server (OHS) is based on the Apache web server 1.3.28 and is designed to take advantage of the latest optimizations and security features.

Oracle Enterprise Manger (EM)   The Oracle Enterprise Manager (EM) is a GUI tool to manage the Oracle environment, which includes a database, host server, listener, HTTP Server, and web applications.

Oracle Management Agent   The Oracle Management Agent is used by Oracle Enterprise Manager to monitor the database and server. The Oracle Management Agent is responsible for monitoring all targets on the host, for communicating that information to the middle-tier Management Service, and for managing and maintaining the host and its targets.

Oracle Universal Installer (OUI)   The Oracle Universal Installer (OUI) is a GUI tool to install the Oracle software. The OUI performs the necessary OS and hardware resources before the install.

ORBn   In an ASM instance, this performs the actual extent movement between disks in the disk groups managed by the ASM instance. n can be from 0 to 9.

P

partial workload   An option within the SQL Access Advisor to specify that a workload is only a single SQL statement or a group of problematic SQL statements, as opposed to all SQL statements run during a typical business cycle.

Partition change tracking   Partition change tracking (PCT) is the ability to identify which rows in a materialized view are affected by certain detail table partitions.

Partitioned outer join   A method in Oracle 10g to convert dense data to sparse data in order to better utilize some analytical functions.

program   Determines what task needs to be performed. The program is a collection of metadata information about the name of the program, its type, and its arguments.

R

RBAL   In an ASM instance, this coordinates the disk activity for disk groups.

Redo Logfile Size Advisor   An advisor within the Oracle advisory framework that analyzes redo logfile usage and recommends an optimal redo logfile size to minimize I/O and logfile switches.

recycle bin   A logical structure available in all locally managed tablespaces (except for the SYSTEM and SYSAUX tablespaces) that maintains dropped versions of tables. The recycle bin is purged either manually or whenever space pressure exists in the tablespace.

Regular expressions   A method of describing both simple and complex patterns for searching and manipulating.

RVWR   A background process that writes data from the *flashback buffer* in the SGA to flash-back logs in the flash recovery area.

S

Sample schema   Sample schemas are schema objects with sample data in them. The sample schema installation has five schemas: HR, IX, OE, PM, and SH. Most of the examples and sample code provided in the Oracle documentation are based on these sample schemas.

Segment Advisor   A tool available either via a PL/SQL package or within the EM Database Control that analyzes a segment or all segments within a tablespace and recommends remedial action to optimize the space within the segments.

schedule   Specifies when and how often a task (job) will be executed.

Segment Resource Estimation   A tool available only within the EM Database Control that can estimate space usage for a new table segment given the column datatypes, sizes, and the estimated row count.

segment shrink   The functionality either using ALTER TABLE or the EM Database Control interface to reclaim wasted space within a segment and optionally move the HWM down.

SET_THRESHOLD   A procedure within the package DBMS_SERVER_ALERT to set the threshold levels for a tablespace or other database resource.

Shared server   A database architecture where user requests are handled by different server processes. This architecture was formerly known as a *multithreaded server*.

smallfile tablespace   The traditional type of tablespace available in both previous releases of Oracle and Oracle 10*g*. Smallfile tablespaces can consist of one or many datafiles. Using all smallfile tablespaces limits the amount of data stored in an Oracle database to 8 petabytes (PB).

sorted hash clusters   A hash cluster, either single table or multiple table, that maintains rows ordered by one or more sort keys for each value of the cluster key to minimize memory usage and sort operations when the rows are retrieved from the cluster. Supports applications that process data in a FIFO manner.

SQL Access Advisor   A component of the Oracle advisory framework and the DBMS_ADVISOR package that helps to determine which indexes, materialized views, and materialized view logs will help the performance of a single query, an entire workload, or a derived workload based on a specified schema.

SQL profile   A collection of additional information about a SQL query that is collected during the automatic tuning of a SQL statement that can be used to improve the execution plan for future executions of the SQL statement.

SQL Tuning Advisor   A component of the Oracle advisory framework that automatically calls the Automatic Tuning Optimizer to perform several different types of analyses on a SQL query.

SQL Tuning Set (STS)   A construct to store and maintain a set of SQL statements along with its execution information.

SQLTUNE_CATEGORY   An initialization parameter used by the SQL Tuning Advisor to specify which category to use when applying a SQL profile to a SQL statement.

stateful alerts   As a category of server-generated alerts, stateful alerts are based on a threshold. Alerts are configured by setting a warning and critical threshold values on database metrics.

stateless alerts   As a category of server-generated alerts, stateless alerts are based on an event. Alert is sent out when an event such as "resumable session suspended" occurs.

Statistics aggregation   Aggregation of key metrics and statistics for problem diagnosis and analysis captured at the session, instance, service, module, or client identifier level.

STS   *See* SQL Tuning Set (STS).

SWITCH DATABASE   A new feature in RMAN used to quickly recover a database by using datafiles in the flash recovery area as the live database, eliminating any copy operations.

SYSAUX tablespace   A companion tablespace to the SYSTEM tablespace designed to offload the metadata from the SYSTEM tablespace as well as to consolidate other applications that previously required their own tablespaces.

T

temporary tablespace group   A database object that represents one or more temporary tablespaces. A temporary tablespace group cannot exist without any members. Temporary tablespace groups can be used anywhere that a temporary tablespace can.

Trcsess   A new utility to combine the trace files generated by multiple sessions based on a common criteria such as client identifier or service name.

tuning mode   A mode of the SQL Tuning Advisor that performs an in-depth analysis of high-load SQL and produces a series of recommended actions to improve the execution plan of the query.

U

Undo Advisor   A tool within the Oracle advisory framework that uses past undo usage to recommend settings for the UNDO_RETENTION parameter as well as an optimal size for the undo tablespace.

V

V$SYSAUX_OCCUPANTS   A dynamic performance view containing a list of the applications whose metadata resides in the SYSAUX tablespace. Along with the space usage for each application, the column MOVE_PROCEDURE provides the name of the procedure or package that can be used to move the application's metadata out of or into the SYSAUX tablespace.

Virtual Private Database (VPD)   Securing privileges of data at a row level. User queries are rewritten by the database to add a WHERE clause to filter rows that are not relevant to the user, which is determined by a policy function.

W

window   In the scheduler, can be used to activate different resource plans at different times. The window represents an interval with a well-defined start and end time.Dump FilesFiles written by data pump (expdp) and export (exp) utilities, which contain data and metadata extract from the database.

Window Group   In the scheduler, a window group represents a collection of windows.

Index

Note to the Reader: Throughout this index **boldfaced** page numbers indicate primary discussions of a topic. *Italicized* page numbers indicate illustrations.

J

O

Q

R